S0-AEM-662

Foreign Relations of the United States, 1964–1968

Volume XXIII

Congo, 1960–1968

Editors Nina D. Howland, David C. Humphrey, Harriet D. Schwar

General Editor Adam M. Howard

United States Government Printing Office
Washington
2013

DEPARTMENT OF STATE

Office of the Historian

Bureau of Public Affairs

For sale by the Superintendent of Documents, U.S. Government Printing Office
Internet: bookstore.gpo.gov Phone: toll free (866) 512-1800; DC area (202) 512-1800
Fax: (202) 512-2104 Mail: Stop IDCC, Washington, DC 20402-0001

ISBN 978-0-16-082002-1

Preface

The *Foreign Relations of the United States* series presents the official documentary historical record of major foreign policy decisions and significant diplomatic activity of the United States Government. The Historian of the Department of State is charged with responsibility for the preparation of the *Foreign Relations* series. The General Editor and the staff of the Office of the Historian, plan, research, select, and edit the volumes in the series. Official regulations codifying specific standards for the selection and editing of documents for the series were first promulgated by Secretary of State Frank B. Kellogg on March 26, 1925. These regulations, with minor modifications, guided the series through 1991. A new statutory charter for the preparation of the series was established by Public Law 102–138, the Foreign Relations Authorization Act, Fiscal Years 1992 and 1993, which was signed by President George Bush on October 28, 1991. Section 198 of P.L. 102–138 added a new Title IV to the Department of State's Basic Authorities Act of 1956 (22 USC 4351, *et seq.).* The statute requires that the *Foreign Relations* series be a thorough, accurate, and reliable record of major United States foreign policy decisions and significant United States diplomatic activity. The volumes of the series should include all records needed to provide comprehensive documentation of major foreign policy decisions and actions of the United States Government. The statute also confirms the editing principles established by Secretary Kellogg: the *Foreign Relations* series is guided by the principles of historical objectivity and accuracy; records should not be altered or deletions made without indicating in the published text that a deletion has been made; the published record should omit no facts that were of major importance in reaching a decision; and nothing should be omitted for the purposes of concealing a defect in policy. The statute also requires that the *Foreign Relations* series be published not more than 30 years after the events recorded.

Focus of Research and Principles of Selection for Foreign Relations, *1964–1968, Volume XXIII, Congo, 1960–1968*

This volume is part of a *Foreign Relations* subseries that documents the most important issues in the foreign policy of President Lyndon B. Johnson. However, this volume also includes documentation on U.S. foreign policy toward Congo-Léopoldville during the administrations of Presidents Dwight D. Eisenhower and John F. Kennedy. It is therefore a retrospective, composite volume, which covers U.S. policy in Congo-Léopoldville from March 1960 until December 1968. It should be read as a supplement to *Foreign Relations,* 1958–1960, Volume XIV, Africa, and *Foreign Relations,* 1961–1963, Volume XX, Congo Crisis. Both volumes provide thorough and detailed coverage of overt U.S. policy toward Congo-Léopoldville during the 1960–1963 period including: U.S. support for UN intervention; diplomatic efforts to bring about a peaceful resolution of the Katanga secessions; and U.S. efforts to promote stability, install a pro-Western regime and limit Soviet influence. The volumes did not, however, contain documentation of the U.S. covert political action program. There were also no records in the two volumes concerning U.S. planning and preparation for the possible assassination of Patrice Lumumba. At the time these volumes were published, Department of State historians had no access to sensitive records still in the custody of the Central Intelligence Agency (CIA). In 1991, however, Congressional legislation was passed and signed into law that affirmed the *Foreign Relations* series "shall be a thorough, accurate, and reliable documentary record of major United States foreign policy decisions and significant United States diplomatic activity" and required U.S. Government departments and agencies to provide Department of State historians with "full and complete access to the records pertinent to United States foreign policy decisions and actions." Department of State historians were therefore able to conduct comprehensive research on the U.S. role in covertly shaping, influencing and implementing U.S. foreign policy for this volume.

Foreign Relations, 1964–1968, Volume XXIII, Congo, was originally conceived as a volume documenting U.S. policy during the Johnson administration. However, in March 1997 the Department of State Advisory Committee on Historical Diplomatic Documentation called into question the completeness and accuracy of the previously released Eisenhower and Kennedy volumes on this topic. At the Committee's suggestion, the Office of the Historian delayed publication of this volume to incorporate all relevant material regarding U.S. covert actions missing in the earlier volumes. This volume consists of a selection of the most significant of those previously unavailable documents.

The first part of the volume, covering 1960 to 1963, contains numerous CIA cables to and from the Station in Léopoldville, which document the chaotic nature of the Congo crisis and the pervasive influence of U.S. Government covert actions in the newly independent nation. They also provide the analysis that is at the core of policy formulation with regard to covert action. A significant portion of this intelligence information is presented in editorial notes, in an effort to release as much of the pertinent information as possible given the extensive declassification challenges. Covert political action was only one part of U.S. policy during this period and must be viewed within the broader context. Thus, this portion of the volume is not intended to stand on its own and should be used in conjunction with *Foreign Relations*, 1958–1960, Volume XIV, Africa, and *Foreign Relations*, 1961–1963, Volume XX, Congo Crisis, in order to gain a comprehensive picture of U.S. policy toward Congo-Léopoldville during this period.

The second part of the volume, covering 1964 to 1968, documents the continuation of the U.S. covert political action programs and their role in providing paramilitary and air support to the Congolese Government in an effort to quell provincial rebellions. While CIA cables are an important component of the documentation, other agency positions are represented in cables, memoranda, memoranda of conversation, and analytical papers. This documentation illustrates a gradual shift in policy to engage other nations in the stabilization of Congo-Léopoldville, including the joint U.S.-Belgian rescue of European and U.S. hostages during Operation Dragon Rouge and the efforts of the Department of State to convince other nations, including Belgium and members of the Organization of African Unity, to support the Congo-Léopoldville Government and condemn outside interference. Additionally, this portion documents efforts by the Department of State, National Security Council, Joint Chiefs of Staff, Department of Defense, and CIA to abandon the ad hoc approach to U.S. relations that characterized the earlier period and develop a more strategic, long-term approach.

Editorial Methodology

The documents are presented chronologically according to Washington time. Memoranda of conversation are placed according to the time and date of the conversation, rather than the date the memorandum was drafted.

Editorial treatment of the documents published in the *Foreign Relations* series follows Office style guidelines, supplemented by guidance from the General Editor and the chief technical editor. The documents are reproduced as exactly as possible, including marginalia or other notations, which are described in the footnotes. Texts are transcribed and printed according to accepted conventions for the publication of historical documents within the limitations of modern typography. A heading has been supplied by the editors for each document included in the volume. Words or phrases underlined in the source text are printed in italics. Abbreviations and contractions are preserved as found in the original text, and a list of abbreviations is included in the front matter of each volume. Spelling, capitalization, punctuation, and place names are retained as found in the original text, except that obvious typographical errors are silently corrected. Other mistakes and omissions in the documents are corrected by bracketed insertions: a correction is set in italic type; an addition in roman type.

Bracketed insertions are also used to indicate omitted text that deals with an unrelated subject (in roman type) or that remains classified after declassification review (in italic type). For this volume, where possible, the editors have used bracketed insertions to indicate names, titles, or agencies in place of cryptonyms that are not declassified. When this is not possible, the amount and nature of classified material is indicated by the number of lines or pages of text that were omitted. In some cases, when more than one individual whose name cannot be declassified is discussed in the body of a document, they have been designated by the editors as "[Identity 1]," [Identity 2]," etc. for clarity. The identity designation of a specific individual is valid for a single document only, and is not consistent throughout the volume. An individual designated as "[Identity1]" in Document 1, for example, may be referred to as "[Identity 2]" in subsequent documents. Entire documents withheld for declassification purposes have been accounted for and are listed with headings, source notes, and number of pages not declassified in their chronological place. All brackets that appear in the original text are so identified in footnotes.

The first footnote to each document indicates the source of the document, original classification, distribution, and drafting information. This note also provides the background of important documents and policies and indicates whether the President or his major policy advisers read the document.

Editorial notes and additional annotation summarize pertinent material not printed in the volume, indicate the location of additional documentary sources, provide references to important related documents printed in other volumes, describe key events, and provide summaries of and citations to public statements that supplement and elucidate the printed documents. In addition, this volume also contains editorial notes that summarize extensively redacted documents in order to provide narrative cohesion. Information derived from memoirs and other first-hand accounts has been used when appropriate to supplement or explicate the official record.

The numbers in the index refer to document numbers rather than to page numbers.

Advisory Committee on Historical Diplomatic Documentation

The Advisory Committee on Historical Diplomatic Documentation, established under the *Foreign Relations* statute, reviews records, advises, and makes recommendations concerning the *Foreign Relations* series. The Advisory Committee monitors the overall compilation and editorial process of the series and advises on all aspects of the preparation and declassification of the series. Although the Advisory Committee does not attempt to review the contents of individual volumes in the series, it does monitor the overall process and makes recommendations on particular problems that come to its attention.

Because of the history and significance of this volume, the Advisory Committee offered advice throughout its lengthy preparation and took the unusual step of delegating a member to review the final manuscript. Although the committee appreciates that some documentation remains classified and does not appear in the volume, it assesses the volume as a reliable guide to the trajectory of U.S. policy toward the Congo from 1960 until 1968 and an exceptionally valuable addition to the historical record. Accordingly, the committee recommended its publication.

Declassification Review

The Office of Information Programs and Services, Bureau of Administration, Department of State, conducted the declassification review of the documents published in this volume. The review was conducted in accordance with the standards set forth in 22 U.S.C. 4353, and Executive Orders 12356, 12958 and 13526 on Classified National Security Information and applicable laws.

The principle guiding declassification review is to release all information, subject only to the current requirements of national security as embodied in law and regulation. Declassification decisions entailed concurrence of the appropriate geographic and functional bureaus in the Department of State and other concerned agencies of the U.S. Government. The declassification review of this volume began in 1994 and was finally completed in 2013. It resulted in the decision to withhold 4 documents in full, excise a paragraph or more in 12 documents, and make excisions of less than a paragraph in 222 documents.

As a result of the sui generis nature of this volume, it has undergone an extensive and prolonged declassification review and appeals process. The Office of the Historian is confident, on the basis of the research conducted in preparing this volume and as a result of the declassification review process described above, that the documentation, annotation, and editorial notes presented here provide a broadly accurate account of the main lines of U.S. policy toward Congo-Léopoldville from 1960 until 1968.

Acknowledgments

The editors would like to acknowledge the assistance of the Historical Staff of the Center for the Study of Intelligence who assisted Nina D. Howland and Harriet D. Schwar in the collection of materials for this volume. The editors extend sincere appreciation to the *Foreign Relations* Coordination Staff and the National Clandestine Service Declassification reviewer at the Central Intelligence Agency for providing assistance to the Office of the Historian and sustained collegial cooperation for a period of years during the production of this volume. The editors would like to thank Cherie Andrews and Patricia Rosendale for their hard work and dedication to the composition and layout of *Foreign Relations* volumes for more than a decade. Nina D. Howland selected and annotated the documentation under the general supervision of Harriet D. Schwar and the then General Editors of the *Foreign Relations* series, Glen LaFantasie and, later, David S. Patterson. David C. Humphrey streamlined the volume, wrote editorial notes, and expanded footnotes. Edward C. Keefer, who succeeded Patterson as General Editor, worked extensively on negotiating declassification decisions. David Herschler, Kerry Hite, David Geyer, Susan C. Weetman and Carl E. Ashley coordinated the declassification review. Do Mi Stauber prepared the index.

Bureau of Public Affairs
December 2013

Stephen P. Randolph, Ph.D.
The Historian

Contents

Sources

Sources for the Foreign Relations *Series*

The Foreign Relations statute requires that the published record in the *Foreign Relations* series include all records needed to provide comprehensive documentation on major U.S. foreign policy decisions and significant U.S. diplomatic activity. It further requires that government agencies, departments, and other entities of the U.S. Government engaged in foreign policy formulation, execution, or support cooperate with the Department of State Historian by providing full and complete access to records pertinent to foreign policy decisions and actions and by providing copies of selected records.

The editors of the *Foreign Relations* series have complete access to all the retired records and papers of the Department of State: the central files of the Department; the special decentralized files ("lot files") of the Department at the bureau, office, and division levels; the files of the Department's Executive Secretariat, which contain the records of international conferences and high-level official visits, correspondence with foreign leaders by the President and Secretary of State and foreign officials and the files of overseas diplomatic posts. All the Department's indexed central files for 1960–1968 have been permanently transferred to the National Archives and Records Administration at College Park, Maryland (Archives II). The Department's decentralized office (or lot) files covering this period that the National Archives deems worthy of permanent retention, have been transferred from the Department's custody to Archives II.

The editors of the Foreign Relations series also have full access to the papers of President Johnson and other White House foreign policy records. Presidential papers maintained and preserved at the Presidential libraries include some of the most significant foreign affairs-related documentation from the Department of State and other Federal agencies, including the National Security Council, the Central Intelligence Agency, the Department of Defense, and the Joint Chiefs of Staff.

Sources for Foreign Relations, *1964–1968, Volume XXIII, Congo, 1960–1968*

This retrospective volume on the Congo, 1960–1968, is a documentary history of U.S. relations with Congo-Léopoldville, including U.S. involvement in the Congo Crisis. As such, the first part of this volume relies heavily on CIA documents. Much of the documentation is in Jobs 78–00435R and 79–00149A, which contain cables between CIA headquarters and the Station in Léopoldville. They also contain field reports and analytical papers. Job 81–00966R contains an extensive collection of papers and memoranda prepared for the Special Group and the 303 Committee. In some instances, names of files and collections have not been declassified. Special Group and 303 Committee meeting minutes and summaries are available in several collections in the National Security Council Intelligence Files, specifically: Special Group Meeting Minutes, Special Group Minutes and Agenda, Special Group Minutes and Approvals and 303 Committee Files Minutes. These collections contain documentation of the deliberations of the high-level interdepartmental groups set up to approve and supervise covert operations. Finally, the Church Committee's Interim Report provides extensive testimony on the plot to assassinate Patrice Lumumba.

The records of the Department of State are crucial to understanding the evolution of U.S. policy towards Congo-Léopoldville in the aftermath of the Congo Crisis. The Department's central files contain the cable traffic recording U.S. diplomatic relations with the Congolese Government and other nations, memoranda of diplomatic conversations, as well as action and information memoranda. The richest collection of cable traffic for 1964–1968 is in POL 23–9 The Congo, which also contains extensive documentation on Operation Dragon Rouge. Defense records in the central files provide documentation on U.S. efforts to train the Congolese National Army and to provide planes and equipment for their use.

The Johnson Library, National Security File, Country Files, Congo, contains interagency memoranda and telegrams regarding ongoing instability in the Congo after 1963, including the hostage situation in Stanleyville which resulted in Operation Dragon Rouge. The file also contains documentation regarding efforts to convince the Organization of African Unity and Belgium to support the Tshombe government and denounce outside interference in the provinces by mercenaries, neighboring states and others.

Unpublished Sources

Department of State

Central Files. See National Archives and Records Administration below.

Lot Files. See also National Archives and Records Administration below.

INR/IL Historical Files:

Files of the Office of Intelligence Coordination, containing records from the 1940s through the 1970s, maintained by the Office of Intelligence Liaison, Bureau of Intelligence and Research.

S/S Files: Lot 68 D 451

Minutes of meetings and memoranda of the Special Group, Counterinsurgency, for July-December 1964, maintained by the Executive Secretariat.

National Archives and Records Administration, College Park, Maryland

Record Group 59, Records of the Department of State

Decimal Central Files. Through January 1963, the Department of State continued to use the decimal central file system familiar to users of previous volumes of the *Foreign Relations* series. The following file was most useful in compiling this volume for the period through January 1963:

770G.00, political affairs and conditions in the Congo (the major file for the Congo crisis)

Subject-Numeric Indexed Central Files. In February 1963, the Department of State adopted a subject-numeric central file system. Under this system, files on the Republic of the Congo (now Zaire) were designated THE CONGO, and files on the Congo Republic (capital at Brazzaville) were designated CONGO.

DEF 1–1 THE CONGO, contingency planning

DEF 6–5 THE CONGO, paramilitary forces, The Congo

DEF 9–7 THE CONGO, service in foreign armed forces, The Congo

DEF 12 THE CONGO, armaments, The Congo

DEF 19 US–THE CONGO, military assistance, U.S.-The Congo

DEF 19–3 US–THE CONGO, defense organizations and conferences, U.S.-The Congo

DEF 19–8 US–THE CONGO, defense equipment and supplies, U.S.-The Congo

POL BEL–THE CONGO, political affairs and relations, Belgium-The Congo

POL THE CONGO–US, political affairs and relations, The Congo-U.S.

POL 1 THE CONGO–US, political affairs, general policy, The Congo-U.S.

POL 3 OAU, regional alignments and groupings, Organization of African Unity

POL 6 THE CONGO, biographic data, The Congo

POL 7 BEL, visits and meetings with Belgian officials

POL 7 RWANDA, visits and meetings with Rwandan officials

POL 7 THE CONGO, visits and meetings with Congolese officials

POL 7 US/HARRIMAN, visits and meetings with W. Averell Harriman

POL 7 US/HUMPHREY, visits and meetings with Vice President Humphrey

POL 9 EURW–TANZAN, intervention, Western Europe-Tanzania

POL 15–1 THE CONGO, Congolese Head of State, Executive Branch

POL 23–9 THE CONGO, rebellions and coups, The Congo

POL 30 THE CONGO, defectors and expellees, The Congo

POL 31–1 THE CONGO, air disputes and violations, The Congo

POL 31–1 THE CONGO–UGANDA, air disputes and violations, The Congo-Uganda

PS 7–6 THE CONGO, protective services, welfare and whereabouts, The Congo

SOC 3 Red Cross, organizations and conferences

Lot Files

AF/CM Files: Lot 67 D 63

Files on Congo (Kinshasa), including administrative, economic, political-defense, social, health, and science for 1964, as maintained by the Office of the Country Director for Central Africa, Malagasy, and Mauritius, Bureau of African Affairs

AF/CWG Files: Lot 65 D 498

Stanleyville POL 23–9 files (rebellions, coups) for 1964, as maintained by the Office of the Congo Working Group, Bureau of African Affairs

AF Files: Lot 69 D 118

Congo (Kinshasa) desk officer's subject files, including administrative, consular, cultural information, economic, defense affairs, intelligence, political affairs, science, refugees and migration for 1966, as maintained by the Office of the Country Director for Central Africa, Malagasy, and Mauritius, Bureau of African Affairs

S/S Files: Lot 72 D 192

Files of Secretary of State Dean Rusk, 1961–1969, including texts of speeches, miscellaneous correspondence files, White House correspondence, chronological files and memoranda of telephone conversations

Central Intelligence Agency, Langley, Virginia

Job 64–00352R
Job 76–00366R
Job 78–00435R
Job 78–00801R
Job 78–01450R
Job 78–02520R
Job 78–02888R
Job 78–03805R
Job 79–00149A
Job 81–00966R
Job 82–00450R
Job 89–00195R
Job 89–00639R
Job 90–01073R

Job 79R00890A
Job 79R01012A
Job 80B01285A
Job 80B00910A
Job 80B01285A
Job 86B00975R

National Security Council

Intelligence Files

- NSC 541212 Special Group Minutes/Agendas
- Special Group, Minutes and Agendas, Congo
- Special Group, Minutes and Approvals
- Special Group Meeting Minutes
- 303 Committee Files, Minutes

Library of Congress, Manuscript Division, Washington, D.C.

Harriman Papers

Special files of W. Averell Harriman, Public Service, Kennedy and Johnson administrations

Washington National Records Center, Suitland, Maryland

Record Group 218, Records of the Joint Chiefs of Staff

9111

Record Group 330, Records of the Office of the Secretary of Defense

OASD/ISA Files: FRC 68 A 4023

Top Secret files of the Assistant Secretary of Defense for International Security Affairs, 1964

OSD Files: FRC 69 A 7425

Top Secret files of the Secretary of Defense, Deputy Assistant Secretary of Defense, and Special Assistant, 1964

OSD Files: FRC 71 A 6489

Miscellaneous files and records of the Secretary of Defense, the Deputy Secretary of Defense and their assistants, 1951–1966

OSD Files: FRC 72 A 2467

Top Secret files of the Secretary of Defense, Deputy Assistant Secretary of Defense, and Special Assistant, 1967

OSD Files: 72 A 2468

Official records of the Secretary of Defense, Deputy Assistant Secretary of Defense, and Special Assistant, 1967

Lyndon B. Johnson Library, Austin, Texas

Papers of Lyndon B. Johnson

National Security File
- Country File, Congo
- Files of McGeorge Bundy
- Files of Edward Hamilton, Congo
- Intelligence Files, Special Group, Minutes & Agendas
- Memos to the President, McGeorge Bundy, Walt W. Rostow
- Name File, Komer Memos
- National Security Council Histories, Congo C–130 Crisis, July 1967

Recordings and Transcripts of Telephone Conversations and Meetings

White House Central Files
- Confidential File, CO 52

Other Personal Papers

Papers of George Ball

Tom Johnson's Notes of Meetings

Published Sources

U.S. Congress. Senate Select Committee to Study Governmental Operations with Respect to Intelligence Activities. *Alleged Assassination Plots Involving Foreign Leaders: An Interim Report.* Senate Report No. 94-9465, 94th Congress, 1st Session. Washington: U.S. Government Printing Office, 1975.

U.S. Department of State. *American Foreign Policy: Current Documents, 1960, 1961, 1962, 1964, 1966, 1967.* Washington: U.S. Government Printing Office.

Abbreviations and Cryptonyms

ABAKO, Alliance des Ba-Kongo
ACOA, American Committee on Africa
ADV, Advance Echelon
AF, Bureau of African Affairs, Department of State
AF/P, Public Affairs Adviser, Bureau of African Affairs, Department of State
AFB, Air Force Base
AFC, Office of Central African Affairs, Bureau of African Affairs, Department of State
AFI, Office of Inter-African Affairs, Bureau of African Affairs, Department of State
AID, Agency for International Development
Amb, ambassador
ammo, ammunition
ANC, Armée Nationale Congolaise, Congolese National Army
AP, Associated Press
ARMA, Army Attaché
ARMISHI/MAAG, U.S. Army Mission in Iran/Military Assistance Advisory Group

BAFM, Belgian Air Force Mission
BALUBAKAT, Association des Baluba du Katanga
BCF, Belgian Congo Franc
BF, Belgian Franc
BLOC, communist bloc
BNA, Office of British Commonwealth and Northern European Affairs, Bureau of European Affairs, Department of State
BRUS, Brussels

CA, covert action
C/AF, Chief, Africa Bureau, Central Intelligence Agency
CAF, Congolese Air Force
CAR, Central African Republic
CAS, controlled American source
CCC, Congo Conciliation Commission
CDA, Comité Démocratique Africain
Chicom, Chinese Communist(s)
Chinat, Chinese nationals
CI, counterinsurgency
CIA, Central Intelligence Agency
CINCEUR, Commander in Chief, European Command
CINCLANT, Commander in Chief, Armed Forces, Atlantic
CINCMEAFSA, Commander in Chief, Middle East/South Asia and Africa South of the Sahara
CINCSTRIKE, Commander in Chief, Strike Command
CIVOPS, Civilian Operations in the Congo (UN)
CJCS, Chairman, Joint Chiefs of Staff
CNA, Congo National Army
CNL, Committee of National Liberation

CO, Commanding Officer
COMINT, communications intelligence
COMISH, U.S. military mission, Congo
COMUSJTF, Commander, U.S. Joint Task Force
CONACO, Comité Nationale du Congo [Tshombe's party]
CONAKAT, Confédération des Association Tribales du Katanga
Contels, consulate telegrams
COQ, Coquilhatville (Congo)
COS, Chief of Station
CP, Communist Party
CRS/CB, Central Reference Service, Collection Branch, Central Intelligence Agency
CS, Chief of Staff
CWG, Congo Working Group

DCI, Director of Central intelligence
DCI/OCA, Office of Congressional Affairs, Office of the Director of Central Intelligence
DCM, Deputy Chief of Mission
DDO/AF, Africa Division, Office of the Deputy Director for Operations, Central Intelligence Agency
DDO/IMS, Information Management Staff, Office of the Deputy Director for Operations, Central Intelligence Agency
DDP, Deputy Director for Plans, Central Intelligence Agency
DDP/AF, Africa Division, Office of the Deputy Director for Plans, Central Intelligence Agency
DEFCON, defense readiness condition
DEFMIN, defense minister
DEL, delegation
DEPCIRCTEL, Department of State, circular telegram
Deptel, Department of State telegram
Deptoff, Department of State Officer
DIR, Director
DOD, Department of Defense
DOD/GC, General Counsel, Department of Defense
DOS, Department of State
DR, Dragon Rouge, U.S.-Belgian military operation into Stanleyville to rescue the foreign community
DRC, Democratic Republic of the Congo

Eliz, Elizabethville
Emboff, Embassy Officer
Embtel, Embassy telegram
EST, Eastern Standard Time
ETA, estimated time of arrival
EUR, Bureau of European Affairs, Department of State
EUR/FBX, Country Director for France, Benelux, Bureau of European Affairs, Department of State
EUR/SPP, Country Director for Spain and Portugal, Bureau of European Affairs, Department of State
EXDIS, Exclusive Distribution (acronym indicating extremely limited distribution or dissemination)

FBIS, Foreign Broadcast Information Service
FI, foreign intelligence
FM, Foreign Minister

FONMIN, Foreign Minister
FMS, Foreign Military Sales
FOL, following
FONOFF, Foreign Office
FRC, Federal Records Center
FY, fiscal year
FYI, for your information

GA, General Assembly (UN)
GDRC, Government of the Democratic Republic of the Congo
GOB, Government of Belgium
GOC, Government of the Congo
GOCL, Government of the Congo at Léopoldville
GOK, Government of Katanga
GON, Government of Nigeria
GOR, Government of Rwanda
GOT, Government of Tanzania
GOU, Government of Uganda
Govts, governments
GRAE, Angolan Revolutionary Government in Exile
GRC, Government of the Republic of China

HIM, His Imperial Majesty
HM, His Majesty
HMG, Her Majesty's Government
HQS, headquarters

IBRD, International Bank for Reconstruction and Development (World Bank)
Iden, identity
ICJ, International Court of Justice
ICRC, International Committee of the Red Cross
IEG, Imperial Ethiopian Government
IMF, International Monetary Fund
INR, Bureau of Intelligence and Research, Department of State
INTEL, intelligence
IO/UNP, Office of United Nations Political Affairs, Bureau of International Organization Affairs, Department of State
ITM, Italian Training Mission

JCS, Joint Chiefs of Staff
JTF, joint task force

KATGENS, Katangan gendarmes
KUBARK, Central Intelligence Agency

Leo, Léopoldville
LEOP, Léopoldville
LIMDIS, limited distribution

M, Under Secretary of State for Political Affairs
MAP, Military Assistance Aid Program
memcon, memorandum of conversation
merc, mercenary
MIL, military

MNC, Mouvement National Congolais
MOD, Minister of Defense
MPC, Mouvement Populaire Congolais
msg, message
MTT, mobile training team

NATO, North American Treaty Organization
NIACT, needs immediate action
NOFORN, No Foreign Dissemination
NSC, National Security Council

OASD, Office of the Assistant Secretary of Defense
OASD/ISA, Office of the Assistant Secretary of Defense for International Security Affairs
OAU, Organization of African Unity
OCAM, Organzation Commune Africaine et Malagache (African-Malagasy Common Organization)
ODACID, U.S. Department of State
ODDI, Office of the Deputy Director of Intelligence
ODYOKE, U.S. Government
OEP, Office of Emergency Planning
OPIM, Operational Immediate
Ops, operations
Org, organization

PARA, paratroop; paragraph
PBPRIME, United States
PBPRIMERS, Americans
PM, Prime Minister
PNG, persona non grata
PNP, Parti National du Progress
POLAD, political adviser
POLIT, political
Polto, series indicator for telegrams from the United States Mission to the North Atlantic Treaty Organization and European Regional Organizations to the Department of State
PRIMIN, prime minister
psywar, psychological warfare
PSA, Parti Solidaire Africain
PUNA, Parti de l'Unité National

QTE, quote

RADECO, Ressemblement des Démocrates Congolaise
Re, regarding
REFTEL, reference telegram
Rep, representative
reps, representatives
RG, Record Group
Roger, channel for communications between the Assistant Secretary for Intelligence and Research (INR) and the chief of mission
rpt, repeat
Rybat, communications indicator that limits the distribution of sensitive material

S, Office of the Secretary of State

S/AH, Office of the Ambassador at Large
SA, South Africa
SAC, Strategic Air Command
SAG, South African Government
SC RES, Security Council resolutions
SC, Security Council (UN)
SCS, Office of Special Consular Services
SG, Special Group
SITREP, situation report
SNIE, Special National Intelligence Estimate
SOV, Soviet
SQ, squadron
Sta, station
STAN, Stanleyville
STEY, Stanleyville
STRCC, Strike Command cable
SYG, Secretary-General (UN)

telcon, telephone conversation

UAMCE, Union for African and Malagasy Economic Cooperation
UAR, United Arab Republic
UEAC, Union des Etats de l'Afrique Centrale (Congo)
UK, United Kingdom
UKG, Government of the United Kingdom
UM, Union Miniere (Congo)
UMHK, Union Miniere du Haut Katanga (Congo)
UN, United Nations
UNDP, United Nations Development Program
UNGA, United Nations General Assembly
UNOC, United Nations Operations, Congo
UNP, Office of United Nations Political Affairs, Bureau of International Organization Affairs, Department of State
UNQTE, unquote
UNREP, United Nations Representative
UNSYG, Secretary General of the United Nations
UPI, United Press International
URTEL, urgent telegram
USAF, United States Air Force
USG, United States Government
USIA, United State Information Agency
USRO, United States Mission to the North Atlantic Treaty Organizations and European Regional Organizations
USSR, Union of Soviet Socialist Republics
USUN, United States Mission at the United Nations

VDW, Frederick Van der Walle
VOA, Voice of America
VP, Vice President

WH, White House
WHO, World Health Organization

Persons and Pseudonyms

Abboud, Ibrahim, President of Sudan from November 18, 1958 until November 16, 1964

Adams, Paul D., General, USA; Commander in Chief, Strike Command, until November 1966; concurrently Commander in Chief, Middle East/South Asia and Africa South of the Sahara, November 1963 until November 1966

Adoula, Cyrille, Prime Minister of the Congo from August 2, 1961 until June 30, 1964; Congolese Ambassador to the United States from January 1967

Anany, Jerome, Congolese Minister of Defense

Appling, Hugh G., Deputy Director, Office of Western European Affairs, Bureau of European Affairs, Department of State

Ascham, pseudonym for Allen Dulles

Attwood, William H., Ambassador to Guinea from April 26, 1961 until May 27, 1963; Ambassador to Kenya from March 2, 1964 until May 1, 1966

Balewa, Sir Abubakar T., Prime Minister of Nigeria from October 1, 1960 until January 15, 1966

Ball, George W., Under Secretary of State, from December 1961 until September 1966; Representative to the United Nations, from May 1968 until September 1968

Bell, David E., Director, Office of Management and Budget, from January 22, 1961 until December 20, 1962; Administrator of the Agency for International Development from late 1962 until 1966

Ben Bella, Ahmed, President and Prime Minister of Algeria until June 1965; concurrently Minister of the Interior, From December 1964 until June 1965

Berlind, Alan D., member, Congo Working Group, Bureau of African Affairs, Department of State

Bissell, Richard M., Deputy Director for Plans, Central Intelligence Agency from 1958 until 1962

Blake, Robert O., Deputy Chief of Mission at Léopoldville/Kinshasa, March 1964 until July 1967

Boigney, Félix Houphet, Prime Minister of Côte d'lvoire, August 7, 1960 until November 27, 1960; President since November 3, 1960

Bokassa, Jean-Bedel, President of the Central African Republic from 1966

Bolen, Charles E., Special Assistant to the Secretary of State until 1962; Ambassador to France, September 1962 until February 1968; Deputy Under Secretary of State for Political Affairs, December 1967 until January 1969

Bolikango, Jean, leader of Parti de I'Unité National (PUNA); Vice Premier in the lleo Ministry; Third Vice-Premier in the Adoula Ministry

Bomboko, Justin, President of the Congolese College of Commissioners and Commissioner for Foreign Affairs from October 4, 1960 until February 9, 1961; Foreign Minister from February 1961 until April 1963; Congolese Minister of Foreign Affairs from 1965; concurrently Minister of Industry and Foreign Trade from 1967

Bourgiba, Habib, President of Tunisia

Bowles, Chester B., Under Secretary of State from January 25, 1961 until December 3, 1961; Ambassador at Large from December 4, 1961 until June 9, 1963

Brown, Elizabeth A., Director, Office of United Nations Political Affairs, Bureau of International Organization Affairs, Department of State

Brown, L. Dean, Director, Office of Central African Affairs, Bureau of African Affairs, Department of State, September 1965 until July 1966; Country Director for Central Africa, July 1966 until November 1967; thereafter Ambassador to Senegal and The Gambia

Brubeck, William H., member, National Security Council Staff, until November 1964

Bunche, Ralph J., Special Representative of the Secretary General for UN Operations in the Congo from July until August 1960; UN Under Secretary for Special Political Affairs until 1967; thereafter Under Secretary General

Bundy, McGeorge, Special Assistant to the President for National Security Affairs until February 1966; Executive Secretary of the Special Committee of the National Security Council from June until August 1967

Burgess, Warren R., Chief of the U.S. Mission to the North Atlantic Treaty Organization until March 23, 1961

Campbell, Stephen, Officer in Charge of United Nations Political Affairs, Bureau of International Organization Affairs, Department of State

Canup, William C., member, Congo Working Group, Bureau of African Affairs, Department of State

Cashin, Richard M., Director, Office of Central African Affairs, Agency for International Development from July 1962 until July 1976; Deputy Director, Agency for International Development, from July 1967 until January 1968; thereafter Director, Agency for International Development

Cleveland, James H., Assistant Secretary of State for International Organization Affairs from February 1961 until September 1965

Clingerman, John R., Consul in Stanleyville, from July 1963 until October 1964; member of the Congo Working Group from November 1964 until 1965

Creel, Robert C., Deputy Assistant Secretary of State for European Affairs

Cyr, Leo G., Ambassador to Rwanda, November 1966 until September 1971

Dayal, Rajeshwar, Special Representative of the U.N. Secretary-General in the Congo until May 1961

Davignon, Viscount Etienne, Chef de Cabinet, Belgian Ministry of Foreign Affairs

Deming, Olcott H., Ambassador to Uganda, January 1963 until June 1966

Devlin, Lawrence, Chief of Station, Congo (Léopoldville) from July 1960 until May 1963 and July 1965 until June 1967

Dillon, C. Douglas, Under Secretary of State from June 12, 1959 until January 4, 1961; Treasury Secretary, January 1961 until April 1965

Dirksen, Everett M., Senator (R-Illinois) from January 3, 1951 until September 7, 1969

Dodds, William A., Colonel, Adviser on counterinsurgency operations in the Congo from February 1964

Dulles, Allen W., Director of Central Intelligence until November 1961

Eisenhower, Dwight D., President of the United States until January 20, 1961

Engulu, Leon, President of Cuvette Centrale from September 1962 until April 25, 1966; Governor of Équateur Province from April 25, 1966 until January 3, 1967; Governor of Kivu Province from January 3, 1967 until August 9, 1968; thereafter, Governor of Katanga

Ferguson, Glenn W., Ambassador to Kenya, November 1966 until April 1969

Fields, Glenn D., Deputy Chief of the Africa Division, Directorate of Plans, Central Intelligence Agency; Chief of the Africa Division, Directorate of Plans, Central Intelligence Agency

Fine, Sydney H., Public Affairs Adviser, Bureau of African Affairs, Department of State

Fitzgerald, Desmond, Deputy Director of Plans, Central Intelligence Agency

Fredericks, J. Wayne, Deputy Assistant Secretary of State for African Affairs, from May 1961 until September 1967

Gallopin, Roger, Director General, International Commission of the Red Cross

Gardiner, Robert K.A., United Nations Representative in the Congo from April 1961 until February 1962; Officer in Charge of the U.N. Operation in the Congo from February 1962 until April 1963

Gaud, William S., Deputy Administrator, Agency for International Development, February 1964 until August 1966; thereafter Administrator

Gbenye, Christophe, Minister of the Interior in the opposition regime in Stanleyville until July 1961; Congolese Minister of the Interior from August 1961 until February 1962; Deputy Prime Minister from February until July 1962

Gilpatric, Roswell L., Deputy Secretary of Defense from 1961 until 1964

Ginzenga, Antoine, Prime Minister of the opposition regime in Stanleyville from December 13, 1960 until August 5, 1961; Deputy Prime Minister of the Republic of the Congo from August 1961 until January 1962; thereafter imprisoned

Godley, G. McMurtrie, Ambassador to the Congo from March 23, 1964 until October 15, 1966

Gonard, Samuel A., President of the International Committee of the Red Cross from 1964 until 1969

Greene, M.J.L., Colonel, Office of the Assistant Secretary of Defense for International Security Affairs; headed Special Military Advisory Team to the Congo from June until July 1962

Greenfield, James L., Deputy Assistant Secretary, Bureau of Public Affairs, Department of State

Grenfell, Georges, provincial president in Stanleyville

Gullion, Edmund A., Ambassador to the Congo from September 11, 1961 until February 20, 1964

Hadsel, Fred L., Director, Office of Inter-African Affairs, Department of State

Hamilton, Edward, member, National Security Council Staff, October 1965 until December 1968

Hammerskjold, Dag, Secretary-General of the United Nations until his death on September 18, 1961

Harmel, Pierre, Belgian Prime Minister, July 1965 until 1966; Minister of Foreign Affairs, 1966 until 1968

Harriman, W. Averell, Ambassador At Large from February 1961 until December 1961; Assistant Secretary of State for East Asian and Pacific Affairs, from December 1961 until April 1963; Under Secretary of State for Political Affairs from April 1963 until March 1965; thereafter Ambassador at Large

Hassan II, King of Morocco

Helms, Richard, Deputy Director for Plans, Central Intelligence Agency from 1964 until 1966; Deputy Director of Central Intelligence from April 1965 until June 1966; thereafter Director

Herter, Christian A., Secretary of State from April 22, 1959 until January 20, 1961

Hickenlooper, Bourke B., Senator (R-Iowa) from January 3, 1945 until January 3, 1969

Hilsman, Roger Jr., Assistant Secretary of State for Intelligence and Research from February 19, 1961 until April 25, 1963

Hoyt, Michael P.E., Consul in Stanleyville from 1964

Humphrey, Hubert H. Jr., Senator (D-Minnesota) until 1964; Vice President, January 20, 1965 until January 20, 1969

Identity 1, 2, etc., Designators supplied by editors for clarity. Identity designation of a specific individual is valid for a single document only, and is not consistent throughout the volume.

Idzumbuir, Theodore, Congolese Ambassador to the United Nations

Ileo, Joseph, President of the Republic of the Congo Senate; Prime Minister from September 5, 1960 until September 20, 1960 and February 9, 1961 until August 2, 1961; Minister of Information and Culture from August 1961 until July 1962; Minister Resident in Katanga from January 1963

Jessup, Peter, member, National Security Council Staff

Johnson, Lyndon B., President of the United States from November 22, 1963 until January 20, 1969

Johnson, U. Alexis, Deputy Under Secretary of State for Political Affairs from May 2, 1961 until July 12, 1964

Kalonji, Albert, President of South Kasai from August 9, 1960 until April 12, 1961

Kamitatu, Cleophas, Head of the Léopoldville provincial government; Congolese Minister of the Interior

Karamessines, Thomas, Assistant Deputy Director for Plans, Central Intelligence Agency until July 1967; thereafter Deputy Director for Plans

Kasavubu, Joseph, President of the Republic of the Congo from July 1, 1960 until November 25, 1965

Katzenbach, Nicholas de B., Deputy Attorney General until February 1965; Attorney General, February 1965 until October 1966; Under Secretary of State, September 1966–January 1969

Kaunda, Kenneth, President of Zambia from 1964

Kayibanda, Gregoire, President of Rwanda

Kearney, Richard D., Deputy Legal Adviser, Office of the Legal Adviser, Department of State

Keita, Modibo, President of Mali

Kennedy, John F., President of the United States from January 20, 1961 until November 22, 1963

Kent, Sherman, Chairman, Board of National Estimates, Central Intelligence Agency

Kenyatta, Jomo, President of Kenya; Chairman of the Organization of African Unity Ad Hoc Commission on the Congo

Ketema, Yifru, Ethiopian Prime Minister from 1961

Kerchove, Charles de, Belgian Ambassador to the Congo (Léopoldville) from April 1962

Kimba, Évariste, Congolese Prime Minister from October 18, 1965 until November 14, 1965

Knight, Ridgeway B., Ambassador to Belgium, June 1965 until April 1969

Kohler, Foy D., Deputy Under Secretary of State for Political Affairs, November 1966 until December 1967

Komer, Robert W., member, National Security Council Staff until September 1965; Deputy Special Assistant to the President for National Security Affairs, September 1965 until March 1966; Special Assistant to the President, March 1966 until May 1967

Korry, Edward M., Ambassador to Ethiopia from April 20, 1963 until September 22, 1967

Landau, George W., Country Director for Spain and Portugal, Bureau of European Affairs, Department of State

Lang, William E., Deputy Assistant Secretary of Defense for International Security Affairs

Lefevre, Theodore, Belgian Prime Minister from 1961 until 1965

Lengema, Marcel, Congolese Ambassador at Large

Looram, Matthew J., Deputy Director, Office of Central African Affairs, Bureau of African Affairs, Department of State from April 1964 until September 1965; Deputy Director, Office of Northern African Affairs from October 1965 until May 1966; thereafter Country Director, Office of Northeast African Affairs

Lumumba, Patrice E., Congolese Prime Minister from June 24, 1960 until September 5, 1960, died January 1961

MacDonald, John W. Jr., Office of Research and Analysis for Africa, Bureau of Intelligence and Research, Department of State

McBride, Robert H., Ambassador to Zaire from June 1967 until May 1969

McCone, John A., Director of Central Intelligence from November 29, 1961 until April 28, 1965

McGhee, George C., Counselor of the Department of State and Chairman of the Policy Planning Council, from February until December 1961; Under Secretary of State for Political Affairs, from December 1961 until March 1963

McKillop, David H., Director, Office of Western European Affairs, Bureau of European Affairs, Department of State

McNaughton, John T., Assistant Secretary of Defense for International Security Affairs from July 1964 until June 1966

Meeker, Leonard C., Legal Adviser, Office of the Legal Adviser, Department of State

Merchant, Livingston T., Under Secretary of State for Political Affairs from December 1959 until January 31, 1961; Ambassador to Canada from March 15, 1961 until May 26, 1962

Miruho, Jean, President of Kivu Province from June 11, 1960 until December 24, 1960 and from September 18, 1961 until May 10, 1962

Mobutu, Joseph Désiré, Chief of Staff of the Congolese National Army; after January 23, 1961, Major General and Commander in Chief of Congolese Forces; President of the Republic of the Congo from November 25, 1965

Moffat, Jay P., Officer in Charge of Belgian and Luxembourg Affairs, Bureau of European Affairs, Department of State

Moyers, Bill, Special Assistant to the President, 1964–1967; Chief of Staff in the White House, October 1964–January 1967; White House Press Secretary, July 1965 until January 1967

Mpolo, Maurice, General, Lumumba associate, assassinated January 17, 1961

Mulamba, General Leonard, Congolese Prime Minister, from November 25, 1965 until October 26, 1966

Mulele, Pierre, leader of the Congolese Committee for National Liberation, President of Kwilu Province from January 1964 until November 1964

Munongo, Godefroid, Katangan Minister of the Interior

Murumbi, Joseph, Kenyan Minister of State; head of delegation to the United States of the OAU Ad Hoc Commission on the Congo

Nasser, Gamal A., President of the United Arab Republic

Ndele, Albert, Chairman of the Board of Commissioners-general from September 20, 1960 until October 3, 1960; Governor of the Central Bank of Congo from 1961; Congo Finance Commissioner

Nendaka, Victor, Head of Security Services, Republic of the Congo from 1960 until 1965; Minister of the Interior from October 1965 until November 1965; Minister of Transport and Communications, November 28, 1965; Minister of Finance and Budget from August 16, 1968

Neuman, Robert H., African Affairs, Office of the Legal Adviser, Department of State

Nitze, Paul R., Secretary of the Navy until June 1967; Deputy Secretary of Defense, July 1967 until January 1969

Nkrumah, Kwame, Prime Minister of Ghana until July 1960; President of Ghana from July 1, 1960 until February 24, 1966

Nogueira, Alberto Franco, Portuguese Foreign Minister from 1961 until 1969

Nothom, Patrick, Belgian Consul to Stanleyville

Obote, A. Milton, Ugandan Prime Minister, April 1963 until April 1966; President from April 1966

Okito, Joseph, Lumumba associate, assassinated January 17, 1961

Olenga, Nicholas, leader of the rebel forces that seized Stanleyville on August 5–6, 1964

Osorio-Tafall, Bibiano F., Officer in Charge of the U.N. Operations in the Congo from April until June 1964

O'Sullivan, James L., Director, Office of Central African Affairs, Bureau of African Affairs, Department of State, from April 1964 until August 1965

Palmer, Joseph, II, Ambassador to Nigeria from October 4, 1960 until January 16, 1964; Director General of the Foreign Service from February 16, 1964 until April 10, 1966; Member of the Congo Working Group, August 1964; Assistant Secretary of State for African Affairs from April 11, 1966 until July 7, 1969

Parrott, Thomas A., Secretary of the Special Group

Penfield, James K., Deputy Assistant Secretary of State for African Affairs from September 21, 1958; Ambassador to Iceland from May 24, 1961 until March 16 1967

Podgornov, Leonid, Soviet Chargé in Léopoldville

Pognon, Gratien, Assistant Secretary General of the Organization of African Unity

Raborn, Admiral William F., Director of Central Intelligence, April 1965 until June 1966

Read, Benjamin H., Special Assistant to the Secretary of State and Executive Secretary of the Department from August 4, 1963 until February 14, 1969

Rikhye, Brigadier General Indar Jit, Military Adviser to the U.N. Secretary-General

Roosevelt, Archibald B., Jr., Chief, Africa Division, Central Intelligence Agency

Ross, Claude G., Ambassador to the Central African Republic from September 16, 1963 until April 22, 1967

Rostow, Eugene V., Under Secretary of State for Political Affairs, from October 1966 until January 1969

Rostow, Walt W., Counselor of the Department of State and Chairman of the Policy Planning Council until March 1966; thereafter Special Assistant to the President

Rowan, Carl T., Director, United States Information Agency, February 1964 until July 1965

Runyon, Charles, III, Assistant Legal Adviser, African Affairs, Office of the Legal Adviser, Department of State

Rusk, Dean, Secretary of State, from January 21, 1961 until January 20, 1969

Russell, Richard B., Jr., Senator (D-Georgia) from January 12, 1933

Salans, Carl F., Deputy Legal Adviser, Office of the Legal Adviser, Department of State

Satterthwaite, Joseph C., Assistant Secretary of State for African Affairs until January 31, 1961; Ambassador to South Africa from May 22, 1961 until November 17, 1965

Saunders, Harold, member, National Security Council Staff

Schaufele, William E., Jr., Officer in Charge of Congo Affairs, Bureau of African Affairs, Department of State from June 1964 until September 1965; Deputy Director, Office of Central African Affairs, from October 1965 until May 1966; thereafter Country Director for West Central Africa

Sidikou, Abdou, Ambassador of Niger to the U.S., U.N. and Canada, 1962 until 1964; Foreign Minister from 1967

Sisco, Joseph J., Director, Office of United Nations Political and Security Affairs, Bureau of International Organization Affairs, Department of State from July 1961 until November 1963; Deputy Assistant Secretary of State for International Organization Affairs from 1964 until August 1965; thereafter Assistant Secretary of State for International Organization Affairs

Soumialot, Gaston E., Head of the provisional government of the People's Republic of the Congo (Stanleyville) from July 21, 1964 until September 7, 1964; President of the Supreme Council of the Congolese Revolution and Chairman of the Revolutionary Government from May 27, 1965 until August 6, 1965

Spaak, Paul-Henri, Belgian Prime Minister and Foreign Minister from April 1961 until 1965; Minister of Foreign Affairs and Coordination of External Policy, from 1965 until 1966

Stebbins, Henry E., Ambassador to Uganda from July 22, 1966 until September 2, 1969

Stoessel, Walter J., Jr., Deputy Assistant Secretary, Bureau of European Affairs, Department of State

Struelens, Michel, Tshombe's personal adviser on foreign affairs, political adviser to the Cogolese Missions to the United States and the United Nations

Strong, Curtis C., United Nations Adviser, Office of Inter-African Affairs, Bureau of African Affairs, Department of State, until 1964; Deputy Director, Office of Central African Affairs, November 1964 until October 1965; Deputy Director, Office of Eastern and Southern African Affairs, October 1965 until July 1966; Country Director for East African Affairs, July 1966 until June 1967

Tasca, Henry J., Deputy Assistant Secretary of State for African Affairs until May 1965; thereafter Ambassador to Morocco

Telli, Boubacar Diallo, Guinean Permanent Representative to the United Nations from September 1958 until June 1964; Ambassador to the United States from April 1959 until June 1961; Secretary-General of the Organization of African Unity from July 21, 1964

Thompson, Herbert B., Deputy Executive Secretary, Office of the Secretary, Department of State

Thompson, Llewellyn E., Career Ambassador from June 24, 1960; Ambassador-at-Large from October 3, 1962 until December 26, 1966

Timberlake, Clare H., Ambassador to the Congo from July 25, 1960 until June 15, 1961

Toure, Sekou, President of Guinea

Trimble, William C., Deputy Assistant Secretary of State for African Affairs, July 1965 until December 1967

Tshombe, Moi'se K., President of Katanga Province in the Republic of the Congo; Prime Minister from July 10, 1964 until October 13, 1965

Tsiranana, Philibert, President of Madagascar

Tubby, Roger W., Assistant Secretary of State for Public Affairs, from March 1961 until April 1962; Representative to the United Nations in Geneva, from October 1967 until September 1969

Tweedy, Bronson, Chief of the Africa Division, Directorate of Plans, Central Intelligence Agency

Tyler, William R., Assistant Secretary of State for European Affairs, from September 2, 1962 until May 18, 1965

Valenti, Jack J., Special Assistant to President Johnson, November 1963 until June 1966

Vance, Cyrus R., Secretary of the Army from July 5, 1962 until January 27, 1964; Deputy Secretary of Defense from January 28, 1964 until June 30, 1967

Van der Walle, Col. Frederick, Tshombe's military adviser and leader of the Belgian mercenary force in the Congo

Wadsworth, James J., Ambassador to the United Nations from September 8, 1960 until January 21, 1961

Wheeler, Earle G., General, USA; Chief of Staff, until July 1964; thereafter Chairman of the Joint Chiefs of Staff

Williams, G. Mennen "Soapy," Assistant Secretary of State for African Affairs from February 1, 1961 until March 23, 1966

Yost, Charles W., Ambassador to Morocco until March 1961; thereafter Deputy Representative to the U.N. Security Council and Representative to the U.N. General Assembly

Zorin, Valerian A., Deputy Soviet Foreign Minister; Permanent Representative at the United Nations from 1960 until 1962

Introduction

The drive for independence in the Belgian Congo began in earnest during the 1950s with the independence of neighboring territories and the formation of a number of Congolese political groups, including ABAKO, BALUBAKAT, and CONACAT. Most of these groups were based upon regional and/or tribal and cultural affiliation, but an exception to this was the Mouvement National Congolais (MNC), a national party whose leadership included Patrice Lumumba. All of these groups sought independence from Belgium, but they were divided over whether the new nation should form a central or federalist government. Belgium granted full independence on June 30, 1960, and set the stage for elections in May.

During the pre-independence period, the Eisenhower administration grew increasingly wary of the potential for Communist-bloc interference in the election process and the new government. The administration was particularly concerned about Lumumba, who it viewed as harboring pro-Communist sentiments. Since Lumumba enjoyed broad national support in the Congo, the administration feared he posed a potential threat to U.S. interests and goals in Sub-Saharan Africa. In response, the U.S. Government began to consider a political action program in March 1960, designed to support pro-Western candidates and marginalize Marxist groups.

Congo, 1960–1968

1. Editorial Note

Within 3 weeks of the day the Congo gained its independence on June 30, 1960, disorder and rioting broke out, Belgium flew in paratroopers to protect its citizens and protect order, and Katanga Province seceded. The new Congolese Prime Minister Patrice Lumumba, whom U.S. officials already believed was a dangerous, pro-Communist radical, turned to the Soviet Union for political support and military assistance, confirming the worst fears of U.S. policymakers. In August 1960, the U.S. Government launched a covert political program in the Congo lasting almost 7 years, initially aimed at eliminating Lumumba from power and replacing him with a more moderate, pro-Western leader. The U.S. Government provided advice and financial subsidies. At the same time, based on authorization from President Eisenhower's statements at an NSC meeting on August 18, 1960, discussions began to develop highly sensitive, tightly-held plans to assassinate Lumumba. After Lumumba's death at the hands of Congolese rivals in January 1961, the U.S. Government authorized the provision of paramilitary and air support to the new Congolese Government.

Operation Supporting Anti-Communist Congolese Politicians

Even before Congolese independence, the U.S. Government attempted to ensure election of a pro-Western government by identifying and supporting individual pro-U.S. leaders. During August 1960, reporting from the Station in Leopoldville warned Washington that unless Prime Minister Lumumba was stopped in the near future, he would become a strongman and establish a government under the influence of, or completely controlled by, Communists. Washington authorized limited funds for an operation in the Congo with the objective of replacing Lumumba with a pro-Western group. These funds were to be channeled in such a way as to conceal the U.S. Government as a source.

On September 14, 1960, Congolese Army Chief of Staff Joseph Mobutu carried out a virtual coup by establishing a College of Commissioners to administer the country on an interim basis. The Station provided the new government with covert funds as part of a general program of covert support, using the previously established, not attributable to the United States, channel. In addition, the covert program included organizing mass demonstrations, distributing anti-Communist pamphlets, and providing propaganda material for broadcasts.

The Special Group (later the 303 Committee), the high-level interdepartmental group set up to approve and supervise covert operations, made its first approval of major funding to strengthen Mobuto's de facto government, in order to prevent Lumumba from regaining control, on October 27, 1960. U.S. covert support continued during the series of political crises that followed.

After the Special Group's authorization in October 1960, a pattern evolved. One of the Congolese leaders urgently asked the Station for funds to avert an imminent crisis, such as the establishment by Lumumba supporters of a rival government in Stanleyville, an army mutiny, or a parliamentary defeat. Expenditure of at least some of the requested funds was almost always authorized. Periodically, the Special Group would meet and approve overall funding and direction of covert operations. On February 14, 1961, following a near mutiny of the Congolese army and police, the Special Group approved an even larger request to the Congolese Government through clandestine channels. President Kennedy's Special Assistant for National Security Affairs, McGeorge Bundy, reported to the Special Group on June 21, 1961, that the President had approved a CIA recommendation, with Department of State concurrence, for a substantial contingency fund. The fund was to be used for a covert political action program to help elect a pro-U.S. prime minister and government during the upcoming parliamentary session at the University of Lovanium scheduled to convene in late July. On August 2, 1961, the Congolese parliament approved a predominantly moderate government headed by Prime Minister Cyrille Adoula.

On November 22, 1961, the Special Group approved additional funding to strengthen the Adoula government as a moderate force and eventually build a new cohesive national political party. This carried the funding through fiscal year 1962 and averted two parliamentary crises: a proposed censure of then Foreign Minister Bomboko in June and a vote of no confidence in the government in late November.

In March 1963, the Embassy warned that terminating U.S. financial support would probably result in the fall of the government. Responding to the warning, the Special Group on April 25 approved funding for FY 1964 for continuation of the covert action program supporting the government. The Congolese were subsequently warned, however, that the United States would not continue the crash ad hoc funding it had provided in the past and wanted instead an organized program leading to formation of a national political party that would act as a political instrument in the forthcoming national elections. On November 6, 1963, the Station in Leopoldville submitted an additional budget to support establishment of a national political party. This was approved on November 8.

On June 1, 1964, a revised budget was approved for the project for FY 1964. Following former Katanga premier Moishe Tshombe's appointment as Prime Minister in July 1964 and the fall of Stanleyville to rebel forces in early August, the program continued to provide limited support to selected Congolese leaders. On June 30, 1966, the program was formally terminated on the recommendation of CIA and Department of State officials that it was no longer necessary to engage in large-scale political funding in the Congo. However, limited funding continued into 1968.

Lumumba Assassination Attempt

On August 27, 1960, Director of Central Intelligence Allen Dulles cabled the Leopoldville Station Chief that there was agreement in "high quarters" that Lumumba's removal must be an urgent and prime objective. CIA's Deputy Director for Plans, Richard Bissell, told a CIA scientist in late summer or early fall 1960 to have biological materials ready at short notice for the assassination of an unspecified African leader and that he (Bissell) had Presidential authorization for such an operation. In September 1960, the Chief of CIA's Africa Division, Bronson Tweedy, instructed the scientist to take the materials to the Congo and deliver instructions to the Station Chief to mount an operation if it could be done securely. The scientist traveled to Leopoldville, but Mobutu's coup on September 14 resulted in Lumumba becoming a de facto prisoner in the Prime Minister's residence guarded by U.N. forces who were in turn surrounded by Congolese troops. The scientist returned to the United States on October 5, but planning continued in Leopoldville to try to implement the assassination operation.

On October 15, Tweedy cabled the Station in Leopoldville that "disposition" of Lumumba remained the highest priority. It was subsequently reported that Lumumba was so closely guarded that he could not be approached. On November 27, 1960, Lumumba escaped but was recaptured by Mobutu's forces on December 1. On January 17, 1961, the Station reported that Lumumba had been removed from the Thysville military camp to Elizabethville in Katanga province and had been beaten. Between January 17 and February 7, Lumumba's fate was unknown, although there was widespread speculation that he was dead. On February 7, a Field Report informed Washington that Lumumba and his two companions had been executed on January 17 by Katangan soldiers and a Belgian officer.

Covert Support of the Congolese Air Force

In October 1962, the Congolese Government asked the United States to provide jet fighters, pilots, several transport aircraft, trucks and other military equipment to fight leftist rebels. It was subsequently authorized for the Congolese Government to contract for the services of pilots. On December 7, 1962, the Special Group approved a proposal to provide additional personnel and logistical support to the Congolese Air Force (CAF).

On April 24, 1964, President Johnson authorized the Department of Defense to provide the CAF with six T–28, ten C–47, and six H–21 aircraft, plus a 6-month supply of parts and ammunition. The Special Group approved a proposal on May 28, 1964, to provide covert support to the CAF for maintaining the six U.S.-provided T–28 aircraft and a minimal helicopter rescue capability, in addition to continued operation of the current six T–6 aircraft. The program was further expanded with 303 Committee approval on August 24, 1964, when rebellion throughout the eastern half of the Congo threatened the government's survival.

On October 28, 1965, the 303 Committee approved a request for continuation of covert support to the CAF at its current funding level. A memorandum for the 303 Committee, dated February 5, 1966, proposed continuing covert funding of the air program through CY 1966 at a reduced level, and on February 17, the 303 Committee reduced the air program again. At Deputy Director of Intelligence Helms' request, the Committee agreed to await the results of a Joint Chiefs of Staff study to determine the Congo's military needs. On July 19, 1966, the 303 Committee approved by telephone contingency air support if a coup were mounted against Mobutu.

On October 10, 1966, the 303 Committee was informed that a State-Defense-CIA working group had been established to draw up plans for the phase-out of the air program. The Committee agreed in early November that a turnover of the U.S.-operated Congolese Air Force to the host government should be effected with all convenient speed, with minimum sacrifice of efficiency and order. On March 3, 1967, a progress report warned that the pace of the phase-out had been delayed and might require underwriting beyond the original estimated date of June 30, 1967, on a month-to-month basis. On March 8, the 303 Committee directed that the project be liquidated as soon as possible.

A June 14 progress report alerted the 303 Committee to the problems arising from the Congolese Government's continued failure to meet its commitment to deposit funds in the account of a maintenance company originally set up under Congolese Government sponsorship to service Congolese aircraft. Finally on June 16, 1967, the Committee refused to authorize further support. The next month, however, a mutiny of white mercenaries and Katangan forces broke out and the 303 Committee directed that the project be extended to December 31, 1967. On November 22, the Committee approved a Department of State recommendation that the contracts of pilots hired on September 4 to fly for the Congolese Government also be extended to December 31. In May 1968, the project was terminated.

Political Action in Support of Tshombe and Maritime Interdiction Program

On August 13, 1964, the 303 Committee approved a proposal to provide covert financial aid and other support to be used periodically as needed for assuring tribal support of pro-Western Congolese leaders in critical areas and also to supplement the pay of white military technicians working for the Congolese Government. In early 1965, a capability was established to interdict supplies going to the Congolese rebels via Lake Albert and Lake Tanganyika, creating a "pocket navy" comprised of eight craft belonging to the Congolese Government and five U.S.-owned craft on Lake Tanganyika, which would be under general U.S. control.

Anticipating the cost of the programs for FY 1966, additional funds were requested to finance a greatly expanded maritime operation based in Albertville, to support selected tribal elements in the Northeast Congo, and to provide a contingency fund for use in preserving the existing political balance. On September 23, 1965, the 303 Committee approved the purchase and manning of six additional boats.

On October 7, 1965, the 303 Committee approved a reduced contingency fund, but on November 26 it approved a request for an expanded program. The emergence of Mobutu as head of a new regime was not deemed to eliminate the need for the program.

On February 5, 1966, the 303 Committee was requested to approve continued covert maritime operations in the Congo, as well as covert political funding. The last covert payment to Mobutu under this program was made in September 1966, and 303 Committee authority to make such payments expired on December 31, 1966. In compliance with a 303 Committee decision on November 4, 1966, to phase out U.S. Government participation in the maritime program, control of the boats was transferred to the Congolese on January 7, 1967. The project was terminated effective December 31, 1967.

The Special Group/303 Committee-approved aggregate budget for covert action in the Congo for the years 1960–1968 totaled approximately $11,702,000 (Political Action, $5,842,000; Air Program, $3,285,000; and Maritime Program, $2,575,000).

2. Editorial Note

In telegram 20521 to Leopoldville, March 21, 1960, the Central Intelligence Agency requested the Chief of Station's views on supporting selected Congolese figures during the pre-independence period. It was important, the Agency believed, to "get as many lines as possible into present and prospective leaders so that we not left on outside looking in while BLOC, ACOA, and others operate at will" without any CIA attempt to "establish covert counter influences." The Chief of Station responded in telegram 518, March 25, that he agreed that the United States should keep the door open but he considered support of the Lumumba wing of the Mouvement National Congolais (MNC) a poor risk in terms of eventual benefits to the United States or the West in general. (Central Intelligence Agency Files, [*text not declassified*], Volume 1)

3. Memorandum From the Chief of the Africa Division, Directorate of Plans, Central Intelligence Agency (Tweedy) to the Deputy Director for Plans, Central Intelligence Agency (Bissell)[1]

Washington, April 1, 1960.

SUBJECT

Request for Assistance in Congo Elections

1. At the request of Jim Penfield we went over to see State at 10:30 a.m. Present were Assistant Secretary Satterthwaite, Deputy Assistant Secretary Penfield, Director Office of Middle and South African Affairs Ferguson.

2. The topic presented is fairly completely covered in our outgoing cable.[2]

3. Satterthwaite said that he had replied to his callers that he would inquire in one or two places as to what could be done. Ferguson said that in an earlier conversation Dhanis[3] had asked whether or not the

---

[1] Source: Central Intelligence Agency Files, Job 64–00352R, DDO/ISS Files, Box 1, Folder 7, AF Division, 1960. Confidential.

[2] Not found.

[3] Baron Dhanis, Belgian Congo Affairs Counselor at the Belgian Embassy in Washington.

Agency could not assist. Our hand clearly would show as far as they are concerned.

4. On the point as to why Belgian financial interests, with much obviously at stake, were not in the fray, Ferguson thought that this was in part a good example of Belgian thrift in getting the other fellow to do it and that the Union Miniere was probably already supporting the Conakat. The Conakat is a regional party consisting of Africans and Europeans who stand for separatism for the Katanga. It has been under the domination of the Union Miniere.

5. Our feeling is that there is so much at stake in preventing the placing of Lumumba in a prominent role, especially becoming the Minister of the Interior (he has already taken over Justice and the Surete) that although we admittedly do not have great resources we should make every effort possible.[4]

B Tweedy
Chief, Africa Division

---

[4] A handwritten notation by Tweedy at the bottom of the memorandum reads: "P.S. Irrespective of any Belgian financial support, it is most important that some CS money and influence get in there quick! BT."

---

4. Memorandum From the Chief of the Africa Division, Directorate of Plans, Central Intelligence Agency (Tweedy) to the Assistant Secretary of State for African Affairs (Satterthwaite)[1]

Washington, April 18, 1960.

SUBJECT

Political Action Operations in the Belgian Congo

Quoted below as received from Brussels and Leopoldville via [CIA] channels are joint [State/CIA] statements on the Belgian Congo political situation.

---

[1] Source: Central Intelligence Agency Files, Job 76–00366R, DDO/ISS Files, Box 1, Folder 7, Congo, 1960–1969, Part 1. Secret. This memorandum was sent via back-channel. For this volume, where possible, the editors have used bracketed insertions to indicate names, titles, or agencies in place of cryptonyms that are not declassified.

a. Brussels

We believe that it is unwise to undertake a major political action program in the pre-election period. The political situation in the Congo is highly fluid. We are new on the Congo political scene and, with few exceptions, do not have sufficient information on which to base a judgment on who will win or who merits support. However, we are not opposed to giving discreet support (provided it is not attributable to the United States Government) to a limited number of candidates if specific justification is provided in each case. In view of the delicacy of the situation and paucity of good information, we believe it is essential that the [CIA] representative consult with the senior [State] representative in Leopoldville on specific cases.

Our view is that pre-election emphasis should be on establishing access to and infiltration of various political groups by both normal political officer contact and [*less than 1 line not declassified*] key militants. The information obtained from both these activities is a necessary basis for planning a sound investment in a limited number of key political leaders.

We are opposed to any "stop Lumumba" campaign. He is one of the few, if not only, Congolese leaders with a Congo-wide appeal and standing. We feel it is almost certain that he will play an important political role in the Congo for at least the next two years. Thus, an anti-Lumumba campaign could backfire. Although we consider him unscrupulous and willing to accept aid from anyone if it would help him, we suggest the possibility of limited funding to Lumumba along with other selected leaders. This would provide relatively more help to other leaders but would also keep the door open for future Lumumba contacts and perhaps avoid alienating him if he learns of our support to other leaders.

[*3 names not declassified*] seem more attractive than many other leaders because their newspaper and trade union ties give them some assurance of a continued role in Congo affairs if they fail as political candidates. Also, [*name not declassified*] may offer a line to [*name not declassified*]. We suggest that consideration also be given to possible assistance to [*1 line not declassified*] who is fighting against the communist sympathizers, [*1 line not declassified*] approached the Brussels senior [State] representative in Bukavu and made a good impression. If the [CIA] representative in Leopoldville agrees, this would seem a particularly good case where a small investment could pay real returns in weakening an existing communist beachhead in East Congo.

Whether or not it is decided to mount political operations, it is strongly recommended that Washington tell the Belgian Embassy that we do not intend to intervene in the Congolese elections. As a matter of interest, the [State] establishment in Brussels considers[2] [*less than 1 line not declassified*].

b. Leopoldville

Whatever action we might undertake, now or at a later date, in the internal politics of the Congo, we should exercise extreme caution in dealing with either [*less than 1 line not declassified*] has always shown certain suspicions regarding our motives and even recently cautioned Ngalula, during the latter's stay in Washington, not to be taken in by the blandishments of U.S. officials (see [State] despatch [illegible], 23 March).[3] In addition, [*name not declassified*] has often tried to minimize to [State] the problems in the Congo. For example, the Belgian Embassy's statement following the January 1959 riots said that they were of little significance. Based on our contacts, we likewise do not believe [illegible] suitable for participation in such negotiations.

The present political situation in the Congo is so fluid that we would be running great risks were we to enter the arena now. At present, there is no single political leader or party which has a majority. After forthcoming elections, it is almost inevitable that cartels and new political groups will be formed for the purpose of obtaining power and planting their own men in key positions.

Since mid-March, there has been growing opposition to Lumumba among the Congolese themselves. They have already set the machinery in motion to stop Lumumba, and they themselves may be able to accomplish this. (See [State] telegram 271 to Washington, 139 to Brussels.)[4]

Pending present fast breaking developments (Joseph Kasavubu's swing around the Congo, the Congolese of the MNC, Lumumba wing, now being held in [illegible—Lulabourg?] we should now reserve our position regarding assistance to certain candidates for limited purposes. In this connection, we shall continue to follow closely the general developments and activities of promising candidates.

[*pseudonym not declassified*][5]

---

[2] Counselor for Congo Affairs at the Belgian Embassy in Washington. [Footnote in the original.]

[3] Not found.

[4] Not found.

[5] Printed from a copy bearing Tweedy's typed pseudonym.

5. Paper Prepared in the Central Intelligence Agency[1]

Washington, undated.

CIA POSITION IN BELGIAN CONGO RE POLITICAL ACTION OPERATIONS

I Objectives

A. The role of KUBARK in the Belgian Congo during the period prior to 30 June 1960, should be to ensure that U.S. aims for the area, both the Congo and the other parts of the continent whose relationship with the Congo will affect our aims, can be implemented. These aims are as follows:

1. The election of a government oriented to the West, friendly to the United States, devoted to ideals which may best guarantee stability and order.

2. The identification, isolation and exclusion of bloc-supported, bloc-oriented and Marxist groups.

B. For the accomplishment of these aims, KUBARK must address itself to a number of goals as follows:

1. The tendency in the Congo is for political groupings to develop on the basis of tribal connections. This has led to an extraordinary fractionalization which, should it continue, can be depended upon to hinder the development of a politically unified state which could provide a secure base for the economic development upon which economic stability depends. In this connection it would seem obvious to support a movement which could cut across tribal lines and which would draw its strength from a wide geographic base. [*6½ lines not declassified*]

2. No one leader has shown himself to be a disinterested statesman. Each of the many party and party-fraction leaders has been utilizing his tribal associations and followers for the purpose of self-aggrandizement. No one seems to have evolved a political platform on the basis of ideology; the only theme with any appeal on a national basis has been that of independence and, since independence is a fore-gone conclusion, there remains only an attempt to identify oneself with its attainment. Although some will have more success than others, it is inevitable that each ethno-political entity will be represented in the government-to-be. Our goal in this connection is to be able to deal with

[1] Source: Central Intelligence Agency Files, Job 64–00352R, DDO/ISS Files, Box 1, Folder 7, AF Division, 1960. Secret. A stamped note indicates that the paper was a DD/P document.

and influence as many as possible of these groups. Our task will be to identify individual leaders whose policies most nearly coincide with ours and offer them some support. We should also attempt to identify other leaders whose views may *not* coincide with ours who are fairly sure of some success in the forthcoming elections. Although we may not support them to the same degree, we should avoid any action which will make enemies of them and take some insurance for future shifts in political power. We should realize that in most cases the political leaders of the Congo today have not matured ideologically. Most have shown themselves willing to take help from any quarter and many have been amenable to bloc blandishments and aid. In our view this should not be interpreted to mean that the bloc-supported groups have committed themselves ideologically either to the East or to communism. Rather than consider these groups as targets for attack, we should prefer to attack, where possible, the bloc sources which are attempting to subvert them.[2]

[Omitted here is further discussion on the situation in the Belgian Congo.]

[2] In CIA telegram 27945 to Leopoldville, May 4, the CIA instructed the Station to develop the widest possible spectrum of contacts and friends and to cultivate people close to the top in all parties who might become important. Given the short time involved, it was unlikely that this could appreciably affect the elections, but it was important to try to create goodwill and means of access during the period of formation of the new government and afterwards. (Ibid., [*text not declassified*], Volume 2)

6. Editorial Note

At a meeting of the National Security Council's 5412 Committee on June 30, 1960, Deputy Director of Central Intelligence Cable made the following comments on the Congo, according to a memorandum for the record prepared the same day:

> Gen. Cabell mentioned briefly the fact of the election of Joseph Ileo to the Presidency of the Congo Senate, [*text not declassified*]. He indicated that we in no way intend to claim full credit for this election but, particularly in view of the very close contest, we might have had some effect; and in any case we may have secured some influence with this potentially useful individual. (National Security Council, Intelligence Files, NSC 5412/2 Special Group, Minutes & Agendas, 1960)

In Dispatch [*text not declassified*] from Leopoldville to the Central Intelligence Agency, July 1, 1960, the Chief of Station wrote that although Lumumba forces had gained a 74 to 58 majority in the election for President of the Chamber of Representatives and thereby had wrested from Joseph Kasavubu the authorization to form a government, the margin had narrowly tilted the other way (41–30 on the third ballot) in the Senate, with [*text not declassified*] Joseph Ileo becoming President of that body. This meant that Patrice Lumumba had not been able to put his own man in as Chief of State, since a two-thirds majority in both houses in joint session was required. Lumumba ultimately supported Joseph Kasavubu. The Chief of Station warned, however, that as Chief of State, Kasavubu posed a continuing threat which Lumumba, "aiming at a dictatorship," could not long tolerate. (Central Intelligence Agency Files, Job 82–00450R, Box 6, Folder 6, Leopoldville, 3 Feb 54–Dec 65, [*cryptonym not declassified*])

---

7. National Security Council Briefing[1]

Washington, July 25, 1960.

REPUBLIC OF THE CONGO

I. Situation within the Congo has apparently eased somewhat in past few days.

A. Half of eventual 12,000-man United Nations Force now on scene are restoring order almost without incident.

B. Belgian Forces, responding to last week's Security Council resolution, pulled back on Saturday to two Congo bases (except in Katanga Province where nearly 2,000 Belgian troops helping keep order).

C. Work progressing toward restoring port facilities at Matadi, dredging Congo river, and restoring vital fuel pipelines.

D. Katanga Premier Moise Tshombe, having failed in secessionist move to obtain recognition as independent state, now proposes loose federation of autonomous states composed of Katanga and five other Congo provinces.

II. Serious problems remain and require prompt action, however.

A. Foremost among these is status of Belgian bases. Agreement of 29 June 1960 (which not yet ratified) granted Belgium two bases at Kamina and Kitona.

---

[1] Source: Central Intelligence Agency Files, Job 79R00890A, Box 13, Folder 1, NSC Briefings, July 1960. Top Secret; [*codeword not declassified*].

1. But Lumumba stated to the press in London on Saturday that: "It is inconceivable that foreign bases should exist in a sovereign state."

B. Katanga Province where Premier Tshombe—apparently egged on by some Belgian groups—opposes strongly unitary state is most important to new Congo state.

1. Landlocked Katanga is richest of Congo's six provinces and adjoins Copperbelt of Northern Rhodesia to the south.
2. Katanga supplies two-thirds of total value of Congo's mineral production—all Congo's copper (7% of world production), cobalt (60% world production), manganese, zinc, cadmium, germanium and uranium. Agricultural resources, however, are poor.
3. Katanga's wealth essential to creation of viable Congo state.
4. Congo's leaders have unanimous support of increasingly vocal African bloc in opposing dismemberment of Congo.

C. Faced with loss of Belgian technicians, Congo in dire need of administrative and economic cadres.

1. UN representative Bunche has approached Morocco and Tunisia—seriously shorthanded in capable administrators themselves—and possibly other African governments for administrators.
2. Congo leaders may resist assignment of "white technicians"; probably will be influenced by other African leaders such as Ghana's President Nkrumah who, although he retains British advisors and technicians, recently declared "our campaign is to drive out the white people from Africa."
3. Inexperienced Congo leaders are "ripe to be taken to the cleaners by the first carpetbagger," according to locally stationed American official.

E. Unemployment and food shortages create immediate problems, may produce some serious localized situations until employment is obtained and distribution problems can be solved.

III. Mercurial Premier Patrice Lumumba is major negative factor in present Congo situation.

A. Described both as "crazy" (by Ralph Bunche) and paranoic. Congo's advance mission to the UN informed African group of Lumumba's "particularly violent character."

B. [*less than 1 line not declassified*] reported that Lumumba planned to visit USSR immediately after conclusion of his 10-day visit to US and Canada.

C. Despite Lumumba's withdrawal of his threat to request Soviet intervention and his remarks concerning his desire for Western assistance, Congo's position appears to be moving toward Soviet-oriented neutralism.

IV. The USSR may have become concerned over Lumumba's appeals for Soviet military support.

A. After proposing a three-day ultimatum from the UN to Brussels, the Soviet delegation supported the moderate Tunisian-Ceylonese resolution in the UN Security Council, probably to avoid becoming isolated from the Afro-Asian position.

B. The hasty dispatch of a small party of Soviet officials to Leopoldville on 21 July suggests that the USSR is anxious to be in a position to coordinate further moves as well as to put some limitation on further Congolese initiatives which would directly involve the USSR.

1. The USSR has also made urgent efforts to establish direct communications facilities between Moscow and Leopoldville.

C. Five Soviet IL–18 transport aircraft have carried Ghanian troops to Leopoldville for the UN force and are also transporting supplies.

---

8. Telegram From the Station in the Congo to the Central Intelligence Agency[1]

Leopoldville, August 11, 1960.

0731 (In 36351). Ref Dir 44012 (Out 55588):[2]

1. Although Congo political situation chaotic and it difficult predict eventual outcome, Embassy and Station believe Lumumba moving left and Commie influence increasing. Unless he stopped near future, believe he will become strongman, eliminating moderate opposition and establishing regime under influence if not fully controlled by Commies. Thus believe fall Lumumba would assist Western objectives.

2. Lumumba faced by mounting but apparently uncoordinated and disorganized opposition in parliament and streets. Opposition appears based on tribal jealousies, fear that Lumumba plans play strongman role eliminating opposition leaders and belief held by many Congolese that he pro-Communist or under Communist control. How-

---

[1] Source: Central Intelligence Agency Files, Job 78–00435R, DDO/ISS Files, Box 1, Folder 3, [*cryptonym not declassified*] Ops. Secret; Rybat; [*cryptonym not declassified*]; Priority. Received at 1737Z. The identity designation for a specific individual is valid for a single document only and is not consistent throughout the volume.

[2] Requested specific suggested plan which might oust Lumumba. [Footnote in the original.] This CIA telegram has not been found.

ever tribal and personal jealousies and lack political acumen opposition leaders preventing concerted action and organized effort defeat govt in parliament. Per Embtel sent Wash 359[3] (anti-Lumumba forces endeavoring embarrass govt and even considering coup d'etat or assassination. Station counseling [Identity 1] and other contacts adhere legal means ousting Lumumba. Urging them to coordinate efforts and obtain sufficient votes topple govt in senate.

Reminding [Identity 1] and others that if they act prematurely it will give Lumumba opening to move against opposition, perhaps arresting leaders and or attempting eliminate senate. Also illegal overthrow would force hand United Nations.

3. Most opposition groups favor some form confederation in place present federal system. This development appears stem from fear of Lumumba and tribal loyalties. View this situation we forced go along with confederation approach if wish work against Lumumba. However, decentralization has many disadvantages such as opening way for Soviets to penetrate one govt at a time, possibility of paramilitary and subversive ops directed against other provinces from Lumumba controlled orientale, possibility of increased anarchy (if this be possible) resulting from division responsibilities which would open way for Communist penetration. Many problems would merely be transferred from Leop to provincial capitals where it would be more difficult for KUBARK and ODYOKE to follow them.

4. View situation Station recommends following steps which coordinated with Ambassador[4] be taken shore up Western position Congo:

A. Use all Embassy and KUBARK contacts particularly [Identity 1] to influence senate to act as balance wheel to Lumumba, Gizenga and other who appear favor bloc. This respect senate would take position against bloc intervention or other acts inimical Western position.

B. Launch extensive [*less than 1 line not declassified*] campaign ([*less than 1 line not declassified*] meetings) by assisting local political groups with the funds and guidance to take anti Commie line and oppose Lumumba.

C. Expand political action operations seeking out and recruiting additional political leaders with view to influencing opposition activities. Would try avoid premature action and organize efforts to mount a no confidence vote in one or both houses of parliament. Presently believe senate offers best chance win such vote. Immediate goal would be replace present govt with more moderate coalition headed by [Identity

---

[3] OCR/CB notified of reference. [Footnote in the original.] This CIA telegram has not been found.

[4] A handwritten notation on the original reads: "have been/when?"

1]. He appears be only opposition leader with hope of rallying opposition groups.

D. Attempt infiltrate govt with KUBARK controlled assets such as [*name not declassified*] to obtain political intel and try limit influence Commies and incompetent Congolese officials, many of whom fail realize gravity situation and do not understand steps taken by them leading Congo to chaos and opening way for future Commie takeover.

E. Bring about call constituent assembly once opposition organized with view writing constitution acceptable majority on basis desires and Congo mores.

F. Cultivate and attempt recruit members current govt to keep foot in Lumumba camp. Although believe would be better oust him, do not want become tied irrevocably to opposition, if it not able achieve goals. Also would use such assets to try moderate Lumumba govt and obtain political intel.

5. Recognize above campaign involves large expenditures and offers no guarantee success. Even if campaign successful our work only beginning as political and economic chaos will continue forseeable future. Also wish stress Lumumba and company well organized, opposition disorganized, Station faced with problem finding, developing and recruiting [*less than 1 line not declassified*] and political action assets, few if any of opposition appear understand parliamentary methods needed change govt. However, all Station efforts concentrated this campaign on crash basis as political pot may boil over any time and action necessary now.

[Omitted here is further discussion of the proposal.]

9. Telegram From the Central Intelligence Agency to the Station in the Congo[1]

Washington, August 12, 1960, 2147Z.

Dir 44972 (Out 57496). Ref: Leop 0731 (In 36351).[2]

1. Discussed ref with heads State African bureau 12 Aug. Prelim discussion naturally largely centered around whether ODYOKE policy should be removal Lumumba from power. State reps, while fully concurring in assessment Lumumba as continuing threat to Western and UN purposes and increasingly susceptible Commie line and tactics, felt his removal might breed more problems than would solve and specifically referred to estimate para three ref re confederation which would run counter to ODYOKE hope of UN-assisted Congo and particularly be opposed by other African states. Your own estimate disadvantages also noted. We also agreed constitutional overthrow Lumumba and preservation unified Congo likely very difficult view lack politicians in opposition Lumumba who can match him in force and appeal. State reps also recognized full rejection your tentative recommendations could result in do-nothing policy which equally unacceptable. State will cable Amb asking additional questions and meanwhile following conclusions reached for your temporary guidance:

A. Concur KUBARK Embassy should not advocate illegal overthrow Lumumba.

B. Concur your continuing efforts along lines para 4 A, B, D, F ref, but main emphasis should be countering Commie line and request anti-Lumumba aspects be underplayed and more implied than specific.

C. Continue give counsel, when asked, re constitutional means available to Lumumba opponents but in such way does not appear this main ODYOKE objective in life.

D. Continually assess and report on likelihood constitutional overthrow coming off and this connection request your best statistical estimate Lumumba and opposition strength in assembly. In addition would like what facts you possess re strength of Lumumba's control of force publique, police or similar paramilitary force. What are these numbers?

---

[1] Source: Central Intelligence Agency Files, Job 78–00435R, DDO/ISS Files, Box 1, Folder 3, [*cryptonym not declassified*] Ops. Secret; Rybat; Priority. Drafted by Bronson Tweedy (C/AF); authenticated by [*name not declassified*] (for Chief/AF); and released by Richard Helms (COP).

[2] The Embassy and the Station believed that Lumumba was moving to the left and that Communist influence was increasing. The Station and the Embassy were of the opinion that the fall of Lumumba would assist Western objectives. [Footnote in the original.] This telegram is printed as Document 8.

2. Realize above is not clear-cut reply but HQ concurs with State final decision still not easy to reach and believes above still leaves you considerable op latitude.

[Omitted here is further discussion of the proposal.]

---

10. Editorial Note

In telegram 0772 to the Central Intelligence Agency, August 18, 1960, the Station in Leopoldville reported the following: "Embassy and Station believe Congo experiencing classic Communist effort take over government. Many forces at work here: Soviets, Czechs, Guineans, Ghanians, Communist Party, etc. Although difficult determine major influencing factors to predict outcome struggle for power, decisive period not far off. Whether or not Lumumba actually Commie or just playing Commie game to assist his solidifying power, anti-West forces rapidly increasing power Congo and there may be little time left in which take action to avoid another Cuba or Guinea." The telegram then outlined a proposal to assist a Congolese effort to organize opposition to Prime Minister Patrice Lumumba with the aim of replacing him with a more moderate and pro-Western government. In addition to propaganda efforts and coordinating the activities of youth groups and trade unions, [*text not declassified*]. The Station emphasized that the plan would go forward whether or not the United States supported it, but without U.S. money and advice it might well fall short of its goal and be shattered by Lumumba's police state response. (Central Intelligence Agency Files, Job 78–00435R, DDO/ISS Files, Box 1, Folder 3, [*cryptonym not declassified*] Ops) In a follow-up telegram, the Station reported that it had discussed the plan in general terms with Ambassador Timberlake, who had expressed his approval. (Telegram 0775, August 18; ibid.)

In telegram 46115, August 19, the CIA authorized the Station to proceed with the operation proposed in telegram 0772 provided the Ambassador still agreed. The Ambassador was also to be told that CIA was informing the Department of State of its authorization and would make every effort to get final policy clearance to continue the operation provided the initial steps proved fruitful. The Station responded in telegram 0782, August 24, that the operation had been discussed again with the Ambassador, who concurred. (Ibid.)

11. Editorial Note

On August 18, 1960, the National Security Council discussed Congolese Prime Minister Lumumba's threats to force the United Nations out of the Congo. Saying that this would be a disaster the United States should do everything it could to prevent, Under Secretary of State Douglas Dillon warned that the Soviet Union might be invited to intervene in the Congo after the United Nations was forced out. Director of Central Intelligence Allen Dulles noted that Lumumba was in Soviet pay. President Eisenhower said that the possibility that the United Nations would be forced out was simply inconceivable, and declared that the United States should keep the United Nations in the Congo, even if it had to ask for European troops or if such action was used by the Soviets to start a fight. Dillon said that the Department of State agreed, but noted that both Secretary General Hammarskjold and Ambassador Lodge doubted whether the United Nations could stay if the Congolese Government were opposed. For a full record of the NSC discussion of the Congo, see *Foreign Relations,* 1958–1960, volume XIV, Africa, Document 180.

On June 18, 1975, former NSC staff member Robert H. Johnson testified before the Church Committee that during an NSC meeting in the summer of 1960 President Eisenhower said something that came across to him as an order for the assassination of Lumumba, following which there was no discussion. Johnson testified that, although he could no longer remember the exact words, he remembered clearly that this came as a "great shock" to him. Presumably the meeting referred to was that of August 18, as there were only two NSC meetings that summer—August 18 and September 7—attended by both the President and Johnson, and the notes of the September 7 meeting have no record of any Presidential comment about the Congo. Dillon and NSC Acting Executive Secretary Marion Boggs testified that they had no memory of any clearcut order from the President for the assassination of Lumumba, although Dillon agreed that it was "perfectly possible" that Allen Dulles might have translated strong Presidential language about "getting rid of" Lumumba into authorization for an assassination attempt. See *Interim Report,* pages 55–60, for a record of the Church Committee's investigation of whether the subsequent CIA plot to assassinate Lumumba was authorized by the President. In August 2000, the National Archives released a memorandum recording a June 10, 1975, conversation between Johnson and the director of the Church Committee concerning the August 18, 1960, NSC meeting. In this memorandum, Johnson recalled Eisenhower turning to CIA Director Allen Dulles "in the full hearing of all those in attendance and saying something to the effect that Lumumba should be eliminated." After that "there was a stunned silence for about 15 seconds and the meeting continued." (National Archives, Testimony of Robert H. Johnson, June 18, 1975; Folder 10-H-02, Box 44, Hearings, RG 46 Records of the United States Senate, Church Committee Records on JFK Assassination; President John F. Kennedy Assassination)

---

12. Memorandum for the Record[1]

Washington, August 25, 1960.

SUBJECT

Minutes of Special Group Meeting, 25 August 1960

PRESENT

Messrs. Merchant, Gray, Irwin, Dulles

1. Congo

Mr. Parrott outlined broadly three (or as Mr. Dulles later described them "2½") operational lines that we are following in mounting an anti-Lumumba campaign in the Congo. These included: operations through the [*less than 1 line not declassified*] Christian Trade Unions; the planned attempt of a [*less than 1 line not declassified*] Senator to arrange a vote of no confidence in Lumumba; and a brand new contact with [*less than 1 line not declassified*] of certain independent labor groups. He emphasized that the latter had just come up and that we are now in the process of assessing the bona fides and capabilities of the individual.

The Group agreed that the action contemplated is very much in order. Mr. Gray commented, however, that his associates had expressed extremely strong feelings on the necessity for very straightforward action in this situation, and he wondered whether the plans as outlined were sufficient to accomplish this. Mr. Dulles replied that he had taken the comments referred to seriously and had every intention of proceeding as vigorously as the situation permits or requires, but added that he must necessarily put himself in a position of interpreting instructions of this kind within the bounds of necessity and capability. It was finally agreed that planning for the Congo would not necessarily

---

[1] Source: National Security Council, Intelligence Files, NSC 5412/2 Special Group, Minutes and Agendas, 1960. Secret; Eyes Only.

rule out "consideration" of any particular kind of activity which might contribute to getting rid of Lumumba.

Mr. Irwin commented that certain individuals in Defense have given thought to the possibility of using high officials [*less than 1 line not declassified*] to promote the general objectives of the West. In this connection, he cited a preliminary assessment which had been made of [*less than 1 line not declassified*]—the assessment being that the individual in question is a man of not outstanding intelligence, ability or drive, but that he is obviously well motivated. Mr. Irwin asked whether there might be other individuals of similar, although naturally lesser, stature [*less than 1 line not declassified*] who could be useful.

Mr. Merchant commented that [*less than 1 line not declassified*] in Black Africa is not a very substantial force. Mr. Dulles concurred in this, but added that this would be something to keep in mind as appropriate.

[Omitted here is discussion of unrelated subjects.]

---

13. Editorial Note

In telegram 0806 from Leopoldville to the Central Intelligence Agency, August 25, 1960, the Station reported that President Kasavubu had been approached at the time of the Force Publique mutiny by anti-Lumumba leaders with a plan to assassinate Lumumba. Kasavubu had refused, saying that he was reluctant to resort to violence and that there was no other leader with sufficient stature to replace Lumumba. However, in telegram 0844 to the Central Intelligence Agency, August 30, the Station reported that it had learned indirectly [*text not declassified*] that Kasavubu had agreed to support a legal move in the Senate to oust Lumumba. Kasavubu said that he "feels Lumumba too far out of line and must go" and he "must have replacement govt ready when Senate topples L[umumba]"; he planned to name Adoula premier of the new government. (Central Intelligence Agency Files, Job 78–00435R, DDO/ISS Files, Box 1, Folder 3, [*cryptonym not declassified*] Ops)

The Station also reported that it had prepared a proposed implementation program, including parliamentary moves, plans to avoid police or army intervention, and propaganda-type activities for [*name not declassified*] consideration as he planned to take over the government. But [*name not declassified*] wanted to act immediately "as political pressure building up and wants take advantage anti-Lumumba feeling. Also afraid K[asavubu] might weaken and withdraw offer support opposition. Station torn between desire implement detailed program leaving little as possible to chance and need strike when iron hot." The Station noted that the Ambassador had been fully briefed. (Ibid.) In telegram 48153 to Leopoldville, August 31, the CIA responded that the situation was such that the Station should support [*text not declassified*] fast action. (Ibid.)

---

14. Telegram From the Central Intelligence Agency to the Station in the Congo[1]

Washington, August 27, 1960.

Dir 47587 (Out 62966).

1. In high quarters here it is the clear-cut conclusion that if [garble—Lumumba?] continues to hold high office, the inevitable result will at best be chaos and at worst pave the way to Communist takeover of the Congo with disastrous consequences for the prestige of UN and for the interests of the free world generally. Consequently we conclude that his removal must be an urgent and prime objective and that under existing conditions this should be a high priority of our covert action.[2]

2. Hence we wish to give you wider authority along lines Leop 0772[3] and Leop 0785[4] and Dir 46115[5] including even more aggressive action if it can remain covert. We realize that targets of opportunity may present themselves to you and in addition to sums heretofore authorized, we further authorize expenditure up to a total of [*dollar amount not declassified*] to carry out any crash programs on which you do not have the opportunity to consult HQS. Advise your cash needs.

3. To the extent that Ambassador may desire to be consulted you should seek his concurrence. If in any particular case he does not wish

---

[1] Source: Central Intelligence Agency Files, Job 79–00149A, DDO/IMS Files, Box 23, Folder 1, African Division, Senate Select Committee, Volume II. Secret; Rybat; Priority. For COS from Ascham. Drafted by Director of Central Intelligence Allen W. Dulles. A typed notation on the telegram instructed the Cable Secretariat to "limit distribution to Mr. Helms."

[2] This paragraph is printed in *Interim Report*, p. 15.

[3] See Document 10.

[4] Telegram 0785 from Leopoldville to CIA, August 22. (Central Intelligence Agency Files, Job 78–00435R, DDO/ISS Files, Box 1, Folder 3, [*cryptonym not declassified*] Ops)

[5] See Document 10.

to be consulted you can act on your own authority where time does not permit referral here.

4. This message has been seen and approved at competent level ODACID.

End of message.

---

15. Telegram From the Station in the Congo to the Central Intelligence Agency[1]

Leopoldville, September 5, 1960.

0888 (In 48185). Ref: Leop 0858 (In 46633).[2]

1. Following joint KUBARK ODACID message. Eyes only for Ascham and for transmittal to chief ODACID.

2. An unimpeachable source (identity) advised [Embassy] that Kasavubu plans to oust Lumumba and name Joseph Ileo premier. As soon as this step taken, he plans to broadcast a message to Congolese people from Radio Congo requesting them to remain calm and accept the new government. Presumably he also will explain his reasons for ousting Lumumba. Concurrently, Kasavubu will order the Force Publique lay down its arms and place itself under the order of the UN.

3. Kasavubu plan includes following steps:

A. For the UN Operation Congo (UNOC) to guarantee his personal safety with UN troops.
B. Request UNOC to guard the radio station, thus guaranteeing his personal safety when he speaks and insuring that Lumumba forces will not be able take control of the radio and mount a propaganda campaign in support of Lumumba.
C. Airports Congo would be closed to all departures.

4. Kasavubu's plan has been coordinated with UNOC at highest levels here. He already has taken the first step, to demand protection by UN troops. The rest of the plan was to be implemented 5 September but timing may well be changed.

---

[1] Source: Central Intelligence Agency Files, Job 78–00435R, DDO/ISS Files, Box 1, Folder 3, [*cryptonym not declassified*] Ops. Secret; Rybat; [*cryptonym not declassified*]; Emergency. Received at 2357Z.

[2] Reported the content of a meeting between Mobutu and [*name not declassified*] on 31 August. [Footnote in the original.] This CIA telegram has not been found.

5. Lumumba suddenly left for Stanleyville 5 September. Not known whether his departure motivated by knowledge plan and desire escape Leopoldville and possible arrest. If so, it entirely possible he plans take position in area where his popularity is greatest to resist overthrow and attempt regain control of Congo. If lost, using troops in Orientale, Equateur and, possibly, Kasai provinces.

6. If he unaware plan, quite possible he intends carry out attack on Katanga, using troops just brought from northern Orientale to Stanleyville and Soviet planes now there or arriving, which he promised during visit last week.

7. Utmost importance this be given maximum protection.[3]

End of message.

---

[3] On September 5, President Kasavubu announced (on the radio) that he was dismissing Lumumba and appointing Ileo as Prime Minister. He asked the army to lay down its weapons and called on the United Nations to maintain law and order. Lumumba subsequently declared (also on the radio) that Kasavubu was a traitor and no longer head of state. Lumumba's Council of Ministers, called into emergency session, accused Kasavubu of high treason and declared him deprived of all presidential functions. U.N. forces proceeded to take control of the airports and radio station, denying their use to both factions. Telegram 901 from Leopoldville to the CIA, September 6, transmitted a message from the Ambassador to Herter and Dulles, saying that he believed that only the most vigorous support of Kasavubu by the United Nations could save the situation. He noted that Kasavubu had apparently jumped the gun, not coordinating his plan with his supporters and not having the radio station secured. (Central Intelligence Agency Files, Job 78–00435R, Box 1, Folder 3)

---

16. Paper Prepared in the Central Intelligence Agency[1]

Washington, undated.

OPERATIONS IN THE CONGO

In the period immediately preceding Congo independence, CIA efforts in the Belgian Congo concentrated on establishing direct contact with as many responsible political figures as possible and influencing their actions. This task was made difficult by the emergence of many new figures and political parties. However, by virtue of having prior

---

[1] Source: Central Intelligence Agency Files, Job 78–00435R, DDO/ISS Files, Box 1, Folder 3, [*cryptonym not declassified*] Ops. Secret. A handwritten notation on the paper reads: "Prepared for Nixon 7 Sept 1960."

contact with certain of the important educated Congolese, [*less than 1 line not declassified*] a precedent had been established which facilitated these efforts. In this period, as it was apparent that no one single political figure or tribe was in a position effectively to lead a unified Congolese state, we encouraged formation of a moderate coalition which adopted a generally pro-Western posture and which rejected Congo separatism. The aggressiveness of Lumumba and the extremist political heat generated at the time prevented this coalition from winning the elections. However, it did emerge as a significant political force with its leader, Joseph Ileo, not only becoming President of the Senate but the only Congolese figure who dared publicly to challenge many of Lumumba's dictatorial actions. [*1½ lines not declassified*]

In the immediate post-independence period, CIA continued to maintain contact with the assets it had been developing and to be on the lookout for new ones for whatever contingencies might arise. [*1 line not declassified*] There followed the mutiny of the Force Publique and the breakdown of public order and government administration. From this time on, CIA concentrated on developing contact with [*less than 1 line not declassified*] assets who were in active opposition to Lumumba or appeared to have that potential. These were developed with the long-range view of possible active use against Lumumba and on a day to day basis in tactical opposition to increasing signs of Soviet Bloc influence in the Lumumba Government and such organs as Leopoldville Radio and the Soviet-inspired line which Kashamura was broadcasting over it. [*3 lines not declassified*]

[*2½ lines not declassified*] To accomplish this and to implement operations to this end, CIA has been steadily reinforcing the Leopoldville station with additional personnel and funds, and the Director of Central Intelligence has given the station authority to take decisions on the spot, in consultation with Ambassador Timberlake, whenever time considerations prevent consultation with Washington. [*2 lines not declassified*]

CIA has been coordinating an effort to have the Senate assemble and pass a vote of no confidence in the Lumumba Government. After the required 48 hours of consideration had intervened, the no confidence vote would have left the way clear for a successor, probably Ileo himself, to be named as Prime Minister. Preparations have been in the making to support this by radio, propaganda and various types of demonstrations. (An example of this was the preplanned demonstration which took place on the day of the recent Congress of African States convened in Leopoldville.) Kasavubu, the President and Chief of State and considered by reason of his primacy in the Abako movement Lumumba's most powerful opponent, was involved peripherally [*1 line not declassified*]. Unfortunately, and for reasons which are not yet fully clear to us, Kasavubu jumped the gun on this operation two days too early and (illegally) declared Lumumba out of office and failed further to implement his action. [*5 lines not declassified*] The key to the power situation in the Congo is the Force Publique, elements of which Lumumba currently controls and which are not subject to U.N. direction. The Secretary General is awaiting a suitable opportunity to disarm or control this group and in connection with Kasavubu's actions of 5 September, Cordier has made an appeal to the Secretary General to meet the Force Publique payroll with a million dollars to be paid directly by the U.N. to the Force Publique. The U.N. has for the time being put the Leopoldville radio station out of operation and has blocked the airfield there.

On the basis of what information we have so far received it would appear that Kasavubu's precipitate action has at least seriously jeopardized the plan for ousting Lumumba by constitutional means. These aspects are currently being examined by our station in Leopoldville and Ileo and Adoula are already attempting to pick up the pieces. Further anti-Lumumba demonstrations are planned. It is still possible that the plan for the Senate to oust Lumumba may be carried out but we are not yet in possession of sufficient facts to state what these possibilities are.

---

17. Telegram From the Station in the Congo to the Central Intelligence Agency[1]

Leopoldville, September 8, 1960.

0905 (In 49679). Ref: Leop 0904[2] [*less than 1 line not declassified*].

1. [*1 line not declassified*] Latter reported following:

A. Ileo missing. Has not returned his home since just after Kasavubu speech night 5 September. [*1 line not declassified*] asking if knew whereabouts Ileo. In reply query, said he doubts Ileo in hands Lumumba.

---

[1] Source: Central Intelligence Agency Files, [*cryptonym not declassified*]; Job 78–00435R, DDO/ISS Files, Box 1, Folder 3, [*cryptonym not declassified*] Ops. Secret; Rybat; [*cryptonym not declassified*]; Priority. Received at 2231Z.

[2] According to Foreign Minister Bomboko, Kasavubu planned to arrest Lumumba on 6 or 7 September. [Footnote in the original.] This CIA telegram has not been found.

B. [*3 lines not declassified*] Mobutu showed him written order from Lumumba ordering him have army ready carry out any Lumumba order. Mobutu said he refused obey and told Lumumba army would not become involved political problems. Said it up Lumumba and opposition settle problem politically, that army would not intervene. (Note: U.N. says troops Camp Leopoldville Two disarmed, all arms and ammo under lock. However [COS] has seen 50 to 100 armed troops Leop. Many roadblocks since youth demonstration.

C. Expects Tshombe publicly support Kasavubu move.

D. Firmly convinced Kasavubu legal right replace Lumumba government without submitting decision to confidence vote parliament.

E. Concerned by premature move Kasavubu [*3 lines not declassified*].

F. [*less than 1 line not declassified*] said nine ministers Lumumba government resigned 5 and 6 September. Did not give names as left hurriedly when convoy armed police passed meeting place.

2. Suggested [Identity 1] do following:

A. [*less than 1 line not declassified*] try get operation back on tracks.

B. [*less than 1 line not declassified*] telegrams all African states and members Security Council justifying Lumumba ouster. [*less than 1 line not declassified*] press conference to try get support world opinion.

C. Get [*less than 1 line not declassified*] leaders on radio soonest to present opposition to people. As Congo Radio now off air, suggested try get statements out Radio Braz.

D. Get old government out of office. [Identity 1] said will be done soon as Ileo government installed office by President. [*less than 1 line not declassified*] To COS comment that Lumumba in opposition is almost as dangerous as in office, [Identity 1] indicated understood and implied might physically eliminate Lumumba.

E. Be prepared influence votes parliament.

F. COS offered assist [Identity 1] in preparation new government program.[3] Also said he sure ODYOKE prepared help with technicians as needed.

3. [*4 lines not declassified*] If opposition fails its efforts, believe ODYOKE and U.N. position Congo undetermined and Lumumba will

---

[3] In a 1967 Agency debriefing, the Chief of Station in September 1960 recalled [*text not declassified*] that he had drawn up a "three-page plan, step-by-step-by-step, as to what should be done and when, right from the time of buying the first senator, etc." All the propaganda was prepared as well as guards to be placed around the radio station and airport. The Chief of Station said he believed he had thought of everything, but Kasavubu had moved the schedule up by two days and just fired Lumumba without waiting for the vote. (16 August 1967 and 20 September 1967 Debriefing: Chief of Station, Leopoldville, 1960–1963; Central Intelligence Agency Files, Job 82–00450R, Box 7, Folder 1, DDO/AF, AF/DIV Historical Files)

have dictatorial power. Also bloc would strongly influence control such government. Ambassador shares this view. Thus Station going all out this crisis. Forced take calculated risks would not normally take in effort pull hat out of fire.[4]

End of message.

---

[4] In CIA telegram 49672 the CIA also said that it agreed with the conclusions of this paragraph and particularly with the Station's attitude as indicated in the last two sentences.

---

18. Telegram From the Central Intelligence Agency to the Station in the Congo[1]

Washington, September 9, 1960, 1654Z.

49671 (Out 67761). State requests that essence of the following message be transmitted [*less than 1 line of text not declassified*] immediately. [*3 lines not declassified*] Please consult Ambassador and implement immediately. Message follows:

1. We [Department of State] are distressed at apparent inactivity Kasavubu at this crucial turning point. Lumumba dominating scene and we believe strong public statements by Kasavubu essential to counter Lumumba's activities. You should approach him soonest recommending in strongest terms he send message to SYG and publish same. Timing is crucial since Kasavubu's message to SYG must be available before SC meeting, now scheduled Saturday a.m., Sept 10.

2. Kasavubu should declare he is Chief of State and that he has, in accordance with legal procedures prescribed in "fundamental law" deposed Lumumba. Latter has no official status.

3. He should appeal to UN in name legally constituted authority to remain in Congo and to assume full control public safety sector including control all armed Congolese units so that people of Congo can freely express their feelings rather than live in fear and intimidation.

4. He should request that all outside unilateral intervention in Congo cease immediately and that all assistance be channeled through

---

[1] Source: Central Intelligence Agency Files, Job 78–00435R, DDO/ISS Files, Box 1, Folder 3, [*cryptonym not declassified*] Ops. Secret; Rybat; Operational Immediate. Drafted and authenticated by [*name not declassified*] and released by [illegible] (DD/P).

UN. In this regard request UN take complete control all airports and ports of entry, as well as communications facilities.

5. He should request UN guarantee safety of all Congolese political leaders, assuring their freedom from arbitrary arrest and permitting full and immediate implementation normal constitutional procedures, and

6. He should appeal to all African states to give complete support to UN, to protest outside interference, thereby keeping Congo for the Africans and denying it to communism or colonialism.[2]

End of message.

---

[2] In telegram 920 from Leopoldville to CIA, September 10, the Station reported that the message had been passed immediately to Foreign Minister Justin Bomboko for Kasavubu, [*text not declassified*]. (Ibid.)

---

19. Editorial Note

In telegram 0927 to the Central Intelligence Agency, September 13, 1960, the Station in Leopoldville reported that it had established an informal channel of communications with [*name not declassified*], had met with Colonel Joseph Mobutu, and was providing both with financial help. The contacts and support had been cleared with Ambassador Timberlake. (Central Intelligence Agency Files, Job 78–00435R, DDO/ISS Files, Box 1, Folder 3, [*text not declassified*])

The Station's contact with Mobutu first took place during a meeting at the Presidential Palace on September 7. As reported in telegram 0927, Mobutu "complained bitterly Lumumba trying involve army in politics" and, in addition, Mobutu made the following points:

"A. Plans refuse admit Camp Leopold Second 15 MNC political organizers assigned camp by Lumumba.

"B. He ordering troops try avoid fighting Kasai. Said bloody fighting there resulted from attack on troops by Baluba tribesmen.

"C. Hopes avoid attack on Katanga to avoid civil war but bragged his troops well armed and could easily defeat Tshombe and Kalonsi forces.

"D. Has ordered one company whose loyalty 'sure' to Leop area. Also said he ordered commanding officer and chief staff Stanleyville area to Leop for talks, indicating wants them under his control during crisis. (They came Leop 8 September.)

"E. Several times said needed help accomplish his objective."

At a follow-up meeting the next day Mobutu "explained he strongly opposed Lumumba but wished avoid arresting him for fear starting civil war. Instead said plan was to have opposition parties mount large demonstration, with police and troops arriving too late to prevent people from getting Lumumba." He was advised that "UN troops would intervene if public order disturbed by mob, but Mobutu refused change plan." Although it doubted the feasibility of the plan, the Station "decided to bet on long shot." More importantly, it felt Mobutu offered long term "political action potential, provided he does not destroy himself in plot." (Ibid.)

In concluding its report, the Station stated in part that it realized the possibility of provocation of the political action program in support of moderate anti-Lumumba leaders and the risk opposition may not achieve its objective. The Station stated: "believe KUBARK should support this long shot operation. Lumumba victory, which quite possible, would mean, at least for near future, govt hostile to ODYOKE interests." The Station reported it was continuing press the operation even though it realized that [*name not declassified*] bungling of the coup and lack guts and imagination of most opposition leaders had greatly limited the chances the operation would succeed. (Ibid.)

In a radio interview 37 years later, the Chief of Station said that at the Presidential Palace Mobutu told him of his plans to mount a coup and asked whether the U.S. Government would support him. The Chief of Station recalled that after finessing for some time he finally had said, "I believe we will." ("The Connection," WBUR, Boston, Massachusetts, March 27, 1997) In his 1967 debriefing, the Chief of Station gave a somewhat different version of this meeting, saying that Mobutu had complained about Soviet penetration of the army and asked him what he should do. The Chief of Station remembers telling him that, as a junior officer, he could not set policy. Finally Mobutu said that he would not act unless the Chief of Station told him that the U.S. Government would back him. The Chief of Station responded that Mobutu should prevent at any cost the Soviets taking over the army. Arrangements were then made to provide funds. The Chief of Station said that this was the beginning of the plan for Mobutu to take over the government. (16 August 1967 and 20 September 1967 Debriefing: Chief of Station, Leopoldville, 1960–1963, Central Intelligence Agency Files, Job 82–00450R, Box 7, Folder 1, DDO/AF, AF/DIV Historical Files)

20. Telegram From the Central Intelligence Agency to the Station in the Congo[1]

Washington, September 13, 1960, 2245Z.

Dir 00369 (Out 69233). Re Leop 0941 (In 12092).[2]

1. Your and Station efforts past few days most impressive and very sympathetic your frustration at lack conclusive results view naivete human material you dealing with. Very difficult for us here make practical suggestions which must depend on hourly contact with the scene and cast of characters which only you know well. Lumumba talents and dynamism appear overriding factor in reestablishing his position each time it seems half lost. In other words each time Lumumba has opportunity have last word he can sway events to his advantage.[3] Many Congolese, including Parliament, however appear vulnerable to almost any talented speaker, as long as Lumumba not there nullify his effect. Do you believe there is any opportunity for repeating an event like 12 Sept Lumumba arrest[4], i.e. anything which will remove Lumumba temporarily from the scene, with sufficient coordinated preparation of such actions as strike demonstrations, radio speeches and, most important, a parliamentary quorum to which Kasavubu, Ileo, Bolikango etc. can talk and reverse latest info we have which is Lumumba's new vote confidence.

2. Realize these not new thoughts to you but they do appear offer only semi-constitutional means achieve our ends.

End of message.

---

[1] Source: Central Intelligence Agency Files, Job 79–00149A, DDO/IMS Files, Box 23, Folder 1, African Division, Senate Select Committee, Volume II. Secret; Priority; Rybat; [*cryptonym not declassified*]. Drafted in C/AF and released by Bronson Tweedy (C/AF).

[2] The footnote in the original describing this reference is illegible. In telegram 941 from Leopoldville to CIA, September 13, the Station reported that the Ambassador and Chief of Station believed that the Kasavubu forces had to act or be ousted, but could not get them to act. They were taking a "hope for the best" attitude, moving with the speed of a snail, and continuing to ignore advice. (Ibid., [*text not declassified*], Mobutu, Joseph Desire, Vol. I)

[3] These two sentences are quoted in *Interim Report*, p. 17.

[4] On September 12, Colonel Joseph Mobutu, Chief of Staff of the Congolese army, had Lumumba arrested, but he was released 3 hours later by other Congolese soldiers.

21. National Security Council Briefing[1]

Washington, September 15, 1960.

CONGO

I. Confusion surrounds coup attempted by army commander Joseph Mobutu.

A. Latest press report is that Lumumba followers claiming Mobutu arrested and he still in control.

B. However, Mobutu told newsmen early on 15 September that both Kasavubu and Lumumba were under guard in their homes in Leopoldville.

C. We also have report from official in Leopoldville airport tower that Lumumba departed for Stanleyville yesterday.

D. If he has indeed gone to Stanleyville, it is probably to organize civil war against Mobutu.

II. Mobutu's coup appears intended to block Congo's slide into Communist orbit.

A. Mobutu proposes that Congo to be run until 31 December by "collect" of students and technicians with political truce in effect to let factions iron out differences.

B. Mobutu announced cooperation with UN, and ordered Soviet and Czech diplomats to get out of Congo within 48 hours.

1. Communist embassies and consulates reportedly being put under military guard 15 September.

C. Kasavubu–Ileo team were proving unable to counter effectively Lumumba and Communist advisors.

1. Moved with "speed of snail" and continued to ignore advice of US embassy officials who characterized Kasavubu as "acting more like a vegetable every day".

D. Mobutu, aged 30, reasonably intelligent but as ex-newspaperman he lacks military background or political training. As army chief of staff he dominated C-in-C Gen. Lundula (ex-sergeant).

E. Appointed by Ileo to be army commander on 14 September, but past close identity with Lumumba political movement may make him suspect in some moderate quarters.

---

[1] Source: Central Intelligence Agency Files, Job 79R00890A, Box 13, Folder 1, NSC Briefings, September 1960. Top Secret; [*codeword not declassified*].

III. UN Security Council postponing action on Hammarskjold's request for stronger action in Congo pending some clarification of situation.

A. On 14 September voted down USSR attempt seat Lumumba delegation.

B. Adjourned late on 14 September after Tunisia suggested good offices committee try to resolve constitutional crisis in Congo. This has not come to a vote. SC will meet again today.

1. Previous session of 12 September adjourned when apparent wavering African support of UN Command in Congo was almost certain to help Lumumba rather than Kasavubu. [*1 line not declassified*]

IV. Prior to Mobutu's coup, Communist nations were becoming increasingly involved in Congo.

A. Khrushchev, in his strongest attack on Hammarskjold's handling of the Congo crisis, charged on 13 September that the secretary general is "consciously working in the interests of the imperialists."

1. Zoria particularly biting in attack on 14 September in Security Council.

B. [*less than 1 line not declassified*] two Soviet cargo ships—*Voroshilov* and *Krasnodar*—off West African coast south of Conakry due in Congo on 18 September. [*less than 1 line not declassified*] Black Sea ports suggests clandestine cargo may be aboard.

1. High level Soviet interest in activities these vessels [*less than 1 line not declassified*].

2. Third ship also on way.

C. Sudanese foreign ministry has received Soviet request for overflight and landing rights for new USSR-Congo air service.

D. However, five Soviet AW–12's have returned to USSR after getting as far as Khartoum on the flight to Congo (probably because UN blocked airports.)

22. Telegram From the Station in the Congo to the Central Intelligence Agency[1]

Leopoldville, September 16, 1960.

0950 (In 13374). Ref: Leop 0944 (In 12931).[2]

1. [COS] tried without success all day 15 September contact Mobutu. Station was flooded with reports re outcome Mobutu coup.[3] Some said Lumumba arrested, others Mobutu arrested. [*less than 1 line not declassified*] generally reliable Station contacts had no idea what was happening. Finally learned Lumumba surrounded by angry troops at Camp Leopold 2. Some wanted shoot him, others to take him prisoner. But per phone call from Kasavubu residence, UN troops had interfered prevent CNA troops from "arresting" Lumumba in accordance with legal warrant issued against him.

2. Still difficult determine whether Mobutu has sufficient control army to enforce decisions announced night 14 September. Station advised [Identity 1] and [Identity 2] try work with Mobutu in effort eliminate Lumumba. Fear UN protection will give Lumumba opportunity organize counter attack. Only solution is remove him from scene soonest.[4]

End of message.

---

[1] Source: Central Intelligence Agency Files, Job 78–00435R, DDO/ISS Files, Box 1, Folder 3, [*cryptonym not declassified*] Ops. Secret; Rybat; [*cryptonym not declassified*]; Operational Immediate. Received at 0155Z.

[2] Devlin would establish contact with Mobutu and try to give direction to the latter's efforts. [Footnote in the original.] In telegram 944 from Leopoldville to CIA, September 15, the Station reported that once the Chief of Station was sure Mobutu was firmly in power, he would establish contact with him and try to give direction to his efforts. (Ibid.)

[3] On September 14, Mobutu announced that the army had decide to "neutralize" the Chief of State, the two rival governments, and the Congolese legislature until December 31. Until that date, he proposed that the Congo be governed by a commission of students and technicians (later the College of Commissioners). Mobutu also announced a policy of cooperation with the U.N., asked that all Soviet and Czech technicians leave the country within 48 hours, and demanded that the embassies of Communist countries be placed under guard. (*New York Times*, September 17, 1960, p.1)

[4] This sentence is quoted in *Interim Report*, p. 17.

23. Editorial Note

For purposes of briefing the National Security Council for its meeting on September 21, 1960, the Central Intelligence Agency prepared a summary in outline form, excerpted below, of telegram 0963 from the Station in Leopoldville, September 18:

"I. Chief of Station states crash operation needed to bolster Colonel Mobutu and opposition to Lumumba.

"A. Mobutu needs financial assistance to pay certain troops and officers, provide gas for troop movements.

"B. Mobutu needs French-speaking economic, political and security advisers.

"C. Mobutu desires security team to work against Lumumba and Communists.

"II. Assassination plot against Mobutu on 18 September almost successful.

" A. Plan was to sound general alarm Camp Leopold II and turn out all troops. Mobutu would be shot when he arrived on the scene.

"B. Mobutu, learning of plot, locked central alarm and called in former friend, a major, who was behind plot.

"C. Major tried to draw pistol but Mobutu grappled with him until guards arrived.

"D. He then ordered arrest of all Communist-influenced ministers in Lumumba government.

"III. Mobutu plans to cooperate with Ileo–Kasavubu group."

A. On urging of Chief of Station, "he agreed to name Bomboko chief Congolese UN delegate with Kanza as his deputy.

"B. Promised to turn over government to Ileo group by end of October but meanwhile must save face by living up to promise which he made to army of neutralizing political factions.

"C. Stated that until end October, the technical council would take orders from Kasavubu. (Central Intelligence Agency Files, Job 79R00890A, Box 12, Folder 9, NSC Briefings, September 1960)

For a record of discussion of the Congo at the NSC meeting on September 21, see *Foreign Relations,* 1958–1960, volume XIV, Africa, Document 223.

24. Telegram From the Central Intelligence Agency to the Station in the Congo[1]

Washington, September 19, 1960, 0919Z.

Dir 01443 (Out 71464).

1. Iden[2] proceeding Brazzaville shortly and should arrive approx 27 Sept. He will make his way Leop soonest thereafter and call you at office on arrival. Will announce himself as "[Joe] from Paris".[3]

[Omitted here is discussion of meeting arrangements.]

2. It urgent you should see Iden soonest possible after he phones you. He will fully identify himself and explain his assignment to you.[4] However his ETA not firm and you should not be concerned by some delay.

3. Acknowledge above soonest, with any revisions you wish make in above procedures. Continue use [*less than 1 line not declassified*] PROP indicator all traffic this op, which you instructed hold entirely to yourself.[5]

End of message.

---

[1] Source: Central Intelligence Agency Files, Job 79–00149A, DDO/IMS Files, Box 23, Folder 1, African Division, Senate Select Committee, Volume II. Secret; Rybat; [*less than 1 line not declassified*]PROP; Priority. Eyes only COS from Tweedy. Drafted and authenticated by Tweedy (C/AF) and released by [illegible] (DD/P).

[2] [*text not declassified*], September 19, stated that "iden" was "Sidney Braun." (Ibid.) The *Interim Report* identifies "Iden" as "Joseph Scheider," Special Assistant to the DDP (Bissell) for Scientific Matters with a degree in bio-organic chemistry. (pp. 20–23) Braun/Scheider was actually CIA scientist [*name not declassified*], who testified before the Church Committee in October 1975. [*text not declassified*] (Central Intelligence Agency Files, Job 79–00149A, DDO/IMS Files, Box 23, Folder 1, African Division, Senate Select Committee, Volume II)

[3] The *Interim Report,* p. 23, included the following excerpts from the first three sentences "['Joe'] should arrive approx 27 Sept." It went on to say: "Will announce himself as 'Joe from Paris.'"

[4] These two sentences are quoted ibid. On October 7, 1975, Scheider testified that Bissell had told him in late summer or early fall of 1960 to have biological materials ready at short notice for assassination of an unspecified African leader and that he had direction from the "highest authority" for such an operation. (Scheider said that he had assumed this meant the President.) He told the Committee that after he had prepared toxic biological materials and accessories for use in an assassination operation, he had a meeting with Tweedy and his deputy in September, during which Tweedy asked him to take the toxic materials to the Congo and deliver instructions to the Chief of Station "to mount an operation, if he could do it securely . . . to either seriously incapacitate or eliminate Lumumba." (Ibid., p. 21) For a more detailed description of Scheider's testimony before the Church Committee regarding the assassination plot, see ibid., pp. 19–30.

[5] According to the *Interim Report,* the codeword "PROP" indicated extraordinary sensitivity and restricted circulation at CIA headquarters to Dulles, Bissell, Tweedy, and Tweedy's deputy. On October 9, 1975, Tweedy testified before the Church Committee that the PROP channel was established and used exclusively for the Lumumba assassination operation. (p. 23)

25. Editorial Note

At the National Security Council meeting on September 21, 1960, Under Secretary of State Dillon reported that Patrice Lumumba had requested a visa to travel to New York as representative of the Congo to the United Nations and also as an official of the Congo Government. Both requests for visas had been denied, but Dillon warned that if Lumumba asked for a visa to visit the United States as a private citizen, it would be difficult to turn him down. Director of Central Intelligence Dulles warned that although Mobutu appeared to be the effective power in the Congo for the moment, Lumumba was not yet disposed of and remained a grave danger as long as he was not disposed of. (*Foreign Relations,* 1958–1960, volume XIV, Africa, Document 223)

In telegram 974 to the Central Intelligence Agency that same day, September 21, the Station in Leopoldville reported the following: "In absence orders to contrary (which arrived much later), Ambassador felt he forced issue visas, but delayed issuance at Station request." With the Ambassador's approval, the Chief of Station alerted [*name not declassified*] and Colonel Mobutu, "pointing out Lumumba could be stopped if legal arrest warrant issued, as UN said it would not prevent legal arrest." The Chief of Station "also suggested as alternative that government lift Lumumba passport at airfield, thus preventing his departure. [*text not declassified*] Mobutu called the Chief of Station to his home immediately, where the latter "urged arrest or other more permanent disposal of Lumumba, [*names not declassified*]. Also warned Mobutu of efforts by UAR, Ghana and Morocco achieve reconciliation between Lumumba and Kasavubu. Mobutu listened but seemed unconcerned; was rather like man in trance." The Station indicated it was "checking recurring reports of Kasavubu Lumumba reconciliation. [*text not declassified*] Believe some substance to rumor but will do best prevent. If Lumumba allowed even minor role, he most apt come out on top." (Central Intelligence Agency Files, Job 78–00435R, DDO/ISS Files, Box 1, Folder 3, [*cryptonym not declassified*] Ops)

26. Memorandum for the Record[1]

Washington, September 22, 1960.

[Omitted here is discussion of unrelated matters.]

6. *Airplanes for Katanga*

Mr. Irwin said that the U.S. Air Attaché to the Union of South Africa had reported a request from Comdt. Hirsch, a Belgian military advisor to the Katanga Government, for covert assistance in obtaining aircraft. The Group agreed that such action would not be appropriate at this time, in view of U.S. backing of the proposition that aid to any part of the Congo should be funneled through the U.N. Mr. Dulles said, however, that this is something that we would want to have as much information on as possible from the attaché, against the eventuality that Lumumba should return to power.

TA Parrott

[1] Source: National Security Council, Intelligence Files, NSC 5412/2 Special Group, Minutes and Agendas, 1960. Secret; Eyes Only.

27. Telegram From the Central Intelligence Agency to the Station in the Congo[1]

Washington, September 24, 1960, 0429Z.

Dir 02521 (Out 73573). From Ascham and Tweedy. Re: Leop 0002 (In 17384).[2]

[1] Source: Central Intelligence Agency Files, Job 79–00149A, DDO/IMS Files, Box 23, Folder 1, African Division, Senate Select Committee, Volume II. Secret; Rybat; [*cryptonym not declassified*]; Operational Immediate. Drafted and released by Dulles.

[2] [*text not declassified*] reported on 23 September that Pierre Mulele, Gabriel Yumbu, and Antoine Gizenga of the PSA were mounting a coup against Mobutu and the Council of Commissioners. [Footnote in the original.] In telegram 0002 from Leopoldville to CIA, September 23, the Station reported that upon learning of a coup plot against Mobutu and the Council of Commissioners, the Chief of Station immediately informed Mobutu and had the Embassy warn Kasavubu. Kasavubu did not act upon the warning, but Mobutu had two of the plotters arrested. The Embassy and Station urged Mobutu and Kasavubu to take action against Lumumba and the other plotters, [*text not declassified*]. (Ibid., Job 78-00435R, Box 1, folder 3)

1. Appreciate excellent reporting your reference [*less than 1 line not declassified*]. We wish give every possible support in eliminating Lumumba from any possibility resuming governmental position or if he fails in Leop, setting himself in Stanleyville or elsewhere.[3]

2. While fully aware of nefarious plotting Ghana, Guinea, UAR, to restore Lumumba, greatly disturbed at reference to Morocco and particularly Tunisia as members of this clique. Can you suggest any action we can propose to ODACID or take otherwise to help detach them from Lumumba camp?

3. Disturbed at possibility that [Mobutu] might lose control of his forces due possible higher pay being offered sources hostile to us as suggested para 4 your reference. [2 *lines not declassified*]

4. Agree position outlined last sentence reference which we assume is fully endorsed by Ambassador.

5. At your discretion, share this message with Ambassador.

End of message.

---

[3] This sentence is quoted in *Interim Report,* pp. 24, 62.

---

28. Editorial Note

In telegram 0026 to the Central Intelligence Agency, September 28, 1960, sent "eyes only" for Bronson Tweedy, the Chief of Station in Leopoldville reported that [*name not declassified*] "contacted 26 September. We on same wave length. [COS] afraid [Mobutu] weakening under Afro-Arab pressure. Hence believe most rapid action consistent with security indicated. Basis 2 talks considering possibilities." The telegram then briefly outlined seven "possibilities," the first of which involved having an agent "take refuge with big brother [Lumumba]. Would thus act as inside man to brush up details to razor edge. Also would provide info on food and agricultural problem." The second possibility involved an unidentified individual who "said he planned action within 8 days. Date passed and no action but if price right might get show on road." The Chief of Station indicated to CIA that he planned to proceed "on basis priorities as listed" unless instructed to contrary. (Central Intelligence Agency Files, Job 79–00149A, DDO/IMS Files, Box 23, Folder 1, African Division, Senate Select Committee, Volume II) In CIA telegram 03094 to Leopoldville, September 28, Tweedy commented briefly on each of the seven possibilities and warned that where the PROP operation (i.e., elimination of Lumumba) was concerned, their primary concern must be concealment of the U.S. role, unless an outstanding opportunity emerged which made a calculated risk a first class bet. Headquarters was ready to entertain any serious proposals the Station made. (Ibid.)

On August 21, 1975, the Chief of Station testified before the Church Committee that Scheider had told him that his instructions were to "eliminate" Lumumba, and that he had received "rubber gloves, a mask and a syringe" along with lethal biological materials from Scheider, who also instructed him in their use. (Scheider testified on October 7, 1975, that the toxic material was to be injected into some substance that Lumumba would ingest, i.e., food or a toothbrush, so that some of it would get into his mouth.) The means of assassination had not been restricted to use of this toxic material, but the Chief of Station emphasized that although selection of a mode of assassination was left to his judgment, it had been essential that it be carried out in a way that could not be traced back either to an American or the U.S. Government. He also recalled he had reacted with great surprise when he realized that Scheider had come to discuss an assassination plan, and said that Scheider had indicated this had been authorized by the President. Both Scheider and the Chief of Station confirmed to the Church Committee that the top priority possibility listed in telegram 0026 involved instructing an agent to infiltrate Lumumba's entourage to explore means of poisoning him. (*Interim Report,* pages. 24–27)

---

29. Editorial Note

In telegram 0057 to the Central Intelligence Agency, October 2, 1960, the Station in Leopoldville reported on a meeting with Colonel Joseph Mobutu the previous day during which he stated that he was under tremendous pressure from numerous "diplomats" to support President Kasavubu, but maintained that, in view of his announced policy of neutralism, he could not show favoritism. He added that he was so fed up that he was ready to throw in the sponge, reopen parliament, and let the politicians fight it out themselves. The Station expressed its great concern at the possibility that Mobutu might carry out his threat and withdraw the army from the conflict, since the field would then be wide open for Lumumba's return to power. In a second meeting later the same day, reported in telegram 0058, October 2, Mobutu appeared more calm and promised to do nothing more against

Kasavubu; at the same time he asked for additional financial aid with the comment that "Lumumba got everything he needed from Communists, whereas I get practically no help at all." (Central Intelligence Agency Files, Job 78–00435R, DDO/ISS Files, Box 1, Folder 4, [*cryptonym not declassified*] Ops)

The Central Intelligence Agency informed the Station in telegram 04697, October 6, that in view of the uncertain outcome of current developments it was conducting contingency planning for the Congo at the request of "policy echelons." The planning was designed to prepare for a situation in which the United States would provide clandestine support for elements in the armed opposition to Lumumba. Although implementation of such a plan posed special problems, it was felt that the "stakes [were] great enough [to] leave nothing untried to maintain acceptable Congo situation." (Ibid., Job 79–00149A, DDO/IMS Files, Box 23, Folder 1, African Division, Senate Select Committee, Volume II)

30. Editorial Note

In telegram 04802, October 7, 1960, Bronson Tweedy, Chief of the Central Intelligence Agency's Africa Division in the Directorate of Plans, informed the Chief of Station in Leopoldville that he had "had good discussion with your colleague 7 Oct.," a reference to Joseph Scheider, who had left Leopoldville for the United States on October 5. "Be assured did not expect [*text not declassified*]PROP objectives be reached in short period," Tweedy stated, "and understand current situation fully warranted return your colleague." Meanwhile, Tweedy reported, "we considering dispatching third national operator who, when he arrives, should then be assessed by you over period to see whether he might play active or cutout role on full time basis. If you conclude he suitable and bearing in mind heavy extra load this places on you, would expect dispatch TDY senior case officer run this op and outside agent full time under your direction." (Central Intelligence Agency Files, Job 79–00149A, DDO/IMS Files, Box 23, Folder 1, African Division, Senate Select Committee, Volume II.)

In telegram 0089, October 8, the Station in Leopoldville informed the Central Intelligence Agency that Scheider had left Leopoldville for the United States on October 5 in "view expiration date his materials. However left certain items of continuing usefulness." The Chief of Station "plans continue try implement op" and wished to "stress necessity provide Station with qualified third country national." (Ibid.) Scheider, however, testified before the Church Committee in October 1975 that he had "destroyed the viability" of the biological material and disposed of it in the Congo River before departing for the United States on October 5. In what the *Interim Report* calls the "only real conflict" between the Chief of Station's and Scheider's testimony, the Chief of Station testified in August 1975 that the toxic material was not disposed of until after Lumumba was imprisoned by the Congolese in early December. The *Interim Report* notes that the central point was that the Chief of Station planned to continue the assassination effort, by whatever means, even after Scheider's departure. (*Interim Report,* pages 29–30)

On November 3, 1960, a Central Intelligence Agency senior case officer, called Michael Mulroney in *Interim Report,* arrived in Leopoldville. In June 1975 Mulroney testified to the Church Committee that he had been asked by Richard Bissell, Deputy Director of Plans, to go to the Congo to carry out the assassination of Patrice Lumumba. Mulroney told the committee that before leaving for Leopoldville he had met with Scheider, who discussed with him lethal means for disposing of Lumumba, including a virus and poison, but Mulroney informed Bissell he would not participate in an assassination plot. Mulroney testified, however, that while in Leopoldville he had been prepared to take action to "neutralize" Lumumba by drawing him away from UN custody and turning him over to the legal Congolese authorities, Mulroney told the committee that he was opposed to assassination but not "capital punishment." For more information on Mulroney's testimony, see Document 45, footnote 5 to Document 46, and the *Interim Report,* pages 37–44.

---

31. Editorial Note

Responding to rumors that President Kasavubu was thinking of replacing or curtailing the authority of Colonel Mobutu, on October 7, 1960, the Central Intelligence Agency asked the Station in Leopoldville to inform the Ambassador that the Department of State's reaction, which the Agency shared, was to attempt to persuade Kasavubu not to replace Mobutu, since obvious legal chaos would follow. (Telegram 04785; Central Intelligence Agency Files, Job 78–00435R, DDO/ISS Files, Box 1, Folder 4, [*cryptonym not declassified*] Ops) In telegram 0092 to the Central Intelligence Agency, October 8, the Station noted that the rumors had come from many sources and in each case it had reacted strongly, pointing out the facts of political life and indicating that such action would torpedo the [*cryptonym not declassified*] effort in support of moderate anti-Lumumba leaders. The Station also reported that, in response to telegram 04785, meetings had been held with the Ambassador and with Georges Denis, Kasavubu's Belgian advisor, who admitted there had been some talk recently in Kasavubu circles of removing or reducing Mobutu's authority but insisted such action was no longer under consideration. Denis agreed such action could be most dangerous and he would do his best to convince Kasavubu of that fact. (Ibid.)

The Station also informed the CIA in telegram 0092 that there was a report that Mobutu had told the College of Commissioners the previous evening that he agreed to the arrest of Patrice Lumumba. Three days later, on October 11, the Station reported in telegram 0107 that the UN Secretary-General's Special Representative in the Congo, Rajeshwar Dayal, had four times refused to allow Congolese authorities to serve an arrest warrant on Lumumba, stating that the arrest was just a trick to assassinate Lumumba. Bomoboko had told the Embassy that Mobutu was prepared to attack UN guards if necessary to take Lumumba. The Station noted that although it had consistently urged [*cryptonym not declassified*] leaders to arrest Lumumba, the Embassy and Station had been trying to prevent a Mobutu attack, fearing that it would not succeed and would jeopardize the position of the moderate [*cryptonym not declassified*] leaders. (Ibid.)

On October 13, Allen Dulles informed the National Security Council that the UN position was that it would surrender Lumumba only if his parliamentary immunity were lifted by the Congolese Parliament, and there was some talk of convening Parliament to get his immunity withdrawn. He said that there were a thousand Congolese troops around Lumumba's house, while the UN guard force was not nearly so strong. Dillon noted that conflict between UN and Congolese forces would create a very bad situation, and said the U.S. Government had suggested that Lumumba be moved from the prime minister's mansion. (*Foreign Relations,* 1958–1960, volume XIV, Africa, Document 242)

32. Telegram From the Central Intelligence Agency to the Station in the Congo[1]

Washington, October 15, 1960, illegible.

Dir 06250 (Out 81396).

1. You will note from cable[2] through normal channel currently being transmitted a para on [*less than 1 line not declassified*]PROP type suggestions. You will probably receive more along these lines as stumbling block [Lumumba] represents increasingly apparent[.] All studying Congo situation closely and his disposition spontaneously becomes number one consideration.[3] [*3 lines not declassified*]

2. Raise above so you not confused by any apparent duplication. This channel remains for specific purpose you discussed with colleague and also remains highest priority.[4] Re Dir 04802,[5] request your reaction to possible directed assignment senior case officer soonest to concentrate entirely this aspect. We still working on third national mentioned that ref, but wonder whether you think early arrival case officer would make sense. Seems to us your other commitments too heavy give necessary concentration [*less than 1 line not declassified*] PROP.[6] Advise.

3. Have discussed [*less than 1 line not declassified*] possibility of commando type group for abduction [*cryptonym not declassified*], either via assault on house up cliff from river or, more probably, if [*cryptonym not declassified*] attempts another breakout into town as recently.[7] Picked

---

[1] Source: Central Intelligence Agency Files, Job 79–00149A, DDO/IMS Files, Box 23, Folder 1, African Division, Senate Select Committee, Volume II. Secret; Rybat; [*less than 1 line not declassified*]PROP; Priority. Eyes only Devlin. [*text not declassified*]. Drafted and released by Tweedy.

[2] CIA telegram 06285 to Leopoldville, October 15, stated that the only direct action the U.S. Government could now stand behind was to support immobilizing or arresting Lumumba, and that desirable as more definitive action might be, any action taken would have to be entirely Congolese. (Ibid., Job 78–00435R, Box 1, Folder 4, [*cryptonym not declassified*] Ops) Quoted in *Interim Report*, p. 31.

[3] These two sentences are quoted ibid.

[4] These two sentences are quoted ibid. On October 9, 1975, Tweedy told the Church Committee that the "specific purpose discussed with colleague" referred to the Chief of Station's discussion of assassination with Scheider, and that the premise of his message had been that "there was no solution to the Congo as long as Lumumba stays in a position of power or influence there." On October 17, 1975, Tweedy's Deputy, Glenn Fields, testified that the cable bearing the PROP indicator would have had controlling authority between the two cables. (Ibid.)

[5] See Document 30.

[6] This sentence is quoted in *Interim Report*, p. 32.

[7] Most of this sentence is quoted ibid.

group of [Mobutu] CNA troops might also be considered. Request your views.

End of message.

B. Tweedy

33. Telegram From the Station in the Congo to the Central Intelligence Agency[1]

Leopoldville, October 17, 1960.

0145 (In 28936). Ref: A. Dir 04802 (Out 78336).[2] B. Dir 06250 (Out 81396).[3]

1. [*name not declassified*] has not been able penetrate entourage. Thus he has not been able provide ops intel needed this job.[4]

2. Believe early assignment senior case officer handle [*less than 1 line not declassified*]PROP ops excellent idea. Although maintaining priority interest this op, able devote only limited amount time, view multiple ops commitments. Situation will be even more complicated when [*name not declassified*] goes Eliz 19 October. If case officer available, [COS] would devote as much time as possible to assisting and directing his efforts.[5]

3. Seriously doubt possibility assault house, view strong guard. Concur op feasible if subject goes out into town but view CNA troops watching house, doubt he will try this in near future. Believe possible to mount commando, per ref B. [*1 line not declassified*]

4. If case officer sent, recommend has pouch soonest high powered foreign make rifle with telescopic sight and silencer. Hunting good

---

[1] Source: Central Intelligence Agency Files, Job 79–00149A, DDO/IMS Files, Box 23, Folder 1, African Division, Senate Select Committee, Volume II. Secret; Rybat; [*less than 1 line not declassified*]PROP. Eyes only Tweedy from COS. Priority. Received at 2348Z.

[2] See Document 30.

[3] Requested Sta views re possibility use commando type group for abduction (subj). [Footnote in the original.] This telegram is Document 32.

[4] All but the first word in this paragraph (#1) was printed in *Interim Report,* p. 32.

[5] The first, second, and fourth sentences in this paragraph (#2) were printed ibid.

here when lights right. However as hunting rifles now forbidden, would keep rifle in office pending opening of hunting season.[6]

End of message.

---

[6] This paragraph (#4) was printed ibid. On October 9, 1975, Tweedy testified that this paragraph clearly referred to sending to the Congo via diplomatic pouch a weapon suited for assassinating Lumumba. The case officer subsequently sent to the Congo testified that he had no knowledge of any such weapon being pouched to the Congo. Tweedy said that he interpreted the cable to mean that "an operational plan involving a rifle" had not yet been formulated and that the "opening of hunting season" would depend upon approval of such a plan by CIA headquarters. (Ibid.)

---

34. Paper Prepared for the Special Group

Washington, undated.

[Source: Central Intelligence Agency Files, Job 81–00966R, Box 1, Folder 11. Secret; Eyes Only. *2 pages not declassified.*]

---

35. Editorial Note

In telegram 0162 to the Central Intelligence Agency, October 22, 1960, the Station in Leopoldville reported that Joseph Mobutu was considering another coup with the objective of a full takeover of the government and the neutralization indefinitely of President Joseph Kasavubu and Patrice Lumumba. However, both the Station and the Ambassador believed such a move would fail and would lead to failure of the program to support moderate anti-Lumumba leaders. Seeking a solution that would be acceptable to Mobutu as well as to other moderate leaders and public opinion yet would coincide with U.S. policy, the Station proposed a program, with the concurrence of the Ambassador, based on Mobutu's remaining in the background as the strong man. (Central Intelligence Agency Files, Job 78–00435R, DDO/ISS Files, Box 1, Folder 4, [*cryptonym not declassified*] Ops)

Immediately upon receiving telegram 0162 the Agency discussed the proposal with the Department of State at the bureau level and reported back in telegram 07606, October 22, that the initial reaction was not at all unfavorable but since it involved basic U.S. policy toward the Congo it would require clearance at least by the Secretary of State. (Ibid.) In an October 24 memorandum Bronson Tweedy submitted the proposal to Joseph Satterthwaite, Assistant Secretary of State for African Affairs, and requested his approval to discuss it with Mobutu. (Ibid., Job 76–00366R, DDO/ISO Files, Box 1, Folder 7, Congo, 1960–1969, Part 1)

In telegram 0192 from Leopoldville to CIA, October 26, the Station reported that the anti-Lumumba leaders, believing they commanded a parliamentary majority, were organizing a new government, and Mobutu planned to open parliament by the end of the month. The Embassy, however, was convinced that the anti-Lumumba leaders did not have a majority. Thus, it was urgent that the Station obtain approval of the proposal in Leopoldville 0162 along with authority to make tactical changes and work through others if Mobutu was not willing to play the part outlined for him. The anti-Lumumba leaders were all anxious to return to power. The Department of State must realize that the Embassy and Station were not able to control events, the telegram stressed, and if they did not have a program such as that proposed, they could not even influence the outcome of events. Even with a program it was not certain they could control events but they would have a much better chance of achieving their objectives. If the anti-Lumumba leaders opened parliament and failed to get a majority, pressures for Lumumba's return would be almost irresistible. (Ibid., Job 78–00435R, DDO/ISS Files, Box 1, Folder 4, [*cryptonym not declassified*] Ops)

The proposed program was considered by the Special Group at its meeting on October 27. See Documents 37 and 38.

36. Telegram From the Central Intelligence Agency to the Station in the Congo[1]

Washington, October 26, 1960, 2259Z.

Dir 08314 (Out 85633). Re Leop 0192 (In 33499).[2]

1. We fully understand and are sympathetic to reference and your basic proposals supporting same. As you know this matter is now in the governmental hopper and is being considered at highest levels. Since receipt of your basic proposal we have been in daily contact with ODACID and to date there has been no suggestion of a negative attitude.

2. However, ODACID is not disposed to push for a government decision this week and we agree that their reasons for this are correct. Basic to this is the fact that ODACID made a strong, high level approach to SYG on the whole question. The outcome of this was unclear but ODACID believes, and we agree, that before we launch into a unilateral program of broad magnitude which per se is in contravention of the UN approach, ODACID should have a second and strong approach to the SYG. [*name not declassified*] was advised by Penfield this date that ODACID has every intention of doing this. We are advised that a summary of the first démarche to the [*less than 1 line not declassified*] has been sent to Ambassador. Urge you study this carefully.

3. In meantime want you and Station to know we consider you right on target and messages appreciated. On your specific proposals suggest patience for a few days but continue send immediately all info bearing on viability and mechanics.

End of message.

---

[1] Source: Central Intelligence Agency Files, Job 78–00435R, DDO/ISS Files, Box 1, Folder 4, [*cryptonym not declassified*] Ops. Secret; Rybat; Operational Immediate. [*name not declassified*] to COS. Drafted and authenticated by [*name not declassified*] and released by [illegible] (DD/P).

[2] A footnote in the original urged Headquarters to pressure the Department of State "for earliest decision" on the anti-Lumumba plan. See Document 35 for additional information on telegram 0192.

37. Memorandum for the Special Group[1]

Washington, undated.

SUBJECT

Covert Action in the Congo

1. *Problem*:

To strengthen the de facto government of Colonel Mobutu, Chief of Staff of the Congolese National Army (CNA), in order to prevent Lumumba from regaining control of the Congo.

2. *Assumptions*:

It is assumed that it is in our interest to support Colonel Mobutu as a counterbalance to Lumumba and encourage him to work towards the eventual formation of a moderate civilian government in the Congo.

3. *Facts and Discussion*:

It is reliably reported that Colonel Mobutu is considering another coup in the Congo with the objective of a full take-over of the government. Although full details of his plan are not available, it is presumed he would act as Chief of State and might try to assume that title. Our representatives in Leopoldville believe that such a move would fail and lead to a general collapse of current operations designed to build up a moderate political opposition to Lumumba. It is considered that Colonel Mobutu does not have sufficient administrative or political ability to run the government and that he lacks political following. A review of other political personalities in the Congo indicates that none of them appear to meet the absolute standards required for leadership at this time. An attempt has therefore been made to develop a course of action that might be acceptable to Colonel Mobutu, to the Congolese, and world opinion.

Colonel Mobutu had advised he planned to fly to New York to make a direct personal appeal to the UN Secretary General for support of his government. He stated that he intended to expose a plot against him by Ghana, Guinea, the UAR, Morocco, and India, through their UN representatives and contingents in the Congo, and that he would insist on immediate withdrawal of military units of those countries. This trip has now apparently been postponed indefinitely.

In spite of Colonel Mobutu's claims to the loyalty of the CNA, it is not clear the extent to which certain elements may still be favorable to

[1] Source: National Security Council, Intelligence Files, Congo, 1960–1965. Secret. The memorandum was prepared for the Special Group meeting on October 27, 1960.

Lumumba. There is also a resurgence of political activity by Lumumba's supporters which tends to weaken Colonel Mobutu's position.

4. Conclusions:

It is concluded that action is advisable at this time to strengthen Colonel Mobutu's position in an effort to prevent the Communist-oriented Lumumba government from regaining control of the Congo. It is also concluded that assistance provided to Colonel Mobutu should be of such a nature as to encourage the establishment of a moderate civilian government.

5. Action Recommended:

It is recommended that authorization be granted to undertake the following steps to bring about a de facto government of the Congo under Colonel Mobutu's leadership, with parliamentary support and participation of leading moderate political elements.

a. It is proposed to approach Colonel Mobutu to convince him of the advantages of remaining in the position of a "strong man" behind the government avoiding an overt role. He would be assured of adequate funds to maintain control over troops in the Leopoldville area and expand his authority in the provinces. It is also proposed to offer a personal subsidy to Mobutu further to insure his continued cooperation.

b. If this proposal is acceptable in principle, a ministerial list would be submitted to Colonel Mobutu asking him for his suggestions and possible changes. Our Leopoldville representatives are currently preparing such a list.

c. Once a ministerial list is accepted, Colonel Mobutu would be asked to meet with the principal political leaders in opposition to Lumumba and indicate to them that they cannot obtain office without his support, and that he needs their help to run the government. He would then suggest the formation of a small inner council, [*1 line not declassified*] to be used as the mechanism to organize support in parliament [*less than 1 line not declassified*]. In this connection it is proposed to maintain direct subsidies to certain major political leaders to provide an additional element of control.

d. As a next step Colonel Mobutu's political inner council would call in parliamentarians one at a time, or in small groups, to discuss the political situation and induce them to sign a petition in support of Colonel Mobutu's government program. All possible pressure to cooperate would be put on these individuals during these discussions.

e. If these steps should succeed, parliament would be convened to obtain a confidence vote in a new government. A vote then would be proposed to lift parliamentary immunity from Lumumba and his more dangerous supporters and collaborators. Finally, a parliamentary vote would be proposed to give the government full powers for an extended period to meet the economic crisis.

It is estimated that funds required to implement these recommendations will amount to approximately [*dollar amount not declassified*] during the period up to 31 December 1960. Approximately [*dollar amount not declassified*] would be required for payments to elements of the CNA, the balance being used to obtain parliamentary support for Colonel Mobutu's government. Adequate funds are currently available in our budget for expenditures of this magnitude. However, if the cost of this program runs higher than these figures during this period, or the program needs to be continued over a longer period, it may be necessary to request additional funds [*less than 1 line not declassified*].

38. Memorandum for the Record[1]

Washington, October 27, 1960.

SUBJECT

Minutes of Special Group Meeting, 27 October 1960

PRESENT

Messrs. Merchant, Douglas, Gray, Gen. Cabell

[Omitted here is discussion of other subjects.]

3. Congo

The paper[2] outlining the proposal to aid Col. Mobutu in working toward the eventual formation of a moderate government was read by the Group.

Mr. Merchant questioned the intent toward Kasavubu. Mr. Parrott replied that the program envisages complete recognition of Kasavubu as the legitimate head of state and that Mobutu would remain in the background. With this understanding, the Group approved the proposal.

---

[1] Source: National Security Council, Intelligence Files, NSC 5412/2 Special Group, Minutes and Agendas, 1960. Secret; Eyes Only.

[2] Document 37.

Mr. Merchant went on to explain that Department representatives had had two discussions with Hammarskjold and that the trend in the latter's thinking has been somewhat disturbing. He has swung away from a feeling that Lumumba must be removed, to a feeling that he is the legitimate prime minister and we must live with him, although acknowledging that his title is somewhat clouded. Mr. Merchant said that a telegram has been dispatched to Ambassador Wadsworth (Department #764)[3] directing him to make another approach to the SYG, expressing the U.S. view that a stable, non-aligned government without Lumumba, and working through Kasavubu, should be established. He concluded—as did the rest of the Group—that our proposal complements the overt State position.[4]

[Omitted here is discussion of other subjects.]

---

[3] For telegram 764 from the Department of State to the Mission at the United Nations, see *Foreign Relations*, 1958–1960, volume XIV, Africa, Document 250.

[4] An October 27 memorandum from Thomas Parrott to "Mr. B" (presumably Bissell) reported that the Special Group had approved the Congo paper and noted that Merchant's principal concern was to assure that they planned to retain Kasavubu. Parrott had explained that this was their intent. The Special Group had unanimously agreed that their program was complementary to the Department of State's policy, as expressed in telegram 764, desiring a stable, non-aligned government without Lumumba, but with Kasavubu. (Central Intelligence Agency Files, Job 81–00966R, Box 1, Folder 11)

---

39. Editorial Note

In telegram 08451 to Leopoldville, October 27, 1960, the Central Intelligence Agency reported that the Special Group had approved the basic proposal outlined in telegram 0162, October 22, with the inclusion of [*name not declassified*], and authorized expenditure of [*dollar amount not declassified*] by the end of the year. The Station was ordered to implement the program in coordination with the Ambassador. (Central Intelligence Agency Files, Job 78–00435R, DDO/ISS Files, Box 1, Folder 5, [*cryptonym not declassified*] Ops) Telegram 0162 is discussed in Document 35. For details of the proposal, see Document 37.

In telegram 09643 to Leopoldville, November 2, the CIA informed the Station that after receiving telegram 1078 from the Embassy in Leopoldville, November 1, the Department of State now endorsed CIA action and, in full coordination with the Ambassador, the Station was authorized to implement the program outlined in Leopoldville 0162. (Central Intelligence Agency Files, Job 78–00435R, DDO/ISS Files, Box 1,

Folder 4, [*cryptonym not declassified*] Ops) For Embassy telegram 1078, see *Foreign Relations*, 1958–1960, volume XIV, Africa, Document 253.

In telegram 0253 from Leopoldville to CIA, November 6, the Station reported that Joseph Mobutu had accepted the plan. (Central Intelligence Agency Files, Job 78–00435R, DDO/ISS Files, Box 1, Folder 5, [*cryptonym not declassified*] Ops)

40. Telegram From the Station in the Congo to the Central Intelligence Agency[1]

Leopoldville, November 3, 1960.

0229 (In 37289). Ref Leop 0162 (In 31811).[2]

1. No action taken ref program view instructions to delay.

2. Although cannot predict next premier, doubt [Identity 1] would be best candidate. He relatively able by local standards but lacks drive and force necessary for Govt Chief. Have asked many locals, [Embassy] personnel and Europeans who they believe would be best premier. [Identity 2] cited by majority as best qualified, although he lacks broad political support. [Identity 3] might provide alternate candidate but many consider him be tarred with Belgian brush and lacking in courage.

3. Station believes plan outlined by SYG will greatly hinder and could render impossible ref plan.

A. If UN assumes de facto control CNA, [*cryptonym not declassified*][3] coalition will lose its primary weapon, [Mobutu] will become just another anti-[Lumumba] leader (and one with little influence as has no political party) and way would be open for civil war and/or [Lumumba] return power. In short, [Mobutu's] control CNA absolutely essential [*less than 1 line not declassified*]. UN control army would play into hands [Lumumba] forces. If ODYOKE gives in on this point, [*cryptonym not declassified*][4] program will have little if any chance in near future. In

---

[1] Source: Central Intelligence Agency Files, Job 78–00435R, DDO/ISS Files, Box 1, Folder 5, [*cryptonym not declassified*] Ops. Secret; Rybat; Operational Immediate. Received at 1648Z.

[2] Station's suggested program of 22 October for supporting Mobutu. [Footnote in the original.] Regarding this telegram, see Document 35.

[3] CIA political action program in support of moderate, anti-Lumumba leaders in the Congo [*text not declassified*].

[4] See footnote 3.

such case it would be just as well to soft peddle [*less than 1 line not declassified*][5]. Station hopes this will not be case, for return [Lumumba] will mean trouble for West and advantages for Bloc. Despite reports by limited number journalists Leop, neither Station nor Embassy have reason believe [Mobutu's] power waning in army. Also we discount exaggerated stories re CNA terrorist activities. There were incidents but some journalists exaggerated them out of all proportions.

B. Agree political realities require some form constitutionality for new govt. However if we to be realistic, must be satisfied with democratic facade as, with possible exception Nigeria, there no real democracy in Africa and Congolese are less prepared than most Africans for true democracy. We have alternatives between [Lumumba] dictatorship which would be anti-Western and pro-Western coalition which would try give Congo stable if not fully democratic govt.

C. Agree parliament meeting must be "full" (that is include Katanga deputies). Although recognize political difficulties UN which would result if [Lumumba] prevented from attending parliament, his presence parliament will endanger our program. He is a convincing demogogue. UN protection parliament meeting will remove lever Station planned use. Had planned place CNA around parliament building in effort convince hesitant deputies it not healthy support [Lumumba]. However placing UN troops around parliament building is not solution to intimidation problem. Many anti-[Lumumba] deputies afraid come Leop or afraid take open stand against [Lumumba]. As they fear MNC and PSA goon squads, attacks on families in provinces, and destruction property. View this, believe it essential [Mobutu] guarantee anti-[Lumumba] deputies protection while Leop, perhaps reserving and guarding hotel for them. Also believe he must form civilian goon squads to counter pro-[Lumumba] squads.

D. [*less than 1 line not declassified*] operation cannot succeed if we do not "put something in pocket" of many people.

4. Station greatly concerned by maneuvering within UN of nations supporting [Lumumba] and apparent cooperation if not actual connivance of Dayal, Rikhye and other UN personnel. They have made no secret of their dislike and contempt for [Mobutu] and Rikhye has stated on many occasions UN objective is to disarm CNA and quoted by some American correspondents as "looking for pretext" effect same. Although recognize need discipline CNA, Rikhye and others know this would give [Lumumba] big trump card. Now appears ODYOKE being outmaneuvered in UN. Our policy oppose [Lumumba] being blocked by small group powers claiming speak for Afro-Asian bloc, despite fact

[5] See footnote 3.

we providing largest part financing for UNOC. Example of maneuvering by pro-[Lumumba] bloc in UN is eight nation resolution to seat Congolese delegation and recommend opening parliament soonest. USUN has suggested compromise resolution and Embassy has recommended delay, for if resolution calling for early opening parliament passed UNGA, Dayal could and probably would use it force open parliament with UN troops. Such action in near future would probably return [Lumumba] to power. Also a compromise which weakened [*cryptonym not declassified*][6] forces would definitely undermine Station relations with [Mobutu].

5. If ODYOKE continues permit tail to wag UN dog, Station believes we will soon find [Lumumba] back in saddle, Bloc reps will return in force, Congo which is key to Central Africa will follow Cuban path with result that all Africa may soon fall under influence if not control of anti-Western nations. In short, Station believes ODYOKE must take stronger UN position, even at risk temporary loss popularity among neutrals. If we continue compromise and permit pro-[Lumumba] nations take initiative our [*cryptonym not declassified*][7] policy will fail and another area will have gone down the drain.

6. View maneuvering within UN, Station in coordination with Ambassador will endeavor implement ref plan. If UN were not in act, outcome would be in the bag. However, view UN presence and role, Hqs must realize this uphill fight.

7. Regret delay reply Dir 09026 (Out 87173).[8] Was not able obtain Niact 142 until (*portion garbled-being serviced*) Nov.

8. Ambassador read clear text version this message and fully approves.[9] He received Roger channel message authorizing ref plan 3 Nov. Will coordinate all steps plan per Dir 09643 (Out 88263).[10]

End of message.

---

[6] See footnote 3.

[7] See footnote 3.

[8] Queried whether any action was taken on Leopoldville's proposal prior to receipt of request to hold off on the proposal. [Footnote in the original.] This CIA telegram has not been found.

[9] In a 1967 Agency debriefing, the Chief of Station in late 1960 said how lucky he had been to work with Ambassador Clare Timberlake, who was "very pro-Agency." He described Timberlake as a man whose object was to get the job done, with no worry about who got the credit. The Chief of Station recalled that he and the Ambassador were the principal parties involved; they agreed on a course and they acted. He argued that this had made the critical difference because "nobody in Washington knew what was going on anyway." (16 August 1967 and 20 September 1967 Debriefing: Chief of Station, Leopoldville, 1960–1963; Central Intelligence Agency Files, Job 82–00450R, Box 7, Folder 1, DDO/AF, AF/DIV Historical Files)

[10] Authorized Leopoldville to implement program of support to Mobutu. [Footnote in the original.] Regarding this telegram, see Document 39.

41. Memorandum for the Special Group[1]

Washington, undated.

SUBJECT

Contingency Planning for the Congo

1. Problem:

To prevent a Communist-oriented government from gaining control of the Congo.

2. Assumptions:

It is assumed that Lumumba, with Communist support, will make every effort to regain control of the Congo and will, if possible, employ force against his political opponents to achieve this end.

In the event that Lumumba regains control of the Congolese National Army (CNA), or obtains paramilitary support from tribal elements, there will be open resistance by opposition political elements to his attempt to establish control.

3. Facts and Discussion:

At present Colonel Mobutu, the CNA commander, is in de facto control of the Congolese government. He has established a group of general commissioners to run the country pending the eventual formation of a moderate civilian government.

An unpredictable factor in the situation is the extent to which Mobutu can retain control of the CNA and utilize it as a force to check Lumumba. There is also the possibility that Lumumba, with support by Ghana, Guinea, the UAR, and the Communist bloc, will be able to raise forces to attempt an open seizure of power.

If there is a split in the CNA, or a weakening in Mobutu's position combined with a resurgence of Lumumba forces, it may be possible to prevent Communist consolidation of power by providing paramilitary support to anti-Communist opposition elements. Our contingency planning is directed toward this end.

Under these conditions, selected opposition elements would be provided with support consisting of arms, ammunition, sabotage materials and training. The establishment of a controlled clandestine radio is also envisaged.

---

[1] Source: National Security Council, Intelligence Files, Subject Files, Congo, 1960–1965. Secret. This memorandum was prepared for the Special Group meeting on November 10, 1960.

The immediate problem is to obtain necessary political clearances to facilitate shipment and the secure storage of radio equipment and an initial stock of arms and ammunition in adjacent areas, and to discuss plans for their covert introduction into the Congo.

[Omitted here is further discussion of the issue.]

42. Memorandum for the Record[1]

Washington, November 10, 1960.

SUBJECT

Minutes of Special Group Meeting, 10 November 1960

PRESENT

Messrs. Merchant, Douglas, Gray, Dulles, Bissell

[Omitted here is discussion of other subjects.]

7. Contingency Plans for the Congo

Mr. Bissell mentioned briefly that we are making certain contingency plans for the Congo against the possibility of a pro-Soviet Lumumba government, or complications arising from a militant Katanga independence movement.

Mr. Scott, who had replaced Mr. Merchant in the meeting, said that the African Bureau of State agrees with CIA's general method of proceeding with these plans.

[*1 paragraph (11 lines) not declassified*]

TA Parrott

[1] Source: National Security Council, Intelligence Files, NSC 5412/2 Special Group, Minutes and Agendas, 1960. Secret; Eyes Only.

43. Telegram From the Station in the Congo to the Central Intelligence Agency[1]

Leopoldville, November 15, 1960.

0304 (In 42478).

1. Target[2] has not left building in several weeks. House guarded day and night by Congolese and UN troops, both groups total about 150 men. Congolese troops are there to prevent target's escape and to arrest him if he attempts. UN troops there to prevent storming of palace by Congolese. Concentric rings of defense make establishment of observation post impossible. Attempting get coverage of any movement into or out of house by Congolese. [*1 line not declassified*] Target has dismissed most of servants so entry this means seems remote.[3]

2. From local evidence it would appear that Egyptians wish to get target out of building so that he can participate in inflamatory political meetings. Ghanians on other hand, according to [*name not declassified*], wish subject to remain in building until arrival of UN good offices mission. At same time subject's political followers in Stanleyville desire that he break out of his confinement and proceed to that city by car to engage in political activity since leaders feel that his popularity is sagging. Approach was made to Ghanians for help in breakout but this refused for reason given above. However, matter still under discussion by subject's followers in Leopoldville and decision on breakout will probably be made shortly. Station expects to be advised [*less than 1 line not declassified*] of decision when made.

3. Station has several possible assets to use in event of breakout and studying several plans of action.[4]

End of message.

---

[1] Source: Central Intelligence Agency Files, Job 79–00149A, DDO/IMS Files, Box 23, Folder 1, African Division, Senate Select Committee, Volume II. Secret; Rybat; [*text not declassified*]PROP; Routine. Eyes alone Tweedy from COS. Received at 0534Z.

[2] Lumumba.

[3] Most of this paragraph is quoted in *Interim Report*, p. 33.

[4] Parts of paragraph two and all of paragraph three are quoted ibid., p. 48.

44. Telegram From the Station in the Congo to the Central Intelligence Agency[1]

Leopoldville, November 16, 1960.

0320 (In 43551). Re Deptel 1372.[2]

1. Ambassador concerned by query para 5 ref re progress on plan approved Deptel 1274 (Deptel)[3] which approved plan outlined Leop 0162 (in 31811).[4] He does not wish (and rightly so) discuss action part this plan via ODACID channels and requests HQS advise ODACID that all communications this subject will be handled via KUBARK channels with HQS passing all information re developments to ODACID.

2. Ref refers to possibility formation interim govt. Embassy and Station wish emphasize plan outlined Leop 0162 did not call for another interim govt. If we tried institute another interim govt effort would be counter productive, annoying parliament, commissioners and certain political leaders. Plan as seen by Embassy and Station is directed toward formation permanent govt. View arrival good offices commission and lack organization Congolese, doubt can implement plan before late December, if then. Thus, Station continuing effort work through [Mobutu] to get firm nose count and signed petition parliamentarians guaranteeing support of new govt. Once this achieved, will enter phase of buying or otherwise attempting swing necessary votes to obtain majority for [*cryptonym not declassified*][5] forces. Only then will we urge [Mobutu] to open parliament.[6]

End of message.

---

[1] Source: Central Intelligence Agency Files, Job 78–00435R, DDO/ISS Files, Box 1, Folder 5, [*cryptonym not declassified*] Ops. Secret; Rybat; [*cryptonym not declassified*]; Priority. Received at 2017Z.

[2] For Department of State telegram 1372 to Leopoldville, November 12, see *Foreign Relations*, 1958–1960, volume XIV, Africa, Document 262.

[3] See footnote 5 to Document 262, ibid.

[4] See Document 35.

[5] CIA political action program in support of moderate, anti-Lumumba leaders in the Congo.

[6] In CIA telegram 12365 to Leopoldville, November 19, Tweedy informed the Station that he had advised Penfield that quick progress on the operation originally envisaged had undoubtedly been slowed down by local events. He urged the Station to advise CIA immediately whenever it believed the original objectives were either unattainable or had to be reached by radically different means in light of the developing local situation. (Central Intelligence Agency Files, Job 78–00435R, DDO/ISS Files, Box 1, Folder 5, [*cryptonym not declassified*] Ops)

45. Editorial Note

On the night of November 27, 1960, Patrice Lumumba, who had been confined to his house since early October, slipped past the United Nations and Congolese National Army troops guarding his residence and set out for Stanleyville, where Antoine Gizenga was regrouping Lumumba's supporters. On November 28, the Chief of Station cabled the Central Intelligence Agency that the Station was working with the Congolese Government "to get roads blocked and troops alerted possible escape route." (*Interim Report,* page 48) The former prime minister was captured in Kasai Province around midnight on December 1 by Congolese National Army troops. On December 2 he was flown to Leopoldville; the next day he was imprisoned at Thysville.

In 1975 the Church Committee looked into the question of whether the Central Intelligence Agency had played any role in either Lumumba's escape or his recapture. A senior case officer called Michael Mulroney in the Church Committee's *Interim Report,* who was in Leopoldville at the time of Lumumba's escape, testified that he had been prepared to "neutralize" Lumumba by drawing him away from UN custody and turning him over to the legal Congolese authorities, but he denied any responsibility for Lumumba's escape or his subsequent recapture. He testified in addition that a CIA operative QJWIN (see Document 46 and footnote 5 thereto), who arrived in Leopoldville on November 21 and worked for Mulroney, also bore no responsibility. The Chief of Station at the time testified that he was "quite certain that there was no Agency involvement in any way" in Lumumba's escape and that he had no advance knowledge of Lumumba's plans. The Chief of Station said he consulted with Congolese authorities about possible routes Lumumba might take to Stanleyville, but he was "not a major assistance" in tracking him down prior to his capture. (*Interim Report,* pages 42–44, 48–49)

In its 988-page report released in 2001 following a parliamentary inquiry into the assassination of Patrice Lumumba, a Belgian parliamentary committee reported that telegrams in Belgian Government files, sent to Brussels by way of the embassy in Brazzaville, did not appear to support as modest a role in the recapture of Lumumba as claimed by officials in their testimony before the Church Committee. The parliamentary committee verified that Belgian advisers at Leopoldville participated actively in the hunt for Lumumba, and, the committee indicated, "indirectly, we can equally confirm that the CIA played, in this hunt, a more important role than the Church Committee report, presented in 1975 by the American Senate, was willing to admit." However, the report does not provide specific documentation on the U.S. role. (Chambre des Représentants de Belgique, November 16, 2001, Enquête Parlementaire, Document 50: 0312/006, Rapport Fair au Nom de la Commission D'Enquête, volume 1, pages 219–225, volume 2, page 595; quotation translated from French)

46. Telegram From the Station in the Congo to the Central Intelligence Agency[1]

Leopoldville, November 29, 1960.

0390 (In 49486).

1. QJWIN[2] arrived Leop 21 Nov. View delicate nature op, Station did not surface him to [Mobutu]. Unilaterally and on own initiative he made contact with Iden[3] who agreed 26 Nov in following plan against target: Iden to supply four UNO vehicles and six Congolese soldiers with UNO brassards and berets. QJWIN posing as [*less than 1 line not declassified*] officer would enter target's home and provide escort out of residence. Iden said could easily provide vehicles and men. (UNO announced fifty-five of its vehicles have been stolen and Station knows where [*less than 1 line not declassified*] uniform available.) Iden organization needed to pierce both Congolese and UNO guards.

2. QJWIN has displayed great initiative, imagination and courage since arrival. Has identified self to Identity as German.

3. View change in location target, QJWIN anxious go Stanleyville and expressed desire execute plan by himself without using any apparat.[4] Would go Stan under his own passport and use business credentials from various German firms and chambers of commerce. When employed QJWIN told he would be paid [*dollar amount not declassified*]

---

[1] Source: Central Intelligence Agency Files, Job 79–00149A, DDO/IMS Files, Box 23, Folder 1, African Division, Senate Select Committee, Volume II. Secret; Rybat; [*text not declassified*]PROP; Priority. Eyes only Tweedy or Fields from COS. Received at 2233Z.

[2] QJWIN was a foreign citizen with a criminal background recruited in Europe. (*Interim Report,* p. 43) [*text not declassified*]. For information about QJWIN's stay in the Congo from November 21, 1960, until late December 1960, see ibid., pp. 43–46.

[3] Not further identified.

[4] This sentence is quoted in *Interim Report,* p. 44.

per month for period one or maximum two months. If HQS concurs he go Stan. Recommend maintain his salary at same rate.[5]

End of message.

---

[5] In CIA telegram 14254 to Leopoldville, November 30, Tweedy concurred that QJWIN should go to Stanleyville. He noted that CIA was prepared to consider direct action by QJWIN, but wanted the Chief of Station's reading on security factors, i.e., how close would this place the United States to the action if he were apprehended. (Central Intelligence Agency Files, Job 79–00149A, DDO/IMS Files, Box 23, Folder 1, African Division, Senate Select Committee, Volume II; *Interim Report*, p. 44) *Interim Report* noted that this language "could have been interpreted as an assassination order," but concluded that "there is no clear evidence that QJ/WIN was actually involved in any assassination plan or attempt." (pp. 44–45) In June 1975, a CIA senior case officer, called Michael Mulroney in *Interim Report*, testified before the Church Committee that following his own arrival in Leopoldville on November 3, he arranged for QJWIN to come to the Congo to work with him on counter-espionage. Mulroney declared, however, that neither he nor QJWIN was responsible for Lumumba's departure from UN custody or his subsequent capture. He also testified that so far as he knew, he was the only CIA officer with supervisory responsibility for QJWIN and that it was "highly unlikely" that QJWIN was ever used by another agent for an assassination operation. (Ibid., pp. 37–44) See Documents 30 and 45 for further information on Mulroney's testimony.

---

47. National Security Council Briefing[1]

Washington, November 30, 1960.

CONGO

I. Lumumba's escape from Leopoldville—presumably towards Stanleyville in Orientale Province—planned since early November.

A. [*less than 1 line not declassified*] —who had been in close contact with Lumumba—told [*less than 1 line not declassified*] 28 November he had not aided Lumumba's escape and had not seen him for a week. Characterized Lumumba as in "disturbed personal condition." [*less than 1 line not declassified*] says Lumumba blamed his remaining on so long in Leopoldville on Afro-Asians. Most of his followers have also fled.

B. Unconfirmed press reports suggest Lumumba is moving overland to Stanleyville.

II. Orientale Province controlled by Lumumba forces since mid-October, despite some opposition from army elements loyal to Mobutu.

---

[1] Source: Central Intelligence Agency Files, Job 79R00890A, Box 13, Folder 2, NSC Briefings, November 1960. Top Secret; [*codeword not declassified*].

A. Lumumba, describing situation Orientale, recently observed that "liberation movement in Congo could be launched from there." Probably hopes to consolidate position there, then build up his following in other areas.

B. Lumumba agents, the UAR, and Soviet Bloc continue active in support of this goal.

1. On 26 November, [*less than 1 line not declassified*] that Lumumba's operations in Stanleyville should be encouraged, "and similar movements started in Kasai, North Katanga and Kivu."

2. In mid-November, Lumumba emissary contacted [*less than 1 line not declassified*] concerning delivery of unidentified shipment which was to transit UAR and Sudan, presumably to Orientale Province.

III. On 28 November, Lumumba partisans in Stanleyville launched sweeping arrests of Europeans, including UN personnel. Most released, but many beaten. UN representative Stanleyville asked for emergency air evacuation of 1,000 Europeans on 29 November, but request dropped on 30 November with UN reporting Stanleyville "quiet."

A. Also on 28 November Congolese district commissioner in Stanleyville instructed all police posts Orientale Province that any European expressing anti-Lumumba sentiments would be expelled.

IV. Should Lumumba arrive safely Stanleyville, where his followers so well established, new phase of power struggle in Congo would begin.

A. According to one report, Mobutu's commissioners decided 29 November to mount military operations against Lumumba forces at Stanleyville. This would be most difficult. If UN unable prevent such action, result would be civil war.

48. Telegram From the Station in the Congo to the Central Intelligence Agency[1]

Leopoldville, December 10, 1960.

0452 (In 15279).

[*4 paragraphs (30 lines) not declassified*]

---

[1] Source: Central Intelligence Agency Files, Job 78–00435R, DDO/ISS Files, Box 1, Folder 5, [*cryptonym not declassified*] Ops. Secret; Rybat; [*cryptonym not declassified*]; Priority. Received at 1704Z.

5. During course meeting with [Mobutu] on 7 Dec, [COS] asked him if it not possible in near future establish legal govt replace college of commissioners and asked about [Mobutu] statement he plans retain commissioners as interim govt after 1 Jan. [Mobutu] expressed contempt for majority political leaders, noting they did little to oppose [Lumumba] when going was rough and that now [Lumumba] out of way they want reap benefits of his work. Expressed view most want benefits of office but few are willing accept responsibilities. Although [COS] could not but concur, he pointed out need to form legal government in near future to satisfy world opinion and to obtain backing of political leaders. After much talk, [Mobutu] agreed to compromise suggested by [COS] ([*less than 1 line not declassified*]) in which [Mobutu] would permit parliament to open 10 Jan 61 providing political leaders can guarantee majority parliamentarians will be present and majority will support government satisfactory to [*less than 1 line not declassified*] forces. ([COS] suggested and [Mobutu] agreed many commissioners should remain in govt as secretaries of state.) As new govt must be acceptable to [Mobutu], [COS] raised possibility of [Identity 1] as premier. [Mobutu] reacted favorably but [COS] did not try push point other than noting that [Identity 1] good man and now trying line up workable coalition.

6. [COS] reported above to Ambassador 7 Dec and obtained latter's okay to try organize new coalition govt. Ambassador agreed help and will see [Identity 1] with [COS] 10 Dec and will also try see [Mobutu] and [Identity 2] same day, [*less than 1 line not declassified*]. However, [Mobutu] called [COS] morning 9 Dec saying he "most disappointed" statements by [Identity 3] and Albert Delvaux criticizing his efforts govern Congo. [Mobutu] was very angry. Said he plans call meeting Leop of all CNA senior officers, to offer his resignation as chief of staff to Kasavubu and let latter try find someone who able control CNA. [Mobutu] made it clear he does not believe such person can be found. [COS] commiserated with [Mobutu] and arranged meet him later in morning. However, [Mobutu] did not call and although [COS] tried reach him many times no contact made. Will continue try see him soonest, as fear statements by [Identity 3] and Delvaux may upset [Mobutu's] agreement to reach compromise per para five. If [*cryptonym not declassified*] forces continue fight over spoils, [Mobutu] might be tempted dump them all and resort to another coup. Trying best to avoid this. Also will try convince him not submit resignation.

7. Ambassador under pressure from ODACID achieve interim solution government situation here to obtain legal facade for regime. Station and [Embassy] doubt interim government will provide more acceptable facade than commissioners govt unless it approved by parliament but we trying. ODACID appears believe we dealing with [*less than 1 line not declassified*] persons with some understanding

niceties parliamentary system. This not the case. [*cryptonym not declassified*] leaders [*1 line not declassified*] have little understanding of meaning world opinion or need for political compromise. Although Station understands pressure now heavy USUN, wish emphasize KUBARK not in position reach an immediate solution. Effort force through interim solution not acceptable key [*cryptonym not declassified*] leaders might result in formation govt which would not be able obtain parliamentary majority when parliament finally opened. Alternative danger might be angry [Mobutu] going for broke with another coup.

8. View political nature this operation, Station working closely with Ambassador and coordinating every step. We trying move as fast as possible and to implement ODYOKE policy but Station does not believe it advisable risk stirring up intramural [*cryptonym not declassified*] fight to try accomplish in week what we hope can be done in one month. We have come long way [*less than 1 line not declassified*] when one considers situation only three months ago. Our position strong with [Mobutu] as we give him help and guidance in early days when his chances were slim indeed. Some [*cryptonym not declassified*] leaders realize they would be occupying [Lumumba's] current quarters today had we not helped them. However, it is their country and they want make final decisions. Also politics is new game which they have not learned to play by our rules. Thus, we can go only so far as they willing go. Station believes we should not risk long term relationship with leaders for possible immediate gain in world opinion. However, will provide regular reports on efforts comply with Dir 15739 (Out 51379)[2] and ODACID cable 1551.[3]

End of message.

---

[2] Requested Leop see ODACID cable 1551 of 8 Dec. and support fully. [Footnote in the original.] CIA telegram 15739 to Leopoldville, December 9, is ibid.

[3] OCR/CB notified of reference. [Footnote in the original.] Regarding this cable, see footnote 1 to Document 280 in *Foreign Relations,* 1958–1960, volume XIV, Africa.

49. Telegram From the Station in the Congo to the Central Intelligence Agency[1]

Leopoldville, December 17, 1960.

0481 (In 18736). 1. [COS] met with [Mobutu] for nearly three hours 16 Dec.

2. When questioned about installation new government, [Mobutu] repeated statements reported Leop 0451 (In 15263).[2] Added he had discussed with [Identity 1] and told latter he willing open parliament soon as political leaders submit sufficient facts indicate they have parliamentary majority to support a government. In short, [Mobutu] says he ready to permit re-establishment legal govt, but only when political leaders prepared provide stable govt.

3. Unfortunately, Station sees few indications that political leaders (with exception [Identity 2] actively working to form coalition. They talk but appear unable work to achieve objectives. Seriously doubt any govt will be formed prior mid-January and suspect will take much longer.

4. Chief [Embassy] cabled ODACID 17 Dec saying he and English and French colleagues believe it advisable have African leaders meeting Brazzaville put pressure on [Identity 1] obtain legal govt. Station heartily concurs.

5. Chief [Embassy] requests paras 2 and 3 this message be passed ODACID soonest.

End of message.

---

[1] Source: Central Intelligence Agency Files, Job 78–00435R, DDO/ISS Files, Box 1, Folder 5, [*cryptonym not declassified*] Ops. Secret; Rybat; [*cryptonym not declassified*]; Operational Immediate. Received at 1848Z.

[2] Compromise plan to establish Congo govt. [Footnote in the original.] This CIA telegram has not been found.

---

50. Editorial Note

In telegram 0478 to the Central Intelligence Agency, December 17, 1960, the Station in Leopoldville reported that WIROGUE, an unidentified asset of the Congo Station, had arrived in Leopoldville on December 2. (Central Intelligence Agency Files, Job 86B00975R, Box 2, Folder 23, Review Staff Files, Assassinations, Vol. II) [*text not declassified*] Envision use as utility agent such as (1) organizing and conducting surveillance team (2) interception of pouches (3) blowing up bridges and/or (4) executing other assignments requiring positive action." (Ibid., Job 79–00149A, DDO/IMS Files, Box 23, Folder 1, Africa Division, Senate Select Committee, Volume II) In its December 17 telegram, the Station reported that WIROGUE had offered QJWIN, a CIA agent then in Leopoldville, "three hundred dollars per month to participate in intel net and be member 'execution squad.'" QJWIN responded that he was not interested. The Station commented that it was "concerned by WIROGUE free wheeling and lack security. Station has enough headaches without worrying about agent who not able handle finances and who not willing follow instructions. If Hqs desires, willing keep him on probation, but if continue have difficulties, believe WIROGUE recall best solution."

In 1975 the Church Committee investigated the possibility that WIROGUE's reference to an "execution squad" was connected to the assassination of Patrice Lumumba, but the committee was unable to substantiate such a connection. A March 14, 1975, CIA memorandum for the record (responding to the CIA Inspector General's request for information on WIROGUE) stated that a search of available documents did not clarify the matter to any great extent. (Ibid., Job 80B00910A, Box 18, Folder 11, Homicides—Lumumba, Patrice, Tab 6)

In a memorandum for the record dated June 20, 1975, another CIA official stated that he had briefed WIROGUE prior to his dispatch to Leopoldville, where WIROGUE was to be available to the Station for paramilitary activities. The official noted that WIROGUE had not followed instructions and had become a handling problem; eventually he had been returned to the United States. The official stated that neither WIROGUE nor QJWIN was in any way involved in Lumumba's arrest and subsequent assassination. (Ibid., Tab 4) For official testimony concerning WIROGUE and QJWIN in the Congo, see *Interim Report*, pages 37–48.

51. National Security Council Briefing[1]

Washington, December 20, 1960.

CONGO

I. Efforts by Gizenga's dissident regime in Stanleyville to secure foreign aid may result in greater Bloc or African intervention in the already explosive situation.

A. The UAR presently providing material assistance through its UN battalion in Equateur province.
B. USSR is probably also preparing to supply dissidents in Orientale Soviet UN delegate Zorin told [*less than 1 line not declassified*] December that "US is making preparations now, and we are making preparations too."
C. Although Sudan on 15 December advised [*less than 1 line not declassified*] that it could not permit transshipping of supplies to dissidents through Sudan, [*less than 1 line not declassified*] subsequently advised [*less than 1 line not declassified*] that there was at least "50 per cent chance" this position will be reversed.

II. Pro-Lumumba African countries, though vague as to how to return Lumumba to power, are now thinking in terms of a joint military command independent of UN to support dissidents. Such a command apparently would consist of military contingents "withdrawn" from UN command but not from Congo.

A. Morocco reportedly plans to delay pullout of its UN contingent until a decision is reached among African states concerning means of aiding dissidents.
B. Similarly, the UAR has made no move to carry out withdrawal of its UN contingent.
C. Hammarskjold has appealed to nations threatening withdrawal to reconsider their decision.

III. Mobutu, meanwhile, is considering military moves against dissidents.

A. Mobutu, under pressure from commissioners to move against dissidents, held council of war with subordinate commanders 14–15 December.
B. Congo Army units loyal to Mobutu scattered throughout Orientale and Equateur provinces evidently outnumber Gizenga's dissident forces.

---

[1] Source: Central Intelligence Agency Files, Job 79R00890A, Box 13, Folder 3, NSC Briefings December 1960. Top Secret; [*codeword not declassified*].

C. UN official in Leopoldville has stated that Gizenga and followers are doubtful of their ability to repel attack by Mobutu, and have made plans to flee in case of attack.

IV. The UN command in Leopoldville, threatened with departure of perhaps third of its 20,000-man force, maintains an anti-Mobutu posture.

A. UN representative Dayal increasingly anti-West. Continues to advocate disarming of Congo Army, blames current crisis on "those who build up Mobutu."

B. Sporadic tribal warfare in northern Katanga not yet controlled by UN forces.

V. Various Congolese political factions continue to work at cross purposes.

A. Mobutu, who earlier indicated he would extend his interim government indefinitely, reportedly is now willing to reconvene parliament in January. Has stated, however, that he will allow restoration of civil government only if its composition to his liking.

B. Kasavubu reportedly plans to call round table conference of Congolese parties in late December. He desires restoration of powers to the Ileo cabinet, and admits to being at odds with Mobutu, who desires to continue commissioners in office under some guise.

VI. We have just received an unconfirmed report that Lumumba had died in prison. I am taking this with a grain of salt until we have confirmation.

52. Telegram From the Central Intelligence Agency to the Station in the Congo[1]

Washington, December 30, 1960, 2358Z.

Dir 18908 (Out 58521). Re Leop 0552 (In 23752).[2]

1. We have been discussing ref recommendations with State at African bureau level and will be discussing further at Undersecretary level at 1100 local time 31 December. In discussion with Penfield, latter brought up recent embtels from Ambassador which have emphasized political settlement rather than military action. As result has asked following be passed Ambassador from him:

"We are having some difficulty reconciling your recommendations re encouragement and assistance to military campaign against Gizenga with your apparent reliance on political settlement as reflected your recent reporting e.g. Embtels 1419, 1432, 1436.[3] We assume you regard military action as essentially show of force to support political settlement but on basis info here one would appear prejudicial to the other. Our principal hesitations re military action are (1) possibility Mobutu forces would find themselves in situation where conflict with UN forces unavoidable, thus forcing UN in effect fight on Gizenga's side and (2) Belgian involvement could turn entire Afro Asian world violently against Kasavubu–Mobutu. Please comment urgently."

---

[1] Source: Central Intelligence Agency Files, Job 78–00435R, DDO/ISS Files, Box 1, Folder 5, [*cryptonym not declassified*] Ops. Secret; Rybat; [*cryptonym not declassified*]; Operational Immediate. Drafted and released by Tweedy.

[2] Station and Ambassador believed it urgent to support operation against Stanleyville. [Footnote in the original.] In telegram 0552 to CIA, December 29, the Station in Leopoldville reported that it had been unable to obtain hard intelligence on the Congolese Government's plans to mount a military operation against Stanleyville. (On December 12, Antoine Gizenga had declared an independent Free Republic of the Congo with Stanleyville as its capital.) Congo Sûreté member [*name not declassified*] said that the details were still not firm, but that the Belgian Government had agreed to support such an operation. He and Bomboko warned that a Stanleyville operation could not be mounted unless U.S. funds were forthcoming. The cable stressed that the Station and Ambassador believed it was urgent that the United States support the Congolese Government in mounting an operation against Stanleyville, and recommended that the Chief of Station be authorized to advise Mobutu or Bomboko that he had been authorized "in principle" to provide aid. (Ibid.)

[3] See footnotes 1, 2, and 3 to Document 292 in *Foreign Relations*, 1958–1960, volume XIV, Africa.

2. A reply prior our meeting tomorrow would obviously be most helpful.[4]

End of message.

---

[4] Telegram 0564 from Leopoldville to CIA, December 31, transmitted Ambassador Timberlake's reply, which stated that military action would be a show of force to support efforts toward a political settlement. He recognized the possibility of a clash between Mobutu's forces and UN forces, but believed the likelihood of such a clash was slight unless the United Nations ordered them to intervene. The Ambassador also believed that Belgium intended to exercise maximum discretion in providing support. Therefore, he believed that this operation should be supported as suggested. (Central Intelligence Agency Files, Job 78–00435R, DDO/ISS Files, Box 1, Folder 4, [*cryptonym not declassified*] Ops)

---

53. Telegram From the Central Intelligence Agency to the Station in the Congo[1]

Washington, December 31, 1960, 2104Z.

Dir 19039 (Out 58858).

1. As result of policy meeting this morning, you authorized as follows:

(A) To advise Congolese we prepared in principle to support financially their efforts to topple Gizenga regime. That we are anxious to avoid as far as possible full-scale fighting and bloodshed and to use troops wherever possible as show of force to produce desired political end.

(B) To inform Belgians of (A) above and that we will continue to deal with Congolese on these matters.

(C) To concert with [*less than 1 line not declassified*] in their planning along lines (A) above, with particular attention to UN capability and resolve to "freeze" Stanleyville and Orientale, and thus avoid risk major CNA–UN military clash. (*Comment:* We have in mind SYG apparent serious reaction to recent USUN démarche and Embtel 1449[2] re UN stopping Ilyushins. If UN purpose firm, about which plenty of room for doubt, we would then hope to see funds used for full-scale subversion

---

[1] Source: Central Intelligence Agency Files, Job 78–00435R, DDO/ISS Files, Box 1, Folder 5, [*cryptonym not declassified*] Ops. Secret; Rybat; [*cryptonym not declassified*]; Operational Immediate. Drafted and released by Tweedy.

[2] OCR/CB notified of reference cable. [Footnote in the original.] This telegram has not been found.

effort against a Gizenga who at least not receiving as much logistic and hardware support as he anticipated).

(D) To request [*less than 1 line not declassified*] to show you detail their arithmetic re [*number not declassified*] francs so we can be in better position decide what our contribution should be. You should forward recommendations on this soonest.

2. While necessity for limited role with [*less than 1 line not declassified*] accepted, wish emphasize need for maximum security this regard order minimize risk of public association with them in this enterprise.[3]

3. State is sending parallel cable via its channels.[4]

End of message.

---

[3] In telegram 0567 from Leopoldville to CIA, January 2, 1961, the Chief of Station reported that he had advised the Ambassador of the decision in telegram 19039, and had briefed Bomboko and [*text not declassified*], who accepted the conditions outlined in paragraph one. (Mobutu was still in Luluabourg.) Considering Mobutu's defeat at Bukavu, the Chief of Station doubted that the Congolese Government would continue its planned moves on Stanleyville until more troops were available. (Central Intelligence Agency Files, Job 78–00435R, DDO/ISS Files, Box 1, Folder 6, [*cryptonym not declassified*] Ops)

[4] See Document 292 in *Foreign Relations*, 1958–1960, volume XIV, Africa.

---

54. Telegram From the Station in the Congo to the Central Intelligence Agency[1]

Leopoldville, January 12, 1961.

0625 (In 30010).

1. [*cryptonym not declassified*][2] situation deteriorating rapidly. Troops and police most resentful because pay low as compared officers and govt leaders. Per [Embassy] cables, police were on verge mutiny 10 Jan. Many local sources say discontent continuing mount but station not able substantiate at present.

2. [COS] returned Leop morning 12 Jan on same plane [Identity 1]. Latter talked with [Mobutu] by phone 11 Jan. Said it his opinion Leop garrison will mutiny within two or three days unless drastic action

---

[1] Source: Central Intelligence Agency Files, Job 78–00435R, DDO/ISS Files, Box 1, Folder 6, [*cryptonym not declassified*] Ops. Secret; Rybat; [*cryptonym not declassified*]; Operational Immediate. Received at 1741Z.

[2] CIA political action program in support of moderate, anti-Lumumba leaders in the Congo [*text not declassified*].

taken satisfy complaints.[3] In reply question said only suggestion at present is offer troops special combat bonus to put down Gizenga "rebellion." However said no GOC funds available this purpose. Literally begged [COS] obtain ODYOKE funds meet this need, pointing out troop mutiny almost certainly would end [Mobutu] control CNA and bring about [Lumumba] return power. [Identity 1] estimates would take about one million dollars per month for several months to achieve objective. He recognizes this not good solution for in way this is accepting CNA blackmail. But believes it better than letting matters drift and facing certain failure [*cryptonym not declassified*][4] objectives. Station concurs.

3. COS and Ambassador seeing [Identity 1] 1500Z, 12 Jan. [COS] also trying contact [Mobutu] and other [*cryptonym not declassified*] leaders to get reading. This message sent warn HQS serious problem exists and to urge immediate KUBARK liaison and discussion this problem. Believe could insert funds clandestinely via [Mobutu], [Identity 1] if necessary.

4. Will cable Station and [Embassy] views on request soonest.

End of message.

---

[3] Part of this sentence is quoted in *Interim Report* p. 49.

[4] See footnote 2.

---

55. Memorandum From the Chief of the Africa Division, Directorate of Plans, Central Intelligence Agency (Tweedy) to the Assistant Secretary of State for African Affairs (Satterthwaite)[1]

Washington, January 14, 1961.

SUBJECT

Political Situation in the Congo

1. [CIA] received the following message from its representative in Leopoldville on January 13, 1961.[2] [Department of State] a Leopoldville

---

[1] Source: Central Intelligence Agency Files, Job 76–00366R, DDO/ISG Files, Box 1, Folder 10, [*text not declassified*], 1960–62. Secret. This memorandum was sent via back-channel.

[2] Telegram 0630 from Leopoldville to CIA, January 13. (Ibid., Job 78–00435R, DDO/ISS Files, Box 1, Folder 6, [*cryptonym not declassified*] Ops)

representative read and concurred with the message. The message is as follows.

2. Both the [Department of State] and [CIA] representatives in Leopoldville recognize that a temporary pay increase does not provide a final or good solution to the CNA problem. However, it now appears we have no acceptable alternative. If the GOC refuses to heed CNA pay demands [CIA] and [Department of State] representatives in Leopoldville believe the present government may fall within a few days. The result would almost certainly be chaos and the return of Lumumba to power.[3] The second alternative would be for the UNOC to disarm the CNA. That step might lead to fighting between CNA and UN troops, which would play into the hands of the Gizenga regime. Also, if the troops were disarmed, Lumumba would probably return to power. Dayal and other UN leaders have directly or indirectly supported Lumumba to such an extent that [CIA] and [Department of State] have little doubt that they would avail themselves of this opportunity to encourage the return of Lumumba to the government. For example, if the CNA were disarmed and the UNOC opened parliament, the combination of Lumumba's powers as a demagogue, his able use of goon squads and propaganda, and the spirit of defeat within the Kasavubu/ Mobutu coalition which would increase rapidly under such conditions would almost certainly insure a Lumumba victory in the parliament. In short, [CIA] and [Department of State] believe the US Government faces a difficult choice. Neither alternative is good, but refusal to take drastic steps at this time will lead to defeat of US policy in the Congo. On the other hand, immediate steps to guarantee troop loyalty by increasing salaries through a combat bonus would give the US a breathing spell during which time we might aid Mobutu and [*name not declassified*] and others to meet the problem of the Gizenga regime and to instill discipline in the CNA.

3. In view of the above, [Department of State] and [CIA] representatives in Leopoldville recommend that the [CIA] representative be authorized to tell Mobutu and [*name not declassified*] that the US is prepared "in principle" to assist them by providing funds on a temporary basis (three or four months) to meet CNA pay demands providing the following requirements are met:

a. Final approval would be contingent upon submission of GOC plans and the view of headquarters in Washington.

b. GOC would immediately prepare plans to counter the moves of the Gizenga regime (if it risks disaster, *sic.*)

c. Mobutu and [*name not declassified*] would coordinate in advance future political and military moves with the [CIA] representative.

[3] Quoted in *Interim Report*, p. 49.

4. It is recognized that many powers would accuse the US of intervention if the GOC suddenly finds extra funds for the troops. However, the [CIA] representative believes he can fund the operation without any appreciable risk of compromise. We have already been accused of doing more than we have done, but to date no one has offered proof of US intervention. [*1½ lines not declassified*]

[*pseudonym not declassified*][4]

---

[4] Printed from a copy that bears Tweedy's typed pseudonym.

---

56. Editorial Note

On April 25, 1963, the Station in Leopoldville reported to Central Intelligence Agency headquarters that it had received and reviewed a "first batch" of Tshombe papers [*text not declassified*] including letters dated January 15, 1961, to Justin Bomboko and Joseph Kasavubu approving Patrice Lumumba's transfer to Katanga, and one dated January 13, 1961, to Joseph Mobutu offering a payment of one million Belgian Congolese francs in the hope that this sum would aid his army. The cable said that Mobutu had advised the Congolese Government of the payment, which was made during the "post-Coquilhatville reconciliation period," and had turned the funds over to the Congolese National Army. (Telegram 6730 to the Central Intelligence Agency; Central Intelligence Agency Files, [*text not declassified*], Tshombe, Moise, Fiche 4) Copies of the letters to Kasavubu and Mobutu, which are in French, are ibid., Fiche 18, and a copy of the letter to Bomboko, also in French, is ibid., [*text not declassified*], Bomboko, Justin, Vol. I.) On April 12, 1966, CIA headquarters, responding to an inquiry from a Chief of Station regarding the authenticity of the January 15 letter to Bomboko, stated that CIA could not state definitely that the letter was a forgery. CIA's dispatch said it was possible that the letter had been prepared by the Soviets or "some other interested party," but noted that there was no contradiction between the contents and date of the letter and the known events leading up to Lumumba's death. (Dispatch [*text not declassified*] to the Chief of Station, [*text not declassified*], April 12, 1966; ibid., [*text not declassified*], Tshombe, Moise, Fiche 41)

57. Memorandum for the Record[1]

Washington, January 16, 1961.

SUBJECT

Political Situation in the Congo (Consideration of payment to CNA Troops)

Based on cable traffic from Leopoldville concerning the possible need to supply additional funds to [*name not declassified*] and Mobutu to cover a proposed increase in pay to CNA troops, Mr. Tweedy had discussions with Department of State on Friday[2] last. On Saturday morning an [CIA/Department of State] note was handed to Mr. Philip Clock.[3] This memo reflected recommendations from COS, Leopoldville and concurred in by the Ambassador that an undetermined amount of money be pledged in principle to [*name not declassified*] or Mobutu for troop payment. Certain provisions and demands would accompany the pledge.

On Saturday, Mr. Clock handed the memo to Mr. Merchant. I had advised Mr. Clock that according to our information the Congo Government had openly pledged an increase in payment to the troops at Thysville and planned to advise all of its commands that a similar increase in payments would be forthcoming. Mr. Clock had wanted to know what CIA thought of the proposal. After discussions in the Division and with Mr. Helms, I told Mr. Clock that in view of the rapidly deteriorating situation in the Congo[4] that anything which could be done to hold it together to give us additional time for planning and action would appear to be worthwhile. Later in the morning (Saturday) Mr. Clock telephoned to say that his office had been in consultation with Mr. Merchant.

Mr. Merchant had stated that the open and public action taken by the Government of the Congo to promise increased payment to the CNA had put the earlier Congelese request for money on an entirely different basis. He said that the matter was now in the open and must be handled that way. He said the question was should the United Nations assume this additional payment or failing this, should the United

---

[1] Source: Central Intelligence Agency Files, Job 78–00435R, DDO/ISS Files, Box 1, Folder 6, [*cryptonym not declassified*] Ops. Secret.

[2] January 13.

[3] See Document 55.

[4] Telegram 0636 from Leopoldville to CIA, January 15, transmitted a report of mutiny developing at Camp Nkoklo (the main CNA camp at Leopoldville), with soldiers saying they had orders to arrest all officers and other troops departing for Thysville with plans to liberate Lumumba. (Central Intelligence Agency Files, Job 78–00435R, DDO/ISS Files, Box 1, Folder 6, [*cryptonym not declassified*] Ops)

States offer to handle the increased payments in a bi-lateral way. If the latter were to be the case, this would be overt and official. The question of a bi-lateral approach for this purpose is one of high policy and is one which Mr. Merchant said that he would not recommend to the President "in the next five days." Mr. Merchant made it clear that the incoming Secretary of State should be given the opportunity to decide whether or not a bilateral approach should be used in this matter.

I told Mr. Clock that I could understand perfectly their rationale in this decision but wondered if it took into account the urgency and time element involved. Mr. Clock said he felt that although the commitment by GOC had been immediate that perhaps there would be a lag period between now and the time additional funds were actually needed on hand.

I asked Mr. Clock how much of the above we were at liberty to cable to COS, Leopoldville. He preferred that we not forward all of the elements in Mr. Merchant's decision but suggested that we tell our man to take no initiative in raising this with either [*name not declassified*] or Mobutu. Should they take the initiative then the COS would take that opportunity to find the answers to such answers as:

a. How many troops are involved?
b. Total sum involved?
c. When is pay day?
d. How long can the Congolese continue payments without outside help?

Mr. Clock said that the Department would be sending the Ambassador instructions on the whole question.

Glenn Fields[5]
Deputy Chief
African Division

[5] Printed from a copy that bears this typed signature.

58. Memorandum From the Chief of the Africa Division, Directorate of Plans, Central Intelligence Agency (Tweedy) to the Assistant Secretary of State for African Affairs (Satterthwaite)[1]

Washington, January 16, 1961.

SUBJECT

Political Situation in the Congo

1. After discussions with [Department of State] on Saturday, January 14, 1961, [CIA] advised its representative as follows concerning recent communications about possible action concerning increased pay for the CNA.

2. The [CIA] representative in Leopoldville was advised that Washington had specifically noted that the GOC had publicly declared its intention to raise CNA pay. This, of course, puts the matter on a different basis and this development is being given further consideration here.

3. In the meanwhile, the [CIA] representative was instructed not to approach either [*name not declassified*] or Mobutu on this subject but to await their initiative. If and when they raise the subject again, the [CIA] representative was instructed to make no commitments but should take this opportunity to find out:

a. How many troops are involved and where were they located,
b. Best estimate of money required,
c. When does GOC expect to make the first increased payment to troops,
d. How long can GOC make payments without additional outside help.

4. The [CIA] representative was instructed that under no circumstances should he indicate that assistance might be forthcoming.

[*pseudonym not declassified*][2]

---

[1] Source: Central Intelligence Agency Files, Job 76–00366R, DDO/ISG Files, Box 1, Folder 7, Congo. 1960–69, Pt. 1. Secret. This memorandum was sent via backchannel.

[2] Printed from a copy that bears Tweedy's typed pseudonym.

59. Telegram From the Station in the Congo to the Central Intelligence Agency[1]

Leopoldville, January 17, 1961.

0646 (In 32132). Supdata [COS] from [Identity 1] and [Identity 2].[2] [Identity 3] advised [COS] 14 Jan that plans being made transfer Lumumba from Thysville [to] Baxwnga [*Bakwangam*]. Also [Identity 4] reported GOC planning move Lumumba. Filed 17164; report class Secret Noforn. [*less than 1 line not declassified*][3] Congo Republic. Subj: ex-premier Patrice Lumumba transferred from Thysville Military camp to prison in Bakwangam DOI 1 Jan 61. Pada Congo Republic, Leopoldville 17 Jan 61. Source: [*less than 1 line not declassified*] (B) [*less than 1 line not declassified*] (C) [*1 line not declassified*] (C). Apr 2.

---

[1] Source: Central Intelligence Agency Files, Job 79–00149A, DDO/IMS Files, African Division, Senate Select Committee, Volume III, Box 23, Folder 2. Secret; Priority. Received at 2307Z.

[2] Unidentified CIA contract agent.

[3] Field Report No. [*text not declassified*], TDCS–3/462,509, January 17, also reported that various Congolese Government officials had indicated some uneasiness at having Lumumba imprisoned in a military camp so close to Leopoldville. (Central Intelligence Agency Files, Job 79–00149A, DDO/IMS Files, African Division, Senate Select Committee, Volume III, Box 23, Folder 2)

---

60. Central Intelligence Agency Information Report[1]

Washington, January 18, 1961.

TDCS–3/462, 691, Field Report [*text not declassified*]

SUBJECT

Arrival of Patrice Lumumba in Elisabethville

1. Patrice Lumumba arrived about 1700 hours 17 Jan via air Congo DC–4 from Moana (near Matadi). His arrival was not expected by GOK

---

[1] Source: Central Intelligence Agency Files, Job 79–00149A, DDO/IMS Files, African Division, Senate Select Committee, Volume III, Box 23, Folder 2. Confidential; Noforn; Continued Control.

and plane had to circle for one hour while security forces were assembled to meet aircraft. Lumumba and two fellow detainees debarked chained together and showing signs of having been badly beaten in flight. All Lumumba teeth have been knocked out beaten after disembarked but not too roughly, then removed unknown prison ([*less than 1 line not declassified*] Comment: One source claimed Lumumba in Jadotville but the other believed Jadotville too insecure and he probably taken somewhere like Sandoa). 2. Field dissem: State.

End of message.

---

61. Memorandum From the Ambassador to the North American Treaty Organization (Burgess) to Secretary of State Herter[1]

Washington, January 18, 1961.

SUBJECT

Message to Secretary of State from Ambassador Burgess concerning the Congo

On January 16, 1961 at the request of Mr. Frederick Nolting, Deputy Chief USRO, [*less than 1 line not declassified*] in Paris met with Ambassador Burgess, Mr. Nolting and Mr. Joseph Wolf to brief them on the general situation in the Congo as background for their deliberations concerning a Belgian proposal that NATO endorse Belgian direct military assistance to Mobutu.

[*less than 1 line not declassified*] conveyed the substance of available reports concerning the Congo and also advised them that [*less than 1 line not declassified*] was discussing contingency planning with the French although no policy decisions regarding any action program had yet been made in Washington. Mr. Nolting requested [*less than 1 line not declassified*] pass the following message to the Secretary of State from Ambassador Burgess:

"Further to Polto 948[2] regarding Bomboko request to Belgians for direct aid, we have had discussions [*less than 1 line not declassified*] in which they gave us gist of recommendations already submitted to Washington for covert operation to bolster Mobutu's forces. As we see

---

[1] Source: Central Intelligence Agency Files, Job 78–00435R, DDO/ISS Files, Box 1, Folder 6, [*cryptonym not declassified*] Ops. Secret. This memorandum was sent via backchannel.

[2] Not found.

the situation in the Congo, in relation to Western interests generally and in relation interests member countries of NATO in African developments, believe covert operation stands best chance of reversing present unsatisfactory situation while avoiding large, obvious dangers implicit in overt bilateral aid by Belgians or any other Western country. While we do not know details of proposed operation and are in no position to evaluate chances of success, we would favor prompt consideration, and fastest possible action if plan is approved. From NATO point of view, believe most member countries would expect U.S. to take action of this kind in present deteriorating situation in the Congo. They would expect us to use sufficient skill, determination and force to make it succeed, without traceable evidence of complicity on the part of any member country."[3]

[*pseudonym not declassified*][4]

---

[3] Transmitted in telegram [*text not declassified*] (Central Intelligence Agency Files, Job 78–00435R, DDO/ISS Files, Box 1, Folder 6, [*cryptonym not declassified*] Ops.)

[4] Printed from a copy that bears Tweedy's typed pseudonym.

---

62. Telegram From [*location not declassified*] to the Central Intelligence Agency[1]

[*location not declassified*], January 19, 1961.

0283 [*less than 1 line not declassified*]. 1. Thanks for Patrice. If we had known he was coming we would have baked a snake.

2. Per [*name not declassified*] GOK had no advance word whatsoever. Lumumba severely beaten at airport by gendarmerie, then taken Jadotville prison where guarded by all white guards. GOK does not plan liquidate Lumumba. [*name not declassified*] fears chances of Balubakat uprising in Eville considerably increased.[2]

End of message.

---

[1] Source: Central Intelligence Agency Files, [*text not declassified*], Folder 3. Secret; Routine. Repeated priority to Leopoldville. Received at 0135Z.

[2] Most of this cable is quoted in *Interim Report*, p. 51.

63. Editorial Note

In telegram 0662, January 20, 1961, the Station in Leopoldville reported to the Central Intelligence Agency that Joseph Mobutu and [*name not declassified*] were "constantly" urging financial aid for the Congolese National Army. Otherwise, they said, their regime would fall. Mobutu insisted that he must have a guarantee of financial aid before he could launch a military operation against the Gizenga regime. The next day, in telegram 21704 to Leopoldville, the Central Intelligence Agency informed the Station that Headquarters was urgently seeking a review of U.S. policy toward aiding Mobutu's forces. Pending the receipt of further instructions, the Station was to continue to accept statements concerning Mobutu's needs without making any specific commitments. (Both in Central Intelligence Agency Files, Job 78–00435R, DDO/ISS Files, Box 1, Folder 6, [*cryptonym not declassified*] Ops) The Station replied on January 22, in telegram 0678, that at a meeting the previous day [*name not declassified*] had again made a pitch for U.S. support for pay and equipment for the CNA. While the government could meet the regular army pay for January, [*name not declassified*] explained, it did not have the funds needed to meet the "special indemnity" promised after the Thysville mutiny. (Ibid.)

64. Dispatch From the Station in the Congo to the Central Intelligence Agency[1]

Leopoldville, January 26, 1961.

[*Dispatch number not declassified*]

SUBJECT

Special Letter from Leopoldville Station

ACTION

None, for your information

1. I regret that the force of circumstances has prevented me from writing the usual [*cryptonym not declassified*] letters to you during the Congo crisis. However, from personal meetings with [Tweedy] and [Bissell], I understand you have received regular and detailed briefings on the operational developments in this area. I am taking the liberty of writing this special letter to you because I wish to call to your attention a matter which I believe is of direct concern to KUBARK.

2. Many rumors have come to the attention of the Embassy and the Station to the effect that, with the change in administration, our policy in the Congo will be reversed and that we will favor a return of Lumumba in some capacity to the Congolese Government. Persons relating these rumors almost invariably add that Ambassador Timberlake will be replaced by a person who favors the establishment of close relations with Lumumba and his supporters. These rumors have been brought to my attention by many Congolese political figures (some of them clandestine contacts of this Station), journalists and representatives of other governments, as well as press reports of which you are undoubtedly aware. Needless to say, these rumors are beginning to have an adverse effect upon our operational efforts, for some assets are afraid the Station will reverse its current policy and that, as a result of their confidential cooperation with us, they will be abandoned to suffer the consequences of their acts. This situation has not reached the state at which Station efforts are hampered appreciably, but in view of the pessimism and defeatism which is so prevalent in Leopoldville at this time, the continued spread of such rumors could undermine the Station's position rather rapidly, should they become accepted by the local population. Thus, any steps which can be taken by the appropriate au-

[1] Source: Central Intelligence Agency Files, Job 82–00450R, Box 6, Folder 6, Leopoldville, 3 Feb 54–Dec 65, [*cryptonym not declassified*]. Secret; Rybat.

thorities to nip these rumors in the bud would be of considerable aid to the Leopoldville Station. In this respect, the inaugural address was well received in the Congo and raised the hopes of many Congolese.

3. The rumors concerning the possible replacement of Ambassador Timberlake also have a direct effect upon Station operations. As I have reported in numerous communications, Ambassador Timberlake has proved to be a strong supporter of KUBARK in general, and, specifically, he has provided the aid, guidance, and support necessary for the implementation of our clandestine operations. Without his strong support, it would not have been possible for the Station to accomplish many of the operational objectives assigned by Headquarters to support ODYOKE policy in the Congo. As a result of Timberlake's dynamic and effective brand of diplomacy, he has been personally attacked by [*less than 1 line not declassified*]. According to journalistic contacts of the Station and the Embassy, [*less than 1 line not declassified*] has launched a campaign against Ambassador Timberlake, accusing him of undermining the objectives and work of the [*less than 1 line not declassified*]. It would appear that [*less than 1 line not declassified*] objective in this campaign is to bring about the recall of the Ambassador and the appointment of a replacement more amenable to his personal influence and policies, policies which do not seem to be in accord with the policy directives received by this Station.

4. While I realize that major policy decisions and the selection of senior government officials are not, and should not be, the responsibility of KUBARK field personnel, I believe this is a situation which warrants your personal attention. Insofar as our Congo policy is concerned, I firmly believe that a drastic change at this time would be both disastrous and ineffectual. A change would not only alienate those persons and assets who support our present policy, but it is my opinion that it would also not be possible to win the support or friendship of the opposition leaders. While they might be willing to accept our financial and technical aid, they also would turn to the UAR and the Soviet Bloc with requests for aid and technical assistance. As their appetites would be insatiable, we would soon reach a point beyond which we would not be prepared to fulfill their requests. At that point, I believe they would turn more and more to the Soviet Bloc for aid and that in a very short time the Congo would fall under the influence, if not the control, of the Soviet Bloc. The opinions which I have expressed herein relative to a possible Bloc take over in the Congo are shared, to the best of my knowledge, by all Embassy personnel and many other qualified observers who have had an opportunity to observe the Congo crisis at first hand. I thus submit these views to you for your personal consideration.

5. Although I am reluctant to raise matters which are not within my field of competence, I feel it incumbent upon me to draw to your at-

tention the unfailing support and cooperation this Station has received from Ambassador Timberlake and to note that one reason he is being attacked by [*less than 1 line not declassified*] is that ODYOKE policy, which is supported by clandestine KUBARK operations, often has appeared to be in conflict with [*less than 1 line not declassified*] personal policy for the Congo. Most of the allegations made against Timberlake by [*less than 1 line not declassified*] are false, but [*less than 1 line not declassified*] obviously suspects some of the political activities of Lumumba's opponents are inspired by covert ODYOKE operations and he blames Timberlake for this. In short, one of the reasons for which Timberlake is under fire is that he has firmly advocated ODYOKE policy in the Congo, including KUBARK operations designed to support such ODYOKE policy. Thus, should it be decided to recall Ambassador Timberlake, as is rumored in Leopoldville, I believe it would be only logical that I, too, be transferred to another post of duty, should the reason for his recall be related to his support of ODYOKE policy and KUBARK operations. In this respect, I should note that my usefulness in this area in the near future would probably be limited, should ODYOKE policy toward the Congo undergo a complete reversal. Many Station assets would almost certainly believe that I had betrayed them and hold me personally responsible for encouraging them to take positions which, with a reversal of ODYOKE policy, would become extremely dangerous. In all probability many would refuse to cooperate with KUBARK or any other ODYOKE agency, in the future, and some might attempt to buy their personal safety by denouncing me or other ODYOKE personnel.

[***pseudonym not declassified***][2]

[2] Printed from a copy that bears Devlin's typed pseudonym.

65. Telegram From the Central Intelligence Agency to the Station in the Congo[1]

Washington, January 26, 1961, 2329Z.

Dir 22503 (Out 67110). Re Leop 0678 (In 34375).[2]

1. All factors in your recent cables concerning requests by [Mobutu] and [Identity 1] for funds were presented on 25 Jan to responsible levels including Idens A[3] and B.[4]

2. KUBARK expressed the view that whereas money alone is not the cure-all it does appear that a quick and sizable contribution is required as a stop gap measure to buy time and slow the rate of general deterioration. KUBARK recognized that the matter of publicly announced increased pay for troops must be handled ultimately in an open and regularized way from whatever source.

3. Based on KUBARK recommendation it was agreed this message be sent asking you to consult with Ambassador and respond as best you can to following questions:

A. How convinced are you that the [*cryptonym not declassified*][5] are in fact in urgent need of funds.

B. Is it possible to state in a fairly precise way what the funds would be used for.

C. How much and how soon would you recommend we contribute.

4. Some of the questions here arise from a variety of opinions and reports on whether, what and how much is needed. For example [Identity 2] is persuaded that the [*cryptonym not declassified*][6] are not in urgent need now. [Identity 3] appears to tend the other way. The full nature and extent of the Belgian input is not clear. The [*cryptonym not declassified*][7] themselves seem to have been unable or unwilling to give sufficient facts with which to document a good case.

---

[1] Source: Central Intelligence Agency Files, Job 78–00435R, DDO/ISS Files, Box 1, Folder 6, [*cryptonym not declassified*] Ops. Secret; Rybat; [*cryptonym not declassified*]; Priority. Drafted and authenticated by Fields (C/AF) and released by DD/P.

[2] [*text not declassified*] [Identity 1] made pitch to Devlin for ODYOKE support to pay and equip the troops. [Footnote in the original.] See Document 63.

[3] Under Secretary of State Chester A. Bowles.

[4] Ambassador at Large W. Averell Harriman.

[5] Moderate, anti-Lumumba leaders in the Congo supported by a CIA political action program called [*cryptonym not declassified*].

[6] See footnote 5.

[7] See footnote 5.

5. We recognize difficulties involved and assure you will use your answers to best possible advantage here.

End of message.

66. Memorandum for the Record[1]

Washington, January 31, 1961.

SUBJECT

Telephone Conversation with James Penfield,[2] 31 Jan 61

At noon on 31 January Jim Penfield called to say that they were having an internal meeting on the policy paper on the Congo.[3] He asked whether we had any further comments on it. I said that there were some bothersome aspects to it. These were the facts that on the one hand we would be taming Mobutu and on the other releasing Lumumba. In essence we were generating a sequence of events which would lead to a political being in the Congo the ultimate orientation of which could not be assured. He said that these risks had been taken into account and believed to be acceptable. I said that I felt that if the UN in fact did neutralize in a strong way the political and military elements in the Congo and did take control in a neutral way, then this, combined with the administrative structure outlined in the third element of the proposal, would indeed make the risk of a pro-Lumumbist takeover more remote. I emphasized that strong neutral UN action would be the key to it. I asked him what he thought Timberlake's reaction would be. He didn't know, but suggested that it would appear that Timberlake had no concrete alternative proposals.[4]

Glenn Fields
AC/AF

---

[1] Source: Central Intelligence Agency Files, Job 78–00435R, DDO/ISS Files, Box 1, Folder 6, [*cryptonym not declassified*] Ops. Secret.

[2] Deputy Assistant Secretary of State for African Affairs James K. Penfield.

[3] See Document 17, *Foreign Relations*, 1961–1963, volume XX, Congo Crisis.

[4] At the 475th meeting of the National Security Council on February 1, Rusk summarized the policy proposals sent to the President. NSC Record of Action No. 2397-d stated that the Department of State's proposal, which was subsequently reviewed and approved by the President, was being submitted after coordination with the Department of Defense and CIA. Dulles subsequently took issue with the record, saying that the recently adopted course of action dealing with Congo problems had not been coordinated with CIA. (Ibid., p. 46)

67. Paper Prepared in the Embassy in the Congo[1]

Leopoldville, undated.

THE ALTERNATIVES WE FACE

I. Support Continuation of the United Nations Effort on Essentially Its Present Basis.

Action Required

1. Keep the Belgians from intervening, on larger scale, and lower the boom on them if they do.

2. Allow the Katanga and South Kasai "situation of fact" to continue essentially unchanged.

3. Be prepared to continue to pay the bulk of the bill while leaving the policy control with Hammarskjold.

Probable Consequences

1. Faint possibility Mobutu might bring off his present offensive with short term favorable results but no guarantee increased stability.

2. Probability Gizenga forces will take over through breakdown Mobutu forces in Leopoldville without actual fighting in face of ruthlessness and forward motion of Gizenga forces.

3. Belgians will either—

a) heed our request not to intervene, but hold us bitterly responsible for unfavorable outcome; or
b) intervene in half-baked way, which is unlikely to stem the tide more likely.

4. If Gizenga takes over, will put himself increasingly under Communist wing, though probably Soviets will be more discreet this time and work throught Czechs, UAR and Guinea. Probable rapid increase of Chicom influence through Mulele in particular.

5. Flight of whites (as in Province Orientale) and consequent economic breakdown, which will assist Communist penetration. Also flight of moderate Congolese.

---

[1] Source: Central Intelligence Agency Files, Job 78–00435R, DDO/ISS Files, Box 1, Folder 6, [*cryptonym not declassified*]. Ops. Secret. The original is attached to a February 2 memorandum from Acting Chief of the Africa Division Glenn Fields to Deputy Director of Plans Richard Bissell, stating that the paper was drafted by Ambassador Timberlake with the assistance of Ambassador to Belgium William Burden and the Chief of Station in Leopoldville.

6. Probable center of Gizenga policy would be military action against South Kasai and Katanga (as Lumumba tried), eventually also Angola, etc.

7. UN would be pushed out gradually as it ceased to serve Gizenga's purposes. Disastrous consequences for UN would only be deferred.

Advantages

None we can think of.

Disadvantages

1. Introduction of more virulent form of Communist satellite in heart of Central Africa, with constant threat to peace and security of all of Black Africa (see above).

2. Serious blow to Belgo-American relations (see point 3 above) and to NATO unity (c.f. Suez crisis).

3. Serious blow to future of UN.

II. Redirect and Beef up UN Effort

A. Minimum solution: Seal off Congo frontiers and airfields in order to isolate Congo from outside intervention, but without further UN intervention in internal affairs.

Action Required

1. Make real effort to obtain Soviet agreement to mutual non-intervention, if this proves feasible.

2. If not, we will need effective support of moderate (non-Casablanca) group in UNGA to outvote Soviets and Casablanca group, as on Kasavubu credentials.

3. UN forces and mixed control groups must be stationed at *all* significant frontier points and airfields and be willing to use force to prevent inflow of military aid.

4. This will require substantial reinforcement of UNOC forces, and in addition more trustworthy ones (Australian, South American, etc., not just African).

5. This will also require full commitment by Hammarskjold to an active policy, which in turn will require Security Council or UNGA resolution (depending on whether Soviets cooperate or not).

6. Dayal must be replaced by an objective, honest and energetic man prepared to use his mandate to the full. Cdr. Jackson, a good Nigerian, etc.

7. Outside aid to Katanga and South Kasai will also have to be stopped, which means

a) Obtain full Belgian cooperation, which will be difficult until mid-April.

b) Scuttling Tshombe's would automatically be seriously weakened.

8. UN must at least help to train Congo Army.

Advantages

1. Reduce chances of hot war involving US and Soviet Union in Congo.

2. Cut ground out from under Gizenga, assuming he is largely dependent on outside help.

3. Make possible at least limited success of UN.

Disadvantages

1. There is real doubt this will work.

2. Makes no provision for longer-term settlement of Congo's problems, which will continue to plague us for a long time.

3. Will require a remarkable degree of continuing support from Europeans and Africans to work.

4. May well cause instability and chaos to spread to Katanga.

5. The major burden of economic support for Congo will fall even more heavily on the US.

B. Intermediate solution: Seal off borders, etc., as in A. but put UN forces in position to help Congolese Central Government to maintain order.

Action Required

1. All action mentioned under A above.

2. Installation of a Central Government which UN can recognize.

3. More troops required, and probably a stronger UN mandate.

Advantages

1. As above, Section A.

2. Speedier elimination of Gizenga and other harmful elements.

3. Better chance of creating long-term stability in Congo.

Disadvantages

1. Difficulty of obtaining a clearly legal government.

2. More difficult to obtain UN mandate and perhaps less support from Afro-Asians.

3. Probability of continued friction between GOC and UN.

C. Maximum solutions: Seal off frontiers, disarm all CNA forces and UN takes over responsibility for creation and maintenance of order.

Action Required

1. All of above, plus.

2. Even more troops.

3. Agreement of Congolese Government or decision to override their wishes.

4. The UN would have to have a real political policy-making body or delegate that power to its Representative.

Advantages

1. If it worked, there might be some real chance of having law and order in the Congo.

2. Hence there might be better chance for longer-term solution.

Disadvantages

1. Difficult to believe Congolese Government would ever accept this "trusteeship". Cannot make it work without or against them.

2. Probably impossible to obtain UN majority because of the precedent involved.

3. UN structure not strong enough to do the political decision-making necessary in fact to govern the Congo.

4. Even more troops and money required.

5. Some difficulties with the Belgians, only worse.

General Comments on Alternative II

1. If we are determined to play the UN card, we must be prepared to throw our assets into the balance, and also to make clear that if the necessary things are not done, we will withdraw our support of the UN effort, which means its termination.

2. Effective action along any of above lines will require several months at least. But within a month or a bit more, if things continue as they are, Gizenga may be in power. This is a fundamental and urgent problem.

III. Active and Direct Western Intervention Outside the UN.

A. Minimum effort: Combined US-Belgian military assistance on quasi-clandestine basis designed to permit Mobutu's forces to stop the advance of Gizenga's troops and if possible to take Stanleyville (essentially what Bomboko has requested).

Action Required

1. Most important, Belgians must provide 100-odd officers to Mobutu on as clandestine a basis as possible.

2. US must provide financial and material support.

3. Belgian-US effort must be closely coordinated in the field.

4. US must give Belgium at least tacit support and cover in UN for their part of the operation.

5. A strong propaganda barrage against UAR and USSR intervention to cover and justify our own action.

Advantages

1. Such action could save situation from complete breakdown in next one-or two-month period.

Disadvantages

1. Harmful effects on our posture in UN and with Afro-Asians.

2. Could call forth an intensification of Soviet and UAR intervention, on their side, which might require our proceeding to next sub-alternative.

B. Intermediate effort: More overtbilateral Western military assistance to Kasavubu, but short of direct involvement of American personnel. Purpose would be to defeat Gizenga forces and help Kasavubu Government to establish its authority in entire Congo.

Action Required

1. Same as above, but will require equipment and training officers who can reorganize CNA over a longer period.

2. US must take leading role in cooperative Western endeavor.

Advantages

1. If it worked, could put our friends solidly in power in Congo.

Disadvantages

1. Would put us in clear opposition to UN and probably require abandonment of UN effort.

2. Could create long-term difficulties in our relations with Africans including our friends there.

3. Pro-Western Congolese leaders are weak reeds, and might not be able to exploit even a clear military advantage. Hence no guarantee of permanent political solution.

C. Direct intervention by US and Western forces. (This is clearly only a last resort possibility in answer to massive Soviet intervention.)

General Comments on Alternative III

1. Difficulty of keeping things really clandestine, especially if Belgians involved.

2. Need for effective coordination of Western efforts in all cases.

3. Need for a strong attack on Soviet and UAR intervention for its own sake and as a cover for our activities.

4. Once we start on the road of military intervention, we may inevitably be led on to the next step.

Conclusion: Because of the time factor, we should be prepared to take at least saving action on military lines—i.e. Alternative IIIA. This can be combined with an effort to beef up the UN effort along the lines of Alternative IIA or IIB. Among the many unpleasant possibilities, this combination seems on balance the best.

68. Central Intelligence Agency Information Report[1]

Washington, February 7, 1961.

TDCS–3/464, 615, Field Report [*text not declassified*]

SUBJECT

Reported death of Patrice Lumumba, Joseph Okito and Maurice Mpolo in Katanga

1. Patrice Lumumba, Joseph Okito and Maurice Mpolo were executed shortly after their arrival in Elisabethville the evening of 17 Jan. Katanga soldiers shot and killed Okito and Mpolo. A Belgian officer of Flemish origin executed Lumumba with a burst of submachine gun fire at 2300Z 17 Jan. An ear was severed from Lumumba's head and sent to Albert Kalonji, President of Sud-Kasai. The three bodies were buried in a common grave. ([*less than 1 line not declassified*] comment: Although a Katanga Government official ([*less than 1 line not declassified*]) (TDCS-3/463,595)[2] reported Lumumba alive as of 17 Jan, no other report has confirmed this. The United Nations command in Leopoldville has been unable to determine the whereabouts or condition of Lumumba. A qualified American observer (B) in Leopoldville who has contacts among the

[1] Source: Central Intelligence Agency Files, Job 79–00149A, DDO/IMS Files, African Division, Senate Select Committee, Volume II, Box 23, Folder 1. Secret; Priority; Noforn; Continued Control.

[2] Not found.

international press corps believes a few of the newsmen recently returned from Katanga have heard rumors of Lumumba's death).[3]

2. Field dissem: State Army Navy Air CINCLANT.

End of message.

[3] Telegram 0785 from Leopoldville to CIA and [*text not declassified*], February 8, reported that Fernand Kazadi, Commissioner General for National Defense, claimed he saw the execution and asked whether [*text not declassified*] could comment. (Central Intelligence Agency Files, [*text not declassified*], folder 3) See Document 70 for [*text not declassified*] response. Telegram 0797 from Leopoldville to CIA, February 9, reported that a Station officer had been told by [*text not declassified*] that Lumumba, Okito, and Mpolo had been executed in mid-January by Katanga officials. The telegram also reported that a Station contact said February 9 that he believed Lumumba was dead, based on a conversation with Interior Commissioner Daniel Kandolo on February 2 in which Kandolo expressed the same opinion. (Ibid.)

69. Telegram From the Central Intelligence Agency to the Station in the Congo[1]

Washington, February 9, 1961, 0137Z.

Dir 24445 (Out 71749). Ref Leop 0783 (In 42022).[2]

1. Whereas policy still undergoing review, you are authorized continue [*cryptonym not declassified*] op until further notice.

2. We believe of utmost importance to reassure and support moderate elements in this interim period. HQS is seeking specific authority in this direction and will advise soonest.

End of message.

[1] Source: Central Intelligence Agency Files, Job 78–00435R, DDO/ISS Files, Box 1, Folder 6, [*cryptonym not declassified*] Ops. Secret; Rybat; [*cryptonym not declassified*]; Priority. Drafted and authenticated by Fields (AC/AF) and released by DD/P.

[2] [*text not declassified*] unhappy with ODYOKE position in the United Nations and Leopoldville anticipates a flood of requests for aid. Unless advised to the contrary, Leopoldville will continue [*text not declassified*] plan. [Footnote in the original.] Telegram 783 from Leopoldville to CIA, February 7, reported that the military situation there was developing rapidly and that the Station suspected that the [*text not declassified*] were trying to move fast for a quick victory before a U.N. decision was taken to disarm the Congolese National Army. (Central Intelligence Agency Files, Job 78–00435R, DDO/ISS Files, Box 1, Folder 6, [*cryptonym not declassified*] Ops)

70. Telegram From [*location not declassified*] to the Central Intelligence Agency[1]

[*location not declassified*], February 9, 1961.

0370. Ref: Leop 0785 (In 43482).[2]

[*less than 1 line not declassified*] has collected various conflicting reports re Lumumba. Three reports obtained week of 6 Feb indicated he dead, two of these reports said he killed by man whose whole family were killed by Lumumbists in July. On other hand [*name not declassified*] (Turkish refugee from Luluabourg) swore he had seen and talked to repentant Lumumba 5 Feb. On balance believe [*less than 1 line not declassified*][3] more likely than [*name not declassified*] story but do not have enough firm data for good intel report.

End of message.

---

[1] Source: Central Intelligence Agency Files, [*text not declassified*], Folder 3. Secret; Routine. Received at 1952Z. Repeated to Leopoldville.

[2] Stated that Kazadi claims he saw the execution of Lumumba. [Footnote in the original.] Regarding this telegram, see footnote 3 to Document 68.

[3] See Document 68.

71. Memorandum for the Special Group[1]

Washington, undated.

SUBJECT

Covert Action in the Congo[2]

1. Problem:

To strengthen the central government of the Congo (GOC) under President Kasavubu to prevent Lumumba/Gizenga forces from regaining control of the country prior to effective implementation of a more vigorous UN operation that will ensure orderly political development along lines acceptable to the U.S.

2. Assumptions:

It is assumed that it is in our interest to ensure that the Lumumba/Gizenga forces, with or without UAR and Sino-Soviet support, do not regain control of the country during the period in which the United Nations is attempting to strengthen its hand in the Congo. It is also assumed that it is our objective to have the Congo emerge as a country unified along acceptable political and economic lines.

3. Facts and Discussion:

At the present time the Lumumba forces, under the leadership of Gizenga, are making every effort to regain control of the Congo by military means from their Stanleyville base. Available intelligence indicates that Gizenga has received support from the UAR consisting of money and weapons, and that further UAR as well as Sino-Soviet Bloc logistic support to the Stanleyville regime will be forthcoming.

The only counter-balance to military action by Gizenga consists of General Mobutu's military forces in Leopoldville and Tshombe's army in Katanga. Reporting from Leopoldville and Elizabethville indicates

---

[1] Source: National Security Council, Intelligence Files, Congo, 1960–1965. Secret. No drafting information appears on this memorandum.

[2] The NSC minutes of the Special Group meeting on February 9 record that Dulles and Bissell "outlined very broadly a proposal to support pro-Western forces in the Congo" but that detailed discussion of the proposal was postponed until the February 14 meeting. Rusk was assured that the proposed channel could be used to induce Kasavubu to cooperate in a broadly-based government, and with the United Nations. (Ibid., Intelligence Files, Special Group—Minutes and Approvals—1961) The minutes of the meeting on February 14 record that Bissell provided more details concerning the project and that the Special Group indicated that it had no objections to the proposal. (Ibid.) On February 11, three days before the formal Special Group authorization on February 14, Bissell sent the Chief of Station a telegram confirming that the Station was authorized to expend the funds recommended in the proposal. See Document 73.

that these forces are currently the target of strong military pressure and subversive efforts directed from Stanleyville. As presently constituted, they are poorly led, in need of weapons, communications equipment, and motor transport, and require, in the case of Mobutu's forces, sufficient funds to ensure the loyalty of troops.

In Leopoldville our official representatives have been requested by Congolese Foreign Minister Bomboko and General Mobutu to provide funds to maintain their forces.

In Elizabethville, Katanga army representatives have requested aid in the form of weapons and aircraft. In view of the support that Tshombe is apparently receiving from Belgian sources, no action on our part in this regard is considered advisable at this time.

The Belgian Foreign Office has advised that Bomboko has made a specific request to Belgium for military assistance consisting of arms, money and training instructors. Bomboko has also approached the French Foreign Office indicating the seriousness of the situation and requesting French assistance, particularly for arms.

At the present time diplomatic initiatives are being taken primarily through the UN to find a consensus which would allow for a solution to the Congo problem. It is expected that whatever final solution evolves at the UN, the implementation of these actions will at least take several weeks or, more probably, months. It is believed that the widespread publicity which has attended the UN considerations, as well as any number of diplomatic feelers which have been put out, cannot help but have a deteriorating effect on the morale and stability of moderate Congolese political and military leaders. It follows that in the interval between the present and the date of reasonably effective implementation of the UN policy, it is desirable to provide, in a quiet but effective way, reassurance and support to these moderate leaders. This, in effect, would constitute a holding action until it became clear that such support was either unnecessary or conflicting openly with generally accepted and effective UN actions.

This support would also enable our representatives to maintain a degree of influence over the leaders of the Congolese Government to obtain their cooperation in any solution worked out by the UN.

4. Conclusions:

In view of these developments, it is concluded that steps should be taken to improve the capabilities of Congolese Government forces to provide a counter-balance to military action by Lumumba forces directed at regaining control of the Congo. Without maintenance in being of these forces there is an imminent risk that military action from Stanleyville, supported by the UAR and the Sino-Soviet Bloc, will regain control of the Congo for the Lumumba forces prior to implementation of any effective action by the UN.

5. Action Recommended:

It is recommended, that in order to preserve General Mobutu's military capabilities and to maintain the integrity of the moderate Congolese leadership supporting Kasavubu, authorization be granted to provide financial assistance to the Congolese Government through clandestine channels, initially up to a total of [*number not declassified*]. It is understood that these funds would be used by the Congolese to obtain transport, arms and communications equipment, to supplement salaries of loyal troops and for action in the political field. Every effort will be made to ensure that the funds are used for this purpose and not diverted to the individual members of the regime.

It is possible that this authorization will have to be increased when the urgent requirements of the Congolese Government are better known, perhaps within the next few weeks.

72. Telegram From [*location not declassified*] to the Central Intelligence Agency[1]

[*location not declassified*], February 10, 1961.

0372. Ref: Dir 24302 (Out 71507).[2]

1. Lumumba fate is best kept secret in Katanga. In addition [Embassy] démarche to Munongo to request humane treatment for Lumumba has caused GOK make every effort deny firm data to ODYOKE.

2. In above context following is review of reports received by [*less than 1 line not declassified*] since 17 Jan:

A. [Identity 1] from Dr. De Coster (pediatrician from Stanleyville, now living in Eville, who got data from unknown doctor who claims verified death). Lumumba, Mpolo and Okito executed just off road from Eville to Jadotville on 17 Jan.

[1] Source: Central Intelligence Agency Files, [*text not declassified*], Folder 3. Secret; Routine. Received at 0328Z. Repeated to Leopoldville.

[2] Hqs. requested any information which might confirm or deny the reports of Lumumba's death. [Footnote in the original.] This CIA telegram has not been found.

B. Doctor Lauveau, Belgian physician with good local contacts, stated on 19 Jan that Lumumba if not already executed was about to be. Mentioned GOK ministers had each been allowed beat Lumumba first. ([*less than 1 line not declassified*]).[3]

C. On 1 Feb Commandant Roger Van der Stock, G–2 Sud Kasai army, stated categorically that Lumumba dead but refused reveal source. Said knows man who executed him.

D. On 2 Feb Dutch local dentist Van Baalen, whose wife is secretary in Tshombe office, stated Lumumba definitely dead, killed by man whose whole family were killed in July by Lumumbists.

E. On 19 Jan British Honorary Consul Georges Cailleau stated believes Lumumba dead because those Belgians originally assigned take care of him had relaxed as if job done. [*less than 1 line not declassified*]

3. Sole recent negative report is that of [*less than 1 line not declassified*][4] which could well be [*cryptonym not declassified*] plant as [*cryptonym not declassified*] met [*name not declassified*] while dining with [Identity 2]. See also [*less than 1 line not declassified*][5] which perhaps also plant.

4. Have avoided direct questioning [*cryptonym not declassified*] or [Identity 3] view delicacy subject and probability they under orders hide or distort truth. [*less than 1 line not declassified*] so far has all been one way in favor KUBARK and believe it best avoid forcing them this early in game on most delicate local question, as they might feel forces cut off [*less than 1 line not declassified*] altogether.

5. Realize importance this question and am still making major effort.

End of message.

---

[3] Dr. Jean Louveaux remarked that Lumumba would certainly be killed by the GOK, if not done already. Louveaux also stated that each GOK Minister had already been permitted to personally beat Lumumba in conformity with ancient tradition. [Footnote in the original.] This CIA telegram has not been found.

[4] [*text not declassified*] a Turkish refugee from Luluabourg, swore that he had talked to Lumumba on 5 February 1961. [Footnote in the original.] This telegram is printed as Document 70.

[5] Reported that as of 27 January 1961, Patrice Lumumba was still alive. [Footnote in the original.] This CIA telegram has not been found.

73. Telegram From the Central Intelligence Agency to the Station in the Congo[1]

Washington, February 11, 1961, 2221Z.

Dir 24946 (Out 72868). 1. Per oral discussions with you HQS, this is to confirm Leop authorized expend up to [*number not declassified*] dollars in clandestine support [*cryptonym not declassified*] operations. These funds to provide military support for [*cryptonym not declassified*][2] ops (purchase of arms, commo equipment, transport, etc) as well as to influence loyalty of GOC military personnel and to bribe [*less than 1 line not declassified*] military and civilian personnel. Sum authorized is in addition to [*cryptonym not declassified*] expenditures already authorized for purely political and propaganda ops.

2. You are instructed advise [*name not declassified*] (and other [*cryptonym not declassified*] leaders at your discretion) of authorization assist them in their efforts to establish GOC control over Congo. You will point out this aid is proof ODYOKE continues support efforts and objectives of [*cryptonym not declassified*] leaders. In discussing aid to be provided, proceed as follows:

A. Advise them you have authority expend immediately substantial sum on this operation and believe more funds can be obtained if necessary after discussion and review their needs. If pressed you may explain initial authority is for [*number not declassified*] dollars.

[Omitted here is additional discussion of this program.]

5. All major steps in implementing this program will be coordinated with Chief [U.S. Embassy].

[Omitted here is additional discussion of this program.]

---

[1] Source: Central Intelligence Agency Files, Job 82–00450R, Box 6, Folder 7, 40 Committee, Congo (K), 1960–1964. Secret; Rybat; [*cryptonym not declassified*]; Routine. Drafted and released in draft by Bissell; coordinated in draft with Fields.

[2] In telegram 0822, February 14, the Chief of Station informed the Central Intelligence Agency that after discussing telegram 24946 with Ambassador Timberlake he had briefed [*text not declassified*] regarding the authorization. [*text not declassified*] was most appreciative and said that without U.S. support "would not be able continue effort resist Gizenga forces"; he continued to believe that a military solution was the only hope of ousting the Gizenga regime. [*text not declassified*] also stated that he had no definite information on Lumumba's execution other than the fact that Mobutu had warned him late in January that Lumumba had been executed. (Ibid., Job 78–00435R, DDO/ISS Files, Box 1, Folder 6, [*cryptonym not declassified*] Ops)

74. Telegram From the Consulate in Elizabethville to the Department of State[1]

Elizabethville, February 14, 1961.

525. Re Contels 420[2] and 507.[3]

Since hardly any thinking person here accepts official Katangan version of death of Lumumba and associates,[4] it appears persistent rumors first reported in Contel 420 were, if not correct, at least prophetic. [*less than one line not declassified*] other Consulate officers have heard many stories including that deaths occurred January 17, 18, or 19 from effects of initial bad treatment, on January 26 as result intentional execution, after February 8 as result of announcement US support of liberation of Lumumba and other political prisoners and finally at time of escape on February 10. Speculating on these versions, I would accept as most likely original stories that Lumumba and associates died on January 17 to 19 as result of miscalculation concerning amount of physical punishment they could endure. Reason for my choice is story given me from creditable source that Lucas Samelenge, Secretary State for Information, told associates in this period they must prepare believable story concerning Lumumba's accidental death. Samelenge and associates immediately silenced by Surete but not before certain of them had leaked story to close friends.

Latest information from ONUC here indicates investigative team composed of Ethiopian General Iyassu and Knecht, Swiss Surete official who worked on Jacquinot case, have made little progress against solid opposition by Katangan authorities. Sole element to date was Knecht's interview with UPI cameraman who alone accompanied Katangan investigating committee to alleged place of escape. Cameraman indicated conditions in farm house cast certain doubt on stories of Ka-

---

[1] Source: Central Intelligence Agency Files, [*text not declassified*], Folder 3. Confidential; Priority. Received at 11:22 a.m. Also sent to Leopoldville; repeated (information) to Brussels.

[2] In telegram 420 from Elizabethville, January 20, U.S. Consul William Canup stated that he thought it was impossible to disregard the persistent rumors that Lumumba had died as a result of mistreatment shortly after his arrival. (National Archives, RG 59, Central Files, 770G.00/1–2061) See Document 6, *Foreign Relations,* 1961–1963, Vol. XX, Congo Crisis, pp. 17–18.

[3] In telegram 507 from Elizabethville, February 11, Canup reported widespread skepticism concerning the Katanga Government's story that Lumumba and his two associates had escaped from custody. (National Archives, RG 59, Central Files, 770G.00/2–1161) See footnote 2 to Document 26, *Foreign Relations,* 1961–1963, Vol. XX, Congo Crisis.

[4] On February 13, the Katanga government announced that Lumumba and his companions had been captured and killed by hostile villagers.

tangan Government concerning escape, although locale provided no conclusive evidence as to truth or falsity of story.

Canup

---

75. Central Intelligence Agency Information Report[1]

Washington, February 15, 1961.

TDCS–3/465, 477, Field Report [*text not declassified*]

SUBJECT

Congo Security Report on Death of Lumumba

1. Two security officers who went Elisabethville 10–14 Feb for purpose investigating death of Lumumba returned Leopoldville 14 Feb and reported they had seen and identified body of Lumumba and his two companions. Bodies were rather badly mutilated and showed evidence of having been dead some time. They could not determine from superficial examination exactly what was direct cause death but they did not notice gun shot wounds.

2. Security officers said no one believes legend of victims having been massacred by villagers 12 February.

3. Field dissem: CINCLANT

End of message.

---

[1] Source: Central Intelligence Agency Files, Job 79–00149A, DDO/IMS Files, African Division, Senate Select Committee, Volume II, Box 23, Folder 1. Secret; Noforn; Continued Control; Routine.

76. Telegram From [*location not declassified*] to the Central Intelligence Agency[1]

[*location not declassified*], February 16, 1961.

0398. Ref A. 0372 [*less than 1 line not declassified*];[2] B. 0382 [*less than 1 line not declassified*].[3]

1. On 14 Feb [Identity 1] stated no Belgian in Katanga had any part in events leading to death Lumumba. Plan advanced by [Identity 2] and [Identity 1] was to have Lumumba make public declaration he paid by Soviets and repents, followed by tribunal before major chiefs. However Tshombe and ministers took matter into own hands. [Identity 1] expressed hope highest levels ODYOKE would realize Belgians had counselled against quick violent action against Lumumba, adding also that [Identity 2] responsible for small losses on both sides in recent Bukama attack despite GOK desire inflict heaviest possible casualties on Balubakat.

2. [Identity 3] states that Doctor de Coster on 14 Feb again flatly declared Lumumba killed 17 Jan within hours after his arrival Katanga. [*1½ lines not declassified*]

3. Ref B confusing. Should read "original source [*name not declassified*] on 10 Feb reconfirmed death occurred 17 Jan etc".

4. Am still inclined accept both [Identity 1] and [Identity 3] version although still no firm evidence available.[4]

End of message.

---

[1] Source: Central Intelligence Agency Files, Job 78–00801R, DDO/ISS Files, Box 1, Folder 8, [*cryptonym not declassified*], Vol. I. Secret; Routine. Received at 0912Z. Repeated to Leopoldville.

[2] Review of reports received by [*location not declassified*] regarding the fate of Lumumba. [Footnote in the original.] This telegram is printed as Document 72.

[3] On 10 February [*text not declassified*] repeated his conviction that Lumumba was dead. [Footnote in the original.] Telegram 0382 from [*location not declassified*] to CIA, February 12, quoted several informants who contended that Lumumba was dead. (Central Intelligence Agency Files, [*text not declassified*], Folder 3)

[4] Telegram 0851 from Leopoldville to CIA, February 20, reported that on February 18 a station officer met briefly with two sources who told him that Lumumba and his two companions had been executed on January 18 by a Belgian officer. They said that the officer shot Mpolo and Okito, and then brought Lumumba into the same room and asked if he repented and was willing to denounce communism. When Lumumba said no, the Belgian shot him. The cable noted that this story and its similarity to other reports would seem to cast some doubt on Belgian innocence. (Ibid.)

77. Telegram From the Central Intelligence Agency to the Station in the Congo[1]

Washington, March 3, 1961, 2040Z.

Dir 27978 (Out 79749). 1. At high level policy meeting[2] three March KUBARK received reaffirmation of authority to expend funds both to bribe [*name not declassified*] forces and supplement pay of selected [Mobutu] forces where needed to assure loyalty.

2. Sense of meeting was that KUBARK could be fairly liberal in these actions when best judgment recommends them. It was recognized at best there would be some slippage.

3. Again urge you canvass all means for using funds securely and effectively for these purposes.

End of message.

---

[1] Source: Central Intelligence Agency Files, Job 78–00435R, DDO/ISS Files, Box 1, Folder 6, [*cryptonym not declassified*] Ops. Secret; Rybat; [*cryptonym not declassified*]. Drafted and released by Fields. (C/AF).

[2] On March 3, President Kennedy, Rusk, Dulles, Secretary of Defense Robert McNamara and National Security Adviser McGeorge Bundy discussed the Congo at a meeting at the White House from 3:15 p.m. to 5:15 p.m. Department of State Counselor George McGhee's record of the meeting noted that the group agreed that the CIA was to expedite its "silver bullets" program in the Congo. (See Document 41, *Foreign Relations,* 1961–1963, volume XX, Congo Crisis, p. 89)

---

78. Editorial Note

An undated and unsigned memorandum entitled the "Death of Patrice Lumumba" was sent to Director of Central Intelligence Dulles under cover of a note dated March 7, 1961, which reads: "You were asking that the Division get together in a memorandum our best estimate of the actual facts and circumstances surrounding the death of Patrice Lumumba. This memorandum is attached and I am not sure whether you intended to send it to the President or not. FMC" A stamped notation on the original indicates that Dulles saw it on March 8, but it bears no indication that it was sent to the President. (Central Intelligence Agency Files, Job 86B00975R, DCI/OCA Registry, Box 2, Folder 18, Review Staff Files, Assassinations, Vol. I) The memorandum is printed as Document 44 in *Foreign Relations,* 1961–1963, volume XX, Congo Crisis, pages 93–94.

79. Memorandum From the Chief of the Africa Division, Directorate of Plans, Central Intelligence Agency (Tweedy) to the Deputy Director of Plans, Central Intelligence Agency (Bissell)[1]

Washington, March 29, 1961.

SUBJECT

Summary of [*less than 1 line not declassified*] Documents

From the documents found in the briefcase [*less than 1 line not declassified*] has cabled selected full texts, all of which are in French. English summaries of these texts follow below. We anticipate receiving the documents themselves through VIP pouch by 10 April.

1. Three interesting notes on Mulele's Moscow trip in early March:

a. In regard to military assistance, the Soviets promise arms for 25,000 of Gizenga's men. A test delivery of arms will be sent to Stanleyville via Accra following verbal instructions to Gizenga. Two or three security experts will come to advise Gizenga, and the Soviets suggest a loyal cadre of eight to ten young Congolese be formed to undergo training by these experts. Necessary equipment for the embryonic security service will be forwarded as soon as communications are opened.

b. In regard to diplomatic action, the African States recognizing Gizenga's government should take action together against the Sudan's refusal to grant transit rights to province Orientale, and the signatories to the resolutions of the Casablanca Conference in early January should put their troops with the UN Forces in the Congo at the disposal of the Gizenga regime.

c. In regard to general Soviet support of Gizenga, the USSR will give all aid necessary as soon as transit rights can be arranged: This is the responsibility of the African leaders, particularly Nkrumah, Sekou Toure, Nasser, Modibo Keita and Hassan II. Furthermore, the Soviet Government

1. Which had agreed to put at the disposal of Stanleyville 6 L 12 planes, agrees to replace these with two to four IL–18's. As soon as transit rights are granted, these planes will be en route to Stanleyville.
2. Will deliver immediately a 30 KW 7 ton radio and within two months will deliver a 150 KW station to be set in operation by Soviet technicians.

---

[1] Source: Central Intelligence Agency Files, Job 78–01450R, DDP Subject Files, Box 1, Folder 7, Area Activity—Africa. Secret.

3. Promises 150 scholarships for the USSR People's Friendship University.
4. Guarantees immediate financial aid in a new proposal carried to Gizenga verbally.
5. Assures that military training is immediately available in the USSR for any number of Gizenga's men.

2. Notes of the final decision of the Czech Government in regard to its posture vis-à-vis Gizenga. Based on Mulele's conversations in Prague 14–15 March, this document states that a five man diplomatic mission will be accredited to Stanleyville with a Congolese delegation welcomed in Prague and that there will be on 18 March the simultaneous announcement in Prague and Cairo of a commercial accord between Stanleyville and the Czech Government which will assist in forcing the Sudanese blockade. The Czechs told Mulele that when the accord is followed by contracts between a Czech company and a genuine firm in Stanleyville, it is a mere formality to demand that the Sudan Government allow transit of goods. The Czechs will also continue their efforts to establish a Congolese air line, based in Stanleyville, and the creation of an air link between Prague–Cairo–Khartoum–Stanleyville and/or Prague–Cairo–Red Sea–Addis Ababa–Uganda–Stanleyville. The Czechs also promise immediate financial aid, the details of which will be relayed to Gizenga verbally.

3. A message from J. Messena, former Minister of Labor in the Lumumba government, sent via Mulele for Gizenga. Datelined 19 February, Bulunga, it is essentially a request for funds and weapons to recruit and arm a private army of 20,000 men in the Kwilu–Kwongo area to replace the UN contingents now there.

4. Some propositions for military aid to the Stanleyville regime, datelined 16 March, Cairo, [*1 line not declassified*]. This recommends the formation of a special two to four man office, including one aide from the UAR and separate from the diplomatic mission yet under the control of Mulele, to study but not implement all possible methods for transporting military equipment into Orientale province. Also proposed is the establishment of a short wave radio link between Stanleyville and Cairo and Stanleyville and Europe, the creation of liaison (personal messengers) between Stanleyville and friendly elements throughout the Congo, the enlistment of a group of military specialists (some from Europe) who will organize Congo-wide operations and the formation of an underground cadre for action in Leopoldville province.

5. In a letter from Andre Eduard Kanza to Gizenga, datelined 23 March, Cairo, Kanza reveals that the position of the "Nationalists" in Leopoldville is very difficult and that his father, Daniel Kanza, is holding his political party together but desperately needs funds. Andre Kanza has had several secret meetings in Leopoldville with various sympathizers, at one of which Kimvay and Kamitatu were present.

Andre Kanza states that he decided it was now necessary to pretend to Kamitatu and Kimvay that he was with the "puppets" and to aver that he himself would attempt to interfere with the effectiveness of Gizenga's activities.

6. A copy of a long, undated letter from Argiry Emmanuel (a Greek Communist long linked with leftist Congolese circles) to Pierre Mulele in Cairo outlining a variety of proposals for establishing secure transportation and mail channels between Stanleyville and the outside world.

According to the list of documents cabled from [*less than 1 line not declassified*], there should be several more interesting pieces of information. All that has been reported to date confirms, or is identical with, documents obtained [*less than 1 line not declassified*] from [*less than 1 line not declassified*] the Mulele mission.

B Tweedy
Chief, Africa Division

80. Editorial Note

In telegram 32898 to the Chief of Station in Leopoldville, April 1, 1961, Bronson Tweedy, Chief of the Africa Division, Directorate of Plans, stated that in view of changing circumstances and the fairly rapid trend of events he believed it was time to review again the whole subject of military and paramilitary aid to moderate anti-Lumumba leaders in the Congo. Many facets of that assistance were still in development or being planned and included the agreement with the Belgians and preliminary talks with other countries. The impetus for those was the apparent Gizenga military advance and the need to shore up the Congolese National Army as soon as possible, but it now appeared that the Gizenga forces posed little threat, and Joseph Mobutu was now conducting at least preliminary negotiations with Victor Lundula. The prospects for a Mobutu–Lundula armed clash were slight. The biggest threat of an armed clash was between the CNA and the United Nations Operations in the Congo (UNOC). If this assessment was approximately right, Tweedy stated, then a question arose as to whether continued emphasis should be placed on third countries as military or paramilitary advisers. Tweedy requested the Chief of Station's views on the subject. (Central Intelligence Agency Files, Job 78–00435R, DDO/ISS Files, Box 1, Folder 6, [*cryptonym not declassified*] Ops)

In telegram 1183 from Leopoldville to CIA, April 14, the Chief of Station responded that he generally concurred with Tweedy but believed that some military or paramilitary advisers would be of continuing use if and when the Congo situation again reached the boiling point. The Station assumed that the Congo situation would remain chaotic for some time. (Ibid.)

81. Editorial Note

On April 15, 1961, the U.N. General Assembly, by a vote of 45 to 3 with 49 abstentions (including the United States), adopted Resolution 1601 (XV) establishing a Commission of Investigation to investigate the circumstances of the death of Lumumba and his colleagues. See *American Foreign Policy: Current Documents, 1961,* page 809, for text of the resolution.

82. Memorandum for the Special Group[1]

Washington, June 5, 1961.

SUBJECT

Covert Action in the Congo

1. *Problem:* To strengthen the Central Government of the Congo (GOC) under President Kasavubu by assisting members of the present government to obtain a working majority in the Congolese Parliament which the GOC is planning to reconvene at an early date.

2. *Assumptions:* It is assumed that it is in our interest to insure the parliamentary victory of individuals in the present government of the Congo to prevent the Lumumba/Gizenga forces of the Stanleyville regime from gaining power in the Congo through legal means.

3. *Facts and Discussion:* The GOC has announced that Parliament will be reconvened at an early date to consider the resolutions of the Round Table Conference which has been meeting at Coquilhatville. The GOC has also announced publicly that a government headed by Joseph Ileo will be submitted for parliamentary approval at that time.

While a parliamentary victory of individuals in the present GOC will not eliminate all the major problems facing the country, the victory of certain members of the government will be essential to permit an approach to the long-term solutions of these problems. More vigorous action by members of the GOC in this regard is required to offset an active program of the Gizenga regime in Stanleyville to dominate Parliament when reconvened. Most recent estimates indicate that Ileo could probably muster 51 votes out of a total of 136 in the Chamber, and probably 31 votes out of a total of 83 in the Senate. Taking into con-

[1] Source: National Security Council, Intelligence Files, Congo, 1960–1965. Secret; Eyes Only. No drafting information appears on the memorandum. The political action program outlined in the memorandum was developed by the Station in Leopoldville at the CIA's request and then presented to the Department of State in a memorandum drafted in CIA on May 29. (Central Intelligence Agency Files, Job 76–00366R, DDO/ISG Files, Box 1, Folder 10, [*text not declassified*], 1961–62) Following talks between CIA and the Department of State, the latter submitted its views on the proposed program to CIA in writing. The views were incorporated into the June 5 memorandum to the Special Group and were transmitted to Leopoldville by CIA in telegram 43140, June 2. (Ibid., Job 78–00435R, DDO/ISS Files, Box 1, Folder 7, [*cryptonym not declassified*] Ops) Both the CIA in its May 29 memorandum and the Department of State in its written comments indicated that they favored Cyrille Adoula for the position of prime minister. Regarding Antoine Gizenga, the Department of State commented that given the choice between his continuing to control a separated Orientale and gaining admission to the central government, the latter appeared to be the lesser evil, but neither he nor his radical lieutenants should obtain a politically sensitive ministry.

sideration current trends, it appears that Ileo will have difficulty in obtaining a vote of confidence if the Gizenga forces attend.

4. *Conclusions:* It is concluded that steps should be taken to support key individuals in the GOC in their efforts to obtain a working majority in the Congolese Parliament. If these individuals fail to obtain parliamentary control, there is a real danger that the country will fall under domination of the Gizenga/Stanleyville regime.

5. *Action Recommended:* It is recommended that the following actions, which have been proposed by our Leopoldville representative with the concurrence of the Chief of Mission, be authorized to support key, friendly elements of the Congo government in their efforts to obtain a parliamentary majority:

a. Attempt to convince leaders of the GOC coalition to agree in advance on candidates for key ministerial positions and on a platform for action that will hold Congo-wide appeal.

b. Urge the GOC leaders to select 10 to 15 Parliamentarians to serve as whips to swing certain selected deputies into line behind the GOC coalition. If pressure is not sufficient, these whips or other reliable contacts will be directed to utilize other methods, such as outright payments of money, promises of foreign travel, scholarships, etc. as required for particular deputies. Funds will also be provided to GOC coalition leaders themselves to enable them to invite selected Parliamentarians to their houses for political discussions.

c. Reliable contacts will be used to influence youth groups, trade unions and tribal organizations to contact and persuade Parliamentary deputies, over whom they may have some measure of control, to line up with the GOC coalition. In this regard, funds may be used to induce regional political, labor union, or other leaders not in Leopoldville to put pressure on deputies from their respective regions. Funds can also be expended to bring key regional leaders to Leopoldville from the provinces to influence deputies from their area or tribe.

d. Demonstrations by youth groups can be organized to support personalities and policies of the developing GOC coalition.

e. Funds may be utilized to discourage the possible shift of allegiances to the Gizenga forces. [*3½ lines not declassified*]

6. No action is to be taken, prior to the opening of Parliament, which could reveal to Gizenga that his attendance and negotiations for reintegration of his areas would be fruitless. The program under discussion should be envisaged as aid [*less than 1 line not declassified*] in organizing a government which will have the allegiance of all areas of the Congo and be controlled by the moderates. If Gizenga does not attend Parliament and maintains his present separate position, no special program such as outlined above is needed and none should be launched.

In this contingency it is expected that highly discreet actions on a much reduced basis would be considered on their merits as opportunities arise. If he attends, the program should be limited day to day to those actions which are required to achieve the above goals. It is not assumed that an all-out effort will be needed; it may be, but activity should rise by escalation, on a strict need-for basis. Extreme care should be taken to avoid prejudicing the future effectiveness of the politicians to be aided.

7. It is recommended that a maximum of [*dollar amount not declassified*] be authorized for this program if Gizenga attends and it appears this amount can be usefully spent. If expenditures of this magnitude are required in FY 1961, it will be necessary to draw on [*less than 1 line not declassified*]. If the large-scale program is delayed until FY 1962, or a limited program is possible, funds are available within existing allocations.[2]

---

[2] On June 6, Deputy Assistant Secretary of State Wayne Fredericks sent a memorandum to Under Secretary of State Bowles recommending that he support the covert action program proposed by the Agency, subject to the following conditions: 1) Gizenga's faction should be represented in the government, although not with any sensitive position; 2) no effort should be spared to protect the security of this extremely delicate operation; and 3) the Department had to be kept currently informed of the development of the program. (National Security Council, Intelligence Files, Special Group, Minutes and Approvals, 1961)

---

83. Memorandum for the Record[1]

Washington, June 8, 1961.

SUBJECT

Minutes of Special Group Meeting, 8 June 1961

PRESENT

Messrs. Bowles, Gilpatric, Bundy, Ralph Dungan, Dulles

Mr. Dungan, Special Assistant to the President, participated in the Special Group meeting for the first time.

---

[1] Source: National Security Council, Intelligence Files, Special Group, Minutes and Approvals, 1961. Secret; Eyes Only.

1. Congo

Messrs. Bowles and Gilpatric agreed with the plan for the Congo.[2] Mr. Bowles conditioned his approval on the acceptance of the three provisions set forth in the State Department internal memorandum dated 6 June 1961 (copy attached).[3] Mr. Dulles indicated that these conditions were accepted by the Agency but he pointed out that the condition which prescribed the inclusion of Gizenga or his representative in the Leopoldville Government involved the danger of bringing in a representative of Moscow who would attempt to subvert and control the government. Mr. Bundy felt that he could not approve this program without reference to higher authority.[4]

Note was made of the possibility that if Gizenga decided to participate in a new Leopoldville Government or Parliament, he had ample resources and a chance eventually to win control of the government.[5]

[Omitted here is discussion of other subjects.]

---

[2] Document 82.

[3] Footnote 2 to Document 82.

[4] On June 10, Tweedy advised the Deputy Director for Coordination in the Department of State's Bureau of Intelligence and Research, Joseph W. Scott, that in view of the fact that the Leopoldville Station was already reporting requests for support, the Agency had decided to see whether Bundy would agree to partial clearance of the proposed CA program for the Congo, even though the whole program might not be reviewed until June 15. Scott gave his approval. (Memorandum for the record, June 12, 1961; Central Intelligence Agency Files, Job 78–01450R, DDP Subject Files, Box 1, Folder 7, Area Activity—Africa) In a memorandum to Kennedy dated June 10, McGeorge Bundy reported that a meeting was being arranged with the President to discuss all U.S. clandestine activities in support of political leaders and parties, including in particular a proposal for action in the Congo. One small aspect of the Congo proposal, however, had been presented with an urgency that had led him to approve it in the President's absence on the basis of clear State Department concurrence—an expenditure of [*dollar amount not declassified*] in support of particular activities designed to strengthen the moderate camp in the Congo. Bundy stated that there was danger of losing an important moderate group if U.S. action were delayed and noted that "very much larger sums have been spent in the past in the same direction, through the same channels and without embarrassment." (See *Foreign Relations,* 1961–1963, volume XX, Congo Crisis, Document 71)

[5] In CIA telegram 44709 to Leopoldville, June 10, the Agency reported that while authority for the whole [*cryptonym not declassified*] program had not yet been received, it had requested and received specific approval for the Station's recommendations that [*amount not declassified*] francs be paid to [*text not declassified*] and [*text not declassified*] francs to [*text not declassified*] through [*text not declassified*]. The cable warned that maximum security had to be observed and that, unless no alternatives were possible, Embassy officers should not handle direct payments. (Central Intelligence Agency Files, Job 78–00435R, DDO/ISS Files, Box 1, Folder 7, [*cryptonym not declassified*] Ops)

84. Paper Prepared in the Central Intelligence Agency[1]

Washington, June 14, 1961.

Our Leopoldville representative has provided the following comment on the proposed covert action program in the Congo.[2]

Although Ileo is currently planning to revise his government and present it to Parliament for approval, most Congolese political leaders are convinced he will not be able to obtain a confidence vote. Other individuals who might possibly form a government include Adoula, Bomboko, Bolikango, Gizenga and Kamitatu. Bomboko has eliminated himself from the race and is currently supporting Adoula. These two individuals have agreed to work together closely to obtain a moderate government.

If Ileo withdraws or fails to obtain a confidence vote, Adoula appears the most likely candidate to form a government. In view of Gizenga's and Kamitatu's opposition to Kasavubu it is doubtful that he would call upon either of them unless no other person was available. Although Bomboko is working closely with Adoula and does not feel that Ileo can form a government, he does not want to appear to be undercutting Ileo at the present time.

Our Leopoldville representative has referred to Embassy Dispatch No. 468 of May 24, 1961[3] which contains revised estimates of potential voting lineup in the Congolese party. This dispatch gives Ileo a probable 60 votes out of a total of 136 in the Chamber and 44 probable votes out of a total of 83 in the Senate. These figures are considered overly optimistic and we have been advised that both the Embassy and our representative are working up a new estimate based upon current consultations with local contacts.

Prospects for Government of Katanga participation in Parliament appear increasingly good, but the final outcome will be dependent on the Milan negotiations and continued efforts by the Congolese government and the UNOC. The question of Gizenga's participation remains uncertain. It is possible that some of his followers will come to Parliament if they are given protection and transportation by the

---

[1] Source: Central Intelligence Agency Files, Job 82–00450R, Box 6, Folder 7, 40 Committee, Congo (K), 1960–1964. Secret. No drafting information appears on the original but it is attached to a transmittal slip dated June 14 from Glenn Fields to Thomas A. Parrott, Secretary of the Special Group, that reads: "More background re Congo paper. Copy of this being handed to State."

[2] The following summary is based on telegram 1465 from Leopoldville to CIA, June 12. (Ibid., Job 78–00435R, DDO/ISS Files, Box 1, Folder 7, [*cryptonym not declassified*] Ops)

[3] Not found.

UNOC, even if Gizenga himself refuses to attend. This does not mean, however, that they would necessarily support a moderate government. It is doubted that Gizenga would personally attend Parliament even though he might send his chief followers. Our representative believes that it is wishful thinking to expect Gizenga and his followers to accept minor positions in the new government. It is considered that he would not settle for less than the post of Vice Premier if admitted to the government.

Our representative recommends that we not go all out in support of Ileo if it appears that he has little chance of forming a government. It is, however, considered that Adoula and Bomboko would vote for and support Ileo in the initial instance even though convinced he has little chance of winning a vote of confidence. Our support [*less than 1 line not declassified*] would therefore not be in opposition to Kasavubu's designation of Ileo as the individual to attempt to form a government.

Both the Ambassador and our representative disagree with the view that a relatively large program will not be necessary if Gizenga does not attend Parliament. The need to undertake such a program at the earliest possible date is emphasized.

It is agreed that the operation should proceed on a strict need-for basis, under the Ambassador's control, and with selected Congolese deciding who is to be aided, and how.

Our representative states that the majority of funds used in the program can be handled so that the U.S. Government can plausibly deny involvement. Frequent status reports will be provided. Every effort will be made to avoid prejudicing future effectiveness of the individuals to be aided. They will be discouraged from taking extreme positions.[4]

[4] CIA telegram 45581 to Leopoldville, June 15, reported that the overall [*cryptonym not declassified*] program had still not been reviewed or approved by higher authority, and would not be prior to June 22. (Central Intelligence Agency Files, Job 78–00435R, DDO/ISS Files, Box 1, Folder 7)

85. Telegram From the Central Intelligence Agency to the Station in the Congo[1]

Washington, June 20, 1961, 2253Z.

Dir 46396 (Out 68390). Re A. Dir 43140 (Out 62171);[2] B. Dir 45581 (Out 66823).[3]

1. Full approval for [*cryptonym not declassified*] program as submitted received 1800 local 20 June. This received ahead of anticipated schedule view reported convening parliament 25 June.

2. To clarify Department position re Gizenga per ref A. African Bureau has given us additional language as follows: Program should allow for representation in govt of group centered around Gizenga, altho no sensitive position should be given this group. We believe such representation necessary order assure new govt obtains loyalty all Congo, including Orientale and Kivu, as well as recognition by African and Asian nations in general as the govt of the Congo. Only in this way can solution all political aspects of the Congo crisis be achieved.

3. Additional points made by Department are:

A. No effort should be spared to protect security of this extremely delicate operation.

B. Department must be kept currently informed of development of program.

4. Look forward your early reports.

End of message.

---

[1] Source: Central Intelligence Agency Files, Job 82–00450R, Box 6, Folder 7, 40 Committee, Congo (K), 1960–1964. Secret; Rybat; [*cryptonym not declassified*]; Operatial Immediate. Drafted and released by Tweedy (C/AF).

[2] See footnote 1 to Document 82.

[3] See footnote 4 to Document 84.

86. Memorandum for the Record[1]

Washington, June 21, 1961.

SUBJECT

Covert Action in the Congo

The Congo paper was presented at the Special Group meeting 8 June[2] and deferred because of the request for an over-all briefing on political action.

On 10 June, Mr. Bissell obtained approval from Mr. Bundy for part of the program, i.e. an expenditure of [*number not declassified*] for support of [*less than 1 line not declassified*]

There was no Special Group meeting on 15 June. On 20 June Mr. Tweedy discussed with State the urgency of getting on with the Parliament program, in view of the impending convening of Parliament (scheduled for 25 June). This was approved by Mr. Bowles. He discussed it with Mr. Bundy, who later reported full approval.

TAP

(Note: At the Special Group meeting on 22 June Mr. Bundy stated that the Congo paper had been personally approved by the President.)

---

[1] Source: National Security Council, Intelligence Files, Special Group, Minutes and Approvals, 1961. Secret; Eyes Only. Prepared by Parrott.

[2] See Documents 82 and 83.

87. Paper Prepared in the Central Intelligence Agency[1]

Washington, June 27, 1961.

CONGO POLITICAL ACTION DEVELOPMENTS

The following has been received from our Leopoldville Station in response to our standing request for periodic progress reports on the Congo Political Action Program:[2]

A. The station is devoting the majority of its time talking with Congolese leaders and other persons of political influence trying to obtain a clear picture of political developments and to encourage support of the United States Government position. As a result of political jockeying, it is not possible to arrive at a definitive opinion regarding the probable outcome of the meeting of Parliament. The political scene is constantly changing and leaders have not yet adopted final positions.

B. Our station is working very closely with the Embassy in Leopoldville passing all political information received. Embassy coverage of developments is considered excellent and as a result our reporting will concentrate on operational developments.

C. At the present time, the parliamentary lineup appears to be fairly even between GOC and Gizenga groups. The release of Tshombe is considered a GOC effort to obtain the support of the CONAKAT Party. Adoula, Mobutu and Bomboko hope to create a Leopoldville/Elisabethville axis to obtain greater bargaining strength in an effort to reach an agreement with Stanleyville. However, GOC is not at all certain Tshombe will keep his word and send parliamentarians to Lovanium now that he has returned to Elisabethville. Adoula continues his previous efforts to pick up MNC/Lumumba and PSA votes. It is still not clear to what extent Adoula is prepared to go to get this support. However, the station and Embassy are urging the GOC to retain control of Foreign Affairs, Defense, Interior, the Premiership and Information. The GOC leaders are also being urged to get together behind Adoula and end bickering and throat cutting. [*less than 1 line not declassified*] Embassy officials and most Belgian advisors agree Adoula is probably the only GOC leader able to command sufficient strength to form a government.

D. Despite our calls for unity, personal ambition and failure to meet political facts of life continues to dominate developments. For ex-

---

[1] Source: Central Intelligence Agency Files, Job 78–00435R, DDO/ISS Files, Box 1, Folder 7, [*cryptonym not declassified*] Ops. Secret. There is no drafting information on the original.

[2] The paper is based on telegram 1554 from Leopoldville to CIA, June 27. (Ibid.)

ample, Bolikango appears ready to support Gizenga at the last moment if he thinks such a move would help him achieve his goal of becoming Chief of State. Ileo refuses to step down; thereby Adoula still is unable to take the necessary negotiating steps preparatory to a parliamentary vote.

E. As GOC leaders have done little to convince fence sitters to support the GOC despite our continuing efforts to influence these leaders since the Coquilhatville Conference, our Chief of Station has been attempting to stimulate action by preparing a listing of probable voting positions as well as a listing of parliamentarians who should be developed. This listing has been passed to GOC leaders who are now stirred into action. To support their efforts a total of [*number not declassified*] francs has been passed to influence key deputies.

---

88. Memorandum for the Record[1]

Washington, June 29, 1961.

[Omitted here is discussion of other subjects.]

7. *Congo*

Mr. Dulles said that we feel Gizenga will probably not come to the Parliamentary session in Leopoldville unless he is sure that his forces will win. He commented that this raises a policy question as to whether an attempt should be made to stop the Assembly. Mr. Bowles said that Mr. Bissell had raised this with him yesterday and that appropriate officials in the Department are considering the matter.

TA Parrott

---

[1] Source: National Security Council, Intelligence Files, Special Group, Minutes and Approvals, 1961. Secret; Eyes Only. Approved by the Special Group on July 20.

89. Telegram From the Central Intelligence Agency to the Station in the Congo[1]

Washington, July 6, 1961, 2318Z.

Dir 49270 (Out 73506). Re Dir 47674 (Out 70677).[2]

1. State in procress cabling Embassy along lines that whatever dangers Gizenga may pose to ODYOKE interests and GOC, failure of latter to press for parliamentary solution will be serious and perhaps fatal blow to its international prestige and to its posture vis-à-vis Gizenga himself. State thus hopes Kasavubu and GOC moderates rethinking their position and again planning convene parliament.

2. In bringing above to our attention State wished point out hopeful possibility early opportunities will be found spend useful money under authorized [*cryptonym not declassified*] program and that strictures in ref would not inhibit Station and Embassy from seeking every opportunity press forward with program. Assured State purpose ref was only to advise spending caution during period complete political uncertainty and that you would move soon as situation permitted.

3. While recognize your heavy load would appreciate somewhat more frequent even if brief bulletins on [*cryptonym not declassified*] program prospects both for us and State.

End of message.

---

[1] Source: Central Intelligence Agency Files, Job 78–00435R, DDO/ISS Files, Box 1, Folder 7, [*cryptonym not declassified*] Ops. Secret; Rybat; [*cryptonym not declassified*]; Priority. Drafted and released by Tweedy (C/AF).

[2] Be careful about any heavy payment outlays on [*cryptonym not declassified*] program until situation clarifies. [Footnote in the original.] CIA telegram 47674 to Leopoldville, June 27, 1961, is ibid.

---

90. Editorial Note

In telegram 1638 from Leopoldville to the Central Intelligence Agency, July 11, 1961, the Station stated that its greatest problem had been to convince the moderate, anti-Lumumba leaders supported by CIA of the need to plan and coordinate activities. Partly as a result of its advice, however, this was now being done by an informal coordination and action group composed of Joseph Mobutu, [*names not declassified*] had asked for U.S. support of the group's parliamentary effort, which was agreed to upon condition that its members maintain a close working relationship with the Station. The chances of the [*text not declassified*] forming a government without Gizenga's participation were thought to be slim; to offset this, the Station constantly emphasized the importance of the [*text not declassified*] retaining the key ministries. (Central Intelligence Agency Files, Job 78–00435R, DDO/ISS Files, Box 1, Folder 7, [*cryptonym not declassified*] Ops)

In telegram 1676 from Leopoldville to CIA, July 20, the Station reported that Joseph Ileo had refused to resign as Prime Minister in order to permit Adoula to form a new government. Joseph Kasavubu and Mobutu had agreed that Ileo stood little chance of obtaining a majority vote and warned that an Ileo failure might well divide the parliamentarians and cause them to turn to Gizenga. It now appeared there would be a "donnybrook" at the parliamentary session at Lovanium, and no one could predict the outcome with certainty. However, the Station continued to believe that the [*text not declassified*] had a good chance of gaining control of the key ministries, including the premiership, of a government of national union. (Ibid.)

91. Telegram From the Station in the Congo to the Central Intelligence Agency[1]

Leopoldville, August 1, 1961.

1748 (In 46333). 1. No matter which group emerges victorious from Lovanium conclave (and it doubtful any political group will be able score major victory under present circumstances) KUBARK will be forced maintain high level of political action ops if ODYOKE wishes avoid eventual defeat this area. If [Identity 1][2] or another moderate obtains premiership, it will provide moderates with 3 to 6 month period of grace. If they fail organize during this time, alternative will be continued chaos and probable return of extremists to power. If [Identity 2] or Gbenye achieve power, expect there will be short period in which

[1] Source: Central Intelligence Agency Files, Job 78–00435R, DDO/ISS Files, Box 1, Folder 7, [*cryptonym not declassified*] Ops. Secret; Rybat; [*cryptonym not declassified*]; Routine. Received at 0409Z.

[2] After finally persuading Ileo to resign, Kasavubu named Adoula to succeed him as Prime Minister on August 1. On August 2, both houses of parliament confirmed Adoula and his government by a nearly unanimous vote. Gizenga was named Deputy Prime Minister.

moderates will have time organize themselves for effort regain power. Thus no matter what the outcome may be at Lovanium, believe KUBARK in conjunction with limited number [*cryptonym not declassified*], should concentrate on building strong [*cryptonym not declassified*] apparat and political machine in provinces. Basis experience past year, believe bribes for limited number politicians in Leop is merely stop gap effort which eventually bound to fail.

[Omitted here is detailed discussion of a proposed program.]

92. Telegram From the Station in the Congo to the Central Intelligence Agency[1]

Leopoldville, August 12, 1961.

1817 (In 12139). SitRep 6–12 Aug 61. Ref Embtel 334.[2]

1. Congo: Station continues view Congo situation with moderate optimism. However believe ref rosier than Station assessment.[3] Leo–Stan split still continues, apparently on very basic and critical point defense ministry portfolio. Furthermore, arms inflow to Orientale may give Gizenga sufficient added strength drive harder bargain with Leopoldville. At very least presence arms stocks Stan a dangerous element. Moderates early statements on undertaking immediate and energetic action to bring Gizenga to heel and throw Communist rascals out have paled over past weeks. Moderates now seem more inclined go very carefully since they may realize their balance of power slimmer than parliamentary vote indicated. Further, there may be developing in Leopoldville camp an opposition which, if allied to Gizengist forces on prime issues, might well make Adoula govt extremely uncomfortable.

---

[1] Source: Central Intelligence Agency Files, Job 78–00435R, DDO/ISS Files, Box 1, Folder 8, [*cryptonym not declassified*] Operations. Secret; Rybat; [*cryptonym not declassified*]; Routine. Received at 1637Z. Repeated to [*location not declassified*].

[2] Document 96 in *Foreign Relations,* 1961–1963, volume XX, Congo Crisis, pp. 189–192.

[3] In telegram 1776 from Leopoldville to CIA, August 5, the Station had written that it was difficult not to be optimistic about the immediate Congo situation in view of the events of the past week. The Gizenga forces seemed to be weakening rapidly and Congolese Government and UN pressures were being brought to bear on Tshombe with what appeared appreciable effect to bring him into the government. Most important of all, the Adoula government was exhibiting amazing self-confidence and energy in its plans to reunify the Congo, although it was too early to determine whether talk would be translated into action. (Central Intelligence Agency Files, Job 78–00435R, DDO/ISS Files, Box 1, Folder 7, [*cryptonym not declassified*] Operations)

Nor has Communist bloc response been indicated. On the positive side, there are indications the moderates' cartel of some 80 parliamentarians (known as Leopoldville bloc) is starting to function. UNOC/GOC relations quite good and the reported military agreement (Leop 1796) (In 10639)[4] between Stan and Leo forces very encouraging. GOC/Katanga relations also seem to be improving although serious trouble could occur at any time. Again Station enthusiasm lessened by frustrating experiences of past year. Imminent release Kenyatta may have emotional nationalistic repercussions here, although we have nothing to base our uneasy feeling on.

[Omitted here is further discussion of the Adoula government and discussion of the situation elsewhere in Africa.]

[4] Not found.

---

93. Telegram From the Station in the Congo to the Central Intelligence Agency[1]

Leopoldville, August 24, 1961.

1878 (In 17916). Ref A Leop 1748 (In 46333);[2] B Dir 07458.[3]

1. Payment deferred per ref B. Regret Leop erred in interpretation spending authority this op.

2. As indicated previous traffic, Leop convinced, despite its overwhelming majority, present govt could fall any time in next few

[1] Source: Central Intelligence Agency Files, Job 78–00435R, DDO/ISS Files, Box 1, Folder 8, [*cryptonym not declassified*] Operations. Secret; Rybat; [*cryptonym not declassified*]; Priority. Received at 1757Z.

[2] Forwarded [*text not declassified*] program. [Footnote in the original.] This telegram is printed as Document 91.

[3] Apparently wrong reference. Possibly Dir 07658 (Out 88688) intended. [Footnote in the original.] Telegram 07658 from CIA to Leopoldville, August 23, is in Central Intelligence Agency Files, Job 78–00435R, DDO/ISS Files, Box 1, Folder 8, [*cryptonym not declassified*] Operations.

months. All [*cryptonym not declassified*][4] contacted by [COS] since return, as well as [Embassy officials], journalists, and other contacts, are of opinion [Identity 1] has only few months in which to solidify his strength. Not possible predict with any degree accuracy time available but estimate three months to one year. Even if [Identity 1] lasts one year, his power will gradually weaken unless shored up. Chief [Embassy] concurs this view.

3. [*cryptonym not declassified*] program no substitute for strong effective govt which meets needs of people but present coalition so big and represents so many viewpoints and ethnic groups there little chance for strong govt despite good intentions and desires various [*cryptonym not declassified*]. Size of coalition almost certain to result in govt program based on lowest common denominator. Thus, continue believe KUBARK must implement long term [*cryptonym not declassified*] program along lines ref A. Although recognize cost and difficulties such program, believe effort necessary unless previous efforts to come to nought. In short, parties and power groups are developing even now and will continue to develop in the Congo. If we do not aid and guide our friends, many if not all will drift into the extremist camps and ODYOKE policy will encounter numerous setbacks at best and at worst a major defeat.

4. Present chief [Embassy] concurs with the premises expressed ref A and more current views outlined herein.

[Omitted here is further discussion of the program.]

---

[4] The moderate, pro-Western leaders in the Congo supported by a CIA political action program.

94. Memorandum From the Chief of the Africa Division, Directorate of Plans, Central Intelligence Agency (Tweedy) to the Deputy Director of the Office of Central African Affairs, Department of State (Eisenberg)[1]

Washington, August 25, 1961.

SUBJECT

Developments in the Congo

Confirming the discussion we had in Mr. Fredericks' office on 23 August, the following are the main points contained in our message from Leopoldville:[2]

a. Our Station Chief saw [*name not declassified*] on 23 August, at the latter's request. [*name not declassified*] expressed his concern and that of many of his colleagues in the former Ileo government concerning pressures from Gizenga on Prime Minister Adoula. [*name not declassified*] stated that Gizenga continued to demand concessions which would give the Stanleyville forces control of additional key government slots and [*less than 1 line not declassified*] Adoula received a phone call from General Lundula on 21 August. Lundula told Adoula that Gizenga demanded Pierre Mulele as the Minister of Defense, Lundula to replace Mobutu as commanding general of the CNA and that Thomas Kanza be named Congolese representative to the UN. When Adoula indicated his inability to comply with Gizenga's demands, Lundula indicated that the Stanleyville population was preventing Gizenga from coming to Leopoldville. [*name not declassified*] and presumably Adoula interpreted Lundula's statement to mean that Gizenga would not come to Leopoldville unless his demands for additional key posts were met.

b. Adoula advised Joseph Kasongo, President of the Chamber, of Gizenga's demands. [*less than 1 line not declassified*] Kasongo promised immediately to send Gizenga a letter requesting him to come to Leopoldville at once and indicated that he, Kasongo, would ask Parliament to lift Gizenga's parliamentary immunity if he refused to comply.

(*Note:* Our Chief of Station reported the above to Mac Godley and it was presumably sent by the latter to the Department through his own channel.)

c. In addition to Gizenga's pressures to obtain key jobs, [*name not declassified*] said that the Stanleyville representatives were using other

[1] Source: Central Intelligence Agency Files, Job 78–00435R, DDO/ISS Files, Box 1, Folder 8, [*cryptonym not declassified*] Operations. Secret.

[2] Reference is to telegram 1870 from Leopoldville to CIA, August 23. (Ibid.)

methods as well to obtain their objectives and he indicated his belief that they would not stop at terrorist methods, if necessary. In the latter connection, noted that Gizenga has received arms shipments and also stated he had information that Gizenga had shipped gold from Stanleyville to Cairo. Under the circumstances, [*name not declassified*] asked our Chief of Station to see Adoula shortly in order to advise the latter of the dangers involved in such concessions. [*name not declassified*] expressed the view that Adoula respected the Chief of Station's opinion and would be apt to accept his advice and suggested that he might cite examples such as the communist take-over of Czechoslovakia in his talk with him. (*Note:* Our Chief of Station discussed this immediately with MacGodley, who approved the visit to Adoula. We do not yet have any information that Adoula has been seen.)

d. [*name not declassified*] was also much concerned about the physical safety of GOC leaders and believed that Gizengists were planning a terrorist campaign and might try to "physically eliminate" Kasavubu, Adoula, Bomboko and Mobutu, and possibly others. [*name not declassified*] said that Mobutu had been asked to select forty-odd hand-picked commandos to serve as bodyguards for these leaders and requested our support in training them. (*Note:* As we discussed the other evening, we will certainly do something to respond to [*name not declassified*] request for the training of "secret service" type bodyguards, but we have serious reservations that any formal training program would have any useful result, this based on experience elsewhere with elements probably more ready to receive this type of instruction than the Congolese.)

e. The final point was [*name not declassified*] request for three and a half million BCF to pay off political debts incurred during the Lovanium conclave. (*Note:* Policy authority was received for this from Mr. Scott's office on 24 August.)

Bronson Tweedy[3]

---

[3] Printed from a copy that bears this typed signature.

---

95. Editorial Note

In telegram 09810 to Leopoldvlle, September 2, 1961, the Central Intelligence Agency stated that it was very conscious of the fact that the Station had submitted a variety of proposals in recent weeks to which it had received for the most part only a preliminary response. While the

CIA realized the Congo and long-range planning were a contradiction in terms, such planning was more feasible now than heretofore but Headquarters felt the need for an overall U.S. approach into which to fit the most meaningful CIA role. This had been discussed with newly appointed Ambassador Edmund Gullion, who planned a country team approach to many problems and hoped to return to Washington with firm field recommendations by the end of the year. Headquarters by no means intended to wait that long to undertake a number of new CIA programs but believed the earliest integration of its efforts into more general U.S. thinking was essential. (Central Intelligence Agency Files, Job 78–00435R, DDO/ISS Files, Box 1, Folder 8, [*cryptonym not declassified*] Operations)

96. Editorial Note

In September 1961, fighting between United Nations (UN) and Katangan forces entered a new phase. At the end of August, UN forces seized key points in Elizabethville and arrested a number of Belgian officers and mercenaries. On September 13, a new UN offensive encountered heavy resistance from European-led Katangan forces. President Kennedy and Secretary of State Rusk sent a message to Ambassador Gullion, instructing him to urge UN Secretary General Dag Hammarskjold, who was in Leopoldville, to end the fighting and begin negotiations. In the wake of Hammarskjold's death on September 17 in a plane crash on his way to meet with Tshombe, the United States agreed to a UN request to position four U.S. transport aircraft at Leopoldville for use in an internal airlift of UN troops within the Congo.

On September 19, President Kennedy issued National Security Action Memorandum No. 97, authorizing the dispatch of U.S. fighter aircraft with the necessary logistical support to the Congo, on a contingency basis. Kennedy specifically directed that their mission would be to support and defend U.S. and UN transports or other UN forces that might come under air attack, and that their use in offensive activities against Katangan forces was not authorized. This authorization would become effective only if no fighter aircraft of other nations were made available to the United Nations. The United Nations obtained fighters elsewhere, however, and the question of using U.S. fighters did not arise again for over a year. See *Foreign Relations,* 1961–1963, volume XX, Congo Crisis, Documents 102–128, pages 201–248 for detailed coverage of the September 1961 Katanga crisis.

97. Dispatch From the Station in the Congo to the Central Intelligence Agency[1]

Leopoldville, October 12, 1961.

SUBJECT

[*cryptonym not declassified*]/Suggested [*cryptonym not declassified*] Program for Leopoldville Station

Reference(s): A. Leop 2176, 2 Oct 61;[2] B. Leop 2180, 3 Oct 61;[3] C. Dir 11649, 11 Sep 61;[4] D. Leop 1748, 29 Jul 61;[5] E. [*less than 1 line not declassified*].[6]

1. Summary. Independence in the Congo has resulted in chaos, great difficulties for the West and an opportunity for the Soviet Bloc to exploit the situation to its own ends. The time for ad hoc KUBARK action to meet the emergency must now give way to a detailed and organized plan of action which looks beyond today to the eventual form that ODYOKE wishes to see the future take in the Congo and, for that matter, in Central Africa. This dispatch is an attempt to place on paper certain "talking points" which will serve as a basis for further discussion in the development of such a long-term program of action. Because the need is so great and the problems are so huge, ODYOKE responses and initiatives must likewise be in heroic proportion. Halfway measures will not suffice and there will be no monetary or personnel shortcuts to whatever victory it may be possible to achieve in the Congo over the next several years. The following paragraphs outline a program divided into two arbitrary time phases. In Phase One, we suggest the implementation of operations which (we believe and hope) are within our capacity to accomplish. The accomplishment of Phase Two will require a beefing up of considerable proportions which is beyond our current capacity (both budgetary and personnel). It is our intent to establish an operational framework, wherein boundaries can be established for the future judging of new operations and for the continued

---

[1] Source: Central Intelligence Agency Files, Job 78–00435R, DDO/ISS Files, Box 1, Folder 8, [*cryptonym not declassified*] Operations. Secret; Rybat; Priority.

[2] Telegram 2176 from Leopoldville to CIA, October 2, transmitted a message from Ambassador Gullion to Assistant Secretary Williams, drafted by the Station, supporting short-term and long-term steps CIA was prepared to take to strengthen the moderates in the Congo and to enable them to counter actions already launched by the extremists. (Ibid.)

[3] See footnote 2, Document 98.

[4] Not found.

[5] Document 91.

[6] Not found.

implementation of already-existing operations. Flexibility must be the touchstone of our work, however, since the Congo—as has been seen in the past several months—is capable of infinite changes of direction and varieties of disintegrative forces. The following outline embraces almost all elements of political and psychological action, [*4 lines not declassified*]. In essence this dispatch represents a distillation of Leopoldville Station's experience and frustrations of the past 15 months as well as our earnest hopes for the future.

[Omitted here is the body of the dispatch.]

98. Telegram From the Central Intelligence Agency to the Station in the Congo[1]

Washington, October 14, 1961, 1729Z.

Dir 18065 (Out 58161). Ref Leop 2180 (In 39391).[2]

1. Within recent weeks prospective action program in Congo has been subject discussion with ODACID. No question that program as detailed ref covers important action fields. However ODACID preliminary view is that program likely suffer from scatter gun approach unless attention directed to specific planks which will build permanent viable assets such as youth and labor groupings which capable action support [*cryptonym not declassified*] govt. There is no objection to psych activity in media field and bribes as such but conclusion which we share is that value is transitory unless such activity follows in wake of strenuous, continuing actions by [*cryptonym not declassified*] activists. Accordingly priorities must be established based on capabilities and need for activity which will pave way for well balanced program as activity picks up steam. Further observation which our experience cer-

[1] Source: Central Intelligence Agency Files, Job 78–00435R, DDO/ISS Files, Box 1, Folder 8, [*cryptonym not declassified*] Operations. Secret; Rybat; [*cryptonym not declassified*]; Routine. Drafted in AF/W and released by Tweedy (C/AF).

[2] Station under constant pressure to support an action program designed to build up the moderates and to undermine the Stanleyville group. [Footnote in the original.] In telegram 2180 to the CIA, October 3, the Station reported that all its contacts among the moderates, without exception, had expressed the belief that a showdown was approaching. Mobutu, [*names not declassified*] had decided to take the initiative against Stanleyville and, with Station guidance and support, were launching a psychological campaign [*1½ lines not declassified*]. (Ibid.)

tainly bears out is that success any aspects such program depends to great extent on our ability place effective operators on scene to handle.[3]

[Omitted here is further discussion of programs for the Congo.]

[3] In telegram 2273 from Leopoldville to CIA, October 17, the Station responded that it fully concurred with the Agency and Department of State view that the short-term program submitted in telegram 2180 would be of transitory value unless followed by a long-term program such as that submitted in the October 12 dispatch from Leopoldville (Document 97). The Station wished to emphasize again that the moderates faced considerable pressure and feared that the extremists were gaining ground, and it urged Headquarters to make every effort to obtain the funds and personnel necessary to support a long-term program. (Central Intelligence Agency Files, Job 78–00435R, DDO/ISS Files, Box 1, Folder 8, [*cryptonym not declassified*] Operations)

99. Editorial Note

On November 11, 1961, the report of the U.N. Commission established by General Assembly Resolution 1601 (XV), April 15, 1961, to investigate the circumstances of the death of Patrice Lumumba and his colleagues, was signed at Geneva. The Commission accepted as "substantially true" the evidence indicating that Lumumba, Joseph Okito, and Maurice Mpolo were killed on January 17, 1961, after their arrival at a villa not far from Elizabethville and "in all probability in the presence of high officials of the government of Katanga province, namely Mr. Tshombe, Mr. Munongo, and Mr. Kibwe." The Commission stated that President Kasavubu and his aides, on the one hand, and the Katanga government headed by Moise Tshombe, on the other, should not escape responsibility for the deaths. Kasavubu and his aides had handed the three prisoners over to Katangan authorities, knowing full well that in doing so they were putting them in the hands of their bitterest political enemies. The Katangan government in turn not only did not safeguard the lives of the prisoners, but also by its actions, directly or indirectly, contributed to their murders. (U.N. doc. A/4964)

100. Memorandum for the Special Group[1]

Washington, November 16, 1961.

SUBJECT

Covert Action in the Congo

1. *Problem:* To strengthen the personal position of Prime Minister Cyrille Adoula as the national leader, and of his closest colleagues as a group, in order to endow the Adoula Government with sufficient political stability to resist leftist pressures aimed at its overthrow and to bring about a successful, peaceful settlement with the Government of Katanga leading to unification of the Congo.

2. *Assumptions:* That it is in our interest to bring about the unification of the Congo by peaceful or moderate means, under the leadership of the present Government, rather than an attempted forcible unification under leftist leadership in cooperation with the Soviet Bloc and at the expense of a major United Nations failure.

3. *Facts and Discussion:* The formation of the Adoula Government on August 2, 1961, following the reconvening of the Congolese Parliament, halted for the moment the strong bid for power by the extremist forces led by Bloc-supported Antoine Gizenga and representing the Lumumba *mystique.* However, the Adoula Government contained two major weaknesses: (1) Katanga representatives did not participate in its formation and Katanga's reintegration into the Congo did not ensue, and (2) Gizenga and a number of his key colleagues obtained important positions in the Adoula Government, introducing a disintegrating and irresponsible force. Reintegration of Katanga is necessary for the future economic viability of the Congo, and only peaceful integration can avoid the destruction of Katanga's economic base and the plunging of the Congo into a chaos from which only the Bloc could profit. Attempts by the United Nations Operation in the Congo (UNOC) to bring about Katanga reintegration by combined police action and negotiations has met with failure due in large part to the untimely death of Secretary-General Hammarskjold. Pressure on Adoula and Tshombe to negotiate by the U.S. and other governments has likewise had no success. Popular pressures fanned by the leftists in both Leopoldville and Stanleyville threaten to force the Adoula Government either to take all-out military action (almost certain to be abortive) against Katanga or to resign in favor of the extremists, in either of which eventuality we may expect

[1] Source: National Security Council, Intelligence Files, Subject Files, Congo, 1960–1965. Secret. There is no drafting information on the memorandum.

to see a rapid deterioration of public order and sharply increased influence of the Bloc. This situation has been exacerbated by Adoula's rather colorless and unaggressive personality plus his and his colleagues' absorption with the problems of the daily administration of the government. The extreme opposition, not burdened with responsibility for the success of the government, has been active in undercutting Adoula's position.

4. *Conclusions:* Prime Minister Adoula and his close colleagues must obtain in the immediate future new sources of strength and expert political advice if they are to remain in power as a moderating and moderate force. Should the Adoula Government be forced to relinquish power or to succumb to extremist policies, the following consequences are likely to ensue quickly: (1) accession by an extremist government committed to a military solution of the Katanga problem, (2) discrediting of the UNOC, (3) a rapid deterioration of internal security leading to chaos, and (4) the ascendency of the Bloc as a major influence in the Congo leading to the possible establishment of a Soviet base of power there.

As our Government is committed to the support of UNOC, normal unilateral aid mechanisms are not usable in the Congo. Hence effective measures must be undertaken by covert means.

5. *Action Recommended:* It is recommended that the following actions, which have in substance been proposed jointly by the Chief of Mission and our Leopoldville representative, be authorized to enhance the political image of Prime Minister Adoula domestically and internationally and to furnish him and his closest collaborators with a base of domestic power sufficiently strong to permit the Government to continue in power as a moderate force, friendly toward the United States, and with the ability to achieve a satisfactory solution of the Katanga problem:

a. Encourage the formation of an Adoula-led political "cartel" designed to bring about the coalescence of the disparate and domestically uncommitted politicians, leading to the eventual forming of a new, cohesive national political party with bases throughout the provinces. Such action, if successful, would assure Adoula of Parliamentary support.

b. [*11½ lines not declassified*]

c. [*7 lines not declassified*]

d. Endeavor to organize in support of the Adoula Government significant "mass" organizations, [*3 lines not declassified*].

e. [*3 lines not declassified*]

f. Assist General Mobutu, moderate Chief-of-Staff of the Congolese National Army, to retain the loyalty of key officers.

6. *Budget:* It is recommended that authority to expend up to [*dollar amount not declassified*] be granted for the implementation of this program.[2]

[2] The NSC minutes of the Special Group meeting on November 22 record that the proposal to support Adoula and his associates was approved. The Chairman said he would inform higher authority, i.e., the President. (Ibid., Special Group—Minutes and Approvals—1961) At a meeting on January 9, 1962, attended by CIA and Department of State representatives, CIA reported point by point on the status of the program approved on November 22, indicating modest progress in the face of much difficulty. See Document 104.

---

101. Telegram From the Station in the Congo to the Central Intelligence Agency[1]

Leopoldville, November 28, 1961.

2501 (In 28695).

1. Since returning from HQS [COS] struck by apparent nearness of chaos and failure in Congo. The situation is not the result of one or more specific events. Rather there has been a general decline in moderates' position, a decline which has sharply increased in recent weeks. The Adoula govt is in a precarious position as it faces problems with which it does not appear able to cope and to which inadequate solutions have been addressed by the UNOC. Although it would be premature to predict the govt will fall if help not provided rapidly, Leop believes it entirely possible govt will fall or come under control of extremist elements hostile to ODYOKE if overt action is not taken soon to shore up Adoula's position.

2. Leop recognizes KUBARK is not directly involved, and should not become involved, in formation of policy. Thus, this message is merely for the background use of senior KUBARKers in discussions with ODACID. It represents Station views and was prepared solely on [COS's] responsibility. It has not been submitted to, nor received approval of, [Embassy] or the country team. In the absence of [Ambassador Gullion], Station doubts deputy chief [Embassy] would approve such a message. (Thus if info and suggestions reported herein are used,

[1] Source: Central Intelligence Agency Files, Job 78–00435R, DDO/ISS Files, Box 1, Folder 8, [*cryptonym not declassified*] Operations. Secret; Rybat; Priority. Bissell and Tweedy from COS. Received at 0159Z.

request HQS not indicate origin.) However, Leop believes urgent consideration must be given to new approaches to the Congo problem as considerable risks are entailed in our present policy. Suggestions and comments herein are not intended as a definitive review of Congolese problems or an overall solution. The serious political situation does not permit the time required to conduct detailed studies, and assets to conduct such studies are not available to Leop. However, if HQS concurs with Station views that immediate action is required, this message will provide suggestions for overt stopgap measures designed to reverse, or delay, the current trend.

3. Prior to independence it was recognized that considerable foreign aid would be required to assist an independent Congo. However, the CNA mutiny in July 60 caused ODYOKE and other Western powers to transfer their hopes to an international solution in the form of UN action. This decision restricted ODYOKE overt efforts in the Congo to the provision of guidance by [Embassy] and a severely limited aid program, thus removing the economic, technical and military programs which might have been used as levers to implement ODYOKE policy in the Congo. With the exception of the PL 480 agreement signed 18 Nov 61, the only unilateral ODYOKE program in the Congo available for political action purposes was (and is) the KUBARK covert action program. In the light of what might have occurred had this weapon not been available, the KUBARK program has been relatively successful. KUBARK can take major credit for the fall of the Lumumba govt, the success of the Mobutu coup and considerable credit for Adoula's nomination as premier. Also, it has achieved a number of other less spectacular but nonetheless important political objectives. Had ODYOKE been able to exploit these openings overtly by means of military, technical or economic aid programs or had the UNOC met its responsibilities effectively, ODYOKE policy in the Congo would not now be hanging in the balance. However, ODYOKE was not able to assist overtly persons and govts favorably disposed toward PBPRIME and the UNOC failed to fill the void. Unfortunately, the KUBARK action program has not and realistically could never have been expected to be a substitute for a strong and effective govt, nor could it provide the guidance and aid necessary to shore up the GOC, retrain the CNA and revitalize the economy. Thus, the GOC, assisted by the UNOC, has limped along with only partial and inefficient approaches to the enormous problems which it faces.

4. The problems of the Adoula govt are the same difficulties which have plagued the Congo since independence: lack of discipline within the army, massive unemployment, absence of civic spirit coupled with tribal rivalries, lack of leadership at all levels and lack of preparation for self govt. Although problems facing the GOC are innumerable, the following major problems now hold the key to the future of the Congo.

A. The army: The July 60 CNA mutiny which led to the UN Congo operation has never been fully contained, as demonstrated by the Jan 61 mutiny in Thysville, the incidents at Kindu, Albertville, Luluabourg, Port Franqui and innumerable lawless acts of troops throughout the Congo, particularly in Orientale and the Kivu. While a part of the CNA provided much needed support for the moderates, helped bring down Lumumba and contributed to maintaining the moderates in power, the CNA has remained a problem as well as a support weapon for the moderates. Instead of becoming a strong force for the preservation of law and order, the army has been divided into factions temporarily loyal to its various paymasters (Mobutu and other moderates, the extremists in Kivu and Orientale and Tshombe). It has taken the law into its own hands, arbitrarily arresting Congolese and foreigners, robbing banks and looting. Its untrained officers are not qualified for command or staff positions and have only a minimum of control over their undisciplined troops. In short the CNA is little more than an armed mob. However, with the exception of a small-scale paratroop training program which lasted only about two months (42 CNA troopers made a training jump) the UNOC has done nothing to meet the key problem of training and reorganizing the CNA. As the result of Mobutu's efforts, the majority of troops in the area responsive to Leopoldville have supported the moderates and this has been a major political lever in maintaining the moderates in power since Sept 60. However, because of its lack of discipline and leadership, the CNA has not provided the support which it might have done if properly organized and trained. Also the danger of the extremists gaining control over the army and using it to gain power remains a potential danger. Finally the fact the army is not under control and must constantly be placated has resulted in large expenditure for the CNA (about half the national budget).

B. Administrative breakdown: Considerable responsibility for the failure to date of all Congolese govts results from the breakdown of the administrative machinery. Few if any GOC leaders have sufficient admin ability to carry out govt decisions in an efficient manner. Thus the govt machine works only at a small percentage of its potential efficiency. UNOC has tried to resolve this problem by assigning technical specialists to various ministries but there are not enough and many are not first-rate types.

C. Unemployment: With the departure of many white employers after the July mutiny and the gradual breakdown in govt, the unemployment problem became massive. (No overall unemployment statistics are now available for the Congo. May 61 statistics for Leop showed 52 percent of the male labor force unemployed. [Embassy] believes figures are even higher in provincial cities.) The GOC has done little to cope with this problem and UNOC efforts in conjunction with the GOC have been limited. As of 31 July 61 (last date for which statistics available to [Embassy], about 160 million BCF had been made available by UNOC for work relief program. (Bulk of financing came from counterpart value from sale of American food supplies.) Of total sum available, 142 million BCF had been allocated for projects throughout the Congo. Thus less than 1 and one half million dollars (at parallel market rate) was allocated for purpose of relief works program by the UNOC during its first year in the Congo. As result of confusion in public finances, detailed info re unilateral GOC expenditures for public works are not available. However, [Embassy] believes such expenditures were minimal. A new joint UNOC–GOC program is now being developed. However, only 4 UNOC officers have been assigned to the program. Even if a program of sufficient magnitude evolves to reduce appreciably the number of unemployed, Leop doubts the UNOC will be able provide sufficient qualified administrators and technicians to carry out the program as there are only 450 persons employed by UNOC civil affairs division, including doctors, educators, etc. However, if implementation is left to the GOC, its lack of qualified administrators will greatly limit effectiveness of the program, if indeed it does not fail altogether. In summation, Leop believes the UNOC has failed to provide a solution or even a partial solution to the unemployment problem, a question with tremendous political as well as economic implications. Also, view quantity and quality of tech advisors available to UNOC, Leop doubts UNOC will be able mount an adequate and efficient program.

D. Katanga: Although important from an economic viewpoint, the GOC desire to reintegrate the Katanga into the Congo has become critical from a political viewpoint. The abortive Sept UNOC operation merely succeeded in spotlighting the problem, thus greatly increasing pressures on the Adoula govt (from moderates as well as extremists) to find a solution at any cost. Adoula was forced to send the CNA into Katanga to prevent his govt from falling. The CNA operation failed miserably, further increasing pressures on the govt. The Katanga problem has thus become an emotion charged weapon in the hands of the extremists with which to attack the govt. It could easily bring about the fall of the govt. At present the GOC has reached an impasse. It doubts anything useful will come from negotiations with Tshombe. Adoula feels he cannot go abroad to meet Tshombe, as he doubts Tshombe's sincerity in offering to negotiate and believes his govt would fall if he undertook such negotiations and failed. (The extremists would almost certainly claim that Adoula had sold out to Tshombe.) Also, the failure of the CNA Katanga operation has convinced the GOC that it cannot, without help, resolve the problem by force. As a result, Adoula is desperately casting about for some solution or stop gap measure. Numerous GOC leaders, including [Identity 1], [Identity 2] and [Mobutu] and [Identity 3] have requested ODYOKE to provide GOC with planes. GOC has also sent a mission abroad to purchase aircraft. They believe GOC planes would raise the morale of their followers and, at least temporarily, serve as "proof" that the GOC is taking positive action to resolve the Katanga problem. To date Adoula has rejected Soviet offers of planes, arms and other aid (see Leop 2452) [*less than 1 line not declassified*][2] but he may soon be faced with a choice of his govt falling or accepting Soviet aid to relieve political pressures. In such a case, Leop believes it entirely possible Adoula might, against his better judgment, accept the proferred aid, particularly as his govt would almost certainly be replaced by extremists. At present the GOC is waiting hopefully for someone to get it off the spot. It hopes the UNOC will use force once again and that this time it will be successful in resolving the Katanga question. Also, Adoula hopes Balubakat and ANC pressure in north Katanga will put sufficient pressure on Tshombe to bring him back into the Congo fold. However, as it doubtful action in the north Katanga will result in such a solution sufficiently soon, the GOC now appears to face the following alternatives: it must obtain strong UNOC assistance or it must accept bilateral aid. If the UNOC is unable to resolve the Katanga question and if Adoula continues to refuse bilateral Soviet aid offers, he will become a sitting political duck. In such a case it is probable his govt would fall (or at the very least be greatly weakened and fall under the influence of the extremists). The resolution of the Katanga problem or early positive steps which point toward its eventual resolution are hurdles which Adoula must cross if he is to remain in power. The 24 Nov Security Council resolution[3] should provide Adoula with respite but if the UNOC fails to solve the problem in the near future, extremist pressures will be even greater.

E. Gizengist activities: Although no longer as strong as when he headed the Stan regime and claimed to be the legal chief of govt, Gizenga remains a threat. Although probably not a communist, he received bloc and Belgian CP support in the past and it is probable bloc elements will help him once again if they do not succeed in their efforts to take over or infiltrate the GOC. They could thus create another secessionist govt or by supporting him they could contribute to Congo chaos, thus weakening the GOC and preparing the way for an eventual

---

[2] Not found.

[3] On November 24, the Security Council passed a resolution completely rejecting the claim that Katanga was "a sovereign independent nation;" deploring Katanga's secessionist activities and armed action against the United Nations; authorizing vigorous action, including the "requisite measure of force, if necessary," to secure the immediate withdrawal of all mercenaries and all foreign military and paramilitary personnel and political advisers not under U.N. command; and recognizing the Government of the Congo as exclusively responsible for the conduct of its external affairs. For text, see *American Foreign Policy: Current Documents*, 1961, pp. 851–852.

compromise govt which would be more favorable to the bloc. As of now Orientale is in a complete state of anarchy with both govt and business at a standstill. Considerable economic assistance and, possibly, force may be required to resolve this situation. If such help is not forthcoming from the UNOC or other outside sources, it is doubtful the GOC will be able to solve the problem alone. Gizenga and his active supporters remain a sore in the side of the GOC and by their vocal opposition and criticism exercise an influence out of proportion to their actual strength. Through their constant criticism they keep the Adoula govt on the defensive and most concessions made to them tend to water down salutary govt programs and actions. If it were not for Katanga and the danger of bloc aid to Gizenga, the latter would not now pose as serious a threat to the govt as is now the case. However, he will remain a serious threat until the Katanga problem is resolved and until the GOC develops a more dynamic program.

F. Political frictions within the GOC: although Adoula received a near unanimous vote of approval at Lovanium, numerous factions exist within the govt. The leaders from Stan and their extremist supporters from other areas remain a constant threat to the govt. The Katanga situation is a political lever in their hands. The extremists tend to neutralize the more conservative elements in the govt. As a result most govt actions are based on compromise or the least common denominator. At present extremist elements are divided by a struggle for power. Interior Minister Gbenye and Chamber President Kasongo are fighting for control of the MNC/Lumumba Party and there is friction between the PSA (Gizenga's party) and the MNC over the creation of a new Unified Nationalist Party (Panalu). Both groups want to control the new party, if and when it is formed. Despite current difficulties of the extremists or so-called "nationalists," they represent a strong force in the country and if they succeed in unifying their efforts under one leader they could become the strongest political force in parliament. At present Adoula is forced to depend upon a loose coalition. The moderates have no effective political structure and have continued in power only because the extremists are divided and are not yet ready to make a bid for power. However, should Adoula or the UNOC fail to solve the Katanga problem, this would provide the extreme nationalists with an opening and a govt less friendly to ODYOKE interests than that of Adoula could easily ride to victory. But if the Katanga problem is resolved satisfactorily, the [*cryptonym not declassified*] program outlined in [*less than 1 line not declassified*] should provide the moderates with a reasonable chance of success.

5. By the foregoing Leop has endeavored to outline several major problems which are threatening the continued existence of a moderate govt in the Congo. We recognize most of these facts and views have

been submitted piecemeal by the Station and [Embassy]. However in view of what appears to be a rapid worsening of the moderates position, the Station feels it incumbent to sum up the situation and to point out that the current ODYOKE policy in the Congo could easily fail. Although we recognize our Congo policy is only one part of a complicated puzzle, we suggest urgent consideration be given to a review of our present policy and a study of alternative steps. In Leop 1748 [*less than 1 line not declassified*][4] dated 29 July [*August 1*] the Station estimated a moderate govt would have a three to six months period of grace in which to solidify its position. Adoula has been in office for nearly four months and the period of grace is running out. (On 21 Nov [Identity 4] opined that Adoula has at the very most three months in which to take steps leading to the resolution of the Katanga situation and major economic problems facing the govt. Other [*cryptonym not declassified*][5] have been less specific in their comments but it is clear the group close to Adoula is frightened, pessimistic and believes only outside help can save the present govt.

6. On the basis of VOA broadcasts of UN debates it appears ODYOKE efforts to assist the moderates by means of strengthened UN action have partially failed. (Leop does not have full details on outcome debate as VOA broadcast faded out at the critical moment.) In view of the fact ODYOKE efforts have been blocked by the Soviets, Leop suggests HQS consider recommending to ODACID that ODYOKE provide aid to the Congo on a unilateral basis, or together with one or more friendly powers. We realize any policy which would result in the withdrawal of all ODYOKE support for the UNOC would not be acceptable but a middle course appears possible. A precedent for bilateral aid agreements has already been set by the signing of the PL 480 agreement.

7. The Station understands that the current ODYOKE policy of working only through the UNOC was based on the following considerations:

A. To interdict the Congo to the Soviets and to try to avoid exporting the cold war struggle to the Congo.

B. To try to avoid ruffling the neutral feathers of the Afro-Asian Bloc.

The reasoning which appeared to justify this ODYOKE policy decision when it was first adopted in July 60 no longer appears valid, we have not interdicted the Congo to the Soviets as witnessed by the Soviet

---

[4] This telegram is printed as Document 91.

[5] The moderate, pro-Western leaders in the Congo supported by a CIA political action program.

offer to provide arms and other aid on a unilateral basis. Although the cold war in the Congo has not reached the same levels as in Asia, we believe this to be a result more of Soviet difficulties in launching a program in the Congo (great distance from Soviet Union, fact Soviets were expelled from the Congo and were absent for nearly one year, the reservoir of good will toward PBPRIME which existed in the Congo, the not altogether fortuitous actions of [Mobutu], etc) than to the fact that ODYOKE abdicated its right to intervene on a unilateral basis. As for the second motive (the sensitivities of the Afro-Asians), Leop recognizes any step by ODYOKE to provide unilateral aid would almost certainly ruffle the neutralists. However the precedent has been set by the PL 480 agreement and it appears probable a sharp break with the neutralists could be avoided if ODYOKE continued its general support for the UNOC while instituting certain bilateral programs parallel and complementary to the UNOC effort. In any case we may be faced with a choice of accepting bad publicity among the Afro-Asians or seeing the Congo swing into the camp of anti-Western powers, possibly falling under the influence of the bloc. We believe overt unilateral assistance could be limited to the fields of military assistance and public works.

8. Most responsible moderate leaders recognize an early solution must be found to the CNA problem. This view is shared by [Identity 1], [Identity 2], and [Mobutu], [Identity 5], and [Identity 3], and [Identity 4] and many others. They wish to remove the CNA sword of Damocles which hangs over them. Whether Adoula would now be prepared to request such assistance if it were not to come through UNOC channels is a question which the Station cannot now answer. However if the political situation continues to deteriorate, we suspect he could be convinced to make such a request. [Identity 4] and [Mobutu] have already put out feelers to [COS] to determine whether ODYOKE alone or in conjunction with other friendly govts would be willing to take the following steps:

A. Provide training outside the Congo for selected CNA officers. (Few if any CNA officers are adequately trained for their present position. The troops recognize the lack of capacity of the officers. This partially explains the mutinous conduct of the troops and the miserable showing of the CNA over the past 16 months.)

B. Provide military technicians qualified to give on-the-job training to officers and men who could not be sent abroad. For example, the commander of the paracommando battalion and the troops at Thysville, the only halfway loyal elements available to the govt in the Leopoldville area, could not be spared for training abroad.

C. Assist the CNA to weed out troublesome and incompetent elements and to train new troops. (Leop doubts it will be possible to do anything with the CNA as now constituted. One solution might be to call up new recruits and train two or more battalions in a training area far from the influence of the present mutinous troops. Once trained the new battalions could replace troops which it would be advisable to eliminate from the CNA. In this fashion it would eventually be possible to create a wholly new army retaining only those officers and men who possess the necessary qualifications and training. In this respect HQS should know [Identity 1] told [COS] on 16 and 26 Nov that he eventually hopes to discharge the great majority of present CNA members and that he counts upon PBPRIME aid to resettle them in the provinces.

D. Provide military equipment to replace matériel which has fallen into disrepair or been destroyed over the past year. (Much CNA equipment is no longer usable because the Congolese through lack of competence or discipline have failed to maintain it properly.)

9. In the field of public works ODYOKE might provide additional administrators and technicians (either on bilateral basis or working through the UN) to supplement those now available to the UNOC. There do not appear to be enough UNOC personnel to handle a large public works program and there are few if any Congolese capable of administering such an effort. Also, it may eventually be necessary to provide additional funds (possibly through PL 480 channels) if the serious unemployment problem is to be resolved.

10. In summation, Leop believes the Adoula govt is in serious difficulty and could fall within the next one to three months unless immediate and effective steps are taken to resolve at least one or more of the major problems in the Congo. While Leop recognizes ODYOKE would have little chance of getting the military aid or public works programs suggested herein off the ground in such a short time, the announcement of such plans might serve to extend Adoula's period of grace. Adoula could claim to be taking positive steps which would give hope to the unemployed and which might convince the population that the govt would eventually be able to solve the Katanga problem on its own initiative. While on the basis of the 24 Nov resolution the UNOC may resolve the Katanga problem, Leop is not sanguine. The UNOC does not now have sufficient troops in the Congo to launch a military operation in the Katanga and concurrently insure the maintenance of law and order elsewhere in the Congo. Thus, it would appear advisable to take steps ASAP to implement alternative action should the UNOC fail or should it appear that its action would come too late. In any case a disciplined and trained army under the control of the moderates would provide them with the force of law and order and with a force which would permit them to resist extremist pressures and/or action against the govt.

11. Leop requests HQS indulgence for overstepping the limits of its responsibilities by suggesting policy changes in the Congo. However it

wishes to emphasize the urgency which it attaches to the need for taking overt steps to meet the current problem, if ODYOKE policy objectives are to be achieved. (Such steps cannot be taken by covert means by the Station as now constituted.) We do not wish to imply that all is lost but we wish to alert HQS to the fact that the situation in the Congo could and may well go against us. Thus we are forwarding our comments and suggestions for the background use of [Bissell] and [Tweedy].

End of message.

---

102. Telegram From the Station in the Congo to the Central Intelligence Agency[1]

Leopoldville, November 29, 1961.

2521 (In 30030). 1. [Mobutu] has urgently requested Station provide him with [*amount not declassified*]. Offered following explanation: When he was in Eliz prior Lovanium endeavoring work out unification of CNA, Tshombe gave him this sum for ANC. [Mobutu] reported receipt funds to GOC on return Leop. Said he later used funds cover multitude smaller CNA expenses for which funds not approved or authorized by finance ministry.

2. [Mobutu] says he fears he soon will be queried re location funds. He fears he will be accused of having pocketed money if he cannot produce it. Says opposition could use argument he paid off by Tshombe.

3. Recognize this is unusual request by view importance to [*cryptonym not declassified*] ops of maintaining [Mobutu] in his present position. Recommend HQS authorize expenditure [*amount not declassified*] from [*cryptonym not declassified*] for passage [Mobutu]. Latter states he will obtain [*cryptonym not declassified*] authorization to retain money for political ops work within CNA. Although Leop cannot be certain [Mobutu] story as to disposition funds received from Tshombe correct, believe it probably true. GOC finances in such confused state that [Mobutu] often forced go into his own (or KUBARK) pocket meet CNA needs. Also view our assessment of him believe he most honest of Station contacts.

---

[1] Source: Central Intelligence Agency Files, Job 78–00435R, DDO/ISS Files, Box 1, Folder 8, [*cryptonym not declassified*] Operations. Secret; Rybat; [*cryptonym not declassified*]; Operational Immediate. Received at 2329Z.

4. Please advise OpIm as do not wish risk fall of [Mobutu].[2]

End of message.

---

[2] CIA telegram 27099 to Leopoldville, November 30, authorized the requested expenditure. (Ibid.)

---

103. Editorial Note

In telegram 2533 to the Central Intelligence Agency, December 2, 1961, the Chief of Station in Leopoldville reported on a meeting with Joseph Mobutu at which Mobutu stated that he considered U.S. Congo policy to be "equivocal." Mobutu explained that he and many other moderates could not reconcile U.S. clandestine support of the [*cryptonym not declassified*] with its overt policy of all out support for the United Nations Operations in the Congo. Commenting that he would not have been able to mount his coup on September 14, 1960, or maintain the commissioner form of government in power without U.S. help, he contrasted that assistance with the refusal by the United States to provide the overt support which would have solidified the moderates' position and avoided the present situation in which the Government of the Congo was dependent upon support of Stanleyville elements. He added that could not understand why the United States continued to funnel all overt aid through the United Nations Operations in the Congo when, in his opinion, the UN supported individuals such as Christophe Gbenye who were unfriendly to U.S. policies. He also indicated that he believed the UNOC to be inefficient, noting that it had done nothing to revitalize the economy or assist him in his efforts to reorganize the Congolese National Army. He concluded with an impassioned plea for unilateral U.S. aid to the GOC. He insisted that such aid would have the advantage of supporting the [*text not declassified*] and thus permitting them to defeat the more extremist forces and establish a government and policy which in the long run would be more favorable to the United States. (Central Intelligence Agency Files, Job 78–00435R, DDO/ISS Files, Box 1, Folder 8, [*cryptonym not declassified*] Operations)

104. Memorandum From Alfred T. Wellborn of the Office of the Deputy Director for Coordination, Bureau of Intelligence and Research, Department of State, to the Director of the Bureau of Intelligence and Research (Hilsman)[1]

Washington, January 11, 1962.

SUBJECT

AF Meeting with Agency Representatives January 9, 1962

Present at the meeting were Governor Williams (who left before the end), Mr. Fredericks and Mr. Eisenberg of AF; Messrs. Tweedy, [*less than 1 line not declassified*] of the Agency; and I.

The Agency representatives reported on the status of the covert action in the Congo program approved by the Special Group on November 22, 1961.[2] In brief, the Agency reported modest progress in the face of much difficulty.

1. [*12 lines not declassified*]

2. *Formation of Adoula-led cartel leading to eventual formation of a national political party.* [*2 lines not declassified*] A large part of the problem is that Adoula has no following of his own; he must depend on maneuvering the support he has from leaders with a following. [*4 lines not declassified*][3]

3. [*11½ lines not declassified*]

4. [*6½ lines not declassified*]

5. *Assist Mobotu to retain the loyalty of key officers.* Mobotu continues to receive funds for this purpose.

6. [*4½ lines not declassified*]

As he left the meeting Governor Williams expressed appreciation for the run down and an understanding of the difficulties facing the Agency in getting on with the program.

---

[1] Source: Department of State, INR/IL Historical Files, AF–CIA 1962. Secret. Sent through Deputy Director for Coordination in the Bureau of Intelligence and Research Joseph W. Scott.

[2] See footnote 2, Document 100.

[3] [*text not declassified*]

105. Editorial Note

Telegram 2939 from the Station in Leopoldville to the Central Intelligence Agency, January 19, 1962, reported that [*name not declassified*] said he had been designated by Cyrille Adoula to conduct preliminary talks with Congolese political leaders in order to determine whether Adoula would retain majority support if he reduced the size of the government and eliminated certain extremist elements. [*name not declassified*] made a plea for funds, saying that, as in the case of Lovanium, it would be necessary to "grease many palms" to achieve the objective of a more moderate government. The CIA authorized funding in telegram 36511, January 19. (Central Intelligence Agency Files, Job 78–00435R, DDO/ISS Files, Box 1, Folder 9, [*cryptonym not declassified*] Operations)

---

106. Telegram From the Central Intelligence Agency to the Station in the Congo[1]

Washington, January 20, 1962, 2346Z.

Dir 36739 (Out 92559).

1. ODACID, and higher authority, concerned re arrival Gizenga (G) Leop and are communicating same to [Ambassador Gullion] via own channel.

2. Insofar as we understand it here, situation as follows:

(A) G held Leop under UNOC guard at Adoula (A) request.
(B) No official action against G possible until parliament lifts his immunity.

3. With G immunity lifted, several courses action open to A and GOC, including:

(A) Court trial and sentence.
(B) Leave G alone as private citizen Leop area.
(C) Banish G abroad or facilitate his legal departure (Cairo, Tanganyika or elsewhere)—medical treatment might be possible excuse.
(D) Permit G "escape," with familiar "Lumumba" consequences.

---

[1] Source: Central Intelligence Agency Files, Job 78–00435R, DDO/ISS Files, Box 1, Folder 9, [*cryptonym not declassified*] Operations. Secret; Rybat; [*cryptonym not declassified*]; Operational Immediate. COS from Tweedy. Drafted by [*text not declassified*] and released by Tweedy (C/AF).

4. If A to undertake G action before Lagos and UN trips will have to work awfully fast. Perhaps present UNOC detention until A return might be best interim solution while political pot continues boil and Tshombe negotiations come to some result. This particularly as G arrival Leop appears vastly reduce our own action capabilities. Request your views.

5. Realize above do not exhaust possibilities and request you and [Gullion] examine these (and others) and give us your views and recommendations, particularly interested A plans re G.

6. In event we should decide take some action, present thinking here that following caveats vital:

(A) Only with a knowledge or consent.
(B) ODYOKE hand not shown.
(C) Nothing should happen to G which could leave him martyr symbol.

7. Your views welcome.[2]

End of message.

---

[2] A handwritten notation on the original reads: "Now moved to camp 1/24/62." In telegram 2964 from Leopoldville to CIA, January 22, the Chief of Station informed Tweedy that, based on his talks with Congolese leaders, he feared that the Congolese Government had no definite plans regarding prosecution of Gizenga. He noted that none of the leaders seemed to have any grasp of the legal problems involved in convicting him. They merely thought it obvious that he was responsible for the gendarmerie revolt and therefore guilty. Nendaka, however, had asked if the United States could help them obtain a group of legal specialists to help prosecute the case. (Ibid.) In telegram 2985 from Leopoldville to CIA, January 23, the Chief of Station reported that Gizenga had left UNOC Headquarters of his own accord and was now established in a house under CNA guard. No incarceration warrant had yet been signed, but Gizenga was for all intents and purposes a prisoner. (Ibid., [*text not declassified*], Folder 1, Gizenga) See Document 195 in *Foreign Relations,* 1961–1963, volume XX, Congo Crisis, for the Embassy's January 25 report on Gizenga's incarceration.

107. Telegram From the Station in the Congo to the Central Intelligence Agency[1]

Leopoldville, January 24, 1962.

3003 (In 16905).

1. [Identity 1], called at [COS] home shortly before midnight 22 Jan.[2] After discussing Gizenga problem he said that although political pendulum currently swinging in favor of the moderates, the great number of unemployed and hungry people throughout the Congo pose a serious problem for the GOC. He suggested it would take little to spark a revolt by these people which could result in [Identity 2] ouster and Gizenga or some other extremist coming to power. Said he had discussed this problem with [Identity 2] and that the latter planned to advise chief ODYOKE of his need for immediate and substantial economic assistance. According to [Identity 1], [Identity 2] said ODYOKE must revise its tactics and stop providing economic aid by "eye dropper" methods. [Identity 1] insisted immediate major economic aid from ODYOKE is essential if the Congo is not to fall under control of extremists and anti-Western political leaders.

2. Although [COS] did not have detailed statistics available, he pointed out ODYOKE has provided large amounts of economic aid and that additional funds are in the pipeline. [Identity 1] seemed to know nothing of this and assumed [COS] was referring to funds budgeted for UNOC use. He commented that according to Bantu custom when one sees a friend in distress he immediately offers aid and does not wait to be asked for help. He said if the situation became more difficult the USSR might take advantage and offer to provide the Congo with large sums of economic aid. He added that Soviet Chargé Podgornov recently told [Identity 2] funds which the USSR normally would have contributed to the UN to pay its share of UNOC are now held in Moscow and that the USSR is prepared to turn these funds over to the GOC.[3] [Identity 1] noted that, if made public, it would be difficult for [Identity 2] to refuse such an offer in view of economic suffering in the Congo.

3. [COS] again insisted upon the magnitude of ODYOKE economic aid to the Congo and to UNOC. He reminded [Identity 1] that, should

---

[1] Source: Central Intelligence Agency Files, Job 78–00435R, DDO/ISS Files, Box 1, Folder 9, [*cryptonym not declassified*] Operations. Secret; Rybat; [*cryptonym not declassified*]; Routine. Eyes only Bissell and Tweedy from COS. Received at 2054Z.

[2] A handwritten notation on the original reads: "[Identity 1] certainly now deeply involved Congo politics involving USA thanks to tie with [COS]."

[3] A handwritten notation on the original reads: "Cynical typical USSR line."

the Congo try play off the USSR and PBPRIME, it could easily kill the golden egg laying goose. He further reminded [Identity 1] that, if ODYOKE ever withdrew its aid from the Congo and/or, UNOC, the GOC would find itself dependent upon and thus under the control of the USSR.

4. In discussing ODYOKE aid to the Congo [COS] reminded [Identity 1] that considerable funds already are on hand and that it is up to the GOC and UNOC to develop and implement plans to launch effective public works projects. [Identity 1] by his reply indicated his lack of confidence in effective action by UNOC and asked why ODYOKE refuses to provide aid directly to the GOC. [COS] offered the usual explanation and expressed the belief that [Identity 2] would not wish to receive aid which did not pass through UN channels. [Identity 1] disagreed, stating he believes [Identity 2] would prefer direct aid in matters relating to the internal economy of the Congo. He concluded the meeting by making an impassioned plea for ODYOKE aid to permit the GOC to resolve its grave economic and unemployment problems.

5. [COS] again saw [Identity 1] late 23 Jan. He provided [Identity 1] with a detailed statement concerning ODYOKE aid which ODYOKE has given or will provide during FY 62. [Identity 1] was surprised by the sums involved and stated he would write memo to [Identity 2] on the subject.

6. [COS] again questioned [Identity 1] relative to the latter's belief that [Identity 2] wants direct ODYOKE aid, rather than aid through UNOC channels. [Identity 1] admitted [Identity 2] had never actually made such a statement but said he had interpreted [Identity 2] comments in this light. [Identity 1] expressed the view that, if all aid must be passed through UNOC channels, the Congo has lost its sovereign status and should be considered a UNOC protectorate. Referring to the original UN mandate to preserve peace and order, [Identity 1] said he understands all efforts in this direction must be channelled through UNOC. However as a sovereign state, he believes Congo should be able to deal with any nation on matters relating directly to its economy or other internal problems. (Note: This view is shared by [Mobutu] who is disenchanted with UNOC because of among other things, UNOC's failure to take positive steps to reorganize the CNA. [Mobutu] has become extremely bitter and is convinced the Congo must look elsewhere for aid and guidance if the army is ever to be brought in hand.) Referring to UNOC's failure to develop and implement an adequate public works program and its failure to do any thing to resolve the problem of the CNA, the problem which first brought UNOC to the Congo, [Identity 1] urged [COS] to bring immediately to the attention of ODYOKE the dire need of the Congo for financial aid, as well as guidance in other fields. He concluded by expressing the view that

UNOC efforts and actions are often in direct contradiction to ODYOKE policy and to the best interests of the Congolese people. He further stated that if ODYOKE continued to place all its Congo bets on UNOC it might well wake up to find this policy had undermined GOC elements favorable to the West and resulted in failure, insofar as ODYOKE objectives are concerned.

7. [COS] showed above message in memo form to [Ambassador Gullion] 24 Jan. Latter was annoyed by content and took position he wished use memo to rub noses [*cryptonym not declassified*] and [*cryptonym not declassified*] reps in fact that ODYOKE aid not receiving adequate publicity.

8. Although recognize ODYOKE can never satisfactorily resolve Congo problem Leop interpretation [Identity 1] statements quite different than that of [Gullion]. Believe as previously reported Leop 2501 (In 28695)[4] that UNOC failure launch adequate public works program to at least partially resolve disasterous unemployment situation involves great hazards for ODYOKE Congo policy. In short, Leop does not believe UNOC is doing adequate job on either military or economic front. With Linner, General Maceoin and other senior UNOC officers scheduled leave Congo near future, UNOC High Command appears be taking even more relaxed attitude than usual. While may be in Cassandra-like mood, cannot help being concerned by ODYOKE failure take all possible steps avoid failure in Congo. Thus Station taking liberty forwarding above message on eyes only basis for [Bissell] and [Tweedy] in hope that concern expressed by [Identity 1] may be brought to the attention of appropriate ODYOKE authorities. For obvious reasons Leop not advising [Gullion] it transmitting this message.[5]

End of message.

---

[4] Document 101.

[5] In CIA telegram 38458 to Leopoldville, January 30, Tweedy advised the Chief of Station that assessment of the request needed to be ironed out locally if at all possible with Ambassador Gullion, since this involved a policy decision in which the Agency could play only a minor role. Whether U.S. aid should be greatly increased would presumably be the product of the Ambassador's recommendation, to which Devlin could contribute, and a U.S. Government policy decision. (Central Intelligence Agency Files, Job 78–00435R, DDO/ISS Files, Box 1, Folder 9, [*cryptonym not declassified*] Operations)

108. Editorial Note

In telegram 39667 to the Station in Leopoldville, February 3, 1962, the Central Intelligence Agency reported that during a meeting on February 1 with Ambassador Gullion he had raised with CIA the question of the removal of Antoine Gizenga from the Congo. Gullion was apprehensive that the pressure to see that no harm came to Gizenga may have gone too far and that there was a danger he might even be released from custody and could thereupon assemble some support. It was generally agreed that any movement if not done by force would require causing Gizenga to fear for his life if he remained in the Congo. (Central Intelligence Agency Files, [*text not declassified*], Folder 1, Gizenga)

Responding in telegram 3096, February 6, Leopoldville reported that Gizenga was now a prisoner on the island of Boulabemba, a move that appeared to have created furor in certain United Nations Operations in the Congo circles. While concurring that it would be advisable to get Gizenga out of the country, the Station warned that this would provide no guarantee he would not return if and when the moment appeared appropriate and once current charges against him had died down. The Station preferred to see him charged with revolt and other crimes, though there was no way of being sure that he would be convicted and sentenced, and if he "were tried and acquitted it would be serious blow for [*cryptonym not declassified*] and would mean that he would soon be back in parliament and perhaps in the govt where he would be in a position to work from within." Efforts to obtain information from the Government of the Congo had produced nothing definite other than the fact that Gizenga had been transferred to Moanda where, according to Victor Nendaka, he was to be held until a judicial investigation preliminary to his trial was completed. (Ibid.)

109. Editorial Note

In telegram 3100 to the Central Intelligence Agency, February 5, 1962, the Station in Leopoldville reported that Joseph Mobutu had asked for financial aid, stating that he particularly needed funds now to try to win back Congolese National Army elements which were previously loyal to Antoine Gizenga and the Stanleyville regime. In requesting aid, Mobutu expressed embarrassment at constantly having to seek aid for various projects but added that he believed he would need aid on a continuing basis. The Station expressed its belief that CIA should continue to subsidize Mobutu as he remained "our anchor to windward" in the implementation of [*cryptonym not declassified*] objectives. (Central Intelligence Agency Files, Job 78–00435R, DDO/ISS Files, Box 1, Folder 9, [*cryptonym not declassified*] Operations) The CIA authorized the expenditure in telegram 40969 to Leopoldville, February 9. (Ibid.)

In telegram 3220 to the CIA, February 24, 1962, Leopoldville reported that Mobutu had requested financial support in connection with the military operation now launched against North Katanga. Mobutu was not happy about the situation, the Station commented, but he had no alternative other than to try his best with an army that was poorly officered, poorly trained, and badly organized. If Mobutu failed he would be wide open for attack by extremist enemies, as would be the Adoula government. It had also been learned from Justin Bomboko that the government intended to take over North Katanga administratively as well as militarily. Adoula was scheduled to visit the area soon in order to show the flag and set up an administration loyal to Leopoldville. In short, the Station stated, the government was wagering its existence on the North Katanga operation. Despite strong reservations about the advisability of the operation, the Station strongly recommended supporting Mobutu. (Ibid.) CIA telegram 43881 to Leopoldville, February 25, authorized the expenditure, on the assumption that it had been discussed with the Ambassador. (Ibid.)

---

110. Telegram From the Station in the Congo to the Central Intelligence Agency[1]

Leopoldville, March 24, 1962.

3470 (In 48189). 1. [Identity 1] requested one million BCF [*less than 1 line not declassified*] said [Identity 2] and [Identity 3] have decided make all-out effort split and weaken extremist political ranks in Orientale just as [*cryptonym not declassified*] have done in Leop. Said extremists making strong bid for regaining political control in Orientale and [Identity 2] wants head them off. [Identity 1] commented ex-

---

[1] Source: Central Intelligence Agency Files, Job 78–00435R, DDO/ISS Files, Box 1, Folder 9, [*cryptonym not declassified*] Operations. Secret; No Night Action; Rybat; [*cryptonym not declassified*]; Operational Immediate. Received at 1106Z.

tremists now lack capable leader and thus [*cryptonym not declassified*] stand good chance accomplishing their objective.[2]

[Omitted here is further discussion of the plan.]

---

[2] CIA telegram 49712 to Leopoldville, March 24, approved the requested expenditure. (Ibid.)

---

111. Telegram From the Station in the Congo to the Central Intelligence Agency

Leopoldville, April 3, 1962.

[Source: Central Intelligence Agency Files, Job 78–00435R, DDO/ISS Files, Box 1, Folder 10, [*cryptonym not declassified*] Operations. Secret; Rybat; Priority. *4 pages not declassified*]

---

112. Telegram From the Station in the Congo to the Central Intelligence Agency[1]

Leopoldville, April 14, 1962.

3632 (In 19993). Ref Leop 3594 (In 17216).[2]

1. Per ref and [Gullion] instructions [COS] met with [Identity 1], [Mobutu], and [Identity 2] on 9, 10 and 11 April. Had several meetings

---

[1] Source: Central Intelligence Agency Files, Job 78–00435R, DDO/ISS Files, Box 1, Folder 10, [*cryptonym not declassified*] Operations. Secret; Routine. Tweedy from COS. Received at 1837Z.

[2] Gullion and [COS] views on what to do to bring [*cryptonym not declassified*] attention ODYOKE displeasure at not being in contact with GOC leaders (specifically [*cryptonym not declassified*]). [Footnote in the original.] In telegram 3594 from Leopoldville to CIA, April 10, the Chief of Station reported a conversation with Ambassador Gullion during which the latter expressed anger with Adoula and other Congolese leaders, saying that the strong U.S. interest in the Congo problem had gone to their heads and that he would not put up with such treatment. Gullion suggested that if the situation were not remedied in the near future, he and the Chief of Station should be recalled for consultations, letting it be known prior to their departure that there might be a change in U.S. policy toward the Congolese Government. (Ibid.)

with first two. Although none of above specifically admitted in so many words, first two made it clear [Identity 3] intentionally ducking [COS]. In reply queries why this the case, [Identity 1] and [Mobutu] insisted ODYOKE policy too closely tied to that of UN. They said [Identity 3] was strong supporter of UN until recently but has now turned against UN because of its failure insist GOC find workable solution to Katanga problem.

2. Gist of [Identity 1] and [Mobutu] remarks as follows:

A. GOC convinced Tshombe will never agree to Katanga reintegration unless military pressure used. GOC has reached conclusion UNOC will not employ military pressures on Katanga.

B. GOC dissatisfied with what it considers ineffective UNOC efforts solve Congo economic problems. GOC leaders believe great percentage UNOC Congo expenditures devoted to salaries, housing and other UNOC overhead costs which do not directly assist Congo economic situation. [Mobutu] commented 84 of every 100 dollars expended by UNOC goes for such overhead expenditures.)

C. GOC leaders distrust UNOC leaders. Distrust based on historical background UNOC such as Dayal's opposition Mobutu regime, Khiari's efforts bring about ouster [Identity 4] and [Mobutu] and other [*cryptonym not declassified*]. [Mobutu] commented "How can you expect us to trust men who have repeatedly tried to destroy us."

D. [Identity 1] and [Mobutu] opined ODYOKE policy would fail so long as it closely allied to UNOC. Thus they urged policy whereby ODYOKE would act outside UN channels to assist GOC in its struggle with Katanga and its efforts restore Congo economy.

E. [Identity 1] said most GOC leaders believe UNOC had Tshombe on ropes during December fighting and blames ODYOKE for stopping fighting in order hold Kitona meetings. He added most GOC leaders interpret this as indication ODYOKE indirectly supporting Tshombe. This respect he recited charges that GOK building up its military strength while current talks continue.

3. [COS] explained ODYOKE policy has always supported GOC and sought bring about Katanga reintegration. Reminded [Mobutu] and [Identity 1] of considerable economic, moral and covert support provided by ODYOKE since Sept 60. They acknowledged this fact but reiterated view ODYOKE all-out support UNOC will in long run result in failure ODYOKE policy and GOC efforts reintegrate Katanga. When [COS] pointed out [Identity 5] and [Identity 3] had often expressed wish all ODYOKE aid be through UNOC channels, interlocutors reminded him these statements made prior [Identity 3] disillusionment with UNOC. [Identity 1] added that, since GOC foreign policy line is one of non-alignment, [Identity 3] would probably continue express many official conversation view that ODYOKE aid should continue be

via UNOC channels. However [Identity 1] and [Mobutu] expressed firm opinion [Identity 3] would welcome bilateral ODYOKE aid.

4. [COS] chided [Identity 1] and [Mobutu] re childishness of [Identity 3] avoiding only man who might be able provide sufficient aid for Congo. Reminded them insult to [Gullion] was indirectly insult to ODYOKE and thus could lead to serious consequences. All agreed and indicated they would call facts to [Identity 3] attention. Per Embtel 2571[3] [Identity 3] called and met with [Gullion] night 11 April. By 12 April [Mobutu] stated call made as result [Identity 1] intervention.

5. Leop regards [Identity 3] action in avoiding [Gullion] as indication former's utter frustration as result failure resolve Katanga problem and other governmental pressures. Basis [Gullion's] comments and comments [*two cryptonyms not declassified*] and [Mobutu] it appears [Identity 3] so overwhelmed by current problems he on verge crack-up. Also as result these pressures appears he seeking almost any solution and in process abandoning many old friends and seeking new ones. (Preparing separate cable re [Identity 3] expressions lack confidence [Identity 4] and [Mobutu] and [Identity 2].) In short fear [Identity 3] rapidly becoming desperate man who willing risk almost anything including turning against old friends in hope of finding solutions which he has not found by working with current political allies. (This respect see Leop 3360[4] for earlier report re [Identity 3] frustrations and his determination achieve Katanga settlement at almost any cost.)

6. In addition to his frustrations which result in his blaming ODYOKE, among others, for his present dilemma, [Identity 3] may also be influenced by lack of personal friendship for [Gullion]. Have received following indications of his feelings to [Gullion] and ODYOKE:

A. [Identity 1] and [Mobutu] commented [Identity 3] would never have avoided [Gullion's] predecessor as he has [Gullion]. They explained that [Gullion] lacks warm personality and apparent sincere desire assist GOC that they found in his predecessor.

B. [*cryptonym not declassified*] told [COS] that Israeli rep at UN showed him dispatch from Israeli Chargé Leo in which latter quoted [Identity 3] as saying he tired [Gullion] playing role of "patron."

C. [*name not declassified*] told [COS] night 12 April he overheard phone conversation re Congolese efforts obtain dollars to buy military vehicles in which [Identity 3] stated he disgusted with PBPRIMERS ("Les PBPRIMERS m'emmerdent").

7. [Gullion] has requested [COS] see [Identity 3] ASAP re means whereby ODYOKE hopes support him. Plan use meeting as means at-

---

[3] Not found.

[4] Not found.

tempt determine [Identity 3] present position vis-à-vis ODYOKE and other [*cryptonym not declassified*] will advise.

8. Above for KUBARK background on Congo situation which may be in early stages of shift away from directions ODYOKE would like to see. Do not wish alarm HQS but Leop now in process trying put various conflicting items information together to outline new situation. In this connection see [*cryptonym not declassified*] Leop 3564 (In 14923).[5]

End of message.

[5] Reported the arrest of journalists and labor leaders by the GOC. [Footnote in the original.] This CIA telegram has not been found.

113. Telegram From the Central Intelligence Agency to the Station in the Congo[1]

Washington, April 17, 1962, [illegible].

Dir 04749 (Out 73718). 1. HQS speculates that Sovs may have reoriented Congo policy, abandoned search for Lumumba heir, and decided support Adoula on govt to govt basis if Adoula can get rid UNOC. It possible Zorin told Adoula during New York meet Sovs prepared give no strings large scale support GOC but can not work thru UN as it imperialist instrument which actually frustrating Congo unity whereas Sovs willing actively help unify country and achieve true national independence. May also have told Adoula that Bomboko and Mobutu Belgian tools, supporting with actual or spurious facts.

2. Supporting above are relative passivity Moscow re Gizenga, willingness withdraw Podgornov, strong push get Aeroflot onward rights from Khartoum and invite to Adoula visit Moscow. That Adoula may have swallowed line indicated by public insistence UNOC terminate by 30 Apr, intransigence re Tshombe negots, ire at Bomboko

[1] Source: Central Intelligence Agency Files, Job 78–00435R, DDO/ISS Files, Box 1, Folder 10, [*cryptonym not declassified*] Operations. Secret; Routine. Drafted and authenticated by [*name not declassified*] and released by Tweedy (C/AF).

megots Brussels, threats fire Bomboko, Mobutu, Ndele, Ileo,[2] refusal see Western diplomats, decision visit Moscow May (after UNOC termination deadline).

3. Above not to imply Adoula changing sides but rather that in his frustration over apparent UNOC unwillingness help solve reintegration, plus pressures from radical nationalists and economic deterioration, he sees some merit in Soviet argumentation. As minimum, it of prime importance Leop do all possible assure full coverage Moscow visit.

4. Realize our speculation overly black and white. Above discussed at desk level ODACID where speculation is parallel. Request Station views above and continued local monitoring order demonstrate whether speculation valid.

End of message.

[2] Telegram 3644 from Leopoldville to CIA, April 16, reported that Adoula told Gullion on April 11 that he was dissatisfied with Bomboko and Mobutu and planned to remove them from their present jobs. The Station had been greatly concerned because it regarded Mobutu as a U.S. anchor. Thus, with the Ambassador's approval, the Chief of Station met with Adoula on April 16, reviewing previous U.S. support for him and pointing out that all U.S. activity in the Congo was based on the objective of trying to maintain a stable, moderate government. He emphasized that without a loyal man to control the army, this political objective would be jeopardized, and warned Adoula that if Mobutu was ousted, his own political position might be compromised. Adoula said that Nendaka and others had expressed similar views, and assured the Chief of Station that he no longer intended to remove Mobutu. (Ibid.)

114. Telegram From the Station in the Congo to the Central Intelligence Agency[1]

Leopoldville, April 21, 1962.

3705 (In 23506). Ref A Leop 3690 (In 22606);[2] B Leop 3687 (In 22493).[3]

1. Per Refs A and B believe current political situation requires contingency planning. Although do not consider it probable govt will fall or army revolt, this remains real possibility. Much depends upon how [Identity 1] handles himself on his return Leop.

2. Leop and [Embassy] encouraging GOC take line that events of 18 April were misunderstanding.[4] Suggesting [Identity 1] state GOC not informed in time of Tshombe (T) departure and that govt leaders Leop misunderstood his instructions. Suggesting he say he did not mean keep T Leop by force but merely do everything possible encourage him remain in order continue talks as soon as possible. Also recommending GOC blame UNOC for failure properly advise GOC of T plans depart. This to be done in such way as not bring great discredit on UNOC. UN also supporting this and has sent GOC message regretting UNOC failure properly coordinate departure with GOC. ([Gullion] fears Gardiner may try upset this ploy.) Finally recommending [Identity 1] take position he regrets incidents and state he looking forward return T and continuation talks.

3. GOC leaders questioned by parliament 20 April on T departure. [Identity 2] and [*cryptonym not declassified*] said 20 April that unpopular GOC members, particularly Bolikango, appeared be taking rap and only limited criticism levelled at [Identity 1]. [Identity 2] had sold ap-

---

[1] Source: Central Intelligence Agency Files, Job 78–00435R, DDO/ISS Files, Box 1, Folder 10, [*cryptonym not declassified*] Operations. Secret; Rybat; [*cryptonym not declassified*]; Operational Immediate. Tweedy from COS. Received at 1708Z. Gullion requested that this message or a summary thereof be sent to Assistant Secretary Williams so he would get the flavor of the local situation before arriving in Leopoldville.

[2] Reported on political unrest in the Congo. [Footnote in the original.] Telegram 3690 from Leopoldville to CIA, April 19, reported that the political situation in the Congo following Tshombe's departure remained highly unstable, and that the Station considered that there was a very real possibility that the government might fall. (Ibid.)

[3] Political crisis resulting from Tshombe departure extremely grave. [Footnote in the original.] In telegram 3687 from Leopoldville to CIA, April 19, Devlin asked Tweedy for policy guidance in the event that Adoula seemed about to fall. (Ibid.)

[4] On April 18, Congolese forces at the airport prevented the departure of a U.N. plane bound for Elizabethville with Tshombe aboard. Ambassador Gullion and U.N. officials attempted to persuade Congolese officials to adhere to previous Congolese assurances that there would be no interference with Tshombe's freedom of movement if he came to Leopoldville for talks. Late that evening, Tshombe was permitted to fly to Elizabethville.

proach outlined para 2 above to GOC members who used it in parliament. However, full reaction to T departure has not yet set in and [Identity 1] still not completely out of woods.

4. During morning session 20 April, censure motion voted against Finance Minister Arthur Pinzi. Justice Minister Remy Mwamba appears be next on list. [*cryptonym not declassified*] said he believes [Identity 2] probably will face censure motion and may well fall. However, [Identity 2] says he not aware such possibility. (See [*less than 1 line not declassified*] and [*less than 1 line not declassified*][5] for reports predicting parliamentary efforts oust specific ministers. Although [Identity 2] name not previously on list ministers to go, he has many enemies as result fact he long in office and has stepped on many political toes. Also per Leop 3644 (In 20526)[6] possibility [Identity 1] may wish get rid of [Identity 2] cannot be discounted despite fact [Identity 2] claims he did not sign tech assistance pact with GOB.) View foregoing, appears parliament has bit in mouth and possibility attempt overthrow govt cannot be eliminated.

5. Leop would appreciate HQS guidance re line to take if one of combination of following possible developments occur:

A. Possibility [Identity 1] may have to put down parliamentary rebellion. (This could involve payments to parliamentarians, revision of govt, concessions of all sorts to opposition leaders, etc.)

B. Possibility opposition may submit censure vote against [Identity 1]. (In such case [*cryptonym not declassified*] would require large financial support in order buy sufficient votes try guarantee majority support for [Identity 1].)

C. Possibility govt may fall and relative moderate (portion garbled-being serviced) man who not known be member Leop or Stan groups will emerge as candidate for premiership.

D. [Identity 1] fall and extremist such as [*cryptonym not declassified*] or one of their followers selected form new govt.

E. Possibility [Identity 1] may require CNA support remain in office. (For example, [Identity 1] might be forced establish military regime, sending parliament home or making it a rubber stamp.)

F. Possibility CNA revolt.

6. Neither Station nor [Embassy] happy with [Identity 1]. He started well but has bungled badly lately. Also Leop has for some time toyed with view outlined para 3, Dir 04749 (Out 73718)[7] or variations

---

[5] Neither found.

[6] See footnote 2 to Document 113.

[7] Possible that Adoula sees some merit in Soviet argumentation. [Footnote in the original.] This telegram is printed as Document 113.

thereof. (Additional comments this subject being forwarded separate cable.) [Identity 1] was never Station's favorite candidate but view alternatives we were forced back him. Unfortunately, this continues be the case. Few if any moderates could obtain sufficient votes replace him. Thus, alternatives probably would be selection of extremist with consequent danger of CNA coup per para 11 or parliament would not be able select successor. This would create power vacuum and open way to "adventures."

7. [Gullion] concurs in foregoing but cites Embtel 2621[8] and Deptel 1801[9] which examine [Identity 1] motives, the reasons for which he may go sour, and to what extent sterility ODYOKE and UN policy as he sees it may be responsible. [Gullion] believes station must be prepared provide [Identity 1] with additional financial aid, [*less than 1 line not declassified*].

[Omitted here is further discussion of contingency planning.]

---

[8] Not found.

[9] Document 220 in *Foreign Relations,* 1961–1963, volume XX, Congo Crisis, pp. 421–423.

---

115. Telegram From the Central Intelligence Agency to the Station in the Congo[1]

Washington, April 23, 1962, 2055Z.

Dir 05822 (Out 75526). Ref: A. Leop 3705 (In 23506);[2] B. Dir 05755 (Out 75339).[3]

1. Have not consulted ODACID since receipt Ref A but following based recent talks and furnishes framework for discussion [Gullion] prior contingency action.

---

[1] Source: Central Intelligence Agency Files, Job 78–00435R, DDO/ISS Files, Box 1, Folder 10, [*cryptonym not declassified*] Operations. Secret; Rybat; Priority. Drafted by [*name not declassified*] and released by Tweedy (C/AF).

[2] Leopoldville believes that the current political situation requires contingency planning. Ambassador Gullion believes Station must be prepared to provide additional financial aid to [Identity 1]. [Footnote in the original.] This telegram is printed as Document 114.

[3] Authorized [*monetary amount not declassified*] for support of [*cryptonym not declassified*]. [Footnote in the original.] Telegram 05755, April 21, is in Central Intelligence Agency Files, Job 78–00435R, DDO/ISS Files, Box 1, Folder 10, [*cryptonym not declassified*] Operations.

2. ODACID accepts nationalism as fact of life support of which is only basis successful long term ODYOKE policy. Thinks artificial injections to uphold conservative forces which do not represent main stream Congo opinion will inevitably alienate and isolate ODYOKE. Similarly support military coup per se or in support [Identity 1] will lead to deep ODYOKE commitment down blind alley. Desires continue support [Identity 1] subject above caveats in belief no other now able seriously challenge him despite errors. HQS largely shares this view.

3. Supplemental HQS thoughts: [Mobutu] span control largely limited Leop Province. His illegal assumption power would most likely result Orientale breakaway with Lundula in better legal position than [Mobutu]. This would open Congo to infusion unilateral aid bloc and Casablanca states. Hence believe best chance [Mobutu] survival as internal force is keep ANC out of politics.

4. [*6 lines not declassified*]. Presume [Gullion] will soon brief ODYOKE contingency plan so [Identity 2] able explain more lucidly to Lundula possible consequences of deterioration middle of road govt.

5. HQS also desires actively seek political action instrument other than large injections funds for each crisis. [*5½ lines not declassified*]

6. Comments invited.[4]

End of message.

[4] Telegram 3756 from Leopoldville to CIA, April 27, responded that the Station concurred, and emphasized that, in its opinion, no main stream of Congo political opinion was yet discernible; the majority of Congolese politicians were still jockeying for personal position. Thus, the Station's objective had merely been to prevent from coming to power those (such as Lumumba) who once in power would turn to the Communist bloc for support and guidance. It was devoting considerable time to analyzing the current political situation, and believed the Station was now in a position to obtain assets responsive to CIA guidance rather than those cooperating only on a self interest basis. (Ibid.)

116. Telegram From the Central Intelligence Agency to the Station in the Congo[1]

Washington, April 28, 1962, 1913Z.

Dir 07103 (Out 77554). 1. Foll responds request Leop 3705 (In 23506)[2] for HQS and ODACID guidance, based talks ODACID bureau level 27 Apr.

2. Given Adoula views per Embtel 2621[3] and others, foll courses action open to him:

A. Continue negotiate with Tshombe in good faith. This unlikely given his conviction Tshombe stalling.

B. Pressure UN and US give him stronger support in terms real or implied threat to Tshombe by threatening seek Afro Asian or bloc support or by threat resign in favor radicals. This course likely.

C. Actually turn to Afro Asians or bloc for support. Could inadvertently drift into this as result above course.

D. Seek mil solution using ANC. This unlikely without C above.

E. Resign. While no sign he considering, continued frustration and deteriorating health might lead to it.

3. Possible ODYOKE courses action:

A. Continue urge Adoula reach agreement with Tshombe under present conditions. View Adoula attitude and political realities, this at best short term holding action.

B. Give Adoula stronger support in terms backing tax plan or similar action. This could lead to round three which, if controlled, could erode Tshombe position to point he willing accept reasonable Adoula terms. However UKG, GOB and segment US opinion abhor action risking round three.

C. Support mil or polit coup leading to GOC willing accept Tshombe terms for loose federation of relatively autonomous provinces. This might serve increase bloc opportunities for penetration and would at best lead to even less stable situation.

D. Withdraw and try isolate Congo from other foreign influence. This considered and rejected as impossible.

---

[1] Source: Central Intelligence Agency Files, Job 78–00435R, DDO/ISS Files, Box 1, Folder 10, [*cryptonym not declassified*] Operations. Secret; Rybat; [*cryptonym not declassified*]; Routine. Drafted by [*name not declassified*] and released by Tweedy (C/AF).

[2] Leop believed current political situation required contingency planning. [Footnote in the original.] See Document 114.

[3] See *Foreign Relations*, 1961–1963, volume XX, Congo Crisis, Document 219.

4. Current ODACID position is ODYOKE will not fully commit self to tax plan without concurrence UKG and GOB. 27 Apr talks indicate this most unlikely be forthcoming.

5. You may share gist above with [Gullion] stressing this result our informal talks at bureau level.

End of message.

117. Telegram From the Station in the Congo to the Central Intelligence Agency[1]

Leopoldville, May 14, 1962.

3892 (In 34672). Ref A Dir 09888 (Out 82083);[2] B Leop 3855 (In 32568).[3]

1. [Identity 1] called [COS] his home [*less than 1 line not declassified*]. Said [Identity 2] had advised him of his 7 May conversation with [COS] and had asked him [Identity 1] for his advice whether to accept ODYOKE offer of aid in formation new party. [Identity 1] explained that he and other [*cryptonym not declassified*] believe ODYOKE has accomplished more in the Congo than could have been expected in that it succeeded in torpedoing [Identity 3] preventing [Identity 4] or [Identity

[1] Source: Central Intelligence Agency Files, Job 78–00435R, DDO/ISS Files, Box 1, Folder 10, [*cryptonym not declassified*] Operations. Secret; Rybat; [*cryptonym not declassified*]; Routine. Received at 1243Z.

[2] Gave guidance to Station for future talks with [*cryptonym not declassified*]. [Footnote in the original.] This CIA telegram 09888 to Leopoldville, May 11, stated that CIA support should be contingent on [Identity 2] producing a specific plan. The Chief of Station's advisory role was desirable, but the plan had to be [Identity 2] own product to be meaningful and have hope of implementation. Also [Identity 2] should not wait for civic spirit to grow among Congolese leaders to supplant venal motivation; his plan should include a school or seminar for leader indoctrination. (Ibid.)

[3] In telegram 3855 from Leopoldville to CIA, May 9, the Chief of Station reported that when he met with [Identity 2] on May 7, the latter had not yet prepared an action plan. The Chief of Station told him he thought the current regime was doomed unless it achieved results on the economic level and instituted a program of political solidarity. [Identity 2] said that a public works program had long been his goal, but he could not launch such a program until the budget was voted. When queried regarding the possibility of attempting to create a political party based on key political leaders from each province, [Identity 2] said that was already his plan. He asked the Chief of Station if he could count on U.S. support, to which the former replied that he thought the United States would support such an effort if it offered the possibility of obtaining a stable government and guaranteed financial control of expenditures. The meeting terminated with [Identity 2] promise to come up with his own organizational planning. (Ibid.)

5] from obtaining control GOC and assisted in establishing [Identity 2] regime. He said [*cryptonym not declassified*] understand reasons behind ODYOKE actions, i.e., that ODYOKE did not wish an unfriendly and pro bloc regime in the Congo. However he added that [*cryptonym not declassified*] concerned by possibility ODYOKE might now or later switch its support to Tshombe (T).

2. [Identity 1] said T popularity is on upswing within Congo and T may go for brass ring and try become premier or president. In such case [Identity 1] said he could understand ODYOKE might prefer T to [Identity 2] view fact both T and [Identity 2] anti Communists. Added support of T might facilitate things for Chief ODYOKE in that T appears be fair haired boy more conservative members Congress. [Identity 1] concluded by saying he and most [*cryptonym not declassified*] strongly favor effort work with ODYOKE but before advising [Identity 2] he needed some assurance from [COS] that ODYOKE would not turn against [Identity 2] and favor T.

3. When [COS] expressed surprise that [*cryptonym not declassified*] could suspect such change in ODYOKE policy, [Identity 1] outlined following points as apparently substantiating such possibility:

A. [Ambassador Timberlake] recalled and replaced by [Gullion] despite fact ODYOKE fully aware [*cryptonym not declassified*] preferred [Timberlake].

B. Conservative congressional leaders have expressed approval of Tshombe and have been critical of [Identity 2] and some of his supporters. [Identity 1] opined Chief ODYOKE might find it convenient for internal political reasons sacrifice [Identity 2].

C. Station has recently cracked down on financial support at time [Identity 2] in trouble.

4. [COS] endeavored reassure [Identity 1]. Held long meeting with him night 10 May and again on morning 12 May. Explained need for tightened financial strings. Pointed out that Station had accepted unorthodox funding methods during continued Congo crisis but explained that neither Station nor HQS believes vote buying to be more than interim step. Assured [Identity 1] that continued KUBARK support would be forthcoming, probably even including use of some bribe money, if the [*cryptonym not declassified*] were concurrently endeavoring establish a more permanent organizational solution (a national political party).

5. [Identity 6] raised similar problem with [COS] 11 and 12 May. [COS] used same arguments in replying.

6. At 12 May meeting [Identity 1] told [COS] he had recommended [Identity 2] make every effort comply with Station recommendations and begin organizational efforts ASAP.

7. Following are Station comments on Reference A:

A. While concur [Identity 2] should provide his own plan, it Station and [Embassy] experience that to get things done in Congo it advisable do as much as possible oneself. Certainly any final program must be worked out by [*cryptonym not declassified*] but to be realistic believe Station must make some contribution.

B. Leop not sanguine re possibility removing Congolese venality by means school or seminar for leaders. As in most backward areas which do not have civic traditions, suspect venal motivation will remain for many generations.

C. Fully concur para 1C Ref A.

8. Leop looking forward receipt materials re civic action. Per [*less than 1 line not declassified*][4] would appreciate any written material or guidance which HQS can provide. Specifically would appreciate any studies re political organizational work conducted by KUBARK in other retarded areas. Wish take advantage KUBARK experience elsewhere in order avoid as many mistakes as possible.

9. [Identity 2] not under [*cryptonym not declassified*] care. Have tried achieve this through [Mobutu] and [Identity 2] but no luck to date.

10. Leop trying obtain list Releve members [*cryptonym not declassified*].[5] Basis talks leaders believe Releve has wide geographical basis and includes members from all provinces but cannot yet categorically confirm this. Will advise.

End of message.

---

[4] Not found.

[5] In telegram 3822 to CIA, May 5, Leopoldville reported that the [*cryptonym not declassified*] team members had decided to try to take over the Releve group as a nucleus for a parliamentary majority. The objective would be to convert Releve, which was composed of representatives of many political parties, into a national party in support of Adoula. (Central Intelligence Agency Files, Job 78–00435R, DDO/ISS Files, Box 1, Folder 10, [*cryptonym not declassified*] Operations)

118. Telegram From the Station in the Congo to the Central Intelligence Agency[1]

Leopoldville, July 26, 1962.

4382 (In 34960). 1. In two separate sessions 24 July [Identity 1] expounded [Identity 2] proposal for creation political party to support [*cryptonym not declassified*] and requested 1.8 million BCF toward this effort.

2. Core of proposed party would be 40 tribal chiefs who members parliament and with whom [Identity 2] feels he on excellent terms. ([COS] knows background.) FYI: Chiefs and [Identity 2] participated formal ceremony 23 June at [Identity 3] residence during which chiefs pledged "everlasting loyalty" to [Identity 3] and [Identity 2]. [Identity 2] thus believes this best psychological moment to launch proposed party.

3. [Identity 1] states [Identity 2] convinced that to weather parliamentary impetuosities, erratic political behavior which bound continue, party must have broadest possible base and be as completely interwoven as possible in fabric of lives of Congolese masses. [Identity 2] equally convinced that essentially moderate, traditionalist, tribally-oriented party is only one which can fill this bill. Thus to him party of tribal chiefs is only feasible approach.

4. In response query whether proposed party—which would probably become known as "traditionalist"—could withstand strains such current issues as leftist-oppositionist maneuvering and creation new provinces, [Identity 1] stated [Identity 2] believes only party such as one proposed would have sufficiently solid footing avoid being swept away by political caprices and crises of moment. [Identity 1] said that among majority non-urbanized masses extremists-oppositionists can make significant headway only by railing against tribal chiefs—a tactic which for considerable time to come cannot possibly succeed. [Identity 1] added that majority those parliamentarians who now afraid return to home districts (see [*less than 1 line not declassified*])[2] are oppositionist, or at least non-tribal politicos. On new provinces question, [Identity 1] said [Identity 2] readily admits such issue bound create certain tribal frictions, but believes these disputes can be far more easily resolved within same party than among number of factions.

---

[1] Source: Central Intelligence Agency Files, Job 78–00435R, DDO/ISS Files, Box 1, Folder 11, [*cryptonym not declassified*]; Operations. Secret; Rybat; [*cryptonym not declassified*]; Priority; Immediate Action. Received at 1530Z.

[2] Not found.

5. [Identity 1] added [Identity 2] argument that in extreme event parliament ever became "ineffective", proposed party could "stand in" as representative body reflecting will of people. He emphasized this only last resort to be considered when all else fails.

6. Proposed sum would be spent to establish national party HQS Leop and small offices in each chief's home town, and to enable chiefs to conduct membership drives in their respective areas.

7. In answer request, Leop said only that idea sounded sensible, but would of course have to consider it before making decision. [Identity 1] then requested answer ASAP since [Identity 2] wishes get machinery in motion before chiefs begin returning home at impending close parliamentary session. Also stated that if total sum not immediately available, would welcome half now, half shortly thereafter.

8. In further discussion proposed party and its place in context ODYOKE/GOC objectives, [Identity 1] stated [Identity 2] fed up with parliamentary bribing as method remaining in power, particularly since many parliamentarians appear create trouble whenever they need money. [Identity 2] convinced proposed party can reduce or eliminate need continuance this practice. Leop said ODYOKE agreed completely on futility continued bribing and therefore welcomed proposals for creation sound [*cryptonym not declassified*] base. At same time, Leop creation [Identity 2] political party only one of many problems facing Congo, and no party however strong can support indefinitely govt which people feel is insufficiently active. [Identity 1] said [*cryptonym not declassified*] agreed completely, and hoped creation [Identity 2] party would remove GOC handicap of having operate in perpetual aura of compromise.

9. While Leop under no illusions proposed party will become greatest political org since Tammany, must admit essential soundness [Identity 2] ideas convincing and prospect of solid action attractive. Experience here seems have shown futility attempting mould and hold together any purely political grouping (i.e. not based on tribal lines) over any appreciable time span. Thus [Identity 2] party to be founded on other than somewhat abstract (to Congolese) politico-social ideals would seem have considerably better chance success than previous attempts. Two hindrances to success proposed party appear possible: trend of rural to urban migration, and fact that cities often centers of political effervescence. Impact of such migration however usually long range, not immediate and Congolese would-be politicos continue attempt draw support from countryside—even in Stey—thus acknowledging importance rural political sentiment. Chances probably less than even that urban politicos would attempt fly in face chiefs in surrounding countryside, particularly if these chiefs enjoyed support GOC.

10. Thus after careful consideration all factors here, Leop recommends approval pass [*monetary amount not declassified*] to [Identity 1] for establishment proposed party. Party may not be final solution to political stabilization [*cryptonym not declassified*] but to Leop it appears decided step forward with very good chance making significant contribution to achievement ODYOKE objectives Congo.

11. Still believe eventual [*cryptonym not declassified*] success dependent on ability combine tribal and urban (labor) support for maximum mass action. In this line, see Leop 4380 (In 33687).[3] [Godley] concurs above proposal while emphasizing (as did Leop to [*cryptonym not declassified*] that proposed party must be part of overall diversified effort generate mass support for [*cryptonym not declassified*].

12. As [Identity 2] considers matter of extreme urgency (due imminent departure chiefs) request reply by 1600Z 25 July.[4]

End of message.

---

[3] Not found.

[4] CIA telegram 25790 to Leopoldville, July 26, approved an initial funding, noting that the plan struck Headquarters and the Leopoldville Chief of Station (who was then in Washington) as a feasible segment of an overall political effort. (Central Intelligence Agency Files, Job 78–00435R, DDO/ISS Files, Box 1, Folder 11, [*cryptonym not declassified*] Operations)

119. Memorandum From the Chief of Station in Leopoldville to the Deputy Director for Plans, Central Intelligence Agency (Helms)[1]

Washington, undated.

SUBJECT

Comments on Overt U.S. Policy toward the Congo

1. This memorandum responds to the Deputy Director/Plans' request for comments on Subject. The short and long-term problems are treated separately.

2. *Short-term Problem*

A. Discussion: Although the Congo is beset with many pressing problems, the issue of reintegrating Katanga Province is emotionally foremost and takes precedence over all others in the minds of virtually all Congolese politicians. Prime Minister Adoula came to office nearly a year ago with a mandate to solve the Katanga problem as his primary task. A UNOC military operation in September 1961 and Congolese National Army (CNA) efforts in October and November failed in this purpose; UNOC's "Round Two" in December was inconclusive. Since then, beginning with the Kitona meeting, Adoula and Tshombe have held a series of negotiations leading to no agreement; these broke off in late June 1962. With each failure of solution, left extremists have been emboldened to take action against Adoula, and the right extreme (Tshombe's Conakat Party) have become more convinced that Adoula's fall would secure Katangan independence. Left and right are currently coalescing in a mutual effort to topple the moderate Adoula government. Ambassador Gullion and other Embassy officers believe Adoula's sands are running out; Adoula has written to President Kennedy that his government may fall in the next few weeks.[2] As U.S. policy is tied to support of the Adoula government and to Katangan reintegration, this policy faces imminent failure unless urgent consideration is given to new approaches to the Congo problem.

---

[1] Source: Central Intelligence Agency Files, Job 78–02888R, DDO/ISS Files, Box 1, Folder 6. Secret. The memorandum was sent though Chief of the Africa Division Bronson Tweedy. It was transmitted under cover of an August 10 memorandum from Tweedy to Bissell stating that the attached memorandum was a condensed version of a paper prepared by the Chief of Station during his recent stay at Headquarters and was responsive to Bissell's request that his comments on this subject be submitted in writing. Tweedy noted that since the Chief of Station, like any Station Chief in the field, was not always able to remain fully aware of the planning of other U.S. agencies, the AF Division had inserted a number of comments intended to clarify or update certain of his statements.

[2] See *Foreign Relations*, 1961–1963, volume XX, Congo Crisis, Document 264.

B. Recommendations: The U.S. should continue to back the U.N. and, if there is a Security Council meeting, should strive for a resolution which it can back. (*AF Comment:* This is being done through urgent consultations with the U.K., Belgium, France, and the U.N. Secretariat.) However, in an effort to insure U.N. success in an early solution of the Congo problem, the U.S. must take a more active role in U.N. planning and program implementation. (*AF Comment:* State is in almost daily contact with U Thant, Bunch, and UNOC Chief Robert Gardiner.) Specifically the U.S. might consider the following:

(1) Urge Belgium, Canada and possibly others to provide the CNA with technical assistance and necessary hardware, possibly under a U.N. umbrella. (*AF Comment:* This has been done. Canada demurred. Belgian offers have been made but Congolese are reluctant to accept them until *after* the Katanga situation is resolved.)

(2) Provide General Mobutu with up to six technical advisors to assist in training and organizing the CNA. The U.S. could also furnish the CNA with transport, commo equipment, rations, armored vehicles, training aids, transport aircraft, medical supplies and medical personnel. (*AF Comment:* An overall recommendation is currently being staffed through JCS preparatory to submission for State concurrence.)

(3) Back the GOC in its desire to install tax collection units in or near Elisabethville. As this could easily lead to "Round Three" in Katanga, the U.S. must be prepared to accept the consequences. Neither the UNOC Command nor U.S. military believe UNOC is capable of a rapid, decisive military campaign in Katanga. If military reinforcements cannot be found elsewhere, Tshombe should be advised privately that the U.S. will assign troops to UNOC unless Katanga comes to terms with the GOC and submits to U.N. decisions. I well recognize the implications of such a step and its probable unacceptability for domestic political reasons, but if we do not throw our full weight into the balance now, we may be forced to accept less palatable decisions soon. (*AF Comment:* Such a move would also cause a *serious* split with the U.K.)

(4) Prior to such a step, Adoula should announce a program for allocation of powers between the Central and Provincial governments, based on federal principles of the U.S. Constitution. He should also submit a constitution to Parliament within three months, state he would support a 50–50 distribution of Katanga revenues, and promise Tshombe and other Conakat leaders positions in the GOC. (*AF Comment:* All these steps have now been taken.)[3]

---

[3] For text of the July 28 communiqué issued by the Congolese Government outlining the principles for a federal constitution, see *American Foreign Policy: Current Documents,* 1962, pp. 877–878.

(5) The U.S. should make it known that it is prepared to offer economic aid to all of the Congo, including Katanga, as soon as reintegration is accomplished.

(6) Economic pressures on Katanga should be explored, although it is recognized that levers for such pressures on Tshombe have limitations. (*AF Comment:* U.S. is urgently consulting with Belgium, France, and U.K. on this subject, exploring unilateral approaches, and giving much press publicity to this effort.)

(7) The U.S. must be prepared to continue relatively large covert expenditures to shore up Adoula and other moderate leaders during the next few months. Without such aid in the past, the moderates would almost certainly have already lost control. Although only a stop-gap effort, I am convinced that there is no alternative, as a long-range political action program cannot be implemented as long as key leaders are concentrating all attention on Katanga. Also, Leopoldville Station lacks sufficient staff/contract personnel to implement and direct a comprehensive action program of the type submitted to Headquarters last October. (*AF Comment:* Adequate funds are available under Project [*cryptonym not declassified*]; Headquarters has addressed itself urgently to the personnel problem for almost ten months with inadequate results.)

3. *Long-term Problem*

A. Discussion: Prior to independence, it was recognized that Congo would need considerable foreign aid. But the mutiny of the CNA caused the U.S. to channel all aid (with minor exceptions) through the U.N. As a result, Agency covert action has furnished the U.S. with its only instrument for unilateral action in the Congo. The Agency's actions have been relatively successful; we can claim major credit for Lumumba's overthrow, the success of the Mobutu coup, and for Adoula's nomination and the survival of his government to date. Had the U.S. been able to exploit Agency-created opportunities through overt military, technical or economic aid programs (or had UNOC met its responsibilities effectively), U.S. policy would not now be hanging in the balance. In addition to Katanga, the GOC faces the following major long-term problems:

(1) The CNA: The 1960 CNA mutiny has never been fully contained. CNA lacks a trained cadre and adequate supplies. The U.N. has done nothing to resolve this problem and will not do so as long as officers unfriendly to the CNA are in charge of U.N. military efforts in the Congo. (*AF Comment:* Some three months ago, the U.N. offered a military training team and sent it to Leopoldville, but General Mobutu seems to have remained convinced that the CNA is quite all right as it is. The U.N. training team finally left, lacking employment. As noted above, DOD has this problem under urgent consideration.)

(2) Administrative Breakdown: Few GOC officials have the training or ability to carry out government decisions effectively. UNOC technical advisors assigned to various GOC ministries are too few in number and many are not competent. (*AF Comment:* Contributing to administrative confusion is the running fight between U.N. technicians and Belgians hired by the GOC.)

(3) Unemployment: With the departure of many Belgian employers in July 1960 and the gradual breakdown of government administration, unemployment rose to 52% of the male labor force in Leopoldville by May 1961; it is probably even higher now, and may be higher still in provincial cities. A problem of tremendous political import, neither the GOC nor the U.N. has been able to take effective measures. (*AF Comment:* Although relief and stop-gap measures can and should be taken, the problem basically depends upon getting the economy moving again. AID is slowly working out a plan to get transport moving, in the belief that the problem is distribution rather than production per se.)

B. Recommendations: The U.S. Government should recognize that the policy of channeling all efforts through the U.N. is not the reason for Soviet difficulties in launching a program in the Congo, and that unilateral U.S. aid to the Congo under a U.N. umbrella would not be objectionable to the Afro-Asians if it contributed to reducing the Katanga secession and restoring order to the Congo. Therefore, the U.S. should, with other friendly governments undertake the following steps, with tacit U.N. concurrence.

(1) Provide training outside of the Congo for selected CNA officers. Until effective cadres control the CNA, it will not be an effective force or a support for moderate political elements. (*AF Comment:* As noted above, DOD is looking into CNA training. Belgium is willing to undertake additional military training, but the GOC has not accepted recent offers.)

(2) Provide a small number of military technicians for training of officers and men in the Congo.

(3) Provide military equipment to replace material destroyed or in disrepair. (*AF Comment:* DOD is willing to recommend this as soon as it has assurances that CNA personnel can use and maintain it.)

(4) Provide public works administrators and technicians to supplement UNOC personnel. (*AF Comment:* This is a complicated problem. Administrators and technicians are now furnished by both the U.N. and Belgium, plus the fairly large number of Belgians employed by the GOC. Each group has a different approach to the problems at hand, and none gets along with the other. U.S. policy, which makes sense to AF, is that such assistance ultimately be provided by the Belgian Gov-

ernment, eliminating UNOC personnel and the cadre of old Belgian *colons* kept on by the GOC. Belgium is generally agreeable to this.)

(5) Provide additional funds to support a public works program. (*AF Comment:* AID has programmed for this.)

(6) Provide technical assistance to the GOC in an effort to make the moderate government more efficient and more effective. (*AF Comment:* Here, too, one hits the problem of the entrenched Belgian *colon* now employed by the GOC and jealously guarding what he considers the last bastion of Belgian influence; also, there is evidence that the GOC does not desire foreign technical assistance in this area.)

4. *Summary*

A. The Adoula government is in political difficulties. Its fall might spell failure of U.S. policy in the Congo. Should it survive, both it and the U.S. must be content with only partial successes unless U.S. policy is changed to permit overt unilateral assistance in key areas. Lacking such a change, the GOC must continue to depend upon the compromise-prone and inefficient UNOC which is subject to influences not always favorable to the U.S. and which no longer has the full confidence of the GOC.

B. The GOC recognizes its need for outside aid in solving its problems. Lacking such aid in the form of a strong, unilateral ally, and lacking solid and effective programs on which to base actions, they believe their regime may well fall and be replaced by the sort of extremist-nationalist regime which has appeared elsewhere in Africa. This would destroy the strategic advantage the U.S. enjoys in the Congo today. The moderate leaders around Adoula do not understand, therefore, why the U.S. withholds unilateral assistance.

C. Should the Congo fall into the hands of extremists, which is likely unless the moderates provide effective solutions, neighboring areas such as Angola, Congo (Brazzaville), the Central African Republic, Sudan, Uganda, Kenya, Tanganyika, Rwanda, Burundi, and the Rhodesias would become vulnerable to Bloc penetration through subversive penetration from the Congo. Also, political leaders in these countries, observing the failure of the West to support friendly governments, might be expected to seek accommodation with the Bloc and with internal extremist elements.

Lawrence Devlin
Chief of Station
Leopoldville

120. Memorandum From H. Bartlett Wells of the Office of the Deputy Director for Coordination, Bureau of Intelligence and Research, Department of State to the Director of the Bureau of Intelligence and Research (Hilsman)

Washington, August 29, 1962.

[Source: Department of State Files, INR/IL Historical Files, AF–CIA, 1962. Secret. *2 pages not declassified*]

---

121. Editorial Note

Telegram 4662 from Leopoldville to the Central Intelligence Agency, August 30, 1962, reported that Justin Bomboko had discussed the development of new provinces in the Congo with the Chief of Station on August 30, emphasizing that considerable political jockeying was now going on to gain control of them and requesting substantial aid to insure continuation of his influence and that of other [*cryptonym not declassified*]. The Station strongly recommended providing support, pointing out that if the [*cryptonym not declassified*] did not have control of their home provinces, they could easily lose their government jobs in Leopoldville. Also the new constitution had to be ratified by a majority of the new provinces prior to its final adoption. Thus, control over the new provinces was important for overall U.S. objectives as well as specific [*cryptonym not declassified*] objectives. The cable noted that Ambassador Gullion concurred with this request. (Central Intelligence Agency Files, Job 78–00435R, DDO/ISS Files, Box 1, Folder 11, [*cryptonym not declassified*] Operations)

The CIA responded in telegram 33362, August 31, that it considered funding for such purposes valid but premature, in that creation of new provinces required parliamentary action and parliament was now recessed. (Ibid.) Leopoldville advised Headquarters in telegram 4676, August 31, that its information on the timing of formation of the new provinces was not correct. Parliament had already approved many new provinces; most provincial governments would be formed within the next few weeks; and the campaign period for formation of the new provincial governments was already in full swing. The cable reiterated that if the [*cryptonym not declassified*] did not have control of their home provinces, they could easily be eliminated from the Leopoldville scene, thus jeopardizing the entire political edifice on which U.S. Congo policy rested. The Station recognized and shared Headquarters' frustrations as a result of continued spending requests to shore up the [*cryptonym not declassified*]. "However, believe we must be realistic and recognize this as fact of life in Congo. There just is no easy and rapid solution to the Congo problem." (Ibid.) CIA telegram 33690 to Leopoldville, September 1, approved funding. (Ibid.)

---

122. Editorial Note

In telegram 4871 to the Central Intelligence Agency, September 28, 1962, the Station in Leopoldville reported that in both its own and the Embassy's opinion, Joseph Mobutu remained the most effective Congolese National Army officer and key figure on the political scene. Based on numerous discussions with attachés and others, the Station did not believe there was any other CNA officer on the horizon with the political and military qualifications to replace Mobutu. Although he was not as effective as Leopoldville would like, he remained the only available asset to control the CNA. If his position fell to someone else this could easily terminate the [*cryptonym not declassified*] program. In view of the continued critical political situation and the possibility of a [*cryptonym not declassified*] coup, the Station recommended continuing support for Mobutu and the CNA, noting that it did not believe the Greene report (see footnote 3 to Document 123) had altered the situation. To date the only steps taken to implement the report, the Station commented, were an invitation for Mobutu to visit the United States and one "impact shipment" which Leopoldville understood was on its way. (Central Intelligence Agency Files, Job 89–00195R, DDO/AF Files, Box 1, Folder 7, [*cryptonym not declassified*] Operations, Volume I)

123. Telegram From the Station in the Congo to the Central Intelligence Agency[1]

Leopoldville, October 26, 1962.

5067 (In 46957). Ref Leop 4942 (In 35772).[2]

1. [*cryptonym not declassified*] have made considerable headway over the past 6 months in extending and strengthening their influence. The political control of MNC/L extremists has been broken in Orientale (the last of the extremist office holders of the Gizenga regime is under house arrest), the Kalonji Autonomous Regime of the South Kasai has been smashed and extremist and separatist movements in other parts of the Kasai and Kivu have been weakened if not fully eliminated. Despite these plus factors, the Congo is again heading into a serious political crisis, a crisis which stems largely from the failure of the UN to implement its much publicized reconciliation plan. It has been nearly 8 weeks since Tshombe accepted the plan (with qualifications) but it has yet to be implemented. Opposition elements within parliament are exploiting this apparent failure of UN plan and blaming [*cryptonym not declassified*] for failure take decisive action resolve Katanga problem.

2. [*cryptonym not declassified*] running scared and fear opposition will be able muster sufficient votes in the chamber to bring govt down or prevent it from implementing its program. [Identity 1], [Mobutu], [Identity 2], and [Identity 3], recently contacted [COS] and presented following views: pointing out serious danger to [*cryptonym not declassified*] if Katanga crisis not resolved soonest, they expressed surprise that ODYOKE has failed act more decisively to support group which friendly to PBPRIME interests and opposed by group composed persons which either under Bloc influence or in opposition for opportunistic reasons. They insisted ODYOKE should provide positive support now, rather than risk govt fall and replacement by unfriendly elements. Comparing Congo to Cuba, they noted that help now could avoid much greater problem in future, insisting any replacement govt would be far to left current govt and almost certainly unfriendly to ODYOKE.

3. Specifically they urged ODYOKE provide GOC with at least five jet fighters (together with mercenary pilots), several transport aircraft,

[1] Source: Central Intelligence Agency Files, Job 78–00435R, DDO/ISS Files, Box 1, Folder 12, [*cryptonym not declassified*] Operations. Secret; Rybat; [*cryptonym not declassified*]; Priority. Received at 1921Z.

[2] Not found.

trucks and other equipment recommended Greene plan[3] and large sums for political propaganda and action. [Identity 1] suggested that if [Identity 4] could give the president of each (or most) of the new provinces [*monetary amount not declassified*] this would go far to build support for GOC, as provincial leaders would get funds only if parliamentarians from their area agreed cooperate with GOC. Also asked for funds bribe parliamentary leaders, provide gifts for disaffected army leaders ([*name not declassified*] and [*name not declassified*]), traditional chiefs, etc.

4. Although basis July confidence vote, [*cryptonym not declassified*] might be able squeak through this political crisis, this by no means sure. Final outcome will depend upon extent parliamentary disaffection as result failure resolve Katanga crisis, funds available to opposition for bribery, military developments if any in north Katanga, degree to which Congolese accept or reject Soviet propaganda efforts (offers planes, arms and funds) and many other imponderables. Per ref, Station regards immediate political problem which will arise with opening parliament on 5 Nov as critical. Even if [*cryptonym not declassified*] squeak through at that time, continued failure settle Katanga bound have unfavorable effect. Thus, Leop considers that ODYOKE nearing end line on its present Congo policy and favors strong and immediate action to try reverse present unfavorable current. Leop not prepared take risk that [*cryptonym not declassified*] will muddle through without our aid and assumes HQS not willing take such risk. Submit that cost providing planes, arms and political action funds now could be small compared to costs if we wait until GOC falls into unfriendly hands. [Omitted here is further discussion of the proposal.]

5. Above message read in clear text draft and approved by [*cryptonym not declassified*].

End of message.

---

[3] A Special Military Advisory Team headed by Colonel M.J.L. Greene of the Department of Defense's Office of International Security Affairs visited the Congo June 7–July 12, 1962. On July 23, the team submitted a report recommending a broad program for modernization and training of the Congolese armed forces under a U.N. umbrella. See footnote 5 to Document 268 and footnotes 2 and 3 to Document 318, in *Foreign Relations, 1961–1963*, volume XX, Congo Crisis.

124. Editorial Note

In an October 27, 1962, telegram to the Central Intelligence Agency, the Station in Leopoldville proposed that the U.S. Government covertly arrange to provide the Government of the Congo with the services of five pilots. The proposal was submitted in response to a Department of State telegram indicating that the Department was searching for a crash action program which the U.S. Government could take prior to the November 5 meeting of parliament to shore up Prime Minister Adoula's position. The Congolese Government had five Harvard trainer aircraft and four transport aircraft but no pilots, the Station noted. If pilots could be made available to the Congolese Government prior to November 5 it would give Adoula a psychological and political lift out of all the proportion to the military value of the aircraft. The proposal was discussed at a meeting of CIA and Department of State representatives on October 29. CIA informed the Department that the most readily available pilots were refugee [*less than 1 line not declassified*] In an October 29 memorandum, Joseph W. Scott of the Bureau of Intelligence and Research briefed Deputy Under Secretary of State for Political Affairs George McGhee on the proposal and recommended that he approve the Department's concurrence in its implementation. (Department of State, INR/IL Historical Files, Congo, Sept. 1962–Dec. 1963)

The Department informed CIA of its concurrence in an October 31 memorandum and added that its understanding was that CIA would handle the matter in such a way that only Adoula and Joseph Mobutu would know of the U.S. Government's role. (Ibid.) On November 2 the CIA notified State that it was proceeding with implementation on an urgent basis, but indicated that although CIA would make every effort to confine knowledge of the U.S. role to Adoula and Mobutu, there could be no assurances that they would not inform other Congolese. (Ibid.)

Three and a half weeks later, in a November 26 memorandum, Scott informed U. Alexis Johnson, Under Secretary of State for Political Affairs, that the Congolese Government now desired to use the pilots for reconnaissance and combat missions in North Katanga. Scott indicated, however, that according to the Agency there were urgent problems of personnel and supply augmentation which must be met before the pilots and the Congolese Government aircraft would have the capability to fly missions outside the immediate area of Leopoldville. In view of the possible financial magnitude of a program giving the Congolese Air Force a combat capability and the possibility that Department of Defense equipment and funds might be required, it appeared to Scott that the proposal should go the Special Group. Johnson approved his recommendation that he ask CIA to prepare a proposal for the Special Group's consideration. (Ibid.)

125. Paper Prepared in the Central Intelligence Agency[1]

Washington, November 16, 1962.

PRECIS

Recommendation to Special Group for the Organization and Training of a Mobile Gendarme Paratroop Unit for the Republic of the Congo (Leopoldville)

1. This memorandum is forwarded for your use as background in the presentation of attached memorandum[2] for Special Group.

2. The attached memorandum proposes that this Agency undertake the organization, training, and, to some extent, the equipping of an airborne company[3] of Congolese gendarmes for the purpose of providing a stopgap internal security and counter-insurgency striking force during the interim between the phaseout of U.N. troops and the long-range training of regular Congo National Army troops. It would also provide an unconventional warfare capability in the event of communist take-over of all or part of the Congo. First year costs would be about [*dollar amount not declassified*]. Subsequent annual costs should be half that amount.

3. On 6 November 1962, the Department of State submitted a contingency plan for the Congo[4] which recommended, among other items, that the U.S. undertake the training of an airborne gendarmerie unit.

---

[1] Source: Central Intelligence Agency Files, Job 78–00435R, DDO/ISS Files, Box 1, Folder 11, [*cryptonym not declassified*] Operations. Secret. The original is attached to a November 28 transmittal memorandum to Director of Central Intelligence John McCone and General Carter that reads: "The President on 7 November approved a State Department plan of action for the Congo. One part of the plan he approved urged the 'training of an airborne gendarmerie unit.' This is the Agency's paper which would provide for such training. It will provide the nucleus for a Congolese force to be used in maintaining order in provincial areas and to serve as a cadre for unconventional warfare activities as required. It would involve training for 125 men. [*name not declassified*]."

[2] Dated November 16, attached but not printed.

[3] At this point "125 men" is written in an unidentified hand.

[4] See footnote 5 to Document 323 and Document 324 in *Foreign Relations,* 1961–1963, volume XX, Congo Crisis.

The President approved this plan on 7 November, without naming an executive agency.[5]

4. The current Department of Defense plan for the reorganization and training of the Congolese National Army, which has been approved by the President, does not provide for an MAP program but recommends that the United Nations attempt its implementation, with the U.S. willing to assume responsibility for an unspecified portion of the overall plan. We do not believe this plan could be revised and implemented on a timely basis to include provision for the program recommended in attached memorandum, nor do we believe that such a revision would be readily accepted by the U.N. For these reasons, it is proposed that C.I.A. be the executive agency.

5. Implementation of attached proposal depends upon its acceptance by Congolese Commander-in-Chief, General Joseph D. Mobutu, who will be visiting the U.S. as a guest of the U.S. Army Chief-of-Staff between 3–15 December. If attached proposal is approved, it would be presented to General Mobutu during his visit to Headquarters.[6]

[Omitted here is further discussion of the proposal.]

---

[5] See Document 325, ibid.

[6] A November 27 memorandum from Assistant Secretary Williams to Deputy Under Secretary of State for Political Affairs U. Alexis Johnson states that the Bureau of African Affairs recommended approval of the proposal, with the only possible caveat being the possibility that the Adoula government might fall within the next few days and be replaced by a leftist government. (Department of State, INR/IL Historical Files, Congo, Sept. 1962–Dec. 1963) On November 29, the Special Group approved the proposal, subject to the caveat that if Adoula fell, the plan should be reconsidered. (National Security Council, Intelligence Files, Special Group—Minutes and Approvals—1962) On June 20, 1963, the Special Group approved a State–CIA proposal to hold the project in abeyance.

---

126. Editorial Note

In telegram 5271 to the Central Intelligence Agency, November 26, 1962, the Station in Leopoldville reported that the opposition had submitted a no confidence motion to Chamber President Mwamba. He had so far refused officially to accept it, but as this position was illegal, both the [*cryptonym not declassified*] and the opposition believed he would be forced to accept it by November 27 at the latest. Joseph Mobutu, Victor Nendaka, and Minister of the Interior Kamitatu were highly pessimistic about the outcome of the crisis. Kamitatu estimated that the opposition should be able to obtain the votes needed to bring the government down. Katanga was widely believed to be the key issue.

Prime Minister Adoula took a slightly more optimistic view in a meeting with Ambassador Gullion and the Chief of Station, the telegram reported, but the Prime Minister expressed strong resentment over U.S. failure to provide sufficient aid earlier to resolve the Katanga crisis. Adoula indicated that last minute help might not do the trick but nevertheless gave the impression of a man intending to fight. He believed that President Kasavubu would agree to prorogue parliament for 30 days providing he was convinced strong action would be taken during the interim to resolve the Katanga problem. Tangible evidence of U.S. intentions was needed, Adoula stated. With Congolese National Army troops in North Katanga under constant attack by Government of Katanga aircraft, the Government of the Congo had an urgent need for aircraft to redress the balance of power. In concluding telegram 5271, the Station emphasized that Adoula was facing his most serious crisis to date, and there were "only days or perhaps hours in which to redress situation." It was doubted that the [*cryptonym not declassified*] could pull the fat out of the fire without receiving hardware immediately, including aircraft and other tactical weapons. In any case, the Station planned to aid Adoula. (Central Intelligence Agency Files, Job 78–00435R, DDO/ISS Files, Box 1, Folder 12, [*cryptonym not declassified*] Operations)

Two days later, in telegram 5297, November 28, the Station reported that the Adoula government had escaped defeat but that its narrow escape—and the 47 votes in favor of the government—had not come easily. The Station had concentrated on the one objective of preventing the government's fall ever since the crisis had come into the open on November 23; it doubted it could continue to hold the present line unless dramatic steps were taken immediately. (Ibid.)

In telegram 5346 to CIA, December 5, Leopoldville reported that although the government had squeaked through on November 28, the [*cryptonym not declassified*] and other government supporters remained greatly concerned by the possibility that the opposition, which now felt it had the government on the run, would continue to try to bring it down. The [*cryptonym not declassified*] appeared to be in a state of confusion regarding which steps to take. Ndele and Nendaka had contacted the Chief of Station to ask whether they could count on U.S. support should the government fall and they tried to maintain Adoula in power by means of a military coup. The Chief of Station replied he could not promise the necessary U.S. aid for a coup, since the U.S. position would depend on many things, including alternative leaders should the government fall, the Bloc position, and the policies followed by the government installed by a coup. (Ibid.)

127. Paper Prepared in the Central Intelligence Agency[1]

Washington, December 7, 1962.

PRECIS

Assistance to the Congolese Air Force (CAF)[2]

1. *Problem*

To determine the advisability of the U.S. Government's furnishing additional personnel and logistical support to the CAF.[3]

2. *Situation*

A. In early November 1962 the Katanga Air Force began bombing Congolese National Army troops in North Katanga. The United Nations has been either unwilling or unable to furnish air protection.

B. General Mobutu has requested that his five Harvard trainer aircraft now being flown by [*less than 1 line not declassified*] pilots supplied by CIA, be augmented by more pilots and ground crews, plus spare parts and armament for planes.

C. Unconfirmed reports indicate that Yugoslavia has offered jet aircraft with pilots to the CAF, and that the Soviets are preparing an offer of other military equipment.

3. *Aims*

A. Provide the CAF with the capability to undertake combat missions anywhere in the Congo using on-hand aircraft.

B. Restore morale of Congolese Army troops in North Katanga.

C. Prevent the Adoula Government from turning from the US/UN to undesirable sources for military assistance.

---

[1] Source: Central Intelligence Agency Files, Job 81–00966R, Box 1, Folder 1. Secret; Eyes Only. There is no drafting information on the original.

[2] The original is a precis of a 10-page, December 7 memorandum to the Special Group, attached to the memorandum but not printed. A note attached to the December 7 memorandum states that the paper was approved at the Special Group meeting on December 13, subject to decisions reached after discussions with the President on overall U.S. policy toward the Congo, and provided the President had no objection. The minutes of the Special Group meeting on December 13 state that it was later ascertained that the President had no objection to this proposal, provided that the Department of State determined that it would be compatible with the overall plan for the Congo. (Department of State Files, INR/IL Historical Files, Congo, Sept. 1962–Dec. 1963)

[3] On December 12, Assistant Secretary of State Williams sent a memorandum to Deputy Under Secretary Johnson recommending that he authorize the CIA to accede to the request set forth in the CIA memorandum of December 7, emphasizing that rapid strengthening of the Congolese air force capability was extremely important if a moderate government and pro-Western chief of staff were to remain in power in Leopoldville. (Ibid.)

4. *Coordination*

A. Ambassador Gullion concurred in the original recommendation. On 27 November 1962 the Department of State requested CIA to "prepare a memorandum which will provide a basis for the Special Group to address itself to the policy and financial consideration inherent in the suggested activity." Mr. Joseph Scott concurs in the submission of this memorandum.

B. The Office of the Secretary of Defense has been consulted. The feasibility of USAF logistical support has not been determined.

5. *Cost*—The total cost of this undertaking for the recommended three months is [*dollar amount not declassified*]. CIA can provide [*dollar amount not declassified*] from programmed funds. The remaining sum of [*dollar amount not declassified*] has not been programmed within CIA. (Note: The attached memorandum makes no special plea for approval of the proposal but recommends means of implementing it should the SG approve.)

128. Telegram From the Central Intelligence Agency to the Station in the Congo[1]

Washington, December 11, 1962, 2259Z.

Dir 04450. Ref: Dir 04151.[2]

1. HQS continues seek guidance re coup which subj under active discussion ODACID. Crux of debate is what can be asked from [Identity 1] in return for ODYOKE coup support e.g. more conciliatory attitude toward Tshombe, agreement not accept Bloc offers, legal amnesty, etc. Expect ODACID position will crystalize next several days. HQS

[1] Source: Central Intelligence Agency Files, Job 78–00435R, DDO/ISS Files, Box 1, Folder 12, [*cryptonym not declassified*] Operations. Secret; Rybat; [*cryptonym not declassified*]; Priority. Drafted and authenticated by [*name not declassified*] and released by Tweedy (C/AF).

[2] Ref gave results of Congo Working Group mtg 10 Dec. [Footnote in the original.] Reporting on the Congo Working Group meeting on December 10, CIA telegram 04151 to Leopoldville, December 10, stated that the Department of State was avoiding focusing on the coup problem, even though it was aware that continued support of the [*cryptonym not declassified*] was necessary and that [*cryptonym not declassified*] survival was probably dependent on some type of extra-legal action; it was also apparent that State decisions would be based more on preempting the Bloc than on supporting the [*cryptonym not declassified*]. (Ibid.)

also injected request for prior guidance event Leop faced with request to support accomplished coup.

2. [Godley] reports ref para 1 B action has lost steam.

3. Should have answers on [aid to Congolese Air Force] by 14 Dec.

End of message.

---

129. Memorandum From Alfred T. Wellborn of the Office of the Deputy Director for Coordination, Bureau of Intelligence and Research, Department of State, to the Director of the Bureau of Intelligence and Research (Hilsman)[1]

Washington, December 12, 1962.

SUBJECT

Meeting with Agency Representatives on Congo

PARTICIPANTS

Governor Williams, Messrs. Fredericks and Tasca (present part of the time) and Mr. Godley, AF; Mr. Wallner, IO; Messrs. Tweedy and [*name not declassified*], CIA and Mr. Wellborn, INR/DDC

Mr. [*name not declassified*] observed that one of the possibilities in the fast moving Congo situation is that the so-called Adoula Group (including Mobutu, Ndaka and Ndele), would stage a coup i.e. prorogue Parliament and carry on without it. If this should happen the leaders would probably come knocking on the Station chief's door for U.S. covert support. The policy question therefore arises whether assistance should be provided to them under the authorization of the program, approved by the Special Group, for political support of the Adoula Government.

Mr. Godley, who had just come from a meeting in Mr. McGhee's office said that, at this point, he could not express an opinion. The McGhee meeting had considered possible courses of action in the Congo, including the pros and cons of the desirability of a coup by the Adoula group. There was a question in his mind as a result of the discussion at the meeting, as to how much further the Department would

---

[1] Source: Department of State Files, INR/IL Historical Files, Congo, Sept. 1962–Dec. 1963. Secret. Sent through the Deputy Director for Coordination, Joseph W. Scott, in the Department of State's Bureau of Intelligence and Research.

be willing to go in assisting the Central Congolese Government without some evidence that it would be more forthcoming in trying to solve the Katanga problem. After some discussion of the critical situation in the Congo, Mr. Tasca suggested that we consult Governor Williams. The meeting then continued in Governor Williams' office where it was joined by Mr. Wallner.

Mr. Godley summarized the situation in the Congo as follows: Because of the personal dangers which the fall of the Adoula Government would pose for them, such leaders of the Adoula group as Mobutu, Ndaka and Ndele were considering a coup. Undoubtedly they would seek to find out what help they could expect from the U.S. We must therefore face up to this question. In the event the Adoula Government falls the alternatives before us in broad terms are to support the Adoula group or face up to the fact that any other group which would come to power would take an even harder position regarding Katangan reintegration and probably would turn to the Soviet bloc for help. It was not realistic to expect that any successor government could take a more conciliatory line on Katanga. If the Adoula group stages a coup we must expect that they will press for solution of the Katanga problem. In all probability they would seek an air force and continuing pressure for action on Katanga. It would be shortsighted to expect less than continuing and very substantial demands. While this is a disagreeable prospect the alternative is even worse; entry of the Soviet bloc into the Congo in a big way.

There followed an extensive discussion of the probable consequences of our looking favorably upon a coup, Governor Williams posing a series of questions designed to explore various aspects. The Agency representatives and Mr. Godley tended to advocate continued assistance to Mobutu, Ndaka et al. emphasizing the need to give the Congolese Government an air capability and pursuing the Thant plan.

At the end, Governor Williams asked Messrs. Wallner and Godley jointly to draft a paper which would serve as a basis for discussion with Mr. McGhee and Mr. Ball.[2]

---

[2] Telegram 5440 from Leopoldville to CIA, December 13, reported that the [*cryptonym not declassified*], disturbed by Adoula's failure to make advance preparations for a possible coup, had called on the Chief of Station for advice as to what preliminary steps would be necessary. The Chief of Station, with Ambassador Gullion's approval, outlined such steps for them, but emphasized that neither he nor the United States Government was specifically recommending this course of action. (Central Intelligence Agency Files, Job 78–00435R, DDO/ISS Files, Box 1, Folder 12, [*cryptonym not declassified*] Operations)

130. Paper Prepared in the Central Intelligence Agency[1]

Washington, undated.

REPUBLIC OF THE CONGO

COVERT ANNEX[2]

CIA Capability to Support Government of the Congo Actions to Dissolve Parliament

1. Assumptions

A. That key members of the Government of the Congo (GOC) will decide to prorogue, recess, or otherwise disperse the Parliament in order to create an environment for the undertaking of positive actions to resolve the Katanga secession within the framework of the U.N. Reconciliation Plan, and to take constructive steps to stabilize the internal situation in the Congo.

B. That actions against Parliament, whether legal or otherwise, will be fully backed by the Congolese National Army and the Sûreté, using force if required.

C. That the GOC decision to take such action will be contingent upon prior assurances of U.S. support of such action, of all phases of the U.N. Reconciliation Plan, and of other pressing internal matters.

2. Pre-Coup Actions

A. [*1 paragraph (3 lines) not declassified*]

B. [*1 paragraph (2½ lines) not declassified*]

C. [*1 paragraph (1 line) not declassified*]

D. [*1 paragraph (1½ lines) not declassified*]

---

[1] Source: Department of State Files, INR/IL Historical Files, Congo, Sept. 1962–Dec. 1963. Top Secret. There is no drafting information on the original.

[2] The paper is apparently a covert annex to an undated memorandum to President Kennedy entitled "Operating Plan for the Congo," printed in *Foreign Relations*, 1961–1963, volume XX, Congo Crisis, Document 362. The annotation to Document 362 states that the original bears no drafting information and that National Security Adviser McGeorge Bundy received a copy from the Department of State on December 17, 1962. For information about Kennedy's discussions of the plan with the NSC Executive Committee on December 17, see ibid., Documents 363 and 366. In a December 21 memorandum to Rusk (ibid., Document 381), Assistant Secretary Williams recommended to Rusk that Ambassador Gullion be instructed to advise the men around Adoula to permit him to rule by extra-parliamentary means. He noted that this would mean that the CIA would proceed to implement the covert annex to the NSC paper approved the previous weekend. Footnote 2 to Document 381 states that the covert annex was not found.

3. Coup Actions

A. [*1 paragraph (2½ lines) not declassified*]

B. [*1 paragraph (3 lines) not declassified*]

C. [*1 paragraph (1 line) not declassified*]

D. [*1 paragraph (3 lines) not declassified*]

4. Post-Coup Actions

A. [*1 paragraph (1½ lines) not declassified*]

B. [*1 paragraph (1½ lines) not declassified*]

C. [*1 paragraph (3 lines) not declassified*]

*D. [*1 paragraph (2 lines) not declassified*]

E. [*1 paragraph (2 lines) not declassified*]

*F. [*1 paragraph (4 lines) not declassified*]

5. Coordination

All actions will be taken in close consultation and with the concurrence of the Ambassador.

6. Budget

A. All items except those marked with an asterisk fall within programmed activities for which funds are available.

B. [*dollar amount not declassified*] in unprogrammed funds is required to stage the Congolese Air Force to North Katanga, as noted in memorandum to Special Group, dated 7 December 1962.

C. An estimated [*dollar amount not declassified*] in unprogrammed funds is required for a training and support program for the [*less than 1 line not declassified*].[3]

---

[3] In telegram 07059 to Leopoldville, December 22, CIA authorized the Station to undertake, in close coordination and with the concurrence of the Ambassador, the following actions outlined in the covert annex: 2A–2D, 3A–3D, 4A–4B. (Central Intelligence Agency Files, Job 78–00435R, DDO/ISS Files, Box 1, Folder 12, [*cryptonym not declassified*] Operations)

131. Telegram From the Station in the Congo to the Central Intelligence Agency[1]

Leopoldville, December 28, 1962.

5576 (In 41537). Ref: A. Leop 5558 (In 41007);[2] B. Leop 5566 (In 40682).[3]

1. [*1 line not declassified*] [COS] met with [Mobutu][4] night 27 Dec. [Mobutu] appeared be particularly annoyed and recognized that continued delay could lead failure implement plan. [COS] advised them reports that Kasavubu has signed decree closing parliament circulating widely in Leopoldville and per local journalist have appeared London papers.

2. Basis this info [Mobutu] phoned Anany [*1½ lines not declassified*] pointed out there no need delay action pending passage resolution creating Moyen Congo and high court. [Mobutu] said this could be done by decree. Anany accepted this advice [*less than 1 line not declassified*]. Anany later phoned [Mobutu] [*4 lines not declassified*].

3. [*3½ lines not declassified*] include paragraph in speech [*less than 1 line not declassified*] promising that parliament would again be opened March in accordance requirements fundamental law. [*3 lines not declassified*]

4. Although [COS] in process of moving will try maintain regular contact [*less than 1 line not declassified*] and advise developments.

End of message.

---

[1] Source: Central Intelligence Agency Files, Job 78–00435R, DDO/ISS Files, Box 1, Folder 12, [*cryptonym not declassified*] Operations. Secret; Rybat; [*cryptonym not declassified*]; Priority. Received at 1147Z.

[2] Not found.

[3] Not found.

[4] Telegram 5552 from Leopoldville to CIA, December 24, reported that [*text not declassified*] Kasavubu had finally signed the decree recessing parliament, but that they had no further information as to when the decree would be implemented. [*text not declassified*] said Minister of Defense Anany wanted parliamentary approval for creation of a Moyen Congo province first. The Station warned that since parliament was not scheduled to meet again until January 2, this gave more than a week for news of the decree to leak and for the opposition to take appropriate action to block it. (Central Intelligence Agency Files, Job 78–00435R, DDO/ISS Files, Box 1, Folder 12, [*cryptonym not declassified*] Operations)

132. Telegram From the Station in the Congo to the Central Intelligence Agency[1]

Leopoldville, December 30, 1962.

5595 (In 42396). Ref: Dir 07926.[2]

1. Prior to and after Lovanium [*cryptonym not declassified*] appeared be only moderate with chance obtain and hold power. This resulted from fact that he consciously sought and obtained middle ground position and thus was in position act as broker between Leop and Stey factions. Such person essential so long as parliamentary govt maintained. However, [*cryptonym not declassified*] abilities as compromiser proving weakness now that time for strong action has arrived. This will be particularly true if parliament closed per plan. At that time a strong and decisive leadership will be necessary and [*cryptonym not declassified*] does not seem be constitutionally capable adopting such role.

2. [*cryptonym not declassified*] team appears realize above facts. However at 28 Dec meeting team decided continue backing [*cryptonym not declassified*]. This based on personal friendship and loyalty toward him but primary factor seems to be their fear that dropping [*cryptonym not declassified*] at this time could lead to situation similar to that which developed when [*cryptonym not declassified*] and [*cryptonym not declassified*] clashed in Sep 60 and world debated constitutionality [*cryptonym not declassified*] action. As long as [*cryptonym not declassified*] and [*cryptonym not declassified*] work together repetition this danger can be avoided. Thus, team does not want take any action against [*cryptonym not declassified*] until parliament closed. At that time they hope Anany [*less than 1 line not declassified*] and [*cryptonym not declassified*] will be able give [*cryptonym not declassified*] some backbone. Also team hopes it will be in position impose its will to greater extent than is now case, for with parliament closed [*cryptonym not declassified*] will be almost com-

---

[1] Source: Central Intelligence Agency Files, Job 78–00435R, DDO/ISS Files, Box 1, Folder 12, [*cryptonym not declassified*] Operations. Secret; Rybat; [*cryptonym not declassified*]; Priority. Received at 1532Z.

[2] A footnote in the original requested the Station's views regarding recent evidence that Adoula was rapidly running out of steam, physically and politically. CIA telegram 07926 to Leopoldville, December 29, noted that the Station's recent messages made it evident that unless an unexpected event occurred which had an adrenalin effect, Adoula was rapidly running out of steam physically and politically. When one added the question of whether he could ever negotiate effectively with Tshombe, the United States had to consider whether there were, or should be, alternatives to Adoula. Under what circumstances might he be replaced and what U.S. actions might foster this? Headquarters' off-the-cuff choice for a replacement would be Anany, although its knowledge of him was superficial. (Ibid., Folder 9, [*cryptonym not declassified*] Operations)

pletely dependent on [*cryptonym not declassified*] and [Mobutu]. (They will control power forces needed maintain him in office.)

3. Leop trying develop [*name not declassified*] but do not yet have sufficient info determine whether he has qualities necessary take over [*cryptonym not declassified*] leadership.

4. Suggest HQS may wish make limited dissem paras 1 and 2. If not advise and Leop will include in dissem.

End of message.

---

133. Memorandum From Alfred T. Wellborn of the Office of the Deputy Director for Coordination, Bureau of Intelligence and Research, Department of State, to the Director of the Bureau of Intelligence and Research (Hilsman)[1]

Washington, January 16, 1963.

SUBJECT

AF Meeting with Agency Representatives, January 15, 1963

PARTICIPANTS

Messrs. Fredericks, Tasca and Ford (item 1), AF; Messrs. Tweedy and [*name not declassified*] (item 1), CIA; and Mr. Wellborn INR/DDC

1. *Congo*. Mr. Tweedy remarked that recently the Agency's activities in the Congo had been very quiet on the political action front.[2] It had been largely a matter of intelligence acquisition. He did, however, wish to raise the question of what should be done about the [*less than 1 line not declassified*] pilots who were now limited to flying in the immediate vicinity of Leopoldville. As he saw it there were two valid alternatives—either pull them out or augment their capability, generally as outlined in the proposal that had gone to the Special Group. Mr. Tweedy said that he was not at this time making any recommenda-

---

[1] Source: Department of State Files, INR/IL Historical Files, AF Meetings, 1963. Secret. Sent through the Deputy Director for Coordination, Joseph W. Scott, Bureau of Intelligence and Research.

[2] Telegram 5614 from Leopoldville to CIA, January 2, reported that the "creeping coup" was crawling to a climax, and that there had been no reaction so far to Adoula's January 1 announcement that parliament was being closed. It appeared that they might have lucked through, despite the [*cryptonym not declassified*] failure to take the precautionary steps recommended by the Station. (Central Intelligence Agency Files, Job 78–00435R, DDO/ISS Files, Box 2, Folder 1, [*cryptonym not declassified*] Operations)

tion—merely raising the question. Mr. [*name not declassified*] observed that he had discussed the matter with Mr. Godley, Director of AFC, who was in favor of expanding the Congolese Government's air capability. The Congolese Government could well use such an instrument to maintain order.[3] The tribal fighting in Kasai was a case in point. Until the Congolese Air Force could develop a native capability under the Greene plan[4] training, which would take months, the [*less than 1 line not declassified*] pilots would be very useful. Mr. Fredericks indicated he also favored providing the Congolese Government with an air force capability. Mr. Wellborn reviewed the status of the proposal—it had been approved by the Special Group but held in abeyance because of the rapid developments in the Congo right after that and the emergence of other considerations.

As Mr. Tweedy was going to get the views of the Embassy and the Station on what to do about the pilots, Mr. Wellborn suggested the field's views and the Agency's recommendations be submitted to the Department by [*less than one line not declassified*] memorandum. This could form the basis of a memorandum to Mr. Johnson, from INR incorporating AF's recommendation.[5]

[Omitted here is discussion of unrelated subjects.]

---

[3] Katanga's secession ended on January 21, 1963.

[4] See footnote 3, Document 123.

[5] At a meeting with Fredericks and G. McMurtrie Godley on March 13, Tweedy noted that the Cleveland Report considered valid the Congolese Air Force's need for a tactical air capability represented by six Harvard aircraft and that to maintain this capability the services of non-Congolese pilots were needed for at least a year, until Congolese pilots could be trained. However, it was quite another matter to work out practical arrangements, Tweedy remarked. The [*text not declassified*] were now there essentially on a crash, short term basis. If their services were to be extended for a year, or probably longer as it was difficult to foresee that Congolese pilots could be trained in that time, the arrangements would have to be on an entirely different basis. (Memorandum from Alfred Wellborn to Roger Hilsman, March 13; Department of State Files, INR/IL Historical Files, AF Meetings, 1963)

134. Dispatch From the Station in Leopoldville to the Chief of the Africa Division, Directorate of Plans, Central Intelligence Agency (Tweedy)[1]

Leopoldville, February 15, 1963.

[*dispatch number not declassified*]

SUBJECT

Operational/[*cryptonym not declassified*]/Transmittal of KUBARK Recommendation on Creation of Political Party

FYI. Transmitted under separate cover for all addressees are copies of a paper[2] written by the undersigned at the request of [Gullion] and passed to [Identity 1] in late January 1963. As Headquarters is aware, the Station has been pushing the [*cryptonym not declassified*] to establish a strong party mechanism for well over a year. While [Embassy] has always accepted the need for such an organization, some of its members previously looked upon such a development with mixed feelings, for some [Embassy] officers objected to the patronage and other "questionable" aspects involved in creating a strong political mechanism. However, [Embassy] views have evolved with the local political situation and all [Embassy] officers are now strong proponents of the plan. The [*cryptonym not declassified*] are the main problem. As a result of the shortage of qualified leaders, they do not have anyone available to work fulltime on this problem, and, although the [*cryptonym not declassified*] favor the creation of a new national party, the project has not got off the ground. Also, the Station has not insisted upon an immediate beginning, for Leopoldville is reluctant to expend the large sums that would be involved in such an operation unless it has one qualified asset to monitor expenditures and provide guidance on a day-to-day basis. In the absence of such direction and supervision, it is doubtful that the operation would succeed and it is probable that considerable funds would be wasted.

[Lawrence Devlin]

---

[1] Source: Central Intelligence Agency Files, Job 78–00435R, DDO/ISS Files, Box 2, Folder 1, [*cryptonym not declassified*] Operations. Secret.

[2] Attached but not printed.

135. Telegram From the Station in the Congo to the Central Intelligence Agency[1]

Leopoldville, March 1, 1963.

6155 (In 77386). Ref Dir 20038.[2]

1. Leop and [*name not declassified*] have discussed full spectrum [*cryptonym not declassified*] programs. Following concensus:

2. [*cryptonym not declassified*] do not constitute team but group leaders whose interests more or less coincide, whose fates more or less interdependent and who have in past tended work in close concert principally in times immediate crisis. [Identity 1] failure use them as team has reduced cohesion of group. [Identity 1] seems least integral member group but at same time most critical member. Of late, has tended decreasingly take others into confidence and appears increasingly susceptible to undesirable advice (which subj separate cable).[3]

3. Per [*less than 1 line not declassified*],[4] general outlines action plan given [Identity 1] late Jan which while well recd has stimulated no action his part. Ditto others in group who assert they anxious implement but cannot do so without [Identity 1] support and leadership. Neither group as such nor individual members capable fleshing out this plan in terms timetable, budget, etc, so this must be done by Leop. Even when fully prepared, plan with details will probably bear only vague resemblance to actions taken, timing and actual expenditures due in part need adapt actions to developing situations and in part to inability Congolese stick to predetermined course.

[Omitted here is further discussion of the plan.]

5. If all preliminary conditions met, believe implementation stands chance initial success of no more than one third total districts Congo. Excluded might be Kongo Central which currently virtually at war with central govt and parts Kivu, Katanga, Kasai and possibly Orien-

---

[1] Source: Central Intelligence Agency Files, Job 78–00435R, DDO/ISS Files, Box 2, Folder 1, [*cryptonym not declassified*] Operations. Secret; Rybat; [*cryptonym not declassified*]; Routine. Received at 1953Z.

[2] Hqs. wished take advantage [*text not declassified*] TDY Leop for detailed discussion [*text not declassified*] Program. [Footnote in the original.] CIA telegram 20038 to Leopoldville, February 23, stated that the Agency wished to take advantage of [*text not declassified*] temporary duty in Leopoldville for a detailed discussion of the [*text not declassified*] program. It recognized the limitations inherent in getting the [*text not declassified*] to plan, but would appreciate the Station's efforts to delineate programs and attempt insofar as circumstances permitted to establish organized bases which could be used in determining the extent to which the CIA should support the tribal chiefs' organization, a new political party, and other [*text not declassified*] political action programs. (Ibid.)

[3] Not found.

[4] Document 134.

tale. Hence in near future wildest success would build [*cryptonym not declassified*] party with large block of votes but which might well fall short of absolute majority. However believe well organized homogeneous group, if such can be formed, will attract numerous other political leaders, as bandwagon movement even stronger in Congo than elsewhere. In summation would not foresee immediate across-board success of [*cryptonym not declassified*] National Party but if early success considerable believe it would then gather steam and achieve desired results.

[Omitted here is further discussion of the plan.]

136. Editorial Note

On March 12, 1963, Bronson Tweedy of the Central Intelligence Agency met with Assistant Secretary of State Wayne Fredericks and G. McMurtrie Godley, Director of the Office of Central African Affairs, to discuss the Congo. According to a memorandum of the meeting prepared on March 13 by Alfred Wellborn of the Bureau of Intelligence and Research, the following conversation took place regarding Prime Minister Adoula:

"*Adoula's Weaknesses and Possible Replacement.* In reply to Mr. Godley, Mr. Tweedy said that Adoula's performance in recent weeks had been very poor as regards those matters on which the Station had had contact with him. He appeared tired, disinterested, and lacking in the fighting spirit he had shown in the past. This led to a discussion of his possible replacement. Mr. Godley and Mr. Tweedy expressed the view that we should stay out of the jockeying attending a political reshuffle in the Congo. A number of political figures were mentioned as having certain assets but these were counterbalanced by serious shortcomings so that no one loomed as a candidate we should support. [*name not declassified*] was considered the brightest of the lot but so utterly unpredictable that it would be practically impossible to work with him. Mr. Fredericks inquired what were the Soviets doing. Mr. Tweedy said that there was no evidence that they were doing anything in particular." (Department of State Files, INR/IL Historical Files, AF Meetings, 1963)

137. Editorial Note

In telegram 6298 from Leopoldville to the Central Intelligence Agency, March 14, 1963, the Chief of Station reported that the Congo Government was in serious political trouble caused by lack of political organization and know-how, [*text not declassified*], and a multitude of nearly insoluble problems which had plagued the Congo since independence. When he warned [*text not declassified*] that the U.S Government did not want to pour money into a lost cause, [*text not declassified*] said it would probably take at least a year for the [*text not declassified*] to create a political organization of the type required to eliminate or reduce constant vote-buying. The Chief of Station noted that the United States had a choice between terminating support for the moderates, which would probably result in their fall, or continuing to provide support over the coming year, [*text not declassified*]. He pointed out that, although frustrating, the [*text not declassified*] operation had maintained a government which was as pro-American as any that could be expected in Africa at that time. (Central Intelligence Agency Files, Job 78–00435R, DDO/ISS Files, Box 2, Folder 1, [*cryptonym not declassified*] Operations)

138. Paper Prepared in the Central Intelligence Agency[1]

Washington, undated.

PROJECT RENEWAL—[*cryptonym not declassified*]

A. Current Objectives

The central objective of this project continues to be the strengthening of the present moderate elements of the Government of the Congo (GOC) in order to permit the GOC a sufficiently strong footing to achieve and maintain unity of the entire Congo, and to ensure that a moderate pro-West, or at least genuinely neutral, government remains in power. The Adoula Government is still in power and the current

[1] Source: Central Intelligence Agency Files, Job 78–00435R, DDO/ISS Files, Box 1, Folder 1, [*cryptonym not declassified*]—Development & Plans. Secret. The original is attached to a Project Action form from the CIA's Congo desk to Deputy Director of Central Intelligence Carter requesting [*text not declassified*] for the [*text not declassified*] project for FY 1963. On March 18, Executive Director Lyman Kirkpatrick signed for the Deputy Director as Approving Authority.

prognosis for re-integration of Katanga is as optimistic as it has ever been. CIA's activities in support of this objective have played a vital role in the current degree of accomplishment; it is in fact doubtful that the objective could have been attained without CIA activities closely coordinated with overall U.S. Government policy and planning.

[Omitted here are operational and personnel aspects of the project.]

C. Intelligence Production

Approximately 200 field intelligence reports were received during 1962, a very large percentage of which were disseminated. Much of the information was semi-overt or highly perishable. Undoubtedly some of this information was slanted since the [*cryptonym not declassified*] clearly knew they were talking to U.S. officials and it is doubtful that they always made a clear distinction between Department of State and CIA officers. Nevertheless, on many occasions valuable information was received in time for the U.S. Government to consider it and act upon it before the GOC itself took certain steps. In addition, it is highly probable that because of the special relationship with the [*less than 1 line not declassified*] developed by Chief of Station, Leopoldville, information was obtained which could not have been obtained by Embassy officers.

CIA was also able to obtain much valuable information not disseminated which has been useful for operational planning, for background purposes, and for counter-intelligence purposes.

D. Effectiveness

(1) Financial support to an unofficial grouping known as the Customary Tribal Chiefs, while it has not as yet led to the forming of a cohesive national political party, has served to bring Premier Adoula a certain degree of political support.

(2) A [*less than 1 line not declassified*] international public relations program has enabled the Adoula Government to project an international image, primarily among Afro-Asian countries, which the government could not have achieved if left to its own resources. The Adoula Government continues to receive general support from those countries which were the principal targets of this activity and this has been of great value in the United Nations. [*3 lines not declassified*]

(3) The Adoula Government has not yet been able to gain complete control of an effective, large-circulation newspaper. However, [*less than 1 line not declassified*] financial support as well as guidance as to content has played a significant role in maintaining both the existence and the effectiveness of a new newspaper which is generally recognized to be a government outlet.

(4) [*less than 1 line not declassified*] support has enabled a major labor union to increase its effectiveness in Congolese labor matters.

This union has supported the Adoula Government policies, or has been constructively critical.

(5) Financial support to General Mobutu, Chief-of-Staff of the Congolese National Army, has been effective in enabling him to retain the loyalty of key officers. At one time Mobutu was able to restrain his officers from action which could possibly have negated U.S. efforts.

(6) [*1 line not declassified*] the development of a cooperative in Equateur province has generated an interest in cooperative activity as a whole and has put a specific cooperative on its economic feet. One of Adoula's principal political supporters has profited from a certain amount of grassroots political support through association with this activity.

(7) The provision by CIA of non-Congolese pilots to the pilotless Congolese Air Force resulted in an increase of local prestige to the Adoula Government at a critical time.

(8) On numerous occasions financial support as well as political guidance to Adoula and his principal supporters have enabled them to survive immediate, short-term crises, failure in which might have resulted in the downfall of the government, or to accomplish certain tactical objectives which enhanced their overall political posture.

[Omitted here is further discussion of the personnel aspects of the project.]

G. Interagency Coordination

Coordination with the Department of State, both in the field and at Headquarters, has been continually close and detailed.

H. Plans

Plans will to a great extent be conditioned by the outcome of the Katanga secession and the ability of the Adoula Government to focus its attention effectively upon internal problems, particularly economic ones. Reasonable achievements in this area should do much to ensure continued political support by the population. Nevertheless, the future stability of the Adoula Government is by no means ensured even with the successful reintegration of Katanga. A slight de-emphasis on public relations in the international arena is possible. The formation of a political organization able to concentrate close local and provincial political support for the Adoula Government is necessary. Increased internal propaganda support is envisioned, and candidates for newspaper and radio jobs are currently being interviewed and assessed.

Special Group authority has been granted for a para-military project which aims to provide a stop-gap internal security and counter-insurgency striking force during the interim between the phase-out of

UN troops and the long-range training of regular Congolese National Army troops.

[Omitted here is further discussion of the personnel aspects of the project.]

As another stop-gap pressure to strengthen internal security, pending results from implementation of the Greene Plan, it is planned to continue and expand support to the Congo Air Force. Provision of qualified pilots, together with a limited maintenance capability, has already converted a previously "paper" Air Force into an airborne one, and the planned expansion will give this new Air Force a nationwide operational capability.

[Omitted here is detailed discussion of the costs of the project.]

---

139. Telegram From the Station in the Congo to the Central Intelligence Agency[1]

Leopoldville, March 22, 1963.

6405 (In 91600). Ref A. Dir 26397;[2] B. Dir 25831;[3] C. [Embassy] telegram 2421 to ODACID.[4]

[Omitted here is discussion of the political situation.]

7. In summation political situation remains even more confused than usual. Opposition apparently has votes to bring down govt, but as opposition lacks cohesion [Identity 1] belief that he can split opposition may yet prove correct. Leop remains pessimistic insofar as possibility

---

[1] Source: Central Intelligence Agency Files, Job 78–00435R, DDO/ISS Files, Box 2, Folder 1, [*cryptonym not declassified*] Operations. Secret; Rybat; [*cryptonym not declassified*]. No time of receipt appears on the message.

[2] Guidance for Leop to strengthen incumbent government. [Footnote in the original.] This CIA telegram has not been found.

[3] Meeting with ODACID on 18 March established the interim policy that in the event of a motion of censure being tabled, ODYOKE would continue to support the incumbent government if there continued to be any indication that it would squeak through. [Footnote in the original.] CIA telegram 25831, March 19, stated that the [*text not declassified*] project had been approved, but with a series of caveats requiring assessment of the project and detailed follow-up on expenditures. (Central Intelligence Agency Files, Job 78–00435R, DDO/ISS Files, Box 2, Folder 1, [*cryptonym not declassified*] Operations)

[4] Summary of lengthy discussion with Adoula, in which he predicted that his reshuffled government would obtain a comfortable majority, noting that the opposition was divided. [Footnote in the original.] This Department of State telegram has not been found.

govt will squeak through but anything possible when dealing with power-hungry individuals who put personal objectives ahead of national good. Should govt fall believe [*cryptonym not declassified*] plan to prolong crisis in order try push their candidate or candidates offers as good possibility as now available. Station endeavoring monitor on continuing basis opposition and [*cryptonym not declassified*] plans. Primary problem is that each opposition leader sets forth his views as opposition policy when in reality these leaders are generally speaking only for themselves or at most their small group. (However Leop continuing report info as received on theory it of use to HQS and ODACID in trying piece together picture confused political struggle going on here. Will continue do so unless advised to contrary.) As for [*cryptonym not declassified*] their views provide more solid intel but even then their statements cannot be accepted en toto. They too are confused and desperately seeking and considering various alternative solutions. As new developments arise their position shifts. In short, Leop proceeding on hypothesis that worst may occur and trying to prepare for any one of a number of possible eventualities.

8. Refs A and B most helpful. Would appreciate continuing guidance whenever feasible.[5]

---

[5] CIA telegram 28182 to Leopoldville, March 27, informed the Station that Headquarters far preferred that the new political organization not be centered on Adoula personally but be based on the inner [*text not declassified*] circle, which should include one or two alternatives to Adoula for the top slot and have enough leadership flexibility to permit party reshuffles without changing party complexion. It suggested that the organization be built at two levels—one (overt) based on the essential tribal structure of the Congo and the second [*text not declassified*] to be a control commission type of inner leadership capable of imposing discipline on key figures. It was also essential that Nendaka and Mobutu be part of the inner circle. (Central Intelligence Agency Files, Job 78–00435R, DDO/ISS Files, Box 2, Folder 1, [*cryptonym not declassified*] Operations)

---

140. Editorial Note

Telegram 6570 from the Station in Leopoldville to the Central Intelligence Agency, April 10, 1963, reported that the political situation there was so murky that it was difficult to determine whether Prime Minister Cyrille Adoula would survive. On April 9, the Chief of Station met with the Prime Minister and told him that he thought that the great mass of the Congolese population was disgusted with the lack of government action and the ostentatious living and corruption of its political leaders. He urged Adoula to take decisive action to terminate the incompetent parliament immediately, suggesting that he select a small government of the most qualified individuals and announce a program with limited objectives such as severe austerity, an anti-corruption campaign, and immediate implementation of a public works program. (Central Intelligence Agency Files, Job 78–00435R, DDO/ISS Files, Box 2, Folder 1, [*cryptonym not declassified*] Operations)

The Agency responded in telegram 31679, April 10, that the disturbing aspect of telegram 6570 was that even though Leopoldville agreed that Adoula had shown himself thoroughly incapable of taking any action—decisive or otherwise—during the crisis, Leopoldville still believed that urging him to take such action would have the desired results. Experience regretfully just did not permit such a hopeful conclusion to be drawn. (Ibid.)

In telegram 6687 to Headquarters, April 20, Leopoldville reported that the [*text not declassified*] were again in trouble and facing a no confidence vote. On the urging of the Ambassador, funds had been passed [*text not declassified*] for use in this vote. The Station requested authorization to expend additional funds to keep the [*text not declassified*] afloat. (Ibid.) The Agency responded in telegram 34111, April 20, that its impression was that Adoula's inept handling of cabinet reorganization, his failure to take other [*text not declassified*] into his confidence, and the fact that he could rely on only 48 chamber votes appeared to make it unlikely he could survive until the end of June. Hence Headquarters, while authorizing additional funds, was reluctant to pour in money with scant hope of success. Due to the past failures of either CIA or the Department of State to influence Adoula's tactics, the Agency was pessimistic that any new radical approach could change the situation and get Adoula out of his self made box. (Ibid.)

Telegram 6708 from Leopoldville to CIA, April 23, expressed the hope that Adoula would close parliament before the end of April, and said that in view of his success in the April 20 no confidence vote, he might make it through. The Station was keeping its fingers crossed. (Ibid.)

141. Memorandum From the Comptroller of the Central Intelligence Agency (Bross) to the Deputy Director of Central Intelligence (Carter)[1]

Washington, April 17, 1963.

SUBJECT

Support for the Congolese Air Force

1. The annexed project[2] covers operation and maintenance of planes and air crews assigned to the Congolese Government. From the funding point of view, the project is all right as the Clandestine Services have funds for the project in both FY 1963 and FY 1964.

2. From the policy point of view, there appears to be ample support for the proposition that the Congolese Government requires this support from the U.S. Government. There appears to be some doubt, however, as to whether CIA must render this support or whether it could come from other sources (the U.S. Air Force or AID). The DD/P believes that practical considerations make it extremely unlikely that another Government Agency could successfully assume this responsibility. I am also informed that the DCI has expressed the opinion that this activity should continue under CIA control.

3. Approval is recommended.[3]

John A. Bross
Comptroller

---

[1] Source: Central Intelligence Agency Files, Job 89–00639R, DO/AF Files, Box 1, Folder 18, Project Removals & Termination, Apr. 63–May 68, [*folder name not declassified*]. Secret.

[2] Attached but not printed.

[3] Executive Director Lyman Kirkpatrick signed the attached memorandum's approval line for the Director of Central Intelligence on April 18.

142. Paper Prepared in the Central Intelligence Agency[1]

Washington, April 19, 1963.

PRECIS

Covert Action in the Congo[2]

1. *Problem*

To determine the advisability of continuing certain covert actions in support of the Adoula Group in the Congo as authorized by Special Group on 17 November 1961.

2. *Situation*

Despite the frustrations and difficulties of operating in the Congo, our actions there over the last 18 months have helped materially to reduce the Katanga secession and to maintain in power a moderate, pro-Western government. If the Congo is to consolidate the gains already made and move into a nation-building phase, it is essential that these actions be carried forward, as outlined below.

3. *Aims*

If the program is approved, following activities will be continued:

A. Direct political support to the Adoula Group, including tactical guidance and help in formation of a national political party:	[*dollar amount not declassified*]
B. Expansion of the successful public relations program which has already proved its worth in supporting the Adoula Group:	[*dollar amount not declassified*]
C. Support to General Joseph Mobutu, Commander-in-Chief of the Congolese National Army, who has maintained control of the Army and assured its continued support to Adoula.	[*dollar amount not declassified*]
Total Funds Requested	[*dollar amount not declassified*]

[1] Source: Central Intelligence Agency Files, Job 81–00966R, Box 1, Folder 11. Secret; Eyes Only. There is no drafting information on the original.

[2] This paper is a precis of an attached 6-page April 19 memorandum to the Special Group. A note attached to the memorandum states that the proposal was approved at the Special Group meeting on April 25, and that the Chairman's only concern had been that there was no cut-off date on funding. McGeorge Bundy said he would mention it to higher authority.

4. *Coordination*

The Chief of Mission and our Chief of Station, Leopoldville feel strongly that the above program must be continued if the Congo is to be prevented from slipping back into chaos with the attendant risk of a Bloc take-over.[3] The Adoula Group strongly favors continuation of these activities and would view any interruption of them as a major and unfavorable change in U.S. policy.

5. *Recommendation*

It is recommended that Special Group approve the continuation of activities listed in paragraph 3, above. Total cost: [*dollar amount not declassified*] for FY 1964.

6. Funds will be available through reprogramming within the Clandestine Services.

[3] A handwritten notation in the original reads: "CIA Hqs & State Dept. concur."

---

143. Memorandum for the Record[1]

Washington, April 25, 1963.

[Omitted here is discussion of unrelated subjects.]

6. Covert Action, Congo

The CIA paper of 19 April[2] was approved with little discussion. The Chairman said that his only concern was whether we are committed to spending money at this rate forever. Mr. Tweedy said first that if the Adoula government should fall, it would probably be in the U.S. interest to support a successor government in a somewhat similar way and, secondly, he pointed out that there are no firm commitments made, although of course the recipients do come to expect a subsidy.

[1] Source: National Security Council, Intelligence Files, Special Group—Minutes—1963. Secret; Eyes Only.

[2] See Document 142, which recommended the approval of activities costing [*dollar amount not declassified*] for FY 1964.

Mr. Bundy said he would mention this project to higher authority.[3]

[Omitted here is discussion of unrelated subjects.]

---

[3] CIA telegram 36265 to Leopoldville, April 30, informed the Station that higher authority had approved continuation of the [*text not declassified*] project and programmed funds for organization of a political party, for propaganda [*text not declassified*], and to support Mobutu. Headquarters, however, saw serious drawbacks to a CIA-sponsored party centered on either Adoula or Bomboko. Thus, it strongly urged the Station to review with the Ambassador the entire concept of a covert U.S. effort to build a party, suggesting as alternatives concentration on building the political loyalty of Mobutu's subordinates, [*text not declassified*] and continuing to search for a better instrument than the presently constituted [*text not declassified*] offered. (Central Intelligence Agency Files, Job 78–00435R, DDO/ISS Files, Box 2, Folder 1, [*cryptonym not declassified*] Operations)

---

144. Editorial Note

On May 23, 1963, Joseph Mobutu visited Central Intelligence Agency Headquarters for discussion and a luncheon. That same day, in telegram 7032 to CIA, the Chief of Station in Leopoldville spoke favorably of Mobutu while offering his last views before leaving the Congo. He said that he continued to regard Mobutu as their best insurance that the [*text not declassified*] effort would not fail, and thought he was the most sincere U.S. friend in the Congo. Although Mobutu had many weaknesses, the Chief of Station believed the United States should continue to bet on him, as there was no alternative with similar power. (Central Intelligence Agency Files, [*text not declassified*], Mobutu, Joseph Desire, Vol. II) While visiting Washington, Mobutu met with President Kennedy. For a memorandum of their conversation, see *Foreign Relations*, 1961–1963, volume XX, Congo Crisis, Document 423, pages 858–862).

145. Dispatch From the Chief of the Africa Division, Directorate of Plans, Central Intelligence Agency (Tweedy) to the Station in Leopoldville[1]

Washington, June 4, 1963.

[*dispatch number not declassified*]

SUBJECT

Political Action in the Congo

Reference: DIR 36265.[2]

1. This dispatch is meant not so much to enlighten the field as to the political realities of the Congo as to clarify our own thinking and commit some specific thoughts to paper. We hope that you will read it thoughtfully, discuss it with appropriate [Embassy] personnel, and comment upon it both substantively and in context of the operational problems it raises. Because of its sensitivity, we are not sending copies to either of the Bases, but hope you will discuss it with Base personnel at first opportunity.

2. With each succeeding political crisis, the Adoula Government has had increasing difficulty in maintaining itself, even with substantial outside help. One result has been that Adoula, to maintain his personal position, has been forced to make compromises with various opposition members at the cost of his partially alienating and breaking the cohesion of the [*less than 1 line not declassified*]. On some occasions he has consulted the Group and rejected their advice, on others he has not consulted them. Further, Adoula has shown no particular aptitude for using compromises to strengthen his position. He talks with the full spectrum of political leaders, excluding the extreme nationalists, and makes or implies numerous and contradictory commitments, many of which he cannot fulfill. The result is that he displeases as many as he pleases and his net gains, if any, are not significant.

4. In our talks with the [*cryptonym not declassified*], as well as by policy authorization, we are committed to support the [*cryptonym not declassified*] effort(s) to organize a national political party and must therefore make at least a gesture to follow through, not only because of our commitments but also as a matter of prudence in hedging bets.

---

[1] Source: Central Intelligence Agency Files, Job 78–00435R, DDO/ISS Files, Box 2, Folder 2, [*cryptonym not declassified*] Operations. Secret. Drafted by [*name not declassified*].

[2] See footnote 3 to Document 143.

However, the various forces in process of coalescence in the post-secessionist era give strong indications that an Adoula Government will probably be challenged with increasing success as time goes on; it behooves KUBARK to extend its range of contacts and to extend political action aid to most individuals and groups whose capability, actual or potential, to challenge Adoula successfully make them potential future allies. Our objective is *not* to perpetuate the Adoula regime indefinitely, but to insure in the Congo a moderate, friendly government capable of getting the Congo moving along the road back. The ultimate purpose is to deny the Congo to the Bloc.

5. In considering the political forces in being or in formation in the Congo, we should identify and give consideration to non-political organizations which can exercise a palpable to decisive influence in politics. These include: the ANC, the Sûreté, the labor unions. They also include foreign governments, UMHK and other large, primarily Belgian, industrial and commercial interests, plus the UNOC and the many individuals therein who are willing and able to intervene in Congolese politics.

6. Among the parties whose actual and potential position should be reviewed are: the Abako, representing the Bakongo tribe exclusively; the Conakat, which traditionally represents the most powerful tribes of Katanga except for the Balubas; the Balubakat, representing the Baluba tribes of Katanga; the Baluba-Kasai; the MNC/L, whose strength is largely regional at this point (Orientale and parts of Kivu) and which is substantially the only identifiable organization left of the original MNC; and the PSA. Other parties either represent smaller tribal groups, are largely the feeble instruments of individuals, or are small but potentially powerful extremists; these include the Puna, Unimo, Reko, Cerka and Kapwasa's nascent party in Katanga.

6. The Traditional Chiefs Organization (TCO) in the Senate is of particular interest. It is the only known political organization which cuts across political lines, and the only one which forms a nucleus for political discussion and decision by important tribal leaders as such. It is assumed that tribalism will be an important if not decisive factor in Congo politics for the foreseeable future.

7. In our thinking, the important facts are whether individuals or groups are pro-West, pro-Bloc or "neutralist"; whether "moderate" or "radical." In many cases, it is easy to identify individuals or groups within these categories. But in Congolese politics, individuals and groups do not nucleate within these categories, i.e., the pro-Bloc groups do not necessarily band together because they are pro-Bloc. Issues are usually quite local, frequently evanescent and very often highly personal; leftists and moderates will band together to undercut an individual too long in office, or to defeat a measure which threatens their

official perquisites. Issues are rarely ideological or philosophical, although they may sometimes assume such as protective coloration. This factor makes our choice(s) difficult from an organizational standpoint. We can select a series of groups who, by our logic, should combine themselves into a potent organization; yet such an organization will inexplicably (to us) shatter itself over an inconsequential issue.

8. The Abako Party for the foreseeable future, will continue to be moderate and pro-West and federalist. It has no potential to become a national party. It is the natural ally of other moderate, tribally-based parties which also favor the continuation of tribal autonomy through fairly to very loose federation within the Congo. Its hold over the significant Bakongo tribal area is unlikely to be challenged. The major bar to its enduring alliance with other tribal parties is the question of spoils of office and regional/national sharing of revenues. Its leaders hold and will continue to hold an important share in the Central Government cabinet and other appointive offices. A major issue is the question of the jurisdiction over Leopoldville city, traditionally Bakongo territory, and with great voting power (population approaching 1,000,000). A secondary issue is Central Government support of the Union of Angolan Peoples (UPA), which support is contrary to the Abako's unrealistic ambition to control the Bakongo tribes of Angola and both Congos and in come mystical fashion to resurrect the old Kongo Empire. The ABAKO probably maintains greater unity between provincial and national leaders than do other parties, primarily because of the location of Leopoldville. However, it can hardly be described as a monolith.

9. The Conakat Party, consisting of the non-Baluba forces of Katanga (plus Kasongo-Niembo' Balubas), is dominated by Lunda and Bayeke leaders. Its virtual exclusion of Balubas is based on the traditional hostility toward the Baluba fostered by Baluba superiority in adapting to Katanga's industrial society. The Conakat has been supported heavily by UMHK and conservative Belgian industrial and intellectual circles, and its views generally favor the continuation of a Belgian presence and of free enterprise; politically, it favors maximum decentralization of central government and a minimal sharing of provincial revenues. The degree to which it still enjoys Belgian support is still undertermined; it is likely to return to secessionism if the final Congolese constitution does not permit a large degree of provincial autonomy or if ANC units in Katanga continue to act in an undisciplined fashion.

10. The Balubakat party is traditionally opposed to the Conakat for tribal reasons, and has in the past been its competitor for power in Katanga. Since the end of Katanga's secession, a large element of the Balubakat has favored a rapprochement with the Conakat and the formation of a United Front in central government parliament, and the

reunification of North and South Katanga. Some elements of the Balubakat, particularly those members now holding official positions in the North Katanga Government, oppose such reunification.

11. There are strong reasons why the United Front should hold together; thereby, they could represent in the central government the largest and richest province, and, with the resources at their disposal, could exercise a decisive influence in national politics. Further, such a United Front would have a natural affinity with the Abako party which has substantially the same political aims, particularly regarding provincial autonomy. The aims of the Baluba/Kasai group should also be substantially similar. So there is the possibility of an alliance of the major parties of the entire southern half of the Congo as a conservative, Western-oriented, coalition representing the majority of the Congolese population, a majority which embodies the highest percentage of skills, and an overwhelming percentage of its wealth. While such a coalition would probably pursue acceptable policies, it would also risk bringing about a sharp North-South cleavage. The extremists of the PSA, MNC/L and Cerea would oppose it by all means, probably including violence. The Mongo/Bangala groups would oppose it as they would be relinquishing the important positions they now occupy, and as—coming from a poor province—they would favor more rather than less central government control of the provinces and their revenues. Similarly, the moderates of Orientale and Kivu would oppose such a coalition as it would seriously reduce their voices in the parliament. Nevertheless, that serious opposition to a Conakat/Balubakat/Baluba–Kasai/Abako coalition would arise should not be over-stressed; there will be serious opposition to any force which threatens to become predominant in Congo politics, and means can always be found to ameliorate the sharpness of such opposition. It appears to us that the emergence of such a coalition is the most probable political development, given the "geopolitical" forces in play.

12. As for the other political groups in the Congo today, it is evident that that formerly strong MNC/L, as well as the PSA, are deeply, perhaps irretrievably split between their moderate and extremist wings; further, that there seems to be less and less identity between party stalwarts at the provincial and national levels. Cerea, if it still exists in fact, is similarly split (Kashamura/Weregemere), and the remaining parties in parliament can hardly be said to exist as such. There is the possibility, of course, that these disparate elements could bury their differences for the immediate, tactical purpose of surviving in the face of a coalescence of the southern tier forces described above. Given the history of efforts elsewhere to form "united fronts" between right and left (or moderate and extremist), and given the ever-presence of Soviet assistance to the extremists, we believe that a "united front" of the

northern tier should be discouraged, and attempts be made to prevent its formation or, if formed, to fragment it, on the grounds that it is likely to fall under radical influence.

13. Assuming that the above analysis has at least a shred of validity, there are several courses of action available:

A. Continued support of the present ruling group. We are committed to do this and have been given specific authority therefor, so some effort will have to be made in this direction. The group, however, has the shortcomings cited in Dir 36265, and it is doubtful if they could withstand the forces of a southern tier coalition.

B. Observe the trend toward the formation of a southern tier coalition with the possibility of supporting it (and fragmenting the opposition) at some future point in time.

C. Re-explore the tribal chiefs approach. Despite the Traditional Chiefs Organization's very poor showing to date, one cannot help but feel that the Congo is going to be tribally-based for some time to come, and that a viable political organization must take this into account and channel it into productive channels.

D. Engage in tactical political action on an ad hoc basis, while reinforcing the ANC's reliability and capabilities through troop indoctrination programs with the aim of placing the ANC in a totally decisive position in internal affairs, at least to the extent that if our interest requires their intervention in political affairs, we may be assured that such intervention will be effective.

E. Approach Congolese political organizational problems on a clandestine basis ([Identity 1]), attempting to build "cells" or "control groups" in the major political entities.

14. Evidently, it is theoretically possible to combine more than one of the above alternatives into a combined approach to the problem. And, it need hardly be said, we must exercise a reasonable economy of effort, consistent with our basic objective to deny the Congo to the Bloc.

15. Lastly, we have addressed ourselves alone largely to the political situation of the immediate post-independence period during which the first generation of politicians continue to dominate—leaders largely elected in 1960. We must be diligent in identifying and developing appropriate relations with the men of the second generation as they emerge.

146. Telegram From the Station in the Congo to the Central Intelligence Agency[1]

Leopoldville, June 13, 1963.

7194 (In 58893). Ref A. Dir 36205;[2] B. Dir 39113.[3]

1. Have discussed refs with [Gullion] and upshot is view that [Identity 1], despite his well-known shortcomings has repeat has succeeded in thwarting parliament by his tactic of taking them by turns into the government, and is probably the best man for the job available in this country. [Gullion] reluctant to contemplate period of rule by reinforced army a la Rhee.[4] Recent election of Grenfell in Stanleyville is evidence of extremist potential, thus believe would be mistake sit back and let nature take its course. This was in fact the policy of the GOC with respect to the election for presidency of Haut Congo Province. Thus conclude that Station should make a significant financial contribution to [Identity 1] current effort to establish a new national party based on a relatively moderate African national platform broadly responsive to ODYOKE interests, with roots in all provinces.

2. [*2½ lines not declassified*]

3. However, we have reservations concerning the extent to which the Belgians will be willing to make the necessary concessions to the letter of African nationalism, particularly as the Belgians most directly concerned with covert political operations are likely to be of the Societe Generale stamp.

4. Re the [*less than 1 line not declassified*], recent evidence indicates that [Identity 1] is again drawing close to them, and we believe it would be a mistake to withdraw our support at this juncture, if, in the course of the actual party congress, other moderate figures emerge to take charge of the key posts, we can still exercise the option of withdrawing our support, yielding to Belgian influence, [*less than 1 line not declassified*].

5. As reported in [*less than 1 line not declassified*][5] [Identity1] has apparently decided to launch an entirely new party, the name of which (Mouvement Populaire Congolais) he reportedly decided on himself. His plan is said to be to make political soundings in all the provinces,

---

[1] Source: Central Intelligence Agency Files, Job 78–00435R, DDO/ISS Files, Box 2, Folder 2, [*cryptonym not declassified*] Operations. Secret; Rybat; [*cryptonym not declassified*]; Priority. Received at 0810Z.

[2] Not found.

[3] Not found.

[4] Syngman Rhee of South Korea.

[5] Not found.

hold a National Party Congress in the course of the next few weeks, and then arrange for a series of friendly parties to fuse with his party. [Identity 2] and [Identity 1] claim that parties which are expected to merge with the MPC are the PDC (Anany) (also Kanany): the Parti de Reconstruction Nationale (Manzikala): Cerea (Miruho and Rudahindwa). Encouraging conversations have reportedly been held with Interior Minister Maboti and Emile Zola. [Identity 3] states that Bolikango represents a force in Lisala which cannot be ignored. Nyembo and Yav are said to be in favor of the [Identity 1] idea. [Identity 1] reportedly intends the MPC to have a revolutionary platform designed to preempt the nationalist area now claimed by the MNC/L.

6. To date we have not discussed with [Identity 1] the plans ascribed to him, and we would as a first and precautionary step, do so promptly upon receipt of a favorable response from HQS to this cable. To date we can only report that [Identity 1] recently demonstrated an active and interested awareness of our plan to bring a political party adviser to Leopoldville on 17 June.

7. If HQS agrees, we would stress the following points in our talks with [Identity 1] on this subject:

A. The importance of establishing party units at the local level in all districts of the Congo, and in all significant institutions in the urban areas, such as the trade unions, student organizations, chambers of commerce, together with a special propaganda campaign directed at the army. A dialogue should also be established with the church organizations.

B. An effective press and publicity section should be organized at once.

C. A provisional National Party Committee should be appointed by [Identity 1], including the designation of a treasurer through whom all receipts and disbursements must pass.

C. A forceful political and economic program should be drawn up, including plans for a public works program and a program for constitutional reform permitting the establishment of a strong executive with an assured term of four years.

D. A fund-raising campaign should be initiated, canvassing business and industry, and collecting dues from party members, [*1 line not declassified*] and other well-wishers.

E. Set up a membership committee to keep out extremist elements who might try to take over the party later on.

F. Plan for the participation of the ANC in supervision of the polling places to ensure honest outcome.

G. Study ways of limiting the number of parties which may compete in the national elections (but not set up a one-party system), perhaps by requiring a certain number of signatures from each province.

H. An independent auditor should be appointed to control mismanagement of funds.

8. Station would appreciate early reaction to above proposal, since local politicoes already beginning to look ahead actively toward elections, and are beginning to press for financial aid; e.g. Miruho, Anekonzapa, [Identity 3] and [Identity 2] and we would like to exercise this leverage to force such applicants to turn to the MPC for their money. This policy naturally would not preclude our disbursing small amounts for purely informational purposes.

9. Station not proposing detailed budget at this time, but if authorized would draw up breakdown by categories of activity, and also a breakdown on installment plan, to retain control.

10. [Identity 3] now pressing for [*amount not declassified*] to enable Engulu to visit all provincial presidents to line up support for MPC. [Identity 3] claims Engulu best man for this job view his role in recent provincial presidents conference in Coquilhatville.

---

147. Paper Prepared in the Central Intelligence Agency

Washington, June 20, 1963.

[Source: National Security Files, Special Group Minutes—1963. Secret; Eyes Only. *1 page not declassified*].

---

148. Editorial Note

In telegram 7612 from Leopoldville to the Central Intelligence Agency, July 24, 1963, the Chief of Station reported that he had had a 2-hour talk with [*text not declassified*] on July 22 which was their frankest session to date. [*text not declassified*] touched on a number of points, which taken together suggested the [*text not declassified*] doubted they could win free elections, were uncertain as to the extent to which CIA would support them against mounting opposition, and were considering running Justin Bomboko for prime minister or the equivalent office next year. [*text not declassified*] did not specify just how unfree elections might have to be to accomplish a [*text not declassified*] victory. He cited a cabinet meeting the previous week during Prime Minister Adoula's vacation at which criticism of Adoula was long and loud. In concluding the telegram, the Chief of Station warned that the Department of State and CIA might well be faced in the next few months with the serious question of whether to support a moderate [*text not declassified*] solution to the Congo's political problems in preference to either an unregenerate conservative Belgian bloc or a Soviet-supported extremist bloc. (Central Intelligence Agency Files, Job 78–00435R, DDO/ISS Files, Box 2, Folder 3, [*cryptonym not declassified*] Operations)

---

149. Dispatch From the Station in the Congo to the Central Intelligence Agency[1]

[*dispatch number not declassified*] Leopoldville, August 2, 1963.

SUBJECT

[*cryptonym not declassified*] Letter for July

1. This is my first monthly letter since assuming charge of the Leopoldville Station from [former COS] on 1 June 1963. These first two months have been characterized by a lull in the normally crisis-ridden Congo political scene. In fact, people are beginning to ask themselves whether Prime Minister Adoula is not more astute than they had supposed, since, despite his much talked-about indecisiveness, his lack of skill in meeting the electorate, and his seeming pedestrian gait in general, he has, as he slyly points out himself, remained in office, he has weathered the parliamentary storms, and he has even increased his international stature on the African scene, mainly by his handling of the Angolan problem.

2. Operationally, the period has been one of reassessment of goals in the light of the end of the Katanga secession. Whatever the final decision may turn out to be on the extent to which we are to "give the country back to the Belgians", the Station is satisfied that KUBARK

---

[1] Source: Central Intelligence Agency Files, Job 82–00450R, DDO/AF–AF/DIV Historical Files, Box 6, Folder 6, Leopoldville, 3 Feb 54–Dec 65, [*cryptonym not declassified*]. Secret; Rybat; [*cryptonym not declassified*].

must as a minimum continue to give strong support to the Army and to the Security Services, as the best guarantee against a takeover either by the Communists or by the more unreconstructed Belgian conservatives, neither of which eventuality would be in the interest of ODYOKE.

[Omitted here is unrelated information.]

[COS]

150. Telegram From the Station in the Congo to the Central Intelligence Agency[1]

Leopoldville, September 30, 1963, 1430Z.

8368 (In 29739). Ref Leop 8359 (In 29379).[2]

1. [COS] had two hour long, relaxed meet with [Mobutu] afternoon 29 Sept at his house [*less than 1 line not declassified*], with no bystanders, relatives etc in evidence. Ref describes subjects mood on eve of Kasavubu decision to close parliament. Although he expressed confidence in his officers and men, he did express feeling opposition would be redoubling efforts to subvert them, and suggested KUBARK should be prepared support sizeable counter-action program within army. As we know from [*cryptonym not declassified*] reports, some officers already infected, and unknown author of leaflet mentioned ref clearly working hard to cause mutiny in army.

[Omitted here is further discussion of Mobutu.]

[1] Source: Central Intelligence Agency Files, [*text not declassified*], Mobutu, Joseph Desire, Vol. II. Secret; Rybat; [*cryptonym not declassified*]. No time of receipt appears on the message.

[2] Re [*cryptonym not declassified*] [COS] telcon with [*cryptonym not declassified*] [Mobutu]. [Footnote in the original.] This CIA telegram has not been found.

151. Editorial Note

On October 1, 1963, representatives of the Department of State and the Central Intelligence Agency met to discuss issues involving Ghana and the Congo. Among those attending were G. McMurtrie Godley, Director of the Department of State Office of Central African Affairs; Glenn Fields, Chief of the Africa Division in CIA's Directorate of Plans; and [*name not declassified*] of CIA's Africa Division. According to a memorandum of the meeting prepared on October 3 by Alfred Wellborn of the Bureau of Intelligence and Research, Godley asked [*name not declassified*] how President's Kasavubu's closure of the Congolese Parliament affected the Agency's political action program in the Congo. "Mr. [*name not declassified*] observed that the Agency had been pursuing the policy of bolstering the [*text not declassified*] and of endeavoring to develop an effective political organization to support Prime Minister Adoula. It had found that the Congolese would not follow the Agency's suggestions on how to go about building a political organization but were handling matters their own way and were apparently not doing badly. For the moment the funds authorized by the Special Group for political action were sufficient. If there were to be elections later on more might be required." [*name not declassified*] also noted that the Agency had been worrying that Belgian funds—both governmental and private—were going to support Anany and other more conservative Congolese and that U.S. and Belgian efforts might be cancelling each other to a certain extent, but a recent development was expected to provided adequate safeguards against that. (Department of State Files, INR/IL Historical Files, AF Meetings, 1963)

In an October 4 memorandum, Fields reported on the covert political action program in the Congo to Deputy Director for Plans Richard Helms. Special emphasis, Fields noted, had been placed "on assisting the Adoula group in the formation of a national party mechanism, initially to enable them to succeed in the upcoming national elections." Ancillary expenses in support of the Adoula group included the "funding of General Mobutu as Army Chief of Staff to help him to insure the loyalty of vital units of the CNA." Fields told Helms that he had reviewed the status and direction of the program with the Department of State on October 1. "They stated they were in full accord with our activities, asked if we needed further authority, and said we were on the right track." Fields also advised Helms that it was "probable we will hit a financial snag sometime after 1 January. National elections will be held and undoubtedly there will be requests both from the Department and the Congolese for intensive covert action support beyond funds presently programmed." (Central Intelligence Agency Files, Job 78–00435R, DDO/ISS Files, Box 2, Folder 6, [*cryptonym not declassified*] Operations)

152. Telegram From the Station in the Congo to the Central Intelligence Agency[1]

Leopoldville, October 16, 1963.

8606 (In 41258). 1. [Identity 1] at 1800 meet 16 Oct said [COS] should get advance authority for money in case of emergency,[2] but despite [COS] best efforts he refused provide any details what sort of emergency might be in offing. [COS] finally said it plain as nose on face that strong measures being readied to thwart extremists, and we preferred know before rather than after steps are taken, so we can better support GOC in international forum. [Identity 1] remained tight-lipped. [COS] impression is that thoroughgoing reshuffle of GOC plus perhaps state of exception for Leop is planned, but not until [Identity 2] returns. FYI, [Gullion] was seeing [Identity 3] concurrently with above meet, and he made out no better than did [COS]

2. One possible clue to mystery is [Identity 1] remark army is disgruntled at [Identity 2] statements designed support retention UN troops in Congo that ANC still unable maintain internal order, for example during upcoming elections. [Identity 1] said ANC accepted argument about possibility invasion by Portuguese or other foreign power, but resented aspersion on its ability within Congo. Still, [Identity 1] did say decision would await [Identity 2] return.

3. Will keep checking. Looks like busy weekend.

---

[1] Source: Central Intelligence Agency Files, Job 78–00435R, DDO/ISS Files, Box 2, Folder 6, [*cryptonym not declassified*] Operations. Secret; Rybat; [*cryptonym not declassified*]; Priority. Received at 1545Z.

[2] During the week of October 14, a substantial number of ANC troops mutinied at the Luluabourg garrison, the teachers' union went on strike, and major union leaders called for the replacement of the current government by a politically neutral government pending the next year's elections.

153. Editorial Note

In telegram 76839 to Leopoldville, October 18, 1963, the Central Intelligence Agency stated that it would appreciate as soon as possible the suggestions of the Chief of Station and Ambassador Gullion regarding the nature of future U.S. support should Cyrille Adoula be disavowed by the [*text not declassified*] group in the immediate future, or should he, in a realignment of the group, receive a position inferior to the one he held now. The Chief of Station and the Ambassador were to include in their consideration such factors as the ascendancy of Belgian political influence, and also extremist nationalist activity. (Central Intelligence Agency Files, Job 78–00435R, DDO/ISS Files, Box 2, Folder 6, [*cryptonym not declassified*] Operations)

In telegram 8639 to CIA, October 19, the Chief of Station and the Ambassador responded that they thought Adoula would pull through again this time, but agreed that they should not be caught without a contingency policy in case he were demoted or removed completely. In case of the latter, their best estimate was that Adoula would be replaced initially at least by a basically moderate leader whose cabinet would reflect roughly the same political spectrum as was now running the country. Whether Adoula survived or not, they recommended that the United States continue to keep a strong hand in the Congolese political picture—partly as a brake on the more baneful aspects of Belgian commercial policy, and partly because creation of a national moderate political party (which the United States was covertly supporting) would make a valuable contribution to future political stability in the Congo. (Ibid.)

---

154. Telegram From the Station in the Congo to the Central Intelligence Agency[1]

Leopoldville, November 1, 1963.

8805 (In 52438). Ref Leop 8780, para 2 (In 50695).[2]

1. [COS] finally contacted [Identity 1] by phone 30 Oct, and he invited [COS] meet him his home at Para Camp 1 Nov 1000. Had twenty minutes alone with [Identity 1] before [Mobutu] and [Identity 2] arrived. [Identity 3] finally arrived at 1215 for last half hour of meet.

2. With [Identity 1] alone, [COS] made point ODYOKE supports him, and does not support anyones efforts to overthrow him by force. [Identity 1] said he understood our attitude on trade unions, although his colleagues do not, said he knows ODYOKE does not support trade unions in Congo, but that such support is private. [COS] then said, in accord [Gullion] instructions, our delay last weekend due to need an-

---

[1] Source: Central Intelligence Agency Files, Job 78–00435R, DDO/ISS Files, Box 2, Folder 7, [*cryptonym not declassified*] Operations. Secret; Rybat; [*cryptonym not declassified*]; Priority. Received at 1604Z.

[2] Not found.

swer wash queries whether locus of power had shifted.[3] Re arrest trade union leaders, assured [Identity 1] our concern was not with right of GOC to arrest people who advocate violent overthrow of government, but whether this move was tactically wise, and in any case pointed out need for consultation before hand view international ramifications.

3. Main substantive point this meet was inadequacy our proposed contribution to [*cryptonym not declassified*] party effort. [Identity 1] left these complaints to his colleagues who carried on manfully.[4]

[Omitted here is further discussion of the meeting.]

---

[3] On October 21, Kasavubu signed a decree putting into effect a "state of exception" imposing martial law in Leopoldville and establishing a ministerial committee of three (Anany, Maboti, and Bomboko) to administer it. Telegram 8709 from Leopoldville to CIA, October 25, reported that Ambassador Gullion was deeply concerned at the consequences of the committee's arrest of four Congo labor leaders who had called for a general strike, apparently without consulting Adoula. The Ambassador was trying to bring home the folly of this decision, and specifically requested a delay in funding for the [*text not declassified*] political party. (Central Intelligence Agency Files, Job 78–00435R, DDO/ISS Files, Box 2, Folder 7, [*cryptonym not declassified*] Operations) However, in telegram 78634 to Leopoldville, October 28, the CIA stated that in view of the tense situation in Leopoldville, the Department of State had now asked that the funds withheld be passed at the earliest opportunity. (Ibid.)

[4] Telegram 8828 from Leopoldville to CIA, November 4, reported that the Ambassador had meet with the [*text not declassified*] group on November 2 and thought the meeting had at least partially allayed the [*text not declassified*] fears that they were being ditched. Gullion believed CIA should increase its contribution to the party. (Ibid.) For Gullion's report to Washington on his and Godley's meetings with the [*text not declassified*] leaders, see *Foreign Relations*, 1961–1963, volume XX, Congo Crisis, Document 433.

---

155. Memorandum From the Chief of the Africa Division, Directorate of Plans, Central Intelligence Agency (Fields) to the Deputy Director for Plans, Central Intelligence Agency (Helms)[1]

Washington, undated.

SUBJECT

Project [*cryptonym not declassified*]

1. Pursuant to policy guidance from the Special Group, the [*cryptonym not declassified*] program has been operative since November

---

[1] Source: Central Intelligence Agency Files, Job 78–00435R, DDO/ISS Files, Box 2, Folder 7, [*cryptonym not declassified*] Operations. Secret.

1961. There was an initial Special Group authorization for [*dollar amount not declassified*]. A progress and status report made in April 1963 requested authority to continue certain covert actions at a cost of [*dollar amount not declassified*] for FY 1964. This authority was approved by the Special Group.

2. The [*cryptonym not declassified*] program has been, in effect, the covert action program to maintain and support the Adoula government in the Congo in implementation of U.S. policy directives. The judicious use of covertly provided funds has kept opposition groups off-balance and uncoordinated to the extent that the incumbent moderate government has survived. This government is now able to focus for the first time on the establishment of a national political party initially to provide an organizational base for the projected national elections next spring. The Station has been urging the incumbent government for sometime to systematize their political activities.

3. The matter at issue is the extent of covert support to the formation of this national political party. The Leopoldville Station has submitted a budget of [*dollar amount not declassified*] for this purpose. This request exceeds the current FY 1964 (within ceiling) operational program funds ear-marked for [*cryptonym not declassified*] activities by [*dollar amount not declassified*]. In anticipation of exceptional demands, [*dollar amount not declassified*] was requested over ceiling for [*cryptonym not declassified*] in the FY 1964 Africa Division Operational Program and on 4 October 1963 a memorandum was addressed to the DDP from Chief, Africa Division alerting him to the possibility of such a request for additional funds.[2]

4. The request for a budget of [*dollar amount not declassified*] was arrived at after exhaustive discussions with responsible members of the Adoula government and reflects a detailed analysis of budget proposals. The Ambassador has participated in these discussions and urges favorable consideration of this budget as a major factor in providing continued support and confidence of the Adoula or [*less than 1 line not declassified*]. The Chief of the Office of Central African Affairs, Mr. G. M. Godley, and the Chief of the responsible African Branch also participated in these discussions in Leopoldville.

Glenn D. Fields
Chief, Africa Division

[2] See Document 151.

156. Telegram From the Station in the Congo to the Central Intelligence Agency[1]

Leopoldville, November 6, 1963.

8842 (In 55582). Ref Leop 8828 (In 53889);[2] Leop 8841 (In 55524).[3]

1. As noted in [Embassy] traffic cited refs, [Identity 1] has emerged from the events of last two weeks, despite his well known shortcomings, as the one figure who by his relative moderation and patience is able to set a limit to impulses of his colleagues in direction ruthless authoritarian regime. Believe [*cryptonym not declassified*], despite their real fear of revolutionary potential of unions, have recognized need consider international ramifications, and particularly effect on PBPRIME public opinion of methods they use. Thus we now again, as after so many previous crises, emerge with only one logical contender, and [*cryptonym not declassified*] have been taught that there is some limit to ODYOKE patience.

2. However, it is clear that Station relations with [*cryptonym not declassified*] would have been strained even without impact of [Embassy] reaction to recent actions of triumvirate in view of what they consider inadequacy our contribution to their political party effort.

[Omitted here is discussion of funding.]

---

[1] Source: Central Intelligence Agency Files, Job 78–00435R, DDO/ISS Files, Box 1, Folder 2, [*cryptonym not declassified*] Support. Secret; Rybat; [*cryptonym not declassified*]. Received at 1305Z.

[2] [*cryptonym not declassified*] [Ambassador Gullion] indicated his belief that KUBARK [*less than 1 line not declassified*] should increase its contribution to [*cryptonym not declassified*]. [Footnote in the original.] Regarding this telegram, see footnote 4 to Document 154.

[3] Telegram 8841 from Leopoldville to CIA, November 6, stated that the Station believed that what had chiefly upset the [*text not declassified*] was the small size of the proposed electoral contributions compared to their hopes, in spite of the fact that they previously had been warned of the U.S. intention to introduce economies and stricter accounting. (Central Intelligence Agency Files, Job 78–00435R, DDO/ISS Files, Box 2, Folder 7, [*cryptonym not declassified*] Operations)

157. Telegram From the Central Intelligence Agency to the Station in the Congo[1]

Washington, December 9, 1963, 1402Z.

Dir 87720. Ref Leop 9211 (In 7478[?]).[2]

1. [former COS] arriving Sabena flt 301 2005 local time 9 Dec. Hope Station can get lodging.[3]

2. ODACID has asked [former COS] in contact [Mobutu] to:

A. Reassure [Mobutu] on continuity ODYOKE policy.
B. Determine attitudes towards ANC retraining, not about equipment.
C. Urge him cooperate with [UN] forces in action against gendarmes, formation joint patrols, and of course in phase out.
D. Urge him cooperate with [*cryptonym not declassified*].
E. Point out necessity avoid appearance of joint ODYOKE in any training [*less than 1 line not declassified*] activity.

3. In any contacts with [*cryptonym not declassified*] team ODACID has requested [former COS] determine their attitude toward [Identity 1] and terms and possibility his return Congo, and also position and role which [Identity 2] currently plays within the [*cryptonym not declassified*].

4. Suggest that [COS] after discussion with [former COS] might wish arrange reception for [*cryptonym not declassified*] group as appropriate opportunity explore above request and permit [former COS] pay respects while avoiding involvement in individual visits to each [*cryptonym not declassified*]. [former COS] will enlarge on above.[4]

End of message.

---

[1] Source: Central Intelligence Agency Files, Job 78–00435R, DDO/ISS Files, Box 2, Folder 7, [*cryptonym not declassified*] Operations. Secret; [*cryptonym not declassified*]; Immediate. Drafted by [*name not declassified*], coordinated with [*text not declassified*], authenticated by [*text not declassified*], and released by Fields [*text not declassified*].

[2] Not found.

[3] CIA telegram 87023 to Leopoldville, December 5, informed the Station that at the urging of the Department of State, the Agency had agreed to have the former Chief of Station stop over in Leopoldville en route to Salisbury and other points in Africa in order to contact Mobutu and enlist his cooperation in pushing the ANC retraining program. (Central Intelligence Agency Files, Job 78–00435R, DDO/ISS Files, Box 2, Folder 7, [*cryptonym not declassified*] Operations)

[4] No record of the former Chief of Station's conversations in Leopoldville has been found.

158. Memorandum From the Joint Chiefs of Staff to Secretary of Defense McNamara[1]

JCSM–63–64 Washington, January 30, 1964.

SUBJECT

Retraining of the Congolese National Army (C)

1. Reference is made to a memorandum by the Assistant Secretary of Defense (ISA), I–17477/63, dated 11 January 1964, subject as above,[2] which requested the views of the Joint Chiefs of Staff "concerning modification of the Military Assistance Program including training which the United States could undertake to assist the Congolese National Army in meeting the possible unstable situation which may exist in a relatively short period of time following the departure of the UN Force in June 1964." The memorandum also informed the Joint Chiefs of Staff that "it is anticipated that the Department of State will request the Department of Defense to take on a portion of the operational training of the Congolese Armed Forces."

2. Attached as the Appendix[3] is a plan to provide individual and unit training for selected units in the Leopoldville and Elisabethville areas, if required. The proposed plan is contingent upon a political decision requiring its implementation. It is proposed to finance the plan within the FY 1964–1965 Military Assistance Program dollar ceilings programmed for the Congo. However, the delivery of some programmed matériel would have to be deferred. If the plan is to be initiated in the Congo by 1 May 1964, the political decision should be made by 1 March 1964. CINCSTRIKE/USCINCMEAFSA will recommend to the Office of the Director of Military Assistance, OASD(ISA), priorities for the deferral of matériel, if this plan is approved for implementation.

3. The Joint Chiefs of Staff consider that, given a political requirement to preserve a pro-Western regime in the Congo (Leopoldville), the retraining of the Congolese National Army (ANC) into a disciplined force responsive to legitimate authority and loyal to the established government continues to be an urgent military task. However, the retraining effort is only one approach to the problem of instability in the Congo (Leopoldville) and is related to US attempts to achieve objectives in the economic and political spheres. Training, by itself, will not insure that the pro-Western Congolese will remain in power. The

[1] Source: Johnson Library, National Security File, Country File, Congo, Vol. I, 11/63–6/64. Secret.

[2] Not printed.

[3] Attached but not printed.

military effort can only be an instrument to aid in the achievement of economic and political goals. This training effort should in no way imply that the United States will commit its forces to military or paramilitary operations in the maintenance of internal security in the country. Further, the Joint Chiefs of Staff view with concern the possibilities that action on the part of the United States to undertake to increase its role in retraining of the ANC might prove counterproductive for reasons enumerated below. They therefore offer the following additional views:

a. The task of retraining should be undertaken by the Belgians and Italians on the basis of policy and planning to date. Diplomatic and political efforts at high level should be intensified by the United States to persuade the Belgians and Italians to initiate, prior to 1 March 1964, an effective retraining program.

b. While the United States should avoid identification with the Israeli retraining program in the Congo (Leopoldville), discreet efforts should be undertaken to contribute to the effectiveness of the Israeli program, as may be appropriate.

c. The UN Secretary General (UNSYG) should be urged to require the present UN Forces in the Congo (UNOC) to reduce lawless activities in coordination with and in anticipation of the turnover of responsibility for internal security to the ANC and, in the meantime, to contribute in any way feasible to the increased effectiveness of the ANC.

d. The United States should not itself undertake direct operational training of the ANC pending:

(1) Further evidence, including a determination at the appropriate political level, that it is demanded by US national interests.
(2) Approval by the appropriate Congolese authorities of training programs at small unit levels as recommended by the United States.
(3) Mutually acceptable coordination with the appropriate Belgian authorities.
(4) Consideration of its impact on other African nations.
(5) Consideration of the possibility that direct participation by the United States might contribute to further internal instability, if exploited sufficiently by communist and other political elements in opposition to the Congolese Government.

e. In the event political considerations require the United States to undertake a portion of the operational training, the United States should offer to train, in priority, a battalion plus supporting units in the Leopoldville area and two battalions plus supporting units in the Elisabethville (Katanga) area, utilizing small Mobile Training Teams (MTTs) plus command and staff personnel to control and coordinate the entire US effort. MTTs would be phased in on a schedule designed to keep the number of US personnel in the country at a minimum.

f. The commitment of these training teams might prove insufficient to maintain a pro-Western regime in power in the light of the history of the Congo (Leopoldville) and the factors now contributing to instability.

4. The commitment of US operational forces as distinct from training forces is beyond the scope of this paper and has not been considered in the formulation of the attached retraining plan.

For the Joint Chiefs of Staff:

Curtis E. LeMay[4]
Acting Chairman
Joint Chiefs of Staff

[4] Printed from a copy that bears this typed signature.

---

159. Telegram From the Department of State to the Embassy in Belgium[1]

Washington, February 10, 1964, 7:51 p.m.

1037. Please deliver following letter from Secretary to Spaak:

Begin verbatim text.

My dear Mr. Minister:

I am increasingly concerned about the prospect of widespread chaos in the Congo which is likely to face us a few months from now when the UN Force must leave. Even as matters now stand, it can hardly be said that the Central Government exercises effective control much beyond the major population centers. The recent insurgency in Kwilu Province,[2] organized by a Congolese trained in Communist China, is I fear but a sample of what we may have to confront.

I know Ambassador MacArthur has spoken to you about this matter several times and I know that I do not need to rehearse the argu-

[1] Source: National Archives, RG 59, Central Files 1964–66, POL THE CONGO. Confidential; Immediate. Drafted by Buffum; cleared by Cleveland, EUR/WE Deputy Director Hugh G. Appling, AFC Deputy Director Alan W. Ford, Harriman, and Tyler; and approved by Secretary Rusk. Repeated to USUN and Leopoldville.

[2] On January 21, Congolese President Joseph Kasavubu declared a state of emergency in Kwilu Province, where rebellious tribesmen had seized control of one-third of the territory.

ment that fundamental cause of instability in the Congo is the lack of a trained and disciplined army. I am mindful of the efforts that you have personally been making to expedite Belgian participation in the re-training efforts and I am aware of many of the difficulties that you have faced in getting officers to the Congo. However, the prospect of a debacle in the Congo putting us back to the days of 1960 is terrible to contemplate.

From where I sit, trying to look at our various responsibilities for free world defense in several parts of the globe, I am impressed both with the potential dangers of communist breakthrough in the Congo and with the special responsibility which Belgium, because of its historical affiliation with the Congo, has to shore up that particular front. With your unique knowledge of and vast investment in the Congo, in manpower, in industry, and in relevant experience, this particular part of the free world defense effort should rest primarily, I believe, with your Government. I think it would not be too much to say that this is the most important security task which Belgium can assume in the common interest.

We share with you a vital interest in stability in the Congo and we are prepared to consider any further step you may think useful for us to take to that end.

For one reason or another, in the three and one-half difficult years since Congolese independence, the ANC has not become a force capable of supporting an effective government and dealing with an internal security problem of great scope and complexity. Retraining the ANC for this task will require, in our best judgement, a substantial increase in your training program in the immediate future. In particular, we would hope to see a substantial number of Belgian officers placed in forward units at least down to the battalion level. I therefore hope you will find it possible to redouble your efforts and intensify the good work you are already doing.[3] *End verbatim text.*

Rusk

---

[3] In telegram 1182 from Brussels, February 15, Ambassador MacArthur reported that Foreign Minister Spaak told him that the Belgian Cabinet had agreed to respond affirmatively to a Congolese request that 100 Belgian officers be sent urgently to the Congo. Spaak wanted to assure the Secretary that Belgium was keenly aware of its responsibilities and would do everything it could to speed up effective ANC training. (National Archives, RG 59, Central Files 1964–66, POL 23–9 THE CONGO)

160. Memorandum From Secretary of State Rusk to President Johnson[1]

Washington, February 15, 1964.

SUBJECT

Training of the Congolese Army (ANC)

There will be a serious security situation in the Congo following the withdrawal of United Nations forces at the end of June 1964, given the size of the country and existence of a variety of actual and potential insurgencies and secessions. The current insurgency in Kwilu province, led by a Congolese long associated with both the Soviets and Chinese, underscores the gravity of the problem. The poorly trained and ill-disciplined Congolese army (ANC) is incapable of coping with that problem and is often a source of disorder itself.

The UN forces in the Congo are greatly reduced in number but still contribute substantially to stability in the two critical urban areas, Leopoldville and Elisabethville. Retention of the UN forces beyond July 1 does not appear feasible since it would require a special session of the General Assembly which would raise the difficult problems of Chinese representation and of applying Article 19 to the USSR. Moreover, the Secretary General and a substantial number of delegations would oppose a continuation of UNOC. In any event, an extension of UNOC would not solve the basic problems because the UN is not engaged in dealing with present insurgency in Kwilu province and is not engaged in training the ANC.

The training problem therefore has to be faced now. While we will continue to look to Belgium to assume primary responsibility for ANC training, we have (with Belgian concurrence) also encouraged other countries to participate. In addition to Belgian plans for training the ANC, Israel and Italy have also undertaken to provide some training to paracommando units and the air force. However, the training programs of these three countries have barely begun. We are doing everything possible to encourage them to accelerate their programs and, in particular, we are encouraging the Belgians to expand their program to include operational unit training and placement of Belgian officers in line units. However, it now seems unlikely that training programs of

[1] Source: National Archives, RG 59, Central Files 1964–66, DEF 1-1 THE CONGO. Confidential. Drafted by Ford on February 13 and cleared by Tyler, Appling, Williams, Colonel Gall in DOD, and Cleveland. A typed note on the original reads: "Approved by White House–Bundy for President 2/20/64. Action Approval sent to AF for action 2/22/64. Follow up action required. Miss Moor and Mr. Mills notified. (WAH)"

those three countries will bear fruit in time both to take on the growing counterinsurgency job and (after June) to provide an effective substitute for the UN forces in maintaining some minimum security in Leopoldville, Katanga, and a few other population centers.

In order to help meet the immediate security problem, the United States could supply tactical mobile training teams (MTTs) in order to provide some training to three battalions and appropriate support units in the two important urban areas of Leopoldville and Elisabethville. The use of these teams would not of course guarantee internal security but they would make an important contribution to the training of a limited number of strategically located units. They would represent an added United States role since our efforts have heretofore been confined to supplying equipment and training incidental to the use of that equipment. However, if tactical MTTs were introduced their job would be clearly limited in time and scope and would be designed to supplement and not supplant the training programs of Belgium.

Naturally, the United States tactical MTTs could not be introduced in the Congo without the agreement of the Congolese Government. Because of the weak position of that Government, its fear of an adverse political reaction to the introduction of tactical MTTs, and its lack of appreciation of the seriousness of the problem it faces, there will be substantial difficulties in getting its concurrence and in making appropriate arrangements for the introduction of the teams. In addition, because of Belgium's primary responsibility for ANC training, such a step should not be taken without full prior consultations with the Belgian Government. Neither Ambassador Gullion nor Ambassador-designate Godley see any satisfactory alternative method of dealing with the immediate problem and both agree that such consultation should be undertaken immediately. Since preparation for the introduction of such teams will consume approximately sixty days, it seems equally important that the Department of Defense begin immediately to make preparations for the introduction of tactical MTTs at the earliest possible time. Once consultation with Belgian and Congolese Governments has begun, we will keep the UN Secretary General and the British Government informed.

The scope of the additional United States training effort that is suggested is outlined in the contingency plan (enclosed)[2] which was prepared by the Department of Defense. It calls for the use of 17 technical and tactical MTTs utilizing 105 men, to be phased into the Congo for varying periods of time (12–20 weeks). This plan is in addition to approximately 7 technical MTTs (33 men) that had already been pro-

[2] Attached but not printed.

grammed for training in the use and maintenance of equipment that the United States is supplying to the ANC. The number and location of American military personnel present in the Congo will, therefore, vary from time to time.

Recommendation

It is recommended that you authorize the Department of State immediately to undertake consultations with the Governments of Belgium and of the Congo with respect to the introduction of a limited number of tactical mobile training teams for the purposes outlined above. This consultation would be conducted on the basis that such teams would be assigned to the Congo on a temporary basis and with a mission clearly limited in scope to the provision of some training to three ANC battalions and appropriate headquarters and support units in Leopoldville and Elisabethville. These consultations would also proceed on the basis that the scope and duration of the activities of such United States teams would be correspondingly reduced or adjusted to the extent that effective additional assistance becomes available from other sources.

It is also recommended that the Department of Defense be authorized immediately to commence preparations for an expansion of the United States effort in accordance with the enclosed contingency plan.[3]

Dean Rusk[4]

---

[3] On February 20, McGeorge Bundy sent Rusk a memorandum stating that the President had approved his recommendation for consultations with the Belgians and the Congolese regarding the use of U.S. mobile training teams (MTTs) in the Congo. Bundy said that the President had asked him to emphasize his own view that time was running out, that July 1 was not far away, and that he felt strongly that "we should either persuade the Belgians to do this job, or find diplomatically effective ways of doing it ourselves." (National Archives, RG 59, Central Files 1964–66, DEF 1–1 THE CONGO)

[4] Printed from a copy that indicates Rusk signed the original.

161. Letter From the Under Secretary of State for Political Affairs (Harriman) to the Deputy Secretary of Defense (Vance)[1]

Washington, March 18, 1964.

Dear Cy:

The internal security problem in the Congo continues to give us the greatest concern. Apart from the question of training the Congolese Army (ANC) which still remains of the utmost importance in terms of our policy goals in the Congo, we are also faced with an insurrection in Kwilu Province which poses a most serious threat to the overall security problem.

Our Embassy in Leopoldville, together with Colonel William Dodds, the specialist on counter-guerilla warfare detailed to the Congo by CINCSTRIKE, believes that if the Kwilu rebellion is not rolled back before the departure of the UN troops at the end of June, when the ANC must accept sole responsibility for internal security in the Congo, there is serious danger that it will act as a catalyst for other similar insurgencies elsewhere in the Congo. Should this happen, and there is a substantial danger that it will, it would be a matter of grave concern to us, for there is little probability that the untrained ANC would be able to contain another insurrection so long as the Kwilu rebellion remains unchecked.

Accordingly, the Embassy has recommended strongly that we take steps to roll back the Kwilu insurrection now. The Embassy believes that the only possibility of the ANC accomplishing this fairly quickly lies in providing it with some additional equipment and transport capacity. The Embassy has recommended a list of equipment which includes inter alia, helicopters, light aircraft, and vehicles for immediate use in Kwilu. (The list is detailed in Leopoldville's cables 1580 and 1754 to the Department.)[2]

The Department of State fully shares the Embassy's views of the imperative necessity of ending the insurrection in Kwilu before the departure of the UN forces in June. We, therefore, urge the Department of Defense to develop as a matter of very high priority a program for the supply of such equipment as may be necessary to do the job in Kwilu. In so doing, we are aware that funds within the FY 1964 MAP program for the Congo will generally not be adequate for this purpose because of important commitments to train the ANC. We are therefore ex-

---

[1] Source: Washington National Records Center, RG 330, OSD Files: FRC 69 A 7425, Congo 353. Confidential. A stamped notation on the letter reads: "Mr. Vance has seen."

[2] Dated February 16 and March 6, respectively. (Both in National Archives, RG 59, Central Files 1964–66, POL 23–9 THE CONGO)

ploring other finance possibilities and request that the Department of Defense will join us on an urgent basis in locating whatever funds may eventually become necessary.

Sincerely,

W. Averell Harriman

162. Telegram From the Embassy in the Congo to the Department of State[1]

Leopoldville, March 27, 1964, 7 p.m.

1897. From Harriman.[2] I called on Adoula on March 26. He was relaxed, appeared unworried and in excellent spirits. He showed great pleasure on receiving President's photograph. Said he was glad to have a chance to talk with me and asked if I had "brought good news." I explained that the President asked me to visit the Congo to show his personal interest in the Congo specifically and Africa in general. He wanted report on the situation and particularly Adoula's own views on how he saw the future. He was prepared to support Adoula and his government if it could be done constructively. Adoula then stated he wished to talk about three subjects: Angola, Congo security, and finance.

1. Angola. He expressed concern over deterioration of Holden's position and threat of radical takeover in GRAE. He had offered to serve as mediator between GRAE and Portuguese to bring about round-table talks but had been unsuccessful and hopes for European and American support. He fears ChiCom presence in Brazzaville will increase likelihood of ChiCom penetration of GRAE which might bring on Holden's overthrow. However, he believes that if Portugal agrees to negotiate, he is prepared personally to guarantee that Holden will maintain a moderate position. However, time is running out, and Holden is under attack as agent of the imperialists for moving too slowly. Adoula is fearful of left wing penetration into Congo through GRAE as well as adverse effect on Congo of Communist revolution in Angola. I mentioned US efforts to revive Portuguese-African talks and

[1] Source: National Archives, RG 59, Central Files 1964–66, POL 7 US/HARRIMAN. Confidential; Priority; Limdis.

[2] Harriman was on a fact-finding trip to the Congo.

reviewed our continuing efforts to bring pressure on Salazar, mentioning Ball visits to Salazar, our pressures on him to accept UN formula on self-determination, etc. I explained the assistance we were giving refugees in education but we did not know what further action we could take.

2. Congo security. In turning to security I expressed our continuing interest in supporting his government and assistance in problem security. Adoula stated after four years of UN presence which was not normal, Congo must now stand on its own without UN forces. I asked Adoula directly whether he trusted his army. He hesitated a moment and then replied "yes and no", but did not elaborate. He said that Spaak had promised substantial increase in Belgian military advisors before June 30 but that greatest need prior to June 30 was not training but transport to assure ANC mobility—helicopters and other air and ground transport. He explained that DOD had sent team here to help in studying these problems looking for early US decision. I said plans for technical training teams to reactivate deadlined vehicles and to train maintenance personnel. He confirmed that he approved this program. In reply to my question as to Belgian encadrement at battalion level, Adoula expressed reluctance for fear of provoking mutiny and indicated introduction of Belgians below staff level would have to be handled carefully. He dismissed the police in giving security and indicated that they must rely on USC. The Nigerian police training program was not he maintained a significant contribution to internal overall security. In reply to my question regarding the threat of Tshombe gendarmerie now in Angola, he agreed that this posed a serious threat to Katanga after June 30 but solidly maintained that the government was consolidating its position in Katanga and could take care of threat. He expressed strong opposition to possibility British giving Tshombe visa. Godley interjected to ask Adoula whether there was a possibility of Tshombe's returning to Congo political scene. Adoula reacted strongly. Said Tshombe had left Congo on his own volition and had not been threatened. He listed number of Tshombists still here, unharmed and many in high government posts. Reviewing Tshombe perfidies he declared Tshombe's own past treacheries made him fear return, not Congo Government threats. He ended by stating that if Tshombe wished to return the initiative was up to him. He seemed quite relaxed about the Kwilu and indicated that the uprising had been contained.

3. Economic situation. Adoula brought up the IMF review just concluded and Mladek's opinion that the economy was improving. (I had had a talk with Mladek the night before and Adoula's statements substantially confirmed what Mladek had told me.) However, Adoula continued, the Congo was not able to do it alone and needed assistance through 1965. I responded that we were willing continue support to

Congo but that Congo's own actions to control inflation, encourage production and exports was essential as well as contributions from other countries. I explained that we were not willing to be the only contributors both because of our Congressional and public opinion at home and also because it was not wise for the Congo to be dependent on one country. As time was running out because of my engagement with President Kasavubu, I said that we could discuss these matters in further detail and that I had another one to add to the list, namely his political problems, the question of the new constitution, the referendum and the elections, and what he was doing to strengthen his own position and that of his party.

Godley

---

163. Telegram From the Embassy in France to the Department of State[1]

Paris, April 2, 1964, 8 p.m.

4614. From Harriman. In one and one-half hour session with Spaak Wednesday afternoon at Consulate, Nice, I covered full range of Congo problems. I began by expressing gratification at Belgian and US military and Embassies in Congo working in complete cooperation.

In course of talks, Spaak made these undertakings:

1. He will talk to Minister of Defense to be sure 100 Belgian officers reach Congo before June 30.
2. He will press Mobutu on forthcoming visit to Belgium to accept Israeli training of two existing battalions immediately.
3. He will undertake to raise problem of ex-Katanga gendarmes in Angola in NATO and request Portuguese agreement to inspection of Katanga gendarme camps in Angola by agency such as International Red Cross.
4. He will attempt to improve Belgian intelligence contacts on Tshombe capabilities and intentions.
5. He will look into political background of certain Belgian professors at Elisabethville and question of Katangan need for Belgian technicians.

---

[1] Source: National Archives, RG 59, Central Files 1964–66, POL 23–9 THE CONGO. Secret; Immediate; Exdis. Repeated to Brussels and Leopoldville and passed to the White House.

6. Belgians prepared explore with us possibilities of providing Belgian crews and perhaps maintenance for possible US-loaned helicopters and combat aircraft.

Full account follows:

I began with brief review of my trip and, when I mentioned Mobutu, Spaak volunteered his concern that Mobutu is over-confident and hard to influence. Spaak thought Adoula had agreed to Israeli training of two battalions, is much concerned at hold up and will talk to Mobutu.

We agreed Colonels Mulambe (Stanleyville) and Bobozo (Elisabethville) quite competent, particularly former, and Spaak seemed interested in my report that Mulambe thinks that in time ANC will accept Belgian advisers at company level. I mentioned excellent relations of Mulambe and Belgian Col. Dacoster. Spaak agreed Belgians will keep Dacoster there for another tour.

I reviewed our present thinking about need for ANC transport and communications; plans for MTTs; motor transport and spare parts supply; and maintenance training program. I stressed we look to Belgians for major tactical training functions with US in supporting role.

I said also we hope to work closely with GOB on problems of Constitution and election. Spaak commented on difficulty of getting Adoula, like other Africans, to look beyond immediate problems to plan few months ahead. Spaak stressed Adoula's complacency regarding his political plans and expressed opposition to early Congolese election.

In reply to my question about Tshombe's activities, Spaak said their intelligence is poor. While some Belgians see him, those who do are unreliable people. He agreed to try to improve intelligence and establish an effective contact.

He thinks Tshombe very mercurial. When Spaak saw him in Brussels he was very reasonable, said he had abandoned Katanga secession and talked of entering Leopoldville political scene. But shortly after, he attacked Adoula regarding Lumumba's death. Spaak feels probably too late now for Tshombe play role in Leo. He thinks Tshombe working with some elements in Brazzaville.

Spaak has only general reports re ex-gendarmes in Angola but disturbed by UMHK report of several hundred ex-gendarmes leaving jobs to go join Angola force. Belgian Consul in Luanda has permission visit camps. Spaak proposes NATO discussion of problem with view to getting Portuguese agreement for International Red Cross inspection of gendarme camps in Angola.

I pointed out Portuguese will probably raise Roberto camps in Congo as other side of issue and we discussed Roberto problem briefly and inconclusively. He said the Belgian Embassy in Leo has no contact with Roberto.

We talked briefly also of SW Africa problem and ICJ case, and of its relation to Article 19 problem. Spaak said MacArthur had talked to him re Article 19 and that GOB "has no clear opinion on problem, it is very difficult."

I then reviewed our analysis of 3-part Congo air requirement—airlift, choppers, and either T–6 or AD–6 type combat aircraft. Spaak agreed it is major factor in ANC ability provide security. I indicated we might supply equipment (on loan basis) and even maintenance but impossible for US provide operating crews and suggested Belgian crews. Spaak showed interest and said GOB willing to explore further possible Belgian role in operation and perhaps maintenance of choppers and AD–6, providing Italians would not do so.

He then listed four short term priorities in this order: more Belgian officers; Israeli training of two battalions; retention of Nigerian troops after June 30; and US supply of air capability. I pointed out Nigerians would require burden-sharing and mentioned that Adoula suggested Tunisians as another possible source. He commented Tunisians would be "second best."

I then mentioned minor matter, regarding allegedly Communist Belgian professors in University, Elisabethville, and need for Belgian technicians in Katanga which he agreed to check.

With regard to French role in Congo, I reported French Ambassador in Leo's interest in cultural affairs and rumor regarding French military aid. Spaak expressed great doubt French prepared to make any substantial contribution in Congo, but would welcome it.

On economic matters, I reported impression that large Belgian plantations recovering to pre-independence production but vicious circle of inadequate consumer goods incentives and consequent low production holding native agriculture at low level as well as inadequate transport. I mentioned also estimate by Mladek of IMF that economy on upgrade, and US intention to continue import credit support. Although he agreed, he appeared reluctant to discuss further commitments regarding Belgian import credits.

He seemed gratified by my report that Adoula had expressed satisfaction over his financial agreements with Spaak.

With regard to Brazzaville, Spaak feels it is dangerous base for subversion of Congo–Leo and that French influence there is diminishing rapidly. However, he will talk with French when opportunity offers about Brazzaville problem.

Comment: I told Spaak I would expect to keep in close touch on African matters of common interest. He was forthcoming and I feel close

US-Belgian cooperation in Congo is on good footing, both in Leo and at government level. Important we follow up promptly on specifics to keep cooperation moving forward.

Bohlen

164. Memorandum of Meeting[1]

Washington, April 3, 1964.

MEETING WITH PRESIDENT RE GOVERNOR HARRIMAN'S REPORT ON TRIP TO GHANA, NIGERIA AND CONGO

PRESENT

Under Secretary Harriman, Assistant Secretary G. Mennen Williams, William Brubeck, White House

[Omitted here is discussion of Libya.]

2. Congo

The President said he had seen Harriman's tentative recommendations and thought we would be doing very well if we could handle the problem with a matériel program of the size indicated.

Harriman said that it would require further discussions with the military to give the President precise recommendations but that the cost of the transport airlift and air combat program being contemplated would probably be under $10 million. However, this will require an increase in the present $3.5 million Congo MAP budget. He also stressed the need for improved intelligence on Tshombe's activities; expressed his concern about the potentiality for subversive from Brazzaville; and indicated he thinks early elections in the Congo would not be a good idea. With a reasonable amount of help from ourselves and other coun-

[1] Source: Johnson Library, National Security File, Files of McGeorge Bundy, Memoranda of Meetings with the President, Vol. I. Confidential. Drafted by William H. Brubeck.

tries over the next several years, Harriman concluded, the Congo *might* pull through.

[Omitted here is discussion of Zanzibar and Ghana.]

William H. Brubeck[2]

---

[2] Printed from a copy that bears this typed signature.

---

165. Summary Record of the 526th Meeting of the National Security Council[1]

Washington, April 3, 1964, 2 p.m.

Summary Record of National Security Council Meeting No. 526 April 3, 1964, 2:00 PM with the Congressional Leaders—Various Subjects

The President opened the meeting with the Congressional Leaders by saying that his purpose was to bring them up to date on recent developments. Various Council members would report on current situations. He first called on Secretary Rusk for a summary of developments in Brazil.

[Omitted here is discussion of unrelated subjects.]

The President then introduced Under Secretary Harriman to summarize his recent trip to Africa. (A copy of Harriman's report to the President is attached.[2] It contains a detailed account which he summarized at the meeting.)

Mr. Harriman said that there was a potentially explosive situation in the Congo because the UN forces would be leaving in June. He reported increased economic stability in the Congo and said that real progress had been made toward restoring economic health. Production of copper and coffee has now almost reached the level of production prior to the departure of the Belgians. He said that Adoula is now governing the State and is a thorough anti-Communist even though he follows a policy of non-alignment.

---

[1] Source: Johnson Library, National Security File, NSC Meetings File, Vol. I, Tab 7, 4/3/64, Various Topics (Panama, etc.). Top Secret.

[2] Not attached, but see Document 166 and footnote 2 thereto.

Mr. Harriman described the program we are undertaking to assist in training native Congo military forces. The U.S. would contribute to the mobility of Congolese forces by providing trucks, jeeps and transport planes. U.S. repair teams would go to the area on temporary training assignments.

Mr. Harriman said the Congo can achieve stability if there is no pressure from outside the country. Leftists in Brazzaville may cause trouble and Tshombe may try a comeback. If both of these forces move against Adoula, he will be in real trouble. There is a possibility, however, that Nigeria may come to his assistance in the event either of these forces seeks to overthrow him.

[Omitted here is discussion of unrelated subjects.]

166. Memorandum From William H. Brubeck of the National Security Council Staff to President Johnson[1]

Washington, April 20, 1964.

Attached are Averell Harriman's specific recommendations for increased military assistance to the Congo, based on his recent trip, and with Defense and AID concurrence.[2] This program will add $5.1 million fiscal 1964 funds to the $3.5 million per year already programmed for FY 1964 and FY 1965.

Main points of the program:

1. Funds are almost all for combat air and airlift capacity—

six T28C fighter aircraft
six H21 coup lift helicopters
ten C47 aircraft
aircraft operation and maintenance costs

2. We will try to get the Belgians to operate these aircraft; if unsuccessful we will try a civilian contract operation; but in any event US military will not take an operational flight or ground crew function.

3. Additional aid may be required if the Congo situation worsens.

---

[1] Source: Johnson Library, National Security File, Country File, Congo, Vol. I. Secret.

[2] Not attached. A copy of Harriman's April 20 memorandum to the President is in National Archives, RG 59, Central Files 1964–66, DEF 19 US–THE CONGO.

4. If Adoula requests temporary loan of military security forces from other Africans (e.g. Nigerians) we may have to contribute to cost.

Recommendation: That you approve the program as outlined above.[3]

B.[4]

[3] President Johnson initialed his approval of the recommendation.

[4] McGeorge Bundy initialed under Brubeck's initial.

167. Paper Prepared in the Central Intelligence Agency[1]

Washington, undated.

ATTACHMENT A

1. On 17 November 1961, Special Group approved a proposal to undertake specific covert actions in the Congo in support of the moderate government headed by Prime Minister Adoula and authorized the expenditure of up to [*dollar amount not declassified*] for this purpose. On April 23, 1963, a progress report was submitted to Special Group which approved the continuation of these covert actions which were programmed for [*dollar amount not declassified*]. The [*cryptonym not declassified*] project outline was initially approved for FY 1962 for [*dollar amount not declassified*], the FY 1963 renewal was approved for [*dollar amount not declassified*].

2. The policy coordination of this project with the Department of State has been singularly close since its inception. The U.S. Ambassador to the Congo has been kept informed at all times and has frequently added his endorsement to station proposals. Coordination with the Chief of the Bureau of African Affairs in the Department of State has been most close and no major steps have been taken without thorough

[1] Source: Central Intelligence Agency Files, Job 78–00435R, DDO/ISS Files, Box 1, Folder 1, [*cryptonym not declassified*]—Development & Plans. Secret. The original is attached to a memorandum, dated April 22, 1964, from Glenn Fields, Chief of CIA's Africa Division in the Directorate of Plans, to Deputy Director of Central Intelligence Carter. Fields recommended that Carter approve amendment of Project [*cryptonym not declassified*] for FY 1964 for a revised funding total of [*dollar amount not declassified*]. Assistant Deputy Director for Plans Thomas Karamessines concurred in the recommendation. Lyman Kirkpatrick, acting for Carter, approved the recommendation on June 1. (Ibid.)

and detailed discussions both with the Department of State and with the Ambassador.

3. The policy guidance laid down by the Department of State to strengthen the moderate elements in the Government of the Congo led by Prime Minister Adoula remains the central objective of Project [*cryptonym not declassified*]. During the first two years of this project the Adoula Government was plagued by a crescendo of political crises which led to a constant recourse to crash ad hoc funding. Because of the immediacy of the crisis of the moment there was never an opportunity to examine a request for support in detail, and the alternative to non-support was the ever present danger that the moderate government would fall, being replaced by extremist nationalists who, without cohesion or program would rapidly reduce the Congo to chaos thereby inviting subversive Communist activities. This approach did succeed in that the Adoula Government has maintained itself in power to some extent through this device of crisis-funding and has survived not only the threat of the Katanga secessionist regime, but several political crises notably in November 1962 and March 1963.

4. *Political Program:* In an effort to get away from this crash funding and bring some order and organization to the political operations of Prime Minister Adoula and his close colleagues [*less than 1 line not declassified*] negotiations were begun with them in the Fall of 1963. It was made abundantly clear to the [*less than 1 line not declassified*] that the U.S. Government was not going to continue the ad hoc funding and would require from them an organized program leading to the formation of a national political party which would act as their political instrument in the anticipated national elections.

5. A detailed budget was hammered out with the [*less than 1 line not declassified*] (the details of which are given in Attachment B) looking towards the formation of RADECO (Rassemblement Democratique Congolaise). The Ambassador participated in discussions on this budget and urged their favorable consideration. The Chief of the Bureau of Central African Affairs also participated in these discussions. Approval was given by the Department of State and a cable was sent to the field on 8 November 1963 authorizing a budget of [*dollar amount not declassified*] for these purposes.

6. The station is satisfied that the funds are being expended for political ends in support of the Adoula Government if not in adherence with the budget outline. The station is obtaining accountings on those hard currency expenditures in Europe, but despite all efforts cannot obtain accountings for funds expended locally. Realistically, even if procured, such accountings would be relatively meaningless. One built-in protection, however, is that the passage of funds is always known to at

least two of the [*less than 1 line not declassified*] thereby limiting the potential for personal profit.

7. This agreement has put an end to the ad hoc funding which in itself is an accomplishment, but it has not led to the effective establishment of RADECO. The results to date have been most disheartening despite all efforts to get RADECO going.[2] [*3½ lines not declassified*] The station has done its utmost in daily and weekly guidance but a 90-day review clearly showed that the RADECO organization had barely gotten off the ground. The Chief of Station has been given authority to suspend payments of funds. Although he has not fully exercised this authority yet, by dragging his feet on the last installment, and giving the recipients a rather blunt lecture, has paved the way for a total suspension or a thorough-going revision of the current budget. Headquarters has also made its dissatisfaction bluntly clear to [*5 lines not declassified*].

8. The dissatisfactions with the organization of RADECO are now well known to all the principals and even the Congolese have admitted its shortcomings. The station is now in a position to examine coldly with the [*less than 1 line not declassified*] without mincing words, the political problem of their future survival.

9. *Military Support:* Nominal direct assistance had been authorized by Special Group in April 1963 for General Joseph D. Mobutu, the Commander-in-Chief of the Congolese National Army. General Mobutu has been able to scotch at least one attempted military coup against the government and has remained loyal throughout to the Adoula Government.

10. The Special Group also authorized in April 1963 support to the Congolese National Army in order to retain its loyalty under General Mobutu to the incumbent moderate regime. This authorization was not called upon until March 1964 when the station requested, with the endorsement of the Ambassador, that support should be provided the Congolese National Army at the rate of [*dollar amount not declassified*] per month at least for the balance of FY 1964, at which time the arrangement would be renegotiated in light of existing circumstances.

11. This support was frankly intended to help maintain this key member of the [*less than 1 line not declassified*] in his present position at a time when he was under fire by the violent exile opposition operating out of Brazzaville, and through his efforts to ensure the continued loyalty of the Army. The funds would be used largely to improve the

---

[2] In telegram 0097 from Leopoldville to CIA, February 21, the station reported on its efforts to get the [*cryptonym not declassified*] "to come up with some sort of businesslike statement of progress" and stated that RADECO seemed to have made little progress organizationally. (Ibid.)

amenities of the officers, for amelioration of messes, and possibly small emergency loans to deserving army personnel.

12. This matter was approved after coordination with the Department of State and cabled authorization was given on 5 March 1964 for the station to expend up to [*dollar amount not declassified*] through June 1964. It was agreed at that time with the DDP/PG/CA that the [*cryptonym not declassified*] project outline would be amended to cover this additional amount.

[Omitted here is further discussion of the project.]

---

168. Report Prepared in the Central Intelligence Agency[1]

Washington, May 5, 1964.

SUBJECT

Status Report on CIA Assistance to the Congolese Air Force

1. This memorandum presents a status report on the CIA program for assistance to the Congolese Air Force.

2. *Summary*

A. From January through March 1963, CIA, with Special Group approval, covertly furnished to the Congolese Air Force (CAF) pilot and maintenance personnel and assorted supplies for the operation and maintenance of 6 Harvard T–6 aircraft which are the property of the CAF. In April 1963, in coordination with the Departments of State and Defense, a determination was made to expand this activity to include additional aircraft, pilot and maintenance personnel. In February 1964, as a result of the Kwilu uprising, the Department of State concurred in shifting the mission of the air support program from a non-combat, psychological effort to an active combat participation.

B. Anticipating the June 1964 withdrawal of the UN forces in the Congo in face of an active Kwilu rebellion, President Johnson, on 24 April 1964, approved a Department of State recommendation to provide to the CAF on a loan basis six T–28 aircraft, and to provide on a grant basis ten H–21 aircraft through the Military Assistance Program. In the absence of Belgian or Italian willingness to fly the T–28s in

[1] Source: National Archives, RG 59, AF/CM Files: Lot 67 D 63, DEF 19–3, Military Assistance, January–June 1964. Secret. No drafting information appears on the original.

combat, CIA has been requested by the Departments of State and Defense to provide the necessary personnel to maintain a T–28 combat capability.[2] CIA intends to add a helicopter rescue capability for the air support program, and to operate the T–28 aircraft as replacements for the original Harvard T–6s for a period of one year beginning 1 July 1964, or to terminate this activity should the Belgians assume responsibility.

3. *Discussion*

A. The continuance of an active air support program for the GOC is necessitated by both political and military considerations. Originated as a psychological effort to enhance the prestige of the Adoula government when it was faced with the politically demoralizing Katanga secession and the militarily superior Katangan air force, this support program was continued after the Katangan conflict when it was determined that withdrawal of this air arm would be interpreted by both Prime Minister Adoula and Commander-in-Chief General Mobutu as a strong indication of a U.S. policy decision to withdraw its support of the present Congolese Government. The advent of the Kwilu uprising in February 1964 added a genuine military significance to this support program, and the decision was made by the Department of State to accede to a GOC request to fly the T–6 Harvards in combat, using .30 caliber machine guns and rockets. Although this force has been an effective deterrent to the Kwilu revolt, the revolt continues. Upon withdrawal of the UN forces in June, the GOC will be faced with the Kwilu situation as well as a possible security threat in the Katanga and Kivu areas.

B. The U.S. Government has attempted to persuade either the Italian or Belgian Governments to furnish pilot and maintenance crews for the aircraft provided by the U.S. Department of Defense. The Italians have deferred flying in combat areas to the Belgians. The latter have agreed to fly the unarmed C–47s and H–21 helicopters in combat areas, but have not reached a decision on operating the armed T–28s.

C. While it is possible that the Belgians would cooperate with CIA personnel and support them with a helicopter rescue unit, there is no way of insuring control over such a unit. CIA is prepared to provide necessary personnel to establish a helicopter rescue capability under the direct control of CIA operational personnel, and to supply the necessary pilot and maintenance personnel to operate the armed T–28 aircraft in lieu of the Harvard T–6 aircraft. The latter aircraft are already

[2] On May 28, the 303 Committee approved the budget of [*text not declassified*] for operation and maintenance of these aircraft by [*text not declassified*] contract personnel through fiscal year 1965. (Central Intelligence Agency Files, Office of Congressional Affairs, Review Staff Files, Job 86B00975R)

considered unsafe to fly in combat conditions and will be retired on or about 1 July 1964. It is anticipated that unless the Belgians agree to fly the T–28s in combat, this activity will continue at least for an additional year at an annual cost of [*dollar amount not declassified*], exclusive of those spare parts and ammunition furnished by the Department of Defense. CIA has the necessary funds for this activity.

4. *Coordination*

This memorandum has been coordinated with the Department of State (Bureau of Central African Affairs) and with representatives in the Office of the Assistant to the Secretary of Defense.

---

169. Memorandum From the Chief of the Africa Division, Directorate of Plans, Central Intelligence Agency (Fields) to the Assistant Secretary of State for African Affairs (Williams)[1]

Washington, May 13, 1964.

SUBJECT

Covert Political Action Program in the Congo

On 28 April 1964 the Station and American Ambassador to the Congo, G.M. Godley, reviewed the six-month-old effort to assist Prime Minister Cyrille Adoula and the [*less than 1 line not declassified*] in the formation of a national political party. They reached the following conclusions, which agree in substance with those of Headquarters:

1. No national political party has yet been formed.
2. A homogeneous national party will not be formed in the foreseeable future. A probable alternative is the formation of one or more election alliances grouping various strong provincial single parties.
3. Adoula has not effectively utilized the funds provided for the organization of a national political party. The Station and Godley recommend cutting in half the political party subsidy in an effort to force Adoula into effective action.

This recommendation is prompted by the belief that Adoula will achieve a more durable party coalition on the basis of straight party program principles than on the basis of the bought or rented loyalties of

---

[1] Source: Central Intelligence Agency Files, Job 76–00366R, DDO/ISO Files, Box 1, Folder 7, Congo, 1960–1969, Part 1. Secret. This memorandum was sent via backchannel.

selected regional strongmen. Predictably Adoula would regard such a cut, as he has past financial denials, as a sign the U.S. has lost confidence in him.

---

170. Paper Prepared in the Central Intelligence Agency[1]

Washington, May 18, 1964.

PRECIS

Covert Action in the Congo[2]

1. *Summary:* On 22 November 1961, the Special Group authorized [*dollar amount not declassified*] for covert actions in the Congo in support of Prime Minister Cyrille Adoula's moderate government. On 23 April 1963, the Special Group authorized [*dollar amount not declassified*] for the continuation of this program. To date covert support of Adoula's government has cost a total of [*dollar amount not declassified*].

2. *Problems and Progress:* Timely application of covert funds has been instrumental in maintaining in power the Adoula government for the past three years. Efforts to organize a moderate national party, however, have been somewhat less successful, and no such party has materialized to date.

The Congolese National Army, currently a potential force for stability in the Congo, will assume even broader significance with the withdrawal of UN forces from the Congo on 30 June 1964. Accordingly, it is planned to increase covert aid to CNA Commander-in-Chief Mobutu. Such aid in the past has helped to retain the loyalty of CNA officers to the Adoula government and to discourage opposition efforts to penetrate the army.

The public relations mechanism established in November 1961 has been providing public relations guidance to Prime Minister Adoula and has been successful both domestically and outside the Congo (L).

3. *Coordination:* All major steps in the covert action program for the Congo have been closely coordinated with the Department of State and

---

[1] Source: Central Intelligence Agency Files, Job 82–00450R, DDO/AF, AF/DIV Historical Files, 40 Committee, Congo (K), 1960–1964. Secret; Eyes Only. A handwritten note reads: "18 May 1964." No drafting information appears on the paper.

[2] This paper is a precis of an attached May 18 memorandum presenting a progress and status report to the Special Group entitled "Covert Action in the Congo."

the U.S. Ambassador to the Congo. The Ambassador to the Congo, G.M. Godley, favors continuation of this program.

4. *Conclusions:* The organization of a national political party has failed to materialize, and a review of the party program and possible alternatives currently is in progress. A generally agreed upon alternative is the creation of a united-front coalition of regional political groups and leaders, rather than the originally-envisioned single, national party.

The moderate, pro-Western Congo regime will continue to require major covert political support for the foreseeable future. The anticipated commitment is estimated at [*dollar amount not declassified*]. Should the postponed national elections be held in FY 1965, an additional [*dollar amount not declassified*] would be required for an election campaign.[3]

[3] The minutes of the May 21 Special Group meeting recorded that the Group noted the paper, and that "Mr. Hughes indicated that Governor Harriman maintained serious concern over the situation in the Congo with particular emphasis on Prime Minister Adoula's failure to establish any real political organization and General Mobutu's equal lack of success in molding a military force of any reliability. Mr. Fields indicated that no new action other than that already approved was being initiated at this time until the effects of the UN222 withdrawal, the adoption of a constitution, and probable national elections are discernible. Mr. McCone indicated that he and Mr. Fields would see Governor Harriman on the Congo problem in the near future." (National Security Council, Intelligence Files, 303 Committee Files, Minutes—1964)

171. Paper Prepared in the Central Intelligence Agency[1]

Washington, May 22, 1964.

PRECIS

Assistance to the Congolese Air Force (CAF)[2]

1. Problem:

To provide covert support to the CAF for manning and maintaining six U.S. provided T–28 aircraft and a minimal helicopter rescue

[1] Source: Central Intelligence Agency Files, Job 81–00966R, Congo, 1960–1964. Secret; Eyes Only.

[2] This paper is a precis of an attached May 22 memorandum for the Special Group entitled "Covert Assistance to the Congolese Air Force."

capability for protection of CIA contract personnel in addition to continued operation of the present six T–6 aircraft.

2. *Situation:*

A. Since November 1962, CIA has been providing covert personnel and logistical support to the CAF. In February 1964, upon the outbreak of the Kwilu revolt in the Congo, the non-combat, psychological mission of the CIA unit was changed with State Department approval to one of active combat participation.

B. On 24 April 1964, President Johnson authorized the Department of Defense to provide to the CAF six T–28, ten C–47, and six H–21 aircraft, plus a six month supply of parts and ammunition. In the absence of Belgian crews to operate the T–28s, the Department of Defense and AF Bureau in State have informally requested CIA to provide the necessary personnel to operate and maintain the T–28s in addition to the T–6s.

C. Expansion of CIA's present program to include operation of the T–28s doubles the potential of air support to the Congolese National Army. At the same time, however, this expansion means doubling the present size of the CIA unit and thus reduces the security of the operation.

3. *Aim:*

To provide the CAF with a combat air capability in order to support the Congolese Government's efforts to quell the current as well as possible future insurgency.

4. *Coordination:*

This proposal has been discussed with the Bureau of African Affairs of the Department of State, with the U.S. Ambassador to Leopoldville, and with representatives in the Office of the Secretary of Defense/International Security Affairs.

5. *Cost:*

The total cost of this program for the recommended one year, to 15 June 1965, is [*dollar amount not declassified*]. For Fiscal Year 1964, funds are available within CIA. Funds for this activity for Fiscal Year 1965 have not been programmed in their entirety but can be made available within CIA through reprogramming.[3]

---

[3] A note attached to the original reads "Approved as presented by Special Group via telephone: 28 May 1964."

172. Telegram From the Department of State to the Embassy in the Congo[1]

Washington, May 26, 1964, 7:10 p.m.

1319. For Ambassadors from Harriman.

Current Congolese Situation

High level interagency meeting held May 22 to review present situation Congo (Leopoldville) and possibilities for further action designed to assist in meeting present crisis. Grave view taken of current developments particularly in Kivu. It appeared that crisis originally expected to occur following UN withdrawal June 30 already underway. Review of present US military program for improving transport and mobility ANC appeared progressing satisfactorily as well Belgian and Italian cooperation this respect. It was concluded following are principal problem areas:

1. *Urgent need for presence Belgian officers in ANC line units.* Fully appreciate background this subject, natural hesitancy of Belgians in light previous experience place officers in local commands and similarly hesitancy of Congolese to request Belgians to do so. Notwithstanding, we of opinion that presence of Belgian officers Kivu might have avoided present disintegration of command.

2. *General Mobutu.* While General has many qualities and has performed effectively in past, his vanity and irresponsibility would appear to have contributed significantly to ineffectiveness and disarray ANC. Remains to be seen how he performs on return Leopoldville and appreciate there apparently no present alternative. Would accordingly seem desirable explore additional channels for communication with Mobutu (possibly through individuals such as Nendaka or Marliere) in order for us to get across our ideas to him. In this connection, opportunities should continue to be sought to induce Mobutu to accept further training by Israelis and Belgian encadrement.

3. *Presence of CNL Brazzaville and Bujumbura and their current and future activities.* Best approach would seem raising this issue with UN SYG or in OAU. As to UN, initiative should be taken by Congolese (L) and/or SYG on recommendation Osorio Tafal. Nigerians or possibly Senegalese might stimulate SYG action. However USUN could be

[1] Source: National Archives, RG 59, Central Files 1964–66, POL 23-9 THE CONGO. Secret; Priority; Limdis. Drafted by AFC Deputy Director Matthew J. Looram; cleared by Appling, Tasca, Director of AID's Office of Central African Affairs Richard M. Cashin, Cleveland, Buffum, and Colonel Gall in DOD; and approved by Harriman. Also sent to Brussels and repeated to USUN, Lagos, Paris, Brazzaville, Bujumbura, and Rome (by pouch).

helpful behind scenes. (Separate message to be sent USUN.) We have made representations regarding this matter to Mwami and Burundi delegation here, but Belgians have greater assets for exercising pressure on Burundi. Reported Burundi intention send Soumialot out of Bujumbura helpful but not enough. Rumored rupture Congo (L) relations with Burundi or retaliatory actions by Congo (L) against Brazza would be highly undesirable. Despite erosion French influence Brazza, French may still be able to take helpful action Brazza re CNL. At same time every consideration must be given to sensitivity of both Congos toward outside interference their affairs.

4. *UN rescue potential.* Additional aircraft now being provided Congo by US presumably will be available for rescue missions UN CivOps and arrival of aircraft should serve bolster confidence such personnel stationed remote areas. However we will continue our discussions with UNNY re separate UN rescue capability.

5. *Nigerian battalion.* Presence Nigerian forces after June 30 would seem desirable, particularly in light present situation Kivu. Most encouraging Adoula reportedly now intends discuss this with Wachuku (Leo tel 2323).[2]

6. *Tshombe.* We still do not have sufficient information re his intentions or full extent his potential in Congo for return to active political role.

Request Ambassadors Godley and MacArthur explore possibilities as they deem best for tackling above items. At same time we should continue keep in mind desirability minimize to extent feasible evidence of active US role in internal Congolese affairs. We face difficult dilemma of needing continuous cooperation Adoula, Mobutu and other key members Congolese government on one hand and of trying to avoid—in Congolese domestic picture, Brazza and other African countries—their appearing to be American puppets on other hand.[3]

Rusk

---

[2] Dated May 23. (Ibid.)

[3] In telegram 1885 from Brussels, May 27, MacArthur reported that he had discussed with Spaak the current Congolese situation along the lines of the Department's telegram. Spaak agreed that the crises expected to follow U.N. withdrawal had already begun. He also agreed in principle that the presence of Belgian officers in ANC line units would be helpful in stiffening them, but pointed out that Mobutu and Adoula had consistently opposed such encadrement. (Ibid.)

173. Telegram From the Department of State to the Embassy in Belgium[1]

Washington, May 31, 1964, 3:30 p.m.

1620. For Ambassadors MacArthur and Godley. Brussels 1886 and 1897; Leopoldville 2368 and 2375.[2] *Request Ambassador MacArthur convey following to Spaak:*

We wholeheartedly endorse concept of Belgian preparedness to act in emergency, and should necessity for intervention arise, our agreement thereto would certainly entail our willingness to stand by Belgians and give full moral and political support.

We fully agree would be most helpful if Belgian Government gave verbal assurances to Congolese Government it prepared assist militarily if necessary. Given special Belgian-Congolese relations, Belgium is in position make unique contribution to security free world by preventing disintegration Congo and possible takeover by elements hostile to West. Belgian willingness give such commitment would undoubtedly bolster morale of Congolese Government now shaken by events Kivu.

We assume, however, that Spaak would first wish make sure that request for secret pact was made on behalf Adoula and Kasavubu and does not simply constitute idea floated by Lengema on own. It seems to us as practical matter that in light present alignment of Congolese political and military forces, were Adoula ever make specific request for Belgian military intervention, request should have firm approval of Kasavubu and concurrence or at least non-opposition of Mobutu.

We of opinion disadvantages outweigh advantages to be gained from existence secret written pact including legal basis prepared in advance for intervention. If document to have any validity would presumably require approval Kasavubu and Adoula cabinet, or at least its key figures, with resultant likelihood matter would become public knowledge as Congolese Cabinet not secure. If this happened it would provoke strong Afro-Asian and Bloc reaction creating unnecessary embarrassment for GOB and jeopardizing position of Adoula Government in Congolese domestic scene and in many parts Africa. Secret verbal assurances would seem sufficient for purpose.

---

[1] Source: National Archives, RG 59, Central Files 1964–66, POL 23–9 THE CONGO. Top Secret; Priority; Limit Distribution. Drafted by Looram; cleared in draft by Williams, Colonel Junkerman in DOD/ISA, Tyler, Meeke, and Sisco; and by Harriman; and approved by Acting Secretary Ball. Also sent to Leopoldville and repeated to USUN.

[2] Telegram 1886 from Brussels, May 27; telegram 1897 from Brussels, May 29; telegram 2368 from Leopoldville, May 28; telegram 2375 from Leopoldville, May 29. (All ibid.)

We believe moreover that GOB would wish qualify such assurances by making clear to Adoula and Kasavubu that military intervention could not be automatic whenever and wherever Congolese requested, but that final Belgian decision would have to be taken in light all factors obtaining at that time. It is assumed that in any event assurances would only apply after June 30. In addition Congolese request would have to be made in writing according Congolese constitutional procedures (i.e. having approval of Chief of State as well as of Government) and Congolese would have to be prepared make such request public in view likely international repercussions.

If Spaak agrees with foregoing, we would expect, were GOB to receive request for military forces and if our moral and political support were desired, that GOB would consult urgently with us in order that we might have chance review with Belgians whether or not such military forces seemed required.

For Ambassador Godley: Believe under circumstances it preferable that you not raise this matter with Lengema. We prefer that it remain a subject for bilateral Belgian-Congolese discussions and that initiative be left to Belgians for present.

Ball

---

174. Telegram From the Department of State to the Embassy in the Congo[1]

Washington, June 2, 1964, 7:55 p.m.

1376. In view imminent departure all UN troops from Congo and deteriorating situation involving ANC in Kivu which could have important repercussions on other potential trouble areas in Congo, we believe GOC should now move rapidly to make bilateral arrangements with one or more friendly African countries to permit stationing of troops in Congo.

We recognize of course that strenuous efforts in support this thesis have already been made with various GOC officials and we aware of problems which presence other African troops might pose for Con-

---

[1] Source: National Archives, RG 59, Central Files 1964–66, POL 23–9 THE CONGO. Confidential; Priority. Drafted by Tienken; cleared by Dorros in AF/W, Polk, Buffum, Galanto, and Colonel Junkerman in DOD; and approved by O'Sullivan. Repeated to USUN, Brussels, CINCMEAFSA, Addis Ababa, Lagos, and Tunis.

golese. We encouraged however by Nendaka's remarks re Adoula's thinking reported Embtel 2438[2] and believe conclusion of bilateral offers quickest means of introducing stabilizing force into Congo at this time.

Since time appears be ripe, Embassy accordingly requested raise matter again with GOC at earliest appropriate time and urge GOC take necessary action quickly. Nigeria of course comes to mind as well as Tunisia and Ethiopia as possible bilateral partners. We suggest you may wish discuss with both Adoula and Kasavubu, although we leave choice to your discretion. We would in any case appreciate rundown on Kasavubu's views on general situation.[3]

Ball

---

[2] Telegram 2438 from Leopoldville, June 2, reported that Nendaka told an Embassy officer that Mobutu was finally prepared to seek assistance for a program to recruit 10 new battalions and provide them with 12 months of intensive training. (Ibid.)

[3] In telegram 2460 from Leopoldville, June 3, Godley suggested that discussions with Africans concerning assistance to the Congolese be discreet and limited to high-level, general discussions until they could see the results of Adoula's approach to the Nigerians. (Ibid.)

---

175. Telegram From the Department of State to the Embassy in Belgium[1]

Washington, June 12, 1964, 7:43 p.m.

1720. Embtel 2007.[2] We fully share Spaak's concern that there be politically effective government in Congo which must very soon assume responsibility for its own internal order. Broader base and more

---

[1] Source: National Archives, RG 59, Central Files 1964–66, POL 23–9 THE CONGO. Secret; Priority. Drafted by Appling and Looram, cleared by Tasca, and approved by Harriman. Repeated to Leopoldville.

[2] Telegram 2007 from Brussels, June 11, reported that Spaak was planning to send letters to Kasavubu and Adoula pointing out that strong opinion existed in Belgium that the Congolese Government needed to take constructive steps to strengthen its political position throughout the Congo. The letters would warn that additional Belgian assistance might in part be conditioned by parliamentary and public opinion of the vigor of the Congolese Government and whether it was representative of the whole nation. MacArthur's response had been that he thought it important that the letters not imply that the Belgians were hinting at replacement of Adoula or that reorganization and broadening the base of the government should involve inclusion of pro-Communist elements supported by Peking or Moscow. (Ibid.)

representative leadership may help. However, we strongly endorse your remarks contained penultimate paragraph reftel. While letters might elicit clearer picture Kasavubu's and Adoula's thinking, important that they not have effect of encouraging Congolese open negotiations with CNL, as Ambassador Godley points out (Leo's 1215 to Brussels).[3] Similarly we of opinion that at this juncture Belgian advice would be taken more constructively if not accompanied by implied threats of reducing support. On balance we agree with Amb Godley that oral approach probably more prudent and flexible than letter unless it of very general nature. At same time appreciate Spaak probably under heavy pressure take some action.

We have Congolese situation under continual review. However given present fluidity of political situation depending in part on outcome day to day military events, Department not yet prepared move as fast and far as Spaak at this juncture. We continue nevertheless believe highly important we and Belgians coordinate thinking and if possible work together towards general objectives. In this connection would be interested in more specific information on Belgian thinking about possible reshuffle or makeup any new government should such occur. Are there indications GOB now considering Tshombe as PM or for other role in government at one end of political spectrum and members CNL including Soumialot at other?

Brussels 2022 and 2023 just received but do not alter our thinking above.[4]

Rusk

---

[3] Telegram 1215 from Leopoldville to Brussels was sent to the Department as telegram 2553, June 11. (Ibid., POL THE CONGO)

[4] Both dated June 12. (Ibid.)

176. Telegram From the Station in the Congo to the Central Intelligence Agency[1]

Leopoldville, June 13, 1964.

1413 (In 05830). Ref: [*less than 1 line not declassified*].[2]

1. Ref plus related lesser developments lead us believe it time consider operational tactics to insure ODYOKE against possible loss of influence in Congo if [Identity 1] falls and his equipe eclipsed by influx [Identity 2] or other entourage. Though we far from certain how present muddle will resolve itself, we reasonably optimistic that with fast footwork and pertinent decisions ODYOKE can maintain its position vis-à-vis any of the more probable successor regimes to that of [Identity 1].

2. Must bear in mind however that ODYOKE has for so long been associated in so many minds with unequivocal [*cryptonym not declassified*] support that if we were to adopt traditional policy of "watchful waiting" toward any new regime such posture would almost certainly be misinterpreted by that regime. We have gone for broke for so long that our reservoir of trust among [*cryptonym not declassified*] is disturbingly low.

3. While we might be able count on Congolese venality and lust for power to enable us to buy our way through any immediate crises, such tactics would seem to return us to mid-62 morass rather than moving us ahead toward goal of united and stable Congo. However difficult a nettle it may be to grasp, it our conviction that there are all sorts of political figures in Congo who while strongly anti-Communist simply do not like [Identity 1] or his associates. Given basically conservative character [Identity 3], it seems highly likely these figures will play key role in new regime.

4. Thus believe it incumbent on us to begin deciding which of these figures we (KUBARK) can work with, can influence, and therefore should support.

[Omitted here is further discussion of the political situation.]

5. While we cannot argue with conviction that CDA has yet become impressive political organization, mass forces it claims to represent may be more formidable than those which [*cryptonym not declassified*] and/or RADECO have rallied up to now. RADECO currently

---

[1] Source: Central Intelligence Agency Files, Job 78–00435R, DDO/ISS Files, Box 2, Folder 10, [*cryptonym not declassified*] Operations. Secret; Rybat; [*cryptonym not declassified*]. No time of receipt appears on the message.

[2] Not found.

negotiating with Conakat and MNC/Kiwewa, but outcome these negotiations remains very much an open question. And this seems to us to be crux of problem. However desirable national party and "apolitical" government may be, neither seem to be in cards for Congo at present time. Strong leader might make these goals feasible, but even [Identity 4] had his problems. Thus inclined believe we should recognize political appeal of regional groupings and alliances, and try to influence and focus them on one objective—unified Congo. [*cryptonym not declassified*] have obviously tried political alliance system, but in terms of mass support they have always dealt from weakness. Popular dissatisfaction with [*cryptonym not declassified*] inability solve overwhelming problems overnight has only underscored this weakness. Ineffectiveness [*cryptonym not declassified*] security forces—ANC and Sûreté—has further undercut their national hegemony.

[Omitted here is further discussion of the political situation.]

---

177. Memorandum for President Johnson[1]

Washington, June 15, 1964.

SUBJECT

Congo

Both the political and military situations in the Congo are very confused. The government is weak, political unrest is growing, the army is unreliable, and insurgency is spreading.

1. *Politically* a "transition government" will take over by June 30, looking to a new constitution and elections. Adoula is at the low point of his power and prestige, and there is a lot of intrigue and maneuver. Adoula seems completely indecisive and incapable of action. However, the best bet for the new government is still Adoula with a broader base to the right and, perhaps, to the moderate left (which the Belgians are demanding). We probably have enough influence to force a change of government but not to control the outcome—and it's doubtful change

[1] Source: Johnson Library, National Security File, Country File, Congo, Vol. I, 11/63–6/64. Secret. The memorandum, on NSC stationery, is not signed. A June 16 memorandum from McGeorge Bundy transmitting two memoranda on the Congo to the President indicates that the "short one" was prepared at his direction by William H. Brubeck of the NSC Staff. (Ibid., Memos to the President, McGeorge Bundy, Vol. 5)

would solve much. We continue, therefore, to play a waiting game, maintaining support for Adoula for want of a better alternative.

2. *Militarily* the Congo army (ANC) has been almost a complete failure in the Kivu rebellion; well armed troops are being routed by Pygmies carrying spears and machetes. The rebellion is largely tribal with no real evidence of foreign intervention or supply. However, rebels now have some arms and equipment captured from the ANC. After taking several towns and routing the ANC the rebels have been quiet the past week. This weekend the ANC began a counter offensive, have gone a few miles south and reoccuppied a town formally [*formerly*?] rebel-held, but now seem to be stalled even though there is no resistance. If the rebels counterattack the ANC will probably run again and there is no significant evidence of ANC leadership or fighting ability. If the rebels take Bukavu, which could well happen, there may well be a serious political crisis in Leopoldville and new fighting in other places, particularly Stanleyville.

178. Editorial Note

A memorandum prepared in the Central Intelligence Agency on June 18, 1964, briefed Director of Central Intelligence McCone on U.S. assistance to the Congolese Air Force. The occasion was a meeting the same day of the Special Group (CI) at which the participation of two American pilots in combat missions in the Congo was discussed. According to the memorandum, on June 11, 12, and 13, "under heavy pressures from the hard-pressed Congolese, these men exceeded their authority and flew operational missions in the Kivu area." On June 8 the field had been "cabled instructions on the limitations on operational involvement of the American pilots, restricting them to reconnaissance." The pilots were contract employees of CIA and had signed contracts with General Mobutu for the Congolese Government. When first questioned about the matter, the memorandum stated, the Department of State had said it had no knowledge that American personnel were engaged in air operational activity in the Congo, but on June 16 the Department indicated it had checked with the Embassy and had been informed that some American civilian pilots under contract to the Congo Government had flown sorties in the last few days. (Central Intelligence Agency Files, Job 82–00450R, 40 Committee, Congo (K), 1960–1964)

In reviewing authorization for U.S. assistance to the Congolese Air Force, the memorandum noted that on December 7, 1962, the Special Group had approved a proposal presented by CIA, based on recommendations from the U.S. Ambassador in Leopoldville and the Department of State, to increase the capability of the Congolese Air Force to the extent of enabling it to operate with armament in the eastern regions of the Congo for morale and reconnaissance purposes. Then, at its meeting on May 28, 1964, the Special Group approved expansion of that assistance with the operational objective of providing "the CAF with a fighter aircraft capability to render combat air support to the Congolese National Army in suppressing the present insurgencies, as well as any possible future insurgencies which might erupt as a result of the withdrawal of UN forces." The memorandum also noted that the Special Group authorization of May 28, 1964, included the following statement: "In February 1964, as a result of the Kwilu uprising, the Department of State, at the request of the Government of the Congo, authorized shifting the mission of the air support program from a non-combat, psychological effort to an active combat participation."

According to the minutes of the Special Group (CI) meeting at 2 p.m. on June 18, the following discussion took place:

"*Congo (L)*—Mr. McCone reported that the two T–28s piloted by Americans had done an excellent job in breaking up the rebel attack on ANC positions in Kamanyola. Without these air strikes, Bukavu would have probably fallen before the rebel advance. He informed the Group that these Americans were hired by the Congolese Government to train [*less than 1 line not declassified*] the use of the T–28s but that training had not been completed at this time and Mobutu had persuaded them to fly the missions.

"Mr. McCone expressed concern about criticism of US citizens under contractual employment with a foreign government participating in combat operations. Governor Harriman, while praising the practical results of the air attacks in saving Kamanyola, added that US policy, as it now stands, is against the use of such US citizens on combat missions." (Ibid.)

DCI McCone's own record of the June 18 Special Group meeting stated that he took exception to the Department of State's comments to the press, saying that he saw no reason to "stand down" the American pilots, whose missions had been very successful. McCone recorded that during the meeting and afterwards, Harriman had taken "violent exception" to his position, stating that the Americans had acted beyond their authority and were subject to sanctions and possible loss of citizenship. McCone said he had countered by saying that the Americans were in the employ of the Congolese government and could do anything they wanted to, and that he was pleased they had taken the initiative they took as they had saved a deteriorating situation. He noted that he had made the same statements on this issue at the 303 Committee meeting and also privately to McGeorge Bundy. (Ibid.)

179. Telegram From the Department of State to the Embassy in Nigeria[1]

Washington, June 19, 1964, 7:58 p.m.

2505. Lagos 2447 to Dept.[2]

For Lagos: Appreciate your efforts press GON take favorable decision on question of troops for Congo. Continued failure ANC assume its responsibilities in Kivu in our view makes presence of Nigerian troops in Congo increasingly imperative.[3] We believe, inter alia, Adoula government will benefit considerably from presence Nigerian troops regardless of their terms of reference simply by being in Congo during this difficult transition period. We naturally leave question of tactics with GON to your discretion. Request however that you continue follow matter closely and urge GON on every appropriate occasion move quickly in response to GOC request.

We have no info substantiate Wachuku's concern about possible British opposition. On contrary all our talks with British reps here have indicated British support for Nigerian troop contingent in Congo including likelihood HMG might be willing provide air transport from Nigeria if asked.

---

[1] Source: National Archives, RG 59, Central Files 1964–66, POL 23–9 THE CONGO. Confidential; Priority. Drafted by Tienken; cleared by Colonel Gall, Thomas A. Thoreson of AFW, and Thomas M. Judd of BNA; and approved by Tasca. Also sent to Leopoldville and repeated to Brussels, USUN, CINCMEAFSA, London, and Paris.

[2] In telegram 2447 from Lagos, June 18, Ambassador Matthews reported that he had discussed the Congolese request for Nigerian troops with Nigerian officials, urging the need to protect the investment Nigeria, the United States, and others had already made in the Congo and stressing that the United States was prepared to assist Nigeria in maintaining troops there. (Ibid.)

[3] Telegram 2511 to Lagos, June 22, transmitted a letter from President Johnson to Prime Minister Balewa in which the President said that he hoped it would be possible for the Nigerian Government to give Adoula an early, favorable reply because he believed that the presence of Nigerian troops in the Congo would greatly improve the situation. (Ibid.)

For Leopoldville: Trust you will continue do what you can with Osakwe and GOC as appropriate obtain favorable GON response ASAP.

Rusk

180. Memorandum From William H. Brubeck of the National Security Council Staff to President Johnson[1]

Washington, June 20, 1964.

SUBJECT

American Pilots in the Congo

For eighteen months a group of [*less than 1 line not declassified*] pilots under nominal contract to the Congo Government [*less than 1 line not declassified*] has been flying US-supplied T6 planes in support of the Congo army. The T6s have now been replaced by T28s. The operation is managed and trained by two American civilians. They were under certain restrictions but did do some reconnaissance and combat missions in the Kwilu this spring, but were subsequently ordered to do no more combat missions.

The two Americans were under heavy local pressure during the past two weeks, however, to fly combat in the Eastern Congo crisis, as the only pilots already trained to fly the T28s. They did so, and their contribution was probably decisive in temporarily saving the Kivu. It would be hard to second guess their decision now by hindsight.

However, our press handling of the problem here is open to criticism. After several days of press rumors, and in response to questions last Monday, State said "The Department's present information is" no American civilian pilots are flying combat. [*1½ lines not declassified*]

As a result, on Tuesday State told the press that we had now learned some American civilians had in fact "flown T28 sorties in the past few days." On Wednesday in response to further questions, State said the contract pilots had violated no US law but that we now had an understanding that the Congo Government would no longer use them for operational missions. After that interest began to die down.

[1] Source: Johnson Library, National Security File, Country File, Congo, Vol. I. Secret; Sensitive Handling.

Comment:

The actual combat flying in the Congo was not the cause of our trouble. Press handling was, even though there was ample high-level consideration of the problem each day, in which I participated.

In retrospect we made three mistakes. We gave a qualified answer before we knew the facts and then had to retract. We were too slow, once the story broke, in giving the press an adequate explanation, so the story snowballed on a speculative basis for several days. Undoubtedly encouraged by some people in State looking for a scapegoat, the press made this into a State–CIA fight; some papers implied, I think unfairly, that CIA had engaged in tricky dealing. The result, in addition to bad publicity on CIA and damage to our general credibility, is of course to cast doubt on our operations not only in the Congo but in Southeast Asia.

In part the handling of the story was just bad judgment and we just have to learn from the experience. Beyond that, State is trying to prevent any further gossip to the press about CIA. Also, because part of our trouble was inadequate briefing of the press, we are systematically back-grounding key reporters so that they will have better information on the Congo and we can avoid speculative stories.

B.

181. Telegram From the Department of State to the Embassy in Spain[1]

Washington, June 22, 1964, 7:44 p.m.

3192. Tshombe. Re Madrid's 2116.[2] We appreciate suggestion contained reftel for contact with Tshombe. Unless Embassy Leo perceives objection we believe that contact should be made but, however, by DCM McBride. We hope that circumstances of meeting can be such as to attract no publicity. We recognize there exists risks that Tshombe will put out his version of why contact was made and what transpired

[1] Source: National Archives, RG 59, Central Files 1964–66, POL 6 THE CONGO. Confidential; Priority; Limit Distribution. Drafted by O'Sullivan; cleared by Williams, Harriman, and McKillop; and approved by Tyler. Repeated to Leopoldville and Brussels.

[2] In telegram 2116 from Madrid, June 18, the Embassy asked whether, in view of the unsettled Congo situation, it should take the initiative and attempt to discover Tshombe's plans. (Ibid.)

either publicly or through political channels. This information probably will reach Adoula and others in GOC very quickly. Consequently important you flash report Washington and Leo results conversation.

Dept hopes that meeting can take place in friendly atmosphere. Principal purposes of meeting should be 1) to ascertain Tshombe views on Congo scene and his plans for future. Department would be particularly interested in Tshombe's version of what transpired in recent Mali visit; 2) to inform him that US policy continues to strongly support a unified Congo. You should point out that GOC is moving to stabilize the political institutions through development of Constitution which issued from Constitutional Commission with participation his lieutenants at Luluabourg earlier this year; that GOC is planning submit Constitution to referendum; and that all patriotic Congolese should work toward greater stability in a unified Congo.

If Tshombe should sound you out on US views re his return to Congo, you should state that his return basically internal Congolese affair. We would strongly hope if he did return would be done legally and without use threat ex-Katanga gendarmes or Katanga secession.

You may also remind Tshombe that his anti-Communist views expressed US officials in past are in contrast with his apparent recent contacts leftist elements of CNL.[3]

For Leopoldville: You may in your discretion inform Adoula and/or other GOC officials of prospective meeting. You might wish to point out that purpose of meeting is to try to probe Tshombe's intentions and to caution him against any moves on his part against Congolese territorial integrity. You may add if you so desire that we will inform PriMin of results.

Rusk

---

[3] In telegram 1791 to Brussels, June 24, Harriman suggested that, in view of Tshombe's travel plans, MacArthur should see Tshombe while he was in Brussels in order to make the points in telegram 3192. (Ibid.) In telegram 2100 from Brussels, June 25, MacArthur reported that he met that morning with Tshombe, who said that he was returning to Leopoldville at the request of Kasavubu and Adoula and that he was willing to play an important and constructive political role in the Congo if this was desired. (Ibid., POL 23–9 THE CONGO)

182. Memorandum From the Joint Strategic Survey Council to the Joint Chiefs of Staff[1]

JCS 2262/145 Washington, June 25, 1964.

THE SITUATION IN THE CONGO (U)

1. The situation in the Congo is deteriorating rapidly, and both the public news and the intelligence reports indicate that the central government has little, if any, control over the course of events. The UN forces, except for some Nigerian troops, have left the country. The Congolese National Army is an almost useless instrument.

2. There are clear signs that the Communists are exploiting the growing chaos. The Committee of National Liberation has had financial aid and guidance from both the Soviets and the Chinese; there are Chinese and Czech agents along the Burundi border in the east; and Mulele, the leader of the revolt in Kwilu, was trained by the Communists in China.

3. Some moves are underway to promote bilateral arrangements by which the incumbent Congo government would receive troop assistance from other countries. It is not yet clear whether such efforts will be fruitful.

4. The consistent US policy has been to support a Congolese government of coalition moderates and attempt to enforce control by UN-supported military efforts. In four years of UN presence, no Congolese government, either under Premier Adoula or his predecessor, has been successful in establishing order.

5. The Council suggests that the situation is now so unpromising that the basic US policy should be reconsidered. It is further suggested that, since the "moderate coalition" concept has failed, the time has come to back a strong leader who is opposed to the Communists. The only man who now meets this description is Tshombe, and if we are to accept the reality that the moderate coalition concept has failed, it would seem that we have little choice but to support Tshombe if we are to improve the political situation. Only if this political situation is stabilized is there any hope that military force (native or other) could be effective in establishing order under a government which would be either neutral or pro-Western rather than Communist.

6. It is perhaps an over-simplification to say that Tshombe is a creature of the Union Minière and of the Belgians, but it is fairly safe to say that he would be "on our side" if we were to help him. Certainly he is a

---

[1] Source: Washington National Records Center, RG 218, JCS Files, 9111 (25 June 64). Secret.

strong leader in Katanga; he does command some loyalties among other Congolese in addition to control of his own gendarmerie; and the chances are that he could establish control and order in Katanga initially, and, from this base, eventual control of the rest of the country. Tshombe could be supported either as a member of, or a replacement for, the present government.

7. There are many facets to a proposal to back Tshombe, not the least of which would be the reluctance of the State Department to support a man who was closely associated with the former Belgian colonialism. But, if we do nothing, we will soon watch the Republic of the Congo disintegrate and then emerge as a Communist-controlled entity. Radical changes are needed if this is to be forestalled, and radical changes in our favor will not be achieved through the Organization of African Unity. The answer lies in a different direction.

8. a. The best solution would be to have President Kasavubu appoint Tshombe as Premier. If this were to happen, the United States should give strong and overt political support to Tshombe as the legal government.

b. If this overt solution does not come about, we should covertly support Tshombe, [*2½ lines not declassified*].

c. The chances of success under Tshombe, one way or the other, appear to be considerably brighter than those under the present course of events.

9. It is, therefore, recommended that the Joint Chiefs of Staff express their concern over the present course of events in the Congo both to the Secretary of Defense and at the next State–JCS meeting, and that, in these conversations, they explore:

a. The apparent failure of the present US policy of supporting the broadly-based moderate-coalition type of government;

b. The prospects of success if Tshombe were to be installed as the head of a strong central government, or covertly supported to replace the present government; and

c. The problems of rendering support through the Belgians.

10. It is further recommended that:

a. This paper NOT be forwarded to commanders of unified or specified commands.

b. This paper NOT be forwarded to US officers assigned to NATO activities.

c. This paper NOT be forwarded to the Chairman, US Delegation, United Nations Military Staff Committee.[2]

---

[2] Attached is a July 8 note signed by Assistant Secretary E.A. Davidson stating that the Joint Chiefs of Staff considered JCS 2262/145 on July 8 and agreed to "Note" it.

183. Circular Telegram From the Department of State to All African Posts[1]

Washington, June 28, 1964, 3:48 p.m.

2451. Return of Tshombe to Congo. Previous US position re ex-Katanga president Moise Tshombe was based on his efforts establish separate, independent state of Katanga thus threatening fragmentation of Congo. There was no US opposition to Tshombe assuming a role to be determined by Congolese people on national political level or even on provincial level within framework Congolese nation.

Tshombe returned to Leopoldville June 26 at invitation of President Kasavubu and Prime Minister Adoula. Speculation is rife as to what role he will play in resolution of current Congo crisis. Possibilities include his becoming Prime Minister, assuming an important Ministry, returning to Katanga, returning to exile but there no firm indication of outcome of present maneuvering. On balance we believe chances are good (but less good than a week ago) that Adoula will remain Prime Minister.

In talks with government officials or other Africans following guidance is provided:

USG views return of Tshombe with some reserve at this point and hopes that he will not be a disturbing factor in Congolese political picture. However determination of his role is a Congolese internal matter.

If he can contribute to internal stability in Congo and strengthen unity of country his presence would be useful. He is still a popular and powerful figure in Katanga and we hope he will anchor that key province to rest of Congo. On other hand if his presence would give rise to secessionist tendencies in Katanga or elsewhere USG would view return with grave concern.

Mr. Tshombe has shown himself to be a gifted opportunist in the past. Recently he has associated himself with extremist and leftist self-exiled Congolese politicians, publicly called for a government of conciliation including elements of all tendencies, and paid visit to Mali. These may be efforts improve his image as an African nationalist and thus gain acceptance from Africans who have always opposed him. He may believe that he can use leftists to come into power and then effectively neutralize and eliminate them. However even if this the case his

---

[1] Source: National Archives, RG 59, Central Files 1964–66, POL 6 THE CONGO. Confidential. Drafted by Schaufele; cleared by Fredericks, O'Sullivan, and James Ozzello of EUR; and approved by Harriman. Also sent to Brussels, Paris, and London and pouched to Constantine, Douala, Durban, Enugu, Ibadan, Johannesburg, Kaduna, Oran, and Port Elizabeth.

willingness accept them even temporarily may serve to provide basis for increased Bloc, and perhaps Chicom influence in Congo.

Obviously US cannot make decision re Tshombe's future but it following situation closely and hopes that results of political palavers in Congo will result in moderate, independent GOC which can maintain internal peace and order, contribute to strengthening of Congolese unity and take necessary steps to establish sound public finance system which will further encourage recent economic upturn.

Rusk

184. Memorandum From Samuel Belk of the National Security Council Staff to the President's Special Assistant for National Security Affairs (Bundy)[1]

Washington, July 2, 1964.

SUBJECT

The Congo

Political maneuvering is continuing in Leopoldville and Tshombe, at the moment, appears to be gaining strength. Mac Godley is less sure today than yesterday that Kasavubu will ask Adoula to take the reins of government. The CAS in Leopoldville also thinks Tshombe has the edge.

Godley and company are continuing to "lay low" but also are discreetly maintaining their usual contacts.

As for how long Kasavubu will wait before appointing a new PM, the best *guess* is that it will be on July 10, when the referendum for the new constitution is finished, or shortly thereafter.

As a backdrop for Kasavubu's final decision are two important considerations: one is that he knows that Tshombe himself wants to be President and, if he got the post of PM, he would be a direct threat to Kasavubu; the second consideration—and Mac Godley takes this very seriously—is that Kasavubu has said many times in the past that Adoula is his man and Kasavubu, for a Congolese, is very consistent.

[1] Source: Johnson Library, National Security File, Country File, Congo, Vol. II, Memos and Miscellaneous, 7/64–8/64. No classification marking.

If things go "normally," as soon as Kasavubu appoints a new PM, I think this will be the time for Governor Harriman to brief the President. Until that time—unless some unforeseen disaster develops in the meantime—we can only continue alert watchfulness.

Both Governors Harriman and Williams are out of town over the holiday. I plan to be here most—if not all—of the time. If I do go away, I will see to it that we are fully covered over here.

Sam

---

185. Memorandum for the Record[1]

Washington, July 2, 1964.

SUBJECT

Meeting of the 303 Committee

Present were

McGeorge Bundy, Secretary Vance, Ambassador Thompson, myself and Peter Jessup
[*1½ lines not declassified*]

[Omitted here is discussion of other matters.]

6. We then went into an inconclusive discussion of what to do about such flaps as the Congo flyers when covert actions became surfaced. I made a strong plea that the whole machinery of Government settle down and not be euchred into going off half cocked every time somebody in the press asked a question. I said it seemed to me we could certainly delay at least 24 hours if we wanted to before attempting to reply to Communist propaganda charges whether true or false. I said I deplored the proliferation of information about covert actions. Bundy thought that perhaps Greenfield (Manning's replacement) should be fully clued in on covert operations. I objected and said that he should be taught to keep his antenna tuned to the possibility that a flap might be as a result of covert operations and in such circumstances

---

[1] Source: Central Intelligence Agency Files, Job 80B01285A, DCI/McCone Files, 303 Committee Meetings (1964). Secret; Eyes Only. A note on the memorandum reads: "Dictated 4 July but not read."

to check immediately with Joe Scott or Joe's successor. I got the impression they all agreed with this but no decision was taken.

Marshall S. Carter
Lieutenant General, USA
Acting Director

186. Editorial Note

In telegram 1711 to the Central Intelligence Agency, July 2, 1964, the Station in Leopoldville reported that the [*cryptonym not declassified*] program as currently authorized appeared finished in view of the split up of the [*cryptonym not declassified*] group. If Cyrille Adoula remained in or returned to his present position, he would have a quite different basis of support, and established channels to him were no longer usable. If he lost his present position his principal role then would become leadership of a political grouping and hence any future CIA support would necessarily be on a different basis and presumably at a greatly reduced level. The very fluidity of the situation indicated that it was time to build or solidify channels over a broad spectrum. The Station expected soon to begin receiving feelers and requests for support from many quarters and should be prepared to respond thereto on an interim basis while seeking guidance from Headquarters. (Central Intelligence Agency Files, Job 78–00435R, DDO/ISS Files, Box 1, Folder 10, [*cryptonym not declassified*] Operations)

187. Telegram From the Station in the Congo to the Central Intelligence Agency[1]

Leopoldville, July 3, 1964.

1737 (In 20904). Ref Leop 1731 (In 20700).[2]

1. Ref meeting not attended by [COS], who temporarily out of action with dysentery. However as background to above, following are [COS] impressions of currents and cross currents among [*cryptonym not declassified*] during past week. First fact of life is that [Identity 1] and [Mobutu] have obviously committed themselves to course of action which designed put [Identity 2] into Prime Minister job. Second fact of life is [Godley] hostility to [Identity 1] whom he considers evil and basically undemocratic. Third element is (somewhat inept) tactics of [Godley] in beating drums around town on [Identity 3] behalf. Present situation is that all concerned are acutely aware that [Identity 2] may end up as Prime Minister and all concerned are trying hedge bets in case this happens as well as in case it does not happen.

2. Re [Identity 1] and [Mobutu] [Identity 1] has been assiduously repeating to [COS] history of [*less than 1 line not declassified*] group, citing ODACID basic opposition to [Mobutu] takeover in 1960, with continuing pressure from ODACID to [*less than 1 line not declassified*] parliament, culminating in recall of Timberlake and in Lovanium reconciliation in July 61. [Identity 1] reminding us of [*cryptonym not declassified*] charter of August 1961 in which power to be controlled by [*cryptonym not declassified*] with [Identity 3] [*less than 1 line not declassified*], as front man as long as he served the purpose. [*27 lines not declassified*]

3. Re [Godley]. [Embassy] reporting describes fully [Godley] activity in passing on word to [Identity 4], diplomatic colony, and local politicoes, his conviction that [Identity 3] should remain in present job.[3] [*5 lines not declassified*]

[Omitted here is further discussion of the political situation.]

---

[1] Source: Central Intelligence Agency Files, Job 78–00435R, DDO/ISS Files, Box 2, Folder 10, [*cryptonym not declassified*] Operations. Secret; Rybat; [*2 cryptonyms not declassified*]; Priority. Received at 0230Z.

[2] Not found.

[3] In telegram 1813 from Leopoldville, July 8, Cushing reported that during a routine meeting, [*name not declassified*] had continued to ask for U.S. Government support for Tshombe, and had assured him that the [*cryptonym not declassified*] group would be capable of "managing" him. (Central Intelligence Agency Files, Job 78–00435R, DDO/ISS Files, Box 2, Folder 10, [*cryptonym not declassified*] Operations)

188. Telegram From the Department of State to the Embassy in Belgium[1]

Washington, July 7, 1964, 12:19 p.m.

23. Brussels tel 2108.[2] Department shares Spaak's analysis of general situation and what our relations with Tshombe should be if he becomes Prime Minister or member cabinet. Would be advantageous for GOB take lead in this respect since it has retained closer contact with Tshombe than we have and because of support for him in non-official Belgian circles.

Our ability to work closely with Tshombe if he becomes PriMin will depend in large measure on Tshombe himself, what commitments he makes to become PriMin and how he and his Cabinet conduct themselves thereafter. It would give us particular concern if GOC under Tshombe were to withdraw recognition of GRC and subsequently recognize Chicoms, which could be condition CNL agreement to support or join Tshombe govt.

Secondly, we would expect Tshombe to show his good faith in working toward a territorially intact, economically viable Congo by ensuring that ex-Katangese gendarmes including mercenaries in Katanga and Angola were effectively eliminated as threat to Congo unity.

Finally we believe it essential that Tshombe or any other prime minister continue economic stabilization and fiscal austerity programs and resist any policy which could lead to inflationary pressure or reverse economic progress made over past eight months.

For Brussels: Suggest that Embassy express foregoing views to Spaak and should occasion arise to Belgian business and financial interests. In talks with Spaak you should draw on forthcoming Leopoldville reply to Deptel 16 to Leopoldville[3] concerning relative acceptability various leftists in Tshombe cabinet. We continue to be concerned over potential danger from leftists who may be included in government and desire Spaak's continuing appraisal of personalities involved, and their objectives.

Ball

---

[1] Source: National Archives, RG 59, Central Files 1964–66, POL 23–9 THE CONGO. Confidential; Limit Distribution. Drafted on July 6 by O'Sullivan and Schaufele; cleared by Appling, Tasca, and EA Director Robert A. Fearey; and approved by Harriman. Also sent to Leopoldville and repeated to London and Paris.

[2] In telegram 2108 from Brussels, June 25, MacArthur reported a conversation with Spaak, who pointed to Tshombe's mounting popularity in the Congo and advised that the United States try to work with him so that he would play "Belgo-American cards" and work with Congolese moderates. (Ibid.)

[3] Dated July 6. (Ibid., POL 1 US–THE CONGO)

189. Memorandum From the Under Secretary of State for Political Affairs (Harriman) to the President's Special Assistant for National Security Affairs (Bundy)[1]

Washington, July 11, 1964.

SUBJECT

Preliminary Comments on New Political Situation in the Congo

President Kasavubu's motives in naming Tshombe as Prime Minister and giving him the responsibility to form a transitional government are unclear. He may be giving Tshombe enough rope to hang himself or he may feel that it is necessary to get Tshombe's support to prevent unrest and instability in Katanga. Kasavubu has alleged that he is keeping Adoula out of the transitional government in order to keep him available for the future.

It seems clear, however, that Kasavubu intends to control the situation more closely than he has in the past and the new constitution which has just been submitted to a national referendum provides for a de Gaulle type of president with the cabinet responsible to him rather than to Parliament. A further indication of this is that he has placed the Defense Ministry in a committee, the membership of which is still unknown, reporting directly to him rather than to Tshombe.

The announced cabinet discards all of the old government, brings in Tshombe's collaborator in Katanga as Interior Minister, makes a gesture to the dissident Committee of National Liberation (CNL) by including one of its leaders and includes representatives of four other political groupings as well as two so-called technicians. It is not so broadly representative as Tshombe seemed to indicate when he called for a government of national reconciliation or as the Belgians wanted. The ability of many of the ministers most of whom do not have high positions in their political parties, is unknown.

Tshombe and his Katangan colleague, Munongo, have concentrated six portfolios and the prime ministership in their hands. Although Tshombe has awakened many Congolese hopes for an effective and unifying government, this fact may soon cause serious difficulties. The individuals and groups not included will probably not wait long to start harassing him.

Immediately after his installation Tshombe called in our Ambassador and complained of breakdowns of the T–28 aircraft and de-

---

[1] Source: Johnson Library, National Security File, Country File, Congo, Vol. II. Confidential.

manded immediate operational availability. We are sending a maintenance mechanic to Leopoldville on Tuesday to work on the planes. Tshombe stated that he planned to repatriate his gendarmes, now in Angola, alleging a strength of 4,000, to restore order in North Katanga and retake the provincial capital from the rebels. Chief of Staff Mobutu was present and raised no objection. Tshombe pointed out these forces would be under Congolese army command. The return of the gendarmes will probably cause strong African criticism of Tshombe to whom the Africans in the past have been hostile. After his first cabinet meeting Tshombe announced that all political prisoners would be released. This presumably includes Gizenga, Lumumba's senior supporter. It is reported that Kasavubu does not want to free him.

We believe that we should support Tshombe in his efforts to promote unity, internal security and economic stability. Our existing economic and military aid programs should be quietly continued. Former Prime Minister Adoula believes that there should be no change in this regard. We should also endeavor to strengthen our ties and relations with President Kasavubu whose position is so much stronger now. However, until we have a clearer indication of Tshombe's intentions by his actions, we should be cautious in not appearing to give him unqualified support.

Averell

---

190. Telegram From the Department of State to the Embassy in the Congo[1]

Washington, July 15, 1964, 7:25 p.m.

70. Embtel 116.[2] Although Department recognizes reasons causing Kasavubu decision not to attend Cairo meeting, in long run absence may prove harmful to Congo and Kasavubu himself. However we believe his presence desirable in terms his African image and to permit him reassure other Africans about future direction Congolese policy.

---

[1] Source: National Archives, RG 59, Central Files 1964–66, POL 3 OAU. Confidential; Immediate. Drafted by Schaufele; cleared by O'Sullivan, Olds of AFI, and Jones of NE; and approved by Williams. Repeated to Brussels and Cairo.

[2] Telegram 116 from Leopoldville, July 15, reported that no one from Leopoldville was going to attend the Organization of African Unity (OAU) Heads of State meeting at Cairo. (Ibid.)

If GOC leaders absent, moderate African resistance to determined steam roller tactics by certain African states to ostracize Congo on basis Tshombe position may well evaporate. On other hand their presence presents fait accompli which hopefully will stiffen moderate attitude and gain at least some initial African acceptability for Tshombe.

Absence could result in isolation of Congo in Africa which will give Tshombe excuse turn further toward Belgians, Portuguese, South Africans for assistance.

Unless in your opinion effort to change Kasavubu's mind is too late you requested in your discretion make urgent representations to Kasavubu based on above considerations urging him to attend OAU meeting as scheduled.

FYI: Reporting from Cairo gives no indication of reported telegram to Kasavubu from OAU foreign ministers asking him not to bring Tshombe to OAU meeting. Conceivably this was rumor planted to bring about Kasavubu–Tshombe decision not to attend. Suggest you take no position re Tshombe attendance. This decision one to be made by Kasavubu. If you approach Kasavubu you should inform Belgians in advance. End FYI.

For Brussels: In your discretion you may approach Belgians requesting them intercede with Kasavubu on above lines.[3]

Rusk

---

[3] Telegram 78 to Leopoldville, July 16, reported that Congo Chargé Pongo called at the Department to get the U.S. reaction to his government's decision not to attend the OAU conference. He was told that the U.S. Government thought Kasavubu should attend the meeting to preserve his image as an African leader and to prevent the Congo from being isolated in Africa. (Ibid.) No Congolese representative attended the Cairo conference, which was held July 17–21.

191. Memorandum From the Chief of the Africa Division, Directorate of Plans, Central Intelligence Agency (Fields) to the Deputy Director for Plans, Central Intelligence Agency (Helms)[1]

Washington, July 20, 1964.

SUBJECT

Personal Communication From Congolese Officials to Director and Africa Division Officer

1. The attached three letters with translations are from [*1 line not declassified*], to DCI; from [*less than 1 line not declassified*] to Mr. Lawrence Devlin, AF Division officer; and from General Joseph Mobutu, Commanding General of the Congolese National Army, to Mr. Devlin.[2]

2. These letters were carried by [*less than 1 line not declassified*] and close confidant of [*name not declassified*] and delivered to Mr. Devlin in New York on the evening of 17 July 1964. [*name not declassified*] instructions are to deliver the original of the letter addressed to the DCI personally to the DCI.

3. While it is not entirely clear what is the exact Congolese purpose in undertaking this action, it seems likely that the letter addressed to the DCI [*1 line not declassified*]. It should be noted that both [*name not declassified*] and Mobutu have been key movers in arranging the return of Tshombe. Further it has been reported recently that Tshombe is sending emissaries to London, Paris, and Brussels possibly to determine what support his government can expect in those countries.

4. [*4 lines not declassified*] Recent reporting shows further that Tshombe is concerned at the lack of support which he has both in the Congo and outside. In the Congo it is confined to Katanga and Leopoldville. On the international scene it is confined to Belgium, France and to a lesser extent Great Britain. Reportedly Tshombe believes that without US public support the British will soon withdraw theirs.

---

[1] Source: Central Intelligence Agency Files, [*text not declassified*], [*folder title not declassified*], Vol. III. Secret.

[2] In his letter to McCone, [*name not declassified*] asked that he send someone enjoying his confidence to spend "about 24 hours" in Leopoldville, and suggested that Devlin was well-qualified for this mission because he had their fullest confidence. In his letter to Devlin, [*name not declassified*] said that he insisted that he return immediately to Leopoldville "before it is too late." Mobutu's letter asked "his old friend" Devlin to tell his Chiefs that the situation as it pertained to relations between their two countries was very serious, and that the U.S. Embassy in its present attitude was endangering everything. Mobutu said that before it was too late, it would be most desirable that he and [*name not declassified*] explain the situation very clearly to Devlin and that this would only take 24 hours. (Ibid.)

5. Given the uncertainties of the situation in the Congo at the moment, it is difficult for the Department of State to reach a policy decision regarding public backing of Tshombe in the immediate future. For this reason, I recommend against [*name not declassified*] being given an appointment with the Director. On the other hand, in the coming period while the Department is determining what commitment it should make in the Congo it is important that some channel to Tshombe be established and maintained. [*name not declassified*] appears to provide this channel. I, therefore, recommend that [*name not declassified*] letter be accepted by a designated representative of the Director. It can be implied that the Director is absent from Washington at this time. I believe further that the [*name not declassified*] proposal that Mr. Devlin meet with him, Mobutu and possibly others be accepted and [*name not declassified*] be told that the Director will give the matter his consideration.

6. The division would like to consider with the Department of State the desirability of such a meeting and work out with them the timing and location. [*2½ lines not declassified*] Tshombe's isolation from African leaders, the Soviet Bloc, and at the same time the United States places him in a rather weak position and in my opinion he is acutely aware of this. We can conjecture that what [*name not declassified*] and Tshombe may be seeking is a public statement by the USG endorsing the Tshombe government. Alternatively, if such a statement is not forthcoming, it may be that [*name not declassified*] will want some indication from CIA as to whom he should back to obtain US endorsement.[3]

Glenn Fields[4]
Chief, Africa Division

---

[3] On July 24, McCone wrote [*name not declassified*] that he had met with [*name not declassified*] and discussed his message. In accordance with his request, the bearer of McCone's letter (Devlin) would consult with him and others he might suggest concerning the questions which lay within the Director's province. McCone assured [*name not declassified*] that Devlin had his full confidence and would be as helpful as possible, adding that he also had complete confidence in his representative in Leopoldville. (Ibid.) In telegram 2071 from Leopoldville to CIA, July 25, the Chief of Station reported that he had informed [*name not declassified*] that Devlin would arrive in Leopoldville on July 28, and that [*name not declassified*] suggested that he, the Chief of Station, Devlin, and [*name not declassified*] spend the afternoon of July 29 at his farm outside Leopoldville to permit full uninterrupted conversation. (Ibid., Job 78–00435R, DDO/ISS Files, Box 2, Folder 10, [*cryptonym not declassified*] Operations)

[4] Waller signed for Fields above Fields' typed signature.

192. Telegram From the Station in the Congo to the Central Intelligence Agency[1]

Leopoldville, July 31, 1964.

2163 (In 40340). 1. [former COS] has met with [Identity 1], [Identity 2], [Identity 3], [*1 line not declassified*] [Mobutu], [Identity 4], [*name not declassified*], and [Identity 5]. All meetings went extremely well. Sending detailed cables 1 Aug on each meeting.[2] [*name not declassified*] present for [Identity 5] meeting and [COS] present at numerous meetings with [Identity 3] and [Mobutu] and [Identity 1] [*cryptonym not declassified*]

2. [*5 lines not declassified*] Full details 1 Aug.

[*4 paragraphs (25 lines) not declassified*]

---

[1] Source: Central Intelligence Agency Files, [*text not declassified*], Fiche 37, Row 5, Frames 2–3, [*text not declassified*]. Secret; Immediate. Received at 1805Z.

[2] See Document 194.

---

193. Memorandum From the Under Secretary of State for Political Affairs (Harriman) to the President's Special Assistant for National Security Affairs (Bundy)[1]

Washington, August 4, 1964.

SUBJECT

The Congo

During Prime Minister Tshombe's month in office various different groups of rebels and dissident tribal elements have taken over much of the eastern Congo threatening to capture three major cities of Stanleyville, Bukavu and Luluabourg and the major Army base at Kamina. Evacuation of Americans from Stanleyville and Bukavu is underway.[2]

---

[1] Source: Johnson Library, National Security File, Country File, Congo, Vol. II, Memos & Miscellaneous, 7/64–8/64. Secret.

[2] The memorandum is attached to an August 4 memorandum from Brubeck to Bundy stating that about 11 a.m. Washington time Godley reported fighting between rebels and the Congolese Army outside the Consulate in Stanleyville, but that the evacuation was proceeding and under control. Brubeck suggested that Harriman go to Brussels the following day to talk urgently with Spaak about what help could be given to Tshombe.

The fall of one or more of the three cities to the rebels, whose operations have little coordination, when added to the territory already lost by the central government, might lead to foreign recognition of a rebel government. A rebel government has already been proclaimed by Soumialot in the eastern Congo. The Congolese National Army (ANC), lacking officer leadership and discipline, has shown itself incapable of stemming the epidemic spread of the rebels despite our current military aid programs and the help the ANC is receiving in advisers, training and matériel from Belgian and other sources. Tshombe has attempted (so far unsuccessfully) to enlist the cooperation of tribal chiefs in support of the central government and to resist the spread of tribal unrest and rebel uprisings.

Action we have already taken includes frequent consultations between Ambassador Godley with President Kasavubu, Prime Minister Tshombe and other Congolese on the internal security threat and how to meet it and instructions to Ambassador MacArthur to urge Mr. Spaak to make additional officers available either as advisers or to command ANC units. We have also asked our Embassy at Paris to attempt to get the French to use their influence in Brazzaville to restrain the Congolese rebels there.

Earlier proposals for the use of foreign troops, preferably from friendly African countries, have not so far appeared feasible because of African reluctance to associate themselves with Tshombe, Tshombe's unwillingness to make a request, and the unlikelihood that other African countries would agree to allow their troops to fight Congolese insurgents.

Recognizing the worthlessness of the ANC, Tshombe has brought back his ex-Katangan gendarmes from the bush and Angola. To be effective they would require white officers. Some mercenaries have already arrived in Leopoldville. While we wish Tshombe would choose mercenaries other than South Africans and Southern Rhodesians, who are unacceptable to other African states, to Tshombe they may represent the only immediately available resources to stiffen the gendarmes and the ANC.

Mr. Tshombe is also faced with political opposition in Leopoldville, since he has excluded many ambitious politicians from his government, especially the Binza group, and his relations with President Kasavubu are not close. With the government as presently constituted, Tshombe is facing growing political opposition with the Binza group, particularly General Mobutu, and President Kasavubu who under the new Constitution has the authority to dismiss the Prime Minister. A coup by the Binza group or Mobutu or violence in Leopoldville to prevent such a coup is possible.

Tshombe has prepared additional military requests designed to arm his gendarmes and integrate them into the police. These requests are being brought to Washington by Michel Struelens, who has been appointed as Tshombe's personal adviser on foreign affairs and political adviser to the Congolese missions to the U.S. and the UN. Godley recommends that no action be taken on this request without consultation with Kasavubu.

Governor Harriman is considering a visit to Brussels at the end of this week to attempt to work out with Mr. Spaak a joint action program to improve internal security both by military and political means. We want to encourage the Belgians to exercise leadership and take responsibility in the critical situation which now exists. We are prepared to work with the Belgians to enlist the cooperation and support of African nations and other European countries in this effort.

Averell

---

194. Telegram From the Station in the Congo to the Central Intelligence Agency[1]

Leopoldville, August 4, 1964.

2224 (In 42515). 1. Following is effort sum up [former COS] and [COS] contacts over past week, to provide some comments on the current situation and to submit some op suggestions for HQS consideration during [COS] TDY. Comments concerning reasons behind [*cryptonym not declassified*] request for [former COS] presence follow by separate cable.[2]

2. [*cryptonym not declassified*] and other moderates greatly concerned by chaotic situation which prevails Congo. Beginning Nov 62 [*cryptonym not declassified*] began voicing fear [Identity 1] lack leadership qualities and tendency seek compromise in all political situations would lead to failure [*cryptonym not declassified*] effort establish moderate GOC. This situation apparently continued for long period and [Identity 2] April 64 PBPRIME trip represented effort by [*cryptonym not*

---

[1] Source: Central Intelligence Agency Files, Job 78–00435R, DDO/ISS Files, Box 2, Folder 11, [*cryptonym not declassified*] Operations. Secret; Rybat; [*cryptonym not declassified*]; Priority. Received at 1500Z.

[2] Not found.

declassified] to obtain ODYOKE guidance and help in finding alternate solution.

3. [Identity 2] effort win presidency RADECO, thus eliminating [Identity 1] control over party, appears represent uncoordinated step by [Identity 2] and [Identity 3] to avoid chaotic political situation and failure [*cryptonym not declassified*] objectives (which they believed would result from [Identity 1] election as party chief). It impossible determine exactly what happened after the RADECO conference but appears following resulted:

A. [Identity 4] suspicions that [Identity 1] seeking replace him were "confirmed" in his mind when [Identity 1] obtained RADECO presidency. These suspicions compounded by [Identity 1] earlier negotiations with Kimbanguists and [Identity 1] efforts obtain modification constitution. Thus, [Identity 4] allegedly again wrote [Identity 5] in early June in effort play off [Identity 5] against [Identity 1].

B. [Identity 4] also became suspicious other [*cryptonym not declassified*]. [Identity 3] and [Mobutu] claim they have set these suspicions to rest insofar as they personally concerned and have made peace with [Identity 4].

C. [Identity 1] on learning of CDA and [Identity 4] overtures to [Identity 5] decided beat others to punch and obtain personal credit for returning [Identity 5] to Congo. Although not confirmed, appears he expected obtain future political credit by this action. Also suspect [Identity 1] hoped obtain [Identity 5] political support, possibly in return for naming [Identity 5] premier. [Identity 1] confirmed this view at 3 Aug meeting. [Mobutu], however, has stated [Identity 1] had already decided give up premiership to [Identity 5] when latter recalled. Difficult determine exact role played by [Mobutu]. Latter insists his merely advisory role and carried out [Identity 1] instructions in arranging [Identity 5] return. However, suspect [Mobutu] role in convincing [Identity 1] turn govt over to [Identity 5] greater than [Mobutu] states, or perhaps greater than he realizes. [Identity 1] could have interpreted [Mobutu's] advice as indication [Mobutu] withdrawing his support, support which [Identity 1] knew he must have to remain in office.

D. Basis info available, believe [Mobutu] only member of [*cryptonym not declassified*] who directly involved [Identity 5] return and negotiations leading thereto.

E. [Identity 2] apparently decided it useless oppose [Identity 5] and thus set out develop close working relationship. Believe this done to try establish foothold in [Identity 5] camp for [*cryptonym not declassified*], to permit [Identity 2] monitor [Identity 5] activities and to serve as holding action pending final evaluation situation. In short, believe [Identity 2] and other [*cryptonym not declassified*] had no long-term plan and thus decided they had no alternative but to go along with [Identity 5].

4. [*cryptonym not declassified*] remain without firm plans other than to hope ODYOKE will be able solve Congo security problem. Only political plans [*cryptonym not declassified*] able suggest were continued support RADECO, together with parallel effort establish voting block in next parliament based on ex-Orientale province, Ubangi and Cuvette Centrale. They hope such minority block would provide swing vote similar that of Abako in previous parliament. It also clear [*cryptonym not declassified*] convinced RADECO stands little or no chance under [Identity 1] leadership, as they believe he lacks political sex appeal and leadership qualities.

5. In addition to appearance of [Identity 5] and his entourage on the local scene, military successes of CNL (or perhaps it more exact to say military failures of ANC) have greatly complicated political situation. The [*cryptonym not declassified*] and probably [Identity 5] are desperately anxious head off the CNL advance. They believe they have little time to do this, for with every chance of the CNL its prestige goes up and the prestige of the govt and indirectly the [*cryptonym not declassified*] (particularly [Mobutu] goes down. This based on old African phenomena that nothing succeeds like success or fails like failure. Thus, [*cryptonym not declassified*] appear be making sincere effort support [Identity 5] in face CNL danger. Believe this support will continue so long as CNL poses actual danger. However, [*cryptonym not declassified*] would prefer find solution to CNL problem which would enhance their prestige, rather than that of [Identity 5]. It to this reason [Mobutu] raised question of obtaining ChiNat, Philippine or South Korean troops to shore up his forces. (Note: This earlier reported [U.S. Embassy] channels.)

6. Although situation too fluid reach positive conclusions on basis one week consultations, suggest following developments may well come to pass:

A. In absence other foreign support, suspect [Identity 5] will resort to use mercenaries in his efforts limit expansion CNL.

B. Use mercenaries, particularly South Africans or white Southern Rhodesians, will cause numerous political problems. Specifically this could well be exploited by CNL as "proof" [Identity 5] serving as front man for neo-colonialists. Also could result in some outside states collaborating overtly with or even recognizing CNL regime. However, use mercenaries might provide extra backbone needed by ANC to defeat revolutionary forces. As of now does not appear [Identity 5] will receive sufficient help from more acceptable outside forces and thus very possibly will turn to mercenaries for needed military assistance.

C. If [Identity 5] succeeds in solving security problems by using mercenaries, it probable he may take advantage this situation to eliminate [Mobutu]. He might relegate [Mobutu] to position minor importance and avoid requesting [Identity 4] agreement to latter's removal. Should this develop would assume [Identity 5] also would try eliminate [Identity 2] thus insuring his control of army and [Identity 6].

D. Assume [Identity 5] and [Identity 4] eventually will clash in effort win presidency. All persons contacted expect this rivalry to result in power struggle. As of now there appears be little coordination between [Identity 4] and [Identity 5].

E. Although anything can happen and much will depend upon [*cryptonym not declassified*] estimate of political power factors, assume they will eventually lean toward [Identity 4] should latter enter open struggle for presidency.

F. Despite foregoing, [*cryptonym not declassified*] currently working with [Identity 5] view their fear that open [Identity 5/Identity 4] clash might lead to CNL takeover.

G. At present [*cryptonym not declassified*] at relatively low political ebb. However, they obviously seeking guidance and support and hope regain old position of political king-makers. However, they greatly worried and unsure what political future holds for them, as they recognize dangers of [Identity 5] and/or CNL regime.

7. It too early determine whether [Identity 5] represents passing political phase or whether latter has chance righting situation and confirming his position as key Congo figure. Much depends upon military, political and economic developments of next few months, but it normal in Congo for govt to lose popularity after several months in office. Thus, expect [Identity 5] do everything within his power achieve political and economic break-through ASAP.

[Omitted here is further discussion of the political situation.]

9. Current security situation extremely serious and could well result in CNL extremists winning control GOC. If Stan falls to CNL, as appears probable, Leop situation will become precarious; would expect snowballing situation to result if Stan falls. Should it appear GOC unable prevent CNL takeover Leop area, suspect [Identity 5] would endeavor return Katanga and establish redoubt there. Thus Congo could once again be split, as during time of Katanga secessionist movement. Difference might be that [Identity 5] would represent legal govt. Much will depend upon [Identity 4] actions and decisions. If CNL victorious and/or Congo again divided, believe KUBARK will be able make strong contribution to implementation ODYOKE policy. However, situation appears considerably different than summer 60. Doubt situation is one which KUBARK alone can change situation. Thus, much will depend upon ODYOKE actions in military and economic fields.

10. General line above message discussed verbally with [COS] prior his departure. Assume this message will be reviewed by him. Views contained herein submitted merely as discussion points and not intended as recommended solutions. Also, wish emphasize these recommendations are for short-term period. Situation so fluid that major operational changes may be required, if and when local political situation stabilizes.

11. Foregoing gone over in detail with [Godley] and his deputy who concur with report and recommendations. [Godley] requests Gov Harriman be informed his concurrence [former COS] assessment situation.

---

195. Special National Intelligence Estimate[1]

SNIE 65–64 Washington, August 5, 1964.

SHORT-TERM PROSPECTS FOR THE TSHOMBE GOVERNMENT IN THE CONGO

The Problem

To examine the prospects for the Tshombe government during the next six to nine months.[2]

Conclusions

A. In recent months, regional dissidence and violence have assumed serious proportions, even by Congolese standards, and produced the threat of a total breakdown in governmental authority. The difficulties confronting Prime Minister Tshombe are enormous. His greatest need is a military force which can handle the various rebellions. His political position will be threatened by other aspirants to

[1] Source: Central Intelligence Agency Files, Job 79R01012A, ODDI Registry. Secret; Controlled Dissem. According to a note on the cover sheet: "The following intelligence organizations participated in the preparation of this estimate: The Central Intelligence Agency and the intelligence organizations of the Departments of State, Defense, and NSA." All members of the U.S. Intelligence Board concurred in this estimate on August 5, except the Atomic Energy Commission representative and the Assistant Director of the Federal Bureau of Investigation, who abstained on the grounds that the subject was outside their jurisdiction.

[2] Under the newly approved constitution national elections are to be held during this period. [Footnote in the original.]

power. We think the chances are about even that he will be able to remain Prime Minister over the next six to nine months. If Tshombe is able to avoid anarchy in the Congo, he will have scored a considerable achievement, but there is little prospect of establishing a central government which will have a substantial degree of authority throughout the country. (Paras. 1–6, 11–13, 15–16)

B. Should Tshombe fall, the prospects are dark. Extremists would be likely to gain increased influence in Leopoldville, secessionist regimes might break off and disorder would spread. (Paras. 14, 18)

C. We believe Tshombe will adopt a generally pro-West orientation within the confines of a pro forma non-aligned policy. He will probably remain close to the Belgians and susceptible to their influence; we believe he will cooperate with the US. Although still suspect by many African leaders, we believe Tshombe would become generally acceptable in Black Africa if he succeeded in providing a workable solution to the Congo's problems. (Paras. 21–23)

[Omitted here is the Discussion section of the paper.]

---

196. Memorandum From the Chief of the Africa Division, Directorate of Plans, Central Intelligence Agency (Fields) to the Assistant Secretary of State for African Affairs (Williams)[1]

Washington, August 5, 1964.

1. At 1 August Tshombe press conference the Ambassador raised with Tshombe the question of a Tshombe–[*name not declassified*] meeting which Tshombe had suggested on 31 July. Tshombe requested that [*name not declassified*] lunch alone with him at his residence on 2 August. The Ambassador concurred.

2. [*name not declassified*] arrived at Tshombe's residence at 1300 hours and introduced himself. He had been dropped off by the Ambassador. After some misunderstanding [*name not declassified*] was ushered into Tshombe's office.

3. After brief interval of small talk, Tshombe, who was obviously turning on the charm, launched into a long discourse on his boyhood,

---

[1] Source: Central Intelligence Agency Files, Job 76–00366R, DDO/ISO Files, Box 1, Folder 8, Congo, 1960–1969, Part II. Secret. This memorandum was sent via back-channel from the Department of State representative in Leopoldville to be passed to Harriman.

the fact that he was educated by U.S. missionaries, and his great affection for the U.S. Government. He concluded by saying that with such a background he could not be suspected of being anti-U.S. Government. However, he noted that U.S. Government authorities had never understood his position and thus, erroneously, misinterpreted his plans and ambitions.

4. [*name not declassified*] thanked Tshombe for his frank statement, adding that such frankness deserved an equally frank reply. [*name not declassified*] informed Tshombe that he had served for nearly three years in Leop, adding that he had done his best as an officer of the U.S. Government to implement the U.S. Government Congo policy and that he had sometimes found himself in opposition to all repeat all efforts to divide the Congo. [*name not declassified*] emphasized that his actions had been based on the general policy decision to oppose the division of the Congo and not on personal motives. Tshombe replied he well aware of [*name not declassified*] background, that he appreciated frankness, that he desired establish a frank relationship with [*less than 1 line not declassified*] all U.S. Government officers and that he had sought this meeting with [*name not declassified*] precisely because he aware of [*name not declassified*] background. He continued saying he understood and respected the reasons for [*name not declassified*] past activities. However, said he must say [*less than 1 line not declassified*] U.S. Government had been ill advised by persons who for selfish or other reasons had failed provide U.S. Government with a clear understanding of realities of Congo situation. Also, he noted [*name not declassified*] and other U.S. officials had failed establish direct contact with him in years past, and he commented that had the U.S. Government conducted frank talks with him at that time that many problems might have been avoided, particularly the current chaotic situation. To keep conversation going on a friendly plane (and Tshombe's remarks were made in an apparently friendly and candid manner) [*name not declassified*] avoided pointing out that Tshombe had always had access to the U.S. Consulate Elisabethville. Instead he noted that he had accompanied Timberlake to Eville in Nov 60 and that in July 61 he had tried without success to contact Tshombe in Brazzaville to urge Tshombe to attend the Lovanium conclave.

5. Tshombe implied there might have been some cause for misunderstanding during period of the Eville secession. However, he expressed view that U.S. Government should have accepted at face value his declaration that he was abandoning secessionist efforts and worked for a reconciliation between the GOC and himself. Added he recognized many persons in the U.S. believe he merely awaiting opportunity lead another secessionist movement, but he explained such a path no longer open to him. He said that, were he to lead again Lunda people in

a secessionist movement and were it to fail, he and his entire family would lose their lives and property, for the tribe would not forgive him for such an error. Said anyone who understood Lunda tribal customs and the danger which he and his entire family would run were he to so act should have understood he had been seeking honest reconciliation with GOC.

6. [*name not declassified*] replied it regrettable that earlier reconciliation had not taken place, but added little could be accomplished by looking to the past. The important point being that Tshombe had finally returned to Leop, that he heading central govt, that he was prepared to put down rebellion in the provinces and that, as Tshombe already aware, U.S. Government was prepared continue its economic and military support to govt headed by Tshombe. [*name not declassified*] also took this opportunity point out that there only one repeat one U.S. Govt foreign policy, that contrary to case in some countries U.S. policy controlled by Washington thus [*name not declassified*] emphasized Tshombe need have no fear that [*less than 1 line not declassified*] seeking undermine govt. This connection, [*name not declassified*] noted Struelens had indicated Tshombe suspected [*name not declassified*] involved in efforts undermine his govt. [*name not declassified*] assured Tshombe this could not be the case as U.S. policy directed by one head and that U.S. policy is as communicated to him by Godley and other U.S. reps. Tshombe did not comment on [*name not declassified*] matter at that time, but at end of meeting he stated that he fully reassured re [*name not declassified*] and that the matter is closed.

7. Taking up the point of U.S. policy, Tshombe said he had found Congo situation much more difficult and dangerous than he had realized it be prior his return Leop. He explained he seeking win back people from "the Communists"; to leave Gizenga, Mulele and other extremists without followers. Said he needs U.S. help to accomplish this, for without U.S. Govt economic help over the next five years there no hope of avoiding chaos and Communist penetration of Congo. After Tshombe had expounded at great length about his need for U.S. help and his desire cooperate with U.S. Govt, and in accordance with suggestions made by Deputy Assistant Secretary Fredericks, urged Tshombe maintain close contact with Godley and other reps of US, noting that U.S. Embassy could support Tshombe only insofar as it fully aware his plans and objectives and thus able to communicate these plans to Department of State. Tshombe acknowledged need for such contact and indicated his willingness work closely with U.S. reps.

8. Tshombe said he had been unsure that such U.S. Embassy collaboration would be forthcoming, stating that he aware U.S. Embassy had done everything possible block his return Leop and his nomination as Prime Minister. He admitted these alleged actions preceeded his ap-

pointment as Prime Minister. [*name not declassified*] again reassured Tshombe that U.S. policy is as reported to him by Godley. When Tshombe implied there might be divergent policies between Washington and U.S. Embassy, [*name not declassified*] repeated there only one Congo policy, and added that were anyone in U.S. Embassy to fail to adhere to this policy line he would face immediate recall.

9. Tshombe next referred to Radeco, implying it supported by U.S. He did not dwell on this point but assured [*name not declassified*] that Adoula finished politically. Tshombe said Adoula's only hope was to cooperate with Tshombe, that he, Tshombe, could and would help Adoula retain some position influence if Adoula played game. Tshombe concluded comments this point saying U.S. had bet on a poor horse and making it clear he has little respect for Adoula as a political opponent.

10. [*name not declassified*] took advantage ref to Adoula to say he, [*name not declassified*] had many friends or contacts in Congo and noted he seeing persons from various political groups in order try provide his superiors with valid appreciation current political situation. Added these contacts made only for purposes obtaining cross section political views and not to oppose Tshombe regime. Also said had urged upon all contacts need for moritorium on political maneuvering until danger posed by CNL rebellion contained. Stressed that contacts based on personal friendship developed over long period and referred to fact that [*name not declassified*] had been able warn various persons of assassination attempts. [*14 lines not declassified*]

11. [*1 paragraph (6½ lines) not declassified*]

12. [*name not declassified*] stressed importance [*less than 1 line not declassified*] collaboration, stating primary objective [*less than 1 line not declassified*] is to prevent Communist penetration Africa. Noted [*less than 1 line not declassified*] objectives thus coincide with Tshombe objectives, particularly in view of "fact" CNL being exploited by ChiComs and Sov. Tshombe concurred this point and again repeated his desire for intel and CI support.

13. Godley joined [*name not declassified*] after foregoing discussed and his report contained Embtel 301.[2]

14. Recognize talks described herein went somewhat beyond listening brief, but wish stress that all points made by [*name not declassified*] cleared in advance with Godley. Latter concurs this report and requests transmit to Governor Harriman.

---

[2] National Archives, RG 59, Central Files 1964–66, POL 23–9, THE CONGO.

197. Telegram From the Department of State to the Embassy in Belgium[1]

Washington, August 6, 1964, 2:01 a.m.

164. Please deliver ASAP following message from the Secretary to Spaak:

It is our judgment that events in the Congo have reached so critical a point that you and we and all our European friends must move immediately and vigorously to prevent total collapse. We estimate that there is no effective internal security force and none in prospect without outside help. Deterioration is so rapid that Elisabethville, Leopoldville and central government may be gone in next several weeks.

Not only is Congo key to central Africa but also chronic instability provides fertile ground for Communist infiltration, prevention of which has been cornerstone our Congo policy last four years. I want you to know that President shares my deep concern over the situation. While appreciating considerations you raised with MacArthur, President and I are convinced that you and we must concert urgently on tangible, specific measures to save the Congo. We agree with you on need to elicit Tshombe's plans and are attempting to do so.

In view of the foregoing we are requesting Averell Harriman to leave tomorrow to discuss with you what can be done on an emergency basis. I very much hope you and we can develop such a program of action adequate to save the immediate situation. I have asked him to discuss with you the following:

1. In view of the vital European interests in central Africa, what assistance might be forthcoming from a joint military force of the Six, or of some of its member nations. What help can we be to you if you should take the lead in the organization of such a European rescue mission. I should think it possible even the French might participate now that UN military presence has been withdrawn.

2. The need for additional military forces in the Congo which we believe Belgium is in the best position to provide. Averell can go into details of what we might be able to do in this connection.

3. The measures which your government can take to ensure continued Central Government control of Kamina, Bukavu and Luluabourg and to strengthen the government of Rwanda which is put in

[1] Source: National Archives, RG 59, Central Files 1964–66, POL 23-9 THE CONGO. Confidential; Immediate. Drafted by Tasca and O'Sullivan; cleared by Williams, Harriman, Brubeck, and McKillop; and approved by Secretary Rusk. Repeated to Leopoldville.

jeopardy by rebel control of the eastern Congo. This probably requires, on an emergency basis at least, that Belgian officers now in the Congo join and exercise de facto command of operational ANC forces in the field.

4. Establishment as soon as possible of gendarmerie force with mercenary officers.

5. Need for joint efforts on the part of all the Western allies to induce Kasavubu and Tshombe to broaden the base of the present government and to gain greater acceptance for it among African states. I do not understand for example why Tshombe does not utilize Adoula, in explaining the Congo problem to the Congo's African friends and to request support both diplomatic and military from them.

FYI Inform Spaak, if he agrees, Harriman arriving Friday morning. Also alert Societe Generale management Harriman wishes speak with them.[2]

Rusk

---

[2] In telegram 176 from Brussels, August 6, MacArthur reported that he delivered the Secretary's message to Spaak, who had said he would be glad to talk with Harriman the following day. MacArthur warned, however, that there had been developments that had further strengthened Spaak's opposition to any direct Belgian military involvement in the Congo. (Ibid.) In telegram 177 from Brussels, August 6, MacArthur said that Spaak told him there was no hope of getting any support from Belgian Government, parliament, press, or business leaders for either encadrement or direct intervention by Belgian military forces. (Ibid.)

---

198. Memorandum From the Deputy Assistant Secretary of Defense for International Security Affairs (Lang) to the Deputy Secretary of Defense (Vance)[1]

I–36,511/64 Washington, August 6, 1964.

SUBJECT

Evacuation of US Consulate Representatives at Stanleyville

Late last night, a message was received from our Consulate at Stanleyville that four of its staff members were in the communications

---

[1] Source: Washington National Records Center, RG 330, OASD/ISA Files: FRC 68 A 4023, 510 Congo 6 Aug 1964. Top Secret.

vault of the Consulate and a fifth was in an apartment building about one mile away (Tab A).[2] The message indicated that in the early hours of the morning the rebels had cut off the Consulate power supply and tried to enter the communications vault. Shortly afterwards, the rebels departed and the Consulate reported that the city seemed quiet before the Consulate staff returned to the communications vault after turning on the power again.

Shortly before midnight, Bill Brubeck asked us to examine whether it would be feasible to evacuate the Consulate personnel by airlift from Stanleyville. After informally alerting CINCSTRIKE of this request, we examined the problem based on information available here. We concluded that no operations involving resources in the Congo could be carried out today. The airport is in rebel hands, and H–21 helicopters could not be flown to the area in sufficient time to carry out rescue operations while daylight remained. More importantly, we could not find any airfield sufficiently close to Stanleyville, from which the H–21s could mount a round trip to Stanleyville. (This also applied to any T–28s that might be used for air cover.)

By Tab B, Embassy Leopoldville reported that it planned to carry out a rescue operation involving T–28s and H–21 helicopters along the lines that we had considered impracticable. As a result, we sent the message at Tab C asking for further details from Leopoldville. We have not yet had a response. Tab D outlines CINCSTRIKE's proposed course of action. It involves bringing in between a platoon and a company of US troops by helicopter, presumably to secure the area around the Consulate while the rescue is carried out. The STRIKE plan would involve three or four days of preparation.

We informed Bill Brubeck this morning of the foregoing. We also raised with him the possibility that the rebels might retaliate against the remaining white population in Stanleyville which is substantial in number if the rescue operation involved any hostilities. We suggested that a more feasible course would be an attempt, through negotiations with the rebels, to arrange for the safe passage of all members of the white population who might wish to leave Stanleyville. The rebels permitted such a safe passage after Albertville fell. Brubeck thought this idea had considerable merit, as did representatives of the State Department with whom we discussed it last evening.

William E. Lang[3]

---

[2] None of the tabs is attached.

[3] Printed from a copy that indicates Lang signed the original.

199. Memorandum From William H. Brubeck of the National Security Council Staff to President Johnson[1]

Washington, August 6, 1964.

SUBJECT

Congo

1. *Situation:* Stanleyville is in rebel hands. All of Eastern Congo may go in next several days; Katanga, Leopoldville and entire Central Government may collapse in next several weeks. Although situation largely the result of tribal violence there is real danger Communists will be able to exploit in near future. Situation is basically power vacuum, could probably be retrieved by small security force (ideally white, at a minimum white-led and, if really good, as few as 1000).

2. *Problem:* No useable force exists or is now in prospect in Congo. *The basic immediate problem is how to get such a force in a hurry.*

3. Although Spaak flatly declares Belgians can take no significant action, Harriman is going to Brussels tonight for a final effort with him. Harriman will offer range of alternatives—

(a) Belgium provide the white military personnel required (Belgians absolutely refuse, from fear of reprisals against Belgian citizens in rebel held territories).

(b) Belgian leadership in organizing a multi-national European force for Congo (very unlikely—other Europeans even less willing than Belgians to commit troops).

(c) US-Belgian cooperation to help Tshombe organize and equip a force of Katanga ex-gendarmes led by white mercenaries (best practical prospect, but Spaak so far refuses to let Belgians serve as mercenaries, which is most critical need).

(d) Try to get African forces into Congo (Nigerians, Tunisians, etc.)—very doubtful, very complicated and would take time. We would have to compel Tshombe to broaden Congo Government in order to get any African help.

4. The Harriman–Spaak talks will probably show Belgians absolutely unwilling to do anything except perhaps supply and equip mercenary-gendarmes force. If so, by this weekend the problem of short run salvage of Congo will be squarely in our laps, raising questions—

[1] Source: Johnson Library, National Security File, Country File, Congo, Vol. III, Memos & Miscellaneous, 8/64. Secret.

(a) How much support are we prepared to give mercenary force (e.g. covert recruiting, US money, etc.) as first choice?

(b) If this fails how tough will we get in ultimatum to Congo Government to compel changes necessary to get African force into Congo?

5. If these efforts fail and/or continued disintegration forces our hand (as is possible) we are reduced to three alternatives—

(a) Go back to UN Security Council and try to make a deal with Russia to permit a new UN force in Congo.

(b) Explore putting in small US force or US-Belgian force on short term basis.

(c) Let the chaos run its course, hoping the Congolese will work out an adjustment without serious Communist intrusion; and rely on Congo's need of our aid and support for influence with the eventual government. This would be hard to explain politically in US, but it is essentially what Belgians and Europeans are doing.

6. My own feeling is the practical alternative offering early results on which we should concentrate now is to help the Congolese in every way to organize a mercenary-led force and, at same time, use our heaviest pressures (including threats to withdraw support) to compel reorganization of Congo Government in order to try to win broader African acceptance, as political basis for mercenary military operation.

William H. Brubeck[2]

[2] Printed from a copy that bears this typed signature.

---

200. Telegram From the Department of State to the Embassy in the Congo[1]

Washington, August 6, 1964, 1:46 p.m.

174. We fully share your concern expressed in recent messages re possible catastrophe in Congo. See septel which conveying our views of situation to Spaak.

[1] Source: National Archives, RG 59, Central Files 1964–66, POL 23–9 THE CONGO. Confidential; Immediate. Drafted by O'Sullivan and Tasca, cleared by Williams and Lang in DOD, and approved by Harriman. Repeated to Brussels, USUN, and CINCSTRIKE for POLAD Tampa.

You should talk to Kasavubu and Tshombe as soon as possible. With all the muscle you can put into it, you should press upon them necessity of maintaining government control where it now exists and particular necessity of preventing rebels from capturing Kamina (which covers approaches to Elisabethville) as well as Bukavu and Luluabourg. To this end you should urge them to use resources immediately available, such as getting into operational units Belgian officers whom they now have in Congo serving as military advisors and using available technicians for this purpose.

Tshombe and GOC should proceed soonest to establish effective gendarmerie-mercenary unit. To minimize training and logistic difficulties, equipment (small arms) should be from Belgian sources. Spaak indicated receptivity this idea (Brussels 172).[2] US prepared assist with transport, communications and other reasonable requirements needed such a force.

You should make clear to them our belief that government should be as representative as possible all responsible, moderate political elements in order to gain widest possible internal support and African sympathy. At same time you should also urge them to begin immediately explaining their problems frankly to and asking help from other African leaders such as but not limited to Kaunda, Balewa, Bourguiba and Emperor of Ethiopia. For this purpose it necessary he and Kasavubu choose Congolese leaders most acceptable other friendly African countries.

You should also ask what plans they have for bringing into Congo military resources other than those now available for it seems clear that situation can become catastrophic unless they immediately are prepared to call for outside assistance. US is prepared to assist in helping with transport and other needed support foreign troops from friendly countries agreeing to Congolese requests.[3]

Rusk

---

[2] Dated August 5. (Ibid.)

[3] In telegram 394 from Leopoldville, August 7, Godley said that in view of his recent conversations with Tshombe, he believed that it was Kasavubu, whom he had been trying to see without success since August 1, with whom he needed to discuss telegram 174. (Ibid.) In telegram 409 from Leopoldville, August 8, the Ambassador reported that he had made every point set forth in the Department's telegram during his meeting with Kasavubu that morning. (Ibid., POL 15–1 THE CONGO)

201. Telegram From the Department of State to the Embassy in the Congo[1]

Washington, August 6, 1964, 5:16 p.m.

178. In conversation with Cleveland, Bunche has indicated receptivity to idea of UN effort to negotiate with Stanleyville authorities for permission to evacuate on UN aircraft all Europeans including all official and non-official US citizens who wish leave city.

You requested discuss matter urgently with Osorio-Tafall offering him all possible assistance.[2]

In meantime you should cease Stanleyville relief operation keeping it on stand-by basis pending outcome this effort. In no case should it be set in motion again without Department's approval.

Rusk

---

[1] Source: National Archives, RG 59, Central Files 1964–66, POL 23-9 THE CONGO. Confidential; Flash. Drafted by Schaufele; cleared by O'Sullivan, Tasca, Lang, and Cleveland; and approved by Harriman.

[2] In telegram 392 from Leopoldville, August 7, Godley reported that he contacted Osorio-Tafall, who greatly appreciated the U.S. offer of assistance and said he would pursue the matter immediately. (Ibid.)

202. Telegram From the Station in the Congo to the Central Intelligence Agency[1]

Leopoldville, August 6, 1964.

2273 (In 44709). 1. [Identity 1] and [former COS] had long meeting with [Identity 2] afternoon 5 Aug and exchanged views on current situation. Intel and ops info obtained cabled earlier messages.[2]

2. Later in evening [Identity 2] phoned requesting immediate meeting. As [Identity 1] occupied other duties, [former COS] covered meeting. In addition [Identity 2], [Identity 3] also present. Both men

---

[1] Source: Central Intelligence Agency Files, Job 78–00435R, DDO/ISS Files, Box 2, Folder 11, [*cryptonym not declassified*] Operations. Secret; Rybat; [*cryptonym not declassified*]; Priority. Received at 1620Z.

[2] Not further identified.

greatly worried by developments, particularly by fall Stan. They believe rebel capture this city, combined with rapid rebel progress in Kivu, Kasai and Katanga, will give rebel movement great psychological lift. Both expressed view that disorders will break out in Leop within one week. They believe bandwagon psychology will encourage rebel supporters already in native city Leop to try all the harder arouse popular disorders and that rebels may not even have to attack city. Comment: Difficult judge whether they being too pessimistic, but view fact it normal Congolese practice for people jump on bandwagon and view general dissatisfaction masses over unemployment, high cost living, lack political maturity people, etc, they may well be correct. If trouble does not come quite as soon as they expect, Station would nonetheless expect disorders within few weeks unless ANC successful in arresting progress of rebels.

3. Both men appeared believe ODYOKE has some secret plan to resolve Congo rebellion. They commented they could not believe ODYOKE which has expended great sums and wagered its prestige on support moderates would sit back and permit men who would be hostile ODYOKE and probably under Commie influence to take over. [Identity 3] who obviously trying plant idea, then suggested following might be ODYOKE policy:

A. Make secret deal with [Identity 4] whereby latter would agree oust [Identity 5] in return for ODYOKE military intervention. [Identity 3] noted that, as [Identity 5] reconciliation policy has failed, [Identity 4] would have good reason to dump [Identity 5]. [Identity 3] suggested [Identity 4] should then be encouraged to appoint member [*cryptonym not declassified*] group as temporary Prime Minister, specifically mentioning [Identity 2] as best possible candidate.

B. Once steps outlined sub-para 3A accomplished, [Identity 3] suggested new govt would immediately arrest [Identity 5] to insure he could not return to home province to launch new secessionist movement.

C. ODYOKE military intervention would take place concurrently with nomination [Identity 5] replacement. Thus new govt would have opportunity crack down on all extremists (right or left) while PBPRIME troops settling rebellion.

4. [Identity 2] and [Identity 3] obviously suggested para 3 plan because they desperately grasping at straws and in typical Congolese fashion seeking place burden responsibility on shoulders of others. [former COS] scoffed at idea, noting he aware [Identity 3] effort plant idea. [former COS] pointed out following weaknesses para 3 plan:

A. ODYOKE does not look with favor on idea intervening militarily in Congo rebellion.

B. Such intervention would be most obvious to entire world.

C. Dumping [Identity 5] might result in yet additional political infighting that would only serve assist rebels.

D. [former COS] not at all sure new govt would be able prevent escape [Identity 5] or other key leaders from his home area.

E. Such coup d'etat could be used as pretext by many persons to withdraw support from central govt.

F. Suggestion no more than outright coup d'etat with local trappings, and would alienate many countries. Such action would particularly upset Belgians and thus might preclude Belgian intervention. [former COS] added that, after African solution, direct Belgian intervention appeared offer good alternative. Took advantage this statement to again run over ODACID policy guidances as [Godley] had requested be done.

5. [Identity 2] and [Identity 3] appeared accept this advice. Both recognized problems involved ODYOKE direct intervention. They also recognized advantages African involvement but flatly stated would much prefer Belgian troops. However, they came around to idea African troops might be used police non-combat areas.

6. [Identity 2] and [Identity 3] volunteered view that CNA with exception first paracommando battalion should be disarmed, if Belgian troops intervened in Congo. Thus they recognized need get rid of current rabble and replace with newly-trained and hopefully disciplined army. This does not mean they favor removing [Mobutu] from his army job.

7. [former COS] and [Identity 1] decided it advisable not pass above report to [Godley]. FYI only: [*cryptonym not declassified*] down on him and Leop fears [Godley] might in some way reveal his knowledge [Identity 2] and [Identity 3] had toyed with ideas reported para 3 above. In any case, believe they have put this idea aside, at least for immediate future. [former COS] and [Identity 1] will endeavor regularly monitor their feelings this subject. Believe we will obtain advance warning if they return to para 3 ideas.

203. Telegram From the Department of State to the Embassy in Belgium[1]

Washington, August 7, 1964, 11:42 a.m.

179. For Harriman from the Secretary. Following has President's full support. You should make clear to Spaak the interest in this program at highest levels of US Government and our hope that Belgians will be able to participate fully.

Interdepartmental working group spent two to three hours with Struelens. Struelens presented copy of Ndele memo to Tshombe dated July 18 estimating partial cost of four thousand man force. Details of package developed in separate cable.

Tshombe plan based initial four thousand man force rolling back rebels beginning Baudoinville, Albertville, etc. and ending up with Stanleyville. In meantime Bukavu must be stiffened and held, and so also Kamina.

Struelens presentation indicated plan not thought out in any detail concerning either organization or use of force. Also some hint Tshombe having difficulties obtaining mercenaries.

Propose you explore following general plan with Spaak:

1. U.S. and Belgium give commitment in principle to creation of mercenary officered gendarmerie force, as only alternative to continued disintegration of security situation, with tentative force level of four thousand gendarmes and two hundred white officers. We recognize and are prepared to share political responsibility this course with GOB and GOC.

2. Immediate objective is at earliest possible time to provide equipment and funds to establish pilot group of about 500 men to meet most urgent security needs in next several weeks.

3. Belgian and American Ambassadors with experts in Leo should develop detailed plan for creation, organization, and use of force and equipment with immediate priority on mounting 500 man force.

4. Points you should particularly explore with Spaak:

A. Belgian acceptance of general plan;
B. Belgian help on mercenary problem including recruitment of Belgians;

---

[1] Source: National Archives, RG 59, Central Files 1964–66, POL 23–9 THE CONGO. Secret; Flash, Exdis. Drafted by Williams; cleared by Lang, Brubeck, and Appling; and approved by Secretary Rusk. Also sent to Leopoldville as telegram 187 and repeated to CINCMEAFSA.

C. What would be Belgian matériel and financial contribution (Belgian supply of arms and ammunition is essential);

D. Belgian personnel for staff and logistics and technical services such as maintenance;

E. Belgian consent for Belgian flying crews to operate in rebel held territory.

For Leopoldville:

Request comments ASAP on above plan. Appreciate also views on political steps desirable to make such a force politically more defensible, e.g. broadening of government by inclusion of Adoula and others. Objective is to have sufficient information on Belgian position and sufficient Embassy guidance to permit detailed consideration in Department by end week.[2]

Rusk

---

[2] In telegram 191 from Brussels, August 7, Harriman informed Rusk that his message had arrived following the conclusion of extensive talks with Spaak, but noted that practically all of its points had been covered, although in a somewhat different context. (Ibid.)

---

204. Telegram From the Embassy in Belgium to the Department of State[1]

Brussels, August 7, 1964, 7 p.m.

184. For Secretary from Harriman; Leoville for Ambassador. After a sticky beginning talks with Spaak went well. Spaak first maintained situation in Congo not as critical as we think. Also he tried to minimize adverse effect to Belgian business of rebel takeover. After I expressed our judgment that rebels would in time be dominated by ChiComs, he modified his position and discussed a step-by-step program (details septel).[2]

---

[1] Source: National Archives, RG 59, Central Files 1964–66, POL 23–9 THE CONGO. Secret; Limdis; Immediate. Received at 3 p.m. Repeated to Leopoldville and relayed to the White House, the Army, and CIA.

[2] Telegram 200 from Brussels, August 8, transmitted the text of the agreement reached by Spaak and Harriman. (Ibid.)

I. Congo

A. In general, Belgian Govt will supply by middle of month 3000 NATO rifles and ammunition for gendarmerie. (Request we supply one flight C–130 to assist in air delivery.)

Belgians request us to add six additional T–28s or armed T–6s. I agreed we would consider promptly. We expected to contribute needed motor vehicles.

B. He is sending Col. Van der Walle with Kasavubu concurrence to become Tshombe's military advisor. Will also consider furnishing additional reliable advisors to strengthen Tshombe's entourage.

C. While maintaining his refusal to have Belgian officers encadred in ANC, we [*he*?] did agree to authorize Belgian advisors to go to Bukavu and critical forward points, and agreed desirability of Congo request for French officers for encadrement of gendarmerie.

D. He agreed instruct his Ambassador to discuss with Kasavubu Tshombe request to friendly African countries for prompt dispatch of troops. I agreed we would support this initiative.

E. We discussed at some length possible necessity of Western peace-keeping forces in which the Belgians would participate. While initially Spaak was reticent he finally offered to talk to British, German, French and Italian Ambassadors over the weekend or latest on Monday stressing gravity of situation, importance of preserving Congo to protect interests of all in Africa and possibility of requirement of some form of Western participation. Spaak assumed that we would also participate. I took no commitment but indicated that our contribution, if any, could better be in an air support unit. On Spaak's insistence I agreed that we would have similar talks with above Ambassadors in Washington early next week.

Thus at the end we appeared to be in full agreement on matters that should be given urgent consideration.

II. Burundi

Spaak agreed to call in Burundi Ambassador and tell him bluntly that Burundi must choose between ChiCom and rebel activity in Congo or assistance from Belgium. He expected us to support this position.

III. Ruanda

Spaak agreed to increase military equipment and encadrement Belgian officers for Ruanda army. Requested we supply one flight C–130 for prompt air delivery.

All in all, I found him surprisingly forthcoming, cooperative and prepared to take effective action.

MacArthur

205. Extract of a Telephone Conversation Between President Johnson and the President's Special Assistant for National Security Affairs (Bundy)[1]

Washington, August 8, 1964, 12:18 p.m.

Bundy: The other one you need to know about is in the Congo where there's shakiness today in Leopoldville. We've had a rather panicky request from the Ambassador to authorize a flyover of jets from the aircraft carrier *Enterprise* to try to scare off rebels. We are not disposed to authorize that and would prefer not to have any U.S. military hand showing there at all and we'll go back to him in that sense unless, against all my expectations, you want to have another aircraft carrier in action in another continent this weekend.

Johnson: No.

Bundy: Finally we've got to go into—

Johnson: Why does he think—

Bundy: Well, he thinks a show of force may strengthen Tshombe's hand but that seems to us the least desirable show of force. We're going to have a couple of cargo planes fly in there landing things and get out some black propaganda about how strong he is, and wait for Harriman to get back here tomorrow morning and then go on with the plan that he and Spaak have put together which, if we have time enough, makes pretty good sense.

---

[1] Source: Johnson Library, Recordings and Transcripts, Recording of Telephone Conversation between President Johnson and McGeorge Bundy, August 8, 1964, 12:18 p.m., Tape WH 6408.12, F64.01, Side A, PNO 2. Secret. This transcript was prepared in the Office of the Historian specifically for this volume.

206. Telegram From the Department of State to the Embassy in the Congo[1]

Washington, August 9, 1964, 12:45 a.m.

212. Ref Brussels tel 200.[2] Department believes it most urgent that GOC request immediate bilateral assistance from African countries likely and able to assist which are part of moderate group in Africa. These countries could include, for example, based on attitudes held during the last days of Adoula government, Ethiopia, Sudan, Tunisia and Nigeria. Because of deep seated African suspicions of Tshombe, it would be most useful in our view, if Adoula and Bomboko, particularly former could be associated with such efforts.

Time is of essence and hope we can earliest—matter of days—obtain some African troop presence Leopoldville (e.g. Ethiopians), and perhaps elsewhere.

You should stress to Tshombe (and Kasavubu if you consider useful) that if US to assist Congo effectively in its most critical moment, it can only do so if GOC cooperates fully by mobilizing all possible forms of assistance required and available.

Rusk

---

[1] Source: National Archives, RG 59, Central Files 1964–66, POL 23-9 THE CONGO. Confidential; Immediate. Drafted by Tasca, cleared by Lang in OSD/ISA, and approved by Tasca. Repeated to Brussels, CINCMEAFSA, and CINCMEAFSA for Ramsey.

[2] See footnote 2, Document 204.

---

207. Telegram From the Department of State to the Embassy in the Congo[1]

Washington, August 10, 1964, 1:13 a.m.

223. 1. As result of Harriman/Spaak discussions, Belgians and we have agreed that the only realistic course is to develop as rapidly as

---

[1] Source: National Archives, RG 59, Central Files 1964–66, POL 23–9 THE CONGO. Secret; Priority; Limdis. Drafted on August 9 by O'Sullivan and Lang; cleared by Tasca, Lang, Brubeck, and Colonel Gall in DOD; and approved by Harriman. Repeated to Brussels and CINCSTRIKE for POLAD.

possible a gendarme force led by military technicians (mercenaries). Belgians have agreed to supply arms, helmets and boots. US will provide vehicles, communications and air support as needed and not available locally.

2. You are authorized immediately to inform Tshombe USG will support the development of a 3000 man force. As first order of business the immediate objective is to have an effective force of up to 500 men in being prepared for operation within seven days.

In this connection you are authorized to take whatever steps are necessary in collaboration with Belgians (i.e. Van der Walle, Logiest) to achieve this objective. Funds for this purpose will be provided through the use of counterpart funds (see AID septel).[2] Problem of foreign exchange for special purposes being dealt with through other channels, as are special recruitment questions. You are authorized to use whatever locally available US matériel you control to equip and support this force (i.e. diversion of matériel from AID programs as well as military).

Obviously a force which can accomplish this objective will require military technician leadership, must be amenable to American and Belgian military advice, and not subject to control or veto by Mobutu. If additional guidance, authority or matériel needed to support your efforts this program please advise soonest.

3. Beyond immediate action to create this first component, planning must be done urgently toward eventual force of 3–4000. You should consult with Belgians, particularly Van der Walle, to determine availability human and matériel resources and how these resources will be organized and used as new force, consulting Congolese as necessary for information. (Struelens' explanation of Tshombe's plan left strong impression that it nothing more than general idea of what he would like to have, and did not have benefit of careful thought on organization or use). As a result your consultation we would also like to get a clearer picture of what matériel requirements could be met out of stocks in the Congo, and what new equipment would be needed.

4. In preparation for discussions, Embassy will want to consider following matters:

A. *Chain of Command*

Should new force be: (a) connected to the ANC or existing gendarmes; (b) separately assigned to control of Defense Committee; or (c) under control of Minister of Interior.

While we want to avoid problem with Mobutu, believe it important he not be able to control or frustrate this force. (Devlin may have

---

[2] Not identified.

some ideas on how he can be kept happy because we want to avoid his active opposition.)

It seems to us also that new force should not be attached directly to Tshombe for the simple reason that he already has too much to do and would not be in position to make decisions even if he were readily accessible. Munongo therefore would seem logical candidate, as Minister of Interior. However, Embassy should consider other alternatives.

B. *Organization of the Force*

Unit organization of new force will depend in large measure on the operational concepts under which it will operate and the resources readily available. In developing first component (para 2) as well as follow-on units, consideration should be given to "attack unit" composed entirely of military technicians to form cutting edge. In addition to combat units, consideration should be given to development of logistical support system, manned by Belgian or military technicians. Thought should also be given to development of logistical base (possibly Kamina).

C. *Concept of Operations*

Consideration should be given to:

(a) How units would be organized and used to capture rebel strong points;

(b) How strong points, when captured, will be held; and

(c) How new force would work with ANC and forces from other African countries. Consideration should also be given to follow-up measures to be taken in areas freed from rebel control. From experience in Baudoinville, building materials in addition to consumer goods and such things as medicines should be brought into the area immediately, with special attention paid to tribal chiefs to obtain their loyalty to central government.

4. Aside from para 2 program would appreciate soonest country team's views on foregoing together with whatever other substantive matters it considers would be helpful to raise with Belgians and Congolese.[3]

Rusk

[3] In telegram 450 from Leopoldville, August 10, Godley reported that he discussed telegram 223 with de Kerchove and other Belgian officials, who agreed that the first discussion with Tshombe should be mainly focused on the first subparagraph of paragraph 2, the development of a 3,000-man force. (National Archives, RG 59, Central Files 1964–66, POL 23–9 THE CONGO) Telegram CX–181 from Leopoldville, August 11, reported that Tshombe, Mobutu, and their Belgian military advisers agreed that the separate force proposed in telegram 223 was impractical because it would require too expensive a logistic system as well as establishment of a headquarters for which qualified personnel could not be spared. (Ibid.)

208. Telegram From the Station in the Congo to the Central Intelligence Agency[1]

Leopoldville, August 10, 1964.

2343 (In 47324). [McCone], [Helms] and [Fields] from [former COS] and [Identity 1].

1. In past few days security and military situation has deteriorated seriously. Rebel capture Stan has given rebels and persons favoring their cause great psychological fillip. This extremely important asset for the rebels, more important than an additional BN, for the bandwagon effect plays even greater role in Congolese politics than in more sophisticated nations. Also, fall of Stan when added to considerable rebel successes Kivu, Maniema, some areas Katanga and Kasai and fact many other areas appear open to subversion has depressed GOC leaders and supporters. Although spirits of leaders fluctuate, a sense of pessimism and defeatism prevails. It stems from recent rebel successes and fact most leaders realize ANC is a weak reed, if indeed not a broken reed, on which to rest the internal security of the Congo.

2. As reported previously, rebel activists already working in Leo, and presumably in other areas not under rebel control, endeavoring to exploit rebel successes by fanning flames of discontent of people and army (based on high unemployment rate, dissatisfaction with incompetent and venal leaders, tribal enmities, etc) and to weaken their will to fight. GOC expects these agitators, some of whom have been trained abroad, to step up their activities and to resort to violent tactics. In 60 Gizenga, Mulele and some others who now CNL leaders did not hesitate to try assasinate opponents; thus such tactics are again expected. Should this come to pass, and should even three or four key GOC leaders be assassinated, it could result in rebel victory, for there are only a few leaders available with capacity and courage to oppose rebel objectives.

3. Leaders such as Nendaka, Bomboko, Mobutu, Kithima, Bolikango and Ndele have stated at one time or another in last few days that they expect security situation continue deteriorate. Specifically, Nendaka and Bomboko, both of whom have been fairly reliable interpretors of the feelings of the people and who have proved their personal courage many times in past few years, fear ANC will collapse under rebel pressure, take easy way out by joining rebels and that Leo will fall from within through subversion and internal disorder. (Inter-

[1] Source: Central Intelligence Agency Files, Job 78–00435R, DDO/ISS Files, Box 1, Folder 1, [*cryptonym not declassified*] Development & Plans. Secret; Rybat; Immediate. Received at 1315Z.

estingly enough Nendaka has sent his family to Europe for "school registration" and Bomboko plans do same with his family. Also Adoula has requested [US Embassy] to pass message to his family in Rome that he hopes to join them 15 Aug.)

4. The ANC is in poor shape. Only a few units have had the courage of capacity to oppose effectively the rebels. Main problems of the army are lack of leadership, discipline, knowhow and motivation. This point driven home to [Identity 1] and other [US Embassy] personnel in Lisala and Bumba during aborted attempt rescue Stan [Identity 2] personnel. They found state of ANC morale precarious and rebel fever beginning seize the area. Troops were restive, surly and near rebellion. Lisala troops appeared dominated by some noncoms and purposeful agitators. Also presence of about three hundred soldiers at Bumba who escaped from Stan creates potentially explosive situation. The virus could easily spread to the limited number of ANC troops remaining in the western Congo and set stage for a domino-like collapse of the army similar to that which occurred in 60. Seriousness of situation can be recognized when one realizes that only troops in Equateur and Leopoldville provinces which now stand immediately between rebel forces in Stan and those in Leo are the fourth gendarmerie BN (whose contingents in Lisala do not instill confidence), one company at Bolobo and disorganized remnants of the Stan garrison. While other organized troops might be flown in, such step would weaken ANC positions other areas.

5. One alternative which being suggested from all sides is encadrement of ANC with mercenaries or officers on loan. However, this assumes that morale of troops is such that they willing and able fight under proper leadership. Many here doubt time exists for imported officers raise troop morale and reinstill discipline and will to fight. One possibility to which some GOC leaders cling is use of Katangan gendarmes (Katgens). Many Katgens available, and if sufficient arms and other supplies could be provided along with proper encadrement, they might be able save the situation. Recognize many believe this would be most palatable solution of various alternatives explored recently. However we and local ODYOKE military doubt Katgens offer rapid short term solution. View fact many of Katgens have been demobilized since Dec 62, they would probably need considerable training before they could be whipped into shape and unfortunate fact that during Katanga secession they did not prove better than average ANC troops (believe mercenaries responsible for majority Katgen victories), cannot help wonder whether this solution can be achieved fast enough and whether it offers a sufficient margin of security, one on which ODYOKE is prepared consciously to base its Congo (and perhaps African) policy.

6. During 8 Aug meeting Cols Williams (Chief COMISH) and Dodds expressed their personal views that the introduction of addi-

tional mercenaries does not offer a sufficiently sure margin of security. Also they doubt additional hardware would, alone, do the job, for if the Congo is to remain a national entity the GOC must regain and occupy the vast territories over which it has lost control. These officers concluded that, to obtain a sufficient margin of safety to permit the GOC to encadre troops, either Katgens or ANC, it would be necessary to station at least one non-African battalion in Leo. They specifically mentioned non-African troops, for they doubted African troops would be prepared intervene directly, in local security problems. Station not qualified militarily to pass judgement on these views, but on the basis of intel available, it shares view that intervention of foreign troops probably would be required to insure Leo held long enough to train and encadre units needed to defeat rebels and occupy lost areas. These views shared by many Station contacts (Kithima, Bolikango and CDA executive committee). Nendaka, Bomboko specifically favor foreign intervention, for they look upon it as only way of disarming rebels, ANC, of securing some semblance of peace in the country and of providing a respite during which GOC could create and train an entirely new army. They convinced this step will be necessary, for even if by a miracle the ANC resolved the current rebellion, peace and order cannot be guaranteed in the Congo until current rabble which passes for an army is reorganized and retrained.

7. One problem of awaiting the encadrement of Katgens is that, per above, it will take time and thus might allow Commies or extremist African states time to recognize rebels. Thus, such military policy could conceivably allow outside powers who oppose Leo govt to supply arms and/or "volunteers" to rebels.

8. Should use of mercenaries and Katgens fail turn tide, foresee Commie field day in the Congo. Although doubt more than a few rebel leaders motivated by Commie ideas and thus trained agents of influence, most rebel leaders have come under some degree of Commie influence. If Commies worked fast enough, they might be able to exploit rebel govt for Commie ends, just as Bloc tried do immediately after independence in July and Aug 60. However, unless Commie civil and military technicians were able to move in behind the rebels, suspect rebel victory would in very short time result in struggle for power between various leaders, factions and tribal groups now closely allied under CNL flag. While an outstanding leader might come to fore and build a monolithic state, one which at very best would be less than friendly and at worst would be actively hostile to ODYOKE interests, believe chances much greater that chaos and anarchy would be the result. Together with many other local observers, suspect Congo would gradually splinter under pressures of personal ambition and tribal rivalries into numerous semi-autonomous states, some of which might

obtain actual or defacto independence. One such state might be Katanga, but to retain its independence, it would probably have to align itself with South Africa, Southern Rhodesia and Portugal. Obviously, such a state would provide Commies, not to mention more extremist African states, with a ready-made opportunity for intervention. Similarly, many of the states which might develop would not be viable and thus would make easy targets for subversion. In short, Congo would become the sick man of Africa. Commie toe holds in petty Congo states would provide bases for subversion ops into many east, central and west African countries, most if not all of which are ripe for subversion.

9. If neither ODYOKE nor other Western states prepared send troops to Congo, believe ODYOKE must face the other alternative, i.e., the almost certain collapse of the central govt and establishment of a regime controlled by rebels. Recognize Belgians believe it possible come to terms with rebels but per above we consider this fallacious thinking. Although recognize few, if any, rebels actual Communists, continue believe their control of govt would open the way to Communist penetration of Congo and possibly undermine ODYOKE's African policy.

10. While recognize KUBARK is not and should not become involved policy decisions, we have prepared this cable to provide HQS with Station appreciation of the intelligence factors. Also recognize some of this message based on speculation. However, this speculation represents a consensus of many local observers, including such Station contacts as Nendaka, Bomboko, Ndele and, partially, of Adoula and Mobutu. Thus we believe it incumbent upon us to submit these views through KUBARK channels to assist HQS in interpreting the many intel items which Station has submitted on the current crisis and to stress urgency which we attach to current crisis.

11. Discussed above informally with [Godley] who states he finds "nothing with which to quarrel" in the preceding message. He specifically requested this message be passed [Harriman] and requested that some of these views be included in a joint COMISH/KUBARK assessment which being sent ODACID 10 Aug.

12. If it decided not to pass this message to [Harriman] pls advise Leop in order that we may advise [Godley].

209. Memorandum From William H. Brubeck of the National Security Council Staff to the President's Special Assistant for National Security Affairs (Bundy)[1]

Washington, August 11, 1964.

SUBJECT

Congo

Situation:

—Over one-sixth of the Congo in rebel hands.

—Rebels on the move, and ANC continues to disintegrate.

—Military and CIA judgment in Leopoldville is that Bukavu may fall any moment and Leopoldville anytime in next two weeks.

—Central Government has almost no reliable military force or capacity to prevent takeover.

Additional Steps US is Taking:

—Sending seven more T–28s immediately (ETA about three weeks).

—Supplying C–130 airlift to Belgian military logistics.

—Offering airlift and assistance to bring in Nigerian and (possibly) other troops.

Steps Under Consideration:

—CINCSTRIKE has operational plan (not yet approved) to put four C–130s plus two helicopters with armed escort platoon into Leopoldville on 38 hours notice.

—Sending two or three of seven Agency B–26s [*less than 1 line not declassified*] to Leopoldville for armed recon (10 day lead time).

—Covert funding to enable Tshombe to strengthen political alliance with tribal leaders.

Questions:

1. Should CINCSTRIKE C–130 force go to Leopoldville immediately to eliminate 38 hour lead time; for logistic support mission and possible evacuation of 500 Americans there?

2. Should US put on short lead time standby a special forces battalion for possible emergency occupation of Leopoldville and Matadi Port area, per Embassy recommendation?

---

[1] Source: Johnson Library, National Security File, Country File, Congo, Vol. III. Secret.

3. Should US begin to cut losses, restrict future commitment present regime, wait for outcome of internal power fight in Congo hoping to develop relations with new regime on basis their need for continuing US aid?

4. Re question three, what is the possibility that Chicoms could and would prevent US establishing effective ties with new regime?

B

---

210. Memorandum From the President's Special Assistant for National Security Affairs (Bundy) to President Johnson[1]

Washington, August 11, 1964.

The attached memorandum to me from Bill Brubeck gives the up-to-date situation in the Congo as we now see it.[2]

What is very unclear is how deep the Chinese hand is in the rebel efforts. Harriman thinks it is pretty deep; most of the intelligence community thinks it is more marginal.

Brubeck raises hard questions at the end of his memorandum, and I think that the dominant judgment at the moment is that we ought not go beyond the steps currently in train, and that particularly we should not now plan on sending a Special Forces of U.S. forces—that could not only come if a lot of other people were willing to act, which is not currently the case. The CINC Strike C–130 force is another matter because of its relation to a possible need for evacuation of Americans.

McG. B.[3]

---

[1] Source: Johnson Library, National Security File, Memos to the President, McGeorge Bundy, Vol. 6. No classification marking.

[2] Not attached; the reference is presumably to Document 209.

[3] Printed from a copy that bears this typed signature.

211. Memorandum for the Files[1]

Washington, August 11, 1964, 12:30 p.m.

NSC MEETING ON THE CONGO

PARTICIPANTS

The President
Department of State—Secretary Rusk, Under Secretary Ball, Under Secretary Harriman
Department of Defense—Secretary McNamara, Deputy Secretary Vance, Mr. McNaughton
CIA—Mr. McCone
OEP—Mr. McDermott
AID—Mr. Bell
Treasury Department—Secretary Dillon
USIA—Mr. Rowan
White House—Messrs. Bundy, Bromley Smith, Reedy, Cater, Valenti, Brubeck

Governor Harriman reported on his talk with Spaak in Brussels and on agreements reached there regarding support for gendarmerie and mercenary forces and additional US military assistance. Harriman felt that these steps while useful would probably not meet fully the military need, and expressed concern with Chicom involvement. He said the Congolese army in most cases has proved useless, that the people in the government are demoralized and Leopoldville in danger.

With regard to possible US-European forces, he said the Europeans are unlikely to participate without US involvement but thought the US role could be limited to an air contribution. He will talk to the Western European Ambassadors in Washington along these lines.

The President asked what countries and how much force are being considered.

Harriman said France, Great Britain, Germany, the Netherlands, Italy and Canada with a maximum of 3,000 men for garrison duty only. Actual combat operations would be left to Congolese army and gendarmes but they would require white officers. Although the Belgians have talked of the possibility of "doing business" with the rebels Harriman believes he convinced Spaak that this is a myth.

McCone endorsed Harriman's stress on the Chicom role and expressed similar skepticism about doing business with the rebels. Al-

[1] Source: Johnson Library, National Security File, NSC Meetings File, Vol. III, Tab 21, 8/11/64, Congo. Secret. Drafted by Brubeck.

though he thought the military problem is quantitatively small, he was pessimistic about the Congolese military capacity and thought Western troops would be necessary.

In response to a Bundy question Harriman said that if Nigerians or other Africans will provide troops, European intervention is avoidable. Without African help, European help might be needed within two weeks. Immediate US efforts should be concentrated on air support and pressure for African assistance to the Congo. UN help is unlikely because the Russians would veto Security Council action and a General Assembly at this time is undesirable.

Rusk said that while the present trouble is tribal unrest and rebel bands moving freely in the absence of effective police, we must assume that if disintegration continues the Communists will take over. The job can be done on a small scale if done now, and it should be put squarely to the Europeans as their responsibility. We should urge them immediately to put troops into Leopoldville, using Presidential pressure if necessary.

Vance reported on the military situation and status of US aircraft being supplied. McNamara expressed his strong agreement with Rusk and suggested that, if the Europeans fail to accept responsibility, we should not continue to carry the burden alone in the Congo.

The President expressed doubt as to whether such a choice is open to us, and said we may have to continue our role regardless of what others do. However, he added, this may be the point at which to make a basic issue with the Europeans of their accepting a share of responsibility in situations such as the Congo.

McNamara indicated his belief that we should be prepared to increase our military assistance to Ethiopia and Nigeria perhaps as much as $10 million, if this would help them in providing military support to the Congo.

Dillon expressed the view that direct American involvement in the Congo should be considered only as extreme last resort. General Wheeler concurred in this as "the long held view of the JCS."

The President said emphatically that we all share this view. He said that Harriman has authority to make strong representations to the Europeans for help and should ask Spaak to make similar approaches. The President asked for a report by Friday, August 14 on our success in getting European or African military help for the Congo.[2]

---

[2] See Document 220.

The President also authorized financial and logistic support to any African countries in meeting the expense of any such help; and air transport assistance for moving European troops.

The President observed that time is running out and the Congo must be saved. When these steps have been tried, he said, we will look at the situation again to consider what further decisions may be required.

WB

212. Telegram From the Department of State to the Embassy in the Congo[1]

Washington, August 11, 1964, 11:01 p.m.

248. For Godley. Ref: Leo's 461.[2] You should inform Kasavubu C–130's are coming in response to GOC need and request. FYI. In view of our repeated difficulties in getting cooperation or realism from Mobutu it is important that continuing U.S. aid—e.g. C–130's and B–26's, etc. not be explained as response to Mobutu requests or permitted to add to his prestige and influence. On contrary, these are efforts to meet needs of Congo Government and people and should so appear publicly in Leo in order to strengthen position of Government and of no particular individual or faction. It should be clear that we expect the increasing U.S. commitments to carry with them U.S. leverage in securing Congo Government cooperation and action in meeting problems that concern U.S. End FYI.

Rusk

[1] Source: National Archives, RG 59, Central Files 1964–66, DEF 19–3 US–THE CONGO. Secret; Immediate; Limdis. Drafted by Schaufele, cleared by Harriman and Brubeck, and approved by Williams.

[2] In telegram 461 from Leopoldville, August 11, Godley said that he believed that the earliest possible arrival of a small task force of C–130s would be highly desirable and that C–130s would be invaluable in moving ANC personnel and necessary supplies throughout the Congo. (Ibid.)

213. Telegram From the Department of State to the Embassy in the Congo[1]

Washington, August 11, 1964, 11:01 p.m.

249. From the Secretary. I am convinced that requests to Governments from Kasavubu and Tshombe for African troops constitutes key to present Congo impasse. Without such requests from GOC, problem of trying assist Congo becomes much more complicated. It is essential US exert every pressure now to this end.

You are therefore instructed to request an immediate audience with Kasavubu and Tshombe to get them to despatch today requests to other African countries, particularly Ethiopia and Sudan. In this connection might be useful to have ready draft text of letter of request. In case of Nigerians letter should be follow up to earlier request. Indicate US will support strongly GOC efforts. For obvious reasons Kasavubu should figure prominently in request to other African governments. Should also follow up if possible with expressions of support from Adoula, Bomboko et cetera (perhaps as special ambassadors).

You should inform Kasavubu that it is essential to our cooperation that he put his cards on table and explain his political objectives, tactics and problems. I believe you should also tell Kasavubu and Tshombe that more evidence of realism and cooperation must be forthcoming from them if our collaboration is to be fruitful.

You should also tell ambassadors of countries receiving requests that US prepared provide necessary airlift and support costs above normal salary, allowances and maintenance.

To maximize chance of African help terms of request should be limited and precise, e.g. that mission is to garrison and secure two or three key cities, not to act as assault troops.

US and Belgian efforts will be frustrated unless you persuade Kasavubu and Tshombe soonest to act with energy in area of African assistance and create image of Congolese Government representative of Congolese people struggling to maintain unity and independence in face of great difficulties and external attempts at subversion.

Rusk

[1] Source: National Archives, RG 59, Central Files 1964–66, POL 23–9 THE CONGO. Confidential; Immediate. Drafted by Tasca and O'Sullivan; cleared by Harriman, Brubeck, and Rusk; and approved by Williams. Repeated to Brussels and CINCSTRIKE for Ramsey.

214. Editorial Note

On August 11, 1964, Ambassador Godley reported that the Embassy had received a commercial telegram in French from Consul Michael Hoyt in Stanleyville stating that Lieutenant General Nicholas Olenga, Commander-in-Chief of the Popular Liberation Army, had told him that because they had seen U.S. troops in action against the Popular Army, the Consulate had to be evacuated. Despite Hoyt's denial that any U.S. troops were engaged in operations against Olenga's army, the General ordered that all the personnel of the Consulate be evacuated by the first available plane. Hoyt asked for instructions. The Ambassador sent a reply asking Hoyt to inform Olenga that he had been misinformed, but nonetheless authorizing Hoyt and other U.S. personnel to depart on the first available aircraft. Godley asked Hoyt to tell Olenga that U.N. Representative Osorio-Tafall was willing to send aircraft carrying WHO doctors and medicine, which could evacuate the Consulate personnel to Leopoldville, but he must have the General's assurance that its landing and subsequent departure would be permitted and that the safety of the doctors and crew would be assured. (Telegram 458 from Leopoldville; National Archives, RG 59, Central Files 1964–66, POL 23–9 THE CONGO)

On August 12, Godley informed Washington that the Embassy had received a message in French from Olenga via public telex, warning that if military or technical aid were furnished to the Tshombe government, he would consider himself obliged, with the greatest regret, to reconsider his position in relation to the nationals of those countries providing aid. (Telegram 471 from Leopoldville; ibid.) The Ambassador reported that he responded to the Olenga's message via public telex, warning the General that the U.S. Government would hold him personally responsible for the security of every American in the Stanleyville region. (Telegram 480 from Leopoldville, August 12; ibid.)

215. Telegram From the Embassy in the Congo to the Department of State[1]

Leopoldville, August 12, 1964, 3 p.m.

472. For the Secretary and Governor Harriman.

1. On receipt Department's 249 to Leo[2] this morning I requested immediate audiences with Kasavubu and Tshombe. Kasavubu received Blake and me at 1330 local time. I reviewed for President in general way Harriman–Spaak discussions saying Belgians and US had agreed important response to GOC request for assistance rapidly and as full as possible.

Relying on Deptel 223 to Leo[3] I then said USG had decided, as requested by GOC support development of 3,000 man gendarme force to be led by military technicians, with US providing vehicles, communications and air support as needed and Belgians providing other arms and other kinds of equipment.

2. In line with this I added four C–130 aircraft would arrive tomorrow in order provide lift capacity urgently requested by GOC. These aircraft would be accompanied, in addition to their crews, by group of soldiers for maintenance and protection of these aircraft. Total number of such soldiers would be about 100 men.

3. I said that Governor Williams would be arriving aboard one of these planes in order discuss with him and PriMin problems of restoring security in Congo and how US might help. Kasavubu said he would look forward to seeing Governor Williams.

4. I then paraphrased for Chief of State first three paragraphs of Deptel 249. At point where I emphasized it essential that if GOC and USG are to cooperate they must put all cards on table. I distressed to say that Department informed by South African Ambassador in Washington yesterday (Deptel 244)[4] that GOC had requested SAG provide two squadrons fighter aircraft ready for action plus officers and enlisted men and various equipment, all within 48 hours. When I pointedly asked Kasavubu whether he knew about request for SA military assistance he gave me distinct impression this first he had heard program, although he was somewhat evasive in answering.

---

[1] Source: National Archives, RG 59, Central Files 1964–66, DEF 19–3 US–THE CONGO. Secret; Flash; Limdis. Received at 11:34 a.m. Repeated to Brussels and CINCSTRIKE and relayed to the White House, DOD, and CIA.

[2] Document 213.

[3] Document 207.

[4] Dated August 11. (National Archives, RG 59, Central Files 1964–66, POL 1 S AFR–CONGO)

5. I once again bore down with Kasavubu on importance US attaches to African participation in process of restoring order in Congo and said we ready provide necessary aircraft and support costs above normal salary, allowances and maintenance for African troops which might come here. I did not discuss penultimate paragraph of Deptel 249 re missions which African troops might have, nor did I point up though that Belgian, as well as our own efforts might be frustrated unless African assistance forthcoming. However, I did return once again to theme that more evidence of realism and cooperation must definitely be forthcoming from Congolese side.

6. Kasavubu then said what I had just told him obviously important since it represented views of highest USG circles. He added he could give me no answer until he had had chance to discuss this whole question of African assistance with Tshombe. Only then could he give US and Belgians, whom he implied had made parallel démarche, re importance of African participation, GOC's considered reply. I tried in several ways draw him out further in order get his own views on subject, but to no avail. He ended audience by saying he hoped have good talk with Governor Williams, whom he hoped would be able stay longer in Congo than during last visit.

7. Upon return to office I found message from Tshombe asking me to call at 1600 local time.[5]

Godley

---

[5] In telegram 481 from Leopoldville, August 12, Godley reported his discussion of this issue with Tshombe, who asked him to report that he agreed with the necessity of obtaining African assistance and not to be misled by his public statements, which were based on his conviction that the Congolese people would react violently against their government if they learned of such requests. (Ibid.)

216. Telegram From the Department of State to the Mission to the United Nations[1]

Washington, August 12, 1964, 8:47 p.m.

374. Confirming Sisco/Yost telecon,[2] you requested take up Congo problem immediately with SYG or Bunche, making following points:

1) We informing UNNY on strictly confidential basis Nigerians have agreed to Kasavubu's request to provide troops by offering one battalion on condition that such action have UN or OAU blessing.

2) We consider immediate follow-through of critical importance in saving Congo from anarchy. Continued deterioration in security situation with further rebel gains and consequent disintegration of morale throughout country could lead to fragmentation of Congo within matter of weeks if immediate and drastic remedial action not taken.

3) As SYG stated in his terminal report June 29, 1964,[3] SC reses re Congo continue be applicable since they have no terminal date. In addition, in same report, he noted that developments in Congo will continue to be of very great concern to UN and to him.

4) Several reses pertinent in this regard. You should draw on Deptel 3364[4] as supporting evidence, emphasizing particularly obligation of SYG to employ resources he has available (a) to seek maintain Congolese territorial integrity and political independence; (b) to help GOC in restoration and maintenance of law and order; and (c) to seek prevent civil war in Congo. In addition, member states have obligation under Res S/5002[5] to lend their support to GOC in conformity with Charter and UN decisions.

5) SYG will readily recognize that military input of responsible African state will also be constructive adjunct to UN efforts through its civilian operations in restoring Congo to stability.

---

[1] Source: National Archives, RG 59, Central Files 1964–66, POL 23–9 THE CONGO. Secret; Priority. Drafted by Buffum, cleared by Harriman and Tasca, and approved by Sisco. Repeated to Lagos, Leopoldville, Brussels, Addis Ababa, Khartoum, and Tunis.

[2] Not further identified.

[3] The text of the U.N. Secretary-General's report of June 29, 1964 (U.N. Doc. S/5784), is printed in *American Foreign Policy: Current Documents, 1964*, pp. 750–759.

[4] Telegram 3364 to USUN, June 22, contained the Department's analysis of continuing responsibilities of the U.N. Secretary-General, U.N. members, and non-members under existing U.N. resolutions on the Congo. (National Archives, RG 59, Central Files 1964–66, POL 23–9 THE CONGO)

[5] The text of U.N. Security Council Resolution 5002, November 24, 1961 (U.N. Doc. S/5002), is printed in *American Foreign Policy: Current Documents, 1961*, pp. 851–853.

6) Under circumstances, we consider minimum action which SYG can take is to issue public statement welcoming Nigerian offer and indicating he finds it fully consistent with UN resolutions.

7) We appreciate that SYG will want direct request from Nigerians before issuing such statement, and once you have established his willingness cooperate this fashion, we will ask Embassy Lagos suggest GON pursue matter through its UN Rep.

Rusk

217. Telegram From the Station in the Congo to the Central Intelligence Agency[1]

Leopoldville, August 12, 1964.

(No Night Action)

2394 (In 49309). Ref: Dir 41328.[2] [Fields] from [former COS] and [*name not declassified*].

1. [former COS] remaining Leop. Will try send [Identity 1] Coquilhatville alone, as believe it important hold that city if at all possible. Per previous cable 11 Aug, [former COS] saw [*name not declassified*] 11 Aug and seeing him again 12 Aug. Regret not able obtain intel on plans for military encadrement. Belgians appear be trying play this one close to vest. Suspect this may stem from Belgian belief they should try reach agreement with rebels as they believe, in short sighted way, that this way protect business interests. However, will push as hard as possible 12 Aug meeting.

2. In brief meeting 11 Aug [*name not declassified*] made following points:

A. Doubts Congo can be preserved as one national entity. With few competent troops could retake any point now held by rebels. But what is the use if Congo does not have qualified cadre to move in behind army and establish civil administration.

---

[1] Source: Central Intelligence Agency Files, [*text not declassified*], Fiche 38, Row 5, Frames 2–4, Tshombe. Secret; Rybat; Priority. Received at 1100Z.

[2] In CIA telegram 41328 to Leopoldville, August 11, Fields requested that Devlin remain in Leopoldville, and stated that the most urgent matter at hand was that he have a clear conversation with [*text not declassified*] in order to determine the present status of the military technician program and what they could do to strengthen it. (Ibid., Fiche 38, Row 4, Frame 12, Tshombe)

B. View above only solution is to create a Congo based on limited number loosely federated provinces or independent states, perhaps along lines previous provinces in Belgian Congo. Perhaps, and only perhaps, Congolese qualified administer such units. In reality, good administration not possible without European cadre. If such cadre not available and area liberated, Congolese troops will merely start looting, stealing, etc once again and situation which we know now will start all over again.

C. Katgens no better than ANC, unless led by European officers, except for fact they have not been exposed to anarchy of Leop.

D. [*name not declassified*] returning [*less than 1 line not declassified*], 14 Aug. Will return only if he believes there chance for viable solution. Regrets ODYOKE did not go along with Katanga experiment. On leaving [former COS], he pointed to area of Katanga, saying it was once a fine area, but "it is finished now."

4. Heartily concur we need numerous contacts in [Identity 2] camp, but this strongly opposed by [Godley] and his deputy. (FYI only: They reluctant have Leop move in direction [Identity 2]. Basically, they do not like or trust him, and prefer not make move in his direction unless this solicited by him. Secondly, believe they hope keep KUBARK tied to [*cryptonym not declassified*] group and insure that ODACID takes over all contacts in "new regime".)

5. [former COS] has not seen [Identity 2] again because [Godley] did not want additional KUBARK contacts: Leop does not concur, but had been going along with this. Thus, basis ref, will begin 12 Aug trying build up such contacts. Believe this can be done in most cases without arousing ire [US. Embassy]. Only cases which would cause too much trouble would be [Identity 2] and minister who is over [Identity 3].

[Omitted here is further discussion of the political situation.]

218. Memorandum for the Record[1]

Washington, August 13, 1964.

SUBJECT

Minutes of the Meeting of the 303 Committee

PRESENT

Mr. Bundy, Mr. George C. Denney, Jr., Mr. Vance, and Mr. McCone
Governor Harriman and Mr. Glenn Fields were present for Items 1 and 2
General Wheeler was present for all items

1. Congo

a. In regard to the Congo proposal ("Covert Support for Moise Tshombe and Selected Congolese Leaders for Restoration of Order in the Congo" dated 12 August 1964),[2] Governor Harriman indicated there were some questions in Ambassador Godley's mind about the uses of funds and felt that the ambassador's approval should be obtained. Mr. McCone indicated that he thought Ambassador Godley could be made to see the urgent need for this assistance. Mr. Bundy summarized the points of view by saying that the proposal was considered approved with Ambassador Godley retaining the right to review and raise any questions now or later in regard to these expenditures. Mr. Fields added that this had been the current procedure in Leopoldville.[3]

b. Governor Harriman then requested that the Agency [2 *lines not declassified*]. Any assistance that could be proffered in Rwanda would be appreciated as well, Governor Harriman indicated.

---

[1] Source: Central Intelligence Agency Files, DCI (McCone) Files, Job 80B01285A, 303 Committee Meetings (1964). Secret; Eyes Only. Drafted by Peter Jessup of the NSC Staff on August 14.

[2] The prososal requested authority to provide covert financial and other support to Tshombe and certain key politicians in the form of a fund to be used periodically as and when needed for assuring tribal support in critical areas to Tshombe and certain other leaders. It also would be used to fill the gap between the hiring and paying of white "Military Technicians" who were prepared to offer their services to the GOC. The total cost was estimated at [*dollar amount not declassified*]. (National Security Council, Intelligence Files, Congo, 1960–1965)

[3] McCone's record of this meeting indicates that he protested Harriman's suggestion that Godley should have veto power over the uses of funds, and that it had been agreed that any proposed action not agreed to by Godley would be submitted to Washington for review and consideration by State and CIA at headquarters level. (Central Intelligence Agency Files, DCI (McCone) Files, Job 80B01285A, 303 Committee Meetings (1964))

c. Mr. McCone outlined for those present some of the psywar type projects presently under way or contemplated for the Congo. [4½ *lines not declassified*]

d. Mr. Denney underscored the serious problems of the introduction of any number of South African or Rhodesian white mercenaries into the Congo if this should be publicized.

[Omitted here is discussion of other matters.]

Peter Jessup

219. Paper Prepared in the Central Intelligence Agency[1]

Washington, August 13, 1964.

CONGO

1. Problem: How to restore order and some semblance of stability in the Congo (Leopoldville).

2. Situation: The so-called rebel forces of the CNL in the Congo have extended their control in a very brief period from Uvira on the Burundi border to Albertville on Lake Tanganyika west to Kabalo and up the Lualaba River and rail line to Stanleyville, the center of Lumumbist dissidence in the Congo. They have done this through the relatively simple tactic of exploiting whatever discontent there may be in each area by the use of advance agitation agents followed by a relatively small but active armed force. The rebel forces are currently in effective control of Stanleyville and are planning to move on momentarily further west to Coquilhatville. Their successes have been loudly broadcast by Stanleyville Radio and their indominability is becoming accepted by both Congolese and Europeans alike. A general attitude of defeatism has set in not only in the towns in their path but even in Leopoldville. As of this date the key city of Bukavu on Lake Kivu in the east is seriously threatened but has not yet fallen. In viewing the extraordinary progress made by the dissident forces it becomes ever more apparent that they are receiving both monetary and advisory support from outside and that there are evidences of the Chinese Communist trademark.

[1] Source: Central Intelligence Agency Files, Job 82–00450R, Box 6, Folder 3, Willis' Notes, Working Papers—Congo. Secret. There is no drafting information on the original. A handwritten notation on the paper reads: "Prepared for DCI."

3. Faced with the above situation and the continued disintegration of Central Government control in the Congo as well as the approaching evaporation of the Central Government itself, the Embassy in Leopoldville is anticipating in the near future the possible fall from within of Leopoldville itself. There has been some speculation among informed Congolese leaders that it could come as early as 15 August 1964. With this in mind the Embassy has urgently recommended the immediate dispatch of non-African troops to guarantee the security of Leopoldville and the port area at the mouth of the Congo River. With this area secured, planning could then proceed for the reacquisition by various means of the territory already in rebel hands. There is a growing feeling that even Mobutu's 8–900 paracommandos cannot or will not hold even Leopoldville. Without first securing this critical area as a base from which to operate, it will be more difficult to carry out a realistic plan for reclaiming the rest of the Congo in the immediate future.

4. Therefore, in simplest terms, the alternatives seem clear and are in descending order or desirability:

A. Dispatch of at least one battalion of Belgian paracommandos to secure and garrison Leopoldville and the port area. These troops would be on the ground for the stated, and not too implausible, purpose of protecting what is left of the Congo from outside invasion. There is precedent for this in Congo (Brazzaville) where a French garrison is still located. Further, there is precedent for dispatch of metropole troops at the request of the government of a former colony, i.e., Tanganyika.

B. A second alternative is obtaining French willingness to provide troops for this purpose.

C. A third and probably unacceptable option is the dispatch of a U.S. force.

5. In order to obtain the military intervention of any foreign power the Congo Government must first make such a request and clearly on a most urgent basis. The three operative elements in the GOC today are Joseph Kasavubu, as President, Defense Minister and Commander-in-Chief of the Congolese National Army (CNA), Moise Tshombe, the Prime Minister, who claims the support of at least 4,000 ex-Katangan gendarmes (Katgens), and General Joseph Mobutu, the Commander of the CNA. Unless these three leaders work together there is little prospect of accomplishing even the first step in a plan to reclaim the Congo, i.e., securing full Belgian assistance. Thus, it is imperative that the USG, presumably through its ambassador, establish a close and confidential relationship with all three of these leaders. To date this is not the case, but it must be developed without delay if we are to be able to provide the necessary assistance. Tshombe, being the most active of the three, is perhaps the key element and must be prepared to keep our Ambas-

sador intimately informed in strictest confidence of his day to day plans and problems.

6. Assuming that the U.S. immediate objective in the Congo is as stated above to take all possible action to restore order in the Congo and establish some semblance of stability in the country after returning the disaffected areas to Central Government control, the following actions can be and in some areas are being undertaken by CIA:

A. Military Action:

(1) Air:

CIA is presently providing air support to the Congo Government. At present this support includes furnishing [*less than 1 line not declassified*] pilots and ground personnel for six T–28's provided by MAP and six T–6 aircraft [*less than 1 line not declassified*]. There are at this moment four of six T–28's flying. One is undergoing repairs, one is being replaced and is expected to be in operation within 14 days. The six T–6's are in flying condition but are currently in the process of being armed. Six additional T–28's provided by MAP have been promised for the Congo and all are expected to be combat operational within 31 days. Seven B–26 aircraft from CIA contingency force [*less than 1 line not declassified*] have been ordered to the Congo. The first two of these are to depart for the Congo within two days and will arrive within one week. These planes will be ferried to Leopoldville by U.S. contract personnel with USAF markings with stops at Takhli, Ganis, and Aden. The [*less than 1 line not declassified*] operational pilots and ground personnel will be provided by CIA ostensibly under contract with the GOC. Experienced B–26 pilots are already on the ground. More will be dispatched shortly. The longer-range B–26 as opposed to T–28's or T–6 are considered necessary to provide greater flexibility of movement in the Congo where many alternate airfields are now in rebel hands. The remaining aircraft will arrive in the Congo within 2–3 weeks.

With the greatly augmented CIA Air Operations in the Congo it will be necessary to procure two C–47's for logistic support and two helicopters for a rescue capability.

Wherever possible qualified [*less than 1 line not declassified*] personnel will be used. However, it may be necessary to have a minimum number of ground U.S. contract technicians where no [*less than 1 line not declassified*] are available. In addition, there will be a total of at least three U.S. contract or staff officers [*less than 1 line not declassified*]. The total number of personnel in this program will reach a total of approximately 120 foreign and U.S. personnel.

(2) Ground:

Since it has now been graphically displayed that the Congolese Army is totally ineffective and unreliable without leadership and it is clear that the army does not have qualified officers to lead the troops, it is apparent that only with Belgian or other white officers can an effective striking force be put in the field. Thus the Belgian Government has been requested by State to assist and has agreed to provide Belgian officers to lead these troops. Fifty such officers have or are being dispatched to the Congo for this purpose. In addition the French Government has been requested similar assistance. However, to date the French have not been forthcoming with direct support. Nigerian troops have also been requested for garrison duty but the response to this request has not yet been received. It is further understood that Tshombe has asked the Government of the Central African Republic (CAR) to provide troop units. The army of the CAR is largely officered by former French Foreign Legionnaires. As of this date it is not known whether an agreement has been signed. At the same time Tshombe has made efforts to obtain the services of white mercenaries from South Africa and Southern Rhodesia. According to Michel Struelens, Belgian Publicist for Tshombe, there are 100 such mercenaries ready to go. It is believed, however, that Tshombe is unable to pay their salaries and has accordingly asked for financial assistance in this matter from both the Belgian and U.S. Governments. In the interest of creating at the earliest possible time an effective strike force it has been agreed that the USG will support the immediate development of a 3000 man force with 200 white mercenaries. In order to avoid official USG involvement with these mercenaries (Military Technicians) CIA has been called upon to [*1½ lines not declassified*] determine what Tshombe needs to establish a force with the least possible delay and to offer to help finance the salaries of these Military Technicians if payment is causing the delay. (A paper has been submitted to the 303 Committee requesting policy approval for this action.)[2]

[Omitted here is further discussion of military actions.]

B. Political and Psychological:

(1) Political:

Recognizing that the tribal allegiances can be the final controlling factor in stabilizing the Congo, it has been proposed that CIA provide [*less than 1 line not declassified*] selected key leaders financial support to reinforce tribal loyalties.

In the Swahili speaking section of the Congo, Tshombe has in the past maintained the support of tribal leaders through periodic application of funds, gifts, and various items such as "Black Powder" for their muskets (which is extremely hard for them to procure on their own). Other political leaders in critical areas who would need support to

---

[2] Not found.

maintain or reestablish control over specific regions would include: (See map attached)[3]

a) [*name not declassified*] in the Bakongo area in the west. [*less than 1 line not declassified*]

b) [*name not declassified*] in the Moyen Congo along the Northern reaches of the Congo River. [*less than 1 line not declassified*]

c) [*name not declassified*] in the Mongo Tribal region of Cuvette Centrale (just south of Moyen Congo). [*name not declassified*] who has in the past shown ability as an organizer is a close friend of Bomboko with whom the State keeps close contact.

d) General Joseph Mobutu in Ubangi, the northernmost province on the border of the Central African Republic. [*less than 1 line not declassified*]

e) [*name not declassified*] has support of the Bakongo who make up approximately half of the native population in the Cite in Leopoldville. [*1 line not declassified*]

f) [*name not declassified*], a CNL leftist presently in the Tshombe government who has good support in Luluabourg in Central Kasai as well as Lualaba in the south and Kwilu Province to the west. Station would establish contact.

g) [*name not declassified*], former Defense Minister, from Lisala in Moyen Congo also has some support in the Kivu area.

h) [*1½ lines not declassified*]

i) [*1 line not declassified*] Kibali-Ituri Province on the Uganda border.

j) [*1 line not declassified*]

k) [*1 line not declassified*]

l) [*1 line not declassified*]

(3) [*sic*] Psychological:

CIA plans certain specific initiatives in the psywar field which can supplement other U.S. action programs. The basic, immediate, and overriding objectives of these activities would be:

(a) To counter and neutralize the highly effective rebel psychological offensive which has succeeded to date in demoralizing the Congolese Army and population.

(b) To create a more favorable climate of opinion toward the Congolese Government throughout Africa.

[Omitted here is further discussion of psychological actions.]

[3] Not reproduced.

220. Memorandum From the Under Secretary of State for Political Affairs (Harriman) to the President's Special Assistant for National Security Affairs (Bundy)[1]

Washington, August 14, 1964.

SUBJECT

Congo

Soundings which Mr. Spaak and I have taken through Ambassadors in Brussels and Washington indicate an adverse reaction to a European force to intervene in the Congo.

The Government of Nigeria has informed Mr. Tshombe that it would be willing to make a battalion available for Leopoldville only in December after the Nigerian elections, although other African participation could speed up this action. Prime Minister Balewa does not wish the troop question to become a Nigerian election issue unless he is sure of African support. Despite our efforts, the Congolese Government has not so far asked any other African country for military forces save South Africa which fortunately refused. Governor Williams is now in the Congo to press as a matter of highest priority the Congolese Government to make such requests. Belgian Ambassador has been taking parallel initiative. If GOC requests to friendly Africans are forthcoming, he[2] will visit the capitals concerned on his return trip.

The Belgian Government appears to be doing more to help the Congolese Government militarily than anticipated. In addition to supplying weapons and some items of personal equipment, Col. Van der Walle, sent by Spaak to Leopoldville as Mr. Tshombe's military adviser, is developing a plan which involves the use of some additional Belgian military personnel in command positions coupled with military technicians (mercenaries) to stiffen ANC and Gendarme units. Col. Van der Walle's plans call for retaining the eastern Congolese air fields to minimize the possibility of air support to the rebels from unfriendly

---

[1] Source: Johnson Library, National Security File, Country File, Congo, Vol. III. Confidential. The memorandum is attached to a transmittal memorandum from Brubeck to the President which reads: "You asked for the attached progress report from State for today on efforts to get European and other African military help for the Congo. Prospects for help from either source are very dim. However, Belgians are working on a plan for a white mercenary-Congolese force with Belgian officers and we are supporting. Also Tshombe seems to be getting 100 or so South African white mercenaries in next few days. We hope to add some other nationalities to avoid the political problem in Africa of conspicuous South African involvement. We will give you a further report on Monday." See Document 226.

[2] A handwritten note next to this word reads: "Gov. Williams."

powers and the recapture of rebel held territory from Bukavu and Kamina.

Col. Van der Walle's recommendations, if rebels can be contained long enough to implement them, offer the best present solution to the security problem. The American Ambassador in Brussels is being instructed to urge Mr. Spaak's concurrence.

The use of military technicians poses problems for Mr. Tshombe in gaining acceptance in Africa. If the mercenaries come solely from South Africa, the risk of Bloc recognition and possibly support of the rebel government will increase.

Averell

---

221. Memorandum From the Director of the United States Information Agency (Rowan) to President Johnson[1]

Washington, August 14, 1964.

SUBJECT

Propaganda Problems Relating to the Congo

No one feels more strongly than I that the immediate security problem in the Congo is the overriding factor in any determination as to what our present policy ought to be. I do believe, however, that we dare not lose sight of the fact that on even a short-term basis much more is at stake than Stanleyville, or Leopoldville, or any amount of real estate in the Congo. There is a real danger that in saving the present situation in the Congo we can suffer psychological and other setbacks that could lose us the longer range struggle for all of Africa.

I am particularly concerned about the damaging implications of possible press reports that United States' planes are hauling in Belgian guns to be used by South African and Southern Rhodesian mercenaries to kill Africans and to protect "Tshombe and European financial interests." *The New York Times* already has had one such story and Communist, and some African, propagandists have seized upon this theme.

This Agency and I are for taking whatever immediate steps are necessary to halt the deteriorating situation in the Congo, but we are

---

[1] Source: Johnson Library, White House Central File, Confidential Files, CO 52: Congo, Republic of (Former Belgian Congo) (1964). Secret.

convinced that long lasting damage to United States interests throughout Africa will result from our becoming closely identified with any operation involving the aforementioned mercenaries. I think it is unreasonable to assume that the label "technicians" will conceal the fact that the hired soldiers are mercenaries.

I call to your attention the enclosed report[2] which spells out propaganda themes being pushed by the Communists with regard to the Congo; the propaganda activities of the Congolese rebels, and reactions in other African countries to United States and other Western activities.

It is our view that the Communist campaign in itself is not as significant as the fact that it is being picked up in other African countries (and is certain to be fed by the debate that began today in the Congress and in the American press).

I believe that there are some things that we can do to make our actions in the Congo more palatable internationally and to make ourselves less vulnerable to Communist propaganda. I recommend that:

1. We seek publicly to justify our activities in the Congo as assistance given in response to requests by President Kasavubu.

2. We do not overpublicize on our initiative relatively small actions that we are taking. I do not advocate hiding facts from the American public, but I do not believe we are obligated to make a press announcement every time an American official confers with Belgian officials; and I believe we can send in transport planes without creating a barrage of press stories that make it appear that we are invading the Congo.

3. If it is possible, we not permit to become public United States activities in transporting arms to the Congo for use by white mercenaries.

4. We avoid, if at all possible, having South African and Southern Rhodesian mercenaries fly United States aircraft in operations against the rebels.

Carl

---

[2] Attached but not printed.

222. Telegram From the Department of State to the Embassy in the Congo[1]

Washington, August 14, 1964, 8:28 p.m.

317. Joint State–Defense–USIA message. *Public Affairs Policy Guidance.*

1. We are disturbed by press here publishing statements today attributed to Leopoldville to effect that US paratroopers will ride "shot gun" on the H–34 helicopters and that these aircraft may be used to support the ANC. Fact that helicopters included in equipment being sent Congo had not up to that point been made public. There is no present thought here of expanding mission of plane guards beyond that established in CINCSTRIKE order covering deployment of four C–130's to Congo.

2. Press and public opinion suspicious and restive that US is undertaking "creeping" commitment in Congo where every move enlarges area US responsibility and draws US closer into expanding role, comparable to that in Vietnam, in Congo military and security situation.

3. We wish to make it perfectly clear that the military personnel which accompanied the C–130s are for the sole purpose of providing ground security for C–130s deployed to the Congo. They are not intended to provide security or to accompany helicopters in any mission which the helicopters might attempt. Departures from foregoing such as to provide guards for helicopter mission contemplated in which the security of helicopters is in doubt will not be flown without JCS approval on a case by case basis.

4. We recognize that Leopoldville is small village and that able aggressive press corps there capable of finding out most US moves. However Embassy and country team should avoid premature disclosure of US moves and contingency plans.

5. Embassy and country team should particularly avoid any comments on what other governments particularly Belgium and African countries are, or may be, planning to do.

Rusk

---

[1] Source: National Archives, RG 59, Central Files 1964–66, POL 23–9 THE CONGO. Confidential; Immediate. Drafted by O'Sullivan; cleared by Colonel Gall, Lewis in USIA, Greenfield, Fine, and Tasca; and approved by Harriman. Also sent to USUN, JCS, and CINCSTRIKE for POLAD.

223. Paper Prepared in the Central Intelligence Agency[1]

Washington, undated.

PROJECT OUTLINE

Cryptonym

[*cryptonym not declassified*]

A. *Identification:*

This is a covert action project designed to reduce the insurgency and restore some semblance of order and stability to the Congo (Leopoldville).

B. *Objectives:*

The objective of this project is to help stem the tide of the rebel advance by two basic covert actions:

A. To assist in reinforcing and re-establishing tribal allegiances in critical areas, by judicious contributions of covert funds, and
B. To assist in financing mercenaries in cases where hard currency is not otherwise available.

Tribal allegiances are of critical importance in stabilizing the Congo under present disrupted conditions. This project will attempt to obtain assurances from local chiefs that they will resist encroachment by CNL agitators as well as attacks by armed bands. Acting through political leaders with known tribal bases, certain monetary contributions to achieve this end will be made. Advice will be provided for reinforcing the will of tribes to resist the spread of insurgency, and efforts made to insure that covert funds are effectively spent. In providing support of this nature to tribal leaders other than Moise Tshombe, the Prime Minister, action may generally but not necessarily be coordinated with him.

In assisting in the financing of mercenaries, where hard currencies are otherwise not available, it is the basic intent of the project to keep to a minimum the number of South African or Rhodesian mercenaries assisted through this mechanism; it is also accepted that some funds might be used for assisting the Belgian technicians directly concerned with the re-establishment of order in the Congo.

---

[1] Source: Central Intelligence Agency Files, Job 78–02502R, Box 1, [*cryptonym not declassified*]/Development & Plans, [*text not declassified*], Aug. '64–Jan. 1967. Secret. There is no drafting information on the original.

The origin of this project followed from the agreement concluded between Under Secretary of State Governor Averill Harriman and Belgian Foreign Minister Paul Henry Spaak on 7 August 1964 which called for the development as rapidly as possible of a gendarme force led by military technicians.[2] The 303 Committee considered the matter of covert support for the restoration of order in the Congo on August 13, and authorized [*dollar amount not declassified*] for these purposes.[3] This authorization was confirmed by a CIA cable to the Leopoldville Station on August 14.[4]

C. *Background:*

The so-called rebel forces of the CNL in the Congo have extended their control in a very brief period from Uvira on the Burundi border, and in Kwilu to a large part of the eastern Congo, including Stanleyville. They have done this through the relatively simple tactic of exploiting whatever discontent there may be in each area by the use of advance agitation agents followed by a relatively small but active armed force. Rebel successes have been loudly broadcast by Stanleyville Radio and their invincibility is becoming accepted by both Congolese and Europeans alike. A general attitude of defeatism has set in not only in the towns in their path but even in Leopoldville. As of this date the key city of Bukavu on Lake Kivu in the east is seriously threatened but so far has stood off concerted attacks. In viewing the extraordinary progress made by the dissident forces it is apparent that they are receiving both monetary and advisory support from Chinese Communist, Ghanaian, Burundi and, tacitly, from Congolese (Brazzaville) sources.

[Omitted here is further discussion of the project.]

---

[2] See Document 204.

[3] See Document 218.

[4] Funds for Project [*text not declassified*] were obligated through June 30, 1965. On July 23, 1965, Karamessines approved an interim extension of the project through October 31, 1965. (Memorandum from Fields to Karamessines, July 16, 1965; Central Intelligence Agency Files, Job 78–02502R, Box 1, [*cryptonym not declassified*]/Development & Plans, [*text not declassified*], Aug.'64 thru Jan. 1967)

224. Memorandum of Conversation[1]

Leopoldville, August 15, 1964.

PARTICIPANTS

Prime Minister Tshombe and
Governor Williams

At the close of the four and one-half hour meeting between Prime Minister Tshombe and his advisors and the country team and myself,[2] I asked the Prime Minister for the opportunity to speak a few words with him alone. I opened the conversation by referring to the point he had made at the beginning of the long conference of the necessity of establishing a firm basis of confidence between us. I said that the President of the United States was most concerned with the grave situation in the Congo and that he wanted to support the efforts of Prime Minister Tshombe and his government to maintain the unity of the Congo and the prosperity of its people. I then made reference to the fact that he had during the larger conference called attention to the doubts expressed by some of his associates and the attitude of some of the country team toward the Tshombe government. I said that it was the President's policy to support the present government of the Congo and that it consequently was the policy of all of us.

I pointed out that in the memorandum which he had given me the day before he had raised certain doubts as to the attitude of the Ambassador toward him. I said that for that reason I was sure he would understand that in all friendship I could not accept the memorandum. I said, of course, that if he had any reason not to want Mr. Godley to represent the United States he had only to say that, and that the matter would be taken care of forthwith. (During the general meeting I had already explained the policy of the United States with respect to our maintaining contact with members of the opposition as well as with the Government, and that this was an obligation of the Ambassador. I had already in the same meeting indicated that the President and I had full confidence in Mr. Godley.) Mr. Tshombe brushed the idea of his being concerned about the attitude of Ambassador Godley completely aside. He said when he had spoken in the general meeting that the abscess

[1] Source: National Archives, RG 59, AF/CM Files: Lot 67 D 63, Box 1778, Congo. Secret. Drafted by Williams. The conversation was held at Prime Minister Tshombe's residence in Leopoldville.

[2] Telegram 543 from Leopoldville, August 15, reported on this meeting. (Ibid., Central Files 1964–66, POL 23–9 THE CONGO)

was drawn, that the whole matter was closed, and that he intended to move ahead with complete mutual confidence.

Mr. Tshombe indicated that he was glad that Ambassador Godley had spoken so firmly and directly in response to Prime Minister Tshombe's bringing up the question of doubts about people in the country team. He said it was very useful for him to have had Godley speak in this fashion before certain of his colleagues who were in the larger meeting. He indicated that he had had some questions raised by them and that Mr. Godley's forthright statement would help him foreclose these questions. Prime Minister Tshombe treated the whole Godley matter in an extremely friendly and understanding manner and showed not the slightest indication of concern or displeasure. In fact, he was smiling and extremely cordial and friendly throughout the entire interview. As we rose to leave, he picked up the memorandum and, I believe, put it in his pocket.

During the talk we had alone, Mr. Tshombe also raised the matter of communicating with other African countries for help. He said that after our meeting of the day before he had prepared letters to a number of other African countries asking for help. He mentioned particularly Tsiranana of Madagascar. He indicated his sympathy with the necessity for Africanization but pointed out that he had certain difficulties with this among his associates, particularly General Mobutu.

On the matter of Africanization, I pointed out to the Prime Minister the great importance of this to the President, both as a matter of international politics and also of domestic politics, in as much as there were some in our country who felt strongly that the United States should not take the lead in trying to solve what might appear to some as a purely African situation. It was important that other Africans be engaged as well.

In discussing the request for direct intervention of American combat personnel. I emphasized to the Prime Minister that this was an exceedingly difficult problem for the President because it involved global and domestic policy considerations. I pointed out that the President had authorized me to go a long way in working out matériel and training assistance so as to help prosecute the war effort against the rebels. I said that the President was really as interested as was the Prime Minister himself.

The Prime Minister confided that he was in a somewhat difficult position with some of his colleagues because they tended to chide him on not getting as much American aid as another leader might or as his predecessor had. He said that he felt a particular duty to his country to prove that he could get as much American aid as anyone else. I told him that the best proof of America's desire to be of help to him and his ability to get aid from the Americans was the fact that we had immediately volunteered to continue all aid programs and that we had then gone ahead and provided even further aid.

I said that I hoped the discussions between General Mobutu and his experts and our American military experts would be successful in nailing down what the Congo needed in the way of matériel, transportation, and training, because I was sure that he would find that we would go a long way to be of assistance to him, and that this in turn would further satisfy those who questioned his relationships with us.

Let me say again, that throughout the entire conversation, Prime Minister Tshombe was exceedingly cordial and, in fact, he spent a great deal of his time trying to ingratiate himself. He went through his whole history of American missionary training, the fact that most of his colleagues had American training or associations, and, indeed, he said, the Belgians frequently reproached them as being too pro-American. In short, he appeared to be as eager as I was to establish a good working relationship, and he constantly reiterated his complete confidence in our cooperativeness and reaffirmed his desire of cooperation.

---

225. Telegram From the Department of State to the Embassy in the Congo[1]

Washington, August 15, 1964, 4:33 p.m.

334. For Williams and Ambassador from Secretary and Harriman. Ref Embtel 540.[2] Shocked at naivete of Tshombe that we would send under any circumstances American forces to attack Congolese. You should make this doubly plain and point out that we have since June been attempting to get Mobutu and Congolese Government to ask other friendly African countries for forces to protect key areas. Action on this must be undertaken at once, preferably in name of Kasavubu. Consideration should be given promptly to special missions by Adoula and Bomboko to selected African capitals both to support troop request and to improve image and understanding of GOC by other Africans.

---

[1] Source: National Archives, RG 59, Central Files 1964–66, POL 23–9 THE CONGO. Top Secret; Flash. Drafted by O'Sullivan and approved by Harriman. Repeated to Brussels and CINCSTRIKE for POLAD.

[2] Telegram 540 from Leopoldville, August 15, reported that Tshombe asked Williams for the immediate dispatch of three U.S. parachute battalions in order to help retake Stanleyville. (Ibid.)

Congolese must understand that attacks to regain territory must be by Congolese forces. Quick implementation of Van der Walle plan with full Congolese support, particularly Mobutu, gives greatest promise to retrieve lost areas.

GOC must use what they have to hold out until African troops arrive. What has happened to consideration movement Katanga gendarmes perhaps from Angola to stiffen Leopoldville and threatened areas?

Feel that your presence should be used to knock some sense into Kasavubu, Tshombe, Mobutu. They have bucked every suggestion that we have made so far and we cannot help them if their failure to cooperate continues. You can quote this directly to Tshombe coming from Harriman if you feel useful.

Rusk

---

226. Memorandum From the Under Secretary of State for Political Affairs (Harriman) to the President's Special Assistant for National Security Affairs (Bundy)[1]

Washington, August 17, 1964.

SUBJECT

The Congo

There are several somewhat favorable developments that have improved the security situation of the Congo and the morale in Leopoldville:

1) The arrival of four C–130's and 3 helicopters with a platoon of U.S. airborne infantry; the imminent arrival of five B–26's for long-range reconnaissance and strafing to strengthen Congolese army limited air capability; the presence of Governor Williams as indicative of high level U.S. interest.

2) The development of a military program by Belgian Colonel Van der Walle (now before Spaak for approval) (a) for introduction of 50 additional Belgian officers to assist in direction of military action and additional Belgian military personnel for logistic support and (b) the reac-

---

[1] Source: Johnson Library, National Security File, Country File, Congo, Vol. IV. Secret.

tivation of Katanga gendarmes, with European military technicians, to be integrated into and to strengthen the ANC. With these additional forces, it is expected that an offensive to recover areas lost to rebels can be initiated in about six weeks.

3) The Military position has improved.

(a) Bukavu has held out due to tenacious defense by ANC. (In this, Col. Dodd's presence has played a key role.) Local Kabare Bashi and Ngweshi Nyaugezi tribesmen have remained loyal and have taken an active part in the fighting. This appears to be a dividend of Tshombe's recent visit. Two T–28's have broken up rebel advances.

(b) The recapture of Baudoinville. The city was found to be in a shambles by looting. GOC with our assistance has sent substantial quantities of civilian emergency supplies.

(c) The recapture of a number of other points in northern Katanga by a column moving up from military base Kamina.

4) Governor Williams has established better communication with Tshombe and other Congolese leaders. At long last the government has appealed for African troops from the governments of Liberia, Senegal, Malagasy and Ethiopia, in addition to an earlier request to Nigeria. Mr. Tshombe has also written the Secretary General of the United Nations requesting he use his personal influence with Burundi and Congo (Brazzaville) to bring these countries "to cease action seriously injurious to the population of my country." He has also written to the Secretary General of the Organization for United Africa requesting African solidarity and support. These steps should be helpful in achieving our objective of Africanizing the Congo's problems, but Tshombe's unpopularity with African leaders may still cause difficulties. Although Ethiopia and Nigeria are the only ones of these countries which could send as much as a battalion, the other countries might send token forces or in other ways support the GOC in its efforts to withstand rebel uprisings. Our missions in the above-mentioned countries have been instructed to support Tshombe's requests.

5) The Belgian businessmen are reconsidering their plan for evacuation of dependents.

It should be recognized, however, that the situation, although less critical, is still fragile and might rapidly deteriorate again by adverse development such as the assassination of one of the key political personalities or the fall of additional significant cities. The Mulele rebels in Kwilu are active again, threatening the provincial capital Kikwit. The situation in Luluabourg is tense due to rebel activity in the immediate neighborhood.

The report of arrival of three Ilyushin planes in Stanleyville is disturbing but it has not yet been confirmed. They may be Ghanaian rather than Soviet.

Averell

P.S. Tshombe asked Governor Williams on Saturday for immediate despatch of three U.S. parachute battalions in order to retake Stanleyville and other important rebel-held cities. This request was bluntly turned down. This was probably an important factor in influencing Tshombe to take subsequent steps to appeal to African countries for support, as well as to UN and OAU.

227. Telegram From the Embassy in the Congo to the Department of State[1]

Leopoldville, August 19, 1964, 8:44 p.m.

616. I have not discussed following with local CIA personnel for I am not clear as to our policy on this problem.

Am reporting separately conversation I have just had with Ndele, Governor National Bank and Roux, his technical advisor, concerning request they received this afternoon from Tshombe for immediate availability $4 million to pay 3 months salary and expenses for 1,000 mercenary officers and noncoms. Ndele also said Nendaka was seeking [*dollar amount not declassified*] Belgian francs to assist Sûreté and he anticipates further hard currency requests for 200 agents for Sûreté that he has been informed are about to be recruited in Europe. (We believe these are Pomploma graduates mentioned frequently by Tshombe.)

Devlin has just informed me of green light having been given by Washington for 10 million Congo franc fund for Mobutu with no accounting or indication where it may be used. Munongo, as Department already aware, seeking up to 35 million dollars create his own police force and I anticipate important shopping list from Nendaka for Sûreté.

Funds involved are, in my opinion, relatively small as compared to principle of [*less than 1 line not declassified*] covert financial support of Tshombe and his current team. I cannot help but have feeling that our aid to current team and its implication of our overall African policy must be given another hard look. If I am wrong, would appreciate urgent instructions.

We could give all-out back stopping to Tshombe. This would, I believe, eventually involve US personnel, for once we get on this slippery

[1] Source: National Archives, RG 59, Central Files 1964–66, POL 23–9 THE CONGO. Secret; Immediate; Roger Channel.

slope, we are more and more captive of the recipient as our political investment increases.

We may now be past point of no return due commitment aircraft of US origin, but am not too pessimistic on this score as of this time. Believe, however, that if Tshombe creates majority white army to retake rebel-held territories and if he and Kasavubu fail bring about effective Africanization of situation, we may well soon find ourselves in all-out support, alone or with Belgians, of minority regime being propped up by US financed foreign military technicians, US financed secret police, again with white encadrement, plus US matériel. This regime undoubtedly does not enjoy wide African support and could well be target of any African states seeking to attack us. With continued local brutal repression and attempts reconquest of rebel areas which would be carried out under banner of anti-Communist action, those rebels not now looking to East would soon turn their attention in that direction. We thus in brief time, I am convinced, would find ourselves aligned with Union of South Africa, Portugal and Tshombe against most, if not all of this vast continent.

Reiterate what I have already recommended [*less than 1 line not declassified*], i.e., that we maintain current, overt, limited support of this Government, but that we not go all out in covert support until we more certain as to longevity and effectiveness Tshombe team. To hold back will (except in limited area of mercenary support) not in my view, pose threat of hobbling war effort against rebels.

I, personally, am convinced that any course we now take involves serious risks but in weighing the risks, I believe that the establishment of a covert all-out support Tshombe is betting on weak reed and once again urge that we not go all out either in overt or covert political support.

Godley

228. Circular Telegram From the Department of State to Certain Posts[1]

Washington, August 19, 1964, 10:24 p.m.

322. Re Leo's 609 and Brazza's 140.[2] Tshombe Retaliation. You should tell Tshombe ASAP that expulsion of citizens Congo (B), Burundi, Mali and Rwandans of Tutsi origin should be cancelled in his own personal and governmental interest. It will bring retaliation which GOC (L) cannot afford, in case Tutsis will complicate problem of Kayibanda who has given Congo real support with use of Kamembe airport (without which defense of Bukavu never could have been undertaken) and worst of all will be interpreted as sign of frustration and weakness throughout Africa.

If Tshombe does not agree to cancel or substantially modify expulsion orders you should tell press upon your departure that you have called upon Tshombe to protest these un-African actions which will only worsen lot of innocent Africans.

For Brazza, Kigali, and Bamako: You may inform Fonoff after receiving Leo's report of action taken.

Rusk

---

[1] Source: National Archives, RG 59, Central Files 1964–66, POL 23–9 THE CONGO. Confidential; Immediate. Drafted by O'Sullivan, cleared by Albert V. Nyren in AFW and Harriman, and approved by Fredericks. Sent to Leopoldville and repeated to Paris, Brussels, USUN, Brazzaville, Dakar, Tananarive, Monrovia, CINCSTRIKE, Bujumbura, Kigali, and Bamako.

[2] Telegram 609 from Leopoldville, August 19, reported that Tshombe's order expelling all nationals of Burundi and Congo-Brazzaville also applied to Mali and Rwandans of Tutsi origin. (Ibid.) Telegram 140 from Brazzaville, August 19, warned that the expulsion of Congo-Brazzaville nationals would bring about retaliatory acts against Congo-Leopoldville nationals, and suggested that heavy U.S. pressure be brought to bear on Tshombe to cease bellicose statements and not act intemperately. (Ibid.)

229. Telegram From the Department of State to the Embassy in the Congo[1]

Washington, August 20, 1964, 11:05 a.m.

390. For Ambassador from Secretary. Regarding your flash 631 you should know that STRCC 8653 was based directly upon Presidential instructions.[2] The point is that we do not intend to be drawn step by step into use of US military personnel for armed action against the rebels while other African nations and all of Western Europe are sitting on their hands. If everyone else in the free world resigns from any serious responsibility for what happens in Africa and we have to face what we do in that circumstance, we will look at it and come to a highest level decision. But we do not wish to have that decision made for us by bits and pieces. STRCC 8653 constitutes a directive for you as well as military and I regret that you were not so informed last night. Regards.

Rusk

[1] Source: National Archives, RG 59, Central Files 1964–66, POL 23–9 THE CONGO. Secret; Immediate; Exdis. Drafted and approved by Rusk and cleared by Fredericks.

[2] Telegram 631 from Leopoldville, August 20, noted that STRCC 8653 precluded any use of force to rescue a party led by Colonel William Dodds, U.S. Strike Command's Senior Representative in Leopoldville, which had gone to inspect the front lines near Bukuvu on the morning of August 19 and been reported missing. Godley assured Rusk and Harriman that U.S. Embassy and military officials in Leopoldville were fully cognizant of the risks involved and would not incur unnecessary ones. (Ibid.) STRCC 8653 has not been found.

230. Telegram From the Department of State to the Embassy in the Congo[1]

Washington, August 20, 1964, 2:50 p.m.

392. Joint State–Defense message. Re Embtel 632.[2] There is full appreciation here for problem you face in finding and extricating Macfarlane, Dodds, and Rattan. We have full confidence in your judgment and you are authorized to use US helicopters and planes in search. Planes to be used in search need not be dearmed. However use of force to effect rescue is not authorized without advance clearance from Washington.

Rusk

[1] Source: National Archives, RG 59, Central Files 1964–66, POL 23–9 THE CONGO. Secret; Flash. Drafted by O'Sullivan; cleared by Fredericks, Vance, and Brubeck; and approved by Harriman. Repeated to CINCSTRIKE.

[2] In telegram 632 from Leopoldville, August 20, Godley stated that he believed that the United States had to be willing to use force if there were to be a serious rescue attempt. He pointed out that if the search aircraft were not allowed to be armed, this would merely condemn more brave men to uncalled-for hazards. (Ibid.) On August 22, Dodds and his two companions returned unharmed to Bukuvu.

231. Telegram From the Department of State to the Embassy in Ethiopia[1]

Washington, August 20, 1964, 4 p.m.

165. Please deliver following message from President to Emperor:

"Your Majesty:

Ambassador Korry has reported to me your deep concern over events in the Congo.[2] We share that concern.

I was personally gratified to learn that Your Majesty was considering a possible initiative in this problem. I believe that an initiative by

[1] Source: National Archives, RG 59, Central Files 1964–66, POL 23–9 THE CONGO. Secret; Immediate; Limdis. Drafted by Newsom; cleared by Brubeck, Fredericks, and the Congo Task Force; and approved by Harriman. Repeated to Leopoldville.

[2] Telegram 200 from Addis Ababa, August 18, reported that Emperor Haile Selassie was considering taking the initiative in consulting with other African states on how to assist the Congolese Government in restoring order. (Ibid.)

Your Majesty would be particularly effective at this time. I recall the dramatic results of your most helpful assistance in the Algerian-Moroccan crisis last fall. Ambassador Korry has, perhaps, already informed you that we would consider most favorably any move which Your Majesty might feel appropriate to strengthen the authority of the central government of the Congo under President Kasavubu and to help establish peace and order under that government.

The events in the Congo are moving rapidly and posing a most serious problem to President Kasavubu and his government. The sacking of Baudouinville by the rebels who destroyed hundreds of dwellings and news of rebel entry into Bukavu highlight the threat of anarchy in the Congo and increase the need for quick and effective action.

The United States has, from the beginning, sought to preserve the unity of the Congo under the central government. To this end, we joined with the African nations, as Your Majesty well knows, in the massive effort of the United Nations. The preservation of the unity of the Congo and the restoration of peace and order remain our basic objectives. We have strongly supported a solution within an African framework and the principal reliance on African security forces. I can assure you that our own efforts in response to requests for assistance from the Government of the Congo are part of our continuing effort to support the unity of this important nation and are designed only to undergird and supplement efforts in the same direction by the nations of Africa.

I wish Your Majesty every success as you deal with this, as well as other, critical problems in the great continent of Africa.

Lyndon B. Johnson."

Rusk

232. Memorandum From the Acting Chief of the Africa Division, Directorate of Plans, Central Intelligence Agency (Waller) to Director of Central Intelligence McCone[1]

Washington, August 21, 1964.

SUBJECT

Special Group (CI) Meeting

1. The following is for the information of the Director of Central Intelligence.

2. Attached hereto is a summary of the report given by Governor G. Mennen Williams, Assistant Secretary of State for African Affairs, based on his recent trip to Leopoldville.[2]

3. The following are the highlights of the Special Group (CI) meeting of 21 August:

A. There is an urgent need for an analysis of the extent and importance of the Chinese Communist assistance to the Congo rebels. Mr. McCone stated he could have a report on this subject available by this afternoon.

B. One of the most important danger spots in the Congo is Leopoldville itself where CNL rebels have been reported planning terrorist activities.

C. CIA will make every effort to provide maintenance for the aircraft being [*less than 1 line not declassified*] through the hiring of non-military contract personnel. If, however, CIA finds itself unable to recruit adequately qualified maintenance personnel, it can call upon the Department of Defense to provide military personnel, recognizing that it is important to keep the total number of military personnel in Leopoldville to a minimum. U.S. Air Force aircraft maintenance personnel now in the Congo to service the three B–26K's supplied by the Air Force may remain as long as necessary to train non-military personnel.[3]

D. The lives of five American Consular Officials in Stanleyville are in danger. Everything possible should be done to effect their release. CIA on a priority basis is currently exploring the feasibility of a covert rescue operation. Ambassador Godley should respond strongly to the

[1] Source: Central Intelligence Agency Files, DCI/McCone Files, Job 80B01285A, Box 2, DCI (McCone) Memos for the Record, 08 Jul–10 Sept 64. Secret. Sent through the Acting Deputy Director for Plans.

[2] Not attached.

[3] On August 24, the 303 Committee approved a proposal to expand its support of Congolese air operations. (Central Intelligence Agency Files, DCI/McCone Files, Job 80B01285A, 303 Committee Meetings (1964))

most recent and threatening communication from the rebel leader, "General" Olenga, in Stanleyville.

E. U.S. approach to the Congo should be:

(1) Advance the Africanization of the Congo problem by quiet diplomacy, but not by publicity or public discussion. In other words, do not "Americanize the Africanization."

(2) To provide a "cutting edge" necessary for military victories, the U.S. should encourage the use of a requisite number of mercenaries. But ostensibly the Belgians should be kept out in front in this and other military matters. The U.S. military contribution should be confined mainly to air support.

John H. Waller
Acting Chief, Africa Division

233. Telegram From the Department of State to the Embassy in the Congo[1]

Washington, August 21, 1964, 8:01 p.m.

408. For Ambassador. Embtels 675, 677 and 679.[2] Subject your views propose following message be sent to Hoyt in reply message transmitted reftels 675 and 677.

Begin text.

I have received the message from Stanleyville with your signature. It has also been transmitted to Washington.

In accordance with normal international practice your consular duties include contact with authorities in control in the localities covered by your consular district. You may so inform General Olenga. You are requested ask him whether he will arrange safe conduct for the

[1] Source: National Archives, RG 59, Central Files 1964–66, POL 23–9 THE CONGO. Confidential; Flash; Limdis. Drafted by Schaufele; cleared by O'Sullivan, Fredericks, Runyan, and Lindsey Grant in M; and approved by Tasca. Repeated to Brussels and to CINCSTRIKE for Ramsey.

[2] Telegrams 675 and 677, August 21, transmitted a message to the Department and President Johnson, purportedly from Hoyt, asking that the U.S. Government reconsider its policy of military assistance to the Congolese Government, and warning that the lives of all Americans resident in Stanleyville, including those of Consulate personnel, were at stake. (Ibid.) In telegram 679, August 21, Godley reported that the Embassy did not believe that Hoyt had written the message, noting that he was obviously under rebel control. He warned, however, that the Embassy was inclined to believe from the tone of the communication that the threat should be taken seriously. (Ibid.)

landing of a plane at the Stanleyville airport carrying official American supplies and personnel. They would confirm that you and your present staff as well as other American citizens in the area are in good health and are allowed freely to come and go and that you have free and unrestricted access to communications with me. Please advise promptly whether it would be useful send US official to consult with you further on these matters.

You should also repeat to General Olenga and the authorities in Stanleyville my earlier message that I hold them personally responsible for the safety and well being of all Americans in the Stanleyville area. *End text.*[3]

You may wish to explain to Tshombe and Kasavubu what we propose to do. Have you any recommendations as to who should go in and by what means. FYI Dept considers proposed message does not imply recognition.

For Brussels: You may wish to keep Spaak informed.

Rusk

[3] Telegram 690 from Leopoldville, August 22, reported that all communications with Stanleyville had been out since early that morning and the Department's message to Hoyt could not be delivered. Telegram 312 to Brussels (414 to Leopoldville), August 22, asked the U.S. Embassies in Brussels and Leopoldville to attempt to have the message to Hoyt passed via ham radio. (Ibid.)

234. Telegram From the Department of State to the Embassy in the Congo[1]

Washington, August 22, 1964, 4:30 p.m.

418. Stan Consular Staff. There follow some suggestions which Emb should explore and comment upon.

1. We need counter hostages. Can GOC (perhaps Nendaka) put under protective surveillance any relatives of rebel leaders such as Olenga (if he is still alive) Soumialot, or any others whom Emb believes may be influential there. It might be possible grab some important rebel leaders in Leo or Bukavu for this purpose.

[1] Source: National Archives, RG 59, Central Files 1964–66, POL 23–9 THE CONGO. Confidential; Immediate. Drafted by O'Sullivan; cleared by Fredericks, Tasca, and Grant; and approved by O'Sullivan. Repeated to Brussels.

2. Explore with Yugoslav Mission Leo whether it has any way of reaching rebels and would it be willing act as intermediary for purpose extricating Hoyt and staff.

3. Indian and Greek missions may have connections with their respective communities in Stan. There is no reason to believe that rebels are immune to carrots that attract other Congolese. In this connection has Alhadeff any ideas?

4. We have considered asking Nkrumah to act as intermediary. This idea temporarily held in abeyance due 1) possibility Quashie may be PNGed and 2) probability that he would try expand his role from extrication of Hoyt to full scale mediation between GOC and rebels.

We are going to approach Aboud (Sudan) (see separate tel)[2] in whose case these drawbacks are not present.

Rusk

---

[2] Not identified.

235. Telegram From the Department of State to the Embassy in Ethiopia[1]

Washington, August 22, 1964, 4:32 p.m.

182. Addis's 227 to Dept.[2] In further conversations with HIM, Katema and others on OAU aspect of Congo problem believe it important you stress following points in way you think most appropriate:

1. US fully supports initiative designed take current Congo problem to OAU forum in context of supporting authority legitimate Govt.

2. We believe however OAU nations will wish give most serious consideration procedures and objectives in considering this problem.

3. Congo problem is essentially question of assisting a legitimate constitutional government to maintain security and integrity of nation

---

[1] Source: National Archives, RG 59, Central Files 1964–66, POL 23–9 THE CONGO. Secret; Priority. Drafted by Newsom, cleared by Williams and Harriman, and approved by Grant. Repeated to Leopoldville, Lagos, and POLAD CINCMEAFSA Tampa.

[2] Telegram 227 from Addis Ababa, August 21, reported that the Ethiopian Government had convinced the Emperor that his proposal for a personal initiative regarding the Congo had been a mistake and that nothing should be done outside the OAU. (Ibid.)

in face of externally assisted insurrection. Whatever may be African views of Tshombe fact remains he is Prime Minister appointed by recognized head of state, President Kasavubu.

4. At center of problem therefore is sovereign government diplomatically recognized by all Africans, established under a constitution approved by national referendum and seeking maintain order in anticipation future national elections. Any effort put present Congo government "in dock" before OAU would establish dangerous precedent of passing external judgment on legally constituted government. (In this connection Dept endorses approach made Ketema in paragraph 5 of reftel.)[3]

Rusk

[3] Ambassador Korry told Foreign Minister Ketema that the matter boiled down to whether the Ethiopian Government was willing to take action in defense of a principle that it had supported in the past: territorial integrity and deterrence of outside subversive forces meddling in internal affairs. (Ibid.)

236. Telegram From the Department of State to the Embassy in the Congo[1]

Washington, August 22, 1964, 6:40 p.m.

420. We have carefully considered matters raised in your tels 615 and 616.[2] We are in agreement with your analyses particularly that we should not become so committed to Tshombe personally that we become his captive as our political and military investment in him increases. While he is Prime Minister, he serves at least in theory at pleasure of Kasavubu whose commitment to Tshombe may not be complete and total. On other hand as long as he is Prime Minister, it is important we support him to extent necessary to achieve commonly held objectives.

Main thrust of our present efforts are to promote Africanization of problem. But we are not prepared to give up such present and potential

[1] Source: National Archives, RG 59, Central Files 1964–66, POL 23–9 THE CONGO. Secret; Priority; Roger Channel. Drafted by O'Sullivan; cleared by Fredericks, Tasca, and Grant; and approved by H. Bartlett Wells in INR.

[2] Telegram 615 from Leopoldville, August 19, is not printed. (Ibid.) Telegram 616 is Document 227.

assets as we have in the Congo to this end. We recognize there is a certain ambivalence in our willingness to see military technicians employed on contract by the GOC and our desire to try to insist that Africans themselves come up with an African solution.

We therefore propose that in giving specific aid for military technicians it should funnel through Van der Walle. This will have advantage not only of better accounting for funds but will also give us a higher level of security.

As for numbers of military technicians involved, we would be willing to accept levels (50 to 100) Belgians (Logiest and Van der Walle) have been talking about. Munongo's scheme involving a thousand simply not practicable as numbers involved are too great to be effectively controlled and their great presence would be not only a very severe drawback in Africa but probably would be a burden if not a plague inside Congo. In any event, it most important to get initial program started immediately.

We see no objection to continuing aid, even slight increase to Nendaka and Sûreté. We would be willing to entertain reasonable projects involving use of Gombloma graduates but Nendaka should realize that to attempt immediately to double size of Sûreté would only involve him in administrative messes.

Overtly, we should have no connection with "technicians" or mercenaries. This must be responsibility of GOCL and Belgians.

Rusk

237. Memorandum for the Record[1]

Washington, August 24, 1964.

SUBJECT

Minutes of the Meeting of the 303 Committee

PRESENT

Mr. Bundy, Ambassador Thompson, Mr. Vance, and General Carter
[*name not declassified*] was present for Item 1
[2 *names not declassified*] were present for Item 2
[*name not declassified*] was present for Item 3

[Omitted here is an item unrelated to the Congo.]

2. *Congo*

The CIA paper entitled "Request for Approval to Expand Covert CIA Participation in Congolese Tactical Air Program," (in response to a meeting on 21 August 1964 chaired by Governor Harriman)[2] asked for authority to expand support to Congolese air operations and for the money to embark on the expansion. The proposal was approved by the Committee. Mr. Vance said that the paper was unclear on some of the ordnance required, and he requested [*name not declassified*] to prepare a detailed shopping list which could be worked out with DOD. General Carter indicated that he would seek the release of the funds from the Bureau of the Budget. Mr. Bundy added that, if necessary, he could readily explain the desires of higher authority to the Director of the Bureau that this support be as covert as possible. He requested progress reports for the Committee from time to time on the recruiting and organizing efforts.

[Omitted here is an item unrelated to the Congo.]

Peter Jessup

---

[1] Source: National Security Council, Intelligence Files, 303 Committee Files, Minutes—1964. Secret; Eyes Only. Prepared on August 25.

[2] Attached but not printed.

238. Telegram From the Department of State to the Mission to the European Office of the United Nations[1]

Washington, August 24, 1964, 7:05 p.m.

489. Brussels 306 Notal.[2] Dept has been informed that Mr. Sens, ICRC Representative at Bujumbura, has been trying to assist in evacuation Europeans from Stanleyville and Kindu.

FYI Sens reportedly not receiving proper support from ICRC in Geneva which seems to have substantial reservations concerning operation in Stanleyville area. End FYI.

We understand Govt of Belgium approaching ICRC Headquarters Geneva to request ICRC help in evacuating Belgians from Stanleyville. There are still five American staff members our Consulate Stanleyville and approximately 20 other Americans (missionaries) trapped by rebel authorities Stanleyville. Recent reports from Europeans who have escaped Stanleyville recount tales of massacres of Europeans and local officials. USG examining all possibilities for evacuation Americans from Stanleyville but current prospects are not bright.

You are requested consult with Belgian colleagues and make similar approach to ICRC Headquarters in favor Americans in Stanleyville area. We realize ICRC cannot give any assurances to take action in our behalf but we wish ICRC Headquarters to know of our very great interest in Sens' efforts and hope ICRC will encourage Sens make every possible effort obtain release evacuation Americans in Stanleyville.

FYI If ICRC should need logistic support such as aircraft for transportation USG ready willing and able provide. End FYI.

Rusk

---

[1] Source: National Archives, RG 59, Central Files 1964–66, PS 7–6 THE CONGO. Confidential; Priority. Drafted by Walker A. Diamanti in AF; cleared by O'Sullivan, Gerald B. Helman of UNP, Alice B. Correll of SCS, and Officer in Charge of Belgian Affairs Allen C. Davis; and approved by Tasca. Repeated to Brussels, Leopoldville, Bujumbura, and Kigali.

[2] Dated August 22. (Ibid., POL 23–9 THE CONGO)

239. Circular Telegram From the Department of State to All African Posts[1]

Washington, August 25, 1964, 8:25 p.m.

364. Department seriously concerned by reported broadcasts from Albertville indicating Europeans held in city by rebel forces will be massacred if ANC retakes city.

This further substantiates earlier report that rebels under "General" Olenga intend make hostages of Europeans in Congo.

USG believes such effort would reflect most seriously on African image in America and Europe and critically affect ability US and others exercise constructive influence in resolution Congo problem.

If useful result can be expected desire recipient posts bring US concern this report immediately to attention African Governments. Department requests Accra, Lagos, Conakry, Addis, Khartoum make special effort encourage governments seek ways not inconsistent with authority Central Government prevent any actions this kind.

Rusk

[1] Source: National Archives, RG 59, Central Files 1964–66, POL 23–9 THE CONGO. Confidential. Drafted by Newsom, cleared by O'Sullivan, and approved by Tasca.

240. Editorial Note

In telegram 2670 [*text not declassified*], August 25, 1964, [*text not declassified*] in Leopoldville reported on his private talks with [*text not declassified*] on August 14 and 21. He told [*text not declassified*] that [*text not declassified*] was reviewing its funding of RADECO (Rassemblement des Démocrates Congolaise, a coalition of some 50 small political groups which had elected Adoula its president in June 1964) and was reluctant to continue supporting an operation which apparently had contributed to dividing moderate political forces. Adoula's only hope was to try to bring as many moderates into the party as possible. [*text not declassified*] reaction was "a hurt and pained one." He reviewed at length [*text not declassified*] close cooperation with the U.S. Government, pointing out that [*text not declassified*] had often taken unpopular positions in its support. After much talk, however, [*text not declassified*] admitted he did not know how he could get many other leaders into the party, but pointed out that a cessation of funding would put [*text not declassified*] in an embarrassing, almost untenable, position as it would mean a complete breakdown of the party organization; and [*text not declassified*]. (Central Intelligence Agency Files, Job 78–00435R, DDO/ISS Files, Box 2, Folder 11, [*cryptonym not declassified*] Operations)

[*text not declassified*] responded that it did not intend to continue funding RADECO but would provide short-term support to [*name not declassified*] to enable him to maintain a personal political presence. (Ibid.)

241. Memorandum From the Acting Chief of the Africa Division, Directorate of Plans, Central Intelligence Agency (Waller) to the Deputy Director for Plans, Central Intelligence Agency (Helms)[1]

Washington, August 26, 1964.

SUBJECT

[*cryptonym not declassified*] Project Renewal
Request for Extension (1 July–31 December 1964)

1. Recent political events in the Congo, culminating in the formation of a government led by Moise Tshombe, have rendered invalid the content of the [*cryptonym not declassified*] Project Outline renewal submitted for FY 1965. The policy guidelines under which the Project has operated have also been overtaken by events.

2. The members of the [*cryptonym not declassified*] group remain, however, important factors in Congolese political affairs. It would be highly inadvisable entirely to cut them off, operationally or financially, during this interim. Were we to do so we would be subject to a charge of "fair weather" expediency and the re-establishment of close relationship at a later date would be severely hampered.

3. When the new lines of political party formation and leadership have substantially clarified and crystallized, the Division will draft a new, if only interim, project outline. A more or less "permanent" type project outline may have to await the outcome of the general elections scheduled for early 1965.

---

[1] Source: Central Intelligence Agency Files, Job 78–00435R, DDO/ISS Files, Box 1, Folder 1, [*cryptonym not declassified*] Development & Plans. Secret.

4. In the meantime, it is requested that approval be given to providing limited support to selected Congolese political figures on an individual basis (see attachment).[2] The Department of State has endorsed such action on an ad hoc basis. As has been customary in the past, there will continue to be discussion with the Ambassador prior to any substantive disbursement.

5. This funding is intended for purposes both of short-term FI and CA exploitation of the politicians concerned and to preserve operational relationships for possible more important employment in the event these assets again return to positions of concrete political power. Any CA exploitation will be coordinated with the Department of State and the Ambassador.

6. These interim relationships will be maintained until new policy guidances have been provided by the Department of State in the light of the changed terms of political reference, and CIA has been able to redirect its operations in consonance with these guidances.

7. The objective of this project is quite separate from project [*cryptonym not declassified*] which is designed to cope with the insurgency situation now engulfing much of the Congo. [*cryptonym not declassified*] is a short-range counter-insurgency effort providing for support to tribal leaders to enable them to strengthen their defense against the various active guerrilla movements which are all being supported to some extent by the Chicoms. The [*cryptonym not declassified*] project, on the other hand, is intended to give KUBARK political capability at the national level. While no political action program can be undertaken until the insurgency situation is settled, it is considered very important to maintain access during this period to members of the [*cryptonym not declassified*] group and other former political leaders, per attachment, who may be expected to play influential roles again when normal political life is resumed in Leopoldville.

8. It is recommended that Africa Division be authorized to expend up to [*dollar amount not declassified*] of the [*dollar amount not declassified*] earmarked for [*cryptonym not declassified*] in the African Division Operational Program for FY 1965. This authority would be for the first six months of FY 1965. This is an arbitrary figure which should cover most contingencies which might arise during this period.[3]

John H. Waller
Acting Chief
Africa Division

---

[2] Not attached; see footnote 2, Document 218.

[3] No action is recorded on the memorandum.

242. Telegram From the Mission to the United Nations to the Department of State[1]

New York, August 28, 1964, 7 p.m.

559. USUN 548 to Dept.[2] Evacuation US personnel Stanleyville. Pursuant Sisco–Yost telcon, Yost called Bunche this afternoon to inquire whether SYG had followed up our suggestion yesterday concerning appeal over Ghana, Burundi and Brazzaville radios for evacuation foreigners in Stanleyville.

Bunche was not certain but believed SYG had been so preoccupied with other matters he had not followed through on this one.

We stated in strongest terms that lives of these persons, including UN personnel, are in danger, that appeal by SYG transmitted through these media would be purely humanitarian, not political, action and that we very strongly urged he go forward with it. Bunche replied that UN had of course already attempted to make arrangements directly with rebels without success, that UN is in bad odor with them and he very much doubts appeal even through three countries in question would be successful, and that, moreover, UN relations with two of these countries, Ghana and Burundi, are also in very bad state of repair.

We replied that even if prospects are not bright, situation is so serious that no stone should be left unturned.

Bunche agreed to communicate our views immediately to SYG in Geneva.[3]

Stevenson

---

[1] Source: National Archives, RG 59, Central Files 1964–66, PS 7–6 US–THE CONGO. Confidential; Priority. Repeated to Leopoldville Priority and Geneva.

[2] Dated August 27. (Ibid.)

[3] Telegram 506 to USUN, August 28, instructed the Mission to urge Bunche or the Secretary-General again in the strongest terms to approach Ghana, Congo (Brazzaville), and Burundi and ask them to bring pressure on the rebels to permit evacuation and to broadcast the Secretary-General's appeal. (Ibid., POL 23–9 THE CONGO)

243. Telegram From the Department of State to the Embassy in the Congo[1]

Washington, August 29, 1964, 10:24 p.m.

521. Re: Urtel 830; Addis 268.[2] Pleased that Gardiner's good advice apparently went down well with Tshombe. There follows additional Dept thinking which you may be able to use in helping inspire realistic planning and scenario for GOC use at Addis.

Attendance:

As respected African leader and embodiment Congolese Government legitimacy, seems indispensable Kasavubu as well as Tshombe attend. Although this technical Foreign Minister session there is precedent in that Nyerere presented Tanganyikan case to similar meeting and Ben Bella represented Algeria at Dakar meeting.

GOC delegation should be strong one designed appeal varying shades African opinion. Bomboko and Lengema would seem be minimum this respect and Idzumbuir and Cardoso might also be useful especially for technical advice and corridor politicking. If Kasavubu wished Adoula along, he might go also preferably as Presidential advisor, but Department cognizant of danger that he may thus be "tarred" by association with Tshombe. There might be some merit in including Midiburo as quasi-representative last legislature if he would not be disturbing factor.

Organization:

Department assumes that, following normal international conference procedure, IEG as host, will as matter of courtesy chair opening session. Suggest that HIM actually open session to give reasonable, moderate tone to proceedings and then Kasavubu give basic presentation GOC position. If necessary achieve this chronology either IEG or GOC request should be used as basis for meeting rather than Mali's or Ghana's which could be interpreted to give them right make initial presentation.

GOC Presentation:

Appears GOC could usefully emphasize following points:

---

[1] Source: National Archives, RG 59, Central Files 1964–66, POL 23–9 THE CONGO. Secret; Priority. Drafted by Schaufele and Operations Center Director Lewis Hoffacker; cleared by Palmer, Brubeck, O'Sullivan, Fredericks, and Helman; and approved by Harriman. Repeated to Addis Ababa, Conakry, Accra, Lagos, London, Brussels, and Paris.

[2] Dated August 28 and August 27, respectively. (Both ibid.)

(1) In accordance OAU principles, action should be based on acknowledgment of Congo sovereignty and designed protect independence and territorial integrity its members.

(2) It is assumed GOC will not raise question its own legitimacy. But if question raised privately or publicly it should be prepared reply succinctly and matter-of-factly on constitutional grounds. GOC should also be careful that no conference document throws any doubt on its legitimacy.

(3) Resort to force by opposition elements to overthrow legitimate democratic GOC cannot be condoned by other African states which themselves may be faced with similar problem.

(4) OAU should reaffirm in positive, forceful way its basic principle that interference in internal affairs in one state by others is inadmissible. Although GOC must obviously be prepared make specific bill of particulars against Congo (B) and Burundi, it appears best that this be minimal in formal meetings if pre-conference and corridor diplomacy assures adoption satisfactory resolution. In any case such indictment these two countries should be done in factual, unemotional manner. Neither Tshombe nor Kasavubu should engage in shouting match with Congo (B). (FYI: Department tends to believe Chicom involvement can be more effectively discussed in selected, private talks than in open debate. End FYI.

(5) GOC should draw on precedent of Tanganyika formula which specifically recognized Tanganyika right to conclude bilateral agreements with African countries of own choice for troops. However, we hope that discussion, or, at least, position on other, non-African sources for material and equipment assistance can be avoided.

(6) GOC could point out that UNGA and SC in numerous resolutions affirmed importance maintaining territorial integrity, political independence and unity of Congo. UN military operations in Congo were conducted to achieve these goals. Members OAU supported and voted for these resolutions and principles. Several resolutions, which UNSYG, in terminal report on UNOC June 29, recognized as still valid, can be cited. (See analysis Deptel 1525 to Leo repeated Addis info 1048.)[3] SC and GA called on "all states to refrain from any action which might tend to impede the restoration of law and order and the exercise by the GOC of its authority and also to refrain from any action which might undermine the territorial integrity and political independence of the GOC." SC also called for "all member states to lend their support according to their national procedures to the GOC in conformity with the Charter and the decisions of the UN."

---

[3] Dated June 21. (Ibid.)

(7) Moderate Africans should also be convinced that care must be exercised that actions and procedures this OAU meeting do not accord any special stature or status to Congolese rebels. Moderates should recognize peaceful solution and Africanization Congo problem could be unduly delayed and seriously prejudiced if any other premise adopted. Other African states with their unlawful internal opposition should be aware that at some future meeting such elements could be heard based on such a precedent. Future political solutions in African context and tradition require restoration lawful authority and peaceful condition throughout country soonest.

Although Gbenye, Soumialot, or others may be present during conference, OAU Charter and rules procedure (Nos. 4 and 5) clearly limit participation Council meetings to representatives lawful government. (Forum for discussions involving rebel leaders could appropriately be provided in commission of inquiry suggested in Deptcirctel 390.)[4] Nor is there provision in OAU rules for hearing witnesses, petitioners, etc.

Any suggestion such hearings should be strongly resisted in advance and in corridors especially to prevent GOC from risking a probably futile floor fight if it finds self in lonely opposition to majority in Council meeting deciding hear such witnesses. In last resort preferable to meet and refute rebel arguments giving first hand demonstrations GOC higher sense of responsibility. We must, however, be prepared for some conciliatory attitudes toward rebels. Moderate Africans should realize dangers in OAU investigation involving rebels, but believe there may be minimum of mischief if such investigations are kept out of hands of radicals, as was done e.g., re OAU investigation of Roberto and rival Angolan organizations in 1963.

(8) Although it doubtful meeting could undertake it, most desirable action which could emerge from meeting would be resolution on Tanganyika formula provided it does not specifically place limit on numbers African troops or a time limit on their stay. GOC could press for such a resolution if climate appeared favorable to it. At same time, GOC should not run risk trying for such resolution and failing, since this would adversely affect GOC political maneuverability.

GOC Bargaining Points:

GOC must obviously be willing make moves to meet African sensibilities, mitigate criticisms and maximize effective support. Following appear to be possible areas in which this can be done:

(1) Assurances that elections will be held within a specified time limit, perhaps January or February, 1965 if security situation permits.

---

[4] Dated August 28. (Ibid.)

(2) GOC will continue make every effort include widest possible spectrum in Government without, however, making unacceptable concessions to rebellious elements which may weaken basic Congolese unity. Tshombe might come to Addis with changes which he able to make in order broaden his government. He could easily therefore "concede" on this point if pressed or in order sweeten atmosphere of Conference.

(3) GOC willing in principle accept OAU-sponsored commissions appropriately charged with mediating international differences between it and its neighbors. (Depcirctel 390)

(4) GOC could state that USG aircraft would no longer be needed when GOC convinced that adequate substitute for purposes served by such planes is forthcoming or internal security situation permits.

(5) Important part of GOC image in Africa closely tied to its attitude toward Angolan nationalists. Without modifying Adoula's policy this subject Tshombe could reap advantage of reiterating it.

(6) As suggested urtel 813,[5] procedure for notification to OAU of agreements reached on military assistance may be important to solution sought. Since forthcoming meeting might not wish establish permanent generalized procedure all future contingencies, which could be difficult and possibly dangerous, resolution might cover all arrangements of African states (with other Africans and non-Africans) for military assistance in support of objectives of present OAU resolution. As emphasized urtel, implication must be avoided OAU permission required for such assistance. Premise is rather that authoritative reporting clears air and meets legitimate OAU interest in developments.

(7) Perhaps biggest obstacle to favorable African attitude is presence of mercenaries in Congo. GOC should be willing state that:

(a) Foreign mercenaries will no longer be sought or permitted enter Congo provided OAU willing take action which will result in satisfactory military support;
(b) Those presently in Congo will be gradually removed as Africans are able to provide capability for maintaining unity, security and independence of Congo.

Rusk

[5] Dated August 28. (Ibid., DEF 19 AFR)

244. Telegram From the Department of State to the Embassy in Belgium[1]

Washington, August 31, 1964, 4:16 p.m.

374. Brussels 349;[2] Deptel 352.[3] Know you will keep Dept fully informed regarding "hard look" at Congo which GOB is expected take this coming week.

With respect to rockets, you are authorized make new démarche, in manner which you regard as most appropriate, along following lines:

1) In line with Spaak–Harriman talks, it is expected GOB will continue assume responsibility for furnishing ammo support including rockets to Congo operations.

2) GOB should arrange transport of same to Congo. US airlift should be requested only in genuine emergency.

3) Suggested US-Belgian-Congolese talks in Leopoldville should be best means resolving:

a) continuing requirements and transport for rockets and other ammo.
b) rules of engagement for pilots carrying rockets.
c) investigation of charges "trigger-happy" pilots.

In interim DOD sending rocket supply to Congo but this supply will be terminated as soon as we can return to original understanding of Belgian supply.

Rusk

---

[1] Source: National Archives, RG 59, Central Files 1964–66, DEF 12 THE CONGO. Secret; Priority. Drafted by Hoffacker and John R. Clingerman of AFC; cleared by O'Sullivan, Williams, Colonel Gall, Davis, and Harriman; and approved by Palmer. Repeated to Leopoldville.

[2] Dated August 28. (Ibid.)

[3] Dated August 27. (Ibid., DEF 19–3 BEL–THE CONGO)

245. Memorandum From the Joint Chiefs of Staff to Secretary of Defense McNamara[1]

JCSM–756–64 Washington, September 1, 1964.

SUBJECT

Internal Security of the Congo (U)

1. The Joint Chiefs of Staff have received the attached staff estimate of the internal security situation in the Congo[2] and consider that it provides an effective basis for evaluation of policy alternatives. The estimate includes a brief explanation of the situation, a list of possible broad military courses of action, and conclusions. These are summarized for convenience on the attached spread-sheet.

2. The courses of action range from one of "wait and see" to one of direct US military intervention. It should be noted, however, that alternatives might be selected in combination and that any one could be refined to show various options. Furthermore, some of the alternatives have already been considered, are being explored, or are in the process of implementation.

3. The Congo has little strategic value from a strictly military point of view. However, in terms of communist strategy and tactics, the Congo has great value from a political point of view. The course of events in the Congo may threaten US objectives of insuring its pro-Western orientation, preventing communist infiltration, and maintaining Congolese unity. The Joint Chiefs of Staff consider that communist-inspired rebellion could lead to the rapid spread of communist influence throughout Central Africa. They recommend that the United States:

a. Provide necessary matériel and financial assistance leading to effective operations by Congolese security forces. Such assistance should supplement Belgian and other Western support, which must continue to be encouraged.

b. Continue to persuade the Belgians to increase and accelerate their support leadership efforts and to assume responsibility for the effective performance of Congolese security forces, including mercenaries.

c. Supplement Belgian support and leadership with limited numbers of US advisory personnel to meet the immediate needs of the

[1] Source: Washington National Records Center, RG 218, JCS Files, 9111 (25 August 64). Top Secret.

[2] Attached but not printed.

Congolese security forces. Continuation of US advisory support should be conditional upon satisfactory Congolese performance.

d. Continue with the Belgians to solicit appropriate assistance from other Western nations.

e. If Belgium does not assume responsibility for the effective performance of Congolese security forces, encourage the concept of intervention by a coalition of Western and African countries to establish internal security. However, implementation of other possible courses of action should not await the outcome of efforts to obtain African support.

f. Accelerate current psychological operations designed to condemn communist aggression, demoralize the rebels, and strengthen the Government of the Congo and the political positions of its pro-Western leaders. A public statement to serve these purposes should be issued promptly by the President or the Secretary of State; however, this statement should guard against committing the United States to "certain victory" in the Congo.

g. Exert increased diplomatic pressure as appropriate to discourage any political, financial, or matériel assistance to the rebels.

4. The foregoing courses of action may fail because of Belgian reluctance to become deeply involved, because of divisive forces and incompetence within the Congolese Government, and/or because of increased external assistance to the rebels. Consequently, the United States could be faced with a hard choice between a basic desire to avoid an increasing US involvement and the need to pursue US objectives. In this regard, the Joint Chiefs of Staff have concluded that:

a. Direct US military intervention with combat forces could suppress rebel military operations, preserve the existence of the pro-Western Government, and provide short-term protection of US objectives. However, this probably would not insure the objective of Congolese unity, and communist infiltration would continue to be a threat. Also, the US Government would be vulnerable to severe international reactions. While US forces might be quickly disengaged, there would be a risk of continuing involvement.

b. A substantial unilateral US support program, to include tactical advisors, might be successful. While international reactions would be less severe, greater risks would be encountered of "another Vietnam," with the United States inheriting a continuing, difficult responsibility for internal Congolese security.

c. Any course of action, to be of lasting value, would require effective diplomatic action to deny the Congo–Brazzaville and Burundi as safe-havens for rebel forces and similar action to discourage other African countries from supporting rebel forces.

d. A decision on extensive US involvement is not justified, pending solidification of Belgian and Congolese plans and intentions and an examination of these proposals for compatibility in the light of US objectives. At the same time, it is apparent that an early decision should be made concerning such US assistance as may be furnished, because delays probably will result in strengthened rebel forces. If intervention becomes necessary, it should be executed without hesitation and with adequate forces to insure rapid success.

5. While military actions can assist in solving the immediate security problems in the Congo, there is also the overriding concurrent requirement for solutions to political problems within the Congolese Government if the US objective of establishing a viable and unified Congo is to be permanently realized.

6. In summary, the Joint Chiefs of Staff recommend that the United States intensify its diplomatic efforts to persuade Belgium to accept responsibility for the effective performance of Congolese security forces and, to the extent necessary to secure this, provide matériel and limited numbers of advisory personnel. Such US assistance is justified in the face of communist encroachment. Although reconsideration may be appropriate as the situation evolves, the United States should avoid the commitment of US combat forces.

For the Joint Chiefs of Staff:

Earle G. Wheeler[3]
Chairman
Joint Chiefs of Staff

[3] Printed from a copy that indicates General Wheeler signed the original.

246. Circular Telegram From the Department of State to Certain Posts[1]

Washington, September 1, 1964, 8:13 p.m.

411. Congo Guidance for AF Posts. All OAU states have indicated they will be represented Sept 5 ministerial council Addis Ababa. Dept instructed certain African posts approach host govts on behalf wholehearted consideration by council of Monrovia initiative. (Presidents Liberia, Guinea, Ivory Coast, and Prime Minister Sierra Leone, meeting at Monrovia, appealed to OAU states to authorize OAU to appoint commission to determine facts and propose joint action by African states re Congo in interests peace.) Posts making presentation are to emphasize that US believes this proposal is good basis for African action but that we not trying to interfere this matter.

We believe US interests would be served by achievement at Addis of: OAU acceptance legitimacy of Congo Govt; OAU commitment undertake constructive inquiry at invitation and under aegis of GOC; OAU engagement in material, political and moral aid to GOC; and prevention formal condemnation US policy and action in Congo. We consider terms of reference and makeup of commission most important, and think it essential moderate Africans exclude if possible radical states—Ghana, Algeria, Mali, UAR—from commission membership.

Belgians in Accord US Approach. Emb Brussels briefed Davignon, Spaak's Chef de Cabinet, re US approach African states on OAU meeting and he indicated agreement. Said Belgian Ambs to African posts being briefed Sept 4 Brussels to assure all will speak as one in various African capitals. Agreed GOC should take initiative in proposing in OAU some kind of commission of inquiry on Congo be established, but suggested calling it "good offices committee" preferable as carrying implication committee designed to assist Tshombe Govt overcome its difficulties rather than to investigate it.

Re possibility OAU might try insist US and Belgian military aid to Congo be channeled through OAU, Emb Brussels pointed out nearly all African states have bilateral aid agreements with non-African countries

---

[1] Source: National Archives, RG 59, Central Files 1964–66, POL 3 OAU. Secret. Drafted by F. Virginia Montague in AF/AFI; cleared by Schaufele, Deputy Assistant Secretary for EUR Robert C. Creel, and Palmer; and approved by Fredericks. Sent to Abidjan, Accra, Addis Ababa, Algiers, Baida, Bonn, Brazzaville, Brussels, Cairo, CINCMEAFSA for Ramsey, Conakry, Dakar, Dar es Salaam, Freetown, Kampala, Khartoum, Lagos, Leopoldville, Lisbon, London, Lusaka, Monrovia, Nairobi, Paris, Pretoria, Rabat, Rome, Tananarive, Tunis, and USUN. Sent by pouch to Bamako, Bangui, Blantyre, Bujumbura, Cotonou, Fort Lamy, Kigali, Libreville, Lome, Mogadiscio, Nouakchott, Ouagadougou, Niamey, Tripoli, and Yaounde.

and indicated strong US belief Congolese Govt should not accept any infringement its sovereign rights in making similar bilateral arrangements. Davignon concurred.

Tshombe confirmed to Emb Leopoldville Aug 28 that he going Addis. Said he sending Foreign Minister Bomboko as advance guard. Agreed necessity high powered GOC delegation. Concurred he must be first speaker and that non-vituperative approach essential. Agreed on statement re Congolese unity. Said question of mercenaries difficult point, but could solemnly promise get rid of them as soon as situation stabilized and this had always been his intention. Agreed necessity obtaining support local African diplomatic colony, and indicated would see all African Ambs in order lay groundwork for Addis meeting, which he has since done.

According Mammo, Ethiopian Emperor's personal representative to GOC on OAU Congo meeting, Mammo urged Kasavubu to lead GOC delegation but Kasavubu noncommittal.

Albertville Retaken. ANC recapture Albertville August 29–30 confirmed. Europeans safe.

Stanleyville Still in Rebel Hands. Emb Leopoldville reported Sept 1 Stanleyville tower has contacted Leopoldville tower and announced Stanleyville airport now open for Air Congo planes.

In response routine welfare inquiry, British Ambassador Bujumbura received message from rebel General Olenga stating all British citizens Stanleyville safe. Emb Leopoldville has asked Embassies Brazzaville, Bangui, Bujumbura send commercial messages inquiring re welfare Americans in Stanleyville.

Rusk

247. Memorandum for the Record[1]

Washington, September 1, 1964.

SUBJECT

Discussion with the President—1 September 1964

Following the NSC meeting (memorandum of the meeting prepared by Dr. Cline and attached),[2] I had a private meeting with the President. This meeting was in lieu of my attendance at the regular Tuesday luncheon which was to involve political matters and therefore my presence was not required.

1. I explained in detail the extent of CIA's support [*less than 1 line not declassified*] which included the operation of 41 combat and transport aircraft, supplying with adequate number of pilots for these aircraft [*less than 1 line not declassified*] obtaining foreign ground crews [*1½ lines not declassified*]. I explained that this was the best means of reducing the "U.S. Presence in the Congo", which was desirable, and met the complaint of Senators Russell and Stennis. I pointed out to the President however that some place along the line CIA would be criticized and accused of operating contrary to U.S. policy and this could not be avoided [*less than 1 line not declassified*]. Nevertheless it would help [*less than 1 line not declassified*] to stabilize the Congo, if doing so is possible, and it was better that CIA take the criticism than have the U.S. Government criticized. The President agreed.

[Omitted here is discussion of unrelated topics.]

---

[1] Source: Central Intelligence Agency Files, DCI/McCone Files: Job 80B01285A, DCI Meetings with the President, 01 May–31 October 1964. Top Secret. Drafted by McCone on September 2.

[2] Not attached.

248. Telegram From the Department of State to the Embassy in the Congo[1]

Washington, September 2, 1964, 8:48 p.m.

573. Reurtel 912;[2] Deptels 560[3] and 561.[4] If Tshombe returns to Leo Sept 3 as scheduled, you should see him soonest. If for any reason he does not return then, you should make plans to fly soonest to wherever he may be and to deliver letter with accompanying argumentation (ref Deptels).

FYI This urgent action is necessary because of:

1. increasing evidence deep resentment African leaders over Tshombe's and Kasavubu's tactics;

2. necessity leave no stone unturned in effort to persuade Tshombe attend Sept 5 meeting;

3. desirability letter be placed in Tshombe's hands before release here. End FYI.

Dept also considers it most desirable you present to Tshombe substance our position on OAU meeting but this should assume secondary importance to your efforts convince him he should attend. Our comments Embtel 887[5] are contained separate message.

Rusk

---

[1] Source: National Archives, RG 59, Central Files 1964–66, POL 3 OAU. Secret; Immediate. Drafted by Hoffacker and Palmer; cleared in substance by Brubeck, Harriman, and Williams; and approved by Palmer. Repeated to Brussels and Addis Ababa.

[2] In telegram 912 from Leopoldville, September 2, Godley reported that, in view of the urgency of getting both Kasavubu and Tshombe to attend the September 5 OAU meeting, he had scheduled a meeting with Kasavubu and would see Tshombe as soon as he returned to Leopoldville on September 3. (Ibid.)

[3] Telegram 560 to Leopoldville, September 2, transmitted a personal message from Rusk to Tshombe, expressing the Secretary's concern over reports that Kasavubu had asked that the OAU meeting be postponed and reiterating the sense of urgency with which he felt that the Congo's problems needed to be faced. (Ibid.)

[4] Telegram 561 to Leopoldville, September 2, instructed Godley to emphasize to Kasavubu and Tshombe that the United States considered the OAU meeting a vital step in obtaining the understanding and cooperation of other African states. If the Congo was not prepared to cooperate in a matter of such importance, the fundamental assumptions under which the U.S. Government was proceeding would be questioned. (Ibid.)

[5] Telegram 887 from Leopoldville, September 1, presented Godley's concerns regarding possible problems that might result from the formation of an OAU commission of mediation or inquiry on the Congo. (Ibid., POL 23-9 THE CONGO)

249. Telegram From the Department of State to the Embassy in the Congo[1]

Washington, September 4, 1964, 5:14 p.m.

600. Re Leo 955.[2] Dept strongly opposed planned air strike on Stanleyville radio which would both jeopardize Americans and other foreigners Stanleyville and result severe damage U.S. position at Addis Ababa as well as worldwide.

For Leo: Under circumstances, U.S. interests necessitate your using every available means prevent strike. You will receive through other channels urgent instructions re measures to be taken to keep planes grounded. Unless you are confident these measures are sufficient assure strike does not take place, you should demand see Kasavubu and Mobutu immediately, inform them we are aware planned strike and that we insist it be cancelled. (As subsidiary argument you should also point out difficulty effectively destroying towers from air and proximity hospitals which, if hit, would further revulse world opinion.) If this does not have desired effect, you should tell them we will withdraw all B–26s unless they countermand order.

For Addis: If Kasavubu and Mobutu unwilling take necessary steps, Godley should flash Addis and Korry should see Tshombe soonest and make same points, using plane withdrawal only as final card.

Although we would hope it would not be necessary reveal source our info, both Leopoldville and Addis should regard this as acceptable risk if necessary to accomplishment our purposes.

Brussels should immediately inform Spaak this development and urge immediate Belgian action in support our position on this matter. Leopoldville should take parallel action key Belgians. Foregoing guidance and instructions should guide Leo with respect any air strikes Stanleyville until further notice.

Rusk

---

[1] Source: National Archives, RG 59, Central Files 1964–66, POL 23–9 THE CONGO. Top Secret; Flash. Drafted by Palmer; cleared by Fredericks, Brubeck, and Ball; and approved by Harriman. Also sent to Addis Ababa and Brussels and repeated to CINCSTRIKE for Ramsey.

[2] Telegram 955 from Leopoldville, September 4, reported that Tshombe ordered an air strike against Stanleyville radio for Sunday, September 6. (Ibid.)

250. Telegram From the Department of State to the Embassy in the Congo[1]

Washington, September 8, 1964, 11:43 a.m.

626. Ref: Addis 372 and 377; Leo's 998.[2]

For Leo: You should see Kasavubu urgently and make clear to him that if he were to veto commission idea, as reported Addis 377,[3] we could not support such action. Moreover, USG would have to review its Congo policy in light of situation created in rest of Africa.

You should use occasion to explain commission idea as envisioned para 5 Addis Ababa's 372 (98 to Leo)[4] emphasizing presence of such commission in Congo would be in cooperation with GOC. Such language we believe would give GOC sufficient control over unacceptable interference Congo internal affairs.

For Addis: You should inform GOC delegation US making above démarche Kasavubu and make every effort encourage Tshombe accept commission idea if does not go substantially further than your draft resolution.

You should also point out that in any event OAU will probably have adjourned before Kasavubu could consider and veto any specific language. If language of resolution is sufficiently flexible, therefore, you should assure GOC delegation that we will assist in subsequently justifying to Kasavubu its acceptance of resolution. We would do so by supporting an interpretation of resolution requiring that activities of commission recognize legitimacy of and be conducted in cooperation with GOC.

Rusk

---

[1] Source: National Archives, RG 59, Central Files 1964–66, POL 3 OAU. Confidential; Flash. Drafted by Schaufele; cleared by Brubeck, Lang, Fredericks, and O'Sullivan; and approved by Rusk. Also sent to Addis Ababa and repeated to Brussels.

[2] Telegram 372 from Addis Ababa, September 7; telegram 377 from Addis Ababa, September 8; and telegram 998 from Leopoldville, September 8. (All ibid.)

[3] Telegram 377 reported that it would be impossible for the Congolese delegation to accept the presence of any OAU commission in the Congo, since Kasavubu had given formal instructions against it. (Ibid.)

[4] Paragraph 5 of telegram 372 described a resolution drafted by Ambassador Korry that would establish two OAU commissions to help bring an end to frictions between the Congo and its neighbors, to make recommendations on ways OAU members could assist the Congolese people and government by material and other means to bring an end to the armed conflict, and to assist the Congo in achieving national reconciliation and in preparing for a general election. (Ibid.)

251. Telegram From the Department of State to the Embassy in Ethiopia[1]

Washington, September 8, 1964, 11:53 a.m.

292. Re Deptel 290.[2] Our ability live with resolution along lines your draft will of course depend in large measure on membership of commissions. Since two commissions are contemplated, we hope that membership of radical states can be so divided between them as to dilute their influence on any one with corresponding increases numbers and influence moderate members. Recognize how little control we have over situation but suggest possibility your encouraging Gardiner and others in this parliamentary maneuver.[3]

Rusk

[1] Source: National Archives, RG 59, Central Files 1964–66, POL 3 OAU. Secret; Flash. Drafted and approved by Palmer and cleared by Brubeck, O'Sullivan, and Fredericks. Repeated to Brussels and Leopoldville.

[2] Telegram 290 to Addis Ababa, September 8, authorized Korry to continue to press for adoption of his draft resolution. (Ibid.)

[3] In telegram 381 from Addis Ababa, September 8, Korry reported that Tshombe had accepted his draft resolution and that negotiations on the draft were continuing. (Ibid.)

252. Telegram From the Embassy in Belgium to the Department of State[1]

Brussels, September 10, 1964, 6 p.m.

433. Deptel 446.[2] Greatly appreciated reftel which I discussed with Spaak at luncheon today and at second more private meeting later. He had seen text of final OAU resolution[3] and concurs with us that it is

[1] Source: National Archives, RG 59, Central Files 1964–66, POL 3 OAU. Secret; Immediate. Repeated to Leopoldville and passed to the White House, DOD, and CIA.

[2] Telegram 446 to Brussels, September 9, reported that the Department shared Spaak's wish that a useful resolution would emerge from Addis Ababa, and noted that the latest reports indicated that the OAU was gradually coming around to a resolution the United States could approve. (Ibid.)

[3] For text of the final resolution adopted by the OAU Council of Ministers, September 10, "Creation of an Ad Hoc Commission of the Organization of African Unity To Help Restore National Unity in the Congo," see *American Foreign Policy: Current Docu-*

generally good, particularly since it confirms legitimacy of Leoville govt. At same time he noted that it is rather "equivocal" on certain points, notably "foreign intervention" and expulsion of mercenaries. While more extreme African states such as Casablanca bloc will doubtless try to exploit equivocal provisions re "no foreign intervention" to attack Belgian and US military aid to GOC, he did not think we had to worry very much about this because substantial majority of African nations would recognize Congo right to receive bilateral assistance. Re expulsion of mercenaries, he felt draft language "as soon as possible" would be generally interpreted in sense that this phrase has been interpreted in UN resolutions which has more meaning "as soon as feasible". While he thought composition of commission could have been more favorable his preliminary thought is that moderates would have at least majority of one and that Kenyatta would make reasonable chairman.

Spaak then went on to say key question on which future evolution of Congo situation largely depends is "what will Tshombe do next?" While Tshombe has certain good and useful qualities he also has his faults and if he is not properly advised he is apt to act impulsively and take steps which are damaging. Therefore Spaak is thinking in first instance of someone who might serve as Tshombe's political advisor. In other words, Spaak wants someone on political side who can supply Tshombe with advice and counsel that Van der Walle is supplying to him on military side.

In strictest and most absolute secrecy Spaak said he was thinking of detailing Rothschild to Congo for period of about three months. He explained that when Rothschild arrived in Addis the initial draft of Tshombe's speech was appalling but as result of Rothschild's work it had been substantially revised in helpful sense. Tshombe apparently likes and respects Rothschild and also knows he has Spaak's full confidence. What Spaak has in mind is, at Tshombe's request, to send Rothschild on preliminary survey trip to Congo (just as Van der Walle was sent) following which Rothschild would return and report to Spaak on political situation and possibilities, and then if Tshombe desired his services he would be detailed for limited period, perhaps three months.

Spaak's second preoccupation is that there be no "spectacular military adventures" undertaken in the immediate future. He explained there is substantial amount of military consolidation to be effected and

---

ments, 1964, pp. 763–765. The Ad Hoc Commission, headed by Kenyan Prime Minister Jomo Kenyatta, consisted of representatives from Ethiopia, Ghana, Nigeria, Guinea, Cameroun, Upper Volta, Tunisia, the United Arab Republic, and Somalia. Its mission was to restore peace in the Congo through helping it to normalize relations with its neighbors and to restore national reconciliation.

one must move steadily rather than spectacularly if ANC is to avoid (a) bloody nose and (b) if gains are to be consolidated and progress maintained. He then said he wished to say on personal but frank basis in keeping with intimacy of our relations that he understood there are some differences between Americans and Belgian military in Congo and that certain American officers are pressing for a swift and spectacular operation against Stanleyville (Embtel 427).[4] He felt this extremely unwise and hoped that any differences in tactics and strategy between Belgian and American military would be resolved in Leoville in a constructive sense.

Spaak concluded by saying that in next few days he and his immediate advisors would be reviewing all aspects of Congo problem and that he would wish to meet with me next Tuesday morning, Sept 15, for full and frank exchange of views.

I expressed appreciation to Spaak for his speaking with such complete frankness about Congo picture including possibility of Rothschild being sent there. I emphasized again, as I had at beginning, that we looked to Belgium to take lead in Congo and that if Tshombe desires Rothschild's services, I thought it would be splendid to send him. I added we fully agree, as Gov Harriman had made clear in his August meeting with Spaak,[5] that one of crying needs of Congo was qualified advisors and Belgium was in best position to supply them. We had great confidence in Rothschild who over past several years had collaborated with us on a basis of complete frankness and friendship and we respected his intelligence and integrity.

Davignon, who was present, expressed reservation about sending Rothschild to Leoville, saying it would in effect mean establishing "two Ambassadors." Spaak brushed this aside saying that if Rothschild went there he would go as an advisor to Tshombe and that this was not incompatible with the presence of a separate Belgian Amb who could ride herd on details of Belgium's multiple interests.

Comment: Other than what Belgians have told us we are not aware of any differences between US and Belgian military advisors. However, if we want Belgians to continue to take lead I strongly recommend they be reconciled at once in accord with Van der Walle plan.

MacArthur

---

[4] Dated September 7. (National Archives, RG 59, Central Files 1964–66, 23–9 THE CONGO)

[5] See Document 204.

253. Paper Prepared in the Central Intelligence Agency[1]

Washington, September 10, 1964.

SUBJECT

Additional Background Information Concerning Certain Significant Political and Military Developments within the Congo Since the Time Project [*cryptonym not declassified*] was Drafted[2]

Moise Tshombe, former President of the secessionist state of Katanga, returned to the Congo during the latter part of June 1964, and at the invitation of Joseph Kasavubu, President of the Congo, (and ostensibly with the agreement of General Mobutu and Victor Nendaka, Chief of the Sûreté Nationale) accepted the task of forming a Government of National Reconciliation as a necessary preliminary step to a general pacification of the Congo. (This took place just before the formal resignation of Prime Minister Adoula on 30 June, when it became necessary to appoint an interim caretaker government which would rule the Congo until national elections could be organized.) (In accordance with the provisions of the new constitution, which is now being submitted to a referendum for ratification, elections are to be held not later than nine months after acceptance of the constitution by the people on 1 August 1964.) Tshombe quickly presented to Kasavubu a cabinet list made up of, for the most part, relatively unknown individuals and was himself named by Kasavubu as Prime Minister.

During the period of maneuver and counter-maneuver by various individuals and political groups leading up to the return of Tshombe and the developments immediately thereafter, General Mobutu and Victor Nendaka played a somewhat devious game, the final element of which was that their support was withdrawn from Adoula and, it is assumed, at least conditionally given to Tshombe. Both Mobutu and Nendaka have retained their positions under Tshombe, but there is now a good deal of evidence that Tshombe is strengthening his hand so as to be able ultimately to wield more influence within the Congolese Army, and needless to say, reduce the influence of General Mobutu therein. Large contingents of ex-Katangese gendarmes are now coming out of hiding in the bush and from neighboring Angola. Recently reports have verified the presence in the Congo of a number of white mercenary officers who formerly commanded Tshombe's gendarmes during

[1] Source: Central Intelligence Agency Files, Job 89–00195R, Box 1, [*cryptonym not declassified*]—Development & Plans, [*text not declassified*]. Secret.

[2] Attached to the paper is a CIA Project Approval Notification form dated September 10, 1964, showing that Project [*cryptonym not declassified*] was approved.

the secession of Katanga, and it is surmised that they may be used to lead ANC troops into battle against the various rebel bands now terrorizing large segments of the country. (The uprisings have spread from Kwilu and Kivu provinces into North Katanga, Maniema, and Lac Leopold II provinces and have met with very ineffective resistance from the ANC.) More than ever Mobutu needs the support of ODYOKE (and particularly KUBARK support in the form outlined in the project objectives):

1. To shore up his authority in the ANC.
2. To assure him sufficient strength to be able to successfully counter any attempt to impose an extreme (whether of the right or left) political solution on the Congo;
3. To maintain the loyalty of his troops in the face of direct attempts at subversion designed to fragment the army's leadership and destroy its morale and confidence in its officers;
4. To carry out the necessary reorganization and training programs to make of his army a reasonably effective fighting force capable of handling the grave threat to civil order posed by the various rebel movements.

---

254. Memorandum for the Record[1]

Washington, September 10, 1964.

SUBJECT

Minutes of the Meeting of the 303 Committee, 10 September 1964

PRESENT

Mr. Bundy, Ambassador Thompson, Mr. Vance, and Mr. McCone
Colonel Ralph D. Steakley was present for Item 1

[Omitted here is discussion of other subjects.]

7. *Congo*

Mr. McCone brought up the subject of covert support [*less than 1 line not declassified*] and said he hoped the time was near when the C–130's could be withdrawn and with them, most of the U.S. military support force. Mr. Vance estimated that withdrawal of the C–130's would result in a reduction of no more than 125 personnel, leaving ap-

---

[1] Source: National Security Council, Intelligence Files, 303 Committee, Minutes – 1964. Secret; Eyes Only. Prepared on September 11.

proximately the same number for other required tasks, including T–28 maintenance. Mr. McCone indicated that two C–54's and several C–46's were earmarked to satisfy the Congolese government lift requirements and handling and maintenance would be supervised by a Panamanian company which was recruiting in Europe; this would reduce the American presence. Mr. McCone added that it was his impression that considering the prejudices against Tshombe in Addis Ababa, both self imposed and otherwise, he had emerged relatively unscathed and with some degree of stature.

[Omitted here is discussion of another subject.]

Peter Jessup

255. Memorandum From the Joint Chiefs of Staff to Secretary of Defense McNamara[1]

JCSM–788–64 Washington, September 12, 1964.

SUBJECT

Evacuation of US Personnel (U)

1. Reference is made to a memorandum by the Deputy Secretary of Defense, dated 4 September 1964,[2] subject as above, requesting the views of the Joint Chiefs of Staff as to appropriate US military courses of action which could be pursued to rescue the 25 Americans presently held by the rebel forces in Stanleyville, Republic of the Congo, and an evaluation of the probability of securing the rescue of the individuals unharmed.

2. Basically, two courses of action are available:

a. The overt use of a joint task force in a parachute/air-landed assault operation, utilizing multiple drop zones and supported by tactical air, to seize and secure the Stanleyville airfield, rescue the US personnel, and withdraw the entire force. Additional details are contained in the Annex hereto.

b. The covert use of military forces to effect a clandestine night parachute landing west of Stanleyville, infiltrate by rubber boat or foot to the US Consulate and/or other known locations of US personnel,

[1] Source: Washington National Records Center, RG 330, OASD/ISA Files: FRC 68 A 4023, 510 Congo 12 Sep 64. Top Secret.

[2] Attached but not printed.

overpower the guards, and move with the rescued personnel to a prearranged exfiltration area for pickup by helicopter or C–46 air commando aircraft.

3. Modifications to either course of action would be required dependent upon the latest enemy intelligence, the location and surveillance/guarding of the personnel to be rescued, US force availability, and the decision as to whether all or only part of the US personnel were to be rescued.

4. Either an overt or covert operation has a reasonable chance of successfully rescuing the personnel unharmed, providing:

a. The precise location of the personnel to be rescued can be determined PRIOR to initiation of the operation.
b. The plan is NOT compromised and complete surprise is obtained.
c. The commander is authorized to use such force as is necessary to accomplish the mission.

5. Both of the courses of action in paragraph 2, above, might prove to be infeasible because locations of US personnel may not be known, because of the opposition of the Belgian Government due to anticipated reprisals against foreigners in the Stanleyville area, or because the element of surprise may be lost. Accordingly a third course of action might be required which would provide for the capture of Stanleyville and its control long enough to transfer control to Congolese security forces and/or evacuate all foreign personnel. This course of action would probably require additional force.

6. From a military viewpoint, if a decision is made to employ US military forces to rescue the US personnel in Stanleyville:

a. The covert operation offers the best chance of successfully rescuing the US personnel unharmed.
b. The covert operation should be backed up by the prepositioning of the overt force for contingency employment, if required.

7. To preclude undue delay in implementation, if directed, immediate authorization to initiate detailed planning and dispatch of covert planners to the Congo is required.

8. The Joint Chiefs of Staff recommend:

a. The broad course of action, envisioning the initial effort being conducted by covert means with the back-up overt force being pre-positioned and ready for contingency employment if required, be selected as the appropriate course of action, if US intervention is directed.
b. Authority be granted for the immediate dispatch of the covert planners to the Congo, if detailed planning is desired.
c. Political coordination be accomplished with Government of Belgium officials and authorization be granted for on-the-scene military

coordination between appropriate US and Belgian military personnel, if US intervention is directed.

d. The above views be transmitted to the Department of State substantially as in the Appendix and Annex hereto.[3]

For the Joint Chiefs of Staff:

Earle G. Wheeler[4]
Chairman
Joint Chiefs of Staff

[3] Attached but not printed.

[4] Printed from a copy that indicates General Wheeler signed the original.

256. Memorandum From William H. Brubeck of the National Security Council Staff to the President's Special Assistant for National Security Affairs (Bundy)[1]

Washington, September 12, 1964.

RE

Congo

There is now an OAU Commission on the Congo which is beginning to operate in Nairobi, Kenya, September 18. Meanwhile, Tshombe has gone home to resume his war and he and rebels are both making intransigent noises.

Tshombe now has enough military power for leverage in political negotiation, OAU Commission very likely wants to and can help produce a negotiated settlement, and the Belgians are obviously taking this line. Neither we nor Belgians can really control situation. However, if we work together, we can provide an essential part of help needed to solve.

The decision making process in State is badly bogged down with Palmer caught between Williams (who wants to deal with *all* Congo policy for long term now, including economic aid) and Harriman (who is still on a cold war wicket as is General Adams). Palmer is getting

[1] Source: Johnson Library, National Security File, Country File, Congo, Vol. V. Secret.

desperate, and the 7th floor is leaving him to cope with Williams and Harriman.[2]

We need a fairly precise policy determination as to whether we are prepared to *join with* Belgians in pressing a political solution, including real pressure on Tshombe and Kasavubu; or alternatively to back a strengthened military solution by Tshombe. This is needed for two reasons: to lay down a clear line for all the cooks in this stew; and to put some energy into the policy fast enough to keep up with the maneuvers of Tshombe and the OAU.

Recommendation

That we request a *short* memorandum for the President from State by Monday, addressed narrowly to the question of how we now proceed, in light of OAU meeting, to attempt to get a settlement in Congo that will permit our reduction of military role, preserve legitimacy of Kasavubu Government, and preserve American position in Congo.

Bill Brubeck[3]

---

[2] On August 28, Secretary Rusk formally established the Congo Working Group (CWG) headed by Ambassador Palmer with representatives from the Department of Defense, CIA, AID, and USIA. A Congo Task Force began meeting informally at the Department of State shortly after the fall of Stanleyville.

[3] Printed from a copy that bears this typed signature.

---

257. Telegram From the Department of State to the Embassy in the Congo[1]

Washington, September 12, 1964, 4:28 p.m.

664. As we see immediate problems which face us in light relatively satisfactory outcome of OAU conference, following are our immediate priority tasks:

1. To assure that Kasavubu, Tshombe and rest of GOC not only remain committed to resolution but cooperate in implementing it in spirit

---

[1] Source: National Archives, RG 59, Central Files 1964–66, POL 23–9 THE CONGO. Secret; Immediate. Drafted by Palmer and Schaufele; cleared by McKillop, Fredericks, Lang, Brubeck, Palmer, and O'Sullivan; and approved by Harriman. Also sent to Brussels.

and as much in letter as negotiating history and Congo's internal security problems require;

2. To take rapid hard look at military and related activities with view toward reducing US visibility and, if possible, changing forms of assistance in ways which might lessen problems with ad hoc committee without incurring unacceptable loss of military effectiveness; and

3. Coordinating diplomatic initiatives by US, Belgians and GOC in African capitals, particularly with those members of ad hoc committee which we have reason to believe will be understanding and helpful, with objective of assuring best possible atmosphere for cooperation between commission and GOC on former's arrival Leopoldville.

Re (1), you should see Tshombe and express to him our great pleasure and admiration at effective manner in which he handled himself and presented his country's problems at Addis Ababa. You should add that in our opinion he has made most heartening progress in establishing his credentials as an African leader and in obtaining the understanding of many of his African brethren of the hard problems which confront his government. You should emphasize importance we attach, and which we are sure he shares, to building on promising beginnings made at Addis Ababa toward obtaining vital cooperation of rest of Africa in dealing with Congo problem. You may tell him at same time that we aware of problems which some of provisions of resolution may pose for him. Nevertheless, we believe resolution constitutes signal victory for principles for which he sought recognition and important thing now is to prepare for commission of inquiry in spirit of Addis Ababa. FYI. Above not a substitution for suggestion contained para 4 Embtel 1022[2] on which we await your further recommendations. End FYI.

Although we believe it would be a mistake to give Tshombe what we regard as reasonable interpretations of questionable parts of resolution you may wish keep following in back your mind in case conversation should turn in that direction.

1. Department does not consider that paragraphs 6 and 7 of resolution prohibit GOC from concluding or continuing bilateral arrangements to assure its own internal security. On same basis USG is not "at present intervening in internal affairs Democratic Republic of Congo" since it assisting GOC at request legitimate government.

2. Although Tshombe committed to expelling mercenaries, Department believes resolution phrase "as soon as possible" and fact OAU did not provide troops which he requested give him considerable flexibility in meeting this commitment. Recognize he will be subject varying degrees of adverse criticism.

---

[2] Dated September 10. (Ibid.)

3. Resolution acceptably recognizes previous GOC efforts bring about national reconciliation and does not confer on commission powers to negotiate with rebels without GOC cooperation.

Re (2), Department suggests following areas should be explored:

(a) Embassy requested examine and suggest soonest any possible means in addition those already taken to reduce visibility and change form US military assistance consistent essential security requirements. In this connection is there anything US could or should do before visit OAU commission?

(b) Embassy should urge Kasavubu, Tshombe and other GOC officials as appropriate to assure that all necessary actions taken to accept individual rebel surrenders and deposit their arms; to prevent any brutal or retaliatory treatment against captured and surrendering rebels; to suspend obvious or unnecessary activities in Leopoldville and elsewhere which could be considered intimidation opposition elements; to examine moves which could be made to broaden government, at least partially.

(c) GOC should undertake all possible steps, without weakening internal security, to reduce mercenaries visibility or otherwise lessen the effect as political liabilities. For example, perhaps repatriation undesirables can be represented as conscious decision reduce numbers.

(d) Embassy requested offer suggestions consistent with internal security requirements to assure against excessive use of force or militarily unimportant actions.

Re (3), continuing guidance will follow as required.

For Brussels: You should summarize above for GOB in effort coordinate our approaches to these problems, making clear we most anxious obtain GOB views thereon.

Rusk

258. Telegram From the Department of State to the Embassy in the Congo[1]

Washington, September 14, 1964, 8:10 p.m.

673. Embtel 1060.[2] While we are glad to learn that Belgian Emboff has been able to reach Stan, we believe you would be justified in expressing your surprise to Belg Embassy at apparent absence of advance coordination with you. This particularly hard to understand in light US-Belgian cooperation on Congo matters and Belgian knowledge of our deep concern over our personnel in Stan.

Hope Belg Emb will provide advance notice any further such trips and that Embassy Brussels will take early opportunity express our surprise and stress our desire for closest consultation this matter. Also appreciate knowing how Nothomb got to Stan and how and when he plans return Leo. Also how message sent.

Can you find out whether Nothomb trip related Gbenye's talks with Belgians?

Rusk

---

[1] Source: National Archives, RG 59, Central Files 1964–66, PS 7–6 THE CONGO. Confidential; Priority; Limdis. Drafted by AFC Deputy Director Mathew J. Looram and Curtis C. Strong, cleared by McKillop, and approved by Palmer. Also sent to Brussels.

[2] In telegram 1060 from Leopoldville, September 14, Godley reported a telephone conversation with the Belgian Ambassador, who told him that he had received several "long" messages from a Belgian Embassy official who had been in Stanleyville and who had reported that all of the persons the Ambassador had inquired about were all right. The Ambassador believed that "all" persons included the Americans, but was not sure. (Ibid.)

259. Circular Telegram From the Department of State to Certain Posts[1]

Washington, September 18, 1964, 3:56 p.m.

497. Ref: Leo's 1039.[2] Joint State/USIA message. While Department completely shares views expressed by Emb Leo re importance African leaders understanding true nature rebel leadership and dissension within its ranks, we believe it most important that we guard against creating impression that US undertaking campaign to discredit rebels either for its own reasons or because we not confident African ability form valid judgments their own.

Although we recognize that members OAU Ad Hoc Commission will indulge in much self-seeking and wishful thinking re rebel leadership, we believe that more responsible members will be at pains protect position GOC and wish examine for themselves true facts re rebel movement. In this connection Dept assumes Bochley–Davidson press conference at Addis Ababa and widely publicized recent statements by Gizenga, Gbenye, Olenga, et al are already known to most African leaders. We believe these statements speak for themselves without necessity for US drawing inferences therefrom for benefit OAU members. In short, we believe that rebel leaders themselves doing good job of discrediting themselves if their statements are widely circulated and that US is in strongest posture by staying in background and avoiding risk of being charged by radicals with effort sabotage commission's efforts at national reconciliation by seeking discredit rebels.

We assume moreover that GOC will be making clear to Commission in strongest terms its own appraisal of rebels. While GOC assessments will undoubtedly be suspect, particularly to radicals, we would hope that they would at least underline importance of Commission visiting rebel areas and assessing leadership on spot before becoming too deeply into national reconciliation. Believe US and Congolese objectives will be most effectively served by encouraging such visits to rebel areas.

---

[1] Source: National Archives, RG 59, Central Files 1964–66, POL 23–9 THE CONGO. Confidential; Priority. Drafted by Palmer and Strong; cleared by Lewis in USIA, Harriman, Carl H. Peterson in AF/P, and Tasca; and approved by Palmer. Sent to Accra, Addis Ababa, Algiers, Bamako, Bangui, Brazzaville, Brussels, Bujumbura, Bukuvu, Cairo, Conakry, Dakar, Dar es Salaam, Elisabethville, Freetown, Kampala, Khartoum, Kigali, Lagos, Leopoldville, London, Mogadiscio, Monrovia, Nairobi, Ouagadougou, Paris, Tunis, Yaounde, and CINCMEAFSA for Ramsey.

[2] Dated September 11. (Ibid.)

Department has no objection to posts responding discreetly and selectively to requests from friendly African governments by furnishing bio data or even appropriately generalized appraisals of rebel leaders and their "movement". Also make available rebels public statements if appropriate. Posts should, however, avoid anything resembling campaign.

USIA may use selectively straight factual reporting on rebels through VOA, wireless file, etc. and posts should be sensitive in utilizing such material to avoid appearance of a U.S. campaign.

Rusk

260. Memorandum From the Deputy Director of the Office of Central African Affairs (Looram) to the Assistant Secretary of State for African Affairs (Williams)[1]

Washington, September 19, 1964.

SUBJECT

Status Report on Recent Developments—INFORMATION MEMORANDUM

American Personnel Stanleyville

The most significant development has been the receipt by the ICRC representative in Bujumbura of a message from the Stanleyville authorities saying that they accept the ICRC proposal to send in a plane to Stanleyville with doctors and medical supplies. We have assured the ICRC of our full support, urging that a Swiss plane and pilots be used for this purpose. The ICRC is working on this matter on an urgent basis and it is hoped that an ICRC plane will be in a nearby position, such as Bangui, by the middle of the week to go into Stanleyville.

Whether or not the plane will be allowed to evacuate people, particularly Americans, remains to be seen. (There are indications that Gbenye's acceptance of the plane is due to his desire to use it for his own transport to Nairobi for the OAU Commission.) However, we

---

[1] Source: National Archives, RG 59, Central Files 1964–66, POL 23–9 THE CONGO. Confidential.

have our fingers crossed and the mission should at least serve to ascertain their welfare and whereabouts.[2]

[2] On September 21, Looram sent Williams a memorandum pointing out that it would be difficult for the ICRC representatives to obtain early permission from the rebel authorities for the evacuation of the U.S. Consulate staff, and that they might find it necessary to obtain authorization for the evacuation of other nationals first. He emphasized that it was essential that the ICRC not give any indication that the U.S. Government was behind the operation. (Ibid.)

261. Telegram From the Department of State to the Embassy in Kenya[1]

Washington, September 22, 1964, 7:37 p.m.

1001. From Acting Secretary. Ref Nairobi's 714.[2] You should see Kenyatta immediately and remind him that U.S. has made it clear that we are anxious cooperate in every appropriate way with OAU and attaches great importance to success its efforts to contribute to solution Congo problem. At same time, we must emphasize that any U.S. assistance to Congo is at request of GOC in exercise its sovereign rights and duty to assure law and order, just as similar assistance given other African nations at their request. We therefore could not agree to any meeting with commission on the subject of U.S. assistance to the Congo without appropriate participation by the Government of the Congo.

If the GOC willing to participate, the U.S. would be prepared to designate representatives to meet with representatives of the GOC and the OAU Commission at time and place to be agreed to discuss matters of common concern and interest according to a previously agreed agenda. We could not however agree participate in any such talks under any circumstances which imply U.S. improperly intervening in

[1] Source: National Archives, RG 59, Central Files 1964–66, POL 23–9 THE CONGO. Secret; Flash. Drafted by Williams and Palmer; cleared by Brubeck, Williams, George S. Springsteen, Jr., and Fredericks; and approved by Palmer. Repeated to Leopoldville, Brussels, Lagos, Cairo, Accra, and Conakry.

[2] Telegram 714 from Nairobi, September 22, transmitted the text of a communiqué issued by the OAU Ad Hoc Commission stating that the Commission had decided to send a special delegation of five Ministers to see President Johnson in Washington. The communiqué also declared that without the withdrawal of all foreign military intervention from the Congo the Commission would not be able to achieve its mission of reconciliation. (Ibid.)

Congo. U.S. also of course stands prepared discuss such matters through normal diplomatic channels at any time.

FYI.

1. It is most important you do everything within your power to prevent mission coming to U.S.

2. President's obvious preoccupations and commitments rule out such meeting. (If useful you may tell Kenyatta this.)

3. Adverse U.S. public reaction to possible commission gaff at this critical point could greatly endanger U.S. Congo and general African policies and programs.

4. Commission should be exposed to Congolese realities in order to assist it reach proper judgments. End FYI.

Ball

262. Telegram From the Department of State to the Embassy in the Congo[1]

Washington, September 22, 1964, 10:24 p.m.

739. Believe you should see Tshombe soonest possible, flying Katanga if necessary, and acquaint him with reply Attwood instructed make to Kenyatta re proposed OAU mission to U.S. You should make clear to Tshombe, in standing on position that GOC should participate in any conversations involving U.S. and OAU commission reps, we are counting on his flexibility and cooperation. You should add that if formula we have proposed should be acceptable to OAU commission, we believe Leo would be most appropriate locus of conversations and we would wish try steer things in that direction. This would have advantages of talks taking place at seat of GOC and, at same time, bringing commission to Congo where we hope it might be persuaded more realistically to face up to Congo realities than is presently case in rarified Nairobi atmosphere.

Regardless whether OAU commission accepts our formula for conversations, we strongly believe Tshombe's best tactic in any event is to encourage commission come to Congo soonest. We concerned in this

[1] Source: National Archives, RG 59, Central Files 1964–66, POL 23–9 THE CONGO. Secret; Flash. Drafted by Palmer, cleared by Fredericks and Brubeck, and approved by Palmer. Repeated to Nairobi and Brussels.

connection at accumulating evidence that commission moving beyond terms of reference laid down Addis Ababa. We believe GOC can help reverse this trend by following means:

(1) GOC should act immediately to send emissaries to friendly African members commission (particularly Nigeria, Upper Volta, Cameroons, Ethiopia, Tunisia and possibly Somalia and Guinea) to express his concern and to urge those governments to instruct their representatives to insist that the commission keep its activities within purview OAU resolution.

(2) To take initiative himself in urging commission to come soonest to Congo to appraise problems on spot and offer place plane at their disposal for this purpose. Believe it important in this connection that Tshombe make clear that he wants commission to visit rebel held areas to assess for themselves nature these regimes, degree of unity (and disunity) amongst rebel leaders and extent their genuine political (as contrasted military) support amongst population. In short, objective would be to encourage commission to undertake realistic survey Congo problems on spot before becoming involved in unrealistic and dangerous approaches to problem of national reconciliation.

You should assure Tshombe we will assist in these efforts as well, but GOC must take lead re (1) and only GOC can accomplish (2).

We are also most anxious obtain Tshombe's version of apparent impasse reported Nairobi's 695[2] re discussions with Gbenye and you should obtain as full details as possible.

New subject: Unless ICRC or Swiss Ambassador interposes objections or new developments make action unnecessary, you should also take occasion urge Tshombe in strongest terms drop his condition re ICRC plane stopping Leo.[3] Report from Nairobi of Gbenye's presence Uganda would seem remove reason for Tshombe insistence this condition.

Ball

---

[2] In telegram 695 from Nairobi, September 21, Ambassador Attwood reported that almost all Africans there thought that Tshombe had let down the Ad Hoc Commission and Kenyatta by refusing to meet with the rebels after telling Kenyatta he would. Attwood recommended that Tshombe, in order to head off severe criticism of himself and his government, invite the Commission to Leopoldville to assess the situation, and that Tshombe state his willingness to cooperate and to meet with any dissidents in the interest of national reconciliation. (Ibid.)

[3] Telegram 352 from Elisabethville, September 22, reported that Tshombe told the Consul in Elisabethville that he agreed that the ICRC plane should go to Stanleyville, provided that it first proceed to Leopoldville to pick up a Congolese Red Cross representative. (Ibid., PS 7-6 THE CONGO)

263. Telegram From the Department of State to the Embassy in Kenya[1]

Washington, September 23, 1964, 5:16 p.m.

1020. For Attwood from the Secretary. Embtel 721.[2] We must reiterate in strongest terms we do not want OAU Mission come to Washington and you should make every effort prevent it. Moreover we do not believe it useful to explain position to Kenyatta, Dialo or others in terms domestic politics. Points we must stand on are (1) that we cannot discuss these matters without GOC for reasons stated Deptel 1001;[3] and (2) that we are not refusing to talk but do not think it unreasonable we should have something to say re time, place, subject matter and level of representation. We leave it to you to put best face possible on this position with Kenyatta and Commission and to put President's unavailability in best possible light.

You should also be aware that, as emphasized Deptel 1007,[4] we are deeply disturbed at present tendencies within Commission. Until Commission may get on more constructive track, we are most anxious not become this much involved with it and certainly not on its terms or in Washington.

We repeat your objective must be to prevent mission coming here.[5]

Rusk

---

[1] Source: National Archives, RG 59, Central Files 1964–66, POL 3 OAU. Secret; Flash; Exdis. Drafted by Palmer, cleared by Williams, and approved by Rusk.

[2] In telegram 721 from Nairobi, Attwood suggested that the fact that Africans wanted the President to win the U.S. election offered the opportunity to exercise leverage in order to make OAU actions look like a victory for responsible African leadership and not an anti-U.S. move. He argued that a categorical refusal to meet with the OAU delegation would destroy U.S. leverage, enabling OAU extremists to attack the United States and thereby giving Senator Goldwater the chance to say that the Johnson administration had lost Africa. (Ibid., POL 23–9 THE CONGO)

[3] Document 261.

[4] Telegram 1007 to Nairobi, September 22, warned that the OAU Commission seemed to be departing from the letter and spirit of the OAU resolution at Addis Ababa, and that it appeared that certain states, such as Ghana and the United Arab Republic, had seized the initiative and embarked on a dangerous course of action that could result in a divided Congo. (National Archives, RG 59, Central Files 1964–66, POL 23–9 THE CONGO)

[5] Telegram 1021 to Nairobi, September 23, instructed Attwood to urge Kenyatta "in the strongest terms" to intercept the OAU delegation, which had already left Nairobi, and instruct it not to proceed. (Ibid., POL 3 OAU) In telegram 738 from Nairobi, September 24, Attwood reported that Kenyatta was adamant about sending the delegation but had agreed under pressure to send a message to Murumbi instructing him to say in public statements that his visit was as the personal representative of the Prime Minister and designed to pave the way for a meeting with U.S. and Congolese representatives, and that he hoped to call on the Secretary and other high officials, if possible. (Ibid., POL 23–9 THE CONGO)

264. Letter From Congolese President Kasavubu to President Johnson[1]

Leopoldville, September 25, 1964.

Mr. President:

The decision taken by the ad hoc Commission of the Organization of African Unity to send a delegation to Your Excellency in order to discuss the bilateral agreements between our two countries, signed in full sovereignty, constitutes such a flagrant violation of the Charter of the OAU that I take the liberty of sending you this message.

The Democratic Republic of the Congo, co-signatory to the Addis Ababa Charter, has subscribed to the following principles: (1) the sovereign equality of all Member States; (2) noninterference in the internal affairs of the States; (3) respect for the sovereignty and territorial integrity of each State and for its inalienable right to an independent existence.

The people and the Government of the Democratic Republic of the Congo will never consent to the Organization of African Unity discussing and calling into question any bilateral agreements that our two countries have the right to conclude and have concluded in full sovereignty.

We shall continue to cooperate with the Government and the people of the United States in the certainty that no political condition which would deprive us of independence is attached to the assistance we are receiving.

The re-establishment of order and peace is still our primary objective in the difficult situation now faced by our country. This task rests solely with the legal government headed by Prime Minister Moise Tshombe.

The first duty of the Commission is to hold a talk with this government and in the Congo. Its principal task is "to support and encourage the efforts that the Government of the Democratic Republic of the Congo is making to achieve national reconciliation; to seek every possible means of normalizing the relations between the Democratic Republic of the Congo and its neighbors, particularly Burundi and the Republic of the Congo (Brazzaville)".

This is the message that I have thought is advisable to send you in the name of the people and the Government of the Democratic Republic of the Congo.

---

[1] Source: National Archives, RG 59, Central Files 1964–66, POL THE CONGO–US. No classification marking. The original is attached to an October 1 transmittal memorandum from Read to Bundy which states that the letter was delivered to Williams by Congolese Chargé Mario Cardoso.

Accept, Mr. President, the renewed assurances of my very high consideration.

J.K.[2]

[2] Printed from a copy that indicates President Kasavubu initialed the original.

---

265. Telegram From the Department of State to the Embassy in Kenya[1]

Washington, September 25, 1964, 11:16 a.m.

1056. Governor Williams reached Murumbi by telephone just prior to his transatlantic takeoff. Governor Williams pointed out that Secretary Rusk could not see Murumbi unless he could make public statement such as included in his prior authorization to wit: Murumbi coming as special representative of Kenyatta without reference American aid to Congo. Murumbi assured Williams Kenyatta statement misunderstood and that last thing in world they wanted was embarrass USG. Williams said USG didn't want embarrass him or OAU. Default requested statement Williams would see Murumbi but could not talk about Congo aid without Congolese present. Murumbi said confident of mutually agreeable meeting. He would not speak press New York or Washington and would see Ambassadors of countries his delegation requesting they do same. Williams asked whether mission could be construed goodwill mission. Murumbi said just about. Murumbi said would look up Williams directly after checking Ambassadors.[2]

Rusk

[1] Source: National Archives, RG 59, Central Files 1964–66, POL 3 OAU. Confidential; Flash. Drafted by Williams; cleared by Brubeck, Harriman, and Palmer; and approved by Williams. Also sent to Leopoldville and repeated to London, Brussels, Accra, Conakry, Lagos, and Cairo.

[2] Telegram 210 to Accra, September 25, reported that Murumbi arrived in Washington that afternoon and that Williams would be seeing him within the framework of the announced U.S. position. Unless Murumbi could meet the principal points in the U.S. position, however, neither he nor the other members of the delegation would be received by higher U.S. officials. Therefore, the U.S. Government hoped that, in order to avoid an embarrassing situation, host governments would instruct their delegates not to proceed to Washington until exploratory talks with Murumbi reached a satisfactory conclusion. (Ibid., POL 23–9 THE CONGO)

266. Editorial Note

An ICRC aircraft departed from Bangui in the Central African Republic at 0623Z on September 25, 1964, and arrived in Stanleyville at 0945Z. Before the final decision to fly was made, Tshombe withdrew his proviso that a Congolese Red Cross representative had to be aboard any ICRC flight to Stanleyville, and the ICRC received assurances from the Stanleyville authorities regarding flight safety and authorization to land. (Memorandum from O'Sullivan to Williams, September 25; National Archives, RG 59, AF/CWG Files: Lot 65 D 498 Rebellion. Coups. Stanleyville 1964) On September 27, O'Sullivan reported to Williams that the ICRC plane had returned safely to Bangui on September 26, but had been unable to bring out any evacuees because the rebel leaders feared they would not be able to guarantee the safety of the foreigners, ICRC personnel, or themselves if the Jeunesse and the Army learned that foreigners were being evacuated. The ICRC mission had also not been able to visit the U.S. Consular personnel, but had been assured by a Belgian who saw the Americans regularly that Hoyt and his staff were safe and well. (Memorandum from O'Sullivan to Williams, September 27; ibid.)

In telegram 151 from Bangui, September 27, Ambassador Ross reported that ICRC officials Rubli and Senn told him that feeling against Americans in Stanleyville was running particularly high and that rebel leaders considered the United States an "aggressor." Rubli emphasized that he greatly feared for the lives of all foreigners in Stanleyville in the event of any bombings or even overflights, and warned that any military action to take the city would have to be sudden and massive enough that key points could be secured quickly or they would run the risk of a general massacre. (Ibid., Central Files 1964–66, POL 23–9 THE CONGO)

267. Telegram From the Department of State to the Embassy in Kenya[1]

Washington, September 26, 1964, 1:55 a.m.

1075. Embassy Nairobi should hold until further instructions following possible message from Secretary to Kenyatta. Other addressees should be prepared pass copies host govts only when and if so instructed:

Dear Mr. Prime Minister:

Your letter to the President[2] has been received and will be brought promptly to his attention on his return to Washington next week. I know you are aware through Ambassador Attwood of the importance my government attaches to the efforts of the Organization of African Unity to contribute to a solution of the Congo problem. I wish to assure you personally that we are, as we have made clear, anxious to cooperate with the Organization of African Unity in every appropriate way. In particular, we desire to work in a friendly way with the OAU Commission over which you preside to achieve results beneficial to all concerned.

As you are also aware, our efforts to assist in a solution of the Congo problem have consistently been directed at helping the sovereign government of the Congo in response to its requests. This has been the case ever since Congo independence irrespective of personalities, both in our support of the UN and subsequently. The principle involved is one which animates us in our assistance to countries throughout the world, including many in Africa, and I am sure you will appreciate that we cannot depart from it in this case. It would therefore be most improper for us to discuss changes in our present limited assistance to the Congo without the Congolese Government's concurrence and participation. I am sure you would agree that every other African nation would expect to be treated with the same consideration.

We sincerely regret, as I am sure you do, the difficulties that have arisen in connection with the proposed delegation from the OAU Com-

---

[1] Source: National Archives, RG 59, Central Files 1964–66, POL 23–9 THE CONGO. Confidential; Immediate; Limdis. Drafted by Palmer and Strong in AF/CWG on September 25; cleared by Williams, Brubeck, and Rusk; and approved by Palmer. Repeated to Accra, Addis Ababa, Brussels, Cairo, Conakry, Lagos, Leopoldville, Mogadiscio, Ouagadougou, Tunis, and Yaounde.

[2] Telegram 760 from Nairobi, September 24, transmitted a message from Kenyatta to Johnson stating that he hoped the President would find a suitable opportunity, at his convenience, to meet with the OAU delegation, and enclosing a copy of his instructions to Murumbi. (Ibid.) Attwood reported on Kenyatta's instructions to Murumbi in telegram 738; see footnote 5, Document 263.

mission. I wish to assure you that my Government wholeheartedly and unreservedly shares the objective set forth in the OAU resolution, i.e., "to support and encourage the efforts of the Democratic Republic of the Congo in the restoration of national reconciliation." We are, in this connection, pleased indeed that you have sent us your personal representative and distinguished Minister of State, Mr. Joseph Murumbi. We hope that his visit will make it possible for our two Governments constructively to direct our energies toward the earliest possible attainment of a unified, peaceful and genuinely independent Congo which will be able to play its full part with other African states in realizing the potential of your great continent.

I appreciate very much the good will which has animated your own efforts in these vital matters and I continue to hope for your success in bringing about an African solution of the Congo problem.[3]

Begin FYI: In course your discussion with Kenyatta you should let him know that reaction our people to these problems is greatly complicated by fact that five of our officials are being held incommunicado by the rebels in Stanleyville.[4]

Also, you should not hesitate to indicate to Kenyatta that objective US policy in Congo since 1960 has been to support the unity and security of the country and in this process we have worked with solidarity and unity of purpose with overwhelming majority African nations. This remains our policy and we are distressed when differences arise because elements foreign to Africa and hostile to freedom attempt subvert unity and independence of Congo. End FYI.

Rusk

---

[3] Telegram 1078 to Nairobi, September 26, instructed the Embassy to deliver the Secretary's message to Kenyatta as soon as possible, but to delete the first sentence and convey this information orally. (National Archives, RG 59, Central Files 1964–66, POL 23–9 THE CONGO) In telegram 788 from Nairobi, September 27, Attwood reported that Kenyatta could not be reached, but that he had delivered the Secretary's message to Cabinet Secretary Ndegwa. (Ibid., POL 3 OAU)

[4] Telegram 1118 to Nairobi, September 29, instructed the Embassy to take no action on this sentence until further instructed. (Ibid., POL 23–9 THE CONGO)

268. Telegram From the Department of State to Embassy in Kenya[1]

Washington, September 26, 1964, 11:49 a.m.

1077. Williams, Fredericks, and Palmer met privately last evening with Murumbi and Nbwera. Williams explained U.S. position re ad hoc commission delegation, emphasizing our desire cooperate appropriately with OAU but problems caused for us by delegation's publicly announced terms reference. Murumbi took line these clarified privately thru Attwood and that there no intention on part Commission embarrass us or question our right maintain bilateral relationships with sovereign GOC. He added in this context that he recognized right of Congo to receive military aid from U.S. just as Kenya itself had from UK. Went on to say purpose delegation simply enlist assistance U.S. in OAU efforts solve Congo problem. Williams said whatever Commission's private intentions, it had either wittingly or unwittingly created awkward situation for itself and for U.S. by public stance it has taken. (Williams also gave him world press summary material critical U.S. and OAU stance this matter.) Williams went on to say that until Murumbi's own terms reference publicly clarified to meet points of principle in our public statement (Deptel 1027 to Nairobi)[2] Secretary unfortunately could not receive him. Urged Murumbi issue public statement based on his instructions from Kenyatta (Nairobi's 738 to Dept)[3] and gave him informally draft text which would meet our points and make possible meeting with Secretary. Murumbi demurred, taking position Kenyatta instructions sent in context his being head delegation as well as Kenyatta's personal representative. Since rest of delegation not here, he would have to consult Kenyatta by telephone this morning and Ambassadors here of other countries represented on delegation which he intended do after leaving Williams last evening. He suggested further

[1] Source: National Archives, RG 59, Central Files 1964–66, POL 3 OAU. Secret; Immediate. Drafted by Palmer, cleared by Williams, and approved by Palmer. Repeated to Accra, Addis Ababa, Cairo, Conakry, Lagos, Mogadiscio, Ouagadougou, Tunis, and Yaounde.

[2] Dated September 23. (Ibid.)

[3] See footnote 5, Document 263.

talk with Williams this morning at 11:00 local, but subsequently postponed meeting since had not yet been able contact Kenyatta.[4]

Rusk

[4] Telegram 1084 to Nairobi, September 26, reported that Murumbi told Williams that Kenyatta was consulting the other members of the Commission. Murumbi insisted that the Commission did not question the U.S. right to give aid to the Congo. Its only objective was to obtain U.S. assistance in getting Tshombe to respect a cease-fire. Williams expressed the U.S. concern that the Commission seemed to equate the legitimate government with the rebels. Murumbi replied that the OAU fully respected the Congo's sovereignty but had a mandate to work for national reconciliation. After a cease-fire, all areas of the Congo would be returned to central government control, and once a coalition government was achieved, there would be OAU-supervised elections. (National Archives, RG 59, Central Files 1964–66, POL 3 OAU)

269. Telegram From the Department of State to the Embassy in Nigeria[1]

Washington, September 28, 1964, 8:16 p.m.

729. In private conversation today with Palmer, Murumbi indicated personal agreement with following formula as basis for meeting of OAU delegation with Williams and undertook to consult other countries represented on delegation. He will advise Dept at 1400 Zulu Sept 29 whether entire delegation agrees. If there is agreement meeting with Williams would be scheduled later same day as Murumbi, Botsio (who arriving here tonight) and perhaps other members of OAU delegation have to leave Washington evening Sept 29. Formula involves advance commitment by delegation to issuance of joint press statement with US immediately after meeting with Williams. On issuance of press statement, delegation would pay courtesy call on Secretary barring unforeseen conflict of schedules).

Text of press statement as agreed by Murumbi follows:

"Mr. Joseph Murumbi, head of the delegation to the United States of the Ad Hoc Commission on the Congo established by the Organization of African Unity and speaking on behalf of his delegation, met

[1] Source: National Archives, RG 59, Central Files 1964–66, POL 3 OAU. Confidential; Immediate. Drafted by Strong and approved by Palmer. Repeated to Accra, Addis Ababa, Brussels, Cairo, Conakry, Leopoldville, Mogadiscio, Nairobi, Ouagadougou, Tunis, Yaounde, and USUN.

with the Assistant Secretary of State for African Affairs, G. Mennen Williams, today, together with M. Pognon, Assistant Secretary General of the OAU, and informed the Assistant Secretary of the efforts of the OAU Commission to help resolve the Congo problem.

Mr. Murumbi made it clear to Assistant Secretary Williams that he had come to the United States on a purely good will visit. Mr. Murumbi also made it clear that the Commission recognizes that in any meetings of the delegation with the U.S. Govt it would be inappropriate to discuss matters affecting the sovereignty of the Dem Rep of the Congo.

In welcoming Mr. Murumbi's assurances, Assistant Secretary Williams asked Mr. Murumbi to convey to Prime Minister Kenyatta the sympathetic understanding of the United States Government that the Prime Minister is engaged in a most significant undertaking in the service of Africa, to the success of which the United States attaches great importance. Mr. Williams asked that, with this in mind, Prime Minister Kenyatta be assured of the desire of the United States to cooperate with the OAU in every appropriate way. Mr. Williams emphasized that the limited U.S. military assistance to the Congo is at the request of the sovereign Government of the Congo to assist it in maintaining law and order. He pointed out that U.S. military assistance has been provided to the Government of the Congo for a number of years, first through the United Nations and, subsequently, under agreements fully consistent with UN resolutions and with the final report of the UN Secretary General on UN operations in the Congo.

In acknowledging the sovereign rights of the Congo to request and accept military assistance from the U.S., Mr. Murumbi assured Mr. Williams that this was not at issue. He explained that the Commission's objective was rather to seek the cooperation of the United States in the Commission's efforts to support and encourage the efforts of the Government of the Congo in the restoration of national reconciliation. In this connection, he welcomed Assistant Secretary Williams' assurances of cooperation.

Mr. Murumbi and Assistant Secretary Williams agreed that the conversation had been most helpful in clarifying the views of the Commission and of the U.S. Government and in establishing a general framework for cooperation between them.

It has also been arranged for Mr. Murumbi and M. Pognon to pay a courtesy call on the Secretary of State before leaving Washington."

If there is agreement by OAU delegation language of first and last paras would be modified to show entire delegation being received. In addition to Botsio, Beavogui (Guinea) also expected. In his consultations Murumbi will suggest other members, Nigeria and Ghana be represented by local Ambassadors.

Nigeria's Chargé informed of above and states present instructions would not permit him participate as Nigeria considers mission to US ultra vires. However, in light of proposed joint press statement recognizing sovereign rights of Congo, is seeking new instructions. Since it obviously desirable have Nigerians present you should point out changed circumstances to GON and urge that Chargé or Adebo be authorized attend. We also strongly prefer entire exercise be completed tomorrow rather than have new round of publicity as would be case if reception of OAU delegation delayed to later date. Also preferable delegation be received before opening of Non-Aligned Conference Cairo. Thus preferable an on-the-spot Nigerian representative be authorized attend rather than have representative sent from Lagos for later meeting.

Rusk

---

270. Memorandum From the Assistant Secretary of State for African Affairs (Williams) to the Under Secretary of State (Ball)[1]

Washington, September 29, 1964.

SUBJECT

Use of U.S.-supplied Aircraft for Attacks on Uvira or other Congolese towns

1. The ANC uses U.S.-supplied aircraft (T–28's and B–26's) piloted by contract personnel [*less than 1 line not declassified*] in connection with military operations in the Congo. These aircraft are loaned to the ANC and are under their operational control but the U.S. can take action to bar their use for missions of which we disapprove.

2. On September 15, ANC Commander in Bukavu, Colonel Mulamba, ordered T–28 pilots not to strike (i.e. strafe) the town of Uvira but to continue attacking concentrations of trucks and other equipment outside the town.

3. We have expressed to our Embassy in Leopoldville our strong concern at the possibility that air attacks on Uvira might result in re-

[1] Source: National Archives, RG 59, Central Files 1964–66, POL 23–9 THE CONGO. Secret. The memorandum does not indicate the drafter, but the memorandum was cleared in draft by Harriman.

prisals against Europeans there and in other rebel held areas. However, we have left it to the Leopoldville Country Team to determine whether strikes within Uvira are essential from a military viewpoint. They are to try to limit air strikes in the area to road and lake traffic until such time as the ANC is prepared to launch a serious offensive against Uvira or the magnitude of the rebel build-up clearly necessitates defensive action involving air strikes on the town itself. Both conditions now prevail.

4. We are concerned over the possible consequences for Americans in Stanleyville if air strikes on Uvira or other towns are permitted at this time. The rebels put our Consular personnel under protective arrest when an earlier air attack on Uvira was reported. They, moreover considered that air attacks on Albertville occurred only after the evacuation of Europeans were evacuated and appear to be determined to hold Europeans in Stanleyville, particularly our Consular personnel, hostage to avoid air attacks on Stanleyville. On the other hand air attacks on truck concentrations, etc. outside of towns appears to have provoked no rebel retaliation against Europeans.

Recommendation: That new instructions be sent to our Embassy in Leopoldville that U.S.-supplied aircraft should not hit targets within Uvira or other towns during the current negotiations of the International Red Cross with the rebels for the evacuation of Americans and Europeans from Stanleyville. This restriction should remain in effect as long as the Americans in Stanleyville are in danger. There would, however, be no bar on air attacks on targets outside towns, including the road from Uvira to Bukavu, a strategic town currently threatened with rebel attack.

271. Circular Telegram From the Department of State to Certain Posts[1]

Washington, September 30, 1964, 10:05 p.m.

569. Ref: Deptel 747 to Lagos; Depcirtel 563.[2] Secretary's remarks are FYI and Noforn, based on uncleared and subject to review.

Secretary received OAU delegation at working lunch today.[3] Composition of delegation as contained Deptel 747 to Lagos and in general ground covered conformed to substance of joint communiqué. Atmosphere of talks was relaxed and friendly with Murumbi and other delegates going out of their way to emphasize that there had been no intention embarrass US Government or President and that OAU regarded US as friend whose cooperation essential to success their mission re Congo. Secretary pointed out US has no important interests in Congo but has consistently supported unity and integrity of country. We however consider Congo an African problem and were therefore glad to see OAU take it up. One reason we welcome efforts OAU to solve Congo problem in African context was that we do not want to see injection Cold War into Congo or elsewhere in Africa. At same time, we would not shrink from our responsibilities if others chose inject it. Best way avoid Cold War confrontation is for African states prevent Chicom intrusion and to assist GOC to solve problem in manner which will make outside military help unnecessary. He pointed out that while there was some hope for peaceful accommodation between Soviet bloc and NATO powers, Chicoms committed to violence in pursuit their national aims. Not in interest Africa and world that their influence take hold in Africa.

In summary we hope Africans will come to assistance of Congo so Congolese will not need assistance from elsewhere.

African reps welcomed Secretary's remarks re keeping Cold War out of Africa and his assurance of cooperation with OAU.

Effort was made by Botsio to inject question of our military assistance to Congo into discussion. He took line grounding of US-supplied

---

[1] Source: National Archives, RG 59, Central Files 1964–66, POL 3 OAU. Confidential; Immediate. Drafted by Strong; cleared by Fredericks, James Ozzello in EUR, Williams, and Nathan Pelcovits in UNP; and approved by Palmer. Sent to Nairobi, Lagos, and Leopoldville, and repeated to Accra, Addis Ababa, Bonn, Brussels, Cairo, Conakry, Lisbon, London, Mogadiscio, New Delhi, Ouagadougou, Paris, Rome, Tunis, Yaounde, and USUN.

[2] Telegram 747 to Lagos, September 30, transmitted the text of a joint press communiqué worked out between Palmer and the OAU delegation. (Ibid.) Circular telegram 563, September 29, is not printed. (Ibid.)

[3] A memorandum of conversation is ibid.

planes used for combat operations essential to success OAU Commission's efforts bring about national reconciliation. He was supported by Kamel (UAR) and others appeared acquiesce his views. Secretary said US-supplied combat planes were under operational control of GOC and Commission should address itself in first instance to GOC on this matter. US would be happy to cooperate with any arrangements worked out between OAU and GOC in this connection.

Both Secretary and Murumbi said meeting had been most useful and expressed hope that it would provide basis for further fruitful cooperation between OAU Commission and the US. Murumbi said that Commission's real work will begin when it arrives Leo early October and he hoped that if Commission runs into difficulties there it may call upon US for assistance.

Several members of delegation expressed appreciation for efforts made by Dept officials to salvage mission to US by arranging meeting thereby avoiding rebuff to OAU while at same time permitting US position of principle. There was a good deal of mutual congratulation that efforts to resolve embarrassing impasse had been successful.

For Nairobi: You may inform Kenyatta our pleasure at successful outcome of mission and our strong hope it will lead continued close cooperation.

For Lagos: You may inform GON we have kept Embassy here closely informed. While we regret Nigeria not present, we entirely understand reasons and wholeheartedly appreciate GON efforts get Commission back on track. We hopeful our talks with delegation and our insistence on principle may help contribute to same objective.

For Leopoldville: You may assure Tshombe and Kasavubu that we have maintained principles our press statement, Sept. 23,[4] steered away from any tripartite meetings, and averted any meeting involving President—all points to which we understand GOC attaches importance. We have kept Congo Embassy fully informed and Murumbi planned to see Cardoso after lunch.

Rusk

---

[4] Telegram 748 to Leopoldville, September 23, transmitted the text of the September 23 press statement issued by the Department concerning the proposed visit of the OAU delegation to the United States. (Ibid., POL 23–9 THE CONGO)

272. Memorandum From the Chief of the Africa Division, Directorate of Plans, Central Intelligence Agency (Fields) to Director of Central Intelligence McCone[1]

Washington, October 2, 1964.

SUBJECT

Status of B–26 K Aircraft in the Congo

1. This memorandum is for the information of the Director of Central Intelligence.

2. During August 1964 the U.S. Air Force furnished three B–26 K aircraft to the Congo, and CIA furnished four B–26 B aircraft. The B–26 K's were furnished for a limited period and are scheduled for withdrawal from the Congo on 17 October 1964. It is Africa Division's understanding that the Department of Defense is prepared to extend this date for an additional period if requested to do so. In discussions with the Departments of State and Defense, Africa Division has taken the position that the extension of the B–26 K's in the Congo is a policy matter and that the request to the Department of Defense for an extension should originate with the Department of State. It was learned on 1 October 1964 that the Department of State intends to submit such a request.

3. From an operational standpoint, Africa Division and Special Operations Division think it necessary that the B–26 K's be retained in the Congo for an additional period of 60 days (or earlier if the situation changes in such a way as to make them unnecessary), and that the 13 USAF maintenance personnel for these aircraft remain until CIA-provided personnel are in position and checked out to maintain them. This view is based on the following considerations:

A. The Congolese Air Force is now operating from four widely dispersed bases (Leopoldville, Kamina, Bukavu, and Lisala). Except for Bukavu, other combat aircraft available (T–28's and T–6's) do not have adequate range to perform all necessary missions in support of the Congolese National Army. The effective T–28/T–6 combat radius under average conditions is 90 miles with little reserve left for time over target. The B–26 under average conditions has a combat radius of up to 500 miles with as much as an hour and a half over target.

B. The CIA senior air operations officer in the Congo has stated that the Congolese National Army troops do not perform effectively without air support visible overhead.

---

[1] Source: Central Intelligence Agency Files, Job 81–00966R, Box 1, Folder 11, Congo, 1960–1964. Secret. The memorandum was sent through Deputy Director for Plan Helms.

C. The B–26 aircraft have the additional advantages of a twin engine safety factor, better armament, a superior all-weather capability, and higher speed.

D. The B–26 B aircraft provided by the Agency are much inferior to the USAF B–26 K's. The Air Force has withdrawn B–26 B's from its inventory, and the Agency is planning to do the same because of certain structural deficiencies in the B–26 B as well as the high maintenance factor due to old age. The [*less than 1 line not declassified*] pilots in the Congo have shown an awareness of the structural deficiencies and a reluctance to utilize B–26 B aircraft.

5. The Director may wish to use the views expressed above should his opinions on the importance of the B–26 K aircraft be sought.

Glenn D. Fields
Chief, Africa Division[2]

[2] A stamped signature on the memorandum indicates that John H. Waller signed for Fields.

---

273. Telegram From the Embassy in the Congo to the Department of State[1]

Leopoldville, October 5, 1964, noon.

1354. Re Department telegram 854.[2]

1. Last night as per reference telegram I told Tshombe we planned withdraw two C–130's soon, suggesting he might wish get some political mileage out of this at Cairo. Tshombe did not react to this suggestion, but predictably expressed disappointment and concern over withdrawal. Since it seemed from his circuitous remarks that he feared we might be starting to pull plug on him militarily in response to OAU pressures, I paraphrased carefully for him Secretary's remarks to OAU group (Department circular telegram 569)[3] indicating that USG would

[1] Source: National Archives, RG 59, Central Files 1964–66, POL 23–9 THE CONGO. Top Secret. Repeated to CINCMEAFSA, DOD, and ARMISH MAAG Tehran.

[2] Telegram 854 to Leopoldville, October 3, instructed Godley to see Tshombe prior to his departure for Cairo to inform him of the U.S. decision to withdraw one C–130 soon and a second C–130 at a subsequent date. (Ibid.)

[3] Document 271.

still be needed for help in civil rehabilitation program. I reminded him GOC had 10 C–47's we had given them and that he should not count on C–130's for civil rehabilitation program. *Comment:* Despite foregoing, there is big psychological payoff for USG when first impact shipment of relief goods can be brought into newly liberated city by US planes, and we intend where priorities permit, continue accede to GOC, Belgian, and UN requests for this kind of lift.

2. Assume reference telegram 854 indicating our proposed C–130 withdrawal program supercedes STRIKE's STRJ 3–OD10372 and that in line with flexibility re withdrawal last two C–130's which we proposed, these will not be pulled out October 18.[4]

Godley

[4] Telegram 879 to Leopoldville, October 7, stated that the first C–130 would leave Leopoldville on October 8 and instructed Godley to make no public announcement concerning the withdrawal of the C–130s in order to prevent the impression that the United States was abandoning Tshombe. (National Archives, RG 59, Central Files 1964–66, POL 23–9 THE CONGO)

---

274. Memorandum From William H. Brubeck of the National Security Council Staff to the President's Special Assistant for National Security Affairs (Bundy)[1]

Washington, October 5, 1964.

SUBJECT

US Nationals in Stanleyville

There is a very real possibility that, at any time over the next few weeks, the rebels in Stanleyville may begin to abuse or kill American hostages there—five official Americans, held briefly in prison and now in house arrest, and up to fifteen other Americans (presumably missionary), precise number and whereabouts unknown. If that happens (and we will probably have little advance warning) we will either have to move quickly with pre-planned force to get our people out or tolerate publicly Americans being killed in a situation of primitive anarchy without timely response on our part to try to prevent it. There are

[1] Source: Johnson Library, National Security File, Files of McGeorge Bundy, "B". Top Secret.

5–800 Europeans also in Stanleyville, mostly Belgian but various others (British, Greeks, Italians, etc.). There will be far less enthusiasm from these countries for contingency planning, both because their people are relatively safe unless and until the US actually uses force to rescue our people, and because they have nationals in other parts of rebel held territory whose danger would be heightened if they intervened militarily in Stanleyville.

While I believe we should consult with Brussels, therefore, and (depending on reactions there) perhaps elsewhere, I do not believe our own, independent contingency planning should wait on consultation. If we delay, we may be caught in a crisis with no capacity to act, or handicapped by Belgian reluctance to act. To be realistic, our planning must include the possible need for quick capture of the city.[2]

Rebel leadership in Stanleyville has made it clear that the official Americans are hostage against air attacks on Stanleyville (they apparently don't blame or threaten Europeans). It is also clear that they don't fully control the Jeunesse guerrillas or the population, and are fearful that air attack on Stanleyville or perhaps even on other towns will cause mob violence they can't control against Americans in Stanleyville (it is widely believed that US planes bombed Albertville *after* Europeans were evacuated and this has terrorized rebels and civilians in rebel-held towns). And indeed, the relatively heavily-armed B–26s represent such an escalation of anything ever experienced in this part of Africa that they have caused a profound psychological shock which contributes to this panicky and potentially dangerous state among the Congolese. There is already some indication of abuse of the official Americans (Khartoum's 138 attached)[3] and much evidence of the acute danger of aerial attacks on towns (see Bujumbura's 333 attached).[4] Also an attaché message from Leo regarding last week's B–26 attack on a military camp at Kindu says that "FBIS intercepts of rebel radio transmissions at Kindu clearly indicate B–26 strikes on Kindu military barracks and attack on military camp at Lofandu had prime effect in shaking up population in and around Kindu. . . . Tone indicates rebels genuinely worried over control of population." JANAF CS–82. See also FBIS 47 attached.[5]

This problem is going to get worse as the Congo army's offensive moves toward Stanleyville and pressure for air attack on towns increases (Tshombe was delighted by the reports of heavy damage and

[2] The last sentence of the paragraph is handwritten.

[3] Telegram 138 from Khartoum, October 4, is attached but not printed.

[4] Telegram 333 from Bujumbura, October 5, is attached but not printed. A copy is in National Archives, RG 59, Central Files 1964–66, POL 23–9 THE CONGO.

[5] Both are attached but not printed.

casualties in B–26 raid on Kindu). If we don't help him, he will shortly be able to use T–6s manned by South Africans, over which we will have no control.

If this analysis is right we should at once start CINCSTRIKE on contingency planning, obviously as discreetly as possible but not waiting for European consultations. At the same time, we can ask State to consider the feasibility of consultations with Belgians and others as appropriate to try to multilateralize planning and to put the total problem before the Secretary, and, if he thinks it necessary, put it before the President at an early date. I am going to a 5:00 PM meeting at State on this problem and would propose to take the above line if you agree.

Yes[6]

See me

B

[6] This option is checked, and a handwritten notation reads: "but it should be made very very clear that any such course is last resort. First we must use & re-use warnings & restraints & cooperation with Europeans. CINCSTRIKE is a damned blunt instrument for this—McGB."

275. Telegram From the Department of State to the Embassy in Belgium[1]

Washington, October 5, 1964, 3:54 p.m.

636. For Ambassador:

You requested communicate following orally to Spaak in Gov. Harriman's name leaving summary memorandum if you consider desirable.

We appreciate continuing efforts which your government has made in furthering our common aims in the Congo in pursuance Spaak–Harriman August talks. Belgian response has been major factor in stiffening internal security of Congo, affording hope that rebellion can be contained and, hopefully, beginning made in rolling it back. Such a posture of strength, coupled with a Congolese attitude of rea-

[1] Source: National Archives, RG 59, Central Files 1964–66, POL 23–9 THE CONGO. Confidential. Drafted by Palmer and Schaufele in AF/CWG, cleared by Lang and Appling, and approved by Harriman. Repeated to Leopoldville.

sonableness and flexibility, may make it possible for progress on political negotiations which would insure a continued moderate, pro-Western government and at same time reduce to a minimum bloodshed and economic and social dislocation arising from rebellion.

We have been particularly encouraged by steps you have recently taken to supply "equipes Polyvalentes" which could ensure a stable administration and development of Congo in future. We have also been pleased at your action in sending Rothschild to Leopoldville which will, we are confident, help greatly in assuring that Tshombe receives sound advice both in dealing with his internal problems and in adopting a cooperative and flexible relationship with OAU Commission.

As you know, we sent C–130's to Congo to meet special emergency. Therefore, because the original purpose for sending them to the Congo no longer obtains, because they have received an inordinate amount of publicity and because of urgent needs to discharge our heavy worldwide commitments elsewhere, we are planning at an early date to begin withdrawal of our C–130's and joint task force which accompanies it. We must be sure therefore that GOC has sufficient logistic support airlift capability to maintain its military effort, including additional responsibilities which will be placed upon it when Van der Walle plan goes into action. It is considered opinion our civilian and military officials in Congo that after necessary positioning of troops and equipment to implement plan, sufficient airlift capability exists in FAC and Air Congo to meet anticipated needs except for possible special heavy hauls. Problem, however, is to assure that existing Congolese airlift capability is operational. We understand problems that you have been having in providing air crews and maintenance and supply personnel for C–47's and H–21 helicopters. We greatly hope that letter which we now understand Tshombe has sent you will make it possible for you to supply required personnel to put these Congolese planes in the air, thereby relieving us of temporary responsibilities we have assumed and which have continued much longer than we had anticipated. This step would make it possible for U.S. to withdraw on a phased basis four C–130's and cease using one or two other aircraft with U.S. markings for unusual missions such as C–47 which has been performing reconnaissance and other functions in defense of Bukavu because of unavailability of FAC aircraft.

A further problem relates to supply of rockets and ammunition. As you know, airlift of such items from Belgium to Congo is expensive, hazardous, and politically delicate in terms of transit through Wheelus Air Base and at Kano, as well as overflight rights other African countries. We are most pleased that our respective representatives have now made progress in determining recurring needs for ammunition in the

Congo and that you are instituting necessary arrangements to supply ammo on a regular basis by sea which would eliminate further emergency airlifts. We strongly hope that it will be possible to continue to proceed on this basis and thereby to eliminate any need for further emergency airlifts.

From recent communications we gather that continued supply of ammo is posing some financial problems for you. We sincerely hope in this regard that you will find it possible to overcome these difficulties in order that flow of rockets and ammunition so necessary for GOC military effort will not be interrupted. In this connection, I would appreciate your thoughts on possibilities of approaching other Western European countries again for possible assistance which they might be able to render both in form of ammunition and otherwise. We realize that our talks with representatives these countries in August were largely inconclusive, but I believe we must continue to impress on them importance of stability in Central Africa and urge them do their part. In this connection, we would most willingly support such approaches as you would find it possible to make in other Western European capitals. As I have said, I would greatly appreciate your views on best way to go about this as matter high priority.

Please be assured that we will continue to accept and discharge our obligations in Congo in closest harmony and consultation with you and your Government. It would greatly assist us in our planning both with respect to Congo and our worldwide obligations, if you could let me have your earliest possible views on foregoing problems, including your estimate as to when we can expect air personnel for C–47's to arrive in the Congo.

Rusk

---

276. Telegram From the Embassy in Belgium to the Department of State[1]

Brussels, October 5, 1964, 8 p.m.

614. Re Deptel 636.[2] Saw Spaak this morning and communicated orally to him Gov Harriman's message per reftel. Re Belgians fur-

[1] Source: National Archives, RG 59, Central Files 1964–66, POL 23–9 THE CONGO. Confidential. Received at 4:05 p.m. and repeated to Leopoldville.

[2] Document 275.

nishing ammo and adequate sealift, tactfully expressed "expectation" rather than "hope" that GOB will continue to supply rockets and ammo regular basis by sea so as to avoid costly emergency airlift. (My feeling was that to use word "hope" might weaken presentation and lead certain Belgian officials to think that if they did not arrange adequate, timely sealift of ammo, we would perhaps supply both airlift and ammo itself.)

Spaak replied as follows:

1. Belgians realize US airlift of ammo to Congo was to meet special emergency and understand reasons why we must soon begin phased withdrawal from Congo of C–130s. He also agrees Belg aircrews should be sent to Congo soonest now Tshombe has signed necessary letter. He does not know schedule for sending such crews but will inquire of MOD and endeavor expedite their departure. He promised to let us know about this ASAP.

2. He agrees Belgium should supply rockets and ammo to meet needs of ANC and adequate and timely sealift and will ask his people to look into this problem with a view to assuring necessary arrangements.

3. Spaak does not believe other Western European countries will be willing at present to provide military or other assistance in addition to what they are now doing because of uncertainties and instabilities in Congo and hostility of certain African and non-aligned states to Tshombe govt. Therefore, he does not believe it worthwhile to approach other Western European countries for assistance at this time.

4. Spaak then made following general comments on Congo picture. While militarily things not going badly politically Congo is chaotic and future most uncertain. Furthermore econ picture is deteriorating. Serious situation will have to be faced in a few months. Spaak understands rebellion has resulted in reduction of about one third of Congo exports with obvious long term effect on Congo foreign exchange budget, especially when rebel territories regained and sizeable additional imports necessary to avoid galloping inflation with serious political and social repercussions.

Despite earlier impression to contrary (Embtel 577)[3] Tshombe does not seem willing to reorganize his govt by end October. He advances number of reasons why this would be very difficult and why Kasavubu would be opposed to including certain Congolese leaders. While Bomboko ready to join Tshombe govt, Adoula much more reserved and insists that Tshombe negotiate with Gbenye. However since Gbenye un-

---

[3] Dated September 30. (National Archives, RG 59, Central Files 1964–66, POL AFR THE CONGO)

willing to have anything to do with Tshombe there obviously no hope of any talks between them. Spaak said he had reached conclusion that GOC Gbenye negotiations neither feasible nor desirable.

While Tshombe has engaging personality and probably considerable public support in Congo he is not a team player. Recently he has shown increasing authoritarian tendencies which in themselves would not be bad if he had the capability of organizing and running Congo. Spaak doubts he has such capability and said Tshombe obviously needs help. However Tshombe does not trust Africans and relies largely on Belgian and other white advisors.

Spaak said this attitude of Tshombe's raised a major question in mind of Belgian Govt. Question is extent to which Belgian advisors and technical assistance should assume authority and hence responsibility for taking over the de facto running of the Congo under plan such as Rothschild has in mind (Leoville 1361 to Dept).[4] Spaak said there is difference of opinion within GOB on this. While all agree that Belgium must supply adequate technical assistance, there are those who have serious reservations about the wisdom of assuming considerable de facto authority and responsibility as this will leave Belgium open to charges of neo-colonialism. Spaak said Belgians must of course act with circumspection and tact so as to reduce vulnerability to such charges.

I asked Spaak whether he meant that concept of "equipes Polyvalentes" might not be implemented because of risk of charges of neo-colonialism. He replied furnishing of technicians not the issue but rather it was degree of their authority and responsibility which raised questions. This issue would be considered rather in the next several days. I commented that while fully agreeing that Belgian assistance should be handled in way to make it least vulnerable to charges of neo-colonialism, I personally did not believe Congo could be stabilized without very substantial Belgian advice and assistance to Congolese which inevitably would carry with it a degree of responsibility. My feeling was that without such substantial Belgian advice and technical assistance the Congo could come apart at the seams since Congolese themselves not yet capable of administering and managing their own affairs.

Spaak replied he inclined to agree but whole Congolese picture chaotic and uncertain and many people in Belgium reluctant to have Belgians assume positions of authority and responsibility, even if camouflaged with Congolese cover, because they remember how entire world had turned on Belgium in 1960.

Comment: Personally believe Spaak will be prepared to see Belgians assume minimum necessary responsibility because alternative

---

[4] Dated October 5. (Ibid., POL 15 THE CONGO)

would seem to be to let Congo go by default. Rothschild with whom we talked separately shares this view. However decision on Rothschild plan will probably not be taken before end of this week or early next week.

MacArthur

277. Letter From President Johnson to Congolese President Kasavubu[1]

Washington, October 6, 1964.

Dear Mr. President:

I thank you very much for your letter of September 25, regarding the visit to the United States by a delegation from the Ad Hoc Commission of the Organization of African Unity.[2]

By now you will have heard from Ambassador Godley that in our discussions with the delegation, we have steadfastly stood on the principles that we could not discuss matters affecting the sovereignty of the Congo, including the question of our aid relationship. When this point was accepted by the delegation, a friendly meeting with the Secretary of State was arranged. It is my hope that this meeting demonstrates that the United States intends to abide by international rules respecting national sovereignty and, at the same time, has emphasized the sincerity of the United States Government in offering any appropriate aid to the OAU Commission in the fulfillment of its task.

The United States continues to believe that OAU participation in the search for solutions to the Congo problem, requested by the Congo itself, can be a valuable contribution to the progress of the whole of Africa, I have been pleased to note that your Government has maintained a calm and constructive attitude by indicating its willingness to cooperate fully with the Commission within the terms of its mandate, and

[1] Source: National Archives, RG 59, Central Files 1964–66, POL 3 OAU. Limited Official Use. A typed notation on the letter reads: "Signed original given to Congo Task Force to dispatch to Embassy. See tel. 664. To Brussels 10/7." Telegram 664 to Brussels, October 7, transmitted the text of the President's letter to deliver to Cardoso, who was en route to Leopoldville, noting that a signed copy was being forwarded to Leopoldville. (Ibid., POL 7 AFR)

[2] Document 264.

by reiterating its earlier invitation to the Commission to visit the Congo.

The Congo's own efforts augmented by those of the OAU and its other friends will soon, I am sure, assure the restoration of order in the Congo, permitting it to proceed on the vital task of economic and social development. In your efforts to accomplish these objectives, you have my continuing best wishes for success.

Sincerely,

Lyndon B. Johnson[3]

[3] Printed from a copy that indicates President Johnson signed the original.

278. Telegram From the Department of State to the Embassy in Burundi[1]

Washington, October 8, 1964, 3:52 p.m.

217. Ref: Bujumbura's 91 to Nairobi, repeated all posts.[2] Americans Stanleyville.

In addition indications contained reftel that Gbenye possibly in Stanleyville, FBIS reports rebel radio Kindu broadcast of October 7 transmitted official telegram from Olenga to "President of the Congolese People's Republic in Stanleyville" and other rebel addressees. Telegram reads in part: "Giving you official order. If NATO aircraft bomb and kill Congolese civilian population, please kill one foreigner for each Congolese of your region."

Please pass above and substance reftel to ICRC reps. You should urge ICRC attempt communicate with Gbenye with view to resuming ICRC mission ASAP.

Rusk

[1] Source: National Archives, RG 59, Central Files 1964–66, POL 23–9 THE CONGO. Confidential; Immediate; Limdis. Drafted by Berlind in AF/CWG, cleared by Diamanti in AFC, and approved by Palmer. Also sent to Nairobi, Leopoldville, and the U.S. Mission in Geneva.

[2] Telegram 91 from Bujumbura to Nairobi, October 8, reported that a radio message from Stanleyville carrying the "usual tirade against Tshombe and American imperialists" received in Bujumbura on October 8 had been signed by Gbenye. (Ibid., SOC 3 RED CROSS)

279. Telegram From the Department of State to the Embassy in Belgium[1]

Washington, October 8, 1964, 6:28 p.m.

669. We are anxious receive on most urgent basis authoritative Belgian (Spaak if possible) appraisal extent of present and future danger to foreign community Stanleyville and degree to which this likely be affected by air strikes and other military actions against rebel positions both inside and outside urban areas. We are of course deeply concerned re public rebel reprisal threats directed primarily against Americans and would be grateful for Belgian assessment re reasons for singling out US. You should also endeavor ascertain whether Belgians have any plans or thoughts re measures which could be taken (beyond current ICRC efforts) to improve security foreign community in Stan, including their protection against reprisals. You should also utilize occasion ascertain whether Belgians in position either overtly or covertly to assist in protecting American lives and whether they have any assets, official or private, which we could utilize for this purpose.

In raising this matter, you should feel free to draw on messages from Leo and Bujumbura which indicate increasingly strident tone of rebel threats against US and to lesser extent other foreign hostages (see particularly FBIS 62 of 7 October "Olenga Telegram" being sent septel).[2] You should also make clear our deepening concern re situation foreigners Stanleyville and dilemma that would be posed for us both if rebels were to carry out reprisals against US and Belgian nationals under their control.

Request reply soonest.[3]

Rusk

---

[1] Source: National Archives, RG 59, Central Files 1964–66, POL 23–9 THE CONGO. Secret; Immediate; Limdis. Drafted by Palmer, cleared by Williams and McKillop, and approved by Palmer. Repeated to Leopoldville.

[2] See Document 278.

[3] Telegram 675 to Brussels, October 8, asked the Embassy to advise urgently whether appropriate Belgian officials (including Davignon and Rothschild) would be available to discuss the Congo with Fredericks and INR/RAF Director Robert Good in Brussels on October 13 and 14. (National Archives, RG 59, Central Files 1964–66, POL 23–9 THE CONGO)

280. Telegram From the Department of State to the Embassy in the Congo[1]

Washington, October 11, 1964, 1:18 p.m.

922. Re: Leo 1394 and 1408.[2] Dept believes use of South African mercenary pilots by Tshombe will become such serious political liability both for GOC and USG and will so endanger US personnel Stanleyville that we must take very firm line with him against their further use. We must make every effort to persuade him abandon project, making clear that we cannot agree to be associated in any way with SA airforce operation.[3] We consider it essential that GOB make equally strong parallel approach.

Embassy Leo: You should see Tshombe soonest after his return. You are authorized to proceed along following lines in attempting achieve objective of getting GOC abandon South African pilot project:

1. You should make clear to Tshombe grave USG concern over venture which can redound only to US and GOC disadvantage and play into hands of extremists who seek to discredit him personally and challenge sovereignty GOC. At time when Tshombe should be seeking strengthen position in OAU, he would be creating opposite impression by introducing additional South Africans, particularly in conspicuous role of killing Africans from air. He should appreciate that mercenaries are probably most vulnerable aspect of his relations with other Africans. We and other qualified observers are convinced that militarily these planes are not necessary for Congolese military success. We convinced planes we have furnished are sufficient to do job. Thus GOC by employing South African pilots would not be adding military strength commensurate with serious political disadvantages.

We recognize that Tshombe may have serious doubts about US intentions in continuing to make available to him air support for ANC operations and thus has undertaken South African pilot project to give himself an independent capability. We suggest you sound him out on

---

[1] Source: National Archives, RG 59, Central Files 1964–66, DEF 6–5 THE CONGO. Secret; Flash; Limdis. Drafted by Palmer; cleared by Lang, Brubeck, Fredericks, Tyler, and Fields in CIA; and approved by Ball. Also sent to Brussels and repeated to Rome, CINCSTRIKE for Ramsey, and Pretoria.

[2] Both dated October 7. (Ibid.)

[3] On October 11, McCone raised with Rusk the question of the prospective Department cable warning Tshombe not to use South African mercenary pilots or face the consequence of U.S. withdrawal of pilots and other forms of support. McCone urged the Secretary to moderate such threats in the final draft of the cable. He pointed out that the United States had provided only 20 pilots [*text not declassified*]. (Memorandum for the record; Central Intelligence Agency Files, DCI/McCone Files, Job 80B01285A, DCI McCone Memos for the Record, 08 Jul–10 Sep 64)

this and, if appropriate, you may reaffirm that US tactical aircraft now on loan to GOC will continue to be fully available for action against appropriate military targets for duration of military need. In this connection, you should make clear our understanding that aircraft will be used only against essential military targets and within spirit of Geneva Conventions, thus avoiding towns and cities. We hope Tshombe would readily accept this line of reasoning, not only for humanitarian reasons but also in interest economic future of country and eventual national reconciliation.

If helpful, you can specifically reiterate that C–130 lift will be phased out only as adequate C–47 lift becomes available and that, with appropriate mutual understanding re South African pilot project, B–26s can be retained beyond present Oct. 17 expiration date. You can also assure him of continued availability of T–28s on basis of similar understanding. FYI In offering such oral assurances you should of course stay strictly within limits of carefully formulated terms of foregoing. End FYI.

2. If this argumentation and these assurances fail to elicit assurances from Tshombe that he will abandon project, you should attempt persuade him at least to defer movement from Leo pending joint resolution of this issue.

3. At any point in this sequence and in order to dissuade him from project or persuade him defer, you are authorized use in ascending order any or all following additional points:

a. US cannot agree airlift additional T–6's from Italy. (If you are sure that we retain title and withdrawal rights over two operational T–6's referred reftel, you may also say we would have to insist on their withdrawal.)

b. Since we cannot agree to be associated in any way with South African airforce operations, we would be forced withdraw US supplied aircraft from Lisala-Coq vicinity so long as T–6's active in that area.

c. In absence of an appropriate mutual understanding re South African pilot project, we would find it impossible extend B–26 agreement covering their loan to GOC beyond Oct. 17 expiry date and aircraft must consequently be grounded beforehand to prepare them mechanically for return to US.

d. You have full authorization of USG to take above steps. In addition, after receiving your report, USG may take such serious view of situation that it may feel obliged to take further steps to dissociate self from this project. At minimum, therefore, Tshombe should hold South Africans at Leo pending further reaction from USG.

4. We leave to your discretion how you use foregoing authorities, i.e. in one session with Tshombe or spread over several. Moreover, you

are authorized take such consequential actions as may be required in connection any moves Tshombe may make, e.g. withdrawing US supplied planes from Lisala area or preparing B–26's for return US if despite your efforts he deploys planes with SA pilots to operational areas. We would of course wish make every effort prevent any of these moves from becoming public at this time.

5. Given present deployment date Oct. 14, it most important we know as soon as possible where we stand with Tshombe on this issue so that we can decide what if any further steps we should take to protect US interests. You may therefore have to play your cards quickly. Objective must therefore be either to get satisfactory assurances from Tshombe or convey advance warning of failure to Dept in time permit us take any subsequent actions before movement actually takes place.[4]

Emb Brussels: You should inform GOB of foregoing soonest—today if possible but otherwise Oct. 12 in Fredericks talks. You should make every effort secure Belgian agreement to make urgent parallel approach to GOB in Leo not later than Oct. 13. Hope also GOB will enlist cooperation Bouzin (who we understand in Brussels) and Van der Walle in trying get GOC to understand importance dropping project or as minimum blocking operational deployment.

Rusk

---

[4] In telegram 1456 from Leopoldville, October 12, Godley stated that he would put the matter firmly to Tshombe after he returned to Leopoldville. The Ambassador pointed out, however, that he was unlikely to get a straight answer, although the Prime Minister would probably agree in principle. (National Archives, RG 59, Central Files 1964–66, DEF 6–5 THE CONGO)

281. Memorandum for the Record[1]

Washington, October 12, 1964.

M. Struelens called me from the Congo Embassy at 7:00 p.m. to say that he had just talked for a half hour to Tshombe in Paris,[2] and told me the following:

1. Tshombe is issuing tonight a statement in Paris denying any intention to use "pilots of South African nation" in their operations in the Congo. Although I tried to discourage this as a little conspicuous, the Congo Embassy here plans to tell reporters about the Paris statement.[3]

2. Tshombe is telegraphing Leo tonight to direct that any plans for use of South African pilots should be suspended pending his return. He will look into the matter as soon as he gets there and is prepared to talk to Godley at the same time.

3. Tshombe professes that he was not really aware of the South African project but agrees that it would be a bad mistake.

4. If in the judgment of his government they have additional requirements for aircraft and personnel, he will take this up with us through Godley.

5. Tshombe plans to visit the UN in November.

6. Tshombe is prepared to set a date for a meeting of his "Council of Chiefs" as soon as "the military situation permits."

7. Tshombe is agreeable in principle to the idea of a preliminary representative or delegation to Leo to pave the way for a full-fledged mission by the OAU Ad Hoc Commission.[4]

B

---

[1] Source: Johnson Library, National Security File, Hamilton File, Congo (B). No classification marking. Drafted by Brubeck. Copies were sent to McGeorge Bundy and Palmer.

[2] Telegram 926 to Leopoldville, October 12, reported that Brubeck and Palmer emphasized the very deep U.S. concern over the South African pilot project and the problems it would create for both governments to Tshombe's special political adviser, Michael Struelens. Struelens readily accepted their points and promised to telephone Tshombe in Paris that evening. (National Archives, RG 59, Central Files 1964–66, DEF 6-5 THE CONGO)

[3] Telegram 2086 from Paris, October 13, transmitted the text of the communiqué released by Tshombe, which categorically denied that pilots of South African nationality had been or would be used in any sort of military operations in the Congo. (Ibid., POL 23–9 THE CONGO)

[4] Telegram 934 to Leopoldville, October 13, informed the Embassy that, in view of Tshombe's press statement, the instructions contained in telegram 922 had been overtaken and the démarche to him on this subject should not be made. (Ibid., DEF 6–5 THE CONGO)

282. Telegram From the Embassy in Belgium to the Department of State[1]

Brussels, October 13, 1964, 3:45 p.m.

666. During Fredericks' conversation with Davignon and other FonOff reps dealing with non-Congolese personnel held in Stanleyville (being reported separately)[2] it was agreed that Belgian and U.S. reps in Leoville meeting in greatest secrecy in limited group would consider hostage problem in light military developments. Davignon stated that Belgians fully understood U.S. concern and that Van der Walle will keep U.S. reps particularly well informed his planning and operations as they affect Stan, keeping in mind ultimate necessity for decision or actions in this area affecting U.S. citizens and personnel.

Davignon further remarked that, of course, Belgian officials in Stan would give as much help as possible to U.S. colleagues in difficult situation. Such Belgian assistance facilitated by fact that Belgians are aware of location of U.S. personnel in Stan.

MacArthur

---

[1] Source: National Archives, RG 59, Central Files 1964–66, POL 23–9 THE CONGO. Secret; Priority; Limdis. Repeated to Leopoldville and CINCSTRIKE/CINCMEAFSA for POLAD.

[2] Telegram 679 from Brussels, October 13, reported Fredericks' discussion of the welfare of the foreign community in Stanleyville with Belgian officials. (Ibid.)

283. Memorandum From the Department of State Executive Secretary (Read) to the President's Special Assistant for National Security Affairs (Bundy)[1]

Washington, October 14, 1964.

SUBJECT

Congo (Leopoldville)

A Congolese rebel message was intercepted this morning from the rebel commander in Stanleyville to the Commander-in-Chief located at Paulis, stating that five American planes had bombed rebel-held Burma and requesting authority to "kill all Americans who are in the liberated zone." We have no indication as yet of what reply, if any, has been made, but we are continuing to monitor.

While there is a possibility that the message may be another of several lesser warnings we have received, the source and nature of the communication lead us to believe that it should be treated as more than a threat.

The Department immediately dispatched an appeal to the Prime Minister of Kenya, Mr. Kenyatta in his capacity as Chairman of the Organization of African Unity Commission on the Congo, asking him to urge the rebel leaders not to harm Americans in rebel-held territories.[2] As a result of Ambassador MacArthur's representations made on telephonic instructions,[3] the Belgian Foreign Office is trying to get a message to the rebel leaders through their Embassy at Bujumbura to use all persuasions to safeguard the lives of our people. Ambassador Godley in Leopoldville has seen Prime Minister Tshombe who states that he will issue an appeal to the rebels not to dishonor the Congo's name by mistreating foreigners in the areas which they control. The GOC has since issued such an appeal over the radio in Leo.[4]

---

[1] Source: Johnson Library, National Security File, Country File, Congo, Vol. V. Top Secret.

[2] Telegram 1341 to Nairobi, October 14, instructed the Ambassador to urge Kenyatta to intervene immediately with the Stanleyville authorities to stop a deed that would shock the conscience of the world and do irreparable harm to Africa. (National Archives, RG 59, Central Files 1964–66, PS 7–6 THE CONGO)

[3] At 12:33 p.m. on October 14, Rusk telephoned MacArthur and asked the Ambassador to see if the Belgians could get a message to their people in Stanleyville and urge the overriding necessity of protecting innocent people. (Ibid., Rusk Files: Lot 72 D 192, Telephone Conversations)

[4] Telegram 1481 from Leopoldville, October 14, transmitted the text of the Congolese Government's appeal, which declared that the killing of any hostages would be a shocking violation of the Geneva Conventions and that such senseless and brutal killings would constitute a shameful stain on the national honor of the Congolese people. (Ibid., RG 59, Central Files 1964–66, POL 23–9 THE CONGO)

We are once again making certain that the T–28 fighters and B–26 bombers now on loan from the United States to the Congolese Government are under adequate control and following current guidance which is calculated to minimize risks against the lives of Americans in rebel-held areas.

Since this matter will be in the news here at any moment we are consulting urgently what to advise the President when it breaks and we will be in touch with you on this subject shortly.

H. Mills[5]

---

[5] Hawthorne Mills signed for Read above Read's typed signature.

---

284. Memorandum From the Deputy Director for Plans, Central Intelligence Agency (Helms) to the Under Secretary of State for Political Affairs (Harriman)[1]

Washington, October 14, 1964.

SUBJECT

Stanleyville

1. I share your deep concern about the official and non-official Americans held as hostages by rebel authorities in Stanleyville. The attached report—the first we have received which contained detail—reminds us sharply of the jeopardy in which the Americans find themselves.[2] Given the mercurial temperament of the Congolese, the specific anti-Americanism of the Stanleyville rebels based on their conviction that the U.S. is responsible for Tshombe's attacks against them, and the likelihood of further rebel reverses, we must, I believe, conclude that Americans are in grave danger. Moreover, as Congolese forces move toward Stanleyville during the coming few weeks, the vulnerability of the American hostages will sharply increase.

---

[1] Source: Library of Congress, Manuscript Division, Harriman Papers, Box 861, Congo (3). Secret.

[2] Attached to the original is intelligence report TDCS DB 315/01019–64, October 14, describing the Congo rebels' mistreatment of U.S. consular personnel since the fall of Stanleyville. It also reported that Gbenye had told ICRC representative Senn in September that he was afraid he could not control the situation and did not know what the reaction of the rebel troops would be if he released the Americans.

2. I know you will agree that this information lends a new urgency to contingency planning for the rescue of the Americans which we and CINCSTRIKE have been conducting. You will recall that we sent a planner to Leopoldville in early September and since then have prepositioned other personnel and equipment in the Congo. It is our understanding that CINCSTRIKE is preparing to send four officers to Leopoldville to do on-the-ground, detailed contingency planning. We, of course, stand ready to help them in any way we can.

3. We are continuing our efforts to acquire information on the Stanleyville situation and will keep you informed of our results.

Richard Helms

---

285. Memorandum From Arthur McCafferty of the National Security Council Staff to the President's Special Assistant for National Security Affairs (Bundy)[1]

Washington, October 15, 1964.

SUBJECT

Planning for evacuation of U.S. personnel from Stanleyville

JCS has requested CINCSTRIKE to prepare to implement either of two plans previously prepared for this evacuation. CINCSTRIKE has replied that neither of the plans was appropriate at present and is forwarding a new plan (USJTF OPLAN 514—Ready Move 3).

The exact details of this plan are not yet available in Washington but from the attached messages the following outline can be seen:

1. Mission is to seize and secure Stanleyville, evacuate non-Congolese, and turn city over to friendly government.

2. Intelligence estimates indicate the enemy situation in Stanleyville represents a greater capability than existed in early September, therefore a larger force is necessary. This would comprise a small air strike force and an airborne battalion for initial assault, with a second airborne battalion ready at a forward staging base to be called forward if required.

---

[1] Source: Johnson Library, National Security File, Country File, Congo, Vol. V, Memos & Miscellaneous, 9/64–10/64. Top Secret.

3. Two routing plans are presented, with plan I–B being recommended.

I–B calls for staging through Wheelus with a D-day, H-hour, 55 hours and 55 minutes after the execution order.
I–C calls for staging through Liberia and Ascension Island with a D-day, H-hour, 59 hours and 50 minutes after the execution order.

4. The forces currently under Defcon 4 alert for this operation consist of

2 battalions from the 101st Airborne Division
16 F4C (fighter) aircraft
60 C–130 aircraft
20 KC 135 SAC Tanker aircraft.

Art

286. Telegram From the Department of State to the Embassy in the Congo[1]

Washington, October 15, 1964, 2:59 p.m.

958. Through other channels we are ordering stand-down T–28's and B–26's. In addition you are hereby directed to suspend any other flights by official US or US controlled aircraft over rebel territory, e.g. C–47's, C–130's or other aircraft.

Without disclosing this action, you should see Tshombe immediately and, against background very deep concern re situation Stanleyville, and on basis of seeking his cooperation urge him to suspend air operations by T–28's and B–26's for 72 hours. FYI—Purpose is to achieve suspension by persuasion without overt resort to assertion of US control. End FYI. You should explain that we find this action necessary in order review with him and at highest levels of USG problems which we face in connection American and other foreigners at Stanleyville, pointing out that it would be neither in GOC, US nor anybody else's interests if continued air strikes by US supplied planes result in reprisals. Purpose of 72 hour suspension is to give US and CongoLeo

[1] Source: National Archives, RG 59, Central Files 1964–66, POL 23–9 THE CONGO. Top Secret; Flash; Limdis. Drafted by Palmer, cleared by Vance in DOD and Brubeck, and approved by Rusk. Repeated to Brussels.

time assess problems connected with use of airstrikes and examine alternative means securing safety civilian population Stan.

You should make every effort persuade Tshombe cooperate with foregoing. If, however, he responds by threatening put T–6's with South African mercenaries into action or to take other steps such as inviting South African intervention, you should warn him that he would thereby precipitate situation in which we might well be forced withdraw our military assistance to GOC.

Related subject: You should also take immediately all possible precautions to assure that no additional official American personnel fall into rebel hands even though this may necessitate evacuation Consulate Bukavu, USIA Luluabourg and Coquilhatville, withdrawal official US military personnel from exposed areas, etc. Further guidance re Leopoldville will follow but meanwhile you should initiate any required actions along foregoing lines with respect personnel outside capital.

For Brussels. You should inform FonOff on closely held basis we are asking Tshombe cooperation in suspension for a few days of air operations over rebel territory. You should explain purpose is avoid provocation any reprisal against Europeans while trying urgently find with Tshombe means of solving European hostage problem. Advise FonOff we will shortly have further message regarding approach we hope use with Tshombe in handling this hostage problem and will be seeking their assistance.

Rusk

---

287. Telegram From the Embassy in the Congo to the Department of State[1]

Leopoldville, October 16, 1964, 6 a.m.

1497. I will, of course, endeavor see Tshombe first thing this morning carry out instructions contained Department telegram 958.[2] Sending appropriate [*1 line not declassified*] insure grounding T–28's and B–26's. Also repeating information contained Department instruc-

---

[1] Source: National Archives, RG 59, Central Files 1964–66, POL 23–9 THE CONGO. Top Secret; Flash; Limdis. Passed to the White House, DOD, and CIA.

[2] Document 286.

tions Bukavu and Elisabethville re grounding of planes, prohibition on overflights rebel-held territory by US planes, and am reinforcing standing orders that every precaution will be taken insure no additional US official personnel fall into rebel hands.

Am deeply concerned, however, by starkness of message I have to deliver and fear reactions of Tshombe, Nendaka and Kasavubu. In fact Tshombe may well know of our decision even before I can see him because of our action early this morning in standing down crucial air strikes scheduled in Burma and Boende areas. Furthermore, while I will obviously not tell Tshombe that US planes no longer flying over rebel held area, Congolese will probably become aware of this during course of day when ANC request for reconnaissance around Bukavu and Uvira, point still under grave rebel threat, is refused. Department will, of course, realize that grounding of planes will mean complete stoppage of all military offensive operations against rebels, as all current operations depend on air support by US furnished planes.

Tshombe is going to ask right away, or at least ask himself, what USG has in mind, i.e., does this mean US proposing give in to rebel blackmail re hostages and thus getting ready pull out military rug from under him, at least as far as crucial support from US-furnished planes is concerned. Or, he will want to know, does this mean USG has something more positive in mind. I can see reasons why we would not necessarily want to take Tshombe into our confidence at this stage if latter is case. However, I believe it very much in our own interest give Tshombe some additional thoughts which would lead him conclude we not abandoning him and not panicking. This would, I believe, keep him from having to consider possibility, which Department has recognized, of reversing his decision re non use South African mercenary pilots. Therefore, I request authorization make clear to Tshombe that limitation on use of planes is temporary measure and does not mean USG considering withdrawal of its aerial support. In other words, I would like be able assure him that phrase "reviewing with him our aerial support" does not mean give in to rebel blackmail.

Re Belgian reaction, I should think Spaak would also have same concerns as Congolese about what we have in mind. Would it not be better be somewhat more frank with him? We will also need full support top Belgian military advisors in ANC. Have, therefore, asked Williams inform VDW and Marliere of grounding of planes as we will need their support keep impulsive Mobutu in line. Am asking them say nothing to Congolese until I have had opportunity approach Tshombe. Foregoing drafted at 0500 local. At 0700 Marliere was scheduled depart for Coquilhatville in B–26 and I have accordingly told Williams send Marliere at once. Thus in matter of hour our decision will be known here to Belgians.

We must face fact that 72-hour stand down, even though not immediately known to rebels, could result in some substantial rebel victories. For example, last time reconnaissance around Bukavu stopped, rebels quickly took occasion launch major attack on that city which nearly fell. Unless Belgians undertake reconnaissance, US could be in position of being blamed for fall of key city which fell under fear rebel threats.[3]

Godley

[3] Telegram 968 to Leopoldville, October 16, instructed the Embassy to assure Tshombe that the stand down was temporary and did not indicate a decision to withdraw U.S. air support. This was to provide a breathing space so both governments could consider how to minimize the risk of reprisals. (National Archives, RG 59, Central Files 1964–66, POL 23–9 THE CONGO) In telegram 1524 from Leopoldville, October 18, Godley pointed out that ANC attacks on Boende and Kindu were being held up indefinitely pending release of air support, and that Belgian pressure would build up if ANC troops suffered counterattacks, since the VDW plans were based on air support. (Ibid.)

288. Memorandum From the Under Secretary of State for Political Affairs (Harriman) to Secretary of State Rusk[1]

Washington, October 16, 1964.

Dean:

I earnestly hope that stand down of all flights in the Congo will be terminated and orders returned to prohibition of attacks on cities but not rebel columns.

If the communist world once realizes they can blackmail the U.S. by the capture of U.S. personnel, we will become impotent.

Godley's message 1497[2] should be carefully analyzed and acted upon as a minimum.

Plans for strike on Stanleyville should in my judgment be expedited so that Americans can be quickly rescued.

[1] Source: Library of Congress, Manuscript Division, Harriman Papers, Box 861, Congo (3). Secret. Attached to the memorandum is a note from Harriman's Special Assistant, Frederic L. Chapin, to Rusk's Special Assistant, Edmund S. Little, that reads: "Ed: Governor Harriman wrote the attached in car while en route to National Airport this morning at eight o'clock."

[2] Document 287.

I wish that I could discuss the situation personally, but I have a committed schedule through Saturday evening.

Averell[3]

[3] Printed from a copy that bears this typed signature.

289. Memorandum of Telephone Conversation Between Director of Central Intelligence McCone and the Under Secretary of State (Ball)[1]

Washington, October 16, 1964, 3:45 p.m.

McCone called to say that he was terribly troubled over this 72 hour timing in the Congo. This could spell the undoing of Tshombe's success. Mr. Ball said that he had talked to Mac Bundy this morning and it seems to him this is a situation where the President has got to have a look. The reason for the 72 hours is to give him a chance to personally review it. They are trying to get some ground rules out. One of our people came back from talking with the Belgians who agree that the five people, apart from the other Americans, are in very serious jeopardy with the use of the planes. What Mr. Ball wants to do and what Bundy agreed to today was that they would try to get the matter to the President and then go ahead and do what they have to.

Mr. McCone said that the only thing that has held those Congolese forces together has been the air support. They would have disintegrated in the absence of same. He said he realized the danger to the 30 people. On the other hand we brought great pressure on the Belgians to do what they have done even though Spaak felt he was putting several thousand Belgians at risk. There is a big stake and while he has every feeling for the 26 people if we establish a Communist cancer in the middle of dark Africa the consequences are going to be many times more serious than 26 people.

Mr. Ball said that he thought the problem is that he (Ball) would feel very reluctant to see this operation go much further until the President knows. He said that we had had word today that the whole story

[1] Source: Johnson Library, Ball Papers, Congo II. Confidential. Transcribed by Helen M. Hennessey.

of the hostages has been filed. The Department is going to try to get somebody out to Chicago to squelch the story—*Chicago Daily News*.

Mr. Ball said that our people back from Brussels say that the Belgians have a somewhat different appraisal of the situation. He said that Godley had a date with Tshombe today and we were waiting for the telegram. Mr. Ball said he appreciated McCone's feelings and said that there were some different views over here.

McCone mentioned that when he had wanted to get the 130's out and put some covert C 54's in Harriman raised hell.

---

290. Telegram From the Department of State to the Embassy in the Congo[1]

Washington, October 16, 1964, 10:51 p.m.

976. Ref: Deptel 968.[2] Following are instructions re further talks with Tshombe:

You should inform Tshombe that, in line with our continuing desire to provide GOC with air support, we want to propose general formula under which GOC and US air operations in Congo can be carried out which meets both GOC and US requirements. Limiting factors of particular concern to us are dangers rebel reprisals against American hostages Stanleyville and possible use South African piloted planes by GOC. Any formula for air operations must take these factors into account. You should emphasize significance USG attaches to safety of hostages and say that danger to them precludes using planes in ways which clearly risk reprisals on them. In similarly frank and realistic vein you should make clear that association with operations in which SA pilots engaged is unacceptable to USG in view effect on both GOC and US images and positions in the world. Against this background you should propose the following formula to Tshombe:

1. He should take an initiative, based on humanitarian grounds, to make clear to rebels and to world that he will not make air attacks against cities or towns, thereby endangering civilian populations. FYI

---

[1] Source: National Archives, RG 59, Central Files 1964–66, POL 23–9 THE CONGO. Top Secret; Flash; Limdis. Drafted by Palmer; cleared by Brubeck, Runyon, Lang, and Ball; and approved by Palmer. Also sent to Brussels and repeated to CINCSTRIKE for Ramsey, Nairobi, and the U.S. Mission in Geneva.

[2] Dated October 16; see footnote 3, Document 287.

This is not intended to preclude attacks on military targets such as highways and bridges near to towns. Precise guidance will be forthcoming, particularly with regard to Stanleyville. In event rebels dig in to hold any town, we would consider case on merits at time. End FYI. He would insist similarly that rebels treat Congolese and foreign civilian communities under their control in accordance with Article 3 of Geneva Conventions.

2. This undertaking would be in form communications, which would simultaneously be made public, to Kenyatta as head OAU Commission and to Gonard, President ICRC, informing them of GOC's self-imposed restraints and asking them to obtain rebel cooperation for the humanitarian purposes of the Geneva Conventions.

3. Communications would also request OAU Commission and ICRC to send representatives to both GOC and rebel territory. The representatives should have complete freedom of movement to check on possible violations of Geneva Conventions or departures from the undertaking of the GOC with respect to air attacks. (You should tell Tshombe we believe establishment such presence in Stanleyville would significantly enhance safety Congolese, American and other civilian population there.)

4. Communications would invite ICRC and Commission reps to Leopoldville to discuss modalities, but would make clear that GOC unilateral undertaking becomes effective immediately.

We believe foregoing not only helps solve problem of hostages but provides Tshombe excellent opportunity to seize initiative, gaining stature in African and world forums for statesmanlike act and putting rebels on defensive. In tactical sense too he gains the initiative. Instead of GOC and its associates laboring under threat of rebels to take punitive act against foreigners if GOC hits cities from air, it is now GOC which implicitly threatens rebels with punitive act if rebels break international law.

Tshombe may argue that proposed formula implies equal status for rebels. You should respond that Article 3 of Geneva Conventions is solely humanitarian, not political, in objective. Article 3 specifically states that its provisions shall not affect the legal status of the parties to the conflict. The Conventions further stated that an impartial humanitarian body such as the ICRC may offer its services to the parties to the conflict. For the OAU Commission to cooperate with the ICRC and the parties to the conflict for the purpose of Article 3 is consistent with the Conventions and carries no political implications. Moreover, you might point out that even in the absence of the Geneva Conventions Tshombe as PM of GOC has full authority to invite ICRC, OAU Commission or anyone he wishes to any part of his territory for any proper purpose. Thus it could be argued that deployment of such representatives for humanitarian ends at GOC request is completely consistent with GOC sovereignty.

If you consider useful you might point out to Tshombe initiative we suggesting would permit him provide statesmanlike rationale for self-imposed restraints which consistent with realities of our unpublicized requirements.

If appropriate in course of discussions with Tshombe, you are authorized to inform him that withdrawal second C–130 will be delayed pursuant to your recommendations. Please advise earliest time you believe withdrawal can take place.

For Brussels: You should inform GOB urgently of foregoing and request GOB instruct De Kerchove consult with Godley re any supporting action Belgian Embassy Leopoldville might take, including possible parallel approach.

Rusk

---

291. Telegram From the Department of State to the Embassy in the Congo[1]

Washington, October 19, 1964, 1:29 a.m.

989. Following Brubeck–Struelens conversation tonight, Struelens is calling Tshombe immediately to urge importance of seeing Ambassador soonest and to impress on Tshombe need to cooperate in our proposal for control of air operations and for public statements thereon.

In light of Struelens proposed approach to Tshombe we believe you should, in first conversation with Tshombe, avoid any implication of threat of US control or withdrawal of aircraft, and you should not ask Tshombe himself to stand-down aircraft. Approach should be confined to stressing importance of problems and imminence of danger to foreign nationals Stanleyville, and to urging, for this reason, need for proposed statement by Tshombe at earliest time.

You should also stress humanitarian concern for all civilians and all foreign nationals affected, avoiding stress on US official hostages at Stanleyville.

---

[1] Source: National Archives, RG 59, Central Files 1964–66, POL 23–9 THE CONGO. Secret; Flash; Limdis. Drafted by Brubeck, cleared by Palmer and in substance by Ball, and approved by Richard Straus in S/S-O. Repeated to Brussels.

You should further make clear that our support for this approach is in part because we believe it is best way to prevent series of escalating blackmail demands by rebels based on threats to foreign nationals. You should point out that, in any event, as stated in Secretary's letter, US is firm in support to GOC and will not withdraw assistance under threat of blackmail.

FYI: This does not, of course, alter instructions to continue de facto stand-down pending solution to problem. If no satisfactory arrangement is reached with Tshombe on this basis we will need consider again a tougher approach. We have, of course, given Struelens no hint that control already being exercised.

New Subject: Struelens expressed surprise regarding difficulty in seeing Tshombe and indicated misgivings about some staff people around Tshombe in handling such matters. In light this comment, we would be interested in knowing, if you can tell us, through whom your request for appointment was relayed. End FYI.[2]

Rusk

[2] Telegram 992 to Leopoldville, October 19, reported that, following his conversation with Brubeck, Struelens talked twice to Tshombe, who agreed to issue a statement that he would order the Congolese air force to limit its operations to military objects. The telegram also transmitted the text of a draft statement and instructed Godley to see Tshombe and urge some revisions in it. (Ibid.)

---

292. Telegram From the Embassy in the Congo to the Department of State[1]

Leopoldville, October 20, 1964, 8 p.m.

1561. Called at Tshombe's office 1900 local and was informed by his secretary he not there and was detained "for a long time" with Kasavubu. She apologized profusely and said Tshombe promises phone me tomorrow morning himself to establish an appointment then. Have since confirmed that he similarly stood up acting UNOC Chief Gilpin (1730 appointment).

[1] Source: National Archives, RG 59, Central Files 1964–66, POL 23–9 THE CONGO. Top Secret; Flash; Limdis. Received at 6:27 p.m. Repeated to Brussels and passed to the White House, DOD, and CIA.

We know from CAS that he was meeting Nendaka and Mobutu at 1500 at Nendaka's hideout near Belgian Chancery. Belgian Ambassador confirmed to me that Tshombe still there at 1745. It is quite logical that they subsequently went to Kasavubu's. We are, of course, not certain what they discussing, but we gave "Christine" text contained in Department telegram 992[2] this morning. We assume that she gave them to Tshombe and that immediately he began consulting with his two closest advisors Mobutu and Nendaka. We also know that Congolese have intercepted telegram sent by Soumialot to Burundi King and believe it is that quoted in FBIS London's R–192025Z. Believe foregoing is all rather ominous for Mobutu and Nendaka, I fear, will be violently opposed to what Department has proposed to Struelens. It is unfortunate that we gave Christine text this morning, but as we were informed Struelens was forwarding them, such action was, of course, essential. (Struelens message received but badly garbled.)

If, as I fear, Tshombe's attitude will be negative, we seem to have painted ourselves into a corner. VDW plan, now highlighted by Boende phase, depends on Congo air support. With arrival equipment from Belgium approximately October 25, columns from Kamina should be about ready move out. Here again, however, it will depend upon air support. By this time rebels, who were being deluged by messages from everyone and who, as indicated in FBIS R–192035, are handling them very adroitly, will certainly be aware of stand down. If Tshombe does not budge and if we do not, valuable time will be lost and there is, of course, ever present danger of recognition of rebels. In this connection have just received following from Matheron dispatch 1500Z: "ANC Bukavu continues to request T–28 combat support for area outside local defense of Bukavu and beyond exceptions granted in Department telegram 975 to Leopoldville.[3] For example, Beni is once again reported under heavy attack and ANC has requested combat support. (In addition, this entails landing at Goma for refueling.) Local ANC (including De Coster) have not been given any indication whatsoever through own channels about T–28 and B–26 grounding. It is extremely difficult for pilots and Col. Bryant to continue to fabricate excuses; e.g. weather, mechanical and radio failure and pilot illness. Recommend Benezetti be given facts through ANC channels."

Please instruct urgently and also indicate precisely what Brubeck and Palmer told Struelens, if anything, about stand down and how at this late date we should handle stand down of which Congolese must be well aware.

---

[2] See footnote 2, Document 291.

[3] Dated October 16. (National Archives, RG 59, Central Files 1964–66, POL 23–9 THE CONGO)

It is difficult make recommendations from Leopoldville, but if nothing has been said re stand down, from Leopoldville vantage point it is essential it be quietly lifted and if, however, something has been said to Struelens, some face saving device should be sought but in this connection believe Soumialot's message to Burundi King gives us fortuitous out.

Godley

293. Telegram From the Department of State to the Embassy in the Congo[1]

Washington, October 20, 1964, 9:36 p.m.

1006. Re Embtel 1561.[2] Struelens was not informed of stand down.

Department fully aware difficulties stand down poses not only militarily but also politically in our relations with GDRC. However, given our concern about safety Americans and other foreigners in Stanleyville, we feel we must continue make lifting of stand down dependent on Tshombe issuing acceptable statement proscribing air attacks on urban areas also lines Deptel 992.[3] If Tshombe aware of stand down, he has simple expedient available to him, namely to see you and to discuss proposed statement and situation that exists. If he issues satisfactory public statement, planes can go back in air. FYI Actual resumption operations will still require Washington approval. End FYI. If he does not, we must reserve our freedom of decision in situation then obtaining.

If Tshombe confronts you with fact of stand down, you should remind him of efforts you have made see him for past five days in effort work out arrangement which would permit continuation operations on mutually satisfactory basis.

Meanwhile, Benezetti should not be informed of facts through ANC or other channels.

[1] Source: National Archives, RG 59, Central Files 1964–66, POL 23–9 THE CONGO. Top Secret; Flash; Limdis. Drafted by Palmer; cleared by Brubeck, Ball, and Jones of EUR; and approved by Palmer. Repeated to Brussels.

[2] Document 292.

[3] See footnote 2, Document 291.

Re Embtel 1562,[4] you should of course be guided by antepenultimate para Deptel 992[5] in event Tshombe proposes unacceptable changes in statement.

Rusk

---

[4] Dated October 20. (National Archives, RG 59, Central Files 1964–66, POL 23–9 THE CONGO)

[5] The referenced paragraph instructed Godley to discourage Tshombe if he wanted to make unacceptable changes in the draft statement and, if necessary, to try to persuade him to withhold it pending further consultations.

---

294. Telegram From the Embassy in the Congo to the Department of State[1]

Leopoldville, October 21, 1964, 7 p.m.

1571. Tshombe appeared at residence alone 1500 local. Although he had his usual smile, conversation got off to merry start with his opening words "You know my people are furious with what you have done with our aviation". I replied that it unfortunate he and I had not been able meet since I requested urgent meeting with him last Friday morning[2] for we were fully aware of difficulty we placing him in, but also wanted him be aware of difficulties presented my Government by detention our citizens in Stanleyville and fact that Opepe desires kill them. Told Prime Minister that everyone in Washington most concerned over Americans Stanleyville. Tshombe said he personally wished do everything he could to help. Told him that recommended message Struelens had sent him essential including modifications contained Department telegram 992. Tshombe understood modifications and said he would issue communiqué immediately but he could not mention OAU. I argued on this point, but he inquired how could we ask OAU send someone Stanleyville when they might select such a rascal (his word much stronger) as Diallo Telli whose capacity for mischief would be unlimited. I had previously read him FBIS R–192035 and told him I thought that his early issuance of communiqué would

---

[1] Source: National Archives, RG 59, Central Files 1964–66, POL 23–9 THE CONGO. Top Secret; Immediate; Limdis. Received at 4:57 p.m. Repeated to Brussels and Nairobi and passed to the White House, DOD, CIA, and CINCSTRIKE for Ramsey.

[2] October 16.

take winds out of Soumialot's sails. He granted this point, but then said "his people" were categorically opposed to running such risk. I said I did not see how he could stop OAU acceding to Soumialot's request and he said this specifically excluded by Addis terms of reference and subsequent discussions Nairobi.

We ended that I personally understood his position as far as OAU concerned and would recommend strongly that my Government not insist on its inclusion in communiqué. Asked if he prepared send letter to ICRC and he said of course. Tshombe excused himself shortly thereafter saying he wished rush back to office to send me immediately his draft. I gave him many copies French text Article 3 emphasizing last sentence. It is now 1830 local and I have just been informed that Embassy official enroute back from Tshombe's office with text which will be telegraphed immediately.[3]

We have just received further information re 21st SQ. 1300 today Mobutu confirmed movement order to Coq. of all elements except S. African. At 1630 Mulamba came in to say that Mobutu insisted all elements 21st SQ move Coq. Believe this significant in that Mobutu for a while at least appreciated problems he creating. If text Tshombe's communiqué satisfactory, would hope stand down can be withdrawn immediately in order that I can endeavor cancel movement 21st SQ.

Godley

---

[3] See footnote 2, Document 295.

---

295. Telegram From the Department of State to the Embassy in the Congo[1]

Washington, October 21, 1964, 11:48 p.m.

1017. Ref: Embtel 1573.[2] For Ambassador from Acting Secretary. Department cannot accept Tshombe's statement as satisfactory re-

---

[1] Source: National Archives, RG 59, Central Files 1964–66, POL 23–9 THE CONGO. Secret; Flash; Exdis. Drafted by Palmer; cleared by Ball, Brubeck, and McNaughton; and approved by Palmer. Repeated to Nairobi.

[2] Telegram 1573 from Leopoldville, October 21, transmitted the text of Tshombe's communiqué limiting the operations of the Congolese air force to military objectives, with the request that it be delivered immediately to Struelens to be issued by him. (Ibid.)

sponse to our very fundamental concerns. Moreover we cannot ignore tactics he has used in refusing us his cooperation in this matter. For us to lift stand down of planes on basis his empty statement would not only fail secure what we have sought in connection civilian populations but lay ourselves wide open to repetition on future matters of importance to us. We do not believe this can in any sense be regarded as satisfactory basis for future relationship.

Struelens is being told tonight the USG will not tolerate a situation in which the Chief of Government of a nation we are trying to help gives the American Ambassador the run-around for six days and then acts in total disregard of our expressed interests.

Of three points on which Tshombe has failed to meet our position in his statement, we attach greatest significance of course to voluntary restraints with respect to air actions over cities and towns. We believe general reference to Geneva Conventions is sufficiently satisfactory that we need not insist on specific reference to Article 3 which in any event has primary applicability to Stanleyville. With regard to OAU, we would be prepared reserve this point for subsequent discussion and negotiation with him. We regard it as essential, however, that he meet our concerns re air activities over towns and cities.

You should therefore see Tshombe again soonest and express our astonishment both with respect to substance of statement (enumerating omissions of important points) and to his extraordinary action in publishing it without full consultation with us despite six days of effort on your part and our part with Struelens to evolve mutually acceptable statement. You should make clear to him that in light level of assistance and support which we are extending to strengthen GOC and accomplishments its objectives, we fail to understand his lack of responsiveness on matter of very fundamental concern to us. In these circumstances, we must make clear to him necessity of finding more satisfactory basis on which to conduct our relationship. Point of departure must be an immediate and satisfactory resolution of problems which communiqué fails to meet. We certain that he too attaches sufficient importance to this relationship that he will be able devote time and effort to understanding and meeting our concern.

Against this background, you should give Tshombe following draft letters:

First should be addressed to President ICRC and should read as follows:

"On October 21, I issued the attached statement in order to make clear the desire of the GDRC to abide by the Geneva Conventions and to show our respect for generous humanitarian measures which would avoid needless suffering by civilians. I similarly called on those who are illegally in rebellion against my Government similarly to respect these conventions and to protect human life.

In the spirit of this announcement, I am directing my air force to limit its actions to military objectives and not to conduct strikes against cities and important localities which would endanger the civilian population. FYI. Language of this sentence is deliberately ambiguous because of unresolved State/Defense issue. State position is that cities and important localities should not be hit at all because such action would endanger civilian populations. Defense position is that military objectives in cities and important localities are legitimate targets and should be hit if in so doing civilian populations are not endangered. State/Defense differences will be resolved Oct 22 in context control guidance which will be sent you through other channels. For purposes this statement, however, it essential that ambiguity be maintained and that sentence structure not be altered by insertion of comma before 'which' or otherwise. To assure precision on this point, following French text of sentence should be used without change. *Begin text.* Dans l'esprit de cette declaration, j'ai donne l'ordre a ma force aerienne de limiter ses actions aux objectifs militaires et de ne pas faire des attaques contre des villes et localites importantes qui mettraient en danger la population civile. *End text.* End FYI. I hereby invite you to designate an impartial observer to come at once to Leopoldville in order to observe and verify compliance of my Government with the undertakings of my announcement of yesterday and of this letter. I assure you of the full cooperation of my Government in providing facilities to carry out its mission.

Similarly, I urge you to make every effort to send an observer to Stanleyville for similar purposes and to verify compliance of rebel authorities there with the applicable provisions of the Geneva Conventions. In order to assist you in this objective I am addressing a letter to the Chairman of the OAU Ad Hoc Commission on the Congo Mr. Jomo Kenyatta asking his assistance in obtaining agreement of the Stanleyville rebels to cooperate in these arrangements."

Second letter is to Kenyatta and reads as follows:

"Dear Mr. Prime Minister: I am enclosing a copy of a letter which I have sent today to the President of the ICRC urging that organization to send impartial observers to Leopoldville and Stanleyville to observe and verify compliance by the GDRC and the rebels in Stanleyville with the applicable provisions of the Geneva Conventions and of other undertakings set forth in my letter to the ICRC.

In your capacity as Chairman of the OAU Ad Hoc Commission, I urge you to assist the ICRC in obtaining the agreement of the Stanleyville rebels to cooperate in these arrangements."

You should urge Tshombe to send and publish these letters immediately.

You should also again make clear to Tshombe in strongest terms that employment of South African T–6's will pose grave problem for US-Congolese relations and put in question continued US military assistance. FYI. You should of course make every effort prevent deployment and deny support of any US airlift or matériel to T–6 operation. End FYI.

You should reaffirm our desire to cooperate fully with GDRC in restoring peace, referring again to Secretary's letter. You should likewise point out that, in fact, air support has continued for urgent needs, despite your inability to see Tshombe and to get solution to problem of overriding importance to US. You can cite, e.g. air ops at Bukavu, reconnaissance at Boende and logistic flights. You should point out, however, that inability to resolve this problem in manner that protects interests of US as well as GDRC will raise serious question as to continued cooperation in air ops. You should again point out that purpose of statement is to put an end to Stanleyville blackmail threat, strengthen position of GDRC, and make possible effective US military and political support, including air ops. It is not our purpose to deny GDRC support essential to its military requirements and as problems arise we willing to consult with GDRC to ensure satisfactory solution. We cannot however accept situation in which with heavy US commitments and risks, there is inadequate consultation and failure to respect interests of US.[3]

Rusk

[3] In telegram 1580 from Leopoldville, October 22, Godley warned against pressing Tshombe so hard to obtain the precise wording that the Department considered necessary to safeguard U.S. personnel in Stanleyville. His concern was that using the stand down as a means of exerting pressure on the Congolese and neutralizing air units whose operations the United States controlled might push the Congolese into reliance on South Africans and other disreputable elements. (Ibid.)

296. Memorandum for the Record[1]

Washington, October 22, 1964.

MEMORANDUM OF CONVERSATION BETWEEN MR. BRUBECK AND MR. STRUELENS OF THE CONGO EMBASSY—11:00 AM, October 22, 1964

We reviewed the events of the past week in the Congo and I explained to Struelens the approach Godley will be making to Tshombe today, regarding letters to the Red Cross and Kenyatta. I explained that we are deeply concerned with two points:

1. That the Congolese Government should make a public record of assurances regarding restraint of attacks against cities, and
2. That we must have some better basis for dealing with the Congolese Government in order to insure candor, cooperation and mutual confidence and ability to consult promptly and frequently when necessary.

I pointed out that the United States Government, with the very great commitments it has made in the Congo, must be assured that its interests are understood and protected and that the events of the past week—our Ambassador tried unsuccessfully for six days to see Tshombe only to be confronted with a fait accompli in the form of a press release on which there had been no consultation—was a very serious matter.

Struelens agreed that the communiqué was unsatisfactory and that the failure to consult and to see Godley was unacceptable. He explained partially in terms of Tshombe's staff preventing Godley's appointment, and partly in terms of Tshombe's problem of dealing with Mobutu, Nendaka and Kasavubu. He insisted that Tshombe does have confidence in the United States commitments to his Government. He believes, however, that Tshombe is much constrained by the difficulties of handling Mobutu, and that in any event the Congolese leaders are not sufficiently experienced or sophisticated fully to appreciate the problems and how to handle them. He believes that Mobutu has become very anti-American and is disposed to turn to the South Africans for air operational support.

It was agreed that Struelens will call me tonight to learn what success Godley has had with Tshombe. Depending on that report, he will probably call Tshombe himself to underline the concern of the

[1] Source: Johnson Library, National Security File, Country File, Congo, Vol. VI. Secret. Prepared by Brubeck. Copies were sent to Palmer, Ball, and Bundy.

United States and to urge Tshombe to work closely with Godley. If Tshombe agrees, Struelens will proceed to Leopoldville Sunday or Monday in order to talk to Tshombe before Brubeck and Palmer arrive. I said, without giving any indication of our other travel plans, that we expected to be in Leopoldville probably Wednesday for "a couple of days" would hope to see Tshombe Wednesday and if necessary again on Thursday and that our primary concern was to assure a close working relationship between the two Governments on the basis of mutual understanding.

Struelens gives every indication of understanding our concern, being prepared to cooperate in his discussions with Tshombe and quite clear where Tshombe's true interests lie. I have the impression, however, that he is not too confident of his own role and the extent of his influence with Tshombe. He may well have used up some of his credit in the effort he has already made with Tshombe on other issues.

B

---

297. Telegram From the Department of State to the Embassy in the Congo[1]

Washington, October 22, 1964, 9:53 p.m.

1030. Deptel 1017.[2] We are sending you through other channels detailed guidance re use of planes. When you have implemented instructions contained para 7 that message, you are authorized lift stand-down on any planes affected.

You should continue your efforts to see Tshombe and carry out instructions contained Deptel 1017 modified to conform to further instructions contained this tel. In urging on Tshombe need for proposed letters to meet our concerns, you should say we are proceeding on assumption problem can be worked out. You authorized to assure him in this connection that US will continue cooperate to insure essential air operations requirements are met. If consistent your earlier talk with him, suggest you avoid any reference to stand-down and merely indicate your understanding that current operational needs will shortly be

---

[1] Source: National Archives, RG 59, Central Files 1964–66, POL 23–9 THE CONGO. Top Secret; Immediate; Exdis. Drafted and approved by Palmer and cleared by Brubeck. Repeated to Brussels and Nairobi.

[2] Document 295.

met. We remain concerned, like GDRC, to meet essential military needs, and at any time problems arise regarding US military assistance, Tshombe should raise them with you immediately so that the two of you can resolve them. You should point out, however, our understanding that as condition of this cooperation there will be no South African T–6 unit in Congo.

You should likewise reiterate that experience of past week has raised serious question both for you and highest levels Washington with regard to effective working relations between US and GDRC. You should emphasize that magnitude and complexity of US commitment to GDRC makes it essential that Tshombe and Ambassador work on continuous, close, and confidential basis. We must have situation permitting prompt and frequent consultation and frank exchange. While we appreciate GDRC has its own political problems, so do we and we believe both sides will benefit if we can work together in spirit of understanding and mutual give and take.

Department concurs fully your handling of situation described Embtel 1591,[3] and your insistence Tshombe must work out problem with you in Leopoldville.

You should reaffirm that position and tell him that Washington strongly concurs.

Rusk

---

[3] In telegram 1591 from Leopoldville, October 22, Godley described his continuing difficulties in arranging a meeting with Tshombe. He also reported that he had received a message from Tshombe stating that Kasavubu wanted to send a special emissary to the United States to meet with the President and discuss the current situation. The Ambassador replied that he did not know whether the President would receive a special emissary but that he personally had to see Tshombe on an urgent matter pursuant to formal orders from the U.S. Government or else U.S. military aid to the Congo might be jeopardized. (National Archives, RG 59, Central Files 1964–66, POL 23–9 THE CONGO)

298. Memorandum From the Department of State Executive Secretary (Read) to the President's Special Assistant for National Security Affairs (Bundy)[1]

Washington, October 23, 1964.

SUBJECT

Compliance with NSC Action 2498 of August 11, 1964

In compliance with paragraph b.(1) of NSC Action 2498 of August 11, 1964,[2] Great Britain, France, Germany, Italy and the Netherlands, through their representatives in Washington, were sounded out by the Department about the possibility of providing assistance, including the provision of limited forces, to the Congo. Foreign Minister Spaak of Belgium made similar approaches. The reactions of the countries concerned were uniformly negative, although they were sympathetic to Belgian-U.S. aims in the Congo.

The Department of State also instructed its representatives in Nigeria, Ethiopia, Senegal, Liberia and the Malagasy Republic to make representations to those governments encouraging affirmative responses to the Congolese request for troops. Their responses were not completely unfavorable, but all preferred that such assistance be made within the framework of multilateral African action in the Congo. The provision of forces, however, was not agreed at the OAU Conference at Addis Ababa in early September.

The President's authorization contained in paragraph c. of the NSC Action to assist in airlifting equipment and men from the United States and other nations to and within the Congo is still being carried out. Four C–130 aircraft went to the Congo August 12 and have since engaged in transporting Congolese troops, military supplies and equipment, food and other relief equipment within the Congo. One C–130 was withdrawn October 8. In addition, the United States has airlifted, as necessary, equipment provided by Belgium to the Congo and Rwanda.

The President's authorization to Defense and AID to consider favorably additional military and economic assistance to African countries providing military assistance to the Congo has not been acted upon since no African country presently provides such aid. However, the five countries from which the Congo has requested military assist-

---

[1] Source: Johnson Library, National Security File, Country File, Congo, Vol. VI. Secret.

[2] Not printed, but see Document 211.

ance have been informed that the United States would consider favorably requests for an airlift of their troops to the Congo. The British have indicated willingness to airlift Nigerian troops.

H. Gordon[3]

[3] Herbert Gordon signed for Read above Read's typed signature.

299. Telegram From the Embassy in the Congo to the Department of State[1]

Leopoldville, October 23, 1964, noon.

1595. Have just had 50 minute meeting with Tshombe at residence. Told him I believed only frankness should exist between us and my principal objective here was keep him informed of my government's thinking and ascertain at earliest possible moment his government's thinking whenever there was possibility of misunderstanding. This having been said, I wanted read to him rather brutally from two telegrams I had received from top officials of Department of State. Then went through practically verbatim Deptel 1017 and 1030[2] omitting only some of strongest adjectives and fuzzing first paragraph of Deptel 1030. (FYIs of course omitted.) Tshombe took it well. In going through 1017, he read carefully letter to President ICRC and I emphasized that this was language prepared in Washington and not a word could be changed without further consultation with me. Tshombe said he understood. I drew his particular attention to phraseology concerning strikes against cities, pointing out I recognized this might cause him trouble, but this precise language had to be included. Tshombe said he understood. He said he would have messages typed up and would request that we forward them to Geneva and Nairobi. Only point I did not emphasize, although I said it, was that these letters must be published. I feel that this might well be rubbing his nose in it too much, although I think they can be published once they are issued. Re S African T–6 unit, I also hit hard on this point. Told him I personally understood pressure he under from Mobutu, but that now that I believed we were

[1] Source: National Archives, RG 59, Central Files 1964–66, POL THE CONGO–US. Top Secret; Flash; Exdis. Passed to the White House, DOD, and CIA.

[2] Documents 295 and 297.

making major step forward, he would have to do likewise. As I have not yet received instructions through other channel, I had in all honesty fuzzed this point and he and I agreed that I would notify him minute I had instructions and that he would give orders to Mobutu to delay T–6 deployment COQ 24 hours. Concerning our personal relations and frankness that must exist between our 2 governments, Tshombe picked on words "continuous close and confidential basis" in Deptel 1030. He agreed that this must govern all our dealings and promised do so. I pointed out to him that such relationship would be mutually beneficial citing that Department had at my request given way on two of major items, i.e. OAU presence Stanleyville and specific reference article 3. Tshombe expressed gratitude and I believe got point. Early in our conversation he apologized profusely for not showing up yesterday blaming Kasavubu's loquaciousness and fact that any conversation with Kasavubu lasts at least two to three hours. These conversations he said, exhaust him physically and emotionally and he claims he under medical care last evening. I do not think this absolute truth, but would hope that we will not once again experience communications breakdown.

Re Malila's junket, I told him I did not think this necessary, but he said that he so impressed with Secretary's recent message and President's to Kasavubu that the President and he agreed it essential they be acknowledged by Special Emissary. He did not indicate that he expected either President or Secretary receive Malila. In mentioning Secretary's message, he said it had been made helpful to him personally in his dealings with Mobutu and others, especially the last sentence (Deptel 982),[3] which he had used with Mobutu in arguing over SAfrican Air Squadron. He said, however, that Mobutu challenged Secretary's "wholeheartedly continue" by stating that U.S. furnished aircraft were on stand down. I cannot, of course, guarantee that all is now well. Believe, however, that at least for moment the boil has been lanced. (These were words used by Tshombe when he, Gov Williams and I had our first set-to. Tshombe and I used them this morning and we agreed that if we got at boil soon enough, we could solve any problems.)[4]

Godley

---

[3] Dated October 18. (National Archives, RG 59, Central Files 1964–66, POL 1 THE CONGO–US)

[4] In telegram 1597, October 23, Godley reported that he had received the guidance referred to in the first paragraph of telegram 1030. He then telephoned Tshombe that the Embassy had received authorization that U.S.-furnished aircraft might be used provided they did not fly within 25 miles of Stanleyville and they implemented his instructions to the Congolese air force not to threaten urban areas. (Ibid., POL 23–9 THE CONGO)

300. Telegram From the Department of State to the Embassy in Belgium[1]

Washington, October 26, 1964, 8:26 p.m.

838. For Palmer. Ref: Embtel 786.[2] We agree that GOB instructions to Belgian Chargé Leo as outlined reftel provide good basis for you and Brubeck carry through in Leo. We assume re point (1) that Belgians in first instance thinking of South African pilots and are not suggesting precipitate departure all other South African mercenaries. We assume what they have in mind re ground mercenaries is GDRC commitment to withdrawal as alternative resources become available or no longer needed. Re point (4) we assume by "something constructive" Belgians mean OAU Commission activity clearly within framework OAU Addis resolution.

We encouraged that Belgian conclusions essentially same as those of USG on main points. Hope since this is case you can productively press Belgians accept leading role implementing package they propose. With this in mind believe parallel approaches in Leo, with Belgians in lead, preferable to joint approach, but leave this to your discretion in light your consultations on package with Godley after arrival Leo.

Rusk

---

[1] Source: National Archives, RG 59, Central Files 1964–66, POL 23–9 THE CONGO. Secret; Flash; Limdis. Drafted by McElhiney in AF/CWG; cleared by Samuel Belk, McKillop, Harriman, Tasca, and Lang; and approved by Ball. Repeated to Leopoldville.

[2] Telegram 786 from Brussels, October 26, reported on a meeting among Spaak, Palmer, and Brubeck, who were in Brussels for discussions on the Congo. Spaak proposed sending a telegram to the Belgian Chargé in Leopoldville with the following Belgian-U.S. proposals for a joint démarche to Tshombe: 1) Tshombe should get rid of the South Africans, who were ruining his reputation; 2) excessive use of force and brutality in military operations would not be accepted; 3) there could be no purely military solution; 4) the OAU Commission should be urged to do something constructive toward a political solution; 5) Tshombe should take no final actions regarding Stanleyville without informing Belgium and the United States; and 6) the two countries would fully cooperate in carrying through with their present commitments. (Ibid.)

Palmer and Brubeck were in Brussels for talks on the Congo October 26–27. Ambassador Palmer's Trip Report is ibid., AF/CM Files: Lot 67 D 63, Political Affairs & Rel. The Congo. POL 7. Visits. Meetings.

301. Memorandum From the Chief of the Africa Division, Directorate of Plans, Central Intelligence Agency (Fields) to Director of Central Intelligence McCone[1]

Washington, October 26, 1964.

SUBJECT

Status Report on CIA Activities in the Congo

1. This memorandum is for the information of the Director of Central Intelligence and is provided as background for the 29 October Special Group (CI) meeting.

2. CIA activities in the Congo are concentrated on (a) conducting air operations against rebel forces, (b) creating a capability to rescue five U.S. officials [*less than 1 line not declassified*] and to support covertly a CINCSTRIKE plan to effect the release of all American personnel held by the rebel regime in Stanleyville (approximately 25) and (c) taking covert action to create a more stable political situation in the Congo.

3. U.S. Personnel in Stanleyville:

A. Nineteen [*less than 1 line not declassified*] have been positioned in the Congo with the contingency mission of conducting a clandestine rescue (by air, overland, or river) of the five Consulate personnel. It will not have the capability to rescue the American missionary personnel dispersed throughout the area.

B. The Chairman of the JCS and CINCSTRIKE have been briefed on the CIA covert planning for Stanleyville and have been advised that, should the CIA covert plan not be authorized by higher authority, CIA is prepared to permit its personnel and equipment to assist CINCSTRIKE in support of its larger effort. Leopoldville Station, including a CIA contingency planner, is working with four CINCSTRIKE planners on the possibility of meshing the overt and covert plans.

C. CIA is prepared to lend covert support to an effort by Deputy Assistant Secretary of State Wayne Fredericks to contact Thomas Kansa, the rebel foreign minister, although a recent report indicates he may be in Stanleyville and in the bad graces of other rebel leaders. (State Department wants this held very closely.)

D. A high priority effort continues to obtain all possible intelligence on the status of Americans in Stanleyville and on the effective

[1] Source: Central Intelligence Agency Files, Job 78–02502R, Box 1, [*cryptonym not declassified*]/Development & Plans, [*text not declassified*], Aug '64 through Jan 1967. Secret. The memorandum was sent through Deputy Director for Plans Helms.

control which the Stanleyville regime has in the area. Numerous refugees from Stanleyville have been contacted and debriefed and efforts continue to introduce clandestine agents into Stanleyville.

4. The following actions continue in support of the Government of the Congo (GOC):

A. *Air military*: There are now [*less than 1 line not declassified*] pilots in the Congo operating from four bases (Lisala, Bukava, Kamina, and Leopoldville), and [*less than 1 line not declassified*] non-American ground maintenance personnel. The Congolese air force has been a major factor in halting the rebel advance and in supporting Congolese National Army operations. The support has been invaluable not only as a strike factor but also psychologically. From 15 October to 23 October all operational aircraft under U.S. control, including CIA controlled T–28's and B–26's were grounded on orders of the State Department. This order was given in reaction to intercepted rebel communications which indicated that American lives would be endangered if air strikes on non-military targets continued. Aircraft are now operating, but under certain new restrictions imposed by the State Department calculated to reduce the risk of retaliation against U.S. personnel held hostage in Stanleyville and to create a better atmosphere for political reconciliation. These restrictions confine air strikes to military targets in non-urban areas, prevent flying within 25 miles of Stanleyville, prevent B–26 strikes at intervals of less than 5 minutes after reconnaissance flights, and prevent reconnaissance over urban areas at less than 3,000 feet.

The grounding order which revealed to certain Congolese commanders for the first time that the combat aircraft was under U.S., not Congo, control created considerable ill feeling between the Congolese military and the U.S. and has greatly irritated Tshombe himself. One result of the grounding action may be that Tshombe will make a greater effort to prepare the mercenary operated "21st Air Squadron" for combat action. For example, an unconfirmed report stated that on 25 October, T–6's of the "21st Squadron" attacked Boende city driving most of the populace into the bush.

B. *Ground Military:* Colonel Frederick Van der Walle, senior Belgian adviser to Prime Minister Tshombe, is aware that CIA is prepared to provide some assistance [*less than 1 line not declassified*] which would not otherwise be available, but so far Col. Van der Walle has presented no specific requests.

C. *Political/Civic Action:* CIA has given support to five leading political figures for the purpose of building up tribal loyalties in Government held areas against rebel incursion. This activity has been particularly successful in the [*less than 1 line not declassified*] Province at a time the rebel advances were threatening the provincial capital of [*less than 1 line not declassified*].

John H. Waller[2]

[2] A stamped signature on the memorandum indicates that John H. Waller signed for Fields above Fields' typed signature.

302. Memorandum From Samuel E. Belk of the National Security Council Staff to the President's Special Assistant for National Security Affairs (Bundy)[1]

Washington, October 27, 1964.

SUBJECT

The Congo

There still is no hard news on what actually happened to William H. Scholter, the U.S. Missionary who reportedly was killed last week. By this time Godley should have an Embassy officer well along the way to the Bomba area to get the real facts.

Yesterday (October 26) we learned from intercepts that Dr. Paul Carlson (who had voluntarily remained in his mission in Yokama) is being held for trial by a military tribunal in Stanleyville as "U.S. Major Paul Carson". We have asked the International Commission of the Red Cross to inform the Stanleyville authorities that Dr. Carlson is not and never has been a U.S. major.

Both the UPI and AP have carried reports of our consular personnel being held as hostages by the rebels on October 26. UPI states: "The Americans apparently were held for possible reprisals for government air attacks against rebel positions". AP gives the names, ages and home towns of each of our staff; says they are in good health, but under house arrest.

[1] Source: Johnson Library, National Security File, Country File, Congo, Vol. VII. Secret.

The dialogue between the Department, Palmer and Brubeck and the Belgians continues but the situation except for some refinements is generally the same as late yesterday.

The military "fronts" are quiet.

SEB

303. Memorandum From the Under Secretary of State for Political Affairs (Harriman) to Secretary of State Rusk[1]

Washington, October 27, 1964.

I am concerned to learn that a decision has been reached to call off aerial reconnaissance photography of Stanleyville. I understand that the military were prepared to have photographs taken at a high altitude and at an angle which would have kept the aircraft 25 miles from the outskirts of the city. If weather conditions were satisfactory, only two runs would have been necessary.

Under these circumstances, I agree with the country team that the risk is minimal. The information is essential to deal with an emergency, should it arise. I have felt strongly that our planning should be such that the President could deal with any situation that arose in Stanleyville with speed and effectiveness.

I have been told that the weather in November becomes worse and the difficulty of getting satisfactory photographs will increase.

I recommend that the matter be reopened.

Averell

[1] Source: Library of Congress, Manuscript Division, Harriman Papers, Subject Files, TS Congo (3). Top Secret; Personal; Exdis. A copy was sent to Ball.

304. Telegram From the Department of State to the Embassy in Belgium[1]

Washington, October 28, 1964, 8:14 p.m.

860. Department has intelligence information that Colonel Opepe, Third Group Commander Stanleyville, has ordered rebel field commanders to arrest and imprison all Belgians, Catholic priests and nuns, Protestants and Americans and, in one case, all whites. If orders carried out, significant change in situation would be to put other foreign nationals, principally Belgian, in same situation as Americans held by rebels in Stanleyville.

For Brussels: You should see Spaak earliest to give him above information and determine if GOB sources aware these messages. In addition to getting Belgian reactions you should attempt ascertain what action GOB plans take, suggesting that it may wish use its channel communication with Gbenye to verify information and, if true, request orders be annulled. You should add that USG wishes be of assistance if possible and would be sympathetic to any specific suggestions this regard.

For Leopoldville: You should give above information to Belgian Embassy which may be able verify it. We would hope that this will give Belgians Leopoldville greater sense of urgency regarding hostages which they could communicate to Brussels. Request Godley and Palmer opinion on advisability modification present guidelines for air operations.

For Nairobi: In your discretion and in most appropriate manner you may give gist above information to Kenyatta, Murumbi or Mathu in hope this will induce in Kenyatta greater sense of urgency in dealing with Stanleyville question.

Rusk

---

[1] Source: National Archives, RG 59, Central Files 1964–66, POL 23–9 THE CONGO. Secret; Immediate; Limdis. Drafted by Schaufele in AF/CWG; cleared by Hughes, McElhiney in AF/CWG, and Ball; and approved by Tasca. Also sent to Leopoldville and Nairobi.

305. Telegram From the Headquarters, U.S. Strike Command to the Joint Chiefs of Staff[1]

Tampa, Florida, October 30, 1964, 0045Z.

STRCC 841/64. Subject is: Conduct of military operations in the Congo (C).

References:

A. STRCC 786/64
B. COMISH Leo 9342 291045Z Oct 64
C. AmEmbassy Leo action SecState 1650, DTG 271847Z[2]

1. This headquarters remains deeply concerned about the serious restrictions which appear to have been placed on the conduct of military operations in the Congo, and particularly with reference to the employment of air power.

2. While it is most regrettable that five Americans and an unknown number of other foreigners are in rebel custody in Stanleyville, this fact should not be permitted to preclude proper conduct of military operations designed for bringing the rebellion to an early end in the shortest time practicable. The importance of air power in relation to the general undertaking is clearly established in numerous reports received from the Congo.

3. Available information indicates that the rebels are apparently fully aware of their success in countering air power by propaganda. If this continues, the only outcome will be the weakening of the Congolese armed forces to the extent that it is doubtful that they can win over the rebellious elements anytime soon. In other words, this prospects a long drawn-out indecisive undertaking which can lead to future complications that could not be even estimated at this time, but none of them would be good.

4. Information available to me indicates that current policy provides for:

A. No aviation of any kind is permitted to operate closer than 25 miles of Stanleyville.

---

[1] Source: Johnson Library, National Security File, Country File, Congo, Vol. VI, Memos & Miscellaneous, 10/64–11/64. Top Secret; Noforn; Limdis. Received at the DOD Message Center at 3:24 a.m. Repeated to DOD and the Secretary of State. A copy was sent to the White House for Bundy. The headquarters of U.S. Strike Command (CINCSTRIKE) was located at MacDill Air Force Base in Tampa, Florida.

[2] Not found.

B. No combat target can be hit within a belt five miles wide, measured from the outskirts, around any large or sensitive urban area, or within similar belts two miles wide around any other urban area.

C. Combat missions conducted outside the prescribed belts around urban areas are authorized, but are confined to strictly military targets such as troop concentrations, military vehicles, military stores and supplies, highways and bridges, guns and emplacements, fortified positions and roadblocks, communications facilities and vessels being used for military purposes, provided that such targets shall not be attacked where there is danger of hitting significant numbers of noncombatants in the target area, such as wives and children in military barracks area.

D. Air reconnaissance is authorized over urban areas and surrounding belts provided plane maintains minimum altitude of three thousand feet and does not open or return fire.

E. In the case of B–26's, there must be a five-minute interval between any combat run on targets outside the urban area and surrounding belt, and any reconnaissance run within the area and belt.

5. Military objectives in the Congo primarily consist of towns and cities held by the rebels, with very little combat taking place other than in and around the towns. The policy now in effect permits the rebels to remain in the towns unmolested, control the communication and supplies that exist in the towns, and to have the comfort of urban facilities. Unless the restrictions on the use of air power are lifted, and a return to the Geneva Conventions adopted as a proper guideline, the rebels will have achieved a significant victory. There is no question that this is the chief purpose for which the rebel propaganda campaign is designed.

---

306. Memorandum From Secretary of Defense McNamara to the Chairman of the Joint Chiefs of Staff (Wheeler)[1]

Washington, October 30, 1964.

You are authorized to order a reconnaissance flight over the Stanleyville area, provided that the flight:

---

[1] Source: Washington National Records Center, RG 218, JCS Files, 9111 (64). Top Secret.

1. Will not be carried out before Monday, November 2nd.
2. Will be made by a C–97 aircraft.
3. Proceed according to a flight plan filed in advance.
4. Fly in an altitude of 10,000 feet or above and no closer than 10 miles to Stanleyville.

Please develop the detailed operational plan for the mission and clear it with State through ISA, and then through the Country Team, before issuing the operational order to the appropriate commander.

If you have any further questions on this matter, please consult with either Mr. Vance or me.[2]

McNamara[3]

[2] During the October 30 meeting of the 303 Committee, Vance emphasized that the Department of Defense was insistent about the necessity of a reconnaissance flight over Stanleyville prior to the activation of any CINCSTRIKE operation in that theatre, and that a lead time of 7 days between accomplishment of the reconnaissance mission and activation of such an operation would be required. (Central Intelligence Agency Files, DCI/McCone Files, Job 80B01285A, 303 Committee Meetings (1964))

[3] Printed from a copy that indicates McNamara signed the original.

307. Telegram From the Department of State to the Embassy in Kenya[1]

Washington, October 31, 1964, 9:04 p.m.

1618. Ref: Addis' 652 to Dept; Nairobi's 1126 to Dept.[2] Dept concerned over mounting evidence that, by pushing line Tshombe's removal is pre-requisite for national reconciliation in Congo, Diallo Telli and more militant members of OAU Commission may be embarked on course that will lead to open break between OAU and GDRC. In our view any effort by OAU to split Kasavubu and Tshombe at this stage (Nairobi's 1101 and 1102 to Dept)[3] would have this effect. We are par-

[1] Source: National Archives, RG 59, Central Files 1964–66, POL 23–9 THE CONGO. Confidential; Priority. Drafted by Strong in AF/CWG, cleared by O'Neil and McElhiney in AF/CWG, and approved by Tasca. Also sent to Leopoldville, Addis Ababa, and Lagos and repeated to Mogadiscio, Cairo, Yaounde, Conakry, Accra, Ouagadougou, Tunis, Brussels, London, Bujumbura, and Geneva.

[2] Dated October 30 and October 31, respectively. (Ibid.)

[3] Both dated October 28. (Ibid.) Telegram 1102 reported Murumbi's statement that, following the meeting of the OAU Ad Hoc Commission in Nairobi during the first week of November, Kenyatta was planning to send two Kenyan Ministers to the Congo as his

ticularly concerned about Telli's presumably anti-Tshombe letter to Kasavubu (Addis 652).[4]

For Addis: Subject advice from Nairobi, you should in manner you deem most effective, follow up with Mammo Tedessa or other appropriate Ethiopian official with view to getting IEG instruct Getachew warn Kenyatta against course of action that could lead to collapse of OAU efforts, particularly sending of anti-Tshombe letter. We believe Getachew is already on right track in taking line (Nairobi's 1126) that proper next step for OAU Commission is to send "feeler mission" he describes to Leo and in opposing possible OAU efforts split Kasavubu and Tshombe. Since next OAU task is to establish satisfactory working relations between Commission and GDRC, letter such as that proposed by Telli would be even more undesirable from this point of view.

There is an immediate additional task which would be highly appropriate for OAU "feeler mission" to Leo. This is to work out with GDRC measures for getting ICRC personnel into Congo, including rebel-held areas, in order carry out Red Cross traditional humanitarian function. In fact, need to establish ICRC presence is strong reason for earliest possible despatch of "feeler mission" to Leo and, in addition to importance this consideration per se, would have advantage of helping get OAU Commission off on relatively non-political footing with Tshombe.

We understand Tedessa's doubts about wisdom of reviving Commission at this time but believe he would agree that in view of forces seeking to push it along wrong track, best tactic would be to concentrate efforts on getting it on right track rather than (probably fruitlessly) resisting its reactivation. (Begin FYI: In any case, despite risks in OAU reactivation we are most anxious to have OAU facilitate ICRC return to Stan and believe on balance advantage still accrues from Africanization of Congo problem through OAU involvement. End FYI)

For Lagos: Recognize there is limit to extent you can press GON re OAU Commission, in view GON lack of enthusiasm for it, but believe much of above argumentation might usefully be presented to GON. It would be most helpful if you could persuade GON to instruct its rep in Nairobi to support Getachew's approach to Kenyatta; however, you should await advice from Addis (which Addis please repeat to Nairobi) as to whether IEG prepared send suggested instructions to Geta-

---

emissaries to see Kasavubu alone in order to discuss the "Tshombe problem." Murumbi also warned that U.S. support of Tshombe was turning Africa against the United States.

[4] Telegram 652 (see footnote 2 above) reported a statement by Diallo Telli that the OAU Commission was planning to deliver a letter from Kenyatta to Kasavubu directed against Tshombe, which he himself had authored.

chew and extent to which you at liberty make use of information given Ambassador Korry by Ambassador Igwe.

For Nairobi: Inform Addis soonest whether appropriate for US Emb Addis to suggest IEG instructions to Getachew. On receipt of advice from Addis you may wish to consult further with Getachew re his approach to Kenyatta, drawing on material in this tel.

For Nairobi and Leo: While most important elements in getting OAU Commission on right track are to avoid anti-Tshombe letter to Kasavubu or OAU mission to Leo charged with splitting Kasavubu and Tshombe, there is also question of composition any "feeler mission" to Leo. While Getachew's comments on this point (Nairobi's 1120)[5] interesting, some aspects not entirely clear to us. Difficult judge best composition from this distance but we somewhat surprised at Getachew's judgment that Koinange–Mathu mission could be "disastrous" and that Kenyatta should send Murumbi. We note in last sentence Nairobi's 1126 that Murumbi's present position is that "Tshombe must go" so, despite his ability and background, he may not be improvement from point of view attitude towards Tshombe. In view of Kenyatta's apparently deepseated prejudice against Tshombe, seems likely any Kenyan sent by Kenyatta might well go Leo with at least informal instructions work in direction of trying drive wedge between Kasavubu and Tshombe. We can see difficulty in sending Mathu in view of his past clashes with Tshombe in Katanga but we not clear why Koinange significantly worse than others. If feasible we can see advantage of formula including non-Kenyan like Getachew along with intelligent trusted Kenyan, like Mungai or Njonjo. Most important other element, of course, is that member or members of "feeler mission" be acceptable to Tshombe. We question desirability of including African Ambs Leo in mission as this would bring in unacceptable elements (e.g. Ghana). Recognize we will have limited influence on composition of mission but would appreciate comments both Nairobi and Leo.

Rusk

[5] Dated October 30. (National Archives, RG 59, Central Files 1964–66, POL 23–9 THE CONGO)

308. Memorandum From the Deputy Assistant Secretary of Defense for International Security Affairs (Lang) to the Deputy Secretary of Defense (Vance)[1]

I–36,907/64 Washington, November 2, 1964.

SUBJECT

Palmer Talks at Brussels and Leopoldville

1. Ambassador Palmer gave a debriefing this morning on his trip last week with Bill Brubeck. He described his talks with Tshombe as being "of only limited utility".[2] On the plus side, Tshombe agreed to dismiss all South African and Rhodesian pilots; to publish his letters to the OAU and ICRC; to issue orders to Congolese military commanders not to call for air strikes against towns; and to invite the OAU Commission to visit Leopoldville. On the negative side, Tshombe proved adamant against negotiating with the rebels for a political solution and against broadening the political base of his present government.

2. At Brussels, Ambassador Palmer found that there were differing views between Spaak and the Foreign Office on how to handle Tshombe.[3] The Foreign Office argued against pushing Tshombe too far, for fear of pushing him into the hands of the South Africans and the Portuguese. Spaak, on the other hand, questioned whether Tshombe has any alternative other than to continue to rely on Belgium and the US over the long term. Spaak reportedly favors a hard line with Tshombe and fears that, unless he is controlled now, Tshombe will develop an authoritarian regime (a view shared by Palmer). The Foreign Office favors letting Tshombe achieve a quick military victory, followed by a broadening of the government which, argues the Foreign Office, Tshombe would recognize as a necessary step in the interests of his own political survival.

3. Ambassador Palmer also discussed the difference of opinion between himself and Mac Godley on how better to safeguard the Americans at Stanleyville. Mac strongly advocates keeping the pressure on the rebels. Palmer fears that the closer the Congolese forces get to Stanleyville, the greater will be the danger to the hostages. He recognizes, however, that a continued adamant stand by Tshombe against a negoti-

---

[1] Source: Washington National Records Center, RG 330, OASD/ISA Files: FRC 69 A 7425, Congo 381 (12 Aug. 64). Top Secret. A stamped notation on the memorandum reads: "Mr. Vance has seen." A copy was sent to McNaughton.

[2] Palmer, Brubeck, and Godley met with Tshombe in Leopoldville on October 28.

[3] See footnote 2, Document 300.

ated political settlement, coupled with a military slowdown, could have dangerous consequences.

4. Palmer gave no clues about what recommendations or suggestions he would make as the result of his trip (although he had spent the preceding hour with George Ball).

Bill

309. Telegram From the Headquarters, U.S. Strike Command to the Joint Chiefs of Staff[1]

Tampa, Florida, November 2, 1964, 1120Z.

STRCC 858/64. Subject is: Possible Belgium contingency planning for Stanleyville.

Reference: JTF Leo Congo 0412 DTG 011050Z, Subject: Possible Belgium contingency planning for Stanleyville (Notal).[2]

1. The reference message was retransmitted this date to the Joint Chiefs of Staff by USSTRICOM. This is the second occasion on which we have had background information pertaining to some planning or proposals relating to the transport of Belgian paratroopers in US aircraft to participate in an air assault on Stanleyville.

2. While the matter of transporting a given number of people from Belgium to the Congo is no particular problem, the complications of conducting an airborne assault with foreign troops is a matter that should receive the most careful consideration before being undertaken. The Belgians do not have the same loading and jumping techniques as do US forces, and a language and communication problem would exist. The problems of staging a coordinated joint air assault would be most complicated without some preliminary training. This would likely consume as much time as is now programmed for the Van der Walle plan to be completed.

3. If any planning or proposals of this nature are being made with any measure of seriousness, I earnestly recommend that experts of this

---

[1] Source: Johnson Library, National Security File, Country File, Congo, Vol. VI, Memos & Miscellaneous, 10/64–11/64. Top Secret; Noforn; Limdis. Repeated to the Secretary of State and DOD, and forwarded to the White House.

[2] Not found.

command be called upon to participate in the discussions of such proposals.

310. Telegram From the Department of State to the Embassy in Kenya[1]

Washington, November 3, 1964, 9:10 p.m.

1649. For Ambassador.[2] Ref: Geneva's 885 to Dept, info Nairobi 41;[3] Geneva's 886 to Dept, info Nairobi 42.[4] FYI Dept deeply concerned that through misunderstandings or inadequate communication between ICRC and Kenyatta, opportunity may be lost for ICRC to establish effective presence in Stanleyville which would afford measure of protection foreign community and constitute foot in door for carrying out wider humanitarian mission. Our concern is sharpened by increasing risks to foreign community as GDRC military progress increases. In this connection, GDRC columns advancing from south should be in position threaten Kindu within few days and, with similar stepped up offenses from west, operations may shortly begin close in on Stanleyville. This undoubtedly accounts at least in part for increasingly strident notes Stanleyville propaganda and restraints placed on foreign community. End FYI.

Clear from reftel that failure ICRC put its message to Gbenye in form ICRC acceptance his invitation is due ICRC uncertainty authenticity invitation and, even if authenticity established, to Kenyatta's failure transmit message to ICRC. Dept therefore regards it as matter greatest importance and urgency that Kenyatta formally forwards to ICRC full text of Gbenye message. (It obviously would be even more

[1] Source: National Archives, RG 59, Central Files 1964–66, POL 23–9 THE CONGO. Confidential; Flash; Limdis. Drafted by McElhiney and Palmer; cleared by Officer in Charge of Kenyan Affairs W. Paul O'Neil, Runyon, Walter B. Gates in SCS, and Ball; and approved by Palmer, Also sent to the Mission in Geneva and repeated to Bujumbura and Leopoldville.

[2] Telegram 1648 to Nairobi, November 3, from Ball to Ambassador Attwood, emphasized the urgency of telegram 1649 and instructed Attwood to impress the urgency on Kenyatta. (Ibid.)

[3] Telegram 885 from Geneva, November 3, reported that ICRC representatives there had confirmed that the ICRC message to Gbenye on October 30 deliberately omitted any reference to Gebenye's alleged invitation to the ICRC to return to Stanleyville and verify conditions because they had doubts as to its authenticity. (Ibid.)

[4] Telegram 886 from Geneva, November 3, reported that the ICRC was very discouraged at the lack of any response to their message to Gbenye. (Ibid.)

helpful if, in forwarding message, Kenyatta would urge ICRC to respond affirmatively to Gbenye's invitation.) If, for any reason, full text Gbenye message to Kenyatta not suitable for forwarding to ICRC, you should endeavor persuade him to transmit to ICRC substance of that portion of message which could form basis for ICRC affirmative response. Since ICRC expected review on Nov 5 situation created by its failure to arrange reentry Stanleyville, most important that Kenyatta inform ICRC of Gbenye invitation soonest.

If, for reasons that may not be apparent here, Kenyatta is reluctant to involve himself or OAU Commission by notifying ICRC of Gbenye message, we hope that you will make every effort to remove his hesitancy. If you are still unsuccessful, we hope as minimum that you will be able obtain text of Gbenye message for such use as we may be able to make of it with ICRC under such circumstances, as well as your recommendations as to what measures we might take with other OAU members or otherwise to try to persuade Kenyatta to seize ICRC of Gbenye message and to encourage and support a favorable response by the ICRC.

We would hope that you could make Kenyatta understand that deteriorating situation with respect foreigners in Stanleyville confronts Africa and OAU Commission (as its duly designated instrument) with major moral and humanitarian problem. You are free to emphasize in this connection that we have done our utmost in Leopoldville to encourage Tshombe to place prudent restraints on his use of air power in order to cooperate in a humanitarian effort with the ICRC and the OAU to protect innocent civilians and secure respect for Geneva Conventions. Similarity of proposals expressed in Tshombe letters to Kenyatta and ICRC (Leopoldville's 169 to Nairobi)[5] on one hand and Soumialot and Gbenye messages to Kenyatta on other hand seem clearly to create a situation where Kenyatta and OAU Commission, with statesmanlike initiative based on humanitarian considerations, could play effective role in mitigating some of worst effects of unfortunate internal conflict and perhaps pave way for even more far-reaching political initiative within terms their mandate to assist GDRC in achieving national reconciliation. It seems clear to us that a vigorous OAU initiative towards these ends would clearly enhance prestige of the organization and of the commission under Kenyatta chairmanship as its agent. We therefore hope that Kenyatta will view this chance to facilitate ICRC presence Stanleyville as a real opportunity which may not recur.

---

[5] Not found.

In making foregoing points, we hope that you will also be able to obtain full text of Kenyatta message to Gbenye (last para Embtel 1157),[6] as well as ascertain whether Kenyatta has replied to Tshombe message and, if so, obtain text.

For Geneva: You should inform ICRC soonest re efforts we are making to confirm authenticity Gbenye message to Kenyatta, to obtain text thereof, and to persuade Kenyatta to forward it to ICRC Geneva. You should express strong hope that in any event ICRC will not take any decisions on Nov 5 which would preclude (1) further exploration of resumption mercy mission, (2) establishment effective ICRC presence in Congo to enhance safety Congolese and foreign civilian populations, and (3) encouragement compliance Geneva Conventions. You should emphasize our belief that even continued position of ICRC plane in Bujumbura and continuing efforts ICRC officials to assert humanitarian responsibility in Congo represents in and of itself a measure of deterrence against excesses by Stanleyville regime. In view importance of problem and degree of very deeply appreciated past informal cooperation between us, we strongly hope ICRC will not take any decisions to terminate its efforts without consulting further with us and other countries affected.

Rusk

[6] Dated November 3. (National Archives, RG 59, Central Files 1964–66, POL 23–9 THE CONGO)

311. Memorandum for the Files[1]

Washington, November 5, 1964.

It is becoming increasingly clear that our incautious broadcasting of our concern about the fate of the Americans in Stanleyville has increased the rebel appreciation of the value of the hostages, thereby increasing the danger to them. The country team's judgment in these matters and that of our Embassy in Belgium have so far been consistently sound, and it is clear that we should have paid more attention to their views. I have on several occasions registered this opinion, in-

[1] Source: Library of Congress, Manuscript Division, Harriman Papers, Box 448, Congo (3). Confidential. Drafted by Harriman.

cluding my objection to the stand-down of the aircraft in the Congo for seven days.

W.A.H.

---

312. Telegram From the Department of State to the Embassy in the Congo[1]

Washington, November 6, 1964, 9:18 p.m.

1165. Ref: Kampala 716, Leo 1760, Dar es Salaam 916.[2] FYI Dept gravely concerned over confirmed report of *Ilyushin* offloading cargo in Uganda which may contain arms for onward shipment to Stanleyville rebels. Another agency is reasonably certain this is Algerian *Ilyushin* recently seen in Dar es Salaam (Dar es Salaam 884).[3] If this and similar actions continue, tide which now against rebels could turn decisively and could prolong Congolese insurgency indefinitely contrary to US interests (including security of US hostages in rebel hands), as well as Congolese and general African interests. End FYI.

For Leopoldville: You should share gist of first paragraph of ref Kampala tel [*less than 1 line not declassified*] with Tshombe and urge that his representative at Kampala (special envoy if necessary) make dignified but forceful démarche to GOU protesting this aid to rebels and requesting assurances that same will not occur in future. You should also suggest that Tshombe send urgent message to Kenyatta underlining fact that such aid will only prolong Congolese conflict and will jeopardize peaceful solution which he earnestly seeking. Embassy may assist GDRC in preparation of message to Kenyatta in order ensure it is discreet and will create optimum desirable effect if published. You should discourage Tshombe from public denunciation of any African govt at this stage and at least until confidential diplomacy with GOU and Kenyatta is given opportunity to produce desired effect. You

---

[1] Source: National Archives, RG 59, Central Files 1964–66, POL 23–9 THE CONGO. Secret; Priority. Drafted by Hoffacker in AF/CWG on November 5; cleared by McElhiney in AF/CWG, AFE Deputy Director Edward W. Mulcahy, [*text not declassified*], Newsom, and Leonard F. Willems in WE; and approved by Tasca. Also sent to Addis Ababa, Lagos, and Brussels, and repeated to Nairobi, Kampala, Dar es Salaam, Algiers, London, Khartoum, Bujumbura, CINCSTRIKE for Ramsey, and DOD.

[2] Telegram 716 from Kampala, November 4; telegram 1760 from Leopoldville, November 5; telegram 916 from Dar es Salaam, November 4. (All ibid.)

[3] Dated October 30. (Ibid.)

should stress importance of prompt action by GDRC in both channels in order attempt nip in bud possible mounting of supply operation.

You should share same report (Kampala 716) with your Nigerian and Ethiopian colleagues and suggest that this is sort of mischief which radical Africans will continue to engage in unless moderate elements like Nigerian and Ethiopian govts take more spirited action in OAU and elsewhere in support of earliest peaceful solution of Congo problem.

For Addis Ababa and Lagos: You should take line with GON and IEG, at level you deem most appropriate, similar to guidance which Embassy Leo is authorized to use with Nigerian and Ethiopian diplomatic reps. You might ask for suggestions as to how this apparent radical African activity might be countered.

For Brussels: You may inform GOB of Kampala report, may describe action which USG is taking to counter this new development, and, if you perceive no objection, may ask GOB to support USG approach to Tshombe as outlined above.

Rusk

---

313. Memorandum of Conversation[1]

Washington, November 8, 1964.

SUBJECT

Congo

PARTICIPANTS

Governor Harriman
H.E. Paul-Henri Spaak, Belgian Minister of Foreign Affairs
Belgian Ambassador Scheyven
Viscount Etienne Davignon, Chef de Cabinet of Belgian Foreign Minister
Emile Indekeu, Political Counselor of Belgian Embassy
G. Mennen Williams, Assistant Secretary for African Affairs
Wayne Fredericks, Dep. Asst. Secretary for African Affairs
Joseph Palmer, Director General of the Foreign Service
Ambassador Llewellyn Thompson
Henry Tasca, Dep. Asst. Secretary for European Affairs

---

[1] Source: Library of Congress, Manuscript Division, Harriman Papers, Subject Files, Spaak, Paul-Henri. Confidential. Drafted by McKillop. Belgian Foreign Minister Spaak was in Washington November 8–9 to discuss the crisis in the Congo.

David McKillop, Director, Office of Western European Affairs
Frederic Chapin, Sp. Assistant to Governor Harriman
William Brubeck, White House
Ambassador to Belgium Douglas MacArthur

Governor Harriman opened the discussion after dinner by pointing out that we felt that Tshombe or Kasavubu should be induced to make some gesture as a contribution to the security of foreigners in Stanleyville and to improve relations with other African countries. Since, as Mr. Spaak had earlier pointed out, Tshombe had recently made a statement which was not helpful, being somewhat too belligerent in tone, he would like to have Mr. Spaak's further thinking on what should now be done.

Mr. Spaak replied that the military situation was better and if it were not for the hostages in Stanleyville, he would say let the military situation take its normal course. However, we do not know what may happen to our nationals if the rebels lose their heads completely. In Leopoldville the problem is not with Tshombe himself but lies in the fact that a number of people have influence upon him, such as Munongo, as well as a number of Belgians who do not fall under the Belgian director of technical assistance. They are former friends of his from the Katanga and they do not always give him the best of advice.

Mr. Spaak went on to say that after Kindu a few days will be needed to consolidate the ANC forces. He knew that Gbenye had been telegraphing messages in all directions to the effect that the Americans and Belgians are bombing civilians, but as far as he knew there have been no air attacks on towns except very limited action on Boende. Gbenye's messages show that he is losing his head completely.

Mr. Spaak concurred that we should take advantage of the breathing spell after the taking of Kindu. He had read the text of the proposed declaration and felt that it should be made by Kasavubu rather than Tshombe since the former enjoyed better standing with the Africans; however, it would be better to have it made by Tshombe than to have no statement at all. After first reading the text he thought it was well put together and met the requirements of the situation. He had one comment. There was a sentence on page 3 which we would never get Kasavubu to accept. This was the sentence about sending OAU personnel to observe the elections. However, the most important thing was to get Kasavubu personally to make the declaration. Perhaps both embassies in Leopoldville could jointly try to "sell" this to Kasavubu.

In view of the enormous importance of this text Mr. Spaak wondered whether its delivery to Kasavubu should perhaps be entrusted to someone special other than our Ambassadors (there was at present no Belgian Ambassador in Leopoldville). Governor Harriman asked him if he had anyone particular in mind and Mr. Spaak indicated he would prefer that person to be an American. The Governor pointed out that we would prefer that special person to be a Belgian. Mr. Spaak stressed that it was not a refusal on his part to assume such a responsibility, rather the question was who was in a position to influence Kasavubu and he didn't know the answer to that question. It developed that Mr. Van Bilsen, Director of Belgian technical assistance in the Congo, who had been Kasavubu's adviser in earlier days, was the person Mr. Spaak had in mind. It was agreed that Mr. Van Bilsen, who is now in Brussels, would be contacted by Mr. Spaak upon the latter's return to Brussels on November 10.

Turning to the military situation Governor Harriman said that the Van Der Walle column in Kindu would be reinforced as soon as possible so that it could then be decided whether it would launch an attack against Stanleyville. He understood that Mr. Spaak thought a direct attack would be better if it were not for the hostages whose security was a paramount consideration.

Mr. Spaak pointed out that for an attack on Stanleyville timing was very important because of the 800 Europeans there, some 30 of whom were Americans and about 500 Belgians.

Governor Harriman said that Tshombe knows that he must have Belgian-U.S. agreement before he makes an attack. The question was whether one should keep pressure against the rebels or not since experience shows that when the rebels are under pressure generally they do not mistreat foreigners but tend to be rough when things are going well for them.

Mr. Spaak said that Van Der Walle knew he must make no move against Stanleyville without warning us first. However, we have very little control over the column approaching Stanleyville from Boende, as this column is led by South African mercenaries. We must confirm to Van Der Walle that he can make no move on Stanleyville without letting us know. The distance of 250 miles that separates Kindu from Stanleyville is a very important factor because as the ANC troops advance Gbenye may lose control over the rebels who may panic and lose their heads completely. Mr. Spaak stated very strongly that Tshombe must be told emphatically that he can make no move against Stanleyville without prior notification. To a question about safety of the hostages in Stanleyville, Mr. Spaak replied that the danger in Stanleyville was not so much from Gbenye or Soumialot personally but rather that they might lose control over the forces they had unleashed. It could well be that ANC troops advancing against Stanleyville would create general panic over which rebel leaders would have no control. He had thought of recalling Van Der Walle to Brussels for consultation and for an appraisal of the Stanleyville situation. So far we had been extremely fortunate in Albertville, Uvira and Kindu. The action had been so fast the rebels had not had time to kill hostages.

Mr. Brubeck suggested that we find out Van Der Walle's estimates of the value of an air strike on Stanleyville using blank ammunition at the time of his column's land attack on the town.

Returning to his thought of recalling Van Der Walle to Brussels for consultation, Mr. Spaak expressed his uncertainty over this idea, as well as his feeling that the operation against Stanleyville must be a lightning fast strike.

Davignon suggested that the Belgians send their military attaché to talk to Van Der Walle, after which he would come to Brussels to make his report. Davignon commented that Tshombe dislikes Van Bilsen and that Rothschild could conceivably accompany Van Bilsen when he calls on Tshombe. This could be considered a normal step because both have responsibilities for technical assistance.

Mr. Spaak indicated he might suggest that Rothschild accompany Van Bilsen. He went on to say that we should tell Kasavubu that we are always ready to help technically and militarily but that the proposed declaration was an essential preliminary to the military operation and needed to create doubt in the minds of the rebels. Monmart (Belgian Military Attaché in the Congo) would be sent to Kindu to see Van Der Walle to explain to him that if he moves on Stanleyville it must be a lightning fast strike because delays can have very grave consequences. Mr. Spaak believed that we had time for such consultation since Van Der Walle will require a few days to reorganize his forces.

Governor Harriman said that we welcomed these Belgian initiatives.

Mr. Spaak also indicated that another danger was that in Leopoldville there were people who were not greatly concerned over the fate of the 800 Europeans. Munongo was one who advocated a policy of brute force. Mr. Spaak thought that the U.S. and Belgium should hold fast and tell Kasavubu that the declaration must be made.

After summing up the procedures outlined above Mr. Spaak indicated that there were other things that could also be done by the Congo Government, such as sending some emissaries to other African countries on explanatory missions.

Returning to the questions of Tshombe, Governor Harriman was assured by Davignon that Montmart in previous talks with Tshombe had gained Tshombe's acceptance of the idea that no operations against Stanleyville would be undertaken without letting us know. Montmart had also talked with Mobutu and Kasavubu. They as well as Tshombe agreed that the military must proceed to Stanleyville but they fully appreciate the problem that we (U.S. and Belgium) are faced with.

Ambassador Palmer suggested getting the Nigerians to support the idea of a Kasavubu declaration. Davignon suggested the Ethiopians in addition. Tshombe, he asserted, respects the Ethiopians who helped him at Addis Ababa. Mr. Brubeck suggested that in addition to the Nigerians, the Tunisians and the Ethiopians be asked to recommend to Kasavubu that he make the proposed declaration. Davignon pointed out that Arab countries such as Tunisia are out as far as Tshombe is concerned. Governor Harriman agreed that Tunisia should not be approached but that the Nigerians and Ethiopians should be urged to tell Kasavubu that it is essential he make such a declaration.

On the question of individuals to be sent by the Congo Government as emissaries to other African countries, Mr. Spaak thought it was all right to send Langema as he was on good terms with Tshombe and had performed missions for Tshombe before, but we should guard against being too specific about whom we should like to have sent and merely point out in general terms that we feel such missions would be most useful. For example, if we should mention Bomboko, Tshombe, Nendaka, and Mobutu might object.

Mr. Fredericks suggested getting the Zambians to play a part also.

---

314. Memorandum From William H. Brubeck of the National Security Council Staff to the President's Special Assistant for National Security Affairs (Bundy)[1]

Washington, November 9, 1964.

SUBJECT

Stanleyville Hostage Problem

The mercenary (Van der Walle) column that took Kindu last week is preparing for final attack on Stanleyville in two to three weeks. Meanwhile the situation of foreigners in Stanleyville (five official and 20 unofficial Americans, 6–800 Europeans) is increasingly precarious. All Belgians and Americans are now under house arrest and labeled "prisoners of war." At any time during these next several weeks, as the situation in Stanleyville deteriorates, the rebel "Jeunesse" may get out of control and start killing Europeans. The danger will be particularly

---

[1] Source: Johnson Library, National Security File, Country File, Congo, Vol. VI. Top Secret; Sensitive Handling.

acute at the actual time of Van der Walle's attack on Stanleyville (at Kindu last week 80 Europeans were nearly killed by rebels when Van der Walle took the town).

In talks on Sunday[2] to meet this problem, Spaak and Harriman arrived at the following tentative agreement (Spaak asks great secrecy because this is politically very touchy in Belgium):

1. Belgian paratroop force (probably company size) should be on standby alert in Brussels with a corresponding US C–130 transport force on alert in Europe ready to go into Stanleyville on a few hours notice and seize the town long enough to evacuate by air all Europeans. Belgians will obtain pro forma request for evacuation mission from Congo Government.

2. Spaak will tomorrow (Tuesday) attempt to secure Cabinet approval for this project. We will then send a single, high ranking military officer in civilian clothes to Brussels to work out air transport requirements with the Belgians and then implement (probably half a dozen C–130s at most, for troop transport and evacuation). This to be handled on strictest need-to-know basis.

Recommendations:

1. That the President approve this project with the specific understanding that any actual use of the force would require decision by both governments in the particular case.

2. That Secretary McNamara designate a responsible official in Defense with whom Harriman can deal in making arrangements, to get maximum security.

B

[2] November 8; see Document 313.

315. Memorandum From William H. Brubeck of the National Security Council Staff to President Johnson[1]

Washington, November 9, 1964.

SUBJECT

Congo Situation Report

Last week Tshombe's Belgian-led (Van der Walle) mercenary force took Kindu, the most important rebel city short of Stanleyville. Within two or three weeks it will take Stanleyville, 250 miles away, and the present rebellion will be ended.

Our biggest immediate problem is how to protect the foreign hostages in Stanleyville (5 official and 20 unofficial Americans, 6–800 Europeans) both during this several weeks and when the mercenaries attack. We have gotten Tshombe to agree and to announce publicly that his airplanes will not hit towns, in order to minimize the risk that the rebels will kill the Stanleyville hostages in retaliation for air attacks. However, the hostages are in acute danger—first, because there is a squadron of T–6 aircraft, flown by mercenaries, which we do not control and which is a real threat to attack Stanleyville in the next several weeks; second, because the rebels may well slaughter hostages at the time Van der Walle actually attacks Stanleyville.

The military move on Stanleyville is a calculated risk and a real one. To minimize it, we are trying to compel Tshombe to withdraw the mercenary T–6s and may need a tough Presidential message to Tshombe for this purpose. We are working with the Belgians on a contingency plan to drop Belgian paratroops in Stanleyville on short notice, to evacuate foreigners, if the situation gets out of control. And we are working with the Belgians on a program of political pressures and covert negotiations to try to get the rebels to capitulate and surrender Stanleyville without a fight. Realistically, however, this will be a dangerous two or three weeks, it will probably end in the military conquest of Stanleyville, and there is a real chance that some Americans and Europeans will be killed.

Looking beyond the immediate military problem and the problem of our hostages, our aim is to avoid the US again being involved so deeply in the Congo. We are trying to get the other Africans to take over the Congo problem politically; we are trying to get the Belgians to take responsibility, with the US limited to a supporting role, in helping

---

[1] Source: Johnson Library, National Security File, Country File, Congo, Vol. VI. Top Secret.

the Congo; we want to withdraw our military assistance and leave it to the Belgians; we want to pressure Tshombe to make a sensible political compromise among the forces in the Congo, and not get stuck propping up Tshombe in an authoritarian regime without any power base in the realities of the Congo.

B

---

316. Telegram From the Department of State to the Embassy in the Congo[1]

Washington, November 9, 1964, 9:22 p.m.

1182. Following are agreements reached on Congo with Belgians during discussions Washington November 6–9:

1. Two American officials, one of them military, and a Belgian diplomat will be sent from the Embassies in Leopoldville to Kindu (a) to consult with the military operations commander to elicit his opinions on the time to begin and the time required to carry out the operation against Stanleyville and to determine more precisely the logistical support requirements of the columns, and (b) to survey the situation to assemble information which would be helpful in determining the composition and functions of an equipe polyvalente for Kindu.

2. The Belgian Government will form an equipe polyvalente for Kindu in the shortest possible time.

3. In consideration of the large foreign community in Stanleyville, the two governments will emphasize to the Congolese Government the necessity of consultations with the two governments before an operation against Stanleyville is undertaken.

4. The United States Government will supplement existing air transport in the Congo to provide adequate airlift capability to supply the columns of the military operations commander at Kindu. The rapid supplying of these forces is intended to create as soon as possible a situation in which a decision on his further advance can be taken. The supplying does not prejudge that decision.

---

[1] Source: National Archives, RG 59, Central Files 1964–66, POL 23–9 THE CONGO. Secret. Drafted by McElhiney in AF/CWG, cleared by Davis in EUR/WE, and approved by Palmer. Also sent to Brussels and CINCSTRIKE for POLAD.

5. It would be useful for Kasavubu, before the capitulation of the rebels, to make a public declaration outlining a broad program to resolve the Congo problem that would be transmitted to the OAU. Lengema would be a suitable emissary to the OAU to seek its acceptance of the program.

6. The Belgian Government will attempt to get Congolese agreement to the essential elements of the Rothschild Plan. The United States Government will fully support these efforts. In instituting the Plan, the Belgian Government will as far as possible work closely with the UN chief of civil operations in the Congo to assure maximum UN support of its efforts.

7. Since the Belgian Government is unable to provide all of the crews required for the C–47 planes in the Congo from its own military forces, it will endeavor to obtain non-military personnel for these crews on the basis of commercial contracts.

Spaak has agreed to points in general terms and Davignon has agreed to specific language.

Re point 3, our original formulation was "The two governments (i.e., U.S. and Belgian) will consult and jointly decide when the military operations commander at Kindu should advance further." ("Military operations commander" is standard GOB euphemism for Van der Walle.) Davignon agreed that our formulation was entirely accurate, but said GOB preferred have nothing in its files which made clear that any military operations in Congo, even those of VDW, under Belgian control.

Re point 7, Davignon said he could not promise secure non-military personnel but he would make real effort do so.

Ball

317. Telegram From the Department of State to the Embassy in the Congo[1]

Washington, November 9, 1964, 9:23 p.m.

1183. For Ambassador from Secretary. Following telegram contains text instructions jointly developed and agreed between Belgians and ourselves during Spaak visit here past two days.[2]

I know that you are fully aware of the deep concern which is felt at the highest levels of the Government with the safety of the American community at Stanleyville. Both Spaak and I are strongly convinced that the proposed program will, if accepted and vigorously implemented by Kasavubu and Tshombe, undercut the morale and disrupt the unity of the insurgents, enhance the possibility of a peaceful resolution of the Stanleyville problem and at the same time contribute to a better atmosphere in which to undertake the gigantic tasks of reconstruction and reconciliation which face the Congo.

We realize that with the military effort moving so satisfactorily, there may be a reluctance on the part of the Congo's top leaders to temporize, however marginally, with the rebels. I know that you will make every effort, however, to overcome any such hesitancy, emphasizing the minimal nature of the government offers which are contemplated and the fact that they are intended to supplement and not supplant the continuance of a sustained military effort. While it is not our present intention to threaten or apply specific pressures on the GDRC in order to encourage acceptance of this program, you should not hesitate to make clear as necessary that our attitude towards future cooperation with the Congo will inevitably be affected by Kasavubu's and Tshombe's cooperation on a matter of such fundamental importance to us.

I know that we can count on you to press these proposals in coordination with your Belgian colleagues with all possible vigor and imagination.

Ball

[1] Source: National Archives, RG 59, Central Files 1964–66, POL 23–9 THE CONGO. Secret; Exdis. Drafted and approved by Palmer in AF/CWG and cleared by Read and Harriman. Rusk is also listed as clearing the text.

[2] Presumably reference is to telegram 1182, Document 316.

318. Telegram From the Chairman of the Joint Chiefs of Staff (Wheeler) to the Commander in Chief, European Command (Lemnitzer)[1]

Washington, November 11, 1964, 0051Z.

JCS 001745. From CJCS.

1. Confirming telecon between Lt General Burchinal, Director, Joint Staff, and Maj General Oberbeck, J–3, USEUCOM, you are authorized to send Brigadier General Dougherty, Lt Colonel Gray and Captain Brashears to Brussels without delay. Mission of these officers will be to plan with appropriate Belgian officials use of US airlift for approximately one company of Belgian paratroopers for possible emergency parachute assault on Stanleyville, Congo, in order to free US and European hostages. C–130 aircraft for this purpose will be drawn from those available to you. It is possible that Belgians may request small airlift capability additional to that required for assault drop in order to evacuate Europeans and Americans from Stanleyville area.

2. Officers will proceed to Brussels in civilian clothes and report to Ambassador MacArthur who will put them in touch with appropriate Belgian officials. Maximum discretion in carrying out this mission mandatory.

3. Lt Colonel James E. Dunn from Joint Staff proceeding in civilian clothes ASAP to join group at American Embassy, Brussels, for purpose of keeping JCS and Secretary of Defense informed and providing any required assistance.

4. Repeat that purpose of party is planning only. Decision to execute operation is reserved to highest US governmental level.

[1] Source: Johnson Library, National Security File, Country File, Congo, Vol. VI, Memos & Miscellaneous, 10/64–11/64. Top Secret; Immediate; Limdis. Drafted by Wheeler. Repeated to CINCSTRIKE/USCINCMEAFSA, the Embassy in Brussels, the Department of State, and the White House.

319. Telegram From the Department of State to the Embassy in Belgium[1]

Washington, November 13, 1964, 6:44 p.m.

989. Ref: Leopoldville's 1869, rptd Brussels 1045.[2]

For Brussels and Leo: Dept wishes assure that Washington, Brussels and Leo all equally understand that our willingness to engage with GOB in joint contingency planning does not indicate that we predisposed towards intervening militarily in Congo. Purpose of planning is simply to be prepared for any contingency. It would only be in event demonstrated imminent peril to foreign community Stan that we would consider rescue operation involving US military participation and then only after decision at highest levels USG. Believe this was made fully clear to Spaak and Davignon when they were here but if Brussels or Leo believes there is slightest reason for misunderstanding, they should immediately make this clear to their Belgian colleagues.

For Brussels: Against foregoing background Dept fully concurs your action in seeing Spaak to express concern re De Kerchove's instructions (Embtel 933, rptd Leo 370).[3]

We understood De Kerchove's primary mission on arrival Leo was to secure Tshombe's and Kasavubu's assent to Kasavubu's issuance declaration. (In addition, he would of course deliver Spaak's letter re Rothschild Plan.) We regard it as matter greatest importance that time provided by VDW's pause to regroup and resupply should be used as agreed with Belgians. Time is rapidly running out and we hope GOB will urgently instruct De Kerchove, as we are Godley, to initiate approaches to Kasavubu and Tshombe immediately.

Additional instructions on control of military operations follow in separate tel.

For Leo: Re penultimate para reftel, your assumption does not accord with what Dept believes should be relative priorities based on talks with Belgians here. First priority emphasis in terms of timing is on

---

[1] Source: National Archives, RG 59, Central Files 1964–66, POL 23–9 THE CONGO. Top Secret; Flash; Exdis. Drafted by Palmer and McElhiney in AF/CWG; cleared by Harriman, Colonel Gall in DOD, Brubeck, and Fredericks; and approved by Palmer. Repeated to Leopoldville.

[2] Dated November 13. (Ibid.)

[3] In telegram 933 from Brussels, November 13, MacArthur reported that he expressed to Spaak his personal doubts about the wisdom of prematurely informing Tshombe regarding their contingency plan for Stanleyville. Spaak agreed and instructed De Kerchove to concert with Godley upon arrival in Leopoldville as to when to inform Tshombe. Spaak also told the Ambassador that his own feeling was that the sooner Stanleyville was liberated the better in terms of the safety of the foreign hostages. (Ibid.)

earliest possible political initiative, with any approach to GDRC connected with contingency planning coming at such time as circumstances require. You should therefore see De Kerchove soonest and concert with him re your parallel recommendations as to when Tshombe should be informed of contingency plan. Dept's view is GDRC should not be consulted until last possible moment after need for drop clear.

You should then coordinate with De Kerchove at once re earliest possible approaches to Tshombe and Kasavubu to seek agreement on issuance Kasavubu declaration. If De Kerchove not prepared for any reason to move before you, you should not any longer delay your démarche but should act at once, following Tshombe to Congo Central if necessary to accomplish this mission. Reply your 1353[4] in separate tel. Advise re your plans soonest.

Dept regards both importance and urgency of your démarche and of issuance Kasavubu declaration as being underlined by disturbing developments reported Dar's 1013[5] and possibly by [*telegram number not declassified*],[6] both of which being repeated to you separately.

Rusk

---

[4] Dated October 5. (Ibid., POL 8)

[5] Dated November 13. (Ibid., POL 9 EUR W–TANZAN)

[6] Telegram not found.

320. Memorandum From William H. Brubeck of the National Security Council Staff to the President's Special Assistant for National Security Affairs (Bundy)[1]

Washington, November 15, 1964.

SUBJECT

Congo-US-Belgian Military Contingency Plan

Belgian and US military yesterday completed a contingency plan under which 12 US C–130s would fly battalion (545) of Belgian paratroops from Brussels to Stanleyville via Spain, Ascencion and Kamina

---

[1] Source: Johnson Library, National Security File, Country File, Congo, Vol. VII. Top Secret.

(in Katanga) to seize city and evacuate foreigners (600 Belgians, 200 other Europeans, 30 American). Plan calls for 12 hour warning to alert Belgian paras, departure from Belgium at 1840Z any given day, then following schedule:

Minimum lead time—

Brussels–Stanleyville—57 hrs. 30 mins.
Ascencion–Stanleyville—22 hrs. 30 mins.
Kamina–Stanleyville—3 hrs.

Plan would be used a) if violence began in Stan during next 10–15 days before Congo mercenary (Van der Walle) force can attack, or b) simultaneous with Van der Walle attack in order maximize chance of securing Europeans rapidly so as to prevent reprisal. Such a US-flown Belgian paratroop assault on Stan would cost us heavily in African politics (including Chirep, base rights, etc.), is contemplated only because neither we nor Belgians could afford to stand helplessly enduring slaughter of foreigners in Stan.

Van der Walle now plans tentatively to begin move toward Stan about 17th, final (150 mile straight good road) dash to begin 24th and arrive Stan 25th. This schedule may slip several days. Once it becomes visible moving on Stan, situation there will be very dangerous for hostages, particularly 5 US diplomatic personnel believed in military prison.

Secretary Rusk thinks (Vance and Wheeler concur) that this is primarily Belgian responsibility and Belgian stake, with acute Belgian political consequences for Spaak, difficult for us to refuse or second guess him. Spaak has asked immediate US agreement to launch force Brussels 17th, holding at Ascencion on 18th, with lead time of 22 hours Ascencion to Stan via Kamina if decision made to go. (Obviously, in situation contemplated, lead time may be critical.) We have replied that while disposed to meet his request, would like his comment on several questions (what kind of cover story to maintain security; why not preposition at Kamina instead of Ascencion, with only 4 hours lead time to Stan; why not delay departure from Belgium several days in order to limit period of preposition to shorter, critically important period thus minimizing security risk) but we will probably have to make a decision tomorrow.

The President may therefore be asked tomorrow for a firm decision to move to a preposition base (Kamina or Ascencion) = still deferring the go/no go decision on Stan till need arises.

Addendum—(misc. points and info)

1. With Spanish and French overflight clearances required, local personnel at air bases en route and at Kamina and conspicuous absence

of paratroop battalion from Brussels, likelihood of security leak very great.

2. With a security leak, or if Stanleyville actually hit, political repercussions in Africa hard to over emphasize (political contingency planning is underway).

3. If we hit Stanleyville, there is increased danger of reprisal against additional foreigners (perhaps 30 Americans, several hundred Belgians) scattered throughout Northeast Congo as well as (less probably) attacks on US Embassies and nationals in other African countries (problems under study).

4. Existence and movement of this force will generate heavy Belgian and Embassy Leo pressures to use, particularly at time when Van der Walle reaches Stanleyville.

5. We continue to seek better alternatives including these political moves aimed at collapse of Stanleyville without violence:

a. Tshombe has agreed to help persuade Kasavubu to issue "reconciliation manifesto" offering amnesty, participation in elections, etc.

b. We have sent [*less than 1 line not declassified*] to East Africa to explore with rebel contact there possibility of a deal with the rebel leaders (money and safe conduct to exile).

But these are faint hopes, and a Van der Walle military conquest of Stanleyville in next two weeks is most likely prospect with very real chance US-Belgian intervention will be needed to rescue hostages.

B

321. Memorandum From Arthur McCafferty of the National Security Council Staff to Bromley Smith of the National Security Council Staff[1]

Washington, November 16, 1964.

SUBJECT

Planning for Stanleyville Operation

I have put together a small package of cables which I hope will assist you in understanding the complexities of this operation.

Tab 1 (Leo 1895)[2] contains an excellent résumé of VDW plans and coordination for use of air drop (Dragon Rouge) and [*less than 1 line not declassified*]. VDW plans to jump off from Lubutu, approximately 225 KM from Stanleyville, about 24 November. Hopefully he will reach Stanleyville in 24 hours. He would call for air drop according to resistance capability shown by rebels as he advances. [*less than 1 line not declassified*] will be joined with VDW forces and act in accordance with instructions in Deptel 1235[3] (Tab 2). You will note that Col. Rattan will act as communicator for VDW and will communicate VDW's views and/or desires re air drop, etc.

Tab 3 (Brussels 937)[4] contains an outline of operation Dragon Rouge and Tab 4 is USCINCEUR OPLAN 319/64 (nickname Dragon Rouge). Briefly this operation calls for a U.S. airlift of approximately 550 Belgian paratroops and *equipment* to Stanleyville. The U.S. will supply 12 C–130E aircraft with crews, support and maintenance personnel totalling approximately 200. The force will be pre-positioned at Ascension for deployment on call by VDW (after top level decision in U.S. and Belgium). The planning is flexible at this point to permit deployment to Kamina in the Congo for refueling and final briefing and coordination with VDW or direct deployment to Stanleyville. Belgian CO plans drop on golf course, then a three-pronged attack to: A—block and control access to airport; B—clear and occupy tower and Sabena guest house; C—clear airfield. Following airstrip clearing, paratroops

[1] Source: Johnson Library, National Security File, Country File, Congo, Vol. VII, Memos & Miscellaneous, 11/64. Top Secret. A handwritten "S" on the memorandum indicates Smith saw it.

[2] None of the tabs is attached. Telegram 1895 from Leopoldville is dated November 15. (National Archives, RG 59, Central Files 1964–66, POL 23–9 THE CONGO)

[3] Dated November 13. (Ibid.)

[4] Dated November 13. (Ibid.)

will proceed into city proper to other known areas of hostage imprisonment.

Art McCafferty[5]

[5] Printed from a copy that bears this typed signature.

322. Memorandum From the President's Special Assistant for National Security Affairs (Bundy) to President Johnson[1]

Washington, November 16, 1964.

SUBJECT

Congo Situation

1. The question: Do we concur in the Belgians' desire to preposition Belgian paratroopers at British Ascension Island in the South Atlantic, 22 hours from Stanleyville?

2. Recommendation: State, Defense, and Bundy recommend concurrence.[2]

3. The situation: Mercenary advance on Stanleyville begins tomorrow and should drive rebels out within 3 or 4 days. In this period the safety of 30 Americans and 800 other foreigners, mostly Belgian, will be endangered. Spaak and Prime Minister LeFevre wish to reduce our reaction time from three days to one.

4. As we agreed at the Ranch, it seems best to let Belgians take the lead on this and to be guided by their judgment. They know the Congolese better, and their nationals outnumber ours by 30 to 1. Nevertheless, it is our officials who have been directly threatened, and all the transport will be U.S. Air Force. So it is an important decision.

5. We can still hope that the rescue operation will not be necessary, because any action of this kind will have real political costs in the

[1] Source: Johnson Library, National Security File, Country File, Congo, Vol. VII, Memos & Miscellaneous, 11/64. Top Secret.

[2] A handwritten notation reads: "BKS: P agreed to this & told Brubeck. McGB." Telegram JCS 001903 to CINCEUR, November 16, authorized execution on November 17 of that portion of OPLAN 319/64 (Dragon Rouge) necessary to position forces at Ascension Island but stipulated that no deployment beyond Ascension was authorized except as directed by the Joint Chiefs of Staff. (National Archives, RG 59, Central Files 1964–66, POL 23–9 THE CONGO)

Congo and may involve the death of innocent Americans by panicky rebel reaction. Nevertheless, the possible cost of opposing the Belgian recommendation seems clearly greater than the cost of concurrence.

6. The requirement for your consent to further movement of this force will remain. It is probable that the next recommendation will be to move the paratroops to Kamina in the Katanga Province of the Congo. This will put them only 4 hours from Stanleyville, and while it increases risk of rebel panic, it will also increase the warning signal that we are ready to act if necessary. This decision may come tomorrow, and Secretary Rusk will bring it to you directly if necessary.

McG. B.

---

323. Memorandum From the Under Secretary of State for Political Affairs (Harriman) to the Chairman of the Joint Chiefs of Staff (Wheeler)[1]

Washington, November 16, 1964.

SUBJECT

Dragon Rouge

1. With reference to General Lemnitzer's telegram of November 15 to Ambassador MacArthur regarding the Dragon Rouge operation,[2] the Department of State:

A. Considers Dragon Rouge to be a Belgian operation with U.S. logistical support; and

B. Agrees that if and when the necessary joint US/GOB decision to implement the plan has been made, the military commander responsible for making the "go/no-go" and timing decisions from Kamina onward should be the Belgian paratroop commander.

2. The plan now provides that, following completion of the mission and refueling and crew rest at Leopoldville, the 12 C–130's "will prepare to return to home station via Wheelus". As was the case with the movement to Stanleyville, overriding political considerations make the use of Wheelus for the return trip impossible. The plan should be

---

[1] Source: National Archives, RG 59, Central Files 1964–66, POL 23–9 THE CONGO. Top Secret. Drafted by McElhiney.

[2] Not found.

amended to provide for return without overflying African countries, none of whom would be likely to grant overflight clearances even if we were prepared to request them. The most direct politically acceptable route would be the one used by the C–130's for the flight from Brussels to Stanleyville, i.e. via Ascension and Las Palmas to Europe.

3. The plan makes no provision for the evacuation of Belgian paratroopers from Stanleyville after completion of the mission. We are asking the American Embassy in Brussels to ascertain Belgian intentions in this regard.

W. Averell Harriman[3]

[3] Printed from a copy that indicates Harriman signed the original.

324. Telegram From the Embassy in the Congo to the Department of State[1]

Leopoldville, November 16, 1964, 4 p.m.

1911. Re Embtel 1907.[2] Kasavubu told Belg Amb noon today there was no question of his making proposed statement Deptel 1894[3] as subsequently modified. He very polite but extremely firm in his negative attitude. He said he had already made appeal to rebels. His own population dead-set against forgiveness due wanton destruction life within rebel areas. If he were to make appeal it would be misconstrued here as weakness and would thus weaken his own position and that of his govt. Furthermore futility of such appeal should be obvious in that rebels allege "I do not exist." He also worried regarding non-Congolese in that rebels would interpret his appeal as sign of success of their hostage policy and that they were on way to international recognition and eventually negotiation with central govt thanks to their policy

[1] Source: National Archives, RG 59, Central Files 1964–66, POL 23–9 THE CONGO. Secret; Flash; Limdis. Received at 10:57 a.m. and repeated to Brussels, Addis Ababa, Lagos, London, and Lusaka. Passed to the White House, DOD, and CIA.

[2] Dated November 16. (Ibid.)

[3] Telegram 1894 to Leopoldville, November 9, transmitted the text of a proposed Kasavubu declaration calling on the rebels to lay down their arms, accept his government's guarantees of amnesty, and join in constructing a great nation in peace and order. (Ibid.)

of cruelty and reprisals. Therefore, it essential that military action move ahead as fast as possible.

When De Kerchove mentioned Katangan precedent, Kasavubu said that situation today totally different in that Katangans recognized they were in succession from central govt. Thus they recognized Kasavubu as head of central govt. Rebels, however, do not recognize Kasavubu as head of central govt and are making every effort take over govt and destroy Kasavubu. De Kerchove then said that while Kasavubu looking at this purely from internal Congolese point of view, Belgium and other friendly govts were concerned with international ramifications of situation. Belg Govt representing Belgian people, wants maintain Kasavubu's international position and peaceful image that he now has in minds of all Belgians. Belgians like peaceful people and if he acquired image of someone who can resort only to arms, it will not improve his standing throughout world. Kasavubu made no substantive comment. De Kerchove then referred to Congo's loneliness in African family and bespoke necessity having recourse to OAU. Kasavubu said that he had done everything possible to get OAU here and had recently heard from Kenyatta who inquired whether OAU would have liberty of movement here. Kasavubu said he had informed Kenyatta that Commission certainly would have complete liberty of movement, but he could not guarantee whether they could get into Stan because unfortunately he did not control that city today. Kasavubu reiterated that he thought there nothing more he could do in OAU domain.

In conclusion Kasavubu repeated he would not make any statement. He said, however, he would discuss matter further with PriMin and would of course let De Kerchove know results. He implied, however, that anyone who makes such statement would be endangering his position here and De Kerchove got impression that he would advise Tshombe against such action. I asked De Kerchove whether he had associated USG with his démarche and whether he thought there anything I could do at this time. De Kerchove said that he told Kasavubu several times that draft had been prepared by our two govts but that as Belgium had largest human stake Stan, it had been agreed that he should make first démarche. He repeatedly referred in his conversation to the 5 official Americans Stan and to the presence of American, as well as other, missionaries in rebel territory. As for my seeing Kasavubu this afternoon, De Kerchove personal opinion is that it would be waste of time for Kasavubu knows that we feel as strongly as Belgium does on this issue.

Finally De Kerchove said that he mentioned to Kasavubu what he understood to be VDW's timetable for recapture Stan for he used timetable as means to emphasize urgency of statement.

Notwithstanding apparent futility of such action, am seeking meeting with Kasavubu. Am asking it on urgent basis but I personally would hope it would occur only after Tshombe has discussed this action with Pres which I believe will occur this afternoon. Meanwhile, De Kerchove and I are coordinating our backup démarche to Tshombe for which we have not yet been given appointments.

Godley

325. Telegram From the Department of State to the Embassy in Belgium[1]

Washington, November 16, 1964, 1:58 p.m.

1006. Ref: Brussels 950 rptd Leo 380.[2] You should inform Spaak that President and Secretary agree to prepositioning of Dragon Rouge at Ascension and that deployment should take place November 17 as he requests. We are instructing our military commands accordingly.

You should reiterate that any move beyond Ascension requires joint decision by US and Belgian Governments. In this connection, we agree to procedure and proposed use US communications channel for any further movement this force as suggested final para reftel.

We fear Spaak's proposed cover story so transparent as to blow security on whole operation.[3] We are sending septel alternative proposals and believe vital reach agreed position before any cover story used.[4]

For Leo: De Kerchove and you should coordinate arrangements for forwarding your recommendations in accordance with foregoing understanding.

Rusk

---

[1] Source: National Archives, RG 59, Central Files 1964–66, POL 7 BEL. Secret; Flash; Exdis. Drafted by Palmer; cleared by McGeorge Bundy, Lang in DOD, and Williams; and approved by Harriman. Repeated to Leopoldville, CINCSTRIKE, CINCEUR, and London.

[2] Telegram 950 from Brussels, November 16, reported a discussion of the proposed operation with Spaak and Prime Minister Lefevre. (Ibid., POL 23–9 THE CONGO)

[3] Spaak's proposed cover story was that Belgian troops were involved in a regular training exercise being conducted with the assistance of the U.S. Air Force. (Ibid.)

[4] Telegram 1014 to Brussels, November 16, proposed two cover stories: 1) The Belgian paratroopers were engaged in a joint training exercise with the British and 2) the C–130s were departing for England as part of a mission to fly electronic equipment from England to Ascension Island. (Ibid.)

326. Telegram From the Department of State to the Embassy in Belgium[1]

Washington, November 16, 1964, 5:53 p.m.

1013. Subject: Dragon Rouge. We assured by Col Dunn that Belgian assault forces will give priority attention rescuing five official Americans Stanleyville, who Belgians aware are in greater danger than other foreign nationals. We understand also that Belgian assault force includes some personnel who familiar with Stanleyville area and possibly even some who speak local native languages. We consider both high priority requirements since ability find out where Americans are and disposition get to them quickly may well be life-or-death matter. As opportunities arise in discussion Dragon Rouge, you should make clear importance we attach to these two points.

In further effort along these lines, we sending Clingerman, former Stanleyville consul, to Brussels tonight (arriving 1100 PanAm 108, Nov 17). His mission in Brussels will be to consult with Belgians in order assist in planning specific measures to be taken to rescue Americans. If as we assume Belgians have no objection, he will then accompany Belgian forces from Brussels to Ascension and, if decision taken to execute Dragon Rouge, on to but not beyond Kamina. He will have all info re location Americans Stan available to us and be authorized function in general capacity of political liaison and adviser to Dragon Rouge. (*For Leo:* You should take whatever steps possible in advance on contingency basis to assure that latest info on location Americans and on Stan generally would be made available to Clingerman in Kamina and Ascension to include in briefing there of Belgian forces. We are assembling info on communications with Ascension.)

We note Spaak and Lefevre concerned re foreign nationals in rebel territory outside Stan and are giving thought rescue operations there also. We agree fully on importance contingency planning for such operations. CINCEUR is being instructed be prepared provide planners for this purpose immediately. Advise when they should come Brussels.

Dragon Rouge makes no provision for evacuation Belgian paratroopers from Stanleyville after mission completed there. If GOB has in mind use paratroopers for missions other than rescue foreign nationals, please advise soonest. In absence overriding considerations believe it desirable C–130 force evacuate Belgian force ASAP on completion of

---

[1] Source: National Archives, RG 59, Central Files 1964–66, POL 23–9 THE CONGO. Top Secret; Immediate; Exdis. Drafted by McElhiney; cleared by Lang in DOD, Colonel Dunn in JCS, Palmer, and McKillop; and approved by Harriman. Also sent to Leopoldville and repeated to USCINCEUR, CINCSTRIKE, and London.

evacuation mission in order preserve most defensible public record that mission was strictly confined to evacuation, without military or political overtones. If Belgians agree, CINCEUR planners available immediately to work out with Belgians necessary modifications of plan.[2]

Rusk

---

[2] In telegram 960 from Brussels, November 17, MacArthur reported that Spaak said Belgium did not intend to use paratroopers except to rescue foreign nationals, and that he thought it desirable that C–130s evacuate Belgian forces from Stanleyville as soon as possible after completion of their mission. Spaak hoped that CINCEUR would send planners to Brussels as soon as possible to make the necessary modifications in the current plan and to engage in further contingency planning for evacuation of foreigners from areas other than Stanleyville. (Ibid.)

---

327. Telegram From the Department of State to the Embassy in the Congo[1]

Washington, November 17, 1964, 11:35 a.m.

1268. Embtel 1923.[2] We would have wished that proposed statement by Tshombe and letter to Kenyatta had been closer to suggested US-Belgian text. However, tendency is in right direction and you may inform him that USG reluctantly accepts his wording with minor changes. Sentence after "instigated rebellion" should read as follows: "We renew to all these compatriots the assurances that have been offered to them as affirmed in our solemn undertaking to our fellow Africans in Addis Ababa Sept 10, namely the guarantee of the security of those who lay down their arms." Last sentence should read: "We appeal to them to lay down their arms and in full liberty and the spirit of national reconciliation join their fellow citizens to develop our great country with them in peace and order. FYI: Changes do not constitute

---

[1] Source: National Archives, RG 59, Central Files 1964–66, POL 23–9 THE CONGO. Secret; Flash. Drafted by Schaufele, cleared by Williams and Palmer, and approved by Harriman. Also sent to Brussels and repeated to London, Nairobi, Lagos, and Lusaka.

[2] Telegram 1923 from Leopoldville, November 17, reported a meeting with Tshombe and transmitted the text of a proposed Tshombe statement declaring that the Congolese Government was in the last phase of actions that would result in the restoration of order throughout the country, calling upon those who had permitted themselves to be "led astray" to lay down their arms, and vaguely referring to previously offered guarantees. It also transmitted the text of a proposed letter from Tshombe to Kenyatta. (Ibid.)

conditions for USG approval but you should make every effort achieve meaning expressed in them.[3]

Brussels should attempt establish GOB views on texts Tshombe statement, including above revisions, and letter to Kenyatta. GOB may be informed that we believed this about best which can be obtained and we urge that it communicate its approval to De Kerchove using our communications facilities if necessary so that texts can be issued ASAP.

Rusk

---

[3] In telegram 1960 from Leopoldville, November 18, Godley reported that he gave a Belgian Embassy officer the text of the revised statement and instructed him to try to see Tshombe, who was currently north of the Congo River. (Ibid.) In telegram 1292 to Leopoldville, November 18, the Department responded that although the Embassy should make every effort to get the changes suggested in telegram 1268 included, the main emphasis should be on publication of the statement and transmission of the letter to Kenyatta as soon as possible. (Ibid.)

---

328. Telegram From the Embassy in Belgium to the Department of State[1]

Brussels, November 17, 1964, 6 p.m.

966. Immediately following telegram[2] contains Spaak's instructions to De Kerchove re Dragon Rouge. You will note that 7th paragraph these instructions directs De Kerchove after liaison with Godley to see Tshombe Wednesday (November 18) and lift veil in general way. Spaak feels that before Dragon Rouge can be implemented it essential to have something in writing from Tshombe to cover us politically and asks De Kerchove to obtain Tshombe's agreement in writing on any intervention towards purely humanitarian ends. If we believe approach to Tshombe premature, Davignon thought Spaak would agree to delay it a day or two.

Assume you will send word to Ambassador Godley as soon as possible instructing him on position to take with De Kerchove. We would appreciate substance these instructions by Flash message if De-

---

[1] Source: National Archives, RG 59, Central Files 1964–66, POL 23–9 THE CONGO. Top Secret; Flash; Exdis. Received at 12:20 p.m. and repeated to Leopoldville. Passed to the White House, DOD, and CIA.

[2] Telegram 967 from Brussels, November 17. (Ibid.)

partment does not agree with Spaak on this so that we can also inform him here.

Have informed Davignon that we have asked for Department's views.

MacArthur

---

329. Telegram From the Department of State to the Embassy in the Congo[1]

Washington, November 17, 1964, 6:05 p.m.

1275. Subject: Dragon Rouge. Brussels 966 and 967.[2] We agree approach in general terms to Tshombe is matter some urgency. We giving urgent consideration to form of request from Kasavubu or Tshombe designed inter alia assure best possible position in UN and will send our views soonest to Brussels for coordination with GOB.

Meanwhile you should not give consent to de Kerchove for approach by him to Tshombe.

For Brussels: You may inform Spaak and/or Davignon foregoing, adding we hope send our views later tonight.

Rusk

---

[1] Source: National Archives, RG 59, Central Files 1964–66, POL 23–9 THE CONGO. Top Secret; Flash; Exdis. Drafted by McElhiney and Hoffacker; cleared by Deputy Assistant Secretary for EUR Robert C. Creel, Sisco, Williams, and Palmer; and approved by Harriman. Repeated to Brussels.

[2] See Document 328 and footnote 2 thereto.

330. Notes of a Telephone Conversation Between President Johnson and Secretary of Defense McNamara[1]

Washington, November 17, 1964, 7:00 p.m.

McNamara: It'll be dangerous if the paradrop is carried out, but it'll be dangerous if it isn't and under the circumstances, the danger of carrying it out is less than the danger of not carrying it out.

Johnson: Well now you've got this feedback all over town, I think from the same source that claims that every man in State is against it. Oh hell, the Secretary came in and from Harriman down to the bottom one, they thought it [unintelligible], everybody thought it was terrible.

McNamara: Well I thought—

Johnson: And that Rusk came in and said that he rather thought it ought to be done and that everybody around the table—but they're going around town peddling this kind of stuff. I just had a fellow come into me. I haven't called anyone else. The next man I'm going to call is Rusk, but I'm not going to tell him I've discussed it with folks, but I don't like for him to be [unintelligible].

McNamara: I don't think it's fair to do that, Mr. President, because I am just positive that Harriman was in favor of this. At least he led me to believe he was and Harriman's taken a pretty firm line on the Congo situation. For example, it was he over the objections of another group at State who pressed for a reconnaissance plane to fly over Stanleyville or at least ten or fifteen miles off the center of Stanleyville so we could get back photographs of the area, and this because we said if they wanted a U.S. military operation over there we couldn't possibly carry it out unless we had some photographs of the area and knew what we were dropping into or knew what we were sending troops into. So much over the objections of others at State, Harriman strongly urged that this be done and Dean approved it, which we did. I think this is only to illustrate that he's been a very firm individual and it was my understanding that this Belgian paradrop operation evolved out of his talks in Belgium, although it didn't come up at that particular time. It came about as a result of his conversations and if Spaak was in favor of it, and therefore from my point of view, State was proposing it and we went along with it because I valued Dean's judgment on this issue. Dean has been very much concerned about the lives of the Americans in Stanleyville and his—his—.

[1] Source: Johnson Library, Recordings and Transcripts, Recording of Telephone Conversation between President Johnson and Secretary McNamara, November 17, 1964, evidently already underway when the recording began. This transcript was prepared in the Office of the Historian specifically for this volume.

Johnson: I think we've got to be. I think that flag's got to go to that person, and we've got to stand up and not let the Afro-Asians run over us. And I just took that position when these folks talked to me about it, and I said I'm just damn tired of a bunch of folks like this, and they've got a right to kill American people and we haven't even got a right to furnish a plane to try to get them out and so forth. But the State Department group is putting out some bad stuff and their thing that's coming to my desk is that all of them are against this from Harriman down except Rusk, and he came into me late and they ran under the table but—.

McNamara: Well Rusk is definitely in favor of this. There's no doubt about that, but I'm perfectly willing to stand with him and be known as being in favor of it in the press. I know he's very much concerned about the lives of these people. He has proposed policies that I would not have proposed in order to save their lives. [gap]—but in any case that was his proposal and I supported him on it. And I think this only indicates that he's taken a damn firm hard line in trying to preserve the lives of these people and he strongly believes that this paradrop will act in the course of that objective and I'm strongly in favor of supporting him therefore.

Johnson: Now when you—, when it's leaked though and they have advance notice, does that change—

McNamara: Well I noticed the leaks and I saw some cables referring to them today. I don't think it does. It's just terribly hard to evaluate the psychology of these rebels. I don't know whether you noticed a cable that came in here about a week ago but it told of one of the rebel leaders in Stanleyville going up to the former mayor of the city and taking a knife out and slitting him down the front, reaching in and picking out his kidney and eating it when the man was alive. Now, I don't know how you deal with people like that. I don't know how you interpret what they'll do if we fly an airplane over there or if we drop some paratroopers. I talked to General [Tecuma (sp?)], who is currently head of the Standing Group here in Washington and who was formerly General Wheeler's counterpart in the Belgian army, and he personally has carried out operations in the Belgian Congo. And he says he thinks the rebels are more affected by a show of power such as a drop of Belgian paratroopers and would be less likely to kill the Americans under those circumstances than they will be if we appear weak. And so I'm taking his view plus Dean Rusk's, but I can't guarantee it's a proper interpretation of their psychology.

[Omitted here is discussion of another subject.]

331. Circular Telegram From the Department of State to Certain Posts[1]

Washington, November 17, 1964, 9:03 p.m.

949. Text of proposed Concilium appeal (recent Depcirtel 948)[2] is as follows:

"The Governments of ______ welcome the humanitarian efforts of PM Jomo Kenyatta of Kenya, who is Chairman of the OAU Ad Hoc Commission on the Congo, to save lives in the Congo including foreign civilians. Despite the steps which Prime Minister Kenyatta has taken and the assurances of safety for foreigners which have been made to him from Stanleyville, it has become clear that the lives of civilians in Stanleyville remain in grave danger.

In furtherance of the objectives of Mr. Kenyatta's humanitarian initiative, we the undersigned representatives of Governments, being signatories to the Geneva Conventions of 1949 for the Protection of War Victims, which govern the treatment of civilians and others in the present conflict in the Congo, and being concerned for the safety of all the civilian population, appeal to all concerned to facilitate an immediate and safe arrival at Stanleyville of personnel of the ICRC, in order that they may perform their humanitarian services throughout the whole Congo including those parts of the Congo to which they do not now have access. If it would help to insure the success of this mission, we are, for our part, prepared forthwith to designate our own representative to accompany the ICRC mission to Stanleyville, and if any

[1] Source: National Archives, RG 59, Central Files 1964–66, POL 23–9 THE CONGO. Limited Official Use; Immediate. Drafted by Runyon in L/AF on November 16, cleared by Schaufele, and approved by Williams. Sent to Ottawa, Brussels, London, Nairobi, Addis Ababa, Mogadiscio, Lagos, Yaounde, Ouagadougou, Paris, Athens, The Hague, Rome, New Delhi, Karachi, Port au Prince, Buenos Aires, Bern, Oslo, Canberra, Bonn, Copenhagen, and Geneva. Repeated to Leopoldville and Bujumbura.

[2] Circular telegram 948, November 17, sent to 22 Embassies, instructed them to seek the support of their host governments as soon as possible for a humanitarian appeal by an ad hoc concilium of Geneva Convention signatories on behalf of all civilians in the Congo conflict. (Ibid.) Rebel leaders in Stanleyville had announced that they were planning to execute "Major" Paul Carlson as a U.S. spy on November 16. Secretary Rusk's November 16 appeal to Kenyatta to intervene on behalf of Dr. Carlson, which stated that Carlson had been a medical missionary in the Congo for 3½ years and had no connection with the U.S. military is printed in Department of State *Bulletin*, December 14, 1964, pp. 838–839. Ambassador Godley's November 17 appeal to the rebels is printed ibid., p. 839. On November 18, Kenyatta appealed to the rebels to spare Carlson on humanitarian grounds. Radio Stanleyville subsequently announced that Carlson's execution had been postponed until November 23.

OAU member states wish to designate a representative to accompany the mission, we would welcome this."[3]

Rusk

---

[3] Circular telegram 996, November 21, reported that the appeal was being released that day at Geneva by the following 13 governments: Australia, Canada, United States, Haiti, Argentina, Greece, United Kingdom, Belgium, Netherlands, Germany, Denmark, and Norway, all signatories to the Geneva Convention. (National Archives, RG 59, Central Files 1964–66, POL 23–9 THE CONGO)

---

332. Memorandum From Director of Central Intelligence McCone to the President's Special Assistant for National Security Affairs (Bundy)[1]

Washington, November 18, 1964.

Pursuant to our telephone conversation Friday, I am attaching a memo from Mr. Abbot Smith, Acting Chairman of the Board of National Estimates, on the possible repercussions of the Stanleyville rescue operations.[2] The paper indicates the reaction among African states, principally those critical of our Congo policy, as well as propaganda stirred up by the Communists, would be vigorous although its extent would be inversely proportionate to the time consumed in the operation.

It should be noted that the lack of precise knowledge as to the location of the Americans and most Europeans at Stanleyville, and the fact there are several hundred Europeans and some Americans in rebel-held territory outside of Stanleyville, principally in Paulis, Watsa and Bunia, increases the possibility of rebel massacres even if the operation (irrespective of how carefully it is planned and executed) should accomplish its mission.

John

---

[1] Source: Johnson Library, National Security File, Country File, Congo, Vol. VII. Top Secret. A copy was sent to Rusk.

[2] Attached but not printed.

333. Telegram From the Department of State to the Embassy in Belgium[1]

Washington, November 19, 1964, 1:41 a.m.

1063. Dragon Rouge. Ref: Brussels 986.[2] We cannot of course question GOB decision to delegate authority to de Kerchove re activation of Dragon Rouge, and we are prepared on basis reftel to accept his notification of Godley of code word "Punch" as constituting GOB decision to implement Dragon Rouge plan. For its part, however, USG must continue reserve right take final decision in Washington at highest Governmental level. We therefore propose following "GO" procedure in order preclude misunderstanding or confusion in possibly fast-moving circumstances:

1. US channels will be used exclusively for necessary consultations and communication of decisions.

2. Without questioning GOB delegation to Belgian Ambassador Leo, procedures outlined below assume Belgian "Punch" signal could come from either Brussels or Leo.

3. If "GO" originates Leo: Amembassy will communicate simultaneously to Washington and Brussels "Punch" and US Embassy recommendation. If USG concurs, JCS will be informed and will transmit "Punch" and appropriate instructions to US force commander through military channels. If USG nonconcurs, it will consult with GOB immediately.

4. If "GO" originates GOB Brussels: If US concurs, US will signal Dragon Rouge force through JCS as (3) above. If US nonconcurs, it will consult Brussels and Leo urgently.

5. If "GO" originates Washington: USG will Flash Brussels and Leo and accept "Punch" from either, then proceed with "GO" to Dragon Rouge force through JCS as (3) above. If GOB or Belgian Ambassador Leo nonconcurs, US will expect GOB and/or Belgian Ambassador Leo to consult with USG urgently regarding nonconcurrence and reasons.

---

[1] Source: National Archives, RG 59, Central Files 1964–66, POL 23–9 THE CONGO. Top Secret; Immediate; Exdis. Drafted by Palmer and Brubeck, cleared by Creel and Lang and Alexander in DOD, and approved by Harriman. Repeated to Leopoldville, CINCMEAFSA, and USCINCEUR.

[2] In telegram 986 from Brussels, November 18, MacArthur reported that the Belgian Government had delegated to de Kerchove the authority to recommend initiation of Dragon Rouge on the basis of Van der Walle's recommendation. (Ibid.)

Believe above conforms generally with Belgian understanding described reftel. Please confirm soonest that GOB accepts above more specific procedure.

Rusk

334. Memorandum From the Deputy Assistant Secretary of Defense for International Security Affairs (Lang) to the Deputy Secretary of Defense (Vance)[1]

Washington, November 19, 1964.

SUBJECT

Congo Developments—Wednesday

1. *Operation Dragon Rouge.* The last of 14 C–130s (including 2 spares) landed at Ascension about 4:30 Wednesday[2] afternoon (our time). The force commander reports he is ready to proceed when instructed.

2. *"GO" Procedures.* Spaak has delegated discretion to the Belgian Ambassador at Leopoldville to trigger the move of Belgian forces from Ascension. On the US side, the decision will be made by the President. Detailed procedures on channels of communications to be used in the decision-making process have been sent to Brussels and Leopoldville. (For reliability and speed, only US channels will be used.)

3. *Air Operations.* New guidelines have been set which will permit the use of air operations within 25 miles of Stanleyville in support of Van der Walle's drive. Air operations will be geared to Van der Walle's advances and will be permitted over the city itself when he begins his final assault. Separate guidelines have also been set for the use of air operations in support of Operation Dragon Rouge. The Joint Staff is satisfied that both sets of guidelines meet operational requirements.

L.

---

[1] Source: Washington National Records Center, RG 330, OASD/ISA Files: FRC 69 A 7425, Congo 381 (12 Aug. 64). Top Secret. A stamped notation on the memorandum reads: "Mr. Vance has seen." A copy was sent to McNaughton.

[2] November 18.

335. Telegram From the Joint Chiefs of Staff to Headquarters, Strike Command and Headquarters, Middle East/South Asia and Africa South of the Sahara[1]

Washington, November 19, 1964, 1250Z.

JCS 002044. Subj: US presence in Dragon Rouge (S). In view highly sensitive nature Dragon Rouge, request that action be taken to minimize the appearance US role therein, particularly if and when operations are conducted in the Stanleyville area. Every effort should be made to ensure that US personnel avoid incidents, fire-fights, mob or riot actions and do not leave the airfield.

---

[1] Source: National Archives, RG 59, Central Files 1964–66, POL 23–9 THE CONGO. Top Secret; Noforn; Limdis. Also sent to USCINCEUR and repeated to the Department of State, where it was received at 8:27 a.m., and the White House. General Paul D. Adams served concurrently as Commander in Chief, Strike Command (CINCSTRIKE) and Commander in Chief, Middle East/South Asia and Africa South of the Sahara (CINCMEAFSA).

---

336. Memorandum by the Assistant Secretary of State for African Affairs (Williams)[1]

Washington, November 19, 1964.

SUBJECT

Meeting Notes with the President, Secretary Rusk, et al[2]

Secretary Rusk opened by saying that the Van der Walle column was moving to within short distance of Stanleyville, and that Belgian paratroopers were now in position on Ascension Island and would probably not be called on before November 24, but that in no event would they move further without the decision of the President and Minister Spaak. However, if there were massacres, etc., they might move more quickly.

---

[1] Source: National Archives, RG 59, Central Files 1964–66, POL 23–9 THE CONGO. Top Secret; Exdis.

[2] Other records of this meeting are in Johnson Library, National Security File, Files of McGeorge Bundy, and Central Intelligence Agency Files, DCI/McCone Files, Job 80B01285, DCI Meetings with the President, 01 October–31 December 1964.

Gbenye by radio has offered to negotiate on the safety of American prisoners.[3] The Secretary indicated he thought the terms would likely be unacceptable to us. He said the Stanleyville people might be trying for time to get help from Egypt, etc.

Secretary Rusk said that we placed a high value on the hostages, but that we couldn't give up all of our position and policy because of them.

Secretary Rusk said he thought it was good to accept the offer and that we proposed to send a message today offering to talk and asking when and where.

Our next step would be to get clearance from the Belgians for a program offering amnesty, no prosecution for political crimes, etc., in return for recognition of the authority of the Central Government and release of hostages. The Secretary said it was his personal belief that the rebels would not accept the offer. However, it was important for the record in the United States and in Africa.

This discussion would not put on ice or interfere with military operations.

If this track succeeds, the Secretary continued, we would have difficulties with Kasavubu and Tshombe who want an outright military victory.

The Secretary concluded that he thought this was the best thing to do.

Governor Harriman agreed with what he said was a clear statement by the Secretary. He then added that it was important to take this action in view of world opinion and UN opinion.

Secretary McNamara agreed.

The President said it would put us in a bad light if we didn't act.

John McCone said this is the thing to do. He said the palaver would increase the safety of Americans in the rest of Africa.

The President then asked how many Americans there were in rebel territories, what they were doing and how many were government employees. He was given the answer.

McGeorge Bundy then pointed out that the missionaries were a very determined people. When they were asked to get out they refused

---

[3] Following Gbenye's radio announcement, Godley responded on November 19 that his government had instructed him to state that it was ready at any time for discussions to ensure the safety of the U.S. citizens in Stanleyville. He asked Gbenye to name place, time, and representative, and said that a U.S. representative would be prepared for discussions in Nairobi or any other capital. On November 20, Gbenye announced that his "Foreign Minister," Thomas Kanza, had been charged with carrying out preliminary negotiations in Nairobi and asked the U.S. Government to set a date. See Department of State *Bulletin*, December 14, 1964, p. 839.

to get out because they wanted to continue their work, and when something happened, they were insistent upon protection.

The President then asked the Vice President for his views and he said he was in accord with what had gone on before. The President then asked Governor Williams if he was as pessimistic as the Secretary as to the chances of success in the negotiations. He said that he agreed with the Secretary's position except that he thought that there was some chance that if the rebels could be made to see how desperate their position was, that there would be some give. The President then wondered when the decision to move ahead with Dragon Rouge would have to be made. The Secretary indicated that it would be about the 24th, however, Secretary McNamara indicated that it might come earlier. He pointed out that De Kerchove had been delegated the authority by Brussels to decide when to go. McNamara indicated the President might have to make a decision within 48 hours. The President asked if he ought to stay in Washington. Everyone thought that it wasn't necessary, in fact it would be counter productive as we wanted to keep the matter as low key as possible. The President said he thought it was wise to let Van der Walle go ahead but to hold up the decision on Dragon Rouge.

McGeorge Bundy then raised the question whether the President shouldn't make a broadcast to Gbenye instead of Godley but again everyone agreed that the matter should not be so accelerated. The President asked if there was any dissenting views on the whole matter and there were none expressed.

---

337. Memorandum From the Deputy Assistant Secretary of Defense for International Security Affairs (Lang) to the Deputy Secretary of Defense (Vance)[1]

Washington, November 19, 1964.

Here is a copy of the message that was dispatched as a result of your meeting at the White House.[2] In brief, it tells Mac Godley to an-

[1] Source: Washington National Records Center, RG 330, OASD/ISA Files: FRC 69 A 7425, Congo 381 (12 Aug. 64). Top Secret. A stamped notation on the memorandum reads: "Mr. Vance has seen." A copy was sent to McNaughton.

[2] Telegram 1303 to Leopoldville, November 19, is attached but not printed. A copy is in National Archives, RG 59, Central Files 1964–66, POL 23–9 THE CONGO.

nounce to Gbenye that we are prepared to discuss with him the safety of US nationals in the Stanleyville area. Other African posts are told to get word to Kanza, the rebels' representative in East Africa, that Fredericks is en route prepared for sustained discussions.

The message reflects one recommendation of a briefing paper that went to Mr. Rusk for the meeting (which we got after you had left). The purpose of the proposed discussions, according to the briefing paper, is to keep contact with the rebels alive, and the rebels presumably in a false state of expectation, during the next few days when they will be growing increasingly desperate as Van der Walle approaches Stanleyville.

I don't quarrel with this approach, although I see in it certain dangers when the rebels realize that they've been tricked. I have serious reservations, however, about another recommendation of the paper. This would call for discussions with key OAU personnel (Kenyatta, Diallo Telli) proposing a political package under which we and the Belgians would jointly undertake to compel Kasavubu and Tshombe to take certain actions, such as offering amnesty to the rebels, which might induce them to lay down their arms. The OAU would hopefully join with us in trying to sell this package to the rebels.

I do not yet know whether this approach will be included in Wayne Fredericks' instructions but I see serious dangers in it. First, we are suggesting to influential OAU representatives that we can control Tshombe and Kasavubu. (You will recall that we denied this vigorously when the OAU pressed us to ground the T–28s and B–26s.) More importantly, if we make this approach and then go forward with Dragon Rouge, we would be accused by the OAU of having acted in bad faith. (Diallo Telli, who is no friend of the US, would wring this for all it's worth.) The alternative, which is equally as bad, would be to find ourselves committed to a "negotiated" solution.

I understand that State is now preparing Wayne Fredericks' instructions. I will keep you advised of any significant developments.

L.

338. Telegram From the Department of State to the Embassy in Belgium[1]

Washington, November 19, 1964, 8:15 p.m.

1107. Following are tentative rationale and guidelines for Fredericks talks with Kanza and/or OAU, subject to Belgian concurrence. When final version agreed, including any changes Belgians may propose, Dept will transmit guidelines as basis and framework for all discussions, including exploratory talks authorized Deptel 1303 (to Leopoldville).[2]

For Brussels: Fredericks will be prepared discuss this text urgently with you and GOB on Friday morning with goal of getting agreed guidelines in time proceed Nairobi Friday evening.

Begin text of guidelines. First objective of Godley to Gbenye message emphasizing willingness to negotiate is to avoid accusation in US and Africa that US unwilling respond initiative which could affect life US citizen. Second objective, equally important, is to use confrontation with rebels, if it can be arranged, to test whether rebels are ready to accept restoration of GDRC authority under terms which 1) would make unnecessary invasion Stanleyville, 2) would offer prospect of extracting hostages at minimal risk, 3) could be imposed on GDRC by concerted US-Belgian pressures, and 4) would help rehabilitate US–OAU relations.

While our primary effort is to try to bring about rebel acceptance restoration GDRC authority Stanleyville which would make military solution unnecessary, we do not envisage this initiative as replacing present military efforts. We believe it is only credible threat of GDRC capability and will to decapitate rebellion by military means which might predispose rebels to end hostilities under acceptable terms. Further, this initiative does not presuppose any delay of military thrust. We recognize, however, rebels will seek delaying action in order renew build-up of rebel confidence, increase possibility of external military support to rebel forces. These factors make it imperative adopt hard line with rebels, stressing tight deadlines and, if necessary, a take-it-or-leave-it approach with consequences clearly spelled out of rebel refusal to sign-on.

Political deal we would propose picks up themes from aborted Kasavubu declaration as agreed by Spaak during his visit to US: GDRC guarantee of personal safety to all rebels who lay down their arms,

[1] Source: National Archives, RG 59, Central Files 1964–66, POL 23–9 THE CONGO. Secret; Immediate; Exdis. Drafted by Palmer, cleared by Brubeck and Creel, and approved by Ball. Repeated to Leopoldville, Nairobi, Addis Ababa, Dar es Salaam, and London.

[2] Dated November 19. (Ibid.)

public offer of political amnesty, no prosecution of political crimes, full freedom to engage in political activity in preparation for forthcoming early elections, and right of all to hold office if elected. If rebels indicate any interest, we are prepared to offer, in concert with Belgians and possibly OAU, a major effort to win GDRC acceptance and to examine possibility of arranging some sort of neutral presence (e.g. US-Belgian-OAU) in Stan to assure physical safety and order during transfer to GDRC control and further presence (e.g., OAU observers) to assure other undertakings are fulfilled. This might even include token forces—hopefully from OAU, though possibly even US-Belgian with OAU blessing.

Precise terms and modalities of course might be made to conform in some degree to specific, perhaps even personal, rebel demands. Therefore, would be most helpful, if talks with rebels materialize for Belgium to position an officer in whom Spaak has full confidence to consult with our negotiator on the spot. Hennequiau would be a possibility.

We recognize that keystone to whole enterprise would be US–GOB concerted démarche to GDRC in event rebels seem forthcoming in meaningful and realistic sense. The US and GOB must be prepared clearly indicate that present and future relations with Congo in jeopardy unless GDRC is willing to end hostilities under settlement terms outlined above. Our objective, therefore, is to gain GOB go-ahead with clear understanding that negotiations are ad referendum but that both governments prepared to consider such a deal seriously, including potential heavy pressure on GDRC, if our exploration with rebels so warrants.

We believe this final effort absolutely essential to build irrefutable record of US–GOB attempts to gain political settlement as well as being one final effort to secure safety of hostages short of perilous military solution.

Nor do we entirely discount possibility that even at this late date such a maneuver might work. We have never had any illusions that political deal could be consummated except at point when all possible alternatives to rebels had been slammed shut. That time has now arrived. It is crucial we try to test rebel response. *End of guidelines text.*[3]

Rusk

---

[3] In telegram 1011 from Brussels, November 20, MacArthur reported that Spaak considered the proposed negotiations with the rebels dangerous. Kanza would immediately request a cease-fire as quid pro quo for evacuation of the hostages, but the Congo could not be forced to accept a cease-fire, and refusal to accept a cease-fire would be exploited internationally. (Ibid.) In a telephone conversation with Ball on November 20, Harriman said he had just talked with MacArthur, who told him the Belgians thought it would be a great mistake to send Fredericks to Nairobi for negotiations, which should be conducted locally. If the United States made too much of this, it would be more difficult to handle. (Library of Congress, Manuscript Division, Harriman Papers, Kennedy–Johnson Administrations, Subject Files, Box 448, Congo (1))

339. Draft Message From the President's Special Assistant for National Security Affairs (Bundy) to President Johnson[1]

Washington, November 20, 1964.

Our only very hot spot at the moment is the Congo. Here is where we are:

1. Van der Walle mercenary column is on its way with little opposition so far and could reach Stanleyville in two or three days with luck.

2. Rebels have broadcast another threat to American hostages using the name of U.S. Consul Hoyt who is held in Stanleyville.

3. At the same time rebels have agreed to discuss with a U.S. representative in Nairobi. We are publicly accepting this offer and proposing talks at noon tomorrow (3 a.m. Washington time) with Ambassador Attwood speaking for us.[2]

4. The Belgians are resistant to any concessions that Tshombe and Co. might find unacceptable, and accordingly Attwood's instructions will be quite general and directed at maintaining the palaver while warning strongly of consequences of any hostile act. Attwood is a skillful negotiator and we hope very much that these talks will help protect hostages while the Van der Walle column advances.

5. Very weak security has now forced the Belgian Government to announce that the troops with air support are at Ascension Island as a precautionary measure. We have confirmed this announcement.[3]

6. Tomorrow, Saturday, we shall need to consider whether it is wise to advance paratroopers to Kamina or to execute against Stanleyville. George Ball and I are both very cautious at this point and would probably recommend against action when what we face is threat, not

---

[1] Source: Johnson Library, Memos to the President, McGeorge Bundy, Vol. 7. Top Secret. The message, headed "To the President From Bundy," is an unsigned draft with handwritten insertions. The text was presumably sent to the President at the LBJ Ranch, where he was November 19–29.

[2] Telegram 1916 to Nairobi, November 20, instructed Attwood to inform Kenyatta immediately that, in response to the rebel request to fix a date for negotiations in Nairobi, he was requesting a meeting at noon on November 21, and to ask him to arrange for participation by Kanza and any other participants decided upon by himself or by the rebels. (Ibid.)

[3] On November 20, a Belgian Government spokesman announced that the First Paratroop Battalion had been transported to Ascension Island with the aid of U.S. planes, and that, in view of the danger to their nationals in Stanleyville, both governments considered it their duty to take preparatory measures in order to be able to effect, if necessary, a humanitarian rescue operation. (Department of State *Bulletin*, December 14, 1964, p. 840)

open act of violence. Harriman may be marginally more activist.[4] All of us will be much affected by Spaak's judgment at the time. Belgium Government alarm appears to be increasing.

Bromley Smith and George Ball are here and fully informed, and can tell you more by telephone if you wish.

I will also be fully informed and participate by telephone in discussions tomorrow and Sunday as needed.

The talks in Nairobi, and the unobstructed course of the Van der Walle column so far give me considerable hope that we can avoid the hazards of actual execution of paratroop drop, but this situation is subject to change at very short notice.

---

[4] The sentence originally began: "Rusk and Harriman;" the first two words were crossed out.

---

340. Telegram From the Department of State to the Embassy in Kenya[1]

Washington, November 20, 1964, 5:32 p.m.

1922. Septel contains text our reply to Gbenye re his proposal discussions between US and Kanza with Kenyatta present.[2] Our purpose in agreeing to these discussions is (1) to avoid public stance of rebuffing offer negotiate; (2) to buy time which might permit VDW to take Stan without requirement use Belgian-US force; and (3) explore every possible means of peaceful resolution of hostage problem. Embassy will note these objectives far more limited than those set forth Deptel 1077 to Brussels to which Belgians have objected.

In discussions with Kanza, Attwood should be guided by following:

---

[1] Source: National Archives, RG 59, Central Files 1964–66, POL 23–9 THE CONGO. Secret; Flash; Exdis. Drafted by Palmer; cleared by Ball, Harriman, Williams, Creel in EUR, and Brubeck; and approved by Palmer. Also sent to Brussels and repeated to Leopoldville, Dar es Salaam, Addis Ababa, Bujumbura, Bangui, and Kampala.

[2] Document 338.

1. Objective of discussion is safety civilian population Stan, including all foreigners. We cannot discuss our current problems under threats of executions. If any foreign resident of Stan is killed for political reasons, we shall terminate discussions at once and resort to such other measures as may be necessary.

2. We can not entertain any proposals whatsoever for cease fire, which is in fact completely in control of Congo Government.

3. If Kanza raises matter of "bombings" by US aircraft, you should make clear to him no bombs in Congo, aircraft are responsibility GDRC, and that at our instigation on humanitarian grounds, Tshombe has given undertakings which are being respected not to attack cities and towns which would endanger civilian populations.

4. You should make clear to Kanza hopelessness rebel position. It is everywhere on defensive and cause is lost. Moreover he should be aware there no split between Tshombe and Kasavubu and he therefore cannot bank on this development. Under circumstances he should grasp realities of situation and persuade his colleagues give up and salvage what they can. If he has proposals or suggestions which fall short of cease fire or removal foreign military assistance and which would result in peaceful resolution of conflict and safety foreign population Stan, we prepared to examine them and if feasible take them up with GDRC and GOB to obtain their compliance. Obviously, we not in position guarantee anything, but you should make clear that USG would make strongest efforts obtain GDRC and GOB agreement to reasonable and realistic proposals which result in restoration GDRC sovereignty over northeast Congo, liquidation rebellion and safety civilian population.

5. In event Kanza responds affirmatively and makes any specific proposals, you should immediate inform Dept repeating Leo and Brussels. While you should not take any initiative in proposing political amnesty, right participate political life of Congo, national reconciliation, etc., you should indicate willingness inform Dept such possibilities if Kanza proposes them.

6. In any event you must not break off talks but insure that at end of meeting you have agreement to meet following day for further discussion.

For Brussels: You should immediately inform Davignon and Spaak of foregoing. You should make clear that this effort primarily to exhaust all possibilities no matter how remote and to gain time, adding that we accept completely that VDW columns should not be held up but should proceed with assault on Stan with all possible speed. In off chance discussion with Kanza should yield anything promising, we would of course wish consult again.[3]

Rusk

[3] Attwood met with Kenyatta and Telli at the appointed time on November 21, but Kanza did not appear for the meeting.

---

341. Telegram From the Department of State to the Embassy in the Congo[1]

Washington, November 20, 1964, 10:35 p.m.

1335. Leopoldville's 1136 to Brussels.[2] Confirming Palmer–Godley telecon, we are gratified at reported progress with Tshombe and Kasavubu on documentation for DR.[3] We will not, of course, issue any statement here in advance of Kasavubu statement. We wish, however, underline importance Kasavubu not releasing public statement unless and until we request him to do so through you. Also particularly important you obtain physical custody signed letter to UNSYG and GDRC instructions to Congo rep in New York.

We also understand GDRC has no rep in New York at present. You should urge GDRC arrange soonest for strong representation at UN during this important period.

For Brussels: Foregoing refers telecon in which Godley reported he having satisfactory meeting with Tshombe re GDRC documents in connection DR and hoped get everything we requested. Please inform GOB.

Ball

[1] Source: National Archives, RG 59, Central Files 1964–66, POL 23–9 THE CONGO. Top Secret; Immediate; Exdis. Drafted by Palmer; cleared by Sisco, Percival in EUR, and Brubeck; and approved by Palmer. Also sent to Brussels.

[2] Dated November 20. (Ibid.)

[3] Telegram 1328 to Leopoldville, November 20, instructed the Embassy that it was essential to secure immediately a Congolese letter requesting Dragon Rouge assistance on a contingency basis. (Ibid.) Telegram 2020 from Leopoldville, November 20, reported that Tshombe agreed to submit his letter requesting such assistance to Washington for concurrence, and that Kasavubu agreed to send a message to the U.N. Secretary-General. (Ibid.)

342. Memorandum for the Record[1]

Washington, November 21, 1964.

SUBJECT

Summarizing discussions at meeting at 10:30, Saturday morning, 21 November, presided over by Secretary Ball

ATTENDED BY

Ball, Vance, Wheeler, McCone, Harriman, Williams, Palmer, Cleveland and a number of others

Also a meeting at 9:00 Saturday evening, presided over by Rusk, with all of the above in attendance

1. The morning's meeting was devoted to the question of moving the Belgian paratroopers from Ascension to Kamina. There were divergent views with Williams favoring not moving them until the last minute and then staging through Kamina in order to give maximum element of surprise. Cleveland, while not taking a strong position either way, expressed greatest concern over the fact that the paratroopers would move without a written invitation and request from Kasavubu and Tshombe, and also some recognition at the U.N. that the movement was humanitarian. All others favored the move. As a matter of record, I took a very strong position that we should move up to a point nearest to Stanleyville but reserved as to whether we should move immediately from Kamina to Stanleyville, should coordinate the move with the Van der Walle column which would involve a delay at Kamina or alternatively should hold at Kamina permitting the column to take Stanleyville.

2. There was no decision made concerning operations from Kamina onward, however, the decision was reached that the column should be moved from Ascension to Kamina and orders were given to that effect after clearing with President Johnson by telephone.

3. The evening meeting was called to make the decision concerning an immediate move on Stanleyville from Kamina. Information was presented to show that the stopover time at Kamina could be as little as three hours and if the entire operation went without hitch or interruption, then it was possible to drop at Stanleyville at 4:00 o'clock Stanleyville time. This would give three hours of daylight for the paratrooper operation. It was decided that this would be unsatisfactory as it would be impossible to organize the paratroopers in the three hours and to ef-

[1] Source: Central Intelligence Agency Files, DCI/McCone Files, Job 80B01285A, DCI (McCone) Memos for the Record, 01 Nov.–31 Dec. 64. Secret; Eyes Only. Dictated by McCone on November 23.

fectively rescue the hostages. Hence, it would give the rebels a full night for their reprisal operations which in all probability would be disastrous.

4. It was noted that a final decision to move for the drop at the first hour of daylight on Monday would have to be taken by 6:00 p.m. on Sunday. The decision for the Sunday afternoon drop would have to be taken by 3:00 a.m. Sunday morning, e.s.t.

5. Rusk questioned Wheeler at length about the backup. He expressed concern that if the Belgian paratroopers get into trouble, then we have answered nothing and we will have a real problem on our hands. Also he was concerned about the incoming transports meeting ground fire with disastrous consequences. Wheeler noted that there was no backup for the paratroopers. It would be impossible to deploy the U.S. brigade in less than 66 hours. There was no further Belgian resources as the one paratrooper battalion was all that they had and no approach had been made to the French, Germans, etc. With respect to this problem, it was agreed to deploy a squadron of C–130's to a base in Spain so this could be available to move in any one of several directions. An effort should be made to secure French, Italian or Belgian battalion in position as a backup.

6. With respect to the danger of running into ground fire, Wheeler assured Rusk the B–26's and the T–28's would ferret out any ground fire or anti-aircraft equipment which was in position and, hence, the paratrooper operation would be reasonably safe. Wheeler pointed out there had been severe limitations on operation of B–26's and T–28's and also in the use of two American pilots who were working with [*less than 1 line not declassified*] in the operation of these planes. Rusk ordered that all inhibitions on the use of these planes be immediately removed and that they be authorized to support the battalion. This included the use of the two American pilots on the T–28's.

7. With respect to the drop, Wheeler expressed very positive views that we must have, at best, a full day of daylight and he therefore recommended the brigade be held until early Monday morning and the drop take place on Monday unless information that developed on Sunday indicated it wise to hold for another day.

8. This view coincided with the unanimous view of those present and also with Spaak's very strongly expressed view.

10. Throughout the day I carefully advanced DDP's position that while any course of action was dangerous, the least dangerous course of action would be to have the Van der Walle brigade take Stanleyville and to hold the paratroopers to support them if they got into trouble or if a massacre started.

343. Memorandum of Telephone Conversation Between President Johnson and Acting Secretary of State Ball[1]

November 21, 1964, 11:40 a.m.

Ball said that the situation in Stanleyville is deteriorating rapidly. Reports indicate whatever responsible leaders were there are fleeing. The decision we have to make is whether we move planes from Ascension to Kamina, where they would be four hours away from Stanleyville. Spaak wants to do it. It was delayed last night because we were concerned about creating hysteria before we were prepared to have the paratroops drop over Stanleyville. This morning we are in agreement we ought to do that. Averell, Vance, Ball and Wheeler all agree this does not mean the decision to use paratroops but to move them up within four hours to Stanleyville. Our position regarding the Congolese government is we have an oral request to do this from Tshombe, but they're sitting on the written request in Stanleyville. There would be a few things to sweep up if this is done. Ball has talked to the Secretary, who is in agreement.

President asked Ball to touch base with McNamara. If he agrees, go ahead.

[1] Source: Johnson Library, Ball Papers, Congo III, 11/7/64–3/17/66. No classification marking. Prepared by Velma Heine of Ball's staff. Ball was in Washington; President Johnson was in Texas.

344. Telephone Conversation Between President Johnson and Secretary of State Rusk[1]

November 21, 1964, 9:42 p.m.

Johnson: Yes.

Rusk: This is Dean Rusk. I have here on my end a conference call with Cy Vance, General Wheeler, John McCone, George Ball, Averell Harriman, and myself. We want to talk a moment about the Congo situation. I think you were informed earlier today that the situation in Stanleyville apparently deteriorated somewhat further. The leadership that we've been trying to bicker with apparently is not in the city. The venue apparently is over on the border of Uganda. The military man Olenga is apparently up on the border of Sudan, and the elements in Stanleyville appear to be the most irresponsible group there, the so-called *jeunesse*, the rebel private personnel, that is the troops.

Now we've been talking about this operation that you're familiar with and we would like to send a message tonight saying that upon arrival at Kamina, the aircraft and forces should prepare to execute the operation at first light on Monday morning, November 23. Do not execute unless directed by the Joint Chiefs of Staff. The order to execute would be sent prior to a given hour here unless developments in the next 18 hours indicate the desirability of further postponement. Then we tell them in a second paragraph that the aircraft should be refueled immediately upon arrival in Kamina in case further marked deterioration in Stanleyville requires us to have them go earlier, that is the afternoon before. Now this coincides with the views of the Belgians, who are taking the major burden here and have the major responsibility. We have had a thorough discussion here. The Chiefs of Staff are fully on board with this line of action. So is Cy Vance. There is one—.

Johnson: Where is McNamara?

Rusk: He is in town but I talked to him before I came over here, sir.

Johnson: All right, is he on board?

Rusk: Yes sir.

Johnson: Where's he been all day, Cy?

Vance: He's been here. He's been in budget meetings at the Pentagon.

[1] Source: Johnson Library, Recordings and Transcripts, Recording of Telephone Conversation between President Johnson and Secretary Rusk, November 21, 1964, 9:42 p.m., Tape WH 6411.26, 6439, Side A, PNO 16. Ball was in Washington; President Johnson was in Texas. This transcript was prepared in the Office of the Historian specifically for this volume.

Johnson: Yeah, OK, all right.

Rusk: There's some differences down the line in CIA that I think John McCone ought to mention to you. John, would you speak to that point?

McCone: Yes, Mr. President. The difference at CIA is there is one group that feel that probably the consequences on the hostages would be lessened if the particular operation were held up and moved only in the event that things broke out before the Vanderwaele [*Van der Walle*] column went in. They feel that the most advantageous situation from the standpoint of the hostages would be for the column to take Stanleyville rather than to resort to this drop. Now there is a difference within the Agency on this point, and really it's a matter of opinion more than anything that you can really prove.

Rusk: Mr. President, I think that all of us feel that we should say to you that we can't think of any line of action here that would be sure to pick up live hostages throughout, and if we don't do anything, we'll find corpses and some corpses if we take an action of this sort by execution order tomorrow, that we're likely to find some corpses. But we don't have any feeling at all that there's any responsible authority in Stanleyville that can give anybody any protection. Now our Embassy in Brussels will be talking with Spaak tomorrow to get his final judgment before we recommend whether to push the button for an actual move. But this will get us in a position to move quickly if we have to move with the least possible warning and to get them thoroughly prepared to move at first light on Monday.

Johnson: What does this do, Dean? Move them up a few hours?

Rusk: Well, all this does is to give them in effect an alert time for the most probable hour of commitment, but it does not—, it specifically says do not execute unless directed by JCS.

Johnson: Does it move—, does it physically move them from where they are?

Rusk: It doesn't move them from where we've already ordered them, that is in Kamina.

Johnson: All this does is just say: "get ready."

Rusk: That's right.

Johnson: Now John, do you agree this ought to be done?

McCone: Yes sir, I do.

Johnson: Do you—, then you've got a minority opinion in your own staff?

McCone: Yes, that's correct.

Johnson: But you—

McCone: Based on their appraisal of the situation.

Johnson: But you don't share their view?

McCone: No, but I can't ignore it.

Johnson: No, I'm not saying you ignore it, but you don't agree with it?

McCone: No, I can't agree with that totally.

Johnson: You agree with what Dean's saying?

McCone: Yes, I do.

Johnson: OK. Go ahead, Dean.

Rusk: Well, I do think we ought to give as much weight as we can to the Belgian [predominance]. And they have several hundred hostages, and they're putting in the paratroopers and are going to take casualties, and Spaak seems to feel that it's important to move. I think the Belgians—.

Johnson: How many people, how many paratroopers are they putting in?

Rusk: Approximately a thousand, sir.

Johnson: Now all we're doing is furnishing the planes?

Rusk: That's right, sir, and 200 American military aircrews on those planes. In other words, we're running some risk ourselves.

Johnson: Now wait a minute. Repeat that. How many Americans?

Rusk: It'll be about 200 American air crews on those planes, but no combat troops.

Johnson: How're they going to—, they'll shoot the planes down you mean, that's the danger?

Rusk: Well, we could lose some Americans if they shot the planes down. That's right, sir. But these will be given cover with T–28s and B–26s that are already in the Congo, and they will use these planes to go ahead of the drop and also to help them deliver suppressive fire if anything comes out of the ground at them.

Johnson: Do they have any anti-aircraft?

Rusk: We're not absolutely certain what is at Stanleyville at this point. They had some. Some of the anti-aircraft that they had at Stanleyville turned up in Bukavu, so we know that some of it was moved away, but we don't know what is there or who's there to man it. But these planes should be—, these T–28s and B–26s should be able to find that out before the paratroop-carrying planes actually arrive on the scene.

Johnson: A thousand men in the paratroop group?

Rusk: That's right, sir. Now this is a highly trained elite group that is actually the palace guard in Belgium. This is the best outfit they've got. The Belgians are very confident that if they get down and if they get there, that they will not run into serious problems. They've had a lot of experience in the Congo and they feel certain that if it is necessary to commit these troops that the troops will take care of themselves.

Johnson: Where's Harriman?

Rusk: He's sitting right here.

Johnson: Does he agree?

Rusk: Yes, he agrees very much.

Johnson: All right. Go on then.

Rusk: All right, sir.

Johnson: Good night.

Rusk: We'll call you tomorrow.[2]

---

[2] At 10:56 a.m. on November 22, Rusk phoned the President to report that U.S. and Belgian political and military people were meeting at Kamina and that Washington should have a report by 3 p.m. He said Spaak was waiting for a report from that meeting before making a final decision and the United States would go along with the Belgian decision, whether to postpone or to go ahead. If there was any news from Attwood, they could take that into account as well. Rusk hoped the President would be available between 4:15 and 5 so they could get in touch with him. Johnson asked when they had to decide, and the Secretary said if there were to be a drop the next morning, i.e., November 23, they would have to decide by 5 p.m.—4 p.m. at the Ranch and midnight in the Congo. In response to Johnson's question regarding the purpose of the operation, Rusk stated that the only purpose was the humanitarian one of evacuating those being held hostage and that we would withdraw as soon as that was done. (Ibid., Recording of Telephone Conversation between President Johnson and Secretary Rusk, November 22, 1964, 10:56 a.m., Tape WH 6411.26, Side A, 6442, PNO 19)

---

345. Telegram From the Embassy in the Congo to the Department of State[1]

Leopoldville, November 21, 1964, midnight.

2036. Re Embtel 2022 to Dept, 1140 to Brussels.[2] De Kerchove and I were given at 2115 local following all signed by Tshombe: 1) Letter dated Nov 21 to me, 2) letter dated Nov 23 to UNSYG (which we solemnly promised to [garble] and 3) draft long statement to be released just before troops parachute into Stan, if they do. Translations letters

---

[1] Source: National Archives, RG 59, Central Files 1964–66, POL 23–9 THE CONGO. Top Secret; Flash; Exdis. Received at 6:39 p.m. and repeated to Brussels. Passed to the White House, DOD, and CIA.

[2] Dated November 21. (Ibid.)

and statement follow separate telegrams.[3] Texts of letters essentially those given Tshombe last evening with one major change, i.e. all speak of GDRC authorizing rather than requesting Belgian Govt send humanitarian force and authorizing USG furnish means of transport. De Kerchove and I both cited to Tshombe and to Mobutu, who only other person present, this major difference but both said that Kasavubu at first would not countenance any force coming here and only with great reluctance acquiesced to authorizing humanitarian effort. Reason for reluctance was "Kasavubu's ire" and that of "all Congolese press and many others" re Spaak's premature press release. Tshombe and Mobutu recognize and accept reasons that obliged Spaak make release, but Mobutu pointed out that even he who favors Belgian action was annoyed when he first heard of it over radio.

Mobutu and Tshombe both pled with us to preposition troops Kamina soonest. In view Deptel 1346 to Leo, 1111 to Brussels,[4] we did not indicate troops on way but said that we would endeavor obtain their earliest arrival Kamina. Military here estimate ETA Kamina beginning 0600 Zulu. I intend, unless instructed otherwise, phone Mobutu and Tshombe 0500 Zulu that I have just been informed planes may be landing shortly at Kamina. We also told Mobutu and Tshombe that if troops were to go to Kamina, maximum security must be maintained. They both said this went without saying. We and Belgians of course doing everything possible assure security.

Finally upon departure I emphasized to both Tshombe and Mobutu that it should be clearly understood that if troops were to go to Kamina, this ipso facto did not mark USG's agreement to their being lifted to Stan. I said that lift from Kamina to Stan must have Washington further approval. They both said they understood.

Re statement, we again argued at some length for original text, because Tshombe had changed "requested" in their statement to "authorized". Although they offered release short text of declaration (Embtel 2022) tomorrow morning with "authorize", we noted that this would tip hand to world and would violate security, for press would immediately ask what was being done pursuant to the authorization.

---

[3] Telegram 2037 from Leopoldville, November 21, transmitted the translations of Tshombe's letters and statement. (Ibid.)

[4] Telegram 1111 to Brussels (repeated as telegram 1346 to Leopoldville), November 21, instructed the Embassy in Brussels to inform Spaak that the U.S. Government agreed to move the Dragon Rouge force to Kamina as soon as possible and issued the necessary instructions. Leopoldville was instructed not to inform Tshombe or other Congolese officials until shortly before the planes were due at Kamina in order to minimize the security problem. In the meantime, it was essential to obtain written requests from Kasavubu or Tshombe. (Ibid.)

Ad referendum De Kerchove and I agreed that in view firm position on "authorize" it better not issue statement for time being.[5]

Godley

[5] Telegram 1356 to Leopoldville, November 21, informed the Embassy that Tshombe's letter of authorization was acceptable, and approved Godley's proposal to notify Tshombe and Mobutu at 0500Z of the imminent arrival of the planes at Kamina. He was to request urgently that they hold this information until, and unless, Dragon Rouge actually moved on Stanleyville. (Ibid.)

346. Telegram From the Department of State to the Embassy in Belgium[1]

Washington, November 22, 1964, 1:24 a.m.

1124. For MacArthur from Harriman. After Belgians have had opportunity review morning reports from Congo relative situation Stanleyville and advance VDW, you should see GOB and obtain Spaak's latest judgment on whether DR should proceed daylight Monday[2] morning or defer on possibility VDW arrival Stan Tuesday (see Leo's 2038).[3]

We want GOB judgment on action which would give best chance security of hostages.

We want answer by 11 A.M. our time Sunday. Telephone is necessary using code name Felix for Monday daylight and Harold for delay until Tuesday.

We are inclined to give maximum weight to Belgian judgment in reaching decision.[4]

[1] Source: National Archives, RG 59, Central Files 1964–66, POL 23–9 THE CONGO. Top Secret; Flash; Exdis. Drafted and approved by Harriman and cleared by Palmer. Repeated to Leopoldville and to DOD.

[2] November 23.

[3] Dated November 21. (National Archives, RG 59, Central Files 1964–66, POL 23–9 THE CONGO)

[4] Telegram 1037 from Brussels, November 22, reported that Spaak's current feeling was that Dragon Rouge should proceed on November 23 as planned but that he would seek the latest information before giving the Belgian Government's judgment. Telegram 2060 from Brussels, November 22, reported that although Belgium was reserving its final decision on Dragon Rouge, Spaak recommended that it not take place before November 24. (Ibid.)

For Leo: We require urgently prior 11 A.M. Washington time Nov 22 fullest assessment current situation Stan, and position and timetable VDW.[5]

Rusk

---

[5] Telegram 2057 from Leopoldville, November 22, reported that a conference that day at Kamina among Williams, Godley, De Kerchove, and the Dragon Rouge military leaders agreed to recommend a November 24 paratroop drop on Stanleyville and a November 26 drop on Paulis and Bunia. (Ibid.) At 4:45 p.m., Ball telephoned Rusk to inform him of the Kamina recommendation and said he would call the President at the Ranch. (Johnson Library, Ball Papers, Congo III, 11/7/64–3/17/66)

---

347. Transcript of Telephone Conversation Between President Johnson and Acting Secretary of State Ball[1]

November 22, 1964, 5 p.m.

B: Mac Bundy is on the line with me. We have had a report now from the meeting that took place at Kamina. The military has recommended that the operation be held up one more night to coordinate with the column.

J: How far are you by air from . . .

B: 3 hours.

J: How many miles?

B: About 1,000.

J: Where is the column?

B: It is at Labutto. It then, by moving all night, can reach there Tuesday morning. It would reach there at the same time that the drop would occur.

J: How many in the column?

B: 600.

J: There are 800 in our outfit?

B: 800 to be dropped and 600 in the column. There is enough force there to take care of the situation. Wheeler is clear on this.

J: What do they have?

---

[1] Source: Johnson Library, Ball Papers, Congo III, 11/7/64–3/17/66. No classification marking. No drafting information appears. Ball was in Washington; President Johnson was in Texas.

B: It is hard to tell.

J: Then, how does he know he can take care of it?

B: They are finding that the forces have largely left. It has been the experience of coming in and finding the troops on the run when they encounter the column or any kind of air cover. On the basis of all the experiences there would seem to be no likelihood of meeting resistance, and there is no indication that they are likely to meet much. The expectation is, and it seems to be agreed by all, military on both sides, that they will have an easy time of it.

M. Bundy: In military terms either force can win a battle in Stanleyville. The Kamina–Stanleyville distance we have checked is 2 hours in the air. The theory is to get them in Tuesday morning early. That has an advantage of putting the paratroopers in. We have some ease on the scene as to what is going on. In military terms, to do the two things at once seems very clear. This is the Belgian military in Brussels concurring with their own advisors in the field. There is no reason to think that the hostages may be in great danger for one more day.

B: The only new element that will increase the danger is that there has been a leak through London that the planes have left Ascension. We will have to use the fall-back release that we had worked out with the Belgians, confirming the fact that the planes have left Ascension but simply say they have moved up to a point closer to Stanleyville and are not presently en route to Stanleyville. I think this is not a very serious matter but there is always risk in one more day, but there is ability of mobility and seeking out the hostages because the column will have wheels and transport.

J: Had we anticipated that the paratroopers to go in first?

B: We had thought that might be done and we decided on their recommendation to put the two together. There is an advantage in not having this look like a military operation but a humanitarian operation. We were motivated by the fact that the situation in Stanleyville was deteriorating so rapidly that we wanted to get the quickest force in. During the day there has been no evidence that the situation is falling apart any more. There have been no radio intercepts. There is a meeting later tonight between Attwood and Kanza. We may have some further light on the situation when that meeting takes place. I think there is a good deal for arguing for accepting the Belgian view. This is a unanimous consent here by Wheeler, McNamara, Rusk.

J: O.K. Go ahead.

348. Telegram From the Department of State to the Embassy in Greece[1]

Washington, November 22, 1964, 5:04 p.m.

783. Belgians have now informed President Security Council about situation with respect hostages in Stanleyville and surrounding areas, asking letter be circulated to members SC, reserving right call urgent meeting SC if necessary, and urging each UN member to call for immediate release of hostages. US has sent supporting letter. Purpose help mobilize world opinion in hope influencing moderation on part rebels. Would be extremely helpful if Government addressee posts whose nationals also involved would send supporting letters and/or public statements to same effect to SC President (who happens to be Stevenson this month) or SYG. Request you urge host government do so soonest.

Texts Belgian and US letters follow in septel.[2]

Rusk

---

[1] Source: National Archives, RG 59, Central Files 1964–66, POL 23-9 THE CONGO. Confidential; Immediate. Drafted by Jones, cleared by Cleveland, and approved by Palmer. Also sent to Bern, Bonn, Brussels, Buenos Aires, Dublin, Karachi, Khartoum, London, New Delhi, Ottawa, Paris, Port au Prince, Rome, The Hague, and Vienna. Repeated to Leopoldville and USUN.

[2] Telegram 784 to Athens, November 22. (Ibid.)

349. Telegram From the Commander in Chief, Strike Command, and Commander in Chief, Middle East/South Asia and Africa South of the Sahara to the Commander of the Joint Task Force in the Congo[1]

Tampa, Florida, November 22, 1964, 2136Z.

STRIKE 1089/64. Subject is: Sequence of events on order to execute Dragon Rouge (S).

---

[1] Source: Johnson Library, National Security File, Country File, Congo, Vol. VIII, Cables, Memos & Miscellaneous, 11/64. Top Secret; Limdis; Noforn Except to Belgian Nationals on a Need to Know Basis. Received at the DOD Message Center at 2239Z. Repeated to COMUSJTF Leo Main Leopoldville, and JCS.

1. (TS) The following gives you a time sequence of execution of Dragon Rouge in order that there be no misunderstanding during this crucial phase. This discussion is based on the fact that you are considered to be on a [*less than 1 line not declassified*] with a 2 hour ready to launch alert time, and that the tentative launch hour from Kamina is 0100Z.

2. (TS) The decision time in Washington to order execution should be no later than 2200Z. Safe transmission time of the execute message to you is considered to be one hour. Therefore, the order to execute should be in your hands at Kamina at 2300Z.

3. (TS) In spite of the optimum conditions stated above, the decision to execute may run up to the last minute and perhaps beyond the 2200Z deadline. Therefore, you should be prepared to react in the minimum possible time after receipt of order to execute.

4. (TS) You will be directed to increase your readiness posture using the STRIKE MEAFSA emergency action file (SMEAF) by flash STRIKEOPS 2A message by teletype. These messages will include instructions as follows:

A. [*less than 1 line not declassified*] (to be effective 2300Z). Load all equipment on C–130 aircraft. Prepare personnel for loading. Ready B–26 and T–28 support aircraft for launch. Tentative D-Day H-Hour will be announced in blanks 6 and 7 of STRIKEOPS msg. Blank 6 will be D-Day; blank 7 will be H-Hour.

B. [*less than 1 line not declassified*] (to be effective 0030Z). Load personnel on aircraft, taxi and prepare to launch troop carrier and tactical aircraft. Launch hour will be confirmed as 0100Z. You will not launch until told to execute.

C. Order to execute will be by unclassified words Big Punch, transmitted in the clear. The word Punch, in accordance with a US/Belgian agreement, indicates that the order to execute is a combined US/Belgian decision.

5. (TS) After order to execute has been given, there may be reason to rescind the order and call off the assault. The unclassified words for this will be Dragon Rouge Blue Fish, and will be given you by voice in the clear. Upon receipt of Blue Fish, you will return all aircraft to Kamina and await further instructions.

6. (TS) Prior to launch from Kamina and prior to receipt of the order to execute, the decision may be made to either cancel or delay the planned assault. The unclassified words Blue Fish will be used for this event also. You will then return to a [*less than 1 line not declassified*] readiness posture with a 2 hour alert time and await further orders.

7. (U) Acknowledge.

350. Telegram From the Embassy in Kenya to the Department of State[1]

Nairobi, November 23, 1964, 2 p.m.

1399. Reference: (A) Deptel 1922.[2] (B) Deptel 1957.[3] Americans Stanleyville.

Met Kanza at 0800Z at Gatundu. Kenyatta present, as he put it, in capacity Chairman Ad Hoc Commission.

I covered first and second points instructions (reference A). Kanza then made it plain his instructions were to discuss Congo in general, including ceasefire not just "prisoners of war." Kenyatta broke in with strong pitch for ceasefire as only solution permitting OAU go to Stanleyville and save lives.

I carefully explained not authorized discuss anything but safety hostages and reminded Kenyatta discussion between Kanza and me. Suggested best way prevent killings now would be action in line point four instructions. Said time had come all concerned to be realistic.

Kenyatta and Kanza both returned to ceasefire argument, denouncing mercenaries (who must leave Congo forthwith) and stressing total Tshombe dependence US and Belgian support. Kanza added Gbenye in full control Stanleyville though under great popular pressure execute Carlson.

Realizing no headway possible, I then suggested that in view conflicting instructions and critical situation, only way we could continue would be for me report immediately to my government and meet Kanza again when I had reply. Present meeting had at least clarified our positions. Kanza and Kenyatta agreed.

I took this action only to avoid break in discussions in accordance point six instructions.

Kenyatta said he hoped US would understand and cooperate with OAU on ceasefire, and that I would get quick reply from USG.

Kanza said Carlson alive and he would immediately notify Gbenye in Stanleyville to postpone execution while our discussions in progress.

---

[1] Source: National Archives, RG 59, Central Files 1964–66, POL 23–9 THE CONGO. Secret; Exdis. Received at 7:39 a.m. and repeated to London, Addis Ababa, Bujumbura, Brussels, USUN, Leopoldville, Geneva, and Ottawa. Passed to the White House, DOD, and CIA.

[2] Document 340.

[3] Dated November 21. (National Archives, RG 59, Central Files 1964–66, POL 23–9 THE CONGO)

With concurrence Kanza and Kenyatta, I then made following statement to press:

"I have had a preliminary discussion with Mr. Kanza, Prime Minister Jomo Kenyatta attended our meeting in his capacity as Chairman of the OAU Ad Hoc Commission on the Congo. On the basis of today's discussion, Mr. Kanza and I have agreed to meet again as soon as I have consulted my government."

In response to question about Carlson, I replied, "Mr. Kanza assures me he is still alive."

After meeting with Kanza, I requested few minutes alone with Kenyatta. Mathu and Koinange also remained. Outlined actual situation in line reference B and said if rescue operation becomes necessary as last resort it would be just that, with minimum loss of life, quick withdrawal, non-discriminatory, etc., aim only to prevent massacre which also disaster for Africa.

Kenyatta looked pained at prospect but I assured him this was contemplated only if all other efforts failed. Explained I told him this in confidence as Ambassador to his country. He understood, thanked me for confidence and reiterated hope our next meeting with Kanza would make paratroop action unnecessary.

Previously, while drafting my statement, we considered adding "meanwhile Kanza assured me no harm will befall civilians in Stanleyville while discussions in progress." Kanza first agreed, then refused on grounds "mercenary" attack on Stanleyville would result in fighting and general bloodshed which would not be responsibility Stanleyville authorities. Kenyatta backed him up, using this as further argument for ceasefire.[4]

Attwood

---

[4] In telegram 1978 to Nairobi, November 23, the Department sent Attwood a flash response, informing him that the decision had been made to execute Dragon Rouge at 0400Z November 24 and instructing him to inform Kenyatta as soon as possible that he had received a response from Washington that Kanza's proposals, which used outrageous threats against the lives of innocent civilians as blackmail to achieve a military objective, i.e., a cease-fire, were totally unacceptable. As soon as the Ambassador received the flash announcement of Dragon Rouge, he was to call Kenyatta and inform him that in view of the increased threats, the absence of adequate assurances from Kanza, and the need to protect innocent lives, it had been necessary to launch a rescue operation into Stanleyville. (Ibid.)

351. Telegram From the Embassy in Belgium to the Department of State[1]

Brussels, November 23, 1964, 8:14 p.m.

1057. Embtel 1048 and Brubeck–MacArthur telcons.[2] Saw Spaak and put to him as requested by Palmer and Brubeck fol courses of action: (1) VDW column assault on Stan Nov 23 without DR; (2) DR drop Nov 24 coupled with VDW arrival Stan sometime same day; (3) DR Nov 24 with VDW arrival Stan suspended until Nov 25.

Spaak said he had given much thought to these alternatives. There was no easy, simple course of action and each of above alternatives held risks and serious political inconveniences. However, time had come when lives of 1000 foreign women, children and men were in mortal danger and we must face up to our responsibility and make a decision based on A) elements of problem as Belgian and US knew them and B) which alternative offered best chance of survival for hostages.

1. Re alternative one above, if DR not implemented, VDW forces will have to be rested at least briefly tonight for assault tomorrow and may not arrive until perhaps midday. This means that there would be entire morning for irresponsible elements to massacre hostages before arrival of column. Furthermore, if VDW arrives without DR it will enter Stan from east and have to make its way all across city against resistance to west of city where hostages are believed concentrated, obviously increasing risks for hostages. However if DR implemented resistance expected to be very slight.

2. Re alternative two (arrival of VDW and DR at Stan Nov 24), if DR is implemented, VDW column will be given minimum rest and should be in position outside Stan reasonably early tomorrow morning (Nov 24). If DR para drop occurs (west of city where hostages believed to be), with VDW outside city, estimate is there will be little if any real resistance and maximum VDW–DR resources will be available to rescue hostages soonest.

3. Alternative three (DR on Nov 24 with VDW arrival Nov 25). In view of present rate of progress of VDW column, it will arrive in Stan sometime tomorrow whether or not DR implemented. Belgians have no reason to believe that VDW column can be held up 24 hours and are

---

[1] Source: National Archives, RG 59, Central Files 1964–66, POL 23–9 THE CONGO. Top Secret; Flash; Exdis. Received at 3:14 p.m. and repeated to Leopoldville. Passed to the White House, DOD, and CIA.

[2] Telegram 1048 from Brussels, November 23. (Ibid.) No record of the telcons has been found.

certain that efforts to be so would be bitterly and very probably successfully resisted by GOC. Furthermore, in terms of safety of hostages there will obviously be less resources if DR is implemented alone than if VDW column is there to assist.

Spaak said that from the beginning of planning of DR basic criteria of whether we would implement it was whether it would give maximum survival possibility for foreign hostages. He firmly believes this must be the criteria. His conclusion is that hostages will have maximum chance of survival if alternative two (DR and VDW arrival Nov 24) is implemented. Furthermore, he understands that both Belgian and American Embs and military in Congo share this view. He recognizes that coincidental arrival of VDW and DR in Stan Nov 24 will be exploited by those who will try to portray DR as assistance to ANC rather than humanitarian effort but feels that this is something we will have to accept since hanging in the balance are lives of 1000 men, women and children. He said it would be "grotesque" if we should take the risk of holding up on DR 24 hours with resultant massacre of hostages. While DR cannot guarantee safety of hostages, he believes its implementation gives them maximum chance.

Spaak said I should inform US Govt that Belgian Govt view (concurred in by PriMin and DefMin) is that DR should be implemented as planned Nov 24. The decision was a very difficult one, charged with heavy responsibility but Belgians felt it had to be faced up to. He asked that I inform Washington of Belgian decision, making clear that final decision was joint decision with each of us assuming equal responsibility for it. (I assured him that from the very beginning we had understood it was joint decision with equal responsibility.) Spaak said if we concur in implementation of DR we send "Punch" at once and inform him soonest through Emb Brussels so that he can inform PriMin, DefMin and so that Belgian military can also confirm "Punch" through their military channels to Belgian military in Congo. (Brubeck in telecon at 7:40 P.M. tonight Brussels time informed me "Punch" has been sent and Spaak immediately informed through Davignon.)

MacArthur

352. Telephone Conversation Between President Johnson and Secretary of State Rusk[1]

November 23, 1964, 12:24 p.m.

Johnson: Hello.

Rusk: Hello. Yes, sir.

Johnson: Yes, Dean.

Rusk: Mr. President, I'll put you on with George Ball here in just a moment. [inaudible] he's been meeting with Bob McNamara about the Congo, but the essence of it is that the Belgian cabinet is now meeting at this moment to decide their view on whether it is in the best interest of the hostages to go ahead and drop these fellows tomorrow morning. But let me put you on with George Ball to bring you—, to give you a little more detail on it. Hold on just a minute.

Johnson: [inaudible]

Ball: [inaudible] Spaak's own view is that it's necessary to go ahead with the drop tomorrow morning. He feels that not to do so when that force is assembled would in his words be grotesque. The situation is that the column is moving by road and should be there not later than mid-morning. The drop would take place at the first light of dawn, but the combination of these two would,—one would reinforce the other.[2] And we're expecting within the next half hour word that the Belgian cabinet has made this decision. It's,—we have to make a final decision in order to get the word there by not later than 5 o'clock this afternoon our time here, which is about three and a half hours from now. So we wanted to get your reaction to this situation as it's now developing, Mr. President.

Johnson: I don't think we've got any choice, have we?

Ball: I beg your pardon.

Johnson: I don't think we've got any choice, have we?

Ball: I wouldn't think so. We're all unanimous. Bob McNamara is right here and standing by, as well as Dean, and we're all in agreement as to what we have to do if the Belgians decide, as appears to be the case now, that they want to go ahead.

---

[1] Source: Johnson Library, Recordings and Transcripts, Recording of Telephone Conversation between President Johnson and Secretary Rusk, November 23, 1964, 12:24 p.m., Tape WH 6411.28, 6451, Side A, PNO 2. This transcript was prepared in the Office of the Historian specifically for this volume. Rusk was in Washington; President Johnson was in Texas.

[2] See Document 347, for a record of Ball's November 22 telephone conversation with the President in which he reported that the military had recommended holding up the paradrop operation one more night so it could be coordinated with the arrival of the column at Stanleyville.

Johnson: What domestic reaction are we going to get from the Negroes in this country?

Ball: I think that what we have prepared, Mr. President, is a dossier of the kind of messages that we have been getting out of Stanleyville about the killing and the threats to eat and burn and so on these hostages. I think that this could be represented quite properly as a strictly humanitarian effort and I don't think that it should create any problem of that kind. We've made it clear that our rescue efforts are directed towards the Congolese as well as toward our own people. That is, that it's not solely a matter of saving the white hostages.

Johnson: Is this in any way going to involve us in getting us in there and getting us tied down there?

Ball: Well, we're very conscious of that and of course these are not our troops that are being—.

Johnson: I understand that. I understand that.

Ball: And we're all sensitive to the idea that we get out just as fast as we can, that this is not a commitment to get into a land fight in the middle of Africa.

Johnson: OK. We'll talk a little later, I gather.

Ball: Now we've just had a message while I've been talking to you. I was just handed a note saying that the Belgian cabinet has formally approved the Spaak recommendation and that if the United States concurs, they would give the order for tomorrow morning.

Johnson: Well, you're in agreement then.

Ball: We're all in agreement.

Johnson: Well, all right. Let's go.

Ball: Right.

Johnson: You don't think we need to check any more?

Ball: Not unless there's some new development, Mr. President. Would you like to speak to Bob McNamara? He's right here.—Hello.

Johnson: How are you?

Ball: I said, do you want to speak to Bob McNamara?

Johnson: Yes, yeah.

McNamara: Yes, Mr. President. How are you?

Johnson: Very well, sir.—

[Omitted here is discussion of an unrelated subject.]

Johnson: Any other troubles?

McNamara: No sir, other than this one George was talking about, which is a very great trouble, but which we're all agreed on. We should go ahead if the Belgians request that we do so. They have so requested.

353. Telegram From the Department of State to the Embassy in the Congo[1]

Washington, November 23, 1964, 4:24 p.m.

1391. Punch plus US-concurrence sent through military channels to Dragon Rouge 1900Z November 23 for 0400Z November 24. You should in concert with Belgians assure VDW is informed soonest and GDRC at latest possible moment assuring maximum security.

Other points:

1. While recognizing limitations on how much control we can exercise, you should try to minimize press access to Stan until Dragon Rouge completed and DR forces withdrawn.

2. Both we and Spaak feel strongly that there must be some Congolese brought out to Leo in DR evacuation and rely on you to accomplish.

3. No US personnel or planes except Dragon Rouge to enter Stan till city secured by VDW.

4. We emphasize again our posture is humanitarian evacuation not military collaboration with GDRC.

5. There is concern here to assure that VDW has given thought and is taking action to attempt block remaining northeast escape routes out of Stan to prevent removal hostages.

6. Since DR and VDW assault will inevitably be linked and front page news, VDW must be impressed with necessity highest degree discipline and behavior his forces in order US and Belgium not incur additional liabilities GDRC military excesses.[2]

Rusk

---

[1] Source: National Archives, RG 59, Central Files 1964–66, POL 23–9 THE CONGO. Top Secret; Flash; Exdis. Drafted by Brubeck, cleared by Harriman, and approved by Palmer. Repeated to Brussels, CINCSTRIKE, CINCEUR, DOD, and CIA.

[2] In telegram 2085 from Leopoldville, November 23, Godley reported that he and De Kerchove had informed Tshombe, who said this would save many European and Congolese lives. Tshombe agreed to make a radio statement in the morning once the drop was confirmed. (Ibid.) Telegram 1397 to Leopoldville, November 23, instructed Godley that he and De Kerchove should act to ensure the coordination of the VDW and Dragon Rouge operations, but not allow their public position to reflect any such coordination, since Dragon Rouge should appear to be a strictly humanitarian operation. The Ambassador was also instructed to ensure that the Congolese Government's letters to the U.S. and Belgian Governments authorizing Dragon Rouge were published as soon as the drop was confirmed. (Ibid.)

354. Memorandum Prepared in the White House Situation Room for the President's Special Assistant for National Security Affairs (Bundy)[1]

Washington, November 24, 1964.

This is a telecon with DCM Blake in Leo at 8:45, Number 7.

Clingerman in Stanleyville advises all Americans contained on special lists of Americans in Stanleyville area have now been located and are safe with the exception of (a) the Loewen family who are presumed O.K. and have not yet been picked up since they live out of town, and (b) the two killed in action. Except for the two big dramas, the casualties have been limited. Apparently when the paras started coming and the Simbas heard the shooting, they began to herd Europeans to the hotel. When the group of 250 being herded to Lumumba Square realized what was happening, they broke and dispersed and went over the wall. Casualties were those hit trying to get over the wall. Contrary to CBS 8:00 reports, there is no real fighting in the airport area. Very few Congolese casualties. About 30 Simba dead observed so far. No major killing of Congolese civilians. Two ANC's dead. None of the rebel leaders caught so far. Wounded Congolese being evacuated by C–130 to Leo. City being sectored with Belgian paras operating one area for evacuation and Van der Walle another area for cleanup, with Belgians moving back more and more toward the airport. Stiff fighting still going on in European residential areas. At rough estimate, 35–40 foreigners still unaccounted for. Apparently some rebels have escaped to NE but no mass exodus. Although move to take European hostages into bush began several days ago, few, if any, actually taken away. All wounded due out tonight. About 200 evacuees awaiting transportation at Stanleyville airport now. 350 taken out so far today. 350 more expected out before the end of today. Planes being used in shifts to rest crews. Lumumba Square incidents—when Simbas heard the firing of paras coming into town, they began herding foreigners out of houses toward Lumumba Wall for execution. When foreigners realized what was happening, they broke and dispersed, going over a nearby wall. Those who got over wall found themselves safe in hands of paras; those wounded and killed were hit trying to get over the wall. Paras sticking solely to humanitarian mission with Van der Walle and paras' operations strictly separate. Leo will give us another report just before noon

---

[1] Source: Johnson Library, National Security File, Country File, Congo, Vol. VIII, Memos & Miscellaneous, 11/64. Confidential. No drafting information appears on the memorandum. A handwritten notation states that it was relayed to the President's Special Assistant, Jack Valenti, and Press Secretary George Reedy at the LBJ Ranch.

briefing here. Also checking earliest possible estimates as to when Stanleyville will be cleared up re evacuation and also what is happening to foreigners outside Stanleyville and whether evacuation operations throughout NE will be necessary.

---

355. Telegram From the Department of State to the Embassy in the Congo[1]

Washington, November 24, 1964, 9 a.m.

1405. (a) *Control of GDRC Forces at Stanleyville.* Spotlight world opinion will be focused by all news media on Stanleyville after its recapture. Parallel to news of surviving hostages, search for others and conditions Stanleyville under rebels will be spot news on present events there. Should GDRC fail take effective steps control its forces or should it permit summary rather than proper judicial proceedings with respect trials, if any, of principal rebels for treason or offenses against Geneva Conventions, support for GDRC position will be further undercut and Tshombe's African antagonists will have field day.

GDRC has two possibly advantageous reasonable courses it can follow (1) amnesty followed by consolidation support for central government; (2) proper judicial trial with all safeguards for dealing with all aspects problem of offenses of rebel leadership.

If GDRC indulges simple killings or improper trials, opens self to changes illegal and inhumane conduct and runs risk adding one or more Lumumbas to opposition's pantheon.

Our position also vulnerable in absence reasonably effective restraints, good judicial procedures. US support humanitarian rescue mission will contrast sharply with its support of GDRC if latter pursues officially illegal and inhumane policies or tolerates atrocities or improper trials.

Concerting with Belgian Emb and others in its discretion, suggest Emb seek persuade GDRC adopt immediate and special precautions. Seek urgently through Belgian Ambassador utmost restraint by VDW of Katanga gendarmes. Primary requirement is presence in Stanleyville

---

[1] Source: National Archives, RG 59, Central Files 1964–66, POL 23–9 THE CONGO. Secret; Priority. Drafted by Schaufele and Runyon, cleared by Morris J. Amitay in EUR, and approved by Williams. Repeated to Brussels.

of responsible officials, Congolese or foreign, who understand problem and can exercise restraining influence on excesses.

(b) *Adequate Courts.* Dept recognizes that lack of capable judges and prosecution and defense lawyers will make reasonably fair trials difficult to expect. One possibility would be to assure that those available elsewhere in Congo be assigned Stanleyville for temporary judicial and legal service. In this matter, Emb requested give its views on other possibilities e.g. bringing in outside personnel especially African, calling upon UN for assistance, etc.

Rusk

---

356. Memorandum of Telephone Conversation Between the President's Special Assistant for National Security Affairs (Bundy) and the Under Secretary of State (Ball)[1]

Washington, November 24, 1964, 10:05 a.m.

Ball informed Bundy of his talk with the Belgian Amb. who said this had been the most important and moving experience in Spaak's life. Ball thought some kind of message should be sent out. Ball told Bundy of the efficient job the paras were doing in Stan. This has been a model operation.

Bundy suggested that the President could call Spaak if someone would dictate 3–4 lines on what he should say. Ball was not sure the call should go to Spaak. Bundy suggested as an alternative, Rusk might call Spaak and say the President had asked him to express the warmest congratulations.... Ball thought Spaak might like to have something he could put out. Bundy then suggested a message to the PM or to the King. Ball said we would get something up and send it over. Bundy suggested the message be telephoned over and action would be taken on it.[2]

Bundy asked if there had been any preliminary thought on "what next". Ball said nothing had come through about whether it would take another drop or whether the column would go up the road.

---

[1] Source: Johnson Library, Ball Papers, Congo III, 11/7/64–3/17/66. No classification marking. Prepared by Jacquelyn Taylor.

[2] Telegram 1176 to Brussels, November 24, conveyed a message from Rusk to Spaak expressing his "personal compliments and gratitude." (National Archives, RG 59, Central Files 1964–66, POL 23–9 THE CONGO)

Bundy asked about Gbenye. Ball said there had been no mention at all. Ball told Bundy about his short backgrounder for the press. Ball said this morning he fed out the story from Hoyt which said one, if there had been another 24 hour delay, he thinks there would have been a massacre; two, that the air drop was what saved them—only that saved them. Bundy thought this would be very good therapy for us. The fact that some of the hostages were shot justified the movement.

Ball said that Spaak did not want a SC meeting[3] and things were relaxed there. Ball said he was trying to reach Humphrey and fill him in, before his luncheon.

[3] In telegram 1065 from Brussels, November 24, MacArthur reported that since Spaak continued to have serious reservations concerning a request for a Security Council meeting, they had agreed to send a full written report to the Security Council without requesting a formal Council meeting. (Ibid.)

357. Memorandum Prepared in the White House Situation Room for the President's Special Assistant for National Security Affairs (Bundy)[1]

Washington, November 24, 1964.

SUBJECT

Telecon From Leopoldville

The following is a report of a telephone conversation with American Embassy Leopoldville at 11 EST.

Mr. Blake, Deputy Chief of Mission in Leopoldville, reported that the paratroopers have completed their mission and have withdrawn to the airport, leaving the rest of the city to the ANC. Considerable fighting is taking place on the left bank of the river with the probability that some Europeans are located in that area. Van Der Walle is dealing with this. There is a probability there is still considerable fighting going on within Stanleyville itself and the clean up operation may take a number of days.

The radio in Stanleyville is not yet in ANC hands.

[1] Source: Johnson Library, National Security File, Country File, Congo, Vol. VIII, Memos & Miscellaneous, 11/64. No classification marking.

At this time the transmission was broken off. It was evident they have disturbing reports about conditions in areas outside Stanleyville and are sending reports and recommendations regarding further actions to Washington.

International Situation Room

---

358. Memorandum From the Deputy Assistant Secretary of Defense for International Security Affairs (Lang) to the Deputy Secretary of Defense (Vance)[1]

Washington, November 25, 1964.

SUBJECT

Congo

1. I understand that a meeting will be called this morning to decide two questions—

(i) Whether Dragon Rouge forces should be withdrawn to Kamina.

Basically this seems a political question. Leopoldville reports that Stanleyville is secure enough for the Dragon Rouge forces to withdraw, and Dragons Noir and Blanc could be launched from either Stanleyville or Kamina. Those favoring withdrawal argue that it will emphasize the humanitarian aspects of the Stanleyville drop. Others argue to the contrary, fearing that the OAU meeting tomorrow will interpret a move to Kamina (as opposed to a withdrawal from the Congo) as an indication that the Belgian forces intend to remain indefinitely.

(ii) Whether Dragons Blanc (Bunia) and Noir (Paulis) should be launched tomorrow. Earlier, Leopoldville strongly recommended both drops. Leopoldville wants to take no chances with what appears to be an established rebel pattern of executing hostages. Subsequently, the Belgian para commander recommended going forward only with Noir. Apparently, he feels that his forces are tired and he wants to use two companies against Paulis instead of one originally planned. (This would leave him one assault company and one headquarters/support company.)

---

[1] Source: Washington National Records Center, RG 330, OASD/ISA Files: FRC 69 A 7425, Congo 381 (12 Aug. 64). Top Secret. A stamped notation on the memorandum reads: "Mr. Vance has seen." A copy was sent to McNaughton.

2. Incidental Intelligence. The commander of JTF Leo reports that the rescued hostages feel that Stanleyville could have been taken "without a shot," if Dragon Rouge had been launched two weeks earlier. After the fall of Kindu, Boende and Bumba, the rebels were "psychologically defeated." They began discarding uniforms, etc., but after several weeks they became brave again.

L.

359. Memorandum of Telephone Conversation Between President Johnson and the Under Secretary of State (Ball)[1]

November 25, 1964, 12:15 p.m.

Ball explained Spaak feels strongly there ought to be another drop at a place called Paulis, where there is a big concentration of refugees. There are only 7 Americans but 450 other Europeans, mostly Belgians. What would be involved would be half the force used at Stanleyville—270 paras, 40–50 Americans, air crews for 7 planes. The final decision doesn't have to be made until this afternoon. The inclination here (McNamara, Rusk, McCone, Wheeler) is to do it because the Belgians do feel there is a great obligation to their lives.

President said he wanted very much to accept this advice. His strongest inclination, however, is against it. He had grave doubts about the other one. He didn't want to do it unless there are very compelling reasons felt by everyone. Then he wants to know why we can't get somebody to help us with the Europeans. He doesn't want to get tied in on the Congo and have another Korea, another Viet-Nam, just because of somebody wandering around searching for "Jesus Christ". We made a mistake first of all running the Belgians out and taking the position we did on Tshombe and then embracing him, wrapping the colonial flag around us and acting unilaterally, becoming labeled as aggressors. He said he wanted all of them to consider these things. Then he wants to see why the British won't send planes, why the French won't send planes. He doesn't like the unilateral operation of letting the Belgians bring us in. He doesn't want that image of running them out of the Congo and coming back with them. He asked if Rusk were here and

[1] Source: Johnson Library, Ball Papers, Congo III, 11/7/64–3/17/66. No classification marking. The President was in Texas; Ball was in Washington.

Ball told him he was in the White House at the moment at a meeting on sugar.

President said he was upset about the leaks in the papers about what he is going to do, and the way some good sources make it look like coming out of the White House . . . The Alsop column, about Ball's memorandum, was very degrading to Ball. He said he has not seen the memorandum and knows nothing about such a memorandum. If we can't run a Government better than that . . . Ball replied we were annoyed; President said annoyed, but we will have to put in effect a regulation like McNamara did, how instead of letting the press run the Department, or some little FSOs. . . . He thought Ball should have a high-level meeting and work on these Assistant Secretaries. Some of it may come from the White House. He thought Taylor's report was disgraceful. He is coming in to tell the President how . . . that *Life* magazine article—has Ball seen it? Ball replied he had not. "If you're going to approve something as Administration policy. . . ." He asked if Ball had seen it first. Ball replied he had not. He asked if Rusk had seen it. Ball replied he did not know. President asked Ball to tell the Secretary he wanted to know; that those who approve Administration's policy are President; then Rusk; then Ball. He is tired of Luce telling him what the decision will be. We had to be gentlemanly three weeks ago, but now we have to be patriotic. It's inexcusable—these people telling what he is going to do. Rusk should sit down with these newspapermen. Get it in proportion. No dramatic announcements and no idea we are pulling out. Where is the proper perspective. Forrestal has gone out. Sullivan is in and out. Bundy was there. Rusk was there. McNamara was there. But blowing it up saying he is going to do it—it isn't going to happen. Ball agreed. Of course the purpose of the meeting was that it was intended to be played down as much as possible. Secretary should "get Bundy, Mac Bundy and tell them I don't want this happening where Taylor at all his stops (unless they pay him heavily) should not be getting them (stories) in *Life*." Ball replied he would run it down.

President said to set up whatever precaution needed. Nobody is going to speak for Johnson without letting him know. He thought our political needs needed another new look or we will have all the Africans after us, all the Senators and others, etc.

Ball said he had conditioned this on an immediate evacuation and getting the planes and paratroops out. All we intended to do was an evacuation. The military was afraid this morning to take them out until we were certain the airport was secured. In any event, the idea would be, this force would go to Paulis only to evacuate the people—in and out in 24 hours. President said suppose a plane would be shot down. Ball replied there was a risk—that can't be denied. President said to get somebody else—get the British. Ball replied as far as he was aware they had no nationals in the Congo. President said then let's not have any. Tell them this is it. Ball said we had given warnings they were there at their own risks. President asked if Spaak had any planes at all, and Ball replied none to do this operation. Unless it is done quickly, it should not be done. If we let it go for a week, the people will be lost. President said his instinct would be to give it further exploration.

[Omitted here is discussion of an unrelated subject.]

Ball said on the question of the other matter, we will have to decide this afternoon. We will have further talks here and either Rusk or he will call the President. President said to ask other people to participate—the French. Ball said there were no French there. There may be some Greeks and Turks and other Europeans in very small numbers. President said everybody was smarter than we were then. He doesn't want to get hung in the Congo. Give alternatives.

360. Memorandum of Telephone Conversation Between Secretary of State Rusk and the Ambassador to Belgium (MacArthur)[1]

November 25, 1964, 5:15 p.m.

TELEPHONE CALL FROM AMB. MacARTHUR (BRUSSELS)

M said he was here with the Prime Minister and friends. M said they recognize that neither of us have precise information on all details of what is happening to the people in that next place; they feel if it does not go tonight and we go back to stop 5, the chances are very slim that one would be able to do something; they feel that given the circumstances it would not be understood if a force so close stopped; they feel that subject to the possibility of getting out very quickly by the day after tomorrow, if there is certitude we do not get stuck, their desire and inclination is to go ahead with it; they would like to get out in the next 2–3 days. Sec said he would talk to his principal then on the basis that they would like to do it. M said unless it is very dubious that we can get out by Friday night. (There was much conferring with and in the background on both sides during the call.) M reported to Spaak that we do not have any judgment and we believe the Belgians would have more knowledge on that factor than we. M said they think we should

---

[1] Source: National Archives, RG 59, Rusk Files: Lot 72 D 192, Telephone Conversations. No classification marking. Prepared by Carolyn J. Proctor.

put it right away to the two military there whether they can give a reasonable guarantee we can be out in 48 hours; if not, they would not be inclined to go ahead. M said the Prime Minister said we should ask a guarantee; if not, let's put it off and think about it and have 24 hours . . . ; if they can give the guarantee, we should go and go quickly; if impossible to give that guarantee tonight, postpone for 24 hours, return to Kamina and see how it looks; it would not be much more difficult from there than from a secured Stan. They discussed communications possibilities; not possible to get an answer back in 35 minutes. Sec said we are the junior partner here but it might be hard to explain why this force moves back before the job is done; if we say nothing, we will still make the decision, which will be not to do it. Sec said you could always give the order to come out. M said on the military responsibility, their people say it is feasible if our air people continue to agree it is feasible. Sec said our people say on strictly military side it is feasible. M said if military feel it is feasible to wind up in 48 hours, and be out, they would like to go. Sec will call back.[2]

[2] At 5:45 p.m., Rusk telephoned MacArthur and said that "the boss" shared their feelings, that he hoped it could be done as quickly as possible, and that this was the last one. There should be no waiting around for anyone to join them on the ground and no taking of local prisoners. It was to be purely a rescue operation. MacArthur agreed and said that they were very grateful on this. Rusk said that Washington would flash the word. (Ibid.)

361. Telegram From the Department of State to the Embassy in Belgium[1]

Washington, November 25, 1964, 8:03 p.m.

1185. With decision to go ahead on Dragon Noir, we anxious assure complete understanding with Belgians on following points mentioned in general terms in Secretary MacArthur Telcon:

1. Operation to Paulis would be strictly in and out lasting no more than 24 hours, subject of course to overriding military US-Belgian exigencies affecting safety of forces.

[1] Source: National Archives, RG 59, Central Files 1964–66, POL 23–9 THE CONGO. Top Secret; Immediate; Exdis. Drafted by Palmer and Brubeck, cleared by Rusk, and approved by Palmer. Also sent to Leopoldville.

2. Dragon Noir force would not under any circumstances delay its departure from Paulis to permit ANC to reoccupy city. Nor would it take any rebel Congolese political or other prisoners.

3. As soon as Paulis evacuees returned Stanleyville and replaned to Leo, Dragon Rouge force would immediately redeploy Kamina.

4. Within shortest possible time, force would then redeploy from Kamina via Ascension, Las Palmas, Spain to Belgium.

Please see Spaak soonest and confirm foregoing understandings.[2]

For Leo: Pending Spaak's approval, essential you be guided by foregoing.

Rusk

[2] Telegram 1082 from Brussels, November 26, reported Spaak's approval of the points in telegram 1185. (Ibid.)

362. Memorandum for the Record[1]

Washington, November 27, 1964.

SUBJECT

Telephone Discussion with Secretary Rusk

I called Secretary Rusk to discuss the air drops on Bunia and Watsa. Rusk told me that after careful deliberation the Department and the Belgian Government had decided they would not go forward with the drops. He said they did not feel the recommendations of the embassies in Leopoldville were valid because there was no meaningful inventory of the number of European refugees in either city. Furthermore, there were no Americans there. I dissented sharply from this decision. I said that I felt neither Leopoldville nor the State Department knew very much about how many refugees were in these two cities and that probably the statements of the people from Stanleyville and Paulis were most authoritative. Furthermore, there was evidence of atrocities that I did not think should go on. Finally, if we did not conduct the drops, it would become obvious that our actions against Stanleyville

[1] Source: Central Intelligence Agency Files, DCI/McCone Files, Job 80B01285A, Box 2, DCI (McCone) Memos for the Record, 01 Nov.–31 Dec. 64. Secret; Eyes Only. Dictated by McCone.

were in effect in support of the Congolese Army and humanitarian excuse could not be supported. Rusk responded that the Paulis operation might change this appraisal. I said it might, but, nevertheless, history would record it differently. I therefore said it was my unreserved and very strong recommendation that we go forward. I could see no excuse for not doing so. I thought the drops would be successful and felt it was incumbent upon us to do so. Rusk said, "thank you very much," he would think the thing over and reappraise the situation prior to the withdrawal of the paratroopers from Kamina.

---

363. Memorandum From the Under Secretary of State for Political Affairs (Harriman) to Secretary of State Rusk[1]

Washington, November 27, 1964.

SUBJECT

Congo Rescue Mission

We have just been informed by CINCSTRIKE that the Paulis evacuation has now been completed with the evacuation of nearly 400 refugees. The planes are safely back in the air with the Belgian paratroopers and on their way to Kamina. Meanwhile, there has been a partial redeployment to Kamina of the remaining paratrooper force at Stanleyville; this redeployment will be completed tomorrow.

Present plans are that the entire paratrooper force will leave Kamina on November 29 via Ascension, Las Palmas and Spanish bases to Belgium. This delay from previous plans to begin the move on the 28th is occasioned by Spaak's desire to have the entire unit arrive in a group for appropriate ceremonies in Brussels.

Late yesterday afternoon, you suggested to Joe Palmer that we should have a final look at the question of possibly utilizing the force for other rescue operations in the Congo before it is finally withdrawn. In the absence of any Belgian request for further operations and in view of the fact that our information indicates that the few remaining Americans are in locations which would not be affected by paradrops, both Joe Palmer and I believe that the force should be withdrawn on the 29th according to the foregoing plan.

---

[1] Source: Library of Congress, Manuscript Division Harriman Papers, Kennedy–Johnson Administrations, Subject Files, Box 448, Congo (3). Secret.

Would you kindly let us know urgently whether you concur in this judgment.

Approve withdrawal on the 29th[2]

Believe we should reconsider possible further use of force before withdrawal

W. Averell Harriman[3]

---

[2] Rusk initialed his approval of this option. The 10 U.S. C–130s and the Belgian paratroop battalion that had carried out the rescue missions at Stanleyville and Paulis left the Congo at dawn on November 29.

[3] Printed from a copy that bears this typed signature.

---

364. Circular Telegram From the Department of State to Certain African Posts[1]

Washington, November 27, 1964, 4:27 p.m.

1043. Department deeply concerned by distortions in Africa of Stanleyville–Paulis rescue missions of foreign hostages and endangered Congolese civilians during past few days, especially (1) tendency ignore humanitarian aspect of mission, (2) fact it saved hundreds of innocent Congolese from death or torture in addition to Europeans, and (3) prevalence of assumption mission intended as political imperialism. These attitudes contribute to African sympathy for rebels, make task OAU Commission more difficult and work against reconciliation Kasavubu government with other African governments. They also are giving field day to Communist and radical African propaganda.

Department believes it extremely important African leaders publicly express (1) their recognition of humanitarian aspect of rescue operation, (2) condemnation of atrocities against innocent Congolese teachers, other educated as well as foreign missionaries, and if possible (3) express opposition African association with rebels who perpetrate such atrocities. FYI. Hoyt reports rebel leaders, Simbas, etc., are directly

---

[1] Source: National Archives, RG 59, Central Files 1964–66, POL 23–9 THE CONGO. Secret; Immediate. Drafted by Hadsel in AFI; cleared by Fredericks, Palmer, and Jaegar in EUR; and approved by Harriman. Sent to Addis Ababa, Freetown, Lome, Monrovia, Niamey, Rabat, Tunis, Tripoli, Dakar, Lagos, Blantyre, Abidjan, Tananarive. Repeated to all African posts and to Brussels.

responsible for many of those atrocities to Congolese as well as foreigners. End FYI.

Department also recognizes that this delicate task, requiring you to deploy arguments and information given you by Deptels and USIS file within framework situation your country. Extremely desirable to stimulate African statements as much along lines of above as feasible, but it is important you elicit such statements without getting rebuff which would curtail your influence in following days.

If situation in host countries permits, Info Addressees should seek such statement as feasible along above lines.

Rusk

---

365. Editorial Note

Following an extraordinary meeting in Nairobi on November 27 and 28, 1964, the OAU Ad Hoc Commission issued a communiqué on November 28 strongly condemning foreign military intervention in the Congo by the Governments of the United States, Belgium, United Kingdom, and all other countries who made such intervention possible. It recommended that the OAU Secretary General call an extraordinary meeting of heads of state and government in Addis Ababa on December 18. The Commission also agreed to make an interim report to the Secretary General requesting that steps be taken to effect: A) withdrawal of all mercenaries; B) an immediate end to foreign military intervention; C) a cease-fire; D) granting of a general amnesty; E) sending an Ad Hoc Commission fact-finding party; F) a round table conference of all Congolese leaders from all parties under OAU auspices; and G) holding free elections throughout the Congo supervised by the OAU. (Telegram 1484 from Nairobi, November 30; National Archives, RG 59, Central Files 1964–66, POL 23–9 THE CONGO)

On November 28, the Department issued a press release rejecting the Commission's charge that it had intervened militarily in the Congo and reiterating its previous statements that the United States participated in the rescue missions to Stanleyville and Paulis for purely humanitarian reasons and with the authorization of the Government of the Congo. (Circular telegram 1053; ibid.)

366. Report Prepared in the Department of State[1]

Washington, undated.

According to reliable sources, during the past few days Algeria, Ghana, the UAR, and Sudan have been actively collaborating to provide military supplies to the Congolese rebels via Khartoum and Juba. On November 27 a Soviet manufactured UAR plane (an AN–12) arrived at Juba, in southern Sudan, where it unloaded so-called medical supplies destined for the rebels. Early in the morning of December 3rd a Ghanaian IL–18, which had left Accra the previous day, arrived in Khartoum with a load of small arms. It transferred its cargo to an Egyptian AN–12, which flew the load to Juba very early on the morning of December 4. At least four Algerian AN–12 military aircraft carrying arms had completed their mission flying roundtrip from Khartoum to Juba by December 4. Additional Algerian AN–12 aircraft flew to Juba that same day from Khartoum carrying cargo destined for Congolese rebels.

We also have information that prior to the fall of Stanleyville other African states were assisting the rebels. These included not only Congo-Brazzaville and Burundi but also Uganda. During October high Uganda Government officials visited Stanleyville to confer with rebel authorities. They supplied Stanleyville Radio with equipment and technicians. They also allowed more than 35 trucks from the UAR to pass through Uganda to Stanleyville and later provided the rebels with gasoline. Furthermore, on October 31 Uganda permitted an IL–18 to use its airfield at Arua to discharge arms for the rebels.

---

[1] Source: National Archives, RG 59, Central Files 1964–66, POL 23–9 THE CONGO. Secret. The memorandum, which bears no drafting information, is attached to a December 5 transmittal memorandum from Robert D. Baum, Deputy Director of the INR Office of Research and Analysis for Africa, to Palmer that reads: "In response to your request to Bob Good yesterday, we have prepared the attached statement [3 *lines not declassified*]."

367. Circular Telegram From the Department of State to Certain Posts[1]

Washington, December 7, 1964, 7:38 p.m.

1091. We have been informed that UAR has made formal request for Security Council meeting on Congo pursuant to written request submitted last week.[2] Consultations in New York indicate Wednesday, December 9, as possible date. In connection with SC proceedings, we believe important that primary focus of debate be on outside assistance being provided rebels. We, therefore, believe it advantageous have separate complaint sent to SC by Congolese representative prior to Dec. 9 meeting. Our assumption is that both African and Congolese counter-complaint would be discussed in SC simultaneously. While evidence we possess is still fragmentary, we believe it sufficient to justify placing considerable focus on it during Council proceedings.

We request you see Tshombe immediately with view to getting him to instruct Congolese UN Representative to submit separate complaint to SC along lines described below.

You may tell Tshombe we do not envisage this initiative as a mere tactical device to counter African complaint against us. On contrary, we had been seriously considering suggesting this to him regardless of whether Africans pursued their request for meeting. We feel campaign should be waged, privately and publicly, in order to focus on problem of outside support of rebels and deter supporters of rebel regime from continuing such assistance. Believe it would be particularly useful for Congolese in separate SC complaint to stress that Communist and radical African intervention on side of rebels constitutes threat to sovereignty, stability and internal security of other African states.

---

[1] Source: National Archives, RG 59, Central Files 1964–66, POL 23–9 THE CONGO. Confidential; Flash. Drafted by Sisco and Buffum; cleared by Williams, Davis, Meeker, and Palmer; and approved by Harriman. Sent to Brussels and Leopoldville, and repeated to Abidjan, Algiers, Cairo, Congo (Brazzaville), Kigali, Khartoum, La Paz, London, Moscow, Oslo, Paris, Prague, Rabat, Rio de Janeiro, Taipei, Mogadiscio, Tunis, Addis Ababa, Lagos, Monrovia, Ouagadougou, Freetown, Tripoli, Tananarive, Libreville, Lome, and USUN.

[2] On December 1, the representatives of 22 U.N. member states sent a memorandum to the President of the Security Council calling the Belgian and U.S. actions a flagrant violation of the U.N. Charter and a threat to the peace and security of the African continent, and requesting an urgent meeting of the Security Council to discuss the situation in the Congo. It was endorsed by Afghanistan, Algeria, Burundi, Cambodia, the Central African Republic, Congo (Brazzaville), Dahomey, Ethiopia, Ghana, Guinea, Indonesia, Kenya, Malawi, Mali, Mauritania, Somalia, Sudan, Uganda, the United Arab Republic, Tanzania, Yugoslavia, and Zambia. (U.N. Doc. S/6076)

Following is suggested text of letter:

"Dear Mr. President:

A number of developments have recently occurred affecting the sovereignty and independence of DRC which, if continued, would threaten the maintenance of peace and stability not only in the Congo but throughout Africa.

Contrary to provisions of the UN Charter and SC Resolution S/4405 of July 22, 1960,[3] which "requests all States to refrain from any action which might tend to impede the restoration of law and order and the exercise by the Government of the Republic of the Congo of its authority and also to refrain from any action which might undermine the territorial integrity and political independence of the Republic of the Congo," a number of States have been giving assistance to rebel groups in the eastern part of the Congo.

The position of the Algerian Government is particularly disturbing in this regard. Not only has the Algerian President publicly announced his country is assisting the rebel movement with arms and men, but planes with Algerian markings have been observed in the Sudan near the Congo border. Moreover, the Government of the Sudan has admitted that certain shipments have been made to the rebels without the approval of the legitimate central Government of the Congo. There is also evidence that the Governments of Ghana and UAR are involved in providing assistance.

In addition to the known political support of the Chicom regime for the rebels, my Government has uncovered Chicom arms and ammunition in the Congo. Moreover, we are disturbed at press reports which indicate that the USSR has agreed to provide weapons and to help pay for airlift of arms to the Congolese rebels by the United Arab Republic and Algeria.

The violations of the sovereignty of a UN member in defiance of international law and the Charter of the United Nations are an inadmissible intervention in the internal affairs of my country and should be halted immediately.

Accordingly, I request you to convene an urgent meeting of the Security Council to consider the problem of outside interference in the internal affairs of the Congo which, if it is permitted to continue, will pose a serious threat for the peace of Africa.

---

[3] For text of Security Council Resolution S/4405, July 22, 1960 (U.N. Doc. S/4405), see *American Foreign Policy: Current Documents, 1960*, pp. 538–539.

I am also sending this communication to the Secretary General of the Organization of African Unity and requesting that it be circulated for the specific information of the membership of the OAU."[4]

We note that Tshombe planning to come to New York December 10. In the upcoming SC exercise, we intend to make effort to try to get a moderate African such as Nigerian to speak up on behalf of GDRC. Africans are already divided on Congo, but Tshombe's presence in NY is likely to unite both radicals and moderates in opposition to him as an individual and therefore not be helpful to GDRC either in Council or in relationship to broader problem of getting African support against outside intervention.

Using whatever argumentation you believe most persuasive, you should seek to dissuade Tshombe from coming to NY at this time. It seems to us that continued uncertainty regarding success of military operation in eastern Congo is most convincing and acceptable rationale, but, if necessary, you should not hesitate to tell him frankly we believe Congolese case in SC will be harmed rather than helped by his presence.[5]

If these arguments not adequate you should put forward as your personal view on confidential and informal basis, the following: For Tshombe to come US at this time will stir up propaganda and trouble in Africa. Very likely that American Negro and other liberal groups here unsympathetic to Tshombe would engage in demonstrations and publicity adding further to adverse propaganda in Africa. For US most effectively to help Congo, therefore, and in our mutual interest, Tshombe should postpone visit. You should stress this is purely a matter of timing.

If in spite of these arguments Tshombe insists he is coming to New York you should say nothing re prospects of meeting with President, but should inform Dept urgently for further instructions.

We think Idzumbuir is a reasonably effective representative, but we leave to your discretion whether you feel you can suggest that Tshombe send Bomboko or Lengema to plead Congolese case.

Foregoing message prepared prior ticker report from Leo saying Tshombe was complaining to SC re outside assistance to rebels. How-

---

[4] Tshombe's December 9 letter to the President of the U.N. Security Council called for an urgent meeting of the Council on the basis of direct and indirect intervention in the Congo's domestic affairs by external powers, including Algeria, Sudan, the United Arab Republic, Ghana, the Soviet Union, and Communist China. (U.N. Doc. S/6096)

[5] In telegram 2334 from Leopoldville, December 8, Godley reported that he told Tshombe the Department had doubts as to the advisability of his being in New York at the opening of the Security Council debate on the Congo, and that the Prime Minister said he would accommodate himself to whatever the Department suggested. (National Archives, RG 59, Central Files 1964–66, POL 23–9 THE CONGO)

ever, as of early afternoon New York time, Congo UN Del had received no instructions from Leo. Accordingly, you will wish tailor your approach to Tshombe re initiative in SC in light of circumstances existing at time. We assume that even if he has already decided request SC meeting, foregoing draft letter may be of assistance.

For Brussels. You should inform GOB immediately of contents of this instruction.[6]

Rusk

---

[6] In telegraph 1166 from Brussels, December 8, MacArthur reported that the contents of telegram 1091 were conveyed to Spaak. (Ibid.)

---

368. Telegram From the Department of State to the Embassy in the Congo[1]

Washington, December 10, 1964, 6:02 p.m.

1578. Ref: Rome's 1603 to Dept.[2] Congratulations on job well done.

FYI. There is no disagreement here as to disastrous effect Tshombe visit at this time. White House contacted Struelens who in total agreement and promised so advise PM. Indications are that SC debate will continue on for some time and it will require further time to clarify and re-assess situation. Thus although eventual visit January or later not ruled out, timing will depend on what transpires in interim. End FYI. Blake can tell Tshombe that Nigeria has asked to be heard in SC.

For USUN: Pls continue pass Rome slugged for Blake pertinent msgs per reftel.

Ball

---

[1] Source: National Archives, RG 59, Central Files 1964–66, POL 7 THE CONGO. Confidential; Priority. Drafted by Special Assistant for the Congo Working Group Robinson McIlvaine; cleared by Brubeck, Sisco, O'Sullivan, and Harriman; and approved by McIlvaine. Also sent to Rome for Robert Blake, Deputy Chief of Mission of the Embassy in Leopoldville, and repeated to USUN.

[2] In telegram 1603 from Rome, December 10, Blake reported that he saw Tshombe that morning immediately after the Prime Minister's audience with the Pope and, after considerable argument, obtained his agreement not to proceed to New York. (Ibid.)

369. Memorandum for the Record[1]

Washington, December 12, 1964.

SUBJECT

Discussion with the President on Saturday, 12 December

In addition to personal [*personnel*?] matters, covered in a separate memo, the following subjects were discussed:

1. The Congo. I told the President that I felt the Tshombe Government might be in real trouble because of assistance given to the rebels by a number of South African countries, including Algeria, UAR, Ghana, etc. as well as Communist China and possibly the Soviet Union. This assistance was taking the form of financial aid, military equipment and possibly mercenaries. I indicated that concurrently Tshombe's forces were disintegrating somewhat as mercenary strength was only now about one-half of the peak and air support had reduced substantially. I predicted that we might begin to see Tshombe's forces lose their ground, conceivably Stanleyville and Paulis could be retaken by the rebels and the situation would worsen in the months ahead.

I raised the question of our aid to countries, i.e., military air, grants and loans, PL–480 and Peace Corps aid and then witness the countries opposing a legitimate government and criticizing the U.S. policies. The President asked for a report on aid given these countries and the critical statements and positions taken by their leaders.

Action: This report has been prepared and submitted to the President on December 17th.

[Omitted here is discussion of unrelated subjects.]

---

[1] Source: Central Intelligence Agency Files, DCI/McCone Files, Job 80B01285A, DCI Meetings with the President, 01 October–31 December 1964. Secret; Eyes Only. Drafted by McCone on December 17.

370. Draft Memorandum From the Former Chief of Station in Leopoldville to the Chief of the Africa Division, Directorate of Plans, Central Intelligence Agency (Fields)[1]

Washington, December 14, 1964.

SUBJECT

Adoula's Views Concerning Viability of the Current Congo Government

(1) Adoula is convinced that the Tshombe government will fall within three months, unless drastic action is taken to enlarge the government. He reasons as follows:

(a) The revolt in the Northern and Eastern sections of the Congo is primarily a social revolution and, thus, a revolt which cannot be put down and held down by force alone.

(b) The only hope of putting down the revolt is for the Central Government to provide the necessary governmental services for the area.

(c) Tshombe is not an effective administrator and, thus, is not capable, working with his present government, of providing good government in the provinces.

(d) Tshombe is anathema to all other African leaders. Thus, all African states will cooperate, even with the Soviets and Chicoms, to bring down the Tshombe government.

(e) Tshombe does not have the personal contacts, nor does he have sufficiently clear understanding of African politics to convince the other African leaders to cooperate with his government or, at the very least, to adopt a neutral attitude toward the GDRC.

(2) Adoula advised [*less than 1 line not declassified*] that representatives of various radical African states have urged him to accept the leadership of the rebellion. It is evident from Adoula's statements that he is sorely tempted by this possibility, for it was equally evident that he bitterly resents Tshombe's accession of power. However, the undersigned doubts that Adoula will accept such an offer, at least for the present. Adoula has always maintained his position as a compromise leader, and it is doubtful that he would wish to accept the leadership of an extremist group. Also, Adoula must suspect that such a step on his part would result in his losing the support of the U.S. government. He also must realize that it was the support of the United States government which won for him the premiership in 1961, and

---

[1] Source: Central Intelligence Agency Files, Job 90–01073R, [*text not declassified*], Box 29, Folder 893, [*text not declassified*], Vol. 2 of 5, January 1964–March 1965. Secret.

that without U.S.G. support he would have been unable to maintain himself in office for more than a few months. Thus, it is doubtful that Adoula would agree to accept a position which would place him in direct conflict with the United States government.

(3) Although Adoula would dearly love to see Tshombe fail, he also recognizes that the rebels do not offer a viable alternative. Thus, he recognizes that the fall of Tshombe would contribute to further anarchy within the Congo. He agrees that one possible alternative would be to create a government of public welfare which would include moderate elements not presently in the government. Specifically, he is thinking of himself, Bomboko, Ndele, Kondolo, etc. He believes that if such a government were to be formed, even with Tshombe as premier, it might be feasible to slowly reverse the current situation in the Congo and to achieve a solution to the Congo problem which would be acceptable to other African states. Such a government would be created to carry out the following limited objectives:

(a) To revamp the administrative apparatus of the government.
(b) To achieve a solution to the current rebellion.
(c) To re-establish friendly relations with the other African states.
(d) To prepare for free elections.

(4) Adoula would be willing to enter such a government of public welfare on the following conditions:

(a) Tshombe would have to agree to accept and to work with the moderates added to the government.

(b) Adoula would agree to enter the government only if President Kasavubu were to take the responsibility for appointing him to the government.

(c) It would have to be understood that Adoula, by entering the government, was not going bond for Tshombe as an individual.

(d) A mechanism would have to be created which would permit the Congo government to locate and hire a core of public administrators to work with Congolese civil servants, to train these Congolese civil servants, and to insure the functioning of effective governmental mechanisms in the provinces.

(e) The army must be completely revamped in order to eliminate the incompetent elements.

(f) United States government would have to maintain pressures on Tshombe to insure that the latter would not sabotage the efforts of the government of public welfare.

(g) Similarly, the United States government should guarantee to provide financial support for Adoula and other moderates. Adoula recognizes that should a government of public welfare be successful, it might well guarantee the continuation of power of Tshombe. However, he believes that continued financial support for other moderates would be necessary in order to convince Tshombe that he must cooperate with all moderate groups.

Lawrence Devlin[2]

---

[2] Printed from a copy that bears this typed signature.

---

371. Telegram From the Station in the Congo to the Central Intelligence Agency[1]

Leopoldville, December 14, 1964, 0945Z.

5435 (In 41884). Ref ODACID tel 1507, 1 Dec.[2]

1. In aftermath of Stan recapture, and with ref as backdrop, mtg was held 2 Dec to discuss question of elections and support to pol parties. Present were [Godley], his deputy, [Embassy] pol section chief, [COS], [*name not declassified*]. [Godley] asked [COS] to summarize discussions and consensus arrived at. Foll is draft which [COS] prepared. [Embassy] still pondering draft but eventually presumably will send it or revised version in through its own channels:

A. National elections are scheduled to be held during the first half of February 1965. However, Tshombe's enemies and even some of his warmest supporters have often suggested that Tshombe does not intend to have elections at all. In discussing the importance of holding elections on schedule, [Embassy] officers pointed out that the institution of parliament has in the past served as a valuable safety valve for radical and eccentric politicians, and that it would be particularly important now, when the main military effort of the rebels seems to be crushed, to further take the wind out of their sails by offering to the electorate a means whereby they might peacefully change their leaders rather than be obliged to risk their lives for this purpose.

B. It will probably not be possible to have elections in some areas of the Congo by mid-February because local pockets of rebels will still not have been mopped up yet. (This holds true for the Kwilu area as well as for the Northeast Congo). However, it is thought that the very fact of

---

[1] Source: Central Intelligence Agency Files, Job 78–00435R, DDO/ISS Files, Box 1, Folder 1, [*cryptonym not declassified*] Development & Plans. Secret. No time of receipt appears on the message.

[2] Not found.

offering an opportunity for elections in liberated areas might hasten the collapse of these pockets.

C. We believe that the [Embassy] should use its influence with Congolese authorities to see that elections in fact are held at about the time they have been scheduled. At the same time, we believe that no material support should be provided to the competing political parties for election purposes, and that we should concert with our German and Belgian friends to pursue a like policy. One reason for refraining from such support is that we still do not know what political constellation is favored by Tshombe, nor which by Kasavubu, the leading contenders for the two top jobs under the new constitution. We do have a collection of moderate provincial party groupings, such as PSA/Kamitatu, Unimo (also Azimo)/Bomboko, Puna/Bolikango, Abako/Kasavubu, Conakat/Tshombe, Luka/Delvaux, etc, which have already begun to solicit large sums of money for use in holding party congresses and in dispensing election propaganda.

D. With little more than two months to go before elections, it seems unlikely that any new national party will be able to make an impact on the electorate, and the results of the elections will probably be favorable to the regionally-based groupings. At least this appears to be the way Kasavubu is betting, and Tshombe too, to judge from his lack of effort to organize a national party. It would appear that both Kasavubu and Tshombe believe they will be able to dominate the electoral college sufficiently to ensure their election to the two top jobs. We believe that both these gentlemen are astute enough politicians that they will probably be able in fact to dominate the college.

2. No index.[3]

[3] In his monthly dispatch to CIA, December 31, the Chief of Station commented that one major problem with which the Station would have to come to grips in the next few months was the solution of the political problem posed by the rebellion. The U.S. Government should insist insofar as it was in its power that elections should be held on schedule in February 1965, and the Station should stand ready to assist a broad, national, moderate, pro-Western coalition at election time. But for the time being the Station was refraining from dealing with individual elements which might eventually make up such a coalition in the hope that the several elements may recognize the necessity of rallying around an acceptable national leader. The Station wanted to avoid enabling regional political figures to hold out against such a coalition since the urgent need at the time was for unity. (Central Intelligence Agency Files, Job 82–00450R, DDO/AF, AF/DIV Historical Files, Box 6, Folder 6, Leopoldville, 3 Feb 64–Dec 65, [*cryptonym not declassified*])

372. Telegram From the Department of State to the Mission in Berlin[1]

Washington, December 15, 1964, 4:22 p.m.

489. For McGhee from Williams. USBER 790.[2] Dept believes would be useful for you see Tshombe.

Spaak has asked Tshombe come Brussels from Germany but we understand Tshombe had intended return Leopoldville from Bonn. Since important Spaak see Tshombe soonest, you should urge Tshombe go Brussels. You might say you aware Spaak's desire see him and have been instructed tell him USG attaches greatest importance to his seeing Spaak at this stage in developments in Congo because our aid is dependent on Belgian assistance in many fields. (FYI. U.S. interest is to have Spaak see Tshombe soonest to reach understanding re GOB–GDRC econ/fin relations so we and Belgians can put to Tshombe certain political conditions we consider important to continued assistance for GDRC. MacArthur, who now in Washington, will let Spaak know you urging Tshombe visit Brussels. End FYI.)

Additional object your conversation with Tshombe should be elicit info re his activities in Germany, particularly whether his trip useful in uncovering additional sources assistance to GDRC.[3]

Believe would serve no useful purpose at this stage for you take initiative discuss Congo in general but we would be interested in views Tshombe may volunteer.

Ball

---

[1] Source: National Archives, RG 59, Central Files 1964–66, POL 7 THE CONGO. Secret; Priority. Drafted by McElhiney; cleared by McIlvaine, Harriman, and MacArthur; and approved by Williams. Repeated to Bonn and Leopoldville.

[2] In telegram 790 from Berlin, December 15, Ambassador McGhee reported that Tshombe had requested that McGhee call on him in Bonn on December 17. (Ibid.)

[3] In telegram 2320 from Bonn, December 17, McGhee reported that he met with Tshombe and strongly urged him to alter his itinerary to include a meeting with Spaak in Brussels. After raising some initial objections, Tshombe agreed to do so, saying, "If your government wants me to do it, I will do it." (Ibid., POL 23–9 THE CONGO)

373. Memorandum for the Record[1]

Washington, December 18, 1964.

SUBJECT

Minutes of the Meeting of the Special Group (CI) 3 p.m., Friday, December 18, 1964

PRESENT

Governor Harriman, Mr. Rowan, Mr. McCone, Mr. Komer, Mr. Gaud vice Mr. Bell, Mr. McNaughton vice Mr. Vance, Colonel Loberg vice General Wheeler
Mr. Fields was present for Item 2
Mr. Montenegro and Mr. Meyer were present for Item 3
Mr. Maechling was present for the meeting

[Omitted here is discussion of an unrelated subject.]

2. Congo

Mr. McCone began by saying that the estimate of the situation in the Congo is a dreary one; that the government forces have a very tenuous hold on Stanleyville, that the main mercenary force is surrounded at Paulis, and that other government forces are under heavy attack in Uvira and Albertville. He informed the Group that the amount of arms and ammunition to the rebels thus far has been 25 plane loads, or about 175 tons plus "volunteers." He stated that these arms alone may not be sufficient to swing the military balance, but that the arrival of trained ground forces could and that the government position would deteriorate rapidly unless additional military assistance is provided to the Congolese forces. Mr. McCone suggested that we should investigate ways to interdict these supplies.

Mr. McCone said that he had just come from a meeting with Ambassador Godley, who is of the opinion that Tshombe's broadening his government at this time would not accomplish much, but that additional programs to provide services to liberated areas are desperately needed.

The Group generally discussed the pros and cons of using aid in other countries as a lever to obtain more support for the Tshombe government and to stop the flow of arms to the rebels. Mr. Gaud informed the Group that AID continually reviews existing programs and reminded the Group that there are other issues in Africa which must be considered. The Group expressed its appreciation of the fine job that

[1] Source: National Archives, RG 59, S/S Files: Lot 68 D 451, Special Group (CI) Minutes of Meetings, July–Dec. 1964. Secret. Prepared on December 21.

USIA has done and is still doing to counteract the violent statements of the radical nations and to present the true picture of brutality and atrocities.

Governor Harriman noted that Tshombe is unpopular even with our best friends in Africa and that the job now is to get Tshombe to work with other political parties, indicating that he is prepared to hold elections. He expressed the hope that additional assistance would provide Tshombe with time to work out a solution. Mr. McCone warned that to lose the Congo to the Communists would be like a "cancerous growth which would soon spread." He suggested that we provide additional B–26's of a later model to replace the poorly maintained B–26's presently in the Congo. The Group strongly supported Mr. McCone's recommendation for additional B–26's.

Mr. Rowan agreed that we must take steps to prevent the fall of the Congo into Communist hands and asked what we are prepared to do if the "volunteers" do appear in sizeable numbers. He warned that if the presence of the "volunteers" threatens the legitimate Government of the Congo, Tshombe might well ask for US military assistance.

[Omitted here is discussion of unrelated subjects.]

C.G. Moody, Jr.
Executive Secretary
Special Group (CI)

374. Telegram From the Department of State to the Embassy in Belgium[1]

Washington, December 22, 1964, 7:14 p.m.

1381. For Ambassador from Harriman. Request you deliver following personal oral message from me to Spaak soonest:

I have very carefully re-examined our proposals for the addition of a cease-fire appeal to the Usher resolution[2] in light of your comments today.

---

[1] Source: National Archives, RG 59, Central Files 1964–66, POL 23–9 THE CONGO. Secret; Flash. Drafted by Komer, Sisco, and Buffum; cleared by Palmer, Appling, Fredericks, and Harriman; and approved by Sisco. Repeated to Leopoldville and USUN.

[2] Telegram 2247 from USUN, December 17, transmitted the text of a draft U.N. resolution given to Yost by Ivory Coast's Representative to the United Nations, Arsene Assouan Usher. (Ibid.) On December 28, a revised version of this draft was submitted to the Security Council by Usher and Ambassador Dey Ould Sidi Baba of Morocco. (U.N. Doc. S/6123)

I gather we agree in principle that a cease-fire would, on balance, be advantageous to us especially if it could be effectively policed. I regret we have not had more time for full consultations on this point, but we now are faced with an immediate deadline in New York with great pressure among the delegations to get home for the Christmas holidays which offers an opportunity to get this important point across quickly. My major concern in suggesting this addition is to consolidate the GDRC victory in the northeast Congo before the inevitable erosion sets in.

Reports from Leopoldville including our most recent talks with De Kerchove and Van der Walle indicate the GDRC has reached the end of forward thrust and is holding too thinly everywhere to permit confidence it can resist a growing rebel counterattack. You appreciate as well as I that adequate reinforcements for GDRC are not quickly available now, while men and supplies appear to be pouring in to the rebels.

Thus, it seems imperative to erect a political umbrella over Congo which will help forestall rebel recapture of a solid base for a competing government. The cease-fire seems best suited for this purpose. While covert rebel operations may be difficult to observe, they will have to come out in the open if they are to attack towns.

I am most sympathetic to your concern lest foisting a cease-fire resolution on Tshombe without conditioning him lead to a violent reaction. However, we believe that Tshombe back in Leopoldville must be getting the same gloomy picture that we have. So Godley and I are confident that we can quickly show Tshombe the wisdom of this tactic. In the last analysis, however, can we afford to bargain with Tshombe over a move which we think so essential?

In sum, I believe that the clear advantages of getting on to a political negotiating basis and putting the onus on the rebels and their supporters outweigh the valid risks you cite. To wait might be to lose this opportunity, or to have to try for a cease-fire later when our position is visibly deteriorating and it will be interpreted as showing weakness.

We will not go ahead unless you concur, but I hope you will join us in assuming the risks. We have much to gain and relatively little to lose. *End message.*

Regarding some of Spaak's specific concerns on Usher resolution, we have following comments:

1) Present text does not inhibit freedom of movement of GDRC; believe it would be mistake to raise this issue in res since doing so would appear to call GDRC's competence this regard into question.

2) Re mercenaries (operative para 4 of Usher draft), Ambassador Yost believes we can get reformulation which will not be troublesome based on Tshombe's earlier agreement discharge mercenaries as soon

as possible. (Believe our respective UN Dels should be given flexibility this point.)

3) Re alleged problem of abandoning SC responsibility to OAU, we could meet this by reformulation of cease-fire paragraph to read "calls for an immediate cessation of hostilities and requests UNSYG, in concert with OAU, to develop urgently appropriate machinery to assure observance cease-fire and report to SC as soon as possible."

Spaak should realize there now likelihood USSR will introduce condemnatory resolution. This underscores increased importance that moderate Africans have viable alternative which Usher would be willing press. (Moroccan Del has just told us sponsors of SC complaint will not agree Usher should introduce his resolution unless it is strengthened and will otherwise request Soviets introduce condemnatory res.) In our judgment addition cease-fire element provides that necessary additional attraction.

Request you draw on all your well-known persuasiveness to get Spaak signed on to this cease-fire operation, to which we attach both long-term strategic as well as immediate tactical importance.

If and only if your best efforts in this regard fail to bring Spaak around, our ultimate fallback, which you should give him only as last resort would read as follows:

"*Encourages* the OAU to continue its efforts to attain national reconciliation in conformity with OAU Res CM/RES 5 (III) of 10 September 1964 and to bring about an early cease-fire which would facilitate these efforts.

Requests the SYG to lend his assistance as appropriate.

Requests the OAU and SYG to keep the SC informed of their efforts."

We need answer from Spaak 9:00 AM Washington time, tomorrow, December 23.[3]

Rusk

[3] In telegram 1239 from Brussels, December 23, MacArthur reported that he delivered Harriman's message to Spaak, whose initial reaction was that the resolution was both dangerous and misleading. Spaak also expressed unhappiness with the extent of U.S. commitment to the Usher resolution without what he considered full and adequate consultation with Belgium. After further discussion, Spaak indicated reluctant acceptance of the proposed text if the cease-fire paragraph was modified as suggested in the third paragraph of telegram 1381, and if the paragraph on mercenaries was replaced with a reformulation based on Tshombe's earlier statements that he intended to discharge them as soon as possible. (National Archives, RG 59, Central Files 1964–66, POL 23–9 THE CONGO)

375. Memorandum From Harold H. Saunders of the National Security Council Staff to the President's Special Assistant for National Security Affairs (Bundy)[1]

Washington, December 24, 1964.

McGB:

State is more relaxed this morning about the possibility of new military outbreaks which we had feared might take place in the next couple of days in the Congo. However, the situation in Bukavu is still serious and Rusk has told his people to do as much as possible to get the missionaries out of the area lest we lose more hostages to the rebels.

In New York Usher has just received instructions from Houphouet-Boigny to table a resolution including the cease-fire if he thinks he has eight SC votes.[2] So he will probably go ahead today. But there's little hope of a vote before Monday.[3]

Spaak wants to have a NATO Council meeting on Jan. 5 before he sees Tshombe again. Harriman has volunteered to go so we're beginning to put together the points he should hit Spaak with.

H.

---

[1] Source: Johnson Library, National Security File, Country File, Congo, Vol. X, Memos & Miscellaneous, 12/64. Confidential.

[2] In telegram 2512 from Leopoldville, December 25, Godley reported that he discussed the proposed resolution with Tshombe, noting that its key point was its call for a cease-fire. He pointed out that although the ANC had now achieved victory, it faced the probability of substantial military reverses in the near future if the supply of arms to the rebels was not stopped. The U.S. Government thought that the cease-fire would make it possible to stop aid to the rebels by establishing OAU and U.N. inspection machinery. (National Archives, RG 59, Central Files 1964–66, POL 23–9 THE CONGO)

[3] December 28.

376. Memorandum From the Joint Chiefs of Staff to Secretary of Defense McNamara[1]

JCSM–1071–64 Washington, December 24, 1964.

SUBJECT

Congo Cease Fire

1. The Joint Chiefs of Staff have noted that certain political actions are being discussed in attempting to improve the situation in the Congo. These actions are intended to encourage constructive actions by many nations, including the Congo, and to explore the possibilities of an effective cease-fire agreement.

2. The Joint Chiefs of Staff agree that political solutions to the Congo problem are needed to supplement security operations, and that constructive efforts to bring about a cessation of hostilities could be advantageous. They are concerned, however, that implementation of a cease-fire could provide the environment for a substantial military advantage accruing to communist inspired and supported forces and thus could preclude attainment of favorable political objectives. Specifically, they do not agree with that portion of a draft United Nations resolution which calls for withdrawal of the mercenaries. Rebel forces will gain an immediate advantage if the cease-fire requires such withdrawal, the withdrawal of US aircraft, or decreases other Western support of the Congolese Government. This advantage will be compounded if radical African states are enabled to continue furnishing arms and advisors to the rebels. Under these circumstances, the United States would eventually be faced with a choice between acceptance of a communist supported victory or extensive US military involvement.

3. It should also be recognized that a cease-fire agreement could be construed as according legitimacy and recognition to the rebels. Further, experiences in Laos, Vietnam, and Yemen give evidence of communist and radical tactics of utilizing cease-fire agreements to their advantage.

4. The Joint Chiefs of Staff believe that political negotiations will have the best chance for success if they are conducted against a back-ground of military advantage in the Congo. Specifically, they believe that the Congo military situation should be characterized by:

a. Congolese Army control of principal cities, towns, and communications points now held.

[1] Source: National Archives, RG 218, JCS Files, 9111 (22 Dec. 64). Secret.

b. Continued strengthening of the Congolese forces with the required mercenaries, military matériel, and air support, both tactical and airlift.

c. A demonstrable ability to make rebel resupply by communist aligned countries costly and ineffective and to deal effectively with any rebel counterattack.

5. A CINCSTRIKE/USCINCMEAFSA appraisal of the Congo situation is currently being considered and will be the subject of separate action by the Joint Chiefs of Staff. Meanwhile, they recommend that the Secretary of State be advised of their concern that a cease-fire in the Congo could result in a net advantage to rebel forces unless:

a. The military base of the Tshombe government continues to be strengthened.

b. Appropriate military force is available to enforce cessation of any serious rebellious activity in the Congo.

c. The effective interdiction of arms traffic to the rebels and the denial of rebel safe-havens is assured.

d. Effective nonradical inspection machinery is established in the Congo and surrounding countries.

e. The political strategy has the concurrence in advance of the Belgian and Congolese Governments.

For the Joint Chiefs of Staff:

Earle G. Wheeler[2]
Chairman
Joint Chiefs of Staff

[2] Printed from a copy that indicates General Wheeler signed the original.

377. Telegram From the Embassy in the Congo to the Department of State[1]

Leopoldville, December 26, 1964, 9 p.m.

2519. 1. Tshombe called in Belgian Chargé Puttevils and myself this afternoon to officially inform us that after long consideration by "President and Cabinet," GDRC had decided it could not go along with cease-fire as proposed in SC resolution. Puttevils quickly told Tshombe he had message from Spaak (text of which we repeating separately) which urged GDRC accept resolution but leave to SYG and OAU responsibility for working out concrete proposal, during which time GDRC would reserve full freedom. Spaak's principal point was that rebels would have to lay down arms first and then allow GDG freedom of movement in rebel-held territory.

2. I told Prime Minister that I had no instructions on points raised in Spaak's memo but in line with memo could envisage procedure whereby combined effect of statements by Western members of SC plus statement of intention by GDRC Rep would establish interpretation of resolution which would make it possible for Tshombe accept. Explained this often is done in SC, as resolution is only what members of Council say it is.

3. Tshombe listened carefully and then repeated all arguments against cease-fire which he had used with me on Thursday and as recorded (ourtel 2512).[2] Both Puttevils and I tried to combat these arguments, urging him to be forthcoming with both Western members of SC and moderate Africans in New York. To no avail.

4. Tshombe said firm decision had been taken by GDRC to ask US and other friends of Congo in SC amend resolution to eliminate cease-fire plus certain other objectional points (mercenaries), and if this not possible not to support resolution. *Note:* Tshombe working on basis text I had given him Thursday, not actual draft tabled by IC and Morocco. Tshombe said he wanted USG and GOB to realize that GDRC took very grave view of cease-fire proposal and, even as explained by Spaak, it not acceptable. Mere use of words "cease-fire" imply legal existence of two parties. He insisted again and again that proposal had been given most serious consideration but said USG and GOB must not underestimate dangers which would stem from passage of SC resolution embodying cease-fire. He then gave us both copies of GDRC memo

---

[1] Source: National Archives, RG 59, Central Files 1964–66, POL 23–9 THE CONGO. Secret; Flash. Repeated to Brussels, CINCSTRIKE, and USUN and passed to the White House, DOD, and CIA.

[2] See footnote 2, Document 375.

on subject, which being repeated by septel.[3] Tshombe reminded us that he had successfully fought proposal for cease-fire in Addis long and knew what radical Africans had in mind when they proposed this measure. Nothing which US or other might say in SC would change fact that radical Africans and other enemies of Congo would put interpretation on resolutions unfavorable to Congo and would use cease-fire to build up rebels.

5. Since it clear after more argument that Tshombe adamant in rejecting cease-fire, I urged him instruct Idzumbir to make statement in SC which would emphasize all the positive things Kasavubu [garble—and?] he had said publicly about GDRC's program for national reconciliation. Also urged him instruct Idzumbir work closely with USUN and Belgian Del in drafting GDRC statement to SC, so that statements all three dels would follow same line as far as possible. Tshombe said he would so instruct Idzumbir. Also recalled that he had accepted OAU resolution passed at Addis and positive line contained in that resolution still represents policy of his government.

6. As we left Tshombe again emphasized that GDRC takes very grave view of fact USG and GOB asking it to accept cease-fire, which President and all members of Cabinet were convinced would result in participation [*partition*?] of Congo.

7. *Comment:* Tshombe tired and grave but at no point did he resort to threats. Puttevils and I judge that although GDRC have taken firm decision against SC resolution, we may be able get relatively positive declaration of intention from Idzumbir in SC.[4]

Godley

---

[3] Not found.

[4] Telegram 1687 to Leopoldville, December 28, reported that a revised resolution was tabled that afternoon. The revised text continued to contain an appeal for a cease-fire, but the U.S. Delegation succeeded in getting a specific reference to the September 10 OAU resolution included as a way to meet Tshombe's concern. The Department emphasized that it was essential that Tshombe not place himself in the position of rejecting or violating the Security Council resolution, since this would give the enemies of the Congo a basis for continuing their assistance to the rebels. (National Archives, RG 59, Central Files 1964–66, POL 23–9 THE CONGO)

378. Telegram From the Department of State to the Embassy in the Congo[1]

Washington, December 30, 1964, 7:07 p.m.

1692. As you know Security Council adopted resolution on ceasefire 10–0–1.[2] You should see Tshombe and tell him we believe Congolese representative handled Security Council deliberations today effectively, particularly his comments on ceasefire.[3]

While we will be following up in more detail with further guidance for you re GDRC posture in relation to implementation of SC resolution, we believe Tshombe has excellent opportunity to exploit it fully, particularly as a deterrent to outside intervention by placing onus for violations of ceasefire on rebels. In addition GDRC actions will be watched closely as to steps taken to bring about reconciliation emphasized in operative para 4 of resolution.

As first step we believe Tshombe might well make general statement as follow up to one made by Idzumbir indicating GDRC welcomes SC action and expressing intention to cooperate fully with UN and OAU. You should also explore with him what other initiatives he thinks he might take to exploit the present situation.

Rusk

---

[1] Source: National Archives, RG 59, Central Files 1964–66, POL 23–9 THE CONGO. Confidential; Priority. Drafted by Sisco and approved by Palmer. Also sent to Brussels and repeated to USUN.

[2] Resolution S/6129 requested states not to intervene in the domestic affairs of the Congo, appealed for a cease-fire in accordance with the OAU resolution of September 10, considered that the mercenaries should be withdrawn in accordance with the OAU resolution, encouraged the OAU in its efforts to help the Congolese Government achieve national reconciliation, requested all states to assist the OAU, asked the OAU to keep the Security Council informed, and requested the U.N. Secretary-General to follow the situation and keep the Council informed. (U.N. Doc. S/6129) For text, see *American Foreign Policy: Current Documents, 1964*, pp. 786–787.

[3] In telegram 2569 from Leopoldville, December 31, Godley reported that he emphasized to Tshombe the constructive points in the resolution and expressed his personal conviction that the resolution finally adopted was a remarkable victory for the moderates and much better than might have been expected, and that Tshombe had appeared to concur. (National Archives, RG 59, Central Files 1964–66, POL 23–9 THE CONGO)

379. Memorandum From the Joint Chiefs of Staff to Secretary of Defense McNamara[1]

JCSM–1090–64 Washington, December 31, 1964.

SUBJECT

Appraisal of the Congo Situation (U)

1. The Joint Chiefs of Staff have reviewed an appraisal of the Congo situation which was provided by CINCSTRIKE/USCINC-MEAFSA by letter, dated 18 December 1964, and supplemented by message STRCC 1294/64, 25 December 1964. A copy of the letter and the appraisal are attached as Appendix C hereto.[2] His principal recommendations are as follows:

a. Joint US-Belgian agreement on programs to be developed, responsibilities of each country, and the assistance they will press for from other Western-oriented countries, primarily NATO.

b. Western support of improved and expanded Congolese Armed Forces to include an increased mercenary force.

c. Strongest possible diplomatic, political, and economic measures against nations providing support to the rebels.

d. [*1½ lines not declassified*]

e. [*1½ lines not declassified*]

f. Initiation of large scale social, economic, and cultural programs in the Congo.

2. The Joint Chiefs of Staff consider that actions such as those proposed by CINCSTRIKE/USCINCMEAFSA would be required to attain US objectives of insuring the Congo's pro-Western orientation, preventing communist infiltration and maintaining Congolese unity. At the same time, they recognize that these proposals are inconsistent with stated US desires of limiting US involvement in the Congo, keeping the cold war out of Africa, and placing principal reliance on former metropole countries. In effect, CINCSTRIKE/USCINCMEAFSA has formulated his proposals in a manner which leads to the following important questions concerning US cold war strategy and US policies toward all of Africa:

a. Should the United States concentrate resources in support of pro-Western governments and in opposition to forces attempting to destroy or subvert such governments?

b. With respect to key countries, such as Egypt, Algeria, Ghana, and South Africa, what changes in US policy and courses of action

[1] Source: Washington National Records Center, RG 330, OSD Files: FRC 69 A 7425, Congo 381 (12 Aug. 64). Secret.

[2] None of the attachments is printed.

should be initiated to protect US interests in Africa generally and the Congo in particular?

3. Faced with such important policy questions, the serious threat to the Congo's security, and the aggressive anti-American actions of radical African states, the Joint Chiefs of Staff conclude that two action programs should be initiated without delay:

a. An intensive high-level State/Defense reappraisal of US cold war strategy and US policies toward Africa should be accomplished to include a political assessment of the Congo problem and of the threat this poses to US interests. It should be initialed [*initiated*] and completed urgently because of the rapid deterioration of Western influence in Africa and because events in the Congo are leading toward deepening US involvement in a difficult politico-military situation. Additional views on such a reappraisal are contained in Appendix A hereto and in JCSM–775–64, dated 5 September 1964, subject: "US Policy Toward Africa."

b. If this reappraisal results in a firm policy decision to take positive political and military action in support of the Congolese Government, the United States and Belgium should consider, in conjunction with the Congo and other Western nations, appropriate steps to strengthen the military base of the Tshombe Government. Supporting rationale and specific views are contained in Appendix B hereto and in JCSM–756–64, dated 1 September 1964, subject: "Internal Security of the Congo."[3] Meanwhile, current efforts should be continued to assist the Congo to counter the communist-supported rebel threat.

4. The Joint Chiefs of Staff have also reviewed a letter, dated 18 November 1964, from CINCSTRIKE/USCINCMEAFSA in which he recommended that early consideration be given to establishing negotiations with Belgium, Italy, and the Congo to define an appropriate program for providing air support for the Congolese Army. A copy of his letter, including a study entitled "Concept for the Employment of Congolese Air Capability," is attached as Appendix D hereto. The Joint Chiefs of Staff consider that:

a. Decisions resulting from the aforementioned reappraisal should be reached before long-range plans for the Congolese Air Force are completed.

b. Action should be taken, however, to arrest the deterioration of present Congolese air capabilities and to improve effectiveness. To this end, discussions should be initiated with the Belgians, Italians, and Congolese along these lines. Such discussions should not prejudice courses of action which might result from the reappraisal outlined in subparagraph 3 a, above. Appropriate US military personnel should be included as participants in these discussions.

[3] Document 245.

5. The Joint Chiefs of Staff recommend early initiation of the actions suggested in paragraphs 3 and 4, above. In this connection, the Joint Chiefs of Staff on 5 September 1964 advised that they considered it timely and prudent to reappraise our objectives and policy in Africa in the light of developing communist strategy and tactics. While the Joint Chiefs of Staff are aware that studies treating aspects of this problem have been initiated, it does not appear that these will constitute the concentrated interdepartmental effort to conduct a substantive reappraisal of US objectives toward Africa which they believe to be required. They continue to be seriously concerned over the deterioration of US national security interests and the lack of a common policy with regard to Africa and accordingly request your personal support in initiating the reappraisal, which should be characterized by such stature and authority that it can, if necessary, lead to major and prompt changes in US cold war strategy and US policies toward Africa.

For the Joint Chiefs of Staff:

Earle G. Wheeler[4]
Chairman
Joint Chiefs of Staff

[4] Printed from a copy that indicates General Wheeler signed the original.

---

380. Telegram From the Department of State to the Embassy in the Congo[1]

Washington, January 5, 1965, 1:25 p.m.

1718. Komer of White House staff had long chat with Struelens and discussed among other things Tshombe's projected visit to U.S. in January.

The conversation ended with apparent agreement between the two that a U.S. visit at this time would not repeat not be in Tshombe's interest due continued likelihood Negro demonstrations plus further African charges that he "tool of imperialists" etc. It was therefore agreed Struelens, who leaving here for Leo the 5th, would urge

[1] Source: National Archives, RG 59, Central Files 1964–66, POL 7 THE CONGO. Secret; Immediate. Drafted by McIlvaine, cleared by Komer and Fredericks, and approved by McIlvaine. Repeated to Brussels and London, and to Paris for Harriman.

Tshombe postpone visit, concentrate on mending his African fences and organizing elections. If, as expected, he emerges as head of newly elected government, would be welcome here at mutually convenient time.

Struelens will contact you in Leo and hopes you will see Tshombe with him on this and related matters. Leave this to your discretion but believe you should encourage present constructive approach.[2]

Rusk

---

[2] In telegram 2619 from Leopoldville, January 6, Godley reported that Tshombe, who was "aware of the American Negro leadership's aversion to him," had not mentioned to him any visit to the United States since his return from Europe. (Ibid.)

---

381. Telegram From the Department of State to the Embassy in the Congo[1]

Washington, January 6, 1965, 8:36 p.m.

1729. Fredericks and Komer saw Struelens again separately today and once more stressed our belief GDRC must take more active steps improve its diplomatic and public relations. Fredericks briefed him on attitudes East African leaders to illustrate kind of efforts needed in that quarter. In sum, it was pointed out Tshombe's survival potential, indeed our ability to continue assist him effectively dictate that he do all he reasonably can to enhance acceptability of his regime to as many other African states as possible.

Struelens expressed complete agreement on need GDRC diplomatic efforts in East Africa and Zambia and promised he would attempt influence Tshombe this subject. Added he not leaving today as expected and planned phone Tshombe to make plans.

Dept aware of difficulties convincing Tshombe himself of facts of international life but expects you and country team to continue to exploit every opportunity to get word around in areas where it could be played back to him. In addition to political initiative it seems to us im-

---

[1] Source: National Archives, RG 59, Central Files 1964–66, POL 15-1 THE CONGO. Confidential; Priority. Drafted by McIlvaine; cleared by Fredericks, Komer, Harriman's Staff Assistant John D. Rendahl, and Judd; and approved by McIlvaine. Repeated to Brussels and to London for Harriman.

portant pay more attention day to day propaganda—for example play down to extent possible role mercenaries, US and Belgian military aid.

Rusk

---

382. Memorandum From Robert W. Komer of the National Security Council Staff to President Johnson[1]

Washington, January 8, 1965.

We are trying our best to get some kind of a political umbrella erected over the *Congo*, to help forestall a rebel counter-offensive and to protect us against military overcommitment. Since the Northeast Congo is really being held by only 110 mercenaries, supported by a peanut airforce, we are greatly worried lest outside aid to the rebel remnants lead to a counter-offensive which could even retake Stanleyville. The Belgians, especially Spaak, feel the same way. They and we are also doing what we can to help Tshombe beef up his forces (he's recruiting his own mercenaries) but we doubt they could hold if rebels started using mercenaries too.

During Harriman's trip to Europe, Spaak proposed that we both try to get Kasavubu and Tshombe back into touch with the OAU. Since we want an "African" political solution, or at least an extended negotiation in lieu of renewed fighting, we're inclined to favor this course. However, it may require some pressure on Tshombe to get him to make the necessary gestures to get more African states on his side. Spaak will work on Tshombe when he comes to Brussels next week.

At the NATO Council, Spaak and Harriman seemed to make a dent in urging our allies (except for the French) to join us in supporting the Congo regime. Harriman himself did rather better in London; we can probably count on more UK help in weaning the East Africans away from the radical Arabs and Nkrumah.

Harriman gets back today at 4. You might want to get a brief report directly from him. If not, you might want a half-hour meeting on the Congo sometime next week to brief you on our strategy. I have my fingers crossed on this one, but I now see a 50/50 chance that we'll be

---

[1] Source: Johnson Library, National Security File, Country File, Congo, Vol. X, Cables, Memos & Miscellaneous. Secret. A notation on the memorandum indicates that the President saw it.

able to disengage somewhat from the Congo and get it off the crisis list, while still keeping our legitimate friends in power.

R.W. Komer[2]

[2] McGeorge Bundy initialed below Komer's signature.

383. Memorandum for the Record[1]

Washington, January 8, 1965.

SUBJECT

Discussion with Secretary Rusk—8 January 1965

[Omitted here is material unrelated to the Congo.]

4. In connection with the Congo, Rusk suggested after considerable discussion that CIA do everything possible covertly to stimulate and incite resentment on the part of the Black Africans against the Muslim slave traders of Egypt, Algeria and elsewhere in the Middle East and that conversely incite resentment among the Muslims over supplying arms to the Black Africans which would ultimately be used against the Muslim population in the Sudan. Rusk stated that it was his understanding that one convoy of arms from Khartoum to the Congo had been taken over by the Sanu tribesmen and would be used in the Sudan conflict.

Action: Carefully prepare a dynamic program to meet these requirements.

5. Rusk said that he was informed that Tshombe and Nkrumah were in contact with one another. This information had come from Wayne Fredericks. I said I knew of no such contact. Rusk said he thought that perhaps this information had not gotten up to me.

Action: I wish to be informed, to review the reporting, and also CIA evaluation of the reliability of the reports, and the probable courses of action.

[1] Source: Central Intelligence Agency Files, Job 80B01285A, DCI/McCone Files, DCI (McCone) Memo for the Record, 01 Jan.–28 Feb. 65. Secret; Eyes Only. Drafted by McCone on January 9. Paragraphs 8 and 9 were originally an addendum, but are printed as part of the memorandum of record.

6. [Omitted here is material unrelated to the Congo.]

7. At the close of the meeting, Governor Harriman came in, having just arrived from Europe, and reported briefly on his talks in Paris, purpose of which was to insist upon European participation in the Congo and other African problems. He apparently leveled pretty heavily on the British to use their influence with the East African states. Stated that Spaak handled the meeting in superb fashion. I asked Harriman what he meant by "twisting Tshombe's arm"—what did he expect Tshombe to do? He retorted "write to the Emporer" (presumably Haille Salassie).

Action: I should meet early next week with Harriman to be sure that we are together on the Congo policy and that we are working on parallel tracks.[2]

Addendum to Discussion with Secty Rusk on 1/8/65:

8. Rusk had a [*less than 1 line not declassified*] on his desk and made reference to the paragraph on the Congo in which it was stated that Kasavubu supported Tshombe, was against broadening the government, was in favor of mercenaries and couldn't care less where they came from. It interested me that the report had been so carefully studied, as it was heavily underlined with red pencil and there were a number of questions and comments in the border. In answer to my question, the Secretary said that the Brief was extremely useful, very well done, and he hoped we would continue it in its present form.

With respect to the Congo, I stated to the Secretary that I felt we had no choice except to insure victory for Tshombe, that I thought the covert support we were giving had turned the tide of the battle in the last 2 weeks and if we continued our help, we had a good chance of stabilizing the situation within 60 to 90 days. I said we should not be deterred from this by the persuasion of do-gooders, by reactions from African states in the United Nations who didn't like us anyway, or from the vote in the OAU. Rusk said he agreed completely and that he felt that once Tshombe had established control, the attitude of the neighboring African states, which was now antagonistic, would change. I concurred, stating this had been my viewpoint right along. Harriman who entered the meeting somewhat later, however, expressed the view that "Tshombe would be cut to pieces" by rebels assisted by the soldiers of a great many of the antagonistic African states supplied with modern weapons from China and the Soviet Union. I intend to discuss this matter in depth with Harriman next week.

---

[2] See Document 385.

Addendum #2 to Discussion with Secretary Rusk on 1/8/65

9. Rusk stated that he had been informed that Kanza, rebel Foreign Minister, had been approached by Tshombe and was to come over to Tshombe. I pointed out that Kanza had been associated with Tshombe until Tshombe took over as PM. I said that we had reports that Kanza and Gbenye had split, that I could not verify the rapprochement between Kanza and Tshombe.

Action: I would like this thoroughly checked and if necessary communicate with Station for report on Monday.

10. [*1 paragraph (5½ lines) not declassified*]

[*1 paragraph (1 line) not declassified*]

11. [*1 paragraph (9 lines) not declassified*]

[Omitted here is material unrelated to the Congo.]

---

384. Memorandum From Robert W. Komer of the National Security Council Staff to the Under Secretary of State for Political Affairs (Harriman)[1]

Washington, January 12, 1965.

I very much fear that we're in the eye of the storm over the Congo. The present deceptive lull strikes me as most likely a buildup period, during which those aiding the rebels are preparing a major counter-offensive to retake Congo Orientale. Given the thin screen of mercenaries and peanut airforce which is all that's really between the rebels and Stanleyville, the rebels could probably retake it with "volunteer" support.

Such a counter-thrust would present us with a cruel dilemma. We probably couldn't stop it without a much larger Belgian/US or other military commitment than at present. Equally bad, it would split Africa, forcing us to put great pressure on the radical supporters of the rebels, unless we were willing to see the GDRC lose. So we would face either a major setback to our Congo policy (and our prestige as well) or greater involvement in the Congo with all the costs involved.

These alternatives are both so unpalatable as to justify an all-out effort to forestall a new Congo flareup by promoting some kind of polit-

---

[1] Source: Johnson Library, National Security File, Country File, Congo, Vol. X, Memos & Miscellaneous, 12/64. Secret. A handwritten notation at the top of the memorandum reads: "Mac—I may be too Cassandra-like again but I'm worried. Trying to get Africans to move is like molding mush. RWK."

ical settlement. From our standpoint a political track, tricky as it might be, is infinitely preferable to a military one. Since we *don't* want to get more entangled in the Congo, we want if possible an *African* political solution (which means the OAU), with the US disengaging to the extent feasible without sacrificing the GDRC. What are the key elements?

1. First, we want to erect as many *political barriers* as possible to rebel counterattack. At the moment the GDRC hold most key centers in the Northeast Congo. For this reason we saw a UNSC cease-fire resolution as putting the onus on the rebels if they started to attack again. Building on the SC resolution, and its 10 September 1964 OAU precursor, we must try to isolate the rebels and their supporters politically, and lay the ground-work for charges of violation and "aggression" against a rebel counterattack.

2. Second, we need to get some kind of conciliation or mediatory effort going, so that if the rebels attack again, they are undermining this. If we can get an OAU majority moving in this direction, it's worth the risk.

3. Third, we want to *reinforce the political legitimacy* of the GDRC by getting it to improve its acceptability in Africa. This involves a whole series of action we'd like the GDRC to undertake—de-emphasis of South African mercenaries, broadening the cabinet, elections, etc.

Our problem on all three counts is the reluctance of Tshombe and Kasavubu to take actions which seem to them to show weakness. They also suspect that these moves mask a US/Belgian disengagement. We must first try to get their confidence and overcome these suspicions. If this fails, then pressures are essential, since without them we'll be in the soup again.

Shouldn't we develop a more systematic plan of action to carry out all these aims? I know that we're doing many of them ad hoc already, but we need a more systematic and coordinated approach. Moreover, desirable as it is to hide behind the Africans, I doubt that they will be self-starters. We'll have to cajole and prod them even at risk of showing our hand.

In sum, my real fear is that unless we can draw some political umbrella over the Congo soon, we're either going to be sucked into another war, or have to retreat ignominiously. I realize that I'm only illuminating the problem, not offering concrete solutions. But I have a number of further suggestions on a political track, which I'll come discuss with you.

R.W. Komer[2]

---

[2] Printed from a copy that bears this typed signature.

385. Memorandum for the Record[1]

Washington, January 14, 1965.

SUBJECT

Discussion with Governor Harriman—14 January 1965

Following the Special Group CI Meeting, I met with Governor Harriman to discuss U.S. policy objectives in the Congo.

At the CI meeting I had read [*less than 1 line not declassified*][2] noting particularly the agenda items 3a. through d., all of which were directed against the United States and indicated a fear of an attack on East African states by the Congolese. Harriman stated that in his discussions with representatives of Tanzania, Uganda and Kenya that a very great concern had been expressed that if the Congo situation was cleaned up by large numbers of South African mercenaries under Tshombe, they would continue on into the East African states as means of disrupting them and thus stop the southward trend of the independent Black African movement. They predict that the South African mercenaries would be heavily supported by the Portuguese and would not be manageable by Tshombe. It is this attitude which Governor Harriman feels represents a real and sincere fear that influences the anti-Tshombe attitude in many African states, particularly the East African states.

I reported to Harriman the Rebels had received 39 plane loads of matériel from the North and had established three training and training-holding centers in Southern Sudan and were moving arms by motor trucks from the Sudan into the Congo. I stated several convoys had been intercepted, one involving 18 trucks had been destroyed and some apparently had turned around under orders from the Sudan Government, but nevertheless, the Rebels were being supplied and we expected this to continue. Furthermore, Chinese arms had come into the Burundi via Dar es Salaam, but these had been impounded by orders of the King of Burundi, and as far as we know had not reached the Congo.

I stated there is no evidence of Malian, Algerian or Egyptian "mercenaries" operating in the Congo with the Rebels. There are unconfirmed reports of Algerian and Ghanaian fighters in Brazzaville, but this had not been confirmed. Also reports of Chinese and Soviet arms in Brazzaville, but these also had not been confirmed.

---

[1] Source: Central Intelligence Agency Files, DCI/McCone Files, Job 80B01285A, Box 2, DCI (McCone) Memos for the Record, 01 Jan.–28 Feb. 65. Secret; Eyes Only. Drafted by McCone.

[2] Not found.

Referring to the U.S. policy objectives I expressed no disagreement with the objectives stated in the attached paper of 13 January,[3] except to emphasize that there is no alternative to Tshombe in the Congo and therefore Tshombe must win.

I then reviewed the 13 January comments on some aspects of the U.S. policy, emphasizing each one of the points made in the attached paper.[4] Harriman questioned me concerning the number of mercenaries and Mr. Karamessines responded by stating that in an itemized list as of 10 days ago, there were some 220 South Rhodesian, South African types, 200 Belgian and other Europeans and en route now are 60 Belgian and other European types with possibly 90 additional, making a total of 150.

The following points were agreed upon:

1. There is no alternative to Tshombe and we must help him to win.

2. It would be in our interest to increase the number of Belgian and European mercenaries and phase out the South Africans.

3. Attempts should be made to have Tshombe give assurances concerning the integrity of East African states and also express his hope that he could dispense with South African mercenaries at the earliest practical time.

Note: In this connection Harriman disagreed with our position that "African opinion opposes White mercenaries from any source," stating that certain African leaders, including Nyrere had told him that they would not oppose European mercenaries, indeed they would not oppose United States military, but they would oppose South Africans.

4. Belgium must be kept in the forefront and every possible pressure must be placed on Spaak to assist Tshombe. In this connection Harriman felt that Tshombe either was en route to Brussels or would depart Leopoldville in the immediate future to consult with Spaak.

5. Harriman explained a meeting was planned with Bottomley and Thompson of the British Foreign Office to deal with the East African states problem. [*4 lines not declassified*]

6. Harriman favored recruitment of additional European mercenaries and European pilots. He does not favor the use of [*less than 1 line not declassified*] mercenaries and feels the [*less than 1 line not declassified*] pilots are so closely identified with the United States, that they invite the same criticism as though we had American pilots.

---

[3] Attached but not printed is a paper entitled "U.S. Policy Objectives in the Congo." No drafting information is indicated on the paper.

[4] Attached but not printed is a paper entitled "Comments on Some Aspects of Current U.S. Tactical Policy Objectives in the Congo." The attachment states that the comments represent a consensus of an OCI, ONE, and DDP/AF Working Group.

7. Harriman spoke of demobilization of several thousand of the French Senegalese Army and raised the question as to whether some of them could not be recruited as mercenaries. He admitted this would create problems for Tshombe.

8. Harriman believes that Tshombe should make every gesture to mollify the criticism and proposed such things as a letter from Kasavubu to the Emperor, rapprochement between Tshombe and Holden Roberto, holding the elections as scheduled, and a few other things but none of which would alter Tshombe's position as Head of Government or include Rebel leaders in his government. Harriman was most positive that we could not advocate courses of action by Tshombe which would weaken him and strengthen the Rebels. Harriman is very strong on this point but apparently is having some difficulty within the Department.

---

386. Memorandum From the Chief of the Africa Division, Directorate of Plans, Central Intelligence Agency (Fields) to the Assistant Secretary of State for African Affairs (Williams)[1]

Washington, January 14, 1965.

SUBJECT

Limitations of [CIA] Tactical Air Capability in the Congo (Leopoldville)

1. [CIA] has noted with increasing concern the potential for expansion of the military situation in the Northeast Congo. The radical African states have not only made public declarations of their support for the Congolese rebels, but there are also detailed classified reports delineating the plans and intentions of these states. There are recurring reports of "volunteers" or of specific troop support for the rebels from several African states, notably Kenya, Algeria, and Mali, as well as the UAR, and possibly from Belgium. The radical African states also have the capability of providing high-speed tactical air support to the Congolese rebels. The UAR and Algeria, for instance, both have MIGs of various categories at their disposal.

---

[1] Source: Central Intelligence Agency Files, Job 76–00366R, DDO/ISO Files, Box 1, Folder 8, Congo, 1960–1969, Part II. Secret. This memorandum was sent via backchannel.

2. [CIA] does not have the capability in the Congo to conduct covert operations of a scope and nature commensurate with opposing high-speed tactical aircraft or concerted military troop support to the rebels.

3. Present tactical air support forces in the Congo under the control of [CIA] cannot stand up to high-speed jet aircraft, and if such aircraft are introduced into the Congo, [CIA] would have to withdraw the air support forces under [CIA] control since their continued operations under such conditions would not be feasible.

4. [CIA] considers that if such high speed aircraft or extensive troop support are introduced into the Congo conflict, the alternative to withdrawal will be to call upon extensive Belgian support.

---

387. Memorandum From Robert W. Komer of the National Security Council Staff to the President's Special Assistant for National Security Affairs (Bundy)[1]

Washington, January 18, 1965.

McGB:

You should know that Ball and Harriman now approve Leoville request to let "our" planes hit truck convoys and arms depots in "villages."[2] We've held off on this previously, in order to avoid scare stories of US planes massacring civilians from the air (and also further murders of hostages).

But hostages now apparently mostly gone (except possibly Watsa and Aba, which would still be off limits). Also rebels know our policy so are travelling at night and holing up in village "safehavens" during day. So there is real need to go after them, if we're to have a decent chance of holding (we can always change back later). Finally, we're already so damned that any likely increase in anti-US propaganda would be marginal.

---

[1] Source: Johnson Library, National Security File, Country File, Congo, Vol. X, Cables, Memos & Miscellaneous. Secret.

[2] In telegram 2695 from Leopoldville, January 14, Godley recommended that the restrictions still in effect on using T–28s and B–26s be modified to permit attacks on clearly identifiable targets of military importance in all rebel-held territory except Watsa and Aba, where the Embassy believed hostages might be held. (National Archives, RG 59, Central Files 1964–66, POL 23–9 THE CONGO)

I'm for this, as one of desperate measures to scare off rebels before their counteroffensive starts. But I've asked WH clearance so you can see.[3]

RWK

[3] Komer added a handwritten postscript that reads: "Note also that everybody dives for bush when our planes come over, so field thinks big civilian casualties quite unlikely." It is followed by the handwritten notation: "OK. McGB." Telegram 1831 to Leopoldville, January 18, informed the Embassy that permission was granted, but that pilots should be carefully briefed on the need for careful identification of targets so as to avoid indiscriminate damage to civilians or their property. They should also use great care not to strafe villages within 10 miles of the Uganda border. (Ibid.)

388. Memorandum From Robert W. Komer of the National Security Council Staff to the Under Secretary of State for Political Affairs (Harriman)[1]

Washington, January 19, 1965.

If the Congo rebellion flares up again, as is all too likely, we'll almost certainly be under great Congressional and public pressure to cut off any US aid to nations supporting the rebels. Since this will be aggression as defined by the Gruening Amendment, plenty of anti-Nasser congressmen will raise a howl. And if we suspend aid to Nasser and Ben Bella what grounds will we have for not suspending aid to the other countries as well?

Ergo, if a confrontation like this is likely to develop anyway, why don't we use this stick as a threat in an effort to forestall having to apply it in fact? What I have in mind is quietly getting the word around to the UAR, Algerians, Malians, Sudanese, and East Africans along following lines: If there is another Congo flare-up, openly supported by these countries, the US Congress will almost certainly insist on cutting off aid. The US doesn't want to do this, but the Administration fears that it would have no choice, since charges of aggression would certainly be brought in the UNSC as well as the OAU, and the radicals would be accused of violation of the recent SC Resolution. The GDRC is already touting this line. The USG would deplore such an eventuality, so is

[1] Source: Library of Congress, Manuscript Division, Harriman Papers, Subject Files, Komer, Robert. Secret.

most anxious that the parties concerned move toward some kind of political solution (in line with the SC and OAU Resolutions) which will obviate the risk of an open break between the US and the rebel supporters.

I am not suggesting that our Embassies should use this as an official line. Rather, this thought could be dropped in casual conversations (thinking out loud about the future), [*less than 1 line not declassified*] and unofficial channels, e.g. an Edgar Kaiser letter to Nkrumah. It seems to me that we must exhaust every recourse to forestall resumption of a rebel offensive. The above idea may not seem terribly persuasive, but it wouldn't cost us much. If the rebellion flares up we'll probably have to cut off aid anyway, so why not let this word get around?

Bob K.

---

389. Memorandum From the Joint Chiefs of Staff to Secretary of Defense McNamara[1]

JCSM–48–65 Washington, January 21, 1965.

SUBJECT

Restrictions Upon Air Operations

1. On 27 October 1964, the Joint Chiefs of Staff forwarded JCSM–903–64[2] which expressed the views of the Joint Chiefs of Staff regarding restrictions imposed by the United States upon the use of air support in military operations in the Congo. Such restrictions were deemed to be militarily unwise and establish a political precedent in which are inherent dangers to adequate US military support of US policies and objectives world-wide. Except for support of the Van der Walle attack on Stanleyville in November 1964 and Operation Dragon Rouge, the restrictions remain in effect.

2. The situation in the Congo has changed drastically since last October. The state purpose of the restrictions at that time was to protect the rebel-held US hostages. This condition no longer obtains with the rescue of the hostages by the Dragon Rouge/Noir and subsequent op-

---

[1] Source: National Archives, RG 218, JCS Files, 9111 (25 October 1964). Top Secret.

[2] Enclosure A to JCS 2262/155. [Footnote in the original.] JCSM–903–64 is attached but not printed.

erations. Additionally, the provision of Soviet-made weapons through the Sudan and Uganda is strengthening the rebel forces. Continued restrictions on air operations increasingly jeopardize a satisfactory military conclusion in the Congo and could contribute to the escalation of the present rebellion into a major conflict within Africa.

3. The American Ambassador in Leopoldville on 14 January 1965 recommended[3] to the Secretary of State that the restrictions be appreciably modified to accord discretionary authority to attack clearly identifiable targets of military importance in all rebel-held territory except where hostages are believed held.

4. The Joint Chiefs of Staff reiterate the views they expressed in JCSM–903–64 and recommend that:

a. Restrictions be modified immediately as proposed by the US Ambassador in Leopoldville on 14 January 1965.

b. The attached proposed State/Defense message be coordinated with the Department of State and approved for dispatch.[4]

For the Joint Chiefs of Staff:

Earle G. Wheeler[5]
Chairman
Joint Chiefs of Staff

---

[3] Leopoldville to State msg 2695, DTG 141540Z Jan 65; on file in Joint Secretariat. [Footnote in the original. Regarding telegram 2695, see footnote 2, Document 387.]

[4] Draft telegram, undated, "Use of Aircraft," is attached but not printed.

[5] Printed from a copy that indicates General Wheeler signed the original.

---

390. Memorandum for the Record[1]

Washington, January 23 1965.

SUBJECT

Discussion with Governor Harriman

[Omitted here is discussion of an unrelated subject.]

2. With respect to the Congo, Harriman mentioned a recent set of recommendations made by General Adams which are now being held

---

[1] Source: Central Intelligence Agency Files, Job 80B01285A, DCI (McCone) Memo for the Record, 01 Jan.–28 Feb. 65. Secret; Eyes Only.

by the Joint Chiefs, and resulting in the Joint Chiefs directing an inquiry to State, a copy of which the Governor showed me.[2] I said we had not seen the Adams' recommendations.

Action: We should review the Adams' recommendations and, at an appropriate time, prepare comments.

3. The Governor mentioned there were 500 mercenaries in Europe ready to go to the Congo but the U.S. was not ready to provide transport of their supplies nor to furnish uniforms, etc. I do not know what this problem is. The Governor was vague on details.[3]

Action: DDP should check *immediately* with State to determine what the problems are and see if we should, and can, help. If not, lend an effort to secure appropriate action by DoD or other Departments of the U.S. Government if action on our part is in order and desired.

4. Harriman showed me a long message from Spaak to Tshombe which he thought was most helpful and which in effect told Tshombe to come to Brussels and settle their problems at once if he were to look for any more help from Belgium. Also he showed me excerpts from a statement that Tshombe made to the African Ambassador in the Congo which he thought was both constructive and would be most useful.

[Omitted here is discussion of an unrelated subject.]

5. [*1 paragraph (10½ lines) not declassified*]

[*1 paragraph (6 lines) not declassified*]

6. During the discussion with Gov. Harriman I expressed grave misgivings concerning the outcome in the Congo. I referred to the various reports of training in Algeria, UAR, the Sudan, and, more particularly, [*less than 1 line not declassified*] the establishment of rebel training camps in Algeria. I said that it was very doubtful in my mind whether the Tshombe government could win the game unless there was a reversal of attitude of the neighboring States. It appeared to me that Tshombe himself could not bring about a revision of thought by the Heads of neighboring States; however, if Kasavubu stepped out in front, he might have some effect. Also, if we could publicize the reduction and final elimination of South African mercenaries and the pres-

---

[2] See Document 389.

[3] On January 25, Fields sent a memorandum to Helms commenting on Harriman's information that some 500 mercenaries were in Europe ready to go to the Congo, but that the United States was not prepared to transport their supplies or furnish uniforms. Fields said that mercenaries were currently arriving in the Congo without supplies. He noted that supplies were normally provided by the Belgians and/or Mobutu, but the Belgians were apparently withholding such supplies in an effort to bring pressure on Tshombe to negotiate sensibly on economic and financial matters. Fields stated that up until now, it had not been U.S. policy to equip mercenaries, [*text not declassified*], he did not see where any Agency action was called for. (Central Intelligence Agency Files, Job 78–03805R, DDO/IMS Files, Box 1, Area Activity—Africa)

ence of European mercenaries, this likewise might help. In summary my view was most pessimistic. I gave Harriman a copy of our January 19th weekly summary of the Congo. I told him that I thought it should be read by all of those in the Department who were testifying on the Congo prior to the time they made statements. I pointed out Rusk's statement to the Leadership at the White House was quite in error because it was overly optimistic and this was due to the fact that he had not seen reports, or been briefed. (*Note:* In fact, he admitted afterwards he had received no briefing on the Congo for the past two weeks.)

---

391. Memorandum From Robert W. Komer of the National Security Council Staff to the President's Special Assistant for National Security Affairs (Bundy)[1]

Washington, January 26, 1965.

Mac—

To counter all the gloom I've been purveying, *I do see a bit of blue sky in the Congo*. Not much as yet, but with all our sweat to get a political track going, and Tshombe finally saying what we told him,[2] we now see signs the East Africans and OAU secretariat at least want to get a political reconciliation going too.

First big hurdle is 29 January OAU ad hoc (Congo) commission session in Nairobi. If our moderate friends stand tall there (as we've urged), and East Africans are halfway reasonable, we may get something started. Most important is to *get the fighting stopped and the palaver underway*, before a rebel counter-offensive puts us back in the soup.

---

[1] Source: Johnson Library, National Security File, Country File, Congo, Vol. X, Cables, Memos & Miscellaneous, 12/64. Secret.

[2] Telegram 4331 to Cairo, January 26, described Tshombe's January 21 speech to the African Ambassadors in Leopoldville as generally conciliatory in tone and one that should help to improve his image with other African leaders. The Ambassador was instructed to bring the speech to Nasser's attention as evidence of Tshombe's desire to cooperate with other African states and to emphasize the following points: 1) Tshombe's firm intention to hold elections in March; 2) the Congolese Government's willingness to extend "full collaboration" to the OAU; 3) his invitation to Kenyatta to hold the next Ad Hoc Commission meeting in Leopoldville; and 4) his statement that the Congolese Government had no objection to the recent Security Council resolution. (National Archives, RG 59, Central Files 1964–66, POL 23–9 THE CONGO)

After this comes the big OAU Foreign Ministers meeting in late February. Here we'll try behind-the-scenes to marshal all our friends in favor of an OAU-sponsored political settlement.

Any number of things could go wrong, but what's important is that we at last see an African way to reach an African solution of an African problem. If it only gets underway, we can disengage discreetly behind its cover, and with a fairly good chance of retaining in Leoville a government which serves U.S. and Belgian interests. It may or may not include Tshombe, but at the moment he's still front runner.

RWK

---

392. Memorandum for the Record[1]

Washington, January 26, 1965.

SUBJECT

Meeting with Secretary Rusk. Mr. Helms in attendance. (Gov. Harriman joined latter part of meeting)—26 Jan 65

[Omitted here is discussion of unrelated subjects.]

5. With reference to the Congo I told the Secretary that the situation was deteriorating, that large quantities of arms were coming in, that the rebels were demonstrating some evidence of improved operations resulting from training, that there were three sites in the Sudan which we suspected to be rebel training sites, that three training areas in Algeria had been allocated to the rebels, that we could expect an increased rebel vitality in the future. On the other hand, the ANC troops were practically worthless unless led by mercenaries and that there is deep trouble with the South African mercenaries. I read the Secretary a cable [*1 line not declassified*] (In 67046). At this point Mr. Harriman walked in and we reviewed the cable. After sanitizing it by removing the pseudonyms I left the cable with Harriman, who planned to communicate immediately with the Ambassador, urging that he insist that the problem with the mercenaries over pay and allotments be straightened out at once.

---

[1] Source: Central Intelligence Agency Files, DCI/McCone Files, Job 80B01285A, Box 2, DCI (McCone) Memos for the Record, 01 Jan.-28 Feb. 65. Secret; Eyes Only. Drafted by McCone on January 28.

6. Harriman then again asked whether we had any more information on the possibility of MiG's from the UAR being flown by [*less than 1 line not declassified*] pilots. I said nothing more than I had reported to him on Friday. He then again suggested the prospect of a covert "Chennault Flying Tiger" type of a Congo air force to combat this eventuality. It was agreed on Friday we would do some thinking and planning and perhaps, if appropriate agreement could be reached at policy level, get such a unit in being, but not apply it to the Congo unless and until it was actually needed.

Action: This matter should be discussed.

[Omitted here is discussion of unrelated subjects.]

---

393. Memorandum of Conversation[1]

London, January 29, 1965.

SUBJECT

The Congo

PARTICIPANTS

United States:
W. Averell Harriman
Wendell B. Coote
William L. Eagleton, Jr. (Interpreter)

Congo:
Prime Minister Tshombe
Albert Kalonji, Minister of Agriculture, Water, and Forests
Joseph Kabemba, Chargé d'Affaires, London

After an exchange of greetings and reference to his last meeting with Governor Harriman in Geneva in 1961, Tshombe turned to his recent departure from Leopoldville where he had seen an American negro leader, Mr. Farmer.[2] Mr. Farmer had come to the Congo with distorted impressions but had quickly seen that he had been mistaken. Tshombe had invited Mr. Farmer to visit towns in the interior.

---

[1] Source: National Archives, RG 59, Central Files 1964–66, POL 23–9 THE CONGO. Secret; Limited Distribution. Drafted by William L. Eagleton, Jr., First Secretary of Embassy. Approved in M on February 3 and approved in S on February 8. The conversation was held at the Ambassador's residence.

[2] Civil rights leader James Farmer.

Governor Harriman referred to the problem of aid from certain African states to the rebels which originated in the Soviet Union. Tshombe replied that several things could be done about this problem. One was the diplomatic offensive in which the U.S. had been helpful. Next were Tshombe's contacts with the King of Burundi who had promised to influence Parliament to change the government. It was bad luck that the Prime Minister was killed just as he was about to normalize relations with the Congo. The new Prime Minister, however, has already seized a large quantity of rebel armament. Next were Congolese efforts among the southern Sudanese who were willing to fight rebel arms traffic. They had already been helpful.

In reply to a question about Uganda, Tshombe said he was trying to work with that country; but in any case if he could move his troops to the frontier quickly the frontier could be closed. Tanzania presented a more difficult problem because it was difficult to control traffic across the lake. If the Congo had more military material traffic on the lake it could be controlled.

Governor Harriman asked what could be done to contribute to the diplomatic offensive. Tshombe replied that U.S. could be helpful with its friends as could the UK which had influence in Commonwealth countries. Tshombe observed that there could not be peace in Africa if rebel activities continued. If he wanted to, he said he could himself cause trouble in Uganda.

Governor Harriman asked Tshombe's opinion of his ex-Ambassador to London, Thomas Kanza. Tshombe replied that Kanza was known as a thief in the Congo. He had taken advantage of contacts made as a Congolese diplomat in order to aid the rebels in East Africa.

Governor Harriman stated that Gbenye and Kanza had won a diplomatic victory over him in East Africa and urged that Tshombe should make contacts with the three East African countries which were now opposing the Congo but were perhaps still amenable to persuasion. He also stressed the importance of a Congolese effort to influence the OAU Ad Hoc Committee which is now meeting in Nairobi to discuss the Congo. In reply to Governor Harriman's question on why he had not sent a high level representative such as Leguma, he replied that Leguma had declined because he was afraid for his personal security. Instead, Tshombe had sent a bright and dynamic young student from Belgium, Jean Gouza. Governor Harriman commented that he should not have been fearful of Leguma's safety as the rebels would have done themselves irreparable damage if they had killed an Ambassador.

Governor Harriman asked whether Tshombe personally knew East African leaders such as Obote Kenyatta and Nyerere. Tshombe had only met Nyerere once but knew Kenyatta well. In reply to a question he said his government was about to send an Ambassador to Tanzania. With regard to the Commission meeting, Tshombe did not know what would happen, but he did not expect much with countries such as Algeria and the UAR participating. Nigeria, he said, had sent a good representative with firm instructions but the Upper Volta, while not opposing the Congo, was influenced by radicals, such as the Algerians, who did all the talking.

Governor Harriman suggested that Tshombe should spend more effort himself and send special ambassadors to make contacts with African countries which could be influenced.

Tshombe said his efforts in French Africa had been very successful. The real problem was in English speaking Africa, but he was encouraged by indications that Nkrumah was beginning to modify his position slightly.

Governor Harriman inquired regarding the Congo's military forces. Tshombe replied that the morale was good but there was a shortage of material. The T–28's sent by the United States had been a great help but they were not enough. More air power was needed to prevent the kind of ambushing of Congolese forces that had occurred recently. There was also the problem of Belgian officers who were needed for training and whose contracts would expire in three months time. He would discuss this in Brussels. Governor Harriman stated that it was better for the Congolese to get their volunteers from Europe rather than South Africa. Tshombe replied that he was trying but it was difficult to find qualified Europeans. Many of the French, for example, were working under better conditions for the King of the Yemen. The Congo had an office in Brussels and the Belgians were not interfering with recruiting but only small numbers were volunteering. In reply to a question Tshombe said he needed 1,000 volunteers. This would permit him to station some of them in agricultural and mining areas to give confidence to the people and insure security. Governor Harriman referred to the fact that some volunteers had left the Congo claiming they had not been paid. Tshombe replied that this was true and that malicious propaganda had been circulated among them.

Governor Harriman inquired about plans for the election. Tshombe said he was determined to hold them between the 15th and 31st of March. They would be held province by province so as to insure they would be well regulated and held in a secure atmosphere. Governor Harriman urged that observers and journalists should be invited from other countries to observe the election and Tshombe agreed. He went on to mention his invitation to Diallo Telli who had not come to Leopoldville because of ill health.

In reply to Governor Harriman's question regarding Holden Roberto, Tshombe explained that their relations were now good but that Holden Roberto was having trouble with rival groups backed by the

Algerians and UAR who were demanding that he leave the Congo. He was also having difficulties with some of his soldiers who were not well paid. Tshombe had told him that he should discuss these problems with him so that he could help to solve them.

Governor Harriman inquired regarding the Congo's relations with Brazzaville. Tshombe replied that Chinese influence there was very strong and rebel camps were in existence there. In reply to the suggestion that President De Gaulle might exert some influence in Congo Brazzaville, Tshombe noted that the French were having troubles there too. He did not consider Massamba-Debat to be a real communist but the Foreign Minister Ganao was an out-and-out communist. Tshombe agreed with Governor Harriman that President De Gaulle had not served his own or African interests by recognizing Communist China. The Chinese, said Tshombe, were a greater danger to Africa than the Russians because they were more formidable in numbers and because they used a simple approach that appealed to Africans.

In response to Governor Harriman's suggestion that he present his views re the Congo. Tshombe made the point that the Congo was a particular problem because of its geographic and economic importance. The Congo could be strong and stable under a strong government. Because the people had suffered greatly under communism, they now represented a positive anti-communist force which could be useful in Africa. The Congo could be saved and the Congo's friends should see to it that it did not fall.

Governor Harriman returned to the suggestion that Tshombe should make an effort to establish useful contacts in East Africa. Although no mention was made of negotiating with the rebels, Tshombe raised this subject. When he had become Prime Minister he had invited rebel leaders to Leopoldville. He had even gone to Bujumbura to see the entourage of Soumialot but he had found no representative person to talk to. There was a Congolese public opinion which held Gbenye and others responsible for massacres. How could such persons come to Leopoldville?

Governor Harriman stressed the importance of the Congo's obtaining a victory in the current OAU Ad Hoc Committee session in Nairobi. The Congolese Government's position, he noted, was the right one and if they made the effort they should be able to establish the responsibility of the OAU to contribute to Congolese stability. It would be a tough fight but Tshombe had the skill to do it and he also had friends. World public opinion could be brought to his side if elections were held and outsiders invited to observe them. (At the present time President Kasavubu represented the legitimacy of the Congolese Government. Until he won an election, Tshombe had his position only from Kasavubu.) It was felt in Washington, he said, that President Kasavubu should write more letters to chiefs of state and make public statements more often. Tshombe replied that he agreed that greater efforts should be made. He noted, however, that it was difficult for President Kasavubu to write letters to persons who did not answer the letters or even read them.

Governor Harriman commented that the Emperor of Ethiopia would answer his letters. He observed that the Congo had a good friend in Mr. Spaak and that Belgium could be helpful in ways not open to the U.S.

Governor Harriman asked whether it would not be possible to enlist African military help to replace white volunteers whose presence offended public opinion. Tshombe replied that the only countries in Africa with real armies were the UAR and Algeria. When asked about the soldiers recently released by the French, he said he was continuing to make efforts to enlist them and that he had some encouragement in Upper Volta, but many of these countries were afraid of the outcry of the OAU.

Governor Harriman closed the conversation by assuring Mr. Tshombe that the U.S. wished to help him and the Congo achieve stability and prosperity. Tshombe expressed his thanks and said he very much hoped his friends would not abandon the Congo since its stability and economic progress were essential to the peaceful development of Africa.

At this point Governor Harriman asked Secretary Rusk and Senators Fulbright, Hickenlooper and Jackson to come in. They were introduced to Prime Minister Tshombe and the other Congolese. After an exchange of greetings the Secretary assured Mr. Tshombe of the deep interest of Americans including the President in the well-being of the Congo. He also said he hoped every effort would be made to improve the Congolese image in Africa and the world. Tshombe replied that he agreed entirely with the need for a great effort and he welcomed U.S. support in this regard.

394. Telegram From the Station in the Congo to the Central Intelligence Agency[1]

Leopoldville, February 1, 1965.

6705 (In 71125). 1. At his urgent invitation, [COS] called on [*1 line not declassified*] also present at meet, which apparently arranged jointly by [Identity 1] and [Identity 2]. Subject of conversation was renewed plea for [CIA] to subsidize [*cryptonym not declassified*] electoral program. They made it even plainer than ever before that they fear [Identity 3] eliminate them from political scene. They also claim [Identity 4] is sympathetic to their plans which are to organize "moderate" bloc of provincial parties and create counterforce both to Conaco and to MNC/L groups. [COS] went over same arguments as used on previous occasions, that ODYOKE unwilling subsidize one good Congolese leader against another and that [*cryptonym not declassified*] role is to bring [Identity 4] and [Identity 3] together. Both [*cryptonym not declassified*] were unhappy with our conclusion, and [COS] believes they will be actively looking for support elsewhere. Big question is who will invest money against [Identity 3].

2. Station discussing above situation with [Godley], who points [*4 lines not declassified*].

[1] Source: Central Intelligence Agency Files, Job 78–00435R, DDO/ISS Files, Box 2, Folder 11, [*cryptonym not declassified*] Operations. Secret; [*cryptonym not declassified*]. No time of receipt appears on the message.

395. Telegram From the Department of State to the Embassy in Belgium[1]

Washington, February 6, 1965.

1667. This tel provides basis for discussion with Belgians of kind of OAU political solution we could both accept and persuade GDRC to accept without damage to any of our basic interests. It should be regarded as indicative of our current thinking, not as plan to which we committed in every detail. Moreover, it does not deal with tactics for its implementation, which would be subject subsequent discussions once elements of an acceptable plan were agreed. It also does not deal with actions we should take to get Tshombe to take further steps to improve his relations with OAU and African leaders. (We attach great importance to this aspect and believe, for example, that it would be useful for him to contact not only moderate leaders but also Nkrumah to take advantage of possible favorable developments.)

Combination of circumstances now exists offering reasonable opportunity for political settlement in Congo consonant with GDRC's basic interests and not inimical those of GOB and US. Main elements these circumstances are: (1) GDRC's position of relative military strength vis-à-vis rebels and (2) new initiative by OAU Congo Commission to cooperate with GDRC in dealing with Congo problem.

Failure of Tshombe to exploit present generally favorable circumstances would leave him with no alternative but to seek additional military aid to suppress rebellion strengthened by continuing assistance from radical Africans (and indirectly from Communists), thus raising problem escalation. As thinly disguised South African and Portuguese military aid to Tshombe becomes more apparent, it is possible more and more African countries would side with rebels. Thus, unless GDRC gets on political track promptly, we are likely be confronted with following highly undesirable prospects: escalation; increasing isolation of US and Belgians in de facto alliance with Tshombe, South Africans, Portuguese and Rhodesians; and difficult choice between increasing aid and disengaging, both of which would involve risks we wish avoid. In light these considerations and fact that even if we took on increased military and political burden we would still have no assurance solution

---

[1] Source: Johnson Library, National Security File, Country File, Congo, Vol. XI, Memos & Miscellaneous, 1/65–9/65. Secret; Priority. Repeated to Leopoldville. The telegram is attached to a February 8 memorandum from Komer to Bundy. Komer stated that this was the outline plan he had stimulated for a political settlement of the Congo issue which protected the essential position of the GDRC, although many aspects would be painful to Tshombe and Kasavubu. He noted that the important thing was to find a way to close out this affair without letting it escalate or the United States get over-committed.

to Congo problem would result, we strongly favor seeking political solution and desire maximize chances of achieving one.

Crucial period will be between arrival of OAU subcommittee in Leopoldville, anticipated Feb. 7, and Feb. 26 meeting of OAU FonMins. During this period OAU Commission will be developing national conciliation plan for Congo. Sooner we and Belgians can decide on elements we could accept in such plan, more likely we are to be able influence GDRC and OAU in right direction.

It is evident that to obtain political solution some political concessions would have to be made to radical countries supporting rebels. Believe, however, plan could be worked out which would keep both military and political risks for GDRC within acceptable bounds. Moreover, chances for gaining acceptance for such plan would be greatly increased if GDRC could take forthcoming attitude toward OAU efforts and give moderates something to work with. Even if effort failed, GDRC would have enhanced its position with moderates and shifted onus for intransigence to rebels and their supporters.

Any plan will presumably be based on four principal elements of OAU and SC resolution: (1) nonintervention, (2) cease-fire, (3) withdrawal of mercenaries, and (4) national reconciliation. Maximum objective of rebels and their supporters would be plan which would (1) call for discontinuance of all military assistance to GDRC without interfering with covert military assistance to rebels; (2) place responsibility for initiating cease-fire on GDRC; (3) insist on immediate, unconditional withdrawal of mercenaries; and (4) propose government of national reconciliation excluding Tshombe as Prime Minister and including rebel leaders which would set date and determine conditions for national elections. On other hand, maximum objective of GDRC and its supporters would be plan which would: (1) bar aid to rebels but permit continued assistance to GDRC; (2) place responsibility for cease-fire on rebels; (3) allow GDRC to maintain effectiveness of its armed forces, including mercenaries as long as militarily necessary; and (4) retain Tshombe as PM but exclude rebel leaders from pre-election government and proceed with elections only where GDRC fully in control.

Both we and Belgians have consistently advocated political solution which recognizes GDRC sovereignty and territorial integrity of Congo. Political solution means negotiations between GDRC and OAU and therefore inevitably compromise between positions set out above.

Following are some ideas which we believe acceptable from point of view of GDRC basic interests as well as Belgo-US interests. They should be viewed as package since neither GDRC nor rebels could be expected to accept elements adverse to them without compensating concessions from other side, nor could either be expected to accept cease-fire plan without machinery to police it.

(1) *Cease-fire*: GDRC and rebels would declare publicly their willingness to abide by cease-fire as soon as all parts of OAU plan for implementing it were agreed to by all parties concerned and observers were in place. (Cease-fire would, of course, not prevent either party from dealing with disturbances of public order in territories under their control. Nor would it prevent GDRC, perhaps in consultation with OAU, from securing help to develop long-run capability for maintaining internal security on its own.)

(2) *Nonintervention*: Plan for implementing cease-fire would call on all OAU members on one hand to cooperate with cease-fire by not supplying or permitting supply of arms or ammunition to rebels, and on other hand call for suspension of all further outside military assistance to GDRC's combat forces as long as cease-fire in effect. For their parts, GDRC and rebels would agree neither to request nor receive military assistance for duration of cease-fire. Plan would also provide for agreement of GDRC, rebel authorities, and neighboring countries to permit stationing in areas under their control of observers from OAU, and possibly UN, to check on implementation of these agreements. Suspension of all outside military assistance would be effective as soon as observers in place and cease-fire in effect. To assure that individual observers were acceptable to GDRC and other party concerned, lists would be presented in advance for their approval.

(3) *Mercenaries*: GDRC would agree to phase out mercenaries as rapidly as it could obtain substitutes to help maintain internal security, which it would agree to try to obtain from OAU countries of its own choice. OAU Commission would urge countries receiving GDRC requests for troops or police to comply promptly to extent possible. (We would like Belgian views on what countries would be acceptable to GDRC and estimate of number of troops they could provide.)

(4) *National Reconciliation*: GDRC would agree to proceed with national reconciliation by holding national elections in March as announced in all areas where security situation permits. It would reiterate its offer of amnesty to those who laid down their arms and allow all citizens to participate in elections on same basis, including rebels who are abiding by cease-fire. In rebel areas, ad hoc arrangements for temporary administration during pre-election period would be worked out on local basis with approval of central government. For their part, rebels would agree to seek representation in government of national reconciliation through electoral process. They would not insist on "round-table" or formation, before elections, of government of national reconciliation excluding Tshombe and including rebels. (However, part of the bargaining process may result in some commitment by

GDRC to include "rehabilitated" rebels in post-election cabinet.) GDRC would also inform OAU of its intention to invite certain OAU countries, as well as UN SYG, to send observers. All parties would agree in principle to accept results of elections.

Presumably, there would need to be sweeteners on both sides. On GDRC side, in light of apparently satisfactory settlement of contentieux, one sweetener might be acceleration and expansion of Belgian technical assistance to Congo. This might place particular emphasis on prompt introduction "equipes polyvalentes" to help maintain order in all areas where circumstances permit their employment. On OAU side, sweetener might include US offers of logistical support for OAU observer teams, airlift to bring African troops to Congo and some financial support for African troops and/or police while in Congo. (We are not in position to make any commitments on these points but would explore ways and means once general agreement on plan reached.) On rebel side, effort to sell this package may take form of some enticement to disenchanted rebels to break away from Gbenye leadership. It would also include assurances to OAU that US would take steps to assure that cease-fire was not broken through use of US-supplied aircraft for combat operations.

Clearly it would be unwise to put forward at this or any other time a "Belgo-US plan". It seems to us essential that there be considerable African palaver on this subject as means of educating both sides to realities. Meanwhile it is equally essential that we and Belgians in first instance and perhaps British at a later date determine in our own mind limits to which we feel we can go and still get a livable political solution. We should also consider means of persuading, when the time comes, both the GDRC and the OAU to agree on a reasonable solution as well as to take into account the alternatives. Approach to OAU would be through selected moderates. We would also have to consider what steps we might urge moderates to take outside OAU if OAU effort should break down.[2]

With this in mind you should, as soon as feasible, explore these ideas with appropriate Belgian officials, stressing rationale and need to keep discussions strictly confidential to avoid leaks, and seeking their views and suggestions.

Ball

---

[2] In telegram 2899 from Leopoldville, February 9, Godley agreed that early Congolese discussions with other African states and the OAU regarding a political solution in the Congo could be desirable, but commented that it would be extremely hard to convince the Congolese to accept any cease-fire to which the rebels were legally a party or to allow rebel leaders like Gbenye to stand for election. (National Archives, RG 59, Central Files 1964–66, POL 23–9 THE CONGO)

396. Memorandum From the President's Special Assistant for National Security Affairs (Bundy) to President Johnson[1]

Washington, February 10, 1965.

About ten days ago you called my attention to a bad story in the *Herald Tribune* about the White House and Tshombe.[2] We traced this sharply and clearly to Senator Dodd, and still more to his assistant, David Martin. (Martin admits that both Dodd and he spoke to Freidin in London.)

Nevertheless, I think you will want to know that in fact Dodd's meeting with Tshombe worked out very much to our advantage. We have our own transcript from Dodd, and the Senator said all the things we asked him to say about how Tshombe should widen his circle of friends, play ball with the OAU, broaden his Cabinet, and be responsive to the Belgians. Dodd even told Tshombe that the State Department—and of course the White House—were his friends.

At least partly as a result, Tshombe has paid some real attention to these matters in recent days, and the mess in the Congo looks less discouraging than at any time during recent months. (Cross your fingers.)

Nevertheless, Bob Komer has had a good time beating up Dodd's assistant, who has made all sorts of apologetic noises. As a result I think we got some considerable net help from Dodd, and at the same time have left his people feeling that they owe us something.

McG. B.

---

[1] Source: Johnson Library, National Security File, Country File, Congo, Vol. XI, Memos & Miscellaneous, 1/65–9/65. Secret.

[2] On February 2, the *Herald Tribune* printed a critical story about U.S. Congo policy alleging that the Department of State was opposed to Tshombe, although the White House supported him. That same day, Komer and Bundy sent a memorandum to the President stating that these allegations, which reiterated previous complaints by Dodd, could be traced to the Senator's assistant, David Martin. They also reported that Dodd had agreed to urge Tshombe to be more conciliatory toward his African colleagues when the Senator met with him in London at Churchill's funeral. (Ibid., Memos to the President, McGeorge Bundy, Vol. 8)

397. Memorandum for the Record[1]

Washington, February 11, 1965.

SUBJECT

Meeting of the Special Group (CI) on Thursday, 11 February 1965

1. The meeting was primarily devoted to a presentation by the three ambassadors to East Africa of their views on the current situation in each of the three countries. They were respectively William Attwood, ambassador to Kenya; William Leonhart, ambassador to Tanzania; and Olcott Deming, ambassador to Uganda.

2. In the latter part of the meeting, Governor Harriman opened debate on what measures might be taken by Tshombe to make his regime more acceptable to the East Africans and conversely what steps might be taken to persuade the East African states to cease their assistance to the Congolese rebels. In the course of this discussion, Ambassador Attwood commented that if Tshombe could not be persuaded to take the steps that would make him acceptable, we might consider withdrawing our aid to him since the resulting chaos might be preferable to our ever deepening involvement in an unpopular cause. Governor Harriman asked in Mr. Helms's absence if we had any comment on this point. I said that if chaos alone was all we had to fear, then a strong case could be made for our disengagement. I went on to say, however, that we had firm evidence that the Chinese Communists saw in the Congo rebellion a great opportunity and were determined if possible to gain a position of commanding influence by support to the rebels. They did not underestimate both the Congo's mineral wealth and its strategic position. Governor Harriman supported my view and restated it even more strongly, warning that nobody should have any illusions as to what a rebel victory might mean. He said at best we could expect something like the Ben Bella regime in Algeria, and perhaps something a good deal worse.

3. Governor Harriman concluded the meeting by requesting that each of the three ambassadors draw up a list of the minimum concessions Tshombe would have to make to gain acceptance in East Africa.[2]

Cordmeyer, Jr.
Chief
[less than 1 line not declassified]

---

[1] Source: Central Intelligence Agency Files, Job 78–03805R, DO/IMS Files, Box 4, Folder 14, U.S. Govt.—Special Group CI & 303. Secret. Drafted on February 12.

[2] The minutes of the Special Group (CI) meeting on February 11 state that the Special Group agreed to take the recommendations of the three ambassadors under consideration. (Ibid.)

398. Telegram From the Department of State to the Embassy in the Congo[1]

Washington, February 17, 1965, 1:05 p.m.

2042. It is evident that we are approaching another very crucial phase of Congo situation. Failure thus far of Ad Hoc Subcommission to go to Leo[2] and encouraging sounds out of Nouakchott[3] reinforce our belief that we must continue our pressure on GDRC to maintain forthcoming, reasonable stance in order encourage moderates and fix blame for intransigence on radicals.

Current East African clamor over alleged bombing Uganda border towns[4] is probably due mixture genuine fear plus concerted effort scare us into dropping Tshombe and/or goad him into extreme stance. Also perhaps to justify Uganda support of rebels. Our position on Tshombe is unchanged. We did not, repeat not, put him in power—Kasavubu did. Only Kasavubu can remove him and unless that happens he remains head of govt as far as we are concerned. Meanwhile we are being required pay heavy political price in some parts Africa for our support GDRC. Our ability to continue will depend therefore on Tshombe's capacity to politic in next two weeks.

Ambassadors Deming, Attwood and Leonhart are all returning their respective posts within a week. All three agree that further concil-

---

[1] Source: National Archives, RG 59, Central Files 1964–66, POL 23–9 THE CONGO. Confidential; Immediate. Drafted by McIlvaine; cleared by Trimble, AFE Director Jesse M. MacKnight, Davis, and Amitay; and approved by Harriman. Repeated to Nairobi, Kampala, Dar es Salaam, Lagos, Abidjan, Addis Ababa, Dakar, Monrovia, Paris, London, Brussels, USUN, DOD, CINCSTRIKE for Ramsey.

[2] Airgram A–594 from Nairobi, February 19, reported that the OAU Ad Hoc Commission met on February 13 and issued a communiqué stating that representatives of revolutionary leaders from the Congo were available for talks but no government representatives were present. The communiqué also expressed the hope that the subcommittee that was mandated to visit the Congo would carry out its mandate and report to the last scheduled session of the Commission on February 22. (Ibid., POL 3 OAU)

[3] The 13 French-speaking members of the Common Organization of African and Malagasy States (OCAM) meeting February 10–12 at Nouakchott, Mauritania, adopted a resolution opposing outside interference in the internal affairs of African countries and supporting the legal Government of the Congo.

[4] Telegram 1360 from Kampala, February 13, reported that the Ugandan Government complained that a plane believed to be American had bombed two Ugandan border villages on February 13. (National Archives, RG 59, Central Files 1964–66, POL 31–1 THE CONGO) Telegram 1380 from Kampala, February 16, reported that the alleged incident involved two aircraft not further identified. (Ibid.) Telegram 1452 to Kampala, February 16, transmitted a note to the Ugandan Foreign Office stating that its concern over reports that towns on the Uganda side of the Uganda–Congo border had been attacked by unidentified aircraft should appropriately be expressed to the Congolese Government. The note also stated that no Americans, official or otherwise, were operating combat aircraft in the Congo. (Ibid.)

iatory gestures from Leo will strengthen their hands as it will those of moderates at FonMin conference Nairobi Feb 26. While we will have further suggestions for GDRC stance at Nairobi later immediate problem is Uganda border incident. You are requested to see Tshombe at earliest convenience, review philosophy outlined above and endeavor persuade him to take initiative soonest, if possible before week end. You may point out that ideas which follow are basically tactical and probably will not be accepted.

A public statement accompanied by specific messages to appropriate chiefs of state to effect GDRC desires good relations with all neighbors including Uganda. As entire world knows GDRC engaged in putting down armed rebellion and unfortunately that rebellion being supplied and directed via safe-havens in neighboring countries. Congolese army and air force have strict instructions respect international boundaries regardless provocations. This not always easy in heat of battle near a border. Question of sanctity of borders has greatly concerned GDRC for some time. It appears that Uganda is now equally concerned therefore it would seem appropriate time to reach mutual agreement to assure no further border violations from either side. GDRC willing discuss with GOU at any time and place how to remove this irritant to their relations. Specifically GDRC would propose stationing of small observer force along common border, force to be supplied by mutually agreed upon OAU member or members. This solution would have additional advantage, once aid to rebellion had been stopped and other African security forces are made available, of permitting the GDRC to begin fulfilling its desire to send South African mercenaries home in accordance with Addis and SC resolutions. Or, if GOU has other suggestions, GDRC would like to hear and consider them. Interests of peace and African solidarity require that two countries come to agreement.

Comment: While recognizing psychological hazards to be overcome in Congo to get agreement to offer such program it is clear that something like it or worse may come out of meetings ahead and advantages of their taking initiatives are great. If pattern could be set with one neighbor, rest could be handled separately. GOU refusal to consider is possible if not probable but would certainly put the burden on them. Furthermore Tshombe owes it to his new UAMCE supporters to keep ball rolling and to put opposition on the defensive.

Rusk

399. Memorandum for the Record[1]

Washington, February 18, 1965.

When Struelens came in yesterday to report on his trip to Leoville, I was suitably complimentary. We then discussed the gains Tshombe had made since our last meeting. I underscored how important it is now, with the African moderates gaining strength, for Tshombe to be as responsive as possible to the OAU. If the radicals try to back off, Tshombe must move closer. We want either to tie the radicals to a reasonable peacemaking proposition or pin on them the blame for failure. Struelens seemed to get the point and I agreed with him that this tactic would have its problems since the OAU is unpredictable (to wit, the failure of Guinea and Ghana to show up for the ad hoc commission exercise in Leoville).

Struelens agreed that we had made gains recently. He cited especially the Belgian financial settlement. (In an aside, he said that he had found Spaak highly impressed with Tshombe's performance during the Brussels talks). Tshombe's meeting with the African Ambassadors in Leoville had also been quite successful. (He said he had "watched" this performance from behind a curtain.) He didn't think we had gained too much from Farmer's visit, but thought that Tshombe had impressed Farmer and that Farmer would hesitate now to speak out against Tshombe personally. Struelens was also pleased with the results of the conference at Nouakchott.

Tshombe's next big domestic problem, Struelens said, is his election campaign next month. Struelens pointed out that Tshombe is under constant pressures to support local politicians. However, he seems to be bearing up and Struelens expects him to do very well in the election. The current plan is to hold elections in the safe areas first and then to move out later on.

I urged that Tshombe invite observers to come in for the election. Struelens said he didn't know how many would accept such an invitation and thought there was some problem in having formal observers from the UN. I said I thought it really didn't matter who came. The important thing was to be able to say after the election that everyone had been invited. Struelens nodded assent.

He said that Tshombe is extremely grateful for US aid. However, one additional point had occurred to him: Would it be possible for us to

---

[1] Source: Johnson Library, National Security File, Country File, Congo, Vol. XI, Memos & Miscellaneous, 1/65–9/65. Secret. Prepared by Komer. Copies were sent to McGeorge Bundy, Fredericks, McIlvaine, and Lang.

send one or two patrol boats to hamper the flow of arms across Lake Tanganyika? I said this sounded like a sensible idea and asked Hal Saunders to look into it.

He said confidentially he wanted me to know that Congolese Chargé Cardoso has apparently been involved in some sort of embezzlement here. Struelens said he didn't want to get involved in this and didn't know what Tshombe intended to do about it. However, he thought if we knew in advance there would be less chance of misreading if Tshombe called Cardoso home. I told him to take this up with State; Fredericks wanted to talk with him. Struelens also mentioned present plans to settle in Washington after the Congolese election if all goes well for Tshombe.

I worried several specifics: First, I wished the GDRC could keep its planes away from the Ugandan border. He asked exactly what had happened and I replied that we aren't sure yet. However, the point was that the GDRC had so much more to lose diplomatically than it could gain militarily by taking chances on its planes bombing the wrong side of the border. So I thought it imperative that the GDRC give the border a wide berth.[2]

Second, I said we had heard rumors that the Congolese forces might be getting ready to use napalm. I had no idea whether these rumors were true, but I wanted to take no chances and mentioned this because Tshombe would get a terrible black eye if his planes, piloted by whites, were to be accused of dropping napalm on "innocent Africans." Struelens took all this in, and I got the impression that he would weigh in against it.

Third, we agreed that the mercenary problem was still very much with us. Struelens said that Tshombe was quite willing to get rid of the South Africans and accept other Africans in their place as soon as he could find them. He deplored Major Hoare's public statements about mercenary recruiting. I urged that Tshombe tell Hoare to stick to fighting and leave public statements to the government.

In parting Struelens said he would be in town for the next couple of weeks and would welcome hearing from us any time we had thoughts on these problems.

RWK

---

[2] Circular telegram 1539, February 20, reported that the Congolese Government responded to the Ugandan protest note in firm but conciliatory language attributing the border incidents to an ill-defined frontier and proposing a mixed Congolese-Ugandan commission to make an on-the-spot study and establish responsibility. The telegram also reported that Tshombe in a February 19 Leopoldville press conference denied that ANC aircraft had attacked Ugandan territory and charged that the incident was a Ugandan fabrication to cover up for rebel incursions into the Congo from Uganda. (National Archives, RG 59, Central Files 1964–66, POL 31–1 THE CONGO)

400. Telegram From the Department of State to the Embassy in Belgium[1]

Washington, February 18, 1965, 7:08 p.m.

1754. Spaak–Harriman breakfast conversation this morning served to continue consultations and re-affirm identity of views on importance Tshombe's African image and desirability him playing conciliatory OAU game to the finish; need to get friendly African troops into the northeast as deterrent to rebel operation from neighboring sanctuary; desirability US–GOB meeting Brussels mid-March coordinate military supply and technical assistance roles. He had not heard the napalm rumor but was most positive about the need for us both to do whatever necessary to prevent the use of this weapon.[2] Gov Harriman told him that we would have to withdraw our operational planes even if napalm used on T–6s.

Spaak clearly had more optimistic view of the potential of new OCAM Nouakchott grouping than we. He and Davignon also believe French now inclined encourage OCAM members cooperate with GDRC and would at least not oppose their sending troops.

Gov Harriman pressed Spaak for views on Burundi and what need be done to capitalize on present situations. Spaak, who appeared tired and without sense of urgency on this or Congo matters, said he thought we should wait several weeks before making up mind. Later Davignon was asked to have situation in mind and let us know their thinking.

Spaak also admitted Van der Walle–Mobutu difficulties but thought they would be ironed out when Tshombe returned.

Rusk

---

[1] Source: National Archives, RG 59, Central Files 1964–66, POL 23–9 THE CONGO. Confidential. Drafted by McIlvaine, cleared by O'Sullivan and McKillop, and approved by Harriman. Also sent to Leopoldville, and repeated to Paris, London, Bujumbura, and CINCSTRIKE for POLAD Tampa.

[2] Telegram 1637 from Brussels, February 19, reported that the Belgian Defense Ministry was sending instructions to the Belgian military in the Congo not to have any connection with any napalm project, and that Spaak had instructed De Kerchove to tell Tshombe of Spaak's unalterable opposition to using napalm in the Congo. (Ibid.) In telegram 3017 from Leopoldville, February 20, Godley reported that he had told Tshombe that the U.S. Government was unalterably opposed to the use of napalm in the Congo and that any military advantage would be more than overcome by the political risks. (Ibid.)

401. Memorandum for the Record[1]

Washington, February 24, 1965.

Struelens came in urgently at 2:00 p.m., having just talked to Tshombe on the phone. Tshombe had just returned to Leopoldville from the political conference at Luluabourg full of what he considered his great success there in wrapping up extensive political support for the coming election.

Tshombe called Struelens "as soon as he returned" to ask whether we'd answered his request through Struelens for money to bolster his election campaign. Struelens then launched into a real pitch to the effect that now is the crucial time for Tshombe; a big election victory would give us a unified Congo by spring and win respect for Tshombe in other African capitals. He urged that help in the "next 20 days:" would really pay off for us.

I reassured him that Komer had put his request into the right hands and simply promised to find out where we stand. I said I would give him an idea before day's end (he'll be calling Tshombe again tonight) when he might expect an answer one way or the other. I did *not* say anything about what the answer might be, though he said he'd like to give Tshombe some notion of whether it would be favorable.

The second point Tshombe had raised—definitely secondary to the first in Struelens' pitch—was the need to replace the two T–28's downed last week. I said we were still searching for them and were keenly aware of the need for aircraft but would have to wait until we concluded our search before we thought any further about replacements.

Third, Struelens mentioned again that Tshombe's "comptroller" had verified Chargé Cardoso's "embezzlement" of funds here. He said Tshombe would probably recall Cardoso. He said, as he had last week, that he wanted us to know this simply so we wouldn't misinterpret Cardoso's recall.

At one point, in an aside, Struelens intimated that I probably had seen the tape of their conversation. I shook my head negatively, but he was already off to his next point.

He left with another quick plug for help and my agreement to call him.

---

[1] Source: Johnson Library, National Security File, Country File, Congo, Vol. XI, Memos & Miscellaneous, 1/65–9/65. Top Secret. Prepared by Harold Saunders. Copies were sent to McGeorge Bundy and Fredericks.

After talking with Twining/Fields and McIlvaine, at 5:10 p.m. I phoned Struelens this message: "I have thoroughly checked progress on your request. I'm satisfied that the people working on it fully understand its urgency. However, they are not quite ready to make a decision. I don't have any indication what the decision will be, but I do expect we will have an answer one way or the other by the first of next week." He said he'd tell Tshombe, and I reiterated that we don't know yet what the answer will be. He thanked me for checking.

McIlvaine and Twining had arranged to send the gist of Struelens' pitch to Leoville for Godley's recommendation. All agree that, if we do anything, we'll do it in Leoville, not through Struelens. However, we thought that mentioning Leoville now would only put Ambassador Godley on the spot if we decided negatively.

Harold H. Saunders[2]

[2] Printed from a copy that bears this typed signature.

---

402. Telegram From the Department of State to the Embassy in Uganda[1]

Washington, February 24, 1965, 8 p.m.

1546. For Deming. You should inform Obote following:

(1) On basis evidence which has come to attention USG in past 48 hours, we reasonably sure that Congolese planes violated Ugandan airspace and attacked Nyapea on Feb 22 and may have attacked Goli, probably without overflying Uganda, on Feb 13.

(2) Therefore, in accord Secretary's assurance to Obote, US Amb Leo has been instructed support GOU protest delivered to GDRC Chargé in London.

(3) At same time, USG has equally good evidence that Ugandan troops have crossed Congo frontier and participated with Congolese rebels in actions against Mahagi and Kasindi.

[1] Source: National Archives, RG 59, Central Files 1964–66, POL 31–1 THE CONGO–UGANDA. Confidential; Immediate. Drafted by McElhiney, cleared by McIlvaine and MacKnight, and approved by Tasca. Also sent to Leopoldville and repeated to Nairobi, Addis Ababa, Brussels, Paris, Lusaka, Dar es Salaam, and London.

(4) USG believes that, with hostile acts being committed both sides (whether by error, initiative local commanders, or whatever), GDRC and GOU should do everything in their power to control border area more strictly and thus avoid further incidents which can only exacerbate situation. USG therefore most strongly urges that GOU and GDRC enter into direct negotiations to arrive at some mutually acceptable arrangement for border control.[2] US Amb Leo instructed make same suggestion to GDRC.[3]

Rusk

---

[2] In telegram 1508 from Kampala, February 26, Deming reported that he presented the substance of the Department's telegram to Prime Minister Obote and Acting Foreign Minister Onama in the form of a first person note. (Ibid.)

[3] Telegram 2101 to Leopoldville, February 24, instructed Godley to inform Tshombe of U.S. support of the Ugandan protest and to urge Tshombe to take a conciliatory line, such as attributing the incident to pilot error, expressing regret, and proposing bilateral negotiations to avoid further incidents. (Ibid.)

---

403. Memorandum From Harold H. Saunders of the National Security Council Staff to President Johnson[1]

Washington, February 25, 1965.

Before he left, Bob Komer asked me to bring you up to date on the *deteriorating situation in the Congo.* Tshombe has gained some ground since the UN sessions in December, but we've made no progress toward a cease-fire.

Now the *rebel counter-offensive* we've feared may have begun. Last week Congolese rebels bolstered by Ugandan regulars crossed into the northeastern Congo and took several towns. Shipments from Algeria and the UAR have swelled rebel arms caches, and rebel fighters are training with Arab mentors in East African safe havens.

The Ugandan Prime Minister, panicked by two alleged air strikes on Ugandan border towns, has asked for planes from Communist China and Algeria. We've rejected hysterical charges that we're responsible and are plugging for negotiations which would seal off the border.

---

[1] Source: Johnson Library, National Security File, Country File, Congo, Vol. XI, Memos & Miscellaneous, 1/65–9/65. Secret.

So far, the Congolese army and mercenaries have contained the incursions, and Tshombe with our encouragement has offered to negotiate. To keep on a political track, we're trying to build on his offer by floating the idea that pacifying the border with UN or African observers could be a first step toward the cease-fire which we badly need. Tshombe's forces would be no match for a well-run rebel push supported from outside, and we don't want to face that kind of escalation.

We may see another round of radical propaganda from the *African foreign ministers' meeting which meets this weekend.* However, the moderates there are stronger than at any time since the rebellion began last summer. We've done a substantial amount of diplomatic spadework and hope they'll produce some reasonable proposals for controlling hostilities.

You might want to ask Secretary Rusk about this. With Harriman no longer overseeing our Congo effort, we suffer from lack of persistent attention from State's seventh floor.

Hal Saunders

404. Telegram From the Department of State to the Embassy in Israel[1]

Washington, February 28, 1965, 1:14 p.m.

844. For Gov Harriman. Congo. We have thus far been unable get Tshombe commit himself to go to Fon Min meeting, despite strong appeals from Amb Godley, UK, Zambians, and GDRC Del Nairobi. Meeting will apparently run through first week of March, with Congo item inscribed towards end of agenda. Zambians claim they can rally adequate support for GDRC if Tshombe arrives to coordinate with moderates and present case. Meeting opened with mild statement by Kenyatta, who appears ready adopt moderate stance in effort find Congo solution.

Obote reacted emotionally to Amb Deming's revelation of Ugandan incursions onto Congolese soil. While GDRC appears prepared accept some form of mediation or border commission, chances for Ugandan agreement not favorable at this time. Meanwhile, we have

[1] Source: National Archives, RG 59, Central Files 1964–66, POL 23–9 THE CONGO. Secret; Priority. Drafted by Alan D. Berlind and approved by McIlvaine.

asked Embassy Leo whether ANC cannot effectively seal off northeast corner without actually advancing on border towns, thereby avoiding new incidents.

Houphouet has told us that OCAM grouping formed at Nouakchott is best vehicle both for assisting legitimate GDRC and for persuading Tshombe take steps to improve his African image. Houphouet confident Tshombe can get African police troops from OCAM members but stressed that arms would have to come from US and France.

Davignon informed us that GOB has instructed De Kerchove to refrain from meddling in Kasavubu–Tshombe affair, in line with Spaak belief it best adopt hands-off policy on domestic matters. Belgians see reported rift as predictable phenomenon of electoral period. Nevertheless, our Embassy in Leo is discreetly but firmly pointing out to both elements the mutual disadvantages of a split and the concomitant effect on US ability to cooperate with GDRC.

Rusk

---

405. Memorandum From Harold H. Saunders of the National Security Council Staff to the President's Special Assistant for National Security Affairs (Bundy)[1]

Washington, March 3, 1965.

McGB:

Attached is the latest on one bit of Congo byplay.[2] Just before you and RWK left, Struelens—then just back from Leoville—made a pitch "at Tshombe's request" for financial support to Tshombe's election campaign chest.

RWK asked Glenn Fields in CIA for an informal opinion. CIA is willing (though certainly not to the extent of the $3.3 million Struelens

---

[1] Source: Johnson Library, National Security File, Country File, Congo, Vol. XI, Memos & Miscellaneous, 1/65–9/65. Secret.

[2] The attachment is a March 3 memorandum for the record by Saunders stating that Struelens had phoned him at 9:15 a.m. to ask whether a decision had been made regarding Tshombe's request for financial help in his election campaign. Saunders had responded that the matter would be handled in Leopoldville and that they were sympathetic, although a decision had not yet been made. At 10:30 a.m., Struelens called back to report that Tshombe was leaving for Nairobi that night and would wait for an answer there.

mentioned) but defers to State guidance. State hasn't made up its mind yet, but is wary of getting involved.

The big problem is that Kasavubu's characteristic suspicions of potential rivals are cropping out again. He fears Tshombe will use the election to unseat him. If we do anything for Tshombe, we'll want to be sure he's in good odor with Kasavubu, so we don't end up backing an ex-Prime Minister. However, if they're together a little help might be useful in improving our leverage or achieving limited objectives.

The most dangerous immediate consequence of this rift is that Tshombe is afraid to go to the OAU Foreign Ministers' meeting now sitting in Nairobi for fear Kasavubu will fire him while he's away. We've pulled all the stops to get him there because the African atmosphere is better than at any time in the past six months, and it would be a great loss not to take advantage of it.

If State decides this is a good idea, CIA could probably work on a small scale within its present authority. My feeling is that we wouldn't want to get involved buying votes for Tshombe on any grand scale (Fredericks believes he has enough money for this). However, it might be worthwhile giving limited help *IF* Godley has something specific in mind to accomplish by it.

Hal

---

406. Telegram From the Department of State to the Embassy in India[1]

Washington, March 4, 1965, 5:56 p.m.

1832. For Governor Harriman. Congo. Tshombe arrived Nairobi today. Press reports he had talk with Kenyatta described by Tshombe as very satisfactory. OAU Ad Hoc Commission concluded meetings and issued bland communiqué reaffirming faith in Addis resolution. We have initial report that Kenyatta and Commission arriving Leopoldville March 8 and will be received by Kasavubu. Deptel on pro-

[1] Source: National Archives, RG 59, Central Files 1964–66, POL 23–9 THE CONGO. Secret; Priority; Limdis. Drafted by Berlind, cleared by Franklin J. Crawford in SOA, and approved by McIlvaine.

gram presented Nairobi's 2433 and 2456[2] (repeated New Delhi) being repeated to New Delhi.

Sudan has charged Congolese with recent overflights its territory, but no details given. GDRC has not yet replied. Dept querying Embassy Leo.

Ambassador Godley is skeptical re practical value of African troops for Congo and claims they would not permit removal of mercenaries without jeopardizing military effort and general security situation. Moreover, Godley doubts Tshombe willing surrender leverage on both West and Africa which he believes Portuguese and Southern African ties give him.

There is no additional info on Congolese domestic rifts.

Rusk

[2] Dated March 1 and March 3, respectively. (Ibid.)

407. Editorial Note

In telegram 90199 to the Station in Leopoldville, March 5, 1965, the Central Intelligence Agency reported on a consensus reached regarding the political divisions within the Government of the Democratic Republic of the Congo (GDRC). There was no doubt such schisms existed, the telegram stated. President Kasavubu suspected Prime Minister Tshombe, Tshombe complained to Ambassador Godley concerning Joseph Mobutu, and Victor Nendaka was disturbed over the proliferation of intelligence agencies in the GDRC. Regardless of the degree to which the split had gone or was going, it seemed clear that the [*cryptonym not declassified*] were at least taking out reinsurance by siding with Kasavubu against Tshombe. All this activity was bound to have a disruptive effect on an already chaotic GDRC, the telegram stated, and the U.S. Government must attempt to minimize it. Thus it should undertake selective, modest, ad hoc funding of specific individuals, not parties, for specific purposes, to keep all lines open and to provide some leverage in counseling moderation [*text not declassified*]. (Central Intelligence Agency Files, Job [*text not declassified*], Fiche 44, Row 2, Frames 4–7, [*text not declassified*])

On the other side of the coin, the telegram continued, Tshombe was suspicious of the [*cryptonym not declassified*] or any other power block that he could not completely control. His request for election funds was probably made not because he needed money but rather to test U.S. willingness to stand behind him personally. If the U.S. response was negative or too little he could be expected to interpret the lack of support as a manifestation of an active anti-Tshombe position. CIA believed, albeit reluctantly, that the U.S. could not risk such an interpretation. In its initial approach, the U.S. could assure Tshombe it would make every effort to obtain the [*cryptonym not declassified*] support for the GDRC and Tshombe in the critical pre-election period. The "net message" to Tshombe should be that the greatest danger to the Congo was the creation of feuding factions would lead to an internecine struggle similar to that in Vietnam. (Ibid.)

Telegram 7516 from Leopoldville to CIA, March 8, transmitted Ambassador Godley's response to telegram 90199. The Ambassador emphasized the fluidity of the present situation in the Congo and said he definitely did not believe that the U.S. Government should undertake widespread financing of many additional specific individuals, noting that they could not guarantee that funds so disbursed would not go to parties. (Ibid., Frames 8–11)

408. Memorandum From the Joint Chiefs of Staff to Secretary of Defense McNamara[1]

JCSM–185–65 Washington, March 16, 1965.

SUBJECT

Use of Napalm in the Congo (S)

1. The Joint Chiefs of Staff have noted a recent telegram from the Secretary of State to Embassy Leopoldville, State 2023, dated 15 February 1965,[2] which expressed grave concern regarding the use of napalm in the Congo. They have noted in particular that the American Ambassador to Leopoldville has been directed to inform Premier Tshombe that it is not in the best interests of the Government of the Democratic Republic of the Congo (GDRC) to employ napalm and that its use would require the withdrawal of US operational planes.

2. CINCSTRIKE/USCINCMEAFSA has informed the Joint Chiefs of Staff that he views with concern the apprehensions held in certain

[1] Source: National Archives, RG 218, JCS Files, 9111 (18 Feb. 65). Secret.

[2] Not printed. (Ibid., RG 59, Central Files 1964–66, POL 23–9 THE CONGO)

circles concerning the possible use of napalm in the Congo. He has pointed out that these apprehensions appear to stem from undue sensitivity over the effect of this weapon, and that, if these apprehensions and opposition to usage continue, we risk, through self-imposed limitations, the denial to tactical air forces of one of their most effective weapons.

3. The Joint Chiefs of Staff agree with the views of CINCSTRIKE/USCINCMEAFSA and consider that restrictions on the use of conventional air support weapons are militarily unwise and the use of napalm should be based upon military considerations. They believe that sovereign governments should be permitted to utilize the best conventional weapons available to them in their defense. In this regard, napalm is considered to be conventional ordnance which produces highly effective results with greater efficiency in effort against appropriate military targets. The use of napalm could provide the GDRC with an element of superiority which would unquestionably be most useful in combatting the present externally supported rebel insurgency in the Congo.

4. Accordingly, the Joint Chiefs of Staff recommend that:

a. The present policy restricting the use of napalm by the GDRC be rescinded.[3]

b. A memorandum, subsequently the same as that in the Appendix hereto, be forwarded to the Secretary of State.[4]

For the Joint Chiefs of Staff:

Earle G. Wheeler[5]
Chairman
Joint Chiefs of Staff

---

[3] A memorandum from Vance to Wheeler attached to the original states that JCSM–185–65 was discussed informally with Harriman, who indicated that the Department of State would not concur at that time in the introduction of napalm in the Congo because the psychological reaction of the African states would favor the rebels and the radical states would harden their support of the rebels. The Department's position did not rule out future reconsideration of the use of napalm, if there was a specific and highly important military need.

[4] Not attached.

[5] Printed from a copy that indicates General Wheeler signed the original.

409. Memorandum From Robert W. Komer of the National Security Council Staff to the President's Special Assistant for National Security Affairs (Bundy)[1]

Washington, March 16, 1965.

McGB:

Possible item for Thursday. Before I left, I had a direct pitch from Tshombe via Struelens for money to help his election campaign. Tshombe then put it to Godley. Our best guess is that he's looking for a sign of personal support. Though he can use the money, it's probably not vital.

The biggest risk is further charges of making Tshombe a US puppet if Africans find out. [*1½ lines not declassified*] We'd also have to be careful not to give suspicious Kasavubu the idea we're backing Tshombe to unseat him. In fact, Godley opposed CIA's original proposal for aid to both separately because he didn't want to involve us in that squabble.

However, Godley argues the risks would be worth taking and the money well spent if we could cement the Tshombe–Kasavubu relationship and stave off the mess we'd have if they fell out in the heat of election maneuvering. So he would agree to a [*dollar amount not declassified*] total for both (plus a [*dollar amount not declassified*] contingency fund) if he can get firm assurances that Tshombe and Kasavubu will each support the other's continued tenure.

Soapy is nervous about being involved, but Fredericks [*less than 1 line not declassified*] would go ahead on Godley's conditions. *They fear that Tshombe will, in Bantu fashion, read a negative answer as a sign that we're turning away from him.* They'll take it up with Harriman and, if he approves, bring it to your group.

I share Soapy's wariness, but think we can have the best of both worlds if we play our cards right. If we stick closely to Godley's conditions (which serve both men) and they don't come through, we still get some credit for the offer. If they agree, we're a step closer (even allowing for holes in their promises) to keeping as effective drivers as we'll find at the wheel.

RWK

---

[1] Source: Johnson Library, National Security File, Country File, Congo, Vol. XI, Memos & Miscellaneous, 1/65–9/65. Secret.

410. Memorandum From Harold H. Sanders of the National Security Council Staff to the President's Special Assistant for National Security Affairs (Bundy)[1]

Washington, March 24, 1965.

McGB:

We've gained some ground in *the Congo* since year's end. Tshombe has won wider support among the non-interventionist Africans, and together they stood off the interventionists at the recent OAU foreign ministers' meeting. We now think the only reason they didn't vote a moderate Congo resolution was that they preferred no resolution to a showdown that might have split the OAU.

At home, Tshombe's elections will run through April, and half a dozen African governments have already named observers. There will be a lot of political pulling and hauling between Tshombe and Kasavubu, but we hope each realizes his need for the other. In the northeast, Col. Hoare's offensive to cut rebel supply routes from Uganda and the Sudan is moving ahead steadily. Cutting the line from Tanzania is tougher. Rumors of a rebel counteroffensive continue to fly; we know almost 60 planeloads of arms are stockpiled for them in the area; we've seen two new airfields in rebel territory. So far the rebels haven't marshalled serious opposition, but even if this push succeeds, there's still a lot of mopping up to do.

We're concentrating now on putting together an African political umbrella for the Congo. This is the only sure way to turn off aid to the rebels. Moreover, Hoare's forces are too thin to hold against another big rebel push, so we'd want to fall back immediately on political defenses. Although we've gained substantial African support since December's UN resolution passed, we haven't gone past first base in setting up machinery to close the Congo's borders. We've given State a skeleton action program for doing this and have asked them to come up with a refined version by the end of the week.

Our longer range purpose is to disengage somewhat so as to restore balance to our African policy. The Congo tail has wagged too much of the African dog over the last six months. African machinery would help fill some of the vacuum, and Harriman and RWK should come back with a clearer view of how much cooperation we can count on from the UK and Belgium.[2] All this won't solve the Congo problem,

---

[1] Source: Johnson Library, National Security File, Country File, Congo, Vol. XI, Memos & Miscellaneous, 1/65–9/65. Confidential.

[2] Harriman and Komer were in Brussels for talks on the Congo March 25–27. Telegram 1882 from Brussels, March 27, transmitted the text of a memorandum setting forth the details of the agreement reached by Spaak and Harriman on continued U.S. and Bel-

but it might bring the level of instability within ranges the Congolese can manage and we can accept.

Hal

gian military assistance to the Congolese army. (National Archives, RG 59, Central Files 1964–66, POL 23–9 THE CONGO)

411. Memorandum From Robert W. Komer of the National Security Council Staff to the President's Special Assistant for National Security Affairs (Bundy)[1]

Washington, March 26, 1965.

McGB:

On our first go-round Ball vetoed the idea of our contributing [*dollar amount not declassified*] to Tshombe's campaign fund. He's afraid of publicity. So I agreed to let the matter ride awhile.

But Tshombe has brought it up again with Godley,[2] which makes it an issue of confidence. So we're going back to Ball with following arguments for going ahead: (1) We're already doing so much in the Congo that's obvious (planes, military mission) that a few rumors about political meddling won't add noticeably to the din; (2) *This is the only handle we have for getting Tshombe not to angle for Kasavubu's job*. Africans are beginning to accept the Kasavubu–Tshombe team; if Tshombe knocked off his mantle of legitimacy, it would cost us plenty; (3) Tshombe will surely read a turndown as a sign that we're backing away from him.

After making sure we can handle the transfer without leaving visible tracks, I plan to argue the case again with Ball tomorrow. I'd like to use your proxy again.[3]

RWK

[1] Source: Johnson Library, National Security File, Country File, Congo, Vol. XI, Memos & Miscellaneous, 1/65-9/65. Secret.

[2] On March 24, the Leopoldville Station transmitted a message from Godley to McIlvaine, reiterating Tshombe's request for U.S. financial assistance and quoting Tshombe's assurances that he was collaborating closely with Kasavubu who had no objection to such assistance. The Ambassador thus recommended that [*text not declassified*] be made available to CONACO. (Central Intelligence Agency Files, [*text not declassified*], Fiche 44, Row 4, Frames 2–5, [*text not declassified*])

[3] A handwritten notation in the margin of the original reads: "OK."

412. Telegram From the Central Intelligence Agency to the Station in the Congo[1]

Washington, April 1, 1965.

Dir 97695. For Ambassador or Blake from McIlvaine. Finally took campaign contribution matter up with Secretary who pointed out that it had been very useful for him in his meetings with African Foreign Ministers to be able to say we had no responsibility for individuals in Congo but had nonetheless supported the successive legitimate govts. No matter who involved and that he did not wish to compromise the situation or give Tshombe any handle with which blackmail us. Secretary decided therefore that you should go to Tshombe and tell him frankly that there no question our support as evidenced by our aid and diplomatic activity but that it neither in our interest or his for USG to get involved in this kind of internal political activity.

Having made this point clear to Tshombe Sec. sees no objection to indicating to him that if he really does need campaign money you know that he has many private friends in the states some of whom might be disposed to help him out and that you would be glad to see that this word is passed to them if he, Tshombe, could provide a bank act. no. [*less than 1 line not declassified*] to which such contribution could be sent.

FYI: With this info [*less than 1 line not declassified*] will see that the money is transferred [*less than 1 line not declassified*]. While this rather round about way handling matter am sure you will agree it has merit of accomplishing the aims and keeping skirts clean.[2]

End of message.

---

[1] Source: Central Intelligence Agency Files, [*text not declassified*], Fiche 44, Row 5, Frames 1–2, [*text not declassified*]. Secret; Immediate; [*cryptonym not declassified*]. Drafted by [*name not declassified*] (AF/S), authenticated and coordinated with C/AF, and released by McCone.

[2] Telegram 8015 from Leopoldville to CIA, April 1, reported that the COS had informed Godley, who authorized Blake to brief Tshombe accordingly. (Ibid.)

413. Memorandum From Robert W. Komer of the National Security Council Staff to the President's Special Assistant for National Security Affairs (Bundy)[1]

Washington, April 3, 1965.

Mac—

Unless the President is already up to date, attached might be a useful weekend summary.

[Omitted here is discussion of Cyprus.]

Rusk did a beautiful job of letting Soapy down easy by vetoing a direct US payoff to Tshombe (we didn't intend this anyway), but then agreeing with us that if some private [*less than 1 line not declassified*] supporters wanted to help Tshombe out (at no cost to them), this was OK.

State is becoming quite leery of Struelens, who talks too much. They tend to forget that he's the one who has produced for us at least twice in a pinch, when regular channel had failed. At least we know he talks directly to Tshombe, and the fact that he blows up to twice normal size everything we tell him, doesn't bother me too much (as long as *you* know I'm not really saying what he claims). Rest assured I'm watching myself, and am prepared to disengage when necessary. If *you* hear any grumbles, do let me know.[2]

RWK

Attachment

MEMORANDUM FOR THE PRESIDENT

Progress Report on Congo and Cyprus. Though it hasn't gotten much press play, things are looking up in the Congo. Tshombe's mercenary columns finally took all of the key towns along the northeast border through which the rebels were getting outside supplies. This should have a considerable damping effect, even though there are still several pockets of rebel strength. Moreover, the Northeast Congo was retaken by less than 200 mercenaries, and 200 well-trained "enemy" mercenaries could conceivably take it all back again. Meanwhile Tshombe's elections are proceeding well, despite a snafu in Leopoldville because the ballots for 50-odd different parties simply couldn't be printed fast

---

[1] Source: Johnson Library, National Security File, Name File, Komer Memos, Vol. I (2). Secret.

[2] A handwritten notation in the margin of the original reads: "I'm not worried. He's a plus, net, when well used. McGB."

enough. Finally, the moderate African states are coming out more and more in Tshombe's favor. It's not too much to hope that the active phase of the Congo rebellion may be down to manageable proportions in a few months. We continue to work hard behind the scenes rallying support for our Congo friends, and embarrassing those states still backing the rebels.

[Omitted here is discussion of Cyprus.]

R.W. Komer

---

414. Telegram From the Department of State to the Embassy in the Congo[1]

Washington, April 12, 1965, 12:29 p.m.

2357. Ref: Leopoldville's 3484 to Dept, info Brussels 2025 (also rptd London).[2] Dept shares your concern over reports Kasavubu may be planning shift Prime Ministers as open split now could undermine pacification campaign and, as Embassy points out, raise spectre of renewed Katanga secession.

Of utmost importance in dealing with this threat that USG and GOB take same line. Initial step, therefore, should be for you to coordinate approach with De Kerchove and possibly Mason if you believe HMG can play useful role. In Dept's view, best strategy at this time is to stress to all concerned paramount need for unity, avoiding discussion of personalities. Binza group could be told that any split in moderate forces could turn clock back to the chaos of the post-independence years and complicate efforts of friends of GDRC to be of assistance. Pacification effort plus diplomatic campaign with other Africans now going well. With rebels quarreling in Cairo, this no time to let political feuding break out Leo.

Since reports so far not yet definitive, Dept believes you should avoid any implied threats re USG commitments to GDRC. Also believe

---

[1] Source: National Archives, RG 59, Central Files 1964–66, POL 15–1 THE CONGO. Secret; Immediate; Limdis. Drafted by Frank C. Carlucci in AF/CWG; cleared by Davis, McIlvaine, Judd, Williams, and Fredericks; and approved by McElhiney. Repeated to Brussels and London.

[2] In telegram 3484 from Leopoldville, April 10, Blake reported that the Embassy was very worried about assertions by Ndele, Nedaka, and Bomboko that Kasavubu was thinking of replacing Tshombe with Ileo as Prime Minister at the end of the month. (Ibid.)

it inadvisable slam door on future contingencies involving Binza group by stating flatly we see no alternative to continuation Kasavubu–Tshombe cooperation. Best approach would be emphasize that present GDRC has met with success and deserves loyal support of all moderates during critical transition period, particularly now that elections under way.

In addition to approach to Binza group and Kasavubu, if latter grants appointment, you may wish raise subject again with Tshombe. You could re-emphasize to him our support of GDRC and our hope that his cooperation with Kasavubu would continue. At same time we feel it appropriate point out that Binza group (you may wish include Adoula) represents significant power faction which it dangerous ignore indefinitely. Now that his personal popularity has reached new peak through success in northeast and through favorable initial start in elections, Tshombe may wish again consider possibility broadening his government, if only by filling ministerial vacancies as they occur (Munongo?). A broader government could give added boost to his campaign win African support. Would be particularly valuable if inclusion of member of Binza group could be used as lever to get Adoula return Leopoldville.

Dept leaves possible approach to Tshombe along these lines to your discretion. It should not be made if you believe it would further complicate situation by raising suspicion in Tshombe's mind that USG backing Binza group.[3]

Rusk

---

[3] In telegram 3518 from Leopoldville, April 16, Blake reported that he mentioned these rumors to Tshombe and told him that the Embassy was concerned about the need for unity among moderate political factions in the Congo. Tshombe said he thought this was very helpful, adding that all reports that Kasavubu wanted to dismiss him seemed to come from Bomboko and that he had discussed this with Bomboko the previous evening, hoping to "lance the boil." Blake said he intended to emphasize the U.S. desire to see national unity maintained when he saw Kasavubu on April 17. (Ibid.)

415. Memorandum From the Chief of the Africa Division, Directorate of Plans, Central Intelligence Agency (Fields) to the Assistant Secretary of State for African Affairs (Williams)[1]

AF 397 Washington, April 28, 1965.

SUBJECT

Phasing Out of [CIA] Air Effort in the Congo

1. During the past two months there has been a considerable reduction of rebel effectiveness in the Congo, particularly the northeast Congo. The Ugandan and Sudanese borders have been cleared of rebel pockets and all major roads leading from Uganda and the Sudan into the northeast Congo have been seized by Congolese Government forces. Even if the Ugandan and Sudanese Governments decide to resume shipments of arms and supplies to the rebels, such shipments will of necessity have to go via circuitous routes and will, in most instances, have to pass through areas now under Congolese Government control. The potential of the rebel forces to foment disorder still remains high but it now appears that these rebel groups are no longer under the effective control of their leaders and their ability to regroup and seriously threaten the security of the northeast is definitely declining. The area of current rebel activity most likely to post a problem for the Congolese government in the next 30–90 days in the western shore of Lake Tanganyika, from Albertville in the south to Uvira in the north.

2. A major contributing factor to the reduction of effective rebel activity in the northeast Congo in recent months has been the employment of aircraft in support of the Congolese Army units, and the mercenaries of the 5th Commando. The aircraft now being used, the B–26's and the T–28's, are being utilized and maintained through mechanisms under the control of [CIA]. The tactical deployment of these aircraft in support of ground units is, however, under the operational control of the ANC.

3. As of 27 April 1965, U.S. Government owned aircraft employed in tactical support of ground operations in the northeast Congo and along the western shore of Lake Tanganyika were as follows:

B–26—Five are in the Congo, all of which are based in Stanleyville. These aircraft are manned by [*less than 1 line not declassified*] crews.

---

[1] Source: Central Intelligence Agency Files, Job 76–00366R, DDO/ISO Files, Box 1, Folder 8, Congo, 1960–1969, Part II. Secret. This memorandum was sent via backchannel.

T–28—Ten of these aircraft are now in the Congo and two more are enroute. These aircraft are based in Bunia, Paulis, and Stanleyville. Except for four Belgian pilots, all of these aircraft are manned [*less than 1 line not declassified*].

Helicopters—Two enroute to be manned [*less than 1 line not declassified*].

4. As [Department of State] is aware, the maintenance of these aircraft is carried out by an organization which [CIA] was instrumental in setting up. In addition to the maintenance mechanism, [CIA] has facilitated the assignment of air operations officers to Bunia, Paulis, Stanleyville, and Leopoldville to insure that U.S. aircraft employed in the counter-insurgency program in the Congo are used efficiently, effectively, and within policy limitations established by our government. All of these air operations officers are U.S. citizens.

5. Should the U.S. withdraw the above aircraft, the [*less than 1 line not declassified*] crews, and the maintenance facility, the ANC would have no effective tactical air capability. However, since it is U.S. Government policy to reduce at the earliest practical date U.S. involvement in the air operations aspect of the counter-insurgency program, particularly the use of the B–26 aircraft and the [*less than 1 line not declassified*] crews, [CIA] requests that [Department of State] inform [CIA] what course of action [CIA] should follow in the next six months to effect the withdrawal.

6. [CIA] submits for consideration by [Department of State] the following as a general approach to the problem of reducing U.S. presence in the Congo while at the same time maintaining a tactical air capability in the Congo for the next year to 18 months.

A. At the earliest practical date, consistent with the improvement in the general military situation in the Congo, remove the B–26 aircraft and those [*less than 1 line not declassified*] crews that fly them. We believe, however, that so long as B–26 aircraft are in the Congo [*less than 1 line not declassified*] crews will be required to fly them. Past experience has indicated that only a small number of third country nationals are available to fly this particular type of aircraft.

B. Retain in the Congo twelve T–28 aircraft, or an acceptable substitute, for the foreseeable future. This will be in addition to the six T–6 aircraft now in the 21st Squadron and the four T–6 now enroute from Italy.

C. Recommend to the Belgian Government and to Col. Bouzin, the Belgian air adviser to the ANC, that Belgian pilots be recruited to take the place of the [*less than 1 line not declassified*] pilots, and that Belgian air operations officers be recruited to replace U.S. air operations officers. Col. Bouzin has informally stated that Belgian pilots can be recruited for the above purpose. We believe that he should be encouraged to make the attempt.

D. As Belgian pilots become available from the recruiting effort of Col. Bouzin or the Belgian Government they should be assigned to the 21st Squadron or a new squadron. We feel it unwise to integrate the Belgian pilots into the current U.S. sponsored program.

E. As the Belgian pilots are recruited, increments of three T–28 aircraft to be transferred from the U.S. sponsored unit to the new squadron or the 21st Squadron. With each transfer of T–28 aircraft there will be an equivalent reduction of [*less than 1 line not declassified*] pilots in the U.S. sponsored program until a point is reached where all T–28 aircraft have been transferred and all [*less than 1 line not declassified*] pilots have been returned to [*less than 1 line not declassified*].

F. We believe that the U.S. will have to provide funds to maintain the current aircraft maintenance facility until such time as the Belgians or the Congolese assume this responsibility. We feel that the Belgian Government should pay the salaries and all expenses connected with the recruitment and employment of the Belgian pilots.

If the above program is approved the U.S. will be able to phase out the B–26 aircraft, the [*less than 1 line not declassified*] crews and the U.S. air operations officers, but a tactical air capability will still exist in the Congo. U.S. involvement in the Congo on completion of the above program would be that of providing aircraft and funds to maintain them.

7. To further reduce U.S. involvement in the Congo these funds for the maintenance facility could be passed to the Belgian or Congolese Government for use in paying for the services of the maintenance facility. It is implicit in the above proposal that with the reduction of U.S. involvement there will be a concomitant reduction of U.S. control over and influence on air operations and deployment of tactical aircraft in the Congo.

8. For planning purposes, [CIA] requires policy guidance on what course of action it should pursue in the next six months in regards to [CIA] phasing out the air effort in support of the counter-insurgency program in the Congo.

416. Telegram From the Embassy in the Congo to the Department of State[1]

Leopoldville, June 30, 1965, 1539Z.[2]

4031. President Kasavubu greeted 5th anniversary Congo independence in pretaped radio broadcast last evening. Major portion speech devoted to call for national unity and sense responsibility on part public and politicians, praise of OCAM, pledge of allegiance to Charter African unity and OAU, desire for friendly relations with all nations, particularly neighbors, on basis equality and non-interference with affairs of others.

Brief portion of speech dealt with certain aspects government question. Said that composition of government should conform to "principles of Constitution and political necessity," that presentation of the government to Parliament is personal obligation of President, that Parliamentary approval assures that formation of government is effected not by the personal will of President but by will of nation, and that during the present period of transition constitutional provision requiring government minister give up Parliamentary seat does not apply.

Kasavubu formula on government question should go far assuage fears Tshombe and company re early showdown. We and Belgians interpret Kasavubu to mean that new post-election transitional government not necessary (though this not absolutely clear) and that Tshombe and Ministers can keep seats in Parliament during period provisional government.[3] It would seem only remaining element of earlier Kasavubu formula is submission of government to Parliamentary approval, which should be formality.

In comment to DCM last night Tshombe said Kasavubu's new formula doesn't bother him. In fact, Tshombe said he not disturbed by any aspect speech except Kasavubu failure include praise for work Tshombe and his government in defeating rebels and setting country in order.

Godley

---

[1] Source: National Archives, RG 59, Central Files 1964–66, POL 15–1 THE CONGO. Confidential; Priority. Repeated to Brussels, Elisabethville, and Bukavu.

[2] Beginning in spring 1965, the dates and transmission times of all incoming Department of State telegrams were in 6-figure date-time-groups. The "Z" refers to Greenwich mean time.

[3] During the national and provincial elections, March 18–April 30, Tshombe's CONACO party and its political allies won two-thirds of the 166 national deputy seats and gained control of a majority of the 21 provincial assemblies.

417. Telegram From the Central Intelligence Agency to the Station in the Congo[1]

Washington, July 8, 1965, 2027Z.

Dir 26090. Ref: A. Leop 9903 (In 06673);[2] B. Leop [Embassy] 43 to ODACID.[3]

1. Imbalance between ODYOKE relations with [*cryptonym not declassified*] as opposed to [Identity 1] group is matter of growing concern here. While we should presume [*cryptonym not declassified*] know political and psychological forces at work in Congo better than we, difficult escape conclusion that regardless of [Identity 1] true intentions toward [Identity 2], [*cryptonym not declassified*] in fact have taken offensive rather than alleged defensive position vis-à-vis [Identity 1] and that they underestimating the consequences of eliminating him.[4] Wonder if they not wishfully and unrealistically comparing [Identity 1] situation today to that of [Identity 3] of year ago, when [*cryptonym not declassified*] were discredited in own country, rebellion out of control, and they dramatically saved skins with recall [Identity 1]. Today [Identity 1] has largely stolen [*cryptonym not declassified*] thunder, has "heroic image," fair bit of popularity at home, credit for having put down rebellion, and (in Leop at least) credit for improving supply consumer goods for masses. In view of this, cannot help but think they laboring under an obsession rather than objective analysis.

2. Above leads us to fact that ODYOKE relations with [Identity 1] far from cordial (did our contribution go unnoticed?) and in urgent

---

[1] Source: Central Intelligence Agency Files, Job 78–00435R, DDO/ISS Files, Box 2, Folder 11, [*cryptonym not declassified*] Operations. Secret; [*2 cryptonyms not declassified*]. Drafted by [*name not declassified*], authenticated by [*text not declassified*], and released by Fields (C/AF).

[2] In telegram 9903 from Leopoldville to CIA, July 7, the Station reported that it was working closely with Godley in an effort to prevent the political pot from boiling over, and noted that the basic problem was mutual distrust between the [*cryptonym not declassified*] and Tshombe and his entourage. Both groups agreed that an open political fight would undermine what little stability remained in the Congo. Each group, however, also appeared convinced that the other was out to get them. (Ibid.)

[3] Not printed.

[4] CIA telegram 13571 to Leopoldville, May 24, authorized the Station to respond to [*text not declassified*] recent requests for additional funding by assuring him that CIA supported him solidly as a [*text not declassified*] figure in future Congolese politics, and by offering him a funding program to help defray election costs and provide financial support over the next 3 months. It instructed the Station to make it clear, however, that such payments and any other financial support were contingent on [*text not declassified*] positive actions to encourage and reinforce a close relationship between Tshombe and Kasavubu and that any indications to the contrary would result in immediate suspension of payments. (Central Intelligence Agency Files, Job 78–00435R, DDO/ISS Files, Box 2, Folder 11, [*cryptonym not declassified*] Operations)

need overhaul. If appears personal intel relationship between Station and [Identity 1] feasible, request [COS] pick earliest appropriate opportunity discuss with [Godley]. Suggest this also good time review entire [*cryptonym not declassified*] program and, in view [Godley] statement about [Mobutu] in ref B, [*cryptonym not declassified*] project as well.

3. Queried [*cryptonym not declassified*] today re promised letter to [Godley] citing need for [COS] to be presented early to [Identity 1] to allay latter's suspicion. [*cryptonym not declassified*] advises he wrote letter and had a recent note from [Godley] stating that he had mentioned to [Identity 1] [COS] impending arrival. [Identity 1] apparently observed that he had heard of [COS's] assignment. In view current situation believe particularly important [Godley] to either present [COS] or agree to [COS] call on [Identity 1] without undue delay.

End of message.

---

418. Telegram From the Department of State to the Embassy in the Congo[1]

Washington, July 10, 1965, 12:40 p.m.

30. Embtel 46.[2] Department commends your efforts keep Kasavubu–Tshombe relationship from falling apart at this particular time.

Considerable thought has been given here to method and timing of use in this exercise of threat to cut aid suggested last sentence para 3 reftel. On negative side is question credibility due to our well-known concerns about re-establishment of stability and Kasavubu's sensitivity to interference. On other hand while not always successful, on occasion properly applied pressure has worked. Furthermore it certainly a fact of life that constant Congolese infighting—even among those sharing same aims—is having a bad effect on US public and congressional opinion. Thus further serious upheavals could very credibly affect

---

[1] Source: National Archives, RG 59, Central Files 1964–66, POL 15-1 THE CONGO. Secret; Limdis. Drafted by McIlvaine and approved by Williams. Repeated to Brussels, London, and CINCSTRIKE.

[2] In telegram 46 from Leopoldville, July 7, Godley reported that he and De Kerchove conferred about the sharply deteriorating relations between Kasavubu and Tshombe, and agreed it would be useful to take a very strong line with Kasavubu and Tshombe, and with other political leaders as well. The Ambassador recommended emphasizing that internecine warfare could only work to the advantage of the Congolese rebels and the Congo's enemies, and would cause a crisis of confidence that could hurt the Congo's ability to mobilize external assistance. (Ibid.)

levels and kinds of US aid. It also should be noted that rebels and their supporters making as much hay as they can over Kasavubu–Tshombe infighting.

Department concerned to leave no stone unturned and concurs that this useful chord to play. Leave to your judgment how it should be handled.[3]

Rusk

[3] In telegram 153 from Leopoldville, July 21, Godley reported that he told Kasavubu he was extremely worried over the tension between him and Tshombe and was convinced that if this developed into an open break, everything they had worked for in the Congo would fail. Godley added that although much progress had been made in quelling the rebellion, the United States had hard information concerning continuing rebel activity and possible forceful intervention. (Ibid.)

419. Telegram From the Station in the Congo to the Central Intelligence Agency[1]

Leopoldville, July 20, 1965.

0133 (In 15351). Ref: Leop 0111 (In 14484).[2]

1. [COS] dined with [Godley] and [*name not declassified*] night 19 July. Per previous arrangement with [Godley], [COS] carried most of conversational ball and followed plan outlined para five ref.

2. [*name not declassified*] welcomed [COS] back to Congo and immediately asked how he liked the climate. As [*name not declassified*] obviously referring to the political climate, [COS] took following line:

[1] Source: Central Intelligence Agency Files, [*text not declassified*], Fiche 47, Row 1, Frames 6–10, [*text not declassified*]. Secret; Rybat; [2 *cryptonyms not declassified*]; Priority. Received at 1750Z.

[2] Telegram 0111 from Leopoldville to CIA, July 19, reported that Mobutu told the Chief of Station that afternoon that he strongly supported the U.S. Government position that Kasavubu and Tshombe must both remain in the government. After reviewing the mutual suspicions separating Tshombe from the [*cryptonym not declassified*], Mobutu said he would do everything within his power to get Kasavubu to agree to retain Tshombe as Prime Minister. The Chief of Station informed Headquarters that when he met with [*text not declassified*] that evening he planned to tell him that he had talked with all members of the [*text not declassified*] and that they were all willing to support him. He would also point out to [*text not declassified*] that the present political conflict was based to a large extent upon the mistrust and fear on the part of the [*text not declassified*], based partly on some of the actions of Tshombe's entourage. (Ibid., Job 78–00435R, DDO/ISS Files, Box 2, Folder 11, [*cryptonym not declassified*] Operations)

A. ODYOKE policy is to avoid split between Tshombe on one hand and Kasavubu and [*less than 1 line not declassified*] on other. Such split which now appears possible, could only redound to the advantage of the rebels.

B. Main problem seems to be one of personalities and mutual distrust between the two groups.

C. [COS] pointed out that while Tshombe may in all good faith have tried to work with Kasavubu and the [*less than 1 line not declassified*], some of his entourage had erred in their actions. [COS] cited fact that Mobutu aware of efforts bribe senior army officers and promises that these officers would gain promotion if Mobutu were removed from control of the army; fact that creation of competing security services, and specifically the general incident, had upset Kasavubu and the [*less than 1 line not declassified*] who feared that Tshombe entourage wished to liquidate them physically.

3. All above was said after many protestations on part both [COS] and [*name not declassified*] that frank speech was desirable and useful. In this vein [COS] said (with prior permission [*less than 1 line not declassified*] he had carefully checked all members of [*less than 1 line not declassified*] and that he was convinced that an entente between the Kasavubu and [*less than 1 line not declassified*] and Tshombe was both feasible and desirable. [COS] cited statements by all members of the [*less than 1 line not declassified*] to the effect they wished work with Tshombe and maintain him as prime minister, provided he does not seek the presidency. [COS] added that he fully convinced that the [*less than 1 line not declassified*] as such would be willing to cooperate and he recommended that Tshombe enter into negotiations with General Mobutu, the latter to speak on behalf of the [*less than 1 line not declassified*]. Tshombe had already stated that he found it easier to deal with Mobutu than with Kasavubu in that Mobutu never failed to be frank in his dealings with Tshombe. [*less than 1 line not declassified*] it would be possible to reach an agreement with the [*less than 1 line not declassified*], [COS] was careful to note that he not in contact with Kasavubu.)

4. In making the above statements [COS] stressed ODYOKE policy favored such an entente and underlined that he was in the Congo to help achieve this objective, not to support the [*less than 1 line not declassified*]. [COS] referred to stories that had circulated that he was in the Congo to support the [*less than 1 line not declassified*] and denied them.

5. During the conversation [Godley] and [COS] repeatedly stressed that ODYOKE believes Tshombe must remain as prime minister. In this context [COS] referred to his most recent conversations with Governor Harriman and repeated the latter's hope that Tshombe would remain in the govt. (The governor had authorized this.)

6. [*7 lines not declassified*] and [COS] hit hard on the consequences which would result were Tshombe to resign. He acknowledged seriousness of such a step but indicated that he was not far from resigning. [*5½ lines not declassified*] the fact that he has just brought all of his family back to Leo, convinced both [Godley] and [COS] that Tshombe does not now intend to resign.

7. [*name not declassified*] stated he was delighted with the more than frank conversation, said he hoped [COS] would continue to advise him, and said he would look forward to seeing [COS] again. While recognize this probably polite talk from an accomplished politician, [COS] will make every effort to renew contacts with [*name not declassified*] as often as is feasible and/or as often as [Godley] will permit.

8. See Leo Embtel 137 to Dept (66 to Brus and 52 to Eliz)[3] for [Godley's] report on the conversation.

9. After the talks [Godley] expressed the view that the frank approach had been the proper one, and he noted that [*name not declassified*] interest had never once lagged. Apparently this is not always the case.

[3] Not printed.

420. Telegram From the Central Intelligence Agency to the Station in the Congo[1]

Leopoldville, July 22, 1965, 2242Z.

Dir 29959. 1. On 2 July KUBARK presented foll proposal to ODACID: A) To provide limited financial support to certain political figures who are now or may soon again be in positions power. Purpose twofold: 1) To maintain existing and develop new relationships with persons of varying political tendencies who are or will be useful as sources info or covert channels influence. 2) Attempt influence internal balance power. [Godley] to be consulted in each case. (Sample listing persons with whom relations might be established included [*2½ lines*

[1] Source: Central Intelligence Agency Files, Job 78–00435R, DDO/ISS Files, Box 2, Folder 11, [*cryptonym not declassified*] Operations. Secret; Rybat; [*cryptonym not declassified*]. Drafted by [*name not declassified*] authenticated by [*text not declassified*], and released by Fields (C/AF).

not declassified]. Basis proposal is that such individuals will continue play important roles in Congo politics. Financial support during period flux would ensure continued access to them, while refusal accede requests might hinder establishment productive relationships in future.

B). Transmitted text Leop 9499, (In 91255) 16 June 65[2] with recommendation that [Identity 2] be supported because of high probability he will continue be a most important factor in Congo and because past cooperation indicates he will continue serve as useful and effective channel influence.

C). Recognition security risks with statement of belief funding can be handled securely.[3]

D). Statement of firm belief that unless some form of positive program such as IA above is sustained, ODYOKE options will be severely restricted with each change in Congo power structure. Request for ODACID concurrence or alternative recommendations for assuring ODYOKE capability covertly influence most conceivable power combinations in Congo.

2. In discussions 15 July, ODACID officers expressed concern implied concept of "retainer" for various assets and suggested could possibly accept, on case by case basis, alternative approach of support based on "services rendered." That is, action program for each individual in question. With regard [Identity 7] ODACID deferred to [Godley] but suggested "services rendered concept should be applied specifically to [Identity 7]."

3. In formal reply 20 July, ODACID stated A) prepared consider specific proposals designed attain specific objectives. Requested each proposal set forth objective, amount involved, and other particulars which would help ODACID excercise valid judgement. Also requested [Godley] views on each proposal.

B. With regard [Identity 7] took note [Godley] comments and not prepared concur in KUBARK proposal without further information regarding courses action which [Identity 7] might be urged support.

---

[2] Not found.

[3] CIA telegram 30414 to Leopoldville, July 23, agreed with the Station that this was the most opportune time to place assets in key positions within the Congolese political structure, but pointed out that they must maintain sufficient flexibility to be able to work with any combination of forces which might develop in the Congo. If one individual or grouping were to fall from power, they must still have assets in positions of influence. Thus, the Agency preferred not to put all its money on [*name not declassified*] (or any other single individual or power group), thereby becoming so dependent on him that without him it could not implement necessary programs. (Central Intelligence Agency Files, Job 78–00435R, Box 2, Folder 11, [*cryptonym not declassified*] Operations)

4. Above is condensed quotes formal correspondence and may be shown [Godley] as basis further discussions.

End of message.

---

421. Telegram From the Department of State to the Embassy in the Congo[1]

Washington, August 6, 1965, 4:39 p.m.

142. Embtels 228[2] and 232;[3] Deptel 2520;[4] STR J–3 OM 5730 (June 9).[5] You requested inform Tshombe that due to other commitments and under utilization aircraft US regrets it unable reply favorably to his request retain C–130's in Congo. You should remind him of arrival C–123 which will help fill gap. FYI only. US willing if sufficient prior notice given and in your judgment sufficient urgency exists to allow C–130's which regularly transit Leo to stop over briefly to provide internal lift. Obviously if real crisis occurs USG willing consider request temporary detail one or more C–130's to Congo. End FYI.

Rusk

---

[1] Source: National Archives, RG 59, Central Files 1964–66, DEF 19–8 US–THE CONGO. Secret. Drafted by Schaufele; cleared by Colonels Kennedy and Lang of DOD, Officer in Chargé of Belgian Affairs Jay P. Moffat, and McElhiney; and approved by Fredericks. Repeated to Brussels, CINCSTRIKE, and DOD.

[2] Telegram 228 from Leopoldville, August 4, transmitted the text of a letter from Tshombe stating that General Mobutu informed him that the United States had decided to withdraw the C–130 aircraft that had been assisting the Congolese forces for many months. Mobutu emphasized the grave consequences that would result from their departure, and Tshombe asked U.S. authorities to review this decision and agree to prolong their stay until the end of the year. (Ibid.) The remaining two U.S. C–130s left the Congo on August 18.

[3] Dated August 4. (Ibid.)

[4] Dated May 12. (Ibid., DEF 19–3 US–THE CONGO)

[5] Not found.

422. Telegram From the Station in the Congo to the Central Intelligence Agency[1]

Leopoldville, August 6, 1965.

0404 (In 27046). Ref Leop 0403 (In 26995).[2]

1. [COS] had exceptional frank and friendly conversation with [Mobutu] when he obtained ref info. [Mobutu] greatly concerned by [Identity 1/Identity 2] conflict and appears be doing everything possible to avoid open break. At previous meeting on 4 Aug [Mobutu] complained that his efforts to achieve a political compromise were complicated by fact [Identity 2] is tribalist and thus does not see consequences of open break with [Identity 1] and [Identity 1] is untrustworthy person who promises one thing and does another. In support of latter statement, [Mobutu] noted at very time [Identity 1] was using [Mobutu] as intermediary with [Identity 2] and promising support latter's candidacy for presidency, he was also promising support [*cryptonym not declassified*] candidly [*candidacy*].[3]

2. Of all the [*cryptonym not declassified*] Leop regards [Mobutu] as being far the best person to try to achieve a political entente.

3. [COS] will see [Mobutu] soonest after he returns from Albv [Albertville] night 7 Aug. Will advise.

---

[1] Source: Central Intelligence Agency Files, [*text not declassified*], Mobutu, Vol. III. Secret; [*cryptonym not declassified*]; Priority. Received at 1015Z.

[2] Not found.

[3] In telegram 0497 from Leopoldville to CIA, August 10, Devlin reported that Godley was strongly opposed to Tshombe's request that the U.S. Government support him unconditionally. (Central Intelligence Agency Files, Job [*text not declassified*], Fiche 47, Row 3, Frame 5, [*text not declassified*])

423. Telegram From the Department of State to the Embassy in Belgium[1]

Washington, August 11, 1965, 2:45 p.m.

176. Following message should be delivered either orally or in writing to Spaak from Harriman:

"Since our meeting in Brussels July 23 I have continued to follow the Congolese scene closely. Although I had hoped that the political maneuvering between Messrs. Kasavubu and Tshombe would subside, information received during the last few days leads me to believe that we may be approaching yet another and more serious crisis between the two men.

We have been informed from reliable sources, on the one hand, that Mr. Kasavubu, encouraged by his tactical successes over Mr. Tshombe in recent months, is determined to force the resignation of the latter's government before the Congolese Parliament convenes. On the other hand, we have been told Mr. Tshombe has concluded that it would be impossible for him to continue to work with Mr. Kasavubu and that he plans to contest the presidency.

Both Belgium and the United States, convinced that continuing cooperation between the two men is most important to the immediate future of the Congo, have tried to impress upon Mr. Kasavubu and Mr. Tshombe, as well as other Congolese leaders, their concern in this matter.

However, it seems doubtful that simple expressions of concern will suffice given the volatile nature of Congolese politics and the aspirations for power of the principals as well as others, including the Binza Group. If you share these views, I suggest that Belgium and the United States explore immediately what methods we might employ singly and jointly.

Given the nature of the Belgian and US commitments in the Congo, I think we can best achieve our common aim through coordinated action, since there will undoubtedly be a temptation on the part of those who oppose that aim to divide us in favor of one group or the other.

We have asked our Embassy in Leopoldville for its comments on what steps the United States could best take to prevent a split between Kasavubu and Tshombe. In the interim I would welcome your views

[1] Source: National Archives, RG 59, Central Files 1964–66, POL 23–9 THE CONGO. Secret; Priority. Drafted by Schaufele; cleared by Komer, McKillop, Fredericks, and McElhiney; and approved by Harriman. Repeated to Leopoldville.

including, if possible, an estimate of what actions Belgium might take to this end. I request Amb De Kerchove to consult again with Amb Godley."[2]

Rusk

[2] Telegram 158 from Brussels, August 12, reported that Spaak's response was that the reports he was receiving from the Congo did not indicate that the situation was worsening. He thought it unlikely that Tshombe would have decided to leave the Congo now if the situation was as critical as Harriman implied and he was inclined to concur with De Kerchove's opinion that this was an armistice period with each side watching the other. (Ibid.)

424. Memorandum From Robert W. Komer of the National Security Council Staff to President Johnson[1]

Washington, August 18, 1965, 8:30 p.m.

Congo Troubles. We are busting a gut to prevent a split between our two Congolese prima donnas—Tshombe and Kasavubu. Tshombe wants Kasavubu's job as President and Kasavubu is talking of sacking Tshombe.

Our policy is crystal clear. We've been providing all-out support to both in an effort to finally close out the rebellion. Our line is that they must stick together till the war is won, or they'll hang separately. A Kasavubu–Tshombe split just now might easily cause the whole rebellion to flare up again.

But Tshombe is bidding desperately for our favor. He got hold of Senator Dodd in Europe and gave him an earful about how at least our people in the Congo are anti-Tshombe. Dodd says he intends to see you as soon as possible. This is an old story and sheerest nonsense—[*less than 1 line not declassified*]. The fact is Tshombe wants us to back him against Kasavubu, and we say we insist they pull together, not against each other. I hope you'll say so to Dodd, if he calls you first. If we can catch him first, we will.[2]

R.W. Komer[3]

[1] Source: Johnson Library, National Security File, Memos to the President, McGeorge Bundy, Vol. 13. Secret.

[2] The last 13 words were added in Bundy's handwriting.

[3] Bundy initialed the memorandum under Komer's signature.

425. Telegram From the Department of State to the Embassy in the Congo[1]

Washington, August 19, 1965, 7:55 p.m.

190. Ref: Leo's 320 to Dept.[2] Neither Tshombe nor Struelens has yet approached USG requesting support for Tshombe but we assume Struelens will soon do so to either White House or Dept. Therefore, hard line suggested reftel may be premature.

You should see Tshombe ASAP after his return to:

1. Inform him your departure on routine consultation;
2. Make points enumerated Deptel 201 to Brussels, rptd 179 to Leo,[3] which he has presumably already heard from Ambassador Knight, adding that they represent view of all parts USG concerned with Congo and indicating in passing your knowledge that he has seen Senator Dodd in Brussels;
3. Ask him if he has any message which you could carry back to Washington or anything further he would like to convey to you about his intentions re continuing collaboration with Kasavubu.

Although there some risk Tshombe may assume your recall on consultation result his conversation with Senator Dodd, we see advantage in leaving him in uncertainty this point.

When and if Struelens makes démarche here, same line as in point 2 above will be taken with him.

If you wish, you may depart on consultation immediately after seeing Tshombe.

If it appears that you will be unable see Tshombe within two to three days after his return, you should inform Dept.

Rusk

---

[1] Source: National Archives, RG 59, Central Files 1964–66, POL 23-9 THE CONGO. Secret; Immediate; Exdis. Drafted by Schaufele; cleared by Komer, Williams, and McElhiney; and approved by Ball. Repeated to Brussels.

[2] In telegram 320 from Leopoldville, August 19, Godley complained about Tshombe's "recent maneuvers." He thought that when Tshombe saw Dodd in Brussels he had asked for Dodd's support for U.S. assistance to him and had attacked the "partiality" of the U.S. Embassy in Leopoldville. The Ambassador said he hoped he would be instructed to speak severely to Tshombe. (Ibid.)

[3] Telegram 201 to Brussels, August 17, summarized the Department's views: 1) a split between Kasavubu and Tshombe would encourage the rebels and their supporters to renew their activities: 2) close Kasavubu–Tshombe cooperation was essential for administration of the country; 3) the U.S. role in the Congo had been the subject of domestic and international controversy, and U.S. commitments elsewhere would seriously affect its ability to bail out the Congo once more; and 4) the U.S. Government did not intend to shift to a policy of supporting personalities. (Ibid.)

426. Memorandum From the President's Special Assistant for National Security Affairs (Bundy) to President Johnson[1]

Washington, August 25, 1965.

Here's the *letter from Senator Dodd on our Congo policy*[2] that Bob Komer warned you about. Dodd's meeting with Tshombe in Brussels last week triggered it.

Dodd alleges that State is working against Tshombe, whom he views as the key to Congolese stability. Dodd has been a Tshombe man ever since Tshombe led Katanga province into secession and we opposed in order to keep the country together as a viable unit. He says he thought State had accepted Tshombe after he returned as prime minister last July and we helped him put down the rebellion. But now Dodd sees signs that we're ditching Tshombe and backing President Kasavubu against him. Dodd hopes the Kasavubu–Tshombe rivalry will quiet down, but if it doesn't he feels strongly we should back Tshombe.

The problem is that Dodd gets most of his information from Tshombe and Struelens, his Washington lobbyist. Bob Komer and the State people clued him fully last winter and thought they'd won him over (as he admits in his letter). But every time Tshombe or Struelens gets to him, he swallows their line again.

I'm attaching a point-by-point comment on his facts,[3] but the basic point is that *we have backed Tshombe solidly and still are*. It's fair to say that we've done more for him in the past year than for any other African leader. We agree with Dodd that the Congo could easily become our number one African headache, so we made a major military, covert, diplomatic and economic effort to help Tshombe put down the rebellion, cut off outside support, improve his African image and begin rehabilitation. Now, the back of the rebellion is broken (though one area is still to be liberated), and we're getting down to business with the new Belgian government on longer range military and administrative programs to get the Congo on its feet.

Since the current Kasavubu–Tshombe sparring began in earnest last February, we've turned ourselves inside out to keep Kasavubu from firing Tshombe and to keep Tshombe from trying to take the presidency from Kasavubu. We agree with Dodd that this sparring could

---

[1] Source: Johnson Library, National Security File, Country File, Congo, Vol. XI, Memos & Miscellaneous, 1/65–9/65. Secret.

[2] Dodd's letter to Johnson, dated August 24, is ibid., White House Central Files 1964–66, Confidential Files, CO 52, Republic of Congo (1964) (1965) (1967) (Restricted).

[3] Attached but not printed.

trigger a major political crisis. We also agree that Tshombe is indispensable to getting the Congo on its feet, because he's more of a doer than anyone else on the scene. However, *we believe he's helpful only if he works with Kasavubu since these two represent the two main power bases in the Congo*. Unless they stick together, the Congo will split as it did when Tshombe went it alone in Katanga. *So we don't agree with Dodd that we can keep the Congo together by backing Tshombe alone.*

I ought to mention, since Dodd attacks him, that Ambassador Godley has been a prime innovator and pusher of this policy. He has worked on the Congo since independence and naturally backed US and UN policy in opposing the Katanga secession, so Tshombe may well harbor lingering suspicions. It's entirely possible too that Godley has his reservations about Tshombe as an individual. However, Governor Williams talked this problem out with Tshombe during his visit to the Congo last August, and Tshombe assured Williams that he could work with Godley. The record shows that Godley has accepted Tshombe as indispensable and has worked well with him. He has spent as much effort behind the scenes since February to persuade Kasavubu and his followers not to dump Tshombe as he has trying to keep Tshombe in line. Tshombe in Brussels last week told Ambassador Knight that he counts Godley as a "good friend" and says he told Dodd the same.

Komer and Wayne Fredericks at State had already asked Dodd for an appointment (probably early next week) before this letter arrived. So you could let them straighten Dodd out on his facts. We've had virtually no other Congressional flak on the Congo.

McGeorge Bundy[4]

---

[4] Printed from a copy that bears this typed signature.

427. Memorandum From the Chief of the Africa Division, Directorate of Plans, Central Intelligence Agency (Fields) to the Deputy Director for Plans (Fitzgerald)[1]

Washington, August 30, 1965.

SUBJECT

Discussions at the Department of State on the Congo

1. The following is for your information. Discussions were held on the Congo at the Department of State, 26–27 August 1965. State Department representatives were Wayne Fredericks, Deputy Assistant Secretary for African Affairs; Dean Brown, Director of Office of Central African Affairs; Thomas McElhiney, Congo Working Group; William Schauffele, Office of Central African Affairs; and Ambassador G. McMurtrie Godley. ISA, Department of Defense representatives were William Lang and Col. Richard Kennedy. White House Staff representative was Harold Saunders. CIA representatives were Glenn Fields, John Waller, Lawrence Devlin, and [*less than 1 line not declassified*].

2. *Maritime Operations*[2]

With reference to the Country Team recommendation that two 50 foot Swift boats be dispatched to Lake Tanganyika, CIA described the problem of crewing these boats and stated that our only immediate solution was to man them with 20–25 [*less than 1 line not declassified*] personnel who were familiar with boat operations and specifically with the Swift. If this were agreed to, it would be our understanding that the [*less than 1 line not declassified*] would be replaced with [*less than 1 line not declassified*] crews as quickly as such crews could be recruited, trained and dispatched. However, it was noted that this would require several months to accomplish and that such a time frame was unacceptable in terms of our immediate needs. Mr. McElhiney stated that he and Ambassador Godley had discussed this matter with Assistant Secretary Williams the morning of 26 August. Governor Williams had

[1] Source: Central Intelligence Agency Files, Job 78–03805R, DDO/IMS Files, Box 3, Folder 11, US Govt.—Dept. of State. Secret.

[2] On April 1, Fields sent Deputy Director for Plans Helms a memorandum on the status of maritime assets on Lake Tanganyika, reporting that there were currently on the lake eight craft of various sizes belonging to the Congolese Government. Five Agency-owned craft were scheduled for deployment on the lake by April 5. (Ibid., Job 78–02502R, DDO/ISS Files, Box 1, [*cryptonym not declassified*] Operations (Jan. 65–Apr. 65), [*text not declassified*]) A May 5 memorandum to the 303 Committee reported that the five boats had been covertly supplied to the Congolese Government by CIA and placed on the lake. (National Security Council, Intelligence Files, Congo 1960–1964)

agreed to the dispatching of the craft but was apprehensive about adding more [*less than 1 line not declassified*] to the paramilitary program in the Congo. State representatives present accepted the need for [*less than 1 line not declassified*] and agreed that if assured that every effort would be made to replace [*less than 1 line not declassified*] they would present this proposal to Assistant Secretary Williams. CIA explained that in addition to the Swift, it was our intent to add four seacraft to the four already present in Albertville. Since this part of the proposal was not included in the Country Team message, Ambassador Godley questioned whether a total of eight seacraft was really necessary. After some discussion of proposed utilization of the additional seacraft, it was left that this would be reconsidered. There seemed to be no objection to their use if they are really needed.

2. *Air Operations*

A. Addition of three T–28's to present complement of 12. In response to a proposal by Ambassador Godley and Mr. Devlin that the absolute minimum number of T–28's needed for air operations in the Congo is 15, Mr. Lang stated that although T–28D's are available, they are extremely difficult to come by and for budget reasons it seemed unlikely that they could provide the three additional T–28's. Mr. Lang noted that adding three T–28's would require a reduction in the MAP budget for the Congo. Such a reduction was unacceptable to Ambassador Godley. The matter was left that Mr. Lang would look further into the matter and see whether some alternative solution was possible. He did, however, spend considerable time describing the light aircraft—Cessna 206—presently being tested by the Air Force for use in counterinsurgency operations. Mr. Lang restated his previous position that the 206 or a similar aircraft could replace the T–28. Devlin noted that the [*less than 1 line not declassified*] pilots as well as U.S. air operations officers in the Congo feel that the 206 is totally inadequate for the job to be done and cannot replace the T–28.

B. CIA stated that with the withdrawal of the C–130's and the possible increase in CIA commitments as the result of any expanded maritime operations program, an additional transport plane has become necessary. Unless there were any serious objections on the part of State, we planned to dispatch an additional C–46 to the Congo. It was agreed that the C–46 be sent. There was discussion of the inadequate use by the Belgians of the C–47's presently in the Congo, but when boiled down, it appeared that we must ask but doubted if we could get their support of the air and maritime operations being run by the Agency. It was agreed that at the planned meetings in Brussels with the Belgians, pressure would be put upon the Belgian Government to result in better utilization of available air transport in the Congo. Mr. Lang's office will prepare a paper on this topic.

C. With regard to replacement of the [*less than 1 line not declassified*] pilots, it was agreed that CIA would attempt to recruit European pilots immediately, and that at the September meetings in Brussels the Belgians would be asked to supply Belgian contract pilots for the 21st Squadron. If pilots could be made available by the Belgians, T–28's would be transferred to the 21st Squadron as previously proposed by CIA.

D. In connection with U.S. air operations in the Congo, it was explained by CIA that in view of worldwide Agency commitments, it was becoming difficult to continue providing air operations officers for TDY assignment to the Congo. CIA stated that we would have to find some other solution to obtaining air operations officers who were willing to remain for longer periods of time. This generally involved allowing families to join air operations officers and remain in Leopoldville. A possible solution could be that the air operations officers would be dispatched TDY and allowed to have their families in the Congo for the duration of their stay. Ambassador Godley felt this would create considerable personnel problems. It was agreed that this matter would be further discussed and some solution worked out in the field between Ambassador Godley and Devlin.

3. *Ground Operations*

In connection with ground operations note was made of the apparent lack of unified direction of military operations in the Congo. The unfortunate pay problem appeared to be hampering the Fifth Commando preparations for the Fizi-Baraka campaign and seemed to be the result of mismanagement rather than intentional obstruction. Noting a previous informal conversation with Ambassador Godley on the subject, Devlin mentioned the idea of bringing Col. Dodds (now retired from the U.S. Army) back to the Congo primarily to help out in Albertville. It was observed that Dodds was well received by Congolese military figures Mobutu and Mulamba and could be of considerable assistance to Lt. Col. Michael Hoare in planning and executing the campaign as well as coordinating the operation with the local Congolese commanders and Belgian advisors. Ambassador Godley was receptive to the idea but felt that he should first consult Col. Williams, the COMISH chief. It was also agreed that if the idea has merit, General Adams would have to be consulted. (Col. Williams has since turned this down.)

4. *Political*

Upon completion of discussions of paramilitary activity the Defense Department representatives withdrew, and the discussions turned to political matters. CIA presented the proposition that in order to carry out the U.S. policy objectives of maintaining Kasavubu and

Tshombe in tandem, we should be in a position to fund both factions on the understanding that such funding would continue only as long as each faction worked in agreement with the other. Specifically, Mr. Devlin described our approach as the following:

Contact with Tshombe by CIA [*less than 1 line not declassified*] and in return for his agreement to do all possible to support the present arrangement with Kasavubu, we would offer him certain financial assistance. It would be understood that the other faction would become aware of such funding, and consideration would be given to advising them shortly after the offer to Tshombe. The Kasavubu faction would be funded on the same basis through General Mobutu on the grounds that he is the one individual most nearly acceptable to both contingencies.

Ambassador Godley took issue with the above proposal in strongest terms, stating that he was dead against giving either side anything at this time. He was opposed to giving anything to Tshombe after his behavior with Senator Dodd, i.e., end-running Godley. He felt that such funding would be clear evidence that such end-running payed off and would be an encouragement to Tshombe to by-pass the Ambassador, thereby making his position untenable. In addition he was equally dead set against establishing any more channels to Tshombe either by CIA or others. He stated that he considered Tshombe his particular preserve, and that if anything should happen to him, his DCM was fully able to carry on the relationship. After considerable further discussion, the meeting closed without any satisfactory conclusion. Mr. McElhiney did, however, state that it was the Bureau's position that the 303 Committee should be requested to approve a contingency fund of [*dollar amount not declassified*] for use in maintaining a political balance between the two factions.

The meeting resumed on 27 August. The matter of a CIA/Tshombe relationship was reopened and with equal fervor Ambassador Godley once more spoke out against the proposal to establish another channel for Tshombe to the U.S. Government, stating that he felt that this was not in the best U.S. interest. Further discussions of this proposal did not seem worthwhile. However, Mr. Fields presented a proposal that we attempt, in any case, to establish a controlled penetration of the Tshombe office by providing Tshombe with a public relations advisor. Mr. Devlin reminded Godley of Tshombe's request for such an advisor approximately a year ago. Ambassador Godley stated that he did not look favorably on such a proposal on the grounds that it would not only not be effective, but would probably not be acceptable to Tshombe. After further discussion, however, Ambassador Godley noted that what Tshombe needed in the worst way was a fully competent economist as an advisor, observing that Tshombe had from time to time mentioned this problem to Ambassador Godley. Godley stated that if we could come up with a fluent French speaking economist with a good political head, he (Godley) could offer such an individual to Tshombe. [*1 line not declassified*]

The subject of a contingency fund was raised next by Mr. McElhiney who stated that he had discussed this matter with Assistant Secretary Williams and that it was acceptable to him. It was agreed that all the matters discussed in the past two meetings would be presented to Assistant Secretary Williams for his concurrence, and that if the contingency fund was still agreeable to Williams, the Agency would be asked to prepare a paper for the 303 Committee. The meeting concluded on this note.

Glenn Fields
Chief, Africa Division

---

428. Memorandum From Harold H. Saunders of the National Security Council Staff to the President's Special Assistant for National Security Affairs (Bundy)[1]

Washington, September 13, 1965.

McGB:

Kasavubu and Tshombe have finally agreed to a scenario whereby Tshombe would continue as prime minister in the new government to be formed when Parliament meets 20 September.[2]

While this opens a safety valve on current maneuvering, tension will probably continue. Though Kasavubu seems disgruntled and Tshombe pleased, we don't know how much Kasavubu has given away. Tshombe wanted more power as prime minister, but he may have had to settle for crumbs since Kasavubu had him in a corner. Chances are that Tshombe hasn't given up his long range goal of more power for himself either as prime minister or as Kasavubu's successor.

During this long summer's infighting, economic problems have been mounting. We're shooting for another round of talks with the Bel-

---

[1] Source: Johnson Library, National Security File, Name File, Komer Memos, Vol. II (2). Confidential.

[2] A handwritten notation in the margin reads: "Dodd will claim credit, but steady US/Belgian pressure is the real answer. RWK."

gians on our economic and military programs to get them moving faster in sending out the technicians to tackle these problems.

Hal

429. Telegram From the Central Intelligence Agency to the Station in the Congo[1]

Washington, September 17, 1965, 2040Z.

Dir 43716. Refs A. Leop 1116 (In 53591);[2] B. Leop 1098 (In 52840).[3]

1. HQS disturbed by Ref B plan, which if put into effect could seriously damage [Identity 1] prestige, strengthen tendency other Congolese to join his enemies, and thus cause new flare-up [Identity 1/ Identity 2] conflict. However, difficult evaluate degree of probability plan will be implemented. Request Sta views.

2. In any case, refs taken together indicate [Identity 3] following vigorously anti-[Identity 1] line that hardly coincides ODYOKE objectives. Request Sta seek early opportunity restress importance we attach to continuation of tandem, and danger of [Identity 3] pursuing efforts keep [Identity 1] from becoming president to point where present delicate balance destroyed.[4]

End of message.

---

[1] Source: Central Intelligence Agency Files, [*text not declassified*], Vol. IV, [*text not declassified*]. Secret; [*cryptonym not declassified*]. Drafted and authenticated by [*name not declassified*] and released by [*name not declassified*].

[2] Ref. A concerns plan undermine [*cryptonym not declassified*] position as prelude to his removal. [Footnote in the original.] In telegram 1116 from Leopoldville to CIA, September 16, the Station reported that a group of Congolese politicians opposed to Tshombe (including Nendaka and Ndele) had met in early September to decide on ways and means to block him if he were to run for the presidency at that time. (Ibid.)

[3] Ref. B concerns [*cryptonym not declassified*] plan to create special squad to hinder [*cryptonym not declassified*] efforts become president. [Footnote in the original.] This CIA telegram has not been found.

[4] In telegram 1154 from Leopoldville to CIA, September 18, the Station reported that it was seeing the [*cryptonym not declassified*] almost daily in an effort to push the line that the Kasavubu–Tshombe tandem must be maintained. It was also stressing this with all other contacts, including members of the entourages of Kasavubu and Tshombe. The cable noted that the Station had cautioned [*name not declassified*] and [*name not declassified*] not to use "bully boy" tactics and had warned them that resort to such tactics could seriously compromise their relationship with the U.S. Government. (Central Intelligence Agency Files, Job [*text not declassified*], Vol. IV, [*text not declassified*])

430. Memorandum for the 303 Committee[1]

Washington, September 24, 1965.

SUBJECT

Contingency Authority for a Program of Action to Maintain an Equilibrium between Congo President Kasavubu and Premier Tshombe

1. The conflict between President Kasavubu and Prime Minister Tshombe that has been developing over the past few months could lead to a serious deterioration of the situation in the Congo unless kept within acceptable limits. If it erupted into an open confrontation prior to the successful completion of the impending military campaign against the Fizi-Baraka area, the last center of organized rebel military strength, the stability of the Central Government could be severely threatened. In addition, the Congolese rebels would be heartened and the radical African States encouraged to return to their policy of active interference in Congolese internal affairs. If Tshombe were forced out of the government, there is the possibility of another Katanga secession. At the very least, his removal would lead many European technicians and businessmen to leave the Congo, with disastrous results for the country's fragile administrative and economic structure. If on the other hand Tshombe gained the upper hand there is an equally clear possibility that members of the [*less than 1 line not declassified*], feeling their personal security menaced, would make some violent countermove.

2. It now appears that both parties to the dispute have concluded that for the present at least the existing relationship should continue. However, it is clear that rivalry and deep suspicion persist. Therefore, at recent Washington discussions attended by representatives of the Department of State and CIA, including Ambassador Godley and the CIA Station Chief from Leopoldville, the proposal was put forward and later approved by the Assistant Secretary of State for African Affairs that a contingency fund of [*dollar amount not declassified*] be established, from which covert payments to Congolese leaders could be made for the preservation of the Kasavubu–Tshombe tandem, the primary goal being to avert an open confrontation. These payments would be made only with the approval of the Ambassador at Leopoldville and

[1] Source: National Security Council, Intelligence Files, Congo 1960–1965. Secret; Eyes Only.

of the Department of State.[2] Furthermore, approval to make such payments would be requested only when there existed a threat to the existing balance of power so serious as to require immediate action to avert a major political crisis and possibly another collapse of internal security throughout the Congo. The payments would be made through certain long-established contacts of the CIA Station who from past experience are judged to be reliable and secure. The risk of embarrassment to the United States Government as a result of such payments is considered minimal.

3. A contingency fund of the kind proposed follows logically from the approval by the 303 Committee on 13 August 1964 of a program of covert support for [*name not declassified*] selected moderate Congolese leaders to seek to achieve the restoration of stability and order in the Congo. Funds for this purpose have been requested from the CIA [*less than 1 line not declassified*] fund as part of a comprehensive request for funds for paramilitary and other counterinsurgency operations in the Congo.

4. It is recommended that the 303 Committee approve the program described above to maintain the existing Kasavubu–Tshombe tandem at the head of the Central Government of the Congo, in support of which a contingency fund of [*dollar amount not declassified*] will be established.[3]

---

[2] In his [*cryptonym not declassified*] letter to CIA for September 1965 (dated October 9), the Chief of Station reported that the Station was continuing its efforts to convince Godley of the need to engage in political action operations, but unfortunately the Ambassador continued to oppose such actions for moral and practical reasons. The Station, on the other hand, was convinced that failure to engage in such operations was greatly handicapping the achievement of U.S. objectives in the Congo. The Chief of Station noted that U.S. influence and leverage in the Congo had decreased measurably in the past few months. (Central Intelligence Agency Files, Job 82–005450R, Box 6, Folder 6, Leopoldville, 3 Feb. 54–Dec. 65, [*cryptonym not declassified*])

[3] A handwritten notation on the original indicates this proposal was approved on October 7, "with the stipulation that funds be cut from [*dollar amount not declassified*] to [*dollar amount not declassified*]."

431. Memorandum for President Johnson[1]

Washington, September 29, 1965, 11:55 a.m.

SUBJECT

U.S. Covert Support for Congolese Government on Lake Tanganyika

On 13 August 1964, the 303 Committee approved a large scale program for covert support to [*name not declassified*] and selected Congolese leaders for the restoration of order in the Congo.

Although the rebels have not been able to establish any cohesion or permanent country-wide appeal, the ability of the Tshombe regime to reestablish stability in areas many miles away from Leopoldville is negligible. Main population centers have been captured and garrisoned but outlying areas remain chaotic and filled with marauding bands.

In recent weeks, rebel concentrations in the Fizi-Baraka area (see map)[2] have given grave concern to the State Department. These rebels are being supplied across Lake Tanganyika by Russians and/or Chinese, and the rebel units are well armed and undergoing extensive training by Cuban guerrillas.

The CIA has made a beginning in interdicting this support by the establishment of several boats based in Albertville to harass this supply route. Because of the size of the lake (40 miles wide, 300 miles long) it has been determined that a more substantial pocket Coast Guard is necessary. The 303 Committee approved on 23 September 65 the purchase, transport by air, and armament and manning of six additional boats (two swifts and four seacraft) at a cost of [*dollar amount not declassified*]. The only available nucleus of reliable covert boat operators is presently [*less than 1 line not declassified*]. It is planned to eventually replace them with Europeans. Mercenary adventurers and various Congolese tried thus far have proved disastrous as to discipline and ability to carry out their missions, to say nothing of maintaining the equipment.

Thus far, the pocket fleet has forced the rebels and their supporters to operate at night. The addition of radar to the new boats will make rebel runs more difficult, although intelligence reports indicate the Russians are supplying the rebels with power launches of their own (see picture). Diplomatic efforts to dissuade Tanzania from helping the rebels have not proved successful to date.

Peter Jessup

---

[1] Source: National Security Council, Intelligence Files, Congo 1960–1965. Secret; Eyes Only.

[2] None of the attachments is printed.

432. Telegram From the Department of State to the Embassy in Belgium[1]

Washington, October 5, 1965, 6:53 p.m.

393. We believe working-level talks on Congo[2] served useful purpose in identifying problem area, imparting greater sense of urgency to GOB, accelerating latter's planning timetable and indicating the magnitude of Belgian internal problems which we recognize.

We are sure Spaak and others will not arrive in US under impression USG satisfied with progress on joint planning on Congo. Believe nevertheless "special relationship" with GOB this subject gives us, in our opinion, responsibility to talk frankly.

Therefore, before Spaak departs request you see him to express tactfully our disappointment over meager results Brussels talks. We appreciate and respect confidence in Delperdange and welcome his authority to coordinate Belgian military effort in Congo. We also gratified about enlargement administrative teams and encouraged GOB considering easier terms for one billion BF credit. Believe, however, GOB should give greater weight and more urgent consideration to precarious Congolese balance of payments position.

On military side, with Congolese military cupboard practically bare, a decision in December about filling ANC requirements is woefully late, especially considering time it takes to get supplies in pipeline and delivered to combat units.

We particularly concerned by Belgian inability provide more personnel (1) for air transport which, other than initial provision aircraft, has been wholly Belgian operation vital to Congolese security; and (2) for increased training and encadrement of ANC.

You may wish voice above thoughts to other GOB officials who might be receptive and exercise salutary influence in right direction. Our hope is that in time remaining before his departure Spaak will be

---

[1] Source: National Archives, RG 59, Central Files 1964–66, POL 23–9 THE CONGO. Secret; Priority. Drafted by Schaufele; cleared by Moffat and WE Deputy Director Robert Anderson, AID/AFR/CA Director Richard Cashin, Harriman, Colonel Kennedy, and AFC Director L. Dean Brown; and approved by Fredericks. Repeated to Leopoldville, CINCSTRIKE for POLAD Tampa, and USUN for the Secretary.

[2] U.S.-Belgian working-level talks on the Congo were held in Brussels September 30–October 2.

able do groundwork within GOB to establish beginnings of clearer, firmer and greater Belgian commitment in line with GOB interests.[3]

Ball

[3] Telegram 392 from Brussels, October 7, reported that because of Spaak's absence due to illness, the Ambassador raised the matters contained in the Department's telegram with Davignon. (National Archives, RG 59, Central Files 1964–66, POL 23–9 THE CONGO)

433. Telegram From the Department of State to the Embassy in the Congo[1]

Washington, October 9, 1965, 1:04 p.m.

390. Embtel 642,[2] Deptel 384 to Leo.[3] We concur Embassy's intention channel most of its present efforts retain Kasavubu–Tshombe team through Mobutu who, of all Congolese politicians, has apparently demonstrated greatest understanding of problem.

Assuming that situation approaching decisive point, perhaps in form Kasavubu speech to Parliament, you should explore carefully other steps, preferably in coordination with Belgians, Embassy could take at this juncture to assure continuation of team. If, in your opinion, approaches to Kasavubu, Tshombe, Nendaka, Bomboko or others might be productive you should make them, basing your remarks on previous messages this subject (e.g. Deptels 193 rptd Brussels 212, 179, rptd Brussels 201, 151, rptd Brussels 173).[4] Suggest also that Embassy officers in contact with other politicians who largely supporting players in this situation emphasize advantages to Congo in continuing

[1] Source: National Archives, RG 59, Central Files 1964–66, POL 15–1 THE CONGO. Secret; Priority; Limdis; Noforn. Drafted by Schaufele and approved by Fredericks. Repeated to Brussels, Dar es Salaam, and Accra.

[2] Telegram 642 from Leopoldville, October 8, reported that Blake told Mobutu that the U.S. Government applauded the constructive role he was playing politically. Mobutu said this role was not easy and he had never seen Kasavubu more unhappy about Tshombe. Mobutu had strongly advised Tshombe not to seek the Presidency now, saying he could easily have it in 5 years. (Ibid., POL 23–9 THE CONGO)

[3] Dated October 8. (Ibid., POL 15–1 THE CONGO)

[4] Telegrams 179 and 193 to Leopoldville, August 17 and August 20, are ibid., POL 23–9 THE CONGO. Telegram 151 to Leopoldville, August 10, is ibid., POL 15–1 THE CONGO.

present Kasavubu–Tshombe team which would not exclude expanded government.

We also concerned about Mobutu's report of Nendaka's efforts to turn self and Kasavubu toward Africans particularly Ghanians as means shoring up internal position. Questionable whether they really equipped play this game skillfully enough to avoid being burned. African interventionists would probably exploit Congolese internal disarray for own ends.

Ball

434. Telegram From the Station in the Congo to the Central Intelligence Agency[1]

Leopoldville, October 12, 1965.

1560 (In 71225). Refs: A. Leop 0409 (In 27047);[2] B. Leop 1522 (In 69742);[3] C. Leop 1523 (In 69741);[4] D. Leop 1553 (In 70982);[5] E. Leop 1554 (In 71090).[6]

1. Current political impasse is result, to considerable extent, of ODYOKE failure to play active role in endeavoring mold political events. Per ref A it was predictable that [*cryptonym not declassified*] would go all out to remove [Identity 1] from office in absence of some guarantee of support by a major power. Leop continues believe that it would have been possible to guide them and to avoid present situation whereby there is odds on chance [Identity 2] will remove [Identity 1] from office.

2. Leop's reasoning as follows:

---

[1] Source: Central Intelligence Agency Files, [*text not declassified*], Fiche 49, Row 2, Frames 11–12, [*text not declassified*]. Secret; [2 *cryptonyms not declassified*]; Immediate. Received at 1435Z.

[2] Not found.

[3] Not found.

[4] Dated October 10. (Central Intelligence Agency Files, Job [*text not declassified*], Fiche 49, Row 2, Frame 2, [*text not declassified*])

[5] Dated October 12. (Ibid., [*text not declassified*], Vol. II, Mobutu)

[6] Telegram 1554 from Leopoldville to CIA, October 12, reported that the current political picture in Leopoldville remained extremely murky. On October 11, when Devlin urged Mobutu to work with Kasavubu to maintain the tandem, Mobutu responded that in his opinion it was too late to achieve this objective and said Kasavubu had already decided to remove Tshombe and appoint another person. (Ibid., [*text not declassified*], Fiche 49, Row 2, Frames 6–10, [*text not declassified*])

437. Telegram From the Department of State to the Embassy in the Congo[1]

Washington, October 18, 1965, 7:56 p.m.

428. At opening meeting joint US-Belgian discussions Congo attention primarily directed to political situation resulting from dismissal Tshombe.

Spaak said Kasavubu Parliamentary speech causes concern for several reasons. First was brutal manner Tshombe dismissed. Second is absence any mention rebellion at all coupled with no mention job ANC doing. Third was willingness go to Accra while entirely omitting any mention OCAM. He thought Tshombe had reacted well. Surprised at choice Kimba and considers it form of defiance to Tshombe. Foreign affairs seems to have played little part in Kasavubu action; basically it has been struggle for power with astute Kasavubu once again getting rid of PriMin who threatened take on more power. But one result may have been some deflection foreign policy; this needs careful assessment.

Spaak referred to just-received press reports of Kimba cabinet. Was surprised to see names close Tshombe associates, especially Kibwi and Litho. Wondered if their presence means Kasavubu–Tshombe split is as wide as we had all assumed or whether some long-term deal in offing. As for reaction, suggested we wait a bit to see what develops as there no guarantee Kimba govt will receive Parliamentary approval. Said Belgium concerned by several points in addition to those raised by Kasavubu speech. First is manner Kasavubu action and fact he had misinformed GOB of his plans. Second is question Belgian technicians. Already some of Tshombe advisers being thrown out of Congo. If this extends to men like Cordy, in whom GOB has much trust, situation would become difficult. GOB already reacting against these expulsions and will take firm line. In this case what happens to Delperdange mission and administrative teams? There has been economic stagnation in past 3–4 months, and situation worsening. Concluded with statement we can make no firm decisions now on aid for the future. Must involve IMF but more important make point to Congolese that aid is not a right but given as assistance to serious govt.

Gov. Harriman agreed with general lines Spaak analysis, saying we must study situation closely and be prepared to continue joint efforts in Congo. Military situation has improved and border control more effective with East Africa leaders, such as Nyerere, more aware of

---

[1] Source: National Archives, RG 59, Central Files 1964–66, POL 23–9 THE CONGO. Confidential. Drafted by Brown, cleared by Harriman and Moffat, and approved by Williams. Also sent to Brussels and repeated to CINCMEAFSA/CINCSTRIKE.

real nature rebellion. New govt is puzzle. Essential we cope with budgetary and foreign exchange problems, probably through IMF, and in response to request of new GDRC govt. We cannot allow economic or military situation to collapse. Spaak agreed our assessment that Mobutu continues to be important stabilizing factor.

Accra meeting discussed. It decided GOB would instruct De Kerchove see Kasavubu before his departure (separate cable).[2] Consideration will also be given passing on to certain key African countries our views of new GDRC govt with suggestion they make approaches to Kasavubu at Accra.

Afternoon meeting will concern itself with financial/economic problems and military assistance.[3]

Rusk

[2] Telegram 424 to Leopoldville, October 18, reported that Spaak agreed to instruct De Kerchove to see Kasavubu before the latter's departure for Accra in order to tell him that the Belgian Government was unhappy with the events of the previous week but was prepared to continue its current programs if Kasavubu gave assurances that all previous agreements with Belgium, including those concluded by Tshombe, would be respected. (Ibid., POL 15–1 THE CONGO)

[3] Telegram 470 to Leopoldville, October 26, reported that during the Spaak–Harriman talks the United States and Belgium agreed that in the immediate future their major objectives in the Congo should be to maintain the momentum of the Congolese Government's military campaign to suppress rebellion and to get that government to develop and follow sound financial and economic policy under IMF guidance. (Ibid.)

438. Telegram From the Department of State to the Embassy in the Congo[1]

Washington, October 20, 1965, 8:19 p.m.

445. Reur 730, rptd 357 to Brussels;[2] and 725, info to Brussels 353.[3] Dept concurs general line you propose take with Kimba as reported

[1] Source: National Archives, RG 59, Central Files 1964–66, POL 15–1 THE CONGO. Secret; Immediate. Drafted by Canup in AF/CWG; cleared by Cashin in AID, Moffat in WE, and Brown in AFC; and approved by Williams. Repeated to Brussels.

[2] In telegram 730 from Leopoldville, October 20, Godley reported that Kimba asked him to call on October 21. (Ibid.)

[3] In telegram 725 from Leopoldville, October 20, Godley stated that he did not see any point in discussing with Kasavubu whether it was he or Tshombe who had broken faith. He thought the primary U.S.-Belgian objective should be to get along with the new government and hoped De Kerchove's instructions would be softened. He thought a

your 725, rptd Brussels 353. Following represents items we consider most important this time but their inclusion does not imply you should omit subjects raised in your 725.

Dept believes you should begin your relationship with Kimba by citing past US efforts support and bolster legally constituted Congolese Governments regardless of personalities directing them. We sincerely hope governmental change will not entail alterations GDRC policies toward US. While we will continue pursue policy nonintervention in internal matters, we hope period ahead will not see settling old accounts among political antagonists, thus providing basis subsequent disorders. In this regard, we can only applaud Tshombe's reported pledge of support to Kimba (AFP today) based on principle of respect for majority and willingness place Congolese interests above personal or party considerations.

You may wish to remind Kimba of gigantic tasks remaining both in establishing internal security and speeding rehabilitation of formerly rebel-held areas and on economic side in redressing budgetary disequilibrium and balance of payments difficulties. We believe you should refer to advisability that GDRC call upon IMF for further counseling in governmental fiscal efficiency and that, if IMF responds favorably, he create receptive climate in GDRC calculated assure expert suggestions re fiscal discipline be implemented fullest extent. Future of GDRC may well depend on re-establishing equilibrium and solvency Congolese finances.

You may assure Kimba our willingness continue economic aid only in context serious financial program and firm assurances by GDRC take needed measures stabilize economy.

With regard to discussion of GDRC's external policies, it would seem advisable not to pinpoint Nendaka or other officials purportedly dealing with Ghana, who might misuse or misinterpret such admonishments if passed on by Kimba.

At your discretion you may wish to emphasize importance we attach to GDRC efforts to effect good working relationships with GOB and Belgian authorities in Congo, without however referring specifically to contentious items presently causing strain.

Rusk

---

tough or defiant Belgian stance was not likely to produce the results both countries were hoping for: a more settled situation and military and economic progress. (Ibid., POL BEL–THE CONGO)

439. Memorandum From Robert W. Komer of the National Security Council Staff to Ambassador at Large (Harriman)[1]

Washington, October 21, 1965.

As the toughest Congo-fighter of them all, you're the one with whom I want to share my mounting worries.

I feel in my bones that, just as we close off the tag end of the last rebellion, we're sliding into another all too familiar political crunch that could tear the Congo wide open again.

Tshombe is not just going to sit back and bide his time. He'll probably try either: (1) to gain power legitimately by running for President or scaring Kasavubu into making him PM again; (2) run a coup while his SA mercenaries are still around; or (3) retreat again toward Katanga separatism, perhaps as a threat to get him back into power in Leo.

Meanwhile Kasavubu and Nendaka are proceeding apace to box in Tshombe, and playing with the dangerous idea of seeking radical African support against what they may believe is US/Belgian support of Tshombe. When the Belgians (with our backing) tell the GDRC that we won't give any new economic aid unless it puts its financial house in order this will powerfully reinforce their suspicions. Now Adoula's return adds to the confusion. In sum, a new struggle for power is already well underway.

I suspect Tshombe will be at us and Brussels shortly to back him. Tom Dodd will doubtless weigh in too. We'll be confronted soon with a policy decision on whether to: (a) press for a Kasavubu/Tshombe reconciliation; (b) back Tshombe; (c) back legitimacy and let the chips fall where they may.

The last course has many attractions, but I doubt that it will give us or Belgium the reasonably stable Congo toward which we at least are contributing over $50 million a year.

So without prejudice to our ultimate decision, wouldn't you agree that we should start contingency planning now to anticipate this problem. Otherwise we're at the mercy of the Congolese.

Bob

[1] Source: Library of Congress, Manuscript Division, Harriman Papers, Subject Files, Congo (4). Secret. A copy was sent to McGeorge Bundy.

440. Memorandum for the 303 Committee[1]

Washington, October 22, 1965.

SUBJECT

Request for Approval for Continuation of CIA Covert Tactical Support for the Congolese Air Force

1. *Summary*

This memorandum contains a request for approval of the continuation of covert CIA participation in the Congolese tactical air program at the existing level.

2. *Problem*

The Congolese Government is faced with the formidable task of restoring political and economic stability to the rebel-ravaged eastern and northeastern sections of the Congo. Rebel bands and gangs of outlaws still move freely through much of the area, harassing lines of communication and attacking isolated villages. Relative security exists only in those towns garrisoned by government troops. The area involved is so extensive and the resources of the Central Government in dependable troops are so limited that the use of aircraft will for some time to come be essential for discouraging anti-government activity.

In an effort to crush the last organized rebel resistance in the eastern Congo, Central Government forces are engaged in a major campaign in the Fizi-Baraka area. Even assuming these forces will be successful in achieving their major objectives, we can expect persisting disorder there, as elsewhere in territory once under rebel control.

3. *Factors Bearing on the Problem*

a. *Origin of the Requirement*

On 13 December 1962, the 303 Committee approved a proposal to provide additional personnel and logistical support to the Congolese Air Force in order to give it a limited combat capability, on the condition that the State Department determined that such action was compatible with overall U.S. policy for the Congo. The proposal had its origin in the need to provide air support for Congolese National Army troops then operating in the eastern Congo against Katanga. Subsequent to the approval, it was determined that Congolese Air Force units covertly supported under this program should engage only in flights of a morale or reconnaissance nature. On 30 January 1964, this

[1] Source: Central Intelligence Agency Files, Job 81–00966R, Box 1, Folder 12, Congo, 1965. Secret; Eyes Only.

limited mission was modified with the approval of the Department of State, to one of active participation in combat, to meet the need of the Congolese Government for extensive air support against the rebels in Kwilu Province.

On 28 May 1964, the 303 Committee approved a marked increase in the number of planes to be made available to the Congolese Government still fighting the rebellion in Kwilu Province, and faced with new uprisings in Kivu. The Department of Defense and the Department of State requested CIA to provide the necessary personnel to operate and maintain the additional planes.

The program was again expanded with 303 Committee approval on 24 August 1964, when rebellion throughout the eastern half of the Congo threatened the existence of the Central Government. Subsequently, on 6 April 1965, a periodic report was forwarded to the 303 Committee advising it of a budgetary adjustment which brought the level of support for the program to an estimated [*dollar amount not declassified*] for FY 1965.

b. *Pertinent U.S. Policy Considerations*

It is U.S. policy to support the present Congolese Government in its efforts to defeat the rebels, who have in the past received external support from the Soviet Union, Communist China, Cuba and the radical African states. Recent events indicate, however, that African assistance to the rebels has greatly diminished. President Nyerere of Tanzania has privately expressed his disillusionment with the rebel leadership and stated his intention of halting Soviet, Communist Chinese and Cuban assistance to rebels in refuge on Tanzanian territory.

c. *Operational Objectives*

The major operational objective of the tactical air support program is to give the Congolese Air Force an adequate capability to support, through reconnaissance and combat action, the Congolese National Army in its efforts to destroy rebel resistance and restore order in the countryside.

d. *Cover Considerations*

To reduce to a minimum the visibility of the U.S. official presence in the Congo, efforts have been made to present this program as one sustained and directed by the Congolese Government. The pilots are ostensibly hired by that government. [*less than 1 line not declassified*] The combat aircraft are supplied through the Military Assistance Program. Support aircraft are overtly leased by the Congolese Government [*2½ lines not declassified*]. While these cover mechanisms have served to disguise, to some extent, U.S. official involvement, the necessary use of [*less than 1 line not declassified*] pilots and of American air officers has led to a general assumption in the Congo, reflected from time to time in the international press, that this is in fact a U.S. Government program. However, there has been little comment linking it with the U.S. Government in recent months.

e. *Risks Involved*

Despite the decreased press interest, the widespread assumption that the United States is responsible for the program means that it continues to be potentially embarrassing for the U.S. Government.

f. *Alternative Courses of Action*

In September 1965, U.S. Government proposals made to representatives of the Belgian Government in Brussels, that the Belgians assume responsibility for the tactical air support program, were rejected for political and financial reasons, despite a U.S. offer to transfer the T–28's now in the Congo to Belgian control and to maintain the support facility for several months. Nevertheless, these proposals were raised again during the October 1965 talks in Washington but to date with no more favorable response from the Belgians than previously.

g. *Funding*

[*1 paragraph (6 lines) not declassified*]

h. *Support Required by Other Agencies*

The Department of Defense has provided strong support since the outset of the program. It has supplied all combat aircraft through the Military Assistance Program.

4. *Coordination*

This program has been fully coordinated with the Departments of State and Defense. The U.S. Ambassador to the Congo favors its continuation.

5. *Recommendations*

It is recommended that approval be granted to continue CIA covert support to the Congolese tactical air program at its present estimated level of [*dollar amount not declassified*] per annum. This approval is to be subject to review (1) if talks with the Belgians result in Belgian agreement to assume all or part of this support, and/or (2) if actions by the new Government of the Congo make it inappropriate to continue such support.[2]

---

[2] A handwritten notation on the memorandum reads: "Approved at the 28 Oct 65 meeting of the 303 Committee. Quarterly reviews asked and a consistent effort to cut back wherever possible." An extract from the 303 Committee minutes in CIA files indicates that before the [*dollar amount not declassified*] was approved, McGeorge Bundy hit hard at "the Santa Claus motif" and said he felt that they should be getting something in return for this largesse and apparently were not doing so at that time. He recommended a strong statement from the Department of State to the Embassy in Leopoldville urging "a considerable quid pro quo" from Kasavubu. (Ibid., Job 82–00450R, 40 Committee, Congo (K) 1965)

441. Telegram From the Station in the Congo to the Central Intelligence Agency[1]

Leopoldville, October 25, 1965.

1820 (In 79567). Ref Dir 48684.[2]

1. General comment: KUBARK should not be overly optimistic as to what it alone can accomplish in reducing insurgency and achieving pacification in the countryside. To achieve such an objective KUBARK would have to approach it on a scale similar to that employed in Vietnam. As recognize this not realistic, recommend KUBARK funds and assets be limited to developing ops intel (there is no place in Congo Govt where detailed information on this problem is pulled together); developing access to tribal leaders for purpose of convincing them to lay groundwork for large program of pacification; funding spot requirements (such as provision of small number of arms, key foodstuffs, etc); trying influence key GDRC leaders to launch and implement overall program of pacification (economic and military) and providing technical guidance to responsible GDRC officials in implementing any such program. However, implementation of any large program should be covered by [*cryptonym not declassified*]. In short, covert KUBARK role would be limited to obtaining basic information on which program would be built, influencing GDRC and tribal leaders to take necessary steps to implement program, to providing limited support during early stages, to filling in any gaps not covered by [*cryptonym not declassified*] or GDRC and providing covert assets to guide and assist GDRC in carrying out program. In this respect it should be noted that GDRC lacks qualified personnel and any program left entirely to GDRC direction is destined to failure from start.

2. Recommend marops[3] program, which funded under [*cryptonym not declassified*] be funded as separate project as are [*cryptonym not declassified*][4] and [*cryptonym not declassified*].[5] Marops, [*cryptonym not declassified*] and [*cryptonym not declassified*] are direct paramilitary ops

---

[1] Source: Central Intelligence Agency Files, Job 78–02502R, [*cryptonym not declassified*]/Dev. & Plans, [*text not declassified*], Aug. '64 thru Jan. 1967. Secret; [*cryptonym not declassified*]. No time of receipt appears on the message.

[2] [*cryptonym not declassified*] and [*cryptonym not declassified*] were extended until 31 Oct to allow [COS] time get clear picture of ops needs. Now require Leop views and recommendations for renewal these projects. [Footnote in the original.] This CIA telegram has not been found.

[3] Maritime operations.

[4] Operation supporting the Congolese air force.

[5] Program set up to service aircraft in the Congo.

conducted under KUBARK auspices and, while they contribute to pacification, believe they should be handled separately.

[Omitted here is further discussion of the pacification program.]

442. Telegram From the Station in the Congo to the Central Intelligence Agency[1]

Leopoldville, October 25, 1965.

1834 (In 79991). Ref Leop 1833 (In 79998).[2]

1. Although recognize contingency fund approval by [303 Committee] per Dir 49147[3] may no longer be applicable, strongly recommend HQS approve ref request.

2. As result ODYOKE decision not to engage in political action, ODYOKE influence within GDRC councils has never been lower since departure of Lumumba. Leop now preparing detailed cable this subject but suffice it say for purposes this message [Mobutu] remains almost our only anchor to the windward. Thus, do not believe we can afford risk possibility of his losing his current job or his being discredited by possible revelations of fact he expended [Congolese army] "psychological action" funds to support [*cryptonym not declassified*] efforts to build balancing force in parliament. Failure provide these funds would probably confirm idea which now prevalent among [*cryptonym not declassified*] group that ODYOKE is opposed to them and hopes to bring about their political demise. While [Godley] stipulation that [*cryptonym not declassified*] must agree not to tell other [*cryptonym not declassified*] of this gift will partially limit its value, [Mobutu] would know of it and would continue to work with [*cryptonym not declassified*] group to try ensure group's continued cooperation with ODYOKE. Wish stress importance of obtaining cooperation of [*cryptonym not declassified*] for whether

---

[1] Source: Central Intelligence Agency Files, [*text not declassified*], Vol. III, Mobutu. Secret; Rybat; [*cryptonym not declassified*]. No time of receipt appears on the message.

[2] Telegram 1833 from Leopoldville to CIA, October 25, transmitted a message from Godley to Fredericks recommending that the Station be authorized to provide Mobutu with funds that would permit him to replace what he took from the army's "psychological action" account to fund Nendaka and Bomboko. The Ambassador regretted that Mobutu had done this, but agreed that he continued to be the key to the Congolese situation. Although his efforts to maintain the Kasavubu–Tshombe team failed, the United States had to depend upon him to keep any future government in line and to avoid a drift to the left. (Ibid.)

[3] Not found.

or not ODACID approves of them, they continue to play key role, probably a predominant role, on Congolese political scene. For example, in nineteen-man Kimba govt, [*cryptonym not declassified*] group controls six ministers and one secretary of state and should be able exert considerable influence over six other ministers and one other secretary of state.

3. Please advise if additional supporting info necessary.

4. Hope HQS will obtain approval ref request as soon as possible.[4]

---

[4] In CIA telegram 53496 to Leopoldville, October 26, the Agency transmitted a message from Fredericks to Godley approving his recommendation for assistance to Mobutu. (Ibid.)

---

443. Telegram From the Department of the State to the Embassy in the Congo[1]

Washington, October 29, 1965, 1:19 p.m.

490. Following represents our tentative thinking and guidance on present Congolese situation. Kimba government was successfully and rather speedily formed, it is functioning, apparently with public acquiescence, and may gain parliamentary approval. We will want to maintain influence with government in accordance our legitimate interests and scope our assistance. We should therefore be prepared to do business as before on basis our past policy of support for unity of Congo and legitimate national government in power.

So far Kimba has given series of satisfactory policy assurances; performance is yet to be measured. He has indicated mercenaries are still necessary, he desires improved relations with other Africans, he welcomes African assistance but not intervention in Congo and he believes European technicians will be essential for considerable time. These statements are in accord with our general policies. Kimba appears realistic concerning both internal and external problems, with his greatest merit residing in his understanding of and attitude toward rebellion and necessary rehabilitation afterward.

---

[1] Source: National Archives, RG 59, Central Files 1964–66, POL 15–1 THE CONGO. Secret. Drafted by Canup; cleared by Brown, Moffat, Harriman, and Merriam of S/S; and approved by Williams. Repeated to Brussels, CINCSTRIKE for POLAD Honolulu, and Paris.

This analysis adds up to policy of cooperation with Kimba so long as he retains confidence Kasavubu on one hand and can resist parliamentary encroachments his power on other. While we want Belgians to continue to take lead in Congo and, in fact, to step up their assumption of responsibilities, we would not want necessarily to follow lead they have taken vis-à-vis Kimba because their discouragement with Kasavubu.

With regard to Tshombe, given unknown magnitude his parliamentary and popular support at present, as well as possibility he may someday return to power, we should continue our contact with him and urge him to play game within "role provided for in framework constitutional system."

As to foreign advisers, we cannot deplore departure of some. It would seem advisable for us not to take attitude GDRC cannot expel Belgian technicians per se but rather to use our potential influence in cases of individuals (such as possibly Brassine) whose continued presence of great importance to GDRC.

Our attitude toward Kimba government and Kasavubu subject to evolution imposed by circumstances, but, bearing in mind that Kimba's fortunes can fluctuate momentarily, we see no objection (or alternative) to dealing with him frankly and confidently on assumption GDRC's past policies will not change radically to detriment our goals or interests. It includes impressing on him and other Congo leaders necessity of continued vigorous action against rebels and of financial and economic measures essential to Congo progress. It also includes efforts to associate Kasavubu as closely as possible with GDRC decisions and policies.

Good working relationship with Kimba would also, we hope, help dampen efforts by others to engage in nonproductive, devious politics with various African factions. Mobutu still appears to provide strongest continuity for stability in Congolese foreign and domestic policies.

Pleased to have Embassy comments on above.

Rusk

444. Telegram From the Department of State to the Embassy in the Congo[1]

Washington, November 17, 1965 4:12 p.m.

564. Leo's tels 915 and 921.[2]

1. Dept concerned by implication that Kasavubu's redesignation Kimba[3] may result in strong-arm tactics to assure Parliamentary approval. Chain reaction could be set off with grave repercussions for all Congo.

2. *For Leopoldville*: In your talks with protagonists, you should indicate seriousness with which US views potential for violence. Collapse in public order could endanger foreign assistance to GDRC and increase level rebel activity. You should stress necessity coping with financial and economic problems and rehabilitation liberated areas as essential priorities for all political leaders, failing which we can foresee increased internal disorder.

3. *For Elisabethville*: Trust you will continue watch carefully for signs local reactions and counsel moderation with local officials as situation warrants.

4. *For Brussels*: Request that US concern and line taken be discussed with GOB in order elicit Belgian assessment of situation and steps it may have in mind.

Ball

[1] Source: National Archives, RG 59, Central Files 1964–66, POL 15–1 THE CONGO. Confidential. Drafted by Berlind; cleared by Stearns of S/AH, Walsh of S/S, Anderson, and Brown; approved by Williams. Repeated to Brussels, Elisabethville, Bukavu, and CINCSTRIKE for POLAD Honolulu.

[2] Both dated November 16. (Ibid.)

[3] On November 14, the Congolese Parliament voted to reject the Kimba government. On November 16, Kasavubu asked Kimba to try again to form a government.

445. Memorandum From Harold H. Saunders of the National Security Council Staff to the President's Special Assistant for National Security Affairs (Bundy)[1]

Washington, November 19, 1965.

McGB:

The third round of the *Congo's political imbroglio* has just started. After losing his job in the first, Tshombe came back in the second to block parliamentary approval of Kasavubu's candidate. Now Kasavubu has announced he'll resubmit the same candidate.

Since Kasavubu is staking a lot on sticking to his guns, Godley fears he may turn loose his police to arrest enough Tshombe backers (or even Tshombe himself) to tip the balance. That would force a quick showdown. I think he's more likely just to stall past the parliament's early December adjournment date and ride with a caretaker government either until he sees things going his way or until the February presidential election. Our only indication so far which way the battle will turn is an unconfirmed British report that Kasavubu decided earlier this week not to jail Tshombe yet.

Godley has confined himself to commending Tshombe's restraint, warning Kasavubu's people against strong-arm tactics and trying to find someone in the caretaker government to do business with. The Belgians are staying on the fringes of the fight too, and there may be little more we can do in this melee. Our aid doesn't buy us much when Kasavubu puts his own political future above the Congo's mounting economic problems.

However, if the game gets rougher, we'll face some tough, quick decisions. The hardest would be how to react if Tshombe ends up in jail. Even if Kasavubu shies away from that kind of showdown now, we'll at least have to decide who, if anyone, to bet on in the presidential race. Since the pipeline of our import program is almost dry, we will have some leverage that the Congolese business community and the more sensible politicians will understand, even if Kasavubu doesn't. On the military front, the likely departure of Rhodesian and South African mercenaries mid-December could allow a few limited rebel successes while the Belgians find replacements, so Belgian-US military aid might be worth something.

I readily admit the Congo often limps along despite our worst fears. However, RWK and I have consistently worn our most worried

[1] Source: Johnson Library, National Security File, County File, Congo, Vol. XII, Memos & Miscellaneous, 10/65–10/66. Secret.

faces in State, because this one is worth running scared on. Largely to look as if they're worrying too, they're turning out some contingency plans to clarify our options, but we'll continue to look gloomy.[2]

Hal

[2] A handwritten notation at the bottom of the page reads: "My hunch is that we're going to have to choose between Tshombe and Kasavubu fairly soon. RWK."

446. Telegram From the Station in the Congo to the Central Intelligence Agency[1]

Leopoldville, November 19, 1965.

2385 (In 98411). Ref Leop 2381 (In 98325).[2] Ambassador Godley requests that following information be passed soonest to Governors Harriman and Williams and Ambassador Knight.

1. After a general discussion of political situation with Mobutu on 19 Nov, Mobutu turned to Devlin and stated he wished seek latter's personal advice. He emphasized he speaking to Devlin as friend and not as USG rep and insisted that latter not discuss with anyone matters which he wished to raise. After preface, Mobutu stated following:

A. Both Kasavubu and Kimba have requested he place Tshombe under house arrest. Mobutu has refused carry out this request (it never phrased as direct order). He added that both Nendaka and Bomboko favor this solution and said he no longer fully trusts them.

B. Mobutu asked Devlin if he realized seriousness of present solution. Without waiting for answer he added that current political crisis is rapidly coming to a head and expressed view there does not seem to be any easy solution. He stressed that Kasavubu's popularity is waning but also said he could never bring himself to serve under Tshombe, were latter to become president. Mobutu explained that he considers Tshombe to be an opportunist and liar. He also added that were Tshombe to become president, it would place Congo in hands of wrong type of Belgians and thus would eventually lead to new racial crisis.

[1] Source: Central Intelligence Agency Files, [*text not declassified*], Vol. III, Mobutu. Secret; Rybat; Immediate. Received at 20:05Z.

[2] Reported Mobutu's refusal to arrest Tshombe. [Footnote in the original.] This telegram dated November 19 is ibid.

C. Mobutu stated that on 17 Nov, after luncheon for General Stone, Congolese officers present remained after departure of American group and recommended that army intervene in current political crisis to avoid an explosion. Those present were Colonel David Nzoigba, commanding officer of second groupement headquarters in Leo; Lt Colonel Fredinand Malila, chief of staff of ANC; and Lt Colonel Nonore Nkalufa, G–3 of ANC. These officers stated that, while army wants to maintain parliament and various provincial assemblies in being, they see no solution to current conflict between Kasavubu and Tshombe. Thus, they asked Mobutu if it would not be possible for army to resolve conflict, possibly by eliminating offices of president and prime minister and for army to give central direction to govt formed by parliamentarians. Mobutu added that on following day he met with his senior paratroop officers. He said these officers also urged him find solution to current political problem.

D. Mobutu stressed he does not repeat not wish to stage another coup d'etat. However said he believes it to be his duty to try find compromise solution to current political impasse. Thus, he asked Devlin if he could suggest a solution.

2. Devlin replied that he concurred with the general's view that compromise solution would be required if Congo is to avoid another political crisis which can only advance cause of rebels and other extremist groups. He also insisted upon need to find a place in govt for Tshombe, pointing out that elimination of Tshombe from political scene would almost certainly increase problem, rather than resolve it. Devlin also concurred with Mobutu's views that Kasavubu's popularity has diminished sharply over last month. Devlin concluded by stating one possible alternative would be for Mobutu to select compromise candidate for presidency, one who would be responsive and acceptable to both FDC and Conaco, and for Mobutu then to convince Tshombe that for good of country he must agree to such compromise and accept position of prime minister.

3. Mobutu stated that he would want to discuss this problem again with Devlin, probably on Sunday 21 Nov, but again stressed that he wished Devlin's personal views and he asked that conversation not be discussed with Embassy or Washington.

4. Station concurs that present political impasse is rapidly reaching critical stage. Neither FDC nor Conaco has actual or lasting parlimentary majority. Balance is such that either side could win a narrow majority by purchasing a few votes. On other hand, Tshombe appears to be most popular leader in country. However, Mobutu has repeatedly stressed that he would never agree to work under Tshombe. At 19 Nov meeting he again stated he would resign were Tshombe elected president. Since Station knows of no satisfactory alternative to Mobutu as

commander of army, and in view of Mobutu's long-time cooperation with USG we do not believe that a solution which would remove Mobutu from governmental scene would be advisable. Thus, Station believes it is incumbent upon USG to try help Mobutu find compromise solution. Failure to take this step would, in long run, almost certainly lead to even greater political crisis and contribute to undermining seriously USG position in Congo.[3]

5. Embassy will submit its views by separate cable through this channel, as will Station, morning 20 Nov.[4]

---

[3] Telegram 2408 from Leopoldville to CIA, November 19, transmitted a message from Godley to Harriman, Williams, and Ambassador Knight stating that he believed the time had come for him to see Kasavubu. He asked for the Department's views and instructions, suggesting that he tell Kasavubu that he must not underestimate the U.S. conviction that only a government of national unity could succeed in giving the Congo the stability and security it so desperately required until a presidential election. Such a government need not include Tshombe but should include a strong CONACO contingent with Tshombe's approval. Godley also intended to warn Kasavubu that the United States would not tolerate violent repressive measures against the opposition. (Ibid., Job 78–00435R, DDO/ISS Files, Box 2, Folder 12, [*cryptonym not declassified*] Operations)

[4] Telegram 59745 from the CIA to Leopoldville, November 20, transmitted a message from Williams to Godley, stating that the Department agreed that the situation had reached the point that he should call on Kasavubu. It believed, however, that this approach should be based on the expression of U.S. concern over the potential for trouble which the current situation portended. The Department preferred to hold in abeyance a tougher démarche pending future developments. (Ibid.)

---

447. Memorandum From Robert W. Komer of the National Security Council Staff to the President's Special Assistant for National Security Affairs (Bundy)[1]

Washington, November 22, 1965.

Mac—

Crisis in Congo. What we feared seems to be happening—instead of hanging together Tshombe and Kasavubu are moving toward a showdown. If Belgians and we can't help patch up a compromise we face a painful choice.

---

[1] Source: Johnson Library, National Security Files, Country File, Congo, Vol. XII, 10/65–10/66. Secret.

Tshombe, with all his flaws, is probably the better from our standpoint. All Kasavubu has ever really wanted is to stay in power. So now Kas is playing with the radicals.

The hell of it is that if we backed Tshombe now we'd be going—for the first time—against our principle of legitimacy. We'd be backing the outs against the ins. This might please Dodd, but few others (especially in AF).

Mobutu is the key; perhaps he can force a compromise. You'll probably have a new plea at 303 for baksheesh to this end.

Am going over the jumps with Soapy tomorrow (and playing devil's advocate—it's the only way to move State).

RWK

448. Telegram From the Station in the Congo to the Central Intelligence Agency[1]

Leopoldville, November 22, 1965.

2436 (In 99421). Ref Leop 2429 (In 99075).[2]

1. [Mobutu] visited [COS] briefly 21 Nov. During brief conversation he made following points:

A. He calling two day meeting beginning 24 Nov of six group commanders plus senior staff officers and commanders Thysville camp, paratrooper instruction center and Kitona base. Purpose of meeting is to obtain general consensus of army opinion concerning present political impasse.

---

[1] Source: Central Intelligence Agency Files, [*text not declassified*], Vol. III, Mobutu. Secret; Rybat; [*cryptonym not declassified*]; Immediate. Received at 0905Z.

[2] Resume of current political situation. [Footnote in the original.] In telegram 2429 from Leopoldville to CIA, November 21, the Station reported that the political crisis was coming to a head rapidly. Tshombe appeared to be the most popular political figure in the Congo, while Kasavubu's popularity had diminished sharply since his open break with Tshombe in mid-October. Within parliament, the two major groups, CONACO and the FDC, were nearly equal in strength so it was unlikely that either could elect a president with a strong majority, and compromise would be difficult because so few of the Congolese leaders trusted each other. The Station also expressed concern because, in the absence of U.S. financing, which the [*cryptonym not declassified*] confidently expected after the Chief of Station's return, the Kasavubu–FDC group had been gradually drifting left. (Ibid.)

B. He extremely upset over absence GDRC rep during ChiRep vote in UNGA. He repeatedly remarked that there something rotten in Denmark and that he could not understand how Congo had failed support its friends, as well as to defend its own natural position, during this vote.

C. He repeated his concern re [Identity 1] lack of initiative and commented that latter's popularity has diminished sharply. However he again stressed his lack of trust in [Identity 2].

D. He repeated statements previously made concerning his distrust of the Brazza govt (GOCB) and expressed worry concerning probability that GOCB will endeavor to subvert GDRC.[3] Needless to say Leop encouraged him in his view.

2. In reply [COS] questions concerning steps, if any, [Mobutu] plans take at upcoming meeting in effort achieve solution to present political crisis, [Mobutu] stressed that much will depend upon outcome of his talks. He made it clear that he must use this meeting to try ensure loyal army support. (Unfortunately [Mobutu] had only few minutes and thus [COS] was unable review alternatives with him as outlined para 3 ref.)

[Mobutu] said he believes it imperative that he have funds at his disposition for passage to senior officers. Said these funds would be used to ensure their personal loyalty and for distribution to officers and key enlisted men at all army commands. Also funds would be used to purchase certain personal items for troops in combat areas such as soap, razor blades, etc. Specifically he asked for CF thirty nine million, explaining that he would give CF five million to each group commander and CF three million to Thysville, Kitona and paratrooper training center commands.

3. Leop discussed above request with [Godley] who concurs that [Mobutu] remains key element in our effort to achieve a peaceful and workable solution in present crisis. Both Leop and [Godley] believe ODYOKE should accede to [Mobutu] request with caveat that none of

[3] In telegram 2444 from Leopoldville, November 22, the Chief of Station reported that Mobutu told him that morning that Nendaka and Anany had received a payment of 2.5 million BCF when they first visited Brazzaville to reestablish relations and had been promised an equivalent sum every month for political expenses involved in defeating Tshombe. Mobutu said that he considered this a subversive movement by the Brazzaville government against the Congolese Government. The Chief of Station emphasized the danger of the present situation, pointing out that although the payments were relatively small now, eventually many Congolese ministers and political leaders could be on the Brazzaville payroll. Mobutu recognized that such payments must come from the Chinese Communists or Soviets. He also stated that Kasavubu would almost certainly be a loser in his political conflict with Tshombe, but, the Chief of Station noted, Mobutu was still not ready to accept the fact that he should reach a political understanding with Tshombe and drop Kasavubu. (Ibid.)

these funds be employed to fund specific candidates, politicians or parties. While both [Godley] and Leop believe it would not be advisable for [Mobutu] to pay out such a large sum in one payment, request authority expend equivalent of up to USD one hundred thousand for this purpose. Tentatively, Leop plans recommend that [Mobutu] give CF two or possibly two and one half million to each group and one million to three other separate commands, but to advise him that additional funds would be available if and when necessary. View fact events moving rapidly and could move even more rapidly here, [Godley] and Leop desire have sufficient flexibility to meet emergency funding needs for [Mobutu]. If funds approved, will naturally consult HQS in advance making any additional expenditures beyond CF 18 million if time and events permit, but wish stress importance we attach to having this funding authority for [Mobutu].

4. [Embassy] and Station convinced that [Mobutu's] continued control over army is essential to implementation ODYOKE's Congo policy. Also wish stress importance we attach to finding an early solution to present impasse. At present no one is devoting any time or attention to even the most serious counter-insurgency, military, economic or social problems. In short, the country is going to hell in a hand basket. All efforts are devoted to political in-fighting. Thus an eventual solution to long term Congo problems depends upon resolving immediate political problem. Leop and [Embassy] believe [Mobutu] is best, and possibly only, person on whom ODYOKE can depend to find satisfactory solution. Failure answer his request for funds would obviously weaken his position and could result in his inability to achieve a solution. This, in turn, could leave way open for extremists who appear to be moving even more rapidly than expected. In this respect, Leop wishes note that in its opinion over past year ODYOKE influence has diminished proportionately to ODYOKE refusal to take positive position supplemented by active covert support in seeking solutions to the admittedly tiresome and frustrating Congo problem. Leop convinced that, had we earlier entered arena in covert capacity, current crisis might have been avoided or at very least would have been greatly attenuated. Also submit [Mobutu's] requests for funds may well be our last opportunity to influence outcome of events in Congo.

5. View above, request HQS approval expend up to [*less than 1 line not declassified*] view fact [Mobutu's] meeting begins morning 24 Nov, request reply if at all feasible by COB 23 Nov.

449. Memorandum From Harold H. Saunders of the National Security Council Staff to Robert W. Komer of the National Security Council Staff[1]

Washington, November 23, 1965.

RWK:

THE CONGO

Kasavubu's request that Mobutu jail Tshombe and Nendaka's simultaneous trumpeting of Belgian plot charges now looks like a hand-in-hand ploy to frame Tshombe as an enemy of the Congo. The immediate crisis could still break either of two ways:

1. This first test of strength may already be over. Mobutu's refusal may have convinced Kasavubu that jailing Tshombe now would backfire; Kasa must know that Mobutu is under pressure to unseat him. Kasa's ploy was not phrased as an order and is not public, so he can back off from it without losing face. Reports this morning suggest that CONACO has decided to take part in a government of national union and that Tshombe is talking with FDC leaders along these lines. So the current political impasse could break into a government that would preside over longer term maneuvering leading toward the presidential election.

2. Kasavubu may push ahead by having Nendaka jail him. In doing this, he would risk a coup by Mobutu and (of less concern to him) suspension of US and Belgian aid. He should also realize that Tshombe is popular so jailing him could provoke a boomerang reaction. Even if Kasa decides not to act now, he could continue laying the groundwork for jailing Tshombe when the time is riper.

If Kasa jails Tshombe, our choice will be between simply suspending all our programs and going farther to back a Mobutu coup. We could easily suspend aid on grounds that it's wasted under present circumstances. Whether we could justify backing a coup would probably depend on how good a case we could muster that the coup was necessary to restore constitutional government. In any case, we'd probably end up opposing the radical Africans again because Kasa has been working feverishly to bring them to his help in just such an emergency. We just don't know how tough a combination that would be to beat, though its prospects are ugly enough to underscore the importance of trying to head things off from going that far. So one important job to be

[1] Source: Johnson Library, National Security File, Files of Edward Hamilton, Congo (B). Secret.

done right now is for Mobutu to make clear to Kasa that he won't get away with jailing Tshombe.

What are our choices over the next few months if we get out of this mess whole?

1. We can back legitimacy. This is what Dodd accuses us of doing—hands-off, let the Congolese fight it out. This would leave us flexible to cut off aid if Tshombe goes to jail or to aid him covertly to win a "free" election. But it wouldn't necessarily assure us that the best man would end up running the Congo.

2. We can back Tshombe. He looks like the best man to govern, but there are disadvantages too. The greatest of these right now is that Mobutu wouldn't buy him as president, though the general is drifting in that direction.

3. We can back Mobutu. We could either back him in a coup or let him put together the best formula he can and get behind it. This is where I come out for the moment (as does Godley). He is already our man. He controls the army (with our help). He has shown himself the most sensible leader in the current mess. At the moment, he knows the ins and outs of the situation better than we do.

So I'd recommend shifting our current tactics slightly away from banking so much (as Godley and State seem to be doing) on Godley's talk with Kasavubu. I'd also recommend going back to the tougher line Godley recommended. With authority in hand to talk about the end of our aid, Godley should have a frank talk with Mobutu. This isn't radically different from what we're doing, but thinking this way does (a) make doubly important the case that will be made to 303 (much as I personally hate to think we have to spend our money this way) and (b) focus our pressures on the guy who can accomplish most rather than hoping for too much from Kasa (other than making a record with him).

H.

450. Memorandum for the 303 Committee[1]

Washington, November 23, 1965.

SUBJECT

Request for Increased Contingency Fund Authority to Meet Continuing Political Crisis in the Congo

REFERENCE

24 September 1965 Request for Contingency Authority for a Program of Action to Maintain an Equilibrium between Congo President Kasavubu and Premier Tshombe

1. On 7 October 1965 the 303 Committee considered reference request for a [*dollar amount not declassified*] contingency fund to maintain a political balance between President Kasavubu and the then Premier Tshombe. At this meeting the 303 Committee authorized a reduced contingency fund of [*dollar amount not declassified*] with the understanding that additional funds could be obtained at a later date should the need arise.

2. Events moved quickly in the Congo and on 12 October 1965 Tshombe was dismissed from his post as Premier by President Kasavubu. However, a payment of [*dollar amount not declassified*] was made to General Mobutu on 26 October in recognition of his efforts in support of the U.S. aim of maintaining the Kasavubu–Tshombe team even though his efforts had not been successful. This payment was considered desirable and necessary by the CIA and the U.S. Ambassador to the Congo since Mobutu had used his own official funds in his attempts to stop the break between Kasavubu and Tshombe.

3. The political situation in the Congo remains critical even though Tshombe is no longer Premier and the basic conflicts between Kasavubu and his group and Tshombe continue to threaten to throw the Congo into chaos if some solution to the problem is not soon found. General Mobutu has emerged as perhaps the one man, by virtue of his position as Commander of the Army and his understanding of the realities of the Congolese internal and political situation, who can possibly take steps toward assuring a balance between the opposing political leaders. Further, Mobutu remains the best man to head the military forces in the Congo and to act as a balance wheel between the contending political leaders.

---

[1] Source: Central Intelligence Agency Files, Job 81–00966R, Box 1, Folder 12, Congo, 1965. Secret; Eyes Only.

4. Mobutu is presently concerned by reactions of his senior military area commanders to the state of political unrest in the Congo. The recent dealings of the Kasavubu government with radical African countries such as Ghana and Congo (Brazzaville) together with their requests to Mobutu that Tshombe be placed under arrest for unconstitutional activities while he was Premier, have created a situation wherein the senior officers believe that military rule might be preferable to continued political strife. On 21 November 1965 he made a request to CIA for $100,000 to enable him to make payments to these officers to assure their loyalty to him and keep them from taking any unilateral action in connection with the political situation. CIA and the Bureau of African Affairs with the Ambassador's recommendation supported this request and approval has been granted to the CIA field representative to make an immediate covert payment of [*dollar amount not declassified*] to Mobutu under authority previously granted by the 303 Committee. This amount will exhaust the [*dollar amount not declassified*] contingency fund approved on 7 October 1965.

5. Since the political balance in the Congo is even graver now than in September and October of 1965, it is requested that the 303 Committee approve an expanded program at an additional cost of [*dollar amount not declassified*]. This amount would allow for the passage of an additional [*dollar amount not declassified*] to Mobutu as he requested and also make available funds to meet probable future political funding requirements considered by the Ambassador and the Department of State as necessary to maintain stability in the Congo.

6. The proposal has the concurrence of the Bureau of African Affairs of the Department of State.

7. It is recommended that the 303 Committee approve this proposal.[2]

---

[2] On November 26, the proposal was approved by the 303 Committee by telephonic vote. The emergence of General Mobutu as head of the current regime was not deemed to alter the need for the program. (Ibid., Job 82–00450R, 40 Committee, Congo (K), 1965)

451. Telegram From the Central Intelligence Agency to the Station in the Congo[1]

Washington, November 23, 1965, 2330Z.

Dir 60320. Ref: Dir 60319 1. View [*name not declassified*] increasingly intemperate and ill-advised actions in current political crisis plus growing hard evidence that he and his group heading into dangerous waters in their involvement with Communist dominated radical Africans, we wonder whether time has not come for [COS] to have a tough talk with [*name not declassified*].[2]

2. [COS] line might be that while political conflict in Congo was between two moderate political factions ODYOKE viewed it as internal affair and thus felt it improper to take sides in the natural and legal interplay of political forces. Now appears as a result largely of [*name not declassified*] own initiatives with the left that conflict is moving away from internal politics and approaching a confrontation between east and west. When such a situation develops [*name not declassified*] can easily understand that ODYOKE must take sides. Thus at that point, despite the long and mutually profitable association which we have had with [*name not declassified*] and his colleagues, ODYOKE would be forced to take all-out action against former friends and throw full effective support on the opposing side.

3. [COS] could explain to [*name not declassified*] that his recent actions are extremely dangerous but that there is still time for him to pull back and salvage the situation. If he does not he is lost both ways, since even if his group wins it will do so only with Communist backing and [*name not declassified*] should know full well where that will lead. If the opposing faction wins [*name not declassified*] and his group will have irrevocably lost the support of their former ODYOKE friends and natural allies.

---

[1] Source: Central Intelligence Agency Files, [*text not declassified*], Vol. IV, [*text not declassified*]. Secret; [*cryptonym not declassified*]. Drafted by [*name not declassified*], authenticated by [*text not declassified*], and released by C/AF.

[2] In telegram 2483 to CIA, November 23, Leopoldville reported that the Chief of Station met with [*name not declassified*] that morning and told him he was alienating the U.S. and other foreign governments, which until recently had regarded him as a moderate and constructive Congolese leader. The Chief of Station brought up the allegation that Nendaka had received 2.5 million BCF when he visited Brazzaville on November 4, [*text not declassified*], although [*text not declassified*] Anany might have accepted funds. The Chief of Station pointed out that Kasvuubu would need tremendous funds for his reelection campaign and that such funds would only be forthcoming from the Soviets or Chinese Communists if Kasavubu agreed to take the Congo into the radical African camp. [*name not declassified*] agreed and asked for the Chief of Station's personal advice. The latter said that he doubted Kasavubu could win reelection [*text not declassified*]. (Ibid.)

4. Above or some version thereof could be presented by [COS] as the friendly advice of an old collaborator but would have to be a firm and unequivocal statement. Would clearly need [Godley] concurrence particularly as to timing. Have only informal agreement in principle from ODACID bureau. Appreciate [*cryptonym not declassified*] and [*cryptonym not declassified*] views.[3]

End of message.

---

[3] In telegram 977 from the Embassy in the Congo to the Department of State, November 24, Godley reported that he met with Nendaka that afternoon and told him he was deeply concerned at recent developments in the Congo and that the inflammatory and venomous remarks he and his friends had been making in the press and on the radio had made the Ambassador disappointed in his judgment and wisdom. If the present diatribes continued, blood would undoubtedly flow and the losers would be moderates such as himself. Nendaka agreed that he had gone too far and said he had already ordered the national radio to tone down its comments. He also swore that he would do everything possible to bring about rapprochement, but blamed Kasavubu for his lack of leadership. (Ibid.)

452. Telegram From the Embassy in the Congo to the Department of State[1]

Leopoldville, November 25, 1965, 0638Z.

983. 1. 07:00 Devlin and I phoned Mobutu. He was very pleased with way things have occurred[2] stating Presidents both houses, i.e. Kimpiobi and Mudingayi had already telephoned their congratulations. He had also received telegram from Bolikongo stating latter was praying for his success. Mobutu said he had spoken briefly with Tshombe but did not indicate details of conversation. When I told him of what Tshombe had told us (Embtel 968)[3] he said "that is very good".

---

[1] Source: National Archives, RG 59, Central Files 1964–66, POL 23–9 THE CONGO. Confidential; Immediate. Repeated to Brussels, CINCSTRIKE for POLAD, Bukavu, Elisabethville, DIA, DOD, CIA, Dar es Salaam, Kigali, Bujumbura, London, Paris, Dakar, and Lagos. Passed to the White House and USIA.

[2] In telegram 981 from Leopoldville, November 25, Godley reported that the Congolese National Army had announced at 5 a.m. local time that it had assumed control of the government with General Mobutu in charge, and that Kasavubu had been deposed as President and Kimba as Prime Minister. The Ambassador said that Leopoldville and its suburbs were quiet with no extra police or military patrols in the streets. (Ibid.)

[3] Telegram 968 from Leopoldville, November 23, reported that Tshombe told Godley he had just had a long talk with Mobutu and the two were "in full agreement" about the grave dangers facing the Congo. (Ibid., POL 15 THE CONGO)

He is meeting with press at 10:00 A.M. local and Devlin is calling on him discreetly at 11:30 local.

2. I asked Mobutu what he was going to do with Kasavubu and he said absolutely nothing and Kasavubu was free to go wherever he wished. Also inquired whether among his congratulators was anyone from Abako and he said not yet. Further inquired if he had heard from Nendaka and he said "No, he may still be asleep".

3. We following things closely but I have told CAS personnel, US military, and EmbOffs be extremely discreet. Believe we must avoid any impression we had anything to do with this coup.

4. Have just spoken to De Kerchove who had 09:00 A.M. appointment with Kasavubu. He is relaxed and says has heard of no troubles in Belgian community and confirms our view that all is quiet. In this connection should not aram [*sic*] passed Camp Kokolo and vicinity ANC HQs and could only observe clerical duty personnel going quietly to work.

Godley

453. Telegram From the Embassy in the Congo to the Department of State[1]

Leopoldville, November 25, 1965.

990. Ref: Embtel 983 (Notal).[2]

1. [*less than 1 line not declassified*] Devlin called on Mobutu this morning at 1130 local. He was not observed by press. Mobutu made following points in conversation which lasted over an hour but which was often interrupted by phone calls:

A. Fully understands USG will be unable recognize his regime immediately. In this connection he concurs it would be preferable for USG await action by several African states prior to extending recognition. He hopes, however, American recognition will not be overly delayed.

[1] Source: Central Intelligence Agency Files, [*text not declassified*], Vol. III, Mobutu. Secret; Immediate. Received at 1110Z. Repeated immediate to Brussels, Bukavu, Bujumbura, Dakar, Daressalaam, Cairo, Kampala, Khartoum, Kigali, Lagos, Luanda, Lusaka, Elisabethville, CINCSTRIKE for POLAD, Paris, Nairobi. Telegram 2526 from Leopoldville to CIA, November 25, transmitted the text of telegram 990, noting that Leopoldville was sending it through CIA channels to ensure immediate receipt by Headquarters.

[2] Document 452.

B. Mobutu repeatedly stressed that, in conjunction with army, he had overthrown govt in order avoid prolonged political crisis which, in his opinion, would have eventually led to chaos and redounded to profit only rebels and would have also resulted in major economic crisis. Mobutu further stated that, while thought of coup d'état had been in his mind, he had not intended act so precipitously. He explained, however, that all senior officers in attendance at his Nov 24 meeting had unanimously insisted that the army intervene in order insure governmental mechanism was put to work once again. Col. Ferdinand Malili, ANC Chief of Staff, in separate conversation with Devlin, confirmed decision had been unanimous and none of the officers would hear of delay in implementing coup.

C. Mobutu said that, while he will endeavor maintain good relations with all African States, his regime will insure that Communist influence is not felt in Congo.

D. Mobutu wants create govt of senior party and regional officials all of whom must be extremely competent in their given ministries. Said he had been in telephone communications with Tshombe, who, Mobutu alleges, supports his action. Mobutu said he has not yet decided identity of persons to be included in new govt but indicated he might well name Tshombe as Min Econ Affairs and possibly Vice Premier. He also stated he is considering Bomboko FonMin. He noted that Bomboko has better understanding of African and UN affairs than any other Congolese with possible exception of Adoula. He also implied he might ask Adoula serve as roving ambassador to other African States. Mobutu plans retain Defense Ministry and said he would ask Gen. Delperdange remain as his Chief Advisor Military Affairs in ministry. He also strongly implied that although Gen. Bobozo will serve as Chief of Army, he (Mobutu) intends retain personal control of army.

E. Mobutu repeatedly stressed he is counting on American friendship and support and commented that if his govt fails, it will result in complete chaos in Congo, a situation which, he thought, would almost certainly spread to neighboring countries. Although time did not permit Mobutu to be more specific, if indeed he does know exactly what he wants at this time he said he is counting on American support in providing food and advice as to how resolve critical economic and financial situation faced by GDRC. Elaborating on this thought, he referred to food shortages in certain areas which must be eliminated to forestall further serious price increases. Said what he needs most at this moment is top-notch economic advice.

F. When Devlin took his leave, Mobutu urged him cable Washington immediately explain that GDRC is prepared work in close cooperation USG in effort resolve serious problems in Congo.

G. Mobutu believes he has support of Presidents of House and Senate. Said both officials have promised try to organize parliament in order obtain parliamentary approval for coup. They told him they would schedule such meetings of both houses of parliament for 1500 local Nov 25. Mobutu added he had told presidents of chambre and Senate he hopes create stable regime with continuity and added for example that if things worked out he would expect presidents of both houses remain in office at least five years.

H. Mobutu said that while Kasavubu is free Mobutu does not expect him leave his residence. When Devlin asked what would happen if Kasavubu were to move to Bas Congo area, Mobutu merely shrugged and repeated that he did not expect Kasavubu leave Leo.

2. Atmospherics: Mobutu appeared relaxed despite fact that he said he had not slept for approximately 36 hours. He was surrounded by all his senior officers most of whom seemed tired but satisfied with developments. One exception appeared to be Col. Yamasaki, Kasavubu's military aide. Latter had a rather long face and looked even worse than he usually did.

3. *Comment:* Request immediate instructions on how Dept wishes contact be maintained with Mobutu. During Devlin's conversation with General, Mobutu said he looked to me personally for friendship, advice and guidance. I realize that until recognition is accorded, it is impossible for me to call officially but trust Dept would have no objection to informal, discreet meetings when and if requested by Mobutu. In meantime, Devlin will remain in contact but I do not believe it is wise that this be sole contact for protracted period. Re this point should note that Devlin is as close personally to Mobutu as any non-Congolese I know of.

Godley

454. Telegram From the Station in the Congo to the Central Intelligence Agency[1]

Leopoldville, November 25, 1965.

2527 (In 01864). Ref Leop 2526 (In 01858).[2]

1. Ref reports majority of info obtained by [COS] during hour meeting with [Mobutu] late morning 25 Nov. In addition to points reported ref, [Mobutu] stated following:

A. He sincerely apologized for not having warned [COS] in advance on his plans. Asked that this apology be transmitted to [*name not declassified*] explained his failure advise Station in advance by saying he would have called if [COS] phone had been installed. [COS] just completed move to new quarters. As [Embassy] unable arrange for phone, [Mobutu] sent his commo chief to phone company morning 24 Nov with order that phone be installed soonest. Unfortunately phone not installed until 25 Nov.

B. In addition to requesting food and an economic advisor, [Mobutu] said he would appreciate receiving all advisors that KUBARK can provide. He specifically cited need for advisor to guide information ministry, a political advisor to provide him with guidance and additional assistance for [Identity 1]. When he commented on need for aid for [Identity 1], he called in new chief of [*less than 1 line not declassified*] who was in next room and instructed him to work closely with and to depend upon [COS] for guidance.

C. [Mobutu] received [COS] most cordially. He broke off meeting with senior [Congolese Army] officers and stated he wanted have personal talk. He stressed he looking to KUBARK for advice and guidance now and in future. He added even though he recognizes that he will be dealing with [Godley] regularly once ODYOKE recognition obtained, he wants to maintain close working relationship with Station. He instructed his secretary prepare permanent pass for [COS] which will permit him enter any [Congolese Army] installation any time.

D. [Mobutu] repeatedly stressed he needs help and that without ODYOKE support his efforts will fail.

2. Although recognize that ODYOKE must wait for discreet period before extending recognition and that ODYOKE would prefer have some African countries take lead, Leop sincerely hopes ODYOKE will recognize that, if [Mobutu] fails in his effort bring order out of chaos, all

---

[1] Source: Central Intelligence Agency Files, [*text not declassified*], Vol. III, Mobutu. Secret; Rybat; [*cryptonym not declassified*]; Immediate. Received at 1300Z.

[2] See Document 453 and footnote 1 thereto.

efforts to date will be wasted and Congo will almost certainly slip down drain into chaos. Leop cannot stress sufficiently its belief that [Mobutu] represents ODYOKE's last hope for relatively stable regime.

[Omitted here is further discussion of the new regime.]

455. Telegram From the Department of State to the Embassy in the Congo[1]

Washington, November 26, 1965, 4:11 p.m.

594. 1. You authorized deal informally at all levels new regime, though you should at this point avoid formal acts. If question of recognition is raised you should state that subject remains under study in Washington.

2. Dept requests you continue report as extensively as possible following areas:

(a) Indicia of degree effective control being exercised by new regime.
(b) Extent and nature of visible opposition, if any.
(c) Any declarations or statements by new regime that civil liberties and rights to be safeguarded.
(d) Any indications that regime intends take punitive action against deposed leaders or their supporters.

3. Please report ASAP any actions re recognition taken by other members diplomatic community. Request you consult with your diplomatic colleagues, especially African states, on their intended actions this subject.

FYI. Department will probably formally recognize within one week, if situation appears stable and assuming other states, particularly Africans, recognize. End FYI.

Rusk

[1] Source: National Archives, RG 59, Central Files 1964–66, POL 23–9 THE CONGO. Secret; Limdis. Drafted by R.H. Neuman of L/AF; cleared by Brown, Walsh, and Trimble; and approved by Richard D. Kearney of L. Repeated to Brussels, London, and Paris.

456. Circular Telegram From the Department of State to All African Posts[1]

Washington, November 26, 1965, 8:15 p.m.

1025. On November 25 General Joseph Mobutu, head of Congo (Leo) armed forces, staged a bloodless coup d'etat deposing GDRC President Kasavubu and Prime Minister Kimba. Twenty-four hours after coup capital and principal cities in Congo remain quiet and military presence scarcely apparent. In 13 point announcement, Mobutu said he had assumed all prerogatives of President, and will guarantee continuance national institutions including Parliament, safeguard personal rights and property Congolese citizens, respect all international agreements, continue adhere international bodies particularly UN and OAU and maintain GDRC's adhesion to OCAM unless Parliament decides otherwise. Mobutu also said recent measures against foreigners, expulsions, newspaper suspensions, etc. rescinded and editors of opposition newspapers whose offices recently sacked will receive compensation.

Mobutu announced he will retain presidential prerogatives for five years, during which Colonel Leonard Mulamba (Military Governor Stanleyville area) will serve as Prime Minister and General Bobozo (Commanding Officer Elisabethville garrison) will be Commander in Chief Armed Forces (probably nominally). Mobutu also claimed support from presidents Congolese Parliament chambers and confirmed them in their positions for five years.

New leader of GDRC has announced that "Government of National Union" will be formed by Colonel Mulamba today and presented to Parliament November 27, claiming support former Prime Minister Kimba and his ministers for this move. He predicted approval by acclamation. New government reportedly will be composed one Minister from each province and Leopoldville.[2]

Reaction in political circles to Mobutu's power seizure ranges from outright though qualified approval to wait-and-see attitude. Significant there no known opponents this move so far and no restrictive measures against former leaders, notably Kasavubu, who apparently have free

[1] Source: National Archives, RG 59, Central Files 1964–66, POL 23–9 THE CONGO. Confidential; Priority. Drafted by Canup; cleared by Richard J. Peltier of AF/P, Strong, Root, Ben Thirkield of P, Deputy Assistant Secretary for EUR Walter J. Stoessel Jr., Schaufele, and AFW Director G. Edward Clark; and approved by Trimble. Also sent to Cairo, Brussels, Rome, London, Paris, Bonn, Lisbon, Luanda, and Salisbury.

[2] Circular telegram 1033, November 29, reported that the Congolese Parliament approved the Mobutu government on November 28 by 256 votes to 2 abstentions with no opposition. (Ibid., POL 15–1 THE CONGO)

movement but are presumably expected remain Leopoldville. Former Prime Minister Tshombe reportedly reacted favorably at overthrow Kasavubu, but is less enthusiastic over five years duration Mobutu's position, which eliminates presidential elections scheduled next March.

Mobutu's actions raised internal Congolese constitutional problems as well as question recognition new regime by foreign states. Power seizure clearly unconstitutional regardless how justified it may prove to be in preventing political and military disintegration stemming from increasing possibility of violent confrontation between Kasavubu and Tshombe. Although new regime reportedly will include only two military leaders, i.e. Mobutu and Mulamba, it issues from extraordinary reunion armed forces regional commanders Leopoldville on November 24 and maintenance of regime in power will in last analysis rest upon armed forces. Also, Mobutu will oblige Parliament modify constitution by 1) reducing presidential age requirement from 40 to accommodate 35-year old Mobutu; 2) confirming his own and Prime Minister Mulamba's tenure for five years; 3) enabling increase in number of ministers from present 19 (including State Secretaries) to at least 22; 4) acquiescing in cancellation next year's presidential election.

No state has yet openly announced recognition new regime although France and Belgium have made clear no overt recognition required from them since their diplomatic representation is to state rather than to GDRC. African reaction slow in developing. Noting Mobutu's effective control of machinery of government, apparent lack overt opposition, reported pledges of support from leaders both houses of Parliament, restoration free press, failure so far to take punitive action against former leaders, and announcement new government will respect all African and international agreements, Department will maintain discreet and informal contacts with new leaders pending completion our study this question.

Dept answering press inquiries by saying USG following events closely, studying question recognition, and was not involved in coup or informed in advance.[3]

Rusk

---

[3] The United States recognized the Mobutu government on December 7.

457. Telegram From the Central Intelligence Agency to the Station in the Congo[1]

Washington, November 26, 1965, 2023Z.

Dir 60858. Ref: Para 5 Leop 2527 (In 01864) et al.[2]

1. Wish commend [COS] and Station for outstanding coverage and handling current situation.

2. Understand ODACID has approved [Godley] discreet unofficial contact with [Mobutu] but that they prefer avoid too hasty recognition. Initial informal KUBARK reaction is to support [Mobutu] to utmost. At same time do not wish prejudice [Mobutu] govt chances of success by too open PBPRIME involvement. Must recognize radical Africans, [*cryptonym not declassified*], and certain Belgian advisors will be out to assure [Mobutu] failure. Thus must proceed carefully in what presently appears welcome development and favorable atmosphere.

3. Specifically, consider that added funds for [Mobutu] more applicable now than ever and hope we'll have approval 26 Nov.[3] However, in anticipation of any possible desire have [Godley] views prior final decision, would be helpful have [Godley] recommendation to support position.[4] FYI: KUBARK has proposed to [303 Committee] with ODACID concurrence adding [*dollar amount not declassified*] to previously approved [*dollar amount not declassified*] contingency fund.

4. Advise [Identity 1] reaction and likely role new govt.[5]

---

[1] Source: Central Intelligence Agency Files, [*text not declassified*], Vol. III, Mobutu. Secret; Priority. Drafted and authenticated by [*name not declassified*], coordinated with Waller (AC/AF), and released by [*name not declassified*].

[2] See Document 454; paragraph 5 is not printed.

[3] See Document 450.

[4] Telegram 2561 from Leopoldville to CIA, November 26, reported that the Chief of Station had discussed this with Godley, who heartily concurred in the advisability of adding [*dollar amount not declassified*] to the previously approved [*dollar amount not declassified*] contingency fund. (Central Intelligence Agency Files, [*text not declassified*], Vol. III, Mobutu)

[5] Telegram 2559 from Leopoldville to CIA, November 26, reported that the Chief of Station had [*text not declassified*] impression that the coup had caught Nendaka by surprise, but he had rallied in support of Mobutu, [*text not declassified*] seemed delighted by the fact that the coup apparently was succeeding. The Chief of Station also reported that Mobutu had asked him whether he thought Nendaka should be maintained in his current position, and that he had suggested that he see if the Congolese army would support this. (Ibid., [*text not declassified*], Vol. IV, [*text not declassified*])

458. Telegram From the Department of State to the Embassy in Belgium[1]

Washington, December 1, 1965, 7:21 p.m.

696. Leo's 1028 repeated Brussels 551.[2] De Kerchove's views reported reftel show realistic appraisal potential for positive Belgian action in Congo as well as inherent pitfalls. Reports from Leo give us cause for concern about Delperdange's ability walk tricky tightrope Congolese politics.

Therefore keeping in mind caveats expressed para 6 reftel[3] and our desire not to get involved in question Delperdange's effectiveness Embassy Brussels requested express USG views to GOB, preferably Spaak, along following lines:

1. Assumption of power by Mobutu may be last real opportunity in short-run for Congo to gain political stability which has eluded it since 1960. Welcome given Mobutu coup shows basic awareness by Congolese politicians that country tired of instability;

2. However politicians out of power cannot be expected in long run accept system which denies them fruits of power. Over period of time opposition to present regime will probably build, possibly making Mobutu, unless he able to strike balance and adjustment with most political groups, revert to increasing repressive measures;

3. Therefore it seems important that regime make good start, within limitations its present resources, to resolve outstanding problems or begin to do so;

4. GOB appears to have unparalleled opportunity with maximum Congolese cooperation to make constructive contribution to resolution security, administrative, economic and financial problems;

5. US hopes therefore that GOB can show maximum flexibility in meeting needs for technical, economic and military assistance to present government. In many ways military assistance in terms increased number military advisors, which apparently desired by Mobutu, is easiest method of assistance. Although we believe ceiling on

---

[1] Source: National Archives, RG 59, Central Files 1964–66, POL 23–9 THE CONGO. Confidential; Limdis. Drafted by Schaufele; cleared by Brown, Moffat, and Stearns; and approved by Williams. Repeated to Leopoldville and CINCSTRIKE.

[2] In telegram 1028 from Leopoldville, November 28, Godley reported that De Kerchove was desperately worried about the situation in the Congo because Mobutu was looking to Belgium for assistance and he feared that Belgium might not come through. (Ibid.)

[3] In paragraph 6, Godley reported that De Kerchove had spoken to him frankly and in confidence, but that he had told Spaak he would be discussing his views with Godley.

numbers Belgian military personnel should be raised we suggest this should be gradual process. Too rapid build-up would not only give Belgium bad image Congo and elsewhere but in long run also make Mobutu vulnerable to domestic and international criticism. More fundamental method help Congo probably lies in field technical assistance especially strengthening administrative teams. Finally balance of payments assistance (including but not restricted to proposed $20 million credit) is needed to fill FX gap and contribute to stability we seek for Congo. Latter, we realize, is predicated on more effective performance by GDRC in putting financial house into better order;

6. In summary we believe GOB should seize opportunity offered it to be forthcoming toward reasonable, realistic, well documented requests for assistance. At same time it would be best avoid precipitous action which could be interpreted as Belgian re-colonization or neocolonialism.[4]

Rusk

[4] In telegram 655 from Brussels, December 3, Knight reported that he had given Spaak a full rundown on Washington's thinking concerning the new situation in the Congo as reflected in this telegram. Spaak stated that he concurred in the basic thrust of the Department's assessment, although he did not comment directly on specifics. He said he had sent a warm letter to Mobutu. The Mobutu government represented a last chance and every effort must be made to take advantage of it. (National Archives, RG 59, Central Files 1964–66, POL 23–9 THE CONGO)

459. Dispatch From the Station in the Congo to the Central Intelligence Agency[1]

[*Dispatch number not declassified*]. Leopoldville, December 13, 1965.

SUBJECT

[*cryptonym not declassified*] Letter for October and November 1965

1. Although the Leopoldville Station continued to work on many fronts, particularly in support of paramilitary operations, it concentrated on the political crisis which became more critical during the

[1] Source: Central Intelligence Agency Files, Job 82–00450R, DDO/AF, AF/DIV Historical Files, Box 6, Folder 6, Leopoldville, 3 Feb 54–Dec 65, [*cryptonym not declassified*]. Secret; Rybat.

months of October and November. The Station preached moderation to its numerous political contacts but it proved impossible to control the game. As noted in [*less than 1 line not declassified*][2] from this Station, ODACID's decision not to permit Leopoldville to engage in political action greatly handicapped the Station in its efforts to support ODYOKE objectives.

2. The coup d'etat of 25 November 1965 resolved, at least temporarily, the political crisis which had resulted in a complete breakdown in governmental functions and which, had it continued, would almost certainly have led to even greater chaos. We believe the successful coup d'etat represents the best possible solution to a problem which placed ODYOKE's objectives in Africa in serious jeopardy. The Mobutu regime represents the best government which ODYOKE might expect to obtain. Mobutu is moderate and pro-West in his outlook; our relationship with him is good and he is generally willing to accept advice. On the debit side, however, the Station, the Embassy and most knowledgeable Belgian and Congolese observers here are of the opinion that the Mobutu government represents the last hope for the West in the Congo (and possibly throughout Black Africa). There is little chance that, should his regime fail, it will be replaced by a regime acceptable to the West. Should he fail, we believe it more than probable that the Congo would split into a number of small client states, some of which would fall under Bloc influence. Few, if any, of these states would be economically viable and many would be in conflict, one with the other. Thus, Leopoldville believes that all ODYOKE agencies should do everything possible to ensure the success of the Mobutu regime. The Station has already made a number of recommendations, particularly as concerns the provision of advisors, and further recommendations will be forthcoming.

3. In summation the Station believes that Mobutu's coup d'etat represented the only feasible solution to the political crisis. It provides ODYOKE with time to try, in cooperation with the Congolese Government, to find solutions to the nearly insoluble Congo problem. The Station does not believe that the solutions will be facile. KUBARK must be prepared to take the initiative and to engage in a major effort which, if it fails, would almost certainly result in defeat of ODYOKE objectives in the Congo and, probably, in most of Black Africa. However, the final outcome will not depend upon KUBARK alone. If other ODYOKE agencies fail to take decisive action or if the Congolese themselves are unable or unwilling to take the necessary steps, a new and even more serious crisis will develop. In view of the foregoing, the Leopoldville Station is devoting considerable time and energy to [*less than 1 line not*

[2] Not found.

declassified] operations designed to provide early warning, should the opposition try to launch another coup d'etat. These operations also are designed to provide ODYOKE with operational intelligence. In addition, the Station is emphasizing its [*cryptonym not declassified*] operations in an effort to shore up and assist the present government.

[COS]

460. Information Memorandum From the Deputy Director of the Office of Central African Affairs (Schaufele) to the Assistant Secretary of State for African Affairs (Williams)[1]

Washington, December 27, 1965.

SUBJECT

Status of the Congo (L) Rebellion

The launching of a military campaign last September against the large rebel concentration in the Fizi area was expected to end the last major rebel threat to the country as a whole. Still in progress, the campaign has been successful in recapturing key towns and dispersing rebel forces. Nevertheless, recent reports from the Congo indicate significant rebel activity in the region around Albertville, the Northeast sector, and the Stanleyville area. Locations of rebel strength and activity are marked on the attached map[2] and described in some detail below.

In the Northeast sector alone, the number of rebels has been reported to be as high as 17,500, grouped in about ten locations. Further west, the cities of Ango and Bondo are still in rebel hands. To the south, the area between Buta and Banalia is infested with rebels and has recently been the scene of sharp battles. During the period December 12–18 in this area, the ANC killed 23 rebels and took 84 prisoners. The ANC suffered at least seven dead and 18 wounded. Rebel discipline and determination in this area and the Stanleyville region are reported to be increasing. The ANC lost seven men in recent fighting within 15

---

[1] Source: National Archives, RG 59, Central Files 1964–66, POL 23–9 THE CONGO. Secret. Drafted by Berlind and sent through Fredericks. The memorandum contains several handwritten revisions by an unidentified person who may have used it as the basis for a briefing paper.

[2] Not reproduced.

miles of Stanleyville, and rebel bands continue to infiltrate into the suburbs of the city.

The area where rebels have been most active is located to the west of Albertville. In contrast to other areas where the rebels usually confine themselves to defensive action and ambushing patrols, rebel groups in the Albertville area have been attacking ANC positions and displaying a high degree of sophistication, most notably in the destruction of two solid bridges and use of mines to sabotage railway lines. An ANC communiqué reported that 150 rebels were killed in a pitched battle on December 2 just 25 miles south of Bukavu on the Rwandan border.

Rebels in all areas usually do not possess enough weapons to arm every man, but they have been effectively using automatic rifles, mortars, and mines in addition to the traditional "poo-poo" guns. Although Gbenye, Soumialot and Olenga are generally discredited, rebel field leadership seems to be improving, as evidenced by increased discipline, sophisticated tactics, and improved morale. Foreign advisory assistance is probably a factor, but none of the Cubans alleged to accompany rebel forces in the East has been captured. Support from neighboring countries has diminished considerably over the past several months, but there are still unconfirmed reports of rebel movements in Tanzania and large groups of armed rebels in the southern Sudan. In addition to Rwandan Tutsis, some Burundi nationals have been involved in the fighting in the Bukavu–Fizi region.

The ability of the ANC to defeat or even contain the rebels will depend, as always, upon outside leadership. There are currently some 750 mercenaries in the Congo. Many of these are ineffective, and approximately 100 contracts will expire before March 15. Ambassador Godley has suggested that we consult with the Belgians and perhaps the British on ways of finding replacements for departing mercenaries.

461. Memorandum From the Director of the Office of Central African Affairs (Brown) to the Assistant Secretary of State for African Affairs (Williams)[1]

Washington, January 28, 1966.

SUBJECT

Situation and Outlook in the Democratic Republic of the Congo

General Joseph Mobutu's assumption of power on November 25 stemmed from the increasingly dangerous confrontation between President Kasavubu and Prime Minister Tshombe following the latter's dismissal, October 13, by Kasavubu. Kasavubu named Evariste Kimba as Prime Minister-Designate but the latter was defeated in the Congolese Parliament owing to the opposition of Tshombe and his substantial following. Kasavubu's reappointment of Kimba, coupled with the efforts of members of Kimba's government to discredit Tshombe and his followers, rapidly led to political tension and mounting crisis. General Mobutu, considering the situation dangerous for the country, decided, with his senior officers, to seize power and depose both the President and the government-designate. He named Colonel, now General, Mulamba as Prime Minister, suspended certain provisions of the Constitution, and declared that his government and the national Parliament would sit in for five years.

Mobutu instituted government by decree with the tacit approval of Parliament. His declared program is to substitute hard work and unity of purpose in the reconstruction of the rebellion-devastated country and the rehabilitation of its economy in place of political maneuvering, corruption and lack of direction. While obviously sincere, it is too early to discern where Mobutu will draw the line between corruption and the "normal" use of payments and patronage to facilitate governmental operations. His declarations on behalf of better government and improved popular morale have been ringing, and have been accepted thus far with little visible opposition. Many persons are still grateful that his seizure of power resolved a dangerous situation which appeared to threaten the Congo's existence. The accent is presently on hard work and determination rather than unrest and uncertainty. Rebel activity, while far from dead, has declined.

The principal conclusion is that, in fairness to the new regime, it is too early to predict its success or failure. Mobutu's motivation appears

---

[1] Source: National Archives, RG 59, AF Files: Lot 69 D 118, POL 2–5 Information Summaries 1966. Secret. Drafted by Canup.

quite different from that of the run of Congolese politicians of the last five years. Mobutu's political sense should, hopefully, lead him to pull back from the pitfalls inherent in certain ill-advised decrees aimed at conserving foreign exchange, slashing government expenditures, and sending urban employment back home to assist in his agricultural improvement program. Nevertheless, the following are possible trends:

1. The General's army-led regime could lead to the exclusion of civilian leaders and the withering away of opposition parties;

2. Resistance to the Government could grow among civil servants whose perquisites and power have been reduced, as well as among the population wearying of measures involving austerity, hard work and discipline;

3. The major role assigned to the military could lead to factionalism and competition for political power both among senior officers close to the seat of power and among middle grade officers tasting political power for the first time;

4. Mobutu's over-reliance on Belgian advisors, primarily military, could lead to charges of the regime's manipulation by foreign, European interests, despite present trends in the regime toward an accentuation of Congolese nationalism;

5. The political leaders, especially Moise Tshombe who is apparently the principal opponent of the regime, may become active against Mobutu, leading to an open contest for power involving the General's supporters and Tshombe's broad parliamentary and popular following or a political coalition of varying groups seeking power.

---

462. Memorandum for the 303 Committee[1]

Washington, February 5, 1966.

SUBJECT

Request for Approval to Continue [*less than 1 line not declassified*] Maritime, Air and Covert Funding Operations in the Congo

1. *Summary*

This memorandum recommends that:

---

[1] Source: Central Intelligence Agency Files, Job 81–00966R, Box 1, Folder 12, Congo, 1966. Secret; Eyes Only.

(1) [*less than 1 line not declassified*] maritime activities in the Congo be maintained at their present level through 30 June 1966, after which [*less than 1 line not declassified*] participation would be sharply reduced. The reduction may be possible earlier (and would then be greater) if even before that date the Congolese Government accepts responsibility for crewing the boats. The expected level of expenditure for CY 1966 is [*dollar amount not declassified*].

(2) The [*less than 1 line not declassified*] air program be continued through CY 1966 at an expected level of expenditure of [*dollar amount not declassified*].

(3) Supplementary authorization for [*less than 1 line not declassified*] covert funding activities in CY 1966 be granted in the amount of [*dollar amount not declassified*].

The objective of these programs, at an estimated total cost for CY 1966 of [*dollar amount not declassified*], is to strengthen the pro-Western regime of General Joseph Mobutu and to provide further needed support to the Congolese Government in its efforts to stamp out the rebellion and restore order in its aftermath.

The air program will be reviewed quarterly (the next review to take place in May 1966), with the intent of reducing its level wherever feasible, consistent with U.S. interests at the time. At present, no feasible alternative to its continuation is seen. Following the Belgian Government's refusal to fund the tactical air program in the Congo, reiterated at recent U.S.-Belgian talks in Brussels, the U.S. Ambassador to the Congo has expressed his deep concern lest the air operation be phased out precipitously or appreciably reduced in the coming months.

2. *Problem*

Despite the continuing defeats suffered by rebel military forces and the disarray of the rebel leadership, the Congolese Government has not been able to reestablish administrative control and consequently the free movement of commerce in much of the area once overrun by the rebels. Rebel bands are still active in the northeastern and eastern Congo and, in the latter area, north of Albertville, still mount successful ambushes and other harrassing actions against Central Government forces. There are large groups of rebels in the southern Sudan, Uganda, Burundi and Tanzania. The governments of the Sudan, Tanzania and Uganda have officially ceased active support of rebel efforts to mount offensive action within the Congo and have taken steps to suppress rebel military activity based on their territories. However, as late as November 1965, a small action was fought at night between boats belonging to the [*less than 1 line not declassified*] maritime unit on Lake Tanganyika and rebel boats approaching the Congo from the Tanzanian shore.

In January 1966, there were reliable reports of Congolese rebel activity based in Uganda and directed against the Congo, and during this same month, the growing radical-Tutsi influence over the Burundi Government has raised the very real possibility of a renewal of significant Chinese Communist influence in Bujumbura, including the reopening of their Embassy which served in 1964 as one of the major sources of aid to rebels operating in the eastern Congo.

Of real importance and apart from continuing rebel military activity and the possibility of renewed Chinese Communist or other Bloc support is the failure of the Congolese Government, to date, to take effective action directed at the political, economic and social factors that were the principal causes of the rebellion. On 25 November 1965, fearing that the conflict between then President Kasavubu and former Premier Moise Tshombe threatened political chaos and the loss of all the gains recently made against the rebels, Congolese National Army Commander-in-Chief General Mobutu seized power. He thus provided the Congo with what many informed observers believe to be its last chance to resolve its problems in the framework of a unified nation under a pro-Western government.

3. *Factors bearing on the problem*

a. *Origin of the Requirement*

The [*less than 1 line not declassified*] maritime, air and covert political funding operations in the Congo have been carried out at the request of the Department of State and the Ambassador and with the approval of the 303 Committee. The Ambassador at Leopoldville and the Bureau of African Affairs of the Department of State have recommended a continuation of these operations at the levels indicated in the initial paragraph above.

b. *Relationship to Previous 303 Committee Actions*

On 23 September 1965, the 303 Committee approved a proposal, presented in a status report on the Lake Tanganyika maritime interdiction program, dated 21 September 1965, to add two armed, radar-equipped, 50-foot high-speed boats (Swifts) and up to five smaller boats (Seacrafts) to the existing limited maritime capability at Albertville. The Committee also approved the initial manning of these boats by [*less than 1 line not declassified*] crews, with the understanding that the [*less than 1 line not declassified*] would be replaced by other third-country nationals as soon as qualified personnel became available.

On 28 October 1965, the Committee approved the continuation of [*less than 1 line not declassified*] covert tactical support for the Congolese Air Force at an annual level of [*dollar amount not declassified*], but requested quarterly reviews and a sustained effort to modify and cut back whenever possible.

On 26 November 1965, the Committee approved a request for [*dollar amount not declassified*] to meet existing and potential appeals for funds by General Mobutu.

c. *Accomplishments*

(1) *The maritime program*

The maritime program now consists of the two Swifts (which have been in operation on Lake Tanganyika since the first week of November), six Seacraft, and the *Ermens*, a 75-foot diesel-powered trawler requisitioned locally by the Congolese authorities. As crews for the Swifts there are 15 [*less than 1 line not declassified*].

The boats have been used extensively in interdiction patrols to prevent supplies and men from reaching rebels fighting on the eastern shore of Lake Tanganyika and to prevent rebels from escaping across the lake to Tanzania. Although direct contact with the enemy on the lake has not been frequent, it is known that two Soviet-supplied 35-foot armed launches have been on the lake since September 1965. As a result of the Congolese maritime force, most of the traffic between Tanzania and the rebels has had to move by night. In November 1965, the Congolese force engaged five rebel craft after dark, apparently proceeding from Tanzania to the Congo. Throughout the current military campaign against the last centers of organized rebel resistence in the eastern Congo, the boats have carried out reconnaissance patrols; escorted other boats transporting personnel, supplies of food, ammunition and arms; and evacuated wounded. The presence of the boats on the lake has continued to have a salutary effect on the morale of the local population, both African and European.

[*less than 1 line not declassified*] continuing efforts to find suitable replacements for the [*less than 1 line not declassified*] crews of the Swifts, it is expected that several European seamen will be recruited shortly and proceed to Albertville. With the approval of the Department of State, [*less than 1 line not declassified*] exploring the possibility of gradually turning over the manning of the boats to Congolese troops and mercenaries. At the time of writing, discussions on this subject have begun. If they are successful, it appears likely that Congolese and mercenaries will in the near future assume most of the duties now carried out by [*less than 1 line not declassified*]. This would make possible a further reduction in the cost of the maritime program, [*less than 1 line not declassified*] to supply operational direction for the boats and the necessary spare parts and specialized maintenance.

(2) *The air program*

The air operation now maintains aircraft at the following level: twelve T–28's, five B–26K's, one B–26B, three C–46's, one C–45 (10–2) and three Bell helicopters. The third C–46 was acquired in October 1965 because of the increased transport burden borne by the air operation since the withdrawal in mid-August of the Joint Task Force C–130's formerly stationed in Leopoldville. Efforts to have the Belgian-piloted C–47's of the Congolese Air Force provide the necessary support were unsuccessful. Flying the aircraft are 29 pilots [*1 line not declassified*] who operate under the supervision of six American air operations officers. There are also 130 ground maintenance personnel, 127 of whom are Europeans; the other three, Americans.

The [*less than 1 line not declassified*] air operation has made a significant contribution in the campaign in the eastern Congo north of Albertville. The campaign opened on the night of 27–28 September 1965 with an attack on the rebel stronghold of Baraka and continues in the form of cleanup operations requiring close air support for the ground forces. The other primary area of air activity is in the northeast out of Stanleyville. In general, neither Congolese nor mercenary troops are willing to move without air cover.

The slowly improving military situation is permitting a reduction in the pace of tactical air activity. Thus, it is planned to withdraw the B–26B from service. It is also planned to reduce further the use of tactical aircraft and eventually eliminate more planes in this category, by providing light aircraft which are less costly to operate and maintain, more efficient for reconnaissance work (which until now has had to be carried out by tactical aircraft), and less visibly U.S. military aircraft.

The above reduction in pace and change in character of air activities as well as planned changes in logistical procedures have permitted an initial lowering of the annual cost level from [*less than 1 line not declassified*].

The gradual replacement of the [*less than 1 line not declassified*] pilots by other third-country nationals is a continuing effort.

(3) *Funding*

Of the [*dollar amount not declassified*] supplemental contingency fund programmed and approved by the 303 Committee on 26 November 1965 to meet the continuing political crisis in the Congo, [*dollar amount not declassified*] has been expended in payments to General Mobutu, the last payment—of [*dollar amount not declassified*]—having been authorized in January 1966, leaving a balance of [*dollar amount not declassified*] on hand. This money has been spent to ensure the support of the principal officers of the Congolese National Army and particularly of the First Paracommando Battalion, which is the key to the security of Leopoldville; to provide funds to important political leaders; and to furnish assistance to provincial leaders and tribal chiefs when they visit Leopoldville. It is the belief of the Ambassador at Leopoldville and the CIA Chief of Station that the provision of these funds was an important element in ensuring the support of ranking Congolese officers and their commands during the crisis brought on by the conflict between former

President Kasavubu and former Premier Moise Tshombe, a crisis which ended when General Mobutu seized power in Leopoldville on 25 November 1965. The timely provision of these funds when they were most needed greatly assisted Mobutu in his effort to reestablish a functioning government. He has stated that without them he would have been unable to consolidate his position.

c. [*sic*] *Pertinent U.S. Policy Considerations*

Since the outbreak of the Congo rebellion in 1964, it has been U.S. policy to support the pro-West Central Government against the rebels, who have received aid and encouragement from Communist China, Cuba, the radical African states and the Soviet Union. African and Soviet assistance to the rebels greatly diminished during the latter part of 1965. Also, it seems probable that by now most if not all the [*less than 1 line not declassified*] formerly with the rebels have left the Congo. Nevertheless, pockets of rebel resistance still remain on Congolese territory, rebel groundfire still hits Congolese Air Force planes, shorefire is drawn by Congolese patrol boats on Lake Tanganyika, rebel mines are laid with more proficiency in the path of advancing Congolese troops, and recent reports indicate that rebel leaders maintain continuing contact with Chinese, Soviet, and [*less than 1 line not declassified*] in East Africa. Thus, it is logical to assume that Communist China, the Soviet Union, Cuba and possibly other Bloc powers would take advantage of any weakness of the Congolese Government to encourage a new round of insurgency in the Congo.

d. *Operational Objectives*

The major objectives of the [*less than 1 line not declassified*] maritime, air and covert funding operations in the Congo are (a) to assist the Congolese Government in maintaining a maritime patrol capability designed to discourage further assistance reaching the rebels from the outside and to contribute to stability in the eastern Congo, (b) to give the Congolese Air Force an adequate capability to support the Congolese National Army in its efforts to locate and eliminate rebel resistance and to restore and maintain order in the countryside, and (c) to assist General Mobutu in his effort to keep the support of the army and of key political leaders and factions.

e. *Risks Involved*

Although visible U.S. involvement has been kept to a minimum, it is generally assumed in the Congo that the U.S. Government is responsible for the air and maritime operations. They thus continue to be potentially embarrassing for the U.S. Government. However, the potential for embarrassment has been markedly reduced by the fact that Tshombe is no longer Prime Minister and the Congolese Government is thus no longer a primary target of hostility from other African states.

Passage of funds to Mobutu or other key Congolese officials can be accomplished securely, and minimal risks are involved.

f. *Alternative Courses of Action*

The U.S. Government failed in its efforts during talks held in Brussels in September 1965 and early February 1966 to persuade the Belgian Government to assume responsibility for the tactical air support program or even for logistical support of the [*less than 1 line not declassified*] air operation.

Mobutu has no political organization which, as an alternative to the U.S. covert funding program, can provide him with the funds needed to ensure his continuation in office. Nor is there any wealthy managerial or commercial class to whom he can turn to finance his political efforts. If the U.S. Government refuses to help him, he has the alternative of seeking help from other Western states. To date, other Western powers have been unwilling to provide political action funds in sufficient quantity. Another alternative would be for him to try to squeeze such funds from the local European business and commercial community by a form of blackmail or resort to graft. Such devices might easily backfire, particularly if attempted before Mobutu is firmly in power. A third alternative would be for him to turn to the French, Soviets, Chinese Communists or radical Africans. While he probably would not accept direct Soviet or Chinese Communist funds, he might in desperation accept funds from the radical African states or the French. CIA has no evidence that the French Government would be prepared to accept the financial burden involved. If the radical African states did so, the ultimate source of the funds they provided would almost certainly be one of the Bloc powers.

g. *Support Required from Other Agencies*

Continued support from the Department of Defense is required for the air program. The Department of Defense has provided the five B–26K's, the T–28's and replacements for the T–28's as needed.

4. *Coordination*

a. *Intragovernmental*

This proposal has been coordinated with the Bureau of African Affairs of the Department of State, which recommends approval.

b. *U.S. Ambassador*

This proposal has been concurred in by the U.S. Ambassador at Leopoldville.

5. *Recommendation*

It is recommended that approval be granted for the following, at a total estimated cost for CY 1966 of [*dollar amount not declassified*]:

(1) Continuation of the [*less than 1 line not declassified*] maritime operation on Lake Tanganyika through 30 June 1966 with the understanding that the [*less than 1 line not declassified*] role will be reduced sharply thereafter to a point where [*less than 1 line not declassified*] providing only operational guidance, spare parts and specialized maintenance, at an estimated cost of [*dollar amount not declassified*].

(2) Continuation of [*less than 1 line not declassified*] covert support to the Congolese tactical air program at a level of [*dollar amount not declassified*] per annum.

(3) Provision of a supplementary contingency fund of [*dollar amount not declassified*] for political purposes in support of General Mobutu and the stability of the Leopoldville Government.[2]

---

[2] A handwritten notation on the original reads: "17 Feb 1966: 303 Committee decided a plan should be presented in March (air portion emphasized) with financial cut-back."

---

463. Memorandum From Robert W. Komer of the National Security Council Staff to the President's Special Assistant for National Security Affairs (Bundy)[1]

Washington, February 16, 1966.

Mac:

[*dollar amount not declassified*] *for Congo.* I cannot understand why we still have to spend so much to cope with a rebellion that is practically over. Nor do I find the papers Jessup has at all illuminating on future needs, as opposed to history.[2]

With your O.K., I had a deal with Helms to review the whole program by March and see what economies possible. They cut a whole half million off the air bill—peanuts.

The air force ([*dollar amount not declassified*]) is the nub. I'd give 'em half this ([*dollar amount not declassified*]) for use through 30 June and tell

---

[1] Source: National Security Council, Intelligence Files, 303 Committee, Minutes 1967. Secret.

[2] On February 11, Peter Jessup sent Komer the Congo paper for the 303 Committee (Document 462) attached to a memorandum stating that Mobutu needed what help he could get and noting that overall prospects were bleak for the long run because there was nobody else in the wings to relieve U.S. Government of its support role. (National Security Council, Intelligence Files, 303 Committee, Minutes 1967)

them to cut back to no more than [*dollar amount not declassified*] for the second half year. Believe me, my horseback guess is just as good as theirs.

RWK

---

464. Memorandum for the Record[1]

Washington, February 17, 1966.

SUBJECT

Minutes of the Meeting of the 303 Committee, 17 February 1966

PRESENT

Mr. Bundy, Ambassador Johnson, Mr. Vance, and Mr. Richard Helms

Mr. Glenn Fields and Mr. Lawrence Devlin were present for Item 1

Colonel Ralph D. Steakley, Lt. Cdr. Donald Forbes, and Lt. William McCall were present for Item 3

1. Congo—Request for Approval to Continue [*cryptonym not declassified*] *Maritime, Air and Covert Funding Operations.*

a. On the request for approval to continue [*cryptonym not declassified*] maritime, air and covert funding operations in the Congo,[2] Mr. Bundy pointed out that the proposal hardly represented compliance with the committee's expressed wish that a substantial reduction be made. The new request represented only a half million dollar slash from the earlier high rate of expenditure [*dollar amount not declassified*].

b. Mr. Glenn Fields and Mr. Lawrence Devlin, CAS Chief in Leopoldville, took pains to point out that a reduction would result in a sizable cutback of missions, fewer aircraft spare parts, and no resupply after attrition. They further felt that the rebels, though somewhat more somnolent in their recent behaviour, had still not been eradicated, that Mobutu's ground troops just won't move without air support, and that any withdrawal of support at this time would seriously jeopardize Mobutu's fragile resolve. They emphasized that they would be glad to off-load this heavy paramilitary burden but there were absolutely no

---

[1] Source: National Security Council, Intelligence Files, 303 Committee, Minutes 1966. Secret; Eyes Only. Prepared on February 21.

[2] Document 462.

takers. They warned of a possible collapse of central government authority and a rapid Balkanization of the country with the only profiteers being neighbouring countries and communist opportunism and adventures.

c. Mr. Bundy responded that higher authority took a most negative attitude toward open-end drains on USG funding without hard-nosed efforts to make recipients tighten their own belts. He stated the 303 Committee had decided earlier to reduce, and this proposal seemed to be taking the line of least resistance via perennial handout. The committee agreed that for the next 60 days funds could be expended in proportionate allotments from existing budget levels, but in March a plan should be presented—the air portion was emphasized—with a substantial slash from the proposed [*less than 1 line not declassified*] million to no higher than [*less than 1 line not declassified*] with the full intention of slashing the latter figure in half again for the last part of the year.

d. The issue was decided less on analysis of the murky Congo situation and more on the basis that the proposal did not follow earlier 303 directives, the language of which was as follows: "The committee asked for quarterly reviews and a consistent effort to modify and cut back wherever possible." (Minutes of 29 October 1965, Item 3.b.).[3]

[Omitted here is discussion of other subjects.]

Peter Jessup

[3] See footnote 2, Document 440.

465. Telegram From the Department of State to the Embassy in the Congo[1]

Washington, March 3, 1966, 6:17 p.m.

944.1. Conjunction of discouraging IMF view and Lelyfeld article raises question of outlook for Congo and Mobutu government over next few months.

2. Impression which emerges is that of rudderless administration furnishing even less guidance and authority than heretofore and lack of

[1] Source: National Archives, RG 59, Central Files 1964–66, POL 15–1 THE CONGO. Confidential; Priority. Drafted by Schaufele and approved by Trimble. Repeated to Brussels.

coherent and unified government direction. There seems to be little question that Mobutu well-intentioned and sincere but unable cope with problems or even decide where to start. On financial side IMF indicates utter despair over Litho and his deleterious influence and actions. Mission saw little likelihood that GDRC willing and able take necessary action put its house in order.

3. In conversation with Deptoff French counselor Dubois, presumably reflecting general GOF opinion, gave his impression that things going from bad to worse and that Mobutu could not continue present ineffectiveness and remain in power. He wondered about undesirable or at least unhelpful role of Belgian military advisers in non-military field.

4. Mobutu's ineptness in public relations as evidenced in visits to Bukavu and Elisabethville also discouraging. Mulamba's sharp, possibly justified reaction to attitudes toward Congo and Congolese shown by Belgian—and presumably other foreign—individuals adds another dimension to apparent malaise.

5. We realize magnitude of seemingly perennial Congo problem often leads, on part of some observers, to feeling of hopelessness which not necessarily justified. However on the basis information available we too have impression Mobutu government seems to have lost its headway and is operating from day to day avoiding the hard decisions and actions required of it.

6. Therefore would appreciate as soon as possible Embassy assessment of: (1) effectiveness present government; (2) prospects for economic stabilization; (3) overall efficiency provincial administration; (4) longevity Mobutu–Mulamba government; (5) cohesiveness of senior army officers, including Mulamba; (6) plans which major potential opposition figures—Tshombe, Kasavubu, Nendaka etc.—may have to increase their influence or assume power, their strength, weakness and resources; and (7) other items which may affect future course of events.

Rusk

466. Memorandum From the Chief of the Africa Division, Directorate of Plans, Central Intelligence Agency (Fields) to the Deputy Director for Plans, Central Intelligence Agency (FitzGerald)[1]

Washington, March 3, 1966.

SUBJECT

Termination of Project [*cryptonym not declassified*]

1. It is requested that Project [*cryptonym not declassified*] be formally terminated effective 30 June 1965 [*1966?*].

2. The primary objective of Project [*cryptonym not declassified*], from 1 July 1962 to termination, was to promote political stability in the Congo by strengthening moderate political elements. This objective was pursued through funding of key assets who could provide a political action capability at the national level.

3. This request for termination is, in a sense, a product of Project [*cryptonym not declassified*] success. ODACID and KUBARK believe it is no longer necessary to engage in the large-scale political funding authorized by Project [*cryptonym not declassified*]. The objectives of promoting stability and moderation remain the same, but the means needed to pursue these objectives are now different.

4. All commitments and quit claims have been settled.

5. [*dollar amount not declassified*] was approved for Project [*cryptonym not declassified*] for FY 1965. [*dollar amount not declassified*] was actually spent. [*dollar amount not declassified*] was turned back to Africa Division funds. There are no residual assets, funds or personnel to be disposed of as a result of this project termination. KUBARK continues to have an operational relationship with selected assets previously funded under Project [*cryptonym not declassified*]. The purpose of such association is now primarily for collection of foreign intelligence information and to maintain an equity for the future; not for political action.

6. There is no risk to KUBARK or other ODYOKE elements in the termination of this project.

---

[1] Source: Central Intelligence Agency Files, Job 78–00435R, DDO/ISS Files, Box 1, Folder 1, [*cryptonym not declassified*]—Development & Plans. Secret.

7. There are no special costs involved in terminating this project.

8. No additional funds are needed to liquidate this project.

Glenn D. Fields[2]
Chief, Africa Division

---

[2] [*name not declassified*] signed for Fields above Fields' typed signature.

---

467. Memorandum for the Record[1]

Washington, March 28, 1966.

SUBJECT

Minutes of the Meeting of the 303 Committee, 28 March 1966

PRESENT

Ambassador Johnson, Mr. Vance, Admiral Raborn, Mr. Richard Helms, and Mr. Peter Jessup

Mr. Desmond FitzGerald was present for Items 1 and 2
Mr. John Waller was present for Item 1
Mr. William Broe was present for Item 2

1. *Congo*

a. On the question of continued air support to the Congo (see minutes dated 21 February 1966, Item 1),[2] Ambassador Johnson kept probing for some method to reduce the seemingly endless assistance, some way in which to shift the burden to the Congolese so that they could do more to help themselves.

b. Mr. FitzGerald reviewed the problem and emphasized that the Ambassador, the Air Attaché, the CINCSTRIKE representative, and the Chief of Station were unanimous that, without air support, the Congolese effort against the rebels would evaporate.

c. He pointed out that although the revolt was not one in which a mobile rebel army was on the rampage seizing cities, the ANC, never-

---

[1] Source: National Security Council, Intelligence Files, 303 Committee, Minutes 1966. Secret; Eyes Only. Prepared on March 29.

[2] See Document 464. On March 21, Helms approved release of a memorandum to the 303 Committee requesting a reconsideration of the decision to reduce the air program in the Congo. (Central Intelligence Agency Files, Job 81–00966R, Box 1, Folder 12, Congo 1966)

theless, was not eliminating the rebels and revitalizing the northeast. They were holding the rebels in pockets, but neither mercenaries nor the ANC would budge without the modest umbrella of a dozen or so T–28's and a handful of B–26K's. He pointed out that some economies could be effectuated with the withdrawal of the longer range B–28K's, which were more expensive to maintain, and some economies might be made by cutting the number of sorties. However, he warned that the outlook for even a minimal Congolese air force was at best lugubrious. The Belgians were convinced you couldn't make the Congolese into pilots, period; the Italians thought they could but were far from proving it with their own flabby program. If we pulled out, it was emphasized, the Congolese just didn't have the means to achieve results on their own.

d. It became apparent that the current expense was not the main problem but rather the Congolese themselves; [*1 line not declassified*].

e. Ambassador Johnson wondered about the embarrassment potential, for example in Rhodesia, stemming from the present state of affairs. Mr. FitzGerald pointed out that under present circumstances the USG was in a position of control over these assets.

f. Mr. Vance stated that, in his opinion, the military requirements must continue to be met. He therefore suggested a prompt survey by the JCS on what the minimum military requirements should be. The committee agreed to this. The committee will examine these findings when ready and review the problem late in April.[3]

[Omitted here is discussion of other subjects.]

Peter Jessup

---

[3] At the 303 Committee meeting on April 22, Vance was asked if the JCS had come up with a definitive opinion on necessary air support to the Congo. He replied that they had not and were not able to assess the need largely because the size and status of the rebel threat was thoroughly opaque. It was suggested that two JCS officers in civilian dress, perhaps accompanied by a CIA Headquarters officer, proceed to the field and determine this aspect on the spot. (Extract from the Minutes of the 303 Committee meeting on April 22; ibid., Job 82–00450R, 40 Committee, Congo (K) 1965–)

468. Telegram From the Department of State to the Embassy in the Congo[1]

Washington, April 28, 1966, 12:39 p.m.

1138. 1. Lt. Colonel Puati, GDRC military attaché, called requesting Department's assessment Tshombe's activities Brussels and accuracy current accusations against him. Puati indicated GDRC concerned and seeking friendly government's advice re Tshombe situation.

2. Deptoff replied by reviewing USG attitude toward Tshombe when he President of Katanga and later Prime Minister of Congo. Said since Tshombe relinquished power USG has maintained only correct, respectful attitude toward him as toward other ex-premiers. Department had no information bearing on reliability reports Tshombe's activities since arrival Europe.

3. Puati then asked what USG attitude would be if it develops Tshombe conspiring against Mobutu. Deptoff said that our correct and frank relationship with Mobutu and others in GDRC would continue in accordance our known policy toward Congo. Deptoff then asked whether Puati believed Tshombe engaged subversive activities and received reply that Tshombe sufficiently supported by powerful elements in Brussels to assure credibility such suspicion.

4. Puati's manner indicated belief Tshombe conspiring and fear Tshombe's base may be broad enough to cause considerable trouble to Mobutu. He doubted Tshombe could now return Leopoldville. Subsequent conversation with Chargé Nzeza revealed latter unaware of Nendaka's charges against Tshombe, not directly concerned with Puati's activities and presumably ignorant of latter's visit to Department.

Rusk

[1] Source: National Archives, RG 59, Central Files 1964–66, POL 6 THE CONGO. Secret; Priority. Drafted by Canup, cleared by Moffat and Colonel Kennedy, and approved by Brown. Also sent to Brussels and repeated to CINCSTRIKE for POLAD Tampa.

469. Action Memorandum From the Director of the Office of Central African Affairs (Brown) to the Assistant Secretary of State for African Affairs (Palmer)[1]

Washington, May 17, 1966.

SUBJECT

Belgian Aid to the Congo

You will meet with Belgian Foreign Minister Harmel at 1600 hours on May 19.

Issue:

There is currently considerable strain on Belgo-Congolese relations centered in the negotiations in Brussels over the financial settlement between the two countries reached in February 1965. The Congolese delegation led by the Prime Minister and Foreign Minister has made charges of insulting behavior by Belgian officials and presented what the Belgians consider unacceptable proposals for reopening and revising the settlement. This action, preceded as it was by financial measures detrimental to Belgian interests in the Congo, could create a public and government climate unpropitious for the continuation of Belgian assistance to the Congo at present levels.

Discussion:

We are inclined to regard President Mobutu, Prime Minister Mulamba and Foreign Minister Bomboko as still basically pre-Belgian and favorable toward continued Belgian assistance to the Congo and the role of Belgian enterprises in the country's economy. If this is true, the current strain between the two countries can be expected to subside, whether or not present talks on the financial settlement are broken off or pursued to a satisfactory conclusion. Therefore it would be unfortunate if the Belgian Government, acting on the basis of the present atmosphere, were to revise its plans for assistance to the Congo in the economic, technical and military fields.

The Belgian Government's position in the Congo is an extremely influential one. Despite momentary lapses, Belgian military advisers to General Mobutu and Prime Minister Mulamba are among the most influential in the entourage. Similarly Belgian economic and other ad-

[1] Source: National Archives, RG 59, AF Files: Lot 69 D 118, Box 3828, POL 7 Visits, Meetings, 1966, Harmel. Confidential. Drafted by Canup.

visers throughout the government play significant parts as counselors and usually have the confidence of their Congolese principals. The Belgians have no reason to expect a change in this situation on the basis of events to date, since in most cases—but not all—they are aware of the necessity of not playing too obvious a role in Congolese internal affairs. Nevertheless the Mobutu regime is undergoing a spasm of nationalist feeling tinged with xenophobia which expresses itself in outcries against foreign influence, insistence that foreign enterprises must become Congolese entities and emphasis on the "Congolization" of government and business. This campaign is presently carried on mainly at the highest level, although it is beginning to be translated into agitation for the replacement or effacement of Europeans in various areas and positions. Since complete "Congolization"—like nationalization of large industries—has never been a characteristic trend of the Congolese scene, there is no cause to expect that the process will be other than steady and gradual, but recurring difficulties are likely.

Mr. Harmel will probably note the recent deterioration in Belgo-Congolese relations and place the blame on the Congolese. He will explain that recent Congolese demands for reopening the financial settlement issue are largely unacceptable and even extreme. He will, however, probably indicate that the Belgian Government is not planning a serious revision of its policy toward assisting the Congo, although Belgian public opinion and certain large mineral exporting corporations in the Congo are experiencing disillusionment as a result of the Brussels negotiations and recent rises in taxes on exports and business operations and increases in the minimum wage levels in the Congo.

Recommendation:

I recommend that you urge Harmel to continue official Belgian assistance policies and aid levels toward the Congo, and carry out actions discussed and agreed to in last February's U.S.-Belgian bilateral talks, especially the increase in Belgian military instructors and cadres, technical experts and administrative advisory teams in the Congo. The Belgians also agreed to contribute 100 million francs for purchases of military hardware through the Tripartite Logistics Group in Leopoldville with the possibility existing of increasing this amount next year. They also agreed to approach the Italian Government to urge the latter to continue the Italian military pilot training program in the Congo and to seek ways to eliminate frictions which have developed between the Belgian and Italian military missions in Leopoldville. Since the Italian Government is in the final stage of decision-making concerning President Mobutu's request for the Italians to continue their training program, the Belgians could perhaps indicate at an appropriate high level their strong belief that this training should continue in the Congo.[2]

[2] No memorandum of conversation recording Harmel's talks with Harriman and Palmer on May 19 has been found. A May 23 memorandum from Schaufele to Palmer states that Harmel said he did not understand the sudden deterioration in Belgian-Congolese relations. The memorandum states that the talks were very harmonious and that the Belgian and U.S. views of the Congo situation seemed very close. (Ibid., POL 2–5 Information Summaries 1966)

470. Telegram From the Station in the Congo to the Central Intelligence Agency[1]

Leopoldville, May 28, 1966.

5775 (In 26612). For Palmer from Chargé.

1. You have probably seen Embtel 2234[2] reporting proposed coup by senior ANC officers plus civilian faction headed by ex-finance minister Bamba. CAS has just found out that coup, which was scheduled for two weeks hence, now scheduled tentatively for Sunday or Monday. Reason: Fear of possible Tshombe coup of which we know nothing.

2. Whatever problems we have with Mobutu, coup at this time would be against US interests, just at time Congo beginning settle down. Strong possibility forces unfriendly to USG could take advantage this plot, although no sign coup group anti US. Also believe we have leverage to gain with Mobutu from having Devlin inform him of all we know about the coup. Therefore, propose send Devlin to see Mobutu this evening and share with him all information we have about coup. Devlin will not make contact until 1600 hours Zulu in case you have other thoughts on matter.

[1] Source: Central Intelligence Agency Files, Job 78–02502R, DDO/ISS Files, Box 1, [*cryptonym not declassified*] Operations, Jan.–Dec. 1966, [*text not declassified*]. Secret; [*cryptonym not declassified*]; Flash. Received at 1331Z.

[2] Not printed. (National Archives, RG 59, Central Files 1964–1966, POL 23–9 THE CONGO)

3. Meanwhile, Emboffs have strict instructions stay away from Bamba and his fellow conspirators.[3]

---

[3] Telegram 5776 from Leopoldville to CIA, May 28, transmitted more details of the plot and stated that to avoid the risk of chaos, it was urgent that the Chief of Station brief Mobutu as soon as possible and obtain details of the information in his possession. (Central Intelligence Agency Files, Job 78–02502R, DDO/ISS Files, Box 1, [*cryptonym not declassified*] Operations, Jan.–Dec. 1966, [*text not declassified*]) Telegram 5781 from Leopoldville to CIA, May 28, reported that the Chief of Station had met with Mobutu and briefed him on the information in the Station's possession concerning the plot, explaining that his source was not directly involved but was close to Bamba. The Chief of Station said it now appeared that the coup might be imminent and he considered it imperative to ascertain if Mobutu was fully aware of and monitoring developments, and if in fact some military elements were really opposed to him. Mobutu indicated his full awareness of virtually all of the details of the plot and stated that all of the military officers involved were under his control and, under his instructions, playing a double game. (Ibid.)

---

471. Information Memorandum From the Deputy Assistant Secretary of State for African Affairs (Fredericks) to Secretary of State Rusk[1]

Washington, May 31, 1966.

SUBJECT

Coup Plot Exposed in Leopoldville

In the early hours of May 30 the Congolese Government exposed a rather childish plot to overthrow the Mobutu regime. Four former national ministers were arrested through the loyalty to Mobutu of several high-ranking Congolese military officers (notably Colonel Bangala, Governor of Leopoldville) who by pretending to join the conspirators foiled the plot and demonstrated the solidity of Mobutu's position.

The arrested conspirators are: (1) Evariste Kimba (a BALUBAKAT politician from North Katanga who served as Tshombe's Foreign Minister during secession and whose brief designation as national Prime Minister last fall was interrupted by Mobutu's November 25 coup), (2) Jerome Anany (a PNP politician from Bukavu who served as Defense Minister under Cyrille Adoula), (3) Alexandre Mahamba (member of the MNC/Lumumba and CEREA parties from North Kivu, who

---

[1] Source: National Archives, RG 59, Central Files 1964–66, POL 23–9 THE CONGO. Secret. Drafted by Brown and Canup.

held several ministerial portfolios under Adoula), (4) Senator Emmanuel Bamba (an ABAKO politician from Kongo Central and close associate of former President Kasavubu and a Finance Minister under Adoula).

Further arrests of Congolese politicians are expected; former Ministers Cleophas Kamitatu, Paul Bolya and Albert Delvaux and provincial politicians Andre Kapwasa and Jean Miruho have been implicated.

Government spokesmen accused the plotters of high treason and predicted that they will be tried immediately and executed publicly.[2] A proclamation which the conspirators had purportedly drawn up called for the overthrow of the Mobutu regime mainly for mishandling of the country's economic and financial situations.

Government statements claimed that four unidentified, non-African Embassies in Leopoldville were approached by the conspirators. We have been told by the Congolese that the Belgian and French Embassies were involved somehow with the conspirators, while our Embassy and the West Germans behaved correctly. A Belgian First Secretary, whose contacts were quite indiscreet, has been declared PNG.

We were approached by Senator Bamba directly late last week [*less than 1 line not declassified*] in an effort to obtain our support for the coup. Our Chargé warned Bamba against the coup attempt. After receiving Departmental approval he had the CAS Station Chief tell Mobutu of our knowledge of a plot. The latter said he already knew of it. The Chargé's prompt action put us in the clear. The Belgians, however, are in a difficult position. The mere existence of the plot has strengthened Mobutu's belief that the Belgians are out to get him. We are doing our best to calm him down and prevent an even further deterioration of strained GOB–GDRC relations.

---

[2] Telegram 2270 from Leopoldville, May 31, reported that the four men had been found guilty of high treason and sentenced to death. (Ibid., POL 29 THE CONGO) Telegram 1266 to Leopoldville, June 1, transmitted a message from Harriman to Mobutu urging that he demonstrate his government's magnanimity by commuting the death sentences. (Ibid., POL 23–9 THE CONGO) In telegram 2292 from Leopoldville, June 2, Blake reported that he delivered Harriman's message to Bomboko in Mobutu's presence. (Ibid., POL 29 THE CONGO) In telegram 2293, June 2, Blake reported that Bomboko telephoned and said very serious consideration had been given to Harriman's message, but it was not possible to commute the death sentences. (Ibid.) On June 2, the four men were hanged in a public execution.

472. Memorandum From the Deputy Secretary of Defense's Military Assistant (Greenleaf) to the Deputy Secretary of Defense (Vance)[1]

Washington, June 3, 1966.

SUBJECT

General Wheeler's Report on Air Operations in the Congo[2]

The principal findings of the Report on Air Operations in the Congo are:

(1) Maintenance of air support at present levels to the Congolese military forces is essential for several more years; and

(2) A coordinate, multi-national approach to resolution of many Congolese problems is long overdue and could well provide alternatives to the current U.S. level of effort in that country.

At least two major arguments are advanced for the development and maintenance of an air capability in the Congo. The first concerns the importance of tactical air support (including air transport) to reduce the effectiveness of rebel or insurgent elements (which, in the main, have been supported by the radical African states and the Chinese Communists). The Report also suggests that tactical air support seems to provide a necessary psychological "prop" to the poorly-trained and poorly-led Congolese Army units. The second major argument concerns the importance of an air transport capability to the extension and maintenance of the Central Government's control and the continued existence of the Democratic Republic of the Congo as a nation.

Much of the Report is an analysis of the fragmented air operations in the Congo which finds the Congolese, but mainly the Belgians, the Italians, mercenaries, [and CAS] all sharing functions and responsibilities with no effective integration of effort or centralized control.

Three alternative arrangements for continued Congolese air operations are discussed:

(1) Integrate as early as possible Congolese pilots and mercenary pilots, technicians, and aircraft with the [CAS air support] Operation to facilitate the gradual withdrawal [of CAS personnel and aircraft];

(2) Transfer control of mercenary pilots, technicians and aircraft to the Italian Training Mission (ITM) and make the ITM responsible for the combat training of the Congolese Air Force so as to permit the Congolese MOD to assume control of combat air operations; and

---

[1] Source: Washington National Records Center, RG 330, OSD Files: FRC 71 A 6489, Congo 385 (Sensitive), 4 Jun 66. Secret; Sensitive.

[2] Attached but not printed.

(3) Integrate as early as possible mercenary pilots, technicians and aircraft and Congolese pilots under the Belgian Air Force Mission (BAFM) with limited U.S. MAP support of this effort.

General Wheeler recommends:

(a) Support of alternative (1) above, and
(b) State initiating—as a matter of priority—high level discussions with Italian, Belgian and Congolese officials to obtain agreement on functions, responsibilities, means, and goals for the development of a satisfactory Congolese Air Force.

A copy of General Wheeler's report already has been forwarded to Admiral Raborn and General Paul D. Adams. Frank Hand believes Des FitzGerald will react negatively (for "NIH" reasons) to the Report's suggested alternatives to the current program.

I have had three copies of the report reproduced and recommend you make copies available to Mr. Rostow, Ambassador Johnson, and possibly Bill Moyers. It can subsequently be scheduled for 303 discussion. Attached is a memorandum of transmittal as well as two letters commending the OJCS and CIA personnel who developed the Report.[3]

G

---

[3] Attached, but not printed. The minutes of the 303 Committee meeting on June 9 record that the Committee generally appreciated the JCS report for its thorough examination of the issue. Mr. FitzGerald emphasized that "the Agency was not anxious to get into a long-term nursemaid or MAAG type role with the Congolese." The Executive Secretary noted that the paper established two points quite clearly: first, the Congolese Government definitely needed some air support and second, there was no short cut for CIA to divest itself of this task in the immediate future. (Central Intelligence Agency Files, Job 82–00450R, 40 Committee, Congo (K) 1965–) A CIA memorandum for the record dated June 28 noted that the initiative for further 303 Committee action on the Congo paper was with the Department of State. As for internal project handling for Project [*text not declassified*] and Project [*text not declassified*] both projects were due to be renewed on June 30, 1966, and the Africa Division was in the process of writing project renewals for both projects for FY 1967 funds. (Ibid.)

473. Memorandum for the Record[1]

Washington, July 8, 1966.

SUBJECT

Minutes of the Meeting of the 303 Committee, 8 July 1966

PRESENT

Mr. Rostow, Ambassador Johnson, Mr. Vance, and Mr. Helms

Mr. Bill Moyers and Mr. Cord Meyer were present for Items 1 and 2

Mr. Leonard Marks and Mr. Robert Kintner were present for Item 1

Mr. John Waller and Mr. [*name not declassified*] were present for Item 4

[Omitted here is discussion of other subjects.]

4. *Congo—The Air Support Problem*

a. On the question of the Congo, the committee punted again on third down. Ambassador Johnson noted that Ambassador Godley, who had recently been in Washington and had just returned to Leopoldville, was to see Mobutu shortly on where he was headed with plans for a Congolese Air Force. Ambassador Godley was to point out to Mobutu that the [*less than 1 line not declassified*] Air Force was ginned up for an emergency but now the threat from neighbours and rebels had dwindled markedly. There was some need to cut back and become realistic. Ambassador Johnson mentioned that via Ambassador Reinhardt we were pressing the Italians to step up their training, but they had their own domestic political problems in agreeing to any long-range aid commitment. The Belgians were pretty well written off as far as concrete assistance at this time.

b. It was agreed to await the results of the Mobutu–Godley talks before facing the subject again.

[Omitted here is discussion of other subjects.]

Peter Jessup

---

[1] Source: National Security Council, Intelligence Files, 303 Committee, Minutes 1966. Secret; Eyes Only. Prepared on July 9.

474. Memorandum From Edward Hamilton of the National Security Council Staff to the President's Special Assistant (Rostow)[1]

Washington, July 13, 1966.

SUBJECT

Possible Explosion in the Congo

Joe Palmer asked me to come over this afternoon to be briefed on a possible Tshombe attempt to overthrow Mobutu. If it develops, it could be messy—involving all of the worst elements of the Congolese history along with the most disruptive of the Southern African factors. The facts are as follows:

1. The CIA has information from a middling reliable source that Tshombe plans a military coup beginning July 21. The 200–250 *white* South African and Rhodesian mercenaries are reportedly preparing to move against government troops, starting in Katanga. (This number seems small, but it is sufficient to take over at least the eastern part of the country very quickly.)

2. A new contingent of 75 South African mercenaries is scheduled to arrive in Elisabethville on July 21. Normally, such recruits would not be very useful for awhile. But if it is true, as alleged, that South Africa is involved, they may be first-class troops which would make the rebel forces much stronger. Needless to say, all of these mercenaries are well-armed, including the only armored cars in the country.

3. Tshombe is now in Brussels, reportedly putting the final touches on the plot.

If the revolt comes off, it will (1) put us back into a Congolese Civil War, without much hope of an effective UN intervention, (2) cause great consternation in Zambia, Tanzania, Kenya, and other surrounding countries, (3) aggravate tensions with Rhodesia and South Africa, and (4) create serious pressure for us to move in. Further, if Mobutu finds out that we know about this plot and have not told him, it will cut our influence substantially.

Thus, I agreed with Palmer's suggestion that we very quietly give Mobutu the information we have (as we did six weeks ago when he stifled another incipient coup), and advise him to take precautionary steps to head the rebels off. This does not, in my judgment, involve us

---

[1] Source: Johnson Library, National Security File, Country File, Congo, Vol. XII, 10/65–10/66. Secret; Sensitive.

too deeply and it protects our interest as much as possible, The cabled instructions will be going out tonight, unless you think otherwise.

I also asked Palmer to put four or five sentences on this into the Department's night-reading paper for the President so that he will know the fundamentals.

EH

---

475. Telegram From the Department of State to the Embassy in the Congo[1]

Washington, July 14, 1966, 10:59 a.m.

7251. If you have not yet seen Mobutu suggest you limit your comments to him to following:

(A) We have heard rumors of a plot that may take place within the next few days. These have come from sources of questionable reliability and we wonder what he may know about it.

(B) Our information is that Tshombe may be behind the plot and that it may involve both the mercenaries in the country and the new mercenaries from Rhodesia and South Africa who will arrive shortly at Elisabethville airport.

(C) It is possible these rumors are being spread simply to create mischief. Would be most harmful his image and our interests if he lashed out widely in all directions and initiated series of reprisals against Congolese or Europeans. We would not wish see repetition June 2 hangings. You should therefore avoid speculating with him on possible involvement certain Congolese within country.

In any event you should impress upon Mobutu that it is essential he react rationally and calmly if he learns any real evidence of a plot. Guidance contained paras 4, 5 and 6, Deptel 7084 remains valid.[2]

Report reaction, Flash.

Rusk

---

[1] Source: National Archives, RG 59, Central Files 1964–66, POL 23–9 THE CONGO. Secret; Flash; Exdis. Drafted and approved by Ball.

[2] Paragraphs 4, 5, and 6 of telegram 7084 to Kinshasa, July 13, listed some possible concrete suggestions for Mobutu if requested. The Congolese Government should consider preventing the entry of the 75 additional South African mercenaries, seizing control of the craft on Lake Tanganyika, and ensuring the neutralization of the ex-Katanga forces in Kisangani (formerly Stanleyville). Mobutu should be told that air action involving use of U.S.-controlled aircraft should be reserved as a last resort. (Ibid.) On May 2, the major cities in the Congo had been renamed, and Leopoldville became Kinshasa.

476. Memorandum for the White House Chief of Staff (Moyers)[1]

Washington, July 19, 1966.

SUBJECT

Contingency Air Support to Mobutu in Case of Coup in Congo

The 303 Committee, at the request of Alexis Johnson, held a telephonic vote on Tuesday, 19 July, in favor of contingency air support should a coup be mounted against Mobutu in the Congo. *The principals all voted yea.*

Nobody was very enthusiastic but felt we had to be ready. Secretary Rusk is preparing a brief memo to the President on this subject.

The CIA made the following reservations on the enclosed sheet.[2]

The general feeling is that nothing could be worse than a Belgian-backed and mercenary-reinforced coup by Moise Tshombe at this time due to the political climate in Black Africa. The British soft line on Rhodesia and the recent unwelcome decision of the World Court have exacerbated sensitive African neighbours' feelings.

Although Mobutu is somewhat inept and his chances of pulling the Congo up by its own bootstraps are indeed remote, the Department and others feel that we have no other choice than to go along with this Congolese for the time being.

I call this matter to your attention because of a possible future embarrassment potential should the CIA-backed air force ever actually go into action against South African and other white mercenaries. Although unlikely, the strafing and killing of a Major Hoare or so would make a big story and an unfavorable one, depending on the journalist's slant.

PJ

---

[1] Source: National Security Council, Intelligence Files, Congo, 1966–1968. Secret; Eyes Only. Prepared by Jessup on July 21.

[2] Attached but not printed.

477. Telegram From the Department of State to the Embassy in the Congo[1]

Washington, July 29, 1966, 4:42 p.m.

17942. Kinshasa 602 (Notal).[2]

1. If Mobutu does discuss with you idea of requesting African nations supply troops to replace 6th Commandos, you should not respond negatively but should discourage any idea US can finance such arrangements or take on transport of forces involved.

2. We do not think here that Tunisians or Ethiopians would respond favorably and we have no intention acting as intermediary for Mobutu with these governments. Bourguiba seems disenchanted with Sub-Saharan Africa and it is doubtful he would be willing send Tunisian forces to area where problems—from his point of view—are so intractable. Ethiopia likely to be equally negative and refer Mobutu to OAU. Comments Addis and Tunis would be appreciated.

3. We are not prepared undertake financing or support for African units. As you point out, logistic and supply problems would be most difficult. Obligation for airlift forces, which would probably involve continuous use of aircraft for resupply and replacement, is one we cannot assume particularly at time such heavy demands already placed on available resources.

4. We have no suggestions where else Mobutu might turn for African forces. While his relations with East African countries have considerably improved, see no prospect of his obtaining troops from any of them. In general believe we should limit ourselves to discouraging any hope for US assistance and avoid advising re possible African sources of assistance.

5. Realize above will put you in somewhat awkward position vis-à-vis Mobutu but agree with you that it is a little late to seek African troops and possibilities any real assistance from African sources dim.

---

[1] Source: National Archives, RG 59, Central Files 1964–66, POL 23–9 THE CONGO. Secret; Priority. Drafted by Brown; cleared by Moffat, Strong, Ambassador to Ethiopia Edward M. Korry, Colonel Kennedy, McElhiney, Cashin, Root, AFNE Country Director Matthew J. Looram, Judd, and Colonel Alba of the Joint Staff; and approved by Trimble. Repeated to Brussels, Paris, London, Addis Ababa, Tunis, and CINCSTRIKE.

[2] On July 23, the Katanga gendarmes and elements of the mercenary 6th Commandos rebelled in Kisangani and seized parts of the town. In telegram 602 from Kinshasa, July 23, Godley reported that a deeply distressed Mobutu told him that he had to get rid of the mercenaries, particularly Belgian nationals, and was thinking of replacing them with African troops who could do garrison but not combat duty. Mobutu asked what the U.S. Government thought of his seeking African troops, what troops did it believe he should use, and if it would contribute toward the cost. (Ibid.)

6. Also foresee problems with Belgians on this subject, especially if final outcome is dismissal Belgian mercenaries and maintenance French. Assume you will inform Bihin if, in fact, Mobutu returns to question.

Rusk

478. Circular Telegram From the Department of State to All Posts[1]

Washington, August 2, 1966, 8:21 p.m.

20361. Congo Situation: For Information Only.

1. Congo again in grip of political convulsions as Mobutu regime gravely threatened by mutiny July 23 of Katangan forces in Kisangani.

2. Situation complicated by coincidence with reported Tshombe plot, with connivance some South African and Rhodesian mercenaries, to depose Mobutu government and reinstall Tshombe as Prime Minister.

3. Existence of separate Katangan units probably loyal to Tshombe has been disturbing to many political foes of Tshombe. Mutiny may have been triggered by ill-advised order to disarm them but other factors such as arrears in pay, homesickness for Katanga and discrimination against Katangan units also factors. Although mutineers hold city Mobutu decided to negotiate with them by sending Prime Minister Mulamba and Katanga governor and Tshombe supporter Munongo to Kisangani. No progress has been reported.

4. Situation also linked to continuing friction with Belgium characterized by GDRC stubbornness in settling economic issues with GOB and private companies, official attacks on Belgium, petty GDRC snubbing of GOB negotiators, harassment of Belgian advisers and escalation of already vituperative press warfare between two countries. GOB has also contributed to friction by its occasional lack of responsiveness to Congolese sensibilities.

5. Now Mobutu apparently thinks Belgians may be involved in plot and mutiny. Order for Belgian military assistance personnel in Ki-

[1] Source: National Archives, RG 59, Central Files 1964–66, POL 23–9 THE CONGO. Confidential; Noforn. Drafted by Schaufele; cleared by EUR/FBX, Strong, Brown, Edward W. Holmes in AF/SE, Peter C. Walker in AF/NE, and James A. Parker in AF/CW; and approved by Trimble.

sangani and Bukavu areas to withdraw to groupement headquarters and to refrain from participation in ANC operations apparently reinforces his belief as does neutral position of mercenaries in city, some of which are Belgians. Belgian Consul General in Lubumbashi has been PNG'd.

6. Following on heels increasing deterioration in Belgo-Congolese relations since May present fracas has disturbing connotations. GOB is awaiting GDRC reply to stiff note seeking more moderate Congolese attitude and is prepared threaten suspend all technical assistance if satisfactory reply not forthcoming. Possibility of break in relations cannot be excluded.

7. We have followed course of attempting exert moderating influence on Mobutu and remind him that USG cannot be expected fill any gap left by complete or partial Belgian withdrawal.

8. Given nature of Congolese politics it is almost impossible to predict outcome of current crisis. However, despite strong hand he has shown since assuming power and although he may surmount immediate problem, Mobutu is faced with essentially fragile situation net effect of which may weaken his hold.

Rusk

---

479. Telegram From the Department of State to the Embassy in the Congo[1]

Washington, August 4, 1966, 10:04 p.m.

22145. Brussels 573.[2]

1. We believe it entirely possible that Mobutu has been peddling line that US would substitute for Belgians in Congo and that Belgian technicians in Congo could well have overheard Mobutu's recent phone calls to Mulamba and Munongo.

---

[1] Source: National Archives, RG 59, Central Files 1964–66, POL 23–9 THE CONGO. Secret; Priority; Exdis. Drafted by Brown and Palmer, cleared by Edgar J. Beigel in EUR/FBX, and approved by Ball. Repeated to Brussels.

[2] Telegram 573 from Brussels, August 3, referred to a *Libre Belgique* story allegedly based on statements by Mobutu to members of his government that they need not worry about the possibility of a Belgian departure from the Congo since he had been assured by a U.S. representative of the CIA that if the Belgians left, the Americans would take their place. (Ibid.)

2. Further believe there could be several explanations why Mobutu would peddle this line:

a) He entirely aware US position but willing run risk of using this line in effort force Belgians concede GDRC demands;
b) He may have bloc offers assistance as alternative to Belgians and is using alleged US assurances as smokescreen;
c) Despite your several efforts convince him otherwise, he may, either through wishful thinking or failure comprehend firmness US position, continue harbor conviction US will bail him out.

3. Whatever possible explanations, Dept considers it vital we make further démarche to Mobutu to make it crystal clear to him that US not willing under any circumstances to substitute in part or in whole for GOB.

4. Only way we see to scotch this is for you and Devlin jointly to see Mobutu. Without mentioning Davignon, you should say you understand story is circulating and apparently gaining credence that U.S. intelligence has said US willing fill Belgian shoes. You should say US cannot fill gaps which departure of Belgians would cause, that you urge him reach acceptable arrangements with Belgians, and that American assistance, even on present scale, would not be effective if Belgians forced leave.

5. You should try find opportunity to add that any turn to left and search for bloc assistance would do Congo no good and should not be thought of as valid alternative to policies followed up to now. There ample evidence in Brazzaville and elsewhere that substantial Soviet or other communist assistance inevitably turns sour. Moreover any such development would create entirely new situation in Congo which US would have to take into account in its future relationships with him.

6. You should also ensure foregoing views are clearly and currently known to other key members of Government.[3]

Rusk

[3] In telegram 970 from Kinshasa, August 5, Godley reported that he and other Embassy officers told both Mobutu and Bomboko that they should not expect any additional aid from the United States. (Ibid., POL THE CONGO–US)

480. Telegram From the Department of State to the Mission to the United Nations[1]

Washington, September 29, 1966, 7:17 p.m.

56984. 1. Dept believes USUN should follow up on job begun by Embassy Kinshasa on Congolese with following objectives in view:

(A) Urge Congolese to take as moderate a position as possible, urge them not to insist on res or to content themselves with mild resolution pointing to dangers of situation but without trying to condemn Portugal;[2]

(B) Make clear to Congo del that, given flimsy nature their case, we unable to assume leadership in Council efforts to negotiate resolution; and unwilling to go along with any except moderate, balanced resolution, and then only in case rest of Council supports it.

2. Accordingly we suggest mission contact Bomboko as soon as possible after his arrival to review our position with him. In addition our position should be explained fully to other friendly dels on SC in hopes they also will try to influence Congolese along lines of para 1. (A) and (B) above. We believe special effort should be made with Nigerian who stands best chance, it seems to us, of countering immoderate attitude which Mali, Soviets, and perhaps Uganda likely to foster.

3. Suggest you also notify Congolese that any U.S. statement will be low-keyed and very carefully balanced in light of facts, most of which, according to our information, do not support Congolese allegations.

Rusk

---

[1] Source: National Archives, RG 59, Central Files 1964–66, POL 23–9 THE CONGO. Confidential; Priority. Drafted by Campbell in IO/UNP; cleared by Elizabeth Ann Brown in UNP, L. Dean Brown in AFCM, and Funseth in EUR; and approved by Sisco. Repeated to Lisbon, Kinshasa, London, and Luanda.

[2] On September 21, the Congolese Government formally requested a Security Council meeting to consider its charges that the Portuguese Government was harboring in Angola and Cabinda mercenary forces hired by Tshombe whose mission was to overthrow the legitimate and lawful government of the Congo.

481. Memorandum of Conversation[1]

New York, October 6, 1966.

SUBJECT

Exchange of Views with Congo (K) Foreign Minister Bomboko

PARTICIPANTS

U.S.
Joseph Palmer 2nd, Assistant Secretary of State for African Affairs
W. Paul O'Neill, AFI

Congo (Kinshasa)
H.E. Justin Bomboko, Foreign Minister and two assistants (?)

Foreign Minister Bomboko opened the conversation by saying that he had taken certain measures so that action on the Congo Parliament's resolution on the closing of foreign consulates would be suspended until his return to Kinshasa. This had already been announced on the radio. Mr. Palmer said he had received the same news from the American Embassy in Kinshasa and he wished to thank Mr. Bomboko for his helpfulness.

Mr. Bomboko then turned to the Congo complaint in the Security Council against Portugal on the subject of Portugal's alleged training of mercenaries for action against the Congo.[2] The Foreign Minister said that the Congo had taken into account the opinions of Security Council members and that the first draft resolution, which was too strong, had been amended. The Congo Delegation had itself been a Devil's Advocate and had persuaded its African friends to put together a resolution which demanded the minimum and had a better chance to pass. Mr. Bomboko said it would be difficult to go back to the Congo without a resolution and he was therefore asking Mr. Palmer as one who understood the situation to help so that he could return as soon as possible to Kinshasa where he wanted to protect President Mobutu from dema-

[1] Source: National Archives, RG 59, Central Files 1964–66, POL THE CONGO–US. Confidential. Drafted by O'Neill, Jr., and cleared in draft by Palmer. The meeting was held at USUN.

[2] On September 30, the Security Council met to begin consideration of the Congolese complaint. On October 14, it voted on a four-power (Jordan, Mali, Nigeria, and Uganda) draft resolution. The first operative paragraph urging Portugal not to allow foreign mercenaries to use Angola as a base of operation for interfering in the domestic affairs of the Congo was adopted 11–0 with 4 abstentions (France, New Zealand, the United Kingdom, and the United States). Resolution 266 (1966), which also called upon all states to refrain or desist from intervening in the domestic affairs of the Congo and requested the Secretary-General to follow closely the implementation of the resolution, was then adopted unanimously. (U.N. Doc. S/7539) For text, see *American Foreign Policy: Current Documents, 1966*, pp. 558–559.

gogic pressures. The Foreign Minister said he would return immediately after the Security Council's intervention was completed. Reemphasizing the importance of his returning to Kinshasa, Mr. Bomboko explained that was why he had asked to see Mr. Palmer today even though they were lunching together tomorrow. He reiterated that the Congo was trying to arrive at a minimum resolution and needed U.S. help. The Africans, he said, had rejected the idea of a consensus put forward by the President of the Security Council. This would not be understood in Kinshasa. Mr. Bomboko then handed Mr. Palmer a copy of a draft resolution acceptable to the Congo.

Mr. Palmer thanked the Minister for his explanation and said that as the latter knew the U.S. was doubtful as to whether there was enough evidence to make a case in the S.C. As Mr. Palmer understood it the U.S. Delegation felt nothing had been proven and this presented difficulties for the U.S. He said that he would, of course, have to discuss the matter with Ambassador Goldberg and our other representatives as he had not actively followed the debate. From what he did know, Mr. Palmer continued, the best resolution of the problem would be a resolution permitting the case to end as gracefully as possible. The Foreign Minister said it would not be understood at home if there were no resolution. The Congo had proof and Portugal had agreed in the Security Council debate that there are weapons for mercenaries in Angola. Mr. Palmer asked if this did not go back several years. The Foreign Minister answered negatively stating that Portugal admits weapons are there and if Tshombe returned he would get them. Paragraphs one and three of the proposed resolution were the minimum that the Congo could accept. Mr. Bomboko said the Congo could show that such and such planes in Angola were Congolese. He repeated that Portugal had agreed in its last speech in the S.C. that the arms were there. Mr. Palmer said he could sympathize with Mr. Bomboko's desire to return to Kinshasa, that he would discuss the matter with Ambassador Goldberg and would follow up with Mr. Bomboko tomorrow. Mr. Palmer stated that in this connection he understood that not only the closing of foreign consulates had been suspended but also the Congo's break with Portugal. The Foreign Minister confirmed this.

Mr. Palmer reminded the Foreign Minister that a previous resolution of the S.C. urged the Congo to get rid of its own mercenaries. He thought that if the Congo eliminated reference to Portuguese territory in its own resolution, it would make the problem of getting it through easier. Mr. Bomboko did not seem to take kindly to this suggestion although he did not altogether dismiss it.

482. Memorandum of Conversation[1]

Washington, October 10, 1966.

SUBJECT

Harmel–Palmer Talks

PARTICIPANTS

Belgian Foreign Minister Harmel
Viscount Etienne Davignon, Chef de Cabinet, Ministry of Foreign Affairs of Belgium
Ambassador Scheyven, Belgian Ambassador to the US
Mr. Lion, Minister, Belgian Embassy, Washington
Mr. de Schoutheets, Member of Foreign Minister Harmel's Party
Mr. Rens, Press Aide, Belgian Embassy, Washington

US Side
Mr. Palmer
Mr. Anderson, EUR/FBX
Mr. Schaufele, AFCM
Mr. Katzen, AFCM

Foreign Minister Harmel and his aides called on Mr. Palmer to discuss relations among our two countries and the Congo (Kinshasa).

Mr. Palmer and Minister Harmel agreed that "emotionalism" has been the basis for many recent decisions by President Mobutu. Mr. Palmer characterized the Congolese President as possessed by an "impetuous" tendency to carry things to the extreme without paying any attention to the consequences. He cited the difficulties which friendly powers such as Belgium and the United States have experienced in extending advice to Mobutu, who often arrives at decisions without consulting his Foreign Minister and others. Mr. Palmer underscored the Congolese clumsiness in their effort to indict Portugal at the Security Council, noting that such was especially foolish given the Congolese and Zambian need to use the Benguela Railroad.

Foreign Minister Harmel noted that poor administration and economic instability remain the Congo's endemic long-range problems. According to Harmel, there are already "too many Belgians" helping in Congolese administrative functions. He prescribed the establishment of a "government planning office", with an international staff, to cope with the myriad of Congolese administrative and economic woes.

Mr. Harmel was pessimistic concerning the next ten years for the Congo. Mr. Palmer added that, despite the need for such institutions as

[1] Source: National Archives, RG 59, Central Files 1964–66, POL THE CONGO–US. Confidential. Drafted by Jay K. Katzen on October 13.

"planning offices", short-run stability remains a key problem. For this reason, the USG supports continued assistance to the ANC and public safety programs. Mr. Schaufele cited the ANC's recent performance in Kisangani as an example that such assistance pays off. Viscount Davignon indicated that the Belgian military technicians would not share this view but agreed that their standards were unrealistically high. Mr. Harmel noted that Belgium is agreeable to continuing support in these fields, despite the fact that Belgian officers seem always to be accused by the Congolese as representing various rival factions rather than being considered as neutral advisors. For this reason in the future, Belgian military are to serve strictly in training and advisory capacities, although military transport pilots and others are to remain. Similarly, the Belgian police program is expected to continue at its present level.

Concerning other aid, Foreign Minister Harmel advised that Belgium will retain its 3.5 billion Belgian franc global support to the Congo. Of this amount, approximately 1 billion BF will go for education, health, and agriculture. Should the Congo cause Belgium to incur expenses without the latter's concurrence, however, these costs will be deducted from the remaining approximately 2.5 billion BF. The GDRC has agreed to seek to fill the 250 million BF "gap" between the 3.5 billion BF Belgian aid and the anticipated Congolese budget, by turning to international organizations or through budgetary acrobatics.

Secretary Palmer noted that one positive measure of the Mobutu regime has been the improvement in the Congo's relations with its neighbors. Mr. Palmer saw the return of Tshombe as leading to a setback of these good relations, with the possibility that dissident movements again would start up at the Congo's borders. Mr. Harmel stated that Belgium seeks to continue good relations with all former Congolese prime ministers, recognizing that one never can be sure who next may become Premier. Mr. Harmel emphasized that the GOB nevertheless continues to dissuade Belgian support for Tshombe from whatever quarter. As evidence of this attitude, Mr. Harmel cited the fact that Brussels has asked Tshombe not to reside in Belgium because of his continuing proclivity to engage in political activities. Harmel was particularly laudatory about Mr. Adoula, who is "realistic and intelligent," and recommended him to the U.S.

Mr. Harmel suggested that the USG might prevail upon friendly participants at the forthcoming OAU conference in Addis Ababa in an effort to urge a moderate Mobutu stance towards Europeans. Mr. Palmer agreed that this was advisable, but noted that extreme caution was necessary in order to prevent such an effort from becoming known to the GDRC. He added, moreover, that Africans on their own are beginning to counsel Mobutu moderation, as witnessed by their advising modification of the Congolese resolution against Portugal at the UN.

Mr. Harmel thanked Mr. Palmer for the USG's moral and political assistance. He concluded that, with hopeless elements such as Litho, the key need for the Congo was to translate written reforms and idealistic statements into action. He added that his meetings with Bomboko seemed to be going along nicely although it appeared that we were more optimistic over the Congo than he, Harmel, was. Mr. Palmer noted that the USG has no desire to replace the Belgians in the Congo and expressed the hope that this has been made adequately clear to Mobutu. In parting, both agreed that it is most important at the present time to bolster the Congolese confidence in the Belgians and the Americans and for us "to get on the same wave length" as the Congolese.

---

483. Memorandum for Director of Central Intelligence Helms[1]

Washington, undated.

SUBJECT

Status Report—Air Program in the Congo

1. *Operational Summary:* The attached memorandum[2] informs the 303 Committee of the establishment of a State–Defense–CIA working group to draw up plans for the phase-out of the [*less than 1 line not declassified*] air program from the Congo, and sets forth the major factors to be considered. Following oral instructions from the Department of State for an early phase-out, the Ambassador at Kinshasa has recommended that the program end by 15 February 1967. This date cannot be met if a condition of the phase-out is to be prior establishment by the GDRC of an adequate replacement program.

2. *Previous 303 Committee Approvals:* On 17 February 1966, the 303 Committee requested that [*less than 1 line not declassified*] air program in the Congo be substantially reduced. On 28 March 1966, the Committee reconsidered its decision pending the results of a study by the Joint Chiefs of Staff. On 8 July, the Committee agreed to await the results of impending talks between the U.S. Ambassador at Kinshasa and Presi-

---

[1] Source: Central Intelligence Agency Files, Job 82–00450R, DDO/AF, AF/DIV Historical Files, Box 6, 40 Committee, Congo (K), 1965-. Secret; Eyes Only.

[2] Attached to the original is an October 10 memorandum for the 303 Committee, "Status Report—Air Program in the Congo."

dent Mobutu before reaching a decision on the future of the air program.

3. *Cover and Personnel:* Pilots in the air program are ostensibly on direct hire to the GDRC. The T–28's and B–26K's are MAP loan to the GDRC. The [*less than 1 line not declassified*] aircraft maintenance company [*less than 1 line not declassified*] under contract to the GDRC. [*less than 1 line not declassified*].

4. *Coordination:* The attached memorandum has been brought to the attention of the Bureau of African Affairs, Department of State.

5. *Security:* The widespread knowledge that the United States Government is responsible for the tactical air program presents a continuing potential for embarrassment.

6. *Cost:* The program is currently operating at an annual cost of about [*dollar amount not declassified*]. The cost of the phase-out will depend on the findings of the working group.

Chief, Africa Division[3]

Concur:

Deputy Director for Plans Date

Release of the attached item to the members of the 303 Committee is authorized:

Director of Central Intelligence

Date

[3] The original is printed from a copy of the memorandum that is unsigned.

484. Telegram From the Station in the Congo to the Central Intelligence Agency[1]

Kinshasa, October 11, 1966.

8296. Ref Kinshasa Limdis 2426.[2]

1. Ref reports essence of [COS] conversations with [Identity 1] and [Mobutu] in which [Mobutu] demanded that [Godley] leave the Congo.

2. Station currently reassessing its relationship with [Identity 2] and [Mobutu], [Identity 1] and assessing current GDRC foreign policy developments in light of certain of [Mobutu's] recent actions. Cable on this subject will follow shortly.[3]

3. [Mobutu's] insistence that [Godley] must go represents complete reversal of his 8 Sept statements to [COS] that his ([Mobutu's]) disagreements with [Godley] had been completely resolved. While there are no doubt numerous factors which motivated [Mobutu] in reaching this decision, believe [Mobutu] was sincere when he patched up relations with [Godley]. However, [*cryptonym not declassified*] decision to withold air support during the late Sept Kisangani crisis was interpreted by [Mobutu] as "proof" that [Godley] did not support the govt. Despite the Station's many assertions to the contrary, [Mobutu] continues blame [Godley] for the decision to withold an air strike and the resulting danger in which the regime was placed by this decision.

4. In addition to the Kisangani problem, Station suspects [Mobutu] endeavoring establish himself as a leader of the African states. In order achieve this objective, he probably believes he must prove that he is not a "[U.S.] puppet". Thus by demanding recall [Godley] suspect he thinks he will be able demonstrate that he not under [U.S.] influence. This move may well be followed by other actions designed to support the thesis that [Mobutu] is truly an independent African nationalist, and some of his moves will almost certainly appear [anti-U.S.] in nature.[4]

---

[1] Source: Central Intelligence Agency Files, [*text not declassified*], Vol. IV, Mobutu. Secret; Rybat; Priority, Director. Received at 1345Z.

[2] Not found.

[3] Not found.

[4] A Central Intelligence Agency Intelligence Information Cable from Kinshasa, TDCS DB–315/02971–66, October 14, reported that Mobutu told a close associate that he was tired of what he believed to be excessive U.S. Government pressure on him on various questions concerning the Congo. He said American aid was designed for the benefit of the United States rather than the recipient country. He also complained of the problems he had with the U.S. Embassy over the use of aircraft in the Kisangani affair. (Central Intelligence Agency Files, [*text not declassified*], Vol. IV, Mobutu)

5. [*name not declassified*] told [COS] that [Godley] now believes it would be advisable for [COS] to be recalled to mark [USG] displeasure with [Mobutu]. While Station disappointed by turn of events, it does not concur with this view. Believe logic which motivated HQS decision to maintain [COS] in Kinshasa for completion his tour continues be applicable in current situation. Should developments convince Station otherwise, Kinshasa would immediately so advise HQS.

6. Paras 1–4 above shown to [*name not declassified*] in draft but not yet coordinated with [Godley] who will be tied up with deputy chief CINCSTRIKE until late afternoon. Will advise if he disagrees with points outlined paras 1–4. Thus request that contents this message not be mentioned to [Department of State] pending Kinshasa's follow-up cable indicating [Godley's] approval or disapproval.[5]

7. No index.

[5] Ambassador Godley left the Congo on October 15.

485. Telegram From the Station in the Congo to the Central Intelligence Agency[1]

Kinshasa, November 4, 1966.

8761 (In 33138). 1. Have not submitted request for payment to [Mobutu] of [*cryptonym not declassified*] funds for September and October 1966. Station immediate reaction when [Mobutu] requested [Godley's] departure was that we should cut off all future payments. On reflection, however, Station reached following conclusions:

A. Cutting off payments to [Mobutu] would almost certainly be interpreted by him as an indication that [USG] no longer supports him. Political repercussions resulting from terminating [*cryptonym not declassified*] payments would be almost as severe as if [USG] were to cut off [AID] funds.

B. Since [Department of State] has indicated it wishes retain all options, Station believes it would not be advisable cut off [AID] payments. This particularly true since [AID] assistance must, view budg-

[1] Source: Central Intelligence Agency Files, Job 78–02502R, DDO/ISS Files, Box 1, [*cryptonym not declassified*] Operations, Jan.–Dec. 1966, [*text not declassified*]. Secret; Rybat; [*cryptonym not declassified*]. No time of receipt appears on the message.

etary cuts, be reduced. [AID] reductions can be explained on the basis of budgetary reductions. However, cutting off [*cryptonym not declassified*] funds probably would convince [Mobutu] that [AID] reductions are punitive in nature, rather than the result of a budgetary cut.

2. Station has discussed above thinking with [Blake]. Latter is reluctant approve additional [*cryptonym not declassified*] payments to [Mobutu]. Just prior his departure [Godley] expressed view that [Mobutu] should be taught lesson by having [*cryptonym not declassified*] funds cut off. Since [Mobutu] has not raised the issue, Station has not pushed the matter with [Blake]. However, suspect we will have to face this problem eventually, as [Mobutu] probably will query Station concerning [*cryptonym not declassified*] funds next time he short of cash for political action ops.

3. Above views submitted for headquarters information in any discussions it may have with [Godley] and [Department of State] on subject of [*cryptonym not declassified*] funding.

4. Would appreciate Headquarters guidance as to position Station should adopt in future discussions of [*cryptonym not declassified*] funding.[2]

5. No index.

---

[2] Not found.

---

486. Memorandum for the Record[1]

Washington, November 4, 1966.

SUBJECT

Minutes of the Meeting of the 303 Committee, 4 November 1966

PRESENT

Mr. Rostow, Ambassador Thompson, Mr. Vance, and Mr. Helms

Ambassador Godley and Mr. John Waller were also present

---

[1] Source: National Security Council, Intelligence Files, 303 Committee, Minutes 1966. Secret; Eyes Only. Prepared on November 10.

1. *Congo—Air and Maritime Program*

a. The long-standing desire to turn over the U.S.-operated Congolese Air Force and pocket Navy to the host government came under discussion on Friday, 4 November. Tabled were two papers from the DOD, one from CIA, and two draft cables from State Department to Kinshasa.

b. Without a paragraph by paragraph overhaul, it was abundantly clear that the Committee was in agreement that a turnover be effected with all convenient speed but with minimum sacrifice to efficiency and order.

c. All agreed that the key to the question was to find an airline executive or experienced operations officer to manage the air force for Mobutu. The candidates, of course, would have to be satisfactory to Mobutu. It was also agreed that a non-American would be preferable and that CIA would undertake the "talent scouting."

d. Declining to be bound by any deadlines, the Committee principals pointed out that with the Congolese penchant for failing to meet payrolls, the Agency might be some time in getting out from under. The pocket Navy was believed to present a somewhat less complicated problem in transfer.

e. Following the meeting, State drafted four Roger channel cables to Kinshasa (Nos. 81702, 81703, 81709, and 81710)[2] offering general guidance on the intent of the Committee. The Executive Secretary believes that these messages contain an umbrella of accurate guidance under which the parties concerned can proceed to search for solutions.

f. It was further agreed that the steps envisaged would, when necessary, be discussed in confidence with both the Belgian and Italian governments.

(References: Minutes of 303 Committee meetings held on 28 October 1965, Item 3; 17 February 1966, Item 1; 28 March 1966, Item 1; 22 April 1966, Item 9; 9 June 1966, Item 2; 8 July 1966, Item 4; and 5 August 1966, Item 8.)[3]

[Omitted here is discussion of another subject.]

Peter Jessup

---

[2] None found.

[3] For text or summaries of the minutes for the first six meetings, see footnote 2 to Document 440, Document 464, Document 467 and footnote 3 thereto, footnote 3 to Document 472, and Document 473. The minutes for the August 5 meeting are in National Security Council, Intelligence Files, 303 Committee, Minutes 1966.

487. Telegram From the Department of State to the Embassy in the Congo[1]

Washington, December 15, 1966, 2:23 p.m.

103125. 1. Ramiro Rodriguez and Mike Pons, self-styled Tshombe emissaries, approached DOD December 13 with letter to President from Tshombe. The two men stated Tshombe had told them avoid Department of State since DOD could be expected be more sympathetic Tshombe's aims. In initial contact, they informed DOD officials they wished to furnish oral briefing and request US support and assistance for Tshombe.

2. After checking with Department for guidance, Rodriguez and Pons received morning of December 14 at DOD in presence State officer (not identified as such to them). They furnished long rambling briefing about satisfactory state Congolese affairs when Tshombe was Prime Minister and how bad they are now, as well as list of benefits which would accrue to West and capitalism if Tshombe returned. They requested loan of $4 million to assist Tshombe, who, they claimed, expected return Kinshasa no later than December 31.

3. In line with State guidance, DOD officials informed them of following:

a) US does not intervene in internal affairs of other nations.
b) US has supported every central government of Congo since independence and continues that policy.
c) Communications re foreign affairs should be submitted to Dept of State and if letter given to DOD officials latter would transmit it to State for forwarding.
d) US will not support or assist in any plot or scheme to overthrow the present government.

4. In view this negative response to request for assistance, emissaries decided not to give letter to DOD. They added that other sources, notably France, had offered support which Tshombe had earlier refused but intimated they would turn back to such sources. Added that when Tshombe comes to power, he will be friendly with US but refusal to assist him now would affect relations with US.

4. [*sic*] At time original contact Dec. 13, DOD officials actually saw unsigned copy of letter which they said was essentially recital of conditions in Congo. Net impression of those attending Dec. 14 meeting was that this not a serious undertaking which leads us to wonder whether

[1] Source: National Archives, RG 59, Central Files 1964–66, POL 30 THE CONGO. Secret; Priority; Exdis. Drafted by Schaufele, cleared by Godley in AF/CM, and approved by Fredericks. Repeated to Brussels, Madrid, and Paris.

two men actually reflecting Tshombe's views on anything other than letter itself.

5. On Dec. 15 Deptoff saw Struelens, who, although he claims no present association with Tshombe, may be in communication with him. He was informed in general terms of this approach. Deptoff suggested Struelens might clearly inform Tshombe that the US will not support any plot or scheme to depose Mobutu government.

6. Embassy should inform Mobutu in general terms this approach and of US reaction. We do not exclude the possibility that Rodriguez and Pons will attempt to peddle letter elsewhere in Washington for delivery to the White House.[2]

Katzenbach

[2] Telegram 110241 to Kinshasa, December 29, reported that Rodriguez and Pons called at the Department on December 28, asked for U.S. support of a future Tshombe government, and left a letter for the President. They said they were not seeking active U.S. support for a move against Mobutu, but asking for "benevolent neutrality" if Tshombe forces attempted a coup, i.e., a commitment not to let U.S.-controlled aircraft in the Congo be used against Tshombe forces. They were informed that the United States continued to support the central government and did not support plots to overthrow it, and that the aircraft in the Congo were part of the Congolese forces and Tshombe should not assume they would not be used against forces attempting a coup. (Ibid.) No copy of the letter to the President has been found.

---

488. Memorandum From the Board of National Estimates to Director of Central Intelligence McCone[1]

Washington, January 27, 1967.

SUBJECT

A Worrisome Contingency in the Congo

The situation in the Congo continues to deteriorate. It may become grave, and the lives of Belgians and other whites may be endangered to the point where some kind of rescue operation may be required.

1. The crisis in the Congo has become worse. Severe economic dislocations now seem almost certain, with possible attendant dangers to

[1] Source: Johnson Library, National Security File, Country File, Congo, Vol. XIII, Memos & Miscellaneous, 11/66–8/67. Secret.

the Belgians and other whites. Given the intransigence of the Union Minière and the ill-considered and erratic actions of the Congolese, eleventh-hour efforts by the Belgian Government to arrange a deal between Mobutu and the Union Minière have only faint prospects of success.[2] Though copper production in Katanga continues, none is exported, and the Congo's foreign exchange reserves are gone. The lack of foreign exchange to replenish low stocks of mining equipment and spare parts, as well as to meet the payroll, is likely to bring mining operations to a halt fairly soon.

2. In these circumstances, one of the most serious eventualities which looms ahead is the threat of violence against the 2,000 Belgian employees of Union Minière and their families in Katanga. Most are eager to leave the Congo as soon as possible, and have been encouraged to do so by the Union Minière though it would take weeks to move all the 6,000 or so people involved. If Mobutu permits a substantial number to leave, the copper industry will close down very quickly. It would be virtually impossible to replace key employees for many months. If the Congolese attempt to prevent the departure of the Belgians, racial tensions will mount, and incidents are likely to arise which will endanger lives. If the copper industry comes to a halt, Congolese officials will probably accuse local Belgians of sabotage, and the already strongly anti-Belgian Congolese press and radio will probably take up the cry. The Congolese army, thus far under orders to prevent harassment of Belgians, may get out of control, and such order as exists may break down.

3. We believe the chances are increasing that anti-Belgian or anti-white incidents will lead to a situation wherein the lives of many Europeans in Katanga, and perhaps in the rest of the Congo, would be in danger. There are some 40,000 Belgians in the Congo (including about 15,000 in Katanga); there are also some 40,000 other whites, including 1,000 to 1,500 US citizens, most of whom are scattered in other parts of the country. Clearly, a rescue operation to evacuate even US nationals would be very difficult, and an effort to remove all Europeans vastly more so. The situation may not deteriorate this far; it is impossible to predict Congolese events with confidence. But in view of the recent turbulent history of the country and the critical nature of the present troubles, such a contingency should be kept in mind.

For the Board of National Estimates:

Sherman Kent
Chairman

---

[2] In December 1966, the Congo had announced the takeover of the Union Minière company without compensation. The company retaliated by stopping remittance of foreign exchange, putting the Congo on the verge of economic collapse.

489. Memorandum From Edward Hamilton of the National Security Council Staff to the President's Special Assistant (Rostow)[1]

Washington, January 31, 1967.

WWR:

SUBJECT

CIA Memorandum on the Congo

You asked me to comment on the attached CIA information memo.[2] I haven't much to add. It is an accurate picture of the present situation, and the inferences it draws for future developments are entirely plausible. The only compensating fact is that one could have as plausibly predicted imminent disaster for the Congo on any given day for the past six months, but nothing catastrophic has happened.

However, there is no question that danger has reached a new octave in January. We now have a very real threat of mass departures by Belgian whites critical to the mining industry—because of unwillingness to work for the new Congolese firm and/or because the Congolese have no foreign exchange to pay them. This will magnify pressures on Mobutu to refuse to let them leave. (He has already issued and rescinded one directive forcing them to give a year's notice.) If he acts, Union Minière will have the Belgian Government right where it wants them, and there will be great pressure on us to help the GOB guarantee the safe departure of what will by then probably be the majority of whites in the Congo. Nothing could be worse for Congolese economics and politics.

The way out is to:

1. Find a way to settle the money issues between the GOC and Union Minière—probably through arbitration—so that UM will stop blocking sales of Congolese copper.
2. Set up a new marketing mechanism to replace Union Minière.
3. Get UM or other experienced corporations to sell technical assistance to the new Congolese corporation so that production continues at a reasonable level.

The arbitration of outstanding issues is, once again, beginning to look possible. A consortium of experienced copper producers and purveyors is now in the process of (quiet) formation to deal with the

---

[1] Source: Johnson Library, National Security File, Country File, Congo, Vol. XIII, Memos & Miscellaneous, 11/66–8/67. Secret.

[2] Document 488.

other problems. Meanwhile, however, copper builds up in the Congo and 70% of her foreign exchange income does not flow in. Unless we have a breakthrough soon, the consequences foreseen in the CIA memo could well occur.

I have followed this one fairly closely, putting my oar in from time to time as it seemed necessary. I am satisfied that we are playing our role—moderator, conciliator, go-between—with skill and relative effectiveness. In my view, we should continue to do what we can to promote reason on both sides, and sweat it out.[3]

EH

[3] In February 1967, the two sides reached an agreement to submit the legal questions involved in the Union Minière takeover to arbitration, and the Congo signed a contract with a company affiliate to continue to produce and sell copper.

490. Telegram From the Department of State to the Embassy in the Congo[1]

Washington, February 13, 1967, 8:51 p.m.

136429. Subject: Tshombe Plot. Ref: State 103125, 110241.[2]

1. Deptoff asked self-styled Tshombe emissary Michael Pons to call Feb 13 to receive reply to his oft-repeated request for USG support for Tshombe coup. Pons was told:

a) USG will continue support central govt in Congo, including Mobutu, just as it did all central govts since independence;
b) USG believes Mobutu expresses same nationalist aspirations any independent Congolese Govt could be expected demonstrate;
c) USG believes another coup at this stage Congo's development could be disastrous for Congo and free world interests in Africa.

2. Pons said he anticipated reply and appreciated frankness with which it given. Nevertheless, he added, Tshombe still plans carry out coup some time during next three to four months. Pons said he familiar with principal aspects of coup planning which he judged sound.

[1] Source: National Archives, RG 59, Central Files 1967–69, POL 23–9 THE CONGO. Secret; Exdis. Drafted by Haverkamp and Brown, cleared by Palmer, and approved by Brown.

[2] See Document 487 and footnote 2 thereto.

3. You should inform Mobutu of pertinent points this message as well as State 110241 as soon as possible and inform Dept when message conveyed.[3]

Katzenbach

[3] In telegram 5314 from Kinshasa, February 18, Blake reported that he gave Mobutu the substance of the points in this telegram, and that Mobutu was obviously pleased. (National Archives, RG 59, Central Files 1967–69, POL 30 THE CONGO)

491. Telegram From the Department of State to the Embassy in the Congo[1]

Washington, March 8, 1967, 3:50 p.m.

150921. For Blake from Palmer. Subj: Tshombe Trial.

1. While we do not yet know verdict in trial of Tshombe, Tshipola and others,[2] believe you should see Bomboko soonest in order make following points:

2) We continue support Central Govt in Congo as we always have and cannot condone extra legal attempts overthrow that govt. At same time we believe that if GDRC is to project desirable image as progressive, stable African leader, full and careful consideration should be given to possible international reaction to trial. Repeat of trials followed by summary executions of last spring could well have adverse effect on Congo's image throughout world.

3) You should make it plain we are not trying to give any opinion or exert any type of influence on outcome of trial. Our hope is that Congo Govt aware implications of trials and possible public executions on its good name as well as possible effect on general attitudes towards African states. Basic questions will be asked such as was there adequate opportunity for defense with independent legal assistance and did ju-

[1] Source: National Archives, RG 59, Central Files 1967–69, POL 29 THE CONGO. Confidential; Immediate. Drafted by Roy T. Haverkamp of AF/CM; cleared by Brown and Runyon; and approved by Palmer. Repeated to Brussels, Bukavu, London, Lubumbashi, Lusaka, Madrid, and Nairobi.

[2] In September 1966, the Congolese Government formally charged Tshombe, who was in exile in Madrid, with high treason for endangering the security of the Congo. In March 1967, a special military tribunal tried Tshombe in absentia along with several others.

dicial proceedings take place free from public pressures and executive interference.[3]

4) FYI Above instruction predicated on belief defendants are military involved in Kisangani mutiny for whom we hold no brief; if defendants should include civilians, such as Kishwe or other former Tshombe supporters, summary justice even less justified. End FYI.

Rusk

[3] In telegram 5708 from Kinshasa, March 9, Blake reported that he went over the points in this telegram with Bomboko, who said he would discuss them with Mobutu. (National Archives, RG 59, Central Files 1967–69, POL 29 THE CONGO)

492. Memorandum for the Record[1]

Washington, March 8, 1967.

SUBJECT

Minutes of the Meeting of the 303 Committee, 8 March 1967

PRESENT

Mr. Rostow, Ambassador Kohler, and Admiral Taylor
Mr. Vance, absent in hospital, registered his views by telephone

General Ralph D. Steakley was present for Item 1
Mr. Glenn Fields was present for Item 3
Mr. [*name not declassified*] and Mr. [*name not declassified*] were present for Item 4
Mr. William Broe was present for Item 5

[Omitted here is discussion of other subjects.]

3. *Progress Report on Phaseout of Air Program in Congo.*

a. The committee approved the proposal of JCS to turn over two C–46's to the GDRC but with the Agency requested modification that the C–46's be leased to [*less than 1 line not declassified*] on behalf of the GDRC since the Congolese have no facility themselves for adequate maintenance. Ambassador Kohler emphasized that the Agency should move with all convenient speed to transfer the responsibility and costs of [*less than 1 line not declassified*] to the Mobutu government. He urged

[1] Source: National Security Council, Intelligence Files, 303 Committee, Minutes 1967. Secret; Eyes Only. Prepared on March 10.

that the committee live up to its commitment and get out by no later than the end of the fiscal year. Mr. Glenn Fields indicated that the Agency was in no way trying to hold on but only to ensure an efficacious turnover.[2] He said that Mobutu had been unable to address himself to the "air force" problem because of his total involvement with the Belgian holding companies. He had not yet made any final agreement with the retired Turkish air force general who would hold the position of "air manager". Mobutu had not yet held talks with [*less than 1 line not declassified*] representatives on payment of salaries to pilots and mechanics. There was more than a possibility that he would not be able to meet this payroll with hard currency. In such a case, the embassy would have to pick up the tab to prevent a total incapacity for flight operations.

b. Despite these clouds, the committee felt that the transfer should proceed as rapidly as possible. Should difficulties emerge they could be referred back to the committee. In any event, a progress report was called for by mid-May 1967.

[Omitted here is discussion of other subjects.]

Peter Jessup

---

[2] A March 3 CIA progress report to Helms on the phaseout of the air program in the Congo noted that the report was being submitted in time to alert the 303 Committee to the fact that the pace of the phaseout had been delayed somewhat by circumstances beyond the Agency's control and thus might require underwriting beyond the originally estimated date of June 30, 1967. Since it was impossible to say with any degree of certainty how long the CIA subsidy would have to be continued, the report proposed that it be extended on a month-to-month basis, but estimated that it seemed likely that the extension period would not exceed 3 months. (Central Intelligence Agency Files, Job 81–00966R, Congo, 1967–68)

493. Memorandum From the Department of State Executive Secretary (Read) to the President's Special Assistant (Rostow)[1]

Washington, March 18, 1967.

SUBJECT

Letter to the President from Moise Tshombe

We recommend that no reply be made to the letter to the President from Moise Tshombe of March 9.[2]

You will recall that Mr. Tshombe, for his own political purposes, has used several methods and individuals to try to establish contact with the President. Any reply to this letter, no matter how innocuous, would lend itself to exploitation by Mr. Tshombe for those political purposes and could thus seriously affect our friendly relations with the present GDRC. The trial of which Mr. Tshombe has written has been concluded, resulting in death sentences for Mr. Tshombe, Colonel Tshipola, who is specifically mentioned in the Tshombe letter, and one other officer and sentences of various lengths for four other people, including Mr. Tshombe's brother. One officer was acquitted.

At our instruction, before the conclusion of the trial, our Chargé in Kinshasa impressed upon the Congolese Foreign Minister, the necessity of avoiding the kind of kangaroo court procedures and brutal executions which followed the discovery of the pentacost plot in 1966. Nevertheless, with the exception of Tshombe, his brother, and possibly the other civilian involved, Colonel Tshipola and the other officers were essentially tried for a mutiny which resulted in the death of the Congolese Army Commander, Colonel Tshatshi, in Kisangani, as well as other military and civilian personnel.

We believe it serves no useful purpose to make any additional efforts with the Congolese Government concerning an essentially domestic matter. There is little question that the verdict against the two Tshombe brothers is a political one and cannot be justified especially since no true defense was permitted. Both Tshombes are in Europe and

---

[1] Source: National Archives, RG 59, Central Files 1967–69, POL 30-2 THE CONGO. Secret. Drafted by Schaufele on March 16 and cleared by Palmer.

[2] A typed notation on the original reads: "White House (Mr. Hamilton) agreeable no reply necessary (Judy Stewart to jmj, 5/17/67)." A copy of Tshombe's letter to the President is ibid.

it is unlikely that any country would permit their extradition even if the Congolese Government requested it.

C. Brown[3]

[3] Printed from a copy that bears this stamped signature indicating that Brown signed for Read above Read's typed signature.

494. Paper Prepared in the Central Intelligence Agency[1]

Washington, April 3, 1967.

PROJECT TERMINATION[2]

CRYPTONYM

[*cryptonym not declassified*]

1. It is requested that Project [*cryptonym not declassified*] be terminated on 31 March 1967. The project was first approved on 13 August 1964, in partial implementation of a 303 Committee decision 13 August 1964, approving covert aid at a level of [*dollar amount not declassified*] to support the Congo (Kinshasa) central government against the rebels. To this end, a wide variety of activities were mounted under this project, but by the renewal for FY 1967 they had been reduced to two: covert support of President Mobutu and the maintenance of a maritime patrol capability on Lake Tanganyika.

2. Termination of this project is requested because changed political conditions in the Congo have eliminated the need for a continuation of the above activities. Rebel activity in the eastern Congo has all but ended. Mobutu is seeking to project an African nationalist image of himself and his government and has not requested further covert funding since the payment due him for September 1966. 303 Committee authority to make such payments expired on 31 December 1966, and there are no present plans to request authority for a new series of

[1] Source: Central Intelligence Agency Files, Job 78–02502R, DDO/ISS Files, Box 1, [*cryptonym not declassified*]/ Dev. & Plans, [*text not declassified*], Aug. '64 thru Jan. 1967. Secret. There is no drafting information on the original.

[2] On May 5, Karamessines signed a CIA Project Action Form approving termination of the project effective March 31, 1967. (Ibid.)

payments. In compliance with a 303 decision of 4 November 1966, to phase out U.S. Government participation in the maritime program, control of the boats was transferred to the Congolese authorities on 7 January 1967. All [*less than 1 line not declassified*] personnel exclusively connected with the maritime program have been withdrawn from the Congo.

3. Unused funds revert to the [*less than 1 line not declassified*].

4. There have been no risks to any elements of [*less than 1 line not declassified*] including [*cryptonym not declassified*] arising out of this termination. All equipment involved in the operation has either been turned over to the Congolese Government or withdrawn. There are no outstanding commitments.

495. Telegram From the Department of State to the Embassy in the Congo[1]

Washington, April 25, 1967, 1:43 p.m.

181618. Ref Kinshasa 5104; 5105 Notal.[2]

1. If you agree you should find suitable occasion deliver over your signature following written reply to Bomboko's letter to you of January 26 (reftels). Any changes, however, should be cleared with Department. "Dear Mr. Minister: Your letter of January 26 expressing the concern of the Congolese Govt over rumors that forces have been gathering in adjacent territory to launch an aggression against the Congo, has been carefully considered by my Govt.

2. I have been instructed to assure you that, while my Govt cannot confirm reliability of these rumors, it nevertheless hopes that the efforts and accomplishments of the GDRC to achieve stability and security

[1] Source: National Archives, RG 59, Central Files 1967–69, POL 23–9 THE CONGO. Secret; Exdis. Drafted by Haverkamp; cleared by Runyon, Deputy Legal Adviser Carl F. Salans, Beigel in EUR/FBX, Portugal Country Director George W. Landau, Palmer, L. Dean Brown, Schaufele, UNP Director Elizabeth Ann Brown and, Lang; and approved by Acting Secretary Katzenbach. Repeated to Brussels, Lisbon, and Kigali.

[2] Telegram 5104 from Kinshasa, February 10, transmitted a translation of a confidential letter from Bomboko to the Chargé requesting information on the U.S. attitude toward rumors of the formation of a mercenary group for attack on the Congo as well as its attitude if the Congo became the object of an external attack. (Ibid.) Telegram 5105 from Kinshasa, February 10, is also ibid.

and assure political, economic and social development will not be thwarted by renewed threats of violence in the Congo.

3. You further expressed a desire to ascertain the attitude of the USG in case the Congo should become the object of external aggression organized by foreigners or Congolese. As you know it has been the policy of the USG, through the UN and in consultation with the GDRC and its friends and supporters, to support the maintenance of the territorial integrity and political independence of the Congo against external aggression. This policy is fully consistent with the U.N. Charter. Actions taken in the U.N. were the basis for the consultation and cooperation by the USG with your Govt in its efforts to maintain the territorial integrity and unity of the Congo after, as well as before, the departure of UN forces. You may recall I have made this attitude of my Govt unmistakably clear in earlier conversations. It was reaffirmed most recently in the statement issued by the Embassy on February 24 of this year. I wish to take this occasion to reiterate in this same context that the USG remains ready to consult with the GDRC on all such questions of common interest.

4. The Congolese Govt's appreciation of the value of US assistance, also noted in your letter, has been warmly received by my Govt and interpreted as a reflection of the traditionally close and friendly relations existing between our two countries."[3]

5. French translation follows.

Katzenbach

---

[3] In telegram 6878 from Kinshasa, May 2, Blake reported that he presented the text of the letter to Bomboko that day. He told the Foreign Minister that the U.S. Government believed on the basis of present information that the threat to the Congo from Tshombist mercenaries was limited, and that such reports appeared to be a psychological warfare campaign on the part of Tshombe. (Ibid.)

496. Memorandum of Conversation[1]

Washington, May 5, 1967.

SUBJECT

Congo General

PARTICIPANTS

Congolese Ambassador Cyrille Adoula

The Secretary
Roy Haverkamp, AFCM
Alec Touamayan, L/S interpreter

The Secretary began the conversation by telling Ambassador Adoula that the Congo continues to be an important preoccupation of the United States Government, that what happens there is of the deepest interest to us and is followed very closely. The Ambassador said that he had recently been in Kinshasa where he was asked by Foreign Minister Bomboko to bring greetings and best wishes to the Secretary and to the American people. As a result of his stay in Kinshasa the Ambassador was optimistic over the future prospects of his country. Thanks to U.S. aid and the success of the Mobutu regime, the situation has been stabilized and the rebellion is disappearing despite several remaining pockets. The Congo now has friendly relations with its neighbors and must now make an effort to improve its economic situation. The Mobutu regime has deep popular support and its reforms have been well received by the people. The net result of the reforms already instituted and those contemplated will be the creation of a new base of confidence for foreign investment, particularly American foreign investment. The Ambassador said that he had been asked by his government to convey its thanks and those of the Congolese people to the American Government and people for their indispensable help in creating these favorable conditions.

Aftermath of November 1964 U.S.–Belgium Paradrop on Stanleyville

The Secretary asked if there was any residue of ill will toward the United States as a result of our involvement in the November 24, 1964 rescue operation in Stanleyville. Ambassador Adoula replied that the general population was certainly afraid when they heard of the paradrop on Stanleyville but that they soon realized that the rescue operation benefited not only foreign hostages of the rebels but also Con-

[1] Source: National Archives, RG 59, Central Files 1967–69, POL THE CONGO. Limited Official Use. Drafted by Haverkamp and approved in S on May 17. The memorandum is labeled "Part I of IV." The meeting was held in Secretary Rusk's office.

golese hostages. It was a humanitarian act benefiting everyone involved. Now the people have forgotten the incident and no longer talk about it except for a few interested individuals. There is no discernible resentment against the United States and Belgium for this operation.

497. Editorial Note

In anticipation of the 303 Committee meeting the following day, Department of State and Central Intelligence Agency officials met at the Department of State on May 11, 1967, to discuss termination of the U.S. Government air program in the Congo. Dean Brown of the Bureau of African Affairs indicated that the bureau's position would be that the U.S. Government could not afford to lose air capability in the Congo through the loss of effective maintenance organization. Both Brown and John MacDonald of the Bureau of Intelligence and Research proposed that CIA provide funds for [*less than 1 line not declassified*] to get it started if the Congolese Government failed to do so and that such a recommendation be made to Deputy Under Secretary of State for Political Affairs Kohler for use at the 303 Committee meeting. (Central Intelligence Agency Files, Job 82–00450R, DDO/AF, AF/DIV Historical Files, Box 6, 40 Committee, Congo (K), 1965–)

At their meeting on May 12, members of the 303 Committee had the following discussion of the air program in the Congo, according to the minutes of the meeting:

"The progress report dated 10 May 1967 on the phaseout of the air program in the Congo (Kinshasa) was noted. Mr. Vance had several questions regarding the role of [*text not declassified*]. Admiral Taylor stated that Senator Russell had reiterated his concern to avoid a total loss of capability in that area. Ambassador Kohler repeated his plea that no one lose sight of the ultimate objective of transferring in toto the air program to the GDRC." (Peter Jessup, Memorandum for the Record, May 18, 1967; National Security Council, Intelligence Files, 303 Committee, Minutes—1967)

Earlier, in telegram 1557 to the Central Intelligence Agency, April 26, the Station in Kinshasa had reported that operational control of all [*text not declassified*] T–28 aircraft had been turned over to the Congolese Government in a low-key ceremony on April 24. The cable noted that with this turnover, CIA was no longer involved in the Congo's combat air program. (Central Intelligence Agency Files, Job 81–00966R, Box 1, Folder 12, Congo, 1967–68)

498. Memorandum From the Chief of the Africa Division, Directorate for Plans, Central Intelligence Agency (Roosevelt) to the Deputy Director for Plans (FitzGerald)[1]

Washington, May 29, 1967.

SUBJECT

Kinshasa Station Contact with Mobutu and [*name not declassified*]

1. CIA's relationship with Mobutu and [*name not declassified*] dates back to pre-Congolese independence (1960) contacts between Devlin and a number of Congolese nationalists in Brussels. The relationship has been strengthened by seven years of close and continuing contact in Kinshasa since independence. Mobutu and [*name not declassified*] have become accustomed to and to some degree dependent on the informal channel to the U.S. Government thus provided. On a number of occasions, Mobutu has sought an extension of Devlin's tour in Kinshasa (most recently in a conversation with Under Secretary Katzenbach) and has said that after Devlin leaves he will expect to maintain close contact with his successor, [*name not declassified*].[2]

2. Mobutu and [*name not declassified*] would interpret the termination of this relationship—particularly if termination were more or less coincident on Devlin's departure—as evidence of a desire on the part of the U.S. Government to disengage from the close and friendly relations that have characterized dealings between the governments of the two countries for most of the period since 1960. Mobutu's regime is essentially a personal one. Relationships between non-Africans and Africans are essentially of a personal, non-institutionalized nature. Since Mobutu has himself personally appealed for a continuation of the relationship, he would almost certainly interpret its termination as evidence that forces within the U.S. Government hostile to him personally had

[1] Source: Central Intelligence Agency Files, [*text not declassified*], Vol. II, [*text not declassified*]. Secret.

[2] In telegram 0952 from Kinshasa to CIA, March 14, the Chief of Station reported that he told Blake that Mobutu was planning to make a formal request that his recall to Headquarters be delayed until November. Blake then told him that it had been decided at the "highest levels" that after the Chief of Station's departure, CIA must terminate all contacts with Mobutu and [*name not declassified*]. Noting that Mobutu was already suspicious concerning the reasons behind his scheduled departure, the Chief of Station said that the Station believed the Department of State edict represented a serious error in judgment which could jeopardize CIA's whole position in the Congo, the position of the new Ambassador (whom Mobutu would almost certainly blame for the decision), and even overall U.S.-Congolese relations. The Chief of Station pointed out that Mobutu had been in regular and close contact with CIA for nearly 7 years and might not permit CIA contact to be maintained at subordinate levels. (Ibid.)

gained strength. He would also almost certainly identify Ambassador McBride with these hostile forces, since the termination would occur shortly after the Ambassador's arrival in Kinshasa, and since the only way the termination could be explained to Mobutu would be to tell him that orders to this effect had been received from Washington.

3. From a more parochial point of view, the termination of the Station's contact with Mobutu under these circumstances would immediately be reflected in a weakening if not a rupture of the [*less than 1 line not declassified*] relationships established [*less than 1 line not declassified*], relationships that would play an essential role in planned efforts to improve our coverage of the Bloc target in Brazzaville and to provide adequate coverage of the Soviets when they reestablish themselves in Kinshasa. The end of the Mobutu relationship would also probably remove what has amounted to a protective umbrella over Station [*less than 1 line not declassified*] operations in the Congo, [*1½ lines not declassified*].

4. Thus it is our conviction that such a termination would have serious adverse effects on U.S. Government relations with the GDRC. On the other hand, a continuation of the present relationship, carefully coordinated with the Ambassador in the future as it has been in the past, would avoid any such adverse effects while providing the Ambassador with a useful additional means of explaining U.S. policies and bringing U.S. influence to bear on the GDRC.

Archibald B. Roosevelt, Jr.
Chief, Africa Division

---

499. Editorial Note

In telegram 2002, June 1, 1967, the Station in Kinshasa informed the Central Intelligence Agency that it had been shown a Department of State telegram stating that the Station was no longer to have contact with either President Mobutu or [*name not declassified*]. The change in policy, the Station indicated in telegram 2002, would make it more difficult to operate successfully across the board.

CIA replied in telegram 06540, June 1, that during a briefing in Washington on CIA personnel and programs in the Congo, newly-appointed Ambassador Robert McBride had stated that the Department of State and he personally felt that contact with officials in the positions held by Mobutu [*text not declassified*] should be restricted to the Chief of Mission. McBride recognized, however, that the situation in the Congo might not fit his preconceptions and would not make a decision on this point until after he had a chance to assess the situation on the ground. He said that if he decided that there should be no CIA contact, he personally would explain the decision to Mobutu. (Central Intelligence Agency Files, [*text not declassified*], Vol. V, Mobutu) In telegram 2205 to CIA, June 26, the Station in Kinshaha reported that McBride, who had arrived in Kinshasa but had yet to present his credentials, still planned to inform Mobutu that further contacts with the U.S. Embassy were to be exclusively with McBride. McBride had indicated, however, that he might modify his position with respect to [*name not declassified*]. (Ibid.)

---

500. Memorandum for the Record[1]

Washington, June 16, 1967.

SUBJECT

Minutes of the Meeting of the 303 Committee, 16 June 1967

PRESENT

Mr. Rostow, Ambassador Kohler, Mr. Vance, and Admiral Taylor

Mr. Archibald Roosevelt was present for Item 4
Mr. Boris Ilyin was present for Item 5

[Omitted here is discussion of other subjects.]

4. *Congo—Progress Report on Phaseout of Air Program*

a. On the question of the progress report on the phaseout of the air program in the Congo (Kinshasa)[2], the committee stonewalled on any further support to Mobutu and asked that a cable be sent instructing

---

[1] Source: National Security Council, Intelligence Files, 303 Committee, Minutes 1967. Secret; Eyes Only.

[2] The June 14 progress report summarized action taken in phasing out U.S. Government covert support of the Congolese air force since the report of May 10, and alerted the Committee to the problems arising from the Congolese Government's continued failure to make the initial deposit of [*text not declassified*] to the [*cryptonym not declassified*] account as stipulated by the contract. (Central Intelligence Agency Files, Job 82–00450R, Box 6, 40 Committee, Congo (K), 1965–)

[*cryptonym not declassified*] to give its 30-day notice to employees. Only a tough approach would galvanize the Congolese into action.[3]

b. Ambassador Kohler took a put-your-money-where-your-mouth-is attitude toward the flibbertigibbet behavior of the Congolese and asked for no further deadlines. Mr. Rostow particularly disliked the alleged Mobutu sense of humor (Mobutu said on 9 June that he believed the USG would be able to cough up the annual cost of the contract for the coming year).

[Omitted here is discussion of other subjects.]

Peter Jessup

---

[3] A July 24 CIA memorandum to the Director of Central Intelligence stated that the Department's Bureau of African Affairs had informed the Africa Division on July 21 that it was recommending a further postponement of the date on which [*cryptonym not declassified*] would send out dismissal notices to its employees if it had not by that time received from the Congolese Government the [*text not declassified*] stipulated in the contract. Under the terms of its contract with [*cryptonym not declassified*], the GDRC had agreed to fund [*cryptonym not declassified*] operations as of July 1, but the initial deposit had not yet been made. (Ibid., Job 81–00966R, Box 1, Folder 12, Congo, 1967–68)

---

501. Memorandum From the President's Special Assistant (Rostow) to President Johnson[1]

Washington, June 21, 1967, 4:45 p.m.

SUBJECT

17 Million Loan to the Congo

In the attached, Messrs. Gaud and Schultze recommend approval of a $17 million loan to the Congo. Schultze's memorandum (Tab A)[2] gives you a concise summary of the proposal, the self-help conditions, and the economic outlook. Gaud's memorandum (Tab B) provides greater detail. At Tab C is a summary of the economic stabilization program of which this loan would be a part.

This loan is proposed in the following policy framework:

---

[1] Source: Johnson Library, National Security File, Country File, Congo, Vol. XIII, Memos & Miscellaneous, 11/66–8/67. No classification marking.

[2] Neither tab is attached. Copies of these memoranda are ibid., Memos to the President, Walt Rostow, Vol. 32.

1. Having helped to achieve a reasonably stable and unified Congo, we are now gradually shifting from a very close paternal connection with the GOC to a more standard relation between independent nations. This makes very good sense for the interests of both countries.

2. A major part of this shift is a trend away from slush funds and toward genuine development aid. In 1962 and 1963, we were making huge grants to the Congo. We later shifted to loans. We are now making the loans smaller (this is $2 million smaller than last year's). Within two years, we plan to eliminate supporting assistance loans altogether.

3. As the loans grow smaller, the self-help terms grow tougher. This loan is conditioned on a complete monetary and economic stabilization program, administered by the IMF. With luck, it will put the basically-strong Congolese economy back into self-sustaining shape.

4. We are a minority financier in the Congo. Even including food, we are providing less than one-fourth of her aid. The great bulk of it comes from the Belgians, the Italians and the EEC, along with the IMF.

Despite these trends, and the very real economic progress the Congo has achieved during the past two years, we should not give you the impression that the sailing is smooth. The Congo survives more perils every week than Pauline ever dreamed of. Mobutu is particularly susceptible to the urge to cut his own throat by finding new ways to kick the Belgians. Thus, the Congolese stability we talk about is very fragile.

It is fair to say, however, that this loan is necessary for any stability, and that, whatever its weaknesses, the present situation is the most stable in recent history. Therefore, I recommend that you approve.

All government agencies, including Treasury, join in the Schultze/Gaud recommendation.

Walt

Approve loan[3]

Disapprove

Speak to me

---

[3] This option is checked.

502. Telegram From the Embassy in the Congo to the Department of State[1]

Kinshasa, July 3, 1967, 1235Z.

46. Subj: Tshombe kidnapping.[2]

1. Bomboko told me this morning that Tshombe's kidnapping and arrival in Algiers had come as surprise to GDRC. MPR Political Bureau had met at length on Sat night and had decided under circumstances it essential that Tshombe be extradited and punished. Basis of extradition, papers for which had been carefully prepared, was common crimes committed by Tshombe. There strong popular pressure now to wipe out Tshombe who is center of or excuse for continuing disorder and sabotage in Congo. Pro-Tshombists were responsible for Lubudi bridge bombings and economic sabotage. Tshombe has continuously plotted overthrow Mobutu govt and elimination of its principal leaders from President down, even if this were to throw Congo into new crisis. It now in vital interest Congolese to eliminate Tshombe, as doing so will remove center around which so much that is troubling Congo revolves.

2. Re details extradition. Bomboko said he had tried discuss matter by phone with Algiers yesterday, but no one could be found in Algerian FonOff. He had then had discussion with Algerian Amb from Brazza who had given GDRC to understand extradition possible but had concurrently also mentioned importance GDRC voting with Arabs and GA (Kinshasa 47)[3] as tacit condition. GDRC also in touch with GOA through Algerian Amb in Madrid who had suggested GDRC send delegation. This morning Mungul-Diaka (Congolese Amb to Algeria and First Secretary MPR), Alcidor Kabeya (Chief Prosecutor (Procuror General)), and his own Assistant Chef de Cabinet, left for Algiers via Athens and Rome (note ACL 5708 which reports Security Chief Singa and group of paratroopers also accompanied above group). Bomboko said he expected Tshombe to be brought here for trial directly and in matter of days.

3. Told Bomboko that he should recognize there likely be strong American public outcry against Tshombe kidnapping. Said basis for

---

[1] Source: National Archives, RG 59, Central Files 1967–69, POL 30 THE CONGO. Confidential; Immediate. Repeated to Brussels, Madrid, and Algiers and passed to the White House and USIA.

[2] On June 30, Tshombe was kidnapped on his way to Majorca in a chartered British plane and taken to Algiers.

[3] Dated July 3. (National Archives, RG 59, Central Files 1967–69, POL 27 ARAB–ISR/UN)

strong negative reaction would be means by which Tshombe seized plus reaction against further political hangings. Recalled we had assured Mobutu on several occasions that USG supported his regime and had no brief for Tshombe. Reminded him that when French kidnapped Ben Bella in 1957, there had been similar reaction and USG had protested to French.

4. Bomboko said he recognized this but urged that we in turn recognize that GDRC had no other alternative but to demand Tshombe's extradition once Tshombe in African hands. I told Bomboko that I had no desire interfere in internal affairs of Congo and that I not acting on instructions, but as friend of Congo. I felt personally obliged to warn him of strong reaction I expected and to urge him to handle Tshombe affair quickly, with justice and without starting what would seem to be extensive purge trials. Bomboko took all this very seriously and said he would report at once to Mobutu.

5. *Comment:* Occasion offered by Bomboko comment on relation GA vote to Tshombe extradition gave me perfect opportunity to knock home what I was sure would be US views on Tshombe affair. Am convinced however that we have not slightest chance of changing Tshombe's fate and in fact I do not think this would be appropriate course of action for us to attempt. We have plenty of evidence that Tshombe has done everything he can to overthrow Mobutu govt through subversion, mercenaries, etc. Furthermore what Bomboko told me is basically true, namely that if Tshombe had had chance to regain political power through violent means, he would not have shrunk from causing deaths of many Congolese or from wiping out present govt. Seems to me that only constructive course open for us at this point is to try ensure that Tshombe's trial and inevitable execution don't get out of hand. We will continue act quietly in that sense unless Dept objects.

McBride

503. Central Intelligence Agency Intelligence Information Cable[1]

TDCS DB–315/02519–67 Washington, July 4, 1967.

SUBJECT

[*name not declassified*] Comments on the Kidnapping of Moise Tshombe

1. ([*less than 1 line not declassified*] comment: [*less than 1 line not declassified*] and [*less than 1 line not declassified*][2] reported that the kidnapping of former Prime Minister Moise Tshombe was a Congo (Kinshasa) operation mounted primarily by Minister of Transport and Communications Victor Nendaka in collaboration with the Algerians and that the Congolese had sent a mission to Algiers to take custody of Tshombe and to return him to Kinshasa to be tried and executed.)

2. In a private conversation [*less than 1 line not declassified*] admitted that the kidnapping of Tshombe was a Congolese operation. He stated that the operation had its origin some months ago. [*name not declassified*] however, did not volunteer any details regarding the operation other than to state that the key individual in the hijacking of Tshombe's aircraft was an unidentified European but not former Five Commando Mercenary Leader Lt. Colonel John Peters whose name has often been linked with Tshombe. [*less than 1 line not declassified*] comment: [*2 lines not declassified*] collaboration with the Algerians.

3. [*name not declassified*] also stated that an official Congolese delegation had departed for Algeria on 3 July which included Colonel Alexandre Singa, Chief Administrator of the Sûreté Nationale. He said that the Congolese expected to obtain custody of Tshombe and return him to Kinshasa for trial and execution. [*name not declassified*] emphasized that such action was purely and simply an act of self-defense on the part of Congolese President Joseph Mobutu's govt against an individual who has repeatedly sought to subvert and overthrow the Mobutu regime and who has plotted the assassination of its leaders.

4. Although [*name not declassified*] tended to minimize the effect of possible adverse international reaction to the Tshombe affair, he did express interest bordering on concern in what the Spanish reaction might be to the kidnapping. [*name not declassified*] stated that the Congolese Chargé in Madrid had informed Kinshasa that Spanish officials had unofficially indicated that Tshombe would not be permitted to reenter Spain should he extricate himself from his current predicament. [*name*

---

[1] Source: Central Intelligence Agency Files, [*text not declassified*], Fiche 60, Row 1, Frames 3–5, [*text not declassified*]. Secret.

[2] Not found.

not declassified] however remarked that all of the Congolese "agents" had fled Spain after the kidnapping in fear of being arrested by the Spanish authorities and that he suspected that those Congolese remaining in Spain were under close surveillance.[3]

5. [*less than 1 line not declassified*] dissem: State (Amb, DCM, POL Chief only) Defense (Attaché) CINCMEAFSA (personal) (also sent Chiefs of Mission only Madrid Lubumbashi Algiers Bukavu).

---

[3] A July 9 CIA report stated that the Congolese Government mounted the kidnapping operation against Tshombe. The Algerian Government was privy to the operation and willing to have Tshombe landed secretly in the country and be spirited out of the country to Kinshasa. The operational plan went afoul when the co-pilot of the aircraft announced to the airport control tower that Tshombe was aboard. (Central Intelligence Agency Files, [*text not declassified*], Fiches 60–61, Rows 5 & 1, Frames 8–9; 2–4, [*text not declassified*])

---

504. Telegram From the President's Special Assistant (Rostow) to President Johnson, in Texas[1]

Washington, July 6, 1967, 0231Z.

CAP 67671. Herewith a message and request for aid from Mobutu. We will be developing a draft response tomorrow morning.

Kinshasa 135[2]

Foreign Minister Bomboko just delivered to me (Ambassador McBride) the following message from Mobutu to President Johnson.

"Mr. President, we must unhappily inform Your Excellency that Democratic Republic Congo today was object of aggression from group of foreign mercenaries in service of groups hostile to peace and security of our country.[3]

This morning at 6:30 local time two unidentified airplanes parachuted group of commandos on Kisangani Airfield. Simultaneously, mercenaries in employ of Army Nationale Congo launched hostilities at Bukavu. Just prior to this peace and tranquility existing throughout

---

[1] Source: Johnson Library, National Security File, Memos to the President, Walt W. Rostow, Vol. 33. Confidential. Received at the LBJ Ranch at 3:13 a.m.

[2] A copy of telegram 135 from Kinshasa, July 5, is in National Archives, RG 59, Central Files 1967–69, POL 23–9 THE CONGO.

[3] On July 5, mercenary units in Kisangani and Bukavu mutinied and took over the two towns.

Democratic Republic Congo for nineteen months were disturbed by acts of economic sabotage in Katanga Province.

You will easily understand that this situation can compromise not only tranquility of Congo but also peace of all central Africa.

In view of gravity of situation we, like all people devoted to peace and liberty, hasten to appeal to friendly people of US, champions of international solidarity.

We, therefore, ask Your Excellency to make available to us as quickly as possible necessary men and material to permit us to rid ourselves once and for all of this group of brigands.

We know that we can count on aid of your government and of American people as well as upon that of governments of friendly countries.

With deep gratitude in advance for consideration which you will give to our request, we renew to you, Mr. President, our high and friendly consideration. Signed J.D. Mobutu, President of Democratic Republic of the Congo."

---

505. Telegram From the Embassy in the Congo to the Department of State[1]

Kinshasa, July 6, 1967, 1120Z.

152. 1. Mobutu made urgent appeal to me this morning in presence Bomboko and Blake that USG immediately make available to DGRC three C–130s for up to one month. Said purpose these planes would be carry troops and material to ANC units throughout country and to get in position launch early counter-offensive against rebels. Made clear that receipt early American military assistance also vital psychologically and politically, if his pro-Western policy to be continued.

2. Mobutu emphasized that he as pro-Western Congolese leader with particularly close relations to us, in very difficult situation. Most of troubles which Congo has had since independence have come from West, and particularly from Belgium. Right now Belgian, French, Spanish and English mercenaries, backed by Belgian financial interests,

---

[1] Source: National Archives, RG 59, Central Files 1967–69, POL 23–9 THE CONGO. Secret; Flash; Limdis. Received at 8:55 a.m. and repeated to CINCSTRIKE, DOD, CIA, Kigali, Brussels, Kampala, Bujumbura, Nairobi, USUN, Bukavu, and Lubumbashi. Passed to the White House, NSA, USIA, COMAC, and CINCLANT.

are engaged in all-out effort to overthrow Mobutu govt. These groups will spare no efforts to overthrow DGRC. On July 4, DGRC found out through its intelligence sources in Belgium that 200 Belgian mercenaries in pay of Tshombe about to depart from Belgium for Congo. When this info brought to attention Belgian Govt, latter prohibited group from leaving. Mobutu said he not accusing Belgian Govt of being responsible for this latest mercenary rebellion, but fact is that two plane loads of Belgian mercenaries arrived in Kisangani on morning July 5 from someplace.

3. Mobutu said there tendency his own entourage but more strongly throughout Congo to blame these latest difficulties not only on Belgians but on all whites. Gen Basongo in Luluabourg had requested permission arrest all Belgians which permission was denied. He, Mobutu, making every effort calm down situation, but he under strong pressure. MPR had wished to hold rally against Belgians and West, but he, Mobutu, denied requests as he did trade union request hold anti-Belgian general strike and Louvanium students request hold major demonstration in front Belgian Emb. Bomboko chimed in to say anti-white feelings running so strong that he feared unless something done to redress balance and show that at least USG stands squarely with DGRC against rebels, there is distinct possibility that security situation in various parts of Congo could get out of hand and many whites might be massacred.

4. Mobutu said he also under pressure, "and not only from young radical intellectuals," to reverse pro-Western foreign policy and move to align Congo with African countries who have close relations with Communists. Said it often pointed out to him that countries like Congo (Brazza), Guinea and Tanzania have no problems with mercenaries; only Western-oriented country like Congo faces these troubles. Said if he could not get immediate aid from West, he will be faced with strong pressures to re-orient his policies. In this respect, time is of essence.

5. In response to my question as to whether other countries and particularly Belgium had been asked for aid, Mobutu replied in negative. Said it would be politically impossible for him under present conditions to request help from Belgian paratroopers or to otherwise use Belgian soldiers. He has asked for and received assurances of Belgian political support plus Belgian assurances they will deny use Belgian territory by pro-Tshombe Belgian groups. However, only real military aid on which he could count was from USG.

6. On political side, Mobutu said he hopes SC will meet soonest to consider what steps UN can take to deny support to mercenaries. Also said he has requested total African support from every African state through OAU channel. Finally, he has also kept Chiefs of State of 13 countries which had participated in Kinshasa summit conference fully

informed and has asked them take urgent measures deny use their territories, airfields, etc. to allies of mercenaries.

7. Mobutu said military situation in East remains nearly static but he must very quickly show that he is able to take counteroffensive against rebel mercenaries. For this he particularly needs immediate help from USG. I said I would transmit this request urgently to Washington. I had started meeting by reading him message contained State 1291;[2] Mobutu very pleased but said it was American matériel assistance which now of utmost importance.

McBride

[2] Dated July 5. (Ibid.)

506. Telegram From the Department of State to the Embassy in the Congo[1]

Washington, July 6, 1967, 2:02 p.m.

1625. Kinshasa 152 and 154.[2]

1. All evidence points to conclusion that GDRC is mesmerized by supposed mercenary invulnerability. We see little indication that GDRC taking any steps in its own defense but is largely engaged in closing airports, imposing curfew, arresting FAC pilots and making statements about imperialist aggression. Even if aid were forthcoming there no evidence that GDRC has any idea of how to use it.

2. Although we have no illusion about capabilities of ANC we nevertheless believe it could be doing more than it is. Therefore you should on appropriate occasions try to instill sense of confidence in Congolese leaders that numerically superior, better-equipped ANC can handle situation.

3. You should strongly discourage any mention of US troops. In view our commitments elsewhere and US policy not to engage its own

[1] Source: National Archives, RG 59, Central Files 1967–69, POL 23–9 THE CONGO. Secret; Immediate. Drafted by Schaufele, cleared by Brown and Walt Rostow, and approved by Trimble. Repeated to Brussels and CINCSTRIKE for POLAD Tampa.

[2] Telegram 152 is Document 505. Telegram 154 from Kinshasa, July 6, is in National Archives, RG 59, Central Files 1967–69, DEF 19 US–THE CONGO.

forces in Africa it most unlikely that they would be forthcoming under any circumstances.

4. As you have correctly pointed out major military problem, as usual, is logistical. We are urgently considering recommendations of your 154. You should suggest to GDRC that its military reps consult with US and Belgian military to make best and most effective use of significant amount of air transport it already has.

5. We realize that this provisional response to Mobutu appeal will probably not be considered very forthcoming but at this stage suspect hand-holding operation is in order. In some manner idea must be gotten across that Congolese in first instance must depend on themselves.

6. We doubt GOB disposed send combat troops to Congo which Mobutu says he would not request in any case. But we see no reason that GDRC should not ask GOB for equipment and supplies. Eventual US response could also depend on other sources of supply.[3]

Rusk

[3] In telegram 252 from Kinshasa, July 7, McBride reported that he discussed the points in this telegram at some length with Bomboko that morning. (Ibid., POL 23–9 THE CONGO)

---

507. Memorandum From the President's Special Assistant (Rostow) to President Johnson[1]

Washington, July 6, 1967, 9 p.m.

SUBJECT

Help for the Congo

In the attached, Secretary Rusk[2] —supported by Paul Nitze, Dick Helms, and the Joint Chiefs—recommends that you authorize the use of three U.S. C–130 aircraft to help Mobutu put down the current mutiny of white mercenaries in the Congo. The State memorandum con-

[1] Source: Johnson Library, National Security File, Country File, Congo, Vol. XIII, Memos & Miscellaneous, 11/66–8/67. Secret. A notation on the memorandum indicates it was seen by the President.

[2] The memorandum is signed by Gene, but approved by the Secretary, who had to leave while it was being typed in final form. [Handwritten footnote in the original.] For Eugene Rostow's memorandum, see Document 508.

tains a good summary of the background of this decision and the costs and benefits involved.

There is little visceral satisfaction in helping Mobutu. He is irritating and often stupid. By our standards, he can be cruel to the point of inhumanity. It is perfectly true that he is trying to get his hands on Tshombe, and if he succeeds there is an excellent chance Tshombe will hang. However, we have to balance these facts against some others—just as hard, cold, and unattractive:

1. Political stability in the Congo is the key to manageable African politics. The Congo is almost as large as India and has much the same dominance over the tone of African politics that India does on the sub-Continent. It would be disastrous to retreat to the Congo of a few years ago where warring regional factions created chaos simply begging for big-power involvement which could spread the arms race to Africa and lead to an eventual big-power confrontation.

2. Mobutu's regime is by far the most stable and widely-supported in Congolese history. It is the first that has some semblance of mass support. It is vigorously supported (and Tshombe rigorously hated) by every country of black Africa.

3. There is no other Congolese leader in sight who stands a reasonable chance of holding the country together, much less maintaining the present friendly relations with us.

4. Whatever Mobutu's personal faults, he has made some impressive economic steps. The IMF is now about to install and support—with help from us and other countries—a comprehensive economic stabilization program which is by far the best hope yet of changing a land basically rich in resources from an international beggar (which costs us on the order of $50 million per year in aid) into a cohesive, productive economy.

5. Mobutu does have alternatives. He is under great pressure to denounce us and throw in his lot with the radical Africans and, by implication, the Soviets and/or the Chicoms. Though this would give the communist brethren some problems, it would be a major political problem for us—foreign and domestic.

With these facts in mind, your advisers have arrived at the recommendation that we supply three transport planes and crews. This recommendation is a result of a careful examination of our four major options: to do nothing; to try to finesse the problem through clandestine help to Mobutu; to provide the aircraft he has requested; and to throw the whole problem into the lap of the UN, taking no bilateral action in the meantime.

We are agreed that to do nothing would risk very serious dangers ranging from the splintering of the Congo to a sharp turn to the left in

Congolese political orientation, perhaps involving military operations by the Algerians and other hostile forces now smarting from their defeat in the Middle East and looking for a way to recoup. As to the second alternative, there just doesn't seem to be a way that we can covertly give Mobutu what he needs. He simply doesn't have the air transport capability to move his men and vehicles in the numbers and with the speed necessary to snuff out the mutiny quickly. The UN is already addressing the problem—the Security Council met this afternoon. But UN action would undoubtedly take time, particularly if it involved blessing American assistance. The Soviets might well block any such resolution in the hope that meanwhile their friends could get into the act and get the credit. (Obviously, this does not mean we would oppose UN action in any event, but it does not appear to us that we can lean on the UN as a substitute for modest bilateral help to Mobutu.)

The C–130's would be provided on the following conditions:

—that we make it crystal clear to Mobutu that this is *not* the first step in anything. We are talking about three C–130's and that's all. We would specifically rule out combat forces.

—that planes will be used only for the transport of men and material in operations we think are soundly planned and have a reasonable prospect of success.

—that Mobutu will not execute Tshombe, on pain of withdrawal of our planes.

One further condition was left out of the State memorandum by mistake, but will be enforced if you approve: that Mobutu will stop seeming to lump the U.S. and Belgium under the heading "Western white colonialists" in his public statements.

There are risks to this approach. We don't know whether the mutiny is part of an organized plot to overthrow Mobutu. We don't know whether or how it is related to the Tshombe incident. Most important, we don't know how well the regular Congolese troops will do against these rough and ready freebooters. Even though the mercenaries are small in number—apparently about 200—they are formidable military forces in the Congo.

Nevertheless, it seems to me that these risks are outweighed by the benefits. This move would be hailed by all the Africans, along with the other poor countries and most of the industrialized world. (The Soviets are already committed publicly against the mercenaries.) By quick action, we may be able to avoid a painful, drawn-out conflict in the bush which could negate all the progress made in the Congo over the past two years. And in doing so, we could preempt large opportunities which this crisis could present for the communists.

Therefore, I would vote that you approve the Secretary's recommendation.

Walt

Approve State memorandum; go ahead and use 3 C–130's

Disapprove

Speak to me[3]

[3] None of these options is checked.

---

508. Memorandum From the Under Secretary of State for Political Affairs (Rostow) to President Johnson[1]

Washington, July 6, 1967.

SUBJECT

C–130's for the Congo

Recommendation:

We recommend that we agree to return to the Congo temporarily three C–130 aircraft with US crews for use in ferrying Congolese army troops and matériel. If you concur, we would instruct our Ambassador to exercise the tightest possible control over these aircraft to ensure they are used only for the transport of men and matériel under safe conditions and not subject to interdiction by rebel-controlled aircraft. The Ambassador would also make clear to Mobutu that the United States is not prepared to make combat forces available to the Congo.[2]

Background

On July 4, approximately 160 white Congolese mercenaries, largely French and Belgian, leading 1,000–2,000 Katangese troops of the Congolese Army, seized several towns in the northeast area of the Congo. These mercenaries, originally recruited by Mobutu, and currently paid by the Congolese Government, are now obviously in a state of mutiny. Apparently their actions were prompted either by a Tshombe plot to overthrow the Congolese Government or by the kid-

[1] Source: National Archives, RG 59, Central Files 1967–69, POL 23–9 THE CONGO. Secret. Drafted by Rostow and cleared by Fredericks, Brown, Sisco, and Stoessel. Rusk approved the memorandum; see footnote 2, Document 507. A handwritten notation at the top of the memorandum reads: "Planes sent—7/8. Removed from WH pending 7/13. pw"

[2] The approval line is checked, indicating the recommendation was approved.

napping of Tshombe and by attempts of the Congolese Government to extradite Tshombe from Algeria. It is not clear to what extent they are receiving support from forces outside the Congo, although we suspect they are backed by individual Belgians in financial and mining circles.

Although the present situation is extremely fluid, Mobutu considers it a serious threat to his regime. The mercenaries have a reputation of toughness, and the Congo Army of about 20,000 is reluctant to engage them. Mobutu believes that in order to defuse the situation he must very quickly show he is able to take a counteroffensive.

To prepare for such a counterattack, Mobutu has asked the US Government for three C–130 aircraft on an urgent basis to transport Congolese troops and matériel within the interior. His present aircraft capability is extremely limited. The eleven armed T–28's we previously provided Mobutu are operational but the pilots are mercenaries and Mobutu seems unwilling to chance using them now. His transport fleet, consisting largely of C–47's, lacks sufficient maintenance and flying personnel; the pilots include some Italian trained Congolese and some Belgian aircraft crews on loan. Past experience has shown that the existing transport fleet cannot provide the vehicle and personnel lift over long distances in the Congo necessary to meet this need.

Mobutu has requested African support from every African state through the OAU. He feels it is politically impossible at the present time to ask for Belgian military support although he has asked for and received assurances of Belgian political support. He views the US as historically the only source on which he can count.

Mobutu has also requested an immediate emergency session of the UN Security Council which is being held tonight.

The Soviet press has denounced the mutiny and the French and Belgian Governments have announced their complete support of the Mobutu Government. We know of no government taking sides with the mercenaries. If we should send C–130's to the Congo, we expect little if any difficulty with the Soviets as they could not behave as if they supported Tshombe or European mercenaries. On the other hand if we let the situation deteriorate without helping Mobutu, we could expect the Soviets to try and take advantage of the situation in unhelpful ways.

Ambassador McBride believes a quick delivery could have a critical psychological effect in the Congo, both with the central government which needs bucking up and as a deterrent to the mutineers. He strongly recommends that we supply the aircraft.

Supplying the aircraft would have the following advantages:

—US support for an African Government against an uprising led by white mercenaries and supported by foreign right wing groups would strengthen the US position among Black African countries. Help for a Black African state would be particularly timely now against the background of the Middle East crisis.

—Quick symbolic action by the US could help prevent the situation from growing out of hand by bolstering Mobutu and deterring the mutineers.

—We helped the Congolese in 1964 by making available four C–130's when they faced the threat from the left. Assisting them now when they face a threat from the right would be another demonstration of our even-handedness.

—US support would help to counter the Congolese racist feeling which is mounting rapidly against white mercenaries and which may grow to include all whites. It would enable us strongly to urge Mobutu to desist from anti-white propaganda, and propaganda against us, the Belgians, and others as "imperialists".

—US support would reassure Mobutu that his pro-Western policy was correct and would enable him to keep from turning in extremis to Arab states, such as Algeria or the UAR, or other African states, who might be willing to intervene.

—US support could make it easier for us to deal with the Security Council situation where we might otherwise face a sweeping Congolese indictment of "Western imperialism" or of individual Western countries. Our assistance would give us leverage to persuade the Congolese to moderate their claims.

—The availability of the C–130's in the Congo would facilitate large scale evacuation of Americans, should this become necessary.

Supplying the aircraft also involves certain risks:

—There is danger in moving military equipment before we know precisely whether there is a real need for it, how it would be used and the dangers to which it will be exposed.

—We may be confronted with a follow-on request for U.S. combat troops if Mobutu judges the ANC would not alone be able to defeat the mercenaries.

—Even though the aircraft would be supplied at the request of the Congo Government, our action could be viewed by some as unilateral US intervention.

—Furnishing military transport planes might encourage future requests for direct assistance from other countries in similar situations. (The distinguishing characteristic here, however, is that foreign white mercenaries are involved.)

—In helping Mobutu put down an insurrection that is sympathetic to Tshombe, we recognize that an early extradition and execution of

Tshombe will provoke strong adverse reactions from his traditional supporters. If we comply with the request for C–130's we would use the opportunity to urge Mobutu strongly not to execute Tshombe. We would make it clear that if the execution occurred, we would be obliged to withdraw the planes.

Action Already Taken

—We have established an inter-agency task force composed of State, DOD, JCS, CIA, and USIA representatives to deal with the Congo crisis.

—We have contacted the Belgians today to explore the possibility of joint action and to see if the GOB can increase the number of air force crews in the Congo.

—We have determined that the three C–130's are available.

—We are talking to African Ambassadors to determine climate of opinion among African states.

—We are asking American Consul in Bukavu to ascertain the mercenaries' motivations and intentions.

Secretary Rusk, Acting Secretary Nitze and DCI Helms concur in this recommendation.

Eugene V. Rostow

509. Telegram From the Department of State to the Embassy in the Congo[1]

Washington, July 7, 1967, 12:19 p.m.

2402. Ref: Kinshasa 135.[2] Please deliver following reply to Mobutu's letter of July 5 to President:

"Dear Mr. President:

I have received your letter of July 5 about the situation in the Democratic Republic of the Congo. I am consulting urgently with my advisers here to determine how, within the limitations of our own re-

[1] Source: National Archives, RG 59, Central Files 1967–69, POL 23–9 THE CONGO. Confidential; Immediate; Limdis. Drafted by Schaufele; cleared by Fredericks, Walt Rostow, and Thompson of S/S; and approved by Eugene Rostow. Acting Secretary of Defense Nitze was informed. Also sent to Brussels.

[2] See Document 504.

sources, we can help your government at this difficult time. We shall communicate with you as soon as possible through my Ambassador to the Congo, Robert McBride. We are confident you will succeed in restoring order and resuming the path on which you have already embarked toward stabilization and progress in the Congo. The Congolese National Army, backed by the Congolese people, acting together under your courageous leadership will, I am sure, reestablish the calm necessary to that task.

Sincerely, Lyndon B. Johnson"

Rusk

---

510. Memorandum for the Record[1]

Washington, July 7, 1967.

Mr. Walt Rostow called me this date and said that the President was mulling around in his mind whether or not he should accede to Mobutu's request for assistance in air transportation to move his troops around, and said the President asked him to ask me the following three questions:

1. Does he need the equipment to move his troops around or not? I said it was my understanding that he's got in the neighborhood of 7 operational C–47s over there which he could use to move them, except for the fact that he is loath to trust his crews for fear they might defect. Mr. Rostow said that he had the same information. I said that if there is a requirement to move troops around and Mobutu is afraid of his own crews because they might defect, the only way he could move his troops would be to get some aircraft with crews he could trust, in which case I would say he would need the C–130s.

2. Mr. Rostow then asked about the danger involved. I said of course there is always danger involved in a situation as unsettled as that, when you don't know who has control. Also, there is always the danger of sabotage, and we might be subject, of course, to actual combat and get the equipment or crews shot up. I said, however, we went in there before to pull the refugees out and we were fortunate

---

[1] Source: Washington National Records Center, RG 330, OSD Files: FRC 72 A 2467, Congo 580 (7 July 67). Top Secret. Prepared by General McConnell. Typed notations on the memorandum read: "Dictated but not read" and "Sec Def has seen."

enough not to suffer any casualties or damage to equipment, except normal operational damage.

3. Mr. Rostow then said he had been told to ask me if the Ambassador would have the competence to determine whether or not the fields that will have to be operated out of are satisfactory for the use of this equipment and whether or not they are secure. I said I couldn't pass judgment on the capabilities of the Ambassador in that respect, but that he does have an Air Attaché there who, in my opinion, would certainly be qualified to determine if the fields could handle the equipment and, given proper intelligence, determine whether they are secure. He could then give the Ambassador appropriate advice. I said I assumed if we sent aircraft we wouldn't just send pilots and crews, but would send a task force commander who would be qualified.

Mr. Rostow thanked me and that concluded the conversation.

J.P. McConnell[2]
General, USAF
Chief of Staff

[2] Printed from a copy that bears this typed signature.

511. Memorandum From the Department of State Executive Secretary (Read) to the President's Special Assistant (Rostow)[1]

Washington, July 7, 1967.

SUBJECT

Further Information on the Congo Situation

1. Belgian Position. We have asked the Belgians here and in Brussels for further air crews for the Congo. They know that we have had a request for C–130s and have agreed to delay replying to a Congolese request for matériel assistance until they learn our reaction. Mr.

[1] Source: Johnson Library, National Security File, Country File, Congo, Vol. XIII, Memos & Miscellaneous, 11/66–8/67. Secret. This memorandum is apparently a response to a note dictated by the President at 11:10 a.m. on July 7, referring to Eugene Rostow's July 6 memorandum (Document 508) requesting further information. (Johnson Library, National Security Council Histories, Congo C–130 Crisis, July 1967 [Tab 1])

Rostow will discuss the subject again with the Belgian Ambassador at 2:45 today.[2] The Belgian position is a bit shaky. The abduction of Tshombe was badly received in some Belgian circles. More importantly, the GOB is smarting under Congolese press and radio attacks lumping the mutineers, many of whom are Belgians, with the rest of the Belgian population of the Congo and with Belgian financial interests. Brussels has said that Belgian air crews now in the Congo will carry out GDRC orders, that other Belgian military personnel (training troops) will stand by, and that a request from the Congo government for arms and munitions has been received. The Belgians may act favorably on the latter request, if we provide assistance and if Congo press attacks abate. However, their initial reaction indicates that they would insist on a moderation of anti-Belgian propaganda as precondition to such aid. Our Ambassador in the Congo is pointing out to the Congolese the dangers of over-exciting the Congolese population. We have made the same point to Ambassador Adoula here. We are keeping the Belgians informed of these actions.

We do not, in summary, expect the Belgian government to consider taking the lead in providing assistance to the Congo until it is sure that the US is ready to help and until it is sure that a wave of anti-Belgian and anti-white propaganda in the Congo is brought under control and possible incidents avoided. Internal political considerations in Belgium dictate this cautious stand. Should there be an unprovoked slaughter of Belgians (and such may have just occurred in Katanga) then the Belgians will pull back from assistance.

2. Mercenary Objectives. Mercenaries in the Congo, even though in the pay of the Congolese government, always represented a potential Trojan horse because their political sympathies were essentially very conservative, even colonialist, and often pro-Tshombe. No single leadership of the various groups has been clearly identified nor has there apparently any public statement which could be attributed to the rebels.

Embassy Kinshasa speculates that mercenary objectives may be to establish control over the Eastern Congo as a base to channel in reinforcements and eventually take over mineral-rich Katanga. Presumably they would welcome the Congolese (or Katangan) leadership of someone like Tshombe or other pliable Congolese elements willing to go along with them.

In the absence of further information it is uncertain exactly what the mercenaries seek. It is perhaps significant that they have not used the radios at Kisangani or Bukavu to broadcast their aims. However, as

---

[2] Memcon will be LDX'd to WH as soon as it is completed. BHR. [Handwritten footnote in the original.]

the rebellion of 1964–65 showed, a very few determined, well-trained and well-armed mercenaries can take over large parts of the Congo and this is the threat that the GDRC now faces.

The Belgians tell us that they are unsure what the exact motivations were. They say it could have been part of a long-planned pro-Tshombe plot, a sudden move to thwart the extradition of Tshombe, or perhaps only a dissatisfaction with lack of pay.

3. African Reaction. Zambia condemned the mercenary rebellion and offered assistance. Kaunda said: "The Congo aggression means there will be no peace for countries small in terms of military might." He congratulated the US and USSR for condemning the mercenaries.

Rwanda has condemned the mercenaries, pledged support to Mobutu and opened the airport of Kamembe to US aircraft for the evacuation of American citizens and to the Congo Government, should it need it.

Congo (Brazzaville) has strongly castigated the mercenary actions and pledged assistance, including troops if necessary, to help suppress the rebellion.

The Nigerian Ambassador here has expressed the view of many of his colleagues in strongly condemning the mercenaries. The Somalis and Ethiopians have told us that they are horrified that foreign mercenaries are trying to disrupt the unity of the Congo.

At the UN, the non-permanent members of the Security Council (including Ethiopia, Mali, and Nigeria) met Friday morning and unanimously agreed to support the Congolese proposed resolution calling on all countries to refrain from assistance to the mercenaries.[3]

4. Military Situation. For an as yet undertermined cause, dissident elements which have held Bukavu for two days left the town in three columns on their own volition early this morning and Congolese troops returned. There seems to be some danger of anti-European acts by the ANC.

Despite GDRC claims that an ANC paracommando unit dropped on Kisangani early this morning, destroyed dissident-held T–28 aircraft, and occupied most of the city, another more reliable report indicates that Kisangani still is partly in mercenary hands and that the T–28s were not destroyed.

The Congolese police report that Kindu radio went silent this morning, which may mean that town is in rebel hands.

Anti-white tensions are reported high in Lubumbashi and we have just learned that 13 Europeans were massacred by the army.

---

[3] July 7. On July 6, the Congolese Representative asked for an emergency meeting of the Security Council to consider the question of aggression against the Congo on July 5.

5. Assessment of Russell/Rivers Reaction. In Bill Macomber's absence, Tully Torbert talked with Mr. Stempler, DOD Legislative Liaison. Stempler feels that neither Russell nor Rivers would be enthusiastic about the return of the C–130's to the Congo but would go along if the move were explained in a clear, well considered policy statement. In general, it would be important to have something to show for the assistance, for example a better public posture by Mobutu toward white Westerners and/or a deal on Tshombe. Torbert defers to Stempler's judgment on the reaction of the House and Senate armed services committee chairman.

BHR

512. Telegram From the Department of State to the Embassy in the Congo[1]

Washington, July 7, 1967, 10:18 p.m.

3258. 1. Although rapid improvement in racial situation is highest immediate priority in our relations with Mobutu, you should be aware that USG would face great political difficulties in continuation of assistance to Congolese regime which summarily executed Tshombe in repetition of Pentecost affair.

2. We leave to your judgment whether repeating to Mobutu your earlier warning regarding the handling of Tshombe issue could be raised in Saturday[2] talk without further jeopardizing critical racial situation. In any case you should get message across to Mobutu at earliest appropriate time and under circumstances most likely to achieve favorable reaction.[3]

Rusk

---

[1] Source: National Archives, RG 59, Central Files 1967–69, POL 23–9 THE CONGO. Secret; Flash; Nodis. Drafted and approved by Fredericks.

[2] July 8.

[3] In telegram 300 from Kinshasa, July 8, McBride reported that he would discuss Tshombe with Mobutu at the appropriate time, but warned that any special démarche at this time could hurt U.S. efforts to protect U.S. citizens during the current crisis, and that any sign of U.S. concern for Tshombe as a person after what had happened in the eastern Congo would be greatly misunderstood. (National Archives, RG 59, Central Files 1967–69, POL 23–9 THE CONGO)

513. Telegram From the Embassy in the Congo to the Department of State[1]

Kinshasa, July 8, 1967, 1100Z.

304. 1. I am acutely aware of difficult moral, human and public relations position in which US Govt has been placed over Congolese C–130 request because of repulsive brutality ANC in Lubumbashi and excesses elsewhere. Incidentally, experience would indicate first day or two ANC reoccupies a town are most critically dangerous. Present situation is of course exacerbated by fact that ANC is retaking towns (they may simply have been evacuated) which were occupied by white mercenaries, so situation would be critical even without Congolese Govt's action in arousing anti-white sentiment which, as reported, was less extreme over last night's television and radio; though this morning's radio not good.

2. As of this moment there are no new elements in situation. Kisangani partly in hands of ANC but this does not include airport where apparently large group of Europeans have been gathered under mercenary control. There is likewise nothing new from Lubumbashi. Fate of rebellion itself is hazy in extreme. However, there little doubt that some mercenary–Katangese bands remain in operation despite reports at least one planeload of mercenaries and others has landed in Rhodesia.

3. I am now attempting to reach Mobutu to convey contents paras 2 and 3 Dept's 3252[2] but have not been successful yet. I will of course not clarify to him all purposes for which C–130s may be pre-positioned but simply indicate as Dept instructs that they are being placed in readiness. Report about readiness of C–130s will not satisfy Mobutu long and he will be pressing to know when they might be available for his missions. I will discuss in as non-inflammatory way as possible, question of their availability in context his need take urgent measures all aspects of racial situation. At same time, it must be realized that not making available C–130s risks causing deterioration of Congolese will to take determinant measures to improve position of European population. On other hand, I am sincerely convinced arrival of C–130s will be kind of demonstration of Western support which would help quickly settle down situation.

---

[1] Source: National Archives, RG 59, Central Files 1967–69, POL 23–9 THE CONGO. Secret; Immediate; Limdis. Received at 10:30 a.m. Also sent to CINCSTRIKE, and repeated to Lubumbashi, Brussels, Kigali, Kampala, Bujumbura, Nairobi, and DOD. Passed to the White House, CIA, USIA, NSA, COMAC, and CINCLANT.

[2] Dated July 7. (Ibid.)

4. Finally, there are no new elements in evacuation situation since last night and considerations about effective presence C–130s here on American morale remain pertinent. Obviously, it is of course essential that Congolese not know evacuation is a factor in our despatching planes to Congo and indeed evacuation from areas controlled by ANC is a highly delicate factor in itself.[3]

McBride

[3] A copy of this telegram was transmitted to the President by Walt Rostow attached to a note that reads: "This cable from McBride gives the flavor of the Congo scene today and of his thinking about the C–130's." (Johnson Library, National Security File, Memos to the President, Walt Rostow, Vol. 33)

---

514. Telegram From the Department of State to the Embassy in the Congo[1]

Washington, July 8, 1967, 11:42 a.m.

3301. Eyes only for Ambassador from Secretary. You have been informed that as a precautionary matter we have displaced three C–130s forward to Ascension. I want to give you some feel of the problem back here which must be taken into account in considering any final decisions about the forward movement of these planes to the Congo. In my talks with Senate leaders great emphasis has been placed once again on the question "who else is doing something about it." We have just been through a Middle Eastern crisis in which there was passionate objection in our Congress to unilateral action by the United States. This feeling runs very deep and is related to a chagrin that not enough help is coming from others in Viet-Nam.

All this means that we should weigh very seriously indeed a forward movement of these planes in the absence of tangible assistance from somewhere else. This would be particularly important if the C–130s are to become involved in ferrying ANC troops with the risks of military incidents as distinct from being there for possible evacuation purposes.

I am not at the moment prejudging the decision here because we will want to take into fullest account your own most sober assessment

[1] Source: National Archives, RG 59, Central Files 1967–69, POL 23–9 THE CONGO. Secret; Immediate; Eyes Only. Drafted and approved by Rusk.

of the situation. But I am dubious about committing aircraft for what might prove to be temporary psychological reasons when we shall run into some quite severe psychological reactions here. If the object is psychological, would one C–130 be as effective as three? Any details with respect to operational use, duration of presence in Congo, and possibility of publicly known assistance from other friendly sources would be very helpful.

Much appreciate the job you are doing.[2]

Rusk

[2] In telegram 331 from Kinshasa, July 8, which crossed this telegram, McBride reported that he had told Mobutu that the three C–130s had been placed in readiness, and warned him again that the deterioration of the racial situation was the cause of deep concern at the highest levels of the U.S. Government. McBride urged early and positive U.S. action on Mobutu's request and emphasized that the need was greater than ever because of press reports of Mobutu's appeal for U.S. assistance. He also noted the vital importance of convincing the Congolese population that their fears of a Western plot against the Congo were unfounded and that the United States was ready to help suppress the white mercenary revolt. (Ibid., DEF 19 US–THE CONGO)

515. Telegram From the Department of State to the Embassy in Belgium[1]

Washington, July 8, 1967, 5:56 p.m.

3380. Please deliver following message from Secretary to Harmel.

"Dear Mr. Minister:

Once again we are both confronted by difficult days in the Congo. I am taking the liberty of sending you our thoughts, for as always I attach the highest importance to consultation and cooperation between us. I am most appreciative of assurances from Viscount Davignon to Ambassador Knight that you await these thoughts before replying to President Mobutu's request for material assistance.

I agree fully with the concern of your government that some Congolese actions and statements are creating a difficult and potentially dangerous situation for foreign nationals in the Congo. We have re-

[1] Source: National Archives, RG 59, Central Files 1967–69, POL 23–9 THE CONGO. Secret; Flash; Limdis. Drafted by Moffat; cleared by Belgian Country Director Robert Anderson, Stoessel, and Fredericks; and approved by Rusk. Repeated to Kinshasa.

viewed at the highest level the possible actions we might take to counter this alarming trend and to bolster the Government of the Congo as it traverses one of its most serious national crises and indeed faces a threat to the Congo's very existence as a nation. As you know we have sent 3 C–130s to Ascension Island as a precautionary measure for possible use in ferrying Congolese army troops and material. We have also instructed Ambassador McBride to persuade President Mobutu that he must end the provocative anti-white, anti-West turn in Congolese propaganda and actions, an effort which I understand may already have had a beneficial effect.

We are aware of the risks and of the significance of sending these aircraft to the Congo but we urge you to make a similar gesture, perhaps the furnishing of additional air-crews.

In my conversations on the Congo with various Senators during the past few days I found passionate interest in what others were doing to help. Specifically, the question was asked, 'why cannot the Belgians do more?' If, in fact, aircraft from outside the Congo are required to restore order and racial peace, our ability to help would be deeply affected by the willingness of others to take similar action.

Ambassadors Knight and McBride and the Department of State will continue to keep in close touch with you and your representatives.[2]

Sincerely, Dean Rusk"

You may tell Harmel orally that we also attach importance to the Tshombe case and that at appropriate times and in appropriate situations we will use our influence in talks with the GDRC to persuade it observe internationally accepted norms of legal and human behavior in handling the Tshombe affair.

Rusk

---

[2] In telegram 144 from Brussels, July 9, Knight reported that he gave the message to Harmel that morning. Harmel and Prime Minister Boeynants expressed willingness to send two or three transport planes to assist in transporting the ANC in operations against the mercenary revolt, if the Congolese Government publicly and officially requested such assistance and if it were agreed that their return flights would carry Belgian civilians. (Ibid.) Telegram 3438 to Kinshasa, July 9, instructed the Embassy to give Mobutu the substance of telegram 144 and urge him to make an immediate request to the Belgian Government for aircraft and crews. (Ibid.)

516. Telegram From the Embassy in the Congo to the Department of State[1]

Kinshasa, July 9, 1967, 0913Z.

388. 1. After careful consideration this morning in light situation here, Lubumbashi, and elsewhere, I must with deep regret take action of calling forth C–130s as authorized State 3420.[2] I cannot conceive of any other alternative available to me which would:

A. Encourage Mobutu and assist him effectively in cleaning up present situation so that we can begin get country back to normal and resume forward progress. Although excesses of ANC are ghastly, in long run our presence here cannot but be advantageous to Europeans, and to reject Mobutu request especially after it had been publicized would undoubtedly further endanger entire foreign community.

B. Give encouragement and modicum protection to large American colony in what remains highly tense situation.

2. Therefore, with respect State 3420, I would like to call forward C–130s with hope they could proceed from [garble—Ascension] immediately.

3. I will notify Mobutu as soon as possible.

4. Press aspect covered separately.

McBride

---

[1] Source: National Archives, RG 59, Central Files 1967–69, DEF 19 US–THE CONGO. Secret; Flash; Limdis. Received at 5:16 a.m. Also sent to CINCSTRIKE and Brussels and passed to the White House, DOD, CIA, USIA, NSA, COMAC, and CINCLANT.

[2] Telegram 3420 to Kinshasa, July 9, authorized the Ambassador to call forward the C–130s at his discretion by Flash request to the Department. (Ibid.)

517. Telegram From the Department of State to the Embassy in the Congo[1]

Washington, July 9, 1967, 9:03 p.m.

3469. Brussels 148 and 150.[2]

1. Agree that we do not want acrimonious debate or unfounded allegations by GDRC UNREP during Monday[3] session. Hope that you will be able to make this point to Bomboko so that he can get appropriate instructions to Idzumbuir immediately.

2. Suggest that USUN see Idzumbuir soonest and give him briefing on what US doing for GDRC while making point that we do not believe that denunciation GOB called for.

3. Suggest that Brussels discuss problem once more with FonOff and the GOB instruct its rep at New York to get in touch with Idzumbuir to give him briefing on Belgian offer. If we can judge from past experience, Idzumbir will probably not know of offer nor have knowledge that Bomboko has thanked GOB for offer. Briefing might deflect him a bit.[4]

Rusk

---

[1] Source: National Archives, RG 59, Central Files 1967–69, POL 23–9 THE CONGO. Secret; Immediate; Limdis. Drafted by Brown, cleared by Gleysteen in IO and Moffat, and approved by Fredericks. Repeated to Brussels, USUN, and CINCSTRIKE.

[2] Telegram 148 from Brussels, July 9, is ibid. In telegram 150 from Brussels, July 9, Knight expressed his concern that the Congo, having turned down the Belgian offer of assistance, might press its complaint against Belgium in the Security Council. He pointed out that the mutiny in the Congo had been instigated by mercenaries recruited largely by Mobutu. If the Belgian Representative were to bring this out in the debate, however, Mobutu would be infuriated, which could have grave repercussions on the situation in the Congo. Therefore, Knight suggested that McBride try to get Bomboko to avoid acrimonious charges and counter-charges when the Council met again on July 10. (Ibid.)

[3] July 10.

[4] On July 10, the Security Council unanimously adopted Resolution 239 (1967), which condemned any state that permitted or tolerated the recruitment of mercenaries, and the provision of facilities to them, with the objective of overthrowing the governments of U.N. member states. It also called upon governments to ensure that their territory was not used for the recruitment, training, and transit of mercenaries designed to overthrow the Congolese Government. (U.N. Doc. S/RES/239) For text, see *American Foreign Policy: Current Documents, 1967*, p. 250.

518. Telegram From the Embassy in the Congo to the Department of State[1]

Kinshasa, July 10, 1967, 1145Z.

492. 1. I told Bomboko as soon as I arrived in town from airport after greeting C–130s this morning how shocked I had been by last night's radio and television attacks against whites. He reiterated what he had told Blake earlier when latter complained violently about the same thing to the effect that Mobutu had personally already given orders that this sort of thing must cease.

Comment: I am of course deeply discouraged at Congolese treachery on this subject but have no other course of action except to keep hammering on Mobutu and Bomboko. I have also asked Case to stress this subject with his contacts. Natural course of action would be for high level Dept officer to berate Adoula severely and perhaps this should be done for record, but I understand Adoula is virtually an exile in Washington and little appreciated by Mobutu.

McBride

---

[1] Source: National Archives, RG 59, Central Files 1967–69, POL 23–9 THE CONGO. Secret; Immediate. Received at 8:36 a.m. Also sent to Brussels and repeated to Lubumbashi, Kigali, Kampala, Bujumbura, Nairobi, DOD, USUN, and CINCSTRIKE. Passed to the White House, CIA, USIA, NSA, COMAC, and CINCLANT.

519. Memorandum From the President's Special Assistant (Rostow) to President Johnson[1]

Washington, July 10, 1967, 5:15 p.m.

SUBJECT

Talking Points on C–130's to the Congo

1. The President's action followed a unanimous positive recommendation from the Secretary of State, the U.S. Ambassador to the Congo (Robert McBride), the Acting Secretary of Defense, the Joint Chiefs of Staff, and the Director of Central Intelligence.

2. Ambassador McBride recommended the C–130's after the most sober reflection. He cabled that he was "acutely aware of the difficult moral, human, and public relations" problems involved. But he recommended "that Mobutu's request be met on basis of extreme urgency on which he has made it." McBride's reasons:

—"It is important in present most shaky state of Congolese Government to give some specific symbol of support as we have in the past. It is difficult to overestimate the urgency of this matter."

—"Assistance from U.S. at this timely juncture would assist in counterbalancing menacing racist feeling which is mounting. Understandably, man in street is incensed at actions of foreign, white mercenaries against his country, and this sentiment regrettably risks running to all whites. Fact that U.S. assisted Congolese Government at this time could be a key element in defusing this dangerous situation."

—"It is important to assist Mobutu now that he faces threat from right . . . since we helped Congolese when they faced threat from left." This would also be important "in the broader African context."

—"It would be most desirable to have C–130's in event local situation deteriorates and it is necessary to evacuate all Americans from Congo."

---

[1] Source: Johnson Library, National Security File, Memos to the President, Walt W. Rostow, Vol. 32. No classification marking. A notation indicates that a copy was sent to the Department of State for Read. The memorandum is attached to a transmittal note from Rostow that reads: "Mr. President: Herewith the full Congo memo you requested, with direct quotations from advisers. In dealing with Scotty Reston (who just called), I made three simple points: If we had not responded to the request: —racial tragedy was almost certain. (We have damped it. We may prevent it.) —Mobutu would almost certainly have turned for help to the Communists. —We would not have the planes there to get our people out, if it comes to a crunch. W.W.R." At 3:08 p.m. on July 10, Rostow called Rusk and reported that the President was "pretty shook up" by the way Congress had erupted on the Congo. (National Archives, RG 59, Rusk Files: Lot 72 D 192, Telephone Conversations)

—In the course of further urgings that the aircraft be sent (the first recommendation was made July 6), McBride commented that the C–130's must be provided if the rebellion were to be put down quickly and "the Congo is not to be set back many years economically and psychologically."

—As the racial problem worsened in the days before the C–130's were announced, McBride cabled that "the American colony, diplomatic and otherwise, in effect is being held hostage in its entirety."

3. All of the abovementioned advisers to the President supported McBride's position. In addition to his arguments, they made the following points in a joint memorandum:

—"If we should send C–130's to the Congo, we expect little if any difficulty with the Soviets as they could not behave as if they supported Tshombe or European mercenaries. On the other hand, if we let the situation deteriorate without helping Mobutu, we could expect the Soviets to try and take advantage of the situation."

—"U.S. support would reassure Mobutu that his pro-Western policy was correct and would enable him to keep from turning in extremis to the Arab states, such as Algeria or the UAR, or other African states, who might be willing to intervene."

—"U.S. support could make it easier for us to deal with the Security Council situation where we might otherwise face a sweeping Congolese indictment of 'Western Imperialism' or of individual Western countries. Our assistance would give us leverage to persuade the Congolese to moderate their claims."

—"Help for a Black African state would be particularly timely now against the background of the Middle East crisis." (The black Africans were heavily pro-Arab.)

4. It is important to note what the action was and what it was not. It was a favorable response to Mobutu's request for long-range logistical support needed to transport his men and matériel across a country nearly as large as India.

—It was *not* the supplying of combat forces. Mobutu was specifically told that the U.S. would *not* supply combat troops. (The contingent of paratroops which came with the planes is the normal security guard for the aircraft, without which the JCS will not send a plane to any danger spot in the world. They are there to protect the aircraft and that is all.)

—It was *not* the first step in growing U.S. military commitment. Mobutu understands that this is all we can do.

—It was *not* an example of callous disregard for the lives of our soldiers. The aircraft commanders have clear orders that the ruling criterion in any decision about their use is to be the safety of our men and equipment.

—It was *not* an indication that the U.S. intends to leap into every internal problem in every African country. The Congo is a special case. It is not a civil war, it is an uprising of foreign mercenaries. The principle involved does not require us to get involved in civil conflict elsewhere on the continent. (This is an oblique reply to the charge that we must now move into the Nigerian problem. You may want to make *private* use of the fact that we turned down an arms request from the Nigerian central government last week.)

5. One can make a decent case that the President's action has already provided us with one major accomplishment—the avoidance of major racial violence on Sunday in Lubumbashi (formerly Elisabethville). The stage was set for serious trouble on Saturday. With the help of the leverage provided by the C–130 decision, we were able to get things quieted down. The lives of 100 Americans and 12,000 European whites were involved.

W.W.R.[2]

[2] Printed from a copy that bears these typed initials.

520. Memorandum From the President's Special Assistant (Rostow) to President Johnson[1]

Washington, July 11, 1967, 11:30 a.m.

SUBJECT

Congo Situation Report

1. Contrary to ticker reports out of Brussels, no U.S. plane has flown to Kisangani (formerly Stanleyville) to attempt to rescue hostages held by the rebel mercenaries. Such an operation had been planned, but was scrubbed by Secretary Rusk last night because of the risks that the landing of our plane might stimulate or get our people involved in a blood bath.

[1] Source: Johnson Library, National Security File, Country File, Congo, Vol. XIII, Memos & Miscellaneous, 11/66–8/67. Secret.

2. We have queried McBride about: (i) paratrooping a single negotiator (perhaps an American) into Kisangani to try to work out an evacuation deal with the mercenaries, and (ii) if successful, bussing the hostages 40 miles to an airport the Congolese army controls and where our aircraft could land safely.

3. We have made a strong pitch to the International Red Cross to take over the hostage problem. They are now deliberating. We are giving them all the communication and transport help we can. You should know, however, that our African experience with this organization is not encouraging.

4. The Secretary is now considering two further moves:

—a Mobutu-ordered and highly publicized mercy drop of food and supplies to Kisangani.

—an approach to Mobutu to suggest a private offer of a deal to the mercenaries for their immediate departure from the Congo in return for a safe passage.

5. We still have no hard information on the situation in Kisangani. The mercenaries remain in control of at least the airport and perhaps the city. Mobutu has not ordered the Congolese army to advance on the airport, but has indicated that he will have to do so soon.

6. As you know, Secretary Rusk will appear at a closed session of the Foreign Relations Committee this afternoon. We are trying to do some ground work on the Hill; Wayne Fredericks has already talked to Senators Moss and Muskie, who have been friendly to our Congo policy, as well as Representatives Brademas, Adair, and others.

7. An additional thought which has occurred to us is that the Vice President has in the past been a solid and effective advocate of the Congo policy. If it is agreeable to you, it might do some good if he could make some phone calls. I will await your guidance on this one.

Walt

521. Memorandum From the President's Special Assistant (Rostow) to President Johnson[1]

Washington, July 12, 1967, 11 a.m.

SUBJECT

Congo Situation Report

1. Our C–130's flew two missions yesterday, dropping ammunition and supplies to Congolese forces.

2. At 10:00 A.M. today, our time, a C–130 left Kinshasa on the first of the humanitarian missions you discussed with Secretary Rusk. This one is carrying 6 tons of AID foodstuffs to Bukavu. It will stop at racially-tense Lubumbashi (formerly Elisabethville) on the way back to buck up the frightened white community. Other such missions are in the works.

3. The situation in Kisangani (formerly Stanleyville) remains unchanged. We have been wracking our brains to think of a way to start negotiations with the mercenaries to free the hostages. The present plan is to send a clearly-marked Red Cross plane, flown by Swiss Red Cross personnel who have been designated International Red Cross representatives. The plane would approach Kisangani, try to raise the mercenaries on the radio and proceed to land whether or not the mercenaries had given their clearance. We have ICRC authorization, and the mission will probably be flown tomorrow.

4. The Red Cross mission will use a non-U.S. plane. If it works, however, we can expect a request to use the larger U.S. aircraft to make the actual evacuations.

5. We have a third-hand report this morning that the mercenaries may be trying to get word to us that they would allow an evacuation of the hostages. This is only a fragmentary report of a Congolese contact with an unidentified aircraft which had passed over Kisangani. However, we will follow it up.

6. We may get trouble on the Hill today because of an A.P. ticker item this morning (A.P.–3) quoting the Congolese Minister of the Interior that there have been instances of Congolese cannibalism of whites in Lubumbashi. This is the Minister whom Mobutu has sent on a grand tour of the Congo to quiet down racial fears. It is most unlikely that he would have said this, particularly since we have no indication from our excellent consul in Lubumbashi that any such thing has occurred. The

---

[1] Source: Johnson Library, National Security File, Country File, Congo, Vol. XIII, Memos & Miscellaneous, 11/66–8/67. Confidential.

Congolese Embassy in Paris has already issued denial that the Minister said anything of the kind. We have sent a flash inquiry to our people in the places involved.

7. Our best guess is that what the Minister of the Interior really did was to refer to the bayoneting of 8 Europeans last week. That incident is known to the press, and things have been pretty quiet in Lubumbashi since. Of course, neither of these fine points will keep our brethren on the Hill from using this news against us.

8. The list of other countries helping Mobutu is growing slowly. Ethiopia has promised some jet fighters; Ghana will send pilots and crews; and Guinea has offered to send 12 MIGs. Mobutu is wrestling with the Guinean offer because of Sekou Toure's strong leftward leanings and possible trouble with the other Africans if he accepts.

Walt

522. Memorandum From the President's Special Assistant (Rostow) to President Johnson[1]

Washington, July 12, 1967, 4:30 p.m.

SUBJECT

Congo Situation Report

1. Mobutu has reported to McBride that the mercenaries in Kisangani (formerly Stanleyville) fled the city by truck convoy at noon today our time. Destination unknown.

2. McBride has refused Mobutu's suggestion that we supply a C–130 for reconnaissance to find out where the mercenaries are going. Congolese planes can and should do this job.

3. The Red Cross mission to Kisangani is now fully set up and will leave at 10:00 tonight our time. We have no word on what happened to the hostages when the mercenaries fled. If they were unharmed, the job of the Red Cross plane will be to forestall any Congolese excesses as the Congolese army occupies the city.

4. McBride has made a strong démarche to Mobutu that a great deal depends on his ability to keep his soldiers from harming the white

[1] Source: Johnson Library, National Security File, Country File, Congo, Vol. XIII, Memos & Miscellaneous, 11/66–8/67. Confidential.

population in Kisangani and other cities. Mobutu has responded with a radio announcement that restrictions on travel by foreigners, curfews, and other measures directed against the white community will be lifted tonight.

5. McBride has worked up several more proposed mercy missions for the C–130's in addition to the food flight now on the way to Bukavu. The first would be another food delivery to the Kisangani area tomorrow.

6. All C–130 missions not required for emergency protection of Americans must now be approved in Washington by the Joint Chiefs.

Walt

---

523. Notes of Meeting[1]

Washington, July 13, 1967, 12:08–12:40 p.m.

NOTES OF THE PRESIDENT'S MEETING WITH THE NATIONAL SECURITY COUNCIL STAFF

[Omitted here is discussion of unrelated subjects.]

On matters affecting the Congo, Secretary Katzenbach reported:

—There is no local competence.

—Despite this Communist influence, U.S. policy has been successful.

—There is no alternative to the current government. Mobutu is "the end of the line." There is no better alternative.

—Since World Way II there has been considerable evidence that the U.S. will not intervene against whites. We did recently, supporting Mobutu against the white mercenaries. Katzenbach said he thought this would have a substantial pay-off in Africa.

—The Secretary reported a Red Cross Plane (C–130) was bringing out a mixture of Congolese soldiers and white Americans.

—The use of the U.S. aircraft is important in protecting and rescuing the whites who are in danger.

General Wheeler reported to the President on the military aspects of the Congolese operation. His report follows:

—Today's airlift was a diversion of a communications plane.

---

[1] Source: Johnson Library, Tom Johnson's Notes of Meetings, July 13, 1967—12:08 p.m., NSC Meeting #592. Eyes Only. Drafted by Tom Johnson of the NSC Staff.

—There were no mercenaries found in the town according to a report received at 6 a.m. today.

—There were 300 wounded refugees and hostages, including some Americans.

—The mercenaries had taken off with 27 truck loads including 300 troops and an unconfirmed report of 20 American women held as hostages.

—Mobutu has asked for U.S. air surveillance to try to find the units. For the time being, the government was asked to use its own planes by the U.S. Ambassador.

—The President asked for a full report on this situation, particularly how many women hostages were being held, from CIA Director Richard Helms. Helms said he would get the report to the President as soon as prepared.

The President then asked for an appraisal of the political situation on Capitol Hill in relation to U.S. actions in the Congo. The President said he believed that the Administration had lost some good will, particularly with the Foreign Relations Committee in the Senate.

He asked, was it true that the House Foreign Relations Committee had applauded Secretary Rusk when the Secretary testified before that committee yesterday. Secretary Katzenbach said that was true.

Secretary Katzenbach said there seems to be a lack of understanding of the Congolese situation by Congressional members. He said some of the criticism has been a result of racial prejudice and a hesitancy to get into any action anywhere in the world because of what is happening in Vietnam.

The President said that a general effort should be made to keep the Congress better advised on anticipated actions.

---

524. Memorandum From the President's Special Assistant (Rostow) to President Johnson[1]

Washington, July 13, 1967, 5:30 p.m.

Mr. President:

Attached are the figures you requested on U.S. economic and military assistance to the Congo:

---

[1] Source: Johnson Library, National Security File, Country File, Congo, Vol. XIII, Memos & Miscellaneous, 1/66–8/67. Confidential.

—At *Tab A* is a breakdown of economic assistance since the Congo became independent, arranged by category of economic aid.[2]

—At *Tab B* is a breakdown of military aid.

—At *Tab C* is a summary of aid to the Congo from other nations.

The grand totals are as follows:

—U.S. economic and military assistance from FY 1960 to FY 1967: $543 million.

—Of this total, $349 million is economic and $194 million is military.

—Another $44 million in U.S. aid is planned for FY 1968.

—We have good figures for other donors only through FY 1966. As of the end of that year, other nations—bilaterally and through the U.N.—contributed a total of $574 million.

W.W. Rostow[3]

---

[2] The tabs are attached but not printed.

[3] Printed from a copy that bears this typed signature.

---

525. Telegram From the Embassy in the Congo to the Department of State[1]

Kinshasa, July 15, 1967, 1115Z.

984. 1. I am restricting distribution on this message since it ventures into realm of prognostication, which is always risky in the Congo.

2. It seems to me that present rebellion falls into three phases. First phase of course ended with mercenary seizure of Bukavu and Kisangani, which gave rise to almost hysteria against foreign elements in Congo. Most extreme danger of this phase was mitigated with US announcement of assistance to Congo. While tension remained high, this decision was a watershed. Shortly thereafter, restrictions against foreigners were terminated. This phase of course ended with mercenary evacuation of Kisangani.

---

[1] Source: National Archives, RG 59, Central Files 1967–69, POL 23–9 THE CONGO. Secret; Priority; Exdis. Repeated to Brussels, CINCSTRIKE, DOD, and JCS and passed to the White House.

3. Second phase was local Congolese reaction against mercenary actions which resulted in unbearable tension in Kisangani following its occupation by ANC which resulted in necessity evacuating virtually all foreigners. Although Congolese cooperation has been spotty, this morning situation looks promising that Red Cross planes and C–130 will complete evacuation with full Congolese assistance. This will terminate second phase.

4. We then pass into obvious third phase which will be Congolese effort to strangle mercenaries who are apparently holed up in Punia area. We cannot predict how long this period will last but some experts feel logistic problems will bring end one way or another to mercenary activity within a couple of weeks. Others of course feel it will take longer. In any event, this phase will probably see Mobutu adopt tactics of attrition rather than attempting any direct attacks on mercenaries. With any luck it should be considerably less hysterical than situation up to now, and permit Mobutu gradually begin to work this country back onto its flimsy tracks. His message to his countrymen on TV today is start of this process.

5. Purpose of speculation in para above is background for consideration when we should schedule departure C–130s. If Kisangani evacuation completed today successfully, I would like Dept to consider if I should not on Monday seek appointment with Mobutu and lead into question of departure C–130s. This may of course be extremely sticky but I could point to new and improved situation. Perhaps Dept can furnish other reasons that could be used to justify departure of planes perhaps on some date in about 10 or 12 days. JTF Commander has reported separately on technical situation, but he feels that by middle of next week most supplies and men needing long-range transport will be positioned as Congolese want them. Congolese own capabilities should be able to take over thereafter.

6. I would be eager to have Dept's view on this subject and instruction upon touching upon subject.[2]

McBride

---

[2] Telegram 7604 to Kinshasa, July 16, instructed McBride to inform Mobutu that the U.S. Government would like to set July 24 as the departure date for the C–130s, which would by then have been in the country for 2 weeks. (Ibid.)

526. Report Prepared in the Department of Defense[1]

Washington, undated.

CONGO—WITHDRAWAL OF C–130s

Steps Taken

—Ambassador McBride was instructed Sunday[2] to arrange with Mobutu for the departure of the C–130s on July 24th—two weeks after the planes' arrival on July 10th. (See Tab A for details.)[3]

—Mobutu reacted strongly and negatively, stating that the planes should stay for one month (his original request). (See Tab B for details.)

Discussion

—The original tasks of the C–130s are largely done: the intense anti-white feeling in the Congo has abated; Kisangani has been evacuated; Congolese Army forces and logistics support are being positioned to contain the mercenary threat.

—The Congo has adequate air transport resources (C–46s, C–47s, and C–54s) in the Congolese Air Force, Air Congo, and other commercial air activities. The Congolese Air Force aircraft are grounded, however, since they were manned by Belgian crews which were expelled by Mobutu on grounds of conspiring with the mercenaries. (See Tab C for list of available aircraft and crews.)

—There are two probable consequences if Mobutu continues to force out Belgian military assistance: (1) he will turn to the U.S. to fill the gap; and (2) he will feed the fears of the European population (largely Belgian) who are vital to the Congo's economy.

—The foregoing points argue for the immediate or early withdrawal of the C–130s. However, there are several points to consider on the other side. Mobutu is not completely rational on the subject of C–130s. He views them as tangible evidence of US support. He could well react emotionally and unpredictably if he felt that the withdrawal of the C–130s meant that the U.S. was withdrawing its support. It is not inconceivable that he would lash out by whipping up again anti-white reaction in the Congo. Just as conceivably, he could decide to cast his

---

[1] Source: Washington National Records Center, RG 330, OSD Files: FRC 72 A 2468, Congo 1967. Secret. No drafting information appears on the original, which is attached to a July 18 transmittal memorandum from Acting Assistant Secretary Townsend Hoopes to Secretary McNamara stating that the paper had been prepared for McNamara's meeting with the President and Secretary Rusk that afternoon.

[2] July 16.

[3] The tabs are attached but not printed.

lot with the radical Africans (and their Communist supporters) and turn to Algeria and East Europeans for support.[4]

—There are several options we should consider.

Option 1— Withdrawal of all three C–130s on July 24th (our original deadline).

Option 2— Withdrawal of all three C–130s on August 7th (giving Mobutu his month).

Option 3— Withdrawing one C–130 on July 24th, and one C–130 each succeeding week (or withdraw both remaining C–130s simultaneously during the second two-week period).

Option 3 probably gives us the best chance to start withdrawing the C–130s without engendering a violent reaction by Mobutu.[5]

—Regardless of which option is chosen, we should press Mobutu not to foreclose Belgian military assistance (which he will need over the long term) and to assure the safety (and hence continued presence) of the European population which is essential to the Congo's economic future.

[4] A handwritten notation in the margin reads: "I doubt this. T. Hoopes."

[5] The first two C–130s left the Congo on July 24 and August 3. The third remained until December 10.

527. Notes of the President's Meeting With Secretary Rusk, Secretary McNamara, Walt Rostow, McGeorge Bundy, and George Christian[1]

Washington, July 18, 1967, 6:06–7:30 p.m.

[Omitted here is discussion of other subjects.]

On the matter of cargo planes to the Congo, the President wanted to know what had happened.

Secretary Rusk said there had been 21 movements of the aircraft, to haul out wounded, to drop food, and to move ammunition.

Secretary Rusk said that there is no deal to save the life of Tshombe. The Secretary said that if Tshombe is executed, we might as well forget about the Congo as far as our people in Congress are con-

[1] Source: Johnson Library, Tom Johnson's Notes of Meetings, July 18, 1967–6:06 p.m. Literally Eyes Only. The meeting was held in the Cabinet Room.

cerned. The Secretary said it was extremely important that something be done about Tshombe's fate while he is held in Algeria.

[Omitted here is discussion of other subjects.]

528. Telegram From the Department of State to the Embassy in the Congo[1]

Washington, July 19, 1967, 7:44 p.m.

9612. For Ambassador from Secretary.

1. We see an acute political problem arising here in US if Mobutu executes Tshombe. It could affect adversely Congressional reaction to our entire African assistance program and, more specifically, might force revision of our aid policy to Congo, which has been its mainstay since independence. As you know, aid program already in deep trouble as result Middle East, Nigeria and other problems.

2. With Algiers indication that Supreme Court will hand down its decision on Congo demand for Tshombe extradition this Friday[2] and Congo statements that no further trial needed in Congo as Tshombe already found guilty, time is pressing in.

3. I know that it will be most difficult for you to approach Mobutu on this matter, that he may deeply resent your raising subject and that the close working relationship you have so quickly worked out with him could be seriously jeopardized. Nevertheless I believe that we must have record clear with him and he know that the execution of Tshombe will have a strong, adverse political effect here in US.

4. I know that you will have to tailor approach to him as you see fit but believe following are points which could enter into your presentation. You should make it plain that you are doing this under instructions:

a. US has no desire interfere with Congo's judicial processes nor in its internal affairs.

b. US has no brief for Tshombe and understands Congo's desire to end his plotting against govt of Congo. Reaction US public opinion,

---

[1] Source: National Archives, RG 59, Central Files 1967–69, POL 30 THE CONGO. Secret; Immediate; Nodis. Drafted by Brown; cleared by the Under Secretary, Meeker in L, and Palmer; and approved by Rusk.

[2] July 21.

however severe it might be, is not aimed especially at the Congo or this particular case, but derives from a strong aversion to politics by violence. Political exile and political asylum are deeply entrenched in the thinking of a nation with our historic background. The difference between exile or imprisonment on the one side and summary execution on the other is a very important distinction.

c. US continues to support the govt as evidenced by its prompt reply to Mobutu's request for assistance in meeting the threat of mercenary mutiny, an action taken by the US despite the political problems it caused for the Administration.

d. US is concerned however that summary execution of Tshombe, following on Pentecost hangings of 1966, will evoke serious adverse political effect in US and thereby seriously threaten steady support US has been able to give Congo since independence.

e. US therefore strongly urges Mobutu that, if Tshombe extradited, he not carry out any planned execution and thus avoid arousing political protests in US and elsewhere which would damage good name of Congo on international scene.

f. Forbearance on this issue, while politically difficult in Congo, could confound Mobutu's and our critics and enable Mobutu to capitalize on stature gained as result of monetary reform and skillful leadership during crisis caused by mercenaries.

5. Since we cannot be sure Tshombe may not be transferred to Kinshasa even before Algiers announcement, you should act on this message soonest.[3]

Rusk

---

[3] In telegram 1329 from Kinshasa, July 20, McBride reported that his staff was convinced that the Embassy could not persuade Mobutu not to execute Tshombe; he suggested a letter from the Secretary to Bomboko. (National Archives, RG 59, Central Files 1967–69, POL 30 THE CONGO) In telegram 10369 to Kinshasa, July 20, Rusk responded that McBride should give Bomboko a personal, oral message from him, drawing on the points in telegram 9612. (Ibid.) McBride reported in telegram 1425 from Kinshasa, July 21, that he delivered the oral message to Bomboko. (Ibid.) In telegram 1453 from Kinshasa, July 22, McBride reported that Bomboko discussed the U.S. démarche with Mobutu who believed he had no alternative but to go ahead with the execution. (Ibid.) Algerian President Boumediene did not sign the extradition order.

529. Telegram From the Embassy in the Congo to the Department of State[1]

Kinshasa, July 28, 1967, 1435Z.

1741. For the Secretary from McBride:

1. I will in separate message be making certain specific recommendations about possibilities for US actions in Congo now. Purpose of this message to you is unfortunately to signal what appears to be failure of local military situation to improve, partially it must be frankly stated, due to failure of Congolese to cope with their operational problems. I hate to add gloom but facts must be faced. While C–130 mission has achieved its immediate purpose of assisting Mobutu psychologically and materially, in calming dangerous racist situation and presence in case of need for total US evacuation, it must be faced that original problems have not gone away. Second issue of anti-white sentiment is dormant for moment but could flare up again. One possibility would be return of Tshombe, his execution followed by outcry in US and Europe (and in part of Africa) followed by anti-foreign outbursts here that would be more serious than events of early July. Insofar as crushing mercenary rebellion is concerned, little progress has been made. C–130s have efficiently transported matériel and men to periphery of area affected, but there is no evidence ANC, in part for lack of air cover, dares yet to tangle with mercenaries. On contrary, Consulate Bukavu reports panic conditions there in ANC when mercenaries made a couple of distant feints two days ago. It is apparent that all of help ANC has received has not converted its officers or men into force that puts its back into anything with relish except looting and beating civilians. Old hands here insist, however, there is some improvement in that ANC did fight mercenaries for a while in Kisangani, though other reports are discouraging.

2. Worst we fear is that second C–130 and even third will depart without any improvement in military situation. Then the irrational man with whom we are dealing will, far from showing gratitude, turn on us. In state of near-hysteria in which Mobutu finds himself, this is real possibility. Simplest solution by far locally would be maintenance of two C–130s until back of mercenary rebellion is broken, but since this may be long-term matter and knowing problems at home, I have refrained from recommending this as I did not want to pose this again. A single C–130 would have some effect militarily and considerable effect

[1] Source: National Archives, RG 59, Central Files 1967–69, POL 23–9 THE CONGO. Secret; Immediate; Nodis.

psychologically, and I would of course like to retain one if this were possible, but I fear even this poses grave difficulties for Department.

3. Despite all this, I am still genuinely concerned at immediate prospect of C–130 departure and we have been seeking some way mitigate this problem. These detailed thoughts will be contained in a separate message, but I just wanted to point out that despite efforts on our part, Congolese have not overcome their inability to utilize what assets they have. Their hand-wringing and tendency to panic are chronic. By far the, easiest course would be to wash our hands of this country. But this would of course be basic reversal of our policy to assist present Congolese Govt in its slow progress towards stability which unfortunately has been severely shaken by this latest outbreak—though it must be admitted this one is not of Congolese making. Furthermore, no alternative to Mobutu appears on horizon and he still in spite of everything seems our best bet as pro-Western Congolese leader. It is with conviction in mind that basic policy should not be reversed that we are recommending separately a series of possible courses of action, some of them controversial and some ramshackle, but the best we can devise bearing Washington problems in mind.

McBride

---

530. Telegram From the Department of State to the Embassy in the Congo[1]

Washington, July 29, 1967, 10:32 p.m.

14267. For Ambassador from Secretary.

1. I have read your recent cables with close attention and understanding of the problems you face. In turn you know how difficult the situation is here.

2. The President has just received a letter from 18 Republican Senators, including Senators Hickenlooper and Dirksen, protesting our action in the Congo. The pressures to have the C–130s return have not abated.

3. I do not see how we can carry the entire burden in the Congo without some effective assistance from others, especially those Euro-

---

[1] Source: National Archives, RG 59, Central Files 1967–69, POL 23–9 THE CONGO. Secret; Immediate; Exdis. Drafted by Brown and approved by Rusk.

pean powers whose direct interests in the Congo are far larger than our own. You will note my preoccupations in the letter I have just sent to Harmel[2] and in the cables we are sending to certain European capitals. The aim of all these is to seek a greater acceptance of responsibility for assistance in the Congo; failing these efforts, I do not see how we can continue.

4. I have asked that orders go forth putting off the Monday[3] departure date for the C–130. We are only thinking of a 24 to 48 hour delay to permit us to get a reading of what others may do. You should not anticipate any substantial delay.

5. I consider it essential for you to condition the Congolese this weekend to the withdrawal of the second C–130 early in the week. I am sure that you will also pass on to them our own preoccupations and problems. You should urge them in the strongest way possible to broaden their search for support elsewhere in Western Europe as in Africa, making it plain that the US cannot carry burden virtually alone.[4]

Rusk

---

[2] The Secretary's message to Harmel was transmitted in telegram 14255 to Brussels, July 29. (Ibid.)

[3] July 31.

[4] In telegram 1786 from Kinshasa, July 30, McBride reported that Mobutu reacted calmly when he informed him that the second C–130 would be leaving in a day or two, and that the final one would probably follow some days later. The telegram expressed the Ambassador's regrets that the C–130 issue had been such a source of anguish to the Department, but he emphasized that the presence of the C–130s had been invaluable locally. (National Archives, RG 59, Central Files 1967–69, POL 23–9 THE CONGO)

---

531. Telegram From the Embassy in the Congo to the Department of State[1]

Kinshasa, August 5, 1967, 1220Z.

2066. 1. I just talked to Mobutu and told him he was enormously complicating task of US in aiding Congo by permitting anti-American broadcasts. He said hastily he had just given order to High Commissioner for information to withdraw offending broadcasts.

---

[1] Source: National Archives, RG 59, Central Files 1967–69, POL THE CONGO–US. Secret; Flash. Repeated to CINCSTRIKE.

2. Mobutu then asked again for C–130 mission to east and I said I would see what could be done. It is conceivable that we could undertake mission to Goma tomorrow as reports from there indicate all quiet.

3. Bukavu situation however obviously reaching crisis and I suppose it will be impossible to recommend mission there though Mobutu strongly urges it on ground there is no danger because airport is in Rwanda.

4. During same conversation I reported to Mobutu C–46 had sighted 41 trucks heading towards Bukavu approximately 40 miles from city. Mobutu was grateful for this piece of intelligence.

5. Mobutu did not sound agitated over telephone and perhaps he may be having second thoughts about wisdom of provoking us, but it is too early to say. I believe this tempest might be calmed definitively if we offered a run or two to Goma. On other hand if mercenaries cross into Rwanda, revolt might be over though probably not in manner Mobutu intended.[2]

McBride

[2] Telegram 16755 to Kinshasa, August 5, stated that the Department would have no objection in principle to a mission to Goma. (Ibid., DEF 19 US–THE CONGO)

532. Extract From Minutes of the 303 Committee[1]

Washington, August 7, 1967.

An excerpt from the Minutes of the 303 Committee meeting held Monday, 7 August 1967, is set forth below for your information.

"Congo—Mr. Hughes circulated a memorandum from Ambassador Palmer to Mr. Hughes dealing with one more extension of CIA support [*less than 1 line not declassified*]. This memorandum is attached as a part of the record.[2] The committee saw no other solution other than to approve this request. It was recognized that frustration is an endemic disease for any representatives of the USG in Kinshasa. It was

[1] Source: Central Intelligence Agency Files, Job 82–00450R, DDO/AF, AF/DIV Historical Files, Box 6, 40 Committee, Congo (K) 1965-. Secret; Eyes Only. The original was forwarded from the CS/Special Group Office to the Chief of the Africa Division.

[2] Attached but not printed.

hoped that this would be the last hurrah in a long musical comedy—one with a potential tragic finale.

---

533. Telegram From the Department of State to the Embassy in the Congo[1]

Washington, August 9, 1967, 1950Z.[2]

18100. Ref: Kinshasa 2251, 2273.[3]

1. You may inform Mobutu that, in part on basis his request for mission to Goma reported Kinshasa 2251, USG will retain remaining C–130 in Congo for short additional period.

2. You should not make any commitment for specific time limit or encourage Mobutu to believe that it will stay for any longer than matter of days.

3. Assume request for mission to Goma August 10 will be forwarded through JTF channel.

4. Concur with line you taking on flights to Bujumbura.

Rusk

[1] Source: National Archives, RG 59, Central Files 1967–69, POL 23–9 THE CONGO. Secret; Flash; Limdis. Drafted by Schaufele; cleared by Palmer, Colonel Hart in JCS, and Brown; and approved by Katzenbach. Repeated to CINCSTRIKE for POLAD Tampa.

[2] Beginning in 1967, the dates and transmission times of all outgoing Department of State telegrams were in 6-figure date-time-groups. The "Z" refers to Greenwich mean time.

[3] Both dated August 9. (National Archives, RG 59, Central Files 1967–69, POL 23–9 THE CONGO)

534. Telegram From the Department of State to the Embassy in the Congo[1]

Washington, August 10, 1967, 0007Z.

18561. Ref Bukavu 29.[2]

1. Believe you should do everything possible discourage Bontemps, Shyns or any others from thinking US could be channel for any Schramme proposals to Mobutu or GDRC.

2. Not only is this unacceptable political risk for US position in Congo but also, we believe, unrealistic to expect Mobutu show any receptivity to such proposal at this time.

3. We assume that it equally impossible for GOB to be channel for proposal. If Kinshasa believes there is some value in getting these proposals to GDRC we would welcome any suggestions it may have. Our initial impression is that only present possibility might be private person who has access to Mobutu.

Rusk

---

[1] Source: National Archives, RG 59, Central Files 1967–69, POL 23–9 THE CONGO. Secret; Immediate; Exdis. Drafted by Schaufele, cleared by Brown, and approved by Palmer. Also sent to Bukavu.

[2] Telegram 29 from Bukavu, August 9, reported that Bontemps, a friend of mercenary leader Major Jean Schramme, warned that the mercenaries had the capability to wreak havoc in the eastern Congo indefinitely if Mobutu refused to negotiate. Bontemps said that he knew the mercenaries' demands: safe departure via Rwanda to Europe and the guaranteed safety of the North Katangan troops who had joined the rebellion, either abroad or in Katanga. He offered to put these on a paper for Schramme's signature. The Consulate asked permission to accept Schramme's demands and pass them to the Embassy in Kinshasa for transmission to Mobutu. (Ibid.)

535. Telegram From the Department of State to the Embassy in the Congo[1]

Washington, August 10, 1967, 2 a.m.

18571. Ref: Kinshasa 2283.[2] Authorization contained Deptel 18800,[3] being kept open pending receipt detailed reasons for judgment expressed reftel. Meanwhile it may be useful for you to have following elaboration reasons which led to decision give you this additional latitude. Complete withdrawal at time mercs threatening move south[4] could produce following major dangers:

1. Encouragement of mercenaries in their resolve, including sweep south.
2. ANC morale would be even further weakened with loss airlift capability.
3. Others assisting GDRC, e.g., Ethiopia and Ghana, might be less willing remain and help. F–86s would be handicapped by lack air transport of fuel.
4. Stimulate Europeans to depart, thus disrupting economy and causing GDRC reprisals.
5. Anti-white campaign, leading to widespread racial violence.
6. Greater difficulty in obtaining GDRC cooperation in evacuating US nationals if that proves necessary.
7. GDRC might turn to radical African and/or communist sources of assistance thereby nullifying six years Free World effort.
8. With outside help mercenaries might set up new secessionist Katanga, with consequences similar to 7 above.

Rusk

---

[1] Source: National Archives, RG 59, Central Files 1967–69, POL 23–9 THE CONGO. Secret; Flash; Limdis. Drafted by Palmer, cleared by Katzenbach, and approved by Palmer.

[2] Telegram 2283 from Kinshasa, August 9, suggested departure of the last C–130 after completion of a mission the following day. (Ibid.)

[3] Reference is presumably to telegram 18100, Document 533.

[4] In telegram 2349 from Kinshasa, August 10, McBride stated that he was pleased with the prospect that the last C–130 would remain in the Congo on a day-to-day basis, adding that the problem of suitable missions could be worked out locally. (National Archives, RG 59, Central Files 1967–69, POL 23–9 THE CONGO)

536. Telegram From the Department of State to the Embassy in the Congo[1]

Washington, August 11, 1967, 1730Z.

19352. 1. Under instructions Adoula called on Palmer today and informed him that GDRC had sent message to UN Secretary General which asks all members of the Security Council and friends of the Congo for logistic assistance and any other assistance which could help maintain order.[2]

2. Palmer emphasized problems inclusion USSR and other Communist countries would cause not only for US but for objectives which GDRC seeks. Even introduction of matter could elicit Soviet offer which would put GDRC in difficult position. Also expressed concern that matter not been discussed with USG in advance.

3. Adoula interpreted GDRC request as meaning such assistance would have to be requested by GDRC but stated he would seek ASAP clarification and if possible delay in case letter has not been forwarded.[3]

4. Palmer stated he hoped two governments could consult before any further action taken.

5. Hope you can take this up immediately with Mobutu or Bomboko to point out pitfalls in this approach. USUN states letter already transmitted.

Rusk

---

[1] Source: National Archives, RG 59, Central Files 1967–69, POL 23–9 THE CONGO. Secret; Flash. Drafted by Schaufele, cleared by Elizabeth Ann Brown, and approved by Palmer. Repeated to Brussels, USUN, and Moscow.

[2] U.N. Doc. S/8118, August 10.

[3] Telegram 19353 to Kinshasa, August 11, reported that Adoula phoned Palmer to inform him that the President of the Security Council had said that if the Congo were asking for aid from the United Nations, it would have to request a meeting of the Security Council. If it were asking only that U.N. members be informed of its need for assistance, however, he had done this by circulating the Congo's letter. (Ibid.)

537. Telegram From the Department of State to the Embassy in the Congo[1]

Washington, August 12, 1967, 0049Z.

19840. 1. Adoula called on Palmer again this afternoon after talking with Mobutu.

2. According to Adoula, Mobutu concurs with his interpretation of Congolese request contained in message to President of SC, i.e. that such assistance should be given upon the specific request of GDRC. FYI Adoula informed Deptoff after call on Palmer that at first Mobutu did not seem averse to assistance from USSR until Adoula reminded him of past history USSR-Congolese relations. End FYI.

3. At Mobutu's request, Adoula raised Tshombe matter. Palmer explained serious concern in US about legal and humanitarian principles as well as manner in which Tshombe apprehended. He went on to say that summary execution of Tshombe would cause serious problem in US-GDRC relations.

4. Adoula defended Govt point of view but FYI in subsequent conversation with Deptoff indicated his unhappiness over course GDRC following in this case although he did not hide his anathema for Tshombe. End FYI.

5. Adoula said Mobutu had stated that primary problem was to get rid of mercenaries. Palmer agreed, stating that if they could be gotten rid by means other than force present problem would be well on way to solution. Adoula indicated his agreement.

6. Hope you able elicit similar interpretation GDRC request contained in letter to SC president so that there is no ambiguity on this point.

Rusk

---

[1] Source: National Archives, RG 59, Central Files 1967–69, POL 23–9 THE CONGO. Secret; Priority; Exdis. Drafted by Schaufele, cleared by L. Dean Brown, and approved by Fredericks. Repeated to USUN.

538. Telegram From the Department of State to the Embassy in the Congo[1]

Washington, August 14, 1967, 0426Z.

20184. Kinshasa 2502.[2]

1. Appreciate what you have already done but believe there might be additional effect if you called Mobutu, even at this hour, to tell him you under instructions to inform him of following:

A. Kind of demonstration reported reftel would be most difficult explain outside Congo. Arrest of diplomatic chiefs of mission would not only be violation diplomatic usage but would also demonstrate that GDRC unable differentiate between Governments concerned and acts of their citizens. To arrest chiefs of mission is very serious step.

B. Such action appears be contradictory to mission we understand Litho has just undertaken in Katanga. It could effectively nullify progress made in assuring European technicians that their presence and contribution desired in Congo.

C. We have not received message regarding Soviet offer but kind of action reported reftel is bound to alienate sources of assistance, including US, which have been most effective in past in helping Congo. Our considered opinion is that lashing out at Belgians and others does not serve help situation but only exacerbate it.[3]

D. Therefore we hope Mobutu will take necessary steps call off actions described reftel if they indeed planned.

2. Brussels requested inform GOB above instructions to Kinshasa.

Rusk

---

[1] Source: National Archives, RG 59, Central Files 1967–69, POL 23–8 THE CONGO. Confidential; Flash. Drafted and approved by Schaufele. Also sent to Brussels and repeated to London and Paris.

[2] In telegram 2502 from Kinshasa, August 13, McBride reported that Belgian Ambassador Bihin informed him that loudspeakers in downtown Kinshasa were broadcasting that the British, French, and Belgian Ambassadors would be arrested the next day. Bihin later called to say that he had been informed that the sacking of the Belgian Embassy was planned for 7 a.m. on August 14. (Ibid., POL 12 THE CONGO)

[3] In telegram 2505 from Kinshasa, August 14, McBride reported that Bomboko informed him of his August 13 talk in Kinshasa with the Soviet Ambassador to the Congo (Brazzaville), who had said he was responding to the Congolese appeal at the United Nations and asked what kind of support the Congolese Government wanted. (Ibid., DEF 19–6 USSR–THE CONGO)

539. Telegram From the Department of State to the Embassy in the Congo[1]

Washington, August 14, 1967, 2312Z.

20600. 1. In view series of events last few days, believe it most important that you seek appointment with Mobutu ASAP and speak to him along following lines:

2. Under instructions you requesting clarification Congolese intentions for immediate future.

3. We aware of discussions which Mobutu had held with Belgian Amb about security Belgian citizens and also of Litho efforts calm foreign population Katanga. Therefore we find violence which took place Kinshasa Aug 14[2] inconsistent with GDRC's own assurances of safety for foreigners and with what we considered to be sincere Belgo-Congolese efforts to find mutually acceptable formula re security Belgian citizens in Congo. It seems to us that incident of Aug 14 in large part due to inflammatory output Govt-controlled communications media.

4. We also concerned by Congolese appeal to President SC which, contrary to our usual frank and full discussions, was carried out without prior knowledge USG. We struck by fact that at very time Adoula under instructions to inform USG of this step Soviet Amb in Brazzaville appeared in Kinshasa to offer assistance in response to it.

5. More than any Congolese leader Mobutu is aware of US policy toward Congo and assistance US has provided Congo. We have worked closely together for seven years. Therefore we at loss to explain recent Congolese actions especially since Mobutu also aware strong domestic reaction which our most recent assistance has caused in U.S.

6. Violence of Aug 14 in which American citizens were badly beaten, especially if combined with assistance from Soviet or other countries backed by Soviets, bound have adverse results in U.S.

7. US policy toward Congo remains unchanged but in view our close and cordial relationships we would welcome Mobutu's comments on above.

---

[1] Source: National Archives, RG 59, Central Files 1967–69, POL 1 THE CONGO. Secret; Immediate. Drafted by Schaufele, cleared by Brown, and approved by Palmer. Repeated to Brussels.

[2] On August 14, the Belgian Embassy was sacked and many Europeans and Americans in Kinshasa were attacked and beaten.

8. If Mobutu queries you about status his requests for assistance you should limit yourself to stating that you have had no response as yet.

Rusk

540. Memorandum From Edward Hamilton of the National Security Council Staff to President Johnson[1]

Washington, August 19, 1967, 11 a.m.

SUBJECT

Congo situation report

1. As you know, the Congolese Foreign Minister seemed on the verge yesterday of working out a scheme with Schramme whereby the mercenaries would "surrender" and be evacuated from the Congo via Rwanda.[2]

2. Last night, however, after listening for hours to the mercenary radio inciting Congolese troops to desert, the Foreign Minister told our people he couldn't go through with the plan without some dramatic move against the mercenaries first. Without some show of government strength, he said, the effects of public announcement of a negotiated settlement would be disastrous for Congolese army morale, and perhaps even threaten Mobutu's future as President.

3. Specifically, the Foreign Minister proposed to give Schramme an ultimatum: give up within 48 hours or the town of Bukavu (where Schramme is headquartered) will be "razed to the ground" by Congolese bombs. If the bluff were called, he would carry out the raids with Ethiopian F–86's based in the neighboring country of Burundi.

---

[1] Source: Johnson Library, National Security File, Files of Edward Hamilton, Congo (B). No classification marking.

[2] Telegram 22134 to Kigali, August 17, instructed the Ambassador to Rwanda, Leo G. Cyr, to deliver a note to Bomboko, who was in Kigali attempting to negotiate the departure of the mercenaries through Rwanda, stating that the U.S. Government was prepared to cooperate as appropriate to facilitate the peaceful withdrawal to Rwanda and the safe and voluntary repatriation or resettlement of certain foreign and Congolese elements. Cyr was told to make it clear to Bomboko that the U.S. Government could not guarantee the security of persons who were not U.S. nationals and not under U.S. control, and that neither the note nor U.S. cooperation involved a financial commitment. (National Archives, RG 59, Central Files 1967–69, POL 23–9 THE CONGO)

4. Our people went at him hard to show him the lunacy of this course. We pointed out that (i) it would probably destroy the Congo's last chance to end the mercenary problem with minimum political disruption and loss of life, and (ii) the threat would be incredible and probably impossible for the Congolese to carry out. (These F–86's are not equipped for bombing; the best they could do would be rockets, and God knows whom they would hit. More important, the airfield in Burundi is under repair and there is no F–86 fuel there.)

5. McBride also went to Mobutu (more than 1000 miles away, in Kinshasa) and asked him to instruct his Foreign Minister to stop the nonsense and get back to working out the settlement. Mobutu complied.

6. By the time Mobutu's instructions arrived this morning, however, the Foreign Minister had left for Burundi, presumably to investigate for himself whether his plan is feasible and whether the Burundians will allow themselves to be implicated in such an operation. Our man in Burundi will try to intercept him and talk some sense into him, as well as relaying Mobutu's instructions.

541. Telegram From the Department of State to the Embassy in Rwanda[1]

Washington, August 19, 1967, 2324Z.

24081. Request Embassy deliver following message from President to President Kayibanda; dated August 19, 1967:

"Dear Mr. President:

It was a great pleasure to see you during your recent visit to Washington[2] and I deeply valued the opportunity to exchange views with you on a number of subjects of importance to our two countries.

I am prompted to write you at this time because of our mutual concern about the situation in the Congo and our common interest in seeing an early end to the mercenary-led rebellion.

[1] Source: National Archives, RG 59, Central Files 1967–69, POL 7 RWANDA. Secret; Limdis. Drafted by Palmer, cleared by Katzenbach and President Johnson, and approved by Rusk.

[2] President Kayibanda was in the United States August 13–14. He met informally with President Johnson at the White House on August 14.

I have viewed with considerable hope the Congolese plan to permit the withdrawal of the mercenaries and Katangans to Rwanda, the evacuation of the mercenaries out of Africa and the eventual voluntary repatriation of the Katangans. I believe this plan is eminently designed to meet the objective which you and we both seek and we have therefore given it our full support.

If the plan can be successfully carried out, it would eliminate the mercenary presence, end the specter of further bloodshed and permit the resumption of normal activity in the Congo. Most important to you is that an unsettling situation on your border will be ended. We are convinced that if the rebellion is not ended as quickly as possible, the future effects in both Rwanda and the Congo could be very serious.

The United States is, as you know, interested in the stability, security and development of central Africa. Therefore, even though we have no nationals among the mercenaries, we are prepared to cooperate with Rwanda, the Congo, Belgium, France, and other countries and international organizations to facilitate the implementation of this plan. Meanwhile, I would like to assure you that we will make every effort to assist in the feeding of the Katangans while they remain in Rwanda through the provision of available PL 480 foodstuffs.

Since time is of the essence, I strongly hope you will be able to give your approval to this plan so that this threat to the security and well-being of the area can be brought to an end.

Lyndon B. Johnson"

Rusk

542. Telegram From the Department of State to the Embassy in Belgium[1]

Washington, August 22, 1967, 1039Z.

24841. 1. We believe time has come for GOB to issue public statement, reiterating its support for GDRC, condemning mercenary-led rebellion, and expressing hope for rapid, bloodless end to strife. Realize that GOB has condemned mercenaries in past but think another state-

[1] Source: National Archives, RG 59, Central Files 1967–69, POL 23–9 THE CONGO. Confidential; Immediate. Drafted by Brown, cleared by Moffat, and approved by Palmer. Repeated to Lisbon, Kinshasa, Kigali, Bujumbura, and CINCSTRIKE for POLAD Tampa.

ment is called for. It should be aimed both at reassuring Mobutu and warning Schramme that he cannot expect assistance or encouragement from official Belgian circles. It should serve take some of sting out of Belgian press articles, sympathetic to Schramme, which disturb Mobutu.[2]

2. Above becomes more urgent as result collapse Rwanda evacuation plan.[3]

Rusk

[2] In telegram 1101 from Brussels, August 23, Knight reported that he conveyed the Department's suggestion to Davignon, who readily agreed. (Ibid.)

[3] Telegram 371 from Kigali, August 21, reported that the Rwandan Government refused to let the mercenaries transit Rwanda. (Ibid.)

543. Telegram From the Department of State to the Embassy in the Congo[1]

Washington, August 25, 1967, 2320Z.

27382. 1. We believe effort must be made to keep GDRC headed toward path of pacific solution to mercenary problem. Therefore, at such time as you feel appropriate keeping in mind Schyns' request (Kinshasa 5480)[2] you should speak with Mobutu and Bomboko, and possibly, Nendaka along following lines:

2. We appreciate political considerations which make it difficult for Congo to resume negotiations, even indirectly, on merc withdrawal and evacuation. We also regret GOR's action in refusing cooperation and issuing communiqué.

3. Nevertheless we continue believe kind of solution which commendable Congolese initiative envisaged seems to be most desirable, i.e. peaceful withdrawal of mercs and Katangans either through Rwanda or from Congolese territory.

[1] Source: Department of Stare, Central Files, POL 23–9 THE CONGO. Secret; Immediate; Limdis. Drafted by Schaufele, cleared by Brown, and approved by Palmer. Repeated to Kigali, Bujumbura, and Brussels, and CINCSTRIKE for POLAD Tampa.

[2] Reference should be to telegram 3251 from Kinshasa, August 25, which reported that Dr. Charles Schyns, a Belgian businessman who had offered to act as an informal intermediary between the Congolese Government and the mercenaries, made a personal plea to Mobutu for one last effort to evacuate the mercenaries peacefully, and asked that there be no other U.S. or Belgian efforts until August 27. (Ibid.)

4. If GDRC insists on military solution it obvious there could be considerable loss of life, danger that confrontation would spill over into other parts of Congo and neighboring countries, confirmation to international opinion that Congo is site of recurring violence and bloodshed, and jeopardizing of OAU conference.

5. If merc/Katangan force determined stand fast GDRC would need further resources which would increase already heavy burden on GDRC budget and whole economy. Even if successful effects would be long-lasting.

6. Mobutu too wise and experienced not to realize that turning to other sources such as Massamba-Debat's Cubans or Soviets for assistance will in long run lead only to undermining his regime and endangering long-run Congolese stability.

7. Whatever short term political disadvantages Mobutu might see in peaceful withdrawal and evacuation, he should realize that, with goodwill and cooperation, actually it likely to be accomplished more rapidly than military reduction of mercenary force. In long run it will have proved his statesmanship in getting rid of element disruptive to Congolese internal security, and saving his country from further bloodshed. If, as we assume, peaceful solution faster than military, internal pressures on him will be relieved much sooner and interracial harmony will have been preserved.[3]

Rusk

---

[3] In telegram 3286 from Kinshasa, August 26, McBride reported that he discussed this with Mobutu, who was very bitter about the mercenaries at the outset, but whose thinking had seemed to evolve somewhat in the direction of a negotiated settlement as the conversation continued. Mobutu said he would meet Schyns with an open mind the following day. (Ibid.)

544. Memorandum From the President's Special Assistant (Rostow) to President Johnson[1]

Washington, August 31, 1967, 9:35 a.m.

SUBJECT

CIA-paid Pilots for the Congo

Messrs. Rusk, McNamara, and Helms have signed off on a small *covert* step to strengthen our negotiating position with Mobutu for a peaceful (evacuation) solution to the mercenary problem in the Congo. I support their decision, but I thought you should be aware of the operation and that we should have your guidance before proceeding.

In substance, the proposal is that we:

—authorize CIA to recruit five pilots, experienced in the Congo and with T–28 aircraft. (The Agency has already located 10 such pilots—[*less than 1 line not declassified*] who are willing to go back to the Congo on such a mission.)

—authorize a three-month CIA contract with the pilots whereby they would, under *covert* direction of an American officer, fly Mobutu's T–28's for him. [*1½ lines not declassified*]

—authorize McBride to use this as a bargaining counter (1) to preempt acceptance of Soviet or Chinese aid (which has been offered and is very hard for Mobutu to refuse), and (2) to push Mobutu toward another try at an evacuation plan of the sort which came within inches of success last week.

Situation

The mercenaries are still holed up in Bukavu on the Eastern border of the Congo, 1200 miles from Mobutu in Kinshasa. Schramme agreed last week to a plan to evacuate them through Rwanda to Europe, but the plan fell through because of Belgian vagueness about precisely how the evacuation would be carried out and Rwandan fear of agreeing to anything which would put the mercenaries on Rwandan territory without absolute assurance that they would leave immediately. Mobutu is under heavy political pressure from his own firebrands—including a good share of his army—to "do something" about the mercenaries. But as of now he is helpless; his troops won't fight them, at least without air cover, and he has no pilots to operate the seven T–28 trainer/fighters which represent his total tactical air force.

The situation is complicated by the fact that the Chinese-influenced Congo Republic (Brazzaville) across the river has made it

[1] Source: Johnson Library, National Security File, Country File, Congo, Vol. XIV, Memos & Miscellaneous, 8/67–10/68. Top Secret.

clear to Mobutu that if he says the word they can and will supply enough Castro Cuban troops to mop up the mercenaries. In addition, the Soviet Ambassador to Congo (B)—there is now *no* Soviet representation in Congo (K)—has asked Mobutu to give him a list of his military requirements, with the strong implication that the Soviets are prepared to help him. In the light of their action in Nigeria, it seems likely that they would jump at the chance, particularly since 150 mercenaries do not represent a very difficult problem for any reasonable military force. The Algerians are also waiting in the wings.

Mobutu has given us several signals that he can't hold out much longer against his internal critics unless he has some further token of Western support that he can point to as good reason for not accepting communist help. Moreover, he must be able to present at least some credible threat to the mercenaries as a deterrent to keep them from marching south to Katanga, a move which could well recreate in precise and painful detail the secession situation of 1962–64—which we have invested more than $500 million to avoid. And it is clear to any Congo veteran that if the Brazzaville Cubans or Soviet troops ever get into the Congo, it will be very hard to get them out. At the very least, we could expect a whole new East-West dimension to the chronic problem of the Congo, with dark implications for the rest of Africa.

Purpose of the Operation

The pilots would be a political bargaining counter, both within Mobutu's councils and for McBride in dealing with Mobutu. They would *not* constitute a decisive military factor. We would hope they would give Mobutu a marginal capacity to present some threat to the mercenaries, give him some evidence of Western support to counter pressure to accept Bloc aid, and give us the leverage to get him to be an active force in moving toward a new evacuation plan. (We are also working on the Brussels end of this problem; we may need to come back to you on it later this week.)

Risks

Like all covert operations, this one runs the risk of exposure. Until a few months ago, the CIA financed and controlled pilots, aircraft and maintenance for the entire Congolese air force. (These operations are now entirely financed and controlled by Mobutu.) The pilots we would supply would be veterans of those days. It is conceivable that an enterprising reporter (of whom there are very few in the Congo) could blow the cover, which could be highly embarrassing here—though it would not have much effect, abroad, in my judgment. It would be even more embarrassing if, after receiving the pilots, Mobutu kicked over the traces and let the Bloc in and then the cover blew. Obviously, we would maintain that the Congolese had hired and paid the pilots, but these are serious risks, which you should take carefully into account.

Recommendation

On balance, I would recommend we go ahead. We got away for several years, through thick and thin, with covert operation of Mobutu's entire air arm. I think the odds are very good that we can get away with quiet support of five pilots now. Moreover, although it may seem implausible to argue that giving Mobutu fighter pilots will make him more peaceful-minded, I think it is our best chance of maximizing the chances of an evacuation solution, while at the same time avoiding Bloc access to the Congo. The costs of mercenary-inspired disintegration of the Congo and/or Sino-Soviet involvement would be infinitely greater than the money cost and political risk involved in this proposition. I would vote that you accept the risks and approve the operation.

Walt

Go ahead with the operation

No

Speak to me[2]

[2] None of these options is checked.

---

545. Telegram From the Department of State to the Embassy in Belgium[1]

Washington, August 31, 1967, 2310Z.

30697. Literally eyes only for Ambassador from Secretary. This message is a personal thought about your 1235,[2] the cogency of which I fully appreciate.

[1] Source: National Archives, RG 59, Central Files 1967–69, POL 23–9 THE CONGO. Secret; Priority; No Distribution Outside the Department. Drafted and approved by Rusk and cleared by Palmer and Leddy.

[2] In telegram 1235 from Brussels, August 30, Knight discussed the possibility of a massacre of large numbers of whites, mostly Belgians, in the Congo by the ANC if the mercenary impasse were not resolved. Noting that Belgium would find it most difficult, if not impossible, to carry out a military-type rescue of its nationals, he pointed out that the Belgians would probably turn to the United States with a fervent eleventh-hour plea for help if such an event occurred. (Ibid.)

We would be greatly concerned if we got an emergency message from the Belgians calling upon us for major assistance in the Congo in the absence of a serious effort by a group of nations to play their part. We would be even more concerned if the Belgians were to take our reactions to such a request as a test of our loyalty to NATO or to them as a NATO ally.

It is easy and convenient for other governments to think that all they have to do is to call on Uncle Sam to meet their necessary requirements in an emergency. But we are not the mercenaries of NATO. To begin with, it is simply not true that the US is the only nation physically able to provide such assistance. The Canadians, the British, the French, the Turks, and perhaps other NATO allies all have transport aircraft. Most of them have Boeing 707s or similar aircraft in their civil airlines which could, in an emergency, be diverted for such purposes. Secondly, the fact that it may be politically inconvenient or difficult for others to assist simply cannot impose upon the US an obligation to act unilaterally.

If it is politically impossible for the Belgians to give Mobutu military help to dispose of the mercenaries, it is no less politically impossible for the US to go rushing in unilaterally to bail them out in the absence of a serious effort by other governments. The day has passed when the US can take on such responsibilities regardless of what others are doing, and what others are willing to do for themselves.

Belgium is a member of the Common Market and has five partners who are fully capable of making a significant contribution toward their common stake in what happens in Africa. It is more than flesh and spirit can bear to suppose that a prosperous, safe and lazy Europe can sit in comfort while calling upon the US to do their disagreeable jobs for them.

The purpose of this message is to alert you to the seriousness of this problem as far as we are concerned. I do not in this message wish to ask you to take any specific step but I would be glad to have your advice as to whether you should go to the Belgians and press upon them the urgent need for doing some contingency planning with other members of NATO, most especially Western European members, if a sudden emergency should develop in the Congo.

We need not be apologetic about this problem. We are carrying a major struggle in Southeast Asia with a half million of our own forces to which two Western European signatories of SEATO are making no contribution. At the same time we are maintaining our forces in NATO unimpaired. Even the prospective rotation of two brigades has not been put into effect.

I know that we have important interests in Africa and that we ourselves are concerned about what happens in the Congo. But we should not be expected to be more concerned about what happens in that vast continent than those who live next door in the small peninsula called Western Europe.

Please give me your best thinking on these matters. One possibility would be for me to send a frank and somewhat more tactfully worded message along the above lines to Harmel. Personal regards.

Rusk

546. Memorandum From the President's Special Assistant (Rostow) to President Johnson[1]

Washington, September 1, 1967, 3:30 p.m.

Mr. President:

I have carried out consultations on the Congo problem and have the following to report.

1. *Nick Katzenbach* (with whom I doubletalked—he is at Martha's Vineyard) says he is for the action so that McBride will have some leverage over Mobutu. We have given McBride little to work with; but he has done a good job with what we have given him. In particular, Katzenbach is afraid of a threat to the lives of the 10,000 or so whites in the Congo. He is not wholly clear about how big the risk is of the operation blowing; or how much trouble it would make if it did blow. But, on balance, he believes we should proceed.

2. Sec. Rusk feels quite strongly that we ought to do this thing. If the Congo goes into an anti-white pogrom, we have already been warned by our Ambassador in Brussels that the Belgians will press us very hard to preserve and fly out the Belgians who are there. If we fail to do this, our Ambassador warns, the Belgians may regard this as letting down a NATO ally. Sec. Rusk wishes to have the record show that we did everything in our power to prevent that kind of situation from coming about and that kind of choice staring at us.

3. Dick Helms recommends against seeing Sen. Russell, mainly because he is now at Winder, Georgia, recuperating. He has not responded to efforts to engage him. For example, Scoop Jackson cannot get him to respond on a matter which Sen. Russell asked Sen. Jackson to

[1] Source: Johnson Library, National Security File, Country File, Congo, Vol. XIV, Memos & Miscellaneous, 8/67–10/68. Top Secret.

undertake. So far as substance of the matter is concerned, Helms believes Russell would support it because he was against pulling the pilots out in the first place. He was not enthusiastic about the commitment of the pilots in the Congo, but he told Dick personally that he thought pulling them out was unwise because "you will probably need them again." Therefore, Dick guesses that if the matter were put to him, he would remind him of his previous position and say "I guess you have got to do it."

With respect to the risk of the pilots becoming publicly known, Dick Helms thinks the probability is quite high that they will become known but he does not believe it will make much noise because the use of foreigners to fly aircraft in that part of the world is widespread.

Walt

Proceed[2]

No

See me

---

[2] This option is checked. On September 1 the 303 Committee approved recruitment of five pilots to fly for the Congolese Government under the direction of a CIA air operations officer for a period of 90 days. (Memorandum to Helms, October 10, 1967; Central Intelligence Agency Files, Job 82–00450R, Box 6, 40 Committee, Congo (K), 1965–)

547. Telegram From the Department of State to the Embassy in Portugal[1]

Washington, September 6, 1967, 1501Z.

32529. Ref: Lisbon's 257 (Notal).[2]

1. Dept Asst Sec Trimble called in Portuguese Chargé September 5 to express our concern over situation in Congo, particularly reports of mercenaries gathering in Angola and plotting against Mobutu, along lines para 4 reftel. After noting information that has been brought to our attention concerning mercenary presence and activities in Angola, and report that 30 or more mercenaries landed Bukavu from unknown destination September 1st, Trimble pointed out that failure settle mercenary problem could mean serious risk of Mobutu accepting proffered Communist aid and realigning his policy, not only to detriment Free World interests in Congo, but also to detriment Portuguese interests. Further, Trimble stressed that continued merc presence in Congo or arrival reinforcements would result in increased racial tension in Congo threatening lives of Africans and foreigners, including Americans and Portuguese.

2. In reply Chargé's question as to sources our information, Trimble said it came from many sources in many countries and directly from mercenaries and not repeat not from Congolese Government. In conclusion, Trimble requested Chargé inform his government of knowledge that had come to our attention as we share mutual interest in encouraging stability and doing whatever possible to prevent further violence and bloodshed in Congo.

3. Chargé promised to report conversation and asked if anything being done to get mercenaries out of Congo. Trimble outlined our views on present evacuation proposals. Chargé then said his government had considered what attitude to adopt toward mercenaries if they go to Angola but did not indicate that any decision had been reached.

---

[1] Source: National Archives, RG 59, Central Files 1967–69, POL 23–9 THE CONGO. Secret; Priority. Drafted by Haverkamp, cleared by Schaufele and Landau, and approved by Trimble. Repeated Priority to Brussels, Kigali, Kinshasa, London, Madrid, Paris, Pretoria, Luanda, Johannesburg, Salisbury, Lubumbashi, and CINCSTRIKE for POLAD.

[2] Telegram 257 from Lisbon, September 5, recommended that if the Department decided to call in the Portuguese Chargé, it emphasize that it had information concerning mercenary presence and activities in Angola which, in light of Portugal's official assurances, it believed should be brought to the Portuguese Government's attention. The telegram also recommended that the Department not base its approach on any accusations by the Congolese Government, since this would merely anger the Portuguese. (Ibid.)

4. *Comment:* We confident Chargé got message and hope his report will discourage GOP from permitting any mercenary adventure from Angola.

Rusk

548. Letter From the Ambassador to Belgium (Knight) to Secretary of State Rusk[1]

Brussels, September 7, 1967.

Dear Mr. Secretary:

I appreciated your frank reply to my 1235[2] concerning possible unilateral contingency planning on our part should the Belgians turn to us for cooperation after they would have done all they could to bring out their nationals in the Congo under conditions of the utmost gravity.

My only fear is that I did not make sufficiently clear in my telegram the emphasis which I have placed in several talks both with Foreign Minister Harmel and Davignon on the fact that they could not in a new crisis turn to us to bail them out. I have done so in pointed terms, stressing not only Vietnam and what we are doing there in the common cause with no help from our NATO Allies, but also our own grave and varied difficulties at home.

The responsiveness of the Belgians in our current project of developing a plan for the departure of the mercenaries would seem to show that my message had carried home.

As to whether we should go further now, I recommend that we let the present effort to eliminate the mercenary problem run its course. If this does not succeed, then I think I should go to Harmel and press upon him the urgent need for contingency planning by the Belgians with other members of NATO, most specially Western European members.

---

[1] Source: National Archives, RG 59, Rusk Files: Lot 72 D 192, Secretary's Miscellaneous Correspondence. Secret; Nodis.

[2] See Document 545 and footnote 2 thereto.

I would hope that the above action, added to the warnings which I have given, should suffice and that we could hold in reserve the option of a personal message from you.

Sincerely,

Ridge

549. Telegram From the Department of State to the Embassy in the Congo[1]

Washington, September 15, 1967, 2236Z.

38356. 1. We are encouraged by developments reported Kinshasa's 4201[2] and 4203.[3] OAU seizure leadership on question peaceful evac of mercs[4] gives promise problem can be grappled with and that Congo's neighbors, as well as Mobutu, will receive political cover they need. Realize that, of course, there many problems still to be faced and that, ultimately, merc agreement needed. Still some unknowns and would appreciate comments.

2. What is ICRC initial reaction? Has it been informed and by whom? Will it receive formal request to act from OAU? Does it still believe that SYG must make formal request or does it share our view that this need overtaken by OAU action?

Rusk

---

[1] Source: National Archives, RG 59, Central Files 1967–69, POL 23–9 THE CONGO. Secret; Immediate; Limdis. Drafted by Haverkamp and Brown, cleared by Arthur R. Day in IO, and approved by Brown. Also sent to Brussels and the Mission in Geneva, and repeated to USUN, CINCSTRIKE, Kigali, Bujumbura, Lusaka, and Bangui.

[2] Telegram 4201 from Kinshasa, September 15, reported on a meeting of African leaders commissioned by the OAU to implement the September 13 OAU resolution on peaceful evacuation of the mercenaries. After some pressure from the other Chiefs of State, Rwandan President Kayibanda agreed to let the mercenaries be evacuated via Rwanda under the auspices of the ICRC, Zambian President Kaunda offered the use of two C–130s for the evacuation, and Central African Republic President Bokassa offered troops for security during the evacuation. (Ibid.)

[3] Dated September 15. (Ibid.)

[4] The fourth meeting of the OAU Heads of State took place in Kinshasa September 11–14. On September 13, the Organization of African Unity adopted a resolution calling on the mercenaries to depart under the supervision of "an international body" and pledging assistance to the Congo in the event the mercenaries did not take advantage of the offer.

550. Memorandum of Conversation[1]

Washington, October 2, 1967, 12:30 p.m.

SUBJECT

Congo

PARTICIPANTS

United States
The Acting Secretary
Mr. L. Dean Brown, Country Director, AFCM
Mr. Robert Anderson, Country Director, France–Benelux Affairs
Mr. Arthur A. Hartman, Special Assistant to the Acting Secretary

Belgium
Foreign Minister Pierre Harmel
Ambassador Louis Scheyven, Embassy of Belgium
Baron Van der Straten-Waillet, Director General for Political Affairs, Belgian Foreign Ministry
Viscount Etienne Davignon, Chef de Cabinet to the Foreign Minister
Mr. Rene Lion, Minister, Embassy of Belgium

Foreign Minister Harmel thanked the Acting Secretary for the personal interest he had taken in the problem of the mercenaries in the Congo, and said that he wished to register his Government's deep appreciation for USG support to the Belgians during this difficult period. He also made special mention of the excellent collaboration given by our Ambassadors in Brussels and Kinshasa.

The Foreign Minister said that his Government had no intention of disengaging because of its fidelity to the Congolese people, its desire to prevent further disorder and its wish to contribute to the peaceful development of the country. In his view, after three months of acute difficulties the operation looking towards the evacuation of the mercenaries now appeared to be proceeding satisfactorily.

The Acting Secretary said that we appreciated this Belgian recognition of our efforts in the Congo, and that we were particularly grateful for Belgian efforts there to seek a peaceful withdrawal of the mercenaries. He, too, hoped that the mercenary evacuation plan would be successful and that the International Red Cross would not insist on dotting every "i" and crossing every "t", as undue delay might jeopardize its success. In commenting on the plan, he said that he was par-

[1] Source: National Archives, RG 59, Central Files 1967–69, POL 23–9 THE CONGO. Confidential. Drafted by Anderson and approved in U on October 12. The original is labeled "Part I of III." The meeting was held in Acting Secretary of State Katzenbach's office.

ticularly encouraged by the recent OAU summit meeting in Kinshasa, which represented a major effort by African leaders to deal with their own problems.

As for future Belgian technical assistance in teaching and health, Harmel said that a decision to return Belgian technicians depended on satisfactory security guarantees from the Mobutu government.[2] He hoped that a solution would be found in the following days so that the uncertainties and dangers which Belgian nationals have traditionally faced would be removed. As one element in giving Belgians the necessary sense of security, the Foreign Minister was particularly interested in the establishment of a permanent Belgo-Congolese Commission to deal effectively with future crises as they arose.

The Acting Secretary said that he was pleased to note the Belgian desire to continue its assistance to the Congo and hoped that satisfactory guarantees could be worked out to ensure the safety of the Belgians in the Congo. He thought future crises inevitable but hoped that in the ups and downs of Congolese politics they would become less and less serious. In his view, the seriousness of any particular crisis would probably rest on the question of how much power General Mobutu has throughout the country at any given time.

In conclusion the Foreign Minister said that while the Congo was of almost constant concern to Belgium, his Government was in the final analysis far more preoccupied with the evolution of Europe and the future of the Atlantic Alliance.

[2] Telegram 47323 to Brussels, October 2, reported that Bomboko told Bihin on September 29 that the Congolese Government had decided against providing the Belgian Government with written assurances about security in the Congo. (Ibid.)

551. Telegram From the Embassy in the Congo to the Department of State[1]

Kinshasa, October 6, 1967, 1750Z.

4738. Subject: Mercenary evacuation.

1. I am becoming increasingly concerned at snail-like way in which mercenary evacuation operation moving. Dept knows as well as I highly unstable nature of Mobutu and his tendency to lose his temper. Just because he has been sweet and patient over recent weeks since OAU resolution on mercenaries does not mean he will not revert to type. Furthermore, he is under pressure from variety of sources within his own govt and especially in army to reject negotiated settlement and insist on military solution. Bomboko has frankly admitted to me he remains personally opposed to implementation of OAU resolution.

2. In light this background, I consider it currently rather unlikely lid can be kept on during considerable time it will apparently take ICRC representative to visit a lot of African capitals, which have no communication with each other, and while there is interminable haggling as to who will pay expenses of operation.

3. Furthermore if we want operation to succeed, it is imperative to keep Belgians in background. Surfacing of fact D'Ursel is coaching from sidelines in Geneva would be enough to enrage Congolese as he is particularly disliked here, along with Davignon. While it is hard to ask Belgians to pick up tab and at same time be inconspicuous, this is precisely view of Belgian Amb Bihin here.

4. I would hazard guess operation can still have chance of success if carried out in next week or ten days. Otherwise, I would consider chances fairly remote. Furthermore, we are at mercy at any moment of having entire operation blown up if mercenaries are reinforced.

5. On specific points, we agree Rubli suggestion (Geneva 1084)[2] it would be better to skip Burundi phase of operations which seems fraught with dangerous possibilities. We also agree with Geneva's point that more matter in hands of ICRC the better.

6. Obviously we have made no commitments to Congolese for US assistance, but we may receive requests in next few days. While it is easy for me to sit here and say Dept should do something, I cannot in all conscience not state my profound hope that if requests are made of

---

[1] Source: National Archives, RG 59, Central Files 1967–69, POL 23–9 THE CONGO. Secret; Priority; Limdis. Also sent to the Mission in Geneva and repeated to Brussels, Bangui, Kigali, Khartoum, Lusaka, Bujumbura, and CINCSTRIKE.

[2] Dated October 5. (Ibid.)

US by Congolese or ICRC, we can carry them out in interest of preventing collapse of operation. If this occurred, we might all be in very serious difficulties indeed in the Congo.[3]

McBride

[3] Telegram 50588 to Geneva, October 7, stated that the Department shared McBride's concern about the slow pace of arrangements for evacuation of the mercenaries. It urged the Mission to convey this concern to the ICRC and to encourage it to take advantage of Kaunda's offer of C–130s as soon as possible. (Ibid.)

552. Telegram From the Department of State to the Mission in Geneva[1]

Washington, October 10, 1967, 1723Z.

51385. For Ambassador from Secretary.

1. Please deliver following message from me to ICRC DirGen Gallopin.

2. "You know of our concern over the situation in the Congo. We have believed that the peaceful evacuation of the mercenaries along the lines proposed by the Organization of African Unity is essential if the Congo is not to experience another tragedy. For this reason we have been gratified with the actions the International Commission of the Red Cross has already taken to put into operation a workable plan to evacuate the mercenaries and the Katangese.

We hope that you will be able to move rapidly to put this plan into effect. It seems to me that each day's delay makes more difficult the final solution. Each of the vitally interested parties, the Congolese government and the mercenaries, may be tempted to take other actions which might bring about the tragedy we all want to avoid. It might be useful for you, while working out final details, to try to send representatives to Kinshasa and Bukavu so as to keep up the momentum towards a peaceful solution.

I know that you have financial problems in handling this task. As Ambassador Tubby told you the other day, we are seeking and hope to

[1] Source: National Archives, RG 59, Central Files 1967–69, POL 23–9 THE CONGO. Secret; Immediate; Exdis. Drafted by Brown, cleared by Katzenbach, and approved by Rusk. Repeated to Kinshasa and Brussels.

have shortly an additional $200,000 to help cover the extraordinary expenditures the ICRC has already encountered in its recent operations. I hope to be able to confirm this contribution soon.

We consider the Congo evacuation essential if there is to be peace and stability in Central Africa and would not want your mission to fail, especially for lack of funds. I therefore want to assure you that my government will make sure that the ICRC does not suffer financially from its humanitarian mission in the Congo. As you know, the Belgian Government is seeking to find additional money and is in touch with other countries which may be prepared to help. If the results of this effort are insufficient, we will do what we have to, in addition to the large contributions we have or are about to make, to assure your success. If there are other problems, such as transport, we will try to be helpful.

With this thought in mind, I want to restate our hope that you can move forward promptly on this urgent problem.

Sincerely yours, Dean Rusk"

3. *For Ambassador*: In delivering above message, tell Gallopin orally that he has my personal commitment on above assurance that USG will guarantee ICRC against financial loss from proposed Congo operation.

Rusk

553. Memorandum From the President's Special Assistant (Rostow) to President Johnson[1]

Washington, October 18, 1967, 7 p.m.

SUBJECT

PL 480 Sales to the Congo

In the attached,[2] Messrs. Schnittker, Gaud and Schultze recommend a $13.4 million PL 480 agreement with the Congo. State and Treasury concur. The specifics:

[1] Source: Johnson Library, National Security File, Memos to the President, Walt W. Rostow, Vol. 46. Confidential.

[2] An October 2 memorandum from AID Administrator William Gaud and Acting Secretary of Agriculture John A. Schnittker and an October 13 memorandum from Budget Director Charles L. Schultze are attached but not printed.

Commodities:

Wheat flour—48,000 tons (equal to 67,000 tons of unmilled wheat)
Cotton—19,000 bales
Tobacco—3,000 tons

Credit Terms:

Repayable in dollars, 20-year maturity with a 2-year grace period, 2½% interest rate.

Budgetary Costs:

These amounts *are* provided for in our export targets and budget estimates. No additional cost.

This food is frankly designed to tide the Congo over the current crisis. There are no new self-help terms attached. The mercenary problem has created a critical supply situation for the Congolese. Production and transport of agricultural products have fallen off badly. They haven't gotten as much copper out of Katanga as they had hoped, so their export earnings are likely to be quite a bit lower than planned. Despite all this, Mobuto has put into effect a comprehensive program of economic reforms—including a devaluation. He badly needs this support to hold the line.

As soon as it is safe, we will send out an AID/Agriculture team to survey the self-help situation and will determine where we can usefully put more leverage.

Walt

Approve[3]

Disapprove

Speak to me

---

[3] Next to this option is a notation on the original in Johnson's handwriting that reads: "I suppose that's all right."

554. Telegram From the Department of State to the Embassy in the Congo[1]

Washington, October 21, 1967, 0055Z.

57958. Ref: Kinshasa 4945,[2] 4992.[3]

1. Have seriously considered your suggestion that C–130s positioned Ascension Island be brought forward now to Kinshasa for possible evacuation needs and as clear indication to mercenaries of US support for GDRC.

2. With great reluctance we unable respond favorably your suggestion at this time for following reasons:

a) Sudden appearance two more aircraft in Kinshasa without thorough and adequate briefing key members of Congress could arouse additional antipathy here. We reluctant to give out sensitive information about possible mercenary activity from Angola.

b) C–130s not most suitable aircraft for mass evacuation although they ideal for gathering US citizens from interior. More useful C–141s or commercial counterparts would require decision to evacuate.

c) If mercenary invasion from Angola to be successful we suspect it will be so rapid that full evacuation may be impossible.

d) We doubt, without adequate publicity, which we do not wish see generated, that word would get to mercenaries rapidly.

e) C–130s might be called forward on "resupply" mission but their withdrawal after two or three days might nullify effect you wish create.

3. We willing of course reconsider if further info becomes available which would indicate that C–130s presence in Kinshasa necessary.

Rusk

---

[1] Source: National Archives, RG 59, Central Files 1967–69, POL 23–9 THE CONGO. Secret; Priority. Drafted by Schaufele, cleared by Brown and Palmer, and approved by Katzenbach.

[2] In telegram 4945 from Kinshasa, October 16, McBride stated that in the event of a mercenary attack on Kinshasa, its entire white population would be in danger. He pointed out that the best way to avoid a potential disaster would be to deter any projected mercenary invasion, and noted that one way to do this might be the return to Kinshasa of the two C–130s at Ascension. (Ibid.)

[3] In telegram 4992 from Kinshasa, October 18, the Ambassador reported that he had just seen CINCSTRIKE's proposal to withdraw one C–130 from Ascension and, referring to the views he had expressed in telegram 4945, said he did not believe that this was an appropriate time to reduce the number of aircraft at Ascension. (Ibid.)

555. Memorandum From the President's Special Assistant (Rostow) to President Johnson[1]

Washington, October 25, 1967.

Mr. President:

My prejudice is to go along with the attached proposed message to McBride in Kinshasa.[2] But I want to be sure that I am reflecting your wishes.

The message has been cleared by Messrs. Katzenbach and Nitze and General Wheeler. It authorizes McBride and our Ambassador in Geneva to tell the International Red Cross that we would respond favorably to a Red Cross request to use the three U.S. military aircraft now in the Congo to help evacuate the mercenaries and their Congolese henchmen. The three planes involved are the one C–130 still in the Congo, the C–123 assigned to our Military Advisory Team, and our Air Attaché's C–54. (We would *not* bring back the two C–130's we pulled out in late summer.)

We would insist that the Red Cross request be strongly worded and that we have the right to make it public. We would also tell them that our favorable response is primarily designed to make it easier for them to get other countries to make similar contributions.

This decision arises because, after endless haggling, the Red Cross has finally negotiated an evacuation plan acceptable to all parties. It involves three steps:

1. A battalion is flown in from the neighboring Central African Republic to supervise the evacuation and guarantee safe passage for the mercenaries.
2. The mercenaries are flown to Malta.
3. The 1,000 plus Congolese (Katangans) now with the mercs are flown to Zambia.

All this must be done quickly. The operation will be mounted from an airport in Rwanda, the only nearby field large enough to take big

---

[1] Source: Johnson Library, National Security File, Memos to the President, Walt W. Rostow, Vol. 48. Secret.

[2] The draft telegram is attached but not printed. After some revision, it was transmitted on October 27 as telegram 60775 to Kinshasa and Geneva. The message expressed willingness to make available to the ICRC not only the C–130 and C–123 currently in the Congo, but also the two C–130s at Ascension. In discussions with the ICRC, the Mission in Geneva was to indicate that the final availability of such aircraft would depend upon formulation of a workable scenario for evacuation, an adequate total commitment of aircraft from other sources, and satisfactory measures to assure the security of the aircraft, as well as a formal ICRC request to the U.S. Government. (National Archives, RG 59, Central Files 1967–69, POL 23–9 THE CONGO)

transports. Rwandan President Kayibanda insists that the job be done in a period of no more than four days so as to minimize the risk of trouble while the evacuees are in his country. This is a big job—about 20 C–130 round trips at about 8 hours per round trip. It would probably take five C–130's to do the job in four days.

The only non-U.S. aircraft now in sight are two Zambian C–130's which we are now reasonably certain will be available. We are scouring the landscape for other planes from African countries and from Europe, as well as looking into other kinds of transport. But prospects are bleak. McBride has concluded that the evacuation probably won't happen without our logistic support and has requested "earnest consideration" of bringing the two U.S. C–130's back to the Congo for this purpose.

The request to bring back the two C–130's has been denied. This message tells McBride that he is free to use the planes now in the Congo. Nobody can guarantee that we will not have to make the C–130 decision again if the evacuation effort breaks down, but McBride understands that the chances of reversal are very slim.

We have a considerable stake in a successful evacuation. If the mercenaries can be peacefully spirited out of the Congo, there is reasonable chance of relative stability for sometime to come. If they remain, every day increases the chances that there will be an attempt to reinforce them (we have intelligence that strongly suggests a Portuguese-backed reinforcement effort in neighboring Angola), and/or that they will decide to march south to Katanga. The latter would almost certainly lead to civil war and a real threat that the country would come apart. In short, we would be back in the same situation we have spent more than half a billion dollars over the last six years to escape.

I think we should go ahead with this limited step. I doubt that it will hurt us much in the Congress to respond to a Red Cross appeal to use planes already on the ground in an evacuation effort which is clearly an attempt to avoid more fighting. I recommend you approve the message.

W.W. Rostow[3]

Approve message

Have Katzenbach and Nitze talk to Russell, Fulbright, Morgan, et al. and come back to me

---

[3] Printed from a copy that bears this typed signature.

Approve message, but make sure Congressional conversations happen before any action is taken

Disapprove message

Speak to me[4]

---

[4] None of these options is checked, but the message was sent; see footnote 2 above. In telegram 1413 from Geneva, October 28, Roger W. Tubby reported that he informed ICRC representatives of the U.S. offer and conditions, and that they had been most appreciative. (National Archives, RG 59, Central Files 1967–69, DEF 9–7 THE CONGO)

---

556. Telegram From the Department of State to the Embassy in the Congo[1]

Washington, October 31, 1967, 0010Z.

61969. Ref: Kinshasa 5250.[2]

1. We believe it preferable that first indication to Mobutu that USG may be willing furnish aircraft for Kat airlift come from ICRC rather than ourselves. We gather from your 5261[3] that Gafner is prepared do this whenever he next sees Mobutu. Gafner of course should mention subject to Mobutu only in context our 60775.[4]

2. Desirability immediate cease-fire daily becoming more pressing in light info Kigalis 749 and 750.[5] We hope Gafner will get to Mobutu quickly on this matter and not only urge cease-fire at earliest possible moment but also withdrawal ANC from Bukavu perimeter.

---

[1] Source: National Archives, RG 59, Central Files 1967–69, POL CONGO. Secret; Priority; Exdis. Drafted by Tienken, cleared by Brown, and approved by Palmer. Repeated to the Mission in Geneva, Brussels, and CINCSTRIKE for POLAD Tampa.

[2] In telegram 5250 from Kinshasa, October 28, McBride raised the question of informing Mobutu of the possibility that the U.S. Government might be willing to furnish aircraft for the evacuation. (Ibid.)

[3] In telegram 5261 from Kinshasa, October 29, McBride described a lengthy talk with the ICRC team operating in Kinshasa under the leadership of Gafner. He reported that Gafner planned to be cautious in his talk with Mobutu regarding transporting the Katangans, but would indicate that the U.S. Government would probably be willing to assist if other countries also played a part. (Ibid.)

[4] See footnote 2, Document 555.

[5] Telegrams 749 and 750 from Kigali, October 30, described the fierce fighting between the ANC and the mercenaries around Bukavu. (National Archives, RG 59, Central Files 1967–69, POL CONGO)

3. Believe you should then see Mobutu at which time you may confirm our position re aircraft. Hopefully you can then find appropriate opportunity to urge cease-fire and possibility withdrawal with Mobutu, pressing home point that continued ANC attacks may jeopardize entire evac scenario and risk calling into question GDRC's sincerity in seeking peaceful solution within terms OAU resolution.

4. Do not believe a concerted diplomatic approach to Mobutu on cease-fire would be productive. Leave to your judgment, however, whether Apostolic Delegate could play useful role.

Rusk

557. Telegram From the Department of State to the Embassy in the Congo[1]

Washington, November 2, 1967, 2345Z.

63987. Ref Kinshasa 5359.[2]

1. Realize you have a problem with Mobutu.

2. Note that Bomboko wants intervention with Portuguese. You may tell him that we have done so in strong terms.[3] We also planning issue press statement which thereafter would be carried by VOA. You can also assure him we will give Congo vigorous support in UN.

---

[1] Source: National Archives, RG 59, Central Files 1967–69, POL 23–9 THE CONGO. Secret; Immediate; Limdis. Drafted by Brown; cleared by Day in IO, Landau in EUR/SPP, and Colonel Kennedy in OSD/ISA; and approved by Palmer. Repeated to Brussels, Kigali, Lisbon, Bujumbura, Lusaka, Addis Ababa, Lubumbashi, Luanda, the Mission in Geneva, USUN, and CINCSTRIKE.

[2] On November 2, a mercenary force from Angola crossed the Congo border and entered western Katanga. In telegram 5359 from Kinshasa, November 2, McBride reported that with mercenaries "running wild" in Katanga the Congo was in for a grave period. Mobutu and Bomboko would undoubtedly ask for some U.S. action, and the Ambassador suggested a strong U.S. statement in the Security Council. He said Bomboko had already asked for another U.S. démarche with the Portuguese. Noting that Mobutu might turn to a OAU multilateral force, McBride suggested U.S. encouragement of formation of such a force and possible assistance in transporting elements to the Congo. (Ibid.)

[3] Telegram 63827 to Lisbon, November 2, reported that Deputy Under Secretary Kohler told Portuguese Ambassador Garin on November 2 that the U.S. Government took the gravest view of reports that mercenaries had entered the Congo from Angola. Kohler pointed out that this action, which must have been known to the Portuguese Government, might gravely prejudice the ICRC operation and endanger the lives of all Europeans living in the Congo. (Ibid.)

3. If your Belgian colleague approves, you might also say that Harmel has acted.

4. Concur with thought Mobutu may turn rapidly in direction OAU and this seems to be a good idea. Without making any commitments re transport, you might encourage this idea.

5. Meanwhile, of course, ICRC goes on. You should try to make sure Mobutu does not suddenly call it off.

Rusk

558. Memorandum From Edward Hamilton of the National Security Council Staff to the President's Special Assistant (Rostow)[1]

Washington, November 6, 1967, 10:30 a.m.

WWR:

SUBJECT

Congo Situation Report (10:30 AM)

1. Our C–130's have not moved from Ascension. We have told the Red Cross that we are prepared to use them in an international evacuation operation if (a) the plan is workable and (b) there are reasonable security safeguards for the aircraft.

2. The mercenaries and Katangans (about 2,000 with families) are just over the border in Rwanda. They are largely disarmed, but some still wear sidearms.

3. The Congolese are feeling their oats. (After all, this is the first victory in the history of the Congolese army.) Mobutu and this Foreign Minister have told us that they are now against any evacuation and will petition Rwanda to extradite the mercenaries "for trial" in the Congo. They are trying to get the Red Cross to give up and go home.

4. The Red Cross has not given up on the evacuation, nor have the Belgians who are very worried (a) that the mercenaries—who are mostly Belgians—will be massacred and (b) this will bring on racial disaster in the Congo.

[1] Source: Johnson Library, National Security File, Country File, Congo, Vol. XIV, Memos & Miscellaneous, 8/67–10/68. Secret.

5. Thus, the Belgians have arranged to send a Sabena 727 to Kigali, Rwanda, today. This plane could take most of the mercenaries to Europe in one load if the Rwandans will allow them to proceed from their present location to the City of Kigali and then to leave the country.

6. An airlift for the 1800 Katangans has yet to be arranged. Ours is the only firm offer the Red Cross has. The Canadians and several other countries are thinking over similar offers. Mobutu's attitude suggests that he may be more receptive to letting the Katangans go than he is about the mercenaries.

7. McBride is having second thoughts about a U.S. role in an evacuation. He recommends we keep our planes at Ascension and wait to see what happens today—whether the Belgian plane actually arrives at Kigali, whether Mobutu softens on letting the mercenaries out, whether other aircraft for the Katangan evacuation actually materializes and whether the Rwandans hold to their willingness to let the evacuation happen rather than driving the group back into the Congo.

8. The consensus here is to go along with McBride, but to be ready to act very quickly if a truly international evacuation effort does jell. Congolese victories, heretofore entirely unknown, are likely to be very fragile.

EH

559. Telegram From the Department of State to the Embassy in the Congo[1]

Washington, November 6, 1967, 2156Z.

65312. Ref Brussels 2675.[2]

1. Although GOR appears be retaining some independence of action re merc/Katgen evacuation, it nevertheless is increasingly clear successful operation can only be undertaken with GDRC open acquies-

[1] Source: National Archives, RG 59, Central Files 1967–69, DEF 9–7 THE CONGO. Secret; Flash; Limdis. Drafted by Palmer; cleared by Stoessel, IO Deputy Assistant Secretary David H. Popper, and L. Dean Brown; and approved by the Under Secretary. Repeated to Kigali, Paris, London, Ottawa, CINCSTRIKE for POLAD, Brussels, Lusaka, Bujumbura, Lubumbashi, Kampala, Lisbon, Luanda, the Mission in Geneva, and USUN.

[2] In telegram 2675 from Brussels, November 6, Knight reported that Harmel gave him the latest information on Mobutu's position, which was agreement that the Katangans should be evacuated, but insistence that the mercenaries be turned over to him. (Ibid.)

cence and secret cooperation. This appears to us minimum required to make possible overflight and transit rights for European aircraft evacuating mercs and for Katgens relocation Zambia. Without these elements, whole operation seems doomed to failure.

2. We recognize extreme delicacy of this problem for you and deeply appreciate efforts you have already made to bring Mobutu around. Believe however you should make further effort, stressing following points as emanating from very high levels in USG and put forth to Mobutu in spirit of friendship and consistent support which has characterized US-Congolese friendship.

a) ANC has won remarkable victory at Bukavu and appears be meeting heartening successes in dealing with latest merc incursion from Angola. This is remarkable development in history of Congo and underlines progress army is making under his leadership in contributing to strong viable nation. Major task is now to liquidate remnants of problem and return to peaceful development as quickly as possible. Towards this end, Mobutu's strongest position would be to take following line:

(1) Merc forces with rebel support have been routed in Bukavu and Congo is now rid of this cancer. Mobutu regrets GDRC victories have created problem for fellow African state of Rwanda and he wishes only see this problem liquidated as soon as possible.

(2) Elements presently in Rwanda are worthless and GDRC wishes nothing more to do with them. So far as mercs are concerned, it only wishes assure they do not return Congo, as notorious Denard and others have done.

(3) Therefore GDRC would have no objection to GOR permitting repatriation to Europe of these elements on following conditions: (i) ICRC would obtain appropriate assurances that mercs will not return to Africa, (ii) ICRC would transmit such assurances to countries of which they are nationals in order that they may take steps within their power prevent mercs return to Congo.

(4) Re Katgens, Mobutu should take posture that these are poor misguided people against whom he has no grudge but only feels sorrow. If they desire return Congo, they can do so under absolute guarantee of amnesty which he has already signed. Otherwise he has no objection their settlement in Zambia until such time as they may wish return.

(b) In putting foregoing to Mobutu you should stress that in eyes of world he has won remarkable military victory. Moreover, strong public position which US has taken against Portugal (at considerable expense to other aspects of our relationship) has created considerable embarrassment to that country and appears have forced it on defensive. It would be great pity for Mobutu to lose sympathy which Congo presently enjoys and to obscure onus which presently rests on Portugal by taking vindictive line. (You may wish show Mobutu texts recent *NY Times* and *Wash Post* editorials.) In this connection Mobutu should be aware that Nogueira presently visiting US (trip arranged some time ago without relation current developments), and that it would be unfortunate if Congo position played into his hands by actions which ignore humanitarian and practical aspects of present situation.

(c) Mobutu should also understand that USG has, at considerable domestic expense, strongly supported GDRC both through C–130s and its military and economic aid programs. We have undertaken extensive consultations with Congress re participation in humanitarian operation to liquidate merc and Katgen problem. Congress and American people will not be able understand hard and vindictive position by Mobutu which might obviate any possibility peaceful resolution of problem without further bloodshed, and this inevitably will affect what we are able to do for him in future.

(d) Although Mobutu may be able risk adverse international reactions on humanitarian grounds which likely to follow mass extradition of merc/Katgen group to Congo, he should be aware that, if he successfully pressures GOR to agree to extradition, he would open Rwanda to same charges. Rwandan copy book already blotted by Tutsi massacres of 1963 and we doubt it would wish be linked with extradition or involuntary repatriation effort. Putting strong pressures on Rwanda could conceivably force GOR cooperation but might also be harmful to future of GDRC–GOR relations.

3. In short, you should try convince Mobutu that he has unprecedented opportunity take statesmanlike, humanitarian posture at this moment which would contrast markedly with very tarnished Portuguese image. We strongly hope he can see problem this way, taking appropriate advantage of OAU resolution, his military victories and his strong position in SC toward this end.

4. In light foregoing, we strongly hope he can find way to facilitate ICRC operation at least by acquiescing in it.

5. Suggest you inform Gafner and Bihin of approach you instructed to make.

Rusk

560. Editorial Note

On November 15, 1967, the U.N. Security Council adopted without objection Resolution 241 (1967) condemning Portugal's failure to prevent mercenaries from using the territory of Angola under its administration as a base for armed attacks against the Congo. (U.N. Doc. S/RES/241) The resolution was passed in response to a November 3 Congolese appeal to the Council that it take the necessary measures to stop aggression by armed mercenaries based in Angola against the Congo, and to ensure the safety of persons and property in the threatened areas. (U.N. Doc. S/8218) For text of both resolutions, see *American Foreign Policy: Current Documents, 1967*, pages 250–253.

561. Information Memorandum From the President's Special Assistant (Rostow) to President Johnson[1]

Washington, November 15, 1967, 3 p.m.

SUBJECT

Congo Situation Report (3:00 PM)[2]

1. The mercenaries (around 120) and the Katangans (about 2,000 with families) are still sitting in what amounts to internment camps across the border in Rwanda. Our three C–130's (2 still on Ascension, 1 in the Congo) are waiting to help in an international evacuation provided (a) the plan is workable and (b) there are reasonable security guarantees for our aircraft.

2. The Red Cross has other promises for aircraft on the same conditions. The Canadians have a C–130 also on Ascension. The British have pledged an Argosy transport (about C–130 size) which is still in the U.K. There's a Belgian DC–6 waiting at the scene. And the French have a DC–3 ready to move in.

3. Consequently, the Red Cross could conceivably begin in 48 hours or so to fly out the *Katangans*. Mobutu has told us he approves this part of the evacuation, and claims the Zambians are ready to take them. But the Zambians say they can't move without "express request" from the Congo to take the Katangans. Zambia thinks that request will come out of an OAU Commission meeting tomorrow in Kinshasa. Flying the 2,000 Katangans to Zambia would involve our C–130s and probably all the other air craft except France's DC–3, which the French

[1] Source: Johnson Library, National Security File, Country File, Congo, Vol. XIV, Memos & Miscellaneous, 8/67–10/68. Secret.

[2] A handwritten notation in the margin of the original reads: "as requested yesterday."

have earmarked for white (French) mercenaries. The operation ferrying the Katangans would take several days.

4. The tougher problem is evacuating the white mercenaries who would then be left in Rwanda. It's anybody's guess how soon they'll get out to Malta.

5. A week ago Mobutu was in the flush of victory (a first for the Congolese army) and calling for "extradition" of the whites. He has since fallen back to a face-saving formula which was adopted over the weekend by the OAU Commission on Mercenaries.[3] But the conditions of this formula are still exacting and could mean delay in completing the evacuation. To let the whites go, Mobutu is requiring:

—some "compensation" for damages from the parent countries (read Belgium and France)
—written assurances from the mercenaries themselves *and* their parent countries that they'll never enter the Congo again
—an ad hoc OAU tribunal to screen and question the mercenaries before they leave Rwanda, trying to find out who planned their operation, who financed them, etc.

6. McBride thinks these conditions make it "obvious" that the mercenary problem will drag on "for weeks at best"—even if we get the Katangans out to Zambia this week. He reports that Mobutu sees these conditions as minimum punishment for the mercenaries, and will be in no mood for any short cut.

7. State is a little more hopeful that a quick and sensible response from the Belgians and French might satisfy Mobutu and thus put the whites on the planes. They point out:

—The Belgians have already offered to help in Red Cross relief for Bukavu and we think the French can be persuaded to do likewise. Mobutu just might accept this token compensation as sufficient.
—The Belgians have a suitable anti-mercenary law already in Parliament, and State thinks the French could meet Mobutu's demands for assurances with some new passport regulations restricting French nationals who were involved.

Walt

[3] A special session of the OAU Commission on Mercenaries meeting in Kinshasa November 11–13 decided to place the mercenaries in Rwanda under the "jurisdiction" of the OAU and send a delegation to Kigali to interrogate them. It also decreed that the governments of which the mercenaries were nationals must compensate the Congo and give guarantees that the mercenaries, once repatriated, would never return to Africa.

562. Telegram From the Department of State to the Embassy in the Congo[1]

Washington, November 17, 1967, 0223Z.

70801. For McBride from Katzenbach.

1. We deeply share concerns expressed in your recent messages re dilemma in which we may be placed as result recent GDRC and OAU decisions and actions re Katgens and mercs. Problem arises most immediately in connection Mobutu's request for US planes to repatriate those Katgens who have expressed willingness return to Congo. Any refusal on our part likely immediately jeopardize our relationships with GDRC; at same time, our agreement could be tantamount to delivering some or all to highly arbitrary future.

2. As I am sure you are also aware, problems posed for us transcend any decision re use US aircraft. While it remains to be seen what position is taken by ICRC/Geneva re procedures followed in consulting Katgens Cyangugu [*sic*] and re future ICRC role, all current indications are that these procedures would not bear international scrutiny on humanitarian lines. From this viewpoint, therefore, it is largely irrelevant whether Katgens return to Congo in US, Congolese, or other aircraft, or whether they proceed by surface. To US and world opinion principal concern will be whether they go back of their own free will and are accorded genuine protection under meaningful amnesty arrangements.

3. I recognize how difficult it is to get Mobutu and members his government to look at this problem from foregoing point of view. I realize also extreme strain to which US-GDRC relationship and your own personal relations with Mobutu have been put as result developments last few months. At same time, I believe it essential that Mobutu should be fully aware of public outcry that will undoubtedly result in this country and elsewhere in Western world if he deals with these people summarily. (Among important elements here, any such summary treatment will inevitably be complicated by concerns re summary justice accorded to Tshombe.)

4. Any such development as foregoing would be unfortunate at any time but it would be doubly so at moment. GDRC, with strong US support, has just won important victory in SC and Portuguese have re-

[1] Source: National Archives, RG 59, Central Files 1967–69, POL 23–9 THE CONGO. Secret; Immediate; Exdis. Drafted by Palmer; cleared by Katzenbach, Colonel Kennedy, Congo Country Director John A. McKesson, Admiral Moore in JC Staff J–3, and Colonel Bachtell in JC Staff J–5; and approved by Palmer. Repeated to Brussels, the Mission in Geneva, Kigali, and CINCSTRIKE.

ceived strong setback. Any arbitrary actions at this time by GDRC would be bound to jeopardize much of sympathy and good will which Congo has gained and would play directly into Portuguese hands. We do not believe this in interest of Congo or its friends.

5. Drawing as appropriate on foregoing, you should see Mobutu soonest. You should make following points clear on instructions from your government:

(A) Mobutu must find means in his own interest of making unmistakably clear to world that Katgens are being given free choice re their destinations, that those who elect to return to Congo will have full amnesty and complete protection and that those who proceed to other African destinations will similarly be protected.

(B) Towards this end, he must do everything required to reengage ICRC in impartially ascertaining desires of Katgens, leaving to ICRC determination whether they return to Congo or accept asylum in some other country.

(C) He must take whatever diplomatic steps are required to request receiving African countries to accept Katgens.

(D) Under these conditions and if other countries participate, USG will assist ICRC with transport for movement of Katgens.

(E) In absence such arrangements, USG can neither furnish aircraft nor utilize existing aircraft in Congo in way which would release Congolese transport for this purpose.

(F) Mobutu should be fully aware that any effort to repatriate Katgens under circumstances which do not meet humanitarian considerations involved will probably provoke reaction in US which will render impossible continuation level of support we have rendered Congo in past. As hard as we find this to say to him, we must make point in frankness and friendship.

6. I realize this is strong medicine but I see no alternative. However your conversation turns out, I want you to know how greatly we have admired patient and skillful way in which you have dealt with these elusive and frustrating problems. Good luck.[2]

Rusk

---

[2] In telegram 5718 from Kinshasa, November 17, McBride stated that after he carried out the instructions in telegram 70801, he doubted he would be of much further use in Kinshasa. (Ibid.) Telegram 70931 to Kinshasa, November 17, responded that the Department deeply appreciated the problems this posed for the Ambassador and that paragraph 5(F) was not a threat but a prediction of the possible consequences of the domestic situation the U.S. Government might face. (Ibid.)

563. Telegram From the Embassy in the Congo to the Department of State[1]

Kinshasa, November 18, 1967, 1111Z.

5723. For Under Secretary from McBride:

1. Mobutu received me Saturday morning on board boat. I outlined in full Dept's instructions as contained in State 70801.[2] I stressed Dept's view about public outcry in US in event Katangese harmed after their return to Congo. I made all six numbered points contained in paragraph five.

2. Mobutu said he was deeply shocked and disappointed in Dept's refusal to help him. He said ICRC had withdrawn from operation and there was no possibility of calling them back into game. I said that under my instructions, I was therefore forced to tell him US could not furnish any aircraft assistance whatever in connection with resettlement of Katangese. Mobutu replied simply in that event, Congo would have to take care of transport problem herself by other means.

3. With regard to Katangese, Mobutu gave me lengthy description of his plans for handling them. He insisted that they had all decided to return to Congo and that Bomboko had held personal conversation with Monga who wished to be reintegrated into life of Congo. He said he had decided to place Katangese for a period of a few months in Iberu near Mbandaka and he wanted to start movement by air from Kigali as soon as possible. He said he felt Katangese might be in some danger if they went to Katanga while so many ANC units were still in Kamina area and it was for reason of guaranteeing their protection that he was sending them to Iberu where only soldiers were a few Katangese. Mobutu added that if Dept was so worried about future of these men, he was willing to establish an international commission that could visit them every two weeks to see they were not being harmed.

4. Mobutu added that furthermore full prestige of OAU was behind this resettlement of Katangese. He said they would be permitted to resettle elsewhere in Congo after brief period. Mobutu stated he was going on radio later today to read his full declaration on this subject and to explain to Congolese people why it was essential these Katangese be peacefully reintegrated into life of country even though they had borne arms against ANC. He said he felt very deeply about this.

---

[1] Source: National Archives, RG 59, Central Files 1967–69, POL 23–9 THE CONGO. Secret; Exdis. Repeated to Brussels, Kigali, the Mission in Geneva, and CINCSTRIKE.

[2] Document 562.

5. With regard to para 5(A) of Dept's instruction, Mobutu said he could give most categoric assurances on this point. He said full weight of Africa was behind this solution and effective implementation of amnesty. Reverting to ICRC, Mobutu said they had withdrawn and it was not possible to consider having them again interrogate Katangese after OAU had already done so, and important point was to get Katangese resettled in Congo. Mobutu insisted that he was satisfied pressure had not been used on Katangese. I said we had reports to contrary, but he denied these.

6. I reiterated Dept's concern at reaction in US both publicly and in government circles if Katangese were mistreated. Mobutu said he was profoundly hurt Dept doubted his word as to their safety. He said amnesty decree was a law of the nation and must be observed. Mobutu continued saying that, far from adding to his difficulties, Dept should be helping him with problem of resettling Katangese. He said he simply failed to understand Dept's attitude regarding an internal Congolese problem which he thought could achieve a satisfactory solution especially if Congo's friends could help. I repeated Dept's refusal to assist with aircraft in any way under circumstances he outlined. He repeated Congo would simply have to proceed with her own resources ("se debrouiller").

7. Mobutu concluded with fairly impassioned statement about his surprise that his word as Chief of State was being doubted by Dept, and expressed regret US was not helping in this operation. He said apparently Dept did not trust him, and this of course was blow to him.

8. Comments follow.

McBride

564. Memorandum for Director of Central Intelligence Helms[1]

Washington, November 21, 1967.

SUBJECT

State Department Recommendation that 303 Committee Approve Extension of Contracts of CIA-supplied Pilots Flying for the Congolese (Kinshasa) Government

1. This memorandum contains a recommendation for the approval of the Director. The recommendation is contained in paragraph five.

2. Transmitted herewith is a proposal to Ambassador Kohler prepared by the African Bureau of the Department of State recommending that he approve a telephonic request to the 303 principals for extension through 31 December 1967 of the contracts of five pilots hired by the CIA to fly for the Congolese Government.[2]

3. When recruited on 4 September 1967, these pilots signed contracts effective through 4 December 1967 but agreed orally to extend for an extra month if requested to do so. Preliminary indications are that some of the pilots may not wish to extend their contracts for personal reasons. The African Bureau believes that if as many as three pilots remain they would be sufficient. But if less than three remain, replacement pilots will be required.

4. President Mobutu was recently upset by the Department of State decision that the U.S. would not supply aircraft for evacuating the Katangese rebels from Rwanda. Since then Ambassador McBride has been asked to undertake a very difficult démarche with Mobutu in connection with the return of these rebels. The African Bureau believes and we agree that the withdrawal of the U.S.-supplied pilots at the 30 November 1967 termination of their contracts would tend only to further alienate Mobutu, especially since these pilots are presently the only ones in the Congo capable of flying combat and support missions.

5. For the reasons outlined in paragraph four, we recommend that the proposed extension be approved.[3]

Archibald B. Roosevelt, Jr.
Chief, Africa Division

---

[1] Source: Central Intelligence Agency Files, Job 81–00966R, Box 1, Folder 12, Congo, 1967–68. Secret.

[2] Attached but not printed.

[3] The memorandum indicates the DDP approved on Nov. 21 and Helms approved Nov. 22. A handwritten notation on the attachment indicates that the 303 Committee approved the proposal telephonically on November 22.

565. Telegram From the Embassy in the Congo to the Department of State[1]

Kinshasa, November 29, 1967, 1100Z.

5919. Ref: Kinshasa 5899.[2]

1. I had long talk with Mobutu and Bomboko this morning about withdrawal of JTE. I explained JTE has long since accomplished its original mission in connection with mercenary revolt and had assisted in ferrying troops to put down Angolan invasion as well. These threats had been met and situation was back to normal now. Therefore we believe that time to withdraw JTF had now come.

2. Mobutu explained at great length his continued preoccupation with situation and especially with security situation in Kivu. He felt it was essential to move virtually all forces out of that area and he pleaded for C–130 to complete this task as well as bring first paras back from Katanga. I said C–130 was already vigorously engaged in this task and I was sure would complete it in few days.

3. Mobutu said it was difficult to set a date for departure of JTF but finally proposed December 15. I said I had thought in earlier terms perhaps of early next week. Mobutu then made firm suggestion of December in which he pointed out would round out five months of JTE response to his original appeal. I indicated that this seemed agreeable to me and that this would be acceptable unless he heard to the contrary.

4. Mobutu is obviously reluctant to see JTF go but I believe has accepted our reasoning. He has formally committed himself to date of December 10 for departure of final C–130. I strongly hope this date will be acceptable to Dept and to Defense. I would be most extremely reluctant to go back and ask for earlier departure date. Furthermore, I think actual task Mobutu has in mind can be accomplished in just about this time. It seems to be an entirely reasonable and amicable way of terminating a highly successful operation.

5. I explained to Mobutu that we would wish some publicity on occasion of departure JTF and that we would be in touch with Bomboko with draft release in few days.[3]

McBride

---

[1] Source: National Archives, RG 59, Central Files 1967–69, DEF 19 US–THE CONGO. Confidential; Immediate; Limdis. Repeated to CINCSTRIKE.

[2] Dated November 28. (Ibid.)

[3] Telegram 77170 to Kinshasa, November 30, said that the Department considered December 10 an acceptable date for final departure of the remaining C–130 and the last elements of the JTF from the Congo. (Ibid.)

566. Memorandum From the President's Special Assistant (Rostow) to President Johnson[1]

Washington, December 18, 1967.

Mr. President:

SUBJECT

Your Meeting with Ambassador Robert McBride (Congo) (12 noon today)

This meeting can be as long or as short as your schedule permits.[2] McBride is home on consultation. He will want to report to you on the success of our C–130 operation,[3] and tell you where we now stand on the mercenary problem. It will also be useful for McBride to be able to tell President Mobutu that he talked to you.

The 100-plus white mercenaries are still sitting in an internment camp in neighboring Rwanda. All along, Mobutu has insisted on two conditions for letting the whites go back to Europe: (1) guarantees from parent countries (Belgium and France) that they would not return to the Congo; and (2) some compensation for damages. The problem is being discussed this weekend at an East African Chiefs of State meeting in Uganda. Mobutu is at this meeting to press his case.

You may wish to sound out McBride along the following lines:

1. What are the prospects for future stability in the Congo.

2. If things look uncertain, what can and should we do to avoid another C–130 crisis? The C–130 experience on the Hill indicates how tough it will be in the future to bail Mobutu out of some emergency.

W.W. Rostow[4]

---

[1] Source: Johnson Library, National Security File, Memos to the President, Walt W. Rostow, Vol. 54. No classification marking.

[2] No record of this meeting has been found.

[3] The last C–130 left the Congo on December 10. During its 5 months in the Congo, the JTF flew 179 missions (412 sorties carrying 7,657 persons and 1,632 tons of cargo).

[4] Printed from a copy that bears this typed signature.

567. Telegram From the Department of State to the Embassy in Uganda[1]

Washington, December 19, 1967, 0207Z.

86428. 1. Démarche to Mobutu should be made soonest by Stebbins or by Burns if time precludes seeing Mobutu in Kampala. Following points should be made.

(a) U.S. gravely concerned over possibility Congolese may take military action against Rwanda as intimated by Bomboko to Ambassador Cyr.

(b) US hopes problem of mercenaries can be solved to satisfaction of all interested parties, but does not believe that military solution, under any circumstances, can serve interest of Congo. Issue would inevitably go to Security Council and cause great difficulties for Congo and its friends.

(c) In any case T–28 aircraft precluded from use outside Congo by terms of MAP agreement. (Under terms of US–Congo MAP agreement T–28's can only be used for internal security or legitimate self defense. Use for any other purpose would require USG approval which could not be given in this case.)

(d) US not involved in mercenary problem and believes GDRC should continue to attempt resolve directly with parties concerned.

2. If asked whether US has approached Belgians or others in matter, Ambassador should reply that we have not for reasons stated in (d) above.[2]

Rusk

---

[1] Source: National Archives, RG 59, Central Files 1967–69, POL 23–9 THE CONGO. Confidential; Immediate; Exdis. Drafted by McKesson; cleared by Palmer, Colonel Kennedy, and Meagher; and approved by McKesson. Also sent to Dar es Salaam and repeated to Kinshasa, Kigali, Brussels, Addis Ababa, Bujumbura, Paris, London, Lubumbashi, USUN, and CINCSTRIKE.

[2] In telegram 1119 from Kampala, December 19, Ambassador Stebbins reported that he made the démarche contained in this telegram to Bomboko, who had said he would convey this to Mobutu en route to Dar es Salaam. (Ibid., POL 7 THE CONGO)

568. Telegram From the Department of State to the Embassy in Belgium[1]

Washington, December 29, 1967, 2307Z.

91251. Ref: Brussels 3731,[2] 3732.[3] Subject: Letter from Secretary to FonMin Harmel.

1. Following is Secretary's reply to Harmel letter contained your 3731:

Dear Mr. Minister:

It was a great pleasure to see you again in Brussels and participate with you in a NATO Council Meeting. The success of this meeting was due in large part to your efforts and I want you to know how much we all appreciate the time and thought you have given to making our Alliance an effective instrument for dealing with our common problems.

I have your message of December 23 regarding the renewed problems of the mercenaries and I wish to assure you of our concern and our realization of the seriousness of this situation as it affects Belgo-Congolese relations.

Our experience with the difficult and complex Congolese situation has taught us that our influence can only be productive when used with the greatest care and when we have taken the fullest account of the appropriate role for the United States. With regard to the present mercenary problem, we believe that the European governments whose nationals are involved should take the lead. This is not because we believe the situation is any less serious than you do but merely reflects our judgment as to how we can be most useful in attempting to resolve this complex problem.

I want to assure you that we will look for every opportunity to be of assistance. While the Vice President[4] will be aware of the situation

---

[1] Source: National Archives, RG 59, Central Files 1967–69, POL 23–9 THE CONGO. Secret; Immediate; Exdis. Drafted by Palmer, cleared by Leddy in EUR and Katzenbach, and approved by Rusk. Repeated to Kinshasa, Kigali, London, Paris, and Niamey.

[2] Telegram 3731 from Brussels, December 23, transmitted a letter to the Secretary from Harmel expressing his concern over the fate of the mercenaries in Rwanda. Harmel emphasized that turning the mercenaries, including 52 Belgian citizens, over to the Congo with the risk that they might be executed would constitute an act of extreme gravity. Various European and African governments had already agreed to approach Mobutu, but without U.S. participation Harmel feared this action would be fruitless. Therefore, he asked that Vice President Humphrey speak to Mobutu during his visit to the Congo on January 4. (Ibid.)

[3] Dated December 23. (Ibid.)

[4] Vice President Humphrey made a 13-day trip to Africa, December 29–January 11, during which he visited nine African nations, including the Congo.

regarding the mercenaries, I do not think that it would be useful or wise for him to make a special démarche on this subject. If the opportunity arises as the result of Mobutu raising this matter, the Vice President will state that, while we hold no brief for the mercenaries, as a practical matter, we feel it would be to everyone's best interest, including the Congo's, if the mercenaries were permitted to return to Europe and thus rid Africa of this difficult problem.

One additional thought has occurred to us. Would it not be possible for private interests in Europe to launch a public appeal for funds to help rebuild Bukavu? A generous, dramatic effort of this kind might help to lift this entire problem from its present stale-mated political level to a new humanitarian plane. If this idea has merit and is practical, we should be glad to see what we can do informally with private interests on this side of the Atlantic.

Once again let me assure you that we will be looking for every opportunity to be of assistance and hope that your efforts with the other European states will be successful.

I sincerely hope that the new year will bring solutions to these difficult problems. Although our tasks are often hard, it is always a great pleasure to be able to work with you, and I look forward to our continued close cooperation. With warmest regards for the coming year.[5]

Sincerely, Dean Rusk

Rusk

[5] In telegram 3793 from Brussels, December 29, Knight reported that he delivered the Secretary's letter to Harmel. (National Archives, RG 59, Central Files 1967–69, POL 23–9 THE CONGO)

569. Telegram From the Embassy in the Congo to the Department of State[1]

Kinshasa, January 5, 1968, 0106Z.

6752. VIPTO 71. Subject: Vice President's trip to Africa, Congo (K). Conversation with President Mobutu, January 4.

[1] Source: National Archives, RG 59, Central Files 1967–69, POL 7 US–HUMPHREY. Confidential; Priority.

1. Accompanied by Ambassador McBride, Van Dyk, Hadsel and McGuire, Vice President met with President Mobutu, FonMin Bomboko, Ambassador Adoula and Vice Minister Lutete for almost two and one half hours of discussion emphasizing primarily internal security and economic problems. Question of evacuation of mercenaries was not discussed.

2. After receiving warm welcome from President Mobutu, VP presented letter from President Johnson,[2] referred to recent advance of the Congo in solving its problems, and assured Mobutu that US shared with Congolese the devotion to self-determination opposition to apartheid and dedication to independence and integrity of Congo nation. Commenting on presence of both Ambassadors McBride and Adoula, he thought that both governments were well served by men of exceptional competence. VP recalled his own days in Senate when he had resolutely supported Congo unity during early years of this nation's life.

3. President Mobutu replied by emphasizing not only the good relations between US and Congo but the genuine American understanding of Congolese problems. He extremely grateful for the help of first, President Kennedy and now President Johnson. He wished in time available for conversations to emphasize particularly two general problems, internal security and economic development.

4. Re internal security, Mobutu noted that each time Congo faced major crisis US had been of decisive assistance, latest example being provision of the three C–130 planes to deal with mercenary rebellion. Now that situation is calm, it extremely important that Congo develop its own internal security, rather than wait for next crisis. He not concerned about direct attack, but there are Cubans, Chinese and Russians just across the river and there is serious danger of subversion. Frankly Congo still young government and not prepared to prevent this kind of disruption.

5. Mobutu continued that there were two essential problems. First, he needed C–130's to provide mobility for approximately 300 men in order that he could rapidly stop rebellious activities, such as recent mercenary efforts. Problems had been studied by US and details were available to General Conway of CINCSTRIKE. VP replied that he thought Mobuto entirely correct in his analysis that period of calm should be used to develop resistance against subversion. It true, of course, that new Foreign Assistance Act had certain restrictions on sophisticated weapons and that cut by Congress of almost one billion dollars entire Act curtailed US funds available for such assistance. He extremely sympathetic to concept of mobile alert force. While he could not foresee exactly all aspects of problem, he promised to present case to President and Dept. of Defense.

6. Secondly, Mobutu referred to ability neighboring countries to overfly Congo with impunity. He had ten or twelve pilots with Soviet training, but badly needed 6 to 8 pursuit planes, probably located at Kamina. With respect to type of equipment VP asked, in light of aid legislation, if propeller planes were appropriate. Bomboko nodded in affirmative but Mobutu replied he preferred jet aircraft. Mobutu hoped for long term purchase arrangements.

7. In elaboration on problem of internal security Mobutu observed that it was contrary to his fundamental beliefs to play the East and West against each other. He believed he should continue to work with friendly Western countries. However, in recent months USSR had been all smiles. Bulgaria and Romania were offering help. At this point VP interjected his personal view was that the Communists became "respectable" when other methods did not work. Perhaps Yugoslavia and possibly Romania were all right, but others probably intended subversive effort. They claim to come to raise vegetables but really raise trouble. He thought European countries, Israel, Canada, etc. were more likely to give genuine assistance. Perhaps in three to five years Congo would be more able to deal with Communist countries with impunity.

8. During comments on security and in course of moving to economic development, it recognized by both VP and Mobutu that internal security and economic development were inter-related. The Vice President moreover, stressed the identity of purpose of the two governments in pursuing these objectives.

9. Mobutu expounded his deep desire to achieve genuine economic independence. This involved economic emancipation from Belgium. For example when he sought spare parts for the Harley-Davidson motorcycles used in the motorcade, he had to go through Brussels and could not deal directly with American company. When he bought American autos for the OAU conference, he had to buy through Belgium and obtain cars on Belgian ships, even though Belgium did not manufacture them. VP replied that this system made no sense. He fully agreed that Congo should have direct access to American firms and that it most desirable there should be a training program so Congolese could become representatives of these firms as soon as possible. He promised to follow up on the study recently done under the applause of the U.S. Department of Commerce to see what could be done, including opening of direct U.S. sales offices in Congo and training Congolese in U.S. to operate own distributionships for U.S. goods.

10. Mobutu added that this year he had declared 1968 the year of agriculture. He did not wish take the time of the VP to go into full details but he would work with the Ambassador on this problem. The Vice President congratulated him on this emphasis. He thought the U.S. Dept. of Agriculture might be able to help Congolese on some of

their problems by sending experts. VP promised that USDA would make contact.

11. The Vice President received with pleasure the news that the agreement with Pan American to build a hotel had just been signed. It was very much in line with his desire to encourage American capital to invest in the Congo. This diversification of assistance was especially important in times when official funds were restricted.

12. Vice President noted that Peace Corps volunteers for Congo had been under discussion on various occasions. As Chairman of the Peace Corps Advisory Council, he personally thought a US assistance of this nature would be a good idea. If Congolese Government desired, he would be pleased to pursue possibility in Washington.

13. The conversation concluded with renewed expression by Mobutu at the pleasure of receiving the Vice President. The Vice President invited General Mobutu to accompany him to see the Lemba housing project.

McBride

---

570. Telegram From the Embassy in Zambia to the Department of State[1]

Lusaka, January 5, 1968, 0904Z.

1112. VIPTO 74. Vice President's Africa trip: Congo mercenaries.

1. In course extensive private conversation between VP and Mobutu (reported septel)[2] subject of mercenaries discussed in some detail. Conversation developed after considerable elaboration by Mobutu of his basic problems of security and his intense personal desire to assure genuine independence of Congo.

2. Mobutu recounted in detail entire mercenary developments since revolt began in summer. He complained most bitterly about the treatment he receiving by right-wing elements in Belgium and right-wing press. He frankly recognized international problem of mercenaries in that manner in which problem was solved would have bearing on attitude of international problem of mercenaries in that manner

---

[1] Source: National Archives, RG 59, Central Files 1967–69, POL 7 US/HUMPHREY. Secret; Immediate; Exdis. Repeated to Kinshasa and Brussels.

[2] Not found.

in which problem was solved would have bearing on attitude of international community towards Congo. He reaffirmed in staunchest fashion that he was not racist in attitude but that situation rapidly developing to point where it would be impossible avoid arousing emotions in Congo unless Belgian right-wing press got off his back. By contrast Belgium King has written him a very good letter.

3. VP recounted that Houphouet-Boigny, Tubman, and Ankrah had all expressed to him their understanding for Mobutu's dilemma but that they were also concerned by international repercussions if mercenaries were returned to the Congo and were tried and shot. They asked VP to discuss matter with Mobutu within framework their sympathetic concern. VP said there no doubt, of course, that mercenaries were criminals. However, recognizing practical problem Mobutu faces, both in relations among Europeans and Congolese in Congo and between Congo and Europeans, we wondered if we could be helpful in any way in this difficult problem.

4. Mobutu explained that if mercenaries left Rwanda by land they would require visas from neighboring African countries and if they were flown out they would require overflight permission. Either would be extremely difficult for African countries to permit in view record of mercenaries. As personal thought, VP wondered whether mercenaries could be tried in absentia. This would tell whole world about their record and would mean that if mercenaries ever returned to African countries they could be arrested as common criminals. Mobutu said he wished to get rid of mercenaries but not have them killed, and would like to find way to be responsive to letter from Belgian King. He was willing to send FM Bomboko to forthcoming OAU meeting at Khartoum to try to work out something. However, if right-wing Belgian press did not reduce its attacks on him and his country, it would be impossible to work out satisfactory solution. He urgently asked that US do whatever it could to get GOB to call off these attacks. He observed that GOB often claimed to have no influence with these interests but that it was not hesitant at all to exercise control when it appeared really necessary.

5. Mobutu gave clear impression that he wished solution short of return and execution of mercenaries. He was eloquent about pressures on him if situation endured for long. He repeatedly said that unless European press attacks stopped he would be unable, possibly unwilling, to avoid emotional reaction within Congo. He very strongly hoped US would be able influence GOB on this matter.

Good

571. Telegram From the Department of State to the Embassy in the Congo[1]

Washington, January 16, 1968, 0325Z.

99130. 1. Secretary met with Foreign Minister Bomboko January 15 and hosted small lunch during which conversations were continued. Bomboko received later in afternoon by Vice President at Capitol. Also met with Palmer and Straus of AID. Bomboko returning NY this evening and proceeding directly to Kinshasa as scheduled arriving January 17.

2. Following is uncleared summary of conversation with Secretary subject to review. Bomboko discussed at some length same problems Mobutu had raised with Vice President in fields of security and economic development. He followed closely lines of memorandum. He stressed need for four C–130s and squadron of fighter planes. Re development he mentioned GDRC desire to have American technicians help Congolese develop projects for increasing production of major crops and importance of direct US–Congo commercial relations to eliminate need for Belgian middlemen.

3. Concerning mercenaries, Bomboko told Secretary problem no longer in Congolese hands and as far as GDRC concerned issue virtually closed matter which would presumably be shortly resolved. (In earlier conversation with Palmer, Bomboko had said that problem is now in hands of OAU and no longer of direct concern to Congo. Fact problem is now an OAU one means Congolese cannot deal directly with Rwandans and GDRC precluded from using force to bring back mercenaries. Bomboko said Congolese had earlier indicated to Rwandans their willingness to see all of mercenaries except for handful of ring-leaders repatriated but GDRC prevented from reaching any agreement with Rwanda owing to Rwandan Government's refusal to discuss matter.[2] Congo interest in matter now terminated and country turning its attention to problems of economic development.)

4. Secretary indicated our understanding of issues presented and our desire to be helpful. He pointed out however many problems connected with acquisition of sophisticated aircraft, and need for having

---

[1] Source: National Archives, RG 59, Central Files 1967–69, POL 7 THE CONGO. Confidential; Priority. Drafted by McKesson and approved by Palmer. Repeated to Brussels, Kigali, CINCSTRIKE for POLAD Tampa, Niamey, Addis Ababa, and Paris.

[2] On January 9, Mobutu issued an angry denunciation of Kayibanda, labeling him a traitor to Africa for refusing to extradite the mercenaries. Kayibanda responded that Rwanda was sticking to the terms of the September OAU resolution. On January 11, the Congo broke diplomatic relations with Rwanda and closed its border. Rwanda followed suit, saying it had no choice but to respond to Congolese provocation.

military experts give careful study to best ways of coping with Congo's security needs.

5. During discussion with Vice President, Bomboko raised security and economic development matters but did not touch on mercenaries. Discussion was extremely friendly and Vice President indicated US interest in assisting Congo with problems presented by Bomboko but made no commitments other than to emphasize our willingness to look into matters and to seek ways of meeting very real needs of Congo in these fields.

Rusk

572. Telegram From the Department of State to the Embassy in Kenya[1]

Washington, March 26, 1968, 2324Z.

136714. Ref: Nairobi 3923,[2] Kinshasa 8301 (Notal),[3] Kinshasa 8313.[4]

1. Dept encouraged by developments reported Nairobi 3923 and Kinshasa 8301 to hope resolution merc problem at long last may now be in sight. We continue believe however that evacuation is primarily matter for governments directly concerned and that ICRC should be

---

[1] Source: National Archives, RG 59, Central Files 1967–69, DEF 9-7 THE CONGO. Confidential. Drafted by Tienken; cleared by Bader in DOD/ISA, McKesson, Day in IO/UNP, Meagher, Moffat, Beigel, Cheslaw in EUR/BMI, and Dozier in EUR/AIS; and approved by Quimby. Repeated to Addis Ababa, Brussels, Bujumbura, Dakar, Dar es Salaam, Fort Lamy, Kampala, Kigali, Kinshasa, Khartoum, London, Niamey, Paris, Rome, Tel Aviv, Luanda, Salisbury, the Mission in Geneva, and CINCSTRIKE for POLAD Tampa.

[2] In telegram 3923 from Nairobi, March 25, Ambassador Ferguson reported that ICRC representative George Hoffman informed him that the Chairman of the OAU Committee on Mercenaries had sent letters to all committee members recommending approval of Mobutu's plan to evacuate the mercenary contingent from Kamembe. Hoffman asked if the U.S. Government would consider use of a U.S. C–130 aircraft with the required military security complement if the French denied use of French military air transport and security guards. (Ibid.)

[3] Telegram 8301 from Kinshasa, March 25, reported that Niger Foreign Minister Sidikou told newsmen that he and Mobutu had had fruitful talks which would probably lead to the early resumption of relations between the Congo and Rwanda. It also reported that according to the Belgian and French Embassies, Sidikou had a full mandate from Mobutu to arrange for the departure of the mercenaries. (Ibid.)

[4] Dated March 25. (Ibid.)

approaching European governments such as French and particularly Belgians without reference to us.

2. We concur completely with Kinshasa's point (para 2 Kinshasa 8313) that we should not give Europeans any reason believe that USG willing get them off hook at last moment by providing airlift and therefore believe it important that Hoffman be set straight before idea gains currency in European, African or ICRC circles that USG might be willing consider furnishing airlift capacity.

3. Accordingly wherever Hoffman next surfaces, Embassy concerned should 1) indicate awareness Hoffman inquiry about possible use C–130, and 2) tell Hoffman that any such request should come to us through ICRC headquarters Geneva but that if he is thinking of making such a recommendation to Geneva, he should know that USG believes any evacuation arrangements should be worked out with governments whose citizens involved, any one of which should be perfectly capable of organizing satisfactory airlift with ICRC. Should ICRC approach Mission Geneva with same proposal, or should Fonoffs Brussels, Paris, London, or Rome request our views, Mission and Embassies authorized make same point without further reference to Dept.

Rusk

573. Memorandum for the Record[1]

Washington, April 8, 1968.

SUBJECT

Briefing of Mr. John McKesson, Director of the Office of Central African and Malagasy Affairs, on CIA Covert Funding of Political Figures in the Congo

1. On 2 April 1968, Mr. John McKesson, Director of the Office of Central African and Malagasy Affairs, Bureau of African Affairs, Department of State, asked me for a briefing on CIA covert funding of Congolese political figures.

2. I told him that such funding was now limited to [Identity 1], [Identity 2], [Identity 3] and [*cryptonym not declassified*]. He asked whether [Mobutu] was still receiving such funds. I said that he had re-

[1] Source: Central Intelligence Agency Files, Job 89–00195R, Box 1, [*cryptonym not declassified*]/Operations, 7–6–58/3. Secret. Drafted by [*name not declassified*].

ceived no funds since September 1966. I explained that the arrangement as it had existed prior to that date as approved by the 303 Committee (in February 1966) was that each month he asked for funds ([*less than 1 line not declassified*]) and that once the Embassy and the Department had given its approval, the Station made the payment. Mr. McKesson expressed surprise at the size of the payment and asked what [Mobutu] did with the money. I said that the funding had been proposed by the Station and the Ambassador to assist [Mobutu] in making the gifts and payments to leading supporters (Army officers, politicians, provincial leaders) expected of an African political leader, at a time when [Mobutu] had seemed the best hope for the preservation of a stable, Western-oriented government in the Congo. [Mobutu] had never asked for a payment after September 1966, probably because he suspected that after his having virtually compelled the Department's withdrawal of the Ambassador, his request would not have been acceded to.

[Omitted here is further discussion of payments.]

[***Name not declassified***]

574. Memorandum From the President's Special Assistant (Rostow) to President Johnson[1]

Washington, April 25, 1968, 6:30 p.m.

Mr. President:

I thought you'd want to know that a stormy chapter has quietly closed in the Congo. Yesterday morning, under an OAU deal with the Red Cross, the 120 white mercenaries interned in Rwanda were finally evacuated to Europe. They flew out in two chartered planes—one to Belgium, the other to Switzerland with a stop in Italy.

We don't know all the details of the evacuation. Our people stayed strictly out of the way while the Africans bargained with the Red Cross. But it's been plain for weeks that everybody concerned, including Mobutu, was tired of haggling and just wanted to be done with it.

[1] Source: Johnson Library, National Security File, Country File, Congo, Vol. XIV, Memos & Miscellaneous, 8/67–10/68. No classification marking. A handwritten notation on the original indicates that the memorandum was received at 6:42 p.m.

You may recall that the sticking point was the Congolese demand for some assurance from the parent countries (mainly Belgium, France, and South Africa) that the mercenaries wouldn't return. Mobutu apparently got some vague promises to this effect and let it go at that.

The job now is to get the Congolese back to serious business in development. No one is betting we've seen the last of these mercenary adventures or that Mobutu will have an easy time holding the country together even without outside interference. But at least we've bought some more time; for the Congo, that's worth celebrating.[2]

Walt

[2] A note at the bottom of the original in Johnson's handwriting reads: "For George C. L."

---

575. Memorandum From the Chief of the Africa Division, Directorate of Plans, Central Intelligence Agency (Roosevelt) to the Assistant Deputy Director for Plans (Karamessines)[1]

Washington, May 1968.

SUBJECT

Request for Termination of Project [*cryptonym not declassified*]

1. On 8 March 1967 the 303 Committee directed that Project [*cryptonym not declassified*] be liquidated as soon as possible "with minimum sacrifice to efficiency and order". On 10 May 1967 the Government of the Democratic Republic of the Congo signed a contract with [*cryptonym not declassified*], the maintenance facility set up under Project [*cryptonym not declassified*] to retain it as the maintenance facility for the Congolese Air Force.

2. Before Project [*cryptonym not declassified*] was in fact liquidated, a mutiny of white mercenaries and Katangan gendarmes broke out in the Congo on 5 July 1967. Congolese forces were unable to control the mutiny and in response to a request from the Congolese Government that the United States provide pilots for the Congolese Air Force, the 303

[1] Source: Central Intelligence Agency Files, Job 89–00639R, DO/AF Files, Box 1, Folder 18, Removals & Termination, Apr. 63–May 68, [*folder name not declassified*]. Secret. Sent through MPS/BG. The month and year are handwritten on the original.

Committee directed that Project [*cryptonym not declassified*] be extended for the period 1 July 1967 to 31 December 1967.

3. The pilots provided under the Project left the Congo before the end of the extension period. The air operations officers connected with the Project departed in February 1968 after the final inventories of equipment were made and the departure of a plane supplied for Project use was arranged.

4. All Project contract personnel have been amicably terminated and have signed quitclaims; there are no residual problems relating to personnel.

5. A considerable amount of material supplied by the Project is presently in the Congo under the control of [*cryptonym not declassified*]; the appropriate offices of CIA are presently negotiating with [*cryptonym not declassified*] to arrange its final disposition as per the attached memorandum.[2] (The disposition of this material is not considered an impediment to the termination of the Project.)

6. It is therefore requested that approval be given for the termination of Project [*cryptonym not declassified*].

Archibald B. Roosevelt, Jr.[3]
Chief, Africa Division

[2] Not printed.

[3] Printed from a copy that bears this typed signature.

576. Memorandum From the President's Special Assistant (Rostow) to President Johnson[1]

Washington, June 19, 1968, 12:45 p.m.

SUBJECT

AID Loan for the Congo (K)

Herewith Messrs. Gaud and Zwick recommend a $15 million Supporting Assistance Loan for the Congo. Joe Fowler concurs. Added to

[1] Source: Johnson Library, National Security File, Country File, Congo, Vol. XIV, Memos & Miscellaneous, 8/67–10/68. Confidential. A handwritten notation on the original indicates that the memorandum was received at 2:55 p.m.

the $13 million PL–480 sales you approved in December, this loan would complete our aid package for the Congo in FY 1968.

The loan will finance imports of U.S. vehicles, machinery, and spare parts. This is primarily a maintenance loan, not a development loan. But President Mobutu is making a serious effort to get back to the development business after the mercenary escapades of last summer and fall. He has taken much needed monetary reforms recommended by the IMF and is working hard to control an unruly budget. Our past aid has given us considerable leverage in urging reforms. We would release this loan in two installments, making the second contingent upon a further show of responsibility on the monetary front.

Other donors (mainly Belgium, France and the EEC) provide 80% of current aid to the Congo. Our share is now down to 20% and will decrease further next year. (Last year's loan was $17 million.) This proposal represents the minimum we can get away with if the Congolese balance of payments is to hold together.

There is no current problem in the Congo with the Conte–Long Amendment, which requires us to deduct economic aid in the amount spent by a poor country on sophisticated weapons. The Congolese haven't made any such purchases so far, but they have been considering buying some Italian jet trainers. We are trying to head this off, and we would warn Mobutu that buying jets would cost him part of this loan.

I recommend you approve.

Walt

Approve loan[2]

Disapprove

Call me

[2] This option is checked.

577. Telegram From the Embassy in the Congo to the Department of State[1]

Kinshasa, August 13, 1968, 1550Z.

10953. Subject: Mobutu and the gold bed syndrome.

1. It seemed prudent at this time to warn the Department of the galloping onset of the gold bed syndrome in conduct of President Mobutu. During my absence on leave, this phenomenon which is never far from the surface in Congolese public figures, came on apace.

2. In first instance it has manifested itself in a development of grandeur which, while not wholly unamusing and vaguely and perhaps deliberately reminiscent of a figure on the banks of a more northern river called the Seine, is hardly appropriate to the harsh realities of even a relatively peaceful Congo.

3. The most spectacular instance of folly so far reported was mentioned to me with fascinated horror by IMF representative Dini who was told by Mobutu that latter had been so impressed by Rome that he was planning to build a replica of St. Peters in Kinshasa. While Dini was still reeling, he added it would be better to build three replicas so Kisangani and Lubumbashi could also have one each.

4. Douglas Aircraft representatives inform us categorically that Mobutu has purchased a BAC–111 aircraft for private Presidential use which British Ambassador states will cost two million pounds fitted with bar, salon etc. not to mention details like spare parts. Neighbors of President on Mount Stanley report conversations with Belgian gardeners concerning five-million dollar Versailles-like parks. *Der Spiegel* and other European magazines have heavily publicized President's purchase of a luxury villa near Lausanne for one million Swiss francs.

5. Dewilde of IBRD who is now here is appalled at Presidential expenditures. Unfortunately Mobutu seems to have lost touch with reality and economics, never a strong suit of the President's, seems to have flown out the window.

6. I believe there is nothing which can be done to restrain these frivolous Presidential expenditures because Mobutu has apparently risen in souffle-like grandiloquence. I feel that to call his attention to the dangers of this type of thing although his budget expenses have already risen more than fifty percent over what was foreseen, would be to incur instant wrath.

---

[1] Source: National Archives, RG 59, Central Files 1967–69, POL 30 THE CONGO. Confidential; Exdis.

7. However, I felt a brief report should be made on his regrettable phenomenon because I believe it is the most serious problem facing Congo at present time and the fault is that of the President and the uncontrollable spending is emanating directly from him. Furthermore, it occurred to me this might have an effect on US policies towards the present regime in the Congo.[2]

McBride

[2] Telegram 224002 to Kinshasa, August 20, expressed the Department's serious concern regarding the situation described by McBride, which was potentially damaging to U.S. programs in the Congo; it asked for suggestions as to how the consequences of such extravagances, such as the danger of losing IMF and IBRD support, could be impressed on Mobutu. (Ibid.)

578. Memorandum From the Assistant Secretary of State for African Affairs (Palmer) to the Deputy Under Secretary of State for Political Affairs (Bohlen)[1]

Washington, September 6, 1968.

SUBJECT

Recommendation for Covert Financial Assistance to President Mobutu, [*less than 1 line not declassified*]

1. President Mobutu has on several occasions since mid-August requested USG financial assistance for his current efforts to encourage moderate military leaders in Congo (Brazzaville) to neutralize radical leftist influences in that country as well as eliminate the Chinese Communist presence. Mobutu has become increasingly insistent in these requests and expresses emphatic disappointment that no USG financial assistance has been forthcoming. Finance Minister Nendaka and Foreign Minister Bomboko have warned that failure to extend substantial financial assistance to Mobutu might seriously impair USG relations with the Congolese Government.

[1] Source: National Security Council, Intelligence Files, Congo, 1966–1968. Secret; Eyes Only. Sent through INR/DDC Trueheart.

2. Ambassador McBride recommended on September 5[2] that [*dollar amount not declassified*] be made available to Mobutu for the purpose of preserving and enhancing the USG's future relations with Mobutu and providing the USG with the opportunity to exploit the rapidly developing situation in Brazzaville in its own interest.

3. It should be noted that Kinshasa [*less than 1 line not declassified*] reports indicates Mobutu has expended in the last three weeks approximately $200,000 of his own funds in his efforts to assist moderate leaders in Brazzaville. Reports from Mobutu and Nendaka, as well as unilateral [*less than 1 line not declassified*] contacts, provided the USG with accurate advance information on political developments in Brazzaville, including the armed conflict of 30–31 August, and on Mobutu's activities vis-à-vis the situation.

4. The Bureau of African Affairs and the Central Intelligence Agency jointly concur in Ambassador McBride's recommendation that [*dollar amount not declassified*] be made available to President Mobutu for the reasons discussed below. [*2½ lines not declassified*]

5. There are basically two issues involved in this request. One is the desirability of lessening Chinese and/or Cuban influence in Congo (B), the other the possible impact on US–Congo (K) relations of a failure to be responsive to Mobutu.

a. Of itself, the lessening of Chicom influence in this volatile part of Africa is a desirable goal through the elimination or curtailment of communist influence in Congo (B) and of communist opportunities to use Congo (B) as an operations base for activities elsewhere. This is a matter of deep concern to Congo (K), whose internal security has frequently been menaced by threats orchestrated from abroad using nearby bases. For this reason, it is also of concern to the USG in pursuance of its policy to aid Congo (K) in combatting these threats.

b. The second problem, namely Mobutu, is complex. He is the ultimate source of power in Congo (K) and ready access to him is vital if we hope to continue our long-standing policy of assisting the Congo to unity, stability and economic progress, with the eventual goal of seeing a stable, western-oriented government in the heart of Africa, capable of exercising important influence not only in the general area of Central Africa, but in the Africa-wide councils as well. Mobutu has asked for our support, rightly or wrongly on the assumption that the interests of the USG in Congo (B) approximate his own. He is an emotional man, and a proud man. Recently he has shown a proclivity towards adventure outside of Congo (K) borders, not all of which are necessarily well-conceived. If he feels he has been let down on this issue of Congo

---

[2] Not further identified.

(B), he is quite capable of translating his annoyance into a broad spectrum of issues not related to the immediate problem of Congo (B).

6. We do not wish to risk the impairment of access to him which if it occurred would very probably be carried over into contacts throughout the Congolese Government [*less than 1 line not declassified*], access to the Foreign Minister and access to a number of government contacts on the economic side whom we consider important for the orderly conduct of our day-to-day relationships and the ultimate achievement of our goals. Impairment of access would also risk a serious adverse impact on our ability to exercise leverage on Mobutu. This applies immediately to his role vis-à-vis Congo (B). It may also apply, however, to other matters of importance to us, both in the foreign and domestic areas. The potential depth of such a development is difficult to judge. It might only be transitory. We would prefer it not occur at all, especially when the immediate issue of Congo (B) is one to which we are favorably disposed. It is clear from Amb. McBride's cables that this aspect and the potential danger of a developing strain in US–Congo relations and in his own relations with Mobutu, weigh heavily on his mind.

f [7]. *Recommendation*

a. That you concur in the attached cable to Ambassador McBride;[3]

b. That you authorize INR/DDC on your behalf to obtain the concurrence of the other 303 principals.[4]

[3] Not attached and not found.

[4] A handwritten notation on the memorandum states that the recommendation was approved by the 303 Committee telephonically on September 6.

579. National Intelligence Estimate[1]

NIE 65–68 Washington, September 27, 1968.

PROSPECTS FOR THE CONGO

Conclusions

A. President Joseph Mobutu is currently providing a greater measure of political stability and internal security to Congo (Kinshasa) than that troubled country has known since independence. But the fabric of government is still fragile. There are persistent popular discontents and frustrations, and no great enthusiasm for Mobutu personally. The opposition to the regime is, however, diffuse and unorganized. We think Mobutu stands a better than even chance of retaining office over the next couple of years, and perhaps longer. His departure, if sudden, would probably result in prolonged political turmoil and a sharp decline in internal security.

B. Mobutu's main base of support is the Congolese National Army (ANC), which holds a virtual monopoly of coercive power but is poorly trained and disciplined and often is as much a threat to, as a preserver of, security. Any significant improvement in the ANC is likely to be gradual and could take many years.

C. The obstacles to a restoration of the economy to preindependence levels of activity are great. If tolerable internal security can be maintained, monetary stability preserved, and foreign aid at about current rates obtained, the Congo will probably be able to function for some time at about the present pace. A considerable improvement in the economy would require a substantial additional input of foreign financing, much of it for the infrastructure.

D. Mobutu has recently shown a tendency to involve himself in the internal affairs of his neighbors. After a period of acrimony, Belgian-Congolese relations are improving, and Mobutu will probably gain limited economic and technical benefits from the détente. Belgium will remain the predominant foreign presence in the Congo, although it is unlikely to be as deeply involved in internal affairs as in the past. Mobutu will continue to look to the US for important military and eco-

[1] Source: Central Intelligence Agency Files, Job 79R01012A, ODDI Registry. Secret; Controlled Dissem. According to a note on the cover sheet, the Central Intelligence Agency and the intelligence organization of the Departments of State and Defense and the NSA prepared the estimate. All members of the U.S. Intelligence Board concurred on September 27, except the Assistant General Manager of the Atomic Energy Commission and the Assistant Director of the Federal Bureau of Investigation, who abstained on the grounds the subject was outside their jurisdiction.

nomic assistance and unless US aid is cut off, he will regard the US as his main foreign backer.

Discussion

I. The Political Order

1. Considering the Congo's chaotic history since 1960, President Joseph Mobutu in his three years in office has had some modest achievements. A major accomplishment has been the mere survival of his regime, which owes something to the exhaustion of the Congolese populace after the prolonged civil strife and to the continued disarray of rival political factions, and a good deal to Mobutu's political skills.

2. Mobutu's regime, like many others in Africa, is characterized by a heavy concentration of authority in the hands of the President. Remnants of earlier regimes, including national and provincial assemblies, have been swept away in favor of a highly personal style of rule virtually devoid of an institutional framework. Mobutu shares power with no one, but he does consult with his old cronies, a group of seasoned and durable politicians known as the Binza Group. This clique forms the core of his cabinet and serves in a few other key administrative posts. None of his civilian associates are in a position to challenge him, and all are kept off balance by cabinet changes and administrative reshuffles.

3. Mobutu has invested time, money, and effort in bolstering his stature as a great national chief—both by displaying the trappings of office (e.g., a yacht, prestige projects) and, more importantly, by being ruthless and decisive. He has shown some response to advice from the International Monetary Fund (IMF) and the US designed to introduce greater financial responsibility. He has also made efforts to grapple with basic internal problems. He keeps in touch with the grassroots by holding informal palavers with groups of clergy, students, labor, businessmen, the army, and others who air their grievances and recommend reforms. He has also established a national political party and has included in it some regional politicians who had been largely excluded from active politics since his takeover. This party is, however, principally an instrument of the regime, and provides a means of dispensing patronage and a cheering section.

4. The capabilities of the central administration in Kinshasa have probably improved slowly under Mobutu. Control of the provinces is probably stronger than under previous regimes. Mobutu selects provincial governors—a fairly competent group on the whole—gives them vice-regal powers, shifts them about, and makes it a practice to send them to areas where they are not native. But this has not necessarily improved provincial government, for the governors frequently lack the expertise, the staffs, and the resources to deal with the complexities of

local situations. Moreover, the governors often do not know the local languages and are regarded as foreigners by the local populace. Corruption, though less flagrant than in earlier regimes, is widespread and has a debilitating effect in the provinces as in the capital.

5. Mobutu's principal base of support is the Congolese National Army (ANC), an organization that is feared and generally hated. Some of the ANC's unpopularity rubs off on the President. He lacks a firm tribal base and is unable to arouse much enthusiasm for himself or his policies. Urban wage-earners, suffering from inflation, grumble at their lot and some resent Mobutu's lavish personal outlays. Many university students are opposed to him, criticize his policies as pro-Western and too moderate, resent his reliance on advisers whom they consider out of tune with the needs of the Congo, and fear that their ambitions for positions of influence will be thwarted. He, in turn, has used the army to put down student demonstrations. The young intellectual elite at one time welcomed Mobutu as a nationalist innovator, and some have lost the important posts they held in the early days of his regime, and have become disillusioned and estranged. In addition, some of the Congo's most important tribes, e.g., Bakongo, Baluba, and Balunda, feel excluded from what they regard as their rightful share of jobs and benefits.

6. There is, however, a considerable difference between the kind of chronic discontent which is prevalent among most Congolese, and active dissidence. Tolerance for corruption, maladministration, and economic failure is high. Moreover, dissatisfied urban masses as well as most of the people in the interior are unlikely to revolt so long as they believe that the ANC would move against them. Thus far, popular discontent and frustration, though persistent, is unorganized and is mainly confined to unarmed civilian elements without allies in the army. Generally speaking, the survival of Mobutu's regime is likely to depend largely on the action or inaction of the ANC at critical moments.

II. Internal Security

7. The ANC holds a virtual monopoly of coercive power in the Congo, but it is a poorly trained and disciplined force and is militarily unreliable. Throughout much of the country, it is as much a threat to security as a preserver of order. Soldiers often set up roadblocks to "tax" travelers, and there are frequent instances in which they beat and rob the populace. Many of the officers line their pockets by organizing rackets. Nevertheless, the ANC generally keeps the provinces under a rough kind of control.

8. No major security problems currently confront the ANC. There are some pockets of rebels in the eastern Congo and in the forests of

Bandundu Province, but these groups act more like bandits than insurgents and tend to avoid contact with the ANC. There is no evidence of any significant resurgence of politically-inspired dissidence which could touch off a new revolt against the government. The rebel leaders have mostly fled the country and have little contact with their former followers in the bush. While some of them are in countries east of the Congo and may have some Cuban or Chinese support, they are at odds with each other and appear to pose little threat of renewed insurgency.

9. The question of the loyalty of the ANC to the regime and its responsiveness to orders from headquarters or field commanders are key considerations in assessing the political stability of the Congo. Officers and men are paid regularly and Mobutu is responsive to their grievances. Under these circumstances the ANC is reasonably loyal. Though Mobutu came to power in 1965 through a military coup, he has carefully excluded the army from participation in government. The top positions in the ANC are largely filled with long-time associates of Mobutu, who are for the most part incompetent, corrupt, and lazy, but are probably more loyal than the younger officers. The latter, particularly those trained abroad, are far more capable and many are thoroughly disgusted at serving under ignorant and corrupt commanders, but they are not a cohesive group and there is little evidence of plotting against Mobutu.

10. Mobutu probably wishes to reform the ANC but he recognizes that any major shakeup might arouse enough discontent among the older group of officers to threaten the stability of the government. He is therefore more likely to tackle the army problem piecemeal through limited and step-by-step reorganizations and reassignments rather than a clean sweep. The foreign training programs will bring some improvement of the capabilities of some units, but it would be unrealistic to expect any significant progress in the discipline, capabilities, or responsiveness of the ANC in the next several years.

11. The national police also has a security role, primarily in the cities. There are several foreign training programs under way, including one supported by the US, and the police force is in general a bit better disciplined than the ANC. It also has better relations with the populace. In times of emergency (as during the mercenary revolt in 1967) it is subject to the authority of the ANC.

12. The fact remains that the ANC is both the main bulwark of the regime and the greatest potential threat to it. Indeed, the most likely challenge to Mobutu would come from within the ANC or from a combination of military and civilian dissidents. So long as he holds the allegiance of the bulk of the ANC, particularly the "elite" First Paracommandos in the capital, he is not likely to be overthrown except by assassination. But there is no assurance that even the elite troops would

stand their ground if confronting an armed and determined opposition. It is difficult to estimate political stability in the Congo with any confidence because in the past the shift from apathy to violence has been abrupt, and major uprisings have stemmed from trivial or unforeseen incidents. But there is currently no indication that Mobutu is heading for serious trouble. On balance, we think he stands a better than even chance of retaining office over the next couple of years, and perhaps longer.

13. If Mobutu were removed from the scene in the near future, it would probably destroy the relative stability and order now prevalent. Any successor, military or civilian, would have to have the backing of the ANC or most elements of it simply to hold office. Moreover, because of the highly personal autocratic type of rule employed by Mobutu, the whole structure of government would be shaken. His successor would probably have to start from scratch, either to fashion a new hierarchy based on personal loyalties, or to begin to construct some institutions of government. In either case there would probably be prolonged confusion and instability.

III. The Economy

14. The overriding economic problem of the Congo has been to halt the downward slide which began just before independence. The natural resources of the country are enormous, but so are the obstacles to their exploitation. Post-independence governments have proved unable to muster the administrative skills needed to operate a complicated and extensive economy. Rebellion, civil disorder, and neglect have hampered production, particularly on plantations, and have also taken a heavy toll of the transport system. Bridges were destroyed, equipment rusted, channels silted, and roads overgrown; reconstruction and repairs have been slow. This is an important factor in a country where the principal mines and the most potentially productive plantations lie some 900 miles from the seaports through which much of their output must move. Finally, in the years immediately preceding the devaluation of June 1967, the currency was grossly overvalued; this dampened the incentive to produce, not only for export but for the domestic market as well.

15. In consequence, current agricultural production is less than half the preindependence level, with cotton, rice, and corn from small farms suffering the most. As for minerals, the output of gold and tin suffered substantial losses. Diamond production was less affected, but a third of the output was smuggled out of the country, thus depriving the government of revenue. A new marketing structure for diamonds has served to cut down this smuggling, and the prospects for both the mineral and the agricultural sectors have been improved by the 1967 monetary reform.

16. Probably the brightest spot in the economic picture is the continued high output of copper, zinc, and cobalt from Katanga. Exports of these minerals have been maintained at about preindependence levels; indeed, copper exports in 1967 exceeded those in 1959, and are rising. Katangan minerals now account for some 80 percent in value of all Congolese exports, and the revenues derived from minerals provide half of government income. Yet revenues have been affected by the drop in copper prices which have fallen from a high of 70 cents a pound in early 1968 to about 45 cents. Prices are unlikely to rise much in the next few years, and may drop further.

17. A complicating factor in the effort to arrest the economic decline is the national financial situation. Years of deficit spending after independence disrupted commerce and hastened inflation. The country has been kept going only by the infusion of over $1 billion in economic and military assistance, 60 percent of it from the US much of it through the UN.[2] Last year the IMF sponsored a sweeping monetary reform. By-and-large the reform has worked, partly because high world copper prices provided a windfall in revenues. Furthermore, Mobutu has taken steps to strengthen the Finance Ministry. But the recent downturn in copper prices and the uncertain outlook for efforts to control governmental expenditures, including Mobutu's propensity for lavish personal and prestige spending, are likely to raise again the spectre of budgetary deficits and perhaps another round of financial instability.

18. Over the years the US has delivered far more economic and military assistance to the Congo than to any other sub-Saharan African country. In the last few years the levels of aid have fallen off, amounting in fiscal year 1968 to only $2.4 million in military assistance and $30 million in economic aid.[3] This included $12 million in PL 480 commodities. The balance financed imports of trucks, spare parts, and industrial supplies. Continued US aid at about this level, together with Belgian and other foreign financial and technical assistance, would probably maintain economic activity at something like the current pace, provided there is no serious decline in internal security, no major deterioration of the monetary situation, and no substantial decrease in the number of expatriate specialists.

19. A program designed to regain the pre-1960 level of economic activity would require massive financing over five years or so. It has

---

[2] Roughly $700 million was economic assistance; the US accounted for about one-half. [Footnote in the original.]

[3] This compares with US economic and military aid of $50 million in fiscal year 1967; $52 million in 1966; $32 million in 1965; $64 million in 1964; $112 million in 1963; $129 million in 1962; and $144 million in 1961. [Footnote in the original.]

been estimated that at least $175 million would be needed to restore the internal transport system alone. An additional sum of at least $125 million would be required to provide other public services. Some outside aid, though far short of the magnitude required for such a program, could be expected from Belgium, the EEC, the IBRD, and other sources, but they as well as the Congolese would look to the US for a major contribution. The success of such a program would depend heavily on the preservation of internal security and political stability, and on the related matter of finding the necessary technical and managerial personnel. Foreign experts willing to work in the bush are hard to find, and the Congolese now being trained for specialized jobs will not be available in sufficient numbers for a decade or more. If these requirements could be largely met, foreign private investors might come forward with the funds to exploit the great natural resources of the country. The economy could then even exceed preindependence levels of activity.

IV. Foreign Relations

20. Mobutu has entered into African diplomatic affairs in a rather erratic and occasionally enthusiastic fashion. He clearly relishes attendance at OAU summit gatherings, where he mingles with other African chiefs in prestigious surroundings. Though he has little interest in more distant parts of Africa, such as Nigeria, he seems to be acquiring a taste for becoming involved in the affairs of his neighbors. He has come to believe that the Congo, as a major African state, has an important role to play in central Africa. For a time he lavished attention on the Union des Etats de l'Afrique Centrale (UEAC), and embryo customs union joining Congo (Kinshasa) with Chad and Central African Republic, though more recently he seems to find Congo (Brazzaville) politics more interesting. We do not know at this stage whether Mobutu's involvement in the activities of neighboring states is a passing fancy or a new phase of foreign policy. We are inclined to believe it is the latter.

21. Congolese relations with Portugal, though normally bad, tend to fluctuate between inactivity and the trading of threats. For some years various Congolese governments have afforded training facilities and safe haven to Holden Roberto's Angolan liberation movement, but Mobutu, like most Congolese, is not deeply committed to the liberation cause. He is aware, moreover, that the Portuguese have the means and occasionally the will to retaliate against the Congo. He has not forgotten the brief foray of mercenaries from Angola into Katanga last year, and has been concerned about bands of Lunda tribesmen from Katanga now in Angola, which he believed were armed and held in readiness by the Portuguese. By-and-large, neither Mobutu nor the Portuguese are keen on worsening relations with each other. The

Congo depends on the Benguela railroad through Angola for the export of Katangan copper, and Angola benefits from the revenues.

22. The Soviet diplomatic mission in Kinshasa, which recently opened for the third time, has been very careful in its relations with Mobutu. Neither trusts the other. It is doubtful that the Soviets really expect to develop close relations with Mobutu's regime. They are likely to offer some aid, and Mobutu will find the Soviet presence useful in his efforts to garner more aid from the West. If he fails to get particularly desired items such as military aircraft from the West he might turn to the USSR.

23. Relations with the Belgians are particularly important for the Congo. After several years of acrimony, Mobutu is now doing what he can to increase Belgian aid and investment. He seems to have learned that no other country or group of countries can replace Belgium, and that the prolonged absence of key Belgian technicians has damaged the Congolese economy and public services. He is therefore willing to risk some domestic displeasure including charges of neocolonialist collaboration in order to regain the services of Belgian specialists and lure Belgian capital back to the Congo.

24. The outlook for the next year or two is for cautiously forthcoming response to Mobutu's overtures. Brussels wants good relations and will continue to provide at least technical assistance but will not quickly forget Mobutu's anti-Belgian campaigns of recent years. Belgian aid has consisted principally of payments on preindependence Congolese debt ($21 million in 1967) and the furnishing of technical assistance ($25 million in 1967). The number of Belgian technicians dropped sharply in 1967 but is now beginning to increase. Belgian private investors will react cautiously to begin with and look for quick returns. Investors will, however, wish expatriate personnel to manage investments and the degree of security and stability throughout the country will be an important factor in determining the availability of such personnel. If relations continue to improve and the Congo maintains reasonable stability, there will probably be some new investment, although mainly for the expansion of existing enterprises rather than the establishment of new ones.

25. With the disappearance of the mercenaries and the liquidation of the issues revolving about the role of Union Minière du Haut Katanga (UMHK), two of the principal sources of friction between the two countries subsided. Belgium has, however, to a considerable extent disentangled itself from the Congo and is unlikely to be as deeply involved in internal Congolese affairs as in the past. Nevertheless, Belgium will remain as the major foreign presence in the Congo.

26. Mobutu's attitude toward the former metropole could change suddenly as it has in the past. It is always possible, therefore, that for

fairly obscure reasons or simply to divert popular discontent from himself, he might launch another hate campaign that would endanger the lives of the 24,000 Belgians in the Congo. In these circumstances other Europeans and US citizens would also be in danger.

27. The US enjoys a high degree of prestige and influence in Kinshasa, based in part on the massive aid provided over the years and on a long working association of US officials with Mobutu. The ANC relies on the US for transport equipment and for some technical training, and the Congolese economy would be in worse shape than it is without US assistance. Mobutu believes that his policies in the Congo and in Africa correspond with those of the US and he is occasionally miffed when the US fails to provide funds for his pet projects. Mobutu would like the US to provide him with some jet aircraft and eventually a few transport planes to move ANC units more rapidly to remote trouble spots. In any future crisis, as in the past, he would almost certainly turn first to the US for military assistance. Unless US aid ceases altogether, Mobutu will continue to regard the US as his most important foreign backer.

580. Memorandum From Roger Morris of the National Security Council Staff to the President's Special Assistant (Rostow)[1]

Washington, October 7, 1968.

WWR:

SUBJECT

Consortium for the Congo

You asked about the prospect of a donors club for the Congo now that her worst birth pangs (hopefully) are over. AID is already well at work on this one.

Over the last few months, we've begun to lay the foundations of a Congo aid group/consortium under the aegis of the World Bank. The first step, of course, was to get the Bank itself involved. They're now ready to begin their first two jobs in the Congo: (a) a management study of a vital water-rail network, and (b) through the UNDP a badly needed

---

[1] Source: Johnson Library, National Security File, Files of Edward Hamilton, Congo (A). Confidential. A handwritten note on the original by Saunders reads: "WWR—per our conversation. Hal." Another handwritten note on the original by Rostow reads: "HS—RM—Good. If & when the IBRD gambit is firm draft a note in sense of final paragraph for the President. WWR."

study to reorganize the Congo's moribund Bureau of Public Roads. AID is working closely with Bank experts on both these projects. We're telling them that we plan to support their efforts directly with an FY '70 program loan in transportation (the first sector loan in Sub-Saharan Africa). Even at this early stage it seems clear the Bank is settling itself into a crucial and long-range problem of Congolese development.

AID has also moved on to the second step and asked the Bank to call a meeting in the next 30 days of the other donors: Belgium, Italy, Israel, Nationalist China, France and the EEC. This session will be only a beginning at the staff level, but at least it ought to: (1) get better coordination of current aid; (2) generally promote the Bank's involvement and leadership; and (3) signal the Congolese that this is the way their benefactors are moving. Soundings tell us that all the donors are for a Bank-sponsored group—except possibly the French, whose aid share and influence are not large enough to kill the idea if they balk. The Congolese think the idea is their ticket to the big leagues in development.

As you well know, the consortium-building business can be slow, hard work. But most of us think these are real beginnings. The U.S. now does roughly 15–20 percent of the Congo's aid bill. By 1970, with a consortium full grown, we would expect our share to drop and level off at a respectable 10 percent.

I'll be following the AID talks with the World Bank and the results of the meeting of the donors. If that session turns out as well as expected, you might want to give the President an incidental report on the Congo aid picture. After all, it's a long and heartening road from Stanleyville paradrop to a club of investors putting their chips on Congolese turnpikes.

RM

581. Dispatch From the Station in the Congo to the Central Intelligence Agency[1]

Kinshasa, December 11, 1968.

SUBJECT

[Identity 1]/[Mobutu]—Meeting (21 November 1968)

For: [*name not declassified*].

1. [Mobutu] granted [Identity 1] an interview on 21 November, 1968 which lasted approximately two hours and which was held at the Presidency on Mount Stanley. [Identity 2] and [COS] also attended. After some introductory remarks by [Identity 1], [Mobutu] did nearly all the talking. Incidentally, it is extremely unusual for [Mobutu] to grant such a long interview to anyone, even to a "personalite de marque." [Mobutu] was extremely frank, although some of the remarks which he expressed were, in several instances, biaised or erroneous (i.e. he described the World Bank as by-and-large US dominated and controlled. He also exaggerated the evils of the Union Minière du Haut Katanga (UMHK) describing its 300 Belgian executives as the worst type of neo-colonialists who perpetually connive against the GRDC and its leadership).

2. After a brief exchange of social amenities, [Identity 1] expressed his appreciation for the interview. He made it clear that the primary purpose of his visit to Africa, including Congo (Kinshasa), was to brief himself on the prevailing political scene. It was not his purpose to negotiate or provide any kind of support for projects or programs. [Identity 1] mentioned that he would be called upon, shortly after his return to [U.S.] to brief certain key members of the new incoming administration on matters having to do with Africa.

3. At this juncture, [Mobutu] began his lengthy expose of Congolese political developments from Independence. The following covers the highlights of his remarks:

A. [Mobutu] expressed his appreciation of past American interest in and support for the Congo dating back to the Kennedy Administration. He emphasized that the US Government had contributed materially and significantly to the achievement and maintenance of Congolese independence. [Mobutu] went on to explain that he and his associates had been faced by powerful opponents both from the right and the left. He mentioned that threats to security still existed primarily

[1] Source: Central Intelligence Agency Files, [*text not declassified*], Vol. V, Mobutu. Secret; Rybat.

from external elements supported by subversive African and Communist States. He expressed the hope that the US would continue to take a major interest in the Congo adding that what was primarily needed from the US at this time was sympathy, understanding and economic rather than military support. He intimated that he wanted to avoid being too dependent on the Belgians.

B. [Mobutu] said that relations with some of the previous [U.S.] Ambassadors had not been ideal. He specifically mentioned [McBride's] predecessor who had on several occasions insisted (i.e. exige) that [Mobutu] undertake certain initiatives in keeping with [USG] desires, rather than those in Congo's best interest. He stated that as a sovereign state the GDRC could not and would not take dictation from anyone, including [USG] and that this should be clearly understood by one and all.

C. [Mobutu] then addressed his remarks to the Belgians. He stated that the rightist Belgian threat (i.e. mercenaries) has been overcome and hopefully for good. He stressed, however, that GDRC was still constantly being threatened with domination by Belgian economic interests. He decried the actual situation in the Congo whereby Belgian subsidiaries of US firms exercise a rigid monopoly over US imports into the Congo. [Mobutu] made it very clear that he wanted US firms to deal directly with GDRC or Congolese businessmen and not to be obligated as is presently the case to deal with Belgian intermediaries. In this way, the Belgians make all the profits.

D. The next topic taken up was the Societe Generale and [Mobutu] devoted nearly ¾ of an hour to this topic but mentioned nothing new ([Mobutu] usually covers this topic with all important visitors and regularly discusses it with [McBride] and other [U.S.] officials). [Mobutu] insisted that the Union Minière du Haut Katanga (UMHK) had always been a Congolese company, but that the Belgians had changed it into a Belgian one just prior to Congolese Independence. [Mobutu] referred to the UMHK being represented by "300 Messieurs" who were highly unscrupulous. [Mobutu] reported time and again that [USG] could not from a moral, or any other standpoint, support "300 Messieurs" against the GDRC and the whole Congolese nation. [Mobutu] insisted that Belgian bankers and businessmen, acting on behalf of the Societe Generale, were besmirching the good name and competence of the GDRC and the Congolese people in the US, and particularly with the World Bank. In [Mobutu's] view, the Belgians are most afraid of economic competition, particularly American.

E. Turning his attention to the World Bank, [Mobutu] flatly stated that it was to all intents and purposes an American creation and instrument, since the US provided 60% of the capital (erroneous—actually 25%).

F. [Mobutu] made it clear that he would continue to do business with the Belgians but that the activities of the Societe Generale would have to be curtailed. He stated that the Societe Generale had confidence in his regime and the future of the Congo, as indicated by its financing the construction of a large commercial business complex in the center of downtown Kinshasa.

G. [Mobutu] finally turned to [*cryptonym not declassified*]-related matters. He stated that he was extensively involved in expensive political action activities. He clearly intimated that some of these activities also served [U.S.] policy interests. [Mobutu] stated that he has given large sums of money to certain Congo (Brazzaville) leaders (Army and civilians), to Bokassa and Tombalbaye to strengthen UEAC, to Zambian President Kaunda for forthcoming elections, Burundi for para-commando training of Micombero's elite batallion and for GDRC propaganda against communist threats.

H. [Mobutu] bemoaned the fact that [*cryptonym not declassified*] in the past had given massive financial assistance to [Identity 3] who, without army support, would never become a real leader worthy of the name.

I. [Mobutu] expressed his appreciation for the current cooperation between [*cryptonym not declassified*] and his services and asked [Identity 1] that this liaison be continued and enlarged. Specifically [Mobutu] asked [Identity 1] to arrange for the early training of [*cryptonym not declassified*] and five others by [*cryptonym not declassified*]. [COS] interjected that [*cryptonym not declassified*] training has already been laid on, but that no commitment had been made about training the other five.

J. [Identity 1] mentioned that he was leaving on 23 November for a visit to the interior of the Congo. [Mobutu] replied that [Identity 1] should remain on in Kinshasa over the weekend for his regime's 3rd Anniversary celebrations. [Identity 1] gracefully declined on the grounds that his tight onward schedule regrettably would not permit a stayover.

4. The meeting was highly successful and contributed effectively to the continued close rapport between Station and [Mobutu].

[COS]

582. Telegram From the Station in the Congo to the Central Intelligence Agency[1]

Kinshasa, December 16, 1968.

7090 (In 55279). Ref: Director 58792.[2]

1. Station has not and does not plan elicit comments from any Station assets concerning [McBride] effectiveness. On contrary, to date, we have refused discuss [McBride] other than to make positive statements in his support.

2. Wish point out in this connection, however, that [Identity 1], [Identity 2] and [Identity 3] would like [McBride], or for that matter any other [Embassy] chief, to exercise a strong advisory influence upon [Mobutu], whom all three claim badly in need good advice. [COS] has repeatedly stressed to all three that [McBride] most influential Mission Chief on [Mobutu] anyway. Possibly these three misinterpret [McBride's] shyness. No doubt these three would like [COS] to play the role of [former COS] with [Mobutu]. [COS] has made it clear repeatedly that times and circumstances have changed radically since [former COS] days and that therefore [COS] cannot and will not play such a role.

3. In sum do not believe this matter constitutes any real problem. It is a fact, nonetheless, that the members of the [*less than 1 line not declassified*] and others are genuinely worried about [Mobutu's] present increasing isolation and what should be done about it.

4. HQS can rest completely assured that no Station member will ever be indiscreet or disloyal in any way regarding [McBride].

---

[1] Source: Central Intelligence Agency Files, [*text not declassified*], Vol. V, Mobutu. Secret; Rybat. No time of receipt appears on the message.

[2] CIA telegram 58792 to Kinshasa, December 13, cautioned the Station not to sound out contacts regarding their attitude toward Ambassador McBride and to refrain from commenting on any adverse statements that were volunteered, other than by commenting positively in McBride's support. The Station should recall the past history of Mobutu's attempts through his cohorts to denigrate McBride's predecessors. (Ibid.)

Index

References are to document numbers

Tshombe government (*1964-65*) (*see also* African hostility toward Tshombe government; Post-Tshombe crisis; Simba Rebellion; Tshombe government period political action operations)—*Continued*

GPO U.S. GOVERNMENT PRINTING OFFICE: 2014—339-370/80002

ISBN 978-0-16-082002-1